Get more mileage out of your money.

AAA members save 10% at more than 2900 domestic hotels.

Here's a major attraction not on your map. Seven different hotels to choose from, all offering at least a 10% discount, and kids stay free with parent or grandparents.

Comfort Inns and Suites feature a free deluxe continental breakfast and a 100% satisfaction guarantee.

Econo Lodge offers special Senior Rooms with in-room coffeemakers, brighter lighting and big button TV remotes.

Quality Inns, Hotels, and Suites offer midpriced, full-service accommodations and a 100% satisfaction guarantee.

Clarion Inns, Hotels, and Resorts offer upscale, full-service lodgings, as well as meetings facilities.

Sleep Inns feature the same unique design that has set a new standard for guest satisfaction, including sensational rooms at sensible prices.

Rodeway Inns offer travelers free local calls and a complimentary newspaper, as well as special rooms designed for the 50-plus traveler.

MainStay Suites is an extended stay hotel featuring studio and one-bedroom suites complete with kitchens.

We help simplify your life by providing AT&T communications in most rooms. And be sure to use the CALL ATT Calling Card for all your calls to access a range of time saving calling features. To order a card dial 1 800 CALL ATT.®

CHOICE HOTELS
INTERNATIONAL

Call 1-800-228-1AAA or your local AAA club

Georgia   North Carolina South Carolina

Published by:

AAA Publishing
1000 AAA Drive
Heathrow, FL 32746-5063

Send Written Comments To:

AAA Member Comments
Box 61, 1000 AAA Drive
Heathrow, FL 32746-5063

Advertising Rate and Circulation Information
Call: (407) 444-8280

Printed in the USA
by Quebecor Printing, Buffalo, NY

Cover: *St. Michael's / Charleston, SC*
©Mark E. Gibson

About Lodgings & Restaurants

Lodgings & Restaurants

Maps

Accommodations:

For Your Information

AAA SUPERNUMBER®
1-800-AAA-HELP

For 24-hour road service when away from home and unable to find AAA or CAA in the phone book. 1-800-955-4TDD for hearing impaired. 3

Index

When traveling away from home...

SUPERNUMBER®

1-800-AAA-HELP

a 24-hour, toll-free, Emergency Road Service information system.

It's easy to use:

Look in the white pages of the telephone book for a listing under "AAA" in the United States or "CAA" in Canada, since road service is dispatched by the local club in many communities.

If there is no listing, have your membership card handy and call:

SUPERNUMBER,

1-800-AAA-HELP, for the nearest road service facility.

SUPERNUMBER, is available in the United States and Canada 24 hours a day, but **only** for Emergency Road Service and **only** when traveling outside the area served by your home club. Contact the nearest club office regarding other services you may require.

NOTE: NOT AVAILABLE WHEN TRAVELING IN MEXICO.

Introduction

*W*E'RE *glad you selected the AAA TourBook to help you plan your trip. You can trust AAA to give you objective information; no attraction, lodging or restaurant pays for a listing. Each is listed on the basis of merit alone after being carefully evaluated by a AAA/CAA inspector or designated representative. An establishment's decision to advertise has no bearing on its inspection, evaluation or rating. Advertising for services or products does not imply AAA endorsement.*

We work hard to give you the most accurate information available. All information in this TourBook was reviewed before publication for accuracy at press time; however, changes often occur between annual editions. We've included phone numbers in the listings so that you can confirm prices and schedules.

Tell us what you think

We encourage you to tell us what we need to improve and what we have done well. We reply to thousands of letters from members every year, and your good ideas are reflected in our products and services.

Please report both pleasant and unpleasant experiences to your local AAA/CAA club, or write directly to AAA Member Comments, 1000 AAA Dr., Box 61, Heathrow, FL 32746-5063.

How the book is organized

The AAA TourBook contains two sections: attractions, and lodgings and restaurants. Both sections list towns or designated places in alphabetical order, and the attractions or facilities are then listed in alphabetical order under the appropriate town. Attractions and AAA RATED® lodgings and restaurants are listed in this book under the name of the city or town in which they physically are located or in some circumstances under the nearest recognized city or town. Use AAA/CAA maps in conjunction with this book when planning a trip.

Major metropolitan areas are organized in separate sections and have expanded treatments. A description of the primary city is presented first, followed by a listing of communities in the vicinity. These AAA/CAA Defined Metro Areas were modeled on U.S. and Canadian government definitions based on economic and social interaction among residents of the core city and surrounding communities. Cities and towns grouped under a metropolitan area's vicinity heading will have cross references where they would typically be alphabetized in the Attractions and Lodgings & Restaurants sections.

Destination areas also have been identified for regions with broad tourist appeal. Towns in these geographic areas are organized alphabetically under the destination area's title. Towns grouped under destination areas have appropriate cross-references inserted where they would normally be alphabetized in the Attractions and Lodgings & Restaurant sections.

Maps created specifically for this book have precise purposes and should be used in *conjunction* with the more complete sheet maps and Triptik maps provided by your AAA/CAA travel counselor. To ensure your complete satisfaction, use book maps as *supplementary* guides only.

What the color bars mean

In TourBooks that contain more than one state or province, you will notice the presence of bars of color along the page edges. The purpose of these bars is to color code corresponding state or province sections. For example, the New Jersey Attractions section will contain the same color bar code as the New Jersey Lodgings & Restaurants section. This coding allows the reader to conveniently flip back and forth between the pertinent sections of the state.

Now AAA can help you shop overseas without any exchanges.

With delivery of foreign cash to your door.

Whether you're going for the shopping, the culture, the cuisine, or to see the sights, the last place you want to end up on your vacation is waiting in line, wasting precious vacation time exchanging your dollars and worrying about the fees. That's why AAA and American Express® are offering this exciting new service. With just a phone call, you can now order all the foreign cash and American Express® Foreign Currency Travelers Cheques you need to take on your trip, and have it conveniently delivered to your home or office before you go.

That way, all you're exchanging is a lot of hassle for more time enjoying the vacation experience of a lifetime. To order foreign cash or American Express® Foreign Currency Travelers Cheques for your next trip, call your local AAA, today.

Travel with someone you trust.®

Travelers Cheques

About Attractions

The Attractions section of your TourBook serves as a guide to selected places rather than as a commercial, geographic or promotional encyclopedia. Communities or areas included offer something for you to do or see that sets them apart from others in the area or nation. We call these "points of interest."

Schedules and prices

All information was reviewed before publication for accuracy at press time. However, changes often occur between annual editions. We regret any inconvenience resulting from such instances, but they are beyond our control. Please use the phone numbers in the listings if you wish to confirm prices. Prices pertaining to attractions in the United States are quoted in U.S. dollars; Canadian province and territory attraction prices are quoted in Canadian dollars.

Reading the listings

Any attraction with a separate heading has been approved by a AAA/CAA field inspector or designated AAA/CAA representative. An attraction's quality is reflected in the length and scope of its general description. We have placed a star (★) before attractions of exceptional interest and quality. An index to starred attractions appears with the orientation map. *(See Maps, below.)* Stand alone casino gambling operations—those establishments that are not contained within hotels—are not inspected and are presented for informational purposes only.

In most cases, distances given are computed from the center of town, unless otherwise specified, using the following highway designations: I (interstate highway), US (federal highway), Hwy. (Canadian highway), SR (state route), CR (county road), FM (farm to market road), FR (forest road), MM (mile marker).

Descriptive information about the attraction follows the location description. Next come the days, hours and seasons the attraction is *open*. These may be preceded by a suggested minimum visiting time. Following are admission prices quoted *without* sales tax; children under the lowest age specified are admitted free when accompanied by an adult. Days, months and age groups written with a hyphen are *inclusive*.

Credit cards accepted for admissions or fares may be indicated at the end of the listing as follows: AE, American Express; CB, Carte Blanche; DI, Diners Club; DS, Discover; JCB, Japanese Credit Bureau; MC, MasterCard; VI, VISA. Minimum amounts that may be charged appear in parentheses when applicable.

Maps

State, province or territory orientation maps appear before the Points of Interest listings in the Attractions section. Their purpose is to illustrate the relative positions of towns, recreation facilities and starred points of interest listed in the TourBooks. Only major road networks are portrayed on these maps.

Coordinates (for example: A-3) following the place or city names in the Points of Interest listings refer to this map; stars next to town names on the maps indicate the presence of highly recommended attractions. An index to starred attractions appears with or adjacent to each orientation map.

City maps show metropolitan areas where numerous attractions are concentrated. While reading an attraction description, refer to this map to see where it is located in relation to major roads, parks, airports, etc.

Walking or Self-Guiding tour maps provide an exceptional level of detail, showing specific routes corresponding to text in the TourBooks. Well-known buildings are often outlined for easier identification. Routes are well-marked with beginning and ending points as well as directional arrows.

National park maps familiarize drivers with the area in and around the park. The main features depicted are mountains, streams, hiking trails, canyons, ice fields, etc. Some of the campground sites and lodges spotted on the maps do not meet AAA/CAA criteria, but have been listed as a service to members who wish to stay at these facilities.

Admission discounts

Your AAA/CAA membership card is the key to reduced prices at many attractions because they value your patronage and respect the AAA/CAA name. A 〔SAVE〕 icon appearing in an attraction listing indicates that a discount is offered to holders of a AAA/CAA membership card, AAA MasterCard, AAA VISA or international Show Your Card & Save discount card. The discount must be at least 10% and must be offered to all age groups. **Note:** If only a senior discount is offered, the attraction will not receive the 〔SAVE〕 icon. Senior citizen rates are already listed in the normal attraction rate structure.

Whether or not a listing shows the icon, present your valid AAA or CAA membership card when purchasing tickets; some attractions not formally enrolled in the program may still give members a discount. A full list of participating attractions appears in the Indexes section of this book. Discounts are offered for the validity period noted on the title page of this book. The discount may not apply if any other price reduction is offered or if tickets are purchased through an outlet other than the attraction's ticket office. In addition, discounts may not apply during special events or particular days or seasons; phone ahead to confirm.

Some AAA/CAA clubs sell tickets for area attractions; phone the local club to confirm.

Golden passports

Citizens or permanent residents of the United States who are 62 and older can obtain Golden Age Passports for a one-time $10 fee. Golden Access Passports are free to citizens or permanent residents of the United States (regardless of age) who are medically blind or permanently disabled. Both cover entrance fees for the holder and accompanying private party to all national parks and historic sites, monuments and battlefields within the U.S. national park system, plus half off camping and other fees. Apply in person at most federally operated areas.

The Golden Eagle Passport is available to everyone, despite country of origin. It costs $50 annually and covers entrance fees for the holder and accompanying private party to all federally operated areas. Obtain the pass in person at any national park or regional office of the U.S. Park Service or Forest Service.

Count on AAA
For Financial Services
You Can Trust

Financial Services

- *Member Select[SM] Prime Access[SM] Card[1]*
- *Member Select[SM] Rewards Card[1]*
- *Auto Financing*
- *Home Equity Loans and Lines[2]*
- *Personal Loans*

- *Student Loans*
- *Market Rate Checking*
- *Money Market Accounts*
- *No-penalty Certificate of Deposit[3]*
- *Vacation Loans*
- *And More*

Products and services provided by PNC Bank, N.A., and its affiliates. Member FDIC. [1]Credit cards provided by PNC National Bank, Wilmington, DE. [2]Where available. (Not available in Texas.) [3]No withdrawal permitted for first 7 days. No penalty thereafter. Partial withdrawals not permitted.

Equal Housing Lender

Available only through participating AAA clubs.

For more information or to open an account, call
24 hours a day, 7 days a week.

1-800-680-AAA4

Chattooga River / Georgia Dept. of Industry, Trade & Tourism

Georgia

An introduction to the state's history, geography, economy and recreation

FACT AND FANCY, PAST AND PRESENT COEXIST WITH
GENIAL EASE IN GEORGIA. SCARLETT O'HARA, UNCLE
REMUS AND POGO—GEORGIANS ALL—INHABIT THE
HALLS OF FANCY. JOHN C. FREMONT, JIMMY CARTER
AND MARTIN LUTHER KING JR.—ALSO GEORGIANS—
DWELL IN THE REALMS OF HISTORIC FACT. WHILE
COSMOPOLITAN ATLANTA'S GLEAMING TOWERS ARE
INDICATIVE OF A HEALTHY PRESENT, SAVANNAH'S
ROMANTIC DEEP SOUTH ATMOSPHERE IS TESTIMONY
THAT THE BEST OF THE STATE'S PAST ALSO IS
ALIVE AND WELL.

HISTORY

Hernando de Soto's 1540 expedition was the first European incursion into the part of Cherokee and Creek lands that would become Georgia. By 1566 Spain had established Franciscan missions on St. Simons and Jekyll islands and the adjacent mainland. The British settlers to the north eyed these Spanish settlements and decided a safeguard was needed against possible encroachment.

General and philanthropist James Oglethorpe was granted a charter for a colony at Savannah in 1733. His plan was to transport imprisoned debtors to Georgia where they could rehabilitate themselves by profitable labor while making money for the colony's proprietors in the process. Oglethorpe directed the affairs of the colony, primarily its military operations.

Government was informal; a hoped-for economy based on wine, silk and spice production was unsuccessful, and the settlers chafed at a highly restrictive economic and social system. As protests against the proprietors' policies mounted, Oglethorpe and his trustees surrendered all power to the British government in 1752. When the crown assumed control, several restrictions—notably one prohibiting slavery—were lifted.

Substantial settlement of Georgia began with the pre-Revolutionary thrust of westward migration. Settlement expanded rapidly after the Revolution, particularly through the cotton counties of central Georgia.

White settlers' acquisition of American Indian land during this period cleared the way for agriculture and transportation development, but it was a traumatic time in the state's history. The forced relocation of the Creeks and Cherokees beyond the Mississippi River came to be known as the Trail of Tears.

Progress in the 19th century was inevitably disrupted by the issue of slavery. Compounding the problem were political actions such as the Compromise of 1850, an uneasy patchwork of concessions designed to placate both the pro-slavery South and the anti-slavery North, and the debate over whether Kansas would be admitted to the Union as a free or a slave state. In January 1861, following the election of Abraham Lincoln, Georgia seceded.

The Civil War in Georgia began and ended in Savannah. When the Georgia volunteers seized the federal defense work of Fort Pulaski at Savannah a few months before secession, the state was rich and confident. Three bloody years later when Gen. William Tecumseh Sherman halted there after his march to the sea, four-fifths of Georgia's wealth and most of its young men had disappeared.

Reconstruction, however, was relatively moderate. The state was readmitted to the Union in 1870; its representatives re-entered Congress in 1871. A home-rule constitution was withheld until 1877 when the threat of Federal military intervention had ended.

Race relations have remained a controlling factor in the state despite the Supreme Court decision to end school segregation in 1954. In 1964 when President Lyndon B. Johnson supported the Civil Rights Act, a Republican won the majority of presidential votes in Georgia for the first time in history.

Amid the turbulence one of the greatest leaders of the civil rights movement, Dr. Martin

Fast Facts

POPULATION: 7,353,200.

AREA: 58,876 square miles; ranks 21st.

CAPITAL: Atlanta.

HIGHEST POINT: 4,784 ft., Brasstown Bald.

LOWEST POINT: Sea level, Atlantic Ocean.

TIME ZONE: Eastern. DST.

MINIMUM AGE FOR DRIVERS: 16.

SEAT BELT/CHILD RESTRAINT LAWS: Seat belts required for driver and all passengers. Seat belts may be used for children over 3; child restraints required for ages 3 and under.

HELMETS FOR MOTORCYCLISTS: Required.

RADAR DETECTORS: Permitted.

FIREARMS LAWS: Vary by state and/or county. Contact the State Attorney General's Office, 40 Capitol Sq., Atlanta, GA 30334-1300; phone (404) 624-4586.

HOLIDAYS: Jan. 1; Martin Luther King Jr.'s Birthday, Jan. (third Mon.); Washington's Birthday, Feb. (3rd Mon.); Confederate Memorial Day, Apr. 26; Memorial Day, May (last Mon.); July 4; Labor Day; Columbus Day, Oct. (2nd Mon.); Veterans Day, Nov. 11; Thanksgiving; Dec. 25.

TAXES: Georgia levies a statewide sales tax of 4 percent, with local options for additional increments.

STATE INFORMATION CENTERS are near Augusta, Columbus, Kingsland, Lavonia, Plains, Ringgold, Savannah, Sylvania, Tallapoosa, Valdosta and West Point; open daily 8:30-5:30.

Luther King Jr., carried his dream for justice from Atlanta to the nation and the world. Jimmy Carter, Georgia native and former governor, brought 4 years of new approaches to Washington, D.C., when he was elected president in 1976.

GEOGRAPHY

The largest state east of the Mississippi River, Georgia sweeps from the Appalachian Mountains to the Atlantic shore. The southernmost portions of the Blue Ridge Mountains extend into north-central and northeastern Georgia, rising to the state's highest elevations. The Appalachian Trail, beloved by serious hikers, begins in Georgia.

In the northwest near the Tennessee border a valley and ridge area predominates. The rolling land slopes gradually southeastward below the mountains, with peaks such as Stone Mountain near Atlanta rising sharply from the generally level terrain.

Most of the state's primary rivers originate in this region—the Chattahoochee, which marks the lower Alabama-Georgia boundary; the Ocmulgee and Oconee, which become the Altamaha, emptying into the Atlantic north of Brunswick; and the many-branched Savannah, which designates the South Carolina border. All are navigable below the fall line.

Along the fall region sandy hills form a narrow, irregular belt. Below these hills the Coastal Plain, covering more than half the state, extends to the 100-mile-long Atlantic coast. Separated from the mainland by a maze of channels, lagoons and inlets are the picturesque Golden Isles, a popular vacation spot.

The 435,000-acre Okefenokee Swamp occupies the southeastern corner of Georgia and spills over into northern Florida. One of the last natural swamp areas in the United States, it is the source of the Suwannee and St. Marys rivers, which drain into the Gulf of Mexico and the Atlantic Ocean respectively. Within the swamp's recesses are many scenic waterways and threatened wildlife species.

ECONOMY

Georgia's rapid industrialization in the second half of the 20th century has redefined such words as "farm" and "machinery," making "agribusiness" a more accurate term. Although there are more industrial workers than farm workers, a great majority of the state's industrial jobs depend on farm or forest products.

The textile plant is the symbol of manufacturing in Georgia, accounting for nearly $10.2 billion in state revenue. Other leading industries in order of importance are tourism, transportation equipment, processed foods, paper and chemicals. Georgia forests, covering approximately two-thirds of the state, help feed a paper-hungry world.

Georgia leads the nation in pulpwood production and naval stores output: turpentine, resin and other pine tree byproducts. The state also produces automobiles, machinery and furniture. Manufacturing is concentrated in Atlanta, Augusta and Savannah; Cairo, Dalton and Marietta are other important industrial centers.

Though justly famous, Georgia peaches do not constitute the sum of the state's agricultural output. The mild climate and long growing season are conducive to a wide variety of crops. Georgia ranks first in the United States in the production of peanuts and pecans and second in the production of eggs and broilers. Also grown on some 49,000 farms are cotton, onions, rye, sweet potatoes, tobacco, tomatoes, sorghum silage and watermelons.

The discovery of gold near Dahlonega in 1828 triggered the nation's first major gold rush, and mining has continued since. Clays and limestone are considered modern gold. Georgia is the largest producer of kaolin, a white clay taken from vast pits in the middle of the state for use in paper coating, ceramics and aluminum.

Limestone from northwestern Georgia is used to manufacture cement and lime. The crystalline rocks of the piedmont in Pickens County yield marble, and fine monumental granite is found around Elberton. Bartow, in east-central Georgia,

For Your Information

FURTHER INFORMATION FOR VISITORS:

Georgia Department of Industry, Trade
and Tourism
P.O. Box 1776
Atlanta, GA 30301
(404) 656-3590 or
(800) 847-4842

RECREATION INFORMATION:

Department of Natural Resources
Division of Parks, Recreation and
Historic Sites
205 Butler St. S.E., Suite 1258
Atlanta, GA 30334
(404) 656-3530

FISHING AND HUNTING REGULATIONS:

Department of Natural Resources
Division of Game and Fish
205 Butler St. S.E., Suite 1258
Atlanta, GA 30334
(706) 557-3024 (fisheries)
(706) 557-3022 (game management)

NATIONAL FOREST INFORMATION:

U.S. Forest Service
1720 Peachtree Rd. N.W.
Atlanta, GA 30367
(404) 347-2384
(800) 280-2267 (reservations)

is in an area containing barite, ochre and some iron. The state also mines fuller's earth, bauxite, talc, asbestos and feldspar.

RECREATION

From luxurious resorts on Jekyll, St. Simons and Sea islands to quiet backwoods trails, Georgia offers a variety of leisure activities and settings. Recreation centers include Tybee Island; St. Simons Island; Callaway Gardens at Pine Mountain north of Columbus; Lake Seminole in the southwestern corner of the state; Lake Lanier, about 45 miles northeast of Atlanta; and Stone Mountain Park near Atlanta.

There is excellent **saltwater fishing** in the labyrinth of coastal channels and in the surf off the fine beaches of the Sea Islands. **Freshwater fishing** enthusiasts will find bass, bream, shad and catfish in the winding southern rivers and marshes. Trout inhabit the northern streams. Most fishing waters offer equally good **boating**, especially the large reservoirs.

Georgia shares West Point and Walter F. George lakes with Alabama, and J. Strom Thurmond, Hartwell and Richard B. Russell lakes with South Carolina. Entirely within the state are Allatoona Lake near Atlanta, Jackson Lake near Jackson, Lake Sidney Lanier near Buford, Lake Sinclair near Milledgeville and Nottely Lake near Blairsville.

The Chattahoochee River National Recreation Area, extending from Lake Lanier to northwest Atlanta, preserves the river's natural beauty and offers fishing, **rafting** and **canoeing.** The Chattooga National Wild and Scenic River threads through the Chattahoochee National Forest, offering opportunities for rafting, canoeing and **hiking.**

The 58 units of the state park system encompass all types of terrain, recreational facilities and historic sites, ranging from picnic locations to highly developed areas with overnight accommodations. Although no entrance fees are charged for state parks, there is a $2 parking fee Thursday through Tuesday, and user fees are levied for swimming areas and campgrounds.

Camping sites in state parks are available on a first-come-first-served basis with a 2-week limit. More than 20 of the state parks also offer housekeeping cabins that can be reserved up to 11 months in advance.

A minimum rental period of 1 week applies from June through August; a 2-day minimum applies during the rest of the year. Plan to set up camp no later than 8 p.m. Reservations for both campsites and cottages are made through the offices of the individual parks between 8 a.m. and 5 p.m.; phone numbers and addresses can be obtained from the Department of Natural Resources main office *(see For Your Information box).*

For detailed information about camping and trailer areas, both public and private, *see the AAA Southeastern CampBook.* **Note:** Pets are permitted in Georgia's state parks only in designated areas.

Throughout the TourBook, you may notice a Recreational Activities heading with bulleted listings of recreation-oriented establishments listed underneath. Since normal AAA inspection criteria cannot be applied, these establishments are presented for information only. Age, height and weight restrictions may apply. Reservations are often recommended and sometimes required. Visitors should phone or write the attraction for additional information, and the address and phone number are provided for this purpose.

RECREATION AREAS	MAP LOCATION	CAMPING	PICNICKING	HIKING TRAILS	BOATING	BOAT RAMP	BOAT RENTAL	FISHING	SWIMMING	PETS ON LEASH	BICYCLE TRAILS	NATURE PROGS.	VISITOR CENTER	LODGE/CABINS	FOOD SERVICE
NATIONAL FORESTS *(See place listing)* Chattahoochee and Oconee 862,368 acres. Central and northern Georgia.		•	•	•	•	•		•	•	•		•	•		
NATIONAL RECREATION AREA *(See place listing)* Chattahoochee River (B-2) 4,100 acres n. of Atlanta.			•	•	•	•		•		•	•	•	•		•
NATIONAL SEASHORE *(See place listing)* Cumberland Island (F-6) 37,000 acres 8 mi. e. of St. Marys.		•	•	•				•	•			•	•		
ARMY CORPS OF ENGINEERS Allatoona Lake (B-2) 25,806 acres 6 mi. s.e. of Cartersville off I-75. Historic. Water skiing.	39	•	•		•	•	•	•	•				•	•	•
Carters Lake (A-2) 3,442 acres 34 mi. n. of Cartersville off US 411 to Old US 411. Water skiing.	40	•	•	•	•	•	•	•	•			•	•	•	•
George W. Andrews Lake (E-2) 1,540 acres 1 mi. e. of Columbia, Ala., on the state line.	56	•	•		•	•		•							•

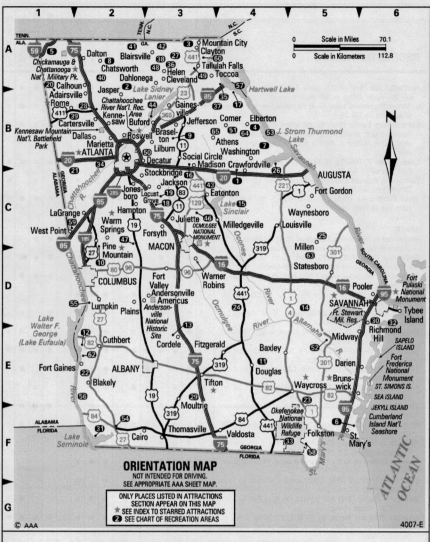

ORIENTATION MAP
NOT INTENDED FOR DRIVING.
SEE APPROPRIATE AAA SHEET MAP.

ONLY PLACES LISTED IN ATTRACTIONS
SECTION APPEAR ON THIS MAP
★ SEE INDEX TO STARRED ATTRACTIONS
❷ SEE CHART OF RECREATION AREAS

© AAA   4007-E

INDEX TO STARRED ATTRACTIONS
ATTRACTIONS AND PLACES OF EXCEPTIONAL INTEREST AND QUALITY

The Antebellum Plantation - see Stone Mountain

Archibald Smith Plantation Home - see Roswell

Atlanta History Center - see Atlanta

Callaway Gardens - see Pine Mountain

Chickamauga and Chattanooga National Military Park -
   see place listing

Fort Pulaski National Monument - see place listing

Georgia Agrirama - see Tifton

Georgia's Stone Mountain Park - see Stone Mountain

Hofwyl-Broadfield Plantation - see Brunswick

Little White House State Historic Site - see Warm Springs

Oak Hill and The Martha Berry Museum -
   see Rome

Ocmulgee National Monument -
   see place listing

Okefenokee Swamp Park - see Waycross

Owens-Thomas House and Museum -
   see Savannah

Savannah History Museum -   see Savannah

Six Flags Over Georgia - see Atlanta

Stone Mountain - see Atlanta

The World of Coca-Cola - see Atlanta

RECREATION AREAS	MAP LOCATION	CAMPING	PICNICKING	HIKING TRAILS	BOATING	BOAT RAMP	BOAT RENTAL	FISHING	SWIMMING	PETS ON LEASH	BICYCLE TRAILS	NATURE PROGS.	VISITOR CENTER	LODGE/CABINS	FOOD SERVICE
Hartwell Lake (A-4) 56,000 acres 6 mi. n. of Hartwell on US 29. Water skiing; power plant tours.	57	•	•		•	•	•	•	•	•		•	•	•	•
J. Strom Thurmond Lake (B-4) 70,000 acres 20 mi. n.w. of Augusta on SR 28.	53	•	•	•	•	•	•	•	•	•		•	•	•	•
Lake Sidney Lanier (B-2) 56,000 acres. Golf (18 holes), miniature golf, tennis, water skiing; horse rental, waterslide. *(See Buford in Atlanta and Vicinity and Gainesville)*	44	•	•	•	•	•	•	•	•	•		•	•	•	•
Lake Walter F. George (E-1) 45,000 acres 2 mi. n. of Fort Gaines off SR 39.	62	•	•		•	•	•	•	•	•		•	•	•	•
Richard B. Russell Lake (B-4) 26,500 acres 20 mi. e. of Elberton on SR 72.	64	•	•	•	•	•		•	•	•			•	•	•
West Point Lake (C-1) 25,900 acres on the Alabama state line at West Point.	59	•	•	•	•	•		•	•	•		•	•		•
STATE															
Alexander H. Stephens Memorial (C-4) 1,189 acres at Crawfordville on US 278 and SR 22. Historic.	1	•	•	•				•	•	•		•	•		
Amicalola Falls (A-2) 1,020 acres 15 mi. w. of Dahlonega on SR 52 near jct. with SR 183. Scenic.	2	•	•	•						•		•	•	•	•
Black Rock Mountain (A-3) 1,502 acres 3 mi. n. of Clayton via US 23/441. Scenic.	3	•	•	•				•		•		•	•	•	
Bobby Brown (B-4) 665 acres 21 mi. s.e. of Elberton off SR 72. Water skiing.	4	•	•		•	•		•	•	•					
Cloudland Canyon (A-1) 2,120 acres 25 mi. n.w. of La Fayette off SR 136. Scenic.	5	•	•	•						•			•	•	
Crooked River (F-5) 1,368 acres 12 mi. e. of Kingsland via SR 40. Water skiing.	6	•	•	•	•	•		•	•	•		•	•	•	
Elijah Clark (B-4) 447 acres 6 mi. n.e. of Lincolnton on US 378. Historic. Water skiing.	7	•	•		•	•		•	•	•		•	•	•	
Florence Marina (D-2) 150 acres 4 mi. s. of Omaha on SR 39C. Water skiing.	55	•	•		•	•	•	•		•		•	•	•	
Fort McAllister (D-6) 1,690 acres 10 mi. e. of I-95 on State Spur 144. Historic. Water skiing.	30	•	•		•	•		•		•		•	•	•	
Fort Mountain (A-2) 1,930 acres 7 mi. e. of Chatsworth off SR 52. Historic.	8	•	•	•				•	•	•		•	•	•	
Fort Yargo (B-3) 1,850 acres 1 mi. s. of Winder on SR 81. Historic.	9	•	•	•	•	•		•	•	•		•	•	•	•
Franklin D. Roosevelt (D-2) 10,000 acres 5 mi. s.e. of Pine Mountain off US 27.	10	•	•	•				•	•	•		•	•	•	
General Coffee (E-4) 1,490 acres 6 mi. e. of Douglas on SR 32.	11	•	•	•				•	•	•		•	•		
George L. Smith, II (D-5) 1,355 acres 4 mi. s.e. of Twin City off SR 23.	63	•	•		•	•		•		•			•		
George T. Bagby (E-2) 300 acres 3 mi. n. of Fort Gaines off SR 39. Water skiing.	12	•	•		•	•		•	•	•				•	•
Georgia Veterans Memorial (E-3) 1,322 acres 9 mi. w. of Cordele on US 280. Historic. Water skiing; exhibits. *(See Cordele)*	13	•	•					•	•	•		•	•	•	•
Gordonia-Alatamaha (D-5) 280 acres on US 280 near Reidsville.	14	•	•		•	•		•	•	•			•		
Hamburg (C-4) 750 acres 6 mi. n.e. of Warthen via Hamburg Rd. on SR 102.	15	•	•		•	•	•	•		•		•	•		
Hard Labor Creek (C-3) 5,805 acres 2 mi. n. of Rutledge off I-20. Golf (18 holes).	16	•	•	•	•	•		•	•	•			•	•	
Hart (B-4) 147 acres 3 mi. n.e. of Hartwell off US 29. Water skiing.	17	•	•		•	•		•	•	•					
High Falls (C-3) 995 acres 11 mi. n. of Forsyth just off I-75 at High Falls Rd. exit.	18	•	•	•	•	•		•	•	•		•	•		•
Indian Springs (C-3) 523 acres 5 mi. s.e. of Jackson on SR 42. Historic. *(See Jackson)*	19	•	•	•	•	•	•	•	•	•		•	•	•	•
James H. "Sloppy" Floyd (B-1) 269 acres 3 mi. s.e. of Summerville off US 27.	20	•	•		•	•		•		•			•		
John Tanner (C-1) 136 acres 6 mi. w. of Carrollton off SR 16.	21	•	•	•	•			•	•	•		•		•	
Kolomoki Mounds (E-2) 1,293 acres. Miniature golf. *(See Blakely)*	22	•	•	•	•	•	•	•	•	•		•	•		•

RECREATION AREAS	MAP LOCATION	CAMPING	PICNICKING	HIKING TRAILS	BOATING	BOAT RAMP	BOAT RENTAL	FISHING	SWIMMING	PETS ON LEASH	BICYCLE TRAILS	NATURE PROGS.	VISITOR CENTER	LODGE/CABINS	FOOD SERVICE
Laura S. Walker (E-5) 306 acres 10 mi. s.e. of Waycross near US 84. Water skiing.	23	●	●		●	●		●	●	●		●			●
Little Ocmulgee (D-4) 1,397 acres 2 mi. n. of McRae on US 441. Scenic. Golf (18 holes), water skiing.	24	●	●		●	●		●	●	●			●	●	●
Magnolia Springs (C-5) 948 acres 5 mi. n. of Millen on US 25.	25	●	●	●	●	●		●	●	●					●
Mistletoe (C-4) 1,920 acres 10 mi. n. of Appling off SR 150. Water skiing.	26	●	●	●	●	●	●	●	●	●			●		●
Moccasin Creek (A-3) 32 acres 16 mi. s.w. of Clayton on SR 197. Water skiing.	27	●	●	●	●	●		●		●					
Red Top Mountain (B-2) 1,950 acres 2 mi. e. of I-75 Red Top exit. Miniature golf, water skiing.	28	●	●	●	●	●		●	●	●				●	
Reed Bingham (E-3) 1,620 acres 6 mi. w. of Adel off SR 37. Water skiing.	29	●	●	●	●	●		●	●	●					●
Seminole (F-2) 343 acres 16 mi. s. of Donalsonville off SR 39. Water skiing.	31	●	●		●	●		●	●	●			●	●	●
Skidaway Island (D-6) 506 acres 6 mi. s.e. of Savannah; take I-16 to SR 21.	32	●	●	●				●	●	●		●	●		
Stephen C. Foster (F-5) 80 acres 18 mi. n.e. of Fargo on SR 177.	33	●	●		●	●	●	●		●			●	●	●
Sweetwater Creek (B-2) 1,986 acres 15 mi. w. of Atlanta off I-20. Historic.	34		●	●	●			●		●					
Tallulah Gorge (A-3) 300 acres at Tallulah Falls. Nature trails, playground. *(See Tallulah Falls)*	60	●	●	●				●	●	●			●		
Tugaloo (B-4) 393 acres 6 mi. n. of Lavonia off SR 328. Water skiing.	35	●	●		●	●		●	●	●		●	●		●
Unicoi (A-3) 1,081 acres 2 mi. n.e. of Helen via SR 356.	36	●	●	●			●	●	●	●		●	●	●	●
Victoria Bryant (B-4) 406 acres 4 mi. w. of Royston off US 29 and SR 327. Golf (nine holes).	37	●	●	●				●	●	●		●	●		●
Vogel (A-3) 250 acres 11 mi. s. of Blairsville on US 19/129. *(See Blairsville)*	38	●	●	●				●	●	●		●	●	●	
Watson Mill Bridge (B-4) 144 acres. Historic. *(See Comer)*	51	●	●	●				●		●					
OTHER															
Earl May Boat Basin and Park (F-2) 600 acres on W. Shotwell St. in Bainbridge. Tennis; exhibits.	54	●	●	●	●	●		●	●	●			●		
Georgia's Stone Mountain Park (B-3) 3,200 acres. Golf (36 holes), miniature golf, tennis; waterslides. *(See Stone Mountain in Atlanta and Vicinity)*	50	●	●	●	●	●	●	●	●	●			●	●	●
Lake Blue Ridge (A-2) 3,290 acres 4 mi. e. of Blue Ridge via US 76 and CR 23.	41	●	●	●	●	●		●	●	●					
Lake Chatuge (A-3) 6,950 acres 3 mi. s.w. of Hiawassee via US 76 and SR 288.	42	●	●		●	●		●	●	●					
Lake Grace (E-5) 250 acres 8 mi. w. of Jesup on SR 203. Water skiing.	52	●			●	●		●	●						
Lake Oconee (C-3) 19,255 acres 7 mi. e. of Eatonton. Water skiing.	43	●	●		●	●	●	●	●	●				●	●
Lake Sinclair (C-3) 15,330 acres n.e. of Milledgeville on SR 441. Marinas.	46	●	●		●	●		●	●	●				●	●
Lake Tobesofkee (C-2) 1,750 acres 12 mi. w. of Macon off I-475 at SR 74 and Thomaston Rd. Tennis, water skiing.	47	●	●		●	●	●	●	●	●	●		●		●
Lake Winfield Scott (A-3) 18 acres 4 mi. e. of Suches on SR 180.	48	●	●	●	●			●	●	●					
Rabun Beach (A-3) 934 acres 13 mi. s. of Clayton via US 23, SR 15 and CR 10.	49	●	●	●	●	●		●	●	●					●
Sandy Creek Park (B-3) 634 acres 2.5 mi. n. of Athens bypass off US 441.	65	●	●		●	●		●	●	●		●	●		
Suwannee Canal Recreation Area (F-5) 396,000 acres. *(See Folkston)*	58		●	●	●	●	●	●		●		●	●		●

CONSULT YOUR LOCAL ⊛ OFFICE
FOR ALL YOUR TRAVEL NEEDS.

Points of Interest

ADAIRSVILLE (B-1) pop. 2,100

[SAVE] **BARNSLEY GARDENS** is at 597 Barnsley Gardens Rd.; go 1.5 mi. w. on SR 140, 5.5 mi. s. on Hall Station Rd., then 2.5 mi. w. The 30-acre estate features rolling hills, English boxwood gardens, water and bog gardens, fruit trees, a fernery and hundreds of roses. A museum housed in an 1850s manor house features Civil War memorabilia. Food is available.

Allow 1 hour, 30 minutes minimum. Tues.-Sun. 10-6, Mar.-June; 10-5, July-Dec.; 11-3, rest of year. Last admission 1 hour before closing. Closed Dec. 25. Admission $6.50; over 61, $6; ages 13-17, $4. AE, DS, MC, VI. Phone (770) 773-7480.

ALBANY (E-2) pop. 78,100, elev. 210'

The site that eventually became Albany was bought in 1836 by a Connecticut man who hired surveyors to plat a town. Later that year Nelson Tift and a group of companions brought supplies up the Flint River from Apalachicola, Fla., and began to construct log buildings. The town took its name from the city in New York that also was at a river's head of navigation.

The River Day Festival, held in April at Chehaw Park, features arts and crafts. The Chehaw Indian Festival, held the third weekend in May, includes native dances as well as hide-tanning and arrow-making demonstrations.

Outside town at Lake Worth, Chehaw Wild Animal Park covers 293 acres of 779-acre Chehaw Park on SR 91, 1.2 miles north of US 19/82/SR 50. The park features animals of the African savannah in surroundings resembling their natural habitat. There also are nature trails and camping facilities.

Off Radium Springs Road is the northern end of 30 miles of fossil sand dunes, considered by some geologists to have once marked the northern edge of the Gulf of Mexico.

Albany Area Chamber of Commerce and Welcome Center: 225 W. Broad Ave., Albany, GA 31701; phone (912) 434-8700.

ALBANY MUSEUM OF ART, 311 Meadowlark Dr., has collections of 19th- and 20th-century American and European art as well as traditional African art. The museum also features temporary traveling exhibits. Tues.-Sat. 10-5 (also Wed. 5-7), Sun. 1-4; closed major holidays. Free. Phone (912) 439-8400.

AMERICUS (D-2) pop. 16,500, elev. 360′

HABITAT FOR HUMANITY INTERNATIONAL is at 322 W. Lamar St. Tours of the international headquarters include a visit to International Village, which has examples of different types of housing used around the world, and a van tour to local sites where the organization has built housing.

Habitat for Humanity works in partnership with volunteers, churches and synagogues, organizations and needy people to help build and renovate affordable housing. Tours are given Mon.-Fri. at 8, 10, 1 and 3. Free. Phone (912) 924-6935, ext. 153.

ANDERSONVILLE (D-3) pop. 300, elev. 394′

ANDERSONVILLE CIVIL WAR VILLAGE, .2 mi. e. on SR 49, is a restored village that once was the point of disembarkation for Civil War prisoners on their way to Andersonville, the Confederate prison. A numbered walking tour of the village begins at the welcome center. Highlights include a pioneer farm, an old log church and the Civil War Drummer Boy Museum, which is open by appointment only.

The Andersonville Historic Fair, the first weekend in October, features old-time craftspeople, a parade, military bands and a flea market. Food and picnic facilities are available. Allow 1 hour minimum. Daily 9-5; closed Dec. 25. Free. Phone (912) 924-2558.

ANDERSONVILLE NATIONAL HISTORIC SITE (D-3)

Andersonville National Historic Site encompasses the Andersonville National Cemetery and the grounds of what was probably the Civil War's most infamous prison. The site is 10 miles northeast of Americus on SR 49.

Begun in December 1863, the Andersonville prison structure consisted of 20-foot logs, 8 to 12 inches thick, set vertically 5 feet in the ground to form an almost impenetrable stockade encircling 26.5 acres. Inside this enclosure was a line prisoners were not permitted to cross under penalty of death. A creek was the main water supply and eventually, because of contamination, a prime source of illness and death among the prisoners.

Although built to accommodate 10,000 prisoners, Andersonville at one time confined more than 32,000. The impoverished Confederate government was unable to supply inmates with the bare necessities, and the mortality rate soared. Although prison commander Capt. Henry Wirz was powerless to prevent the overcrowding, after the war he was convicted by a military tribunal and hanged for conspiring to murder Union war prisoners.

Andersonville commemorates those who have been prisoners of war in defense of this nation. More than 16,000 veterans and their dependents are buried at the site. On the grounds is Providence Spring, which reputedly gushed forth in answer to the prayers of thirsty prisoners. The remains of wells and escape tunnels still exist. Two corners and the north gate of the prison stockade have been rebuilt.

The visitor center at the entrance presents a slide show and displays artifacts related to Andersonville and the Civil War. The National Prisoner of War Museum contains exhibits about prisoners of war from the Revolutionary through the Persian Gulf wars. Picnicking is permitted in designated areas. Site open daily 8-5; museum 8:30-5. Free. Phone (912) 924-0343.

ATHENS (B-4) pop. 45,700, elev. 800′

Athens, the largest city in the rolling piedmont of northeastern Georgia, has many buildings that exemplify the Greek Revival architectural style so popular in the Old South. A house and garden tour is offered in mid-April by the Athens-Clarke Heritage Foundation; phone (706) 353-1801.

The double-barreled cannon in City Hall Plaza was cast at the Athens Foundry during the Civil War. Probably the only one of its kind, this unusual Civil War relic was intended to maximize damage to the enemy by firing two balls joined by a chain. Legend has it that the chain broke during the weapon's only firing and the cannonballs went their separate ways, destroying a cabin and a cow.

Athens' most unusual property owner must be the white oak that stands in a square at Dearing

RackUpThe Miles.
ReapThe Rewards.

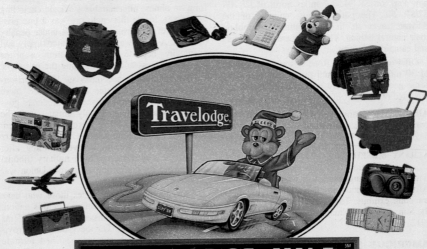

TRAVELODGE MILES℠
The Guest Rewards Program

Hit the road to exceptional value! At Travelodge our great value starts with a comfortable room at a very affordable rate. Then we add lots of special extras* like free fresh-brewed in-room coffee, a free lobby newspaper, free cable TV including movies, news and sports, and no long distance access charges. **And now there's Travelodge Miles,** our new improved Guest Rewards program. Start racking up Travelodge Miles℠ and you can earn a Free Night's Stay,† frequent flyer airline miles, or your choice of dozens of other great new Guest Rewards — everything from cameras to crystal — fast and easy. So call us now for reservations, and get ready for a very rewarding travel experience!

For Reservations Call:
1-800-367-2250

and Finley streets. The owner of the oak deeded the huge tree possession of itself and all the land within 8 feet in appreciation of its beauty and shade. The original tree was destroyed by a storm in 1942 and another was grown from one of its acorns on the same site. The legal rights of "The Tree That Owns Itself" have never been questioned.

Athens Convention and Visitors Bureau: 300 N. Thomas St., Athens, GA 30601; phone (706) 546-1805.

Self-guiding tours: Brochures and maps detailing a walking tour are available at the Athens Welcome Center, 280 E. Dougherty St.; phone (706) 353-1820. The center is in the Church-Waddel-Brumby House, a Federal-style house built in 1820.

NAVY SUPPLY CORPS MUSEUM is 2 mi. e. of the Athens bypass, off the Athens/Jefferson Rd. exit at the corner of Prince and Oglethorpe aves. Housed in the Carnegie Library on the Navy Supply Corps School campus, the museum features ship models, historic uniforms, mess hall cooking equipment, paintings and memorabilia. Allow 30 minutes minimum. Mon.-Fri. 9-5; closed federal holidays. Free. Phone (706) 354-7349.

TAYLOR-GRADY HOUSE, 634 Prince Ave., is a Greek Revival mansion built in the mid-1840s by Gen. Robert Taylor, a planter and cotton merchant. In 1863 the house was purchased by the family of Henry W. Grady, who became managing editor of the *Atlanta Constitution* and was considered by many to be the spokesman of the New South. Grady was an impressive orator who stressed the importance of reconciliation between the North and South after the Civil War.

The house has been restored and is furnished in period style. Allow 30 minutes minimum. Tours are available Mon.-Fri. 9-1 and 2:30-5; closed holidays. Donations. Phone (706) 549-8688.

UNIVERSITY OF GEORGIA campus can be entered from Broad St. through a late 19th-century arch that symbolizes the state seal of Georgia. Founded in 1785, it is among the nation's first chartered state universities. Visitors can stroll the campus and view historic structures, most of which were built before 1850. The Collegiate Tennis Hall of Fame, at Henry Feild Tennis Sta-

dium, pays tribute to collegiate tennis players and is open during tennis matches. Phone (706) 542-3000.

Butts-Mehre Heritage Hall, at Pinecrest Dr. and Lumpkin St., is a modern athletic complex dedicated to two former coaches of the Georgia Bulldogs. The Heritage Museum on the third and fourth floors contains exhibits honoring Georgia athletes. Displays include Heisman and National Championship trophies, retired jerseys and videotapes that replay great moments in the state's sports history.

Tickets to most university athletic events can be purchased on the third floor. Allow 30 minutes minimum. Mon.-Fri. 8-5, Sat. 2-5; closed major holidays. Free. Phone (706) 542-9094.

Garden Club Headquarters of Georgia and Founders Memorial Garden, 325 S. Lumpkin St., honors the founders of the first garden club in America. The grounds include the Serpentine Garden and a restored house with period furnishings. Allow 30 minutes minimum. House open Mon.-Fri. 9-noon and 1-4; grounds open daily dawn-dusk. Donations. Phone (706) 542-3631.

The Georgia Museum of Art is on the East Campus quadrangle. The museum was founded in 1945 when Alfred H. Holbrook donated his collection of 100 American paintings to the university.

Now the collection contains more than 7,000 works: 19th- and 20th-century American paintings, Italian Renaissance paintings and an extensive collection of prints and drawings by American, European and Oriental masters. Allow 1 hour minimum. Tues.-Sat. 10-5 (also Fri. 5-9), Sun. 1-5; closed major holidays. Free. Phone (706) 542-3254.

State Botanical Gardens of Georgia, 2450 S. Milledge Ave., is a 313-acre cultural and recreational facility on the Middle Oconee River. Along the nature trails are many varieties of native plants, flowers and trees. The rose garden usually blooms from May to October.

A visitor center and conservatory complex that displays exotic plants is the site for concerts, lectures and art exhibits. In addition there are many specialty gardens. Food is available. Allow 30 minutes minimum. Grounds open daily 8-dusk. Visitor center open Mon.-Sat. 9-4:30, Sun. 11:30-4:30; closed major holidays. Free. Phone (706) 542-1244.

Atlanta
and Vicinity

Atlanta, capital of Georgia, is the commercial, industrial and financial giant of the Southeast. It is crisscrossed with crowded expressways and throbs with teeming industry, yet manages to maintain a gracious air of Southern living. At its center towering skyscrapers rise along streets with names evocative of the Old South. Throughout the city many trees and shrubs lend an ever present note of green.

Atlanta began in 1837 as a railroad surveyor's stake in a pine clearing. The city rapidly grew into an important railway and manufacturing center, becoming the Confederate arsenal during the Civil War. Reduced to a smoking ruin by Gen. William Tecumseh Sherman's occupation in 1864, the city drew upon its unconquerable spirit and the wise use of carpetbagger money to again become a booming commercial center.

Image Copyright © 1995 / PhotoDisc, Inc.

Rapid growth has continued unabated for more than a century. Due to active urban renewal and the fact that few of its buildings predate the Civil War, Atlanta has suffered less from urban blight than most U.S. cities. Evidence of this good fortune is reflected in the burgeoning skyline; however, there are still reminders of an earlier Atlanta and of a city closer to the Old South and its small towns. The 50-year-old Varsity, a drive-in restaurant near Georgia Tech., stands in stark contrast to the chrome and glass skyscrapers that now surround it.

The CNN Center at Marietta Street and Techwood Drive includes broadcast studios for the Cable News Network as well as shops, restaurants and the Omni sports coliseum. Just across Marietta Street is Centennial Olympic Park, a 21-acre landscaped greenspace that is the focal point of downtown Atlanta; sculptures, walkways and the Fountain of the Rings grace the park, which was the largest single facility of the 1996 Olympics. The World Congress Center on International Boulevard is a huge exhibition hall and convention center. The mammoth Atlanta Merchandise Mart and a complex of skyscrapers comprise Peachtree Center.

Some 1,800 industrial plants manufacture more than 3,500 different commodities including aircraft, automobiles, furniture, textiles, chemicals, food, paper, iron and steel. More than 400 Fortune 500 companies have offices in Atlanta, including the headquarters of Coca-Cola, which was introduced in the city in 1886. Atlanta is the Southeastern headquarters for the U.S. Public Health Service and the national headquarters of the Centers for Disease Control, United Parcel Service and the American Cancer Society.

Atlanta also leads the South in social reform. Civil rights leader Dr. Martin Luther King Jr. worked to eliminate racial discrimination in the city and throughout the nation, and Ralph McGill, publisher of the *Atlanta Constitution,* was a leading force for integration in the early 1960s. Dr. King's birthplace, church and gravesite as well as other buildings are preserved in the Martin Luther King Jr. National Historic Site (*see attraction listing p. 26*).

A tour of the suburbs is a must for any visitor, for the elegant houses and curving, wooded streets make up some of the country's most beautiful residential areas. They are especially stunning in April during the Dogwood Festival, when millions of dogwoods and azaleas burst into red, pink and white bloom.

Atlanta enjoys four definite seasons. Warm summers and mild winters permit nearly year-round golf, fishing and outdoor living—happy distractions from the ambition of a progressive, sophisticated city.

Approaches
By Car

Major highways provide speedy access to Atlanta from nearly all directions. Three interstate highways cross the Perimeter (I-285), which circles the city. I-75 (the Northwest Expressway) joins I-85 (the Northeast Expressway) just north of downtown to become the Downtown Connector (I-75/85), which passes to the east of downtown.

From the southeast I-75 becomes the South Expressway to the point south of downtown near Ted Turner Stadium, where it meets I-20 from the east (the East Expressway) and the west (the West Expressway).

Other roads also run from I-285 toward downtown. I-85 approaches the city from the southwest, joining the South Expressway within I-285. The Lakewood Freeway (SR 166) also connects the southwest portion of I-285 with the South Expressway. US 78 from the east passes Stone Mountain before crossing I-285, after which it runs into Scott Boulevard and Ponce de Leon Avenue.

Additional highways that approach the city include SR 400 (toll 50c) from the north, which crosses I-285 and ends on I-85 just north of the I-85 and I-75 connector; US 41 from the northwest, which runs into the Northside Parkway inside I-285; and US 19, which becomes Roswell Road, Peachtree Street and finally Spring Street as it moves south. Because of the profusion of expressways, be sure to use a detailed map of the city.

Getting Around

Try to time your arrival in Atlanta after rush hours when it is easier to navigate the high-speed expressways and meandering main streets. Rush hours in general are from 6:30 to 9 a.m. and from 3:30 to 7 p.m. The downtown area should be avoided by newcomers at these times; rush-hour expressway traffic both to and in the suburbs is often bumper-to-bumper. Observe posted speed limit signs.

Street System

The center of the downtown area is the Five Points Intersection, where Peachtree, Marietta, Decatur, Edgewood and Whitehall converge near the site of the original surveyor's stake. It also is where the city's four geographical divisions—N.E., N.W., S.E. and S.W.—merge.

Atlanta is not laid out in the traditional grid, so there are few rectangular blocks and square intersections. The main street is Peachtree, extending north and south through the center of the city; North and Ponce de Leon avenues are the principal east-west links. The Downtown Connector (I-75/85) skirts the business district. The East and West expressways (I-20) carry traffic from the city center.

The Informed Traveler

CITY POPULATION: 396,100   **ELEVATION:** 1,050 ft.

Whom To Call

Emergency: 911

Police (non-emergency): (404) 658-6666

Fire: (404) 659-5600

Time and Temperature: (770) 455-7141

Hospitals: Columbia Dunwoody Medical Center, (770) 454-2000; Crawford-Long, (404) 686-4411; Georgia Baptist Medical Center, (404) 265-4000; Piedmont, (404) 605-5000.

Where to Look

Newspapers

Greater Atlanta supports several daily newspapers, including the morning *Constitution*, the evening *Journal* and various suburban papers. *Creative Loafing*, a free weekly available just about everywhere, has extensive entertainment and cultural listings.

Radio and TV

Atlanta radio station WCNN (680 AM) is an all-news/weather station; WABE (90.1 FM) is programmed by National Public Radio.

The major network TV channels are 2 (ABC), 5 (FOX), 8 (PBS), 11 (NBC), 30 (PBS) and 36 (CBS). Cable listings appear in the daily newspapers.

"Teleguide Atlanta," a continuously running cable program offered in several hotels in the metropolitan area, provides information about major tourist attractions, shopping malls, historic sites and restaurants.

Visitor Information

Information about area attractions and events may be obtained from the Atlanta Convention and Visitors Bureau, 233 Peachtree St. N.E., Atlanta, GA 30303, (404) 521-6600; or the Atlanta Chamber of Commerce, 235 International Blvd. N.W., P.O. Box 1740, Atlanta, GA 30301, (404) 880-9000.

What to Wear

Temperate best describes Atlanta's weather. From November to late March, average temperatures range between a minimum of 25 degrees Fahrenheit and a maximum of 60. The thermometer occasionally falls below 15, but snow is infrequent.

Spring and fall are delightful, with temperatures between 50 and the low 70s. June, July and August are warm and humid, and daily highs often exceed 90 degrees. The wettest months are January and March; summer thunderstorms cause another rainy peak in July.

Though Peachtree Street is the main thoroughfare, there are more than 35 other streets, avenues and lanes that include the name. Do not be misled by West Peachtree Street, Peachtree Memorial Drive, Peachtree View, Peachtree Circle, Peachtree Heights, Peachtree Place, Peachtree Battle Avenue, Peachtree Hills Avenue or a similar name.

Parking

On-street parking in the downtown business district is virtually nonexistent. However, garages and lots are plentiful throughout the city, with rates usually 75c for the first half-hour or $7-$8 per day. Rates downtown, especially near the

Transportation

Air travel: Atlanta is served by William B. Hartsfield-Atlanta International Airport 9 miles southwest of the business district via the South Expressway and I-85. Rapid rail transportation to downtown Atlanta and the metropolitan area is provided by the Metropolitan Atlanta Rapid Transit Authority (MARTA). The fare is $1.50.

Limousine service is available to several downtown hotels; the fare is $8 each way or $14 round trip. Taxi fare to downtown Atlanta averages $23—more if traffic is heavy. Travel time to the business district is about 30 minutes.

Rental cars: Hertz, with offices downtown and at the airport, offers discounts to AAA members; phone (404) 530-2925 or (800) 654-3080. For listings of other agencies check the telephone directory.

Rail service: Amtrak train service is provided out of Southern Railway's Peachtree Station, known locally as Brookwood Station, at 1688 Peachtree St. N.W.; phone (800) 872-7245.

Buses: Greyhound Lines Inc., 81 International Blvd. N.W. is the major bus line serving Atlanta; phone (800) 522-6300.

Taxis: Cab companies include Checker Cab, (404) 351-1111, and Yellow, (404) 521-0200. Taxis are metered and base fare is $1.50, plus $1.20 for each additional mile. Other taxi companies are listed in the telephone directory.

Public transport: Atlanta's Metropolitan Atlanta Rapid Transit Authority (MARTA) has a 37-mile rapid rail transit system and extensive connector bus routes. Buses are available to Six Flags Over Georgia and Ted Turner Stadium. Minimum fare is $1.50. For information contact the route information center Mon.-Fri. 6 a.m.-10 p.m., Sat.-Sun. 8-4; phone (404) 848-4711.

CNN Center, the World Congress Center and the Omni complex, exceed $7 per day. Metered parking is available in other areas, but it is usually strictly enforced during business hours and violators' cars are often towed.

What To See

ATLANTA BOTANICAL GARDEN is in midtown's Piedmont Park (RR: Arts Center Station). The garden's 30 acres contain vegetable, herb, Japanese rock and rose gardens as well as walking trails through a 15-acre hardwood forest. In addition the glass-enclosed Fuqua Conservatory features tropical, Mediterranean, desert and endangered plants. Classes and workshops are offered.

Allow 1 hour minimum. Gardens open Tues.-Sun. 9-6; conservatory open Tues.-Sun. 10-6. Closed Jan. 1, Thanksgiving and Dec. 25. Admission $6; over 65, $5; students with ID $3; under 6 free. AE, MC, VI. Phone (404) 876-5859.

[SAVE] ★**ATLANTA HISTORICAL SOCIETY,** 130 W. Paces Ferry Rd. N.W., has an 83,000-square-foot museum housing exhibitions about the history of Atlanta, traditional ethnic celebrations in Atlanta's diverse communities, Southern folklife, the Civil War and African-American history. Some 32 acres of gardens and woodland trails are the setting for two historic houses: The Swan House, a 1928 Italianate villa, and Tullie Smith Farm, an 1840s plantation farmhouse complete with traditional outbuildings.

Allow 3 hours minimum. Mon.-Sat. 10-5:30, Sun. and holidays noon-5:30. Closed Jan. 1, Thanksgiving and Dec. 24-25. Last admission 1 hour before closing. Admission $7; over 65 and students with ID $5; ages 6-17, $4. Admission to historic houses $1 each. Phone (404) 814-4000.

BEN W. FORTSON JR. STATE ARCHIVES AND RECORDS BUILDING is just s.e. of the Capitol at 330 Capitol Ave. S.E. The 17-story building houses historical exhibits, Civil War records and state documents. Stained-glass windows in the auditorium depict the rise and fall of the Confederacy. Mon.-Fri. 8-4:45, Sat. 9:30-3:15. Free. Phone (404) 656-2393.

CARTER PRESIDENTIAL CENTER AND MUSEUM OF THE JIMMY CARTER LIBRARY, off I-75/85 Carter Center/Freedom Pkwy. exit 96, following signs to 441 Freedom Pkwy., contains more than 27 million documents, photographs and other artifacts detailing the Carter administration. The museum offers a multimedia exhibit chronicling major events during the terms of the country's first 39 presidents.

Allow 1 hour, 30 minutes minimum. Mon.-Sat. 9-4:45, Sun. noon-4:45; closed Jan. 1, Thanksgiving and Dec. 25. Admission $5; over 55, $4; under 16 free. Phone (404) 331-3942.

CNN STUDIO TOUR, at One CNN Center, Marietta St. and Techwood Dr. (RR: Omni Station), is

© AAA
CHATTAHOOCHEE   AVE.

To Marietta & Chattanooga

To Marietta

To Gadsden & Birmingham

To Birmingham & Six Flags Over Georgia

To Newman

HOLMES   ST.

HOWELL   MILL   RD.

W.   MARIETTA   ST.

MARIETTA   BLVD.

BANKHEAD   AVE.

78   278

3

Maddox Park

SIMPSON   ST.

ASHBY   ST.

Washington Park

MARTIN   LUTHER   KING   JR.

Morris Brown College

Morehouse College

Clark Atlanta University

Spelman College

RALPH   DAVID   ABERNATHY   BLVD.

RALPH   DAVID   ABERNATHY

LEE   ST.

The Wren's Nest

DONNELLY   AVE.

AVON   AVE.

154   29

DILL   AVE.

SYLVAN

To Griffin & Macon

DERRING   ST.

MECASLIN   ST.

NORTHSIDE   DR.

HEMPHILL   AVE.

14TH   ST.

10TH   ST.

Georgia Tech

FERST   DR.

ATLANTIC   DR.

MARIETTA   PKWY.

NORTH   AVE.

LUCKIE   ST.

THE HIGH MUS. OF ART FOLK ART AND PHOTOGRAPHY GALLERY

Alexander Memorial Coliseum

Institute of Technology

5TH   ST.

Grant Field/Bobby Dodd Stadium

Crawford Long Hosp. of Emory U.

CNN Studio Tour

World Congress Center

Ga. Dome

The Herndon Home

VINE   ST.

UNIV.   PL.

MITCHELL   ST.

Centennial Olympic Park

INTERNATIONAL   BLVD.

MANGUM   ST.

H.W. TECHWOOD

The Omni

P.O.

Five Points

Post Office Underground Atlanta

City Hall State Capitol

PETERS   ST.

WHITEHALL   ST.

DAVID   ST.

FULTON   ST.

WELLS   ST.

W. WHITEHALL   ST.

3

WINDSOR   ST.

PRYOR   ST.

PULLMAN   ST.

Salvation Army College

MC DANIEL   ST.

STEWART   AVE.

UNIVERSITY   AVE.

CAPITOL   AVE.

SOUTH

RIDGE   RD.

PRYOR   RD.

To Hartsfield-Atlanta International Airport, Macon & Montgomery

85   75

19   41

2005-E

To Atlanta Hist. Center

RD.

EXPWY.

14TH   ST.

10TH   ST.

5TH   ST.

19

SPRING   ST.

PEACHTREE   ST.

JUNIPER   ST.

COURTLAND   ST.

PIEDMONT   AVE.

PONCE   DE LEON   AVE.

29   278   78

Rhodes Hall

Robert W. Woodruff Arts Center & High Mus. of Art

PIEDMONT   AVE.

12TH   ST.

SciTrek

Civic Center

RALPH   MC GILL   BLVD.

Georgia Baptist Hospital

HARRIS   ST.

INTERNATIONAL   BLVD.

ELLIS   ST.

HOUSTON   ST.

IRWIN   ST.

AUBURN   AVE.

EDGEWOOD

DECATUR   ST.

GRIMES   ST.

PIEDMONT   AVE.

BUTLER   ST.

Georgia St. Univ.

The World of Coca-Cola

B.W. FORTSON JR. ST. ARCHIVES & RECORDS BLDG.

MEMORIAL   DR.

ABERNATHY   ST.

20

RALPH   ST.

BLVD.

Ted Turner Stadium

ORMOND   ST.

HILL   ST.

To Archibald Smith Plantation Home, Lake Lanier, & Greenville

PEACHTREE   ST.

ATLANTA
RAPID TRANSIT
STATION

Scale in Miles   0.9
Scale in Kilometers   1.4

Atlanta Botanical Gardens

Piedmont Park

PARK   DR.

Piedmont Lake

MONROE   DR.

DE LEON   AVE.

To Georgia's Stone Mtn. Park, Fernbank Mus. of Nat. Hist., M.C. Carlos Mus. of Emory Univ. & The Road to Tara Mus.

To Carter Pres. Ctr. & Museum

S. College of Pharmacy

10

Martin Luther King Jr. Nat'l. Hist. Site

DE KALB   AVE.

75   85

DECATUR   ST.

Oakland Cemetery

154

Grant Park

Cyclorama

Zoo Atlanta

ATLANTA   AVE.

BOULEVARD

To Georgia's Stone Mtn. Park, Covington & Augusta

N

MC DONOUGH   BLVD.

Gammon Theological Seminary

JONESBORO   BLVD.

54

To Jonesboro

SPUR   42

To Forsyth

a 45-minute guided walking tour emphasizing network operations and technical aspects of CNN, Headline News, CNN International and the TBS Collection as well as demonstrations about weather broadcasts. Viewers see newspeople prepare for an upcoming program and watch them in action from an overhead observation booth.

Allow 1 hour minimum. Tours, limited to 35 people, are offered every 15 minutes daily 9-6; closed holidays. Admission $7; over 65, $5; under 12, $4.50. A limited number of same-day tickets is available on a first-come-first-served basis daily starting at 8:30 a.m. (Mon. at 9 a.m.). Under 6 are not admitted. Reservations are suggested. AE, MC, VI. Phone (404) 827-2300.

⟨SAVE⟩ FERNBANK MUSEUM OF NATURAL HISTORY, 767 Clifton Rd. N.E. (RR: North Avenue Station to MARTA bus #2), features dioramas, films and other exhibits pertaining to natural history. "A Walk Through Time in Georgia" portrays the state as a microcosm to illustrate the story of the Earth. Food is available.

Allow 1 hour minimum. Mon.-Sat. 10-5 (also Fri. 5-10), Sun. noon-5. The IMAX® theater presents natural history films on the hour. Closed Thanksgiving and Dec. 25. Museum admission $9.50; over 62 and students with ID $8; ages 3-12, $7. IMAX® theater $5.50; over 62 and students with ID $4.50; ages 3-12, $4. Combination ticket $13.50; over 62 and students with ID $11.50; ages 3-12, $9.50. Rates may be higher for special exhibitions. AE, MC, VI. Phone (404) 370-0960.

GEORGIA STATE CAPITOL, Washington St. between Mitchell St. and Martin Luther King Jr. Dr. (RR: Georgia State Station), was patterned after the national Capitol. Gold leaf mined in northern Georgia covers the exterior dome. Inside, the Georgia State Museum of Science and Industry displays rocks, minerals, fossils, commercial products and American Indian artifacts. The General Assembly is in session from early January to mid-March.

Allow 1 hour, 30 minutes minimum. Mon.-Fri. 7:30-5, Sat. 10-4, Sun. noon-4; closed holidays. Guided tours Mon.-Fri. at 10, 11, 1 and 2. Free. Phone (404) 656-2844.

GRANT PARK is bounded by Atlanta Ave., Sidney St., Cherokee Ave. and the Boulevard. The 144-acre park, near the site of the Battle of Atlanta, includes Old Fort Walker, some Civil War breastworks and miles of scenic trails as well as the Atlanta Cyclorama and Zoo Atlanta. Daily 6:30 a.m.-1 a.m. Free.

Atlanta Cyclorama, in the Civil War Museum at 800 Cherokee Ave. S.E., is a 360-degree painting of the Battle of Atlanta. The painting is 358 feet in circumference. Visitors view the 42-foot-high painting from seats on a revolving platform as sound and light effects, narration and 3-D figures heighten the experience of watching the battle.

Also in the building is the "Texas," a locomotive used in the pursuit of Maj. James Andrews and his Union soldiers during the Andrews Railroad Raid in 1862. Allow 1 hour minimum. Tours offered every 30 minutes daily 9:30-5:30, June-Sept.; 9:30-4:30, rest of year. Closed Jan. 1, Martin Luther King Jr.'s Birthday, Thanksgiving and Dec. 25. Admission $5; over 60, $4; ages 6-12, $3. Phone (404) 658-7625.

Zoo Atlanta, 800 Cherokee Ave. S.E. (RR: Five Points Rail to MARTA bus #97), exhibits more than 1,000 animals on 37 acres. Known for its reptile collection and petting zoo, the zoo also includes the Ford African Rain Forest, where western lowland gorillas live in family groups. Flamingo Plaza is home to 50 Chilean flamingos. Masai Mara, which replicates the East African plains, features browsing giraffes, antelopes and the endangered black rhinoceros. The Ketambe exhibit is home to rare Sumatran orangutans. Changing animal exhibits also are featured. Food is available.

Allow 4 hours minimum. Ticket office Mon.-Fri. 9:30-4:30, Sat.-Sun. 9:30-5:30. Grounds remain open 1 hour after ticket office closes. Closed Jan. 1, Thanksgiving and Dec. 25. Admission $9; over 55, $6.50; ages 3-11, $5.50. Train $1. Phone (404) 624-5600.

HENRY W. GRADY MONUMENT, on Marietta St. near Forsyth St., is a bronze statue of the late 19th-century writer and publisher who coined the phrase "The New South."

THE HERNDON HOME, 587 University Pl. N.W., is a 15-room Beaux Arts Classical house built in 1910 by wealthy businessman Alonzo Herndon, founder of the Atlanta Life Insurance Co. Allow 30 minutes minimum. Guided tours are available Tues.-Sat. on the hour 10-4; closed holidays. Donations. Phone (404) 581-9813.

MARTIN LUTHER KING JR. NATIONAL HISTORIC SITE, 501 Auburn Ave., is a 23.5-acre area that includes the birthplace, church and grave of Dr. Martin Luther King Jr., civil rights leader and Nobel Prize winner. The surrounding preservation district includes the residential and commercial sections of the Sweet Auburn neighborhood, the center of Atlanta's African-American community during most of the 20th century.

Daily 9-5; closed Jan. 1 and Dec. 25. Guided 30-minute tours of Dr. King's birthplace are available on the hour 10-5. Free. Phone (404) 331-3919.

The Martin Luther King Jr. Center for Nonviolent Social Change, 449 Auburn Ave., is housed in the Freedom Hall Complex. Surrounding Rev. Dr. King's crypt are the Freedom Walkway, a reflecting pool, the Chapel of All Faiths and Freedom Hall. The Administration, Program and Archives Building includes an exhibition area and a screening room for educational and historical programs. Daily 8:30-5:30, early Apr.-late Oct.; 9-5:30, rest of year. Tours are available daily 9-5. Archives department open daily 9:30-1 and 2-4:30; phone in advance for appointment. Free. Phone (404) 524-1956.

MICHAEL C. CARLOS MUSEUM OF EMORY UNIVERSITY, 571 S. Kilgo St. on the Emory University campus, contains a permanent collection of artifacts from the Middle and Far East, Greek statues and prints and drawings from the 13th century to the present. The museum also sponsors a variety of changing exhibitions on loan from other major institutions. Tours are available. Mon.-Sat. 10-5, Sun. noon-5; closed Jan. 1, Martin Luther King Jr.'s Birthday, Thanksgiving and Dec. 25. Admission $3. Phone (404) 727-4282.

RHODES HALL, 1516 Peachtree St., was constructed in 1903 for Atlanta businessman A.G. Rhodes. Inspired by European castles, the mansion is made primarily of granite from nearby Stone Mountain. A series of painted and stained-glass windows reflecting historic events of the Confederacy surrounds the carved mahogany staircase. Many original pieces of furniture are on display. The building also houses the Georgia Trust for Historic Preservation. Allow 30 minutes minimum. Mon.-Fri. 11-4, Sun. noon-3; closed holidays. Admission $3; under 12, $2. Phone (404) 885-7800.

ROBERT W. WOODRUFF ARTS CENTER, 1280 Peachtree St. N.E. (RR: Arts Center Station), is dedicated to the 122 Atlanta Art Association members killed in a Paris plane crash in 1962. The four-story center offers visual and performing arts education and entertainment. Within the complex are the Alliance Theater, the Atlanta Symphony and the headquarters for the Atlanta College of Art. Phone (404) 733-5000.

High Museum of Art, part of the Robert W. Woodruff Arts Center, is a four-story building sheathed in white ceramic panels. The museum incorporates large windows and a soaring atrium lit by skylights, allowing glimpses of more than one exhibition area at a time, plus distant or close-up views of individual works of art.

Permanent exhibits include Italian art from the 14th through the 18th centuries, 19th-century French and 19th- and 20th-century American art, African art, photographs, prints, and an extensive collection of decorative arts. Paintings by American artists form the basis of the collection. Visiting exhibitions also are featured. Spectacles, a gallery for young people, offers participatory displays. Guided tours are available.

Allow 2 hours minimum. Tues.-Sat. 10-5 (also fourth Fri. of month 5-9), Sun. noon-5; closed Jan. 1, July 4, Thanksgiving and Dec. 25. Admission $6; over 65 and students with ID $4; ages 6-17, $2; free to all Thurs. 1-5. Metered parking is available. Phone (404) 733-4200.

The High Museum of Art Folk Art and Photography Gallery, in the Georgia Pacific Building at 30 John Wesley Dobbs Ave., is a satellite facility of the High Museum of Art. Exhibits include changing folk art and photography displays. Guided tours, lectures and films also are available. Allow 30 minutes minimum. Mon.-Sat. 10-5; closed holidays. Tours given Wed. at noon. Free. Phone (404) 577-6940.

[SAVE] **SCITREK, THE SCIENCE AND TECHNOLOGY MUSEUM OF ATLANTA** is at 395 Piedmont Ave. N.W. More than 100 exhibits in the main halls—Simple Machines; Light, Color and Perception; Electricity and Magnetism; and Kidspace—provide opportunities for learning about science and technology through hands-on participation. Special activities, demonstrations and exhibits also are featured throughout the year.

Mathematica: A World of Numbers and Beyond, originally designed for the 1964 World's Fair, is an interactive exhibit that illustrates the mathematical foundation of the world and explains models and formulas that scientists use to prove theories.

Allow 2 hours minimum. Mon.-Sat. 10-5, Sun. noon-5; closed Jan. 1, Easter, Thanksgiving and Dec. 25. Admission $7.50; over 65, military with ID and ages 3-17, $5. Prices might be higher during special exhibits. Parking $4. AE, MC, VI. Phone (404) 522-5500.

[SAVE] ★SIX FLAGS OVER GEORGIA is 12 mi. w. on I-20. This 331-acre theme park has more than 100 rides, attractions and shows, including a 10-story free-fall ride, a triple-loop roller coaster and a white-water rafting adventure. NINJA: The Black Belt of Roller Coasters turns visitors upside down five times. In addition, a children's soft play area features roving Looney Tune cartoon characters. The park also has a 12,000-seat concert amphitheater.

There also are Broadway-style musical shows, an audience participation show, a high-diving show and strolling musical groups. Picnic facilities and kennels are available. Open daily at 10, Memorial Day-Labor Day; Sat.-Sun. at 10, mid-Mar. through day before Memorial Day and day after Labor Day-Oct. 31. Closing times vary; the park also may be open extra days in spring. All-inclusive 1-day admission $30.48; over 54 and ages 3-9, $20. Two-day admission $33.33 for all ages. Parking $5. AE, DS, MC, VI. Phone (770) 739-3400.

[SAVE] ★THE WORLD OF COCA-COLA is at 55 Martin Luther King Jr. Dr. and the corner of Central Ave., next to the Kenny's Alley entrance of Underground Atlanta (RR: Five Points Station). The 45,000-square-foot, three-story building houses a museum that pays tribute to Coca-Cola products as well as events that shaped the last century. A neon sign is suspended over the pavilion entrance.

Inside, interactive displays and multimedia exhibits combine with some 1,200 artifacts dating from 1886 to the present. Visitors can walk up to huge Coke cans, press soda "bubbles" and see videotapes of 5-year periods of history, hear radio jingles at a 1930s vintage soda fountain and watch an illusory bottling fantasy. The soda fountain of the future offers sample Coca-Cola products not available in the United States.

Allow 1 hour minimum. Mon.-Sat. 10-8:30, Sun. noon-5; closed Jan. 1, second Sun. in Jan., Easter, Thanksgiving, Dec. 24-25 and 31. Admission $6; over 55, $4; ages 6-12, $3. AE, MC, VI. Phone (404) 676-5151. *See ad.*

THE WREN'S NEST, 1050 Ralph D. Abernathy Blvd. S.W., is the Victorian-style former home of author and journalist Joel Chandler Harris. Best known as the creator of the "Uncle Remus Stories," the author was criticized during the civil rights movement for his use of dialect in writing stories told to him by former slaves. Harris, who died in 1908, has regained popularity as a folklorist who preserved stories that otherwise might have been lost.

The restored house features reproductions of Harris family furnishings and a diorama from the movie "Song of the South." Guided tours are

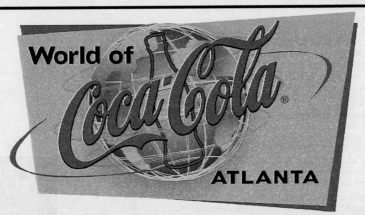

available. Picnic sites are available. Allow 1 hour minimum. Tues.-Sat. 10-4, Sun. 1-4; closed holidays. Storytelling sessions are available; phone for times. Admission $6; over 65 and ages 13-18, $4; ages 4-12, $3. Storytelling sessions $4. Phone (404) 753-7735.

What To Do
Sightseeing

 Bus and Train Tours

American Sightseeing Tours, Gray Line and other companies offer a variety of excursions around downtown Atlanta, to Stone Mountain and through residential areas.

 Walking Tours

House and garden tours of Druid Hills, Ansley Park and midtown are conducted in mid-April. Further information can be obtained at your hotel or from the telephone directory.

Guided tours of Atlanta's historic districts are offered by the Atlanta Preservation Center throughout the year at various locations. Comfortable walking shoes should be worn; phone (404) 876-2040.

Sports and Recreation

Atlanta's leisure activities are many. Visitors can go **rafting** or **canoeing** down the Chattahoochee River, the focal point of the Chattahoochee River National Recreation Area *(see place listing p. 30)*. Affectionately known as The Hooch by natives, the river is usually no more than 5 feet deep. Canoes, rafts, life jackets and shuttle service back to the departure point are provided by the Chattahoochee Outdoor Center early May to mid-September; phone (770) 395-6851. **Jogging** trails border the river.

Golf can be played at six city courses. The Bell South Atlanta Golf Classic and other tournaments attract many spectators each year. The municipal parks also provide **riding** and **hiking** trails, **tennis** courts and **swimming** pools. Piedmont Park, off Monroe Drive and 10th Street in midtown, is a popular spot for **bicycling** and jogging.

Fishing, boating and swimming off a sandy beach are available at Lake Sidney Lanier, about 35 miles northeast off US 23 *(see Buford p. 30 in the Vicinity section and Gainesville p. 44)*.

The National League's Braves play **baseball** from early April to early October at Ted Turner Stadium, off I-75/85 exits 91 or 93 (Ralph David Abernathy Blvd.). **Football** games are played in the Georgia Dome from early September to mid-December when the Atlanta Falcons of the National Football League take the field.

Basketball is the occupation of the National Basketball Association's Hawks, who play downtown at the Omni Coliseum, 100 Techwood Ave.

Racing in Atlanta focuses on horsepower. Fans of the checkered flag can see it waved almost all year at Atlanta Motor Speedway *(see attraction listing in Hampton p. 47)*, 20 miles south, and at Road Atlanta, 39 miles northeast near Braselton. The former is host to NASCAR racing; the latter offers sports car, Formula One, motorcycle and motocross events on its road circuit April through November.

Shopping

The area immediately surrounding the Five Points intersection downtown is a modern bazaar. To the north the Peachtree Center. To the west another megastructure, the Omni, embraces an array of international shops and boutiques. In between is a mix of old and new buildings housing retail stores and other commercial enterprises.

Brooks Brothers and Macy's are prominent department stores that have been a part of Atlanta's downtown for decades. The convenience of MARTA rapid rail and the addition of Peachtree Center's multilevel mall, with stores such as Givenchy and Lanvin, have further enhanced downtown shopping, blending modern elegance with the renovated romance of late 19th-century buildings.

One of the city's novelty shopping areas is somewhat of a misnomer—two of Underground Atlanta's three levels are actually above ground, offering the wares of more than 130 prominent national and local merchants. The underground portion of the nearly 12-acre urban marketplace has existed since before the Civil War, when streets were built over railroad tracks that converged at the heart of Terminus, as Atlanta was then called.

Authentic storefronts and historic buildings below and above the streets have been carefully restored. Visitors can dine in one of 10 varied restaurants, stroll down landscaped pedestrian promenades, or relax on park benches while being entertained by street performers.

At night the district is an entertainment center with nightclubs featuring bluegrass, comedy, Dixieland, rock and jazz. Lying between Peachtree Street and Central Avenue at Alabama Street, Underground Atlanta is next to the Five Points MARTA station and has some 16,000 parking spaces.

Atlanta is not all big-city glitter, for the sophistication of downtown's Five Points has a more casual counterpart in Little Five Points, 3 miles away in Inman Park at the intersection of Moreland and Euclid avenues. The residential Victorian enclave has a mix of shops, boutiques, restaurants and clubs catering to the young and trendy.

Another shopping area worth exploring is fashionable Buckhead, noted for its antique shops and galleries as well as its malls, Lenox Square and upscale Phipps Plaza.

Atlanta also has a number of malls studding its perimeter—Cumberland Mall, the Galleria, North Point Mall and Town Center to the northwest; Outlet Square and Perimeter Mall to the north; Gwinnett Place and Northlake Mall to the northeast; Southlake Mall to the southeast; and Greenbriar Mall to the southwest. An alternative to the mall environment is the 146-acre Atlanta State Farmers Market, popular for both its seasonal selection of fruits and vegetables and its cafeteria.

Theater and Concerts

Atlanta's cultural offerings range from grand opera and fine symphony to summer stock and vintage films. Founded in 1929, the Atlanta Ballet is one of the oldest civic ballet companies in the country. The company performs from September through April in the Civic Center Auditorium, 395 Piedmont Rd.; phone (404) 523-6275. Highlights include a holiday presentation of the Nutcracker; phone (404) 873-5811.

During the fall-winter concert season several other ballet and modern-dance groups stage revues, which are usually presented in the Robert W. Woodruff Arts Center, 1280 Peachtree St. N.E.; phone (404) 733-5000.

The Atlanta Symphony has musical presentations September through May. The series is supplemented by free concerts June through August. The Summer Fest is held in Symphony Hall at the Robert W. Woodruff Arts Center on Tuesdays and Thursdays in July. The Atlanta Symphony Orchestra performs in Chastain Memorial Park Amphitheatre June through August.

The Alliance Theatre, in the Robert W. Woodruff Arts Center at Peachtree and 15th streets, presents productions that range from musicals to new and classic dramas. Dinner theater productions at Agatha's—A Taste of Mystery, 693 Peachtree St. N.E., feature audience participation. The city also is the home of numerous professional, experimental and community theater groups. Daily and weekly newspapers give details about theater and dance productions, concerts and film showings.

Special Events

Atlanta's Dogwood Festival each April features a parade, driving tours of residential areas, a hot-air balloon race and various other events; phone (404) 892-0538.

The Peachtree Road Race, a 10-kilometer event in which 50,000 runners participate, takes place in downtown Atlanta on July 4.

The Atlanta Historical Society's Folklife Festival at the Tullie Smith House is held in early October. The festival includes tours of the house and gardens as well as demonstrations of such 19th-century crafts as blacksmithing, candle dipping, weaving, spinning, yarn dyeing and pottery making, all accompanied by dulcimer music.

In September the Arts Festival of Atlanta in Piedmont Park features painting, sculpture, photography and crafts exhibits as well as puppet shows, children's workshops, and dance, music and theater performances.

The Atlanta Vicinity

BUFORD (B-2) pop. 8,800, elev. 1,205'

Buford Dam is on the Chattahoochee River 5 miles northwest. Above the dam Lake Sidney Lanier *(see Recreation Chart)* extends up both the Chattahoochee and Chestatee rivers, offering some 540 miles of shoreline. Besides recreation, this project provides electricity, flood control, water supplies and supplemental downstream flow during droughts. The powerhouse is open to visitors on weekdays.

LAKE LANIER ISLANDS, n.w. off SR 365, were formed when the waters of Lake Sidney Lanier failed to cover a cluster of heavily forested hilltops. The islands are connected to the mainland by causeways.

Each of the four islands that form this year-round resort area offers different recreational facilities. Amenities include two hotels, campgrounds, tennis courts, boat and bicycle rentals, a beach, water parks and restaurants. Also available are horseback riding, fishing, sailing, hiking and skiing. One island has two 18-hole golf courses. Parking $4 daily. Phone (770) 932-7200. *See the AAA Southeastern CampBook.*

CHATTAHOOCHEE RIVER NATIONAL RECREATION AREA (B-2)

Extending along a 48-mile stretch of the Chattahoochee River from Lake Sidney Lanier to Peachtree Creek in northwest Atlanta, 4,100-acre Chattahoochee River National Recreation Area has preserved the natural riverway within an extensive metropolitan area. Its day-use trails are popular with city dwellers and visitors alike.

Long scenic runs and gentle rapids offer excellent canoeing, rafting and kayaking. Small motorboats are permitted, but there is a limited number of boat ramps. The southernmost public take-out point is Paces Mill on US 41. Watercraft rental and shuttle service are provided through the Chattahoochee Outdoor Center; phone (770) 395-6851.

For information contact the Superintendent, Chattahoochee River National Recreation Area, 1978 Island Ford Pkwy., Atlanta, GA 30350-3400; phone (770) 399-8070, or 952-4419 weekends. *(See Recreation Chart.)*

DECATUR (B-3) pop. 17,300

Legend has it that Decatur became so prosperous after its incorporation in 1823 that 14 years later citizens refused to allow the Western & Atlantic Railroad and its attendant noise and soot to enter the city limits. The tracks were instead laid to a site called Terminus, which was reincorporated as Marthasville in 1843 and 2 years later as Atlanta. Decatur is a suburb of that once lowly terminus.

Although it is only 6 miles from downtown Atlanta, Decatur retains a small town atmosphere that is apparent in its historic complex. The old county courthouse contains the Visitors Center and the DeKalb County Historical Society and Museum.

DeKalb Convention and Visitors Bureau: 750 Commerce Dr., Suite 201, Decatur, GA 30030; phone (404) 378-2525.

FERNBANK SCIENCE CENTER, 156 Heaton Park Dr. N.E., offers science-related exhibits, a planetarium and a 65-acre forest featuring native plants. Allow 1 hour minimum. Displays open Tues.-Fri. 8:30 a.m.-10 p.m., Sat. 10-5, Sun. 1-5, Mon. 8:30-5. Planetarium shows Wed. and Fri. at 3 and 8, Sat.-Sun. at 11 and 3, Tues. and Thurs. at 8. Forest open Sun.-Fri. 2-5, Sat. 10-5. Closed major holidays. Displays and forest free. Planetarium $2, students $1. Under 5 are not permitted in most planetarium shows. Phone (404) 378-4311.

JONESBORO (C-2) pop. 3,600, elev. 917′

STATELY OAKS, 100 Carriage Ln., is an 1839 Greek Revival plantation house furnished with antiques. Guides dressed in period costumes provide tours of the two-story house. Allow 1 hour minimum. Mon.-Fri. 10:30-3:30 (also second and fourth Sun. of the month 2-4); closed major holidays. Admission $5; over 60, $4.50; ages 3-12, $2.50. Phone (770) 473-0197.

KENNESAW (B-2) pop. 8,900, elev. 1,093′

The passengers leaving aboard a train at Big Shanty—modern Kennesaw—on April 11, 1862, had no idea that a dramatic episode in the Civil War was about to begin before their breakfast coffee cooled. While the passengers and crew ate, Maj. James Andrews and 21 Union soldiers, who had boarded in civilian clothes, stole the train and headed for Chattanooga, Tenn.

The conductor and crew chased the stolen train on foot, by handcar and with commandeered engines, catching Andrews just 5 miles from his goal. The major and seven of his men were returned to Atlanta and executed as spies. The Walt Disney movie "The Great Locomotive Chase" was based on the incident.

[SAVE] **KENNESAW CIVIL WAR MUSEUM,** 2829 Cherokee St., houses "The General," the locomotive stolen by Maj. James Andrews and 21 Union soldiers in a daring Civil War raid. A videotape program and art exhibits describe the event. Allow 30 minutes minimum. Mon.-Sat. 9:30-5:30, Sun. noon-5:30, Mar. 16-Oct. 15; Mon.-Sat. 10-4, Sun. noon-4, rest of year. Admission $3; over 65, $2.50; ages 7-15, $1.50; family rate $15. Phone (770) 427-2117 or (800) 742-6897.

KENNESAW MOUNTAIN NATIONAL BATTLEFIELD PARK (B-1)

Kennesaw Mountain National Battlefield Park occupies 2,882 acres 2.5 miles northwest of Marietta off I-75 exit 116, then 4 mi. w. on old US 41. In June 1864, Gen. Joseph E. Johnston's Confederate Army, retreating before Gen. William Tecumseh Sherman's march to Atlanta, took up a strong position on Kennesaw (KEN-i-saw) Mountain in the path of the invading forces. Sherman, however, ultimately forced Johnston and his troops to abandon the mountain and retreat south.

Earthworks from this battle are well preserved. A paved road to the crest of Kennesaw Mountain has fine views; around the crest is a trail with maps illustrating the conflict. The visitor center and park headquarters at the foot of the mountain on old US 41 offer audiovisual programs and exhibits. Picnicking is permitted in designated areas. Allow 2 hours minimum. Mon.-Fri. 8:30-5, Sat.-Sun. 8:30-6, Memorial Day-Labor Day; daily 8:30-5, rest of year. Closed Dec. 25. Free. Phone (770) 427-4686.

LILBURN (B-3) pop. 9,300, elev. 876′

YELLOW RIVER GAME RANCH, at 4525 US 78, is 2.5 mi. e. of Stone Mountain Park. The ranch is a preserve for wildlife, including all species native to Georgia as well as mountain lions, buffaloes and bears. Wild animals are kept in cages but docile, tame animals wander free. A petting area features small barnyard animals. A .5-mile hike over sloping terrain necessitates walking shoes and casual attire.

Allow 1 hour minimum. Daily 9:30-dusk, June-Aug.; 9:30-6, rest of year. Last tour begins 1 hour before closing. Admission $5; ages 3-11, $4. Phone (770) 972-6643.

MARIETTA (B-2) pop. 44,100, elev. 1,118′

Winners of the Cherokee lands lottery settled Marietta in 1834, and the location soon attracted a seasonal population of lowland planters. The town's leisurely serenity was shattered by the Civil War. During Gen. William Tecumseh Sherman's push toward nearby Atlanta, Union and Confederate forces fought a bloody battle just beyond Marietta's boundaries at what is now Kennesaw Mountain National Battlefield Park (see place listing p. 31).

Although Marietta was spared, two of the city's cemeteries bear witness to the bitterness of the war. In 1866 Henry Cole, a local businessman, donated land for the Marietta National Cemetery as a gesture of peace so that the dead from each side could lie in the same ground; however, pride and memories of the war were so strong that Marietta's citizens created a separate Confederate cemetery nearby.

A downtown park complete with an ornate Victorian gazebo recalls the late 19th century, of which few traces remain in this growing city northwest of Atlanta. Quiet walks among courtly old houses, picnics at Kennesaw Mountain National Battlefield Park and rafting down the Chattahoochee are some of the area's recreational possibilities.

Cobb County Convention and Visitors Bureau: P.O. Box 672827, Marietta, GA 30067-0048; phone (770) 933-7228 or (800) 451-3480.

Self-guiding tours: The Marietta Welcome Center, just off the square in the old train depot at Number 4 Depot St., provides brochures outlining a walking/driving tour of the historic district. Highlights include Sherman's former headquarters at Kennesaw House and the Stanley and Marlow houses, now Victorian bed and breakfast inns. Phone (770) 429-1115 or (800) 835-0445.

AMERICAN ADVENTURES, 250 N. Cobb Pkwy., is a 10-acre family amusement park. Highlights include an arcade, bumper cars, a carrousel, Go-Karts, an interactive family fun house, miniature golf and a roller coaster. Food is available. Allow 2 hours minimum. Daily 11-8; closed Thanksgiving and Dec. 25. Hours may vary; phone ahead. All-inclusive admission ages 4-17, 13.99; under 4, $4.99; adults $2.99. Parking $2. DS, MC, VI. Phone (770) 424-9283.

MARIETTA/COBB MUSEUM OF ART, 30 Atlanta St. N.E., features various collections of 19th-century to contemporary art housed in a 1909 Greek Revival building that was formerly a post office. A children's gallery offers hands-on art exhibits. Allow 30 minutes minimum. Tues.-Sat. 11-5; closed holidays. Admission $2; over 64 and ages 6-21, $1. Phone (770) 424-8142.

WHITEWATER PARK, 250 N. Cobb Pkwy., offers more than 40 water-related attractions, including a lazy river, a wave pool, waterfalls, a treehouse and Little Squirt's Island, an activity pool for children. Food is available. Allow a full day. Daily 10-8, June 7-Labor Day; Sat.-Sun. and holidays 10-6, May 1-June 6. Admission $20.99, ages 3 and under 49 inches tall $11.99, over age 62 free. Parking $2. DS, MC, VI. Phone (770) 424-9283.

ROSWELL (B-2) pop. 47,900

Founded in 1839 by businessman Roswell King, Roswell was a leading supplier of cotton and woolen goods to the Confederacy during the Civil War. The restored Roswell Mill, SRs 9 and 120, was the site where Confederate uniforms known as Roswell Grey were made. The mill, which presently serves as an entertainment complex, contains shops and restaurants. Roswell Square's historic storefronts on S. Atlanta Street also house a variety of shops.

The Roswell Historical Society conducts guided walking tours of historic neighborhoods on Wednesday at 10 and Sunday at 1. A walking tour of Mill Village, a supplier of cotton and woolen goods for the Confederate army, is available Saturday at 11. Both tours, which cost $3 each, begin at the Roswell Visitors Center at 617 Atlanta St.; phone (770) 992-1665.

Greater North Fulton Chamber of Commerce: 1025 Old Roswell Rd. #101, Roswell, GA 30076; phone (770) 993-8806.

★**ARCHIBALD SMITH PLANTATION HOME,** 935 Alpharetta St., is the preserved home of one of Roswell's founding families. The 1845 house features original furnishings, clothing and family possessions kept intact by descendents of the Smiths. An 1840s piano, marble-topped washstands and a walnut plantation desk are among the fine antiques and artifacts displayed.

The property also features several original buildings, including a barn, carriage house, greenhouse, corn crib, kitchen, slave cabin and spring house. Docents convey generations of history regarding the house and its inhabitants.

Allow 1 hour, 30 minutes minimum. Guided tours Tues.-Fri. at 11 and 2, Sat. at 11, noon and 1; closed Jan. 1, July 4, Thanksgiving and Dec. 24-25. Admission $5; ages 6-12, $3. Phone (770) 641-3978.

BULLOCH HALL, 1 blk w. of the Old Square at 180 Bulloch Ave., was the childhood home of President Theodore Roosevelt's mother, Martha (Mittie) Bulloch. The 1840 Greek Revival house features restored rooms with some period furnishings. The Great American Cover Up, a large quilt show featuring period and contemporary quilts, is held in March. Osage Orange Festival is celebrated in July.

Allow 1 hour minimum. Tours are given on the hour Mon.-Sat. 10-2, Sun. 1-3; closed Thanksgiving and Dec. 25. Admission $5; ages 6-16, $3. Phone (770) 992-1731.

CHATTAHOOCHEE NATURE CENTER, off SR 120 at 9135 Willeo Rd., encompasses 127 acres and has four nature trails that wind through wetlands and woodlands. The trails are self-guiding, with native flora well marked. Reptiles, a carnivorous plant display, birds—including vultures, bald eagles and many varieties of owls—are exhibited. Pets are not permitted. Allow 1 hour minimum. Mon.-Sat. 9-5, Sun. noon-5; closed Jan. 1, Thanksgiving and Dec. 25. Admission $3; over 54 and ages 3-15, $2. Phone (770) 992-2055.

STONE MOUNTAIN (B-2) pop. 6,500, elev. 1,043'

★**GEORGIA'S STONE MOUNTAIN PARK,** just e. off I-285 via US 78, is a 3,200-acre recreational and historic park encompassing Stone Mountain. Memorial Hall features displays and a videotape presentation detailing the geological and cultural history of the granite mountain. Also in Memorial Hall are large picture windows facing the Confederate memorial carving.

A wide range of recreational facilities includes a 36-hole championship golf course and a lakefront beach. *See Recreation Chart and the AAA Southeastern CampBook.*

"Lasershow '98" is a free laser light show that can be viewed from the memorial lawn each evening from late May through Labor Day (weather permitting).

Park open daily 6 a.m.-midnight. Laser light show daily 1 hour after dark, Memorial Day-Labor Day. Attraction tickets are available at park information and ticket centers. Admission to beach complex $4. Parking $6 (no discounts). AE, DI, DS, MC, VI. Phone (770) 498-5690. *See color ad p. 205.*

SAVE ★**The Antebellum Plantation** is a complex of early 19th-century houses and buildings relocated from throughout the state. The buildings include the main house, overseer's house, slave cabins and a country store, all furnished in period. Allow 1 hour minimum. Daily 10-8, Memorial Day-Labor Day; 10-5, rest of year. Closed Dec. 25. Admission $3.50; ages 3-11, $2.50.

SAVE **Antique Car and Treasure Museum** displays classic cars, brass automotive accessories, a large musical exhibit and toys. Allow 30 minutes minimum. Daily 10-8, Memorial Day-Labor Day; 10-5, rest of year. Closed Dec. 25. Admission $3.50; ages 3-11, $2.50.

The Bells of Stone Mountain, the park's bell tower, is a 13-story spire rising from the lakeshore. The tower uses miniature bell-tone rods and amplification to create its 732 bell sounds. Concerts are given Mon.-Sat. at noon and 4, Sun. at 1, 3 and 5. Free.

SAVE **Riverboat Cruises** on the *Scarlett O'Hara* feature views of the mountain and shoreline. The riverboat offers 30-minute lake cruises daily on the hour 10-8, Memorial Day-Labor Day; 10-5, Apr. 1-day before Memorial Day; 10-5, day after Labor Day-Nov. 30; Sat.-Sun. 10-5 in Mar. and Dec. Fare $3.50; ages 3-11, $2.50.

The Road to Tara Museum, on John B. Gordon Rd., houses one of the country's largest collections of "Gone With the Wind" memorabilia.

Exhibits include a collection of dolls dressed in Scarlett O'Hara costumes as well as original designer sketches and authentic costume reproductions. A 22-minute documentary film focusing on the life of Margaret Mitchell is available.

Allow 30 minutes minimum. Daily 10-5:30; closed Jan. 1 and Dec. 25. Admission $3.50; ages 8-15, $2.50. MC, VI. Phone (770) 465-1939.

SAVE **Scenic Railroad** operates three old-time locomotives on a 5-mile route around Stone Mountain. The locomotives are replicas of those made famous by the great locomotive chase during the Civil War. Allow 30 minutes minimum. Train trips daily 10-8, Memorial Day-Labor Day; 10-5:20, rest of year. Closed Dec. 25. Fare $3.50; ages 3-11, $2.50.

SAVE **Scenic Swiss Skylift** offers a cable car ride to the summit of Stone Mountain. The views of the mountain's equestrian carvings and the countryside are spectacular. The cable car terminal and the Plaza of Flags are on the mountaintop. Allow 30 minutes minimum. Rides daily (weather permitting) 10-8, Memorial Day-Labor Day; 10-5, rest of year. Closed Dec. 25. Fare $3.50; ages 3-11, $2.50.

★**Stone Mountain** is a massive dome of granite rising 825 feet above the surrounding plain. The 300-million-year-old mountain measures 5 miles in circumference and covers 583 acres. A 1.3-mile hiking trail leads up the western flank of the mountain to its summit, and the Stone Mountain Historical Trail offers 5-mile hikes around the mountain.

Three colossal equestrian figures—Confederate president Jefferson Davis, Gen. Thomas "Stonewall" Jackson and Gen. Robert E. Lee—are sculpted on the mountain's sheer northern face. Even though the figure of Lee is the height of a nine-story building and the entire sculpture rests in a niche the size of a city block, the figures seem small compared to the mountain's bulk. The creation of this work of art spanned 57 years.

SAVE **Wildlife Preserve and Petting Farm** allows visitors to see native animals and plants in a scenic wooded setting, complete with running streams. Children can pet and feed domestic farm animals. Allow 30 minutes minimum. Daily 10-8, Memorial Day-Labor Day; 10-5, rest of year. Closed Dec. 25. Admission $3.50; ages 3-11, $2.50.

AUGUSTA (C-5) pop. 44,600, elev. 162′

Georgia's second oldest city, Augusta was one of the main proponents of the New South during Reconstruction. As the resources of the area's leading families were seriously depleted, many

opened their homes to paying guests from the North who were attracted by the region's mild winters. By the 1890s Augusta had become a major resort area.

During this period the owner of one resort hotel built a nine-hole golf course, introducing the game to his wealthy guests. The game was so popular that the following year an 18-hole course was built at what is now the Augusta Country Club. Each April the Masters Golf Tournament, played at the Augusta National Golf Course, attracts the country's best golfers and a number of international champions as well as thousands of spectators.

Augusta also is home to three world-class water-sports events: the Augusta Invitational Rowing Regatta, which highlights international pre-Olympic and open collegiate races by more than 25 college and university teams; the Augusta Southern Nationals drag boat races; and River Race Augusta. The Augusta Futurity, a cutting-horse competition and Western-style festival, is the largest equestrian event of its kind east of the Mississippi.

Renovations in the city's Olde Towne Historic District have returned the splendor that characterized these 1860-1900 homes of Augusta's elite. The Summerville neighborhood, another area of fine old houses, was once the winter retreat of wealthy Northerners but later became the residential choice of affluent Augustans.

Riverwalk, between 5th and 10th streets, comprises five blocks of landscaped lawns and gardens on two levels along the Savannah River. The area is the site of a variety of festivals and events. Riverwalk also features a marina, restaurants, shops and a 1,700-seat amphitheater that plays host to a variety of performances. Phone (706) 821-1754 for events information.

Augusta Metropolitan Convention & Visitors Bureau: P.O. Box 1331, Augusta, GA 30903-1331; phone (706) 823-6600 or (800) 726-0243.

Self-guiding tours: The Bartram Memorial Trail commemorates the 1773-77 journeys of artist and naturalist William Bartram. The trail, outlined in a brochure called "The Augusta Canal," also has a 9-mile wilderness section for hiking, bicycling and canoeing. Pamphlets describing walking and driving tours of Augusta's historic districts and events are available at the welcome center, 32 8th St. at Riverwalk; phone (706) 724-4067.

AUGUSTA-RICHMOND COUNTY MUSEUM, 560 Reynolds St., features a train exhibit, natural history display and exhibits about the city's origin and early history plus details of the Civil War and Revolutionary War. A collection of American Indian artifacts as well as a space exhibit also are housed in the museum. Allow 1 hour minimum. Tues.-Sat. 10-5, Sun. 2-5; closed major holidays. Admission $4; over 65, $3; ages 6-18, $2. Phone (706) 722-8454.

CONFEDERATE MONUMENT, Broad St. between 7th and 8th sts., is a 76-foot-high Italian marble shaft. The monument, dominated by a statue of a Confederate private, includes life-size figures of Gens. Robert E. Lee, Thomas J. "Stonewall" Jackson, W.H.T. Walker, Thomas R.R. Cobb and Barry Benson.

EZEKIEL HARRIS HOUSE is off I-20 Washington Rd. exit, 4 mi. s.e. to Eve St./Crawford Ave., then 2 blks. n. to Welsh Ln. at 1822 Broad St. The 1797 Federal-style house was originally used to house tobacco merchants bringing their crop to market. The house, furnished with period pieces, also contains various archeological artifacts found on the grounds. Allow 30 minutes minimum. Tues.-Fri. 1-4, Sat. 10-1; closed Thanksgiving and Dec. 25. Admission $2; over 59, $1; ages 5-17, 50c. Phone (706) 724-0436.

GERTRUDE HERBERT INSTITUTE OF ART, 506 Telfair St., is a handsome three-story Federal-style house built by Georgia legislator Nicholas Ware in 1818. Because of its huge cost of $40,000, the structure was known as "Ware's Folly." Works by locally and nationally known artists are displayed. Tues.-Fri. 10-5, Sat. 10-2; closed holidays. Donations. Phone (706) 722-5495.

HISTORIC COTTON EXCHANGE WELCOME CENTER, 8th St. and Riverwalk, began a long history of public usage in the late 1800s. Built in 1886 as a center for cotton brokerage, it became one of the largest cotton markets in the world. Today the restored building houses exhibits relating to the farming and marketing of cotton and serves as a visitor center for the Augusta riverfront area. Guided tours are available. Mon.-Sat. 9-5, Sun. 1-5; closed Jan. 1, Easter, Thanksgiving and Dec. 24-25. Free. Phone (706) 724-4067.

SAVE MEADOW GARDEN is near the Augusta Canal at 1320 Independence Dr. The former home of George Walton, a signer of the Declaration of Independence, the museum is furnished with 18th- and early 19th-century antiques. Mon.-Fri. 10-4. Admission $3; grades 8-12, $2; grades K-7, $1. Phone (706) 724-4174.

MONUMENT TO GEORGIA'S SIGNERS of the Declaration of Independence, on Greene St. between 4th and 5th sts., honors George Walton, Lyman Hall and Button Gwinnett.

MONUMENT TO THE POETS OF GEORGIA, in the 700 block of Greene St., honors Sidney Lanier, James R. Randall, Paul Hamilton Hayne and Father Ryan.

MORRIS MUSEUM OF ART, along the riverfront at One 10th St., houses a collection of Southern art from the late 18th century to contemporary pieces, including antebellum portraits and still lifes. The museum also features changing exhibits and houses an art research library. Allow 1 hour minimum. Tues.-Sat. 10-5:30, Sun. 12:30-5:30; closed major holidays. Admission $2; over 65 and ages 12-18, $1; free to all Sun. AE, DS, MC, VI. Phone (706) 724-7501.

SACRED HEART CULTURAL CENTER, 1301 Greene St., was formerly Sacred Heart Catholic Church. The 1900 Romanesque and Byzantine building features intricate brickwork, tall turrets and graceful arches. Nearly abandoned when population patterns shifted in the 1970s, the structure was bought by a private partnership in 1982 and restored to its former grandeur, receiving the National Trust for Historic Preservation Honor Award for 1987.

The former church now serves as a cultural center, reception hall, concert hall and meeting place for local artists and cultural groups. Guided tours are available. Allow 30 minutes minimum. Mon.-Fri. 9-5; closed holidays and during private functions. Pamphlet for self-guided tour $1. Phone (706) 826-4700 to verify availability.

ST. PAUL'S EPISCOPAL CHURCH, 605 Reynolds St., was founded in 1750, but the original building was destroyed during the Revolution. The present structure, a classic example of Colonial-style architecture built in 1919, is the fourth on this site. Interred in the church's cemetery is William Few Jr., Georgia's signer of the U.S. Constitution. Mon.-Fri. 9-4:30, Sat. 9-noon. Donations. Phone (706) 724-2485.

SITE OF FORT AUGUSTA, between St. Paul's Church and the river, is marked by a Celtic cross. One of James Oglethorpe's cannons lies at the foot of the cross.

BAXLEY (E-4) pop. 3,800, elev. 206′

Baxley, a marketing and shipping center for surrounding Appling County, holds large tobacco auctions in late July and early August. Fishing, boating and other water sports are enjoyed on the nearby Altamaha River and Lake Mayers.

Baxley-Appling County Chamber of Commerce: 501 W. Parker St., P.O. Box 413, Baxley, GA 31513; phone (912) 367-7731.

EDWIN I. HATCH NUCLEAR VISITORS CENTER, 12 mi. n. on US 1, explains the concept of nuclear energy through animated displays and films. Allow 30 minutes minimum. Mon.-Fri. 8:30-5; closed holidays. Free. Phone (912) 367-3668.

BLAIRSVILLE (A-2) pop. 600

Blairsville, situated entirely within the Chattahoochee National Forest *(see place listing p. 37),* provides easy access to numerous historic buildings, scenic spots and recreational facilities. The Old Court House in the center of town contains a historical museum. Brasstown Bald, Georgia's highest mountain, provides a panorama of four states, and the Richard Russell Scenic Highway offers 14 miles of overlooks, trails and peaks.

Blairsville-Union County Chamber of Commerce: 385 Blue Ridge, P.O. Box 789, Blairsville, GA 30512; phone (706) 745-5789.

VOGEL STATE PARK, 11 mi. s. on US 19/129, covers 250 acres of the Chattahoochee National Forest in the Blue Ridge Mountains. There are 17 miles of hiking trails, 1 mile of which is interpreted by signs, as well as facilities for camping, fishing and swimming. Organized programs during the summer include guided walks, campfire nights and square dancing. Daily 7 a.m.-10 p.m. Admission $2 per vehicle; free to all Wed. Phone (706) 745-2628. *See Recreation Chart and the AAA Southeastern CampBook.*

BLAKELY (E-2) pop. 5,600, elev. 270′

Blakely and surrounding Early County constitute one of the largest peanut-producing areas in the country. The peanut monument in Courthouse Square's northeast corner was donated by citizens of the town and county.

Other sites in and near Blakely are reminders of the past. In the northwest corner of the square stands the last known Confederate flagpole, erected in 1861. Nine miles southwest, a covered bridge on Old River Road spans picturesque Coheelee Creek. Built in 1883, it is one of the few covered bridges in the South.

Blakely-Early County Chamber of Commerce: P.O. Box 189, Blakely, GA 31723; phone (912) 723-3741.

KOLOMOKI MOUNDS HISTORIC PARK, 6 mi. n. off US 27, is an important archeological site and a popular recreation area. The 1,293-acre park contains seven American Indian mounds. A museum at the west entrance chronicles the area's American Indian cultures from 5000 B.C. to the 13th century. One exhibit shows the interior of a mound as archeologists left it.

Park open daily 7 a.m.-10 p.m. Museum open Tues.-Sat. and holidays 9-5, Sun. 2-5:30; closed Thanksgiving and Dec. 25. Admission $1.50; ages 6-18, 75c. Phone (912) 723-5296 for the park or 723-3398 for the museum. *See Recreation Chart and the AAA Southeastern CampBook.*

BRASELTON (B-3) pop. 400

WINERIES

- **Chateau Elan,** on SR 211 off I-85 exit 48. Daily 10-9; closed Dec. 25. Phone (770) 932-0900 or (800) 233-9463.

- **Chestnut Mountain Winery,** SR 211 to SR 124. Tues.-Fri. 12:30-5, Sat.-Sun. noon-5 and by appointment; closed major holidays. Phone (770) 867-6914.

BRUNSWICK (E-5) pop. 16,400, elev. 14′

Brunswick was founded in 1771 on a peninsula that juts into the Brunswick River; the city was named for King George III of the House of

Brunswick. Streets and parks named after members of England's ruling family and English places help preserve the town's past. Victorian houses remain from the late 19th century, when Brunswick was a busy shipping center for lumber and naval stores.

Shrimp- and crabmeat-processing plants are concentrated along Bay Street (US 341) from Gloucester to Prince streets. Boats unload shrimp onto the street's docks most weekdays in the late afternoon. Charter fishing trips leave from Brunswick, St. Simons Island and Jekyll Island.

Among Brunswick's landmarks are two oak trees. Lover's Oak, at Albany and Prince streets, is thought to date from the late 11th century. Local legend tells of an American Indian and his love, who met beneath its branches. Lanier's Oak overlooks the marshes less than a mile north on US 17. It is said that under this tree the Georgia poet Sidney Lanier was inspired to write "The Marshes of Glynn" and other poems. The James Oglethorpe Monument, on Newcastle Street in Queens Square, honors the founder of Georgia.

Brunswick-Golden Isles Visitors Bureau: 4 Glynn Ave., Brunswick, GA 31520; phone (912) 265-0620 or (800) 933-2627.

Self-guiding tours: Driving tour maps of Brunswick, Jekyll Island, St. Simons Island and Sea Island are available at the Golden Isles Welcome Centers on I-95 off the southbound lanes between exits 8 and 9, on US 17 at the Torras Causeway to St. Simons Island and on St. Simons Island at the visitors center in the village area.

★HOFWYL-BROADFIELD PLANTATION, 10 mi. n. on US 17, provides a glimpse of early 19th-century life on the Georgia rice coast as well as a chance to observe the vegetation and animal life native to this freshwater marsh country.

In 1806 William Brailsford purchased a tract of land and named it Broadfield. Later generations built the present house, which they named Hofwyl, in the 1850s. Hofwyl's rice operation suffered during the Civil War, but recovered by the close of the century. Georgia's rice industry later collapsed and Hofwyl became a dairy farm. The estate remained in the family until 1973.

The plantation is presently a 1,268-acre wildlife preserve with a museum where a videotape presentation details the history of Hofwyl and the rice industry. Exhibits show how slaves, many of them experienced in rice cultivation in Africa, carved a thriving rice plantation from the virgin cypress swamp along the Altamaha River. The house has original furnishings from different periods.

Tues.-Sat. and Mon. holidays 9-5, Sun. 2-5:30; closed Jan. 1, Thanksgiving, Dec. 25 and day after Mon. holidays. Admission $2; ages 6-18, $1.50. Phone (912) 264-7333.

[SAVE] **MARY MILLER DOLL MUSEUM** is at 1523 Glynn Ave. Doll houses, miniature vehicles and more than 3,500 dolls—large and small, antique and modern, straw and china, rag and wooden, bisque and wax—in period costumes represent some 90 countries. Allow 30 minutes minimum. Mon.-Sat. 11-5; closed Jan. 1, Thanksgiving and Dec. 25. Admission $2; ages 5-15, $1.50. Children must be accompanied by an adult. Phone (912) 267-7569.

BUFORD—
see Atlanta and Vicinity p. 30.

CAIRO (F-2) pop. 9,000, elev. 265'

Though the Cairo (KAY-ro) area was supposedly visited by Hernando de Soto in 1540, it was not settled until pioneers from North Carolina founded the Tired Creek Primitive Baptist Church in 1826. By 1870 the local Atlantic & Gulf Railroad station had grown large enough to become a town, and Cairo was born. The town is a food-processing center in a rich farming region.

Cairo-Grady County Chamber of Commerce: 961 N. Broad St., P.O. Box 387, Cairo, GA 31728; phone (912) 377-3663.

RODDENBERY MEMORIAL LIBRARY, 320 N. Broad St., contains area history and wildlife displays and changing art exhibits from national institutions. Mon.-Fri. 9-6 (also Mon.-Tues. and Thurs. 6-7 p.m.), Sat. 9-3. Free. Phone (912) 377-3632.

CALHOUN (A-1) pop. 7,100, elev. 716'

Calhoun and surrounding Gordon County were the home of the Cherokee Indians until 1838, when the Cherokees were forced to sell their land and move to Oklahoma. The town is in a region where poultry and beef and dairy cattle are raised. Resaca Confederate Cemetery, 5 miles north on I-75, was the site of the Civil War battle that opened the way to Atlanta for Gen. William Tecumseh Sherman.

Gordon County Chamber of Commerce: 300 S. Wall St., Calhoun, GA 30701; phone (706) 625-3200.

NEW ECHOTA STATE HISTORIC SITE, 4 mi. n.e. on SR 225, is the site of the last capital of the Cherokee Nation in Georgia. The tribal nation adopted the alphabet devised by the American Indian scholar Sequoyah as the Cherokees' first written language. The *Cherokee Phoenix,* published in 1828, was the first newspaper to use this alphabet. The treaty that moved the Cherokee westward was signed at New Echota under the administration of President Andrew Jackson.

The restored and reconstructed village includes the Worcester House, the courthouse, Vann's Tavern and a newspaper office with a working press that reproduces the *Cherokee Phoenix.* Tues.-Sat. 9-5, Sun. 2-5:30; closed Jan. 1,

Thanksgiving and Dec. 25. Admission $2.50; ages 6-18, $1.50. Phone (706) 624-1321.

CARTERSVILLE (B-2) pop. 12,000, elev. 787′

Only two of Cartersville's houses survived the Federal occupation of 1864, but the town's location in Bartow County's rich mineral belt led to its speedy reconstruction.

Roselawn, the restored Victorian mansion of evangelist Samuel Porter Jones, houses his writings and memorabilia as well as those belonging to Rebecca Latimer Felton, who in 1922 became the first woman to serve in the U.S. Senate. The mansion also is home to the Etowah Historical Society and includes a small museum.

The Etowah Arts Gallery, at 11 Wall St., offers changing exhibitions of works by Georgia artists and artisans.

Cartersville-Bartow Convention and Visitors Bureau: 16 W. Main St., P.O. Box 200397, Cartersville, GA 30120; phone (770) 387-1357 or (800) 733-2280.

ETOWAH INDIAN MOUNDS STATE HISTORICAL SITE, 6 mi. s. of I-75 on SR 61/113, preserves the site of an American Indian settlement occupied more than 1,000 years ago. The earliest published description of the mounds dates from 1817, when a clergyman was guided to the site by a group of Cherokee chiefs who presumably were unaware of the long-abandoned area's significance. A museum displays artifacts excavated from the mounds. Tues.-Sat. 9-5, Sun. 2-5:30; closed Jan. 1, Thanksgiving and Dec. 25. Admission $3; ages 6-18, $2. Phone (770) 387-3747.

WILLIAM WEINMAN MINERAL MUSEUM is at 51 Mineral Museum Dr. N.E. Extensive displays of rocks and minerals from Georgia and the rest of the world interpret the state's geologic history. Included are a walk-in replica of a limestone cave with a waterfall, hands-on exhibits, fossils, mining history displays and cut gemstones, including an amethyst collection. Other highlights include changing exhibits and videotape programs.

Allow 30 minutes minimum. Tues.-Sat. 10-4:30, Sun. 1-4:30; phone for holiday closings. Admission $3.50; over 54, $3; ages 6-11, $2.50. Phone (770) 386-0576.

CHATSWORTH (A-2) pop. 2,900

Chatsworth, formerly an important talc-mining region, is now noted as a major producer of carpet. Just east is Fort Mountain State Park (see Recreation Chart and the AAA Southeastern CampBook); to the south is Carters Lake (see Recreation Chart).

Events that offer a variety of activities for horse enthusiasts include the Beaulieu North American Classic, held in April; Appalachian Wagon Train, spanning 10 days during the July

Fourth holiday; the Georgia State and Red Carpet Championship Mule-Draft Horse Frolic, held in early October; and the North Georgia International Horse Trials, held in October.

Chatsworth also holds the North Georgia Mountain Christmas Parade, a night parade held on the Saturday following Thanksgiving.

Chatsworth-Murray County Chamber of Commerce: N. 3rd Ave., P.O. Box 327, Chatsworth, GA 30705; phone (706) 695-6060.

VANN HOUSE STATE HISTORIC SITE, Spring Pl. 1 mi. s. of US 76 on SR 225, is the restored 1804 mansion of James Vann, a Cherokee chief who sponsored the influential Moravian Mission next to his plantation. The house is part of a memorial to the Cherokee Nation. Tues.-Sat. 9-5, Sun. 2-5:30; closed Thanksgiving and Dec. 25. Admission $2; ages 6-18, $1. Phone (706) 695-2598.

CHATTAHOOCHEE AND OCONEE NATIONAL FORESTS

Elevations in the forests range from 500 ft. in Oconee National Forest to 4,784 ft. at Brasstown Bald in Chattahoochee National Forest. Refer to AAA maps for additional elevation information.

The 749,268 acres of the Chattahoochee National Forest are in northern Georgia, and the 113,100 acres of the Oconee National Forest are in central Georgia. Both areas contribute to the state's timber production. Within the forests are campsites, picnic areas, wilderness areas, trails and the Chattooga National Wild and Scenic River.

The Chattahoochee National Forest includes the southern part of one of the world's most extensive and productive hardwood forests. Its Cohutta Wilderness, covering some 35,307 acres, is a popular area for fishing, hunting and hiking.

Also in the forest are the twin cascades of Anna Ruby Falls, where two creeks converge before running into Unicoi Lake and on into the Chattahoochee River. Anna Ruby Falls Scenic Area offers several hiking trails, a visitor center and picnic areas. The Anna Ruby Falls Visitor Center has exhibits and information about the history and natural resources of the area as well as a trout-viewing pond and trails.

Brasstown Bald Visitor Center, in Chattahoochee National Forest off SR 180 near Blairsville, is open Memorial Day through Labor Day; phone (706) 896-2556. On the summit of Brasstown Bald, the visitor center features a theater, a rooftop observation deck and exhibits about the relationship between people and mountains. The summit also has picnic facilities and three hiking trails.

The forest is open daily 24 hours. Free. Maps of the Cohutta Wilderness and the Chattooga River are available for $3 each, and a set of two maps of the Appalachian Trail is available for $8.95 by contacting the Supervisor's Office, 508 Oak St. N.W., Gainesville, GA 30501. Phone (770) 536-0541. *See Recreation Chart and the AAA Southeastern CampBook.*

CHATTAHOOCHEE RIVER NATIONAL RECREATION AREA—
see Atlanta and Vicinity p. 30.

★CHICKAMAUGA AND CHATTANOOGA NATIONAL MILITARY PARK (A-1)

The 8,113 acres of Chickamauga and Chattanooga National Military Park form the oldest and largest national military park administered by the U.S. National Park Service. The largest section is in northwest Georgia, with the remainder in Tennessee. Several areas within the park commemorate Civil War battles that were fought for control of Chattanooga, Tenn., a strategic railway center.

Early in September 1863, Union general William S. Rosecrans and 58,000 men crossed the Tennessee River southwest of Chattanooga, forcing the Confederate forces of Gen. Braxton Bragg to abandon the city and move south to protect their supply lines from Atlanta. After obtaining reinforcements, Bragg moved back northward, hoping to retake Chattanooga. The two forces clashed at Chickamauga Creek near the Georgia-Tennessee line.

Although victorious, the Confederates suffered heavy losses: 18,000 were killed, wounded or missing out of the 66,000 engaged. The Union forces withdrew to Chattanooga after suffering 16,000 casualties. The ensuing Confederate siege of the city almost subdued the Union army. However, bolstered by reinforcements and a new supply route, they resumed the offensive by November.

The 3-day Battle of Chattanooga began on Nov. 23, with Union forces driving the Confederates back to the base of Missionary Ridge and capturing Orchard Knob. When the Union troops assaulted the remaining Confederates in the Battle of Lookout Mountain the next day, the Confederates chose to evacuate the area rather than risk separation from their main line.

The decisive blow came a day later. Gen. Ulysses S. Grant directed the all-day Battle of Missionary Ridge, in which the Confederates were dislodged from strategic points and Union forces gained the steep slopes above the city. The Confederates withdrew after dark; their defeat opened the way to Atlanta and the heart of the Confederacy.

The woods and fields of this beautiful park are maintained to some degree in their wartime condition. More than 1,600 markers, monuments, cannons and tablets indicate the battle lines of both sides and recount the story of the area. Self-guiding tours enable visitors to explore the battlefields of Chickamauga, Lookout Mountain and Missionary Ridge.

Among points of interest are Orchard Knob, Grant's headquarters during the Battle of Chattanooga; Crest Road, along Missionary Ridge; Wilder Tower, commanding a good view of the Chickamauga Battlefield and its surroundings; the Brotherton House, a prewar farmhouse marking the spot where the Union line was broken; Snodgrass Hill, the scene of the last fighting at Chickamauga; and Snodgrass House, which served as a Union field hospital during the battle.

The park is open daily 8-5:45, Memorial Day-Labor Day; 8-4:45, rest of year. Closed Dec. 25. Free.

CHICKAMAUGA VISITOR CENTER is 9 mi. s. of Chattanooga, Tenn., on US 27, near the n. end of the park on Chickamauga Battlefield. A museum has Civil War exhibits and the Fuller gun collection, a display of American military shoulder arms. Orientation programs are offered.

Daily 8-5:45, Memorial Day-Labor Day; 8-4:45, rest of year. Closed Dec. 25. Visitor center

free. Multimedia presentation depicting the Battle of Chickamauga $3; over 62 and ages 6-16, $1.50. Tape tours relating the history of the park are available to purchase for $7 or to rent for $3. Phone (706) 866-9241.

POINT PARK, on Lookout Mountain, overlooks Chattanooga, Tenn., and the Moccasin Bend of the Tennessee River. The Ochs Memorial Museum and Observatory, the New York Peace Monument and Umbrella Rock are in the park as well as Cravens House, a restored house of the Civil War era. A visitor center at the north end of E. Brow Road contains the restored James Walker painting "Battle Above the Clouds," Civil War flags, code books and telescopes in the signaling exhibit.

Daily 8-5:45, Memorial Day-Labor Day; 8-4:45, rest of year. Park $2, family rate $4. Cravens House admission $2; senior citizens and ages 6-16, $1. Phone (423) 821-7786.

CLAYTON (A-3) pop. 1,600, elev. 1,925′

 RECREATIONAL ACTIVITIES

White-water Rafting

• **Southeastern Expeditions,** 7 mi. e. on SR 76. Write 50 Executive Park S., Atlanta, GA 30329. Daily 8:30-6, Mar.-Oct. Phone (800) 868-7238.

CLEVELAND (A-3) pop. 1,700, elev. 1,570′

CABBAGE PATCH KIDS BABYLAND GENERAL HOSPITAL, 73 W. Underwood St., houses hundreds of Cabbage Patch Kids dolls awaiting adoption. Allow 1 hour minimum. Mon.-Sat. 9-5, Sun. and holidays 10-5; closed Jan. 1, Thanksgiving and Dec. 24-25. Free. Phone (706) 865-2171.

COLUMBUS (D-2) pop. 179,300, elev. 261′

Columbus, once the site of a Creek Indian village on the Chattahoochee River on the western Georgia border, later became a trading post and was the last frontier town of the 13 original Colonies. On April 16, 1865, in one of the final battles of the Civil War, Union troops seized the important Confederate supply depot at Columbus. Remains of the breastworks are still visible.

The restored 1871 Springer Opera House, 103 10th St., is just outside Columbus' 26-block historic district. The opera house, which once featured such prominent figures as Edwin Booth, Oscar Wilde, Lily Langtry and Irving Berlin, now offers productions on a seasonal basis.

The Columbus Historic Riverfront Industrial District consists of 19th-century mills and ironworks in five separate areas along the east bank of the Chattahoochee River from 800 Front Ave. to 38th Street.

The Columbus Iron Works, 801 Front Ave., operated 1853-1964. The breech-loading cannon,

the first successful ice-making machine and the Confederate ironclad CSS *Jackson/Muscogee* were manufactured at the works, which is now a convention and trade center. The Chattahoochee Promenade on Front Avenue borders the river between Fifth and Ninth streets.

Noteworthy among Columbus' events is the Riverfest-Salisbury Pig Jig Festival, held the last full weekend in April, and the Columbus Steeplechase at Callaway Gardens *(see Pine Mountain p. 53)* held in November.

Columbus Convention and Visitors Bureau: 1000 Bay Ave., P.O. Box 2768, Columbus, GA 31902; phone (706) 322-1613.

Self-guiding tours: Brochures detailing a walking and/or driving tour of the original city are available from the Historic Columbus Foundation, 700 Broadway, Columbus, GA 31901; phone (706) 322-0756.

THE COLUMBUS MUSEUM is at 1251 Wynnton Rd. Among the museum's exhibits are works of 19th- and 20th-century American art, prehistoric American Indian artifacts, Yuchi Indian materials, a display of American decorative arts and regional historical items. Guided tours are available. Allow 1 hour minimum. Tues.-Sat. 10-5, Sun. 1-5; closed holidays. Free. Phone (706) 649-0713.

FORT BENNING, s.e. of Columbus, is an Army training center for infantry and airborne troops.

National Infantry Museum, at Fort Benning in Bldg. 396 on Baltzell Ave., is dedicated to the evolution of the infantry since the French and Indian War. Artifacts, weapons, uniforms, battle flags and medals are on display. Guided tours can be arranged. Allow 1 hour minimum. Mon.-Fri. 8-4:30, Sat.-Sun. 12:30-4:30. Free. Phone (706) 545-2958.

HERITAGE CORNER guided walking tours depart from the Historic Columbus Foundation headquarters at 700 Broadway. The tour encompasses five dwellings dating 1800-70; two are on their original sites. All are furnished and decorated in period style. The Walker-Peters-Langdon House, a simple Federal cottage, is believed to be the oldest residence in the city.

The Pemberton House was occupied by Dr. J.S. Pemberton, a druggist and originator of the formula for Coca-Cola. Allow 1 hour minimum. Tours are given Mon.-Fri. at 11 and 3, Sat.-Sun. at 2; closed Jan. 1, Easter, July 4, Thanksgiving and Dec. 25. Admission $3. Phone (706) 322-3181.

WOODRUFF MUSEUM OF CIVIL WAR AND NAVAL HISTORY is at 202 4th Victory Dr., just e. of the Oglethorpe Bridge. The museum depicts the history of the Confederate navy and the efforts of the South to become an important naval power. Displayed are artifacts, ship models and the remains of the ironclad CSS *Jackson/Musco-gee* and the gunboat CSS *Chattahoochee.* Allow 1 hour minimum. Tues.-Fri. 10-5, Sat.-Sun. 1-5; closed holidays. Donations. Phone (706) 327-9798.

COMER (B-4) pop. 900, elev. 573'

WATSON MILL BRIDGE STATE PARK is 3 mi. s. on SR 22 to Watson Mill Park Rd. A 236-foot four-span wooden covered bridge built around 1885 is in the park. Facilities are available for picnicking and camping; wading and fishing in the river are permitted. Daily 7 a.m.-10 p.m. Parking $2 per private vehicle. Phone (706) 783-5349. *See Recreation Chart and the AAA Southeastern CampBook.*

CORDELE (E-3) pop. 10,300, elev. 336'

GEORGIA VETERANS MEMORIAL STATE PARK is 9 mi. w. on US 280. Established in 1946, the park honors Georgia's war veterans. The 1,322-acre park includes an 18-hole golf course, a large lake and outdoor exhibits displaying vintage aircraft and military equipment. A visitor center museum houses a collection of artifacts and relics from different wars. Park open daily 7 a.m.-10 p.m. Museum daily 8-5 (also Fri. 5-10); closed Dec. 25. Free. Parking $2. Phone (912) 276-2371. *See Recreation Chart and the AAA Southeastern CampBook.*

CRAWFORDVILLE (B-4) pop. 600, elev. 589'

A.H. STEPHENS STATE HISTORIC PARK is 2 mi. n. of I-20 via SR 22 exit. Dating from 1830, Liberty Hall was the home of Alexander Stephens, a U.S. congressman who became vice president of the Confederacy in spite of his love for the Union. Stephens later served a second term as congressman and was elected governor of Georgia.

The house contains many of Stephens' possessions; a monument in front marks his grave. The A.H. Stephens Museum depicts life during the Civil War through a collection of weapons, uniforms and civilian artifacts. Tues.-Sat. 9-5, Sun. 2-5; closed holidays. Admission $2.50; ages 6-18, $1.50. Phone (706) 456-2602 for the park or 456-2221 for the museum.

CUMBERLAND ISLAND NATIONAL SEASHORE—

see Golden Isles p. 45.

CUTHBERT (E-2) pop. 3,700, elev. 446'

Cuthbert, founded in 1834, was named for the brothers John A. and Alfred Cuthbert, prominent Georgians of the time. A bustling agricultural center before the Civil War, the town continues to rely on farming as well as lumber and other industries.

Southwest Quarter-Chattahoochee Regional Chamber of Commerce: 219 N. Lumpkin St., Cuthbert, GA 31740, phone (912) 732-2683.

Self-guiding tours: The Cuthbert Historic District, which has more than 30 historic buildings—some dating from before the Civil War—is designated by informational and directional markers. Driving tours start at the chamber of commerce, where maps and brochures are available.

DAHLONEGA (A-2) pop. 3,100, elev. 1,875'

In 1828, nearly 3 centuries after Hernando de Soto sought gold in northwestern Georgia, the area around Dahlonega (dah-LON-a-gah) boomed with the discovery of the ore. A federal mint built in 1838 coined more than $6 million before it was closed at the outbreak of the Civil War. Gold coins minted in Dahlonega are highly prized by collectors.

Gold mining continued in Dahlonega until the early 20th century when the fixing of the metal's worth at $35 an ounce made mining unprofitable. In 1958 gold donated by residents was driven to Atlanta in a mule train and used to re-cover the dome of the Capitol with gold leaf.

Poultry production has replaced commercial gold mining, but Dahlonega and Lumpkin County have considerable riches of the recreational kind.

The price of gold is no longer fixed, and visitors can pan for the metal at Blackburn Park, Old Dahlonega and Crisson Mines. Crisson Mines also offers views of a commercial gold mine and stamping mill. Camping and other activities are available at Blackburn Park.

Dahlonega-Lumpkin County Chamber of Commerce: 101 S. Park St., Dahlonega, GA 30533; phone (706) 864-3711 or (800) 231-5543.

CONSOLIDATED GOLD MINES, 125 Consolidated Gold Mine Rd., offers guided tours of a former gold mine through well-lighted tunnels. An original drill demonstration as well as gold-panning techniques are featured. The underground mine remains at a constant temperature of 60 F. Allow 1 hour, 30 minutes minimum. Daily 10-4; closed Dec. 25. Admission $8; ages 6-12, $5. DS, MC, VI. Phone (706) 864-8473.

DAHLONEGA GOLD MUSEUM STATE HISTORIC SITE, on the public square, depicts America's first major gold rush through exhibits of nuggets and gold dust, mining apparatus and early photographs of mining activities. A 30-minute film, "Gold Fever," describes mining techniques and prospector lifestyles during the gold-rush years. Allow 1 hour minimum. Mon.-Sat. 9-5, Sun. 10-5; closed Jan. 1, Thanksgiving and Dec. 25. Admission $3; ages 6-18, $2. Phone (706) 864-2257.

☀❄❄ RECREATIONAL ACTIVITIES

Canoeing

• **Appalachian Outfitters,** on SR 60, P.O. Box 793, Dahlonega, GA 30533. Mon.-Fri. 10-3, Sat.-Sun. 9-4. Phone (706) 864-7117.

DALLAS (B-2) pop. 2,800

PICKETT'S MILL HISTORIC SITE, 5 mi. n.e. on Dallas-Acworth Rd., then s. to 2640 Mt. Tabor Rd., was the site of the defeat of Union troops advancing toward Atlanta during the Civil War. Walking trails with explanatory signs cross the battlefield; living-history programs, a film, a videotape rendition of the battle and battle artifacts also are featured. Allow 1 hour minimum. Tues.-Sat. and Mon. holidays 9-5, Sun. noon-5; closed Jan. 1, Thanksgiving and Dec. 25. Admission $2; ages 6-18, $1. DS, MC, VI. Phone (770) 443-7850.

DALTON (A-2) pop. 21,800, elev. 767'

In the early 1900s a local farm girl sold a hand-tufted bedspread for $2.50 and unknowingly revived a century-old craft that was to become big business in Dalton. Although the bedspreads are no longer available, the craft is perpetuated in the production of floor coverings. Dalton supplies more than half of the world's tufted carpets.

Another craft is preserved 10 miles northeast of Dalton, off I-75 exit 138 on SR 2, at the restored Prater's Mill. Dating from the 1850s, the mill still grinds cornmeal during country fairs held on the site twice a year. The Prater's Mill Country Fair, which features craft demonstrations, entertainment and traditional Southern food, takes place Mother's Day weekend and Columbus Day weekend; phone (706) 275-6455.

Dalton Convention and Visitors Bureau: 2211 Dug Gap Battle Rd., Dalton, GA 30720; phone (706) 272-7676 or (800) 331-3258. *See color ad.*

DARIEN (E-5) pop. 1,800

Established as a stronghold to protect England's rich Southern holdings from Spanish, French and Indian attacks in the 1720s, Darien was settled by Scottish Highlanders under James Oglethorpe. The town became a prosperous center of timber shipping and trade by the mid-1800s. The Darien River, which determined the town's location, is now dotted with shrimp boats that form the basis of the local economy.

Recreational opportunities, including fishing, swimming and deep-sea charter excursions, are available north on US 17 at Pine Harbor and Shellman Bluff.

McIntosh County Chamber of Commerce: 105 Fort King George Dr., P.O. Box 1497, Darien, GA 31305; phone (912) 437-4192.

Shopping areas: Magnolia Bluffs Outlet Mall at 1 Magnolia Bluff Way features 60 stores, including Levis, Osh-Kosh and Stone Mountain outlets.

FORT KING GEORGE STATE HISTORIC SITE is 1 mi. e. of US 17 on Fort King George Dr. The frontier fort, consisting of a cypress blockhouse and palisaded earthen battlements on a low peninsula in the Altamaha River, was the first English settlement in what is now the state of Georgia, serving as the Southern outpost for the British Empire 1721-36. The 18th-century fort and blockhouse have been reconstructed on the original site and are open to the public.

The museum interprets American Indian, Spanish and British occupation as well as the history of coastal sawmills. Living-history programs are given most weekends. Allow 1 hour minimum. Tues.-Sat. 9-5, Sun. 2-5:30; closed Jan. 1, Thanksgiving and Dec. 25. Admission $2.50; ages 6-18, $1.50. Phone (912) 437-4770.

★**HOFWYL-BROADFIELD PLANTATION—** *see Brunswick p. 35.*

DECATUR—
see Atlanta and Vicinity p. 30.

DOUGLAS (E-4) pop. 10,500, elev. 275'

Named for Stephen A. Douglas, political opponent of Abraham Lincoln, Douglas is a major tobacco market and one of the largest hog markets in Georgia. Tobacco auctions are held from mid-July to mid-September; morning is the best time to attend.

Rodeos and craft fairs attract visitors each spring and fall. The Southeast Georgia Fair is held in April. Recreational opportunities abound

in nearby General Coffee State Park (*see Recreation Chart and the AAA Southeastern CampBook*).

Douglas-Coffee County Chamber of Commerce: 404 N. Peterson Ave., P.O. Box 1607, Douglas, GA 31533; phone (912) 384-1873.

EATONTON (C-4) pop. 4,700

Eatonton was the birthplace in 1848 of Joel Chandler Harris, creator of the popular children's characters Uncle Remus, Br'er Fox, Br'er Bear and Br'er Rabbit. A statue of Br'er Rabbit on Courthouse Square commemorates Harris' works. Eatonton also was home to Alice Walker, author of the 1983 Pulitzer Prize-winning novel "The Color Purple." In April the Color Purple Ball is held to support the Color Purple Scholarship Fund.

April also brings the Spring Tour of Homes, showcasing historic houses and resort houses on Lake Oconee. The Putnam County Dairy Festival, featuring arts and crafts, a parade and other entertainment, is held the first Saturday in June.

Fifteen miles southeast county-owned Oconee Springs Park provides recreational facilities on Lake Sinclair (*see Recreation Chart and the AAA Southeastern CampBook*). Lake Oconee (*see Recreation Chart*), suitable for water skiing and many other water sports, is 7 miles east.

Eatonton-Putnam Chamber of Commerce: 105 Sumter St., P.O. Box 4088, Eatonton, GA 31024; phone (706) 485-7701.

Self-guiding tours: Maps of a driving tour honoring Alice Walker are available at the chamber of commerce.

ROCK EAGLE, 7 mi. n. on US 441, is a 1,500-acre state 4-H center. On the center's grounds is an American Indian mound topped by a huge open-winged eagle made of milky quartz stones pieced together on the ground. Archeologists believe that the Moundbuilders used the effigy in religious ceremonies some 2,000-4,000 years ago. A tower affords a complete view of the structure. Daily dawn-dusk. Free. Phone (706) 485-2831.

UNCLE REMUS MUSEUM, 3 blks. s. on US 441 in Turner Park, is a log cabin built from two slave cabins. In a similar dwelling the little boy in Joel Chandler Harris' tales heard the stories of Uncle Remus, thought to be a fictional composite of two slaves who excelled at storytelling. The fictional house was based on Turnwold, the plantation near Eatonton where Harris was an apprentice on a weekly newspaper. It was at the paper that the author heard the fanciful yarns that later formed the basis of his writing.

The museum is furnished to depict the setting of Uncle Remus' stories, and there are woodcarvings and paintings of Harris' characters. Also displayed are first editions of many of his books.

Allow 30 minutes minimum. Mon.-Sat. 10-noon and 1-5, Sun. 2-5, May-Sept.; Wed.-Sat. and Mon. 10-noon and 1-5, Sun. 2-5, rest of year. Admission 50c, children 25c. Phone (706) 485-6856.

ELBERTON (B-4) pop. 5,700, elev. 708'

ELBERTON GRANITE MUSEUM & EXHIBIT is on SR 17, .5 mi. w. of SR 72. With 45 quarries and more than 100 manufacturing plants, the Elberton area is thought to be the largest granite-producing region in the world. The museum displays interesting granite products of the past, antique working tools and a chart detailing quarrying procedures. Allow 30 minutes minimum. Daily 2-5; closed Dec. 25-Jan. 2. Free. Phone (706) 283-2551.

FITZGERALD (E-3) pop. 8,600, elev. 275'

BLUE AND GRAY MUSEUM, in the Municipal Building, contains artifacts and displays pertaining to both Union and Confederate soldiers' experiences during the Civil War and mirrors the town's beginnings in the 1890s as a Union soldier's colony in the heart of Dixie. Allow 1 hour minimum. Mon.-Fri. 2-5, Mar.-Oct.; by appointment rest of year. Closed holidays. Admission $1; ages 1-16, 50c. Phone (912) 423-5375, or 423-3337 Nov.-Feb.

FOLKSTON (F-5) pop. 2,300, elev. 80'

Folkston is near the eastern entrance to Okefenokee Swamp, an area of more than 600 square miles. The swamp's name refers to the American Indian word for "houses" that are formed when expanding gases raise clumps of partially decayed vegetation above the water level, allowing them to pick up seeds of plants and trees, which germinate and grow, ultimately anchoring the floating islands. Most of the swamp was declared a wildlife refuge in 1937.

Folkston/Charlton County Chamber of Commerce: 202 W. Main St., P.O. Box 756, Folkston, GA 31537; phone (912) 496-2536.

OKEFENOKEE NATIONAL WILDLIFE REFUGE occupies 396,000 acres of the Okefenokee Swamp. It is accessible via the main or eastern entrance at Suwannee Canal Recreation Area, the western entrance at Stephen C. Foster State Park (*see Recreation Chart*) and the northern entrance at the Okefenokee Swamp Park (*see Waycross p. 66*).

Fishing is permitted at the Suwannee Canal, Stephen C. Foster Recreation Area and two unstaffed secondary entrances that provide access to the swamp's interior. Rental boats, motors and canoes are available; rates vary. Camping and cabins are at the western entrance. The swamp's abundant plant and animal life can best be observed on self-guiding wilderness canoe trails.

Canoe trips lasting from 2 to 5 days require permits issued by the refuge manager; reservations can be made up to 2 months in advance.

Contact the Manager, Route 2, Box 3330, Folkston, GA 31537. Fees for the east or west entrance to the refuge are $4 per private vehicle. Fee at the north entrance in Waycross is $10 per person; ages 5-11, $7. Phone (912) 496-3331.

Suwannee Canal Recreation Area (east entrance), 8 mi. s.w. on SR 23/121, then 3.5 mi. w. on Spur 121, is the main or eastern entrance to the refuge. A visitor center offers exhibits, films and information about activities. A wildlife drive provides access to walking trails, a restored swamp homestead and a 4,000-foot boardwalk leading to a 50-foot observation tower.

Unguided visitors are permitted on certain designated waterways during posted hours. A concessioner offers boat trips as well as canoe, boat and motor rentals, fishing supplies and food service. Daily 7 a.m.-7:30 p.m., Mar. 1-Sept. 10; 8-6, rest of year. Closed Dec. 25. A $2.50 launching fee is charged for private boats; motors must not exceed 10 hp. Phone (912) 496-7836. *See Recreation Chart.*

FORSYTH (C-3) pop. 4,300, elev. 704'

Forsyth is named for Gov. John Forsyth, who served as secretary of state to Presidents Andrew Jackson and Martin Van Buren. In 1834 the town became a regional transportation center when it was linked with the railroad. It also served as a distribution point when cotton planters brought their product to Forsyth for shipment to Macon and the southern United States.

The Monroe County Courthouse, in the center of Courthouse Square, was built in 1896 and is an example of Victorian architecture. The courthouse is in the middle of an eight-block historic district that preserves late 19th- and early 20th-century buildings. The Monroe County Museum and Store, Tift College Drive, is a restored 1896 Victorian depot. Its museum features railroad memorabilia and exhibits about local history.

The Rum Creek Wildlife Management Area, 7 miles east on SR 18, comprises 8,100 acres on Lake Juliette. High Falls State Park, 11 miles north on High Falls Road just off I-75, features a scenic waterfall *(see Recreation Chart).*

The Forsythia Festival, held in late March or early April, celebrates the arrival of spring with art shows, crafts, sports tournaments and a parade.

Forsyth-Monroe County Chamber of Commerce: 267 Tift College Dr., P.O. Box 811, Forsyth, GA 31029; phone (912) 994-9239.

Self-guiding tours: Brochures and maps detailing a driving tour of historic houses are available at the chamber of commerce.

FORT FREDERICA NATIONAL MONUMENT—

see Golden Isles p. 45.

FORT GAINES (E-1) pop. 1,200, elev. 163'

At 100 Bluff St. overlooking the Chattahoochee River is Fort Gaines Frontier Village, an open-air museum with log cabins, cane mills, gristmills, a smokehouse and a Civil War cannon. A partial replica of the 1814 frontier fort and a pioneer cemetery are nearby.

Also in the area is Lake Walter F. George *(see Recreation Chart).* The 3-mile-long Walter George Dam has a lock with what is purported to be one of the highest lifts in the world.

Fort Gaines Chamber of Commerce: P.O. Box 298, Fort Gaines, GA 31751; phone (912) 768-2934.

FORT GORDON (C-5)

SIGNAL CORPS MUSEUM, 37th St. and Avenue of the States, is both a research center and a museum for communications and military signal history. Items on display include signal devices from the Civil War, early telegraph keying mechanisms and sophisticated microwave equipment used during the Vietnam War.

A restored World War II Harley-Davidson motorcycle is on display. A section of the museum is devoted to signal corps combat photographers. Tues.-Fri. 8-4, Sat. noon-5; closed holidays. Free. Phone (706) 791-3856.

★FORT PULASKI NATIONAL MONUMENT (D-6)

Fort Pulaski National Monument, 15 miles east of Savannah via US 80, occupies Cockspur and McQueens islands at the mouth of the Savannah River. Fort Pulaski, on the eastern end of Cockspur Island, was preceded by Fort George and Fort Greene, dating from 1761 and 1794-95, respectively.

When the British fleet approached during the Revolution, American patriots dismantled Fort George. A hurricane demolished Fort Greene in 1804. Beginning in 1829, 18 years were required to build Fort Pulaski, a massive irregular pentagon surrounded by a moat crossed by drawbridges. The long galleries are distinguished by fine brick arches.

State troops seized the fort when war between the South and North seemed imminent. Two weeks later Georgia seceded from the Union and the fort was turned over to the Confederacy. Ammunition from newly developed cannons bored through the fort's supposedly impenetrable walls during a 30-hour bombardment in 1862, forcing the post's surrender. Projectiles fired at the fort during the conflict are still embedded in its walls.

The fort offers demonstrations of military arts and garrison life from the Civil War era. The visitor center features artillery exhibits, displays and a videotape presentation detailing the fort's past. Various daily programs are scheduled and self-guiding trails and picnic facilities are available. Allow 1 hour, 30 minutes minimum. Daily 8:30-6:45, Memorial Day-Labor Day; 8:30-5:15, rest of year. Closed Dec. 25. Admission $2, under 17 free, family rate $4. Phone (912) 786-5787.

FORT STEWART MILITARY RESERVATION (D-5)

THE FORT STEWART MUSEUM, Bldg. 814 on Wilson Ave., features an extensive collection of military equipment from World War I, World War II and the Korean War. Exhibits include photographs, uniforms, guns and other weapons. Military equipment used during Operation Desert Storm also is displayed. Allow 1 hour minimum. Tues.-Sun. 10-4; closed Jan. 1, Thanksgiving and Dec. 25. Free. Phone (912) 767-4480.

FORT VALLEY (D-3) pop. 8,200, elev. 525'

Legend has it that the real name of the town was Fox Valley, but when submitted to the Post Office in 1825, illegible handwriting was read as "Fort" and so it has remained.

Cotton was gradually replaced by the peach as a cash crop; in 1875 a new peach variety, the Elberta, was introduced. The new peach and access to railroads made Fort Valley a peach-growing center in the Peach State. The area became so successful that a new county was formed—ultimately named Peach. The Georgia Peach Festival is held in June; for information phone (912) 825-4002.

Peach County Chamber of Commerce: 114 Vineville St., P.O. Box 1238, Fort Valley, GA 31030; phone (912) 825-3733.

MASSEE LANE GARDENS, 5 mi. s. on SR 49, is home to the national headquarters of the American Camellia Society. The 9-acre gardens contain hundreds of camellia varieties that bloom November through March. Highlights include a greenhouse, rose garden and Japanese garden with waterfalls. Two museums and a gallery contain china and more than 300 porcelain sculptures of birds by Edward Boehm. A library of rare books has volumes dating from 1669 as well as works of 19th-century artists. Guided tours are available.

Allow 30 minutes minimum. Mon.-Sat. 9-5, Sun. 1-5, Nov.-Mar.; Mon.-Fri. 9-4, rest of year. Closed holidays. Admission $2, under 12 free. Phone (912) 967-2358.

GAINESVILLE (B-3) pop. 17,900, elev. 1,227'

Gainesville is on the northeast shore of Lake Sidney Lanier (see Recreation Chart). In the early 19th century the city was known as Mule Camp Springs.

Offerings in the Gainesville area range from refined to rowdy. The Green Street Historical District consists of late Victorian and neoclassical revival structures along a broad tree-lined street. The Quinlan Art Center displays exhibits by state and local artists. Road Atlanta, 10 miles south on SR 53, is an SCCA-sanctioned road-racing course.

Greater Hall County Chamber of Commerce: 230 E.E. Butler Pkwy., P.O. Box 374, Gainesville, GA 30503; phone (770) 532-6206.

Self-guiding tours: Maps and brochures detailing walking and driving tours of historic sections in Gainesville and surrounding Hall County are available at the Georgia Mountains Museum (see attraction listing) or from the chamber of commerce.

GEORGIA MOUNTAINS MUSEUM is at 311 Green St. S.E. The museum features nature, arts and crafts and historical exhibits as well as items collected by Ed Dodd, the creator of the "Mark Trail" comic strip. Mementos from the 1996 Olympic rowing competition are exhibited. Also displayed is memorabilia of Gen. James Longstreet. Guided tours are available by reservation. Allow 1 hour minimum. Tues.-Fri. 10-5, Sat. 10-3:30; closed holidays. Admission $2, over 55 and students with ID $1. Phone (770) 536-0889.

Golden Isles

When Spain claimed the lovely subtropical islands along the Georgia coast as the Golden Isles of Guale in the 16th century, habitation was not new to the land. Archeological evidence traces American Indian settlement to about 2500 B.C. Spain ceded the islands to Great Britain in 1763.

The term Golden Isles refers essentially to St. Simons Island, Jekyll Island and Sea Island, all near the city of Brunswick. St. Simons Island is the largest of the three. These are the only islands accessible by car. Other islands in the area include Blackbeard, Cumberland, Little St. Simons, St. Catherines and Sapelo.

Jekyll Island / Georgia Dept. of Industry, Trade & Tourism

Just northeast of Sapelo is Blackbeard Island, where the pirate Edward Teach is said to have hidden his loot. St. Catherines Island is the former home of Button Gwinnett, one of Georgia's three signers of the Declaration of Independence. Southernmost in the chain and once the Carnegie family's private resort, Cumberland Island is now a national seashore.

CUMBERLAND ISLAND NATIONAL SEASHORE (F-6)

The largest and southernmost of Georgia's Golden Isles, Cumberland Island is separated from the mainland by several miles of salt marsh, river and sound. The relatively flat island, 18 miles long by 3 miles wide, parallels the Georgia coast just north of the Florida border. On its eastern side white sand beaches rise to dunes that give way to a forest of magnolias, oaks, palmettos and pines. More than 300 species of birds have been sighted on the island.

Although Cumberland Island exists in a relatively undisturbed state, American Indians inhabited it as early as 4,000 years ago. They called the island Missoe, which meant "sassafras." These American Indians were succeeded by the Spanish in 1566 and the English in 1736. At various times live oaks were cut for ship timbers, and land was cleared for the cultivation of fruits and sea island cotton.

The family of Revolutionary War officer Gen. Nathanael Greene built Dungeness plantation on the island in the late 18th century. Only a small building of tabby—a mixture of oyster shell, lime and sand—and a family cemetery remain, the latter the original burial site of Henry "Light-Horse Harry" Lee of Virginia, the father of Gen. Robert E. Lee and a friend of Greene.

A century later Thomas Carnegie built a lavish 30-room mansion called Dungeness as the centerpiece of an estate that covered 90 percent of Cumberland. Vegetation grows through the remains of the second Dungeness mansion, which burned in the 1950s. Plum Orchard, another Carnegie house, survives on the banks of the Brick Hill River. A small percentage of the island is privately owned and not open to visitors.

Restricted camping is available at developed and backcountry campsites; reservations are required. For further information contact the Superintendent, Cumberland Island National Seashore, P.O. Box 806, St. Marys, GA 31558.

The island is open daily 24 hours. Ferry service provides the only access; just 300 visitors are permitted per day. Private vehicles and pets are not permitted. A National Park Service ferry departs from the visitor center at St. Marys daily at 9 and 11:45, returning daily at 4:45, Mar. 15-Sept. 30. Departures Thurs.-Mon. at 9 and 11:45, rest of year. Ferry $9.50; over 65, $7.50; under 13, $5.65. Reservations are required. Phone (912) 882-4336 for information or 882-4335 for ferry reservations. See Recreation Chart.

FORT FREDERICA NATIONAL MONUMENT (E-6)

Fort Frederica National Monument is on St. Simons Island, which is reached from the mainland via the Brunswick-St. Simons Causeway, a toll road.

In 1736 Gen. James Oglethorpe began construction of an earthwork that became one of the most important British fortifications in America. Next to the fort he laid out the town of Frederica. The settlement and fort were vital in the defense of English interests in the conflict with Spain that erupted in 1739.

On July 7, 1742, the Battle of Bloody Marsh settled the fighting. The entire Colony of Georgia remained under English rule. The Bloody Marsh Memorial Site, a separate area 6 miles south, is open daily. A recording describes the battle.

Oglethorpe's regiment disbanded in 1749, ruining Frederica's economy. A fire in 1758 destroyed most of the town, and the last soldiers left the fort in 1763. Ruins lie atop a bluff on the island's western shore overlooking the Frederica River, and foundations of original houses have been uncovered. Field exhibits explain features of the area.

A visitor center houses pictorial panels, a diorama and excavated objects pertaining to Frederica. A historical film is shown every 30 minutes. Self-guiding and theatrical tape tours are available. Allow 1 hour, 30 minutes minimum. The monument is open daily 8-5; closed Dec. 25. The visitor center is open daily 9-5; closed Dec 25. Entrance fee $2, over 62 and under 16 free. Maximum charge $4 per private vehicle. Phone (912) 638-3639.

JEKYLL ISLAND (F-6)

The most crowded chapter in the history of Jekyll (JECK-el) Island began in 1886 when prominent East Coast millionaires, including Frank Henry Goodyear, Edwin and George Gould, J.P. Morgan, Joseph Pulitzer and William Rockefeller bought the island for $125,000. Naming themselves the Jekyll Island Club, they built a large clubhouse and elaborate cottages for use as a hunting preserve and family getaway.

The activities of some members while staying at this haven changed world events. In 1910 the first draft of the Federal Reserve Act, the foundation of the nation's monetary system, was drawn up. From Jekyll Island in 1915 the president of AT&T made the first transcontinental telephone call, speaking with President Woodrow Wilson in Washington, D.C., Alexander Graham Bell in New York and Bell's assistant Thomas Watson in San Francisco.

By the early 20th century Jekyll Island Club members were said to represent one-sixth of the world's wealth. By World War II, later generations had lost interest and had largely left the island, which was sold in 1947 to the state of Georgia for use as a state park.

Jekyll Island is now one of Georgia's major resort areas. The 10-mile beach offers surf fishing, swimming, bathhouses and a beach walk. Golf, nature walks, tennis, miniature golf, sightseeing cruises and miles of bicycle trails are all available, plus picnic areas, campsites and a water park. Bicycles can be rented.

The Jekyll Island Musical Theatre Festival, in the island's outdoor amphitheater, presents Broadway productions and events from late June to early August.

Jekyll Island Welcome Center: 901 Jekyll Island Cswy., Jekyll Island, GA 31527; phone (912) 635-3636 or (800) 841-6586.

JEKYLL ISLAND CLUB HISTORIC DISTRICT, a cluster of late 19th-century cottages along Riverview Dr., is a reminder of an era when social life revolved around the Jekyll Island Club. Tours begin at the historic district orientation center in the old club stables on Stable Road, where permanent exhibits and a videotape presentation explain the history of the island.

An interpretive ride aboard an open-air tram stops at selected former homes of some of America's wealthiest families. Tram tours depart daily on the hour 10-3. Orientation center open daily 9:30-4; closed Jan. 1 and Dec. 25. Tours $10; ages 6-18, $6. MC, VI. Phone (912) 635-2762.

SUMMER WAVES, 210 S. Riverview Dr., is an 11-acre water park. Featured attractions are six waterslides 30-50 feet high, a wave pool and a lazy river. Food is available. Daily 10-6 (also Sat. 6-8 p.m.), Memorial Day-Labor Day. Admission $12.50; under 48 inches tall, $9.95; over age 60, $6.50. Night Splash, after 4 p.m., $5.50. AE, DS, MC, VI. Phone (912) 635-2074 or (800) 841-6586.

ST. SIMONS ISLAND (E-6)

St. Simons Island has an active Colonial history. The area around Gascoigne Bluff served as the headquarters for English ships after 1736. Land disputes between Spain and England exploded in 1742 with the Battle of Bloody Marsh *(see Fort Frederica National Monument p. 45).* Timber cut on the island was used in the first ships of the U.S. Navy, including the USS *Constitution.*

Aaron Burr sought refuge along the shores of St. Simons Island after his duel with Alexander Hamilton. British actress Fanny Kemble Butler penned many of her anti-slavery letters at the Hampton Plantation. Near the remains of the moat that surrounded the town of Frederica stand ancient live oaks under which John and Charles Wesley, the Anglican ministers who founded Methodism, once preached.

The village, at the island's southern tip, includes a 200-year-old working lighthouse, coastal history museum and fishing pier. St. Simons provides an appropriate setting for such activities as golf, tennis, fishing and boating. Bicycle trails parallel many of the roads on the island.

St. Simons Island Visitors Center: 530B Beachview Dr. W., St. Simons Island, GA 31522; phone (912) 638-9014.

ARTHUR J. MOORE METHODIST MUSEUM is part of the Methodist Conference Center Epworth-by-the-Sea on Arthur Moore Dr. It displays a collection of Methodist artifacts, including two original letters by John Wesley, and has a 5,000-volume library pertaining to Methodist and general church history. Videotape presentations relate to the work of leaders in Methodist ministry and missions. Allow 1 hour minimum. Tues.-Sat. 9-4. Free. Phone (912) 638-4050.

CHRIST CHURCH, just s. of Fort Frederica National Monument, was established in 1736. Charles Wesley, chaplain to Gen. James Oglethorpe's settlers at Fort Frederica, was the first priest. After building the present edifice in 1885 as a memorial to his wife, Anson Green Phelps Dodge Jr. took Holy Orders and served as rector until 1898. His life was the subject of the novel "Beloved Invader" by local writer Eugenia Price. Daily 2-5. Donations. Phone (912) 638-8683.

MUSEUM OF COASTAL HISTORY, 101 12th St., is in a restored 1872 lighthouse-keeper's house. Changing exhibits depict local history. The adjacent lighthouse offers a fine view of the island. Earlier structures on the site have included two forts as well as a lighthouse built in 1810 and destroyed during the Civil War. Mon.-Sat. 10-5, Sun. 1:30-5; closed Thanksgiving and Dec. 25. Admission $3; ages 6-11, $1. Phone (912) 638-4666.

SAPELO ISLAND (E-6)

SAPELO ISLAND NATIONAL ESTUARINE RESEARCH RESERVE is reached by a 30-minute ferry ride from the Meridian Ferry Dock off I-95 exit 9, then 14 mi. n. on SR 99. The visitor center at the dock features exhibits and audiovisual presentations about the area. The tour of the island is by bus and includes the Palladian-style 1925 R.J. Reynolds mansion, the University of Georgia Marine Institute and Hog Hammock, a small community of Sapelo Plantation slave descendents.

Allow 3 hours minimum. Ferry departs Wed. at 8:30 and Sat. at 9, (also Fri. at 9, June 1-Labor Day). Fare $10; ages 6-18, $6. Reservations are required. Phone (912) 485-2251, or 437-3224 for ferry reservations.

SEA ISLAND (E-6)

Seaward of St. Simons Island and accessible from there by causeway, Sea Island is an all-year resort in a lush garden setting of flowering shrubs, ancient oaks, palms and pines. The island lies between the Atlantic Ocean and the marshes of Glynn County, the subject of Sidney Lanier's poem.

Sea Island has long been a favorite with heads of state. Presidents Calvin Coolidge, Herbert Hoover, Dwight Eisenhower, Richard Nixon, Gerald Ford, Jimmy Carter and George Bush all vacationed on the island. John Kennedy Jr. was married on the island. In addition to a smooth 5-mile beach, there are excellent facilities for golf, skeet shooting, horseback riding, tennis and fishing.

HAMPTON (C-2) pop. 2,700, elev. 890′

ATLANTA MOTOR SPEEDWAY is .2 mi. w. of jct. US 19/41. Tours of the motorsport facility allow visitors to experience pit road, the NASCAR garage, victory lane and a VIP suite high above the grandstand. A small garden dedicated to Richard Petty contains a statue of the race car driver. Mon.-Sat. 9-5, Sun. 1-5; closed Easter, Thanksgiving and Dec. 25. No tours conducted during race weeks. Tours $3, under 12 free. AE, DS, MC, VI. Phone (770) 707-7970.

HELEN (A-3) pop. 300

A nearly deserted lumbermill town in 1969, Helen has been remodeled to resemble an Alpine village. Craft and antique shops specializing in foreign items abound in the area.

A number of events are held each year, some with a European theme. The Fasching Karnival occurs in January and February, a wildflower festival in April, a balloon festival in June and Oktoberfest early September to late October. Christmas in Helen begins in late November with the illumination of Alpen lights.

Several state parks and the surrounding Chattahoochee National Forest *(see place listing p. 37)* provide opportunities for recreation. Unicoi State Park *(see Recreation Chart and the AAA Southeastern CampBook)* is 2 miles northeast off SR 356. The Russell-Brasstown Scenic Byway (SR 348), which runs through the Chattahoochee National Forest between Helen and Brasstown Bald, is particularly scenic in autumn.

Greater Helen Area Chamber of Commerce: P.O. Box 730, Helen, GA 30545; phone (706) 878-1619 or (800) 858-8027.

GOLD MINES OF HELEN, GA is 1 mi. s. on SR 75 at 10 Brucken Straus Dr. The 1828 gold mine features displays of mining equipment used during its century of operation. A nature trail traverses a wooded area with creeks and a small waterfall. Daily 10-6, June-Aug.; Sat.-Sun. noon-4, Apr.-May and Sept.-Oct. Admission $4; ages 6-12, $2. Panning for gold or gems is additional. MC, VI. Phone (706) 878-3052.

SAVE **MUSEUM OF THE HILLS,** Main St., uses taped dialogue and wax figures in dioramas to depict the life of those inhabiting Georgia's hilly northern regions. Fantasy Dreamland, the other half of the museum, re-creates imaginative settings from fairy tales and nursery rhymes. Allow 30 minutes minimum. Daily 10-9, June 1-Nov. 7; 10-6, rest of year. Closed Dec. 25. Admission $4.50; over 61, $4; ages 13-18, $3; ages 5-12, $2. AE, DI, MC, VI. Phone (706) 878-3140.

JACKSON (C-3) pop. 4,100, elev. 697′

INDIAN SPRINGS STATE PARK, 5 mi. s.e. on SR 42 off US 23, is on the site of mineral springs in use long before white settlers came to this part of Georgia. Creek Indians once believed the water healed their sick and brought extra vigor to the healthy.

Two major treaties with the Creeks were signed in the vicinity, ceding millions of acres of land to the federal government. The park has been open to the public since 1825. A small museum operates in the summer. Park open daily 7 a.m.-10 p.m. Museum open Tues.-Sun. 10-6, Memorial Day-Labor Day. Hours may vary; phone ahead. Free. Parking $2. Phone (770) 504-2277. *See Recreation Chart.*

JASPER (B-2) pop. 1,800

An itinerant stonecutter traveling through the north Georgia hills in 1835 noticed an outcropping of particularly fine marble. The small quarry he founded near the present site of Jasper was the first exploitation of a vein estimated to be large enough to supply the world's building needs for 3,000 years.

The prominence of marble in construction and art is celebrated during the Marble Festival, held the first weekend in October. The affair combines craft shows, sculpture exhibitions and competitions, musical events and other activities. Tours of nearby Georgia Marble Co. operations are available during the event.

Pickens County Chamber of Commerce: 104 N. Main St., P.O. Box 327, Jasper, GA 30143; phone (706) 692-5600.

JEFFERSON (B-3) pop. 2,800, elev. 850′

CRAWFORD W. LONG MUSEUM, on the public square at 28 College St., honors the doctor who in 1842 used sulfuric ether as an anesthetic to perform the first painless surgical operation. The three-building museum complex occupies the site of Dr. Long's office. Exhibits deal with Dr. Long's life and the history of anesthetics. The complex also includes a 19th-century doctor's office, an apothecary shop, a general store and an herb garden.

Movies are shown upon request. Special programs are presented bimonthly. Crawford W. Long Day, held the first Saturday in November, features crafts, games and entertainment indicative of the mid-1800s. A genealogical library and brochures for a walking tour of Jefferson are available. Allow 30 minutes minimum. Tues.-Sat. 10-4; closed major holidays. Donations. Phone (706) 367-5307.

JEKYLL ISLAND—
see Golden Isles p. 46.

JONESBORO—
see Atlanta and Vicinity p. 31.

JULIETTE (C-3) elev. 376′

The nearly abandoned town of Juliette, a thriving mill town in the 1930s, was revived in the early 1990s with the local filming of the movie "Fried Green Tomatoes." Visitors can sample fried green tomatoes at the Whistle Stop Cafe, a former train depot.

JARRELL PLANTATION STATE HISTORIC SITE is 5 mi. s. on US 23, 3 mi. e. on SR 18, then 3 mi. n. on Jarrell Plantation Rd. An example of a self-sufficient working farm, the 48-acre historic site was settled in the 1840s and belonged to the Jarrell family until 1974. Among the 20 historic buildings on the site are a mill complex, blacksmith shop, barn, sawmill, cotton gin and smokehouse.

Inside the main residence are original 19th-century furnishings, including looms and spinning wheels, a cobbler's bench and a wood-burning stove. The self-guiding tour begins with a slide show. Comfortable shoes are advised. Allow 1 hour minimum. Tues.-Sat. 9-5, Sun. 2-5:30; closed Jan. 1, Thanksgiving and Dec. 25. Admission $2; ages 4-18, $1. Phone (912) 986-5172.

KENNESAW—
see Atlanta and Vicinity p. 31.

KENNESAW MOUNTAIN NATIONAL BATTLEFIELD PARK—
see Atlanta and Vicinity p. 31.

LaGRANGE (C-1) pop. 25,600, elev. 786′

BELLEVUE, 204 Ben Hill St., was the home of Sen. Benjamin Harvey Hill. Built in the early 1850s, the house is a fine example of Greek Revival architecture, featuring Ionic columns, porticos and elaborate millwork and ceiling medallions. Tues.-Sat. 10-noon and 2-5; closed Jan. 1, July 4, Thanksgiving and Dec. 24-25. Admission $4, students with ID $2. Private rentals prevail. Phone (706) 884-1832.

CHATTAHOOCHEE VALLEY ART MUSEUM, 112 Hines St., displays local as well as nationally and internationally acclaimed artwork. Two major shows include the LaGrange National, an art competition held in March and April, and Kaleidoscope, held the third weekend in May and spotlighting the work of Alabama and Georgia artists. Tues.-Fri. 9-5, Sat. 11-5; closed holidays. Free. Phone (706) 882-3267.

LILBURN—
see Atlanta and Vicinity p. 31.

LOCUST GROVE (C-3) pop. 1,700, elev. 837′

NOAH'S ARK REHABILITATION CENTER, 1 blk. s. of the post office, then 2.8 mi. w. on Locust Grove Rd., is a facility dedicated to the care of injured and orphaned animals. Rehabilitated wildlife is returned to its natural habitat; animals that cannot be released are housed permanently. Rehabilitated domestic and farm animals become part of a therapy program for local nursing homes and schools. Guided tours are available Mon.-Sat. noon-3 (weather permitting). Phone for best appointment time. Donations. Phone (770) 957-0888.

LOUISVILLE (C-5) pop. 2,400

In the heart of the cotton belt, Louisville was founded in 1786 and served as Georgia's first capital 1796-1806. Early settlers were reluctant to move away from the coast, so to encourage settlement of the interior an inland site was chosen as the new state capital.

Galphin's Old Town, a trading post older than some of the coastal settlements, was picked because it was in an area of friendly American Indians, had good drinking water and was on high ground above the unhealthy swamplands. This trading post eventually became Louisville. The new town was supposedly modeled after Philadelphia; the Capitol, governor's mansion and some houses were built before it had any residents. Guided tours of the area are available by reservation; contact the chamber of commerce.

Jefferson County Chamber of Commerce: 217 E. Broad St., P.O. Box 630, Louisville, GA 30434; phone (912) 625-8134.

THE OLD MARKET HOUSE, Broad and Mulberry sts., was erected in the mid-1790s, before the town was laid out. Built of great oak timbers, the original structure stands intact. This open-air pavilion, constructed as a slave-trading market, is said to be the only one of its kind still standing in the state.

In the tower hangs a bell cast in France in 1772 for a New Orleans convent. Pirates sacked the French ship carrying the bell; in turn, the pirate ship was captured near Savannah. The bell was later sent to the new capital, where it was rung to celebrate the 13 Colonies' independence. It is now rung only on special occasions. Open daily 24 hours. Free. Phone (912) 625-3166.

LUMPKIN (D-2) pop. 1,300

Lumpkin was named for Wilson Lumpkin, governor of Georgia during the 4 years following the town's incorporation in 1830. Although Lumpkin is in an agricultural region where peanuts are the major crop, the area has not always been suitable for farming. Severe erosion caused by water percolating into the layers of loose clay, sand and blue-marl limestone beneath the topsoil left much of the land unproductive by the mid-1950s. Terracing has helped solve the problem.

Self-guiding tours: A driving tour along the Stage Coach Trail, marked by signs, passes more than 20 antebellum houses.

BEDINGFIELD INN, on the town square, was a stagecoach stop during Lumpkin's frontier days and the residence of Dr. Bryan Bedingfield, Stewart County's first physician. Built in 1836, the restored inn is furnished as it would have been for a prosperous family in the 1840s.

The unusually bright colors found in each room are reproductions of the originals; old wood, glass and brick were used in the restoration, to which many descendants of the county's pioneer families contributed. Guided tours of the house and grounds include the 1900 Hatchett Drug Store, which features apothecary artifacts. Tues.-Sun. 1-5. Admission $2, students with ID $1, under 6 free. Phone (912) 838-6419.

PROVIDENCE CANYON STATE PARK, 7 mi. w. on SR 39C, is known as "Georgia's Little Grand Canyon." The park preserves a 1,108-acre area containing 16 canyons eroded to a depth of 150 feet. The still-eroding walls of the winding gullies exhibit varicolored strata. A trail leads into the canyons from the visitor center, which has interpretive displays. Park open daily 7 a.m.-9 p.m., Apr. 15-Sept. 15; 7-6, rest of year. Visitor center open daily 8-5. Free. Parking $2; free to all Wed. Phone (912) 838-6202.

SAVE **WESTVILLE,** .5 mi. s. on Martin Luther King Dr., is a village of 32 relocated and restored buildings. This living-history museum, including a doctor's office, blacksmith shop, potter's shop, cotton gin, cotton-baling press, farm complex and mansion, depicts pioneer life in Georgia prior to 1850.

May Day, Independence Day, Fair of 1850 and Yuletide festivities highlight the seasons. Costumed interpreters demonstrate how pottery, quilts, gingerbread, candles, syrup and soap were made in 1850. Tues.-Sat. 10-5, Sun. 1-5; closed first week in Jan., Thanksgiving and Dec. 25. Admission $8; over 65, $7; students with ID $4. Phone (912) 838-6310.

MACON (C-3) pop. 106,600, elev. 335'

A blend of Old South culture and New South progress, Macon is near Georgia's geographical center. Laid out in 1823 on the west side of the Ocmulgee River, Macon is said to be the only city in the Southeast that can trace its origin to a frontier fort. The remains of Fort Hawkins on Emery Highway include a replica of one of the original blockhouses.

Other city landmarks include Wesleyan College, founded in 1836 and the first college chartered specifically to grant degrees to women. Mercer University, founded in Penfield in 1833, has been in Macon since 1871.

A highlight among Macon's historic buildings is the 1884 Grand Opera House at 651 Mulberry St. The building's chandelier-illuminated interior is decorated in a style resembling the original decor; the Macon Symphony Orchestra and several

---

– TRAVEL TIP –
On the road, be dependable
and predictable.
Signal your intentions.

professional production companies regularly perform on the large stage, and there is seasonal entertainment throughout the year. Another historic building is the 1836 City Hall. Originally built as a fireproof bank, the Classical Revival-style building also served as the temporary state capitol 1864-65.

The older residential sections are lined with antebellum mansions spared by Gen. William Tecumseh Sherman on his march to the sea. Many are open to the public on a regular basis, including the birthplace of Sidney Lanier, Georgia's foremost poet, at 935 High St.; phone (912) 743-3851. Many of the city's historic buildings are dramatically illuminated at night. Guided tours of Macon's historic downtown area depart from the Macon-Bibb Convention and Visitors Bureau welcome center at Terminal Station at the junction of Cherry and 5th streets.

A number of recreational opportunities are available at nearby Lake Tobesofkee (see Recreation Chart).

Macon celebrates the blooming of some 200,000 Yoshino cherry trees in mid-March. The Macon Cherry Blossom Festival features more than 300 events, including arts and children's festivals, hot-air balloon events, an international food fair, concerts, evening torchlight walks, tours of historic houses and the downtown area, a parade, square dance, ball and a grand finale of fireworks. A cherry blossom trail showcases the flowering trees.

Southern Jubilee, a week-long event celebrating Macon's musical and artistic heritage, takes place in mid-September. The Arrowhead Arts and Crafts Festival occurs the last weekend of October at Lake Tobesofkee. White Columns and Holly—Christmas in Macon, which features tours of historic houses decorated for Christmas special museum functions and holiday activities and performances, is held from the day after Thanksgiving through Dec. 31.

Macon-Bibb County Convention and Visitors Bureau: 200 Cherry St., P.O. Box 6354, Macon GA 31208; phone (912) 743-3401 or (800 768-3401. See ad.

Self-guiding tours: Maps and brochures describing walking and driving tours are available from the convention and visitors bureau or the welcome center north on I-75; phone (912 745-2668.

THE CANNONBALL HOUSE AND MACON CON FEDERATE MUSEUM is at 856 Mulberry St. The Greek Revival mansion, hit by a cannonball on July 30, 1864, contains antebellum furnishings Two rooms re-create the meeting rooms of two sororities, Alpha Delta Pi and Phi Mu, founded at Weslleyan 1851-52. Allow 30 minutes minimum. Mon.-Sat. 10-1 and 2-4, Sun. 1:30-4:30 Admission $3; senior citizens $2.50; ages 13-18 $1; ages 6-12, 50c. Phone (912) 745-5982.

GEORGIA MUSIC HALL OF FAME, 200 Martin Luther King Blvd., features tributes to Georgia musicians. The exhibit hall contains photographs instruments and career memorabilia of nearly 400 music artists, including Ray Charles, Otis Redding and the Marshall Tucker Band. Mon. Sat. 9-5, Sun. and holidays 1-5; closed Jan. 1 Thanksgiving and Dec. 25-26. Admission $7.50 over 60, $5.50; ages 6-16, $3.50. Phone (912 750-8555. See ad p. 51.

HAY HOUSE, 934 Georgia Ave., is a 24-room Italian Renaissance revival villa built by Macon entrepreneur William B. Johnston. Begun in 1855, it took 5 years to complete. The house has modern amenities for that era, including indoor bathrooms, an elevator, a ventilating system and an intricate plumbing system. The entrance hall features 19th-century hand-painted faux marble trompe l'oeil walls.

Mr. and Mrs. Parks Lee Hay bought the villa in 1926 and furnished it much as it presently remains. The antiques and art treasures include plasterwork, porcelains and furniture, crystal chandeliers and hand-carved front doors weighing 500 pounds each. Also displayed is one of William Randolf Rogers' "Ruth Gleaning" sculptures, commissioned by Johnston in 1853.

Allow 1 hour minimum. Mon.-Sat. 10-4:30 Sun. 1-4:30; closed major holidays. Admission $6; over 55, $5; students with ID $2; ages 6-12 $1. Phone (912) 742-8155.

THE MUSEUM OF ARTS AND SCIENCES, 7.5 mi. n. on US 41 at 4182 Forsyth Rd., features two art galleries and a hall of science that present changing exhibits. The Mark Smith Planetarium is in the museum. The Three-story Discovery House features hands-on activities for children and adults. There also are nature trails on the grounds.

Museum open Mon.-Sat. 9-5 (also Fri. 5-9), Sun. 1-5; closed Thanksgiving and Dec. 25. Planetarium shows are presented Mon.-Fri. at 4, Sat. at noon, 2 and 4, Sept.-May; Sat. at noon, 2 and 4, rest of year. Star shows are Fri. at 7 and 8 p.m. Museum admission $5; over 62, $4; age 12 through college with ID $3; ages 2-11, $2; free to all Mon. 9-5 and Fri. 5-9. Planetarium shows free with museum admission. Phone (912) 477-3232.

★OCMULGEE NATIONAL MONUMENT—

see place listing p. 53.

PIEDMONT NATIONAL WILDLIFE REFUGE covers about 32,000 acres 15 mi. n. near the east bank of the Ocmulgee River. The area offers three nature trails, a driving trail and a visitor center with exhibits about the refuge. Address inquiries to the Refuge Manager, Route 1, Box 670, Juliette Rd., Round Oak, GA 31038. Refuge open daily dawn-dusk. Visitor Center open Mon.-Fri. 7:30-5, Sat.-Sun. 9-5; closed federal holidays. Phone (912) 986-5441.

TUBMAN AFRICAN AMERICAN MUSEUM, 340 Walnut St., presents the historic, artistic and cultural contributions of African-Americans. Included in the museum's seven galleries is a mural chronicling the history of African-American people. Exhibits feature inventions and discoveries, local history, and a changing display of African art and artifacts. The center also presents performing arts and other programs.

Allow 30 minutes minimum. Mon.-Fri. 9-5, Sat. 10-5, Sun. 2-5; closed major holidays. Admission $5; under 13, $2. Phone (912) 743-8544.

MADISON (B-3) pop. 3,500, elev. 664'

Incorporated in 1809, Madison's antebellum houses remain virtually intact, possibly due to the efforts of Sen. Joshua Hill, an anti-secessionist who resigned his seat in Congress rather than vote on the issue of secession. When Gen. William Tecumseh Sherman's Union forces approached Madison in November 1864, Hill and two other men worked to spare the town from the torch. Only the train depot, a cotton gin and a cloth factory were burned.

The Morgan County Courthouse in the center of town is a blend of formal and country architectural styles. Many of the historic houses are open during the Madison Tours in May and December.

Madison-Morgan County Chamber of Commerce: 115 E. Jefferson St., P.O. Box 826, Madison, GA 30650; phone (706) 342-4454.

Self-guiding tours: Walking tour maps and brochures are available at the chamber of commerce. A walking-tour audiotape rents for $5.

MADISON-MORGAN CULTURAL CENTER is on US 441 at 434 S. Main St. Built in 1895, it was one of the first brick grade schools in the South. The center includes a museum with 19th-century regional artifacts and decorative arts, a restored auditorium for the performing arts, a restored early 20th-century classroom and four art galleries with changing exhibits. In late July the 4-day Madison Arts Festival offers performances by professional theater companies, tours of historic houses, plus barbecues and lectures.

Allow 30 minutes minimum. Center open Tues.-Sat. 10-4:30, Sun. 2-5; closed major holidays. Admission $3; over 64, $2.50; students with ID $2. Phone (706) 342-4743.

MARIETTA—

see Atlanta and Vicinity p. 31.

MIDWAY (E-5) pop. 900

FORT MORRIS STATE HISTORIC SITE is 9 mi. e. on US 84, then 3 mi. s. on Fort Morris Rd.

following signs. The Continental Congress commissioned Fort Morris in 1776, and American patriots garrisoned the post to protect the port of Sunbury against British forces in the Revolutionary War and the War of 1812. A museum interprets the history of the site. A walking tour and picnic facilities also are available. Allow 1 hour minimum. Tues.-Sat. 9-5, Sun. 9:30-5:30; closed Jan. 1, Thanksgiving and Dec. 25. Admission $2; ages 6-18, $1. Phone (912) 884-5999.

MIDWAY CHURCH, on US 17 in the center of town, was founded in 1792 by Puritans who moved to the area as missionaries to the American Indians. The old slave gallery and high pulpit remain unchanged. From its congregation came two signers of the Declaration of Independence, two Revolutionary War generals and a U.S. senator. Among the church's early pastors were Abiel Holmes, father of Oliver Wendell Holmes, and Jedidiah Morse, father of Samuel Morse.

The church and cemetery can be visited at any time; the keys are kept at the service station next door to the church and at Midway Museum.

MIDWAY MUSEUM, next door to Midway Church on US 17, was built in the 18th-century raised-cottage style and displays furniture, artifacts and documents from the early 18th to the mid-19th centuries. Allow 30 minutes minimum. Tues.-Sat. 10-4, Sun. 2-4; closed holidays. Admission $3, students with ID $1. Phone (912) 884-5837.

MILLEDGEVILLE (C-4) pop. 17,700, elev. 276′

Milledgeville looks much as it did when it was laid out as the capital of Georgia in 1803. The city served as the state capital 1803-68. The Old State House, built in the Gothic style in 1807, contributes a medieval touch; the Victorian courthouse dates from 1885.

Two of Milledgeville's antebellum houses are particularly noteworthy. The 1830 John Marlor House, 201 N. Wayne St., built in a mixture of Federal and early Greek Revival styles, now houses the Elizabeth Marlor Bethune Art Gallery, which has exhibits ranging from paintings to antique furniture. John Marlor was the architect of the Stetson-Sanford House, an 1825 two-story clapboard Federal house that is now the headquarters of the Old Capital Historical Society.

Also historically significant is St. Stephen's Episcopal Church on S. Wayne Street. During Gen. William Tecumseh Sherman's November 1864 occupation, his troops, who stabled their horses in the church, poured sorghum syrup down the organ pipes to prevent the organ from being used to signal Confederate sympathizers.

One notable Milledgeville resident was writer Flannery O'Connor, honored by a room in Georgia College's Dillard Russell Library. Viewed by request, the displays include furnishings from the nearby estate where the writer spent much of her life, as well as manuscripts, clippings and memorabilia.

Guided trolley tours that include stops at the Old Governor's Mansion and the Stetson-Sanford House depart from the convention and visitors bureau Tues. and Fri. at 10.

Some of Milledgeville's events include Brown's Crossing Fall Craftsmen Fair, held the third weekend in October, and the Twelve Days of Christmas Southern Style, celebrated Dec. 1-25.

Milledgeville-Baldwin County Convention and Visitors Bureau: 200 W. Hancock St., P.O. Box 219, Milledgeville, GA 31061; phone (912) 452-4687 or (800) 653-1804.

Self-guiding tours: A free walking-tour map of historic Milledgeville can be obtained from the convention and visitors bureau.

LOCKERLY ARBORETUM, 1 mi. s. on Bus. Rte. 441, features a variety of trees and shrubs, labeled and catalogued for study and enjoyment. Comprising nearly 45 acres, it also contains gardens, trails and forest areas. Mon.-Fri. 8:30-4:30, Sat. 1-5, Oct.-May; Sat. 10-2, rest of year. Free. Phone (912) 452-2212.

OLD GOVERNOR'S MANSION is s. of SR 24 on US 441 at 120 S. Clark St. The home of Georgia's governors 1839-68, the 1839 Greek Revival mansion has period furnishings and a high domed ceiling above the central rotunda. Guided tours of the first two floors are available on the hour Tues.-Sat. 10-4, Sun. 2-4; closed Thanksgiving and Dec. 25. Last tour begins at 4. Admission $5; ages 6-18, $2. Phone (912) 453-4545.

MILLEN (C-5) pop. 3,800, elev. 160′

BO GINN AQUARIUM is 4 mi. n. on US 25 next to Magnolia Springs State Park *(see Recreation Chart and the AAA Southeastern CampBook)*. Approximately 70 species are displayed in 26 tanks and aquariums. The clear water of the adjacent springs allows viewing of native fish, turtles, and other wildlife. Daily 9-4; closed Thanksgiving and Dec. 25. Free. Phone (912) 982-4168.

MOULTRIE (E-3) pop. 14,900

ELLEN PAYNE ODOM GENEALOGY LIBRARY, 204 5th St. S.E. in the Moultrie/Colquitt County Library, houses the archives of 83 Scottish clans. The collection also includes genealogical research materials about families who entered the United States from the Eastern Seaboard and traces their migration routes west. Exhibits feature Cherokee and Creek Indian documents and artifacts as well as a telecommunications display.

Allow 1 hour minimum. Mon.-Sat. 8:30-5:30; closed major holidays and Dec. 24-Jan. 1. Free. Phone (912) 985-6540.

MOUNTAIN CITY (A-4) pop. 800, elev. 2,168′

In 1966 a high school English teacher in nearby Rabun Gap helped his students publish a quarterly magazine dedicated to recording nearly forgotten Appalachian folkways. Called Foxfire after a lichen that glows in the dark, the publication has since grown into a popular series of books, a publishing house and an educational foundation.

FOXFIRE MUSEUM AND COLLECTIONS, 1 mi. n. on US 441, houses exhibits relating to Appalachian culture and the preservation of a vanishing lifestyle. Artifacts and crafts are from an era preceding electricity and running water. Exhibits include the inner workings of an old grist mill, implements for trapping, farming and hunting as well as toys and household items. The 110-acre grounds hold 25 period log cabins.

Mon.-Sat. 9-4:30; closed holidays. Museum free. Cabins and grounds $4.50, students with ID $1. Guided tours of the grounds and cabins $7.50. MC, VI. Phone (706) 746-5828.

★OCMULGEE NATIONAL MONUMENT (C-3)

Ocmulgee (oak-MUL-gee) National Monument is on Macon's eastern limits; take US 80 east from I-16 exit 4 and follow signs. Within the monument's 702 acres are some of the most impressive American Indian mounds and archeological remains in the Southeast. Creeks, early and late Mississippi farmers and Paleo-Indian, Archaic and Woodland hunters and gatherers are known to have inhabited the area from around 10,000 B.C. through the early 19th century.

American Indian farmers migrated to central Georgia about A.D. 900 and built a large village and ceremonial center on the Macon Plateau. Six of their temple mounds, one burial mound and one ceremonial earth lodge remain. The restored earth lodge, which dates from about 1015, was a meeting chamber. The clay floor, benches around the walls, lower portion of the walls and raised bird-shaped platform have survived.

About 1350 a new village, which archeologists named Lamar, was built 2 miles down the river. Around 1690 the Creek Indians built a village, and the Ocmulgee River then marked the southwestern frontier of the Carolinas and Georgia for British colonists. Charleston supported a fur-trading post in the area 1690-1715.

Foot trails connect most of the park's features, and a drive approaches the large mounds. The Opelofa Nature Trail branches off the main walking trail and explores the lowlands of Walnut Creek. The visitor center houses archeological displays and dioramas. The film "People of the Macon Plateau" is shown upon request.

Events are held February through November. Picnic facilities are available. Daily 9-5; closed Jan. 1 and Dec. 25. Free. Phone (912) 752-8257.

OCONEE NATIONAL FOREST—
see Chattahoochee and Oconee National Forests p. 37.

PINE MOUNTAIN (D-2) pop. 900, elev. 1,052′

★**CALLAWAY GARDENS,** with entrances 1.2 and 2.7 mi. s. on US 27, covers 14,500 acres in the foothills of the Appalachians. Founded by industrialist Cason J. Callaway in the 1930s, the area features beautiful horticultural displays. Among these are the John A. Sibley Horticultural Center *(see attraction listing)*, the 45-acre Meadowlark Gardens containing the Day Butterfly Center *(see attraction listing)* and miles of scenic woodland drives. A large man-made sand beach borders Robin Lake.

Other attractions include an early 1800s log cabin, Mr. Cason's Vegetable Garden, the Ida Cason Callaway Memorial Chapel, an information center and facilities for golf, bicycling, fishing, walking, racquetball, sailing and tennis.

The gardens contain what is purported to be one of the world's largest collections of native azaleas, once plentiful in the natural woodlands of the Southeast. These rare varieties, usually more pure in color than cultivated shrubs, display brilliant reds, oranges and yellows. There also are hundreds of cultivated varieties. Some 700 types bloom from late March through the summer.

Each year thousands of new plants are added to preserve the native flora. Greenhouses are filled with native and tropical floral arrangements. The grounds are the site of many events, including a steeplechase, fairs, concerts and the Buick Challenge golf tournament, held in late September.

A 5-mile drive winds around Mountain Creek Lake, where canoes, bicycles and sailboats are available for rent. Robin Lake Beach is the site of shows that include the Florida State University Flying High Circus, daily except Wed., early June to mid-August. Another highlight is the *Robin E. Lee* riverboat, which offers free tours on the lake. Food is available.

Allow 4 hours minimum. Gardens open daily 7-7. Information center open daily 9-7, Mar.-Sept.; otherwise varies. Beach open daily 8-8, June-Aug. Admission $10; ages 6-12, $5. Phone (706) 663-2281 or (800) 225-5292. *See color ad p. 288.*

Day Butterfly Center occupies 4.5 acres within Callaway's Meadowlark Gardens. Tropical plants support and shelter hummingbirds, pheasants and more than 1,000 butterflies of 50 species in the center's octagonal conservatory. The grounds surrounding the conservatory include plantings designed to attract native butterflies and birds. Daily 9-7, Mar.-Aug. Admission is included in Callaway Gardens entrance fee.

John A. Sibley Horticultural Center is a 5-acre greenhouse/garden complex on US 27 within Callaway Gardens. Narrow paths wind among azaleas, ferns, citrus trees and camellias. The Outdoor Garden offers expansive lawns and flower beds displaying spring bulbs, summer annuals and fall chrysanthemums and poinsettias.

Designed using principles of conservation, the center is cooled by shade, ventilation, moving water and misting systems. Solar heat is stored in the greenhouse's rock walls and pool during the day and released at night to warm the interior. Daily 9-7, Mar.-Aug. Admission is included in Callaway Gardens entrance fee.

[SAVE] **PINE MOUNTAIN WILD ANIMAL PARK** is at 1300 Oak Grove Rd. The 500-acre park exhibits animals from around the world. Animals from each continent can be seen in their native habitats. The collection includes alligators, camels, deer, giraffes and zebras. Visitors can drive through the park or ride the tour bus. Food is available.

Allow 2 hours minimum. Park open daily 10-6:30 (also Sat.-Sun. 6:30-7:30 p.m.), early May-early Sept.; 11:30-4, rest of year. Tour bus departs daily at 11:30, 1, 2:30, 4, and 5:30, early May-early Sept.; at 11:30, 2, and 4:30, rest of year. Closed Dec. 25. Admission $11.95; over 55, $10.95; ages 3-9, $7.95. AE, DS, MC, VI. Phone (706) 663-8744 or (800) 367-2751.

PLAINS (D-2) pop. 700
JIMMY CARTER NATIONAL HISTORIC SITE encompasses much of the town of Plains. A self-guiding driving tour begins at 300 N. Bond St. A 15-minute videotape narrated by Jimmy and Rosalynn Carter describes their current home.

Additional stops include the former president's birthplace, boyhood homes, his old high school, brother Billy's service station, Carter's Peanut Warehouse and family homes. The Carters' current residence is not open to the public.

Allow 1 hour minimum. Daily 9-5; closed Jan. 1 and Dec. 25. Free. A 45-minute self-guiding driving tour booklet is available for $1; a cassette tape tour is available for rental ($1) or purchase ($5). Phone (912) 824-3413.

POOLER (D-6) pop. 4,500, elev. 23'
THE MIGHTY EIGHTH AIR FORCE HERITAGE MUSEUM, 175 Bourne Ave., honors those who have served in the Eighth Air Force since its inception in 1942. It features a library, archives, memorial gardens, an art gallery and displays of war artifacts. A moving exhibit lets visitors experience a lifelike World War II mission. Food is available. Daily 10-6; closed Jan. 1, Easter, Thanksgiving and Dec. 25. Admission $7.50; over 59 and ages 6-12, $5.50. AE, MC, VI. Phone (912) 748-8888.

RICHMOND HILL (E-6) pop. 2,900
A few miles north of Richmond Hill, US 17 crosses the Ogeechee River near the site of the Battle of Kings Ferry, an audacious 18th-century defeat of the British by a Colonial colonel, two other officers and three enlisted men. Using widely spaced watch fires and misleading shouts to imaginary sentinels, the Americans convinced the British commander that they vastly outnumbered the five ships and 130 men intended to capture Savannah.

Riding alone into the British camp the next morning, the American leader informed the British commander that the bloodthirsty Colonial soldiers would accept nothing but unconditional surrender. The erstwhile invader handed over his entire force, which was marched away by the lone American while the other five followed behind to restrain their supposedly restless troops.

FORT McALLISTER STATE HISTORIC PARK, 10 mi. e. on US 17, then e. on SR 144 to 144 Spur, is on the bank of the Great Ogeechee River. An example of Confederate earthwork fortifications, it withstood bombardments by the Union navy on Mar. 3, 1863. The only fatality that day was Tom Cat, the garrison's mascot. However, the fort finally fell before Gen. William Tecumseh Sherman's army on Dec. 13, 1864, during Sherman's last artillery exchange of the Civil War.

Exhibits about artillery and the history of the fort are in the museum and the fortification. Mon.-Sat. 9-5, Sun. 2-5:30; closed Thanksgiving and Dec. 25. Admission $2; ages 5-18, $1. Phone (912) 727-2339. *See Recreation Chart and the AAA Southeastern CampBook.*

ROME (B-1) pop. 30,300, elev. 603'

Rome's name is apt, for like its Italian counterpart it is built upon seven hills. The city was founded in 1834 when three men stopped for a drink where the Etowah and Oostanaula rivers become the Coosa River. The men laid out a townsite and drew a name for it from a hat.

Rome's importance to the Confederacy as a rail and manufacturing center led to the 1863 ride of John Wisdom. Wearing out five horses and a mule in 11 hours, Wisdom rode 67 miles from Alabama to Rome to warn of an impending Union attack. A giant cannon lathe atop Civic Center Hill survived even Gen. William Tecumseh Sherman. Marks made by the sledgehammers of Union soldiers who tried to destroy it can be seen on the lathe's sides.

There are other reminders of the past, including Boswell Cabin, a restored mid-19th-century log house next to the lathe, and a cemetery on Myrtle Hill that contains 377 Confederate graves and those of two of Rome's founders. Eileen Axon Wilson, wife of President Woodrow Wilson, also is buried in this cemetery. Atop the water tower on another of the city's seven hills is the Old Town Clock, dating from 1871.

Early 20th-century houses and commercial buildings can be seen in downtown Rome along Broad Street. In front of City Hall is the Capitoline Wolf, a bronze replica of the Roman statue depicting a she-wolf nursing Romulus and Remus, the legendary founders of Rome, Italy. It was received from Benito Mussolini in 1929.

Rome's Mayfest on the Rivers, featuring river activities and concerts is celebrated the first weekend in May. Another notable celebration is Heritage Holidays, held in mid-October. It features a wagon train, riverboat rides, parades, exhibits, concerts, a re-creation of John Wisdom's ride and the Chiaha Arts and Crafts Fair, which draws artisans and visitors from across the Southeast. A variety of holiday events is scheduled from late November through December for A Classic Christmas in Georgia's Rome.

Greater Rome Convention and Visitors Bureau: 402 Civic Center Dr., P.O. Box 5823, Rome, GA 30162-5823; phone (706) 295-5576 or (800) 444-1834. *See ad.*

Self-guiding tours: Brochures and cassette tapes describing walking tours of the Between the Rivers Historic District are available from the convention and visitors bureau.

CHIEFTAINS MUSEUM, 501 Riverside Pkwy., is the late 18th-century home of Cherokee leader Major Ridge, who struggled to maintain his American Indian heritage while adapting to the white man's culture. The original 1790s log cabin remains at the center of this gracious mansion. Displays include dioramas and photographs as well as artifacts dating from 8000 B.C. Tues.-Sat. 10-4; closed national holidays. Admission $3, students with ID $1.50. Phone (706) 291-9494.

SAVE ★**OAK HILL AND THE MARTHA BERRY MUSEUM** are 3 mi. n. on US 27 on the campus of Berry College. Oak Hill, dating from 1847, was the plantation home of Martha Berry, a cotton broker's daughter who began teaching local children in a one-room log cabin in 1902. The cabin eventually developed into Berry College, and Ms. Berry received eight honorary degrees and the praise of statesmen and educators for her work. The house is furnished and maintained as it was during her lifelong occupancy.

The Martha Berry Museum contains memorabilia of the schools and their founder, including paintings owned by the Berry family, furniture made by students and portraits of philanthropists whom Berry persuaded to support her work. A 30-minute film depicts Berry's life.

The estate and the museum, which also serves as a visitor center, are part of a 28,000-acre complex. Structures donated by Henry Ford as well as buildings constructed by students are on the campus.

The Ford Buildings contain collections of Appalachian arts and crafts. A gristmill with a 42-foot wheel is said to be one of the largest in the

world. Nearby are a rose garden, a sunken garden with Japanese cherry trees, a greenhouse and self-guiding nature trails.

Allow 2 hours minimum. House and museum open Mon.-Sat. 10-5, Sun. 1-5; closed holidays. Admission $4; ages 6-12, $2. Phone (706) 291-1883 or (800) 220-5504. *See ad p. 55.*

ROME AREA HISTORY MUSEUM is at 303-305 Broad St. in the historic section. Visitors learn about the founding of Rome and the surrounding area. The museum features artifacts from the Civil War and World War II as well as a historic medical display. It also contains furnishings that belonged to Ellen Axon Wilson, who grew up in Rome and became the wife of President Woodrow Wilson. Guided tours are offered.

Tues.-Sat. 10-5, Sun. noon-5; closed holidays. Admission $2; ages 7-12, $1. Phone (706) 235-8051.

ROSWELL—
see Atlanta and Vicinity p. 32.

ST. MARYS (F-5) pop. 8,200

From treasure-smuggling pirates to commercial fishermen, St. Marys' past blends into its present. Many shrimp and fishing boats line the docks along the St. Marys River. The town is the site of the Cumberland Island National Seashore Visitor Center and ferry dock *(see place listing p. 45).* St. Marys also is home to the Kings Bay Naval Sub Base, the Atlantic Coast home base of Trident nuclear submarines.

McIntosh Sugar Mill Tabby Ruins, on Spur 40 (Crooked River Road), is the largest tabby structure (a material made of oyster shells, sand and water) in the area. Built by John Houston McIntosh in the 18th century, the site was used for cane grinding and the boiling and processing of sugar products.

St. Marys Tourism Council, Inc.: 414 Osborne St., P.O. Box 1291, St. Marys, GA 31558; phone (912) 882-6200 or (800) 868-8687.

Self-guiding tours: A walking tour of the National Historic District features houses dating from 1799. The Braille Trail, within the historic district, highlights 38 historically significant sites marked with raised letters and braille for visually impaired visitors.

ST. SIMONS ISLAND—
see Golden Isles p. 46.

Serving the American traveler since 1902.

SAPELO ISLAND—
see Golden Isles p. 47.

SAVANNAH (D-5) pop. 137,600, elev. 43′

Gen. James Oglethorpe and his settlers founded Savannah and England's 13th and last colony in February 1733. Forgoing the usual village grid system, Oglethorpe and Col. William Bull laid out their new settlement in a series of wards in which commercial and residential buildings centered on a public square. This visionary plan has survived as the city's blueprint because of Oglethorpe's choice of location.

On a bluff overlooking the Savannah River, the new settlement soon prospered as a crossroads of trade with England and the new communities of the interior. Port traffic begun in 1744 experienced a steady increase along with the plantation economy of tobacco and cotton.

Residents eagerly embraced the revolt against England, and Savannah was garrisoned by some 900 Colonial troops under Gen. Robert Howe. British forces captured the city by surprise in December 1778 and made it a base for their operations against the Colonies; they evacuated the city in 1782.

Nineteenth-century Savannah grew and flourished with King Cotton, becoming a vital port. In 1862 Union forces closed the port to all but blockade runners when they captured Fort Pulaski *(see Fort Pulaski National Monument, p. 43).*

Two years later Gen. William Tecumseh Sherman blazed a trail of destruction across Georgia to the city. Confederate forces fought stubbornly, but with the fall of Fort McAllister, Gen. William J. Hardee realized further resistance was futile and evacuated the city to prevent its destruction. Sherman entered Savannah on Christmas Day 1864 and offered it to President Abraham Lincoln as a present.

Cotton again proved to be Savannah's salvation after the war as the city grew into a major trading center. The collapse of the cotton market at the beginning of the 20th century left Savannah languishing until just before World War II when other industries began to develop.

The city almost lost, however, what Sherman had spared some 100 years earlier: its squares, its houses and its heritage. In the drive to reshape the city's skyline, developers began to tear down historic structures. A lost fight to save the old vegetable and fish market sparked the founding of the Historic Savannah Foundation in 1955. This dedicated group of women organized one of the country's first and most successful restoration programs, buying hundreds of properties and selling them to private parties with covenants to restore and repair them.

Presently, 22 of Oglethorpe's original 24 squares survive, bordered by handsome town houses and landscaped with live oaks, azaleas, fountains and statues. The success of Historic Savannah Foundation's early efforts has spawned other civic renewal projects.

The cleanup of the river and the restoration of the warehouses and cotton broker offices along Bay Street, Factor's Walk and River Street have revived the city's historic waterfront. Instead of the bustle of the cotton trade, these 19th-century buildings now house specialty shops, restaurants and nightspots.

Highlights in this area include Solomon's Lodge No. 1, Free & Accepted Masons in the 1886 Cotton and Naval Stores Exchange at 100 E. Bay St. The Masonic lodge, organized in 1734, is the country's oldest in continuous operation, and the old exchange is said to be the first building to straddle a public street according to the legal principle of air rights.

River Street's Waving Girl statue is evocative of Savannah's romantic character. In the early years of the 20th century the city light-tender's sister, Florence Martus, became known to sea-

men all over the world for waving at every ship. One legend maintains that she promised her sailor sweetheart to greet every ship until his return.

Another historic building is Christ Episcopal Church, on Johnson Square at Bull and E. St. Julian streets. The church was the home of the first congregation organized in the colony and what is believed to have been the first Protestant Sunday school in the New World. The present structure was built in 1838; phone (912) 232-4131 or 238-0434. Colonial Park, E. Oglethorpe Avenue and Abercorn Street, is the site of the old Christ Episcopal Church cemetery, for many years the only public burying ground in the colony. Closed to interment in 1853, the cemetery suffered much damage when Gen. William Tecumseh Sherman's troops used it as a stabling ground.

Founded in 1755 by members of the Church of Scotland, Independent Presbyterian Church is at Bull Street and W. Oglethorpe Avenue. This

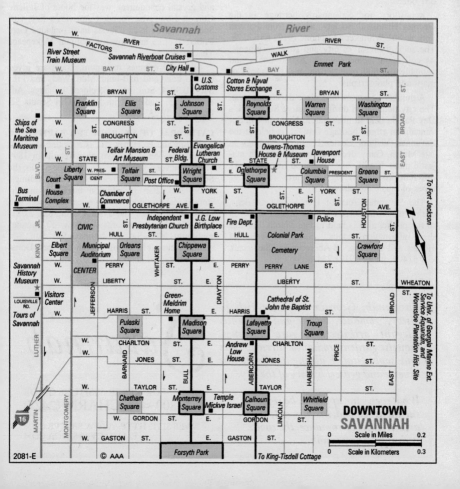

historic church and steeple were modeled after St. Martin-in-the-Fields Church in London's Trafalgar Square. The interior is Georgian; phone (912) 236-3346.

First African Baptist Church, at 23 Montgomery St., was established in 1775. The church is housed in the 1859 brick sanctuary built by congregation members. It is reputedly North America's oldest African-American church, and its museum contains archives and memorabilia dating from the 18th century. The Sunday school, organized in 1826, is said to have been the first African-American Sunday school in North America; phone (912) 233-6597.

The SAVE Historic Railroad Shops, at 601 W. Harris St., constitute what is said to be the nation's oldest railroad repair facility, with construction on the complex starting in 1845. Thirteen of the original structures, including the roundhouse, turntable and smokestack, survive. Several restored locomotives and antique machinery also are displayed; phone (912) 651-6823.

Repository for Savannah's heritage is the Georgia Historical Society, across from Forsyth Park at 501 Whitaker St.; phone (912) 651-2128. The society preserves city and state documents; its collection includes some 20,000 books and pamphlets, 1,500 manuscripts and thousands of maps and photographs.

A number of events take place during the year. The city dons green during a festive St. Patrick's Day Parade held in mid-March. Night in Old Savannah, an ethnic heritage festival, is held at the Savannah Visitors Center on three evenings in late March. Gaily decorated booths beneath majestic moss-draped oaks offer food from some 15 different coastal Georgia cultures as various types of music are played.

The Savannah Tour of Homes and Gardens, during which numerous private houses are open to the public, also is held in late March. For further information contact Savannah Tour of Homes and Gardens, 18 Abercorn St., Savannah, GA 31401; phone (912) 234-8054.

Savannah dresses for the holidays in December with a month-long celebration that includes a Christmas Tour of Historic Inns, the River Street Christmas Festival & Parade, A Holiday Tour of Homes and a Confederate Nog Party and Open House. For a complete list of holiday information contact the convention and visitors bureau.

Savannah Area Convention and Visitors Bureau: 222 W. Oglethrope Ave., Savannah, GA 31401; phone (912) 944-0456. *See ad.*

Self-guiding tours: Information about Savannah's scenic tour route is available at the Savannah Visitors Center, 301 Martin Luther King Jr. Blvd.; phone (912) 944-0455. Driving and walking tape tours from Tours on Tape are available to purchase for $9.95 or to rent for $8.

ANDREW LOW HOUSE, 329 Abercorn St. at Lafayette Sq., was built by Andrew Low, a wealthy cotton merchant. The 1848 stuccoed brick house, noted for its well-proportioned rooms with plaster cornices, carved woodwork and crystal chandeliers, was the home of Juliette Gordon Low, who founded America's first Girl Scout troop in 1912. Guests have included Gen. Robert E. Lee and novelist William Makepeace Thackeray.

Allow 30 minutes minimum. Tours are given on the hour and half-hour Mon.-Wed. and Fri.-Sat. 10:30-4, Sun. noon-4; closed holidays. Admission $5, students with ID $3, Girl Scouts $2. Phone (912) 233-6854.

CATHEDRAL OF ST. JOHN THE BAPTIST, jct. Abercorn and E. Harris sts., is a Gothic-style cathedral completed in 1896, then rebuilt in 1899 after a severe fire. One of the largest in the South, the cathedral features marble railings, floors and altar. In addition there are murals, stained-glass windows, large carved-wood stations of the cross, and a solid white-oak 2,081-pipe Noack tracker organ. Allow 30 minutes minimum. Mon.-Sat. and holidays 9-5, Sun. 8-5; no tours available during church services. Donations. Phone (912) 233-4709.

CITY HALL, 2 Bay St. at the corner of Bull St., was built in 1905 on the site of the 1799 City Exchange. Bronze tablets on each side commemorate the 1834 launching of the *John Randolph*, the first iron ship seen in American waters, and the *Savannah*, the first steam-propelled ship to cross an ocean. Mon.-Fri. 8:30-5; closed holidays. Free. Phone (912) 651-6790.

DAVENPORT HOUSE, 324 E. State St. on Columbia Sq., was built 1815-20 by Isaiah Davenport. In 1955 a group of citizens saved the building, which had become a tenement, from being replaced by a parking lot. Their efforts marked the beginning of the city's concern with preservation. The finely proportioned 1820 Federal house is noted for its American and English period furnishings, delicate ironwork, elliptical stairway and handsome plasterwork.

Tours are given every 30 minutes daily 10-4:30; closed Dec. 25. Admission $5; ages 6-18, $3. Phone (912) 236-8097.

EVANGELICAL LUTHERAN CHURCH OF THE ASCENSION, on Wright Sq. at Bull and E. State sts., combines Norman and Gothic architectural features. The 1741 structure is noted for its stained-glass windows and exhibits about church history. Mon.-Thurs. 9-5, Fri. 9-1; closed holidays. Phone (912) 232-4151.

FACTOR'S WALK, a row of narrow buildings along the river bluff on Bay St., acquired its name in the 19th century when it was the meeting place for cotton merchants and the center of commercial activities. A network of iron and concrete bridgeways connects the buildings to the bluff. The cobblestone streets were made from the ballast of ships from Europe.

FORSYTH PARK, on Gaston St. between Whitaker and Drayton sts., is particularly lovely in early spring during the azalea season. A fountain resembling the one in the Place de la Concorde in Paris, France, is the centerpiece of the original tract, laid out in 1851. The Confederate Monument is in the park extension. Daily 24 hours.

FORT JACKSON, 3 mi. e. via Islands Expwy., was begun in the early 1800s. On the banks of the Savannah River and surrounded by a moat, the fort is one of the oldest remaining brickwork forts in Georgia. Exhibits depict the history of the fort's construction and its garrison during the American Revolution, War of 1812 and the Civil War.

Special demonstrations are given Memorial Day weekend. There are frequent living-history presentations in spring and summer. Allow 30 minutes minimum. Mon.-Sat. 9-5, Sun. noon-5. Admission $2.50; over 62, retired military and students with ID $2. Phone (912) 232-3945.

FORT McALLISTER STATE HISTORIC PARK— *see Richmond Hill p. 54.*

FORT PULASKI NATIONAL MONUMENT— *see place listing p. 43.*

GREEN-MELDRIM HOME, on Madison Sq. at 1 W. Macon St., was Gen. William Tecumseh Sherman's personal headquarters during his 1864 occupation of Savannah. Built in the 1850s, the house is a fine example of Gothic Revival architecture. Tues. and Thurs.-Sat. 10-4; closed holidays. Admission $4, students with ID $2. Phone (912) 233-3845.

JULIETTE GORDON LOW BIRTHPLACE, 142 Bull St. and E. Oglethorpe Ave., is the birthplace of the founder of the Girl Scouts of the USA. The Regency-style townhouse, constructed 1818-21, is restored to the 1886 period, the year of Juliette Low's marriage. The house, which contains many Gordon family furnishings, has a Victorian garden and original outbuildings. The Girl Scouts maintain the house as a memorial to their founder and as a national program center.

Mon.-Tues. and Thurs.-Sat. 10-4, Sun. 12:30-4:30; closed Jan. 1, Mar. 17, Easter, Thanksgiving, Dec. 24-25 and some Sundays in Jan. and Dec. Admission $5; ages 6-18, $4. Phone (912) 233-4501.

KING-TISDELL COTTAGE, 514 E. Huntingdon St., is an African-American heritage museum housed in a restored 1896 Victorian cottage. The museum offers the Negro Heritage Trail Tour, which encompasses 17 historic sites. Museum open Tues.-Sat. noon-5. The Negro Heritage Trail Tour departs from the Savannah Visitors Center, 301 Martin Luther King Jr. Blvd., daily at 1 and 3. Museum admission $3.50. Trail tour $15; under 12, $7. Phone (912) 234-8000.

SAVE ★**OWENS-THOMAS HOUSE AND MUSEUM,** 124 Abercorn St. on Oglethorpe Sq., was designed in the Regency style by English architect William Jay. Influenced by classical antiquity, he created an elegant English villa 1816-19 using domestic and imported materials. The Marquis de Lafayette, while a guest in 1825, gave speeches to the citizens of Savannah.

The house is furnished with rare antiques and contains decorative arts that were owned by Savannah citizens in the 19th century. The carriage house visitor center contains the original slave quarters, a regional art gallery and visitor services. Connecting the carriage house and the main house is a formal garden. Tues.-Sat. 10-5, Sun. 2-5; closed major holidays and Mar. 17. Last tour begins 30 minutes before closing. Admission $6; over 65, $4; students with ID $3; ages 6-12, $2. Phone (912) 233-9743.

RIVER STREET TRAIN MUSEUM, 315 W. River St., is housed in an 1854 building and features O gauge toy train displays dating from 1930, railroad memorabilia and an operating layout with a miniature village. Allow 30 minutes minimum. Mon.-Sat. 11-5:30; closed Thanksgiving and Dec. 25. Admission $1.50; ages 5-12, 50c. MC, VI. Phone (912) 233-6175.

★SAVANNAH HISTORY MUSEUM, in a restored 19th-century train shed behind the visitor center at 303 Martin Luther King Jr. Blvd., occupies the site of a Revolutionary War battle, the 1779 Siege of Savannah. A multimedia exposition chronicles the city's history through a grand museum hall and a videotape presentation.

Exhibits in the museum hall include a model of the SS *Savannah*, an 1890 Baldwin locomotive, a cotton gin, one of the Oscars awarded to Savannah native and composer Johnny Mercer, military uniforms and natural history and transportation displays. Allow 1 hour, 30 minutes minimum. Daily 9-5; closed Thanksgiving and Dec. 25. Last show 30 minutes before closing. Admission $3; over 55, $2.50; ages 6-12, $1.75. Phone (912) 238-1779.

SAVANNAH RIVERBOAT CRUISES, departing from the dock at 9 E. River St., offers 1-hour narrated sightseeing harbor cruises, 1.5-hour Sunday brunch, and 2-hour dinner/dance or moonlight entertainment cruises aboard the *Savannah River Queen*, a replica of a 19th-century stern-wheeler. Sightseeing cruises depart daily at 2 and 4, Apr.-Oct.; daily at 2 in Mar.; Sat.-Sun. at 2, rest of year. Fare $9.95; ages 3-12, $7. Reservations are required for brunch and dinner cruises. AE, DS, MC, VI. Phone (912) 232-6404 or (800) 786-6404.

SAVE SHIPS OF THE SEA MARITIME MUSEUM, 41 Martin Luther King Blvd., is in an 1898 warehouse on Savannah's historic riverfront plaza, once the heart of the city's sea trade. Ships models, artifacts and exhibits depict Savannah's relationship with the sea. Highlights include an extensive ship-in-a-bottle collection, navigational equipment, scrimshaw, figureheads and paintings.

Allow 30 minutes minimum. Tues.-Sun. 10-5; closed Jan. 1, Mar. 1, Easter, Thanksgiving and Dec. 24-25. Last admission is 30 minutes before closing. Admission $5. Phone (912) 232-1511.

TELFAIR MANSION AND ART MUSEUM, on Telfair Sq. at 121 Barnard St., occupies the site of Government House, the residence of Georgia's royal governors from 1760 to the end of the Revolutionary War. Designed by William Jay, the 1818 Regency-style mansion is furnished with period antiques, many of which belonged to Gov. Edward Telfair and his family. The mansion's Octagon Room is considered to be one of the finest period rooms in the United States.

The museum wing contains a collection of American and European paintings as well as rare plaster casts of antique sculptures. Traveling exhibitions also are shown.

Tues.-Sat. 10-5, Sun. 2-5; closed holidays. Admission $5; over 65, $3; ages 13-18, $2; ages 6-12, $1; free to all Sun. Phone (912) 232-1177.

TEMPLE MICKVE ISRAEL is in the historic district at 20 E. Gordon150 St. The Gothic-style 1878 synagogue contains an archival museum displaying the Torah that the founders brought to Savannah from England in 1733. Other items of interest are letters from George Washington, Thomas Jefferson, James Madison and several other presidents. Mon.-Fri. 10-noon and 2-4. Donations. Phone (912) 233-1547.

TOURS OF SAVANNAH, conducted by several different companies, offer sightseeing tours of Savannah's historic district. Some feature nature tours, island tours, coastal low-country tours or specialty tours. Many include admission to one or two historic buildings.

Carriage Tours of Savannah departs the visitors center, 301 M.L. King Jr. Blvd. and several other locations. Narrated 1-hour tours in horse-drawn carriages cover major points of interest in the historic district. Private tours and ghost-story tours also are available. Tours depart daily on the hour 9-3 and 6-9; closed Mar. 17, Thanksgiving and Dec. 25. Fare $13; ages 4-11, $6. Fare for special tours $15-$60; additional person $10 on some tours; under 12, $6. Garage or metered parking at some stops. Reservations are required at some stops. Phone (912) 236-6756.

Classic Historical Tours is in the historic district at the visitors center, 301 M.L. King Jr. Blvd. Tours feature trolleys, buses, double-deckers and river-cruise combinations. Historic area tours and specialty tours are offered. Passengers have unlimited on/off privileges for more than 30 stops in the historic district. Daily 9-4:30; closed Mar. 17, Thanksgiving and Dec. 25. Fare $10-$23; ages 5-12, $6-$13. Phone (912) 234-8128.

Gray Line Tours departs the Gray Line office at 215 W. Boundary St., the visitors center at 301 Martin Luther King Jr. Blvd. and many downtown hotels. Guided tours include 75-minute trolley tours of the historic district and restored waterfront area, with departures every 30 minutes. Air-conditioned minibus tours of the historic district and Isle of Hope low country also are available, ranging from 2-4 hours.

Daily 9-4:20; closed Jan. 1, Mar. 17, Thanksgiving and Dec. 25. Fares $13-$23. Various museum admissions are included. Credit cards are accepted only at Gray Line office. AE, DS, MC, VI. Phone (912) 234-8687.

Old Savannah Tours depart the visitors center, 301 M.L. King Jr. Blvd. Narrated historical, island, nature and specialty tours are conducted on a fleet of trolleys, minibuses and boats. Tours feature unlimited on/off privileges at 13 stops in the historic district. Daily 9-4:30; closed Mar. 17, Thanksgiving and Dec. 25. Fare $12; ages 5-12, $6. Phone (912) 234-8128.

Old Town Trolley Tours depart from various downtown locations. The 90-minute narrated tours feature more than 100 points of interest. Unlimited free reboarding within one loop is permitted on the trolleys, which pass the downtown squares and the historic and waterfront districts. Allow 1 hour, 30 minutes minimum. Trolleys leave every 30 minutes daily 9-4:30; closed Jan. 1, Mar. 17, Thanksgiving and Dec. 25. Fare $17; ages 4-12, $7. Phone (912) 233-0083.

Tapestry Tours, with pick-ups made at local hotels, offers 2.5-hour morning and 4.5-hour afternoon walk-in bus tours of historic Savannah sights. Each tour includes at least two stops, which vary daily. The two tours can be combined into a full-day tour. Lunch is included on the afternoon and full-day tours. Morning tour departs Mon.-Tues. and Thurs.-Sat. at 9:30; afternoon tour departs Mon.-Tues. and Thurs.-Sat. at noon. Fare $25-$80. Phone (912) 233-7770 or (800) 794-7770. *See ad.*

THE UNIVERSITY OF GEORGIA MARINE EXTENSION SERVICE AQUARIUM, 14 mi. s.e. via Waters Ave. and McWhorter Rd. at Skidaway Island, houses 14 aquariums containing local marine life, coastal archeological finds and marine resources, and exhibits of flora and fauna from the South Atlantic continental shelf. A self-guiding trail winds through Maritime Forest and Salt Marsh.

The 680-acre property, formerly portions of two plantations, is shared by the Skidaway Institute of Oceanography. Mon.-Fri. 9-4, Sat. noon-5; closed holidays. Admission $1, under 3 free. Phone (912) 598-2496 Mon.-Fri. or 598-3474 Sat.-Sun.

WORMSLOE PLANTATION HISTORIC SITE, 10 mi. s.e. at 7601 Skidaway Rd. on the Isle of Hope, was received by royal grant in 1756 by Noble Jones, in whose family it remained until 1974. Jones, one of the 114 colonists who came to Georgia with Gen. James E. Oglethorpe, built a fortified house and cultivated a farm. The vestiges of his house, constructed 1739-45, are all that remain of the original plantation.

A 1.5-mile avenue leads to the tabby ruins of the plantation. A visitor center presents excavated artifacts and an audiovisual show about the early settlement of coastal Georgia. Allow 1 hour minimum. Tues.-Sat. 9-5, Sun. 2-5:30. Admission $2; ages 6-18, $1. Phone (912) 353-3023. *See ad.*

SEA ISLAND—
see Golden Isles p. 47.

SOCIAL CIRCLE (B-3) pop. 2,800, elev. 861'

WINERIES

- **Fox Vineyards Winery,** I-20 exit 47, then 1 mi. s. to 225 SR 11S. Mon.-Sat. 10-6, Sun. 1-6; closed holidays. Phone (770) 787-5402.

STATESBORO (D-5) pop. 15,900

GEORGIA SOUTHERN BOTANICAL GARDEN, .5 mi. s. on SR 67 on the campus of Georgia Southern University, features 9.5 acres of nature trails and native flora. A 1920s farmhouse exhibits photographs of native wildflowers and features a display about butterfly gardening. Allow 30 minutes minimum. Mon.-Fri. 9-6, Sun. 2-5; closed holidays and academic breaks. Free. Phone (912) 871-1114.

GEORGIA SOUTHERN MUSEUM is in the Rosenwald Building on Southern Dr. on the grounds of Georgia Southern University, .5 mi. s. on US 301/25. The museum houses fossilized sea animals as well as two large aquariums that depict sea life on the coastal plains. Also displayed is a 2-pound meteorite fragment that fell in a nearby town. The main attraction is a 26-foot Mososaur skeleton believed to be approximately 78 million years old. The museum also is home to an internationally significant whale skeleton reputed to be the oldest in North America.

Throughout the year the museum offers changing exhibits on loan from other museums, including the Smithsonian. Allow 1 hour minimum. Mon.-Fri. 9-5, Sat.-Sun. 2-5; closed holidays. Free. Phone (912) 681-5444.

STOCKBRIDGE (C-3) pop. 3,400, elev. 812'

PANOLA MOUNTAIN STATE CONSERVATION PARK, 9 mi. e. on SR 138, then 4 mi. n. on SR 155, encompasses a 100-acre granite mountain that shelters plants and animals indigenous to the Piedmont region and preserves the granite formation in its natural state. The park offers scenic views, nature trails and an interpretive center with displays about the natural history of the area.

Nature programs and guided hikes are offered. Self-guiding hikes are permitted on three trails, but hikes up the mountain are always guided because of the conservation efforts. Park open daily

7 a.m.-dusk. Nature center and park office open Tues.-Fri. 9-5, Sat.-Sun. noon-5. Free guided hikes are offered Sat.-Sun. at 10, Memorial Day-Labor Day; at 2:30, rest of year. Reservations are required. Free. Parking $2; free on Wed. Phone (770) 389-7801.

STONE MOUNTAIN—
see Atlanta and Vicinity p. 32.

TALLULAH FALLS (A-4) pop. 100, elev. 1,629'

Near the turn of the 20th century, Tallulah Falls was a resort area with scenery and a mountain climate that brought visitors from other parts of Georgia and neighboring states. The American Indian word *tallulah* means "terrible" or "awesome." Local legend maintains that the grandmother of Alabama-born actress Tallulah Bankhead was named for the second meaning of the word.

TALLULAH GORGE STATE PARK, in the center of town, offers a 500-yard walking trail along the rim of Tallulah Gorge, a sheer-walled, 1,000-foot-deep crevice with waterfalls and lush vegetation. Pavilions at various points along the trail offer views of geologic formations as well as native flora and fauna.

An interpretive center has films about history and safety. There also are a hiking trail, a wildflower trail, lighted tennis courts and a children's playground. A beach and campground are open seasonally. Entry to the gorge is by permit only, obtainable at the interpretive center. Park open Mon.-Fri. 8-5, Sat.-Sun. 10-6. Beach area daily 8-dusk, Memorial Day-Labor Day. Free. Phone (706) 754-7970. *See Recreation Chart.*

Kudzu

Kudzu—that leafy green vine that entwines electric poles, decorates porch trellises and overtakes trees—has made the South its home.

The plant arrived in the United States innocently enough; the Japanese brought it to Philadelphia in the late 19th century to decorate their pavilion in the centennial celebration. Kudzu grew in popularity as an ornamental shade plant until the 1930s, when experts at the U.S. Soil Conservation Service discovered how well it stopped soil erosion. Soon Conservation Service workers had planted kudzu on farms all across the South. The plant not only stopped erosion; it sent tendrils in all directions in its quest for more space.

Southerners thought kudzu was pretty and planted it in their yards to hide tree stumps and compost piles. They soon learned kudzu's true nature, however. Growing as much as a foot a day in hot weather, the vine spreads by sending roots into the earth where its leaves touch the ground. In a single season, one plant can creep 100 feet.

So far, kudzu has been successful in its search for space, spreading from Florida as far north as Maryland and as far west as Louisiana. There is good news, though. In Japan, kudzu is ground into powder that is used for cooking and as a medicine. Kudzu adds its flavor to lemonade, sweet and sour sauce, apple pie and fried eggplant. Made into a cream, kudzu allegedly fights influenza, upset stomach, apoplexy and sexual apathy.

In the United States, meanwhile, cattle have found kudzu to be good eating. At the rate it is growing, our cattle will not go hungry.

THOMASVILLE (F-3) pop. 17,500, elev. 290′

Thomasville was spared most of the ravages of the Civil War. Afterward, railroad lines were repaired and Northerners soon were traveling south to enjoy the mild winter climate of the high pinelands; it was believed that the pine-scented air was of therapeutic value. By the 1880s Thomasville had become a popular winter resort with some of the country's finest hotels.

The winter residents brought money to this small town and left behind community improvements and a collection of shooting plantations, as they called their mansions. One such resident, Charles W. Lapham of Chicago, was instrumental in establishing an excellent theater and a park that became one of the nation's first country clubs and golf links.

One of the oldest residents of Thomasville is Big Oak, on the corner of E. Monroe and N. Crawford streets. Dating from the late 17th century, the tree is 68 feet high, with a trunk circumference of 24 feet and a limb spread of 162 feet.

The Rose Festival is held mid- to late April. The town showcases more than 25,000 rose bushes during a week of parades, pageants and parties. Holiday Homecoming Week is held in early December. Highlights include a candlelight tour of houses, street entertainment and residents dressed in Victorian-style clothing.

Destination Thomasville Tourism Authority: 135 N. Broad St., Thomasville, GA, 31792; phone (912) 225-3919.

Self-guiding tours: Brochures describing historic tours of Thomasville and the surrounding area can be obtained at the tourism authority.

LAPHAM-PATTERSON HOUSE STATE HISTORIC SITE, 626 N. Dawson St., bears the names of its first and last owners. Each room in the asymmetrical 1884 house is a different shape and none is square. The house, built as a winter cottage for prosperous merchant C.W. Lapham, has a gas lighting system, a cantilevered balcony and an unusual double-flue chimney with a walk-through stairway. Other innovations included hot and cold running water, indoor plumbing and modern closets, unusual features for those days.

Purchased as a year-round residence in 1905 by James G. Patterson, the house has since been restored and furnished in period, with some original pieces. Guided tours are offered on the hour Tues.-Sat. 9-5, Sun. 2-5:30; closed Jan. 1, Thanksgiving and Dec. 25. Last tour begins at 4. Admission $3; ages 6-18, $1.50. Phone (912) 225-4004.

PEBBLE HILL PLANTATION is 5 mi. s. on US 319. The former winter retreat of the Hanna family of Cleveland, Pebble Hill has extensive grounds and a lavish main house typical of the late 19th- and early 20th-century winter cottages built by wealthy Northerners in the Thomasville area. An extensive collection of prints, paintings and American Indian relics as well as a number of antiques are displayed in the main house.

Other highlights include the stables, carriage house and gardens. Guided tours are available. Allow 2 hours minimum. Tues.-Sat. 10-5, Sun. 1-5, Oct. 2-day before Labor Day; closed Thanksgiving and Dec. 24-25. Last tour begins 1 hour before closing. Grounds $3; under 12, $1.50. Main house $7.50; ages 6-12, $3.50. Under 6 are not admitted to main house. Phone (912) 226-2344.

THOMAS COUNTY HISTORICAL MUSEUM, 725 N. Dawson St., consists of a three-story main building and four outbuildings. The area's history from 1820 to the mid-1900s is depicted through a variety of objects and exhibits, including arrowheads, a patent medicine collection of rare remedies, an 1870 jukebox, a ladies' costume collection and an original Stars and Bars flag with regimental colors.

One of the buildings houses a late 19th-century bowling alley. Also on the grounds are a rural log house and a middle-class frame city house, both furnished in period. Guided tours are offered. Allow 2 hours minimum. Mon.-Sat. 10-noon and 2-5, Sun. 2-5; closed Jan. 1, Easter, the last week in Sept., Thanksgiving and Dec. 24-25. Admission $4; ages 6-18, $1. Phone (912) 226-7664.

THOMASVILLE CULTURAL CENTER, 600 E. Washington St., is housed in a restored 1915 public school. Highlights include 14-foot ceilings and hardwood floors. The center contains a genealogical library, a reading room, an arts workshop and an auditorium. Allow 30 minutes minimum. Mon.-Fri. 9-5, Sat.-Sun. 1-5; closed holidays. Library open Mon.-Fri. 9-noon and 1-5; closed holidays. Free. Phone (912) 226-0588.

TIFTON (E-3) pop. 14,200, elev. 370′

Tifton was founded in 1890 and named for Nelson Tift, Georgia representative to the U.S. Congress 1868-69. Pecans, peanuts, tomatoes and honey are important to the region's agricultural base.

Tifton-Tift County Chamber of Commerce: 100 Central Ave., P.O. Box 165, Tifton, GA 31794; phone (912) 382-6200.

★GEORGIA AGRIRAMA, 8th St. on Whiddon Mill Rd., is an outdoor living-history museum depicting life in an 1890s town, a forest industries complex and two farmsteading communities. Costumed interpreters operate the exhibits and discuss life in the region at the turn of the 20th century.

The 95-acre site includes the Tift House—original home of Henry Harding Tift—a steam-powered sawmill, a cotton gin, farmhouses, blacksmith shop, 19th-century drugstore, masonic hall, water-powered gristmill, newspaper office and turpentine still with cooper's shed. Events include the Folk Life Festival in April, the Old Fashioned Independence Day Celebration on July 4, County Fair of 1896 on Labor Day, Cane Grinding Parties in late November and a Victorian Christmas in mid-December.

The Wiregrass Opry, featuring open-air performances of pop, bluegrass, country and gospel music, performs next to the Agrirama Saturday evenings, May through September. Agrirama open Tues.-Sat. 9-5, Sun. 12:30-5, June-Aug.; Mon.-Sat. 9-5, rest of year. Closed Jan. 1, Thanksgiving and Dec. 22-25. Admission $8; over 55, $6; ages 4-16, $4; family rate $22. Phone (912) 386-3344.

TOCCOA (A-4) pop. 8,300, elev. 1,045′

A mountain community bounded by the Chattahoochee National Forest *(see place listing p. 37)* and Lake Hartwell, Toccoa is in a popular vacation area that offers fishing, hunting, swimming, boating and water recreation.

Toccoa-Stephens County Chamber of Commerce: 901 E. Currahee St., P.O. Box 577, Toccoa, GA 30577; phone (706) 886-2132.

TOCCOA FALLS, 2 mi. n.e. on Alt. SR 17 at Toccoa Falls College, is reached by a short walk. The 186-foot falls are higher than Niagara Falls. Visitors have enjoyed this scenic spot since the early 1800s. Toccoa comes from an American Indian word meaning "beautiful." Mon.-Sat. 9-dusk; Sun. noon-6. Admission $1; over 60, 50c; under 12 free. Phone (706) 886-6831, ext. 5215.

TRAVELER'S REST STATE HISTORIC SITE, 6 mi. e. off US 123 on Riverdale Rd., dates from 1815. Devereaux Jarrett, a Georgia planter and businessman, bought the dwelling in 1838 and expanded it not only to accommodate his family but also to serve as a stagecoach inn. The center of a thriving plantation, the structure became known as Traveler's Rest. The restored inn and plantation house have original pieces of furniture.

Tues.-Sat. 9-5, Sun. 2-5:30; closed Jan. 1, Thanksgiving and Dec. 25. Last tour begins 1 hour before closing. Admission $2; ages 6-18, $1. Phone (706) 886-2256.

TYBEE ISLAND (D-6) pop. 2,800

Tybee Island Visitors Center: 209 Butler Ave., P.O. Box 491, Tybee Island, GA, 31328; phone (912) 786-5444.

TYBEE MUSEUM (FORT SCREVEN) is off US 80E at the n. end of Tybee Island. Housed in one of the gun batteries of an 1885 fort, the museum chronicles the history and multicultural influences of Tybee Island. Exhibits include paintings, dioramas, dolls, artifacts and historic weapons. A continuous film relates the history of the fort. The museum also features ocean views.

Allow 1 hour minimum. Daily 10-6; closed Jan. 1, Thanksgiving and Dec. 25. Combination admission with Tybee Lighthouse $3; over 62, $2; ages 6-12, $1. CB, DS, VI. Phone (912) 786-5801.

Tybee Lighthouse is off US 80E at the n. end of Tybee Island. The 1866 structure, built atop the lower 60 feet of the 1773 light, still has all support buildings intact on the 5-acre site. Among these are three keeper's houses, a summer kitchen furnished with period equipment and a fuel storage building. An ascent of the 178 stairs to the top of the lighthouse affords panoramic views.

Allow 30 minutes minimum. Daily 10-6; closed Jan. 1, Thanksgiving and Dec. 25. Combination admission with Tybee Museum $3; over 62, $2; ages 6-12, $1. CB, DS, VI. Phone (912) 786-5801.

VALDOSTA (F-4) pop. 39,800, elev. 215′

Valdosta's history is linked with transportation growth and a strategic location in the path of early westward expansion. Originally called Troupville, the settlement was designated a county seat in 1837. When it became evident that Troupville would not be on a proposed 1860 railroad route from Savannah to Mobile, Ala., the townsite was moved to take advantage of the potential prosperity. Troupville citizens renamed the town Valdosta for the governor's home Val de Aosta, or "Vale of Beauty."

Valdosta also is known as the gateway to Florida because of its proximity to heavily traveled I-75. Drexel Park, at Brookwood Drive and Patterson Street, offers nature trails and picnic areas. The city has three historic districts featuring commercial and residential buildings of the Victorian era.

Valdosta-Lowndes County Convention and Visitors Bureau: 1703 Norman Dr. #F, P.O. Box 1964, Valdosta, GA 31603-1964; phone (912) 245-0513. *See color ad p. 65.*

Self-guiding tours: A brochure describing a driving tour of Valdosta's three historic districts can be obtained from the convention and visitors bureau.

Shopping areas: The Lake Park Mill Store Plaza *(see color ad p. 307)* and Lake Park Factory Stores, at I-75 exit 2, contain factory outlet shops. Remerton Mill Village, at Baytree Place and Plum Street, offers stores in a historic setting. Anchor stores at the Valdosta Mall on SR 94W are Belk Hudson, JCPenney and Sears.

BARBER HOUSE, 416 N. Ashley St., was built by one of the early bottlers and promoters of Coca-Cola. The restored 1915 neoclassical mansion is decorated with late 19th-century furnishings that include the Barber family piano. Occupied until 1977, the structure now houses the chamber of commerce. Allow 30 minutes minimum. Mon.-Fri. 9-5; closed major holidays. Free. Phone (912) 247-8100.

THE CRESCENT, 904 N. Patterson St., is a stately neoclassical mansion with a crescent-shaped tile and marble porch supported by 13 columns representing the 13 original Colonies. The 23-room 1898 house built by Sen. W.S. West is furnished in period. The house has a large ballroom and orchestra room, ornate woodwork, numerous fireplaces and a wide, curving stairway. An octagonal schoolhouse and five gardens complete the complex. Allow 30 minutes minimum. Mon.-Fri. 2-5; closed holidays. Donations. Phone (912) 245-0513.

LOWNDES COUNTY HISTORICAL SOCIETY AND MUSEUM, 305 W. Central Ave., has photographs, documents and memorabilia reflecting the development of Valdosta and the surrounding area. Among the displayed documents is an original Confederate secession decree. Period clothing, antique handworks, and city directories dating from 1904 are displayed. A genealogical library also is available. Allow 1 hour minimum. Mon.-Fri. 10-5, Sat. 10-2; closed holidays. Donations. Phone (912) 247-4780.

LOWNDES/VALDOSTA CULTURAL ART CENTER, 1204 N. Patterson St., displays various types of art on a rotating monthly basis. The gallery features emerging and recognized local, national and international talent, with an emphasis on professional artists. Allow 30 minutes minimum. Mon.-Fri. 10-6, Sat. 10-4, Sun. 2-4; closed major holidays. Free. Phone (912) 247-2787.

WILD ADVENTURES, off I-75 exit 3A, then 4 mi. s. to 3766 Old Clyattville Rd., is a 170-acre park featuring farm and exotic animals. In addition, there are animal shows, a petting area and rides. Food is available.

Mon.-Thurs. 10-7, Fri.-Sat. 10-9, Sun. 10-6, early June-late Aug.; Sun.-Thurs. 10-6, Fri.-Sat. 10-9, late Aug.-Dec. 31 and Mar. 1-early June; Fri.-Sat. 10-9, Sun. 10-6, rest of year. Admission $14.95; over 54, $12.95; ages 3-10, $10.95. MC, VI. Phone (912) 559-1330. *See ad.*

WARM SPRINGS (C-2) pop. 400

The legendary curative powers of Warm Springs have lured the hopeful for centuries. Wounded American Indian warriors gathered at the springs before Europeans colonized the New World. In the late 1700s the springs were discovered by yellow fever victims, and by 1832 Warm Springs had become a popular summer health resort. The resort survived the torch of Gen. William Tecumseh Sherman only to be reduced to ashes by a runaway bonfire in 1865. Rebuilt, Warm Springs flourished in the 1880s and 1890s and was incorporated in 1893.

Franklin Delano Roosevelt visited the springs in 1924 hoping to improve his health after contracting polio. A few years later he established the Warm Springs Foundation for the care and treatment of fellow polio victims who could not afford such medical help.

Although Warm Springs' popularity as a resort waned after Roosevelt's death, restoration efforts attract visitors who come to browse through the craft shops housed in former grocery and dime stores. Artisans can be seen at work in more than 60 stores, and musicians and cloggers perform on the stage of the old Pavilion during events and on weekends.

Meriwether County Chamber of Commerce: Federal Bldg., P.O. Box 9, Warm Springs, GA 31830; phone (706) 655-2558.

★**LITTLE WHITE HOUSE STATE HISTORIC SITE** is .2 mi. s. on SR 85W. Built by President Franklin Roosevelt in 1932, the Little White House was the site of his death on April 12, 1945, and is now a memorial shrine. A walk flanked by stones and flags from all 50 states leads from the memorial fountain in the center of the grounds to a museum.

Displays chronicle Roosevelt's life and depict his role in history; a 12-minute film also is presented. Picnic facilities are available. Guide service is available in the house and museum. Daily 9-5; closed Jan. 1, Thanksgiving and Dec. 25. Last tour begins 1 hour before closing. Admission $4; ages 6-18, $2. Phone (706) 655-5870.

NATIONAL FISH HATCHERY, s. on SR 41 and US 27A, is a striped-bass hatchery featuring an aquarium and two outdoor display pools. Allow 30 minutes minimum. Daily 7:30-4; closed federal holidays. Free. Phone (706) 655-3620.

WARNER ROBINS (D-3) pop. 43,700

MUSEUM OF AVIATION, SR 247 and Russell Pkwy., displays more than 85 historical aircraft housed in four buildings and a hangar on a 43-acre site. There are exhibits about the F-15 Eagle, a British airfield, hump pilots, P-47 World War II Commemorative, 14th Air Force Flying Tigers and electronic warfare.

Aircraft displays include a MiG-17, British Lightning, Blackbird, Dragon Lady and a 60-foot cutaway replica of a B-17 bomber. A flight simulator allows visitors to experience a lifelike flying mission. The Georgia Aviation Hall of Fame recognizes honored airmen from the state.

Also featured is an American Indian history display. Nearby excavations have unearthed artifacts dating to 8,000 B.C. A theater presents movies. Comfortable walking shoes are advised. Food is available.

Allow 3 hours minimum. Daily 10-5; closed Jan. 1, Thanksgiving and Dec. 25. Museum free. Theater admission $2; ages 4-12, $1. Phone (912) 926-6870.

WASHINGTON (B-4) pop. 4,300, elev. 630'

Established in 1773, Washington has antebellum Greek Revival mansions as well as Colonial-style houses dating from the days following the Revolution; some are occupied by descendants of the original owners. Tree-shaded streets bear such patriotic names as Jefferson and Liberty.

The Battle of Kettle Creek, the decisive battle of the Revolutionary War in Georgia, was fought west of town in 1779. Washington also was the site of a historic moment in the Civil War. A granite marker at the southwest corner of the courthouse indicates the location of the meeting that dissolved the government of the Confederacy on May 4, 1865.

A tour of privately owned historic houses is held in April; for further information contact the chamber of commerce.

Washington-Wilkes Chamber of Commerce: 104 E. Liberty St., P.O. Box 661, Washington, GA 30673; phone (706) 678-2013.

CALLAWAY PLANTATION, 5 mi. w. on US 78, is a restored plantation that includes three restored early American dwellings, a smokehouse, cemetery and surrounding fields. The 1869 red brick Greek Revival house is furnished in period. A 1780s hewn-log house, which was probably a settler's home, features domestic and agricultural implements and primitive furniture. The 1790s two-story Federal Plainstyle house has furnishings characteristic of the period. Surrounding fields are planted in typical 19th century crops. Guided tours are available

Tues.-Sat. 10-5, Sun. 2-5; closed Jan. 1, Thanksgiving and Dec. 25. Admission $4; ages 6-12, $1. Phone (706) 678-7060.

ROBERT TOOMBS HOUSE STATE HISTORIC SITE, 216 E. Robert Toombs Ave., is the former home of the Confederate statesman who was instrumental in leading Georgia to secession and war. The state has carefully restored the structure to its condition at the time of Toombs' death in 1885. The 1797 house now displays numerous furnishings once owned by the Toombs family. Allow 1 hour minimum. Tues.-Sat. 9-5, Sun. 2-5:30; closed Jan. 1, Thanksgiving and Dec. 25. Admission $2.50; ages 6-18, $1.50. Phone (706) 678-2226.

WASHINGTON HISTORICAL MUSEUM is at 308 E. Robert Toombs Ave. on Bus. Rte. 78. Built about 1835, the museum houses antique furnishings and Confederate relics, including Jefferson Davis' camp chest. Tues.-Sat. and Mon. holidays 10-5, Sun. 2-5; closed Jan. 1, Thanksgiving and Dec. 25. Admission $2; ages 5-12, $1. Phone (706) 678-2105.

WAYCROSS (E-5) pop. 16,400, elev. 135'

Known as the "crossing of the ways" in the mid- to late 19th century because of the intersection of several railroad lines, Waycross has maintained its railroad heritage. At Rice Yard, the largest classification facility in the country, freight cars are organized into trains to move shipments across the nation. Other industries in the area include lumber and related concerns, manufactured housing, tobacco and pecan farming, bee culture and the production of honey.

Waycross-Ware Chamber of Commerce: 200 Lee Ave., P.O. Box 137, Waycross, GA 31501; phone (912) 283-3742.

SAVE **OBEDIAH'S OKEFENOK**, US 82W. to Gillmore St., then 8.5 mi. s. to 500 Obediah Tr., offers self-guiding nature walks, a 1,100-foot boardwalk through the Okefenokee Swamp, wildlife exhibits and an 1870s homestead containing various exhibits and displays. Allow 1 hour, 30 minutes minimum. Daily 10-5; closed Jan. 1 and Dec. 25. Admission $4.50; over 55, $3.50; ages 6-17, $3. Phone (912) 287-0090.

OKEFENOKEE HERITAGE CENTER, 2 mi. n.w. via US 1/23, then 4 blks. w. on Augusta Ave., has an art gallery that features permanent and changing exhibits about history and the arts. The museum includes a late 19th-century printshop, a restored 1912 steam locomotive, train cars, a railroad depot and a restored 1840s farmhouse. The Power House exhibit depicts the development of transportation and energy and includes early forms of horse-drawn vehicles and automobiles.

Allow 1 hour minimum. Mon.-Sat. 9-5, Sun. 1-5; closed major holidays. Admission $2; over 65, $1.50; ages 4-18, $1. Phone (912) 285-4260.

★**OKEFENOKEE SWAMP PARK** is 8 mi. s.e. on US 1/23, then 4.7 mi. s. on SR 177. This 1,600-acre wildlife sanctuary on Cowhouse Island is the northern entrance to the Okefenokee Swamp *(see Folkston p. 42).* The park features flower gardens, a wilderness walkway, observation tower, educational centers with exhibits about the swamp and native animals and birds. Optional guided boat tours and canoe rentals offer closer looks at plants and wildlife in the swamp's recesses.

The Swamp Creation Center has dioramas, charts, aquariums and animated exhibits explaining the swamp's evolution. A wildlife observation room and an exhibit of carnivorous plants that feed on insects are features of the Living Swamp Ecological Center. The center also includes a serpentarium, a bear observatory and showings of the film "A Swamp Ecosystem."

Outdoor museum displays at Pioneer Island, accessible by a short boardwalk, pertain to the history of the swamp's early settlers. In addition, there are daily ecology videotape shows and live reptile presentations. Animal habitats feature otters, alligators, turtles, bobcats, deer, foxes, turkeys and other swamp animals.

Park open daily 9-5:30. Optional guided boat tours ranging from 30 minutes to 2 hours depart daily at 10, 1 and 3 (depending on water level and guide availability). Park $8; over 62, military with ID or under 12, $7. Packages including admission and boat tours $12-$20. MC, VI. Phone (912) 283-0583.

SAVE **SOUTHERN FOREST WORLD MUSEUM**, next to the Okefenokee Heritage Center, contains exhibits about the history of forestry in the South. Visitors can walk up the inside of a 38-foot-tall model of a loblolly pine, step inside a giant cypress, listen to a talking tree or sit in the cab of a 1905 logging locomotive. Nature trails are on the grounds. Allow 30 minutes minimum. Mon.-Sat. 10-5, Sun. 1-5; closed major holidays. Admission $2, under 4 free. Phone (912) 285-4056.

WAYNESBORO (C-5) pop. 5,700

Waynesboro, incorporated in 1812, was named in honor of American Indian fighter, patriot and general, "Mad" Anthony Wayne, who fought in Georgia during the Revolution. Though evolved from plantations to tenant and sharecropper tracts to mechanized big-business holdings, farms are still the basis of the area's economy.

Known as the Bird Dog Capital of the World, Waynesboro is the site of the Georgia Field Trials, one of the nation's oldest hunting dog competitions, which is held in January; for information phone (706) 554-2991.

Burke County Chamber of Commerce: 241 E. Peace St., Waynesboro, GA 30830; phone (706) 554-5451.

BURKE COUNTY MUSEUM, 536 Liberty St., presents exhibits about eastern Georgia. A genealogy and local history section is available for research. Allow 30 minutes minimum. Wed.-Fri. 10-5, Sat. 10-4, Sun. 1-4; closed holidays. Free. Phone (706) 554-4889.

WEST POINT (C-1) pop. 3,600, elev. 576'

Because of its strategic location on the Chattahoochee River at the Alabama state line, West Point was considered the key to the granary of the Tennessee Army during the Civil War. Word of Gen. Robert E. Lee's surrender was slow to reach the town, and the last battle east of the Mississippi River, the Battle of Fort Tyler, was fought a week after the war's official end.

Recovery after the war was ensured with the construction of two textile mills that eventually expanded into what is now West Point Pepperell Inc., one of the world's largest textile manufacturing companies.

North of West Point is West Point Lake *(see Recreation Chart),* a 25,900-acre man-made site offering a variety of recreational pursuits. A visitor center, 4 miles north off US 29, contains dioramas, photographs and a slide show describing the history of the region before, during and after construction of the dam that created the lake.

Greater Valley Area Chamber of Commerce: P.O. Box 584, West Point, GA 31833; phone (334) 642-1411.

North Carolina

*An introduction to the state's history, geography,
economy and recreation*

FROM APPALACHIAN VISTAS TO SECLUDED ATLANTIC
SHORELINES, NORTH CAROLINA PRESENTS A VARIETY OF
FACES. THE TARHEEL STATE, RICH IN HISTORY, OFFERS
VISITORS A GLIMPSE OF THE PAST AT BATH, ITS OLDEST
TOWN; AMERICAN INDIAN HERITAGE AT CHEROKEE; THE
FIRST ENGLISH SETTLEMENT IN AMERICA AT FORT
RALEIGH; AND EUROPEAN TRADITION AT THE BILTMORE
ESTATE. MODERN NORTH CAROLINA UNVEILS EXCITING
AUTO RACES AT CHARLOTTE MOTOR SPEEDWAY,
CHILLING SKI SLOPES IN THE BLUE RIDGE MOUNTAINS
AND THRILLING COLLEGE BASKETBALL GAMES.

HISTORY

As early as 1524 the area that is presently North Carolina was explored by such Europeans as Giovanni da Verrazano and Hernando de Soto. In 1585 Sir Walter Raleigh, under the sponsorship of Queen Elizabeth I, established a shortlived colony on Roanoke Island. Two years later, Gov. John White, in charge of a second colony, sailed to England for supplies, and upon his return in 1590 found no trace of the settlement. The only clue to its disappearance was the word "Croatoan" crudely carved into a tree. Among the missing colonists was the first English child born in America, Virginia Dare. The fate of the "Lost Colony" has never been determined.

Virginia colonists made the first permanent settlement in the 1650s on Albemarle Sound. A period of American Indian and pirate raids and misgovernment continued until the territory was officially divided into North Carolina and South Carolina in 1712; North Carolina became a crown colony in 1729.

Although North Carolina residents had fought alongside the British in several previous wars, the colony began to resist British rule in the 1760s. In 1765 North Carolinians were among the first to prevent enforcement of the Stamp Act, a British tax law—thus beginning the fight for independence. On May 20, 1775 Mecklenburg County citizens met in Charlotte and drew up a declaration of independence from England. The following year the first battle of the American Revolution on North Carolina soil took place; Patriots defeated British Loyalists at Moore's Creek Bridge.

Postwar North Carolinians faced many obstacles, including poverty, ineffectual local governments, political unrest and economic depression. Between 1815 and 1835 North Carolina was referred to as the "Rip Van Winkle state" due to its backwards ways and slow growth.

The slavery issue catapulted the state into the Civil War. North Carolina reluctantly seceded from the Union on May 20, 1861, although firmly believing in the preservation of the Union. The most significant events of the war in the state were the battles of Bentonville, Fort Fisher, Fort Hatteras and Plymouth, as well as Gen. William Tecumseh Sherman's 1865 invasion, which blazed a path of destruction through the state.

Following the war North Carolina was devastated. The state supplied more troops than any other, and losses made up more than one-fourth of the South's total casualties. Many farms were destroyed, and the state was in financial despair. Reconstruction brought radical Republican control as well as corrupt carpetbaggers seeking quick gain.

By the turn of the 20th century race relations became a major issue, with many North Carolinians pushing for white supremacy. A constitutional amendment barring all illiterates from voting—except those whose ancestors had voted prior to 1867—effectively prevented many black citizens from voting. This amendment was eventually repealed.

In order to promote the literacy of whites, Gov. Charles Brantley Aycock improved educational opportunities dramatically. North Carolina

Fast Facts

POPULATION: 7,322,900.

AREA: 52,586 square miles, ranks 28th.

CAPITAL: Raleigh.

HIGHEST POINT: 6,684 ft., Mount Mitchell.

LOWEST POINT: Sea level, Atlantic Ocean.

TIME ZONE: Eastern. DST.

MINIMUM AGE FOR DRIVERS: 16.

SEAT BELT/CHILD RESTRAINT LAWS: Seat belts required for driver and front-seat passengers; child restraints required for under 4.

HELMETS FOR MOTORCYCLISTS: Required.

RADAR DETECTORS: Permitted.

FIREARMS LAWS: Vary by state and/or county. Contact Law Enforcement Liaison Section, Attorney General's Office, P.O. Box 629, Raleigh, NC 27602-0629; phone (919) 716-6500.

HOLIDAYS: Jan. 1; Martin Luther King Jr.'s Birthday, Jan. (3rd Mon.); Washington's Birthday, Feb. (3rd Mon.); Good Friday (state and national banks only); Memorial Day, May (last Mon.); July 4; Labor Day, Sept. (1st Mon.); Veterans Day, Nov. 11; General Election Day; Thanksgiving; Dec. 25.

TAXES: North Carolina's statewide sales tax is 4 percent, with local options for an additional 2 percent. Localities may impose a Room Occupancy Tax of varying percentages.

STATE WELCOME CENTERS are on I-85S near Kings Mountain; I-85N near Norlina; I-95N near Roanoke Rapids; I-95S near Rowland; I-77N near Dobson; I-77S near Charlotte; I-26 near Columbus; and I-40W near Waynesville. Information, free brochures and picnic and rest area facilities are available. Centers open daily 8-5; closed Jan. 1 and Dec. 24-25.

was the first state to establish a state university with the 1795 founding of the University of North Carolina. Education for all residents continues to play an important role in the Tarheel State. Other noted institutions of higher learning include Duke University, North Carolina State University and Wake Forest University.

On Dec. 17, 1903 Orville and Wilbur Wright initiated the first flight in a power-driven airplane at Kill Devil Hills. The brothers made more than 1,000 test flights in their 1902 glider before the takeoff of their 1903 *Kitty Hawk* (originally named *Flyer I*). The day's first flight lasted 12 seconds and the last 59 seconds. A memorial to the aviators was dedicated in 1932.

Progress came to North Carolina during World War II as increased industrialization took place. Several military bases, including Ft. Bragg and Camp Lejeune, were established during the war and still remain active. Instead of dependence on a traditional trio—textiles, tobacco and furniture—new industries were introduced, including rubber and plastic-making plants and electrical and non-electrical machinery.

In 1958 Research Triangle Park, between Duke University, North Carolina State University and the University of North Carolina, was founded. The park provides a base for dozens of laboratories that conduct government and business experiments. Present-day tenants include IBM, General Electric and the United States Environmental Protection Agency.

For Your Information

TOURISM INFORMATION:

Travel & Tourism Division
301 N. Wilmington St.
Raleigh, NC 27601
(919) 733-4171 in Raleigh
(800) 847-4862 outside Raleigh

RECREATION INFORMATION:

North Carolina Division of Parks and
   Recreation
P.O. Box 27687
Raleigh, NC 27611-7687
(919) 733-7275 or (919) 733-4181

FISHING AND HUNTING REGULATIONS:

North Carolina Wildlife Resources
   Commission
512 N. Salisbury St.
Raleigh, NC 27604
(919) 733-3391

NATIONAL FOREST INFORMATION:

U.S. Forest Service
P.O. Box 2750
Asheville, NC 28802
(704) 257-4200
(800) 280-2267 (reservations)

By the 1980s the state's diversification programs began to foster growth in the underdeveloped, primarily agricultural regions of eastern North Carolina. With the U.S. government limiting the amount of tobacco that can be grown and sold, however, the emphasis on cigarette smoke's ill effects and an increasing number of Americans giving up smoking, many tobacco farmers are looking at an uncertain future.

Despite a historical dependence on farming diversification continues. Charlotte is headquarters for NationsBank and First Union, two of the largest banks in the nation, as well as the head quarters for other financial institutions, insurance companies and major U.S. corporations. Outdoor recreational activities also abound, making tourism one of the state's largest economy boosters.

GEOGRAPHY

Appalachian highlands, the central Piedmont and the coastal plain make up North Carolina. Along the state's western tier, the Blue Ridge Mountains and the Great Smoky Mountains, master chain of the ancient Appalachian Range, converge. Forty-three summits reach more than 6,000 feet; prominent Mount Mitchell, rising 6,684 feet, is the highest point in the eastern United States.

Covering nearly half the state, the Piedmont descends from a 1,500-foot elevation at the base of the Blue Ridge Mountains to an average of 500 feet at the fall line. To the southeast are the sandhills with sandy soil and longleaf pine. Below the fall line, which wanders from Roanoke Rapids to Rockingham, is the coastal plain, in which lakes are numerous. The largest, Mattamuskeet, covers about 30,000 acres.

Albemarle and Pamlico sounds are the largest of the bays and lagoons that scallop the 320-mile coastline. Between the sounds and the sea are the Outer Banks—long, narrow barrier isles highlighted by Cape Hatteras and Cape Lookout. Though stark shipwrecks bear witness to hurricane tides, the Outer Banks possess a sunny beauty that makes them one of the East's most desirable vacation spots.

A product of this varying terrain is a climate that ranges from subtropical to nearly alpine in the mountains, where snow is no stranger. The sandhills region is noted for its dry, bracing air and mild, invigorating winters.

ECONOMY

Among Southeastern states North Carolina ranks first in value of manufactured products, number of wage earners in industry and wages paid. Major products are textiles, tobacco products and chemicals. The electrical machinery, chemical and pulp and paper industries are expanding. Manufacturing activity is centered in Charlotte, Durham, Greensboro, Raleigh and Winston-Salem.

Income from tourism ranks with that of industrial production. Another dimension of the economy is the renaissance of handicrafts produced in the Appalachian region. Spreading along the Blue Ridge Parkway from a nucleus at Asheville, the timeless arts of basketry, weaving, woodcarving, pottery and furniture making are bringing wide acclaim to the area.

North Carolina produces two-thirds of the nation's bright-leaf tobacco, while corn follows as the state's second largest crop. Fruits, peanuts, potatoes, hay and soybeans are other major harvests. Poultry and livestock also are important.

North Carolina forests cover about 18 million acres; the pine and gum woods of the east and the hardwood stands of the west produce the region's most valuable timber. Commercial fishing takes place in the coastal area, especially on Pamlico Sound. Oysters, shrimp, other edible fish and menhaden, used for making fertilizer, are the main catches.

North Carolina soil yields some 300 minerals, of which 75 are found in commercial quantities. Mica, feldspar, olivine, lithium materials, crushed granite and phosphate are the most significant. One of the world's largest surface granite quarries is in the Mount Airy vicinity. North Carolina also is a rockhound's dream: Franklin is one of the few areas in the nation where rubies and other precious stones can be found.

RECREATION

Beach activities abound along the coastal plain. The 30,000-acre Cape Hatteras National Seashore, on the Outer Banks, has 70 miles of beaches available for **camping, swimming** and **surf fishing.** The barrier islands of the 28,500-acre Cape Lookout National Seashore, only accessible by ferry, offer similar opportunities. Shipwrecks off the coast attract **scuba diving** enthusiasts, and Nags Head dunes afford **hang gliding** sites.

Camping, **fishing, horseback riding** and **hiking** are found throughout North Carolina's four national forests and many state parks. Great Smoky Mountains National Park offers a variety of activities along the 71 miles of the Appalachian Trail that thread through it.

Canoeing and **water skiing** are popular activities throughout the state; the swift mountain streams and rivers are preferred by white-water **rafting** enthusiasts. **Skiing** and other snow sports are available at winter recreation areas along the Blue Ridge Mountains. For further information contact the North Carolina High Country Host, 1700 Blowing Rock Rd., Boone, NC 28607; phone (704) 264-1299 or (800) 438-7500.

State parks offer many areas for fishing, camping, **boating** and swimming. A nominal user fee is charged for activities, but admission and parking are free. Open 8 a.m.-9 p.m. June through August, they close earlier—usually at dusk—the rest of the year. Mount Jefferson and Mount Mitchell are usually closed after heavy snowfalls.

Trailers are permitted in all state park campgrounds, except Mount Mitchell. Utility hookups are available at Falls Lake, Jordan Lake, and Kerr Lake state recreation areas. Reservations for camping in state recreation areas can be made through the superintendent for a 7-day minimum/14-day maximum stay; stays of less than a week are permitted on a space-available basis without reservations. For more information about camping areas *consult the AAA Southeastern CampBook.*

Natural and man-made lakes offer fishing for bass, bluegill, crappie and sunfish. Mountain streams hold both rainbow and brook trout. **Hunting** for bear and deer is allowed in the mountains and the more remote coastal marshes; opossums, raccoons, rabbits and squirrels can be found throughout the state. Waterfowl, quails and turkeys are also prevalent. Consult regulations of the North Carolina Wildlife Resources Commission *(see the For Your Information box).*

Fine **golf** courses and **equestrian activities** distinguish the Piedmont resorts of Pinehurst and Southern Pines. Asheville, in the Appalachian highlands region, offers excellent golf and **tennis** facilities.

North Carolina also plays host to a number of spectator sports. A full program of **races** is highlighted by the Coca-Cola 600 Stock Car Race in May and the United Auto Workers General Motors 500 in October at the Charlotte Motor Speedway. During the academic season there is a full schedule of collegiate team sports throughout the state. Professional **football** watchers in North Carolina have the Carolina Panthers to cheer for, and during **basketball** season the eyes of sports fans focus on the Charlotte Hornets. The state also is noted for its minor league **baseball**, and professional golf tournaments round out the calendar.

Throughout the TourBook, you may notice a Recreational Activities heading with bulleted listings of recreation-oriented establishments listed underneath. Since normal AAA inspection criteria cannot be applied, these establishments are presented for information only. Age, height and weight restrictions may apply. Reservations are often recommended and sometimes required. Visitors should phone or write the attraction for additional information, and the address and phone number are provided for this purpose.

RECREATION AREAS

	MAP LOCATION	CAMPING	PICNICKING	HIKING TRAILS	BOATING	BOAT RAMP	BOAT RENTAL	FISHING	SWIMMING	PETS ON LEASH	BICYCLE TRAILS	NATURE PROGS.	VISITOR CENTER	LODGE/CABINS	FOOD SERVICE
NATIONAL PARK *(See place listing)*															
Great Smoky Mountains (E-2) 520,000 acres. Horse rental.		•	•	•				•			•		•	•	•
NATIONAL FORESTS *(See place listings)*															
Croatan 157,851 acres. Southeastern North Carolina.		•	•	•	•	•		•	•						
Cedar Point (C-8) 260 acres off SR 24 3 mi. s.e. of Swansboro.	66	•	•	•	•	•		•							
Neuse River (C-8) 240 acres 10 mi. s. of New Bern on US 70E.	67	•	•	•		•		•	•						
Nantahala 525,897 acres. Southwestern tip of North Carolina.		•	•	•	•	•		•	•	•		•			
Arrowood Glade (F-2) 4 acres 7 mi. w. of Franklin on SR 1310.	25	•	•					•	•						
Cliffside Lake (F-2) 6 acres 4.5 mi. n.w. on US 64. *(See Highlands)*	52	•	•	•				•	•						
Hanging Dog (F-1) 21 acres 5 mi. n.w. of Murphy on SR 1326.	30	•	•	•	•	•		•		•					
Jackrabbit Mountain (F-1) 28 acres 10 mi. n.e. of Hayesville via US 64, SR 175 and SR 1155.	32	•	•	•	•	•		•	•						
Standing Indian Mountain (F-2) 12 mi. w. of Franklin on US 64, then 2 mi. e. on old US 64 and 2 mi. s. on FR 67.	69	•	•	•				•		•					
Pisgah 500,085 acres. Western North Carolina.		•	•	•				•	•	•	•	•		•	•

INDEX TO STARRED ATTRACTIONS
ATTRACTIONS AND PLACES OF EXCEPTIONAL INTEREST AND QUALITY

Battleship North Carolina -   see Wilmington

Biltmore Estate - see Asheville

Blue Ridge Parkway - see place listing

Cannon Village Visitor Center -
    see Kannapolis

Cape Hatteras National Seashore -
    see place listing

Chimney Rock Park - see Chimney Rock

Chinqua-Penn Plantation - see Reidsville

Discovery Place - see Charlotte

Duke University Chapel - see Durham

Elizabethan Gardens -
    see Fort Raleigh National Historic Site

Ghost Town In the Sky - see Maggie Valley

Grandfather Mountain - see Linville

Great Smoky Mountains National Park -
    see place listing

Greensboro Historical Museum -
    see Greensboro

Historic Halifax State Historic Site -
    see Halifax

"Horn in the West" - see Boone

"The Lost Colony" -
    see Fort Raleigh National Historical Site

Morehead Planetarium - see Chapel Hill

Mount Mitchell State Park - see Asheville

North Carolina Maritime Museum -
    see Beaufort

North Carolina Museum of Art - see Raleigh

North Carolina Museum of History -   see Raleigh

North Carolina Zoological Park - see Asheboro

Oconaluftee Indian Village - see Cherokee

Old Salem - see Winston-Salem

Paramount's Carowinds Theme Park -
    see Charlotte

Pisgah National Forest - see place listing

R.J. Reynolds Tobacco/
    Whitaker Park Manufacturing Center -
    see Winston-Salem

Schiele Museum of Natural History and Planetarium -
    see Gastonia

"Strike at the Wind" - see Pembroke

Tanglewood - see Winston-Salem

Tryon Palace Historic Sites and
    Gardens - see New Bern

Tweetsie Railroad - see Blowing Rock

"Unto These Hills" - see Cherokee

"Worthy is the Lamb" - see Swansboro

Wright Brothers National Memorial -
    see place listing

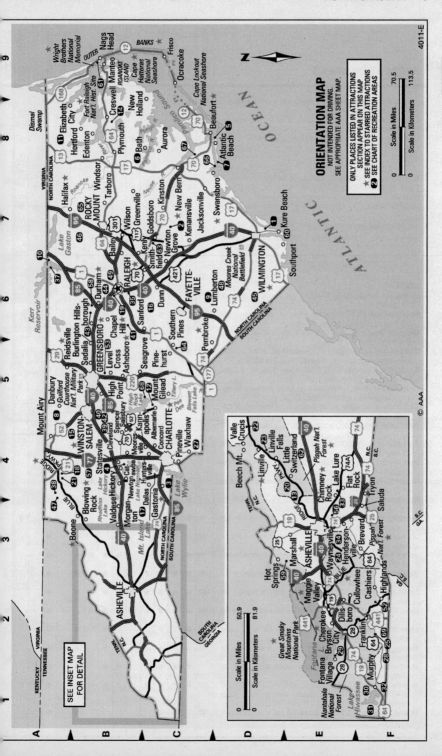

RECREATION AREAS

RECREATION AREAS	MAP LOCATION	CAMPING	PICNICKING	HIKING TRAILS	BOATING	BOAT RAMP	BOAT RENTAL	FISHING	SWIMMING	PETS ON LEASH	BICYCLE TRAILS	NATURE PROGS.	VISITOR CENTER	LODGE/CABINS	FOOD SERVICE
Lake Powhatan (E-3) 30 acres 7 mi. s.w. of Asheville on SR 191 and FR 3484.	34	•	•	•				•	•	•	•				
Rocky Bluff (E-3) 10 acres 3 mi. s. of Hot Springs on SR 209.	59	•	•	•				•		•					
Uwharrie 47,615 acres. Central North Carolina.		•	•	•	•	•		•	•	•					
Badin Lake (C-5) 9,540 acres 10 mi. n. of Troy on SR 109.	68	•	•	•	•	•		•							
NATIONAL SEASHORES *(See place listings)*															
Cape Hatteras (C-9) 45 square miles on the Outer Banks.			•	•	•	•		•	•				•	•	
Cape Lookout (C-9) 55 miles along the Outer Banks.			•	•				•	•				•	•	
ARMY CORPS OF ENGINEERS															
John H. Kerr Reservoir (A-6) 106,860 acres n. of Henderson on the Virginia border off I-85. Water skiing.	37	•	•	•	•	•	•	•	•	•			•	•	
W. Kerr Scott Dam and Reservoir (B-4) 1,470 acres 4 mi. w. of Wilkesboro on SR 268W.	57	•	•	•	•	•		•	•	•					
STATE															
B. Everett Jordan (B-6) 47,000 acres 10 mi. w. of Apex off US 64.	41	•	•	•	•	•		•	•	•		•			
Boone's Cave (B-5) 110 acres 15 mi. n. of Salisbury via US 70 and SR 150. Scenic overlook.	42		•	•				•		•					
Carolina Beach (D-7) 420 acres 1 mi. n.w. of Carolina Beach off US 421.	1	•	•	•	•	•		•	•	•					•
Cliffs of the Neuse (C-7) 751 acres 4 mi. e. on US 70, then 9 mi. s. on SR 111. Scenic. *(See Goldsboro)*	2	•	•	•		•		•	•	•		•			
Crowder's Mountain (C-4) 2,586 acres 6 mi. w. of Gastonia off US 29/74 on SR 1125.	3	•	•	•				•		•					
Duke Power (B-4) 1,458 acres on Lake Norman 10 mi. s. of Statesville via US 77 and US 21.	4	•	•	•	•	•	•	•	•	•					
Eno River (B-6) 2,284 acres 3 mi. n.w. of Durham off CR 1569. Canoeing.	43	•	•	•				•		•					
Falls Lake (B-6) 38,000 acres 13 mi. n. of Raleigh off SR 50.	44	•	•	•	•	•		•	•	•		•			
Fort Fisher (E-7) 287 acres 5 mi. s. of Carolina Beach off Hwy 421.	60		•						•						
Fort Macon (D-8) 389 acres 2 mi. e. on SR 1190. Historic. *(See Atlantic Beach)*	5		•					•	•	•			•	•	
Goose Creek (B-8) 1,596 acres 8 mi. e. of Washington on US 264.	6	•	•	•				•	•	•					
Hammocks Beach (D-8) 736 acres 4 mi. s. via SR 24 and ferry. Scenic. Shelling. *(See Swansboro)*	7	•	•	•				•	•	•					
Hanging Rock (A-5) 6,340 acres 4 mi. n.w. off SR 89. Scenic. *(See Danbury)*	8	•	•	•	•	•		•	•	•				•	
Jockey's Ridge (B-9) 414 acres at US 158 bypass in Nags Head.	61		•	•						•		•			
Jones Lake (C-6) 2,208 acres 4 mi. n. of Elizabethtown off SR 242.	9	•	•	•	•			•	•	•					
Kerr Lake (A-7) 6,200 acres 11 mi. n. of Henderson on the Virginia border off I-85.	10	•	•	•	•	•		•		•					
Lake James (E-4) 585 acres 5 mi. n.e. of Marion on Hwy. 126.	62	•	•	•	•	•		•	•	•					
Lake Norman (C-4) 32, 510 acres n.w. of Huntersville off I-77.	26	•	•	•	•	•	•	•	•	•		•	•		•
Lake Waccamaw (D-6) 10,670 acres 6 mi. s. of Lake Waccamaw off US 74/76.	45	•	•	•				•		•					
Medoc Mountain (B-7) 2,287 acres 15 mi. s.w. of Roanoke Rapids via SR 48, then 2 mi. w. on SR 561.	46	•	•	•				•		•					
Merchants Millpond (A-8) 2,921 acres 6 mi. n.e. of Gatesville on SR 1403.	11	•	•	•	•	•		•		•					
Morrow Mountain (C-5) 4,693 acres 5 mi. e. via SR 24/27/73 and SR 1719 (near Badin). Scenic. *(See Albemarle)*	12	•	•	•	•	•		•	•	•		•	•	•	
Mount Jefferson (A-3) 489 acres 1.5 mi. s. of Jefferson off US 221.	47		•	•						•		•			

RECREATION AREAS

RECREATION AREAS	MAP LOCATION	CAMPING	PICNICKING	HIKING TRAILS	BOATING	BOAT RAMP	BOAT RENTAL	FISHING	SWIMMING	PETS ON LEASH	BICYCLE TRAILS	NATURE PROGS.	VISITOR CENTER	LODGE/CABINS	FOOD SERVICE
Mount Mitchell (E-4) 1,677 acres 35 mi. n.e. via the Blue Ridge Pkwy. and SR 128 at Milepost 355. Scenic. *(See Asheville)*	13	•	•	•						•		•			•
New River (A-4) 1,229 acres 8 mi. s.e. of Jefferson via SR 88. Canoeing.	38	•	•	•	•	•		•		•		•			
Pettigrew (B-8) 17,743 acres 8 mi. s. via US 64. Scenic. *(See Creswell)*	14	•	•	•	•			•		•		•			
Pilot Mountain (B-4) 3,703 acres 24 mi. n. of Winston-Salem off US 52. Mountain climbing.	15	•	•	•				•		•		•			
Raven Rock (C-6) 3,058 acres 6 mi. n.w. of Lillington off US 421. Historic. Scenic. Horse trails.	16	•	•	•				•		•		•	•		
Singletary Lake (D-6) 1,221 acres 12 mi. s.e. of Elizabethtown on SR 53.	48	•	•					•	•	•		•			
South Mountains (C-3) 7,230 acres 13 mi. s. of Morganton on CR 1904.	17	•	•	•				•		•	•	•	•		
Stone Mountain (B-4) 13,434 acres 7 mi. s.w. of Roaring Gap off US 21. Mountain climbing.	18	•	•	•				•		•		•	•		
Waynesborough State Park (C-7) 142 acres off US 117 bypass in Goldsboro.	63		•	•				•		•					
Weymouth Woods-Sandhills Nature Preserve (C-5) 755 acres 2 mi. s. of Southern Pines off US 1 on SR 2074.	64		•							•		•	•		
William B. Umstead (B-6) 5,337 acres 10 mi. n.w. of Raleigh off US 70 or 11 w. on I-40.	19	•	•	•	•		•	•	•	•		•			
BLUE RIDGE PARKWAY *(See place listing)*															
Crabtree Meadows (E-4) 253 acres at Milepost 340.	20	•	•	•						•		•			•
Doughton (B-4) 6,000 acres at Milepost 239.	21	•	•	•				•		•		•		•	•
Julian Price Memorial (D-4) 4,200 acres at Milepost 297. Horse trails.	22	•	•	•	•		•	•		•		•			
Linville Falls (D-4) 995 acres at Milepost 316.	23	•	•	•				•		•		•			
Mount Pisgah (E-3) 680 acres at Milepost 409.	24	•	•	•						•		•		•	•
OTHER															
Cane Creek (C-4) 1,050 acres 14 mi. s. of Monroe off SR 200.	27	•	•	•	•	•	•	•		•		•			
Chatuge Lake (F-2) 7,050 acres 5 mi. e. of Hayesville via US 64.	28	•	•		•	•		•	•	•			•	•	•
Dan Nicholas (B-4) 350 acres 8 mi. s.e. of Salisbury on Bringle Ferry Rd. Tennis; paddleboats.	39	•	•	•	•		•	•	•	•		•	•		
Fontana Lake (E-2) 10,640 acres 2 mi. e. of Fontana Village. Horse rental, nature trails.	29	•	•	•	•	•	•	•	•	•		•	•	•	•
Hagan-Stone (B-5) 409 acres 6.5 mi. s. of Greensboro on US 421, then w. 2 mi. on park road.	53	•	•	•	•			•	•	•		•			
Hiwassee Lake (F-1) 6,090 acres 15 mi. w. of Murphy via SR 294.	31	•	•		•	•	•	•	•	•			•	•	•
Lake Julian (E-3) 10 mi. s. of Asheville off I-26 on SR 280.	56	•	•		•	•		•		•					
Lake Lure (E-4) 1,500 acres 1 mi. e. on US 74. *(See place listing)*	33	•	•		•	•	•	•	•	•		•	•	•	•
Lake Wheeler (B-6) 700 acres 6 mi. s.w. of Raleigh via Lake Wheeler Rd.	35		•	•	•	•	•	•		•		•			
Shelley Lake/Sertoma Park (B-6) 237 acres in n. Raleigh on W. Millbrook Rd. Boating allowed only on boats rented within park. Bicycle rental.	49		•	•	•		•	•		•	•	•			
Tanglewood (B-5) 1,152 acres 10 mi. s.w. of Winston-Salem on I-40. Golf, horse rental, tennis. No motorboats.	40	•	•	•	•		•	•	•	•		•	•	•	•
Tar River Reservoir (B-7) 1,852 acres 5 mi. w. of Rocky Mount on SR 97, then 2 mi. n. on SR 1745.	65		•		•	•		•	•						
West Point on the Eno (B-6) 40 acres, 5105 N. Roxboro St. Historic. *(See Durham)*	58		•	•				•		•		•			

Save $$$ with rent-a-car and special accommodation discounts and the [SAVE] Attraction Admission Discount program.

Points of Interest

ALBEMARLE (C-4) pop. 14,900, elev. 456'

Albemarle is on a crest of the Uwharrie Mountains, the worn slopes of which rise more than 1,800 feet and are older than the Appalachians. Founded in 1841 as the seat of Stanly County, Albemarle is an industrial center for textiles, cottonseed oil, lumber, flour and bricks.

North of the city, in New London, is the Cottonpatch Gold Mine, where rockhounds can pan for gold. Picnicking and camping facilities are available; phone (704) 463-5797.

Stanly County Chamber of Commerce: P.O. Box 909, Albemarle, NC 28002; phone (704) 982-8116.

MORROW MOUNTAIN STATE PARK is 5 mi. e. via SR 24/27/73 and SR 1719 near Badin. In the Uwharrie Mountains on the Pee Dee River banks, this 4,693-acre park is one of the area's outstanding scenic spots. Information is available at the park office. Daily 8 a.m.-9 p.m., June-Aug.; 8-8, Apr.-May and in Sept.; 8-7 in Mar. and Oct.; 8-6, rest of year. Free. Phone (704) 982-4402. *See Recreation Chart and the AAA Southeastern CampBook.*

ASHEBORO (B-5) pop. 16,400, elev. 855'

Once home of the Keyauwee, Saponi and other small American Indian tribes, the Asheboro area was settled about 1740 by German families fleeing European wars. English, Irish and Scottish pioneers soon followed. Asheboro was named for Samuel Ashe, governor of North Carolina 1795-98. The city and its early industries were nurtured by the waters of the Deep and Uwharrie rivers, along which several mills were built.

Asheboro/Randolph Chamber of Commerce: 317 E. Dixie Dr., P.O. Box 2007, Asheboro, NC 27204-2007; phone (919) 626-2626.

SAVE ★**NORTH CAROLINA ZOOLOGICAL PARK,** 6 mi. s.e. off US 64 following signs, contains some 1,600 animals from two continents. African animals include giraffes, ostriches, zebras, lions, elephants, chimpanzees, rhinoceroses, baboons, wart hogs and 13 species of antelopes, all in natural habitats. The climate-controlled African Pavilion, a tropical rain forest setting, is home to 200 rare and unusual animals, including gorillas. A free-flight aviary contains 150 birds and luxuriant tropical plants.

North American exhibits include a red wolf exhibit; The Prairie, featuring bison and elk in a 10-acre enclosure; Rocky Coast, home to polar bears, sea lions and Alaskan seabirds; and black and grizzly bear exhibits. North Carolina Streamside features the state's wildlife from the mountains to the coast and includes fish, snakes, frogs,

otters and bobcats. Visitors can view roadrunners, ocelots and other desert dwellers in the Sonora Desert.

Visitors can stroll around the exhibits on a 4-mile wooded pathway. Special events are held throughout the year. Allow 3 hours minimum. Daily 9-5, Apr.-Oct.; 9-4, rest of year. Closed Dec. 25. Admission $8; over 62 and ages 2-12, $5. Admission half-price Dec.-Feb. Phone (910) 879-7000 or (800) 488-0444.

ASHEVILLE (E-3) pop. 61,600, elev. 2,250'

One of the most popular mountain resorts in the East, Asheville is divided by two rivers, the Swannanoa and the French Broad, and is surrounded by the Great Smoky and the Blue Ridge mountains. Three scenic highways pass through the city: the Blue Ridge Parkway *(see place listing p. 82),* US 74 and I-40.

The Grove Park Inn, north on Macon Street via Charlotte street, was built in 1913 of handhewn boulders hauled by wagon train from nearby Sunset Mountain. The inn has been restored and expanded.

Sections of the French Broad River near Asheville are popular for white-water rafting. Various rafting trips are offered by area outfitters.

From early April to early May Asheville marks spring's arrival with the Festival of Flowers at the Biltmore Estate *(see attraction listing).* During the third weekends in July and October the 4-day Southern Highland Handicraft Guild Fair is held at the Civic Center. Bele-Chere, a downtown 3-day festival with exhibits, music, dance, ethnic food and a children's street, is the last weekend in July. In early August the Civic Center sponsors the Mountain Dance and Folk Festival at which cloggers, banjo pickers and balladeers entertain.

Asheville Area Chamber of Commerce: off I-240 exit 4C at 151 Haywood St., Asheville, NC 28801; phone (704) 258-6109 or (800) 257-1300.

Shopping areas: On US 25 adjacent to the Biltmore Estate entrance, Biltmore Village consists of restored English-style dwellings, housing shops and galleries.

ASHEVILLE CIVIC CENTER/THOMAS WOLFE AUDITORIUM, 87 Haywood St., sponsors a variety of cultural activities throughout the year. Ticket office Mon.-Fri. 10-5:30, Sat. 10-1; closed major holidays. Event prices vary. Phone (704) 259-5736 for event information or (704) 251-9999 for tickets.

★**BILTMORE ESTATE** is on US 25, 3 blks. n. of I-40 exit 50 or 50B. Surrounded by 8,000 acres, the mansion was built at the end of the 19th century by George Washington Vanderbilt, grandson of railroad magnate Cornelius Vanderbilt. Self-guiding tours include the upstairs and downstairs of Biltmore House, the gardens, greenhouse and the Biltmore Estate Winery.

The upstairs of this 250-room French Renaissance-style chateau features three floors containing 26 rooms in which the Vanderbilt family lived and entertained. The downstairs comprises the less formal rooms, including the kitchens, swimming pool, bowling alley and ser-vants' quarters. Vanderbilt provided his servants with labor-saving devices, many of which the general public did not have for years to come, such as clothes washers and dryers, an electric rotary spit and electric dumbwaiters.

In honor of the centennial anniversary four bedrooms have been added to the tour. These tower rooms served as a suite of guest rooms and have been restored to their late 1800s appearance.

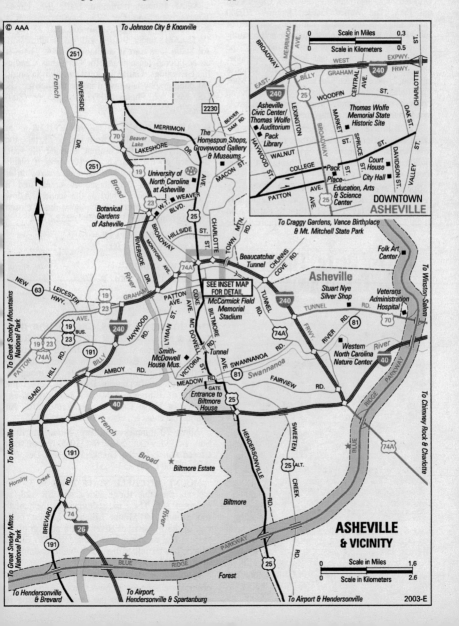

The art collection includes works by Albrecht Dürer, Pierre Auguste Renoir, John Singer Sargent, and James Abbott McNeill Whistler. Also on display are antique Chippendale furniture, the chess table Napoleon Bonaparte took with him to St. Helena and Ming dynasty china. The fireplace mantel in the Breakfast Room was designed by Josiah Wedgwood.

Surrounding the house are 75 acres of formal gardens and grounds designed by Frederick Law Olmsted, who also planned New York City's Central Park. The Walled Garden features 50,000 Dutch tulips in the spring, numerous varieties of annuals and perennials in the summer and a multi-hue display of chrysanthemums in the fall. The Rose Garden blooms in late July and September with some 2,000 roses in more than 100 varieties and the 21-acre Azalea Garden is vibrant in May. The Italian Garden, intended to function as an "outside room," features three symmetrical pools in a Renaissance-style arrangement.

The Biltmore Estate Winery is in the renovated dairy. It produces sparkling, red, white and rosé wines. A tour of the winery includes an audiovisual program, a walk through the vat rooms and a wine tasting.

Special events include the Festival of Flowers, A Victorian Celebration of Spring, held early April to early May; Fall at Biltmore Estate held in September; and Christmas at Biltmore Estate and Christmas Candlelight Evenings, both held mid-November through the end of December; phone for information.

A special behind-the-scenes guided tour of the house is available for an additional fee. Visitors should be aware that the tour involves considerable walking as well as ascending and descending more than 300 stairs. An elevator is available for transportation to the second floor if special assistance is needed. Food is available.

Allow 4 hours minimum. Daily 9-5; closed Thanksgiving and Dec. 25. Last admission 1 hour before closing. Admission $27.95; ages 10-15, $21; under 9 free with adult admission. An audio tape tour is available for $4. There is an additional fee charged for Christmas Candlelight Evenings. Under 10 must be with an adult. No photography is allowed inside the house. AE, DS, MC, VI. Phone (704) 274-6333 or (800) 543-2961.

BOTANICAL GARDENS OF ASHEVILLE is at 151 W.T. Weaver Blvd.; from US 19/23, take the University of North Carolina at Asheville exit. Included on the grounds are 10 acres of plants and flowers indigenous to the southern region of the Appalachian Mountains. A creek and a wooded area also are part of the scenery. Allow 30 minutes minimum. Daily dawn-dusk; closed Thanksgiving. Free. Phone (704) 252-5190.

★**CHIMNEY ROCK PARK—**
see Chimney Rock p. 90.

CRAGGY GARDENS—
see Blue Ridge Parkway p. 82.

FOLK ART CENTER—
see Blue Ridge Parkway p. 82.

THE HOMESPUN SHOPS, GROVEWOOD GALLERY & MUSEUMS are at 111 Grovewood Rd., 2 mi. n. on Macon St. via Charlotte St. next to the Grove Park Inn. Established to preserve the Old World wool-manufacturing skills of mountain people, the crafts museum exhibits depict the history of Biltmore Industries and display examples of North Carolina mountain crafts. An antique car museum also is on the grounds.

Allow 30 minutes minimum. Mon.-Sat. 10-5, Sun. 1-5, May-Oct.; Mon.-Sat. 10-5, rest of year. Closed Jan. 1, Easter, Thanksgiving and Dec. 25. Free. Phone (704) 253-7651.

★**MOUNT MITCHELL STATE PARK** is 35 mi. n.e. via the Blue Ridge Pkwy. and SR 128, at Milepost 355. The park encompasses the 6,684-foot summit of Mount Mitchell, highest peak east of the Mississippi River, and a portion of its slopes. The mountain was named for Dr. Elisha Mitchell, who fell to his death while attempting to prove the mountain's height.

Facilities at this 1,677-acre park include an observation lounge, a tower and a museum. A naturalist is on duty in the summer. Parking is

available near the summit. Food is available in the summer. In spring and fall check road conditions before entering the park. Daily 8 a.m.-9 p.m., June-Aug.; 8-8, Apr.-May and in Sept.; 8-7, in Mar. and Oct.; 8-6, rest of year. Free. Phone (704) 675-4611. *See Recreation Chart and the AAA Southeastern CampBook.*

PACK PLACE—EDUCATION, ARTS & SCIENCE CENTER, 2 S. Pack Sq. in downtown Asheville, 3 blks. s. on US 25 from I-240 exit 5A, combines arts, science, culture and entertainment in one location. The complex contains museums, performance spaces, galleries and shops.

Allow 2 hours minimum. Tues.-Sat. 10-5; also Sun. 1-5, June-Oct. Closed Jan. 1, Thanksgiving and Dec. 25. Admission to each museum $3; over 62 and students with ID $2.50; ages 4-15, $2. One-day pass good for admission to all four museums $6.50; over 62 and students with ID $5.50; ages 4-15, $4.50. Under 12 must be with an adult to visit museums. MC, VI. Phone (704) 257-4500.

Asheville Art Museum presents a permanent exhibit of 20th-century American art. Changing exhibitions include displays of sculpture, paintings, and traditional and contemporary crafts.

Colburn Gem & Mineral Museum displays North Carolina minerals as well as gemstones from around the world.

The Health Adventure is a collection of hands-on health and science exhibits and programs including Nutri-Space, BodyWorks and Brain-Storm. Galleries feature a scavenger hunt through the body and a talking transparent woman.

YMI Cultural Center, commissioned by George Vanderbilt in 1893, celebrates African-American life and history through exhibits and a permanent collection of African artifacts. Cultural insights also are revealed through programs of music, drama and dance.

SMITH-McDOWELL HOUSE MUSEUM is off I-40 exit 50B; take US 25 n. .2 mi. to Biltmore Ave., proceed 1.5 mi. n.e. to Victoria Rd, then .5 mi. w. to 283 Victoria Rd. Built circa 1840 by an affluent businessman, the three-level house contains rooms furnished in various 19th-century styles including an 1850s bedroom, an 1860s sitting room and an 1880s parlor. Antique furniture, photographs, china and cookware are among the items on display. Allow 1 hour minimum. Tues.-Sat. 10-4, Sun. 1-4, Apr.-Dec.; Tues.-Fri. 10-4, rest of year. Admission $3.50; ages 7-15, $2. Phone (704) 253-9231.

THOMAS WOLFE MEMORIAL STATE HISTORIC SITE, 48 Spruce St., was the novelist's childhood home. Furnished with family possessions, the house retains the atmosphere of Dixieland, the boardinghouse in "Look Homeward, Angel." Allow 30 minutes minimum. Mon.-Sat. 9-5, Sun. 1-5, Apr.-Oct.; Tues.-Sat. 10-4, Sun. 1-4, rest of year. Closed Thanksgiving, Dec.

24-25 and on an irregular basis. Admission $1, students 50c, under 6 free. Phone (704) 253-8304 to verify schedule.

WESTERN NORTH CAROLINA NATURE CENTER, 4 mi. e. on SR 81 at Gashes Creek Rd., contains indoor and outdoor exhibits of plant and animal life. Displays include nocturnal animals, freshwater life, snakes, cougars, deer, bears, raccoons, foxes, red and gray wolves, otters, waterfowl, turtles and farm stock. An aviary, petting zoo and self-guiding nature trail also are available.

Daily 10-5; closed Jan. 1, Martin Luther King Jr.'s Birthday, Thanksgiving and Dec. 24-25. Admission $4; senior citizens $3; ages 3-14, $2. Phone (704) 298-5600.

ZEBULON B. VANCE BIRTHPLACE STATE HISTORIC SITE, 12 mi. n.e. via the Blue Ridge Pkwy. or US 19/23N following signs, contains the reconstructed two-story log home in which the state's Civil War-period governor was born on May 13, 1830. The site includes six farm buildings and a visitor center/museum. Guided tours are available.

Allow 1 hour minimum. Mon.-Sat. 9-5, Sun. 1-5, Apr.-Oct.; Tues.-Sat. 10-4, Sun. 1-4, rest of year. Closed Thanksgiving and Dec. 24-25. Donations. Phone (704) 645-6706.

ATLANTIC BEACH (D-8) pop. 1,900

In the late 1800s, "surf bathing" was popular, and beachgoers were transported across the Intracoastal Waterway to Atlantic Beach by sailboat.

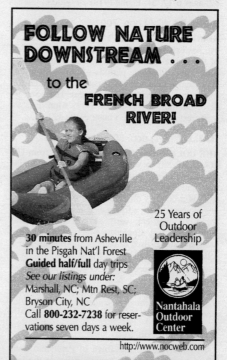

A pavilion was built on the beach in 1887, which included refreshments and a place for changing clothes. Since then, Atlantic Beach has become a popular spot for summer tourists.

The 265-acre Theodore Roosevelt Natural Area is 7 miles northwest of Atlantic Beach; nature trails and observation decks afford views of the coastal woodlands. A Marine Resources Center is nearby off SR 24 on Bogue Sound.

FORT MACON STATE PARK, 389 acres, is 2 mi. e. on SR 1190. Fort Macon was built 1826-34; young Lt. Robert E. Lee designed the garrison's jetties. The fort was captured by the Confederacy during the Civil War. A museum is in the fort. Food is available. Allow 30 minutes minimum. Daily 9-5:30. Guided tours available Memorial Day-Labor Day. Free. Phone (919) 726-3775. *See Recreation Chart.*

NORTH CAROLINA AQUARIUM AT PINE KNOLL SHORES is in the Theodore Roosevelt Natural Area, 5 mi. w. of Atlantic Beach on SR 58N. The aquarium has a large saltwater system and provides a view of animal species found off the coast and in nearby inlets. Visitors can handle live whelks, hermit crabs and horseshoe crabs in the Close Encounters exhibit. The Precious Waters exhibit features alligators. Allow 1 hour minimum. Mon.-Sat. 9-5, Sun. 1-5; closed Jan. 1, Thanksgiving and Dec. 25. Admission $3; senior citizens and active duty military with ID $2; ages 6-17, $1. Phone (919) 247-4003.

AURORA (C-8) pop. 700

AURORA FOSSIL MUSEUM, 400 Main St. at Forest, has exhibits that depict the geological history of the coastal plain. Marine fossils from the Miocene and Pliocene periods—5 to 15 million years ago—are displayed. Visitors can search for fossils in a mound across the street. Tues.-Sat. 9-4:30, Memorial Day-Labor Day; Mon.-Fri. 9-4:30, rest of year. Free. Phone (919) 322-4238.

BAILEY (B-7) pop. 600, elev. 1,728'

THE COUNTRY DOCTOR MUSEUM, s. from US 264 on SR 581 to Vance St., is dedicated to family physicians of the 19th century. Two restored doctors' buildings house an apothecary and library, as well as a doctor's office of the 1880s. On display are apothecary jars; a tilting examination table from the Civil War era; early stethoscopes; medical equipment of a Confederate surgeon, including saws and knives used in battlefield hospitals; and a 1912 Model T used to make house calls.

A medicinal herb garden contains plants used for healing. Allow 1 hour minimum. Tues.-Sat. 10-4, Sun. 2-5; closed major holidays. Admission $2, senior citizens $1, students with ID 50c. Phone (919) 235-4165.

BATH (C-8) pop. 200

Originally called the Town of Pamticoe, Bath was founded along the Pamlico River in the late 17th century. Once a bustling trade center, Bath languished due to continual political friction, epidemics and American Indian warfare. The town boundaries remain about the same as when Bath was incorporated in 1705.

HISTORIC BATH is on SR 92. The oldest incorporated town in North Carolina, Bath was chartered in 1705. It was the colony's first official port of entry and the first meeting place of the Colonial assembly. When he was not plundering in the Caribbean, Blackbeard was a resident. Tours of restored houses depart from the visitor center on SR 92. A film about the town precedes the tour.

Allow 1 hour, 30 minutes minimum. Mon.-Sat. 9-5, Sun. 1-5, Apr.-Oct.; Tues.-Sat. 10-4, Sun. 1-4, rest of year. Closed Thanksgiving and Dec. 24-25. Admission $2, under 12 and students with ID $1. Phone (919) 923-3971.

Bonner House has a collection of period furniture. Behind the 1830 house is the Ruth McCloud Smith Memorial Garden. Guided tours are available.

Palmer-Marsh House is a restored 1795 home. A Colonial kitchen, still in original condition, is in the cellar.

St. Thomas Episcopal Church is at the corner of Craven and Main sts. Built in 1734, it is said to be the oldest existing church in the state. A silver chalice and a pair of silver candelabra from that period are still in use. The walls of the building are 2 feet thick and constructed of solid brick. Allow 30 minutes minimum. Mon.-Sat. 9-5, Sun. 12:30-5. Donations. Phone (919) 923-9141.

Van Der Veer House, built about 1795, is restored and contains exhibits depicting nearly 3 centuries of Bath's history.

BEAUFORT (D-8) pop. 3,800, elev. 12'

First known as Fish Town, Beaufort (BO-fort) was established in the early 1700s. A quaint seacoast town, its historic district is comprised of narrow streets and old houses. One-hour, double-decker bus tours of the town depart from the Beaufort welcome center early April through November.

In the Old Burying Ground, deeded to the town in 1731, the earliest legible date on a marker is 1756. The graveyard was declared full in 1825, yet townspeople continued to use it until the early 1900s. Graves face east in the oldest portion so that the occupants would face the sun on "Judgment Morn." Many interesting characters are buried here, including an English sailor buried upright so that he could salute the king. Maps are available at the welcome center.

Events in Beaufort are historic in theme; the Wooden Boat Show takes place during the first full weekend in May, and the Old Homes Tour and Antique Show, which includes authentic crafts demonstrations, is held the last weekend in June.

Beaufort Historical Association Welcome Center: 138 Turner St., Beaufort, NC 28516; phone (919) 728-5225. Tours are given Monday and Wednesday at 2:15 of the Old Burying Ground.

BEAUFORT HISTORIC SITE offers 1.25-hour guided tours beginning at the Beaufort Historical Association Welcome Center on Turner Street. Included on the tour is the 1767 Joseph Bell House, the former townhouse of a wealthy plantation owner and politician; it has 18th-century furnishings and a formal garden.

The tour also includes the 1796 Carteret County Courthouse with its original 13-star American flag; the 1829 county jail, consisting of one cell and the jailkeeper's quarters; the 1859 apothecary shop with many original bottles and instruments; and the 1778 Samuel Leffers Cottage, a typical early fisherman's cottage. The 1732 Rustell House is an art gallery from mid-April through November 1.

Tours are offered at 10, 11:30, 1 and 3. Open Mon.-Sat. 9:30-4:30, Mar.-Nov.; 10-4, rest of year. Last tour 1 hour, 15 minutes before closing. Fee $5; ages 6-12, $3. Phone (919) 728-5225.

★**NORTH CAROLINA MARITIME MUSEUM,** 315 Front St., depicts the state's maritime and coastal natural history. Exhibits include ship models, area small craft, birds and fish, fossils, decoys and saltwater aquariums. Field trips to coastal habitats are offered year-round for tidal flat and salt marsh exploration. Fossil, mushroom and wildflower hunts as well as birdwatching trips are available. The Wooden Boat Show is held the first weekend in May.

For a schedule of activities and reservations write the North Carolina Maritime Museum, 315 Front St., Beaufort, NC 28516. Allow 1 hour minimum. Mon.-Fri. 9-5, Sat. 10-5, Sun. 1-5; closed Thanksgiving and Dec. 25. Free. Phone (919) 728-7317.

BEECH MOUNTAIN (D-4) pop. 200

Beech Mountain, known for numerous winter recreation opportunities, lies just east of the Tennessee border. The 145-acre Beech Mountain Resort is 4 miles north of Banner Elk via SR 184. At the foot of the slopes, Beech Mountain Village is a center for year-round recreational activities.

Beech Mountain Chamber of Commerce: 403A Beech Mountain Pkwy., Beech Mountain, NC 28604; phone (704) 387-9283 or (800) 468-5506.

 RECREATIONAL ACTIVITIES

Skiing

• **Ski Beech**, off US 321 near the Tenn. border, 1007 Beech Mountain Pkwy., Beech Mountain, NC 28604. Daily mid-Nov. to mid-Mar. Phone (704) 387-2011 or (800) 438-2093.

BLOWING ROCK (B-3) pop. 1,300, elev. 3,578'

Blowing Rock's cool summer temperatures are ideal for golf, fishing, riding and swimming. The region's six ski areas are popular in winter. Moses H. Cone and Julian Price memorial parks, comprising about 8,000 acres on the Blue Ridge Parkway *(see place listing p. 82)*, afford miles of bridle and hiking trails. Bass Lake, .5 mile south on US 221, is a popular spot for walking, jogging and horseback riding. Climbers enjoy Grandfather Mountain in nearby Linville *(see place listing p. 105)* as well as Flat Top.

Blowing Rock Chamber of Commerce: Main St., P.O. Box 406, Blowing Rock, NC 28605; phone (704) 295-7851.

THE APPALACHIAN HERITAGE MUSEUM, 2 mi. n. on US 221/321, is in a 19th-century house displaying 18th- and 19th-century furnishings. Area artifacts and antiques are exhibited, and demonstrations related to mountain culture and crafts are occasionally presented. Daily 9-5; closed Thanksgiving and Dec. 24-25. Donations. Phone (704) 264-1299 for demonstration schedule or (800) 438-7500.

THE BLOWING ROCK, 2 mi. s. on US 321, is a large rock formation 4,000 ft. above sea level overhanging the John's River Gorge. Legend says that a Chickasaw maiden lost her lover as he leapt from the rock; her prayers returned him with an upward gust of wind. The area is said to be the only place where snow falls upward. Lightweight objects cast over the cliff will return to the thrower when uprising air currents are present.

The observation tower affords a view of the gorge and surrounding mountain range. Daily 8-8, May-Oct.; 9-5, rest of year (weather permitting). Admission $4; ages 6-11, $1. Phone (704) 295-7111.

MYSTERY HILL, 2 mi. n. on US 321/221, is home to several optical illusions and other enigmas. The Old Mystery House and the Mystery Platform are among the puzzling yet scientifically explainable phenomena. Food is available. Allow 1 hour minimum. Mon.-Sat. 8-8, Sun. 1-8, May-Sept.; Mon.-Sat. 9-5, Sun. 1-5, rest of year. Closed Thanksgiving and Dec. 25. Admission $5; over 60, $4.50; ages 5-12, $3.50. Under 5 must be with an adult. Phone (704) 264-2792.

SAVE ★**TWEETSIE RAILROAD,** 4.2 mi. n. on US 321, is a Western theme park incorporating a restored narrow-gauge, coal-fired steam railroad that once ran from Boone *(see place listing p. 84)* to Johnson City, Tenn. Fond of the train's whistle, area residents coined the unusual name. Today's passengers experience mock robberies and American Indian attacks during the train ride. The railroad town has an 1880s general store, blacksmith shop, sheriff's office and jail.

Craft demonstrations and live music shows are presented regularly. A chairlift runs to a re-created mining town, where children can pan for gold, visit the animal petting area or board a small train into Mouse Mine No. 9. The park affords scenic views of the surrounding area. Food is available.

Allow 2 hours minimum. Daily 9-6, Memorial Day weekend-Labor Day; Fri.-Sun 9-6, day after Labor Day-Oct. 31. Admission $16; over 60 and ages 4-12, $13. DS, MC, VI. Phone (704) 264-9061 or (800) 526-5740.

 RECREATIONAL ACTIVITIES

Horseback Riding
• **Blowing Rock Stables**, 1 mi. s. on US 221, following signs, P.O. Box 26, Blowing Rock, NC 28604. Rides depart daily approximately every 15 minutes from 9:30-4; closed last week in July and first week in Aug. Phone (704) 295-7847.

★ **BLUE RIDGE PARKWAY**

The Blue Ridge Parkway is a 469-mile scenic road connecting Shenandoah National Park in Virginia and Great Smoky Mountains National Park *(see place listing p. 97, Recreation Chart and the AAA Southeastern CampBook)* in North Carolina and Tennessee. The route follows the crest of the Blue Ridge and other ranges at elevations ranging from 646 to 6,053 feet.

The concept for the construction of the parkway began during Franklin D. Roosevelt's ad-

ministration. The project, in addition to creating a scenic route linking the two new national parks, was a way to provide jobs for many of those left unemployed during the peak of the Great Depression. Begun in 1935, the dedication of the complete parkway did not take place until 1987, although sections of the road have been enjoyed by travelers for many years.

The Blue Ridge Parkway, only 200 feet wide at certain points, is constructed free of billboards and with little residential encroachment, allowing leisurely drives and enjoyment of the surrounding area.

Overlooks offer panoramas of the Southern Highlands. Among the areas of outstanding scenic interest are Humpback Rocks, Otter Creek, Peaks of Otter, Roanoke Mountain, Rocky Knob and Smart View in Virginia; and Crabtree Meadows, Craggy Gardens, Cumberland Knob, Doughton Park, E.B. Jeffress Park, Julian Price, Linville Falls and Moses H. Cone memorial parks, Mount Pisgah and Waterrock Knob in North Carolina.

Hiking trails, varying in length from short strolls to the lengthy and strenuous Appalachian Trail, can be reached from many overlooks and parking areas. During the summer season craft demonstrations and ranger programs at various points along the parkway provide insights into the everyday life and culture of mountain residents.

Many wildflowers are in bloom mid-May to mid-June; fall foliage is at its peak in October. Many visitor accommodations are open May through October only. Pets are permitted if confined or leashed; they are prohibited in overnight facilities. Picnic areas and drinking water are available at intervals along the parkway. Hunting is prohibited.

Food is available at Crabtree Meadows, Doughton Park, Mabry Mill, Mount Pisgah, Otter Creek, Peaks of Otter and Whetstone Ridge. There are overnight facilities at Peaks of Otter Lodge, housekeeping cabins at Rocky Knob and lodges at Doughton Park and Mount Pisgah. Other accommodations are nearby but off the parkway.

Concrete mileposts help keep track of mileage along the road, beginning at Milepost 0 at the northern portion and concluding at Milepost 469 at its southern terminus at Great Smoky Mountains National Park. The speed limit of 45 mph is enforced. To drive the entire length, plan on 3 to 5 days at an average speed of 30 mph. The parkway is open all year, but sections of the road may be closed during icy or snowy weather. Most park facilities close November through April. For weather or other information contact Blue Ridge Parkway, 400 BB&T Building, One Pack Sq., Asheville, NC 28801; phone (704) 298-0398. For emergencies phone (800) 727-5928.

Note: The points of interest below are listed in order, from north to south, according to their nearness to the northern terminus of the road at Shenandoah National Park.

HUMPBACK ROCKS VISITOR CENTER, 5.9 mi. s.e. of Afton, Va., at Milepost 5.8, features a reconstructed pioneer mountain farm. Allow 1 hour minimum. Daily 9-5, May-Oct. Free. Phone (540) 943-4716.

JAMES RIVER VISITOR CENTER, 3 mi. n. of Big Island, Va., at Milepost 63.6, chronicles the story of the James River and the Kanawha Canal. A pedestrian walkway crossing the river leads to a restored canal lock. Daily 9-5, May-Oct. Free. Phone (804) 299-5496.

PEAKS OF OTTER VISITOR CENTER, 10 mi. n.w. of Bedford, Va., at Milepost 86, houses exhibits about forest ecology and the history of the Peaks of Otter area. Nearby are an 1830s cabin that housed early travelers through the region and a historic farm that now offers living history demonstrations. Bus trips and a walking trail to the summit of Sharp Top Mountain are available. Allow 1 hour minimum. Daily 9-5, Apr.-Oct.; Sat.-Sun. 9-5, Nov. 1-15. Free. Round trip bus fare $3.70; under 12, $2.25. Phone (540) 586-4357.

ROCKY KNOB VISITOR CONTACT STATION is 8 mi. n.w. of Meadows of Dan, Va., at Milepost 169. The station provides visitor information daily 9-5, May-Oct. Free. Phone (540) 745-9662.

MABRY MILL is 3 mi. n.w. of Meadows of Dan, Va., just n. of the jct. with US 58 at Milepost 176.1. A display of pioneer items includes a blacksmith shop, sawmill, gristmill and sorghum press. Allow 1 hour minimum. Daily 9-5, May-Oct. Free. Phone (540) 952-2947.

CUMBERLAND KNOB VISITORS CENTER, at Milepost 217.5, marks the site where the Civilian Conservation Corps began construction on the parkway in 1935. Picnic facilities and hiking trails are available. Daily 9-5, May-Oct. Free. Phone (910) 657-8161.

BLUE RIDGE MOUNTAIN FRESCOES are housed in two churches, one in Glendale Springs, 3 mi. n. of the parkway's jct. with SR 16 at Milepost 258, and the other in West Jefferson, following signs from jct. US 221 business route and SR 194. Taped narratives describe the history of the biblical paintings. Allow 1 hour minimum. Open daily 9-6. Donations. Phone (910) 982-3076.

PARKWAY CRAFT CENTER, 3 mi. w. of Blowing Rock at Milepost 294, is in the former manor house at Moses H. Cone Memorial Park. It is operated by the Southern Highland Handicraft Guild. Cone, a wealthy textile manufacturer, built his country estate at the turn of the 20th century. Mountain crafts are demonstrated. Allow 30 minutes minimum. Daily 9-6, Mar.-Jan.; closed Jan 1, Thanksgiving and Dec. 25. Free. Phone (704) 295-7938.

LINN COVE VISITORS CENTER, 6 mi. n.e. of Linville at Milepost 304, offers visitor information. Of interest in the area is the Linn Cove Viaduct, at Milepost 304.6. Completed in 1987, the 1,243-foot-long viaduct is one of the most complicated concrete bridges ever built; it skirts the

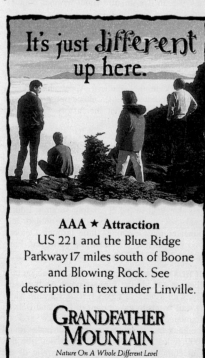

rugged perimeter of Grandfather Mountain. The visitors center has a model of the viaduct. Daily 9-5, May-Oct. Free. Phone (704) 733-1354.

LINVILLE FALLS RECREATION AREA, 2 mi. n.w. of Linville Falls at Milepost 316.4, has trails to the pedestrian overlooks of Linville Falls and Linville Gorge. Picnicking and camping are permitted. Allow 3 hours minimum. Park open daily 24 hours. Information center open daily 9-5, May-Oct. Free. Phone (704) 765-1045. *See Recreation Chart and the AAA Southeastern CampBook.*

MUSEUM OF NORTH CAROLINA MINERALS, on SR 226 5 mi. s. of Spruce Pine at Milepost 331, has samples of many rocks and minerals found within the area. Cutting, polishing and shaping demonstrations are occasionally offered. Allow 30 minutes minimum. Daily 9-5, May-Sept.; Wed.-Sun. 10-5, rest of year. Closed Jan. 1, Thanksgiving and Dec. 25. Free. Phone (704) 765-2761.

★**MOUNT MITCHELL STATE PARK—** *see Asheville p. 78.*

CRAGGY GARDENS is 17 mi. n.e. of Asheville at Milepost 364.6. The Craggy Mountains, at an elevation of more than 6,000 feet, are a colorful sight when the rhododendrons bloom around mid-June. Trails, picnic facilities and a visitor center are available. Daily 9-5, May-Oct.; Fri.-Tues. 9-5, in Apr. Inquire about weather policies. Free. Phone (704) 298-0495.

FOLK ART CENTER is accessible from Asheville via I-40 to US 70W exit 55, following signs to the Blue Ridge Pkwy., then .5 mi. n. to Milepost 382. Operated by the Southern Highland Handicraft Guild, the center celebrates the tradition of craft work in the southern Appalachian region through demonstrations, music programs and changing exhibits about the history and culture of the Southern Highlands.

A parkway information desk is in the center. Allow 30 minutes minimum. Daily 9-6, Apr.-Dec.; 9-5, rest of year. Closed Jan. 1, Thanksgiving and Dec. 25. Donations. Phone (704) 298-7928.

MOUNT PISGAH, at Milepost 408.6, has walking trails that lead to the 5,721-foot summit. Educational programs are presented in an outdoor amphitheater most evenings June through October. Food is available. Picnicking is permitted. Free. Phone (704) 235-8228.

RICHLAND BALSAM, 12 mi. n.e. of Balsam near Milepost 431, is the highest point on the parkway, with a peak of 6,053 feet. A 1.5-mile walking trail winds to the summit of Richland Balsam Mountain, passing through a spruce and fir woodland that is native to climates usually found 1,000 miles north. Trail pamphlets describe this plant community, which is a living relic of the ice age. Free. Phone (704) 298-0398.

WATERROCK KNOB, 8 mi. n.w. of Balsam at Milepost 451.2, commands a 360-degree view of the main ranges of the southern Appalachian Mountains from a 6,000-foot elevation. A visitor information van is in the parking area May through October. Free. Phone (704) 298-0495.

WINERIES

- **Château Morrisette Winery,** between Mileposts 171 and 172 on Blue Ridge Parkway exit SR 726, then s.w. on Winery Rd./SR 777. Daily 10-5; closed Jan. 1, Thanksgiving and Dec. 25. Phone (540) 593-2865.

BOONE (B-3) pop. 12,900, elev. 3,333'

Named after Daniel Boone, who had a cabin in the area in the 1760s, the city is high atop the Blue Ridge Mountains. Boone is at the intersection of two scenic highways: A scenic portion of US 321 runs west across the Tennessee border, and a scenic portion of US 421 runs east to Marler near I-77.

An Appalachian Summer is a multi-arts festival held on the campus of Appalachian State University during the month of July. The festival includes music, dance, theater and visual arts.

Boone Chamber of Commerce: 208 Howard St., Boone, NC 28607; phone (704) 264-2225 or (800) 852-9506.

APPALACHIAN CULTURAL MUSEUM, on University Hall Dr. off US 321 (Blowing Rock Road), .5 mi. s. of jct. SR 105/321, is a regional museum with exhibits and audiovisual aids that interpret the past and present of the land, people, arts and crafts, and industries of western North Carolina. Allow 1 hour minimum. Tues.-Sat. 10-5, Sun. 1-5; closed major holidays. Admission $2; senior citizens $1.75; ages 12-18, $1; free to all Tues. Phone (704) 262-3117.

SAVE ★**"HORN IN THE WEST"** .5 mi. s. of US 421 via "Horn in the West" Dr., is a musical drama portraying the struggle of Daniel Boone and his men to establish freedom in the Southern Appalachian Highlands. Inquire about weather policies. Hickory Ridge Homestead Museum contains a log village typical of the 18th century. Costumed guides demonstrate the lifestyle of the early settlers.

Performances in the outdoor amphitheater last 2 hours and are Tues.-Sun. at 8:30 p.m., late June to mid-Aug. Museum open Tues.-Sun. 1-8:30, late June to mid-Aug. Musical drama $12; over 65, $11; under 13, $6. Museum $2; under 13, $1; free with admission to "Horn in the West." Phone (704) 264-2120.

RECREATIONAL ACTIVITIES
White-water Rafting
- **Wahoo's Adventures,** on US 321, .5 mi. n. of Tweetsie Railroad *(see Blowing Rock p. 81).*

Write Rt. 1, Box 14-A, Brasstown, NC 28902. Other activities are offered. Year-round, weather permitting. Phone (704) 262-5774 or (800) 444-7238.

BREVARD (F-3) pop. 5,400, elev. 2,229′

A popular summer resort at the entrance to Pisgah National Forest *(see place listing p. 113),* Brevard is in an area known as the "Land of Waterfalls." Brevard Music Center offers concerts nightly, late June to mid-August. The town presents a Festival of the Arts during the second week in July.

Brevard is at the northwestern end of a scenic portion of US 64 that passes through the Pisgah National Forest before reaching Highlands.

Brevard/Transylvania Chamber of Commerce: 35 W. Main St., P.O. Box 589, Brevard, NC 28712; phone (704) 883-3700.

BRYSON CITY (E-2) pop. 1,100, elev. 1,740′

Just south of Great Smoky Mountains National Park and east of Fontana Village *(see place listings),* Bryson City is a center for recreational activities. The area offers boating, fishing, skiing, rafting, hiking and camping opportunities.

Swain County Chamber of Commerce: P.O. Box 509, Bryson City, NC 28713; phone (704) 488-3681 or (800) 867-9246.

 RECREATIONAL ACTIVITIES

White-water Rafting

• **Nantahala Outdoor Center,** 13 mi. s. w. on US 19/74W. Write 13077 Hwy. 19W, Bryson City, NC 28713. Guided trips are available Mar.-Oct.; departure times vary. Non-guided trips depart daily 10-3, Mar.-Oct. Phone (704) 488-6900 or (800) 232-7238. *See ad p. 79.*

• [SAVE] **Nantahala Rafts,** 15 mi. s. on US 19W, P.O. Box 45, Bryson City, NC 28713. Trips

depart four times daily, May-Sept. Phone (704) 488-2325.

BURLINGTON (B-5) pop. 39,500, elev. 656′

Burlington is a textile industry center with numerous factory outlet shops that attract bargain hunters from nearby states. Clothing, fabric, yarn, leather goods, towels, blankets, sheets, carpets and furniture are popular products.

Alamance County Area Chamber of Commerce: 610 S. Lexington Ave., P.O. Box 450, Burlington, NC 27216; phone (919) 228-1338. *See ad.*

Shopping areas: The Burlington Outlet Center, at I-85 and SR 49, houses more than 100 stores and is open daily.

ALAMANCE BATTLEGROUND, 6 mi. s.w. on SR 62, commemorates the 1771 battle between Royalist governor William Tryon's militia and an inexperienced army of Colonial reformers known as the "Regulators." The John Allen house, a log home typical of 1780s North Carolina, is on the battlefield near the visitor center. The visitor center offers a 25-minute audiovisual presentation on the battle. Guided tours, special programs and picnic facilities are available. Mon.-Sat. 9-5, Sun. 1-5, Apr.-Oct.; Tues.-Sat. 10-4, Sun. 1-4, rest of year. Free. Phone (910) 227-4785.

ALAMANCE COUNTY HISTORICAL MUSEUM is off I-40/85 exit 143; take SR 62 4.2 mi. s. to 4777 S. SR 62. The museum is inside the 19th-century home of Michael Holt, an early textile manufacturer. The two-story Italianate Revival plantation house contains furnishings and accessories from the mid-1800s as well as changing exhibits.

The Holt family cemetery and several farm buildings constructed immediately after the Civil War also are on the premises. Allow 1 hour minimum. Tues.-Fri. 9-5, Sat. 10:30-5, Sun. and holidays 1-5; closed Easter and Dec. 25. Free. Phone (910) 226-8254.

SAVE **SNOW CAMP OUTDOOR THEATRE**, 15 mi. s. at the Snow Camp Historic Site on SR 1005 e. of SR 49, presents "Sword of Peace," a drama portraying the struggles of the Quakers during the Revolutionary War. Also presented is "Pathway to Freedom," a pre-Civil War drama recalling the events and people involved in the secret transfer of escaped slaves via the Underground Railroad. Children's theater is performed on Saturday.

Presentations are shown on alternate days Wed.-Sat. at 8:30 p.m., June 18-Aug. 24. Children's Theatre Sat. at 10 a.m. Admission $10; over 60, $8; ages 1-11, $5; children's theater $4. Phone (910) 376-6948 or (800) 726-5115.

★**CAPE HATTERAS NATIONAL SEASHORE—**
see Outer Banks p. 110.

CAPE LOOKOUT NATIONAL SEASHORE—
see Outer Banks p. 110.

CASHIERS (F-2) pop. 600

Cashiers is on a plateau surrounded by the Nantahala National Forest and the Appalachian Mountains in the southern crest of the Blue Ridge Mountains. The first European settlers, primarily from the British Isles, arrived in the early 1800s and by the end of the 19th century Cashiers was a summer home for many of the Southern elite. Still a resort town, summer activities include golfing, fishing, swimming, boating, horseback riding and tennis.

Cashiers Chamber of Commerce: P.O. Box 238, Cashiers, NC 28717; phone (704) 743-5191.

WHITEWATER FALLS SCENIC AREA is s. on SR 107 into South Carolina, then n. via SRs 413 and 171 back into North Carolina. The Whitewater River drops more than 400 feet in a series of falls and cascades. A point above the falls offers a view of the mountains and the South Carolina Piedmont. Picnicking is permitted. For further information contact the Jackson County Chamber of Commerce, 116 Central St., Sylva, NC 28779; phone (704) 586-2155 or (800) 962-1911.

CATAWBA (B-4)

HISTORIC MURRAY'S MILL COMPLEX, 2.5 mi. w. on SR 10, then .5 mi. w. on Murray's Mill Rd., contains the homes of four generations of the Murray family. Included on the site are an operating turn-of-the-20th-century general store, a granary adapted as a folk art gallery, and an operating gristmill with a 28-foot water wheel. Guided tours are available. Allow 1 hour minimum. Thurs.-Fri. 10-11 and 1-3, Sat.-Sun. 2-4, Mar.-Dec.; closed major holidays. Admission $2; over 63 and ages 6-17, $1. Phone (704) 465-0383 or 241-4299.

CHAPEL HILL (B-6) pop. 38,700, elev. 502'

Named for the New Hope Chapel that was erected on a hill to denote the crossing of two main roads, the community of Chapel Hill now centers around the campus of the University of North Carolina at Chapel Hill *(see attraction listing)*. The Research Triangle Park, a center for industrial and governmental research, is 12 miles east of Chapel Hill via SR 54 and I-40 *(see Durham p. 92)*. Events include La Fiesta del Pueblo in early September and the Festifall Street Fair in October.

Chapel Hill/Orange County Visitors Bureau: 501 W. Franklin St., Suite 104, Chapel Hill, NC 27516; phone (919) 968-2060 or (888) 968-2060.

PATTERSON'S MILL COUNTRY STORE is off I-40 exit 273B; take SR 54 s.w. to Farrington Rd., then 1 mi. n.w. to 5109 Farrington Rd. The store houses mercantile memorabilia, and many of the items on display have been part of the store's inventory for more than a century. Exhibits include an extensive pharmaceutical collection and tobacco paraphernalia. A furnished, early 20th-century doctor's office and relics from the Patterson's Mill community also can be seen. Allow 1 hour minimum. Tues.-Sat. 10-5:30, Sun. 2-5:30. Free. Phone (919) 493-8149.

THE UNIVERSITY OF NORTH CAROLINA AT CHAPEL HILL, off SR 15, was chartered in 1789. Although not the first state university chartered, UNC became the first in the nation to accept and graduate students. A walking tour of the historic campus is available; visitors may pick up a brochure at the visitor center in the west lobby of the Morehead Planetarium. Visitor parking is available in a number of municipal lots along Franklin and Rosemary streets. Walking tours Mon.-Fri. 10-5. Free. Phone (919) 962-1630.

Ackland Art Museum is on campus on Columbia St., .2 blk. s. of Franklin St. Displays include paintings, drawings, sculpture, photographs, prints, period furniture and artifacts of a wide range of cultures. Edgar Degas, Eugène Delacroix, Peter Paul Rubens, Max Weber and Emanuel de Witte are among the artists represented. Classical, Oriental, 20th-century and North Carolina folk art collections also are exhibited. Allow 1 hour minimum. Wed.-Sat. 10-5, Sun. 1-5; closed holidays. Free. Phone (919) 966-5736.

Morehead-Patterson Bell Tower, on campus, e. off Columbia St. on South Rd., is a brick landmark that has 12 bells duplicating those at West Point. Chimes ring 10 minutes before the hour; songs are played at 8:05, 12:05, 6:05 and 9:05.

★**Morehead Planetarium,** is on campus at 250 E. Franklin St. The planetarium served as a NASA training center and presently contains art and science exhibits, a rose garden and a large sundial. A walk-in model of the solar system is in the building's west wing. Evening planetarium shows are presented daily, and matinees are shown on weekends. Hours and programs vary; phone for schedule.

Allow 1 hour minimum. Sun.-Fri. 12:30-5 and 7-9:30, Sat. 10-5; closed Dec. 24-25. Exhibits free. Program and film admission $3.50; senior citizens, students with ID and ages 2-12, $2.50. Phone (919) 962-1236 or 549-6863.

North Carolina Botanical Garden is on Old Mason Farm Rd. off US 15/501 bypass. This UNC facility consists of more than 600 acres and displays plants native to North Carolina and the Southeast, herb and family gardens and a carnivorous plant collection. A fire ecology section explains the profuse return of vegetation following a burn. Nature trails meander through the gardens. Allow 1 hour minimum. Mon.-Fri. 8-5, Sat. 9-6, Sun. 10-6, mid-Mar. to mid-Nov.; Mon.-Fri. 8-5, rest of year. Free. Phone (919) 962-0522.

The North Carolina Collection, in the Wilson Library on campus, offers a gallery, a reading room and a photographic archive. A gallery contains exhibits pertaining to American Indian and Colonial settlements and the gold rush era. Historic rooms display English antique furniture, maps and statues; of note are the Sir Walter Raleigh rooms. The Hayes Library holds almost 2,000 volumes and imprints dating from the late 1500s.

Guided tours are available. Allow 1 hour, 30 minutes minimum. Gallery Mon.-Fri. 9-5, Sat. 9-1, Sun. 1-5. Reading room Mon.-Fri. 8-5, Sat. 9-1, Sun. 1-5. Photographic archives Mon.-Fri. 8-5. Closed holidays. Free. Phone (919) 962-1172.

CHARLOTTE (C-4) pop. 395,900, elev. 734′

See map page 88.

Charlotte's strong tie with England broke on May 31, 1775, when the Mecklenburg Resolves, a set of resolutions invalidating the authority of the king and parliament, were signed. British general Lord Cornwallis called Charlotte a "hornet's nest of rebellion" as a result of Patriot activity during his occupation of the city. Visitors can see a monument to the signers of the Mecklenburg Resolves at the County Courthouse, 600 E. Trade St.

Modern Charlotte, "The City of Trees," exhibits the same independent spirit. What most cities call downtown is "uptown" in this city. The largest metropolitan area in the Carolinas with more than 1 million residents, Charlotte is a booming financial center as well as a major service and distribution point for the Southeast. Much of the city's prosperity can be attributed to the Charlotte/Douglas International Airport, a transportation hub that opened Charlotte to the world.

Spirit Square Arts Center, 110 E. 7th St., stages concerts and other performing arts programs and sponsors art exhibits throughout the year; phone (704) 372-7469. The Charlotte Symphony, Charlotte Opera Association and Charlotte Repertory Theatre all regularly perform at Blumenthal Performing Arts Center; phone (704) 372-1000.

The Charlotte Coliseum, off the Billy Graham Parkway, is home to the National Basketball Association's Hornets. Ericsson Stadium, 800 S. Mint St., is home to the National Football League's Carolina Panthers. More than 100 parks in Charlotte provide a variety of recreational opportunities. Water sports enthusiasts flock to nearby Lake Wylie for swimming, sailing and water skiing.

NASCAR races take place at the Charlotte Motor Speedway *(see Concord p. 91),* 12 miles north on US 29. The season begins in May with The Winston Select and continues with Goody's Pole Night, CarQuest 300 and the Coca-Cola 600. In October the Winston Pole Night, All Pro Bumper to Bumper and the United Auto Workers General Motors 500 are featured. Other events include national and regional competition and testing, research and development. Phone (704) 455-3200 for information about touring the facility.

Wing Haven Gardens and Bird Sanctuary, 248 Ridgewood Ave., consists of 3 acres of formal gardens and wooded areas offering a respite from the busy city. The center has abbreviated hours; phone (704) 331-0664.

In late February the Southern Spring Show offers the first glimpse of spring with gardens and indoor and outdoor floral displays. Charlotte's summer schedules are filled with ethnic festivals and community events. In late April the Spring-Fest draws hordes of revelers uptown for 3 days of activities welcoming the warm weather.

Fall and winter have their share of festivities as well, including a Thanksgiving Day parade; Kids Day is held the first Saturday in December and culminates in a Christmas tree-lighting ceremony; the Uptown New Year's Eve Street Celebration is a popular way to ring in the New Year.

Gray Line of Charlotte offers tours of the city and various points of interest in the surrounding area; phone (704) 359-8687.

Charlotte Convention and Visitors Bureau: 330 Tryon St., Charlotte, NC 28202; phone (704) 331-2700 or (800) 231-4636.

Shopping areas: The Eastland Mall, 5471 Central Ave., contains 123 stores including Belk, Dillard's, JCPenney and Sears. SouthPark Mall, 4400 Sharon Rd., features such shops as Banana Republic, The Disney Store and Laura Ashley as well as Belk, Dillard's, Hecht's and Sears. The Carolina Place Mall, SR 51 and I-485, contains Belk, Dillard's, Hecht's, JCPenney and Sears.

The Interiors Marketplace, in historic Atherton Mill, resides in a restored building and contains restaurants as well as booths displaying a variety of interior decorating goods. A trolley takes passengers from the marketplace to downtown Charlotte.

CHARLOTTE MUSEUM OF HISTORY AND HEZEKIAH ALEXANDER HOMESITE, 3500 Shamrock Dr., is 3 mi. e. The site includes the 1774 Hezekiah Alexander House, a two-story springhouse, a hand-hewn log kitchen with a working rock fireplace and a museum. Museum and grounds open Tues.-Fri. 10-5, Sat.-Sun. 2-5. Guided house tours Tues.-Fri. at 1:15 and 3:15, Sat.-Sun. at 2:15 and 3:15. Museum and grounds free. House $4; over 64, $3; ages 6-16, $2. Phone (704) 568-1774.

CHARLOTTE NATURE MUSEUM, 2.5 mi. s. at 1658 Sterling Rd., is entered via East Blvd. This

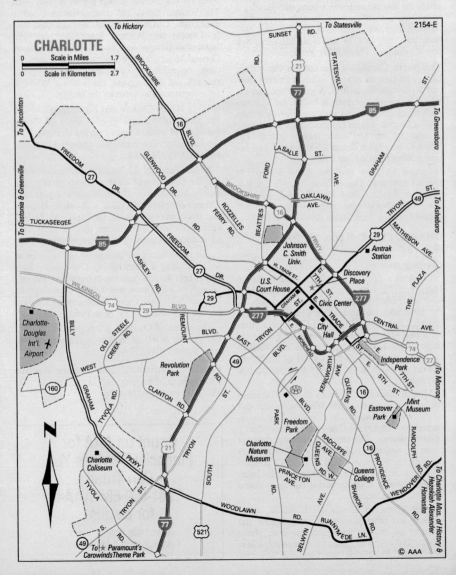

child-oriented nature museum has hands-on exhibits relating to natural history. Allow 1 hour, 30 minutes minimum. Mon.-Fri. 9-5, Sat. 10-5, Sun. 1-5; closed Thanksgiving and Dec. 25. Admission $2, under 3 free with parent. Phone (704) 332-5018.

★DISCOVERY PLACE, 301 N. Tryon St., is an educational complex incorporating an exhibition hall, a planetarium and an OMNIMAX® theater. Exhibits are designed to involve visitors and enhance their perceptions of science and technology. The Science Circus area has hands-on experiments that expose visitors to basic scientific principles. A three-story rain forest has massive rock formations, waterfalls and exotic birds.

Other attractions include the Life Center, which explores the intricacies of human physiology, and the Challenger Learning Center, complete with a space station and mission control. A chemistry hearth allows visitors to enjoy live shows, and the Aquarium Ocean Touch Pool allows visitors to handle live sea creatures. The Kelly Space Voyager Planetarium projects more than 10,000 stars onto one of the country's largest domes. Food is available.

Allow 1 hour, 30 minutes minimum. Exhibit halls open Mon.-Sat. 9-6, Sun. 1-6, June-Aug.; Mon.-Fri. 9-5, Sat. 9-6, Sun. 1-6, rest of year. OMNIMAX® shows Mon.-Sat. at 10:30, 11:30, 1, 3, 4 and 5 (also Thurs.-Sat. at 7 p.m.); Sun. at 1, 3, 4 and 5. Planetarium shows Mon.-Sat. at 9:30 and 2:30, Sun. at 2:30. Show times may vary. Closed Thanksgiving and Dec. 25.

Comprehensive admission to exhibit halls, OMNIMAX® Theater and Kelly Planetarium $9.50; over 59 and ages 6-12, $8.50; ages 3-5, $6.75. Any two areas $7.50; over 59 and ages 6-12, $6.50; ages 3-5, $4.75. Any one area $5.50; over 59 and ages 6-12, $4.50; ages 3-5, $2.75. Parking $3. MC, VI. Phone (704) 372-6261 or (800) 935-0553. *See ad.*

JAMES K. POLK MEMORIAL STATE HISTORIC SITE—
see Pineville p. 112.

MINT MUSEUM OF ART, 2730 Randolph Rd., is housed in what was the Charlotte branch of the U.S. Mint 1837-61 and 1867-1913. Collections include European art dating from the Renaissance, American art, period costumes, pre-Columbian and African items as well as gold coins minted in Charlotte. Changing exhibits also are featured.

The museum's pottery and porcelain collection is reputed to be one of the better in the country. It includes the Delhom Collection, which ranges from ancient Chinese ceramics to late 18th-century Continental and English wares. Allow 1 hour, 30 minutes minimum. Tues.-Sat. 10-5 (also Tues. 5-10), Sun. noon-5; closed Jan. 1, Thanksgiving and Dec. 24-25. Admission $4; over 62, $3; students with ID $2; under 12 free; free to all Tues. 5-10 and second Sun. of each month. MC, VI. Phone (704) 337-2000.

★**PARAMOUNT'S CAROWINDS THEME PARK,** 10 mi. s. on I-77 to exit 90, is on the North Carolina/South Carolina border. Ten theme areas depict different facets of the Carolinas' past and present. Each offers a variety of attractions from quiet stern-wheeler trips to six state-of-the-art roller coasters, water rides and a motion simulator theater.

Yogi Bear, Fred Flintstone, Scooby-Doo and other Hanna-Barbera characters are hosts at Animation Station, which includes rides for children, including a carrousel with 68 wooden horses that were hand-carved in 1923. A three-story jungle gym and various children's shows also are featured.

Plantation Square re-creates the Charleston waterfront of the 1800s, and the Old World Market Place offers foods from around the world. Other areas include Blue Ridge Junction, representing the traditions of the Carolina mountains, and County Fair, which has games, shops and entertainment.

Wayne's World includes a re-creation of sets used in filming the Paramount motion pictures "Wayne's World" and "Wayne's World 2." Among the highlights are Wayne and Garth's hometown of Aurora, Ill. Wayne's World also

features the Hurler roller coaster that treats riders to hills, dips and hair-pin turns at 50 m.p.h.

RipTide Reef, a 6-acre water park, features a giant wave pool, water slides and children's play areas. Guests can experience a 16-story free fall at 56 m.p.h. on the Drop Zone Stunt Tower. Live performances include a variety of comedy and musical entertainment. Headline entertainers perform periodically in the 13,000-seat Paladium Amphitheatre.

Facilities include a first-aid station, wheelchair and stroller rental, food service and a campground. Pets are not allowed in the park; a free kennel is provided. Park open daily at 10, early June to mid-Aug.; Sat.-Sun. at 10, mid-Mar. to early June and mid-Aug. to early Oct. Closing times vary. Closed July 23-24. All-inclusive park admission $28.99; over 55 and ages 4-6 or under 48 inches tall, $15.99. Admission $14.99 for all after 5. Separate admission for Paladium Amphitheatre varies by entertainer. Parking $4. DS, MC, VI. Phone (704) 588-2600, (803) 548-5300 or (800) 888-4386.

CHEROKEE (E-2)

Near the southern entrance of Great Smoky Mountains National Park *(see place listing p. 97)* and the Blue Ridge Parkway *(see place listing p. 82)*, the 56,000-acre Qualla Boundary Cherokee Indian Reservation is occupied by 8,500 members of the Eastern Band of Cherokees, who have made this area and the Smokies their home for centuries. Cherokee history and culture are presented at several museums, an outdoor drama and the Qualla Arts and Crafts Shop.

Cherokee Visitor Center: P.O. Box 460, Cherokee, NC 28719; phone (800) 438-1601.

CHEROKEE MARKER, 2 mi. n. on US 441N, was erected by the United Daughters of the Confederacy in honor of all Cherokee Indians who served with the Confederate Army. Free.

SAVE **MUSEUM OF THE CHEROKEE INDIAN,** jct. US 441N and Drama Rd., has an American Indian art gallery and displays on Cherokee history. Included are crafts, clothing and weapons. Six minitheaters present audiovisual shows describing the Cherokee Nation from prehistory to the present. Allow 1 hour minimum. Mon.-Sat. 9-8, Sun. 9-5, mid-June through Aug. 31; daily 9-5, rest of year. Closed Jan. 1, Thanksgiving and Dec. 25. Museum $4; ages 6-12, $2. Art gallery free. Phone (704) 497-3481.

★OCONALUFTEE INDIAN VILLAGE, 2.5 mi. n. off US 441N, is a Cherokee community where American Indians demonstrate the making of baskets, pottery, canoes, arrows and blowguns. Also of interest are a preserved seven-sided council house and huts and cabins containing articles used two centuries ago. Nature trails and the Cherokee Botanical Gardens are on the grounds. Guided tours are available. Daily 9-

5:30, May 15-Oct. 25. Admission $9; ages 6-13, $5. MC, VI. Phone (704) 497-2315 or 497-2111.

OCONALUFTEE VISITOR CENTER— *see Great Smoky Mountains National Park p. 98.*

SANTA'S LAND PARK AND ZOO, 3 mi. n. on US 19, is a Christmas theme park featuring amusement rides, a mountain heritage section and a zoo. Mon.-Fri. 9-5, Sat.-Sun. 9-6, early May-June 30 and Sept.-Oct.; daily 9-7, July-Aug. Admission $11.95, under 2 free. Season pass $32. AE, DS, MC, VI. Phone (704) 497-9191.

★"UNTO THESE HILLS", .5 mi. n. on US 441N in the Mountainside Theater, is a 2-hour historical drama about the Cherokees. The play covers the period from the arrival of Hernando De Soto in 1540 through the tragic Trail of Tears in 1839. Some descendants of Cherokees who lived the story appear in principal roles. Inquire about weather policies. Mon.-Sat. at 8:30 p.m., mid-June to late Aug. General admission $10; under 13, $5. Reserved seating $12. DS, MC, VI. Phone (704) 497-2111.

CHIMNEY ROCK (E-4)

Chimney Rock lies in a gorge at the foot of its namesake, a giant granite monolith that rises sharply 315 feet. The town serves as an outfitting post for many recreational activities.

Hickory Nut Gorge Chamber of Commerce: Hwy. 64/74A, P.O. Box 32, Chimney Rock, NC 28720; phone (704) 625-2725.

★CHIMNEY ROCK PARK, on US 64/74A, is a 1,000-acre park encompassing the Chimney. For exceptional views, including Lake Lure *(see place listing p. 104 and Recreation Chart)*, visitors can reach the summit by trail and stairs or by an elevator built into the mountain. Three different trails lead to 404-foot Hickory Nut Falls. A sheer drop twice the height of Niagara, the falls were featured as a backdrop in the movie "The Last of the Mohicans." Other points of interest include Devil's Head, Moonshiner's Cave and Needle's Eye.

A myriad of wildflowers, birds and plants are indigenous to the park. One of the trails is steep in places and should be taken only by the surefooted. Guided hikes are led throughout the year by a park naturalist. Facilities include picnic areas, a playground, an observation lounge and a nature center. Visitors can enter their favorite photographs of the park in seasonal photograph contests held throughout the year.

Allow 2 hours minimum. Daily 8:30-7, Apr. 15-Oct. 15; 8:30-6, rest of year (weather permitting). Last admission 1 hour, 30 minutes before closing. Admission $9.50; ages 6-15, $5. MC, VI. Phone (704) 625-9611 or (800) 277-9611. *See color ad p. 78.*

CLEVELAND (B-4) pop. 700, elev. 819'

PETER NEY'S GRAVE, in the graveyard at the Old Third Creek Presbyterian Church, is said to contain the body of Marshal Michel Ney, aide to Napoleon. According to legend, Ney escaped execution in France, came to America, died in 1846 and was buried under the name of Peter Stewart Ney.

CONCORD (C-4) pop. 27,300

In 1775 disagreeing German and Scot-Irish residents of Cabarrus County finally decided on the location of the county seat; they named the site Concord and the main thoroughfare Union Street. A memorial garden on Spring Street between Cabarrus and Corban avenues contains the graves of many Concord founders.

The first gold nugget reputedly discovered in the nation was found nearby by a 12-year-old boy wading in Little Meadow Creek. Stories relate that the 17-pound chunk was used as a doorstop before the boy's father took it to Fayetteville in 1802 and sold it to a jeweler for the "grand price" of $3.50.

Concord/Cabarrus County Chamber of Commerce: 23 Union St. N., P.O. Box 1029, Concord, NC 28025; phone (704) 782-4111.

CHARLOTTE MOTOR SPEEDWAY is 2 mi. s. on US 29. Guided tours of the facility include a history of the track, a tour of the winner's circle and pit areas, and a fast trip around the track to demonstrate the feel of a 24-degree embankment. Allow 30 minutes minimum. Except during race weeks and special events, tours are available every hour Mon.-Sat. 10-5, Sun. 1-4. Last tour begins at 3:45. Closed Jan. 1, Thanksgiving and Dec. 25. Admission $4, under 3 free with parent. Phone (704) 455-3204. See Charlotte p. 87.

REED GOLD MINE STATE HISTORIC SITE, 15 mi. s. via US 601 and SR 200, was the first "placer" (creek) gold mine in the United States; gold was discovered in 1799 on the farm of German immigrant John Reed. A visitor center has an orientation film, exhibits and mining equipment. Guided tours of the mining area, underground workings and the stamp mill are offered.

Panning for gold is allowed April through October. A nature trail is on the grounds. Picnicking is permitted. Allow 1 hour minimum. Mon.-Sat. 9-5, Sun. 1-5, Apr.-Oct.; Tues.-Sat. 10-4, Sun. 1-4, rest of year. Closed Martin Luther King Jr.'s Birthday, Labor Day, Thanksgiving and Dec. 24-26. Museum and tour free; $2 charge to pan for gold. Phone (704) 786-8337.

CRESWELL (B-8) pop. 400

PETTIGREW STATE PARK, 8 mi. s. via US 64, covers 17,743 acres and contains sections of an old plantation. Lake Phelps, a wildlife sanctuary, is lined with cypress trees; it also provides excellent fishing. Nature programs are held in the summer and American Indian artifacts are displayed each September during the park's Indian Heritage Celebration. Daily 8 a.m.-9 p.m., June-Aug.; 8-8, Apr.-May and Sept.; 8-7, in Mar. and Oct.; 8-6, rest of year. Free. Phone (919) 797-4475. See Recreation Chart and the AAA Southeastern CampBook.

Somerset Place State Historic Site is on Lake Phelps. Built in the 1830s, the 14-room plantation house is an example of Greek Revival architecture. Allow 30 minutes minimum. Tours of the mansion, gardens and restored outbuildings are conducted Mon.-Sat. 9-5, Sun. 1-5, Apr.-Oct.; Tues.-Sat. 10-4, Sun. 1-4, rest of year. Closed holidays. Free. Phone (919) 797-4560.

CROATAN NATIONAL FOREST

Elevations in the forest range from sea level to 46 ft. west of Great Lake. Refer to AAA maps for additional elevation information.

Covering 160,000 acres south of New Bern, Croatan National Forest consists mostly of pine and swamp hardwoods. As the most coastal of any national forest in the East, it contains many estuaries and waterfowl nesting areas, as well as public beaches. Three designated areas within the forest provide recreational facilities.

Some of the forest's most interesting wildlife is found in the pocosin ("swamp-on-a-hill"), a wet upland bog with a sponge-like top layer of soil. Among the plant life is the Venus flytrap, which cages insects in its leaves and digests them. The sundew and pitcher plants also supplement their soil diets with insects.

Black bears, alligators, woodpeckers, owls and a small number of bald eagles and falcons are part of the forest's ecosystem. Alligator and osprey habitats can be seen along the White Oak River and other coastal waterways. Canoes or small motorboats are best suited for navigation of the waterways. Both saltwater and freshwater fishing are possible, though fishing in the lakes is generally poor.

Cedar Point Tideland Trail, an elevated boardwalk originating at the mouth of the White Oak River across from Swansboro, winds through tidal marsh areas and hardwood and pine forests. Interpretive signs are found along both the 1- and 2-hour loops of the trail. Most trails within the park open daily 24 hours; ranger station open Mon.-Fri. 8-4:30. Free. For further information contact the U.S. Forest Service, 435 Thurman Rd., New Bern, NC 28560; phone (919) 638-5628. See Recreation Chart and the AAA Southeastern CampBook.

CULLOWHEE (F-2)

Primarily a college town, Cullowhee is the site of Western Carolina University, the University of

North Carolina's mountain campus. Students and visitors alike take advantage of the boating, fishing, canoeing, hiking and backpacking opportunities available in the nearby mountains and lakes.

JUDACULLA ROCK, 3.5 mi. s. via SR 107, then 3 mi. e. on Caney Fork Rd., is a soapstone boulder covered with American Indian pictographs. According to Cherokee mythology, these markings were made by a giant named Tsul'kula when he leaped from his mountaintop home to the Caney Fork Creek. Free. Phone (704) 586-2155.

MOUNTAIN HERITAGE CENTER, in the H.F. Robinson Administration Building on SR 107, chronicles the saga of the Scot-Irish, or Ulster-Scots, whose migrations and settlements opened the country's frontier. Mon.-Fri. 8-5, Sun. 2-5, Apr. 14-Oct. 31; Mon.-Fri. 8-5, rest of year. Free. Phone (704) 227-7129.

DALLAS (C-4) pop. 3,000, elev. 890'

GASTON COUNTY MUSEUM OF ART AND HISTORY, 131 W. Main St., is in the former Hoffman Hotel on Dallas Square. The 1852 building has Victorian period rooms, a carriage and sleigh collection, and changing exhibitions of art, local history and textile history. Brochures detailing Dallas' historic town square are available. Tues.-Fri. 10-5, Sat. 1-5, Sun. 2-5. Free. Phone (704) 922-7681.

DANBURY (A-5) pop. 100

Danbury lies at the foot of the Sauratown Mountains near the Dan River. Union general George Stoneman made his headquarters in Danbury on Apr. 9, 1865, the day Robert E. Lee surrendered at Appomattox.

The *Danbury Reporter* is one of the oldest county weeklies in North Carolina. In the late 1800s the newspaper office was destroyed by fire, but the press was rescued and propped against a young tree. A new press was acquired and the old one forgotten. As the tree grew the original press became embedded in its trunk, and the two remained entwined until the tree died in the 1960s.

HANGING ROCK STATE PARK is 4 mi. n.w. off SR 89. The 6,340-acre park offers rugged mountain terrain, sparkling streams, waterfalls and a lake. More than 300 species of mountain flora are found within the park. Camping is permitted and cabins are available March 15 through November 30; reservations are required. Swimming and bathhouse facilities are open June 1 through Labor Day.

Park open daily 8 a.m.-9 p.m., June-Aug.; 8-8, Apr.-May and in Sept.; 8-7, in Mar. and Oct.; 8-6, rest of year. Free. Phone (910) 593-8480. *See Recreation Chart and the AAA Southeastern CampBook.*

DILLSBORO (E-2) pop. 100

GREAT SMOKY MOUNTAINS RAILWAY operates three sightseeing excursions in the area that depart from Bryson City, Dillsboro and Andrews. The Nantahala Gorge Excursion is scheduled from Bryson City. The 4.5-hour round trip departs from the depot on Everett St. and includes a stopover at the Nantahala Outdoor Center where picnic facilities are available. Seating is offered in the caboose and in open and enclosed cars. A dinner excursion departs on Saturday from Dillsboro; combination trips including the railway and white-water rafting also are available.

Food is available. Departure times vary, Apr.-Dec. Fares begin at $18.95; ages 3-12, $9. Reservations are suggested. AE, DS, MC, VI. Phone (704) 586-8811 or (800) 872-4681.

☀❄ RECREATIONAL ACTIVITIES
White-water Rafting
- **Wildwater Raft & Rail Excursion** meets at the railroad depot on Main St., P.O. Box 397, Dillsboro, NC 28725-0397. Trips depart daily mid-Apr. to late Oct.; departure times vary. Phone (800) 451-9972.

DUNN (C-6) pop. 8,300, elev. 214'

THE GENERAL WILLIAM C. LEE AIRBORNE MUSEUM, 209 W. Divine St., is in the former house of Gen. Lee, known as the "Father of the Airborne." Lee was assigned by President Franklin D. Roosevelt to organize the development of Army airborne units. His efforts led to the establishment of the Airborne Command and earned him the Distinguished Service Medal.

Exhibits include photographs, videotapes, World War II memorabilia, historical documents, and paratrooper equipment and uniforms. Allow 1 hour minimum. Mon.-Fri. 9-5, Sat. 11-4, Sun. 1-4; closed Thanksgiving and Dec. 25. Admission $1, under 12 free. Phone (910) 892-1947.

DURHAM (B-6) pop. 136,600, elev. 406'

Durham, home of Duke University, is known for excellence in medicine, education, research and industry. With five major hospitals, including the Duke University Medical Center, and a physician-to-population ratio five times greater than the national average, the city has exchanged its old identity of "tobacco town" for that of "City of Medicine."

Durham also is part of the Triangle Region, which is anchored by the state's three major universities—University of North Carolina at Chapel Hill *(see attraction listing in Chapel Hill p. 86)*, North Carolina State in Raleigh and Duke. The Triangle is a center for industrial and governmental research and receives support from the nearby educational facilities.

A 6,800-acre wooded tract of land, 4 miles south via US 55, is known as the Research Triangle Park. The park is a research and production district for the county.

Durham Visitor Information Center: 101 East Morgan St., Durham, NC 27701; phone (919) 687-0288 or (800) 446-8604.

BENNETT PLACE STATE HISTORIC SITE is at 4409 Bennett Memorial Rd., 4 mi. n.w. off US 70/I-85 exit 172 southbound or 170 northbound. The site includes the restored Bennett House, where the Civil War ended April 26, 1865. It was here that Gen. Joseph E. Johnston surrendered most of the Confederate armies remaining in the field to Gen. William T. Sherman. A surrender re-enactment is held in April.

Exhibits about North Carolina's contributions to the Civil War are displayed in the visitor center, as well as uniforms, flags, guns and photographs. Guided tours are offered, and an audiovisual presentation is shown by request. Picnic facilities are available. Allow 1 hour minimum. Visitor center Mon.-Sat. 9-5, Sun. 1-5, Apr.-Oct.; Tues.-Sat. 10-4, Sun. 1-4, rest of year. Closed Jan. 1, Easter, Labor Day, day before Thanksgiving, Thanksgiving and Dec. 24-26. Free. Phone (919) 383-4345.

DUKE HOMESTEAD STATE HISTORIC SITE AND TOBACCO MUSEUM is at 2828 Duke Homestead Rd., off I-85 Guess Rd. exit 2. The 1852 main house, two early tobacco factories, a packhouse and a curing barn reflect the historical impact of the tobacco industry on North Carolina. The museum includes a moving mannequin who plants tobacco and explains—with a North Carolina accent—the "13-month crop." The visitor center offers a museum and a movie about the history of tobacco. Special events and living-history weekends are held throughout the year.

Allow 1 hour, 30 minutes minimum. Mon.-Sat. 9-5, Sun. 1-5, Apr.-Oct.; Tues.-Sat. 10-4, Sun. 1-4, rest of year. Closed Jan. 1, Good Friday, Thanksgiving, day after Thanksgiving, and Dec. 24-26. Free. Phone (919) 477-5498.

DUKE UNIVERSITY has two impressive campuses: the West Campus, which has Gothic-style buildings; and the East Campus, formerly Trinity College, with predominantly Georgian architecture. The East Campus is e. off I-85 Hillsborough Rd. exit, then e. on Main St. For the West Campus take US 15/501 bypass to SR 751, then go e. to Duke University Rd. and follow signs.

★**Duke University Chapel,** on the West Campus, is the central and dominant structure of the university buildings. The 50-bell carillon, with bells ranging in size from 10 to 11,200 pounds, plays Mon.-Fri. at 5 p.m. The chapel houses the Flentrop Organ, which contains five keyboards and rises to nearly 40 feet above the gallery floor. Allow 30 minutes minimum. Daily 8 a.m.-10 p.m., Sept.-May; 8-5, rest of year. Closed Dec. 25. Free. Phone (919) 684-2572.

Duke University Museum of Art, on the East Campus off E. Main St., displays Greek and Roman antiquities; Chinese jade; medieval sculpture; American and European paintings, drawings and sculptures; and changing exhibits such as the Far Eastern and pre-Columbian collections. Allow 1 hour minimum. Tues.-Fri. 9-5, Sat. 11-2, Sun. 2-5; closed holidays. Free. Phone (919) 684-5135.

Sarah Duke Gardens, on the Duke University West Campus, encompasses 55 acres of native plants. Seasonal colors can be enjoyed in the formal Terrace Garden. A 300-bush rose garden also is featured. Allow 1 hour minimum. Daily 8-dusk. Free. Phone (919) 684-3698.

NORTH CAROLINA MUSEUM OF LIFE AND SCIENCE, 433 Murray, is off I-85 Duke St. exit, n. on US 501 .7 mi. to Murray Ave., then .2 mi. e. The museum offers nature and science displays and an aerospace exhibit, including an Apollo 15 mock-up and Enos, the first U.S. spacecraft to orbit the Earth. Visitors can see native animals in the Nature Center, hear a rabbit's heartbeat, hold a box turtle in the Discovery Room and pet animals in the farmyard. Picnic facilities are available.

Allow 2 hours minimum. Mon.-Sat. 10-5, Sun. noon-5, Labor Day-Memorial Day; Mon.-Sat. 10-6, Sun. noon-6, rest of year. Closed Jan. 1, Thanksgiving and Dec. 25. Admission $5.50; over 65 and ages 3-12, $3.50; free to Durham residents Fri. 1-5. Miniature train $1. AE, MC, VI. Phone (919) 220-5429.

WEST POINT ON THE ENO, 5105 N. Roxboro St. across from Riverview Shopping Center, is a historic mill community. Tours of West Point Mill, McCowen-Mangum House and the Howe-Mangum Museum of Photography are given Sat.-Sun. 1-5. Traditional craft events are scheduled throughout the year. A 3-day 4th of July festival features entertainment by local performers. Food and picnic facilities are available. Allow 1 hour minimum. Park open daily 8-dusk. Free. Phone (919) 471-1623. *See Recreation Chart.*

EDENTON (B-8) pop. 5,300, elev. 18'

One of the oldest communities in the state, Edenton served as a Colonial center of commerce, society and politics. Named for Lords Proprietary governor Charles Eden, it was the first capital of the colony.

On the courthouse green is a marker commemorating the Edenton Tea Party. On Oct. 25, 1774, a group of 51 ladies voted not to conform "to that pernicious custom of drinking tea" and decided they would not promote the wares of any manufacturer from England.

Historic Edenton Visitor Center: 108 N. Broad St., Edenton, NC 27932; phone (919) 482-2637.

Self-guiding tours: A walking tour begins at the visitor center and includes 28 designated historic sites; maps of the 1.5-mile route are available for 25c. The historic Albemarle region can be explored by a driving tour. Brochures outlining tour sites are available at the visitor center.

HISTORIC EDENTON STATE HISTORIC SITE includes several notable Colonial buildings of the old town. Tours begin at the Historic Edenton Visitor Center, a late 19th-century frame house at 108 N. Broad St. A 14-minute slide show and exhibits about the area are presented. Allow 2 hours minimum for the tours and wear comfortable shoes. Guided walking tours of the town and the buildings listed below depart daily; schedule varies.

The visitor center is open Mon.-Sat. 9-5, Sun. 1-5, Apr.-Oct.; Tues.-Sat. 10-4, Sun. 1-4, rest of year. Closed Jan. 1, Good Friday, Veterans Day, Thanksgiving, day after Thanksgiving and Dec. 24-26. Admission to visitor center free. Guided tour $6; students through grade 12, $2.50; family rate $14. Minitour (includes admission to two buildings) $4, students $1.50. Phone (919) 482-2637.

Chowan County Courthouse State Historic Site, on E. King St., is an example of Georgian architecture. Built in 1767, it is said to be the oldest courthouse in continuous use in North Carolina, and one of the oldest in the country.

Cupola House, 408 S. Broad St., was built in Jacobean style in 1758. Its Georgian interior has elaborate woodwork and windows of wavy glass, with signatures more than 150 years old scratched into the panes.

James Iredell House State Historic Site, 105 E. Church St., was built in 1773 and was the house of Iredell, the first attorney general of North Carolina and a justice of the first U.S. Supreme Court.

St. Paul's Church (Episcopal), at Broad and Church sts., is a Colonial village church. The structure, built 1736-66, was partially burned in 1949 but was restored. Communion silver from 1725 is in use. The graves of three Colonial governors—Charles Eden, Henderson Walker and Thomas Pollack—are in the churchyard.

ELIZABETH CITY (A-8) pop. 14,300, elev. 6′

Elizabeth City is at the Narrows of the Pasquotank River, approximately 12 nautical miles from the Albemarle Sound. The Dismal Swamp Canal connects the Elizabeth River in Virginia and the Pasquotank River. After the canal was dug in 1790, Elizabeth City's development began.

By the early 1800s a vigorous trade with the West Indies was established, and the freshwater, landlocked harbor on the Pasquotank River still remains busy. Nearby are the large U.S. Coast Guard Air Station and the Elizabeth City Shipyard.

Reminders of early days are the old Christ Episcopal Church, the Old Brick House and Hall Creek Church.

The Riverspree Festival, a celebration of life on the river, takes place along the waterfront Memorial Day weekend. Musical entertainment, water races, food and local arts and crafts booths are featured. The ⏺ Albemarle Craftsmen's Fair in mid-October and the Mistletoe Craft Show in mid-November attract artists from many states.

Elizabeth City Area Chamber of Commerce: 502 E. Ehringhaus St., Elizabeth City, NC 27909; phone (919) 335-4365.

Self-guiding tours: A walking-tour map to several historic houses and buildings is available Mon.-Fri. 9-5 from the chamber of commerce.

MUSEUM OF THE ALBEMARLE, 2 mi. s. on US 17, displays American Indian relics and other artifacts reflecting the history of the region. Allow 30 minutes minimum. Tues.-Sat. 9-5, Sun. 2-5; closed state holidays. Free. Phone (919) 335-1453.

FAYETTEVILLE (C-6) pop. 75,700, elev. 135′

North Carolina's most inland port, Fayetteville became an early trade center because of its position at the head of navigation on the Cape Fear River. When water transportation declined, Fayetteville responded by building a system of plank roads that revitalized commerce. Business generated by Fort Bragg *(see attraction listing)* and Pope Air Force Base military installations is Fayetteville's economic mainstay.

Fayetteville's historic sites include the Old Market House, which was built in 1832 in the center of downtown, and Heritage Square. Dick Street features three historic buildings.

A salute to the city's mid-April explosion of blossoms is its 10-day Dogwood Festival, which includes a parade along an 18-mile-long dogwood trail and culminates downtown at Sunday-on-the-Square, a celebration of the arts. The last Sunday in September, ethnic groups don native costumes, demonstrate their national dances and share their traditional foods during the International Folk Festival.

Fayetteville Area Convention and Visitors Bureau: 245 Person St., Fayetteville, NC 28301; phone (910) 483-5311 or (888) 622-4276. *See ad p. 363.*

Self-guiding tours: Brochures outlining Fayetteville's many historic houses and other points of interest are available from the convention and visitors bureau.

FIRST PRESBYTERIAN CHURCH, Bow and Ann sts., was built in 1800, destroyed by fire in 1831 and rebuilt in 1832. It is an example of the classic Southern Colonial style of architecture. The communion silver, crystal chandeliers, hand-wrought-iron locks and hardware and the carving on the galleries are noteworthy. Mon.-Fri. 8-4:30. Free. Phone (910) 483-0121.

FORT BRAGG, off I-95 exit 52 (SR 24) n.w. to Bragg Blvd., is one of America's largest and most important military installations.

82nd Airborne Division Museum, Ardennes St. at Gela St., is dedicated to the division's combat dead. The history of the division is told through pictures and relics of its campaigns from 1917 to the present. Tues.-Sat. and Mon. holidays 10-4:30, Sun. 11:30-4. Free. Phone (910) 432-3443.

John F. Kennedy Special Warfare Museum, at Ardennes and Marion sts. in Building D 2502, serves as the branch museum for the U.S. Army Special Forces Training Group, the Green Berets. Exhibits illustrate the history of special operation units in the U.S. Army. Tues.-Sun. 11:30-4. Free. Phone (910) 432-1533.

MUSEUM OF THE CAPE FEAR, 801 Arsenal Ave., is a branch of the North Carolina Museum of History Division. The museum traces the events that shaped the development of southern North Carolina. Highlights include exhibits about the early settlements of American Indians, the antebellum period, the Civil War and the textile industry. Pottery, a Victorian house and a 1920s general store also can be seen. Tues.-Sat. 10-5, Sun. 1-5; closed major holidays. Free. Phone (910) 486-1330.

FLAT ROCK (E-4) pop. 1,900, elev. 2,214′

Flat Rock is one of the oldest resort towns in western North Carolina. Flat Rock Playhouse, the state theater, presents performances from late May to late September. Matinees are given Thurs. and Sat.-Sun. at 2:15; evening performances are Wed.-Sun. at 8:15 p.m. Phone (704) 693-0731.

CARL SANDBURG HOME NATIONAL HISTORIC SITE (CONNEMARA), on Little River Rd. w. of US 25 following signs, was the house of the poet-historian from 1945 until his death in 1967. The house displays a collection of some 10,000 books as well as the poet's notes. While Sandburg wrote, his wife and daughters managed a 240-acre goat farm, still maintained on the grounds. Hiking trails and picnic areas are available; a visitor center contains exhibits and offers films. Guided tours of the house are offered.

Grounds open daily 9-5. Tour times vary. Closed Dec. 25. Free. Tour $3, under 17 free. For tour schedule phone (704) 698-5627.

ST. JOHN'S IN THE WILDERNESS, on US 25, dates from 1832 and is one of the oldest churches in western North Carolina. Christopher G. Memminger, Secretary of the Treasury of the Confederacy, is buried at the church. Sunday services are held at 9 and 11. Daily 9-4. Free. Phone (704) 693-9783.

FONTANA VILLAGE (E-1)

Fontana Village is a year-round resort at the southern edge of Great Smoky Mountains National Park (see place listing p. 97). Guided nature walks are offered June through October. SR 28 provides a scenic drive west along the Little Tennessee River to Tapoco.

Fontana Dam, 3 miles northeast, is said to be the tallest dam in the eastern United States. The visitor building lobby is open daily 9-5. See Recreation Chart and the AAA Southeastern CampBook.

FORT RALEIGH NATIONAL HISTORIC SITE—
see Outer Banks p. 111.

FRANKLIN (F-2) pop. 2,900, elev. 2,250′

Franklin, on a ridge overlooking the Little Tennessee River, was named for Jesse Franklin, governor of North Carolina 1820-21. The portion of SR 28 leading southeast to Highlands offers scenic views of the Nantahala National Forest (see place listing p. 107, Recreation Chart and the AAA Southeastern CampBook).

The city's major industries—textile production, sawmilling, talc and mica mining and grinding—reflect the region's natural resources. Many precious and semiprecious stones are mined around Franklin. Area towns celebrate the mineral abundance during the Macon County Gemboree in late July when gem and jewelry exhibitors show their wares.

Franklin Chamber of Commerce: 425 Porter St., Franklin, NC 28734; phone (704) 524-3161 or (800) 336-7829.

BIG FIND GEM MINE, 3 mi. s. of Franklin on US 441, is a "salted" or enriched mine. Food is available. Allow 1 hour, 30 minutes minimum. Daily 9-5, May-Oct. Admission free. Dirt-filled buckets, one for $3, two for $5. Phone (704) 524-8931.

HORSESHOE BEND is about 20 mi. n. on SR 28, along the Little Tennessee River. The site offers an excellent panorama with abundant mountain flowers.

RUBY MINES OF THE COWEE VALLEY are gravel beds that have yielded high-quality rubies and sapphires since the turn of the twentieth century. Such minerals as rhodolite garnets, rutile, cyanite and sillimanite also can be found.

Mining companies tried to locate the source of these deposits using costly shafts, tunnels and core drilling, but their efforts were unsuccessful. Today several mines are open to the public, and visitors are invited to wash and screen gravel in search of gemstones. It should be noted that some mines enrich or "salt" their gravel with stones from outside sources while others maintain entirely native, "unsalted" mineral deposits.

[SAVE] **Cherokee Rubies and Sapphires Mine** is 6.5 mi. n. on SR 28; take Cowee Creek Rd. 1.5 mi. e., then Ruby Mine Rd. 2 mi. n.e. to entrance. Gemstones that have been found at this unsalted mine range in size from small chips to several carats. Allow 1 hour, 30 minutes minimum. Daily 8-5, Apr.-Oct. Admission $5, ages 7-12, $3. Phone (704) 524-5684.

Jacobs Ruby Mine is .5 mi. n. on SR 28; take Cowee Creek Rd. 1.5 mi. e., then Ruby Mine Rd. 1 mi. n.e. to entrance. Many high-quality rubies have been found at this unsalted mine on Cowee Creek. Wear comfortable clothes. Allow 1 hour, 30 minutes minimum. Mon.-Sat. 9-5, May-Oct. Admission $6; under 13, $3; bucket of gravel 50c. Phone (704) 524-7022.

SAVE **Old Cardinal Gem Mine,** 5 mi. n. on SR 28, offers panning that has produced a variety of gems. The rubies range in size from small chips to one of 206 carats. Allow 1 hour, 30 minutes minimum. Mon.-Sat. 8-5, Mar.-Jan. Admission $5; ages 5-12, $3; one gravel-filled bag for $1, six bags for $5. Phone (704) 369-7534.

Rose Creek Mine is 5 mi. n. on SR 28 to Bennett Rd., 1 mi. n.w. following signs to 115 Terrace Ridge Dr. Gemstones that have been found at this site include amethysts, garnets, rose quartz, rubies, sapphires and topaz. Allow 1 hour minimum. Daily 10-5, Apr.-Oct. Admission (including 1 gem bag) $5; under age 13, $3. AE, DS, MC, VI. Phone (704) 524-3225.

SCOTTISH TARTANS MUSEUM, 95 E. Main St. in the W.C. Burrell Building, depicts the history of the Scottish tartan from its earliest days in A.D. 325. Exhibits delineate the evolution of the kilt, from function to tradition. Displays include tartans and Highland dress from 1700 to the present and a complete registry of all publicly known tartans. Weaving demonstrations also are given, and visitors may view their family tartan by computer in the research library. Mon.-Sat. 10-5, Sun. 1-5; closed major holidays. Admission $2, senior citizens and students $1. MC, VI. Phone (704) 524-7472.

STANDING INDIAN MOUNTAIN 12 mi. w. on US 64, then 2 mi. e. on old US 64 and 2 mi. s. on FR 67. Noted for purple rhododendron and fine views, this 5,498-foot mountain is a part of the Nantahala National Forest *(see place listing p. 107, Recreation Chart and the AAA Southeastern CampBook).*

WAYAH BALD is 5 mi. s.w. on US 64, then 10 mi. w. on Wayah Bald Rd. and 6 mi. n. on FR 69. At 5,335 feet, Wayah Bald displays an array of mountain flowers in May and June and offers panoramas of the mountains and four adjoining states from the John B. Byrne Memorial Tower. Open daily 24 hours. Free.

FRISCO—
see Outer Banks p. 111.

GASTONIA (C-4) pop. 54,700, elev. 825′
Gastonia is a textile-manufacturing city in the industrial Piedmont west of Charlotte. Nearby are Kings Mountain National Military Park, S.C., *(see place listing p. 165)* and Crowders Mountain State Park *(see Recreation Chart).*

A strike at Gastonia's Loray Mill in the 1920s became the subject of several novels: "A Stone Came Rolling" by Fielding Burke, "Strike" by Mary Heaton Vorse and "To Make My Bread" by Grace Lumpkin. Textile Week is celebrated each October.

Gaston Chamber of Commerce: 601 W. Franklin Blvd., Gastonia, NC 28054; phone (704) 864-2621.

★**SCHIELE MUSEUM OF NATURAL HISTORY AND PLANETARIUM,** off I-85 New Hope Rd. exit, following signs to 1500 E. Garrison Blvd., has a large collection of North American mammals as well as native rocks, minerals, fossils, shells, insects, birds, trees and shrubs. The Trail for All Seasons, a back-country farm complete with sheep and a garden, and a Catawba Village also are featured. Displays depict American Indian lifestyles, artifacts, crafts, costumes and tools. The Hall of Earth and Man interprets the development of life on this planet and houses a mineral collection.

Living-history demonstrations are offered in a restored 1754 log cabin on the last Sunday of each month March through December. A leaflet interprets trees, old wagon roads and flowers to be seen at markers along a nature trail. A planetarium and a 360-degree cinema are housed in the museum.

Allow 1 hour, 30 minutes minimum. Museum open Mon.-Sat. 9-5, Sun. 1-5. Planetarium shows Sat. at 11, 2 and 3, Sun. at 2, 3 and 4. Museum free. Planetarium and cinema $2.50 each; over 65, $1. Under 5 not admitted to planetarium and cinema shows. Phone (704) 866-6900 for the museum, (704) 866-6903 for the planetarium.

GOLDSBORO (C-7) pop. 40,700, elev. 108′
CHARLES B. AYCOCK BIRTHPLACE STATE HISTORIC SITE, approximately 11 mi. n. off US 117, is the birthplace of this former governor and founder of North Carolina's 20th-century public educational system. The restored farmhouse, outbuildings and one-room school date from the mid- to late 1800s. Farm animals are on the grounds. The visitor center offers an audiovisual presentation and exhibits.

Guided tours and picnic facilities are available. Allow 1 hour minimum. Mon.-Sat. 9-5, Sun. 1-5, Apr.-Oct.; Tues.-Sat. 10-4, Sun. 1-4, rest of year. Closed Veterans Day, Thanksgiving and Dec. 24-27. Free. Phone (919) 242-5581.

CLIFFS OF THE NEUSE STATE PARK is 4 mi. e. on US 70, then 9 mi. s. on SR 111. Cliffs and vegetation line the Neuse River. A natural history museum, an 11-acre lake for swimming, fishing and boating, and interpretive nature trails are in the park. Rental boats and camping are available. Daily 8 a.m.-9 p.m., June-Aug.; 8-8, Apr.-May and in Sept.; 8-7, in Mar. and Oct.; 8-6, rest of year. Lake open late May-Sept. Free. Fee for swimming, camping and boat rental. Phone (919) 778-6234. *See Recreation Chart and the AAA Southeastern CampBook.*

★GREAT SMOKY MOUNTAINS NATIONAL PARK

Elevations in the park range from 840 ft. along Abrams Creek to 6,643 ft. at Clingmans Dome. Refer to AAA maps for additional elevation information.

A blue, smokelike haze almost always hangs over the peaks of the Great Smoky Mountains; hence the name. The range runs the entire length of Great Smoky Mountains National Park, which covers more than 520,000 acres almost evenly divided between North Carolina and Tennessee. Newfound Gap Road (US 441) bisects the park, which is 53 miles long and 18 miles wide.

With the exceptions of Mount Mitchell and Mount Craig, the highest mountain peaks in eastern North America are found in the Smokies—the most massive mountain uplift in the East and one of the oldest land areas on Earth. Sixteen mountain summits rise more than 6,000 feet, and the main ridge does not drop below 5,000 feet for a distance of 36 miles.

Few places in the United States have such varied plant life. Because the mountains catch the region's copious rainfall, they support an exceptionally wide variety of vegetation. There are more than 100 native species of trees. A fine stand of Eastern deciduous trees and a large tract of red spruce constitute the park's 120,000 acres of old-growth forest. Much of the remainder is second growth.

Northern conifers, mainly spruce and fir, dominate the higher elevations; at intermediate heights grow hardwoods typical of the Northeast. Some mountaintops are covered only with grass or shrubs and thus are known as "balds."

Many streams are bordered with rhododendron, and in certain areas, such as on Gregory Bald, flame azalea grows in profusion. Rhododendron and sand myrtle are scattered throughout the mountain summits and knife-edged ridges. Dogwood and innumerable wildflowers usually

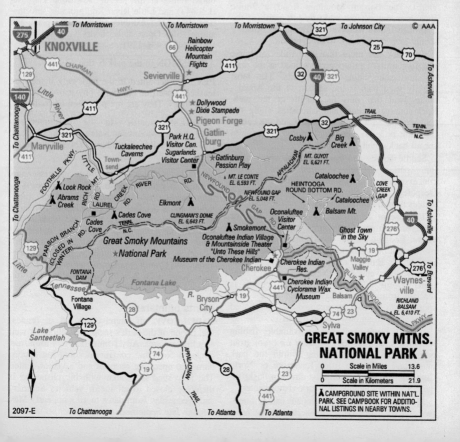

bloom from mid-March to mid-May; other blossoms create spectacular displays into July.

Wildlife was scarce when the park was established in 1934, but hunting has since been outlawed and many species are recovering. Deer are often observed in Cades Cove *(see attraction listing)*, and ruffed grouse, wild turkeys and bears live in the park.

General Information and Activities

The park is open all year. Headquarters and the Sugarlands Visitor Center are 2 miles south of Gatlinburg, Tenn., on US 441. Information on naturalist-led hikes, campfire programs and other park activities can be obtained at both the Sugarlands and Oconaluftee visitor centers, near the Cherokee *(see place listing p. 90)* entrance. Illustrated talks are given from mid-May through October in selected campgrounds and at the visitor centers.

There are 238 miles of paved and 146 miles of gravel park roads. Newfound Gap Road (US 441), a scenic Cherokee-Gatlinburg route with an elevation of 5,048 feet at the state line, crosses the park. The 469-mile scenic Blue Ridge Parkway *(see place listing p. 82)* links the park with Virginia's Shenandoah National Park *(see Virginia)*. The Balsam Mountain Road, a 9-mile spur, branches off the parkway just north of the Cherokee Indian Reservation. Heintooga Road, a scenic loop drive, leads to an overlook.

The park has more than 800 miles of horse and foot trails. Leaflets are provided at the start of short self-guiding nature trails. The most heavily used path is the section of the Appalachian Trail that runs the length of the park. Back-country shelters and campsites along the trail are spaced a day's hike apart and the camping limit is 1 day per site. Permits are required for all back-country camping.

Saddle horses and guides can be obtained in the park. Horseback trails lead from concessioner-operated stables at Smokemont and Deepcreek, as well as Cades Cove and two stables near Gatlinburg, Tenn.

The ascent of Mount LeConte by foot or horseback from Gatlinburg offers awesome views. Lodging on the mountaintop is available by reservation. Also noted for spectacular views is Charlie's Bunion, reached by the Appalachian Trail 4 miles east from Newfound Gap. Clingmans Dome, Tennessee's highest point, is reached from Newfound Gap Road by a 7-mile spur road to the parking area and a .5-mile paved trail leading to an observation tower.

With 735 miles of streams available, fishing for trout is ideal, although fishing for brook trout is prohibited. Visitors fishing within the park must have a license from Tennessee or North Carolina. Fishing is permitted dawn to dusk; inquire about regulations at a park visitor center.

Most of the many developed campgrounds function on a first-come-first-served basis; however, reservations are required May 15-Oct. 31 at Cades Cove and Elkmont in Tennessee and at Smokemont. For reservations at developed campgrounds phone (800) 365-2267. *See Recreation Chart and the AAA Southeastern CampBook.*

VISITOR CENTERS provide information to enhance a visit to the park. Scheduled interpretive activities are posted at all centers. Hours vary; see individual schedule. All are closed Dec. 25. Free. For general information about all centers phone (423) 436-1200.

Oconaluftee Visitor Center is at the south park entrance on Newfound Gap Rd. (US 441) near Cherokee. Exhibits and information about the park are provided. Next to the center is the Mountain Farm Museum, a restored farmstead where visitors may peer into a small farmhouse displaying the essentials of a late 19th-century pioneer house. Craft demonstrations are offered occasionally during the summer as announced.

One-half mile north of the visitor center is Mingus Mill, an old gristmill still in operation. Visitor center open daily; hours vary seasonally. Phone (704) 497-1900.

Sugarlands Visitor Center, 2 mi. s. of Gatlinburg, Tenn., at the jct. of Newfound Gap Rd. (US 441) and Little River Rd., provides information, films and exhibits about native plant and animal life. Open daily; hours vary seasonally. Phone (423) 436-1291.

ADMISSION to the park is free.

PETS are permitted in the park only if they are leashed, crated or otherwise physically restricted at all times. They are not permitted on trails.

ADDRESS inquiries to the Superintendent, Great Smoky Mountains National Park, 107 Park Headquarters Rd., Gatlinburg, TN 37738; phone (423) 436-1200.

AUTO TAPE TOURS allow driver and passengers to enjoy a guided tour at their own pace. A 1-hour cassette tape provides mile-by-mile highlights, and a detailed map is included. The tapes describe history, geology, flora and fauna of the park; the narration is accompanied by music and sound effects. Visitors may purchase a tape for $12.95 at stores and motels in the Gatlinburg, Tenn., and Cherokee areas, or write CCInc. Auto Tape Tours, P.O. Box 227, Allendale, NJ 07401; phone (201) 236-1666.

Points of Interest

CADES COVE, off Laurel Creek Rd. in Tennessee, is one of the park's scenic attractions as well as a historic area. An 11-mile, one-way loop road circles a cove that contains restored log cabins, barns, an operating gristmill and a visitor center. The loop road is popular with bicyclists and is therefore closed to all motor vehicles Saturday and Wednesday from dawn to 10 a.m., early May through late September.

Park rangers conduct free tours of the mill area daily during the summer from the visitor center, as well as present agricultural programs and demonstrations of mountain skills. Allow 2 hours minimum. Cades Cove is open daily dawn-dusk. Free. Phone (423) 436-1200

CATALOOCHEE is about 21 mi. n. of Waynesville via US 276 through Cove Creek Gap, following signs. This secluded area includes several historic buildings and offers good trout fishing.

GREENSBORO (B-5) pop. 183,500, elev. 839'

Until the textile boom of the late 19th century, Greensboro was a quiet Piedmont town. The first steam-operated cotton mill began production in 1833, but real growth in textiles began after the Civil War. Textiles are still important to the economy but are supplemented by tobacco, electronics products and insurance. Greensboro benefits from proximity to Winston-Salem and High Point, with all three forming an urban triangle.

Greensboro was home to several prominent Americans including William Sydney Porter (O. Henry), whose short stories are American classics. Porter's legacy was carried on by another Greensboro native, Wilbur Daniel Steele, winner of the O. Henry Prize for such works as "They Know Not What They Do" and "Can't Cross Jordan." Dolley Madison, wife of President James Madison, also was a native of the area.

The War Memorial Auditorium and Coliseum offers exhibitions, sports events and shows. The Eastern Music Festival, a 6-week series of classical music concerts featuring internationally known guest artists, is held at Guilford College from late June to early August.

Greensboro Area Convention & Visitors Bureau: 317 S. Greene St., Greensboro, NC 27401-2615; phone (910) 274-2282 or (800) 344-2282. *See color ad p. 373.*

Shopping areas: Four Seasons Town Centre, off I-40 at Pinecroft Rd., has more than 200 stores, including Belk, Dillard's and JCPenney. State Street Station features some 35 shops and restaurants housed in refurbished storefronts from the 1920s.

🆂🅰🆅🅴 **BLANDWOOD MANSION** is near downtown at jct. of Edgeworth and Washington. The home of North Carolina Gov. John Motley Morehead, Blandwood was built as a farmhouse in the late 18th century. Redesigned in 1846 as an elegant Italian villa, the house contains many original furnishings. The mansion has been restored and the outbuildings, including the carriage house, have been reconstructed. Allow 1 hour minimum. Tues.-Sat. 11-2, Sun. 2-5, Feb.-Dec.; closed Thanksgiving and Dec. 24-25. Admission $5; over 64, $4; under 12, $2. Phone (910) 272-5003.

EMERALD POINTE WATER PARK, I-85 exit 121 to 3910 S. Holden Rd., contains numerous water-slides, a wave pool, a white-water adventure ride and a children's area. Food is available. Park open at 10, mid-May to mid-Sept. Closing times and days of operation vary; phone ahead. All-day admission $19.95; under 45" tall $13.95; over age 54, $9.95; under age 2 free. After 4, $12.95; under 45" tall $8.95. AE, MC, VI. Phone (910) 852-9721.

GREENSBORO ARBORETUM is in Lindley Park between Ashland Dr., W. Market St. and Wendover Ave. The grounds contain nine labeled plant collections consisting of species indigenous to the Piedmont region of North Carolina. Other features include an arbor, lighted fountain and gazebo. Daily dawn-dusk. Free. Phone (910) 373-2558.

★**GREENSBORO HISTORICAL MUSEUM,** 130 Summit Ave., traces the development of Guilford County. Exhibits include an extensive military history collection, Dolley Madison and O. Henry memorabilia, rare documents, decorative art works and a depiction of the 1960s civil rights movement lunch counter sit-ins. A reconstructed 19th-century Greensboro village displays a doctor's office, drugstore, schoolhouse and antique fire engine.

Other highlights include the 18th-century Christian Isley House and the 19th-century Francis McNairy House. Tues.-Sat. 10-5, Sun. 2-5; closed city holidays. Free. Phone (910) 373-2043.

GUILFORD COURTHOUSE NATIONAL MILITARY PARK—
see place listing p. 100.

NATURAL SCIENCE CENTER, 5 mi. n. on Lawndale via Battleground Ave., displays a Foucault Pendulum and offers hands-on exhibits pertaining to geology, paleontology, energy, health and fitness. On the grounds are a planetarium; a marine gallery; a zoo containing lemurs, snakes and reptiles; and a children's petting zoo.

Center open Mon.-Sat. 9-5, Sun. 12:30-5; closed Thanksgiving and Dec. 25 and 31. Zoo open Mon.-Sat. 10-4:30, Sun. 12:30-4. Planetarium shows daily at 3. Admission $4.50; senior citizens and ages 4-13, $3.50. Planetarium admission $1 extra. Phone (910) 288-3769.

REPLACEMENTS, LTD., is off I-85 N. to I-40, exit 132, heading n.w. to 1089 Knox Rd. A museum holds more than 2,000 unique and rare pieces of china, crystal, flatware and collectibles. Daily 8 a.m.-9 p.m.; closed Dec. 25. Tours are given every 30 minutes beginning at 8:30 a.m. Last tour 1 hour before closing. Free. Phone (800) 737-5223.

WEATHERSPOON ART GALLERY, at Spring Garden and Tate sts. on the University of North Carolina at Greensboro campus, features six galleries of 20th-century works by such artists as Alexander Calder, Willem de Kooning, Louise

Nevelson and Andy Warhol. An entire gallery is devoted to Henri Matisse. An outside exhibit displays sculptures. Allow 1 hour minimum. Tues.-Fri. 10-5 (also Wed. 5-8), Sat.-Sun. 1-5; closed holidays. Free. Phone (910) 334-5770.

GREENVILLE (C-7) pop. 45,000, elev. 75′

One of the largest bright-leaf tobacco markets in the world, Greenville also is an agricultural market and wholesale trading center. The United States Information Agency's Voice of America broadcasting station, the gateway station for programming of all VOA stations around the world, is open to visitors Monday through Friday. Phone (919) 752-7181.

Pitt/Greenville Chamber of Commerce: 302 S. Greene St., Greenville, NC 27834; phone (919) 752-4101.

GREENVILLE MUSEUM OF ART, 802 S. Evans St., displays 20th-century American paintings, drawings, prints and sculpture. Allow 30 minutes minimum. Tues.-Fri. 10-4:30, Sun. 1-4; closed holidays. Free. Phone (919) 758-1946.

GUILFORD COURTHOUSE NATIONAL MILITARY PARK (B-5)

Guilford (GILL-ford) Courthouse National Military Park covers 220 acres in northwest Greensboro, off US 220. A closing engagement of the Revolutionary War, the Battle of Guilford Courthouse pitted Gen. Nathanael Greene's mixed Continental and militia army against Lord Cornwallis' smaller, veteran forces on March 15, 1781.

Cornwallis, eager to avenge the British defeat at Cowpens, S.C., won the battle but took heavy losses and failed to destroy the American force. Although defeated in battle, Greene won his objective and Cornwallis soon moved to Virginia, where he finally surrendered his army at Yorktown on Oct. 19, 1781.

The site includes wayside exhibits throughout the battlefield and a visitor center with displays, films and brochures. A 2.5-mile auto tour leads to many of the monuments, including the graves of John Penn and William Hooper, signers of the Declaration of Independence.

Cavalry Monument honors all American cavalry, including Virginian Peter Francisco, known as "The Goliath of the Revolution." At the Battle of Guilford Courthouse, Francisco—who weighed 260 pounds and stood 6 feet 6 inches tall—supposedly used a 5-foot sword given to him by George Washington.

The visitor center is open daily 8:30-5. For further information contact the Superintendent, Guilford Courthouse National Military Park, 2332 New Garden Rd., Greensboro, NC 27410-2355; phone (910) 288-1776.

Tannenbaum Park is one-quarter mile west on US 220. The park contains picnic areas, two log cabins and a former British military hospital built in 1778.

HALIFAX (A-7) pop. 300, elev. 101′

★**HISTORIC HALIFAX STATE HISTORIC SITE** is on US 301 Bus. Rte. at St. David and Dobbs sts. Halifax was a commercial river port that became a political arena in 1776 when the "Halifax Resolves," recommending independence from England, were ratified by the colony of North Carolina. Founded in 1760, the town has many restored buildings that reflect its early history.

A free 60-minute guided tour through the center of the old town includes the cemetery, Market Square, the 1820 Burgess Law Office, the 1838 jail, the 1833 Clerk of Courts Office and an archeological museum built over the remains of the 1762 Montfort house. Two shorter guided tours are available: one of the 1760 Owens House and another of the 1808 Sally-Billy Plantation House.

Maps of the village and brochures detailing a self-guiding tour are available at the visitor center, which also displays artifacts and shows a 13-minute film. Site open Mon.-Sat. 9-5, Sun. 1-5, Apr.-Oct.; Tues.-Sat. 10-4, Sun. 1-4, rest of year. Closed state holidays. Free. Phone (919) 583-7191.

HENDERSONVILLE (E-3) pop. 7,300, elev. 2,200′

Once a hunting ground for the Cherokee, Hendersonville became a summer resort where many Low Country dwellers came to escape the season's intense heat. Nestled in the mountains of Western North Carolina, Hendersonville continues to offer visitors year-round activities, including hiking, bicycling and antiquing.

The city honors the many apple groves in the area during the Apple Festival on Labor Day weekend. Crafts, food and special activities are featured. Other events include Farm City Day in early October, complete with wagon rides and craft demonstrations; and the Jubilee Main Street Arts Festival in late May.

Visitor Information Center: 201 South Main St., Hendersonville, NC 28792; phone (704) 693-9708 or (800) 828-4244.

Shopping areas: Historic Main Street, in downtown Hendersonville, is home to numerous antique shops and boutiques. For a taste of local flavor, the Henderson County Curb Market, 2nd Ave. and Church St., offers a variety of handmade or locally-grown items. The market is open on select days; phone (704) 692-8012.

JUMP-OFF ROCK is on the summit of Jump-off Mountain, 5 mi. w. via Fifth Ave. Legend holds that an American Indian chief and a Cherokee maiden often met on the rock. When she learned of her love's death in battle, the heartbroken maiden jumped off the ledge. Indian lore say that on some moonlit nights, the ghost of the maiden can be seen on the rock. Today, Jump-off Rock provides visitors with panoramic views of the Blue Ridge and the Pisgah mountain ranges. Free.

HERTFORD (B-8) pop. 2,100, elev. 13'

NEWBOLD-WHITE HOUSE, 1.5 mi. off US 17 bypass on SR 1336 along the Perquimans River, is considered the oldest house in North Carolina. The 1685 house was painstakingly restored by hand, with original workmanship remaining in the two chimneys, 18-inch-thick brick walls and the second-floor woodwork. Seventeenth-century furnishings are exhibited.

Allow 30 minutes minimum. Mon.-Sat. 10-4:30, Mar.-Nov.; by appointment rest of year. Admission $2, students 50c. Phone (919) 426-7567.

HICKORY (B-4) pop. 28,300, elev. 1,165'

Until 1900 Hickory was called Hickory Tavern Station, after the tavern and stagecoach stop that was the town's center of activity. Today Hickory supports a thriving furniture-manufacturing industry.

Catawba County Chamber of Commerce: P.O. Box 1828, 470 Hwy. 70SW, Hickory, NC 28603; phone (704) 328-6111.

Shopping areas: Catawba County is known for its many furniture manufacturers. More than 50 discount furniture retail stores are in the area. For further information contact the chamber of commerce.

ARTS & SCIENCE CENTER OF CATAWBA VALLEY is at 243 Third Ave. N.E., off I-40 exit 125. The center houses the Hickory Museum of Art and the Catawba Science Center. Tues.-Fri. 10-5, Sat. 10-4, Sun. 1-4; closed holidays. Donations. Phone (704) 324-4906.

Catawba Science Center contains hands-on life and physical science exhibits. The Hall of Life Science features a living mountain stream; Body-Works presents exhibits about the human body and wellness; and a Physical Science Arcade emphasizes light, sound and physics. Allow 30 minutes minimum. Tues.-Fri. 10-5, Sat. 10-4, Sun. 1-4; closed major holidays. Admission $2; over 61 and ages 4-16, $1. Phone (704) 322-8169.

Hickory Museum of Art presents changing exhibits and a permanent collection of 19th-century through contemporary American art. Works by Alfred Thompson Bricher, William Merritt Chase and Gilbert Stuart are featured. Allow 30 minutes minimum. Tues.-Fri. 10-5, Sat. 10-4, Sun. 1-4. Donations. Phone (704) 327-8576.

HIGHLANDS (F-2) pop. 900, elev. 4,118'

Highlands is at the intersection of two scenic highways, US 64 running northeast to Brevard and SR 28 running northwest to Franklin. Near Highlands is Whiteside Mountain, accessible from US 64, which has some of the highest sheer cliffs in the eastern United States.

The Highlands District Ranger Station, 5 miles east on US 64, distributes trail maps of Van Hook Glade and Cliffside Lake *(see Recreation Chart and the AAA Southeastern CampBook).* Phone (704) 526-3765, or write Highlands District Ranger Station, 2010 Flat Mountain Rd., Highlands, NC 28741.

Highlands Chamber of Commerce: P.O. Box 404, Highlands, NC 28741; phone (704) 526-2112.

CULLASAJA RIVER GORGE, a deep canyon w. along US 64, has five waterfalls. The road passes under Bridal Veil Falls at the head of the gorge; farther along are Dry Falls and, almost halfway to Franklin *(see place listing p. 95),* Cullasaja Falls. At the head of Dry Falls is a log shelter. A trail leads from it to the foot of the falls.

Note: Because the road is narrow, travelers should pay strict attention to driving; designated overlooks provide ample opportunity for viewing the scenery.

HIGH POINT (B-5) pop. 69,500, elev. 939'

High Point earned its name by being the highest point on the original survey for the old North

Carolina Railroad. The city is the hub of America's furniture-manufacturing industry. Of the more than 125 furniture plants in the area, 15 are among the world's largest. In April and October each year High Point holds an international home-furnishings market. Summers feature the North Carolina Shakespeare Festival, held by the North Carolina School of the Arts.

High Point Chamber of Commerce: 1101 N. Main St., P.O. Box 5025, High Point, NC 27262; phone (910) 889-8151.

SAVE **FURNITURE DISCOVERY CENTER** is downtown at 101 W. Green Dr., just w. of Main St. (US 311). Museum displays depict the furniture manufacturing process from design through finish. Special exhibits include the Furniture Hall of Fame and a miniature bedroom collection. Allow 1 hour minimum. Mon.-Sat. 10-5, Sun. 1-5, Apr.-Oct.; Tues.-Sat. 10-5, Sun. 1-5, rest of year. Closed major holidays. Admission $5; over 65, $4; ages 6-15, $2. Combination ticket with Angela Peterson Doll and Miniature Museum $6. Phone (910) 887-3876.

Angela Peterson Doll and Miniature Museum presents more than 1,700 dolls and miniatures of various styles and from different periods. Featured are a dollhouse village, shadow boxes, displays of childhood toys and dolls and collections of baby, foreign and religious dolls. Tues.-Sat. 10-5, Sun. 1-5. Admission $3; over 65, $2.50; ages 6-15, $1.50. Combination ticket with Furniture Discovery Center $6. Phone (910) 885-3655.

HIGH POINT MUSEUM is 1 mi. e. on US 70A at 1859 E. Lexington Ave. The museum contains local artifacts and military items from the Civil War to the present. Other buildings include the restored 18th-century Haley House, a weaving house and a blacksmith shop. Allow 1 hour minimum. Museum open Tues.-Sat. 10-4:30, Sun. 1-4:30. Outbuildings Sat. 10-4:30, Sun. 1-4:30. Free. Phone (910) 885-6859.

HILLSBOROUGH (B-6) pop. 4,300, elev. 538'

Hillsborough was founded on the site where the Great Indian Trading Path crossed the Eno River. The town was included in many historic events during the colonial and Revolutionary periods, and its architecture reflects that of bygone days; a collection of Colonial, antebellum and Victorian buildings dot the landscape.

The city's historic district boasts more than 100 late 18th- and early 19th-century structures set along streets that retain pre-Revolutionary names, the most unmistakable being King and Queen streets. The Orange County Historical Museum has a gallery featuring the work of area artists and exhibits depicting the daily lives of early Orange County residents. Live musical entertainment, a vintage and antique car show, crafts and a barbecue are a few of the highlights

of Hillsborough Hog Day, held the third Saturday in June.

Orange County Visitor Center: 150 E. King St., Hillsborough, NC 27278; phone (919) 732-7741.

Self-guiding tours: Walking-tour brochures and other visitor information are available at the visitor center.

HOT SPRINGS (E-3) pop. 500, elev. 1,329'

Once a popular health spa, Hot Springs today is a summer resort. Nearby US 70 provides scenic motoring. Rocky Bluff, a recreation area in Pisgah National Forest *(see place listing p. 113)* 3 miles south via SR 209, offers a variety of activities.

HUNTERSVILLE (C-4) pop. 3,000, elev. 819'

Adjacent to Lake Norman *(see recreation chart)*, Huntersville holds a 2-day Lakefest in September that features a fine arts show and strolling Renaissance musicians as well as live bands, a dog show and entertainment for children.

North Mecklenburg Chamber & Visitors Center: in Shops on the Green, 20216 Knox Rd., P.O. Box 760, Cornelius, NC 28031; phone (704) 892-1922.

DUKE POWER'S ENERGY EXPLORIUM, I-77 exit 28, then 6.5 mi. w. on SR 73, features hands-on displays explaining how electricity is produced. The grounds also contain a nature trail and wildflower garden. Picnicking is permitted. Allow 30 minutes minimum. Mon.-Sat. 9-5, Sun. noon-5; closed Jan. 1, Thanksgiving and Dec. 24-25. Free. Phone (704) 875-5600.

LATTA PLANTATION PARK is at 5225 Sample Rd.; from I-77 exit 16B take Sunset Rd. .5 mi. w., then 4.8 mi. n. on Beatties Ford Rd., then w. on Sample Rd. following signs. A 1,063-acre nature preserve bordering Mountain Island Lake, the park has a visitor center, equestrian center and hiking and horse trails. Boating opportunities and canoe access are available. Picnicking is permitted. Swimming is not allowed. Daily 7-dusk. Free. Phone (704) 875-1391.

Carolina Raptor Center, within the park, provides care and rehabilitation for injured and orphaned birds of prey. Educational exhibits and weekend programs about raptors are presented. A nature trail is lined with aviaries containing many varieties of hawks, falcons and owls. Allow 2 hours minimum. Tues.-Sat. 10-5, Sun. noon-5; closed major holidays. Admission $4; over 60 and ages 6-17, $2. Phone (704) 875-6521.

Historic Latta Place is the restored 1800 river plantation house of James Latta, a successful merchant. The two-story Federal-style house is furnished in period; architectural highlights include a finely detailed staircase and elaborate mantels. Outbuildings include the kitchen, a smokehouse, provisions barn, pioneer cabin, wash house and well house. Guided tours are available.

Tues.-Fri. 9-5, Sat.-Sun. 1:30-5, Mar.-Dec. Tours depart Tues.-Fri. at 1:30 and 3:30, Sat.-Sun. at 2, 3 and 4. Closed major holidays. Admission $3; over 65 and students with ID $2; ages 6-12, $1. Phone (704) 875-2312.

JACKSONVILLE (C-7) pop. 30,000, elev. 15'

Jacksonville, at the mouth of the New River and known for its outdoor water activities, is the commercial, banking, cultural and governmental center for the county. The granite Beirut Memorial, built to honor marines and sailors killed in Beirut and Grenada, stands just outside the gate of Camp Johnson on SR 17. Along Lejeune Boulevard, each Bradford pear tree stands for a life lost in Lebanon or Grenada.

Greater Jacksonville/Onslow Chamber of Commerce: 1 Marine Blvd. N., P.O. Box 765, Jacksonville, NC 28541; phone (919) 347-3141.

CAMP LEJEUNE, e. on SR 24, is a 153,000-acre Marine Corps Base, home of Expeditionary Forces in Readiness, the 2nd Marine Division, 6th Marine Expeditionary Brigade, 2nd Force Service Support Group and 2nd Marine Expeditionary Force. To obtain passes, visitors must present a valid driver's license, registration certificate and proof of automobile insurance at the information center next to the main gate on SR 24. Daily 24 hours. Free. Phone (910) 451-2197.

THE GREATEST STORY RETOLD, 106 River Court Plaza, Suite A, is a museum housing religious objects, artifacts from the Christian Holy Land and more than 80 Bible-inspired paintings by George Prout. Items on display include Biblical dolls, crowns of thorns, a 1702 hand-printed Bible, coins from the early Christian era, rocks and soil from Calvary and olive trees descended from the ones that stand today in the Garden of Gethsemane. Allow 30 minutes minimum. Mon.-Fri. 8-4, Sat. 11-4; closed holidays. Free. Phone (910) 455-8011.

KANNAPOLIS (C-4) pop. 29,700

Kannapolis (ka-NA-po-lis) was founded in 1887 as a company town around the Cannon Mills textile headquarters. Before the turn of the 20th century and the marketing of ready-made clothes, Cannon cloth was a staple in Southern homes. The city is still home to Fieldcrest Cannon Inc., one of the world's largest producers of household textiles. Kannapolis' central business district features Cannon Village, which depicts the architectural style of the early 20th century.

Kannapolis Chamber of Commerce: 316 S. Main St., P.O. Box 249, Kannapolis, NC 28082; phone (704) 932-4164.

Shopping areas: Tree-lined West Avenue offers bargain hunters a wide variety of factory outlet stores representing major manufacturers.

★**CANNON VILLAGE VISITOR CENTER,** off I-85 at 200 West Ave., has a welcome center for visitors to the village featuring the Fieldcrest Cannon Textile Museum and Exhibition. Highlights of the exhibit include one of the world's largest towels, an antique hand loom, a hands-on demonstration of sheet fabric printing and samples of textiles that are more than 1,200 years old.

A theater show detailing the manufacturing process as well as a 20-minute film also are available. Allow 1 hour minimum. Mon.-Sat. 9-5, Sun. 1-6; closed Easter, Thanksgiving and Dec. 25. Free. Phone (704) 938-3200.

KENANSVILLE (C-7) pop. 900

Kenansville, in the fertile coastal plain of southeast North Carolina, was settled about 1735 by Swiss, German and Irish immigrants, who called their town Golden Grove. In 1818 Kenansville was renamed for Gen. James Kenan, a member of the House of Commons who fought in the Revolution and helped ratify the Constitution and formulate the Bill of Rights.

Many of Kenansville's old houses have been restored. There are three antebellum churches that have changed little since the 19th century; among them is 1736 Grove Church, the oldest Presbyterian congregation in the state. Brochures of Kenansville are available at the town hall on Rutledge Rd.; phone (910) 296-0369.

Duplin County Tourism Commission: Airport Rd., P.O. Box 929, Kenansville, NC 28349-0929; phone (910) 296-2180 or (800) 755-1755.

COWAN MUSEUM is in the Kelly-Farrior House on SR 11/24/50/903 (S. Main St.). This two-story Greek Revival house contains more than 2,000 items dating mostly from the 18th, 19th and early 20th centuries. A few items, such as a 13th-century slave belt, come from ancient cultures. A blacksmith shop, one-room school, furnished log cabin and smokehouse are on the grounds. Allow 30 minutes minimum. Tues.-Sat. 10-4, Sun. 2-4; closed holidays. Donations. Phone (910) 296-2149.

LIBERTY HALL, on SR 11/24/50/903 (S. Main St.), is a Greek Revival house built in the early 1800s by Thomas Kenan II, son of Gen. James Kenan. The house has been restored as an ancestral memorial. Historical documents were used as references to create the wallpaper and the upholstery and drapery fabric. Many of the furnishings are original.

Other buildings on the estate include the necessary house (bathroom), smokehouse, chicken coop, carriage house and wash shed. Historical exhibits and a 12-minute videotape are presented in the visitor center. Candlelight Christmas Tour, a guided tour of the decorated estate, takes place the second weekend in December. Period music is played on an original 1750 piano forte. Reservations are required.

Allow 1 hour minimum. Tues.-Sat. 10-4, Sun. 2-4; closed Jan. 1, Thanksgiving and Dec. 25. Admission $5; under 13, $2.50. A separate admission is charged for special events. Phone (910) 296-2175.

KENLY (C-7) pop. 1,500, elev. 204′

TOBACCO FARM LIFE MUSEUM, 1.5 mi. off I-95 exit 107 on US 301, offers a history of North Carolina tobacco farming and the economic changes brought about by the introduction of flue-cured tobacco. Displays include artifacts, tools and equipment used in the curing process. Some exhibits illustrate social, educational and religious customs of early families of the area, and a restored farmstead re-creates rural life during the Great Depression. Videotapes show the history of tobacco and some of the phases involved in its production.

Allow 1 hour minimum. Mon.-Sat. 9:30-5, Sun. 2-5, early Jan.-Dec. 31; closed Easter, Thanksgiving and Dec. 25-26. Admission $2; over 65 and ages 5-17, $1. MC, VI. Phone (919) 284-3431.

KINSTON (C-7) pop. 25,300, elev. 43′

Kinston was founded in 1762 and originally named Kingston. After the Revolution Patriots changed the spelling to avoid any reference to England. Today Kinston is one of the nation's leading bright-leaf tobacco markets. East of town on US 70, Lakeside Mills operates a 19th-century gristmill.

Founded in Kinston in 1981, the Eastern North Carolina Bluegrass Association is dedicated to increasing public awareness of bluegrass and its heritage. On the second Saturday of each month the association performs at 6 p.m. in the Lenoir Community College gymnasium on SR 70.

Kinston/Lenoir County Chamber of Commerce: 301 N. Queen St. P.O. Box 157, Kinston, NC 28502; phone (919) 527-1131.

CSS NEUSE STATE HISTORIC SITE AND THE GOVERNOR CASWELL MEMORIAL, 1 mi. w. on US 70A, includes a museum; a memorial to Richard Caswell, first governor of the state of North Carolina; and the CSS Neuse, one of two remaining Confederate ironclads. The museum presents exhibits and a slide show relating the story of the Neuse. Picnic facilities are available.

Allow 1 hour minimum. Mon.-Sat. 9-5, Sun. 1-5, Apr.-Oct.; Tues.-Sat. 10-4, Sun. 1-4, rest of year. Closed Jan. 1, Martin Luther King Jr.'s Birthday, Good Friday, Thanksgiving and Dec. 24-25. Free. Phone (919) 522-2091.

KURE BEACH (E-7) pop. 600

FORT FISHER STATE HISTORIC SITE, about 2 mi. s. at end of US 421, was one of the largest Confederate earthwork fortifications. The Civil War's heaviest land-sea battle was fought Jan. 13-15, 1865; the federal fleet fired more than 2 million pounds of projectiles in two attacks. The site has a monument commemorating the battle, a reconstructed gun emplacement and an interpretive history trail.

The visitor center features an audiovisual show and displays, models and dioramas that illustrate the history of the fort and the role played by the blockade runners. Guided tours are available. Allow 1 hour, 30 minutes minimum. Mon.-Sat. 9-5, Sun. 1-5, Apr.-Oct.; Tues.-Sat. 10-4, Sun. 1-4, rest of year. Closed Good Friday, Thanksgiving and Dec. 24-25. Free. Phone (910) 458-5538.

NORTH CAROLINA AQUARIUM/FORT FISHER, on US 421S, houses live sharks, eels, sea turtles and other marine animals. Visitors can explore the world of humpback whales, view the daily fish feeding and enjoy field trips and a touch tank. Allow 1 hour minimum. Daily 9-7, May 24- Labor Day weekend; 9-5, rest of year. Closed Jan. 1, Thanksgiving and Dec. 25. Admission $3; senior citizens and active duty military with ID $2; ages 6-17, $1. Phone (910) 458-8257.

LAKE LURE (E-4) pop. 700

Lake Lure takes its name from the 1,500-acre man-made lake east of town. It is surrounded by the Rumbling Bald mountain range; faults in the mountains have created landslides, exposing caves in the upper slopes. Scenic coves and inlets of the lake offer access for boating, swimming and fishing. Identified by deep violet blossoms, the paulownia—or empress tree—was brought to the vicinity by George Vanderbilt. See Recreation Chart.

BOTTOMLESS POOLS, off US 74, were created by stream erosion in solid rock. Allow 30 minutes minimum. Daily 9:30-5:30, Apr.-Oct. Admission $2; ages 7-12, $1. Phone (704) 625-8324.

LEVEL CROSS (B-5)

RICHARD PETTY MUSEUM, Level Cross exit off US 220, then 1 mi. e. following signs, is a tribute to stock car racer Richard Petty. Race cars, trophies, photographs, racing signs, letters from government officials and other memorabilia fill the museum. A 25-minute film details the racing legend's life. Allow 1 hour minimum. Mon.-Sat. 9-5; closed Thanksgiving and Dec. 25. Admission $3; ages 7-17, $1.50. Phone (910) 495-1143.

LINVILLE (D-4) pop. 200, elev. 3,800′

Three miles off the Blue Ridge Parkway (see place listing p. 82), Linville is a resort community known for its excellent golf courses. The

Linville River and nearby lakes provide good fishing opportunities, and hiking trails are plentiful on nearby Grandfather Mountain *(see attraction listing)*. In winter the region becomes a ski center.

Two major events entertain summer visitors in the Linville area. Gospel singers perform on the slopes of Grandfather Mountain during Singing on the Mountain, the fourth Sunday in June. Traditional Scottish athletic competitions, dancing, piping, drumming and pageantry are the focus of attention at the Grandfather Mountain Highland Games and Gathering of Scottish Clans, which takes place the second full weekend in July.

★GRANDFATHER MOUNTAIN is 2 mi. n. of Linville on US 221, or 1 mi. s. of jct. US 221 and Blue Ridge Pkwy. The 5,964-foot peak was named by pioneers for its profile when viewed from Foscoe, 7 miles north of Linville. From this vantage point the mountain resembles a bearded grandfather looking toward the sky. Spectacular views and unusual rock formations are visible while ascending the mountain.

The area affords a variety of photographic and recreational opportunities. Dramatic views are visible from Mile High Swinging Bridge. Deer, bald and golden eagles, cougars and black bears can be seen in their natural habitats. A visitor center and a nature museum with a theater have exhibits about wildflowers, minerals and natural history. Food is available. Several picnic areas and 12.5 miles of hiking trails are on the mountain.

Allow 1 hour, 30 minutes minimum. Daily 8-7, Apr. 6-Labor Day; 8-5, rest of year (weather permitting). Admission $10; ages 4-12, $5. AE, MC, VI. Phone (704) 733-4337 or (800) 468-7325. *See ad p. 83.*

LINVILLE FALLS (D-4)

LINVILLE GORGE is a scenic chasm n.w. off the Blue Ridge Pkwy. at Milepost 316.4. The upper falls cascade 50 feet over rocks, disappear through a cleft in the mountainside, reappear as the lower falls and drop about 60 feet into Linville Gorge. Paths to the falls and to lookouts have been cut through great jungles of rhododendron.

Linville Gorge Wilderness, below the falls, is part of Pisgah National Forest *(see place listing p. 113)* and has been set aside for scientific and recreational use. Wiseman's View observation point on the west and Table Rock Lookout Tower on the east overlook the gorge. Hunting and fishing are permitted in season. Permits are available at the district ranger's office in the library building in Marion. The area is reached only by trail or cross-country travel; entry is by permit Sat.-Sun and holidays, May-Oct. Free. Phone (704) 652-2144.

LITTLE SWITZERLAND (E-4)
elev. 3,479'

SAVE **EMERALD VILLAGE** is 2.5 mi. w. on SR 1100. The North Carolina Mining Museum and the Gemstone Mine are two highlights; other features include the Company Store Museum and Discovery Mill, which houses shops and museum displays. A self-guiding tour of the mining museum includes surface and subsurface mines. Daily 9-6, Memorial Day-Labor Day; 9-5, rest of year. Mining Museum admission (Gemstone Mine not included) $4; over 60, $3.50; students in grades 1-12, $3. Phone (704) 765-6463.

LUMBERTON (D-6) pop. 18,600,
elev. 120'

Founded in 1787 by Revolutionary War officer Capt. John Willis, the city began as a shipping point for lumber and naval supplies that were floated down the Lumber River. Today the town's economy is centered around tobacco, farm produce and textile manufacturing. Situated directly off I-95, Lumberton serves as a halfway point between New York and Florida.

Lumberton Area Chamber of Commerce: 800 N. Chestnut St., P.O. Box 1008, Lumberton, NC 28359; phone (910) 739-9999 or (800) 359-6971. *See ad p. 386.*

ROBESON COUNTY SHOWCASE MUSEUM, 101 S. Elm St., displays local memorabilia along with stuffed birds and small mammals that are native to the area. Items on display include a 1909 record player, guns from the early 19th century and fossils found in the nearby Lumber River. Allow 30 minutes minimum. Mon.-Tues. 9-1, Thurs.-Fri. 1-5, Sat. 10-2; closed holidays. Free. Phone (910) 738-7979.

MAGGIE VALLEY (E-2) pop. 200

An all-year resort town, Maggie Valley is off the Blue Ridge Parkway near the east entrance to Great Smoky Mountains National Park *(see place listing p. 97).* The community's name was selected in 1909 by the postmaster general, whose choice for the designation of the new postal district was limited to the name of one of a resident's three daughters.

From late July to early August, nearby Waynesville *(see place listing p. 120)* plays host to Folkmoot U.S.A., which involves musicians and dancers from around the world.

Maggie Valley Area Chamber of Commerce: 2487 Soco Rd., P.O. Box 87, Maggie Valley, NC 28751; phone (704) 926-1686 or (800) 785-8259.

★**GHOST TOWN IN THE SKY** is a western theme park on US 19. A chairlift and an incline railway carry passengers 3,364 feet up the mountain to the main part of the park, where there are saloon shows, thrill rides like the Red Devil roller coaster, gunfights and a country music show. Food is available. Daily 9:30-6, May-Oct. Admission $17.45; ages 3-9, $12.45. AE, DS, MC, VI. Phone (704) 926-1140.

MANTEO—
see Outer Banks p. 111.

MARSHALL (E-3) pop. 800, elev. 1,646'

 RECREATIONAL ACTIVITIES
White-water Rafting
* **Nantahala Outdoor Center,** on Lover's Leap Rd., P.O. Box 488, Hot Springs, NC 28743. Daily 9-1:30, Mar. 11-Oct. 31. Phone (704) 622-3535 or (800) 232-7238.

MOORES CREEK NATIONAL BATTLEFIELD (D-6)

Moores Creek National Battlefield lies about 20 miles northwest of Wilmington and 4 miles west of US 421, on SR 210 near the town of Currie. This 87-acre site was the scene of a brief but decisive Revolutionary War battle on Feb. 27, 1776. Victory by the colonists prevented the Loyalists from controlling North Carolina and helped block a British campaign to conquer the southern colonies.

In the visitor center, displays and an audiovisual program depict the battle; two self-guiding trails with interpretive exhibits originate here. Picnic facilities are available. Daily 9-5; closed Jan. 1 and Dec. 25. Free. Phone (910) 283-5591.

MOORESVILLE (B-4) pop. 9,300,
elev. 911'

D.E. TURNER & COMPANY is 3 mi. e. of I-77 exit 36 on SR 150E to SR 152E, then 1 mi. to 111-115 Main St. Built in 1902, this old-fashioned hardware store has such period features as a hand-crank elevator and rolling ladders. The two-story building also contains examples of 19th- and 20th-century tools and materials. Allow 30 minutes minimum. Mon.-Sat. 8-6; closed Jan. 1, July 4, Thanksgiving and Dec. 25. Free. Phone (704) 664-5145.

MORGANTON (B-3) pop. 15,100,
elev. 1,191'

A series of dams on the Catawba River east and west of Morganton impounds a chain of lakes that provides many recreational opportunities. Optimist Park, 12 miles north on SR 181, offers swimming and picnicking. Nearby Lake James has areas for boating and is stocked with bass, walleye and bluegill. Both South Mountains State Park *(see Recreation Chart)* and Tuttle State Forest are nearby.

Burke County Chamber of Commerce: 110 E. Meeting St., P.O. Box 751, Morganton, NC 28655; phone (704) 437-3021.

OLD BURKE COUNTY COURTHOUSE, off I-40 exit 105, then 2 mi. n. on SR 18, was built in 1837. The Heritage Museum has changing exhibits and a replica of a law office such as Sen. Sam Ervin might have used when he practiced law in Morganton. The adjacent Jailhouse Gallery offers art exhibits. Allow 30 minutes minimum. Tues.-Fri. 9-5; closed major holidays and Dec. 26-Jan. 2. Free. Phone (704) 437-4104.

MOUNT AIRY (A-5) pop. 7,200, elev. 1,014'

Although it was not incorporated until 1885, Mount Airy has had a long history. Originally a riverfront settlement dating from before 1750, its identity was that of a quiet small town until the late 19th century. When the railroad brought in manufacturing interests, Mount Airy began to grow. Now an industrialized city and trading center, it has endeavored to retain some of its old small-town atmosphere.

Despite its growth, Mount Airy still gives evidence that it served as the prototype for Mayberry of "The Andy Griffith Show." Griffith grew up in Mount Airy and later incorporated a number of its features into his fictional hometown. Griffith's former home is in the town's historic district, as is the Andy Griffith Playhouse, a former schoolhouse now used as a theater and arts center.

In late September, fans of "The Andy Griffith Show" flock to Mount Airy to celebrate Mayberry Days, and in October, citizens and visitors welcome fall with The Autumn Leaves Festival.

Mount Airy Visitors Center: 615 N. Main St., Mount Airy, NC 27030; phone (910) 789-4636 or (800) 576-0231.

Self-guiding tours: A brochure outlining a self-guiding driving tour of the historic district is available from the visitor center.

MOUNT GILEAD (C-5) pop. 1,300

TOWN CREEK INDIAN MOUND STATE HISTORIC SITE is 5 mi. s.e. between SR 731 and SR 73. This a 53-acre area was an important cultural, religious and political center, thought to have been developed during the 15th century by a Creek-related people. Several pre-Colonial buildings, including two temples and a mortuary, have been reconstructed. The visitor center offers interpretive exhibits, a film and a slide show. Picnic facilities are available.

Allow 1 hour minimum. Mon.-Sat. 9-5, Sun. 1-5, Apr.-Oct.; Tues.-Sat. 10-4, Sun. 1-4, rest of year. Closed major winter holidays. Free. Phone (910) 439-6802.

MURPHY (F-1) pop. 1,600, elev. 1,578'

Murphy was the site of Fort Butler, built by Gen. Winfield Scott during the roundup of the Cherokee Indians 1837-38. A marble shaft marks

the fort's location. Hiwassee Dam and Lake *(see Recreation Chart and the AAA Southeastern CampBook)* are nearby.

Cherokee County Chamber of Commerce: 115 US Hwy. 64 W., Murphy, NC 28906; phone (704) 837-2242.

FIELDS OF THE WOOD, s. on US 64, then 10 mi. n.w. on SR 294, is a biblical theme park. Highlights include a mountainside where the Ten Commandments are written in 6-foot-high letters made of huge white stones. Food is available. Allow 3 hours minimum. Daily 9-5. Free. Phone (704) 494-7855.

NAGS HEAD—
see Outer Banks p. 112.

NANTAHALA NATIONAL FOREST

Elevations in the forest range from 1,200 ft. on the Tusquetee River below the Appalachian Dam to 5,800 ft. at Lone Bald. Refer to AAA maps for additional elevation information.

The mountainous southwestern tip of North Carolina is overspread by the 515,000-acre Nantahala National Forest. Named after the Cherokee word meaning "land of the noonday sun," the Nantahala gives rise to 10 rivers.

Approximately 600 miles of roads and trails, including the Appalachian Trail, thread through the forest's interior. Scenic drives near Andrews pass Nantahala Lake and Wayah Bald; the "Trail of Tears" crosses the Snowbird Mountains from Andrews to Robbinsville. Joyce Kilmer Memorial Forest, named for the author of the poem "Trees," and Slickrock Wilderness also are in Nantahala. Several recreation areas in the vicinity are designated for public use.

Fishing and hunting are permitted; a license is required. Information is available from the district ranger stations at Robbinsville, Murphy, Highlands and Franklin or from the Visitor Information Center at the Forest Supervisor's Office, Federal Building, Post and Otis streets, P.O. Box 2750, Asheville, NC 28802. For points of interest in the forest, *see Cashiers p. 86, Franklin p. 95, Highlands p. 95 and Murphy p. 107; also see Recreation Chart and the AAA Southeastern CampBook.*

NANTAHALA GORGE is just n.e. of Topton on US 19. The gorge is 8 miles long and in places attains a depth of 2,000 feet.

NEW BERN (C-7) pop. 17,400, elev. 18'

Swiss and German colonists settled New Bern in 1710, naming it for Bern, Switzerland. By

1749 the thriving river port had the colony's first printing press; two years later printer James Davis founded the state's first newspaper, the *North Carolina Gazette.* As Colonial capital 1766-76 and state capital 1776-94, New Bern played an active part in the Revolution.

New Bern's streets are lined with historic sites and outstanding examples of American architecture, especially the early 19th-century Federal style.

Craven County Convention and Visitors Bureau: 219 Pollock St., New Bern, NC 28560; phone (919) 637-9400 or (800) 437-5767. *See color ad.*

Self-guiding tours: Free tour maps are available from the convention and visitors bureau.

CHRIST EPISCOPAL CHURCH, Middle and Pollock sts., is the successor to the old "King's Chapel." The present Gothic Revival edifice dates from 1875 and has a silver communion service, Bible and prayer book presented by King George II in 1752. Mon.-Fri. 9-5. Free. Phone (919) 633-2109.

FIREMEN'S MUSEUM, 408 Hancock St., displays firefighting equipment dating from the early 19th century. Exhibits include maps, old photographs, Civil War artifacts and items from Bern, Switzerland. Mon.-Sat. 10-4:30, Sun. 1-5;

closed Jan. 1, Thanksgiving, Dec. 24-26 and 31. Admission $2; ages 7-12, $1. Phone (919) 636-4087.

FIRST PRESBYTERIAN CHURCH, 418 New St., was built in the Federal style 1819-22 and used as a hospital during the Civil War. Mon.-Wed. and Fri. 9-2. Sunday services at 8:30 and 11. Closed major holidays. Free. Phone (919) 637-3270.

SAVE **THE NEW BERN CIVIL WAR MUSEUM,** 301 Metcalf St., houses an extensive collection of Civil War memorabilia. Objects displayed include one of the largest private collections of Civil War arms in the country, uniforms of the Union and Confederate armies and camp furniture.

Allow 30 minutes minimum. Tues.-Sun. 10-4. Admission $2.50; over 55, $2.25; students $1.50. Phone (919) 633-2818.

SAVE ★**TRYON PALACE HISTORIC SITES AND GARDENS,** a state historic site, is at the corner of George and Pollock sts. Colonial capitol of North Carolina, the palace also was the home of Royalist governor William Tryon. When completed in 1770, it was considered the finest government building in Colonial America. In 1798 a disastrous fire claimed all but one wing of the palace. The remaining area has been reconstructed on its original foundation and is furnished with period antiques.

The grounds of the palace are landscaped in the manner of 18th-century English gardens. Such Colonial crafts as weaving, blacksmithing and cooking are demonstrated. During the summer months, historical drama tours enhance the 18th century atmosphere. The Reception Center shows a 14-minute orientation film. Costumed guides conduct tours every half-hour.

Allow 1 hour, 30 minutes minimum. Mon.-Sat. 9-4, Sun. 1-4; closed Jan. 1, Thanksgiving and Dec. 24-26. Admission (including New Bern Academy Museum) $12; students grades 1-12, $6. Phone (919) 514-4900 or (800) 514-4900. *See color ad p. 108.*

Dixon-Stevenson House, 619 Pollock St., was built about 1828. Antiques from the Federal and Empire periods decorate the interior.

Gardens of the Tryon Palace Complex can be viewed on a self-guiding tour.

John Wright Stanly House, a town house built around 1783, is at 307 George St. Furnishings and the garden are of period design.

New Bern Academy Museum, 508 New St., is housed in an 1809 brick building that was used as a school until 1971. One room contains exhibits pertaining to education and the history of the academy. Other areas of the museum incorporate displays describing the Algonquin people who lived in the area, the German and Swiss settlers who arrived in 1710, the Civil War and the architectural history of New Bern.

Allow 1 hour minimum. Mon.-Sat. 11-5, Sun. 1-5, Jan. 2-Dec. 9; closed Jan. 1, Thanksgiving and Dec. 25. Admission $3; grades 1-12, $1. Phone (919) 514-4874.

NEW HOLLAND (C-8)

MATTAMUSKEET NATIONAL WILDLIFE REFUGE is entered on SR 94, 1 mi. n. of US 264. Covering approximately 50,000 acres and most of Lake Mattamuskeet, the refuge is a wintering area for migratory waterfowl. Within its boundaries is Salyer's Ridge Natural Area, where a mature loblolly pine forest is in the late stage of succession, transforming into a sweetgum and red maple forest. Fishing, best in the spring and fall, is permitted March through October. Daily dawn-dusk. Free. Phone (919) 926-6751.

NEWTON (B-4)

CATAWBA COUNTY MUSEUM OF HISTORY, housed downtown in the former 1924 courthouse, chronicles the development of Catawba Valley. Highlights include agricultural tools; hand-crafted household items; treasured military uniforms, including a 1770s British officer's red coat and silver sword from the Revolutionary War; hand-stitched quilts and clothing; and examples of the furniture, agricultural and textile industries found in the area.

Other exhibits include a 1930 race car, antique medical instruments and Civil War memorabilia. Allow 1 hour minimum. Tues.-Fri. 9-4, Sun. 2-5; closed major holidays. Donations. Phone (704) 465-0383.

NEWTON GROVE (C-7) pop. 500, elev. 155′

BENTONVILLE BATTLEGROUND STATE HISTORIC SITE is 2.5 mi. e. off US 701. The largest land engagement in North Carolina, one of the last conflicts of the Civil War was fought on this site March 19-21, 1865. The Harper House was used as a hospital by both Union and Confederate troops during the war, and is furnished as a Civil War field hospital.

The visitor center offers exhibits and a slide presentation. Battle trenches, a cemetery and a history trail with exhibits also are on the grounds. Allow 1 hour minimum. Mon.-Sat. 9-5, Sun. 1-5, Apr.-Oct.; Tues.-Sat. 10-4, Sun. 1-4, rest of year. Closed Jan. 1, Martin Luther King Jr.'s Birthday, Thanksgiving and Dec. 24-25. Free. Phone (910) 594-0789.

OCRACOKE—

see Outer Banks p. 112.

Outer Banks

The Outer Banks consist of a string of narrow islands and peninsulas that lie between the ocean and the sounds along 125 miles of North Carolina's coast. Through years of storms and shipwrecks, the islands have developed a distinctive culture. Certain areas are resorts, while others retain a relatively primitive charm. Residents closely identified with maritime activity have kept the speech patterns and customs handed down from the 17th century.

The area is rich in history. The first English colony was established on Roanoke Island in 1585. At Kill Devil Hills in 1903, Wilbur and Orville Wright successfully launched the first flight of a power-driven airplane.

The lands of the Outer Banks are constantly shifted by wind and wave action. Some believe the landmass is moving slowly toward the mainland; inlets connecting the ocean and sounds have a lifetime of less than 100 years. The result of storms, they regularly appear and disappear.

Outer Banks Chamber of Commerce: Ocean Bay Boulevard at Mustian Street, P.O. Box 1757, Kill Devil Hills, NC 27948; phone (919) 441-8144.

Cape Hatteras Lighthouse/
North Carolina Travel & Tourism

★CAPE HATTERAS NATIONAL SEASHORE (C-9)

Covering approximately 45 square miles on North Carolina's Outer Banks, Cape Hatteras National Seashore is the most extensive stretch of undeveloped seashore on the Atlantic Coast. Except for a few villages on the islands, the national recreation area includes Ocracoke and Hatteras islands and part of Bodie (Body) Island. The islands are connected by a free bridge and a free ferry.

Vast expanses of sand and water are the main attractions in this area of wild beauty. Bottlenose dolphin sometimes are seen near the beach. The sand is treacherous for motorists; visitors should park in designated areas and only leave the road where indicated.

The lands are public property and residents and visitors have free access to the ocean. State and federal fishing regulations apply to waters inside and outside the boundaries. Regulated waterfowl hunting is permitted within the seashore, excluding Pea Island National Wildlife Refuge.

Day-use facilities are at Coquina Beach, Cape Point and Ocracoke.

The Bodie Island Visitor Center, south on SR 12, provides brochures and a schedule of activities. It is open daily 9-5, Memorial Day-Labor Day; closed Dec. 25. For further information contact Park Headquarters, Rt. 1, Box 675, Manteo, NC 27954; phone (919) 473-2111 or (919) 441-5711. *See Recreation Chart and the AAA Southeastern CampBook.*

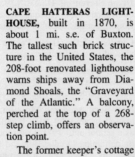

CAPE HATTERAS LIGHTHOUSE, built in 1870, is about 1 mi. s.e. of Buxton. The tallest such brick structure in the United States, the 208-foot renovated lighthouse warns ships away from Diamond Shoals, the "Graveyard of the Atlantic." A balcony, perched at the top of a 268-step climb, offers an observation point.

The former keeper's cottage contains a visitor center and exhibits about area history. Visitor programs are held throughout the summer. A self-guiding nature trail begins near the lighthouse. Allow 30 minutes minimum. Lighthouse open daily 10-4, June-Sept.; 10-2 Apr.-May and in Sept. (weather permitting). Visitor center open daily 9-5; closed Dec. 25. Free. Phone (919) 995-4474.

PEA ISLAND NATIONAL WILDLIFE REFUGE covers approximately 5,880 acres just s. of Oregon Inlet on Hatteras Island. Birds include more than 250 species of local and migratory fowl. Observation decks, about 5 miles south of the Oregon Inlet bridge, permit views of the ocean, wildlife and shipwrecks along the shore. Daily dawn-dusk; information office open Mon.-Fri. 9-4, Apr.-Oct. Free. Phone (919) 987-2394 or 473-1131.

CAPE LOOKOUT NATIONAL SEASHORE

Extending 55 miles along North Carolina's Outer Banks from Ocracoke Inlet in the north to Beaufort Inlet in the south, Cape Lookout National Seashore includes Portsmouth Island, Core Banks and Shackleford Banks. Approximately 28,500 acres of undeveloped barrier islands lie within the national seashore.

Cape Lookout is reached only by boat, and on-island transportation is limited. Passenger and vehicle ferries leave regularly from Harkers Island, Atlantic and Davis; service is generally not available in winter. Charter service to Portsmouth can be obtained from Ocracoke. Rates for round-trip service to the park start at approximately $12 per person, $60-$80 per vehicle.

Popular recreational activities are seashell collecting and surf fishing. Interpretive programs are held in the summer. On Portsmouth Island a historic village is being restored and is open to visitors, and an 1859 lighthouse near Cape Lookout Point is operational. Rustic cabins are available for rent March through November.

A visitor information station at Harkers Island, near the east end of Harkers Island Rd., is open daily 8-4:30; closed Jan. 1 and Dec. 25. For information contact the Superintendent, Cape Lookout National Seashore, 131 Charles St., Harkers Island, NC 28531; phone (919) 728-2250. *See Recreation Chart.*

FORT RALEIGH NATIONAL HISTORIC SITE (B-9)

Covering 143 acres, Fort Raleigh National Historic Site is on Roanoke Island about 3 miles north of Manteo. In 1585 men sent to Roanoke Island by Sir Walter Raleigh attempted the first English colony in what is now the eastern United States. Fort Raleigh was built, but the following year the survivors returned to England.

In 1587 Raleigh dispatched another expedition that included women and children to give permanence to the colony. Led by John White, these settlers rebuilt the fort. On Aug. 18, 1587, White's granddaughter, Virginia Dare, was born in the colony. She was the first English child born in the New World.

Several days later White sailed back to England for provisions, but because of Spanish hostilities was unable to return until 1590. He found no trace of the colonists. Many theories about the fate of the "Lost Colony" have been proposed, but the mystery remains unsolved.

Earthworks representing those that probably were part of the original fort have been reconstructed. A simple granite stone commemorates the birth of Virginia Dare.

★**ELIZABETHAN GARDENS,** reached by the park road into the fort, is a memorial to the first English colonists in America. This re-created, 16th-century formal English garden has antique statuary, period furniture and rose and herb beds in addition to indigenous flowers, shrubs and trees. Allow 1 hour minimum. Daily 9-8, June-Aug.; 9-7, in May and Sept.; 9-6, in Apr. and Oct.; 9-5, in Mar. and Nov. Admission $3; ages 12-17, $1. Phone (919) 473-3234.

THE LINDSAY WARREN VISITOR CENTER, within Fort Raleigh, displays books, charts, pictures, American Indian artifacts and relics from the period of the first colony. A 17-minute film about the English attempt to settle in the New World is shown on the hour in the summer, on

the half-hour off-season. Interpretive programs are held during summer. Allow 30 minutes minimum. Mon.-Fri. 9-6, Sat. 9-5, Sun. 9-8, mid-June through Labor Day; daily 9-5, rest of year. Closed Dec. 25. Free. Phone (919) 473-5772.

★ **"THE LOST COLONY"** is presented in the Waterside Theater, 3 mi. n.w. of Manteo on Roanoke Island via US 64/264. This symphonic outdoor drama is performed Sun.-Fri. at 8:30 p.m., mid-June to late Aug. All seats are reserved. Inquire about weather policies. Tickets $14; senior citizens and active duty military with ID $13; under 12, $7 ($3 on Mon. if with parent). Write to 1409 US 64/264, Manteo, NC 27954; phone (919) 473-3414 or (800) 488-5012.

FRISCO (C-9) pop. 600

FRISCO NATIVE AMERICAN MUSEUM & NATURAL HISTORY CENTER, on SR 12, showcases the history and culture of American Indian tribes. Beadwork, pottery, basketry, Navajo weaving, stone tools and peace pipes are among the items displayed. Highlights include an exhibit featuring the Indians who inhabited Hatteras Island, a Hopi wishing drum and a 10-foot-long dugout canoe. A self-guiding nature trail points out many species of Outer Banks vegetation and wildlife.

Allow 30 minutes minimum. Tues.-Sun. 11-5; closed Thanksgiving and Dec. 25. Donations. Phone (919) 995-4440.

MANTEO (B-9) pop. 1,000

On historic Roanoke Island, Manteo is reached by causeway from the east or west. In 1585 the English tried to establish their first New World colony at Roanoke Island *(see Fort Raleigh National Historic Site p. 111).* Nearby, Gen. Ambrose E. Burnside's Union forces won the Battle of Roanoke Island in 1862. In 1902 the island and Hatteras were the scenes of Reginald A. Fessenden's experiments in wireless telegraphy.

ELIZABETH II **STATE HISTORIC SITE,** across from Manteo's waterfront, is a reproduction of the type of vessel used in Sir Walter Raleigh's Roanoke voyages more than 400 years ago. Interpreters in Elizabethan costume explain the parts of the ship and the lifestyles of those who sailed in such vessels. A visitor center has exhibits in addition to a film about the Roanoke voyages.

Allow 1 hour minimum. Daily 9-7, July-Aug.; 10-6, in May; 10-5, in April; 10-4, in March. Last tour begins 1 hour before closing. Closed Thanksgiving and Dec. 25. Admission $4; students with ID and ages 6-12, $1.50. Phone (919) 473-1144.

★ **"THE LOST COLONY"—**
see Fort Raleigh National Historic Site p. 111.

NORTH CAROLINA AQUARIUM/ROANOKE ISLAND, 3 mi. n. on SR 1116, displays live fish, turtles and other sea animals indigenous to North

Carolina, as well as exhibits about whales, sharks and seabirds. A touch table has starfish, sea urchins, crabs and other small sea creatures; a turtle pond is in the courtyard. A research library also is on the grounds. Mon.-Sat. 9-5, Sun. 1-5; closed Thanksgiving and Dec. 25. Admission $3; senior citizens and active duty military with ID $2; ages 6-17, $1. Phone (919) 473-3493.

NAGS HEAD (B-9) pop. 1,800

An oceanfront resort on the Outer Banks, Nags Head is a hotel and cottage colony. Facilities are excellent for swimming and fishing. According to local legend, the village of Nags Head acquired its name from the islanders' practice of tying lanterns to the necks of ponies and marching them along the dunes at night. The swinging lights simulated anchored boats, thus deceiving ship captains into running aground, where their cargo was seized.

JOCKEY'S RIDGE STATE PARK, off US 158 bypass, contains two of the highest sand dunes on the East Coast. More than 100 feet high, Jockey's Ridge and Engagement Hill are popular takeoff points for hang gliders. Hang gliding permits can be obtained at the park office. Allow 1 hour minimum. Daily 8 a.m.-9 p.m., June-Aug.; 8-8, Apr.-May and in Sept.; 8-7, in Mar. and Oct.; 8-6, rest of year. Free. Phone (919) 441-7132.

OCRACOKE (C-9)

On Ocracoke (OHK-ruh-coke) Island, the fishing village of Ocracoke is adjacent to Cape Hatteras National Seashore on the Outer Banks. Built mainly around Silver Lake, the houses are laid out with Old World irregularity along sandy streets overhung with moss-covered oaks and yaupon. Ocracoke is said to have been a hangout of Edward Teach, alias Blackbeard; the notorious pirate and his crew were killed at Teach's Hole in 1718.

Ocracoke Island is noted for fishing and bird hunting. Bicycle rentals are available in town. The island is reached by a free ferry on scenic SR 12 from Hatteras and by a toll ferry from Cedar Island and Swan Quarter.

Ocracoke Island Visitor Center: Cape Hatteras National Seashore, Ocracoke, NC 27960; phone (919) 928-4531.

Note: Reservations are necessary for the ferries and can be made within 30 days of departure date. Apply in person at the terminal or phone (919) 225-3551 Cedar Island, (919) 928-3841 Ocracoke or (919) 926-1111 Swan Quarter.

★WRIGHT BROTHERS NATIONAL MEMORIAL (B-9)

This 431-acre area on the Outer Banks is on the US 158 bypass, at Milepost 8 in Kill Devil Hills. The Wright Memorial Shaft was dedicated in November 1932 to Orville and Wilbur Wright "in commemoration of the conquest of the air." The first sustained flights by a heavier-than-air powered machine were made nearby on Dec. 17, 1903.

The visitor center exhibits include reproductions of the 1902 glider and 1903 flyer. The grounds have markers showing the distance traveled during the first four flights as well as replicas of the Wright brothers' workshop and living quarters. Allow 1 hour minimum. Daily 9-5; 9-6 in summer. Closed Dec. 25. Admission $2, under 16 free, $4 per automobile. Phone (919) 441-7430.

PEMBROKE (C-6) pop. 2,200, elev. 169'

Pembroke is the center for the approximately 40,000 Lumbee Indians who live in Robeson County. It is theorized that some of these people are descendants of the "Lost Colony." The Lumbee Indians were initially denied full U.S. citizenship, but their protests during the Civil War and the persistence of their leader Henry Berry Lowrie eventually convinced the North Carolina Legislature to extend voting rights to include them.

Pembroke also is the home of Pembroke State University, a constituent institution of the University of North Carolina. The Givens Performing Arts Center, on campus, features various performances September through May; phone (910) 521-6287.

Pembroke Chamber of Commerce: P.O. Box 1978, Pembroke, NC 28372; phone (910) 521-0647.

PINEHURST (C-5) pop. 5,100, elev. 550'

A mild climate and low humidity helped Pinehurst develop into a year-round resort community. The village's New England-style parks and roadways were laid out by Frederick Law Olmsted, designer of New York's Central Park and Asheville's Biltmore Gardens. Handsome estates and other residences, many of Georgian Colonial design, are found throughout the village.

The Pinehurst area is noted for its more than 41 championship golf courses. Tennis competitions are occasionally held in the town. Carriage rides throughout the village are available.

Pinehurst Area Convention and Visitors Bureau: P.O. Box 2270, Southern Pines, NC 28388; phone (800) 346-5362.

PINEVILLE (C-4) pop. 3,000

JAMES K. POLK MEMORIAL STATE HISTORIC SITE, .5 mi. s. on US 521, preserves the birthplace and childhood house of James K. Polk, 11th president of the United States. A 25-minute movie in the museum and displays in the visitor center depict his life. Guided tours of the restored houses are offered. Picnic facilities are available. Allow 1 hour minimum. Mon.-Sat. 9-5, Sun. 1-5, Apr.-Oct.; Tues.-Sat. 10-4, Sun. 1-4, rest of year. Closed Thanksgiving and Dec. 25. Free. Phone (704) 889-7145.

★PISGAH NATIONAL FOREST

Elevations within the boundaries of the forest range from 1,200 ft. at Mulberry Creek to 6,285 ft. at Roan Mountain. Refer to AAA maps for additional elevation information.

Covering 495,000 acres of the Appalachians in western North Carolina are the two segments of Pisgah National Forest. The two main mountain chains and several lesser ranges encompassed by the forest have twenty 6,000-foot peaks, including 6,684-foot Mount Mitchell, highest summit east of the Mississippi River. Mount Mitchell is in a 1,677-acre state park *(see Recreation Chart)* surrounded by the forest and is next to the Blue Ridge Parkway.

A network of roads and miles of trails interlace the forest. Part of the Appalachian Trail winds along the northwestern boundary. US 276, which runs for 37 miles between Brevard and Waynesville, is part of the Forest Heritage National Scenic Byway and affords access to various points of interest.

District rangers are stationed at Marion, Burnsville, Pisgah Forest and Hot Springs. Pisgah headquarters is open Mon.-Fri. 8-4:30 (also Sat.-Sun. 9-5:30, Apr.-Oct.). Information can be obtained at these stations or from the Visitor Information Center at the Forest Supervisor's Office, Federal Building, Post and Otis streets, P.O. Box 2750, Asheville, NC 28802.

Other points of interest within the forest are listed under Asheville, Brevard, Hot Springs, Linville, Linville Falls and Waynesville. *See Recreation Chart and the AAA Southeastern CampBook.*

CRADLE OF FORESTRY IN AMERICA NATIONAL HISTORIC SITE is 14 mi. n. of Brevard via US 276. Two interpretive trails detail the history of forestry in the United States, as well as the history of one of the first schools of forestry. A logging locomotive is displayed on one of the trails. Special events are scheduled throughout the season. Visitor center daily 9-5, Apr. 19-Nov. 2. Admission $4; senior citizens and ages 6-17, $2. Phone (704) 877-3130.

LOOKING GLASS ROCK AND LOOKING GLASS FALLS are 8 mi. n.w. of Brevard via US 276, or 6 mi. from the south park entrance. The rock is believed to be the largest granite monolith in the southern Appalachians.

PISGAH FOREST FISH HATCHERY, on a forest service road 8 mi. n. of Brevard via US 276, is open daily 8-4. Free. Phone (704) 877-3121.

WAGON ROAD GAP, atop the Pisgah ledge, is 20 mi. s.e. of Brevard via US 276, halfway between Waynesville and Brevard. The gap, intersecting US 276 at Milepost 411 on the Blue Ridge Parkway, affords a fine view of the surrounding area.

PLYMOUTH (B-8) pop. 4,300, elev. 6'

PORT O' PLYMOUTH ROANOKE RIVER MUSEUM is n. on Washington St. at 302 Water St. Once a railroad depot, the museum houses memorabilia relating to the Civil War Battle of Plymouth. Photographs, a complete list of Union troops who were stationed in Plymouth, a 1790 loom and a 3,000-year-old American Indian canoe are on display. Especially notable is a weapon collection that includes derringers, a keg torpedo, period rifles and a swivel cannon purchased in Austria by Benjamin Franklin.

During the third weekend in April the museum holds a living-history reenactment of the Battle of Plymouth. Tues.-Sat. 8-5; closed holidays. Admission $1; ages 6-18, 50c. Phone (919) 793-1377.

RALEIGH (B-6) pop. 208,000, elev. 352'

See map page 114.

Founded in 1792 and named for Sir Walter Raleigh, the city was planned as the "unalterable seat of government" for North Carolina. Known as the "City of Oaks," Raleigh was established on land purchased specifically by the state to be used as the state's capital. Laid out in a square grid pattern, the capital city's expansion has slightly deviated from the original plans.

Preservation abounds in Raleigh as the citizens are dedicated to conserving the natural areas found throughout the community. In 1974 a system of public recreational trails was created, including 22 trails covering 34 miles. In 1975, Raleigh was named the first "Green Survival City" in the country.

Raleigh also is known as a cultural and educational center. The Research Triangle area is 15 miles west via I-40 *(see Durham p. 92).*

Pullen Park, next to the North Carolina State University campus via Western Boulevard, has attractions of interest to children, including a 1911 Dentzel carrousel; phone (919) 831-6468.

Raleigh is the site of an International Festival the first full weekend in October. The celebration features food booths, storytelling and cultural exhibits; phone (919) 832-4331.

Greater Raleigh Convention and Visitors Bureau: 225 Hillsborough St., Suite 400, Raleigh, NC 27602-1879; phone (919) 834-5900 or (800) 849-8499. *See ad p. 115.*

Self-guiding tours: An orientation slide program about Raleigh and maps for self-guiding tours that pass the executive mansion and go through the Capitol, the legislative building and the Victorian-style neighborhood of Oakwood are available at the Capital Area Visitor Center in the Andrews-London House at 301 N. Blount St., Raleigh, NC 27601. The center is open Mon.-Fri. 8-5, Sat. and holidays 9-5, Sun. 1-5; closed Jan. 1, Thanksgiving and Dec. 24-25. Phone (919) 733-3456.

Shopping areas: Cary Towne Center, I-40 exit 291, offers 130 stores as well as Dillard's,

Hecht's, Hudson Belk, JCPenney and Sears. Crabtree Valley Mall, SR 70, features more than 200 shops and eateries.

JOEL LANE HOUSE, 728 W. Hargett St., is one of the oldest houses in Raleigh. Built in the 1760s, it has been painstakingly restored and furnished with 18th-century antiques. Col. Joel Lane was a prominent statesman who played an active role in the affairs of first the colony and then the state of North Carolina. His house

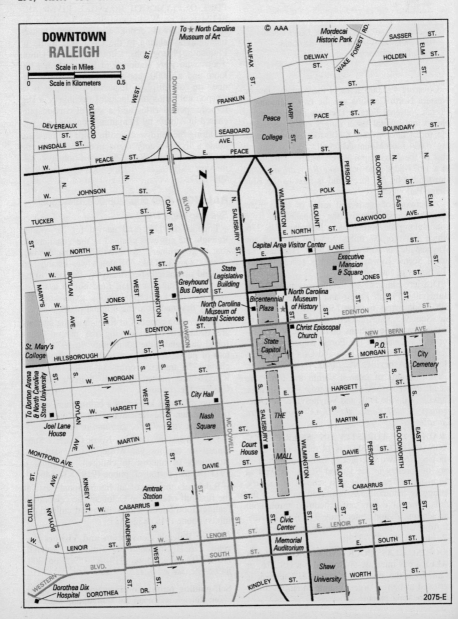

DOWNTOWN RALEIGH

served as the site of many historically significant meetings including the state legislature's selection of Raleigh as the state capital. An 18th-century formal city garden and herb garden are on the grounds. Allow 1 hour minimum. Tues. and Thurs.-Fri. 10-2, Mar. 2-Dec. 19; closed holidays. Free. Phone (919) 833-3431.

J.S. DORTON ARENA, w. at the State Fairgrounds, holds state fairs and concerts and is the home of the Raleigh Ice Caps hockey team. Its roof is suspended from 90-foot parabolic arches and the walls are glass. Allow 30 minutes minimum. Mon.-Fri. 8-5, unless in use. Free. Phone (919) 733-2626.

SAVE **MORDECAI HISTORIC PARK,** n. on Person St. to jct. Wake Forest Rd. and Mimosa St., contains the 1785 plantation house of the Lane and Mordecai families. The house contains original furnishings, portraits and books. A kitchen separate from the house was built in 1842. Also in the park are the relocated 1795 house in which Andrew Johnson, the 17th president of the United States, was born; the Early Raleigh Office Building, thought to have been used in the mid-19th century as Raleigh's post office; an 1810 law office; and the 1847 St. Mark's Chapel.

Allow 1 hour minimum. Guided tours depart every 30 minutes. Wed.-Sat. and Mon. 10-3, Sun. 1-3. Last tour begins 30 minutes before closing.

Closed Jan. 1, Thanksgiving and Dec. 24-25 and 31. Admission $4. Phone (919) 834-4844.

★**NORTH CAROLINA MUSEUM OF ART,** off I-40 Wade Ave. exit following signs to 2110 Blue Ridge Rd., is in a large building designed by Edward Durrell Stone, architect of the John F. Kennedy Center for Performing Arts in Washington, D.C. Works of art are displayed in historical sequence through eight major collections: Ancient, European, American, 20th-Century, Jewish ceremonial art, African, Oceanic and New World.

Representing eight schools and 5 centuries of Western art, the paintings include works by Thomas Hart Benton, Sandro Botticelli, John Singleton Copley, Claude Monet, Georgia O'Keeffe, Raphael, Peter Paul Rubens, Anthony Van Dyck, Andrew Wyeth and Winslow Homer. The Ancient Collection contains art from Egypt, Greece and Rome; the New World Collection displays pre-Columbian works from North and Central America.

Changing exhibits also are presented. The Education Department presents films, concerts and lectures; docents conduct tours at 1:30. Food is available. Allow 1 hour, 30 minutes minimum. Museum open Tues.-Sat. 9-5 (also Fri. 5-9), Sun. 11-6. Guided tours daily at 1:30. Closed Jan. 1, July 4, Thanksgiving and Dec. 25. Free. Phone (919) 839-6262.

★NORTH CAROLINA MUSEUM OF HISTORY is at 5 E. Edenton St. Exhibits depict North Carolina history from pre-Colonial to the present with emphasis on sports, folk life and women's history. Objects on display include period clothing and furnishings, Civil War weapons and flags, a replica of Orville and Wilbur Wright's airplane and one of Richard Petty's racing cars. Allow 1 hour minimum. Tues.-Sat. 9-5, Sun. noon-5; closed holidays. Free. Phone (919) 715-0200.

NORTH CAROLINA STATE MUSEUM OF NATURAL SCIENCES, 102 N. Salisbury St. in Bicentennial Plaza, features living animals, specimens, videotaped presentations and interactive exhibits illustrating the state's biological diversity. Other highlights include the skeletons of four whales as well as the Fossil Lab, Discovery Room and Freshwater Wetlands exhibits. Allow 1 hour minimum. Mon.-Sat. 9-5, Sun. 1-5; closed holidays. Free. Phone (919) 733-7450.

NORTH CAROLINA STATE UNIVERSITY ARBORETUM is off the Hillsborough St. exit of the US 440 beltline at 4301 Beryl Rd. More than 5,000 kinds of plants are in this 8-acre horticultural park. Some highlights are the Japanese Garden, the Rose Garden, the White Garden and the Perennial Border. Allow 1 hour minimum. Daily 8-dusk. Free. Phone (919) 515-7641.

STATE CAPITOL, on Capitol Sq., is a restored neoclassic structure built 1833-40. Reservations are required for guided tours. Allow 30 minutes minimum. Mon.-Fri. 8-5, Sat. 9-5, Sun. 1-5; closed Jan. 1, Thanksgiving and Dec. 25. Free. Phone (919) 733-4994 or 733-3456.

STATE LEGISLATIVE BUILDING, 16 W. Jones St., is a colonnaded, marble-faced building rising from a 340-foot-wide podium of North Carolina granite. In front of the main entrance a 28-foot-diameter terrazzo mosaic of the Great Seal of the State of North Carolina is set in the podium. Interior garden courts and roof gardens complement the dramatic architecture. Allow 30 minutes minimum. Mon.-Fri. 8-5, Sat. 9-5, Sun. 1-5; closed Jan. 1, Thanksgiving and Dec. 25. Free. Phone (919) 733-7928.

REIDSVILLE (A-5) pop. 12,200, elev. 822'

An industrial city, Reidsville has a tobacco market in operation August through November. Three tobacco warehouses hold sales Monday through Thursday from 9 a.m. to mid-afternoon. Penn House, a historical house at 324 Maple Ave., contains a tobacco museum.

Reidsville Chamber of Commerce: 321 S.E. Market St., Reidsville, NC 27323; phone (910) 349-8481.

Self-guiding tours: A brochure outlining a driving tour to several historic houses and buildings in Reidsville is available at the chamber of commerce.

[SAVE] **★CHINQUA-PENN PLANTATION,** 2138 Wentworth St., is a 27-room country manor built in 1925 by Thomas Jefferson Penn and his wife Beatrice. The mansion is filled with the art, artifacts and religious objects that the couple collected on their journeys around the world. Items on display include tapestries, Egyptian winged-phoenix furnishings, Chinese terra cotta sculpture and altarpieces from Nepal. The grounds comprise 22 acres of gardens and lawns with goldfish pools, greenhouses and a replica of a Chinese pagoda.

Allow 2 hours minimum. Tues.-Sat. 9-5, Sun. noon-5, Mar.-Dec.; closed Thanksgiving and Dec. 25. Last admission 45 minutes before closing. Admission $10; over 62, $9; under 6 free. MC, VI. Phone (910) 349-4576. *See color ad.*

ROANOKE ISLAND—

see Manteo and Fort Raleigh National Historic Site in Outer Banks p. 111.

ROCKY MOUNT (B-7) pop. 49,000

In the coastal plain of North Carolina, Rocky Mount was named for a large granite outcropping at the Falls of the Tar River; the Tar River Reservoir offers boating, water skiing, fishing, swimming and picnicking *(see Recreation Chart).* The Down East Festival of the Arts, held in early October, is a celebration of music, food and arts and crafts.

Rocky Mount Area Chamber of Commerce: P.O. Box 392, Rocky Mount, NC 27802; phone (919) 442-5111. *See color ad p. 411.*

CITY OF ROCKY MOUNT CHILDREN'S MUSEUM is at 1610 Gay St. Live animals on display include alligators, snakes and ferrets. Environmental dioramas show regional habitats such as swamps and woodlands. Other exhibits include Tuscarora Indians, Thomas Edison, a Living Marsh and Health Awareness. The Civitan Planetarium has shows about the solar system, the stars and the universe. Picnicking is permitted in a nearby park. Allow 30 minutes minimum. Mon.-Fri. 10-5, Sat. noon-5, Sun. 2-5, holidays noon-4; closed Thanksgiving and Dec. 25. Free. Phone (919) 972-1167.

SALISBURY (B-4) pop. 23,100, elev. 764'

Founded in 1753, Salisbury (SAULS-bur-y) was settled by Scot-Irish and German immigrants. It quickly became a trading, cultural and judicial center because of its location at the junction of two much-traveled routes. At different times during 1781 the city served as headquarters for the British general Lord Charles Cornwallis and Patriot general Nathanael Greene.

Salisbury had one of the largest prison camps maintained by Confederate forces. About 5,000 Union soldiers died there and are buried in a national cemetery nearby, at 202 Government Rd. A highlight of the historic district is the Dr. Josephus Hall House, the home of the surgeon for the prison. Other historic structures are the Thyatira Church, Grimes Mill and the Old Stone House.

Rowan County Convention and Visitors Bureau: 132 E. Innis St., P.O. Box 4044, Salisbury, NC 28145-4044; phone (704) 638-3100 or (800) 332-2343.

Self-guiding tours: Maps and brochures of Salisbury's historic district are available at the Rowan County Visitor Information Center. The center is in the restored Salisbury Railroad Depot, 1 mile west off I-85 exit 76B following signs to 215 Depot St.; phone (800) 332-2343.

A driving-tour audiotape of the Salisbury Confederate Prison Site and National Cemetery as well as a walking-tour tape about the Salisbury historic district are available at the visitor center. The center is open Mon.-Fri. 9-5, Sat. 10-4, Sun. 1-4; closed Jan. 1, Easter, Thanksgiving and Dec. 24-25. For further information contact the convention and visitors bureau.

ROWAN MUSEUM is at 116 S. Jackson St. Displays in this 1819 house include Federal-period furnishings, Civil War relics, 19th-century tools and documents about local history. Thurs.-Sun. 2-5. Admission $3, students with ID $1. Phone (704) 633-5946.

SALUDA (F-3) pop. 500, elev. 209'

PEARSON'S FALLS, 4 mi. n.w. via US 176, offers paths bordered by native plants. The focal point of this lush, natural area is a 90-foot waterfall. Picnic facilities are available. No pets are allowed. Tues.-Sun. 10-6, Mar.-Oct.; Wed.-Sun. 10-5, rest of year. Admission $2; ages 6-12, 50c. Phone (704) 749-3031.

SANFORD (C-6) pop. 18,000, elev. 368'

HOUSE IN THE HORSESHOE is 12 mi. w. on SR 42, then 4 mi. s. on SR 2307 following signs. Built in 1772 on a horseshoe bend of the Deep River, this two-story frame plantation house still bears the scars and bullet holes from a Revolutionary War skirmish. Benjamin Williams, a four-term governor of North Carolina, acquired the house in 1798 and died on the plantation in 1814. The interior is furnished with period antiques and is distinguished by elaborate woodwork.

Allow 30 minutes minimum. Mon.-Sat. 9-5, Sun. 1-5, Apr.-Oct.; Tues.-Sat. 10-4, Sun. 1-4, rest of year. Closed Good Friday, Veterans Day, Thanksgiving, day after Thanksgiving and Dec. 24-26. Free. Phone (910) 947-2051.

SEAGROVE (B-5) pop. 200

The English settlers who moved to Seagrove in the 18th century were potters by trade and were attracted to the area by the abundance of surface clay. Although pottery was produced in Seagrove at least as early as 1750, the craft was adopted by the citizens in earnest during Reconstruction when farmers, who could not market their crops, began marketing whiskey jugs.

Prohibition and the advent of mass-manufactured utensils in the early 1900s greatly reduced the demand for the Seagrove potters' handiwork. Renewed interest in decorative and functional pottery developed during the 1920s. The tradition continues, with more than 40 descendants from generations of potters practicing their craft in Seagrove.

SEDALIA (B-5)

CHARLOTTE HAWKINS BROWN MEMORIAL STATE HISTORIC SITE is 1 mi. off I-85 exit 135 following signs. This is the site of the former Palmer Memorial Institute, a boarding school for blacks, founded by Dr. Brown in 1902. Exhibits and audiovisual presentations document the school's history and Dr. Brown's contribution to black education.

Allow 1 hour, 30 minutes minimum. Mon.-Sat. 9-5, Sun. 1-5, Apr.-Oct.; Tues.-Sat. 10-4, Sun. 1-4, rest of year. Closed holidays. Free. Phone (910) 449-4846.

SMITHFIELD (C-6) pop. 7,500, elev. 153'

AVA GARDNER MUSEUM is off I-95 exit 95, w. on US 70-Business, s. on Fourth St., w. on Johnston St., then s. to 205 S. Third St. Features include childhood memorabilia, film clips and costumes, posters, photographs, large oil portraits, film scripts, magazine covers and other items related to the movie star, who was born and raised in the area. Allow 1 hour minimum. Daily 1-5. Admission $2. Phone (919) 934-5830 or 934-0887.

SOUTHERN PINES (C-6) pop. 9,100, elev. 550'

An all-year resort area in the sandhills region, Southern Pines is known for its dry air, mild winters, outstanding golf courses, numerous equestrian activities and beautiful pine trees. Several professional golf tournaments are played in the area. Other popular sports are bicycling, hunting and tennis.

Pinehurst Area Convention and Visitors Bureau: P.O. Box 2270, Southern Pines, NC 28388; phone (800) 346-5362.

WEYMOUTH WOODS SANDHILLS NATURE PRESERVE, from US 1 take Saunders Rd. 1.2 mi. e., then 1.5 mi. n.e. to 1024 Ft. Bragg Rd. The 525-acre preserve contains hiking trails, a museum relating the evolution of pine trees, ponds and soil indigenous to the area, and a sound-activated "night sounds" display highlighting various animals of the sandhills region. Allow 30 minutes minimum. Mon.-Sat. 9-6, Sun. noon-5; closed Dec. 25. Free. Phone (910) 692-2167. *See Recreation Chart.*

SOUTHPORT (E-7) pop. 2,400

Midway between New York and Miami on the Intracoastal Waterway, Southport's yacht harbor is a popular stopping point for boat traffic. The city also boasts both freshwater and saltwater fishing. Charter boats for deep-sea excursions are plentiful, and several piers accommodate the land-bound angler.

The city's position on a bluff at the mouth of the Cape Fear River made it a strategic location for Fort Johnston, built in 1764, the state's first fort. Today the fort, which was rebuilt after being destroyed by fire in 1775, is occupied by the Commanding Officer of the Sunny Point Military Ocean Terminal.

Southport/Oak Island Chamber of Commerce: 4848 Longbeach Rd. S.E., Southport, NC 28461; phone (919) 457-5787.

CP&L BRUNSWICK VISITORS CENTER, 2 mi. n. on SR 87, contains more than 30 displays on energy. Topics include electricity production, energy conservation and nuclear power. Films and videotapes on energy-related subjects are shown. Picnicking is permitted. Allow 30 minutes minimum. Tues.-Thurs. 9-4; closed holidays. Free. Phone (910) 457-6041.

SPENCER (B-4) pop. 3,200, elev. 760'

NORTH CAROLINA TRANSPORTATION MUSEUM AT HISTORIC SPENCER SHOPS, off I-85 exit 79 at 411 S. Salisbury St., traces the history of transportation in North Carolina. The complex, once Southern Railway's primary staging and repair facility, includes the massive Back Shop, the 37-bay Roundhouse and nine other buildings. Among the displays are Conestoga wagons, antique automobiles, steam locomotives, bicycles and a dugout canoe. Allow 1 hour, 30 minutes minimum.

Separate 30-minute rail tours in restored coaches are available. Departures require a minimum of 10 people. Diesel engine tours run Mon.-Fri. at 11, 1, 2 and 3, Apr.-Oct.; Sat. at 11, 1, 2 and 3, Sun. at 1:30, 2:30 and 3:30, Nov. 1 to mid-Dec. Steam engine tours run Sat. at 11, 1, 2 and 3, Sun. at 1:30, 2:30 and 3:30, Apr.-Oct. Museum and grounds open Mon.-Sat. 9-5, Sun. 1-5, Apr.-Oct.; Tues.-Sat. 10-4, Sun. 1-4, rest of year. Closed major holidays. Museum free. Steam train tour $4.50; over 62 and ages 3-12, $3. Diesel train tour $3.50; over 62 and ages 3-12, $2.50. Phone (704) 636-2889.

STATESVILLE (B-4) pop. 17,600, elev. 925'

ARTS & SCIENCE CENTER is off I-40 exit 150; take SR 115 n. to Millsaps Rd., .5 mi. e. to Museum Rd., then s. to 1335 Museum Rd. Housed in an 1899 former water pump station, the center contains various permanent and changing exhibits. The Egyptian Art and Artifacts Gallery contains a 2,000-year-old mummy and a Lebanon cedar coffin. The museum also houses an antique toy and game collection, a large collection of glassware from the 19th century, a diorama of a North Carolina habitat and many other objects of scientific and historic interest.

The museum grounds encompass 30 acres of forest with nature trails, a paved trail and three log buildings dating from 1790. Picnic facilities are available. Allow 1 hour minimum. Tues.-Sat. 10-5, Sun. 2-5; closed holidays. Trails open dawn-dusk. Admission $1, under 6 free. Phone (704) 873-4734.

SWANSBORO (D-7) pop. 1,200

HAMMOCKS BEACH STATE PARK, 890 acres on Bear Island, is reached by a passenger ferry docked 4 miles s. of Swansboro via SR 24. The beach has unusually high sand dunes. Interpretive displays at the ferry dock describe plant and animal life native to the area. A bathhouse and primitive camping are available.

The ferry operates daily 9:30-5:30, on the hour Mon.-Tues. and on the half-hour Wed.-Sun., Memorial Day-Labor Day; Fri.-Sat. on the hour 9:30-4:30, in Apr. and Oct.; Wed.-Sun. every hour 9:30-4:30, May 1-day before Memorial Day and day after Labor Day-Sept. 30. Park admission free. Fare $2; ages 4-12, $1. Phone (910) 326-4881. *See Recreation Chart and the AAA Southeastern CampBook.*

★ **"WORTHY IS THE LAMB"** staged in the Crystal Coast Amphitheatre off SR 58, 2 mi. n.

jct. SR 24, is a 3-hour musical drama of the
fe of Jesus. The set includes a river represent-
g the Sea of Galilee and replicas of Jerusalem,
olgotha and its nearby garden tomb. Boats,
rses, camels, chariots and a soundtrack re-
rded in England by Shakespearean actors, cho-
groups and a major symphony orchestra
hance performances by local actors.

Performances Thurs.-Sat. at 8:30 p.m., mid-
ne through Sat. of Labor Day weekend; Fri.-
at. at 8 p.m., Labor Day-Sept. 30. Admission
3; over 62, $11; ages 6-12, $6. MC, VI. Phone
19) 393-8373.

ARBORO (B-7) pop. 11,000, elev. 71'

Founded in 1760 as a county government cen-
r, Tarboro became an important tobacco and
tton market. When North Carolina's itinerant
gislature met in Tarboro, the assemblymen
aying at Toole's Tavern were provided with
ming tables and theatrical entertainment. When
e tavern ran out of heating fuel, guests warmed
emselves with doses of spirits. Not surpris-
gly, George Washington later described the
ace as "lively and thriving."

arboro Edgecombe Chamber of Commerce:
8 Main St., Tarboro, NC 27886; phone (919)
23-7241.

elf-guiding tours: The Tarboro Historic District
ational Recreation Trail highlights Tarboro's
any finely preserved Colonial, antebellum and
ctorian houses. Brochures are available at the
ount-Bridgers House and at the chamber of
mmerce.

OUNT-BRIDGERS HOUSE, 130 Bridgers St., is
Federal-style structure built in 1808. Restored
d furnished in period, the house contains the
obson Pittman Memorial Gallery, which dis-
ays a collection of the artist's paintings and
rsonal belongings. Mon.-Fri. 10-4, Sun. 2-4
lso Sat. 2-4, Mar.-Dec.); closed holidays. Ad-
ission $2. Phone (919) 823-4159.

RYON (F-4) pop. 1,700, elev. 1,090'

Tryon is a resort area noted for its horses. The
yon Riding and Hunt Club maintains 500

miles of trails and sponsors equestrian events in
the area. For information about the events contact the Tryon Riding Club, P.O. Box 1095,
Tryon, NC 28782; phone (800) 438-3681.

Shunkawakan Falls, 5 mi. n. via SR 108 off a
private road, near the top of White Oak Mountain, is one of the tallest waterfalls in the Southeast. From Sunset Rock, also on White Oak
Mountain, 16 counties in three states are visible.

Tryon Thermal Belt Chamber of Commerce:
401 N. Trade St., Tryon, NC 28782; phone (704)
859-6236.

UWHARRIE NATIONAL FOREST

Elevations in the forest range from 500 ft. to 1,000 ft. Refer to AAA maps for additional elevation information.

Covering 46,000 acres in the North Carolina
Piedmont region, Uwharrie National Forest was
established in 1961 and is one of the smaller national forests. Named for the Uwharrie Mountains, the forest is traversed by the Uwharrie,
Yadkin and Pee Dee rivers.

Fishing and hunting are permitted in season.
For information about regulations phone the
North Carolina Wildlife Resources Commission,
(919) 733-3391. The forest borders 8,000-acre
Badin Lake, near Troy; campgrounds and boat
ramps are available. For hikers, the 33-mile
Uwharrie Trail runs north to south through the
national forest. The ranger station is 2 miles east
of Troy on SR 27. For further information contact the District Ranger, SR 3, Box 470, Troy,
NC 27371; phone (910) 576-6391. *See Recreation Chart and the AAA Southeastern
CampBook.*

VALDESE (B-3) pop. 3,900, elev. 1,202'

Valdese traces its history to Waldensian settlers, who fled religious persecution in Italy and

emigrated to the new country in the late 19th century. Their story is retold in the outdoor drama "From This Day Forward", presented at the Old Colony Players Amphitheater from late July to mid-August. The season ends with the Waldensian Festival, a street festival of arts, crafts, food and music, on the second Saturday in August. For further information contact the Old Colony Players; phone (704) 874-0176.

VALLE CRUCIS (D-4)

Midway between Banner Elk and Boone, three mountain streams flowing from different directions converge at a valley creek. This intersection of waterways forms the cross for which Valle Crucis (Valley of the Cross) is named.

One of the community's oldest establishments is the Mast General Store, on SR 1112/194, which operates as it did in 1883, complete with antique scales, counters and a potbellied stove. Product advertisements from the 19th century adorn walls along which are stacked such items as overalls, tinware and stone-ground cornmeal.

WAXHAW (C-4) pop. 1,300, elev. 645′

The Old Waxhaw Settlement, on the border of the Carolinas a few miles southwest of present-day Waxhaw, was President Andrew Jackson's birthplace. After the War of 1812, a dispute arose as to whether he was born in North or South Carolina. Jackson maintained he was a native of South Carolina. Attempts to resolve the mystery by finding the remains of the McKemey cabin site, where it is believed he was born, have been unsuccessful.

In June the drama "Listen and Remember" is presented in an outdoor amphitheater. It portrays the history of early settlers of the Old Waxhaw Settlement, including Jackson and his family. Shows are presented Friday and Saturday evenings; phone (704) 843-2300.

Union County Chamber of Commerce: P.O. Box 1789, Monroe, NC 28111; phone (704) 289-4567.

MEXICO-CARDENAS MUSEUM is 5 mi. s. of SR 75, following signs to Davis Rd. The museum, organized in honor of Mexican President Lázaro Cárdenas, contains artifacts from Mexican Indians relating to their customs and languages. Pottery, native costumes, folk art and photographs are on display. A 1938 Chevrolet sedan, a gift from the president, also can be seen. Food is available. Allow 1 hour minimum. Mon.-Sat. 9-4; closed holidays. Free. Phone (704) 843-6045.

MUSEUM OF THE ALPHABET is 5 mi. s. of SR 75, following signs to Davis Rd. The museum is dedicated to the study of written language from the ancient to the present. Included are 10 exhibits about numerous languages from around the globe, including Arabic, Armenian, Brahmi,

Cherokee, Cyrillic, Hebrew, Korean, Romar Thai, Tibetan and Visigoth. Notations of music Braille and sign language also are included.

Visitors can view samples of hieroglyphics, replica of the Rosetta Stone, examples of Ameri can Indian number-writing systems, Chines paper-making and a working model of Guten berg's press. Allow 1 hour, 30 minutes minimum Mon.-Sat. 9-4; closed holidays. Free. Phon (704) 843-6066.

MUSEUM OF THE WAXHAWS-THE ANDREW JACKSON MEMORIAL is 5 mi. e. on SR 7! Named for its first inhabitants, the settlemen was founded by the Scot-Irish about 1755. Th memorial also claims to be the birthplace of th seventh U.S. president. The museum's collectio spans 1650-1900 and contains memorabilia an weapons from the Revolutionary and Civil war a working cotton gin, a display dedicated to Ar drew Jackson, Scot-Irish settlement artifacts an an 1813 Conestoga wagon.

A short film detailing the history of the regio is presented. Picnic facilities are available. Allo 1 hour minimum. Wed.-Sat. and holidays 10-! Sun. 1-5. Admission $2; over 65 and ages 7-1: $1. Phone (704) 843-1832.

WAYNESVILLE (E-3) pop. 6,800, elev. 3,000′

English, Scot-Irish, German and Dutch imm grants who came from the coast to the mountain in search of better hunting and farming settled i Waynesville in the 18th century. Originall called Mount Prospect, Waynesville was rename in honor of Revolutionary War general "Mad Anthony Wayne. The World Methodist Council i headquartered 3 miles from Waynesville at Lak Junaluska.

In late September, Waynesville features mour tain music, clogging and games at the Smok Mountain Folk Festival. This event also feature Southern Appalachian crafts, antiques and a qui show.

Haywood County Chamber of Commerce: 11 Walnut St., P.O. Box 600, Waynesville, N 28786-0600; phone (704) 456-3021.

MILE HIGH HEINTOOGA OVERLOOK, a spur the Blue Ridge Parkway 8 mi. n.e. of Soco Ga affords a view of Great Smoky Mountains Na tional Park (see place listing p. 97).

PIGEON LOOP DRIVE, US 276 e. to Woodro then SR 110 n. to Canton, then US 23/74 w. an s. to US 276, traverses Pigeon Gap past many o chards that are colorful in the spring; the di tance is 24 miles.

SOCO GAP is 13 mi. w. of Waynesville on th edge of Great Smoky Mountains National Par (see place listing p. 97); it affords excellen views.

WILMINGTON (D-6) pop. 55,500, elev. 30'

North Carolina's principal deepwater port, Wilmington is on the Cape Fear River. The city is a leading port for creosote and petroleum products, fertilizer, molasses and wood pulp. Historic areas on the riverfront include the Cotton Exchange and Chandler's Wharf, which have been renovated and house shops and restaurants.

Colonial capital in 1743, Wilmington was the scene of Stamp Act resistance in 1765. British forces took the city and established their headquarters during the winter of 1780-81. As one of the principal ports of the Confederacy, Wilmington maintained communications with foreign governments until 1865 when nearby Fort Fisher *(see Kure Beach p. 104)* fell to Union forces.

Wilmington is ablaze with color during the North Carolina Azalea Festival in early April. Activities include garden tours, parades and a horse show. Riverfest in early October offers arts and crafts shows and music and dance programs. Old Wilmington by Candlelight, a tour of historic houses, occurs the first weekend of December. Wilmington Adventure Tours provides guided walking tours of the city April through October; phone (910) 763-1785.

Cape Fear Coast Convention and Visitors Bureau: 24 N. Third St., Wilmington, NC 28401; phone (910) 341-4030 or (800) 222-4757. *See ad.*

★**BATTLESHIP** *NORTH CAROLINA* is w. on US 17/74/76/421, over the Cape Fear Memorial Bridge on the Cape Fear River. When commissioned in 1941, "The Showboat" was considered the world's greatest sea weapon. During World War II it was in every major naval offensive in the Pacific, earning 15 battle stars. Since 1961 the ship has served as a memorial to the 10,000 North Carolinians of all military services who died during World War II.

The 2-hour self-guiding tour includes visits to the galley, sick bay, engine room, pilot house, crew's quarters, gun turrets, powder and projectile magazine, mess hall and a restored Kingfisher floatplane. A museum displays World War II photographs and artifacts, including the Roll of Honor of North Carolinians who died in the conflict. A 10-minute introductory film is shown.

A river taxi to the memorial leaves Riverfront Park every half-hour between 10 and 5 (except 11:30 and 3:30), June-Aug. *(see Captain J.N. Maffitt River Cruises).* Memorial open daily 8-8, May 16-Sept. 15; 8-5, rest of year. Memorial admission $8; ages 6-11, $4. MC, VI. Phone (910) 251-5797. *See ad.*

BELLAMY MANSION MUSEUM OF HISTORY AND DESIGN ARTS, 503 Market St., is a restored antebellum mansion that showcases several architectural styles including Italianate, neoclassic

and Greek Revival. A slide show provides background information about the mansion and the Bellamy family. Changing exhibits also are featured. Guided tours are available. Allow 45 minutes minimum. Wed.-Sat. 10-5, Sun. 1-5; closed major holidays. Admission $6; ages 6-12, $3. MC, VI. Phone (910) 251-3700.

BRUNSWICK TOWN STATE HISTORIC SITE is on the Cape Fear River, 19 mi. s. via US 17 and SR 133. One of Colonial North Carolina's leading seaports, residents fled at the outbreak of the Revolution and few returned when the war ended. Excavated foundations of Brunswick Town buildings are maintained as archeological exhibits. Throughout the area are explanatory displays. The ruins of St. Phillip's Anglican Church are noteworthy.

Fort Anderson, built near the old townsite by the Confederacy, held out for 30 days after the fall of Fort Fisher but was finally abandoned after a 3-day siege. The earthworks are clearly visible. A visitor center offers exhibits and a slide show. Picnic facilities are available. Allow 1 hour minimum. Mon.-Sat. 9-5, Sun. 1-5, Apr.-Oct.; Tues.-Sat. 10-4, Sun. 1-4, rest of year. Closed Martin Luther King Jr.'s Birthday, Veterans Day, Thanksgiving, day after Thanksgiving and Dec. 24-26. Free. Phone (910) 371-6613.

BURGWIN-WRIGHT HOUSE AND GARDEN, 3rd and Market sts., served as headquarters for Lord Cornwallis during the Revolution. The massive stone walls of the old jail constitute the 1770 house's foundation. Of special interest are the separate three-story cookhouse and the gardens. The house contains 18th-century furnishings and decorations.

Tues.-Sat. 10-4, Feb. 1-day before Good Friday and Tues. after Easter-Dec. 23; closed July 4, Labor Day and Thanksgiving weekend. Admission $3, full-time students with ID $1. Phone (910) 762-0570.

CAPE FEAR MUSEUM, 814 Market St., features a diorama of Fort Fisher; Waves and Currents, an exhibit about the history and culture of the lower Cape Fear area; a 17-foot-by-20-foot scale model of 1863 Wilmington; and an exhibit of the history of regional beaches. Tues.-Sat. 9-5, Sun. 2-5; closed major holidays. Admission $2, senior citizens and students with ID $1, under 5 free. Phone (910) 341-4350.

SAVE *CAPTAIN J.N. MAFFITT* **RIVER CRUISES,** Riverfront Park at the corner of Market and Water sts., offers narrated sightseeing cruises of the Cape Fear River. River taxi rides between Riverfront Park and the Battleship *North Carolina (see attraction listing)* also are offered. Departures for sightseeing cruises daily at 11 and 3, Memorial Day weekend-Labor Day; daily at 3, May 1-day before Memorial Day weekend and day after Labor Day-Sept. 30. River taxi rides depart daily every half-hour 10-5 (except 11:30 and 3:30),

June-Aug. Sightseeing fare $9; ages 2-12, $4. River taxi fare $2. Phone (910) 343-1611 or (800) 676-0162.

FORT FISHER—
see Kure Beach p. 104.

GREENFIELD PARK AND GARDENS, s. end of 3rd St. with entrance on 4th St., is a public park noted for its cypress trees, camellias, azaleas, roses and a 5-mile scenic drive around Greenfield Lake. The gardens are particularly colorful from February through April. Recreational facilities include paddleboats, canoes, playgrounds, and bicycle and nature trails. Picnicking is permitted. Daily dawn-dusk. Free; rental fee charged for paddleboats and canoes. Phone (910) 341-7855.

SAVE *HENRIETTA II,* docked along the riverfront with parking at 301 N. Water St., offers 1.5-hour narrated sightseeing cruises of the Cape Fear River, as well as 2.5-hour entertainment dinner cruises, 2-hour sunset dinner cruises and 1.5-hour moonlight cruises. Throughout the year 1.5-hour special-events cruises also are offered.

Sightseeing cruises depart Tues.-Sun. at 11:30 and 2:30 (also Tues. and Sun. at 6 p.m.), June-Aug.; at 2:30, Apr.-May and Sept.-Oct. Boarding is 30 minutes before departure.

Sightseeing cruise $9; ages 2-12, $4. Entertainment dinner cruise $31-$34. Sunset dinner cruise $24; ages 2-12, $16. Reservations are required for dinner cruises; because moonlight cruises and 11:30 a.m. and 6 p.m. sightseeing cruises may be pre-empted by charters, reservations are advised. DS, MC, VI. For other schedules and prices phone (910) 343-1611 or (800) 676-0162.

ORTON PLANTATION GARDENS are 18 mi. s. on SR 133. Azaleas, camellias, dogwoods, roses and flowering fruit trees are at their peak March through April. Day lilies, oleander, rhododendron, gardenia, magnolia and iris bloom May through June. Summer annuals and crape myrtle peak July through August.

The 1735 mansion, a fine example of antebellum architecture, is closed to the public. Gardens daily 8-6, Mar.-Aug.; 10-5, Sept.-Nov. Admission $8; over 60, $7; ages 6-12, $3. Phone (910) 371-6851.

POPLAR GROVE HISTORIC PLANTATION, 9 mi. n. on US 17, consists of several historic buildings set on 16 acres of land that was once part of a vast, self-supporting agricultural community. Costumed guides conduct tours of the manor house and the outbuildings that include a tenant house, smoke house, herb cellar and kitchen. Built by Joseph Mumford Foy in 1850 and home to Foy family members until 1971, the manor house contains period furniture, clothing and memorabilia. In the Cultural Arts Center craftspeople demonstrate skills that were a part of daily 19th-century life. Food is available.

Allow 1 hour minimum. Mon.-Sat. 9-5, Sun. noon-5, Feb. 2-Dec. 18; closed Thanksgiving. Admission $6; senior citizens $5; ages 6-15, $3. Phone (910) 686-4868.

ST. JAMES EPISCOPAL CHURCH, 3rd and Market sts., originally was built in 1751 and used by the British as a riding school during the Revolutionary War. When rebuilt in 1839, the church structure was designed by T.U. Walter, architect of the U.S. Capitol dome and wings. The church house was designed in 1901 by Henry Bacon, architect of the Lincoln Memorial in Washington, D.C.

An exceptional painting, "Ecce Homo", hangs in the church. Of Spanish origin and probably 400-600 years old, it was taken from a captured ship in 1748 and given to the parish of St. James in 1754. The church interior includes noteworthy wood carvings. Mon.-Fri. 9-4. Free. Phone (910) 763-1628.

ST. JOHN'S MUSEUM OF ART, 114 Orange St. at jct. S. 2nd St., has an extensive collection of 19th-century through contemporary American art and offers changing exhibits. A set of prints by Mary Cassatt is featured. The grounds include a sculpture garden. Tues.-Sat. 10-5, Sun. noon-4; closed Jan. 1, Easter, July 4, Thanksgiving, Dec. 25 and 31. Admission $2; ages 6-17, $1; family rate $5; free to all first Sun. of month. Phone (910) 763-0281.

SAVE **TOTE-EM-IN ZOO,** 10 mi. s. on US 421, has more than 130 different birds, mammals and reptiles. Two small museums contain mounted animals and collections of fossils, currency, arrowheads, seashells and World War II memorabilia. Daily 9-6, June 1-Labor Day; 9-5, early Mar.-May 31; 9-4, day after Labor Day-Nov. 30. Admission $5; ages 2-11, $3. Phone (910) 791-0472.

WILMINGTON RAILROAD MUSEUM, Red Cross and Water sts., commemorates the importance of railroads in local and national history. Exhibits include Wilmington and Weldon Railroad artifacts dating from 1840, as well as items from the Atlantic Coastline and other railroads. A model exhibit of Atlantic Coastline's North Carolina-South Carolina regional routes of the 1940s and 1950s is featured. A steam locomotive, boxcar and caboose can be boarded.

Mon.-Sat. 10-5, Sun. 1-5, Apr.-Oct.; Tues.-Sat. 10-5, Sun. 1-5, rest of year. Closed Jan. 1, Thanksgiving and Dec. 25. Admission $3; ages 6-11, $1.50. Phone (910) 763-2634.

SAVE **ZEBULON LATIMER HOUSE,** 126 S. 3rd St., is a four-story Italianate Revival town residence built in 1852. Empire and Victorian furnishings grace the interior. Guided tours are conducted Tues.-Fri. 10-4, Sat.-Sun. noon-5, May-Oct.; closed July 4, Thanksgiving and Dec. 20-Jan.2. Admission $5; ages 6-18, $2. Phone (910) 762-0492.

WILSON (B-7) pop. 36,900, elev. 145′

Primarily known as a bright-leaf tobacco market, Wilson also is an antique center. The city's central business district boasts many fine examples of late 19th- and early 20th-century architecture, while the older residential areas are noted for their restored bungalows.

Each spring "Another Bloomin' Festival" attracts thousands for music, dancing, arts and crafts displays and a comedy show. In the fall, the Golden Leaf Celebration offers tobacco contests, barbecue cook-offs, musical shows, arts and crafts displays and a parade.

Auctioneers sell thousands of pounds of tobacco during the market season from August through October. Free tours of tobacco auctions in area warehouses are offered Monday through Thursday at 9:30 a.m., August through October.

Wilson Visitors Bureau: 220 Broad St., Wilson, NC 27894; phone (919) 237-0165 or (800) 497-7398.

Self-guiding tours: The Historic Walking Tour of Downtown Wilson offers views of 24 historic houses, churches and public buildings. Brochures are available at the visitors bureau.

IMAGINATION STATION, in the old Court House at 224 E. Nash St., is a science and math learning center geared to children. Hands-on exhibits allow visitors to lift a 500-pound engine, defy gravity, experience a flight simulator and learn in a state-of-the-art computer lab. Live science shows are presented. Food is available. Allow 1 hour minimum. Mon.-Sat. 9-5, Sun. and holidays 1-5; closed Easter, July 4, Thanksgiving and Dec. 25. Admission $3.50; over 62 and ages 4-17, $3. MC, VI. Phone (919) 291-5113.

WINDSOR (B-8) pop. 2,100, elev. 277′

Windsor's beginnings date from 1717, when a plantation named Rosefield was established on 2,810 acres near the Cashie River. The possibilities of river transportation and the plantation's proximity to a road between Edenton and Halifax inspired landowner William Gray to give 100 acres for a new town. In 1773, a bill was passed moving the county seat from Wolfenden, or Hoggard's Mill, to Windsor. The town's streets still bear their old English names.

Windsor Area Chamber of Commerce: 102 N. York St., P.O. Box 572, Windsor, NC 27983; phone (919) 761-1069.

HOPE PLANTATION, 4.5 mi. w. on SR 308, is the restored early 19th-century mansion of David Stone, statesman and governor. It has Georgian and Federal elements and is furnished with period pieces. Also on the grounds are an 18th-century garden; an herb garden; a kitchen garden; and the King-Bazemore House, an early 18th-century rural plantation house. Mon.-Sat.

10-5, Sun. 2-5, May-Sept. Admission $6.50, senior citizens $6, students with ID $2. Phone (919) 794-3140.

WINSTON-SALEM (B-4) pop. 143,500, elev. 868′

Winston-Salem dates from 1753, when a group of Pennsylvania Moravians purchased a large tract of land in the North Carolina Piedmont. Their settlement of Bethabara, meaning "House of Passage" or "Temporary Home," prospered and became a trading and crafts center. In 1766 Salem (from *Shalom*, Hebrew for "peace") was built nearby as the Moravians' permanent settlement.

Winston was founded in 1849. It grew rapidly because of the success of the tobacco and textile industries, and eventually surpassed Salem. The two towns consolidated in 1913.

Textiles and tobacco built the city, but the arts brought new life to a declining downtown in the mid-20th century. The downtown was enhanced with a performing arts center, an arts and crafts school for children and a park and amphitheater. The culmination of the program is the North Carolina School of the Arts, a branch of the University of North Carolina. The Stevens Center, a renovated 1929 movie palace in downtown Winston-Salem, is one of the school's performance centers.

In addition to being the home of Wake Forest University, the town is home to Winston-Salem State University. Founded in 1892 as Slater Industrial Academy, the university's name was changed to Winston-Salem Teacher's College in 1925—it was the first black institution in the country to award degrees in elementary education. Even older is Salem College. Founded in 1772 in the Moravian village of Salem, Salem College is on a 57-acre campus in Old Salem *(see attraction listing).*

Winston-Salem Visitor Center: 601 N. Cherry St., Winston-Salem, NC 27101; phone (910) 725-2361 or (800) 331-7018.

Shopping areas: Old Salem provides numerous shopping opportunities. Several shops adjacent to Salem Sq. offer reproduction furniture and home furnishing reminiscent of the 18th-century Moravians. T. Bagge-Merchant is in the 1775 building where Trangott Bagge once operated the town store. At 1815 Blumhouse is the Furniture and Accessories Shop.

GOD'S ACRE, the Moravian cemetery 1 blk. n. of Salem Sq., contains more than 4,000 graves dating from 1771. The flat white marble markers symbolize the equality of the dead. Open daily 24 hours. Free.

HISTORIC BETHABARA PARK, on Bethabara Rd. 3 mi. n.w. off University Pkwy., is the 1753 site of the first Moravian settlement in the state. The grounds include the 1788 Gemeinhaus, or church; the 1782 Krause-Butner Potter's House, the 1803 Brewers House; excavations of 40 original foundations; a reconstructed 1756 fort in its original trench; the reconstructed 1759 community gardens and a visitor's center with a videotape presentation and exhibits depicting the area's history.

Costumed guides offer tours. The park has more than 6 miles of nature and history trails. Activities include a Revolutionary War encampment Memorial Day weekend and a Fourth of July observance the Sunday before Independence Day. Picnic facilities are available. Park open daily dawn-dusk. Buildings open Mon.-Fri. 9:30-4:30, Sat.-Sun. 1:30-4:30, Apr.-Nov.; closed Thanksgiving. Donations. Phone (910) 924-8191.

HOME MORAVIAN CHURCH, Salem Sq., is the center of Moravian church activities in the South. Services in the 1800 sanctuary are open to visitors; best known are the Easter Sunrise Service, held annually for more than 200 years; the Christmas Lovefeast on Dec. 24; and the Watch Night Service on Dec. 31. Church interpretation is presented daily 1:30-3:30, Mar.-Nov. Phone (910) 722-6171.

[SAVE] ★**OLD SALEM,** on Old Salem Rd. adjacent to downtown Winston-Salem, is a living-history restoration of the Moravian church town of Salem founded in 1766. Many buildings erected 1766-1850 have been restored or reconstructed on their original sites. Family gardens and orchards have been replanted, and streets and lighting have been adapted to re-create an 18th-century atmosphere. Several of the buildings continue to be used as private residences, including the half-timbered 1768 Fourth House, said to be the oldest house in Salem.

Among the events celebrated at Old Salem is Spring Festival, held in late April to mark the arrival of spring. Garden tours, games and special demonstrations are offered during this time. On July 4, during the Torchlight Procession, costumed men, women and children complete a weekend-long celebration when they converge on Salem Square to reenact the nation's first official Independence Day celebration.

The Salem Christmas Season, during which the entire town is decorated with live greenery, wreaths and candles, begins in early November. Costumed guides interpret Moravian Christmas traditions such as illuminated nativity scenes and decorated pyramids. The season culminates just before Christmas with the Salem Christmas festival, complete with craft demonstrations, wagon rides, games and outdoor brass bands.

Self-guiding tours begin with a brief orientation program at the Old Salem Visitor Center, Old Salem Road and E. Academy Street. Costumed interpreters throughout the town are available to answer questions and demonstrate historic trades and domestic activities. Of the more than 90 restored buildings, 15 can be visited Mon.-Sat. 9-5, Sun. 12:30-5. Closed Thanksgiving and Dec. 24-25. Admission to Old Salem $14; ages 6-16, $8. Combination ticket with the Museum of Early Southern Decorative Arts $19; ages 6-16, $11. Phone (910) 721-7300 or (888) 348-4844. *See ad.*

Boys School (Wachovia Museum), facing Salem Sq., was built in 1794 and houses exhibits on various aspects of Moravian life. The second floor displays musical instruments and toys. The third-floor gallery exhibits paintings by Moravian artists, as well as embroideries done by Girls School students 1760-1850.

Market-Fire House, on Salem Sq., is divided into two sections. One portion houses two of the earliest fire engines used in North Carolina; the other is a former meat market. The original fire engines and firefighting equipment are displayed.

Miksch House and Shed, on S. Main St. just n. of Salem Sq., was built in 1771 by Matthew Miksch. An enterprising man, Miksch sold tobacco, candles and gingerbread. Behind the house is a log shed where seasonal activities are often demonstrated.

Museum of Early Southern Decorative Arts is at 924 S. Main St. Displayed in 21 rooms and six galleries are furnishings and art produced 1690-1820. The objects are exhibited within "home-like" settings, and many of the rooms were actually moved from endangered older buildings. Mon.-Sat. 9-5, Sun. 1-5; closed Thanksgiving and Dec. 24-25. Admission $10; ages 6-16, $6. Combination ticket including Old Salem $18; ages 6-16, $10. Phone (910) 721-7300 or (888) 348-4844. *See ad.*

Old Salem Visitor Center, Old Salem Rd. and E. Academy St., includes two theaters where visitors can watch a brief orientation program. The center also contains exhibits detailing the history and lifestyles of the Moravian people.

Salem Tavern, Annex and Barn are on S. Main St. just s. of Salem Sq. The tavern was built in 1784 and accommodated guests until 1850. The guest and gentlemen's dining rooms, bedrooms and kitchen are furnished in period. George Washington was a guest for two nights in 1791. Behind the tavern is an 1840s heavy-timbered

barn, and in the adjacent 1816 Tavern Annex is the Old Salem Tavern Restaurant.

Shultz Shoe Shop, on S. Main St. s. of Salem Sq., is a shoemaker's shop built in 1827. A costumed guide demonstrates 19th-century shoemaking and leatherworking.

Single Brothers House, a half-timbered, brick structure facing Salem Sq., dates from 1769 with a 1786 addition. It served as the home and workplace for the community's single men and older boys. The building includes a dining room, kitchen, meeting hall and trade shops in which costumed artisans can be seen at work. Pewter casting, tailoring and furniture making are among the demonstrations to be seen. On many days, a blacksmith works behind the building.

Vierling House, is at Church and Bank sts. near God's Acre. Once the largest house in Salem, the building was the house of Dr. Benjamin Vierling, a prominent physician. Inside are an apothecary shop, dining room, kitchen and family quarters. A medical and health care exhibit is upstairs. At the rear of the 1802 building is a furnished wash-bake house. Demonstrations of early domestic activities are given.

Vogler House, facing Salem Sq., was the 1819 house and shop of a silversmith. It contains many original 19th-century furnishings, including a Moravian tile stove, several clocks and a silhouette-making device. Silversmithing is demonstrated at the forge in the wash-kitchen.

Winkler Bakery, on S. Main St. n. of Salem Sq., was built in 1800. Inside the restored building, bakers demonstrate early baking methods using historic recipes and a wood-fired brick beehive oven.

SAVE **REYNOLDA HOUSE MUSEUM OF AMERICAN ART** is entered off Reynolda Rd. near Wake Forest University. Built by R.J. Reynolds in 1914-17 on a 1,067-acre estate, this country house offers a fine collection of furnishings and 18th-, 19th- and 20th-century American paintings, prints and sculpture. The works of Mary Cassatt, Frederic Church, John Singleton Copley, Thomas Eakins, Jacob Lawrence, Gilbert Stuart and Andrew Wyeth are represented.

Also of interest is a ladies' costume collection, with items that date 1905-50. Japanese cherry trees on the grounds bloom in late March or early April.

Allow 1 hour minimum. House open Tues.-Sat. 9:30-4:30, Sun. 1:30-4:30; gardens daily 7:30-5. Closed Jan. 1, Thanksgiving and Dec. 25. House admission $6; over 60, $5; students $3. Gardens free. Phone (910) 725-5325.

★**R.J. REYNOLDS TOBACCO/WHITAKER PARK MANUFACTURING CENTER** is 3 mi. n. on US 52, then w. on Akron Dr. and e. on Reynolds Blvd. Guided tours are offered of the plant, which turns out 275 million cigarettes per day.

An exhibit room with historical displays features murals that show the stages of tobacco production, from planting to sale at the auctions. Mon.-Fri. 8-6; closed holidays. Free. Phone (910) 741-5718.

SCIWORKS is 7.5 mi. n. on US 52 to Hanes Mill Rd. exit following signs. The center offers physical and natural science exhibits, nature trails, live animal exhibits, a barnyard, a discovery room and a planetarium. In addition, an outdoor animal habitat contains deer, river otters and wild birds. Allow 1 hour, 30 minutes minimum. Nature center open Mon.-Sat. 10-5, Sun. 1-5; animal habitat open Wed.-Sat. 11-4, Sun. 1-4. Closed major holidays. Admission $7; senior citizens and ages 6-19, $5; ages 3-5, $3. Phone (910) 767-6730.

SOUTHEASTERN CENTER FOR CONTEMPORARY ART, 750 Marguerite Dr. off Reynolda Rd., is in a Tudor-style mansion on 32 acres of landscaped grounds. The center houses works by contemporary American artists. Allow 1 hour minimum. Tues.-Sat. 10-5, Sun. 2-5; closed holidays. Guided tours are available by reservation Tues.-Fri. Admission $3, senior citizens and students with ID $2, under 12 free. Phone (910) 725-1904.

★**TANGLEWOOD,** 10 mi. s.w. via I-40 exit 182, is a 1,300-acre recreation area. Facilities include campgrounds, tennis courts, a 36-hole golf course, a par-three course, stables, swimming pools, picnic areas, and paddleboat and canoe rentals. Special events include a steeplechase the second Saturday in May, a July 4th celebration and fireworks display and The Vantage Senior PGA Tournament the first week in October. A Festival of Lights is held from mid-November through early January.

Daily dawn-dusk. Swimming pools and lake facilities open Memorial Day-Labor Day. Admission $2 per private vehicle; use of facilities extra. Phone (910) 778-6300. *See Recreation Chart and the AAA Southeastern CampBook.*

WAKE FOREST UNIVERSITY is off Silas Creek Pkwy. Campus highlights include the university's art collection in the Benson University Center, the Wait Chapel Carillon and the Scales Fine Arts Gallery. Campus tours can be arranged through the admissions office. Phone (910) 759-4926.

Wake Forest Museum of Anthropology, off University Dr., is North Carolina's only museum devoted to the study of various cultures. Relics from the Americas, Africa, Asia and Oceania are featured and include household and ceremonial items, textiles, hunting and fishing gear and objects of personal adornment. Tues.-Sat. 10-4:30; closed major holidays. Free. Phone (910) 759-5282.

★**WRIGHT BROTHERS NATIONAL MEMORIAL—**

see Outer Banks p. 112.

Charleston Beaches / Courtesy: The Charleston Area CNVB

South Carolina

An introduction to the state's history, geography, economy and recreation

LONG A CRADLE OF INDEPENDENCE, SOUTH CAROLINA ALSO IS A STATE OF UNPARALLELED GRACE AND BEAUTY. FROM THE CHARM OF CHARLESTON'S HISTORIC DISTRICT TO THE ELEGANCE OF THE STATE HOUSE IN COLUMBIA, SOUTH CAROLINA REMAINS A UNIQUE MIXTURE OF PAST AND PRESENT. INDUSTRIAL COMPLEXES AND COMMERCIAL CENTERS EXIST IN TANDEM WITH HISTORIC MANSIONS AND GARDENS. WHILE PROGRESS CLAIMS ITS PLACE IN THE STATE, AVENUES LINED WITH OAKS DRAPED IN SPANISH MOSS EVOKE THE MEMORY OF THE OLD SOUTH.

HISTORY

The first European to explore South Carolina was Spaniard Francisco Cordilla in 1521. Vásquez de Ayllón followed his countryman 5 years later, attempting to establish a permanent settlement near what is now Winyah Bay. Harsh weather, hostile natives and disease soon decimated the settlers, and the fledgling colony summarily was abandoned. Colonization proved equally difficult for the French: Jean Ribault's 1562 venture at Parris Island ended in mutiny.

The English finally succeeded, founding Charles Towne at Albemarle Point on the Ashley River in 1670. Named after the reigning English monarch, the village grew quickly and was moved a decade later to the present site of Charleston.

The colony enjoyed early prosperity, mainly through foresting and trade with the indigenous Indians. The cultivation of rice, indigo and cotton proved successful, establishing an agricultural tradition that soon would transform not only the state, but also the region and even the country.

Also, the often imaginative advertising done by the region's first proprietors attracted many foreigners seeking vast expanses of land and freedom from religious persecution. English, French, Spanish and Scottish pioneers all came in search of the land that early colonist Sir Robert Montgomery described, in an optimistic advertisement typical of the time, as lying "...in the same latitude with Palestine herself...'Tis beautiful with odoriferous plants, green all the year....The orange and the lemon thrive in the same common orchard with the apple, and the pear tree, plums, peaches, apricots, and nectarines bear from stones in three years' growing." With credentials such as these, South Carolina quickly was settled by a diverse, and often contentious, population.

South Carolina played an important role in the American Revolution. Independence-minded South Carolinians fought British imperialism throughout the first half of the 18th century and were among the first to object to the Stamp Act of 1765. Although Charleston was captured by the British in 1780, two pivotal battles were fought in the state: at Kings Mountain that same year and at Cowpens in 1781. The end of the war brought economic success—and economic dependence on slavery.

By the early 19th century, cotton emerged as the pre-eminent crop of the agricultural South; the decline in cotton prices in the 1820s dealt South Carolina a severe financial blow. Laying the blame on harsh tariff policies, South Carolinians began to agitate for more independence from the federal government. Sen. John C. Calhoun successfully argued for states' rights to negate stringent federal laws, and the state nullified the Tariff Act of 1832. Federal military action narrowly was averted by compromise, but the stage was set for deeper conflict.

Fast Facts

POPULATION: 3,698,700.

AREA: 31,055 square miles; ranks 40th.

CAPITAL: Columbia.

HIGHEST POINT: 3,560 ft., Sassafras Mountain.

LOWEST POINT: Sea level, Atlantic Ocean.

TIME ZONE: Eastern. DST.

MINIMUM AGE FOR DRIVERS: 16.

SEAT BELT/CHILD RESTRAINT LAWS: Seat belts required for driver and front-seat passengers, and for all back-seat passengers if the vehicle is equipped with shoulder straps. Child restraints required for under 6.

HELMETS FOR MOTORCYCLISTS: Required for driver and passenger under 21.

RADAR DETECTORS: Permitted.

FIREARMS LAWS: Vary by state and/or county. Contact South Carolina Law Enforcement, Regulatory Services Dept., P.O. Box 21398, Columbia, SC 29221; phone (803) 896-7014.

HOLIDAYS: Jan. 1; Washington's Birthday, Feb. (3rd Mon.); Memorial Day, May (last Mon.); July 4; Labor Day, Sept. (1st Mon.); Veterans Day, Nov. 11; Election Day, Nov. (even years); Thanksgiving (and day after); Dec. 25-26.

TAXES: South Carolina's statewide sales tax is 4 percent, plus an additional 1 percent on all persons under age 85. Counties are authorized to impose an additional 1-percent increment. There is a 5-percent admissions tax on most amusements, and a 2-percent accommodations tax.

STATE INFORMATION CENTERS are at US 17 near Little River, I-85S near Blacksburg, I-26E near Landrum, I-85N near Fair Play, I-20E near North Augusta, I-95S near Hamer, I-95S at Santee, I-95N near Hardeeville, I-77S near Fort Mill, and US 301N near Allendale. Open daily 9-5:30 (also 5:30-6:30, Memorial Day-Labor Day); closed Jan. 1, Thanksgiving and Dec. 25.

Almost 30 years of secessionist sentiment ame to fruition Dec. 20, 1860, when the Ordiance of Secession was passed by the state legis-ture, making South Carolina the first Southern ate to secede. Neighboring states followed and e Civil War began 4 months later, when Conederate forces fired on Fort Sumter. The war as harsh for the Palmetto State: One-fourth of s army was killed, and Gen. William Tecumseh herman literally blazed a trail through the state, urning Columbia in 1865.

Reconstruction was devastating particularly for e birthplace of secession. The established mili-ry rule ignored the needs of the citizens, and orrupt "carpetbaggers"—economic opportunists om the North—raided the treasury and bank-pted the state's economy. The election of emocrat Wade Hampton in 1876 to governor, nd the withdrawal of Federal troops by Presi-ent Rutherford Hayes ended congressional Re-onstruction. However, complete recovery was low. The destruction of the war and the loss of ble-bodied men stifled the state's agricultural utput, and it turned to the textile industry to re-uild. This painful conversion occupied much of e following 4 decades.

World War I slightly boosted the agriculture dustry, particularly cotton farming, and the ten-nt farming system was established. This boost as short-lived, however, as a boll weevil infes-tion and the Depression combined to further ap South Carolina's economy and spirit.

World War II brought heavy industry—and a ew economic base—to the state. Sudden growth the textile industry spurred diversification roughout the industrial sector, a trend that oc-urred also in agriculture. The 1950s and '60s were turbulent time, as the civil rights movement and acial integration led to increased tensions in the tate. Despite some strong resistance, South Caro-nians eventually accepted the reforms.

South Carolina once again was a victim of ardship when Hurricane Hugo—one of the most estructive storms in history—roared through the ow-lying coastal areas Sept. 21, 1989. The storm aused 26 fatalities and more than $7 billion in amages, but the residents' pride and determina-on spurred the rebuilding effort. Once again, outh Carolina exudes the charm and vitality that ave been the state's hallmarks through its often umultuous past.

GEOGRAPHY

As in most Atlantic coastal states, three major eographical divisions—Appalachian Mountain, iedmont and Coastal Plain—are present in outh Carolina. The Blue Ridge in the north-esternmost corner along the North Carolina order gives the state its highest elevations.

From the Blue Ridge the Piedmont rolls south-astward toward the broad, flat Coastal Plain, vhich encompasses about two-thirds of the tate's area and is composed of loosely consoli-

dated aquatic sediments. The outer Coastal Plain saw the first human settlement in the state and is known locally as the Lowcountry. The coast breaks into a spate of islands, which become numerous south of the Santee River.

The Santee River system, comprising the Wateree, Congaree, Broad and Saluda rivers, is the primary watershed, draining the central half of the state. Hydroelectric dams impound such huge reservoirs as Wateree Lake, lakes Moultrie and Marion on the Santee, lakes Murray and Greenwood on the Saluda and Lake Wylie north of Rock Hill.

In the northeast, the Pee Dee River empties into the sea below Georgetown. The Savannah River, flowing through J. Strom Thurmond Lake, Richard B. Russell Lake and Hartwell Reservoir, marks the Georgia-South Carolina boundary.

ECONOMY

The economic havoc brought about during Reconstruction lasted well into the 20th century. Then, spurred by World War II, a shift from agriculture to industry reversed the state's fortunes. The clothing, meat-packing, furniture, chemical, and pulp and paper industries burgeoned. The largest of these was the manufacturing of natural and synthetic textile fibers; the cities of Anderson, Greenville and Spartanburg are the state's principal textile centers.

For Your Information

TOURISM INFORMATION:

South Carolina Division of Tourism
120 Pendleton St.
Columbia, SC 29201
(800) 346-3634

RECREATION INFORMATION:

Dept. of Parks, Recreation and Tourism
1205 Pendleton St.
P.O. Box 5157
Columbia, SC 29250
(803) 734-0122

FISHING AND HUNTING REGULATIONS:

South Carolina Dept. of Natural
  Resources.
Division of Game and Freshwater
  Fisheries
P.O. Box 167
Columbia, SC 29202
(803) 734-3886

NATIONAL FOREST INFORMATION:

U.S. Forest Service
4931 Broad River Rd.
Columbia, SC 29210-4021
(803) 561-4000
(800) 280-2267 (reservations)
(800) 879-4496 TDD

Tourism, the second largest industry, continues to grow, and the state's popularity as a retirement destination has created an economic boom. South Carolina's newest and ever-growing industry is the fabrication of motors, automobile parts and other small steel products. Chemicals and their allied products also are a major industry.

The lands impoverished by the overplanting of indigo, cotton and rice have been rehabilitated; tobacco and sugar cane have overtaken cotton and rice as major crops. However, South Carolina is not primarily an agricultural state. Farms occupy less than half of the state's total area, and only one-sixth of the farmland is used to grow crops. The raising of livestock and the cultivation of the vast woodlands complement South Carolina's agricultural industry. The state's geological resources are kaolin, vermiculite, sand, gravel and high-grade granite. Gold is one of the state's highest mineral yields.

RECREATION

A combination of sun, sand and surf draws thousands of vacationers to the state's beaches and resorts. **Fishing, swimming, sunbathing** and **boating** lure outdoor enthusiasts to Hilton Head Island, Myrtle Beach, Isle of Palms and Seabrook, Kiawah, Fripp and Edisto islands. There is good **saltwater fishing** for mackerel, amberjack, barracuda, grouper and bonito.

Favorite pastimes are **crabbing** and **shrimping** along South Carolina's 2,876 miles of tidal shoreline. Oysters and clams can be gathered at any of several state shellfish grounds; phone the Shellfish Management Program in Charleston, (803) 795-6350, ext. 2027, for locations. Boating enthusiasts launch their craft along the Intracoastal Waterway and on such man-made lakes as Lake Murray near Columbia.

In recent years South Carolina has become known for its numerous championship **golf** and

tennis facilities. Excellent resort and public course are found throughout the state. Myrtle Beach, Kiawah Island and Hilton Head Island are the leading golf and tennis centers. Spring and fall are peak seasons for both golf and tennis.

Spectator sports run the gamut from **steeple chases, flat races** and **polo** at Camden and Aiken to **auto races** at Darlington, and collegiate team sports at Clemson and Columbia.

The state's long **hunting** seasons offer an added inducement for the sportsman. Deer season in some southern counties opens in August or September and runs to Jan. 1. The statewide game season generally opens Thanksgiving and closes March 1.

Whitetail deer, quail, rabbits, squirrels, opossums, foxes and raccoons thrive throughout the state, while wild turkeys inhabit regions characterized by mixed hardwood forests. Edgefield is the home of the Wild Turkey Center, the national headquarters of the National Wild Turkey Federation; phone (803) 637-3106.

Migratory waterfowl are most abundant in the coastal region. Francis Marion and Sumter national forests offer a variety of wildlife. Contact the South Carolina Department of Natural Resources (*see the For Your Information box*) for further information.

South Carolina's state parks are open all year; several have a nominal admission fee during peak seasons. Most of the parks offer a wide range of recreational facilities. Special programs include naturalist-conducted wildflower walks in April and autumn color walks in October. Advance registration is required for the walks; there is a nominal fee. At those parks which have them, furnished cabins rent on a weekly basis between Memorial Day and Labor Day, and a 2-day minimum the rest of the year. Reservations should be made well in advance by telephoning the individual park. Reservations for the *next* calendar year may be made beginning the first Monday following Jan. 1.

For more information write the Programs Section, South Carolina State Parks, 1205 Pendleton St., Columbia, SC 29201; phone (803) 734-0156. For detailed information about **camping** and **trailering** areas, both public and private, *see the AAA Southeastern CampBook.*

Throughout the TourBook, you may notice a Recreational Activities heading with bulleted listings of recreation-oriented establishments listed underneath. Since normal AAA inspection criteria cannot be applied, these establishments are presented for information only. Age, height and weight restrictions may apply. Reservations are often recommended and sometimes required. Visitors should phone or write the attraction for additional information, and the address and phone number are provided for this purpose.

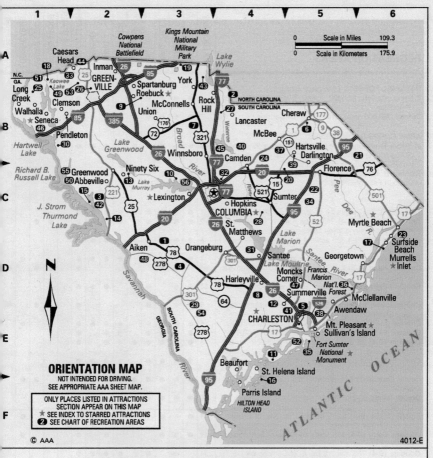

ORIENTATION MAP
NOT INTENDED FOR DRIVING.
SEE APPROPRIATE AAA SHEET MAP.

ONLY PLACES LISTED IN ATTRACTIONS
SECTION APPEAR ON THIS MAP
★ SEE INDEX TO STARRED ATTRACTIONS
❷ SEE CHART OF RECREATION AREAS

INDEX TO STARRED ATTRACTIONS
ATTRACTIONS AND PLACES OF EXCEPTIONAL INTEREST AND QUALITY

Brookgreen Gardens - see Murrells Inlet
Calhoun Mansion - see Charleston
Dixie Stampede - see Myrtle Beach
Dock Street Theatre - see Charleston
Edmondston-Alston House - see Charleston
Fort Sumter National Monument - see place listing
Gibbes Museum of Art - see Charleston
Hampton-Preston Mansion and Garden -
  see Columbia
Heyward-Washington House - see Charleston
Huguenot Church - see Charleston
Joseph Manigault House - see Charleston

Lexington County Museum Complex -
  see Lexington
Magnolia Plantation and Gardens -
  see Charleston
Middleton Place - see Charleston
Nathaniel Russell House - see Charleston
Patriots Point Naval and Maritime Museum -
  see Mount Pleasant
St. Michael's Episcopal Church - see Charleston
South Carolina State Museum - see Columbia
Walnut Grove Plantation - see Roebuck
World of Energy - see Seneca

SEE AND BE SEEN ON THE HIGHWAY.
Turn on your headlights at dusk to help avoid accidents.

RECREATION AREAS

RECREATION AREAS	MAP LOCATION	CAMPING	PICNICKING	HIKING TRAILS	BOATING	BOAT RAMP	BOAT RENTAL	FISHING	SWIMMING	PETS ON LEASH	BICYCLE TRAILS	NATURE PROGS.	VISITOR CENTER	LODGE/CABINS	FOOD SERVICE
NATIONAL FORESTS *(See place listings)*															
Francis Marion 251,000 acres. Coastal Plain n. of Charleston.		•	•	•	•	•		•		•		•	•		
Sumter 360,000 acres. Western South Carolina.		•	•	•	•	•		•	•	•		•			
ARMY CORPS OF ENGINEERS															
J. Strom Thurmond Lake (C-2) 70,000 acres 22 mi. n.w. of Augusta, Ga. on SR 28 or 30 mi. n.w. of Greenwood via US 221. Water skiing; aquarium.	42	•	•	•	•	•	•	•	•	•			•	•	
Richard B. Russell Lake (C-1) 26,650 acres 1 mi. w. of Calhoun Falls on SR 72.	55	•	•	•	•	•		•	•	•			•		•
STATE															
Aiken (D-3) 1,067 acres 16 mi. e. of Aiken off US 78.	1	•	•	•	•	•	•	•	•	•		•			
Andrew Jackson (B-4) 360 acres 8 mi. n. of Lancaster on US 521. Historic. *(See Lancaster)*	2	•	•	•	•	•		•		•		•	•		
Baker Creek (C-2) 1,305 acres 4 mi. s.w. of McCormick on US 378.	3	•	•	•	•	•	•	•	•	•					
Barnwell (D-3) 307 acres 7 mi. n.e. of Barnwell on SR 3.	4	•	•	•				•	•	•				•	
Caesars Head (A-2) 7,467 acres 16 mi. n. of Greenville on US 276 at N.C. state line.	44	•	•	•						•		•	•		•
Calhoun Falls (C-2) 438 acres 13 mi. w. of Abbeville on SR 81. Nature trail.	50	•	•	•	•	•		•	•	•					
Charlestowne Landing (E-5) 664 acres. Historic. Zoo. *(See Charleston and Vicinity)*	5		•	•				•		•		•	•		•
Cheraw (B-5) 7,361 acres 4 mi. s.w. of Cheraw on US 1.	6	•	•	•	•	•	•	•	•	•		•		•	
Chester (B-3) 523 acres 3 mi. s.e. of Chester on SR 72.	7	•	•	•	•	•	•	•		•		•			
Colleton (D-4) 35 acres 11 mi. n. of Walterboro on US 15. Canoeing.	8	•	•	•				•		•		•			
Croft (B-2) 7,054 acres 3 mi. s.e. of Spartanburg off SR 56.	9	•	•	•	•	•		•	•	•		•			
Devils Fork (A-1) 644 acres 16 mi. n.w. of Pickens off SR 11.	51	•	•	•	•	•		•	•	•				•	•
Dreher Island (C-3) 348 acres 6 mi. s.w. of Chapin off US 76.	10	•	•	•	•	•		•	•	•		•			
Edisto Beach (E-4) 1,255 acres 50 mi. s.w. of Charleston on SR 174. Shelling.	11	•	•	•				•	•	•				•	
Givhans Ferry (D-4) 988 acres 16 mi. w. of Summerville on SR 61.	12	•	•	•				•		•				•	
Goodale (B-4) 763 acres 2 mi. n. of Camden off US 1. Golf.	24		•	•		•		•	•	•		•			
Hamilton Branch (C-2) 731 acres 12 mi. s.e. of McCormick off US 221.	14	•	•		•	•		•		•		•			
Hampton Plantation (D-5) 337 acres 8 mi. n. of McClellanville off US 17.	36		•	•				•		•			•	•	
Hickory Knob (C-2) 1,091 acres 8 mi. s.w. of McCormick off US 378. Tennis, golf, archery.	15	•		•	•	•	•	•	•	•		•	•	•	•
Hunting Island (F-4) 5,000 acres 16 mi. s.e. of Beaufort on US 21. Lighthouse complex.	16	•	•	•	•			•	•	•		•	•	•	
Huntington Beach (D-6) 2,500 acres. Birdwatching. *(See Murrells Inlet in The Grand Strand)*	17	•	•	•				•	•	•		•	•		
Jones Gap (A-2) 3,346 acres 3 mi. n.w. of Marietta off US 276.	53	•	•	•				•		•		•			
Keowee-Toxaway (A-1) 1,000 acres on SR 11 at Lake Keowee, 12 mi. n.w. of Pickens.	18	•	•	•	•			•		•		•	•	•	
Kings Mountain (A-3) 6,471 acres 12 mi. n.w. of York on SR 161. Restored 1840s homestead.	19	•	•	•			•	•	•	•		•	•		
Lake Greenwood (C-2) 914 acres 17 mi. e. of Greenwood on SR 702.	13	•	•	•	•	•		•		•		•			
Lake Hartwell (B-1) 680 acres at Fair Play near jct. I-85 and SR 11.	46	•	•	•	•	•		•		•			•		
Lake Warren (E-3) 440 acres 5 mi. s.w. of Hampton off SR 363.	54		•	•				•		•		•			
Lake Wateree (B-4) 238 acres 30 mi. n. of Columbia off I-77.	45	•	•		•	•		•		•					
Landsford Canal (B-4) 244 acres 6 mi. n.w. of Lancaster off US 21.	27		•	•				•		•		•			

RECREATION AREAS

	MAP LOCATION	CAMPING	PICNICKING	HIKING TRAILS	BOATING	BOAT RAMP	BOAT RENTAL	FISHING	SWIMMING	PETS ON LEASH	BICYCLE TRAILS	NATURE PROGS.	VISITOR CENTER	LODGE/CABINS	FOOD SERVICE
Lee (C-5) 2,839 acres 7 mi. e. of Bishopville off I-20.	20	●	●	●	●			●	●	●					
Little Pee Dee (B-6) 835 acres 11 mi. s.e. of Dillon off SR 57.	21	●	●	●	●	●		●	●	●					
Lynches River (C-5) 668 acres 13 mi. s.w. of Florence on US 52.	22		●	●	●			●	●						
Myrtle Beach (D-6) 312 acres 3 mi. s. of Myrtle Beach on US 17.	23	●	●	●				●	●	●			●	●	●
Oconee (A-1) 1,165 acres 12 mi. n.w. of Walhalla off SR 28. Self-guiding auto tour.	25	●	●	●	●	●	●	●	●	●		●			
Old Dorchester (E-5) 325 acres. Historic. *(See Summerville in Charleston and Vicinity)*	41		●	●	●	●		●		●					
Old Santee Canal (D-5) 250 acres 1 mi. e. of Moncks Corner off US 52 bypass. Interpretive center.	47		●	●	●	●	●	●		●		●	●		
Paris Mountain (A-2) 1,275 acres 6 mi. n. of Greenville off US 25.	26	●	●	●	●			●	●	●		●			
Poinsett (C-4) 1,000 acres 18 mi. s.w. of Sumter off SR 261.	28	●	●	●	●	●		●	●	●		●		●	●
Redcliffe Plantation (D-3) 369 acres 3 mi. s.e. of Beech Island on US 278. Historic.	48		●					●		●			●		
Rivers Bridge (E-3) 390 acres 7 mi. s.w. of Ehrhardt off SR 64.	29	●	●	●				●	●	●					
Sadlers Creek (B-1) 395 acres 13 mi. s.w. of Anderson off US 29.	30	●	●	●	●	●		●		●		●			
Santee (D-4) 2,478 acres 3 mi. n.w. of Santee off US 301.	31	●	●	●	●	●	●	●	●	●		●	●	●	●
Sesquicentennial (C-4) 1,419 acres 13 mi. n.e. of Columbia on US 1.	32	●	●	●	●			●	●	●		●			
Table Rock (A-1) 3,083 acres 16 mi. n. of Pickens off SR 11.	33	●	●	●	●			●	●	●		●	●	●	●
Woods Bay (C-5) 1,541 acres 2.5 mi. s. of Olanta on US 301. Canoe rental.	34		●	●	●			●		●		●			
OTHER															
Folly Beach County Park (E-5) 140 acres off Ashley Ave. at w. end of Folly Island.	35		●					●	●	●					
James Island County Park (E-5) 640 acres 7 mi. s. of Charleston off SR 171. Pedal boat rental, playground.	52	●	●	●				●		●	●				●
Lake Murray (C-3) 50,000 acres 9 mi. w. of Columbia.	56	●	●		●	●		●	●	●					●
Lake Robinson (B-4) 2,250 acres 6 mi. w. of Hartsville off SR 151.	37		●		●	●		●		●			●		
Lake Wylie (A-3) 12,455 acres 17 mi. s. of Charlotte, N.C., off SR 49S. Water skiing.	43	●	●		●	●		●	●	●					
Mile Creek Park (B-1) 155 acres 16 mi. n. of Clemson on SR 133.	49	●	●	●	●	●		●		●					
Palmetto Islands County Park (E-5) 943 acres 8 mi. n. of Charleston off US 17 bypass.	38		●	●			●	●	●	●	●	●			●
Prestwood Lake (C-5) 281 acres in Hartsville.	39		●		●	●		●		●					
Wateree Lake (B-4) 13,710 acres 6 mi. n. of Camden on SR 97.	40	●	●	●	●	●		●	●	●					

Points of Interest

ABBEVILLE (C-2) pop. 5,800, elev. 535′

"The Birthplace of the Confederacy" also was its deathbed; both the first organized secession meeting in 1860 and the last cabinet meeting of Confederate president Jefferson Davis in 1865 took place in Abbeville in what is known as Burk-Stark Mansion. John C. Calhoun, statesman and vice president of the United States 1825-32, was born in Abbeville, where he later practiced law.

The historic 1908 Abbeville Opera House on Town Square once presented well-known performers Fanny Brice, Jimmy Durante and Groucho Marx on its stage; today the restored theater offers a broad range of contemporary works.

Abbeville Chamber of Commerce: 107 Court Sq., Abbeville, SC 29620; phone (864) 459-4600.

Self-guiding tours: A map detailing a tour is available at the chamber of commerce.

AIKEN (D-2) pop. 19,900, elev. 490′

The terrain, sandy roads and mild climate of the sandhills region make Aiken an equestrian sporting ground. Thoroughbreds and Standardbreds train on its three racetracks. Carriage roads and bridle paths wind through Hitchcock Woods, a preserve off South Boundary Avenue.

Saturdays the Aiken Chamber of Commerce offers guided bus tours of historic sites. Reservations are requested for the $5 tour; phone (803) 641-1111.

The Aiken Triple Crown, three successive weekends of flat track, steeplechase and harness racing, and the Triple Crown Road Race for human runners are held in March. Other events include Aiken's Makin', a display of arts and crafts in September, and the Christmas Craft Show in December.

Greater Aiken Chamber of Commerce: 400 Laurens St. N.W., P.O. Box 892, Aiken, SC 29802; phone (803) 641-1111.

Self-guiding tours: A map detailing a driving tour past historic landmarks is available from the chamber of commerce

AIKEN COUNTY HISTORICAL MUSEUM, 433 Newberry St. S.W., occupies Banksia, the circa-1930 estate of Richard Howe. Rooms depict late 18th- and early 19th-century life in Aiken County. Displays include military and American Indian artifacts, a drugstore from the former town of Dunbarton and a handmade miniature circus featuring 1,700 pieces. Tues.-Fri. 9:30-4:30, Sat.-Sun. 2-5; closed holidays. Donations. Phone (803) 642-2015.

HOPELANDS GARDENS AND THOROUGHBRED RACING HALL OF FAME, .5 mi. s. off SR 19 at 149 Dupree Pl., are on the grounds of a former estate. A restored carriage house contains racing silks, trophies, photographs and other Thoroughbred racing memorabilia. There also is a changing equine art display. A touch and scent trail lined with identification plaques in Braille leads to the Performing Arts Stage.

Open-air concerts are presented Monday evenings May through August, and outdoor theater is presented in the garden Thursday evenings, mid-July through August. Gardens open daily 10-dusk. Hall of Fame open Tues.-Sun. 2-5, Sept.-June. Donations. Phone (803) 642-7630, 642-7648 for concert information, or 648-1438 for theater information.

AWENDAW—
see Charleston and Vicinity p. 151.

BEAUFORT (E-4) pop. 9,600, elev. 15′

A picturesque old port town, Beaufort (BEW-fort) retains the atmosphere of an earlier day. Its many pre-Revolutionary and antebellum houses surrounded by quiet gardens stand along narrow oak-canopied streets. The oldest is the 1717 Thomas Hepworth House at Port Republic and New streets.

Established by charter from the lords proprietor in 1711, Beaufort is the second oldest town in the state. Its history dates back to Spanish exploration in 1520 and attempted settlements on nearby Parris Island by French Huguenots in 1562 and the Spanish in 1566 and 1577. Areas of early settlement have been the focus of several archeological digs.

In March 1863 the Beaufort National Cemetery was established. Today the remains of more than 7,500 Civil War soldiers as well as those of 6,500 other servicemen killed in action in subsequent wars are interred here. This is the final resting place of Marine Corps PFC. Ralph H. Johnson, who posthumously received the Congressional Medal of Honor for service as a reconnaissance scout in Vietnam. The cemetery is surrounded by a brick wall, with the entrance at 1601 Boundary St.

Moviemakers have made their mark on Beaufort. The city has been the site of filming for several movies, including "The Big Chill," "The Great Santini" and the blockbuster "Forrest Gump."

Facing the Intracoastal Waterway, Beaufort has one of the best natural harbors on the Atlantic coast. The Henry C. Chambers Waterfront Park, on Beaufort River off Bay Street, includes a marina, pavilion and amphitheater. Also in the area is Lady's Island across Beaufort River.

Greater Beaufort Chamber of Commerce: 1006 Bay St., P.O. Box 910, Beaufort, SC 29901; phone (803) 524-0600.

Self-guiding tours: Maps for walking tours of the historic district are available from the chamber of commerce.

BEAUFORT MUSEUM, 713 Craven St., is housed in a 1798 arsenal. Exhibits include local American Indian artifacts, decorative arts, Revolutionary and Civil War relics, cannons and stamps. Guided tours are available. Mon.-Tues. and Thurs.-Sat. 10-5; closed holidays. Admission $2, students with ID 50c. Phone (803) 525-7017.

CARRIAGE TOURS OF BEAUFORT, 1006 Bay St., offers 45-minute horse-drawn carriage excursions through Beaufort's historic district. The tours include a narrated history of the town. Tours depart every half-hour Mon.-Sat. 9:30-5:30. Last tour begins 1 hour before closing. Fare $12.50; over 61, $11.50; ages 3-11, $6.50. Phone (803) 521-1651.

THE JOHN MARK VERDIER HOUSE, 801 Bay St., is a fine Federal-style residence built in the late 1790s by John Mark Verdier, one of Beaufort's leading merchants and planters. The Marquis de Lafayette was entertained at the house during his visit to Beaufort in 1825. During the

Civil War the house served as a headquarters for the Union Army.

The house has been restored and furnished as it would have been between 1790 and Lafayette's visit. Guided tours are available. Open Tues.-Sat. 11-4; closed major holidays. Admission $4; ages 5-12, $2. Phone (803) 524-6334.

ST. HELENA'S EPISCOPAL CHURCH, Church St. between King and North sts., was founded in 1712. The wooden altar was carved by the crew of the USS *New Hampshire*, which was stationed nearby during Reconstruction. In the churchyard are tombstones used as operating tables during the Civil War. Among the interesting grave sites is a brick sepulcher built for a doctor who feared being buried alive. His friends promised to place in his tomb bread, water and an ax to ensure his escape. Mon.-Fri. 10-4. Donations. Phone (803) 522-1712.

CAESARS HEAD (A-1) elev. 3,118′

The small community of Caesars Head is a popular summer resort. Caesars Head State Park *(see Recreation Chart)* is at the foot of its namesake, 3,227-foot Caesars Head Mountain; from the "head," it is a sheer drop of nearly 1,200 feet to the valley. Phone (864) 836-6115 for more park information.

CAMDEN (B-4) pop. 6,700, elev. 222′

Camden is one of the oldest inland towns in the state. The first settlement was made in 1751 by Irish Quakers, who named their town Pine Tree Hill. The name was changed in 1768 to honor Lord Camden, a friend of the Colonies.

More than a dozen Revolutionary War battles, including the Battle of Camden and the Battle of Hobkirk Hill, were fought within 30 miles of Camden. May 8, 1781, the British evacuated Camden after burning most of it.

Camden's mild climate is suited for steeplechases, including the Carolina Cup in March and the Colonial Cup in November. A polo field and 200 miles of bridle paths and country roads also lure equestrians.

Bethesda Presbyterian Church, 502 DeKalb St., was designed in 1822 by Robert Mills, the architect of the Washington Monument. A granite monument in front of the church is dedicated to Baron DeKalb, a Revolutionary War soldier of Austrian descent killed in the Battle of Camden. The cornerstone was laid by the Marquis de Lafayette in 1825. Another local memorial, Monument Square at Broad and Laurens streets, honors Camden's six Confederate generals.

Kershaw County Chamber of Commerce: 724 S. Broad St., P.O. Box 605, Camden, SC 29020; phone (803) 432-2525.

Self-guiding tours: A booklet detailing a driving tour past 63 historic sites, some of which are open to the public, is available from Historic Camden, Camden Archives and Museum *(see attraction listings)* and the chamber of commerce.

CAMDEN ARCHIVES AND MUSEUM, 1314 N. Broad St., chronicles Camden's history through documents, Civil War artifacts and other regional memorabilia. A restored 1825 clock was used in the City Hall tower for some 80 years. Allow 30 minutes minimum. Mon.-Fri. 8-5 (also first Sun. of the month 1-5); closed holidays. Free. Phone (803) 425-6050.

FINE ARTS CENTER OF KERSHAW COUNTY, at Lyttleton and York sts., displays a variety of works of art. Allow 30 minutes minimum. Mon.-Fri. 9-5. Free. Phone (803) 425-7676.

SAVE **HISTORIC CAMDEN,** 1 mi. s. on US 521, is a 98-acre nature trail. On the site are restored buildings, including the Bradley, Craven, Cunningham and Drakeford houses. A trail leads to reconstructions of Revolutionary War fortifications, the powder magazine and the 1777 Kershaw-Cornwallis House, where Cornwallis made his war headquarters. A Revolutionary War Encampment is held the first weekend in November. Picnicking is permitted.

Mon.-Sat. 10-5, Sun. 1-5. Tours are given Tues.-Fri. at 10:30, 1:30 and 3, Sat. 10-4, Sun. 1-4. Last tour begins 1 hour before closing. Closed major holidays. Free. Guided tour $5; over 64, $4.50; students with ID $2. Phone (803) 432-9841.

Area Code Change

The Coastal and Pee Dee regions will change their area code from 803 to 843 effective Mar. 22, 1998, when permissive dialing goes into effect. After Sept. 27, 1998 only the 843 area code will be effective for these regions.

Towns that will be located in the new area code include Beaufort, Charleston, Darlington, Dillon, Florence, Georgetown, Hartsville, Hilton Head, McBee, McClellanville, McColl, Moncks Corner, Mount Pleasant, Murrells Inlet, Myrtle Beach, Pawleys Island, Sullivans Island, Summerville and West Myrtle Beach.

Charleston
and Vicinity

Preservation is a way of life in Charleston. From stately antebellum houses to the more utilitarian "single houses" that shoulder the narrow streets, this 300-year-old city is renowned for its splendid architecture. Embellished with fanciful wrought-iron work as intricate as window frost, and painted sparkling whites, pastels or whimsical rainbow hues, Charleston's houses delight the eye.

Once a cradle of Southern gentility, Charleston is now one of its last bastions. Ancestral pride runs deeper than the Ashley and Cooper rivers that shape the slender peninsula on which the city is built. A story that mány locals tell illustrates the Charlestonian spirit. It concerns a wealthy matron who was asked repeatedly why she didn't spend some of her money on travel. "But my dear," she was said to reply, "why should I travel when I'm already here?" Charleston epito-

Courtesy: The Charleston Area CNVB

mizes the gracious air of the Old South, where life moves at the leisurely pace of a stroll along The Battery.

Though easygoing and elegant, Charleston gave America its first decisive victory in the Revolutionary War and the first defiant shots of the Civil War. A pioneer in civic affairs, the city established the country's first municipal chamber of commerce, municipal college and public museum. In 1931 it passed the first historic district zoning ordinance to preserve its architectural heritage.

Named for King Charles II, Charles Towne was founded in 1670 by English settlers along the marshy shores of nearby Albemarle Point. The settlement relocated to its present site 10 years later. Despite American Indian uprisings, a threat by the French, epidemics and privateers, Charles Towne had developed into a vigorous port and a prosperous and fashionable Colonial city by the mid-1700s.

Though drawn reluctantly into the Revolution, Charles Towne stubbornly repulsed a British attack by sea in 1776 and a second offensive by land 2 years later, before it finally was captured in 1780. The British left in 1782 and the city was incorporated as Charleston the following year.

In 1860, South Carolina passed the first Ordinance of Secession at Charleston, and in April 1861 the Confederates occupied Fort Sumter. For 3 years Union ships blockaded the city, battering Fort Sumter with artillery fire, but the defenders refused to yield. Submarine warfare was introduced in Charleston when the Confederate vessel *Hunley* sank the USS *Housatonic.* The Confederate Army finally abandoned the city late in the war.

Charleston's historic district encompasses more than 2,000 buildings: 73 pre-date the Revolutionary War, 136 date from the late 1700s and more than 600 others were built in the early 1800s. So many church spires poke at the sky that Charleston once was nicknamed "The Holy City." Among the churches which offer tours by appointment are St. James United Methodist Church, 512 St. James Ave., (803) 553-3117; and the Unitarian Church, 8 Archdale St., (803) 723-4617.

Hurricane Hugo's assault in 1989 resulted in massive damages in Charleston, as well as statewide, but 95 percent of the city's structures survived, and the historic district remained intact.

The Battery, the waterfront along the edge of the historic district, offers fine views of the harbor. North of The Battery along E. Bay Street is a particularly colorful collection of houses known as Rainbow Row. A distinctive residential style is the single house, a narrow structure one room wide and two rooms deep whose gabled end, rather than its front, faces the street. Often a single house includes a piazza—the city's version of a veranda—and the pride of any Charleston home: a garden.

Nowhere does Charleston flaunt its beauty more than in its gardens. From the magnificent scale of the nearby plantation gardens to the more modest but equally enchanting walled gardens in the city, the Charleston area's lavish floral displays are famous throughout the world. Charlestonians proudly showcase many of their private residences and gardens during the annual spring and fall tours of houses.

Approaches

By Car

The major approach from the north and south is US 17, which angles into the city proper over the high Cooper River bridges on the east and the Ashley River bridges to the west. US 17 cuts directly across the heart of Charleston and provides easy access to all parts of the city. US 17 links with I-526 to bypass the city.

I-26 approaches from the west, terminating at US 17 near the center of Charleston. It provides a link with several important routes, including I-95, another major north-south highway.

SR 61 is a scenic approach paralleling the Ashley River on the west and giving access to several historic plantations. Other important approaches include US 52, which parallels I-26 immediately west of Charleston; SR 41, which traverses the Lowcountry to the north and terminates at US 17 northeast of the city; and US 701, also from the north, which merges with US 17 and terminates in Charleston.

Getting Around

Street System

Crowded as they are onto a narrow peninsula, most Charleston streets are basically parallel or perpendicular, and many are narrow and/or one-way. While a rough grid is evident, the angle of the grid shifts along the dividing line of Beaufain and Hasell streets in the lower part of town.

Several major north-south streets traverse the city. King Street (US 78), one-way heading south, and Meeting Street (US 52), a two-way street one block east, run through the heart of downtown and the historic districts. E. Bay Street (US 52A) branches off from Meeting Street in the north and winds down the east side, becoming E. Battery Street and then Murray Boulevard as it swings around The Battery. Ashley and Rutledge streets, a block apart and going one way north and south respectively, connect with the western end of Murray Boulevard.

Major east-west streets that cross all of the above thoroughfares south of the US 17 artery include Calhoun and Broad streets, both going two ways, and Tradd Street, one way eastbound. The speed limit is 30 mph unless otherwise posted.

Unless otherwise posted, a right turn on red and a left turn from a one-way street onto a one-way street are permitted after a complete stop.

Parking

Both nonmetered and 50c-per-hour metered parking can be found on downtown streets. Parking garages also are available throughout the

The Informed Traveler

CITY POPULATION: 80,400   **ELEVATION:** 10 ft.

Whom To Call

Emergency: 911

Police (non-emergency): (803) 577-7434

Time and Temperature: (803) 572-8463

Hospitals: Bon Secours-St. Francis Xavier Hospital, (803) 577-1000; Charleston Memorial Hospital, (803) 953-8300; Roper Hospital North, (803) 724-2000.

Where to Look

Newspapers

The major daily newspaper in Charleston is the *Post Courier*. The area also is served by several local weekly newspapers.

Radio and TV

Charleston radio station WTMZ (910 AM) is an all-news/weather station; WSCI (89.3 FM) is programmed by National Public Radio.

The major network TV channels are 2 (ABC), 4 (NBC), 5 (CBS), 7 (PBS) and 57 (FOX). For a complete list of radio and television programs, consult the daily newspaper.

Visitor Information

The Charleston Visitor Center is at 375 Meeting St. Self-guiding tour maps, brochures and information about local events and performance schedules are available. The center is open daily 8:30-5 (also 5-5:30 during DST). Information also can be obtained by writing the Charleston Trident Convention and Visitors Bureau, P.O. Box 975, Charleston, SC 29402. Phone the center or the bureau at (803) 853-8000 or (800) 868-8118.

What to Wear

Charleston enjoys a subtropical climate with a year-round average temperature of 65. Summers generally are hot and humid, with highs in the upper 80s. Winters are mild with occasional cold snaps. March through April and October through November are pleasant months; highs average in the mid-60s and 70s and lows in the high 40s and 50s.

downtown area; fees average 75c an hour with lower daily rates.

What To See

THE BATTERY, also known as White Point Gardens, is on Battery Point. The East, or "High," Battery faces the Cooper River and Charleston Harbor, where some of the settlement's earliest fortifications were. Now planted with palmettos and live oaks, the park contains cannons and other war relics, as well as a monument to the defenders of Fort Moultrie and Fort Sumter. Many walking, motorized and carriage tours of historic Charleston include The Battery on their itineraries. Allow 30 minutes minimum.

BEST FRIEND OF CHARLESTON, 31 Ann St., is a railroad and train museum that includes a replica of the "Best Friend of Charleston", the first engine on the passenger train system. Allow 30 minutes minimum. Mon.-Sat. 9-5, Sun. 1-5; closed Jan. 1, Thanksgiving and Dec. 25. Free. Phone (803) 973-7269.

BETH ELOHIM, 90 Hasell St., is an imposing 1840 synagogue of Greek Revival design. Introducing in 1824 a liberalized ritual that used instrumental music during the service for the first time, the synagogue became the birthplace of Reform Judaism in the United States. Organized in 1749, the temple also is distinguished as the nation's oldest synagogue in continuous use. Archives are available. Open Sun.-Fri. 10-noon. Free. Phone (803) 723-1090.

★**CALHOUN MANSION,** 16 Meeting St., was one of the most elaborate showplaces in the Old South. The Victorian mansion, built about 1876, is embellished throughout with ornate plaster moldings, original tile floors and walnut, cherry and oak woodwork. The gas chandeliers have hand-painted porcelain and hand-etched globes. A skylight built into a 45-foot-high ceiling illuminates the ballroom. The house is furnished in period, with a few original pieces.

Allow 1 hour minimum. Guided 45-minute tours are given continuously Wed.-Sun. 10-4, Feb.-Dec.; closed Thanksgiving and Dec. 24-25. Admission $10; ages 6-15, $5. Phone (803) 722-8205.

CHARLESTON MUSEUM, 360 Meeting St. at John St., was established in 1773 and, although housed in a modern facility, is considered the nation's oldest museum. Focusing on Charleston and the Lowcountry, the museum houses displays about natural history, archeology, ornithology and history. A children's room contains computers and hands-on exhibits. The silver collection includes English pieces, as well as those by Charleston silversmiths dating from the 18th century.

Allow 1 hour minimum. Mon.-Sat. 9-5, Sun. 1-5; closed major holidays. Admission $6; ages 3-12, $3. Combination tickets with the Heyward-Washington House and/or Joseph Manigault House are available; $10 for two sites, $15 for three sites. Phone (803) 722-2996.

SAVE **CHARLESTOWNE LANDING** is on SR 171 between US 17 and I-26 at 1500 Old Town Rd. The site of the state's first permanent English settlement, founded in 1670, is now part of a 664-acre park. Earthworks and a palisade have been reconstructed. Visitors can board the replica of a 17th-century trading vessel moored on a creek or participate in activities in the Settlers' Life Area. A pavilion traces the colony's history. Narrated tram tours and bicycle rentals are available. Picnicking is permitted.

Allow 3 hours minimum. Daily 9-6, June-Aug.; 9-5, rest of year. Closed Dec. 24-25. Admission $5; over 64 and ages 6-14, $2.50. Tram tour $1. Phone (803) 852-4200.

THE CITADEL MUSEUM, is on the third floor of Daniel Library, the first building on the right, inside the main gate of the campus at the foot of Moultrie St. between Hampton Park and the Ashley River. Military, academic, social and athletic

Transportation

Air travel: Most major carriers serve Charleston International Airport, 12 miles west of downtown on I-26.

Rental cars: Hertz, (803) 767-4550 or (800) 654-3080, is located at the airport and offers discounts to AAA members. For listings of other agencies check the telephone directory.

Rail service: The Amtrak train station, (800) 872-7245, is at 4565 Gaynor Ave. in North Charleston.

Buses: Service is provided by Greyhound Lines Inc., (803) 722-7721, at 3610 Dorchester Rd.

Taxis: Cab companies include North Area Taxi, (803) 554-7575, Safety Cab, (803) 722-4066, and Yellow Cab, (803) 577-6565. Taxis are on the meter system; the fare is $1.50 upon entering the cab, and $1 per mile. Fares within the city limits average $2.50 for the first passenger, $1 for each additional passenger; outside the city limits $1 per mile is added to the base rate. Cabs must be ordered by phone.

Public transport: Bus service is provided by South Carolina Electric and Gas Co.; phone (803) 747-0922 for information about routes and schedules. The Downtown Area Shuttle, or DASH, operates daily 8-5 and has many pickup points in the old and historic districts. The fare of $1 provides all-day use; phone (803) 724-7368.

aspects of cadet life are featured through exhibits tracing the history of the college from 1842 to the present. Next to the library is Summerall Chapel which was designed in the spirit of 14th-century Gothic architecture.

A cadet dress parade takes place on the campus each Friday at 3:45 during the school year. Museum open Sun.-Fri. 2-5, Sat. noon-5 while school is in session; closed holidays. Free. Phone (803) 953-6846.

CITY HALL, Broad and Meeting sts., first was used as the United States Bank. Built in 1801, it contains historic relics and a portrait gallery in the Council Chamber. Among the paintings are John Trumbull's 1791 portrait of George Washington and Samuel F.B. Morse's portrait of James Monroe. Mon.-Fri. 9-5. Free. Phone (803) 577-6970.

★**DOCK STREET THEATRE,** Church and Queen sts., opened in 1736 as America's first building

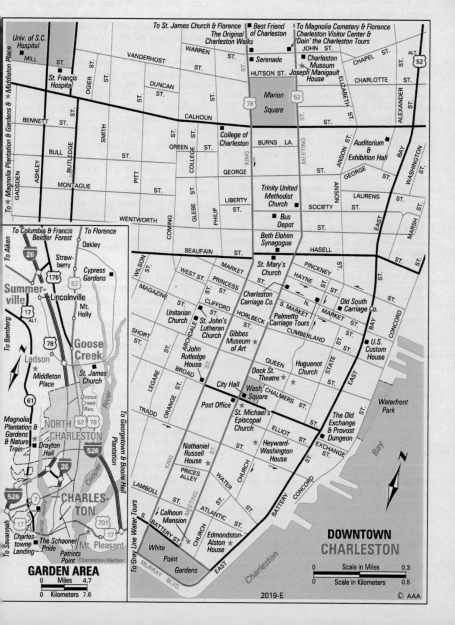

GARDEN AREA

Miles 4.7
Kilometers 7.6

DOWNTOWN CHARLESTON

Scale in Miles   0   0.3
Scale in Kilometers   0   0.5

2019-E   © AAA

designed solely for theatrical performances. The Planters Hotel, built around the original theater's ruins in the early 1800s, was a well-known rendezvous for the local gentry; the drink "Planters Punch" is said to have originated there. In the mid-1930s, the hotel was remodeled into the new Dock Street Theatre. Frequent performances are staged in the theater and foyer. Open Mon.-Fri. noon-6; closed holidays. Theater free; performance prices vary. Phone (803) 965-4032 for theater and performance information.

★EDMONDSTON-ALSTON HOUSE overlooks the harbor at 21 E. Battery St. The house was built about 1828 by Charles Edmondston, a wealthy merchant and wharf owner. Later it was bought by Col. William Alston for his son, Charles, who redecorated it in the Greek Revival style. The house is furnished with family possessions, including documents, portraits, engravings, silver and porcelain. It also contains elaborate and unconventional woodwork.

Allow 30 minutes minimum. Guided 30-minute tours Tues.-Sat. 10-4:30, Sun.-Mon. 1:30-4:30; closed Dec. 25. Last tour begins at at closing. Admission $7, under 6 free. Combination admission to Drayton Hall, Edmondston-Alston House, Gibbes Museum of Art, Middleton Place and Nathaniel Russell House $29; under 12, $19. Phone (803) 722-7171.

FESTIVAL OF HOUSES AND GARDENS features walking tours of private houses and gardens, most dating 1712-1850. For dates of particular events write the Historic Charleston Foundation, P.O. Box 1120, Charleston, SC 29402. Afternoon tours 2-5, plantation oyster roasts 4:30-7:30, candlelight tours 7-10 and candlelight galas 6-9, mid-Mar. to mid-Apr. Fee $25. Reservations are recommended. Phone (803) 722-3405 or 723-1623.

"FOREVER CHARLESTON" is presented in the Charleston Visitor Center, 375 Meeting St. This 24-minute multimedia presentation focuses on the history and flavor of Charleston and comprises more than 2,400 projected images that reveal the beauty of Charleston and the heritage of its people. Shows every half-hour daily 9-4:30; closed Thanksgiving and Dec. 25. Admission $2.50; over 64, $2; ages 6-12, $1. Phone (803) 853-8000.

FORT MOULTRIE—
see Fort Sumter National Monument in the Vicinity section p. 152.

★GIBBES MUSEUM OF ART, 135 Meeting St., has an outstanding collection of American paintings, Japanese woodblock prints, sculpture, engravings and other art objects. Changing exhibits, concerts and lectures are presented throughout the year. Allow 30 minutes minimum. Tues.-Sat. 10-5, Sun.-Mon. 1-5; closed major holidays. Admission $5; over 61, military and college students with ID $4; ages 6-18, $3. Combination admission to Drayton Hall, Edmondston-Alston House, Gibbes Museum of Art, Middleton Place and Nathaniel Russell House $29; under 12, $19. Phone (803) 722-2706.

★HEYWARD-WASHINGTON HOUSE is at 87 Church St. This 1772 house was built by prominent rice planter Daniel Heyward for his son, Thomas Heyward Jr., a signer of the Declaration of Independence. George Washington was a guest here during his visit to Charleston in May 1791. Most of the furnishings are from Charleston. A kitchen house, servants' quarters and a garden behind the main house are included in the tour.

Allow 30 minutes minimum. Mon.-Sat. 10-5, Sun. 1-5. Last tour begins 30 minutes before closing. Closed major holidays. Admission $6; ages 3-12, $3. Combination tickets with the Charleston Museum and/or Joseph Manigault House are available; $10 for two sites, $15 for three sites. Phone (803) 722-0354.

★HUGUENOT CHURCH (French Protestant), 136 Church St., is one of the last remaining Huguenot churches in the nation. For 150 years services were conducted in French, but English now is used; a French Liturgy Service is held each year in the spring. The church is a fine example of Gothic architecture. Guide service is available. Allow 30 minutes minimum. Mon.-Fri. 10-4, Sat. 10-noon, Mar.-June and Sept.-Nov.; closed holidays. Donations. Phone (803) 722-4385.

JOHN RUTLEDGE HOUSE, 116 Broad St., was the town house of John Rutledge, a leading South Carolina statesman and signer of the U.S. Constitution. The restored 1763 house now operates as an inn. It is furnished with antiques and period reproductions. Displayed in the upstairs parlor are relics from the restoration. Allow 30 minutes minimum. Daily 10-4. Free. Phone (803) 723-7999.

★JOSEPH MANIGAULT HOUSE, 350 Meeting St., was designed by Gabriel Manigault for his brother Joseph, a wealthy rice planter, and built in 1803. A notable house of the Adam style, it has fine examples of French-, English- and Charleston-made furniture. A hidden stairway connects the second and third floors.

Allow 30 minutes minimum. Guided tours Mon.-Sat. 10-5, Sun. 1-5. Last tour begins 30 minutes before closing. Closed major holidays. Admission $6; ages 3-12, $3. Combination tickets with the Charleston Museum and/or Heyward-Washington House are available; $10 for two sites, $15 for three sites. Phone (803) 723-2926.

MAGNOLIA CEMETERY, about 1 mi. n. just off US 52 on the banks of the Cooper River, was established in 1849. Among its numerous ornate grave sites are those of South Carolina soldiers who died at Gettysburg and the crew from the CSS *Hunley.* Confederate Memorial Day services include a reading of Henry Timrod's ode, "Magnolia Cemetery," written for the first service in 1866. Allow 30 minutes minimum. Daily 8-5. Free.

MARION SQUARE, or Citadel Green, on Calhoun St. between King and Meeting sts., has monuments to John C. Calhoun, vice president to John Quincy Adams; and to Wade Hampton, Confederate general and governor of South Carolina. The square also contains a part of the Tabby Horn Work, the only remaining section of the bastion system of Colonial defense works. Fronting the square is the Old Citadel Building. Citadel Square Baptist Church and St. Matthew's Lutheran Church also face the green.

★**NATHANIEL RUSSELL HOUSE,** 51 Meeting St., was completed in 1808 for Nathaniel Russell, a wealthy merchant. Set in a spacious garden, the house is a fine example of Federal architecture. Notable features include a free-standing staircase that spirals up three floors, oval drawing rooms and ornate interior detailing. Period furnishings include works by Charleston craftsmen.

Allow 30 minutes minimum. Guided tours Mon.-Sat. 10-5, Sun. 2-5. Last tour begins 20 minutes before closing. Closed Thanksgiving and Dec.24-25. Admission $6, under 6 free. Combination admission to Drayton Hall, Edmondston-Alston House, Gibbes Museum of Art, Middleton Place and Nathaniel Russell House $29; under 12, $19. Phone (803) 724-8481.

THE OLD EXCHANGE AND PROVOST DUNGEON, 122 E. Bay St. at Broad St., was built by the British in 1771 as the Customs House and Exchange for the prosperous city of Charles Towne. In the Great Hall, George Washington was entertained several times and South Carolina ratified the Constitution in 1788. In the original cellars where the British imprisoned prominent patriots during the American Revolution, animatronic "personages" of the past relate events of import to early Charles Towne and the fledgling nation. The excavated Half-moon Battery portion

of the wall which surrounded Charles Towne in the late 1600s is visible in the dungeon.

Allow 30 minutes minimum. Daily 9-5; closed major holidays. Admission $6; over 50, $5.50; ages 7-12, $3.50. Phone (803) 727-2165. *See color ad.*

ST. JOHN'S LUTHERAN CHURCH, Archdale and Clifford sts., was founded and built by German immigrants in 1817 and has been remodeled. It is noted for its wrought-iron gates, fence and steeple. Mon.-Fri. 9:30-3:30. Donations. Phone (803) 723-2426.

ST. MARY'S CHURCH is between Meeting and King sts. at 89 Hasell St. Established in 1789, this is the Mother Church of the Catholic diocese of the Carolinas and Georgia. The church, dating from 1839, contains religious paintings. Daily 7-4:30. Donations. Phone (803) 722-7696.

★**ST. MICHAEL'S EPISCOPAL CHURCH** is at Broad and Meeting sts. Begun in 1751, St. Michael's was the second Episcopal church in Charleston. Designed after the 1720s St. Martin's-in-the-Fields in London, it is considered a notable architectural achievement. Its Palladian Doric portico and storied steeple rise 186 feet above the street. The clock in the tower has marked the time since 1764.

The richly ornamented interior includes box pews and the original pulpit. An old cemetery is on the grounds. Mon.-Fri. 9-5, Sat. 9-noon. Donations. Phone (803) 723-0603.

SERENADE, in Charleston Music Hall at 37 John St., offers 2 hours of music, comedy and dance. Extravagant costumes add to the effect of the variety show. Food is available. Performances are Tues.-Sat. at 8, Feb. 1-late Nov.; at 7, late Nov.-Dec. 31. Admission $25; over 54, $23; students with ID, $18; under 16, $13. AE, DS, MC, VI. Phone (803) 973-3333. *See ad p. 142.*

WASHINGTON SQUARE, or City Hall Park, at Broad and Meeting sts., includes several monuments honoring prominent South Carolinians. Among these are memorials to Henry Timrod, a

noted South Carolina poet; Gen. P.G.T. Beauregard, leader of the city's defense during the Civil War; and the Washington Light Infantry. Also on the square is the Fireproof Building, the nation's first fireproof structure, designed by Robert Mills.

Gardens and Nearby Points of Interest

AUDUBON SWAMP GARDEN, at Magnolia Plantation, 10 mi. n.w. of jct. US 17 on SR 61 (Ashley River Rd.), encompasses 60 acres of blackwater cypress and tupelo swamp accessible by boardwalks, bridges and dikes, with binocular stands for viewing waterfowl, alligators and other wildlife. Allow 1 hour minimum. Daily 8-dusk. Admission $9; ages 13-19, $7; ages 6-12, $4. Phone (803) 571-1266. *See color ad p. 143.*

BOONE HALL PLANTATION—
see Mount Pleasant in the Vicinity section p. 153.

SAVE DRAYTON HALL is 9 mi. n.w. on SR 61 at 3380 Ashley River Rd. Built about 1738 by John Drayton, a member of the Privy Council of the royal governor, this mansion remained in the family for seven generations. The plantation house is an outstanding example of Georgian Palladian architecture. Never modernized with electric lighting, plumbing or central heating, the house is virtually in its original condition. It is noted for its hand-carved woodwork and plasterwork.

Allow 1 hour minimum. Guided 45-minute house tours on the hour daily 10-4, Mar.-Oct.; 10-3, rest of year. Closed Jan. 1, Thanksgiving and Dec. 25. Admission $8; ages 12-18, $6; ages 6-11, $4. Combination admission to Drayton Hall, Edmondston-Alston House, Gibbes Museum of Art, Middleton Place and Nathaniel Rus-

sell House $29; under 12, $19. Phone (803) 766-0188. *See color ad p. 144.*

SAVE ★MAGNOLIA PLANTATION AND GARDENS is on Ashley River Rd. (SR 61), 10 mi. n.w. of jct. US 17. This 500-acre estate was acquired in 1676 by the Drayton family, whose heirs still own it. The 50-acre garden dating from the 1680s contains 900 varieties of camellias, 250 types of azaleas and hundreds of other flowering species providing year-round color. The pre-Revolutionary Greek revival plantation house depicts life since the Civil War and showcases Early American antiques and rare botanical and ornithological prints and books.

Highlights include a petting zoo, waterfowl refuge, biblical garden, topiary garden, herb garden, Barbados tropical garden, a replica of the 16th-century Hampton Court horticultural maze, an antebellum cabin, wildlife observation tower, orientation theater and bicycle, canoe and nature trails. Guided house tours are available. Picnicking and leashed pets are permitted.

Allow 2 hours minimum. Grounds open daily 8-dusk, last admission at 5:30, mid-Feb. through early Nov.; opening time varies while the last admission is at 4:30, rest of year. Guided 30-minute house tours every half-hour 9 a.m.-30 minutes before last grounds admission. Admission to grounds and gardens $9; over 64, $8; ages 13-18, $7; ages 6-12, $4. House tours (in addition to grounds and gardens admission) $5. Under 6 are not permitted on house tours but are permitted on the grounds and on the train. Phone (803) 571-1266. *See color ad p. 143.*

Nature Train, on Magnolia Plantation, offers a narrated 45-minute tour of the wildlife refuge outskirts and focuses on plantation and natural history. Daily (weather permitting) 9-5, mid-Feb.

through early Nov. Fare (in addition to grounds and gardens admission) $4; ages 13-18, $3; ages 6-12, $2.

[SAVE] ★**MIDDLETON PLACE** is on SR 61, 14 mi. n.w. of jct. US 17. The oldest landscaped gardens in America were begun in 1741 by Henry Middleton, later president of the First Continental Congress. It took 100 slaves 10 years to complete the landscaped terraces, camellia-lined walks and ornamental lakes. Azaleas bloom in the spring, magnolias and roses in the early summer, crape myrtle and perennials through the summer and fall, and camellias during the winter.

A restored stableyard has working displays about spinning, weaving, blacksmithing, candlemaking, shingle making, carpentry, pottery making, corn grinding and cow milking. Animals typical of 18th- and 19th-century plantations roam freely.

Special events include Sheep to Shawls in April; Spoleto Finale in June; Africa-to-America Music Festival in October; Plantation Days in November; and Christmas at Middleton in December.

Food is available. Allow 2 hours minimum. Daily 9-5. Admission $14; ages 6-12, $7. Combination admission to Drayton Hall, Edmondston-Alston House, Gibbes Museum of Art, Middleton Place and Nathaniel Russell House $29; under 12, $19. DS, MC, VI. Phone (803) 556-6020.

Middleton Place House, on Middleton Place, was built in 1755. The house originally served as a guest wing; it became the Middleton family residence when the main portion of the house was burned during the Civil War. The house contains furniture, paintings, books and silver. A silk copy of the Declaration of Independence was found among the personal mementos of Henry Middleton's son Arthur, a signer of the document.

Interior photography is not permitted. Allow 30 minutes minimum. Guided tours Tues.-Sun. 10-4:30, Mon. 1:30-4:30. Last tour begins at closing. Admission $6.

What To Do

Sightseeing

Before sightseeing in Charleston, park your car. Trying to negotiate the narrow streets while sightseeing is difficult, and your visit will be much more interesting if you move at a leisurely pace. So, follow one of the TourBook's walking tours or take one of the guided carriage, bus, van or trolley tours. Fort Sumter Tours offers trips to Fort Sumter and cruises around the harbor *(see Boat Tours)*. Other tour operators are listed below.

A good place to begin your exploration is at the Charleston Visitor Center, 375 Meeting St., which is open Mon.-Fri. 8:30-5:30, Sat.-Sun. 8:30-5 during DST; daily 8:30-5, the rest of year. "Forever Charleston" *(see attraction listing)*, a multimedia presentation shown continuously at the center, provides an introduction to the city and its people. Self-guiding tour maps and brochures also are available.

Two of the more prominent features of the historic area are the two major architectural styles: the double house and the single house. The front doors of the double house face the street, with one room to either side. The typical single house is only one room wide with the narrow gable end turned toward the street. To one side is a door that opens onto a porch, which Charlestonians call a piazza. Gardens or courtyards are beside or behind the house.

No one knows why there are so many single houses in Charleston, but there is speculation that the design might have been prompted by taxes levied according to how many feet of a house faced the street. Similar houses were built during the 18th and early 19th centuries in New Orleans for this reason.

Common sights on brick or stuccoed brick buildings in Charleston are metal plates in the walls between stories. These are the decorative ends of "earthquake bolts" used to stabilize buildings damaged in the earthquake of 1886. Rather than rebuild, residents inserted long iron bolts through the walls of their houses in the space between floor joists. These bolts met a turnbuckle, which pulled the building back together as it was tightened.

Many of Charleston's old houses have solid shutters on the first floor windows and louvered shutters on the windows of the floors above. The solid shutters helped keep the noise and dirt from entering the early houses, whose walls often rose from the edge of the street. Next to the street door of many of these old houses are small round plaques, which were awarded by the Preservation Society of Charleston for zealous efforts to maintain a structure's purpose and historic integrity.

Perhaps the most common sight in Charleston is not a thing, but a color. Charleston Green, such an extremely dark shade that it is almost black, is seen on everything from shutters to front doors to piazza trim. The color is said to have been devised during Reconstruction, when only black paint was available in quantity. Residents mixed in a small amount of yellow pigment and were able to use colored paint.

 Bus, Limousine, Carriage or Train Tours

CHARLESTON CARRIAGE CO., 14 Hayne St., offers 1-hour narrated horse-drawn carriage tours of historic Charleston. Mon.-Fri. 9-6:30, Sat.-Sun. 9-9:30, mid-March through mid-Oct. Fare $16; over 54, $14; ages 3-12, $5. Reservations are recommended. AE, DS, MC, VI. Phone (803) 723-8687 or 577-0042.

DOIN' THE CHARLESTON TOURS leave from the Visitor Center at 375 Meeting St. and provide a guided bus-tour of the historic district. The guide brings history to life with 90 minutes of live narration, on-board laser disc images and stories set to music. The 7-mile tour features a stop at The Battery *(see attraction listing).* Free pickup at downtown lodgings is available 30 minutes before tour time. Tours daily at 9:30, noon, 2:30 and 5 (4:30 in the winter). Fare $13; Under 12, $9. Not recommended for under age 6. MC, VI at the Visitor Center only. Phone (803) 763-1233 or (800) 647-4487. *See color ad.*

OLD SOUTH CARRIAGE CO., 14 Anson St., offers 1-hour tours of historic Charleston in surrey-

style carriages. Guides in Confederate uniforms point out the sights. Daily 9-dusk. Fare $16; ages 3-11, $5. Phone (803) 723-9712.

SAVE **PALMETTO CARRIAGE TOURS,** Rainbow Market at 40 N. Market St., offers 1-hour mule-drawn carriage excursions through historic Charleston. Three different tours rotate on a daily basis. Free shuttle van service is available at Wragg Mall across from the Charleston Visitor Center at 375 Meeting St. Daily 9-dusk; closed Dec. 25. Fare $16; ages 4-11, $5. AE, DS, MC, VI. Phone (803) 723-8145.

 Boat Tours

FORT SUMTER TOURS leave from Charleston City Marina at 17 Lockwood Blvd. in Charleston and from Patriots Point Naval and Maritime Museum *(see attraction listing)* in Mount Pleasant. The tours consist of a 75-minute tour of Charleston Harbor and a 1-hour tour of Fort Sumter. National Park Service rangers are available to answer questions. Tours depart from Charleston daily at 9:30, noon and 2:30 and from Patriots Point daily at 10:45, 1:30 and 4, Apr. 1-Labor Day; otherwise varies. Closed Dec. 25. Fare $10; ages 6-11, $5. MC, VI at Charleston City Marina only. Phone (803) 722-1691 or (800) 789-3678. *See ad p. 146.*

Dinner Cruise departs from Charleston City Marina at 17 Lockwood Blvd. The 3-hour cruise offers live music and dancing aboard the *Spirit of Charleston.* There is a dress code. For reservations write Fort Sumter Tours, 205 King St., Suite 204, P.O. Box 59, Charleston, SC 29402. Tues.-Sat. at 7 p.m. (boarding at 6:30 p.m.), Mar.-Jan. (Jan. schedule may vary.); closed Dec. 25. Fare $32.95. AE, DS, MC, VI. Phone (803) 722-2628. *See ad p. 146.*

SAVE **GRAY LINE WATER TOURS** leave from the marina at 196 Concord St. The narrated 2.25-hour cruise aboard the *Charles Towne Princess* includes such sights as a former quarantine station, forts Sumter, Moultrie and Johnson, port facilities, minesweepers, nuclear-powered submarines, the Cooper

River bridges and many of Charleston's fine waterfront houses. Three-hour dinner cruises also are available.

Food is available. Ninety-minute tours depart daily at 9:45, 2 and 3:45, Mar.-Nov. 30; at 2 rest of year. Two-and-a-quarter-hour tours depart daily at 11:30. Dinner cruise departs daily at 7:30 p.m. (boarding begins at 6:30). Ninety-minute cruise $8; ages 6-11, $4. Two-and-a-quarter-hour cruise $10; ages 6-11, $5. Dinner Cruise $25. Under 12 must be with an adult on all cruises. DS, MC, VI. Phone (803) 722-1112 or (800) 344-4483.

HARBOR TOUR departs from Patriots Point Naval and Maritime Museum in Mount Pleasant. The tour consists of a 2-hour narrated cruise around Charleston Harbor, the Cooper River and the Naval Base Harbor. Tours depart daily at 10, 12:30 and 3, Mar.-Oct.; otherwise varies. Fare $10; over 64, $8.50; ages 6-11, $5. Phone (803) 722-1691.

THE SCHOONER *PRIDE*, in the Ripley Light Marina, offers cruises aboard an 84-foot tall ship around Charleston's historic harbor. Guests are permitted to help with the sailing or just enjoy the ride. Coolers are allowed on board. Allow 2 hours minimum. Cruises offered daily Apr.-Oct. Schedule varies; call for departure times. Fare $15; under 12, $10. Phone (803) 571-2486.

Guided Walking Tours

The compact nature of Charleston's historic area makes walking the best way to see the city. Whether you take one of the guided tours outlined below or one of the self-guiding walking tours that follows, walking will give you time to notice the wealth of architectural detail that makes Charleston one of the most picturesque cities in the nation.

ARCHITECTURAL WALKING TOURS OF CHARLESTON, departing from the Meeting Street Inn at 173 Meeting St. and from the Hawthorn Suites Hotel at 181 Church St., provides two guided walking tours through historic Charleston. The 18th-century tour covers the original "walled city"; examples of Georgian architecture are highlighted. The 19th-century tour, covering Meeting St. and The Battery, features Federal, Greek Revival and Victorian architecture.

Tours include private houses and gardens and the interiors of some public buildings and churches. Church architecture is emphasized in December. Allow 2 hours per tour. Both tours depart Mon. and Wed.-Sat. from the Meeting Street Inn at 10 and 2, and from the Hawthorn Suites Hotel at 9:50 and 1:50; closed Dec. 25. Each tour $13, under 13 free. Reservations are requested. Phone (803) 893-2327 or (800) 931-7761.

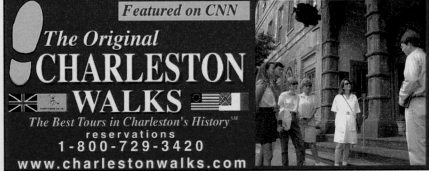

CHARLESTON STROLLS offers three guided walking tours of the historic district. The Battery Tour and the Ghost Walk leave from the Mills House Hotel Courtyard, 115 Meeting St., and the Omni Hotel at 130 Market St. The Market Walk tour leaves from the Charleston Visitor Center, 375 Meeting St. Highlights of The Battery tour include Cabbage Row, the Dock Street Theatre and St. Michael's Episcopal Church. The Ghost Walk includes tales of Charleston's darker personalities and natural and supernatural happenings. The Market Walk explores the 18th-century suburb of Ansonborough and includes Beth Elohim Synagogue, St. Mary's Church and the Market.

Allow 2 hours minimum. Battery tour leaves Mon.-Sat. year-round from the Omni at 9:30 and Mills House at 10. The Market Walk leaves Mon.-Sat. at 10, Mar.-Oct. (weather permitting). Battery tour $12.50, under 13 free. Ghost Walk $12.50; under 13, $6.50. Market Walk $10. Phone (803) 766-2080. *See color ad p. 146.*

THE ORIGINAL CHARLESTON WALKS, departing from the Broad St. entrance of Washington Park, offers various guided walking tours of the city. The Civil War tour concentrates on sites and relics from the 1860s, while the Lowcountry Ghost Hunt explores some of the town's eeriest places. Departure times vary with each tour. Daily 9-6; closed Dec. 25. Fee $12. Phone (803) 577-3800. *See color ad p. 146.*

Self-guiding Walking Tours

Each of the tours outlined below will take about 2 hours, allowing for a leisurely pace and stops for photography and plaque reading. Allow more time for stops at the listed attractions. Parking on the street is scarce, so the tours begin and end at parking lots.

The best way to see the city is to combine the walking tours with stops at the attractions along the way. The names of sites listed in the *What To See* section are printed in **bold** type to help you. Even if you don't tour a listed site, reading the listing when you reach that point will make the tour more interesting.

Tour One (The Battery): *See map following.* Park just north of Broad St. on Meeting St. The intersection of Meeting and Broad is known as "The Four Corners of Law" because the four buildings at the site represent federal, state, local and religious law. The corner on which you are standing is occupied by Charleston County Courthouse **❶**. Straight across Broad St. is the U.S. Courthouse and Post Office. Across from it is **St. Michael's Episcopal Church ❷**, and on the final corner is **City Hall ❸**.

Cross Meeting and Broad sts. to St. Michael's and walk south on Meeting. Just past the church you probably will find the "flower ladies" selling flowers and locally made sweetgrass baskets. Continue past St. Michael's Alley; look ahead across Meeting and note the earthquake bolts on the side of the single house at 69 Meeting St. The building with the white columns on your left is South Carolina Society Hall; the society is a charitable organization founded by French Huguenots in 1737. The Adam-style building was built in 1804.

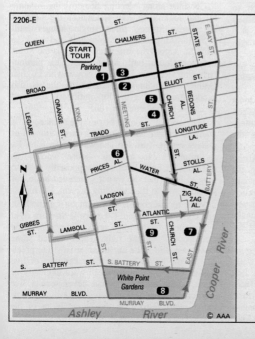

CHARLESTON WALKING TOUR

Scale in Miles   0   0.3
Scale in Kilometers   0   0.5

TOUR ONE
(The Battery)

❶ Charleston County Courthouse

❷ St. Michael's Episcopal Church

❸ City Hall

❹ Heyward - Washington House

❺ Cabbage Row

❻ Nathaniel Russell House

❼ Edmonston - Alston House

❽ The Battery (White Point Gardens)

❾ Calhoun Mansion

© AAA

Walk past Ropemaker's Ln. to Tradd St. and look to your right across Meeting St. at a fine example of a double house. Turn left and walk down Tradd, past its many single and double houses with their earthquake bolts and solid shutters, to Church St., then turn left and continue to the **Heyward-Washington House ❹** at 87 Church St. Note the carriage block (step) and hitching posts in front of this double house.

A few steps farther, at 89-91 Church, is Cabbage Row ❺. This was the model for DuBose Heyward's "Catfish Row" in his novel "Porgy," the basis for George Gershwin's opera "Porgy and Bess." African-American residents gave the building its name by displaying vegetables for sale on the windowsills of the tenement, a term applied in Charleston to any building with more than one set of living quarters. Across the street are some fine single houses.

Retrace your steps to Tradd, cross the street and walk south on Church St. Four doors down on your right is the Robert Brewton House; built in 1720, it is the oldest single house in the city. Next door at 69 Church is the Capers-Motte House, a particularly fine Georgian double house.

Continue down Church St. past the First Baptist Church, crossing Water St. and bearing right. The second house on your right past Water St. at 41 Church St. is the A.W. Todd House; notice the garage entrance through the chimney. To the left is the George Eveleigh House. When it was built in 1721, a creek ran where Water St. is today; the mooring posts in front of the house date from this time.

If you take a slight detour down Water St. to Meeting St., you'll see the **Nathaniel Russell House ❻**. Completed in 1808, the house is a fine example of Federal architecture set in a spacious garden.

Continue walking down Church to Atlantic St., turn left and continue to E. Battery St., glancing down Zig Zag Alley on your left. When you reach E. Battery, turn right and walk two doors down to the **Edmonston-Alston House ❼**. You are now in the area known as the High Battery because of the elevated walkway across the street.

The fourth house past the Edmonston-Alston House is the William Roper House; note the ropelike trim around the front door. When built in 1838, this house was the first on this section of The Battery and its huge white portico was visible from far out in the harbor. The earthquake bolts are covered by decorative plaques in the shape of lions' heads.

Continue down E. Battery, mount the steps across from the corner and stroll down the walkway beside Charleston Harbor, where the first shot of the Civil War was fired April 12, 1861. Here the Cooper and Ashley rivers meet to form the Atlantic Ocean—or so some Charlestonians say. The park straight ahead is White Point Gardens, which was named for the immense mound of oyster shells that covered the area in the settlement's early days.

The park and the nearby residential district often are called **The Battery ❽** for the fortifications that were placed to protect the settlement from sea attack. Continue down the walkway to the bend, where a plaque set in the pavement points out the position of the harbor's forts: Sumter, Moultrie, Castle Pinckney and Johnson. Confederate forces first fired on Fort Sumter from Fort Johnson.

Descend the steps and stroll through the park to the corner of Church and S. Battery sts. A hotel during the early 20th century, the building at 4 S. Battery is now a residence again. At the corner of Meeting and S. Battery sts. is a large Victorian house built by a wealthy banker as a wedding present to his daughter. Not to be outdone, the groom's parents supposedly sent the couple on a 2-year tour of Europe, after which they returned to a house complete with stained-glass windows by Louis Tiffany. The house is now an inn called 2 Meeting St.

Walk about half a block along Meeting St. and look across the street to 11 Meeting; it is covered with stucco scored to look like stone. The huge house on your side of the street is the 1886 **Calhoun Mansion ❾**, which was once the home of the banker who built 2 Meeting St. This 24,000-square-foot mansion was later bought by the grandson of John C. Calhoun. Next door at 18 Meeting is the Thomas Heyward House, a fine Adam-style single house built in 1806.

Continue along Meeting St., crossing Atlantic St. and looking to your left across the street at the Three Sisters, three single houses built 1750-88. At Ladson St., turn left and walk to King St. Across the street at 27 King is the Miles Brewton House, built about 1765. This particularly fine Georgian Palladian House with English Gothic outbuildings was used as the British headquarters during the Revolutionary War, and as Union headquarters in 1865.

The spiked ironwork on the fence is a *chevaux-de-frise* added in 1822 during rumors of a slave revolt. Turn left and walk down King St. to number 21, a huge house known as O'Donnell's Folly because it supposedly took so long to build that the owner's intended bride, for whom it was to be a wedding present, left him.

Walk to the corner, turn right on Lamboll St. and continue to Legare ("Legree") St. Turn right and proceed to the large brick pillars topped by "pineapples" on the right. These carved stone finials are said to be an Italian artist's interpretation of the owner's request for carvings of live oak acorns. The "pineapples" were evidently as close as the artist, who had never seen a live oak, could come. Before you go, notice the vertical *chevaux-de-frise* on the piazza pillar of the single house across the street.

Continue on Legare to the Sword Gate Inn at number 32, whose name comes from the sword and spear motif of the iron gates. Some maintain that the high walls were built after the elopement of a female student from the boarding school that occupied the house 1819-49.

Go to the corner, turn right and walk 2 blocks on Tradd St. to Meeting St., past the old-fashioned gas station building at Tradd and King; while this building isn't as old as the houses of its patrons, it is subject to the same preservation guidelines. About halfway down the next block at 72 Tradd is a tenement built in 1765. Next door is 70 Tradd, a fine single house built 9 years later.

Turn left when you reach Meeting St. You are now a block south of Broad and Meeting, where you began. From here you can easily walk 3 blocks north to Cumberland St. and follow the other tour route; walk 4 blocks north to the shops and restaurants on North and South Market sts.; or go several blocks north and west to the antique shops, stores and restaurants on King St.

Tour Two (Cabbage Row): *See map following.* Park at the lot on Cumberland St., cross the street and walk to the left to Old Powder Magazine ❶ at 79 Cumberland. Continue to Church St. and turn right, stopping at the corner to look back at the earthquake bolts in the wall of the magazine. The large iron crosses might have been used rather than the more common plates because of the extremely thick walls, which were intended to force potential explosions upward through the roof.

Across the street and ahead is St. Philip's Episcopal Church, built in 1835 to replace an earlier structure; the church's congregation was organized in 1680. The churchyard across the street was reserved for "strangers and other transient whites." However, some famous residents came to be buried there, including John C. Calhoun; DuBose Heyward, author of "Porgy"; and Edward Rutledge, one of the signers of the Declaration of Independence.

Continue down Church St. across Queen St., pausing just past the intersection across from the **Huguenot Church** ❷. Next to the church is the Huguenot Church Rectory, a good example of a single house, complete with solid shutters and a restoration plaque. Just past the church is the early 1800s **Dock Street Theatre** ❸. The original theater was built in 1735, when a creek flowed by the site and Queen St. was called Dock St.

Continue to Chalmers St. and turn left onto one of the city's few remaining cobblestone streets. Because stone was scarce in early Charleston, streets were paved with stones brought from Europe as ships' ballast. Continue to State St. and turn right. Across the street is a small two-story brick South Carolina National Bank building, which once housed one of the earliest branches of the Bank of America.

A modern three-story building is to its right on Broad St. Notice how the drive-through addition connecting the two continues the appearance of the building on its right. Walk down the street to Broad St., once called the Wall Street of the South and still the city's main business street. Residents jokingly refer to locations as SOB (South of Broad) or SNOB (Slightly North of Broad).

Turn left and stroll down Broad St. to E. Bay St. Across the street from the **Old Exchange and Provost Dungeon** ❹ is a section of the original wall that once surrounded the early city. As you

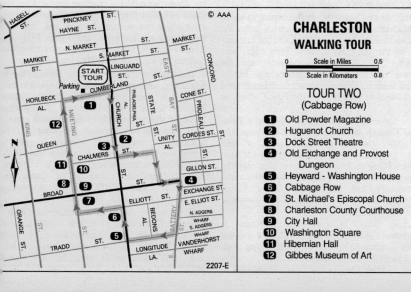

© AAA

CHARLESTON
WALKING TOUR

Scale in Miles   0   0.5
Scale in Kilometers   0   0.8

TOUR TWO
(Cabbage Row)

❶ Old Powder Magazine
❷ Huguenot Church
❸ Dock Street Theatre
❹ Old Exchange and Provost Dungeon
❺ Heyward - Washington House
❻ Cabbage Row
❼ St. Michael's Episcopal Church
❽ Charleston County Courthouse
❾ City Hall
❿ Washington Square
⓫ Hibernian Hall
⓬ Gibbes Museum of Art

2207-E

turn right and walk down E. Bay St. you will pass streets on your left named for the warehouses and wharves that once stood there. At one time E. Bay St. was next to the Cooper River, which can be seen if you peer to the left down Exchange St.

At Elliot St., cross E. Bay and pause just past the service station to look back across the street at the row of houses numbered 79-107. Known as "Rainbow Row," these colorful stuccoed brick houses are a favorite subject of artists. They were built 1723-40 by merchants who had shops in the first floor and living quarters in the upper stories, which were reached by staircases from an inner courtyard.

Walk down E. Bay to Tradd St., turn right and continue to 14 Tradd. To the left of its front door is a fire plaque that showed which fire company the resident subscribed to. Although all fire companies would respond when a house caught fire, only the fire company whose plaque was displayed would be expected to fight the blaze.

Continue to Church St. and turn right. Across the street at 87 Church is the **Heyward-Washington House** ❺, built in 1770 for a future signer of the Declaration of Independence. Hitching posts and a carriage block remain in front of the house. Two doors farther, at 89-91 Church St., is Cabbage Row, the model for Du-Bose Heyward's "Catfish Row" in his novel "Porgy."

Called Cabbage Row ❻ because of the vegetables its African-American residents once displayed for sale on the windowsills, this structure is an example of what Charlestonians call a tenement—any house with more than one set of living quarters. Across the street are several fine single houses. Heyward, whose novel was the basis for George Gershwin's opera "Porgy and Bess," lived at 76 Church St.

Walk down Church St. to the corner, cross to St. Michael's Alley, turn left and walk down the alley to Meeting St. (Watch for cars; the last section of the alley is narrow.) Turn right onto Meeting St. Ahead you'll probably see the "flower ladies," who sell flowers and locally woven baskets. Continue down Meeting toward its intersection with Broad—the Four Corners of Law.

You are standing next to **St. Michael's Episcopal Church** ❼, whose steeple has been visible above the rooftops during parts of your walk. During the Civil War, the tower was painted black to lessen its value as a sighting guide for Northern gunners training their cannon on the city from ships in the harbor. Across Meeting from the church is the U.S. Courthouse and Post Office.

Across Broad St. from the courthouse is Charleston County Courthouse ❽, and the last corner is occupied by **City Hall** ❾. If you wish, you can begin The Battery Tour here, finishing this one when The Battery Tour returns you to this point. If you want to continue this tour first, cross Broad on Meeting and walk north to the wrought-iron fence on the right that encloses **Washington Square** ❿. If you look to the right at the next corner, you'll have another look at cobblestone Chalmers St.

Across Chalmers on Meeting St. is the Frances R. Edmunds Center for Historic Preservation. This building has several exhibits about the city's preservation efforts and is operated by the Historic Charleston Foundation. Across Meeting St. is Hibernian Hall ⓫.

Walk down Meeting and cross Queen St. Halfway down the block on the right is the Circular Congregational Church. Across the street is the **Gibbes Museum of Art** ⓬. The next street is Cumberland. At this point turn right to go to your car or, if you'd like to shop, cross Meeting and walk down Horlbeck Alley to King St. for antiques shops, boutiques and clothing stores. You also can find shops and restaurants by crossing Cumberland and walking up Meeting to Market St. *See Shopping.*

Sports and Recreation

While recreational facilities within the old historic district of Charleston are limited, the surrounding area offers ample choices for the outdoor enthusiast. Nearby state and county parks and the Francis Marion National Forest *(see place listing in the Vicinity section)* provide a variety of activities, such as **picnicking, boating** and **hiking,** and are only a few minutes to an hour drive away. **Camping** is permitted at Givhans Ferry and Edisto Beach state parks *(see Recreation Chart and the AAA Southeastern CampBook).*

The barrier islands that line the coast are the focus of much of Charleston's recreational activity. Once favored as a summer retreat from the threat of yellow fever, many of these islands now sport major resorts. Isle of Palms and Sullivan's Island, east of Charleston, and Edisto, Folly and Kiawah islands, south of the city, all have fine beaches for **swimming, sailing** and **surfing.**

The Charleston area is popular for both **fresh water** and **saltwater fishing.** Surf fishing is permitted on many beaches. Deep-sea fishing charters depart from Charleston City Marina. Some of the best fishing is in estuarine creeks. Bass, sheepshead, flounder and trout can be taken in fall and winter; crabbing is good in spring and summer. For information about fishing regulations write South Carolina Wildlife Resources Department, Division of Game and Freshwater Fisheries, P.O. Box 167, Columbia, SC 29202; phone (803) 734-3886.

Golf can be played at a number of 18-hole courses: Charleston Municipal Golf Course, (803) 795-6517, and Shadowmoss Golf Club, (803) 556-8251, in Charleston; Crooked Oaks and Ocean Winds, (803) 768-2529, on Seabrook Island; Fairfield Ocean Ridge, (803) 723-0325, on Edisto Island; Kiawah Golf Links and Turtle Point Golf Club, (803) 768-2121, ext. 3466, on Kiawah Island; Patriots Point Links, (803) 881-0042, in Mount Pleasant; and Wild Dunes, (803) 886-6000, on Isle of Palms.

Baseball fans can watch the Texas Rangers' minor league team, the Charleston Riverdogs, in action at College Park Stadium, 701 Rutledge Ave.; phone (803) 723-7241.

For a quiet stroll in an urban setting, Charleston has several city parks, including White Point Gardens on The Battery, Waterfront Park along the Cooper River, and Colonial Lake at Broad and Rutledge streets. Many of the parks have trails for **bicycling.** Rentals are available at The Bicycle Shop at 280 Meeting St.; phone (803) 722-8168.

Shopping

It is not surprising that antiques are one of the biggest shopping attractions in Charleston, a city more than 300 years old. An abundance of antiques shops, art galleries, boutiques and specialty stores can be found along King Street downtown, including Saks Fifth Avenue. Shops and stores also can be found along nearby Broad, Church, E. Bay and Meeting streets.

Specialty shops, boutiques and open-sided buildings with vendor and artisan booths can be found along N. and S. Market streets behind Market Hall, 188 Meeting St. This area, known as The Old City Market, was deeded to the city by the owners, who specified that it always must remain a public market.

Reproductions of 18th- and 19th-century Charleston antiques are available at the Historic Charleston Foundation's shop at 105 Broad St. Royalties generated from the sales are used to further the foundation's restoration work.

Such major department stores as Belk, Dillard's and Kerrison's can be found in three nearby shopping malls: Charles Town Square Mall, I-26 exit 213 (Montague Avenue E.); Citadel Mall, US 17 and SR 7; and Northwoods Mall, I-26 at US 52.

Theater and Concerts

Charleston's cultural heritage goes back a long way. By the late 1730s, the city had a music society and the Dock Street Theatre, the first building in the Colonies designed solely for theatrical performances. Today the Footlight Players perform in Dock Street Theatre (*see attraction listing*) at Church and Queen streets. Opera in Charleston also is a tradition: The first opera performance in America was presented here in 1735. Two centuries later George Gershwin wrote the opera "Porgy and Bess" in Cabbage Row, immortalized as "Catfish Row" in DuBose Heyward's novel "Porgy."

Gaillard Municipal Auditorium and Exhibition Hall, 77 Calhoun St., is home to the Charleston Civic Ballet, the Charleston Opera Company and the Charleston Symphony Orchestra. For information phone (803) 577-4500; for tickets phone (803) 577-4502.

Special Events

Oyster season runs September through April in Charleston, but the city celebrates this seafood tradition in January with the Lowcountry Oyster Festival. Oysters by the bucket are the main attraction of this winter event, but activities also include an oyster shucking contest, live music and children's events.

Wildlife connoisseurs of another sort have a month of their own: February in Charleston is Wildlife Month. The Southeastern Wildlife Exposition on the Friday, Saturday and Sunday preceding Presidents' Day is one of the largest wildlife arts, crafts and collectibles shows in the South; phone (800) 221-5273.

Pre-eminent among Charleston's annual events is Spoleto Festival U.S.A., a celebration of the arts beginning Memorial Day weekend and continuing for either 12 or 17 days. During the festival a full schedule of events encompassing music, dance, theater, opera, art, poetry, comedy and crafts takes place throughout the city; phone (803) 722-2764. The Piccolo Spoleto Festival serves as Charleston's companion festival and showcases local and regional performers; phone (803) 724-7305.

Every September a daylong international food festival, The Taste of Charleston, takes place. The cuisine of more than 50 of the city's finest restaurants can be sampled at one location.

Rounding out the year is Christmas in Charleston, celebrated throughout December. Special tours of traditionally decorated houses, churches and public buildings highlight the holiday season. Festivities also include the Parade of Boats in Charleston Harbor.

Many of Charleston's private houses are opened to the public two other times during the year. From mid-March to mid-April the Festival of Houses and Gardens offers afternoon and evening walking tours of houses, gardens and historic sites; phone (803) 722-3405 or 723-1623. The Candlelight Tours of Houses and Gardens, held late September through October, also offer an intimate glimpse of Charleston's architectural heritage; phone (803) 722-4630.

The Charleston Vicinity

AWENDAW (E-5)

Cape Romain National Wildlife Refuge comprises undeveloped barrier islands and sea marshes that lie between the Atlantic Ocean and the Intracoastal Waterway; phone (803)

928-3368. All the islands—including primitive Bulls Island, which is popular with birdwatchers—can be reached only by boat from Moore's Landing.

★FORT SUMTER NATIONAL MONUMENT (E-5)

Fort Sumter, a brick fortification built 1829-60 on a man-made island in Charleston Harbor, is accessible only by boat (see What To Do, Boat Tours). On April 12, 1861, Confederate troops directed the opening shots of the Civil War against Fort Sumter, and after a 2-day bombardment the small Union garrison surrendered.

Confederate forces occupied the fort until February 1865, successfully defying the blockade and foiling Federal attempts to capture Charleston, which remained a major port of the Confederacy. The fort contains some large cannons, and projectiles fired during the war still are embedded in the thick walls.

National Park Service rangers present history talks. A museum displays relics from the fort. Allow 2 hours, 30 minutes minimum. Tours depart daily from Charleston City Marina at 9:30, noon and 2:30, and from Patriots Point at 10:45, 1:30 and 4, Apr. 1-Labor Day; otherwise varies. Closed Dec. 25. Fort admission free. Fare $10.50; ages 6-11, $5.50. Phone (803) 883-3123.

FORT MOULTRIE, across the channel from Fort Sumter and also part of the national monument, is on Sullivan's Island, reached via US 17 and SR 703. A military post for more than 170 years, the fort played an important part in the Revolutionary War as the site of one of the first American victories. The outnumbered Colonial garrison withstood bombardment by the British navy, whose shells were absorbed by the spongy palmetto log and sand defenses. Less than a century later the fort played a role during the Confederate attack on Fort Sumter.

A museum houses military displays. A 20-minute film about the fort's history is shown every 30 minutes. Allow 1 hour, 30 minutes minimum. Daily 9-5; closed Dec. 25. Admission $2. Phone (803) 883-3123.

FORT SUMTER TOURS—
see What To Do, Boat Tours p. 145.

FRANCIS MARION NATIONAL FOREST

  Elevations in the forest range from sea level to 50 ft. Refer to AAA maps for additional information.

Francis Marion National Forest, north of Charleston, covers 251,000 acres of low flatlands, coastal sand areas, black swamp waters, moss-hung oaks, pines and little lakes, or "Carolina Bays," thought to be water-filled meteorite impact depressions. The land had been heavily logged and was in poor condition when it was purchased from private owners in the 1930s. The newly-created forest was named for the Revolutionary War general who engaged British troops in many skirmishes and battles in the area and then took refuge in the deep swamps, thus earning the nickname "Swamp Fox." Much of the painstaking restoration performed over the succeeding 5 decades was undone by Hurricane Hugo in 1989, when more than 1 billion board feet of timber was destroyed.

Home to varied wildlife, the forest is a primary habitat of the red-cockaded woodpecker and of the swallow-tailed kite. At Rembert Dennis Wildlife Center in Bonneau off SR 52, deer, wild turkeys and striped bass fingerlings are raised and studied; the center has free maps of the forest. Visitors can tour the facilities Mon.-Fri. 8:30-5; phone (803) 825-3387. For forest information phone (803) 561-4000. See Recreation Chart and the AAA Southeastern CampBook.

HARLEYVILLE (D-4) pop. 600, elev. 92′

THE FRANCIS BEIDLER FOREST IN FOUR HOLES SWAMP is off I-26W exit 187, following signs. This serene National Audubon Society sanctuary contains the largest known stand of virgin cypress and tupelo trees in the world. A 1.5-mile boardwalk offers a close-up view of trees and plants, as well as occasional glimpses of native wildlife. Self-guiding tours lead to ancient cypress trees up to 10 stories tall and 1,000 years old. Guided canoe trips are offered Friday morning and Saturday and Sunday afternoons, March through May. The visitor center has displays relating to the swamp.

Allow 1 hour, 30 minutes minimum. Tues.-Sun. 9-5; closed Jan. 1, Thanksgiving and Dec. 24-25 and 31. Admission $4.50; ages 6-18, $2. Canoe trip $15; ages 8-18, $10. Phone (803) 462-2150.

MONCKS CORNER (D-5) pop. 5,600, elev. 50′

SAVE **CYPRESS GARDENS,** off US 52, is in a setting of giant cypress trees growing out of a freshwater lake. The profusion of azaleas, camellias and daffodils seen from well-marked paths provides an unforgettable picture. The gardens and lake once were part of a great rice plantation built in 1725. Boat rides are available for those who prefer to see the gardens by water. Allow 30 minutes minimum. Daily 9:30-5:30. Admission Mar.-Apr. $9; over 54, $7; ages 6-16, $3. Admission rest of year $8; over 54, $6; ages 6-16, $1. Air conditioned pet facilities are available. Phone (803) 553-0515.

MOUNT PLEASANT (E-5) pop. 30,100, elev. 24′

SAVE **BOONE HALL PLANTATION,** 8 mi. n. on US 17 at 1235 Long Point Rd., traces its history to a 1681 land grant to Maj. John Boone. Originally a cotton plantation, it also has produced bricks and tiles. Original buildings include the circular smokehouse, the tabby (lime and oyster shell) foundation of the boat dock and nine brick slave cabins. The mansion, rebuilt in 1935, also contains plantation-made bricks as well as woodwork and flooring from an earlier house. Guided tours of the first floor are offered. Food is available.

Allow 1 hour minimum. Guided house tours every 30 minutes Mon.-Sat. 8:30-6:30, Sun. 1-5, Apr. 1-Labor Day; Mon.-Sat. 9-5, Sun. 1-4, rest of year. Closed Thanksgiving and Dec. 25. Last tour begins 30 minutes before closing. Admission $10; over 59, $8.50; ages 6-12, $5. Phone (803) 884-4371.

★**PATRIOTS POINT NAVAL AND MARITIME MUSEUM,** 2 mi. e. on US 17 at 40 Patriots Point Rd., is dominated by the USS *Yorktown,* a retired aircraft carrier that served in World War II and Vietnam. Near the end of World War II, "The Fighting Lady," a film depicting life aboard an aircraft carrier, was shot aboard the *Yorktown;* the ship carried the nickname "Fighting Lady" thereafter. The film is shown regularly in the ship's theater. In the hangar bay there are exhibits of fighter planes and mementos from some of the 3,000 crewmen who worked and lived aboard the carrier.

Visitors can tour the ship's bridge, wheelhouse, flight deck, sick bay and other areas. Seventeen aircraft also are displayed. Exhibits include the Arlington of Naval Aviation, a series of plaques listing all aircraft carrier personnel who have died since World War II; Carrier Hall of Fame; and relics from other carriers.

Also open to visitors are the nuclear merchant ship *Savannah,* an experimental alternative to oil-burning cargo ships; the World War II-era submarine *Clamagore,* which operated in the Atlantic and Mediterranean and patrolled Cuban waters during 1962 Cuban missile crisis; the destroyer *Laffey,* which participated in the D-Day landings of the Allied troops at Normandy; and the Coast Guard Cutter *Ingham,* which sank a U-boat in World War II. The complex also houses the Medal of Honor Museum.

Food and self-guiding tour brochures are available. Allow 3 hours minimum. Daily 9-6:30; closed Dec. 25. Admission $10; over 61 and military with ID $9; ages 6-11, $5. MC, VI. Phone (803) 884-2727. *See ad.*

SULLIVAN'S ISLAND (E-5) pop. 1,600

Near Charleston Harbor, Sullivan's Island was named for Capt. Florence O'Sullivan of the *Carolina,* which, in 1670, was the first English ship to bring settlers. The island is the site of Fort Moultrie *(see Fort Sumter National Monument),* where American troops first triumphed over the British forces during the Revolution. It also was the setting for Edgar Allan Poe's "The Gold Bug." A lighthouse stands at the island's southern tip.

SUMMERVILLE (D-5) pop. 22,500, elev. 75′

Summerville was settled by coastal dwellers who moved inland in the summer to escape malaria. By the early 1890s, the town became a popular health and winter resort. Much of its charm is derived from the natural beauty of its rambling streets, which wind around numerous pine trees protected by a local ordinance prohibiting their removal. Azaleas, camellias and wisteria line the streets and provide seasonal blooms.

OLD DORCHESTER STATE PARK, 6 mi. s. on SR 642, preserves the remnants of the former community of Dorchester, which was settled on the east bank of the Ashley River in 1696 by a small group of Congregationalists. Most moved to Midway, Ga., in the 1750s, and the largely Anglican village left behind ultimately was destroyed by retreating British soldiers in 1781. Ruins of the fort, the bell tower of St. George's Church and excavations are all that remain. Allow 2 hours minimum. Thurs.-Mon. 9-6. Free. Phone (803) 873-1740. *See Recreation Chart.*

CHERAW (B-5) pop. 5,500, elev. 150'

Settled before 1750 and formally laid out in 1768, the town officially was named Cheraw in 1820 after a local American Indian tribe. Its position at the navigational head of the Pee Dee River made Cheraw an important trade center which grew proportionally with increased river traffic.

A historic district encompasses 214 acres in the center of town. It includes more than 50 antebellum houses and buildings and many late 19th- and early 20th-century structures. The original town green and parish church, Old St. David's, still grace Cheraw.

The Cheraw Spring Festival in early April includes arts and crafts, historic house tours, Confederate re-enactments and carriage rides.

Greater Cheraw Chamber of Commerce: 221 Market St., Cheraw, SC 29520; phone (803) 537-7681.

Self-guiding tours: A brochure detailing a tour of the historic district is available at the chamber of commerce.

CHERAW FISH HATCHERY AND AQUARIUM, 6 mi. s. on US 1, raises large- and small-mouth bass; bluegill, red breast and red ear sunfish; and blue and channel catfish for farm ponds and reservoirs in South Carolina. The aquarium exhibits specimens in their natural habitats. Most of the ponds are dry from December to mid-March. Picnic facilities are available. Allow 30 minutes minimum. Daily dawn-dusk. Free. Phone (803) 537-7628.

CLEMSON (B-1) pop. 11,100, elev. 850'

CLEMSON UNIVERSITY, 11 mi. w. of I-85 exit 19B on US 76, was established in 1889 as a scientific college on the former plantation of John C. Calhoun, a prominent South Carolina statesman and U.S. vice president, senator and secretary of state. Maps and information for tours of the 1,400-acre campus can be obtained at the visitor center next to the Alumni Center, Mon.-Fri. 8-4:30, Sat. 9-4:30, Sun. 1:30-4:30; closed University holidays and some weekends Dec.-Jan. Guided 1-hour walking tours Mon.-Sat. at 9:45 and 1:45, Sun. at 1:45. Tours are not offered Dec.-Jan., on home football Saturdays, during final-exam week and when classes are not in session. Free. Phone (864) 656-4789.

Fort Hill, jct. Fort Hill St. and Calhoun Dr., was purchased by John C. Calhoun during his first term as U.S. vice president to John Quincy Adams. His son-in-law, Thomas G. Clemson, founded the university that now occupies the former plantation. Many original furnishings belonging to Calhoun and Clemson decorate the house. Mon.-Sat. 10-5, Sun. 2-5; closed holidays. Donations. Phone (864) 656-2475.

Hanover House, in the Botanical Garden on the e. side of the campus at jct. US 76 and Perimeter Rd., was built in 1716 by Paul de St. Julien, a French Huguenot. Endangered by the construction of a hydroelectric plant in the Lowcountry, the house was dismantled painstakingly in 1941 and rebuilt 250 miles north of its original location. Sat. 10-5, Sun. 2-5; closed holidays. Donations. Phone (864) 656-2241.

Robert Muldrow Cooper Library is at the center of the campus off S. Palmetto Blvd. The James F. Byrnes Room and Edgar A. Brown Room on the main floor exhibit collections of papers, furniture and other memorabilia pertaining to these two 20th-century statesmen. Changing exhibits are presented in the lobby. Mon.-Fri. 7:45 a.m.-1 a.m., Sat. 10-6, Sun. 1 p.m.-1 a.m., during the academic year; abbreviated schedule rest of year. Closed holidays. Free. Phone (864) 656-3027.

Rudolph E. Lee Gallery, in Lee Hall on the w. side of the campus between Perimeter Rd. and S. Palmetto Blvd., displays works by leading architects, artists and craftsmen, as well as works by art and architecture students. Mon.-Fri. 8-4:30 (also Tues. 4:30-8; Sun. 1-5, during the academic year); closed major holidays. Free. Phone (864) 656-3881.

South Carolina Botanical Garden, e. side of the campus off Perimeter Rd., is a 270-acre garden including an arboretum, gristmill, greenhouse, pagoda, teahouse by a lake and the Pioneer Complex, which has exhibits labeled in Braille. The gardens contain 2,200 varieties of plants, including one of the larger shrub collections in the eastern United States. The wildflower, fern and bog gardens contain hundreds of species native to South Carolina. Trails for hiking, jogging and bird watching are available. Daily dawn-dusk. Free. Phone (864) 656-3405.

Strom Thurmond Institute, on Perimeter Rd. next to the parking lot s. of the Robert Muldrow Cooper Library, contains papers and memorabilia documenting the life and career of U.S. Sen. James Strom Thurmond. Also featured are a rare book collection and documents from such important political leaders as John C. Calhoun; the university archives; and manuscript collections, the focus of which is primarily South Carolina. Changing exhibits are presented in the lobby. Mon.-Fri. 8-4:30 (also Tues. 4:30-8; Sun. 1-5, during the academic year); closed major holidays. Free. Phone (864) 656-4700.

★**WORLD OF ENERGY, w.** on US 76 and US 123, then 8 mi. n. on SR 130, is Duke Power Co.'s information center. Next to Oconee Nuclear Station, the center contains exhibits that illustrate the use of water, coal and uranium in creating energy. Displays chart the story of power from lightning to light bulbs, and describe energy conservation programs for the home.

The center also has an aquarium with specimens of local fish and a cold-water habitat, computer games concerning electricity, a Keowee Valley film and a quarter-mile nature trail. Allow 1 hour minimum. Mon.-Sat. 9-5, Sun. noon-5; closed Jan. 1, Thanksgiving and Dec. 24-25. Free. Phone (864) 885-4600.

COLUMBIA (C-4) pop. 98,100, elev. 260'

Originally settled on the opposite bank of the Congaree River, Columbia was created and designated South Carolina's capital by a 1786 act of the legislature, which moved the seat of government from Charleston. On Dec. 17, 1860, a convention met to draw up the Ordinance of Secession, but because of a smallpox epidemic the convention moved to Charleston, where the ordinance was signed.

Gen. William Tecumseh Sherman entered Columbia on Feb. 17, 1865. The same night a fire destroyed three-fourths of the city, including every house on Main Street except that of the French consul. The university, public buildings and the statehouse also were spared. The South Carolina Governor's Mansion, the surviving structure of a destroyed military school, is open by appointment.

Finlay Park, set in the historic Congaree Vista downtown, features lakes, waterfalls, walking trails, a Leland cypress tree, a playground and patios surrounding a plaza; phone (803) 733-8331.

Congaree Vista also is home to the Artista Vista festival in mid-April and the Vista Lights candlelight stroll in mid-November. The South Carolina State Fair is held from mid- to late October.

Columbia Metropolitan Convention and Visitors Bureau and Visitors Center: 1012 Gervais St., P.O. Box 15, Columbia, SC 29202; phone (803) 254-0479 or (800) 264-4884.

ARCHIVES BUILDING, 1430 Senate St., houses governmental records of South Carolina dating

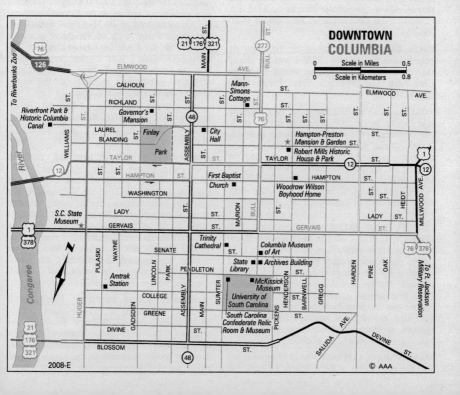

back to 1671. Quarterly exhibits reflect the historic and cultural heritage of the state. Tues.-Fri. 9-9, Sat. 9-6, Sun. 1-6; closed major holidays. Free. Phone (803) 734-8577.

THE COLUMBIA MUSEUM OF ART, Bull and Senate sts., displays the Kress Collection of Renaissance, Medieval and Baroque paintings. Changing exhibits typically display American—especially Southeastern—and European 19th- and 20th-century paintings, works on paper, sculpture and decorative arts. Forty-minute sky shows are presented at Gibbes Planetarium.

Allow 1 hour minimum. Museum open Tues.-Fri. 10-5, Sat.-Sun. 12:30-5. Planetarium shows Sat.-Sun. at 2, 3 and 4. Closed holidays. Museum $2; over 61 and ages 6-18, $1.50. Two and four o'clock planetarium shows $2.50; over 61, military with ID and ages 6-18, $1.50. Three o'clock planetarium show $1; over 61, military with ID and ages 6-18, 50c. Under 5 are not admitted to planetarium show. Phone (803) 799-2810.

CRIMINAL JUSTICE HALL OF FAME, 10 mi. n.w. at 5400 Broad River Rd., focuses on historical and contemporary aspects of law enforcement in South Carolina. Exhibits explore such topics as counterfeiting, moonshining, guns and ammunition and the career of South Carolinian Melvin Purvis, an FBI agent who pursued such notorious criminals as Al Capone and John Dillinger. A restored 1955 state highway patrol car also is displayed. Allow 30 minutes minimum. Mon.-Fri. 8:30-5; closed state holidays. Free. Phone (803) 896-7645.

FIRST BAPTIST CHURCH is on Hampton St. near Marion St. Built in 1856, it was the site of the first Secession Convention, which led to the Civil War. Mon.-Fri. 9-5. Free. Phone (803) 256-4251.

FORT JACKSON MUSEUM is at Fort Jackson; take Devine St. s.e. to Fort Jackson Blvd., turn n. and continue to the post. Fort Jackson is a U.S. Army Training Center established in 1917. The museum details the history of the post and the training of the soldiers. Larger military equipment such as a helicopter, tanks and half-tracks is displayed outdoors. Tues.-Fri. 10-4, Sat.-Sun. 1-4; closed federal holidays. Free. Phone (803) 751-7419.

[SAVE] ★**HAMPTON-PRESTON MANSION AND GARDEN,** 1615 Blanding St., is a restored house reflecting life in antebellum Columbia. The 1818 house, purchased by Gen. Wade Hampton I and occupied by the Hampton family for 50 years, contains family furnishings and memorabilia. Forty-five minute guided tours are offered at quarter past the hour Tues.-Sat. 10:15-3:15, Sun. 1:15-4:15; closed major holidays. Admission $3; military, students with ID and ages 6-18, $1.50. MC, VI. Phone (803) 252-1770.

MANN-SIMONS COTTAGE, 1403 Richland St., was the 1850 home of Celia Mann, a Charleston slave who purchased her freedom and walked to Columbia. The house features the original dining room table with hand-pressed nails, an 1800s midwife room, horse-hair plaster walls and the original brick fireplace. The First Calvary Baptist Church was organized in the basement of the house.

Guided half-hour tours are offered at quarter past the hour Tues.-Sat. 10:15-3:15, Sun. 1:15-4:15; closed major holidays. Admission $3; military, students with ID and ages 6-18, $1.50. MC, VI. Phone (803) 252-1770.

McKISSICK MUSEUM is at the head of the Historic Horseshoe area on the University of South Carolina campus, 2 blks. s. of the State House near Bull and Pendleton sts. Permanent collections, which focus on Southern folk art, culture and the natural environment, include the Howard Gemstone Collection and the Bernard Baruch Silver Collection, as well as items pertaining to the history of the university and South Carolina.

The museum offers changing exhibits from its permanent collections. Other changing exhibits about art, history and natural science also are presented. Allow 1 hour minimum. Mon.-Fri. 9-4, Sat.-Sun. 10-5; closed holidays. Free. Phone (803) 777-7251.

[SAVE] **RIVERBANKS ZOO AND BOTANICAL GARDENS,** at jct. Greystone Blvd. and I-126, is a sanctuary for more than 2,000 animals, including such endangered species as the Siberian tiger and the American bald eagle. Highlights include the Riverbanks Farm, with its variety of domestic animals, and the Aquarium Reptile Complex. The latter encompasses four display areas ranging from the South Carolina Gallery, with a spectrum of native amphibians and fish, to the exotic Tropic Gallery. Food is available.

Allow 2 hours minimum. Daily 9-4; closed Thanksgiving and Dec. 25. Admission $5.75; students with ID $4.50; over 61, $4.25; ages 3-12, $3.25. MC, VI. Phone (803) 779-8717.

RIVERFRONT PARK AND HISTORIC COLUMBIA CANAL, Laurel and Gist sts., centers around the city's original waterworks and hydroelectric plant. A walkway leads to the Columbia Canal. The 1824 canal was an essential means of transportation prior to the railroad. It then became a major source of hydroelectric power. The park features several brick buildings, vintage-style lighting fixtures and wrought-iron fencing. Picnicking, bicycling, hiking and fishing are permitted. Allow 30 minutes minimum. Daily dawn-9 p.m. Free. Phone (803) 733-8331.

[SAVE] **ROBERT MILLS HISTORIC HOUSE AND PARK,** 1616 Blanding St., was designed by Robert Mills and houses a Regency decorative arts collection. The 1823 house features Venetian-style windows, formal English gardens and three floors of rooms furnished in the Regency style. Mills, the first federal architect of the United

States, served seven presidents. His many notable designs include the Washington Monument and the U.S. Treasury Building in Washington, D.C.

Guided half-hour tours are offered at quarter past the hour Tues.-Sat. 10:15-3:15, Sun. 1:15-4:15; closed major holidays. Admission $3; military, students with ID and ages 6-18, $1.50. MC, VI. Phone (803) 252-1770.

SOUTH CAROLINA CONFEDERATE RELIC ROOM AND MUSEUM, 1 blk. s.e. of the State House at 920 Sumter St., contains a collection of military relics reflecting state military history, particularly the Civil War period. Guide service is available. Allow 30 minutes minimum. Mon.-Fri. 8:30-5. Free. Phone (803) 734-9813.

★**SOUTH CAROLINA STATE MUSEUM,** 301 Gervais St., is in the former Columbia Mills building. Built in 1894, the Columbia Mills building was one of the first totally electric textile mills in the world. Today this facility has four floors of exhibits and items chronicling state history, industry and transportation, as well as science and technology and natural history. A laser light show is presented regularly. The museum includes hands-on exhibits. The Lipscomb Art Gallery offers changing exhibits.

Allow 2 hours minimum. Mon.-Sat. 10-5, Sun. and Jan. 1, 1-5; closed Easter, Thanksgiving and Dec. 25. Admission $4; over 61, military and college students with ID $3; ages 6-17, $1.50; under 6 free with adult admission; free to all first Sun. of month. Under 13 must be with an adult. Phone (803) 737-4921. *See ad.*

TRINITY CATHEDRAL (Episcopal), Sumter St. between Senate and Gervais sts., is a beautiful example of English Gothic architecture. Modeled after Britain's York Cathedral, the cathedral has stained-glass windows from Munich and a marble font and altar. Allow 30 minutes minimum. Tours Mon.-Fri. 10-2, mid-Mar. to mid-May and mid-Sept. to mid-Nov.; by appointment rest of year. Free. Phone (803) 771-7300.

SAVE **WOODROW WILSON BOYHOOD HOME,** 1705 Hampton St., was built by Wilson's parents; young Wilson lived in the house 1872-75, from the age of 16 through 19. The house, a Victorian structure in the mode of a Tuscan villa, contains Wilson family memorabilia, original gas lighting fixtures, marble mantels and period furnishings, including the bed in which Woodrow was born. Forty-five minute guided tours are offered at quarter past the hour Tues.-Sat. 10:15-3:15, Sun. 1:15-4:15; closed major holidays. Admission $3; military, students with ID, and ages 6-18, $1.50. MC, VI. Phone (803) 252-1770.

COWPENS NATIONAL BATTLEFIELD
(A-2)

Cowpens National Battlefield encompasses 845 acres 9 miles northwest of Gaffney and 18 miles northeast of Spartanburg, .2 mile east of the junction of SRs 11 and 110. At the battlefield, Patriots commanded by Gen. Daniel Morgan outfought a more experienced British force under Lt. Col. Banastre Tarleton during the Revolutionary War.

After the Battle of Kings Mountain in 1780, British Gen. Charles Cornwallis chose to remain in South Carolina. Gen. Nathanael Greene, commissioned to reorganize the American forces, sent Morgan to divert Cornwallis' attention from the bulk of the American forces. Morgan threatened Ninety Six, where there was a British fort, so Cornwallis dispatched Tarleton to meet him.

When the two forces clashed at the cow pens on Jan. 17, 1781, the British infantry and dragoons outnumbered the Colonials, comprising Continental forces from Maryland and Delaware and militia units from the Carolinas, Georgia and Virginia.

Morgan, a brilliant strategist, divided his troops into three consecutive lines; the first two were meant to engage and slow the enemy, then fall back, leaving the brunt of the fighting to the more seasoned troops in the rear. The plan worked. Within an hour the Colonials sent the British regulars into a disorderly retreat. Morgan's losses were light; Tarleton's amounted to about 75 percent of his command.

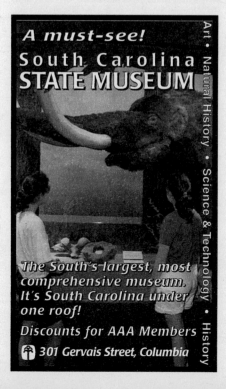

Sites of major action are marked by exhibits along a 1.5-mile walking trail and a 3-mile automobile tour road. A restored 1830 log cabin also is beside the road. Picnic facilities are available.

The visitor center exhibits a lighted map tracing troop movements during the battle as well as oil paintings, woodcarvings and weapons. A multi-image laser disc presentation, "Daybreak at the Cowpens," is shown. Allow 1 hour minimum. Battlefield and visitor center open daily 9-5; closed Jan. 1, Thanksgiving and Dec. 25. Admission free. Laser disc presentation $1; ages 6-11, 50c. Phone (864) 461-2828.

DARLINGTON (B-5) pop. 7,300, elev. 155′

The rich farmland surrounding Darlington produces some of the largest tobacco crops in the state. The city was the site of the "Darlington War" of 1894, a brief citizens' revolt against harsh anti-liquor regulations, which allowed private homes to be searched without a warrant. Gov. B.R. Tillman sent the state militia to restore peace.

Today revving engines shatter the peace at Darlington Raceway, 1.5 miles west on Harry Byrd Hwy. This track is the home of two major stock car races, the Trans South 400 in late March and the Mountain Dew Southern 500 the Sunday before Labor Day.

Darlington/Lamar Department of Tourism: 102 Orange St., P.O. Box 274, Darlington, SC 29532; phone (803) 393-2641.

NMPA STOCK CAR HALL OF FAME/JOE WEATHERLY MUSEUM, .7 mi. w. of US 52 bypass on SR 34, exhibits stock cars, trophies and racing-related items. Daily 8:30-5. Admission $3, under 12 free. Phone (803) 395-8821.

FLORENCE (C-5) pop. 29,800, elev. 137′

In 1853 Florence was an important junction of two newly completed railroads. During the Civil War, the town developed into a shipping center and a point of embarkation for troops. A "prison pen" south of town held more than 8,000 captured Union soldiers. Most of them succumbed to typhoid fever and were buried in what is now a national military cemetery 1 mile east of US 301S on National Cemetery Road.

The railroads continue to play an important role in the town's economy: Florence is a major retail and wholesale distribution center for the various industrial plants in the town and the farms in the surrounding country.

Numerous municipal parks present colorful floral displays in the spring. The 12-mile Beauty Trail is lined with marked gardens that begin to bloom in late March or early April. Timrod Park, at Timrod Park Drive and Coit Street, features test rose gardens and an azalea display in spring. Roses, camellias, azaleas and rhododendrons beautify Lucas Park, at Santee Drive, Azalea Lane and Park Avenue.

The city's floral tradition is celebrated in April with floral presentations during the 4-day Southern Plant and Flower Festival.

Florence Convention and Visitors Center: 3920 W. Radio Rd., P.O. Box 3093, Florence, SC 29502; phone (803) 664-0330.

FLORENCE AIR AND MISSILE MUSEUM is 2.5 mi. e. on US 301 and US 76 at the airport entrance; from I-95 take exit 170 and follow signs. This museum traces the history of aviation and space flight with such memorabilia as a moon rock from the Apollo 12 mission, all launch equipment used for ground control of the Apollo Saturn mission, and 32 rocket missiles, including a bomber torpedo destroyer from WW II. Some 25 pieces of equipment are displayed on the grounds. Allow 1 hour minimum. Daily 10-4; closed Jan. 1 and Dec. 25. Admission $5; over 61 and military with ID $4; ages 8-14, $3. Phone (803) 665-5118.

FLORENCE COUNTY LIBRARY, 319 S. Irby St., contains more than 160,000 books. Its rare historical works include South Carolina genealogical material and family histories. Mon.-Thurs. 9-8:30, Fri.-Sat. 9-5:30, Sun. 2-5. Phone (803) 662-8424.

FLORENCE MUSEUM, Graham and Spruce sts., contains Oriental and Western art as well as a particularly fine collection of Southwestern American Indian pottery. The Hall of South Carolina History traces the development of "The Palmetto State." Tues.-Sat. 10-5, Sun. 2-5. Free. Phone (803) 662-3351.

★FORT SUMTER NATIONAL MONUMENT—
see Charleston and Vicinity p. 152.

FRANCIS MARION NATIONAL FOREST—
see Charleston and Vicinity p. 152.

GEORGETOWN—
see The Grand Strand p. 159.

The Grand Strand

Starting at Little River on the Atlantic Ocean, near the North Carolina border, the Grand Strand runs 60 miles south to the curving banks of the Santee River. Included in its wide path are the inland towns of Loris, Conway, Andrews and Georgetown. But the part of the Grand Strand most visitors know is the sandy coast where numerous towns provide spacious beachfront views. Myrtle Beach is the largest and most traveled, but other communities like Cherry Grove, Windy Hill, Atlantic, Surfside and Pawleys Island also offer beautiful scenery and a warm welcome.

With the Gulf Stream pacing only 40 miles offshore, the temperate climate is perfect for the area's numerous possibilities. Outdoor enthusiasts of all types—from golfers and sailors to snorkelers and divers—will find ample recreational activities.

Courtesy: Myrtle Beach Area Chamber of Commerce

Visitor Information Center: Maps and brochures are available at the center in Planter's Exchange, on US 17 in Pawleys Island.

GEORGETOWN (D-5) pop. 9,500, elev. 12′

In 1526 the Spanish attempted to settle at the head of Winyah Bay where Georgetown now stands but were driven out by disease. The first permanent settlers arrived in the early 18th century; many of their buildings and houses still are in use. With a deep-water harbor that can accommodate oceangoing vessels, Georgetown has developed into an important shipping port.

Georgetown County is the site of numerous events throughout the year. Early in May the town of Andrews goes all out during its week-long Good Ole Days Celebration; topping off the foods, arts and crafts, games and other events is the return of hometown singer Chubby Checker. Plantation Tours, a 2-day tour of private estates, is held in early spring.

Georgetown Harborwalk Celebration, held in late June or early July, features arts and crafts, foods, foot races and entertainment. Around Halloween, take the Ghost Hunt, a 2-day self-guiding tour throughout Georgetown County, and you may stumble into the Gray Man or Drunken Jack, two of Georgetown's late "residents."

Bellefield Nature Center, off US 17 between Pawleys Island and Georgetown at the entrance to Hobcaw Barony, has plant and animal displays, exhibits about the research activities of the Baruch Institutes and a saltwater touch tank with local sea life; phone (803) 546-4623.

Georgetown County Chamber of Commerce: 102 Broad St., P.O. Drawer 1776, Georgetown, SC 29442; phone (803) 546-8436 or (800) 777-7705.

Self-guiding tours: Maps detailing tours past historic sites are available from the chamber of commerce.

CAPTAIN SANDY'S TOURS departs from the floating dock behind Front and Broad sts. Shell Island tours include the 3-hour round trip, in addition to 2 hours of shell-collecting on the barrier island. The narration of the 3-hour Plantation River tour explains the history of the river and its inhabitants and offers plantation views. Island tours leave Wed. and Sat. at 10. River tours leave Tues., Thurs. and Fri. at 1. Island tour $25; ages 3-12, $15. River tour $18; ages 3-12, $10. Reservations are recommended. Phone (803) 527-4106.

HAROLD KAMINSKI HOUSE MUSEUM is at 1003 Front St. Built in the 1760s, the house contains American and European furnishings from the 17th through the 20th century. Tours are given on the hour Mon.-Sat. 10-4, Sun. 1-4. Last tour begins at closing. Closed holidays. Admission $4; ages 6-12, $2. Phone (803) 546-7706.

HOPSEWEE PLANTATION, 12 mi. s. on US 17 at 494 Hopsewee Rd., was the residence of Thomas Lynch, a South Carolina delegate to the Continental Congress, and the birthplace of his son Thomas Jr., who signed the Declaration of Independence. The 1740 plantation house is restored and has period furnishings. Tues.-Fri. 10-4, Mar.-Oct. Grounds, including nature trail, $3 per private vehicle. House $6; ages 5-17, $2. Phone (803) 546-7891.

PRINCE GEORGE WINYAH CHURCH (Episcopal), 300 Broad St. at Highmarket St., dates from 1735. Colonists as well as Revolutionary and Confederate soldiers are buried at the site. Mon.-Thurs. 11:30-4:30, Mar.-Oct. Free. Phone (803) 546-4358.

RICE MUSEUM, Front and Screven sts., chronicles the history of the rice industry in the

United States with maps, dioramas, photographs and artifacts. The museum also has a cross-section scale model of a rice mill. Mon.-Sat. 9:30-4:30; closed major holidays. Admission $2; students with ID free. Phone (803) 546-7423.

McCLELLANVILLE (D-6) pop. 300, elev. 9'

A small fishing village, McClellanville celebrates its livelihood the first week in May when the shrimpboats undergo the Blessing of the Fleet.

HAMPTON PLANTATION STATE PARK is at 1950 Rutledge Rd. The focus of this park is the two-story grand mansion which grew from a six-room farmhouse built 1730-1750 on this former rice plantation. The building is unfurnished in order to show its architectural detail, and walls have cutaway sections to reveal construction techniques. Picnic facilities are available. Allow 1 hour minimum.

Park Thurs.-Mon. 9-6. Mansion Thurs.-Sun. 1-4. Park admission free. Mansion $2; ages 6-16, $1. Phone (803) 546-9361

MURRELLS INLET (D-6) pop. 3,300

According to legend, the marshland community of Murrells Inlet was named for Capt. Murrell, a pirate who used the inlet as a base for his forays along the Atlantic coast. Today the area is known for seafood treasures, including oysters, crabs, clams and shrimp. Fishing boats leave the docks daily.

Shopping areas: Inlet Square Mall, at the junction of US 17 bypass and US 17, includes Belk and JCPenney.

[SAVE] ★**BROOKGREEN GARDENS,** 4 mi. s. off US 17, contains more than 500 sculptures by 19th- and 20th-century American artists. The garden museum is on the site of an old rice and indigo plantation which dates from the mid-1700s. Six large millstones in the gardens once were used for hulling rice on nearby plantations.

Created by railroad heir Archer M. Huntington and his sculptor wife, Anna Hyatt Huntington, in the 1930s, the gardens are among the most beautiful in the South. Moss-hung oak trees, dogwoods, azaleas and other indigenous and exotic plants are among the more than 2,000 species used in the landscape; many are in bloom from early April through September. A sculpture gallery in a loggia around an interior pool and fountain displays small statuary. A wildlife park contains two aviaries, an otter pond, an alligator swamp, nature trails and a picnic area.

Peak color seasons are in early April when the dogwoods and azaleas are in flower and October through November. Free programs and tours are given daily. Allow 2 hours minimum. Daily 9:30-5:30. Last admission 45 minutes before closing. Closed Dec. 25. Admission $7.50; ages 6-12, $3. Phone (803) 237-4218.

HUNTINGTON BEACH STATE PARK, 3 mi. s. on US 17, offers nearly 2,500 acres of natural habitat and wildlife, and camping and recreational facilities. The park features nature trails, beach areas, a saltwater marsh and a freshwater lagoon. Observation decks afford opportunities to view native wildlife, including shorebirds and alligators. Beginning the fourth Friday in September, the park is the site of the 3-day Atalaya Arts and Crafts Festival.

Daily nature study programs are offered June through August. Open daily 6 a.m.-10 p.m., Apr.-Sept.; 6-6, rest of year. Admission Mar.-Nov. $3; 6-12, $1.50. Admission rest of year free. Phone (803) 237-4440. *See Recreation Chart and the AAA Southeastern CampBook.*

Atalaya, the Spanish term for "watchtower," is a 55-room mansion within Huntington Beach State Park. Constructed in a square, the house built 1931-33 features a large open inner court; Anna Hyatt Huntington's sculpture studio; and a 40-foot-high tower that once contained a 3,000-gallon water tank, the height of which created enough pressure to provide running water throughout the house. Guided tours are available daily June through August; the house may be reserved for private functions on off-season weekends. Open daily 9-5. Admission 50c June-Aug.; free rest of year. Phone (803) 237-4440.

MYRTLE BEACH (C-6) pop. 24,800

The central city on the 60-mile-long Grand Strand, Myrtle Beach offers a broad range of entertainment, nightlife and outdoor recreation. A multitude of amusements lines the boardwalk and

---

Area Code Change

The Coastal and Pee Dee regions will change their area code from 803 to 843 effective Mar. 22, 1998, when permissive dialing goes into effect. After Sept. 27, 1998 only the 843 area code will be effective for these regions.

Towns that will be located in the new area code include Beaufort, Charleston, Darlington, Dillon, Florence, Georgetown, Hartsville, Hilton Head, McBee, McClellanville, McColl, Moncks Corner, Mount Pleasant, Murrells Inlet, Myrtle Beach, Pawleys Island, Sullivans Island, Summerville and West Myrtle Beach.

connecting streets. Excellent deep-sea and surf fishing as well as surfing are available. Myrtle Beach State Park *(see Recreation Chart and the AAA Southeastern CampBook)* is 3 miles south.

Myrtle Beach has developed into one of the Southeast's primary golf and tennis resort centers. Especially in spring and fall, pros and duffers alike enjoy the more than 90 golf courses carved from the wooded sandhills within a half-hour's drive.

Country/Western music buffs are beginning to regard this area as Branson East, and new entertainment establishments are popping up faster than prairie dogs in a cloudburst.

One of the largest is Broadway at the Beach, a 350-acre entertainment complex featuring a park, a lake, theaters, nightclubs, restaurants and shops. Celebrity Square in the park features sounds from beach and shag music, to country and blues. Ribs and seafood are among the dishes served in the dining district which surrounds a 23-acre lake. Thrill seekers may enjoy Family Kingdom Amusement Park, 300 Fourth Ave. S., or Pavilion Amusement Park, Ninth Ave. N. and N. Ocean Blvd.

The annual Canadian-American Days Festival takes place in mid-March when Canadian schools are on spring break. Some local attractions offer discounted rates.

In mid-May listen for the loud rumble of the annual Harley Davidson Motorcycle Rally as thousands of Harley owners gather to compete in races, hold contests and swap products. Myrtle Beach celebrates summer with its annual Sun Fun Festival. Held the first weekend in June, the festival includes pageants, parades, entertainment, arts and crafts, a sand-sculpture contest and beach games. For many, the highlight of this festival is the air show which often features the Air Force Thunderbirds precision aerobatics team. Beginning in November the Grand Strand celebrates the holidays with Treasures by the Sea, a festival of lights.

Myrtle Beach Area Chamber of Commerce: 1200 N. Oak St., P.O. Box 2115, Myrtle Beach, SC 29578; phone (803) 626-7444 or (800) 356-3016.

Shopping areas: Barefoot Landing, .2 mi. s. of North Myrtle Beach on US 17, is a waterway marketplace with more than 80 shops and restaurants. Belk and JCPenney are the anchors of the 90 stores in Briarcliffe Mall, about 8 miles north off US 17. Myrtle Beach Factory Stores *(see ad p. 162)* includes more than 60 outlet stores on US 501, 3 miles west of the Waterway. Myrtle Square Mall, 2501 N. Kings Highway, includes Belk, Sears and Peebles among it 92 stores. Waccamaw Outlet Park, on US 501 at the Waterway, appeals to bargain-hunters *(see color ad)*.

ALABAMA THEATRE AT BAREFOOT LANDING, 4750 US 17S, features singing, dancing and comedy. A Celebrity Concert Series also is offered. Shows begin at 8 p.m. Celebrity concerts

begin at 7 p.m. Admission $25; ages 3-16, $10. Concert series $25-$30. Reservations are required. AE, DS, MC, VI. Phone (803) 272-1111 or (800) 342-2262.

THE CAROLINA OPRY, jct. US 17 and US 17 bypass, presents family music and variety shows with an emphasis on country music. Allow 2 hours minimum. Performances Mon.-Sat. at 8 p.m., Apr.-Oct.; Tues.-Sat. at 8 p.m., Feb.-Mar. and in Nov.; Mon.-Sat. at 7 p.m., in Dec.; otherwise varies. Admission $26; students with ID $18; under 16, $13. Reservations are required. DS, MC, VI. Phone (803) 238-8888 or (800) 843-6779. *See ad p. 163.*

★**DIXIE STAMPEDE** is at the n. jct. of US 17 and US 17 bypass. This family-oriented experience combines entertainment with a four-course meal. A performance in the Dixie Belle Saloon precedes the arena event. The main show—which chronicles the North vs. South rivalry—includes feats of horsemanship, special effects and audience participation. Allow 3 hours minimum.

Performances daily Apr.-Dec.; show times vary. Admission $27.95; ages 4-11, $14.95. Reservations are recommended. AE, DS, MC, VI. Phone (803) 497-9700 or (800) 433-4401. *See color ad.*

SAVE **THE GATLIN BROTHERS THEATRE,** e. of US 17 bypass off US 501 at 2901 Fantasy Way, offers family-oriented entertainment with the Gatlins performing their Grammy-winning music. Opening acts vary with time of year. Allow 2 hours minimum. Performances Mon.-Sat. at 8 p.m. (also Wed. at 3). Admission $24.95; over 54, $22.95; ages 3-16, $9.95. AE, DS, MC, VI. Phone (803) 236-8500 or (800) 681-5209.

MEDIEVAL TIMES DINNER AND TOURNAMENT, e. of US 17 bypass off US 501 at 2904 Fantasy Way, lets visitors dine in a European-style castle while watching an 11th-century royal tournament. The action includes jousting, dressage maneuvers, hand-to-hand combat and tests of skill. Allow 3 hours minimum. Performances Mon.-Sat. at 6:45 and 8:45, Sun. at 6:45, June-Aug.; daily at 6 in May and Sept.-Oct.; Mon.-Sat. at 6, Feb.-Apr.; Tues.-Sat. at 6, Nov.-Dec. Admission $27.75; ages 3-12, $15.75. Reservations are required. AE, CB, DS, MC, VI. Phone (803) 236-8080 or (800) 436-4386. *See ad p. 163.*

MYRTLE WAVES WATER PARK is at US 17 bypass and 10th Ave. N. This 20-acre water park features more than 30 rides and attractions, including a variety of waterslides, surfing rides, a lazy river ride, wave pool, children's water park, video arcade and lounge chairs. Life vests, locker rooms, showers and food are available.

Allow 4 hours minimum. Daily 10-7, June-Aug.; 10-5 mid-May through May 31 and Sept. 1 to mid-Sept. Admission $17.99, over age 54 and children

under 48 inches tall $11.99, under age 2 free; after 3 p.m. $11.99, over age 54 and children under 48 inches tall $8.99, under age 2 free. MC, VI. Phone (803) 448-1026 or (800) 524-9283.

SNOOPY'S MAGIC ON ICE, e. of US 17 bypass off US 501 at 2924 Fantasy Way, combines illusions, cabaret dancing and professional ice skating with the costumes and antics of the Snoopy and Friends performers. Allow 2 hours minimum. Performances Mon.-Fri. at 4 and 8, Sat. at 8, May-Dec.; Mon.-Fri. at 3 and 7, Sat. at 7, rest of year. Admission $25.75; over 54, $23.75; ages 3-16, $9.95. AE, DS, MC, VI. Phone (803) 236-8500 or (800) 681-5209.

WACCATEE ZOO, from US 17 bypass, 6 mi. s.w. via SR 707 and Enterprise Rd., is a haven for more than 100 animal species. The 500-acre farm provides a natural habitat for exotic and domestic animals, including miniature horses, leopards, buffalo, llamas and alligators. The zoo also is a wildlife breeding ground for several species

of migratory birds. A nature trail and petting zoo also are featured. Food is available. Allow 2 hours minimum. Daily 10-5. Admission $4; under 12, $2.50. Phone (803) 650-8500.

SURFSIDE BEACH (C-6) pop. 3,800, elev. 10'

LEGENDS IN CONCERT, US 17S and Third Ave. S., presents impressionists re-creating the stage performances of Michael Jackson, Reba McEntire, Marilyn Monroe, Roy Orbison, Dolly Parton, Elvis Presley and others. All the performers play their own instruments and use their own voices. The show also features a live band. Allow 2 hours minimum. Performances Mon.-Sat. at 6 and 9, June-Aug.; Mon.-Sat. at 8 (also Tues.-Thurs. and Sat. at 2), Jan.-May and Sept.-Oct.; otherwise varies. Admission $22.95; under 17, $9.95. DS, MC, VI. Phone (803) 238-7827 or (800) 960-7469.

GREENVILLE (A-2) pop. 58,300, elev. 1,040'

The Blue Ridge Mountains, visible from downtown Greenville, present a compelling lure to many. By the early 19th century, the region had become a summer resort for Lowcountry planters escaping the coastal heat and malaria. The town they built, Pleasantburg, soon was incorporated into Greenville as mills were erected to exploit the falls of the Reedy River in the heart of the community.

Despite the ravages of the Civil War, the city recovered. Greenville soon became known as the "textile center of the world" as many mills relocated from the Northeast. Reedy River Falls Historic Park preserves the site of the city's first settlement and the succession of mills that once stood there. The park offers picnic sites and several paths along the river.

During the Civil War, Greenville was an important hospital center for Confederate soldiers. The city supports the Shriners' Hospital for Crippled Children, which is one of the most modern hospitals of its kind; guided tours are available by phoning (864) 255-7848 between 10 and 3.

Greenville has more than 60 city parks; Cleveland Park includes Greenville Zoo, with exhibits of wild and domestic animals. Cherokee Foothills Scenic Highway, northwest of Greenville, is lined with still lakes, greenery and historic sites.

Prominent events are River Place Festival, a celebration of the arts held in early spring; Freedom Weekend Aloft, with its colorful hot-air balloon race, in early July; and the Back to Nature Festival in November.

Greenville Convention and Visitors Bureau: 206 S. Main St., Greenville, SC 29601; phone (864) 233-0461 or (800) 717-0023.

BOB JONES UNIVERSITY ART GALLERY AND BIBLICAL MUSEUM is at 1700 Wade Hampton Blvd., 3 mi. n. on US 29 at jct. SR 291. The gallery contains more than 400 religious paintings by European artists from the 13th through 19th centuries. Tues.-Sun. 2-5; closed Jan. 1, July 4 and Dec. 20-25. Free. Under 6 are not permitted. Phone (864) 242-5100, ext. 1050.

GREENVILLE COUNTY MUSEUM OF ART, 420 College St., features a permanent collection which includes American art from the Colonial period to the present, with special emphasis on Southern art. Temporary exhibits include contemporary art and explanations of aspects of American art history. Films, seminars and lectures are offered. Guided tours are given by appointment. Open Tues.-Sat. 10-5, Sun. 1-5; closed major holidays. Free. Phone (864) 271-7570.

GREENWOOD (C-2) pop. 20,800, elev. 665'

The test gardens and display plots of George W. Park Seed Co., a seed mail-order house 6

miles north of Greenwood on SR 254, are open to the public. The tours of company's experimental gardens are one of the attractions of the 3-day South Carolina Festival of Flowers, beginning the Friday of the last weekend in June; phone (864) 223-8555 for tour information.

Greenwood Area Chamber of Commerce: 518 S. Main St., P.O. Box 980, Greenwood, SC 29648; phone (864) 223-8431.

CALLIE SELF MEMORIAL CARILLON is next to the Callie Self Memorial Church on US 25. The 37 bells were cast in Holland and displayed as the Netherlands' exhibit at the New York World's Fair in 1939. Open Mon.-Fri. 9-2; concerts daily at 9, noon and 5. Phone (864) 227-2881.

THE MUSEUM, 106 Main St., houses items pertaining to the late 19th century, including such village reconstructions as an early drugstore, a Victorian parlor, a physician's office and a general store. Also featured are natural history displays and objects from Africa, Egypt, Japan and Latin America, as well as changing art exhibits. Tues.-Fri. 9-5, Sat. 2-5. Donations. Phone (864) 229-7093.

HARLEYVILLE—

see Charleston and Vicinity p. 152.

HARTSVILLE (B-5) pop. 8,400

Built on the plantation of Thomas Edward Hart, Hartsville grew into an active trading center largely through the efforts of the Coker family. Arriving in the mid-19th century, Maj. James Lide Coker established several businesses, constructed a railroad and founded Coker College, a 4-year liberal arts college with an enrollment of 950. David Coker, an agricultural expert who bred superior strains of cotton and other crops, also contributed to the town's prosperity.

Today only one-half of one percent Hartsville's population is engaged in agriculture. The town accommodates several major manufacturers, including the international headquarters for a consumer and industrial packaging manufacturer. The town's development is documented at Hartsville Museum, 222 N. Fifth St.; phone (803) 383-3005.

Coker College's Kalmia Gardens, on W. Carolina Avenue, includes mountain and Lowcountry plants grouped around three small lakes on the bluffs of Black Creek.

Greater Hartsville Chamber of Commerce: 214 N. Fifth St., P.O. Box 578, Hartsville, SC 29551; phone (803) 332-6401.

THE NUCLEAR INFORMATION CENTER is 5 mi. n.w. on SR 151 at the site of the Southeast's first commercial nuclear plant. Exhibits pertain to energy, the generation of electricity and nuclear power. Allow 30 minutes minimum. Mon.-Fri. 8:30-4:30; closed holidays. Free. Phone (803) 857-1360.

HILTON HEAD ISLAND (F-4)
pop. 23,700

Hilton Head Island, off the southern coast of South Carolina, is bordered by one of the last major unpolluted marine estuaries on the East Coast. The largest island between New Jersey and Florida, it is 12 miles long and up to 5 miles wide. Hilton Head was named for Capt. William Hilton, an Englishman who sailed into Port Royal Sound in 1663 and wrote about the green headlands of the island.

People lived on the island about 3,800 years ago. Beginning in 1526, Spanish, French and English colonists attempted to settle in this territory but were troubled by American Indian raids and pirates. By the mid-18th century, English plantations were established. They prospered, growing indigo, rice and sea island cotton until the Civil War, when Union troops used the island as a base to block Confederate ports.

After the war the island was left to nature and the freed-slave, or "Gullah," population, which developed a culture based on hunting, fishing and farming. Ruins of historic plantations and forts, including Baynard Ruins, a once-prosperous sea island cotton plantation, still can be seen.

In 1956 the bridge to the mainland was completed, and the island developed into an all-year resort. Recreational facilities include about 25 golf courses, 300 tennis courts, riding stables, bicycle trails and marinas. Harbour Town Links is the site of the MCI Heritage Golf Classic in April. The Hilton Head Island Celebrity Golf Tournament is played at Palmetto Dunes and Shipyard in September.

Wildlife and waterfowl habitats include the Sea Pines Forest Preserve, the Audubon Newhall Preserve and the Pinckney Island National Wildlife Refuge. Daily sightseeing cruises are available on Calibogue Sound, around the island and to Daufuskie Island, where many old Gullah traditions still are observed.

Prominent among the annual festivities on the island is SpringFest. Held throughout March, the festival includes sporting events, concerts, plays, art shows and food.

Hilton Head Island Chamber of Commerce: P.O. Box 5647, Hilton Head Island, SC 29938-5647; phone (803) 785-3673.

HOPKINS (C-4) pop. 1,700, elev. 172'
CONGAREE SWAMP NATIONAL MONUMENT, on SR 48/Bluff Rd., following signs, comprises 22,200 acres of swamp forest along the Congaree River. The area's native wildlife can be seen along two boardwalks. Picnicking, hiking, fishing, canoeing, primitive camping and camping are permitted. Guided nature walks are offered Sat. at 1:30. Allow 1 hour, 30 minutes minimum. Daily 8:30-5; closed Dec. 25. Free. Phone (803) 776-4396.

INMAN (A-2) pop. 1,700, elev. 986'

Inman probably was named after Henry Inman, a local painter. He, along with a few other artists living in the state during the second quarter of the 19th century, contributed some of the earliest genre painting done in America.

HOLLYWILD ANIMAL PARK, 4 mi. s.w. on SR 292, following signs, has a large and unusual collection of exotic, wild and domestic animals in an open-air setting. During the holiday season visitors can drive through the park and see decorations as well as the animals. Picnic facilities are available. Allow 2 hours minimum.

Daily 9-6, Apr. 1-Labor Day; Sat.-Sun. 9-5, day after Labor Day-Oct. 31 and in Mar.; daily 6-10 p.m., Sat. before Thanksgiving-Jan. 1. Admission $6; over 64 and ages 2-12, $4. Holiday drive-thru $2. Phone (864) 472-2038.

KINGS MOUNTAIN NATIONAL MILITARY PARK (A-3)

Kings Mountain National Military Park, south of the town of Kings Mountain, N.C., off I-85, is one of the largest military parks in the United States. Spreading across York and Cherokee counties in South Carolina, this 3,950-acre area is a spur of the Kings Mountain Range. Battlefield Ridge, about 600 yards long, is a narrow hogback 60 feet above the surrounding valleys.

After several years of hostilities, only one Southern region remained undisturbed by the Revolutionary War—the southern Appalachians. That tenuous peace soon came to an end as British troops under Gen. Charles Cornwallis occupied vast areas of North and South Carolina. In September 1780 Maj. Patrick Ferguson raided a mountain town.

The threatened backwoodsmen joined forces with Whigs from Virginia, South Carolina and North Carolina and converged on Kings Mountain, where Ferguson was camped. Although outnumbered by the trained Loyalists, the mountain men advanced steadily against repeated bayonet charges and took the summit. Ferguson, who had threatened "to lay their country waste with fire and sword," was killed.

In the park stand the United States Monument, Centennial Monument and other memorial markers. A self-guiding trail leads to significant battlefield sites. The visitor center offers exhibits, a film and a diorama of the battle. Allow 1 hour minimum. Daily 9-6, Memorial Day-Labor Day; 9-5, rest of year. Closed Jan. 1, Thanksgiving and Dec. 25. Free. Phone (864) 936-7921.

LANCASTER (B-4) pop. 8,900

Settled in the early 1800s, Lancaster became the center of trade for the surrounding mill villages. Instrumental in the city's growth was a series of canals built on the Catawba-Wateree River during the 1820s. The locks made the waterway navigable despite its treacherous shoals and falls. A section of locks at Landsford Canal State Park *(see Recreation Chart)*, northwest off US 21 and SR 330, has been restored.

Lancaster County Chamber of Commerce: 604 N. Main St., P.O. Box 430, Lancaster, SC 29721; phone (803) 283-4105.

ANDREW JACKSON STATE PARK is 8 mi. n. on US 521. Commemorating Andrew Jackson, who was born in the vicinity, the park contains an amphitheater, a museum with documents and relics of the frontier period, and a one-room log schoolhouse with exhibits. Allow 2 hours minimum. Park open daily 9-9 during DST; 8-6, rest of year. Museum open Mon.-Fri. by appointment, Sat.-Sun. 1-4. Free. Phone (803) 285-3344. *See Recreation Chart and the AAA Southeastern CampBook.*

LEXINGTON (C-3) pop. 3,300, elev. 360′

Formed in 1785, Lexington was named for the Massachusetts town where the first battle of the Revolutionary War was fought. However, this Lexington was not as quick to embrace the Patriot cause. The area's population, largely of German descent, was loyal to England's German king George III and his Lutheran queen Charlotte Sophia. The settlers finally did join their fellow colonists late in the war.

Lexington Chamber of Commerce: 321 S. Lake Dr., P.O. Box 44, Lexington, SC 29072; phone (803) 359-6113.

★**LEXINGTON COUNTY MUSEUM COMPLEX** is on Fox St. at jct. US 378. Through period buildings and furnishings constructed by local craftsmen, this complex depicts the lifestyle of the area during the 1830s. The complex houses collections of American Indian artifacts, quilts, coverlets and farm tools and equipment. Spinning and weaving demonstrations and guided tours are conducted. Allow 1 hour minimum. Tours Tues.-Sat. at 10, 11, 1, 2 and 3, Sun. at 1, 2 and 3; closed major holidays. Admission $2; under 12, $1. Phone (803) 359-8369.

LONG CREEK (B-1) pop. 1,500

Long Creek is surrounded by the Andrew Pickens District of Sumter National Forest *(see place listing)*. Whitewater enthusiasts frequent the nearby Chattooga River, where the motion picture "Deliverance" was filmed.

 RECREATIONAL ACTIVITIES

White-water Rafting

- **Nantahala Outdoor Center**, 851 A Chattooga Ridge Rd.; go 2.3 mi. e. on US 76, then 2.5 mi. n. on Chattooga Ridge Rd. Write 13077 Hwy. 19W, Bryson City, NC 28713. Daily mid-Mar. through mid-Nov. Phone (800) 232-7238.

- SAVE **Wildwater Ltd.**, 1 mi. n. of US 76 in the Long Creek Academy Bldg. Write P.O. Box 309, Charleston, SC 29658. Daily Mar.-Oct. Phone (864) 647-9587 or (800) 451-9972.

McBEE (B-4) pop. 700, elev. 490′

McBee traces its origin to 1900, when a barbecue was held and lots were sold at auction. Abandoning cotton and corn farming in favor of more marketable fruit cultivation, area farmers became renowned for their high-quality grapes, which are a favorite with North Carolina winemakers.

CAROLINA SANDHILLS NATIONAL WILDLIFE REFUGE, 4 mi. n. on US 1, is 45,348 acres of forest, stream-side, pond and open-field habitats, supporting nearly 200 species of birds, deer and other wildlife. Sand dunes forming a line from Cheraw to North Augusta are the remains of an ancient coastline that once extended into the middle of the state. The refuge has 1- and 5-mile hiking trails, an automobile route, observation towers and approximately 310 acres of fishing waters. Daily dawn-dusk. Free. Phone (803) 335-8401.

McCLELLANVILLE—
see The Grand Strand p. 160.

McCONNELLS (B-3) pop. 200

York County Convention and Visitors Bureau: 201 E. Main St., P.O. Box 11377, Rock Hill, SC 29731; phone (803) 329-5200 or (800) 866-5200.

HISTORIC BRATTONSVILLE, 4 mi. e. via SR 322 and Brattonsville Rd., following signs, comprises 24 restored structures, including an academy for girls, a pioneer cabin, homestead house and the McConnell family house. The buildings have been restored and furnished to reflect the lifestyle of the Piedmont area during the late 18th and mid-19th centuries. During the Christmas Tour, interpretive skits of life in 1780 and 1850 are presented in the buildings; it is recommended that you bring a flashlight for this tour.

Tues.-Sat. 10-4, Sun. 2-5, the first Sun. in Mar.-last Sat. in Nov.; Christmas Tour Fri.-Sat. 6:30-9, Sun. 4-7, first complete weekend in Dec. Last admission 30 minutes before closing. Closed Easter, Memorial Day, July 4, Labor Day and Thanksgiving. Admission $5; ages 7-17, $2. Phone (803) 684-2327.

MONCKS CORNER—
see Charleston and Vicinity p. 152.

MOUNT PLEASANT—
see Charleston and Vicinity p. 153.

MURRELLS INLET—
see The Grand Strand p. 160.

MYRTLE BEACH—
see The Grand Strand p. 160.

NINETY SIX (C-2) pop. 2,100, elev. 571′

Settled along an American Indian trading route, Ninety Six was named for its distance in miles from the Cherokee village of Keowee in the Blue Ridge Mountains. Patriots and Tories fought the first land battle of the Revolutionary War in the South in November 1775.

Ninety Six Chamber of Commerce: P.O. Box 8, Ninety Six, SC 29666; phone (864) 543-2900.

NINETY SIX NATIONAL HISTORIC SITE is 2 mi. s. on SR 248. In 1781 Patriot general Nathanael Greene laid siege to a force of some 550 British Loyalists entrenched near the village of Ninety Six. Visitors can explore the earthworks, old road beds, traces of the village, a reconstructed stockade fort and an early log cabin along a mile-long trail. The visitor center houses a museum and auditorium. Each October brings the Autumn Candlelight Tour to mark the site's colorful heritage with a portrait of what life was like in the 1780s.

Allow 1 hour, 30 minutes minimum. Park open daily dawn-dusk. Visitor center open daily 8-5; closed Jan. 1, Thanksgiving and Dec. 25. Free. Phone (864) 543-4068.

ORANGEBURG (D-3) pop. 13,700, elev. 252'

Since its settlement in the 1730s, Orangeburg has been an important trade center for Orangeburg County's rich farmland. Such manufactured goods as wood products, textiles, chemicals and machinery sustain the town's economy.

The South Carolina Festival of Roses, usually held the first weekend of May, offers displays of antique and classic cars, golf and fishing tournaments, arts and crafts and a parade and pageant. The week-long Orangeburg County Fair is held in late September.

Orangeburg County Chamber of Commerce: 1570 J.C. Calhoun Dr., P.O. Box 328, Orangeburg, SC 29116; phone (803) 534-6821.

EDISTO MEMORIAL GARDENS is a municipal park along the North Edisto River, one of the longest blackwater rivers in the world. Once a dismal riverbank swamp, the 110 acres of moss-draped oaks, cypresses, dogwoods, crab apples and azaleas are especially beautiful in late March and early April. A rose garden with about 200 varieties provides color from mid-April to mid-November. Within the gardens, Horne Wetlands Park offers 2,500 feet of boardwalk with a view of native plants and wildlife. Daily dawn-dusk. Free. Phone (803) 534-6821.

ORANGEBURG NATIONAL FISH HATCHERY, on US 21 bypass (Stonewall Jackson Blvd.), houses a display aquarium. On the premises blue gills, stripped bass, catfish and shortnose sturgeon are raised. Picnic facilities and guided tours are available. Mon.-Fri. 8-4. Free. Phone (803) 534-4828.

PARRIS ISLAND (F-4) pop. 7,200

The U.S. Marine Corps Recruit Depot has occupied Parris Island since 1915. The Jean Ribault (or Huguenot) Monument marks the site of one of North America's first European settlements.

PARRIS ISLAND MUSEUM is on Panama St., Bldg. 111, at the Marine Corps Recruit Depot. Take I-95 exit 8 to US 17N, then US 21S, following signs. The museum contains displays of uniforms, field equipment, official documents and photographs relating to the history of the Marine Corps and civilian life on Parris Island. Collections of weapons, ordnance and artillery, and scale models of aircraft, ships and amphibious landing craft also are displayed.

Allow 1 hour minimum. Daily 10-4:30 (also Thurs. 4:30-7); closed Jan. 1, Easter, Thanksgiving and Dec. 25. Free. Phone (803) 525-2951.

PENDLETON (B-1) pop. 3,300, elev. 817'

The Pendleton district was formed soon after the Cherokees ceded their territory to South Carolina in 1777. Named for Judge Henry Pendleton of Culpeper, Va., whose Culpeper Minute Men were among the first Revolutionary militia in the South, the town became an important government, business and cultural center because of its location at the crossroads of two major American Indian trading paths.

Pendleton also became popular with wealthy Lowcountry families who built large plantations as summer retreats. Pendleton is the headquarters of one of the largest national historic districts in the country. The first full weekend in April brings the Historic Pendleton Spring Jubilee which features arts, crafts and entertainment.

Self-guiding tours: English and French tape tours of the Pendleton Historic District are available from the Pendleton District Historical, Recreational and Tourism Commission in Old Hunter's Store, 125 E. Queen St. The tape rental fee is $4.

ROCK HILL (B-3) pop. 41,600

The name Rock Hill is derived from the white, flinty rock encountered during the construction of the Charlotte, Columbia and Augusta Railroad. Not much more than a sprawling country crossroads for several decades following 1852, Rock Hill finally blossomed into an industrial town with the spread of cotton mills in the Upcountry and the development of hydroelectric power on the Catawba River.

In 1895, Rock Hill obtained Winthrop College from Columbia, where it had been founded in 1886. Today Winthrop University offers an art gallery, a golf course and a lake for public enjoyment.

Glencairn Garden, at Charlotte Avenue and Edgemont and Crest streets, is a manicured 6-acre city park with a fountain, lily pond and winding paths. In mid-April, the azaleas, dogwoods and wisteria reach their peak; tulips bloom in spring, annuals throughout the summer.

York County Convention and Visitors Bureau: 201 E. Main St., P.O. Box 11377, Rock Hill, SC 29731; phone (803) 329-5200 or (800) 866-5200.

Shopping areas: Outlet Marketplace, I-77 exit 90, houses factory discount stores, including Corning Revere, Van Heusen and Westport.

HISTORIC BRATTONSVILLE— see McConnells p. 167.

MUSEUM OF YORK COUNTY, w. on SR 161 from I-77 exit 82A, then n. on Mount Gallant Rd., offers a planetarium, a large collection of mounted animals from Africa and the Americas, art galleries, an exhibit of Catawba pottery, a nature trail and picnic facilities. Museum open Mon.-Sat. 10-5, Sun. 1-5. Planetarium shows Sat.-Sun. at 2, 3 and 4 (also Sat. at 11 a.m.). Closed major holidays. Admission, including planetarium, $4; over 61, $3; under 6 free. Phone (803) 329-2121.

★**PARAMOUNT'S CAROWINDS THEME PARK—** see Charlotte, N.C. p. 89.

ROEBUCK (B-3) pop. 2,000, elev. 750'

★**WALNUT GROVE PLANTATION**, from I-26 exit 28 (US 221) go s. to Still House Rd. and follow signs, is an 18th-century plantation furnished with pre-1830 antiques. The kitchen building displays 18th-century utensils made from wood, wrought iron and tin as well as earthenware. Other outbuildings include a smithy, school, doctor's office, drover's house and barns. An herb garden, nature trail and family cemetery also are on the grounds.

Tues.-Sat. 11-5, Sun. 2-5, Apr.-Oct.; Sun. 2-5, rest of year. Closed holidays. Admission $4.50; over 64, $4; ages 6-18, $2. Phone (864) 576-6546.

ST. HELENA ISLAND (E-5)

YORK W. BAILEY MUSEUM, off US 21 in the Penn Center Historic District, depicts the culture and history of the Sea Islands' African-American population since the Civil War. Penn Center was founded as Penn School in 1862 to provide formal education and settlement assistance to former slaves. Tues.-Sat. 11-4; closed holidays. Admission $2; under 11, $1. Phone (803) 838-2235.

ST. MATTHEWS (C-4) pop. 2,300, elev. 257'

Originally the site of a trading post on the Cherokee Path, St. Matthews later was settled by Palatine Germans 1730-40. It was one of the first plantation domains in South Carolina beyond the Charleston tidewater region.

Calhoun County Chamber of Commerce: 101 Herlong St., P.O. Box 444, St. Matthews, SC 29135; phone (803) 874-3791.

CALHOUN COUNTY MUSEUM AND CULTURAL CENTER, 303 Butler St., contains local historical memorabilia, period rooms, archeological artifacts, a library, archives and an art gallery. Mon.-Fri. 9-4. Archives open by appointment only. Closed holidays. Free. Phone (803) 874-3964.

SANTEE (D-4) pop. 600

The Santee National Wildlife Refuge, I-95 exit 102, is a 15,095-acre sanctuary for migratory waterfowl; phone (803) 478-2217.

Shopping areas: Santee Factory Stores, I-95 exit 98, includes more than 40 factory outlet stores such as Bass, Fieldcrest Cannon, Izod and Oneida.

SENECA (B-1) pop. 7,700, elev. 950'

★**WORLD OF ENERGY**, w. on US 76 and US 123, then 8 mi. n. on SR 130, is Duke Power Co.'s information center. Next to Oconee Nuclear Station, the center contains exhibits that illustrate the use of water, coal and uranium in creating energy. Displays chart the story of power from lightning to light bulbs, and describe energy conservation programs for the home.

The center also has an aquarium with specimens of local fish and a cold-water habitat, computer games concerning electricity, a Keowee Valley film and a quarter-mile nature trail. Allow 1 hour minimum. Mon.-Sat. 9-5, Sun. noon-5; closed Jan. 1, Thanksgiving and Dec. 24-25. Free. Phone (864) 885-4600.

SPARTANBURG (A-3) pop. 43,500, elev. 875'

One of the South's leading textile-manufacturing cities, Spartanburg also is one of the world's largest peach-shipping centers. Peach orchards and packing sheds can be visited June through August. The city was named for the Spartan Regiment, which represented it during the Revolutionary War. A statue honoring Gen. Daniel Morgan, the hero of the Battle of Cowpens, stands in Morgan Square.

The Spartanburg International Festival is held in late September. Highlights include entertainment, a circus and carnival, arts, crafts and food from a variety of cultures.

Spartanburg Convention and Visitors Bureau: 105 N. Pine St., P.O. Box 1636, Spartanburg, SC 29302; phone (864) 594-5050 or (800) 374-8326.

Spanish Moss

It's not Spanish and it's not moss; it is uniquely American and related to the pineapple. Spanish moss, the silver-green tresses that adorn trees from North Carolina to South America, is one of nature's more picturesque oddities.

Spanish moss is not a parasite but an epiphyte, a type of plant that has no roots but lives off moisture in the atmosphere. Tiny scales on the moss's tendrils trap rain for easier absorption and also keep internal moisture from evaporating. The plants are nourished by mineral-rich cells that wash off the host tree; the greater the number of cells, the more prolific the moss, which is why masses of moss are often found on very old or decaying trees. Also called long moss or vegetable horsehair, it covers more trees than any other type of epiphyte. It does not bear fruit like its spiny distant cousin the pineapple, but it sometimes produces small yellow flowers.

Spanish moss stems can grow as long as 25 feet, with threadlike leaves 1 to 3 inches long sprouting from them. Primarily decorative, the moss sometimes is used as packing material and upholstery stuffing.

THE REGIONAL MUSEUM OF SPARTANBURG COUNTY, 501 Otis Blvd., has exhibits and changing events about regional history, a doll collection and pieces of Spanish Pardo stone used by Spanish explorers to mark trails. Tues.-Sat. 10-noon and 3-5, Sun. 2-5. Admission $1, under 12 free. Phone (864) 596-3501.

★**WALNUT GROVE PLANTATION—** see Roebuck p. 169.

SULLIVAN'S ISLAND—
see Charleston and Vicinity p. 153.

SUMMERVILLE—
see Charleston and Vicinity p. 153.

SUMTER (C-5) pop. 41,900, elev. 174'

Founded in 1785, Sumter was named for Gen. Thomas Sumter, a Revolutionary War hero and statesman. The British, impressed by Sumter's daring "hit-and-run" warfare, nicknamed him the "Gamecock of the Revolution." Settled by a refined citizenry from surrounding plantations, the town developed a reputation as a cultural center. The arrival of road shows packed the old opera house, which now houses the city hall; for information about occasional productions phone (803) 436-2500.

One of the state's leading lumber and agricultural areas, Sumter is known for its furniture and woodworking industry. Further bolstering the city's economy are textile mills, chemical plants, foundries and Palmetto Pigeon Plant, reputed to be the world's largest squab farm. Just west of Sumter is Shaw Air Force Base, home to the F-16 Fighting Falcon and A-10 Thunderbolt II fighter crews.

Greater Sumter Chamber of Commerce: 32 E. Calhoun St., P.O. Box 1229, Sumter, SC 29151; phone (803) 775-1231.

SUMTER COUNTY MUSEUM, 122 N. Washington St., is housed in the 1845 Williams-Brice Home. Displayed are exhibits about the early history of Sumter County, children's period rooms, clothing dating 1840-1940, and works by national and local artists. Formal gardens surround the mansion. Allow 1 hour minimum. Tues.-Sat. 10-5, Sun. 2-5; closed major holidays. Donations. Phone (803) 775-0908.

SUMTER GALLERY OF ART, 421 N. Main St., is housed in the 1850 residence of Elizabeth White, a noted local artist. The gallery features changing exhibits of contemporary artwork in a variety of media and styles. Tues.-Fri. noon-5, Sat.-Sun. 2-5, Aug.-June; closed school holiday periods around Jan. 1, Easter, Thanksgiving and Dec. 25. Free. Phone (803) 775-0543.

SWAN LAKE IRIS GARDENS is at W. Liberty St. These 160 acres of lawns, landscaped gardens, lakes and pinewoods are known for a beautiful collection of Japanese iris, which bloom in late May and June. Seven species of swans float among the waterlilies. Special events take place during Christmas. Picnicking is permitted. Daily 7-dusk. Free. Phone (803) 773-3371.

SUMTER NATIONAL FOREST

Elevations in the forest range from 150 ft. in the Enoree region to 3,000 ft. at Fork Mountain. Refer to AAA maps for additional information.

Divided into three separate units in northwestern South Carolina, Sumter National Forest offers a variety of scenery within its 360,000 acres. The foothills of the southern Appalachians, the Piedmont's rolling terrain and the upper reaches of the Savannah River are enhanced by rhododendron, honeysuckle and azaleas. A particularly scenic route is the 12-mile stretch of SR 107 that runs through the forest. The Chattooga National Wild and Scenic River offers 31 miles of whitewater rapids for canoeing or rafting.

Guided white-water rafting trips can be arranged with operators based in Long Creek (see place listing). Forest facilities include campgrounds, picnic areas, rifle ranges and nature, hiking, canoeing and horse trails. Phone (803) 561-4000. See Recreation Chart and the AAA Southeastern CampBook.

SURFSIDE BEACH—
see The Grand Strand p. 163.

UNION (B-3) pop. 9,800, elev. 641'

ROSE HILL PLANTATION STATE PARK is on 44 acres off CR 2, 8 mi. s.w. via US 176. The former site of secessionist Gov. William Henry Gist's cotton plantation, the park includes the governor's 1832 Federal-style mansion, which features the original wooden-peg staircase, large Renaissance-Revival furnishings and some family clothing and belongings. The landscaped grounds offer boxwood, dogwood and rose gardens, as well as nature trails and magnolia trees planted when the mansion was built. Picnicking is permitted.

Allow 30 minutes minimum. Park open Thurs.-Mon. 9-6. Guided mansion tours Thurs.-Mon. 1-4, holidays by appointment. Park free. Mansion $2; ages 6-18, $1. Phone (864) 427-5966.

WALHALLA (B-1) pop. 3,800, elev. 1,055'

Settled in the mid-1800s, Walhalla was named for Valhalla, the legendary garden paradise of the gods in Norse mythology. One of the area's most scenic spots is just north on SR 28, where Issaquena Falls plunges 200 feet to the valley floor.

Near the falls is Stumphouse Mountain Tunnel, a monument to an unsuccessful but gallant attempt to burrow through 1.5 miles of mountain in the 1850s. After 6 years of chipping and drilling, funds ran out for the project, leaving one-third of the tunnel still to be cut. Despite attempts in 1876, 1900 and 1940, the tunnel was never completed, and was finally closed by a rock slide in the 1990s.

Walhalla Chamber of Commerce: 214 E. Main St., Walhalla, SC 29691; phone (864) 638-2727.

WALHALLA STATE FISH HATCHERY is about 20 mi. n.w. on SR 107 at the entrance to the Ellicott Rock Wilderness in the Sumter National Forest *(see place listing).* The hatchery raises trout. Picnic facilities are nearby. Daily 8-4. Free. Phone (864) 638-2866.

WINNSBORO (B-3) pop. 3,500, elev. 539'

Winnsboro was named in honor of town founder and Revolutionary War colonel Richard Winn. In 1780, British troops under Gen. Charles Cornwallis occupied the town for 4 months before pressing onward to their eventual surrender at Yorktown, Va. In February 1865, Federal troops looted houses and stores and then burned part of Winnsboro.

Many of those buildings not destroyed by the fire are in the town's historic district. This area has several fine examples of early 19th-century architecture, including the Old Town Clock Building, Fairfield County Courthouse and Thespian Hall.

Fairfield County Chamber of Commerce: Town Clock Bldg., Congress St., P.O. Box 297, Winnsboro, SC 29180; phone (803) 635-4242.

Self-guiding tours: Brochures detailing a walking or driving tour of historic Winnsboro, and a walking tour of nearby Ridgeway are available at the chamber of commerce.

FAIRFIELD COUNTY MUSEUM, 231 S. Congress St., was built in 1830 as a private residence. A noteworthy example of Federal architecture, the museum contains period furniture and clothing, local memorabilia, Victorian collectibles, farm and kitchen tools and American Indian artifacts. Of the many special exhibits presented throughout the year, a perennial favorite is the Candlelight Christmas Tour the first Friday and Sunday evenings in December.

Allow 30 minutes minimum. Mon., Wed. and Fri. 10:30-12:30 and 1:30-4:30, every second and fourth Sun. 2-4 for special exhibits. Genealogy services are available Wed. Closed holidays. Donations. Phone (803) 635-9811.

YORK (B-3) pop. 6,700, elev. 756'

York was settled by Scotch-Irish from Pennsylvania. The 340-acre historic district on US 321 and SR 5 contains more than 180 landmarks and structures.

Kings Mountain State Park *(see Recreation Chart and the AAA Southeastern CampBook)* has a re-creation of an 1850s farmstead with log and timber-frame structures. An interpreter is on the site June through August; phone (803) 222-3209.

The fourth Saturday in August visitors flock to Summerfest to enjoy the crafts fair, classic car show, culinary treats and fireworks display.

York County Convention and Visitors Bureau: 201 E. Main St., P.O. Box 11377, Rock Hill, SC 29730; phone (803) 329-5200 or (800) 866-5200.

ENERGYQUEST AT CATAWBA NUCLEAR STATION is next to Catawba Nuclear Station. From I-77 exit 82A, take SR 161 7 mi. to SR 274, then n. 5 mi. to 4850 Concord Rd. This mirrored-glass building contains touch-activated computer terminals that display informative videos about nuclear energy. Visitors also can observe nuclear operators in a control room that simulates the one at Catawba Nuclear Station. There also is a film presentation and a nature trail. Picnicking is permitted.

Allow 1 hour minimum. Mon.-Sat. 9-5; closed Jan. 1, Thanksgiving and Dec. 24-25. Free. Phone (800) 777-0006.

RED ALERT!

When you pick up a AAA TourBook®, be alert for the establishments that display a bright red AAA logo beside their listing. These establishments place a high value on the patronage they receive from AAA members. They are telling you they're willing to go the extra mile to get your business. Some even offer special amenities designed just for you.

And don't forget to look for the establishments that display the familiar **icon to receive discounts.**

So, when you turn to the AAA TourBook to make your travel plans, be on the look out for the establishments that will give you the special treatment you deserve.

About Lodgings & Restaurants

Lodging and restaurant listings appear after this section. Both types of properties are listed alphabetically (with lodgings listed first) under the city or town in which they physically are located or in some circumstances under the nearest recognized city or town. Major restaurant chains are not listed due to their widespread notoriety. To help you plan your trip, towns and cities that contain AAA RATED® lodgings or restaurants are printed in red on AAA/CAA regional, state, provincial and Triptik maps. The TourBook includes special accommodation "spotting" maps to help you find lodgings and restaurants. (See Maps, page 174.)

Using lodging listings

To use this book most effectively, read the sample lodging listing along with the explanation of the terms. The location given to pinpoint a facility is based on major reference points, most often highway junctions. Air conditioning, phones, color TV and private baths are not mentioned if available in all rooms. All showers are tub showers unless otherwise noted. If the term "movie" is denoted in the listing, guests can view the movie through a TV channel; there may be an additional charge. Deposits and fees for pets are stated in the listing. Please verify the property's pet policy when making reservations and inquire about any restrictions.

If parking is provided on the premises at no charge, it is not mentioned in the listing. Other parking conditions such as no parking available, off-site parking, street parking only or off-site valet parking, and any charges, are specifically noted in the listing. **Check-in** times are shown only if they are after 3 p.m.; **check-out** times are shown only if they are before 10 a.m. Service charges are not shown unless they are $1 or more, or at least 5 percent of the room rate.

What the SAVE means

Show Your Card & Save® (SYCS) participants are denoted by the SAVE icon found just below a lodging's name to the right of the AAA/CAA emblem. This icon represents a 10% discount off the published rates printed in the lodging listing for AAA/CAA members.

Only properties that are Official Appointments (see What the ⓐ or ⓒ means) may have a SAVE icon displayed in their listing.

Many properties are part of AAA's chain lodging program. To ensure receiving the best available rate these properties have to offer AAA/CAA members, visit your local AAA/CAA office to make reservations or call the following 800 numbers. Phone (800) 228-1222 for these chain participants: Clarion, Comfort Inn, Econo Lodge, Quality Inn, Rodeway and Sleep Inns; (800) 432-

9755 for Days Inn; (800) 916-2221 for Hilton; (800) 532-1496 for Hyatt; and (800) 221-4731 for La Quinta.

To receive the Show Your Card & Save discount, be sure to identify yourself as a AAA/CAA member when making reservations and show your AAA/CAA card at registration to verify the discount. The Show Your Card & Save discount may not be used in conjunction with other discounts.

Dining establishments that contain a SAVE icon in their listing have agreed to offer AAA/CAA members either discounts or a free item with their purchase. Restrictions may apply; refer to individual restaurant listings for details. Participating locations will also display a Show Your Card & Save decal on their window or door.

What the ⓐ or ⓒ means

Lodgings and restaurants approved by AAA/CAA are eligible for our Official Appointment Program, which permits the display and advertising of the ⓐ or ⓒ emblem. The ⓐ or ⓒ under a property name identifies that property as an Official Appointment establishment with a special interest in serving AAA/CAA members.

Some Official Appointment listings include the following special amenities: free breakfast; early check-in/late check-out; free room upgrade (subject to availability); free local phone calls; free daily newspaper; and preferred room, such as ocean view, poolside, etc. (subject to availability).

This does not imply that these amenities are exclusively offered by these properties. Please remember to identify yourself as a AAA/CAA member when making reservations and present your card at registration.

The ⑭ or ⑭ sign helps traveling members—like you—find accommodations on which they can depend. These properties want AAA/CAA business.

Rate options and discounts

Annually, lodging operators are requested to update rates, rate options and discounts for TourBook publication. Properties are not required to offer a discount to AAA/CAA members. However, if they choose to offer a minimum 10% discount, the SAVE icon appears in the listing. If the property chooses not to offer a discount, then one of the following rate options must be selected:

(1) Guaranteed Rates—The establishment guarantees AAA/CAA members will not be charged more than the maximum rates printed in the TourBook.

(2) Rates Subject To Change—Rates may vary for the life of the TourBook, however are guaranteed not to exceed a 15% increase on rates printed in the TourBook.

To receive the rates noted in the TourBook, you *must* identify yourself as a AAA/CAA member and request them when making reservations. Show your AAA/CAA card at registration and verify the rate.

Rates for Special Events: Lodgings may temporarily increase their room rates or modify their policies during a special event. Examples of such

events range from Mardi Gras and the Kentucky Derby to college football homecoming games, holidays and state fairs.

Senior Discount: Some establishments offer the senior discount with either the **Guaranteed Rates** option or the **Rates Subject to Change** option. Where the words "senior discount" are included in a listing, a minimum discount of 10 percent off the prevailing or guaranteed rates is available to AAA/CAA members who are 60 years of age or older. You *must* identify yourself as a AAA/CAA member *and* request the senior discount when making reservations. Show your AAA/CAA card at registration and verify the rate and discount. **Note:** Members may take the senior discount or the Show Your Card & Save® discount (denoted by the SAVE icon), but not both. The senior discount may not be used in conjunction with other discounts and might not apply during special events.

Rate lines: Rates printed are based on rack rates and last room availability, and are rounded to the nearest dollar. Rates do not include taxes and discounts. Alaska rates are in U.S. dollars; rates for Canadian lodgings are in Canadian dollars.

Maps

Area maps are used for large geographical areas in which there are many towns containing lodgings and restaurants. Because the maps are on such a small scale, lodgings and restaurants are not shown, but the towns that have these types of facilities are printed in magenta type.

Spotting maps are used for large metropolitan areas to assist you in locating the facilities listed in the Lodgings & Restaurants section of your book. These maps locate, or "spot," lodgings with a black-background numeral (⑳, for example); restaurants are spotted with a white-background numeral (⑳, for example). Indexes found near the map match the number symbol to the property. **Downtown/city spotting maps** are provided when spotted facilities are very concentrated.

Starred points of interest also appear on these maps. **Vicinity spotting maps** (Greater, North, South, for example) spot those accommodations that are outside the downtown or city area but are within the metropolitan area. Roads required to find a lodging or dining facility, airports, major landmarks and starred points of interest are shown on vicinity spotting maps. The names of suburban communities that have AAA RATED® accommodations are shown in magenta type.

Driving distance maps located in the For Your Information section of the book are intended to be used only for trip-distance and driving-time planning. Refer to more detailed AAA/CAA maps available from your club for actual route numbers.

Making reservations

When making reservations, you must identify yourself as a AAA/CAA member. Give all pertinent information about your planned stay. Request written confirmation to guarantee: type of room, rate, dates of stay, and cancellation and refund policies. **Note:** Age restrictions may apply.

Most establishments give full deposit refunds if they have been notified at least 48 hours before the normal check-in time. However, when making reservations, confirm the property's deposit, cancellation and refund policies. Some properties may charge a cancellation or handling fee. When this applies, "handling fee imposed" will appear in the listing. If you cancel too late, you have little recourse if a refund is denied. When an establishment requires a full or partial payment in advance, and your trip is cut short, a refund may not be given.

When canceling reservations, call the lodging immediately. Make a note of the date and time you called, the cancellation number if there is one, and the name of the person who handled the cancellation. If your AAA/CAA club made your reservation, allow them to make the cancellation for you as well so you will have proof of cancellation.

When you are charged more than the rate listed in the TourBook, under the option **Guaranteed Rates,** or you qualify for the **Senior Discount** and did not receive it, question the additional charge. If management refuses to adhere to the published rate, pay for the room and submit your receipt and membership number to AAA/CAA *within 30 days (see Tell us what you think, page 5).* Include all pertinent information: dates of stay, rate paid, itemized paid receipts, number of persons in your party, the room number you occupied, and list any extra room equipment used. A refund of the amount paid in excess of the stated maximum will be made when our investigation indicates that unjustified charging has occurred.

Lodging Reservation and Deposit Definitions

RESERVATION: A temporary hold on lodgings, usually until 4 or 6 p.m. on the arrival date.

RESERVATION CONFIRMATION: Once the reservation process is complete, a "confirmation number" is assigned to the guest for future reference. When ample notice is given, a copy of the reservation details and confirmation number is mailed to the guest.

CREDIT CARD GUARANTEED RESERVATION: When reserved lodgings have been secured with a credit card number, the room will be held for the first night regardless of arrival time, but will be billed to the credit card if the guest fails to arrive at all (is a "no show"). Credit card guarantees usually pertain to the first night only.

RESERVATION DEPOSIT: These funds are collected from the guest in advance of arrival to secure reserved lodgings. A reservation deposit can be in the form of cash, check, money order, credit card transaction or other means to transfer funds. One or more days' payment may be required depending on the length of the stay.

PREPAID RESERVATION: Reserved lodgings that are fully paid in advance of arrival.

CANCELLATION POLICY: Published terms/conditions set by lodging by which the guest can cancel a reservation and recover all, or a portion of, the deposit/full payment. Sometimes a "service charge" or "handling fee" is levied regardless of how far in advance the reservation was cancelled.

CANCELLATION NUMBER: Upon receipt of a cancellation, it is customary for lodgings to assign a "cancellation number" that is given to the caller for future reference.

When you find your room is not as specified, and you have written confirmation of reservations for a certain type of accommodation, you should be given the option of choosing a different room or finding one elsewhere. Should you choose to go elsewhere and a refund is refused or resisted, sub-mit the matter to AAA/CAA *within* 30 days along with complete documentation, including your reasons for refusing the room and copies of your written confirmation and any receipts or canceled checks associated with this problem.

Guest safety

In order to be approved for listing in AAA/CAA TourBooks for the United States and Canada, all lodgings must comply with AAA's guest room security requirements. In response to AAA/CAA members' concern about their safety at properties, AAA RATED® accommodations must have deadbolt locks on all guest room entry doors and connecting room doors. If the area outside the guest room door is not visible from inside the room through a window or door panel, viewports must be installed on all guest room entry doors. Bed and breakfast properties and country inns are not required to have viewports. Ground floor and easily accessible sliding doors must be equipped with some other type of secondary security locks.

Field inspectors view a percentage of rooms at each property. Because it is not feasible for the inspectors to evaluate every room in every lodging establishment, AAA cannot guarantee that there are working locks on all doors and windows in all guest rooms.

Travelers are faced with the task of protecting themselves while in a strange environment. Although there is no way to guarantee absolute protection from crime, the experts—law enforcement officials—advise travelers to take a pro-active approach to securing their property and ensuring their safety. A few simple precautions can save a vacation:

- Make sure the hotel desk clerk does not announce your room number; if so, quietly request a new room assignment.

- Ask front desk personnel which areas of town to avoid and what, if any, special precautions should be taken when driving a rental car (some criminals target tourists driving rental cars).

- Never open the door to a stranger; use the peephole and request identification. If you are still unsure, call the front desk to verify the identity of the person and the purpose of his/her visit.

- Carry money separately from credit cards or use a "fanny pack." Carry your purse close to your body and your wallet in an inside coat or front trouser pocket. Never leave luggage unattended, and use your business address, if possible, on luggage tags.

- Beware of distractions staged by would-be scam artists, especially groups of children that surround you or a stranger who accidently spills something on you. They may be lifting your wallet.

- If using an automatic teller machine (ATM), choose one in a well-lit area with plenty of foot traffic, such as one at a grocery store. Machines inside establishments are the safest to use.

- Use room safes or safety deposit boxes provided by the hotel. Store all valuables out of sight, even when you are in the room.

- Law enforcement agencies consider card-key (electronic) door locks the most secure.

Hotel/Motel fire safety

The AAA/CAA inspection program is designed to provide you with the most useful information for selecting the lodgings best suited to your needs. Because of the highly specialized skills needed to conduct professional fire safety inspections, however, AAA/CAA inspectors cannot assess fire safety.

All guest rooms must be equipped with an operational, single-station smoke detector, and all public areas must have operational smoke detectors or an automatic sprinkler system. (**Note:** Some Canadian lodgings are an exception to this requirement. There may be some Canadian proper-ties that were approved prior to 1988 that use heat sensors in place of smoke detectors and/or automatic sprinkler systems.) The type of fire protection a lodging provides is identified with symbols (see the Sample Listing). At each establishment whose listing shows these symbols, a AAA/CAA inspector has evaluated a sampling of the rooms and verified that this equipment is in place.

For additional fire safety information read the page posted on the back of your guest room door, or write the National Fire Protection Association, 1 Batterymarch Park, P.O. Box 9101, Quincy, MA 02269-9101.

Access for disabled

Certain properties listed in this book have symbols indicating they are either *Fully Accessible or Semi-Accessible*. This two-tiered standard was developed to meet members' varying degrees of accessibility needs.

(&) *Fully Accessible* properties meet the needs of those who are significantly disabled and primarily confined to a wheelchair. A fully accessible lodging will provide at least one guest room meeting the designated criteria. A traveler with these disabilities will be able to park and access public areas, including restrooms, check-in facilities and at least one food and beverage outlet. A *Fully Accessible* restaurant indicates that parking, dining rooms and restrooms are accessible.

(f) *Semi-Accessible* properties meet the needs of those who are disabled but have some mobility and are not confined to a wheelchair. Such travelers would include the elderly, people using a cane or walker, or a disabled individual with good mobility but a limited arm or hand range of motion. A semi-accessible lodging will provide at least one guest room meeting the designated criteria. A traveler with these disabilities will be able to park and access public areas, including restrooms, check-in facilities and at least one food and beverage outlet. A *Semi-Accessible* restaurant indicates that parking, dining rooms and restrooms are accessible.

A property with a (⌿) symbol has the following equipment available for *Hearing Impaired* travelers: TDD at front desk or switchboard; visual notification of fire alarm, incoming telephone calls, door knock or bell; closed caption decoder available; text telephone or TDD available for guest room use; telephone amplification device available, with shelf and electric outlet next to guest room telephone.

AAA/CAA urges members with disabilities to always phone ahead to fully understand the accommodation's offerings. Some properties do not fully comply with AAA/CAA's exacting accessibility standards but may offer some property design standards that meet the needs of some guests with disabilities.

AAA/CAA does not evaluate recreational facilities, banquet rooms or convention and meeting facilities for accessibility. Call a property directly to inquire about your needs for these areas.

The criteria used by AAA/CAA do not represent the full scope of the Americans With Disabilities Act of 1990 Accessibility Guidelines (ADAAG); they are, however, consistent with the ADAAG. Members can obtain the brochure AAA Accessibility Criteria for Travelers With Disabilities, which describes the specific criteria pertaining to the *Fully Accessible* and *Semi-Accessible* standards, from their local AAA/CAA club.

The ✺✺✺ Diamonds

Lodgings and restaurants are assigned ratings from one to five diamonds, which reflect the overall quality of the establishment or dining experience.

Lodgings

Properties must satisfy a set of minimum requirements that reflect the basic lodging needs members have identified. Ratings are assigned according to the property's classification, which appears beneath the diamond rating in the lodging listing. A one-diamond property still is better than one-third of the lodgings in operation. Lodgings listed without ratings were undergoing construction or renovation at the time of inspection and are noted as such in the listing. "Best available" indicates the property does not meet AAA requirements, but is listed as a service.

◆ Good but modest accommodations. Establishments are functional, emphasizing clean and comfortable rooms. They must meet the basic needs of comfort and cleanliness.

◆◆ Maintain the attributes offered at the one diamond level, while showing noticeable enhancements in room decor and quality of furnishings. They may be recently constructed or older properties, both targeting the needs of a budget-oriented traveler.

◆◆◆ Offer a degree of sophistication. Additional amenities, services and facilities may be offered. There is a marked upgrade in physical attributes, services and comfort.

◆◆◆◆ Excellent properties displaying a high level of service and hospitality. These properties offer a wide variety of amenities and upscale facilities in the guest rooms, on the grounds and in the public areas.

◆◆◆◆◆ World-class properties exhibiting an exceptionally high degree of service; striking, luxurious facilities; and many extra amenities. Guest services are executed and presented in a flawless manner. The guest is pampered by a professional, attentive staff. The properties' facilities and operation help set industry standards in hospitality and service.

Restaurants

Ratings are assigned based on conditions noted at the time of the evaluation. The condition of one or more aspects may limit the overall rating, which is not an average of the rating criteria. Food quality is the most critical to the overall rating. Restaurants are classified by cuisine type. Some listings include additional information, such as the availability of a senior citizen menu, children's menu or "early bird specials," if offered at least 5 days a week. The dinner price range is approximate and includes a salad or appetizer, an entree, a vegetable and a non-alcoholic beverage for one person. Taxes and tip are not included.

◆ Provides a simple, family or specialty meal in clean, pleasant surroundings. Food is basic and wholesome. Service is casual, limited or self-serve. Decor is informal.

◆◆ More extensive menus for family or adult dining. Food is prepared with standard ingredients. Service is attentive but may be informal, casual, limited or self-serve. The decor presents a unified theme that is comfortable but also may be trendy, casual or upbeat.

◆◆◆ An upscale or special family dining experience. Food is cooked to order and creatively prepared with quality ingredients. A wine list is available. A skilled, often uniformed staff provides service. The usually professional and inviting decor projects a trendy, upbeat, casual or formal atmosphere.

◆◆◆◆ A high degree of sophistication, thus creating an adult dining experience. Complex food is creatively presented. An extensive wine list is offered. The service staff, often formally attired, is professionally trained. The decor is distinctive, stylish and elegant; some establishments are casual while still offering refinement or formality.

◆◆◆◆◆ A memorable occasion—the ultimate in adult dining. Food shows the highest culinary skills, evident in all areas of preparation and presentation. An extensive wine list is available. A professional staff—often in formal attire—provides flawless and pampering service. The decor has classic details, often formal, and reflects comfort and luxury.

Lodging Classifications

BED AND BREAKFAST (limited service)—Usually a smaller establishment emphasizing personal attention. Guest rooms may lack some modern amenities such as TVs, phones, etc., and may have shared bathrooms. A Continental or full hot breakfast is served and is included in the room rate.

COMPLEX (service varies depending on type of lodgings)—A combination of two or more kinds of lodging classifications.

COTTAGE (limited service)—Individual bungalow, cabin or villa that may have a separate living room and bedroom(s). Although basic cleaning supplies must be provided, cottages are not required to offer daily housekeeping service.

COUNTRY INN (moderate service)—Although similar in definition to a bed and breakfast, country inns are usually larger in size. Offers a dining room reflecting the ambiance of the inn. At a minimum, breakfast and dinner are served.

HOTEL (full service)—A multistory building usually including a coffee shop, dining room, lounge, a pool and exercise equipment, room service, convenience shops, valet laundry and full banquet and meeting facilities.

LODGE (moderate service)—Typically several stories with all facilities in one building. Located in vacation, ski, fishing areas, etc. Usually has food and beverage service.

MOTEL (limited service)—Usually one or two stories. Food service, if any, consists of a limited facility or snack bar. Often has a pool or playground.

MOTOR INN (moderate service)—Usually a two or three story facility offering recreational facilities and food service.

RANCH (moderate service)—May be any classification featuring outdoor, Western-style recreation. Accommodations and facilities may vary in size.

Subclassifications

APARTMENT—Usually four or more stories. Each unit typically provides a full kitchen, living room and one or more bedrooms; studios may be available. Although basic cleaning supplies must be available, apartments are not required to offer daily housekeeping service.

CONDOMINIUM—Each unit consists of a bedroom, living room and kitchen. Kitchens are separate from bedrooms and are fully equipped with appliances, cooking utensils and table settings. Although basic cleaning supplies must be available, condominiums are not required to offer daily housekeeping service.

HISTORIC—Accommodations in restored structures more than 50 years old, reflecting the ambiance of yesteryear and the surrounding area. Rooms may lack some modern amenities and have shared baths. Usually owner-operated and food service is often available.

RESORT—Vacation atmosphere offering extensive recreational facilities for such specific interests as golf, tennis, fishing, etc. Rates may include meals under American or Modified American plans.

SUITE—One or more bedrooms and a living room/sitting area which is closed off by a full wall.

Remember

AAA/CAA inspectors assign diamond ratings by evaluating lodging establishments based on their classification. Thus, "Hotels" are rated in comparison with other "Hotels," and so on with all classifications.

Sample Lodging Listing

②   ③   ④

THE HODGES INN   Guaranteed Rates   **Phone:** 555/555-5555   **⓴**
ⒶⒶⒶ **SAVE**   2/1-3/8 [CP]   1P: $59- 79 2P/1B: $59- 79 2P/2B: $59- 79 XP: $6   F18
                 3/9-1/31 [CP]   1P: $49- 69 2P/1B: $49- 69 2P/2B: $49- 69 XP: $6   F18
◆◆◆   **Location:** From I-20 exit 185; just n; intersection US 78 & SR 21S. US 78 & SR 21 36203 (PO Box 5555, OX-
Motor Inn   FORD). Fax: 555/555-5556. **Terms:** Weekly rates; pets. **Facility:** 194 rooms. 2 stories; interior/exterior corri-
           dors; whirlpool; playground, shaded picnic area. **Dining & Entertainment:** Restaurant; 6 am-midnight; cocktail
           lounge; entertainment. **Services:** Fee: coin laundry. **All Rooms:** coffeemakers, free & pay movies.
           Some Rooms: microwaves, refrigerators, safes, whirlpools. **Cards:** AE, CB, DI, DS, JCB, MC, VI.
           Special Amenities: Early check-in/late check-out and free newspaper. 🛏 🏊 🖥 ✈ 📺 ⊠ Ⓓ

①   ⑤

① ⒶⒶⒶ or ⒶⒶⒶ — AAA/CAA Official Appointment (see pg. 173)
   SAVE — Show Your Card and Save (see pg. 173)
   NOTE: the Guaranteed Rates or Rates Subject to Change will not appear when
   the SAVE icon is present
   ◆◆◆ — Diamond Rating (see pg. 178)
   Motor Inn — Lodging Classification (see pg. 179)

② Rate lines show from left to right: dates the rates in that line are effective, any
   meal plan included in the rate (CP=Continental Plan of pastry, juice and another
   beverage or may offer expanded breakfast items; BP=Breakfast Plan of full hot
   breakfast; AP=American Plan of three meals daily; MAP=Modified American
   Plan of two meals daily; EP=European Plan, where rate includes room only),
   number of Persons/Beds allowed/provided for the rates shown, the rates
   charged, the extra person (XP) charge and, if applicable, the family plan
   indicator (F17=children 17 and under stay free; D17=discount for children 17
   and under; F=children stay free; D=discounts for children). The establishment
   may limit the number of children to whom the family plan applies.

③ Rate Options (see pg. 174)

④ ⓴ — Spotting map indicator (see pg. 174)

⑤ 🛏 — Pets allowed   📺 — Extended Cable TV
   🏊 — Outdoor swimming pool   ⑤ — Fully accessible
   🏊 — Swimming pool   ⑥ — Semi-accessible
   🖥 — Dataports and/or business services   ⊠ — Non-smoking available
   ✈ — Airport transportation   🔊 — Hearing impaired
   💪 — Exercise/whirlpool/sauna facilities   Ⓓ — Smoke detectors
   📺 — Cable TV   Ⓢ — Fire protection sprinklers

Lodging Evaluation Criteria

Regardless of the diamond rating, properties listed by AAA/CAA are required to provide:

- Clean and well-maintained facilities
- Hospitable staff
- A well-kept appearance
- Comfortable furnishings and pleasant decor

Each guest room is required to have:

- Comfortable beds and good quality
  bedding
- Adequate towels and supplies
- At least one chair
- Adequate illumination at each task
  area

Look for AAA
Savings on Dining

When using the AAA TourBook® to select places to dine, be sure
to look for restaurants with the bright red (SAVE) symbol beside their
TourBook listing. Why? Because these establishments offer special
savings to AAA members, ranging from discounts and
two-for-one entrees, to a free item with the purchase of a meal.

These restaurants will display the familiar
Show Your Card & Save® symbol — your invitation to savings.

So, to enjoy special savings, quality service and a warm
welcome, look for the restaurants that value the
business they receive from AAA members.

For more information, call or visit your
AAA office today.

GEORGIA

ACWORTH—*see Atlanta & Vicinity p. 227.*

ADAIRSVILLE—2,100

LODGINGS

COMFORT INN
Phone: 770/773-2886
All Year [CP]   1P: $40- 45 2P/1B: $45- 50 2P/2B: $45- 50 XP: $5   F16
Location: I-75 exit 128, just w. 107 Princeton Blvd 30103. **Fax:** 770/773-1964. **Terms:** Reserv deposit; small
pets only. **Facility:** 54 rooms. Near commercial/trucking area. Contemporary room appointments. 2 stories; ex-
terior corridors. **All Rooms:** free movies, combo or shower baths. **Some Rooms:** microwaves, refrigerators.
Fee: whirlpools. **Cards:** AE, CB, DI, DS, MC, VI. **Special Amenities: Free local telephone calls and free**
newspaper.   Roll in showers. ⊟ ⇔ 🖘 CTV ✕ D
Motel

RAMADA LIMITED
Phone: 770/769-9726
4/1-10/31 [CP]   1P: $40- 50 2P/1B: $55- 75 2P/2B: $55- 80 XP: $5   F12
12/1-3/31 & 11/1-11/30 [CP]   1P: $36- 45 2P/1B: $36- 55 2P/2B: $45- 65 XP: $5   F12
Location: I-75 exit 128, 0.3 mi w. 500 Georgia North Cir 30103. **Fax:** 770/769-9728. **Terms:** Reserv deposit,
3 day notice; no pets. **Facility:** 78 rooms. 2 stories; exterior corridors. **Dining:** Restaurant nearby.
Motel   **All Rooms:** free movies, combo or shower baths. **Some Rooms:** microwaves, refrigerators. **Cards:** AE, CB,
DI, DS, JCB, MC, VI. **Special Amenities: Free breakfast and free local telephone calls.**
                                                                           Roll in showers. ⇔ 🖘 CTV ✕ D

ADEL—5,100

LODGINGS

DAYS INN I-75
Guaranteed Rates   Phone: 912/896-4574
All Year   1P: $32- 37 2P/1B: $35- 40 2P/2B: $35- 40 XP: $5   F12
Motor Inn **Location:** I-75, exit 10. 1200 W 4th St 31620. **Fax:** 912/896-4575. **Terms:** Sr. discount; small pets only, $5
extra charge. **Facility:** 80 rooms. 2 stories; exterior corridors. **Dining:** Restaurant; 24 hours; $4-$8.
All Rooms: Fee: movies. **Cards:** AE, CB, DI, DS, MC, VI.   ⊟ ⇔ ✛ CTV ✕ D

HOWARD JOHNSON I-75
Guaranteed Rates   Phone: 912/896-2244
All Year   1P: $30- 35 2P/1B: $32- 37 2P/2B: $32- 37 XP: $5   F17
Motel   **Location:** I-75, exit 10. 1103 W 4th St 31620. **Fax:** 912/896-2245. **Terms:** Sr. discount; small pets only, $4
extra charge. **Facility:** 70 rooms. 2 stories; exterior corridors. **Cards:** AE, CB, DI, DS, MC, VI.
                                                                           ⊟ ⇔ ✛ CTV ✕ D

SUPER 8 MOTEL I-75
Guaranteed Rates   Phone: 912/896-4523
All Year   1P: $30- 35 2P/1B: $32- 37 2P/2B: $32- 37 XP: $5   F12
Motel   **Location:** I-75 exit 10, just e. 1102 W 4th St 31620. **Fax:** 912/896-4524. **Terms:** Sr. discount; small pets
only, $4 extra charge. **Facility:** 50 rooms. 2 stories; exterior corridors. **Cards:** AE, CB, DI, DS, MC, VI.
                                                                           ⊟ ✛ CTV ✕ D

ALBANY—78,100

Airport Accommodations

Listings for these establishments are found under the heading for the city in which they are located.

SOUTHWEST GA. REGION

🖘 Quality Inn-Merry Acres, 4.5 mi n of terminal/ALBANY

LODGINGS

COMFORT SUITES MERRY ACRES
Phone: 912/888-3939
All Year [CP]   1P: $87   2P/1B: $94   2P/2B: $94   XP: $7   F17
Location: 3.3 mi w. 1400 Dawson Rd 31708 (PO Box 3549, 31706). **Fax:** 912/435-4431. **Terms:** Reserv
deposit; no pets. **Facility:** 60 rooms. Modern sandstone colored structure in light commercial area. Guests
Suite Motel have use of the recreational facilities at the nearby Quality Inn-Merry Acres. 2 stories; interior corridors.
Dining: Restaurant nearby. **Services:** valet laundry. **All Rooms:** coffeemakers, microwaves, free movies,
refrigerators. **Some Rooms:** whirlpools. **Cards:** AE, CB, DI, DS, MC, VI. **Special Amenities: Free breakfast and free local**
telephone calls.   Roll in showers. 🖘 ✛ CTV ✕ D

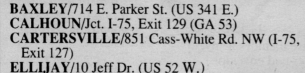

DAYS INN

AAA SAVE

◆◆

Motel

Phone: 912/888-2632

All Year [CP]   1P: $40- 50 2P/1B: $40- 50 2P/2B: $45- 55 XP: $5   F18
Location: 1 mi e on US 19 business route & 82. 422 W Oglethorpe Blvd 31701. Fax: 912/435-1875.
Terms: Weekly rates; package plans; small pets only, $5 extra charge, $15 dep req. **Facility:** 160 rooms. 1-bedroom suite & whirlpool rms, $60-$100; 2 stories; exterior corridors. **All Rooms:** free movies. Fee: safes.
Some Rooms: coffeemakers, microwaves, refrigerators, whirlpools. **Cards:** AE, CB, DI, DS, MC, VI.
Special Amenities: Free breakfast and free local telephone calls.   🐾 🛌 ✈ 🛁 CTV ✕ D

FAIRFIELD INN BY MARRIOTT

AAA SAVE

◆◆◆

Motel

Phone: 912/435-6859

All Year [CP]   1P: $49- 56 2P/1B: $55- 64 2P/2B: $55- 64 XP: $5   F12
Location: From jct 520 bypass, just s. 2586 N Slappy Blvd 31701. Fax: 912/883-5863. **Terms:** Monthly rates; no pets. **Facility:** 122 rooms. Large attractive lawn with pecan grove. 2 stories; exterior corridors; picnic tables & grills. **Dining:** Restaurant nearby. **All Rooms:** free movies. **Cards:** AE, CB, DI, DS, MC, VI.
Special Amenities: Free breakfast and free local telephone calls.   🛌 CTV ✕ 🌀 D

HAMPTON INN

◆◆◆

Motel

Rates Subject to Change   **Phone:** 912/883-3300

All Year [CP]   1P: $55- 59 2P/1B: $63   2P/2B: $59
Location: 7 mi w on Dawson Rd; 0.5 mi s of jct US 82 & SR 520, adjacent to Albany Mall. 806 N Westover Blvd 31707. Fax: 912/435-4092. **Terms:** Reserv deposit, Sun-Thurs; no pets. **Facility:** 82 rooms. Rates for up to 4 persons; 2 stories; exterior corridors. **All Rooms:** free movies. **Cards:** AE, DI, DS, MC, VI.
                                        Roll in showers. 🛌 CTV ♿ ✕ 🌀 D

HOLIDAY INN ALBANY

◆◆◆

Motor Inn

Rates Subject to Change   **Phone:** 912/883-8100

All Year   1P: $68   2P/1B: $76   2P/2B: $76   XP: $9
Location: 7 mi w on Dawson Rd, 0.5 mi s of jct US 82 & SR 520; opposite Albany Mall. 2701 Dawson Rd 31707. Fax: 912/883-8100. **Terms:** Reserv deposit; small pets only. **Facility:** 151 rooms. 2 stories; interior/exterior corridors. **Dining:** Dining room; 6:30 am-1 & 5-10 pm, Sat & Sun 7 am-1 & 5-9 pm; $8-$15. **All Rooms:** free movies. **Cards:** AE, DI, DS, MC, VI.   🐾 🛌 ✈ CTV ✕ 🌀 D S

HOLIDAY INN EXPRESS

AAA SAVE

◆◆◆

Motel

Phone: 912/883-1650

All Year [CP]   1P: $40- 50 2P/1B: $40- 50 2P/2B: $40- 50 XP: $5   F17
Location: 2 mi e on US 19 business route & 82; 1 mi w of US 19. 911 E Oglethorpe Expwy 31705.
Fax: 912/883-1163. **Terms:** Weekly rates; BP avail; no pets. **Facility:** 151 rooms. 4 stories; interior corridors.
Services: Fee: coin laundry. **All Rooms:** free movies. **Cards:** AE, CB, DI, DS, JCB, MC, VI.
Special Amenities: Free breakfast and free local telephone calls.   🛌 🍴 ✈ 🛁 CTV ✕ 🌀 D

KNIGHTS INN

Phone: 912/888-9600

All Year   1P: $35   2P/1B: $41   2P/2B: $43   XP: $6   F18

Location: On US 82, Slappey Blvd exit (US 19 & 82 business route), just n. 1201 Schley Ave 31707. Fax: 912/436-2682. **Terms:** Check-in 4 pm; reserv deposit; weekly rates; pets, $10 extra charge. **Facility:** 119 rooms. Dated, yet well-kept furnishings. 1 story; exterior corridors. **All Rooms:** free movies. **Some Rooms:** microwaves, refrigerators. **Cards:** AE, DI, DS, MC, VI. **Special Amenities: Early check-in/late check-out and free local telephone calls.**

◆   Motel

QUALITY INN-MERRY ACRES

Phone: 912/435-7721

All Year [CP]   1P: $58- 85   2P/1B: $65- 92   2P/2B: $65- 92   XP: $7   F17

Location: 3.3 mi w. 1500 Dawson Rd 31707 (PO Box 3549, 31706). Fax: 912/439-9386. **Terms:** No pets. **Facility:** 110 rooms. Beauty shop on premises. 5 two-bedroom units with kitchen, $141-$151; 1 story; exterior corridors; wading pool. **Dining:** Restaurant; 6:30 am-2 & 5:30-10 pm, Sun 7 am-2 pm; $8-$20; health conscious menu items; cocktails. **All Rooms:** coffeemakers, free movies. Fee: VCP. **Some Rooms:** refrigerators. **Cards:** AE, CB, DI, DS, MC, VI. **Special Amenities: Free breakfast and free local telephone calls.**

◆◆◆   Motor Inn

RAMADA INN

Guaranteed Rates   **Phone:** 912/883-3211

All Year   1P: $49   2P/1B: $55   2P/2B: $55   XP: $7   F18

Location: 4 mi nw on US 19 business route at jct US 19 & 82. 2505 N Slappey Blvd 31701. Fax: 912/883-3211. **Terms:** Sr. discount; pets. **Facility:** 158 rooms. 2 stories; interior/exterior corridors. **Dining:** Restaurant; 6:30 am-2 & 5-10 pm; $8-$14. **All Rooms:** free movies. **Cards:** AE, CB, DI, DS, JCB, MC, VI.

◆◆   Motor Inn

RESTAURANT

VILLA GARGANO   **Lunch:** $5-$8   **Dinner:** $6-$10   **Phone:** 912/436-7265

Location: 3 mi nw on US 19 & 82 business route. 1604 N Slappey Blvd 31701. **Hours:** 11 am-10 pm, Fri & Sat-11 pm. Closed major holidays & Sun. **Reservations:** accepted. **Features:** casual dress; children's menu; carryout; beer & wine only. Family owned. Area delivery avail. **Cards:** AE, MC, VI.

◆   Italian

ALPHARETTA—*See Atlanta & Vicinity p. 227.*

AMERICUS—16,500

LODGINGS

1906 PATHWAY INN BED & BREAKFAST

Rates Subject to Change   **Phone:** 912/928-2078

All Year [BP]   1P: $65- 75   2P/1B: $79- 99   XP: $20

Location: SR 280 0.5 mi s SR 377. 501 S Lee St 31709. Fax: 912/928-2078. **Terms:** Check-in 4 pm; reserv deposit; small pets only. **Facility:** 5 rooms. 2 stories; interior corridors; designated smoking area. **Cards:** AE, DS, MC, VI.

◆◆◆   Historic Bed & Breakfast

THE WINDSOR HOTEL

Phone: 912/924-1555

All Year [BP]   1P: $79- 95   2P/1B: $90- 107   2P/2B: $90- 107   XP: $15   D15

Location: On US 280, in the historic downtown district. 125 W Lamar St 31709. Fax: 912/924-1555. **Terms:** Reserv deposit, 3 day notice; package plans; no pets. **Facility:** 53 rooms. Elegant southern Victorian 1890's decor. Dramatic golden oak, atrium lobby with opera balconies & sweeping verandas. National Trust winner. Nearby parking lot avail. Rates for up to 4 persons. 1-bedroom suite $129, 2-bedroom suite $189, Tower suite $159. Handling fee imposed; 5 stories; interior corridors. **Dining & Entertainment:** Cocktails/lounge; also, The Grand Dining Room, see separate listing. **Services:** valet laundry. **All Rooms:** coffeemakers, free movies. **Some Rooms:** Fee: refrigerators, VCP's. **Cards:** AE, DS, MC, VI. **Special Amenities: Free breakfast and free local telephone calls.** *(See ad below)*

◆◆◆   Historic Hotel

RESTAURANT

THE GRAND DINING ROOM   Historical   **Lunch:** $6-$9   **Dinner:** $12-$24   **Phone:** 912/924-1555

Location: On US 280, in the historic downtown district; in The Windsor Hotel. 125 W Lamar St 31709. **Hours:** 7 am-10 & 11:30-2 & 6-10 pm, Sun-2 pm. **Reservations:** suggested; for dinner. **Features:** casual dress; Sunday brunch; cocktails & lounge; a la carte. Sophisticated dining in an elegant Victorian setting. **Cards:** AE, CB, DI, DS, MC, VI.

◆◆◆   American

ASHBURN—4,800

LODGINGS

COMFORT INN
Phone: 912/567-0080
AAA SAVE
All Year [CP]   1P: $37   2P/1B: $39   2P/2B: $41   XP: $4   F12
◆◆◆ **Location:** I-75 exit 28, just w. 820 Shoneys Dr 31714. Fax: 912/567-0435. **Terms:** Small pets only, $5 extra
Motel charge, $10 dep req. **Facility:** 56 rooms. 2 stories; exterior corridors. **Dining:** Restaurant nearby.
All Rooms: free movies. **Some Rooms:** microwaves, radios, refrigerators, whirlpools. Fee: VCP's.
Cards: AE, CB, DI, DS, JCB, MC, VI. **Special Amenities:** Free breakfast and free local telephone calls.

🛏 🖼 CTV ✕ D

DAYS INN
Phone: 912/567-3346
AAA SAVE
All Year [CP]   1P: $35- 39 2P/1B: $38- 42 2P/2B: $38- 45 XP: $4   F17
◆◆ **Location:** I-75, exit 28, just w. 823 E Washington Ave 31714. Fax: 912/567-0444. **Terms:** Reserv deposit;
Motel pets, $5 dep req, in designated rooms. **Facility:** 68 rooms. 2 stories; exterior corridors; playground.
Dining: Restaurant nearby. **All Rooms:** free movies. **Cards:** AE, CB, DI, DS, JCB, MC, VI.
Special Amenities: Early check-in/late check-out and free local telephone calls. (See color ad below)

🛏 🖼 CTV ✕ D

ATHENS—45,700

LODGINGS

BEST WESTERN-COLONIAL INN
Phone: 706/546-7311
AAA SAVE
3/1-11/30 [CP]   1P: $49- 59 2P/1B: $55- 69 2P/2B: $55- 69 XP: $5   F12
12/1-2/28 [CP]   1P: $49- 59 2P/1B: $49- 59 2P/2B: $49- 59 XP: $5   F12
◆◆◆ **Location:** 0.5 mi w; on SR 15 at jct US Business Rt 78 (Broad St). 170 N Milledge Ave 30601.
Motel Fax: 706/546-7959. **Terms:** Pets, $10 extra charge. **Facility:** 69 rooms. Large, well appointed rooms. 5 blks to
UGA Campus. 2 stories; exterior corridors. **All Rooms:** free & pay movies, refrigerators. **Cards:** AE, CB, DI,
DS, MC, VI. (See color ad below & p 182)

🛏 🖼 🕳 CTV ✕ D

HOLIDAY INN
Phone: 706/549-4433
AAA SAVE
All Year   1P: $84- 139 2P/1B: $84- 139
◆◆◆◆ **Location:** Just w of downtown on US Business Rt 78 (Broad St). Corner Broad & Hull sts 30603 (PO Box
Motor Inn 1666). Fax: 706/548-3031. **Terms:** No pets. **Facility:** 308 rooms. A variety of room types, decors & furnishings
in 2 tower buildings & a motel section nestled on a compact lot. Adjacent to University of Georgia campus. 11
two-bedroom units. Executive suites with wet bars; 2-7 stories; interior/exterior corridors; luxury level rooms;
whirlpool. **Dining & Entertainment:** Restaurant; 6:30 am-2 & 5:30-10 pm; $8-$16; cocktails/lounge. **Services:** childcare;
guest laundry; area transportation. **All Rooms:** coffeemakers, free & pay movies. **Some Rooms:** 5 efficiencies.
Fee: microwaves, refrigerators, VCP's. **Cards:** AE, CB, DI, DS, MC, VI. **Special Amenities:** Free local telephone calls
and free newspaper.

🖼 🕳 🕳 🕳 CTV ✕ 🕳 D S

THE NICHOLSON HOUSE
◆◆◆
Bed &
Breakfast

Guaranteed Rates
All Year [CP]   1P: $75   2P/1B: $75   2P/2B: $75   Phone: 706/353-2200
Location: Business Loop 78/10, exit Prince Ave, 3 mi n. 6295 Jefferson Rd 30607. Fax: 706/353-7799.
Terms: Age restrictions may apply; reserv deposit; no pets. **Facility:** 5 rooms. 2 stories; interior corridors; designated smoking area. **All Rooms:** free movies. **Cards:** AE, DS, JCB, MC, VI.   (CTV) (X) (D)

RAMADA INN
◆◆◆
Motor Inn

Rates Subject to Change   Phone: 706/546-8122
All Year   1P: $61- 67 2P/1B: $67- 73 2P/2B: $67- 73 XP: $3   F18
Location: Downtown on US 78. 513 W Broad St 30601. Fax: 706/546-1722. **Terms:** Sr. discount; small pets
only. **Facility:** 160 rooms. 5 stories; interior corridors. **Dining:** Restaurant; 6 am-9 pm, Sun-2 pm; $9-$16.
All Rooms: free movies. **Cards:** AE, CB, DI, DS, MC.   (🛏) (🖼) (+K) (CTV) (X) (D) (S)

RESTAURANTS

HARRY BISSETT'S NEW ORLEANS CAFE   Lunch: $4-$8   Dinner: $7-$16   Phone: 706/353-7065
◆◆
Regional
American
Location: Downtown, on Business US 78, opposite main entrance to UGA. 279 E Broad St 30601.
Hours: 11:30 am-3 & 5:30-10 pm, Fri & Sat-11 pm, Sun noon-4 & 6-10 pm. Closed: Mon for lunch, 11/26,
12/24 & 12/25. **Features:** casual dress; Sunday brunch; cocktails & lounge; street parking. Specializing in
creative Cajun & Creole cuisine with steak, veal & fresh seafood; featuring oysters. **Cards:** AE, DS, MC, VI.   (X)

R. J. T-BONES STEAKHOUSE   Lunch: $5-$20   Dinner: $5-$20   Phone: 706/548-8702
(Ⓐ)
◆
Steakhouse
Location: 0.5 mi nw of University of Georgia campus. 1061 Baxter St 30606. **Hours:** 11 am-10 pm, Fri &
Sat-11 pm, Sun noon-10 pm. Closed: 1/1, 11/26, 12/24 & 12/25. **Features:** casual dress; children's menu;
carryout; cocktails & lounge. Cheerful dining in a rustic country-western decor. **Cards:** AE, MC, VI.   (X)

Atlanta & Vicinity

ATLANTA—394,000   (See map p. 189; index below)

To help you more easily locate accommodations in the metropolitan Atlanta area, lodgings and restaurants have been divided on the following three indexes and maps between Atlanta, Atlanta Northern Region and Atlanta Southern Region. Listings for these establishments are found under the heading for the city in which they are located. Atlanta Northern Region map comprises: Atlanta North, Austell, Chamblee, Doraville, Marietta, Norcross, Sandy Springs, Smyrna and Tucker; Atlanta Southern Region map comprises: Atlanta South, College Park, Decatur, East Point, Forest Park, Hapeville, Jonesboro, Lithonia, Morrow, Riverdale, Stockbridge and Union City.

Airport Accommodations

Listings for these establishments are found under the heading for the city in which they are located.

The William B. Hartsfield

(Ⓐ) **Atlanta Airport Hilton & Towers, 0.8 mi n of terminal/ATLANTA**
(Ⓐ) **Budgetel Inn-Atlanta Airport, 1.5 mi sw of terminal/COLLEGE PARK**
Club Hotel by Doubletree, 1.5 mi sw of terminal/COLLEGE PARK
(Ⓐ) **Comfort Inn Atlanta Airport, 1.3 mi s of airport terminal/COLLEGE PARK**
(Ⓐ) **Comfort Suites-Atlanta Airport, 1 mi s of terminal/COLLEGE PARK**
Courtyard by Marriott-Airport South, 1 mi s of terminal/COLLEGE PARK
Courtyard by Marriott Atlanta Airport North, 1 mi n of terminal/HAPEVILLE
Crowne Plaza Atlanta Airport, 1 mi n of entrance/ATLANTA
Days Inn Airport South, 1.3 mi s of terminal/COLLEGE PARK
Embassy Suites Hotel at Atlanta Airport, opposite terminal/COLLEGE PARK
Fairfield Inn-by Marriott Airport, 2 mi s of terminal/COLLEGE PARK
Hampton Inn-Atlanta Airport, 1 mi s of terminal/COLLEGE PARK
Holiday Inn Airport North, 1 mi n of terminal/EAST POINT
(Ⓐ) **La Quinta Inn Airport, 1.3 mi sw of terminal/COLLEGE PARK**
Marriott Atlanta Airport, 2 mi sw of terminal/COLLEGE PARK
Microtel Inn, 1 mi s of terminal/COLLEGE PARK
Radisson Hotel-Atlanta Airport, 1 mi n of terminal/COLLEGE PARK
Red Roof Inn Airport, 1.5 mi sw of terminal/COLLEGE PARK
(Ⓐ) **Renaissance Atlanta Hotel Concourse, at the airport/ATLANTA**
Sheraton Gateway Hotel, Atlanta Airport, 1 mi s of terminal/COLLEGE PARK
Sheraton Inn Atlanta Airport, 3.5 mi sw of terminal/EAST POINT
(Ⓐ) **The Westin Hotel-Atlanta Airport, 1 mi s/COLLEGE PARK**

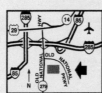

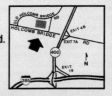

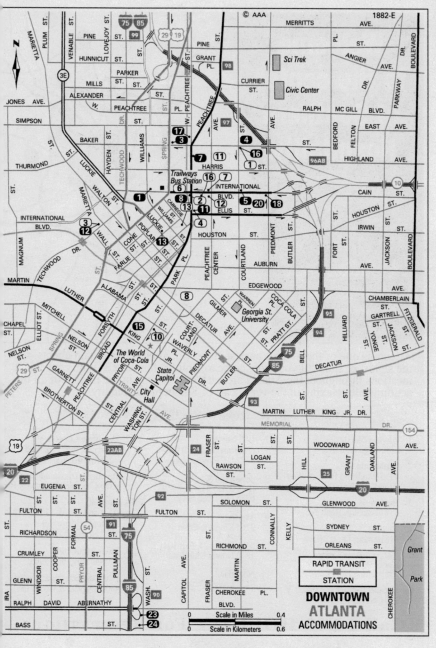

DOWNTOWN
ATLANTA
ACCOMMODATIONS

RAPID TRANSIT
STATION

PATRONIZE
ESTABLISHMENTS

Welcome to the center of Southern Hospitality.

Holiday Inn

On the way.

http:\\www.holiday-inn.com

Atlanta is one of the South's busiest cities. So, after you entertain clients, see the sights, or shop 'til you drop, come to Holiday Inn®hotels. With convenient locations throughout the Atlanta area, it's easy to stay in the middle of all the action while relaxing in the very heart of Southern Hospitality.

Weekend Rates from $49-$99 (1 - 4 Persons)

1. **Airport-North**
   1380 Virginia Avenue

2. **Alpharetta** ◊
   5455 Windward Parkway West
   (Windward Pkwy & GA 400)

3. **Buckhead**
   3377 Peachtree Road, NE

4. **Central**
   418 Armour Drive, NE

5. **Cobb Galleria Centre/
   Cobb Pkwy** ◊
   2855 Spring Hill Pkwy

6. **Decatur** (Conference Plaza) ¥
   130 Clairemont Avenue

7. **I-85 North**
   (Pleasantdale Road) ◊
   4422 NE Expressway

8. **Jonesboro S.**
   (I-75 & US 41)
   6288 Old Dixie Hwy

9. **Marietta**
   2265 Kingston Court

10. **Midtown** (I-75, Exit 104)
    1810 Howell Mill Road

11. **Northlake**
    4156 LaVista Road

12. **Peachtree Corners** ¥
    (Norcross/Tech Park Area)
    6050 Peachtree Industrial Blvd.

13. **Perimeter/Dunwoody Area** ¥
    4386 Chamblee Dunwoody Rd

14. **Roswell**
    (Dunwoody Area-GA 400/
    Holcomb Bridge Rd)
    1075 Holcomb Bridge Rd

15. **Stone Mountain** ◊
    1790 E. Park Place Blvd.

16. **I-20 East** (Snapfinger Woods) ◊
    4300 Snapfinger Woods Dr.

Call 1-800-HOLIDAY For Reservations

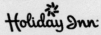

Holiday Inn

Holiday Inn
EXPRESS®

Holiday Inn
SELECT®

(See map p. 189)

LODGINGS

ATLANTA HILTON & TOWERS
Phone: 404/659-2000 [16]
AAA SAVE   All Year   1P: $115- 225   2P/1B: $135- 245   2P/2B: $135- 245
Location: I-75/85; Courtland St exit southbound, International Blvd exit northbound. 255 Courtland St NE
Hotel   30303. Fax: 404/222-2868. **Terms:** BP avail; package plans; small pets only. **Facility:** 1224 rooms. Massive
angular high-rise with rooftop swimming pool & award-winning top floor dining room. 40 suites $350-$1250; 29
stories; interior corridors; luxury level rooms; saunas, whirlpools. Fee: parking; 4 lighted tennis courts.
Dining & Entertainment: Dining room, 2 restaurants, coffee shop, deli; 24 hours; $7-$26; health conscious menu items;
cocktails/lounge; 24-hour room service; also, Nikolai's Roof, see separate listing; nightclub. **Services:** valet laundry.
Fee: massage; valet parking. **Recreation:** jogging. **All Rooms:** honor bars, free & pay movies. **Some Rooms:** refrigerators,
whirlpools. **Cards:** AE, DI, DS, JCB, MC, VI. *(See color ad p 18 & below)*

BEST WESTERN INN AT THE PEACHTREES
Rates Subject to Change   **Phone:** 404/577-6970 [17]
◆◆◆   All Year [BP]   1P: $68- 128   2P/1B: $68- 128   2P/2B: $68-138   XP: $10   F17
Motel   **Location:** I-75/85 exit International Blvd northbound, exit Williams St southbound. 330 W Peachtree St
30308. Fax: 404/659-3244. **Terms:** Pets, $25 extra charge. **Facility:** 110 rooms. 4 stories; interior/exterior cor-
ridors. Fee: parking. **All Rooms:** free movies. **Some Rooms:** A/C, 9 kitchens. **Cards:** AE, CB, DI, DS, JCB, MC, VI.
(See color ad p 193)

COMFORT INN DOWNTOWN ATLANTA
Phone: 404/524-5555 [1]
AAA SAVE   All Year   1P: $79- 159   2P/1B: $89- 179   2P/2B: $89- 179   XP: $10   F18
Location: I-75/85; northbound exit 96 (International Blvd), 0.5 mi w; I-75/85 southbound exit 99 (Williams
Motor Inn   St), 5 blks then dead ends into International, on right. 101 International Blvd 30303. Fax: 404/524-0218.
Terms: Reserv deposit, 3 day notice; package plans; no pets. **Facility:** 260 rooms. Compact, appealing lobby.
Cozy rooms. Courtyard with foliage & seating areas for outdoor seasonal dining. Handling fee imposed; 11 sto-
ries; interior corridors. Fee: parking. **Dining & Entertainment:** Restaurant; 6:30-10:30 am, 11:30-1:30 & 5:30-10 pm; $8-$16;
health conscious menu; cocktails/lounge. **Services:** valet laundry; area transportation, within 5 mi. **All Rooms:** free & pay
movies. **Some Rooms:** microwaves, refrigerators, whirlpools. **Cards:** AE, CB, DI, DS, JCB, MC, VI.

(See map p. 189)

COURTYARD BY MARRIOTT — Rates Subject to Change — **Phone:** 404/659-2727 [18]
◆◆◆   All Year   1P: $71- 139   2P/1B: $81- 149   2P/2B: $81- 149   XP: $10   F17
Motor Inn   **Location:** I-75 & I-85; northbound International Blvd exit, southbound Courtland St exit, 0.3 mi s on Courtland, just e. 175 Piedmont Ave NE 30303. Fax: 404/688-6332. **Terms:** No pets. **Facility:** 211 rooms. 8 stories; interior corridors. Fee: parking. **Dining:** Restaurant; 6 am-11 & 5-11 pm; $9-$16. **All Rooms:** free & pay movies. **Cards:** AE, CB, DI, DS, MC, VI. *(See color ad below)*   Roll in showers.

DAYS INN DOWNTOWN — **Phone:** 404/523-1144 [3]
(AAA) [SAVE]   All Year   1P: $99- 169   2P/1B: $109- 179   2P/2B: $109- 179   XP: $10-25   F17
◆◆   **Location:** At Baker & Spring sts, across from Apparel Mart; I-75/85 southbound exit Williams St, northbound exit 96 (International Blvd), n on Spring St. 300 Spring St 30308. Fax: 404/577-8495. **Terms:** No pets.
Motor Inn   **Facility:** 263 rooms. Attractive public areas. Comtemporary room appointments. 10 stories; interior corridors. Fee: parking. **Dining & Entertainment:** Cocktail lounge; restaurant nearby. **Services:** valet laundry. **All Rooms:** coffeemakers, free & pay movies. Fee: safes. **Some Rooms:** refrigerators. **Cards:** AE, DI, DS, MC, VI. *(See color ad below)*   Roll in showers.

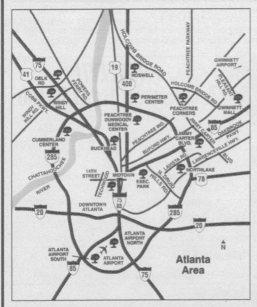

(See map p. 189)

FAIRFIELD INN BY MARRIOTT   Rates Subject to Change   **Phone:** 404/659-7777   20
♦♦♦   All Year [CP]   1P: $56- 94   2P/1B: $66- 104   2P/2B: $66- 104   XP: $10   F12
Motel   **Location:** I-75 & I-85; northbound International Blvd exit, southbound Courtland St exit, 0.3 mi s on Courtland & just e. 175 Piedmont Ave 30303. Fax: 404/659-6518. **Terms:** No pets. **Facility:** 242 rooms. 6 stories; exterior corridors. Fee: parking. **All Rooms:** free & pay movies. **Cards:** AE, DI, DS, MC, VI.
(See color ad p 211 & ad p 194)   Roll in showers. 🛅 ✚ CTV 🛄 ✕ 🔲 D S

HAMPTON INN-DOWNTOWN STADIUM   Rates Subject to Change   **Phone:** 404/658-1961   23
♦♦♦   All Year [CP]   1P: $69   2P/1B: $79   2P/2B: $79
Motel   **Location:** I-75/I-85 exit 90 northbound, exit 91 southbound; 0.3 mi e to Capitol, 0.4 mi s to Abernathy, just w. 759 Washington St 30315. Fax: 404/223-3521. **Terms:** No pets. **Facility:** 87 rooms. 5 stories; interior corridors.
All Rooms: free & pay movies. **Cards:** AE, CB, DI, DS, MC, VI.   🛅 ✚ CTV ✕ 🔲 D S

HOLIDAY INN EXPRESS-STADIUM   Rates Subject to Change   **Phone:** 404/658-1610   24
♦♦♦   All Year [CP]   1P: $69- 109   2P/1B: $79- 119   2P/2B: $79- 119   XP: $10   F19
Motel   **Location:** I-75/85 exit 90 northbound, exit 91 southbound; 0.3 mi e to Capitol, 0.5 mi s to Little, just w. 795 Washington St 30315. Fax: 404/221-1812. **Terms:** Sr. discount; no pets. **Facility:** 89 rooms. 6 stories; interior corridors. **All Rooms:** free & pay movies. **Cards:** AE, CB, DI, DS, MC, VI.   🛅 ✚ CTV ✕ 🔲 D S

(See map p. 189)

HYATT REGENCY ATLANTA IN PEACHTREE CENTER   Phone: 404/577-1234 **7**
(AAA) [SAVE]   All Year   1P: $225   2P/1B: $250   2P/2B: $250   XP: $25   F15
◆◆◆   **Location:** Motor entrance on Peachtree Center Ave. 265 Peachtree St NE 30303. Fax: 404/588-4137.
Hotel   **Terms:** Package plans; no pets. **Facility:** 1264 rooms. Hi-rise mega hotel; part of Peachtree shopping & office
        complex. First atrium hotel in the world. Exciting landmark blue-domed aerial restaurant. Updated room decor.
        24 stories; interior corridors; luxury level rooms. Fee: parking. **Dining & Entertainment:** Dining room,
restaurant, 2 coffee shops; 6 am-1 am; $15-$25; health conscious menu items; cocktails/lounge. **Services:** valet laundry;
area transportation, within 3 mi. Fee: valet parking. **All Rooms:** honor bars, coffeemakers, free & pay movies, safes, combo
or shower baths. **Some Rooms:** Fee: refrigerators. **Cards:** AE, CB, DI, DS, JCB, MC, VI. *(See color ad p 188)*
                                                           Roll in showers. [▤] [▨] [▥] [▦] [CTV] [✕] [▨] [D] [S]

OMNI HOTEL AT CNN CENTER   Rates Subject to Change   Phone: 404/659-0000 **12**
◆◆◆   All Year   1P: $89- 220   2P/1B: $119- 240 2P/2B: $119- 240 XP: $25   F17
Hotel   **Location:** I-75/85 northbound exit Williams St, southbound exit International Blvd; w to jct Techwood &
        Marietta sts. 100 CNN Center 30335. Fax: 404/525-5050. **Terms:** No pets. **Facility:** 458 rooms. 15 stories; in-
terior corridors. Fee: parking. **Dining:** Restaurant, cafeteria; 7 am-10:30 pm; $15-$25; also, Bugatti Restaurant, see separate
listing. **All Rooms:** free & pay movies. **Cards:** AE, CB, DI, MC, VI.   Roll in showers. [▥] [CTV] [✕] [▨] [D] [S]

(See map p. 189)

QUALITY HOTEL   Phone: 404/524-7991 🔟
All Year   1P: $59   2P/1B: $69   2P/2B: $69   XP: $10   F18
Location: I-75/85 exit 97 northbound, exit 96B southbound; 0.3 mi w to Peachtree St, just w at corner of
Luckie & Fairlie sts. 89 Luckie St 30303. Fax: 404/524-0672. **Terms:** No pets. **Facility:** 75 rooms. Appealing
lobby. Contemporary room appointments. 11 stories; interior corridors. Fee: parking. **Dining:** Cafeteria; 7:30
am-8 pm; $3-$10; wine/beer only. **Services:** valet laundry. **All Rooms:** coffeemakers, free movies.
Cards: AE, CB, DI, DS, MC, VI. **Special Amenities: Free local telephone calls and free newspaper.**
Roll in showers. 🛏 🛁 🕃 🕃 CTV ✕ D S

RADISSON HOTEL ATLANTA   Rates Subject to Change   Phone: 404/659-6500 5️⃣
◆◆◆   All Year   1P: $89   2P/1B: $89
Hotel   **Location:** I-75 & I-85; Courtland St exit southbound, International Blvd exit northbound; just w. Courtland &
International Blvd 30303. Fax: 404/681-5306. **Terms:** Reserv deposit, 3 day notice; no pets. **Facility:** 747
rooms. 12 stories; interior/exterior corridors. Fee: parking. **Dining:** Restaurant, deli; 6:30 am-11 pm; $16-$24.
All Rooms: free & pay movies. **Cards:** AE, CB, DI, DS, JCB, MC. *(See ad below)*
Roll in showers. 🛏 🛏 🕃 CTV ✕ 🔊 D S

(See map p. 189)

RITZ-CARLTON ATLANTA   Rates Subject to Change   **Phone: 404/659-0400**   **11**
AAA   All Year   1P: $186- 250   2P/1B: $186- 250   2P/2B: $186- 250
◆◆◆◆◆   **Location:** I-75/85; northbound exit International Blvd, southbound exit Courtland St; 0.5 mi w. 181 Peachtree
Hotel   St NE 30303. Fax: 404/688-0400. **Terms:** No pets. **Facility:** 447 rooms. 27 stories; interior corridors.
Fee: parking. **Dining:** Dining room, restaurant; 6:30 am-midnight; $11-$29; also, The Restaurant, see
separate listing. **All Rooms:** free & pay movies. **Cards:** AE, CB, DI, DS, JCB, MC, VI. *(See ad p 197)*

     ⊕ CTV ✕ 🔌 D S

THE SUITE HOTEL AT UNDERGROUND   **Phone: 404/223-5555**   **15**
AAA SAVE   Sun-Thurs   1P: $120- 160   2P/1B: $130- 185   2P/2B: $130- 185   XP: $10   F16
   Fri & Sat   1P: $89   2P/1B: $99   2P/2B: $99
◆◆◆   **Location:** Peachtree & Alabama sts. 54 Peachtree St 30303. Fax: 404/223-0467. **Terms:** Reserv deposit;
Suite Hotel   package plans; no pets. **Facility:** 157 rooms. Mid-rise boutique hotel located directly in the Underground Atlanta District. Elegant Old World charm in compact lobby; quiet, tastefully decorated suites. Weekend rates for
up to 4 persons; 16 stories; interior corridors. Fee: parking. **Dining & Entertainment:** Cocktail lounge. **Services:** valet
laundry; area transportation, within 2 mi. Fee: valet parking. **All Rooms:** honor bars, coffeemakers, free & pay movies,
refrigerators. **Some Rooms:** Fee: whirlpools. **Cards:** AE, DI, DS, JCB, MC, VI.   🏋 ⊕ 🛁 CTV ✕ 🔌 D S

TRAVELODGE-DOWNTOWN   **Phone: 404/659-4545**   **4**
AAA SAVE   1/1-11/30   1P: $72   2P/1B: $80   2P/2B: $84   XP: $8   F18
   12/1-12/31   1P: $62   2P/1B: $70   2P/2B: $75   XP: $8   F18
◆◆   **Location:** I-75/85; southbound exit 97 (Courtland St); northbound exit 98 (Peachtree St). 311 Courtland St
Motel   NE 30303. Fax: 404/659-5934. **Terms:** CP avail; no pets. **Facility:** 71 rooms. Compact property with covered
parking. Contemporary room appointments. 3 stories; interior/exterior corridors. **Dining:** Restaurants nearby.
Services: valet laundry. **All Rooms:** coffeemakers, free movies, safes, combo or shower baths. **Some Rooms:**
Fee: microwaves, refrigerators, VCP's. **Cards:** AE, CB, DI, DS, JCB, MC, VI. **Special Amenities:** Free newspaper.

     🛆 🏋 ⊕ 🛁 CTV ✕ 🔌 D

THE WESTIN PEACHTREE PLAZA   Rates Subject to Change   **Phone: 404/659-1400**   **8**
◆◆◆   All Year   1P: $148   2P/1B: $148   2P/2B: $148   XP: $25   F18
Hotel   **Location:** I-75 & I-85; Williams St exit southbound, International Blvd exit northbound, just w; in Peachtree
Center. 210 Peachtree St 30303. Fax: 404/589-7424. **Terms:** Reserv deposit; small pets only. **Facility:** 1068
rooms. 73 stories; interior corridors. Fee: parking. **Dining:** 2 dining rooms, cafeteria; 6 am-midnight; $7-$35; also, Savannah
Fish Company, see separate listing. **All Rooms:** Fee: movies. **Cards:** AE, CB, DI, DS, JCB, MC, VI.
     Roll in showers.   🐄 🛆 🛆 ⊕ CTV ✕ 🔌 D S

RESTAURANTS

BUGATTI RESTAURANT   **Lunch:** $8-$15   **Dinner:** $15-$25   **Phone: 404/818-4450**   **3**
◆◆◆   **Location:** I-75/85 northbound exit Williams St, southbound exit International Blvd; w to jct Techwood &
Northern   Marietta sts; in Omni Hotel at CNN Center. 100 CNN Center 30303. **Hours:** 11:30 am-2 & 6-10:30 pm, Sat &
Italian   Sun from 6 pm. **Reservations:** suggested. **Features:** casual dress; children's menu; carryout; cocktails &
   lounge; valet parking; a la carte. Veal & seafood specialties. Fresh items. Cappuccino/espresso, some
table-side preparations. **Cards:** AE, DI, DS, MC, VI.   ✕

CITY GRILL   **Lunch:** $11-$16   **Dinner:** $16-$25   **Phone: 404/524-2489**   **8**
◆◆◆◆   **Location:** I-75 & I-85; exit 95, Edgewood Ave, 0.5 mi w. 50 Hurt Plaza; Suite 200 30303. **Hours:** 11:30
Regional   am-2:30 & 5:30-10 pm, Sat from 5:30 pm. Closed major holidays & Sun. **Reservations:** suggested.
American   **Features:** casual dress; cocktails; fee for parking; valet parking; a la carte. In elegant Federalist-style
   building with dramatic marble rotunda. Modern American cuisine with regional influences. Daily menus might
include blue crab cakes on corn chowder; southern fried quail with raspberry pepper biscuit. **Cards:** AE, DI, DS, MC, VI.
     ✕

DAILEY'S   **Lunch:** $6-$12   **Dinner:** $16-$26   **Phone: 404/681-3303**   **16**
◆◆   **Location:** I-85 S, exit Courtland St, 3 lights s to International Blvd, turn right, 1.5 blks on left; from airport 85
American   N to International Blvd. 17 International Blvd 30303. **Hours:** 11 am-3:30 & 5:30-11 pm, Fri & Sat-midnight,
   Sun from 5:30 pm. Closed major holidays. **Reservations:** accepted. **Features:** casual dress; children's
menu; health conscious menu; carryout; cocktails & lounge; fee for parking. Bring a big appetite to this fun & lively
restaurant. Enjoy a wild decor of old merry-go-round horses, a majestic staircase & a rainforest of vegetation. Downstairs
has a bar & grill with a simpler menu. Parking in nearby lot. **Cards:** AE, CB, DI, DS, MC, VI.   ✕

DELECTABLES   **Phone: 404/681-2909**   **13**
◆   **Location:** Corner Fairlie & Carnegie Way; in Public Library. One Margaret Mitchell Sq 30303. **Hours:** 11
American   am-2 pm. Closed major holidays, Sat & Sun. **Features:** carryout; street parking. Fresh, first-quality
   ingredients. Informal yet sophisticated atmosphere. Variety of tea, soup, hot entrees, full-meal salads &
freshly baked dessert. **Cards:** AE, MC, VI.

HSU'S GOURMET CHINESE RESTAURANT   **Lunch:** $7-$13   **Dinner:** $12-$21   **Phone: 404/659-2788**   **12**
◆◆◆   **Location:** Off I-75 & I-85; Courtland St exit southbound, International Blvd exit northbound; corner Peachtree
Chinese   St & International Blvd. 192 Peachtree Center Ave 30303. **Hours:** 11 am-11 pm, Sat from noon, Sun 5
   pm-10 pm. Closed major holidays. **Reservations:** suggested. **Features:** casual dress; carryout; cocktails &
lounge; fee for parking; a la carte. Hong Kong & Cantonese style gourmet cuisine. Peking Duck a specialty plus fresh fish
daily. Wine list. Validated parking after 5:30 pm. Upscale casual. **Cards:** AE, DI, DS, MC, VI.   ✕

LA FUENTE   **Lunch:** $4-$8   **Dinner:** $8-$17   **Phone: 404/521-0000**   **11**
◆◆   **Location:** I-75 & I-85; Courtland St exit south, just s; Peachtree St exit northbound, just w; in Atlanta
Mexican   Marriott Marquis. 265 Peachtree Center Ave 30303. **Hours:** 11:30 am-2 & 6-10 pm, Sat & Sun from 5 pm.
   Features: casual dress; children's menu; carryout; cocktails; valet parking; a la carte. Fajitas, traditional
Mexican specialties & flan. Warm ambience. Hotel valet parking validated. **Cards:** AE, DI, DS, MC, VI.   ✕

LOMBARDI'S   **Lunch:** $8-$13   **Dinner:** $10-$18   **Phone: 404/522-6568**   **10**
◆◆   **Location:** Pryor & Alabama sts; in Underground Atlanta, street level. 94 Upper Pryor St #238 30303.
Italian   **Hours:** 11 am-10 pm, Sat 5 pm-11 pm, Sun 5 pm-10 pm. Closed major holidays. **Reservations:** suggested.
   Features: casual dress; children's menu; carryout; cocktails; fee for parking; a la carte. High-casual fun
eatery. Pasta & Northern Italian veal entrees, plus brick-oven pizza. Some desserts made on premises. Pay garage, partial
parking validation. **Cards:** AE, DI, MC, VI.   ✕

Twenty flawless diamonds
would of course require two very
spectacular settings.

Is it the lights of the city or our 20 diamonds that give Atlanta such a special glow? Once again, The Ritz-Carlton, Buckhead and The Ritz-Carlton, Atlanta have earned five diamonds each. The Dining Room and The Restaurant have earned five as well. And you, we hope, have earned an opportunity to stay with us. For reservations, please call a travel professional or The Ritz-Carlton at 800-261-3333.

THE RITZ-CARLTON®
ATLANTA
BUCKHEAD

(See map p. 189)

MICK'S   Lunch: $7-$15   Dinner: $7-$15   Phone: 404/688-6425   ⑦
◆◆
American   **Location:** Off I-75 & I-85; Courtland St exit southbound, International Blvd exit northbound; corner of Peachtree Center Ave & International Blvd. 229 Peachtree St 30303. **Hours:** 11 am-10 pm, Fri-midnight, Sat noon-midnight, Sun noon-10 pm. Closed: 11/26 & 12/25. **Features:** casual dress; children's menu; health conscious menu; carryout; cocktails & lounge; fee for parking; a la carte. Casual upbeat atmosphere. Oversize hamburgers, grilled fish, chicken & steak. Homemade pasta & dessert. Parking ticket validated after 5 pm weekdays & all day on weekends. **Cards:** AE, DI, DS, MC, VI.   ✕

NIKOLAI'S ROOF   Dinner: $60   Phone: 404/221-6362   ①
◆◆◆◆
Continental   **Location:** On roof of Atlanta Hilton & Towers. Courtland & Harris Sts 30303. **Hours:** for seatings at 6:30 pm & 9:30 pm. Closed major holidays & Sun. **Reservations:** suggested. **Features:** formal attire; cocktails & lounge; valet parking; prix fixe. Impeccable wait staff in cossack attire. 6-course French-Continental menu with Russian specialties. Beef, fish, wild game & lamb. Menu changes monthly. Extensive wine list. Excellent view of city. **Cards:** AE, CB, DI, DS, JCB, MC, VI.

PITTYPAT'S PORCH   Dinner: $18-$21   Phone: 404/525-8228   ⑥
◆◆
Regional   **Location:** Off I-75 & I-85; Courtland St exit southbound, International Blvd exit northbound. 25 International
American   Blvd NW 30303. **Hours:** 5 pm-9 pm, Fri & Sat-10 pm. Closed major holidays. **Reservations:** suggested. **Features:** casual dress; children's menu; carryout; salad bar; cocktails & lounge; entertainment; fee for parking. Old South decor & regional specialties. Warm ambience. **Cards:** AE, DI, DS, MC, VI.   ✕

THE RESTAURANT   Dinner: $20-$30   Phone: 404/659-0400   ④
Ⓐ   **Location:** I-75/85 northbound exit International Blvd, southbound exit Courtland St; 0.5 mi w; in Ritz-Carlton Atlanta. 181 Peachtree St NE 30303. **Hours:** 6 pm-10 pm. Closed: Sun. **Reservations:** suggested.
◆◆◆◆◆   **Features:** semi-formal attire; health conscious menu; cocktails & lounge; entertainment; valet parking; a la
French   carte, also prix fixe. Gentle lighting, Old World oils, fresh flowers & rich warm wood create private club ambience. Gracious service. Fresh market cuisine with French fusion offerings. **Cards:** AE, DI, DS, JCB, MC, VI. *(See ad p 197)*   ✕

SAVANNAH FISH COMPANY   Lunch: $8-$15   Dinner: $25-$28   Phone: 404/589-7456   ②
◆◆◆
Seafood   **Location:** I-75 & I-85; Williams St exit southbound, International Blvd exit northbound, just w; in The Westin Peachtree Plaza. Peachtree & International Blvd 30303. **Hours:** 11:30 am-2:30 & 5:30-10 pm. **Reservations:** accepted. **Features:** casual dress; children's menu; health conscious menu; cocktails & lounge; valet parking. Sauteed, broiled or blackened fish, steamed vegetables & fish stew. Fresh market seafood & oyster bar. Ornamental poolside location. **Cards:** AE, DI, DS, JCB, MC, VI.   ✕

ATLANTA NORTH   (See map p. 202; index below)

Index of Establishments on the NORTH ATLANTA ACCOMMODATIONS Spotting Map

(See map p. 202)

(See map p. 202)

LODGINGS

AMERISUITES-ATLANTA/BUCKHEAD
AAA **SAVE** — **Suite Motel** — ◆◆◆
Phone: 404/869-6161   **86**
All Year [CP]   1P: $79- 159   2P/1B: $79- 159   2P/2B: $79- 159   XP: $10   F18
Location: From jct of Peachtree Rd NE & Piedmont Rd NE, just w. 3242 Peachtree Rd NE 30305.
Fax: 404/869-6093. **Terms:** Check-in 4 pm; no pets. **Facility:** 172 rooms. Large, tastefully appointed & well equipped units. 8 stories; interior corridors. **Dining:** Restaurant nearby. **Services:** Fee: coin laundry. **All Rooms:** coffeemakers, microwaves, free & pay movies, refrigerators, combo or shower baths, VCP's. **Special Amenities:** Free breakfast and free local telephone calls.
See color ad p 10   Roll in showers. 🛏 🍴 🖨 🛗 CTV ✕ D S

AMERISUITES-ATLANTA/PERIMETER CENTER
AAA **SAVE** — **Suite Motel** — ◆◆◆
Phone: 770/730-9300   **67**
Sun-Thurs [CP]   1P: $99- 109   2P/1B: $109- 119   2P/2B: $109- 119   XP: $10   F18
Fri & Sat [CP]   1P: $65- 75   2P/1B: $65- 75   2P/2B: $65- 75   XP: $10   F18
Location: SR 400 exit 5A (Dunwoody), 0.3 mi e. 1005 Crestline Parkway 30328. Fax: 770/730-9398.
Terms: Weekend rates avail; small pets only. **Facility:** 152 rooms. Large, tastefully done & very well-equipped units. 6 stories; interior corridors. **Services:** complimentary evening beverages, Wed; area transportation, within 5 mi. Fee: coin laundry. **All Rooms:** coffeemakers, microwaves, free & pay movies, refrigerators, combo or shower baths, VCP's. **Cards:** AE, CB, DI, DS, MC, VI. **Special Amenities:** Free breakfast and free local telephone calls.
See color ad p 10   Roll in showers. 🛏 🍴 🖨 🛗 CTV 🛗 ✕ 🏊 D S

ATLANTA MARRIOTT NORTH CENTRAL
◆◆◆ — **Motel**
Rates Subject to Change   Phone: 404/325-0000   **147**
All Year   1P: $129   2P/1B: $129   2P/2B: $129
Location: I-85 exit 32, 0.3 mi nw to Century Blvd, 0.5 mi n. 2000 Century Blvd NE 30345.
Fax: 404/325-4920. **Terms:** Sr. discount; reserv deposit; no pets. **Facility:** 287 rooms. Handling fee imposed; 5 stories; interior corridors. **Dining:** Restaurant; 6:30 am-2 & 5-11 pm; $8-$19. **All Rooms:** free & pay movies. **Cards:** AE, CB, DI, DS, JCB, MC, VI.
🛏 CTV ✕ 🏊 D S

ATLANTA MARRIOTT NORTHWEST
◆◆◆ — **Motel**
Rates Subject to Change   Phone: 770/952-7900   **39**
All Year   1P: $124   2P/1B: $124   2P/2B: $124
Location: I-75 exit 110 (Windy Hill Rd), 0.5 mi se. 200 Interstate North Pkwy 30339. Fax: 770/952-1468. **Terms:** Check-in 4 pm; no pets. **Facility:** 399 rooms. 5-16 stories; interior corridors. **Dining:** Restaurant; 6:30 am-10 pm, Sat & Sun from 7 am; $11-$20. **All Rooms:** free & pay movies. **Cards:** AE, CB, DI, DS, JCB, MC, VI.
Roll in showers. 🛏 🛏 🖨 CTV ✕ 🏊 D S

ATLANTA MARRIOTT PERIMETER CENTER
◆◆◆ — **Motel**
Rates Subject to Change   Phone: 770/394-6500   **66**
Sun-Thurs   1P: $110- 116   2P/1B: $110- 116   2P/2B: $110- 116
Fri & Sat   1P: $79   2P/1B: $79   2P/2B: $79
Location: I-285, exit 21 (Ashford Dunwoody), 0.3 mi n to Hammond Dr, 0.3 mi to Perimeter Center Pkwy NE. 246 Perimeter Center Pkwy NE 30346. Fax: 770/394-4338. **Terms:** Check-in 4 pm; no pets. **Facility:** 400 rooms. Rates for up to 4 persons; 16 stories; interior corridors. **Dining:** Restaurant; 6:30 am-11 pm; $12-$20. **All Rooms:** free & pay movies. **Cards:** AE, CB, DI, DS, JCB, MC, VI.
🛏 🛏 🖨 CTV 🛗 ✕ 🏊 D S

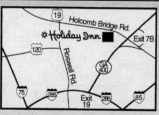

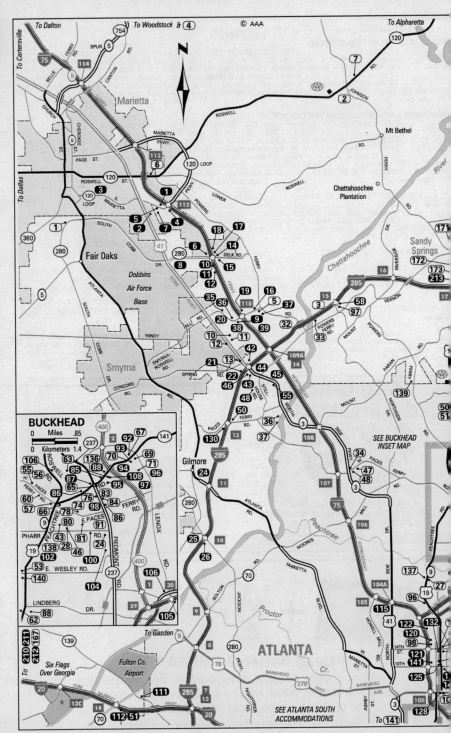

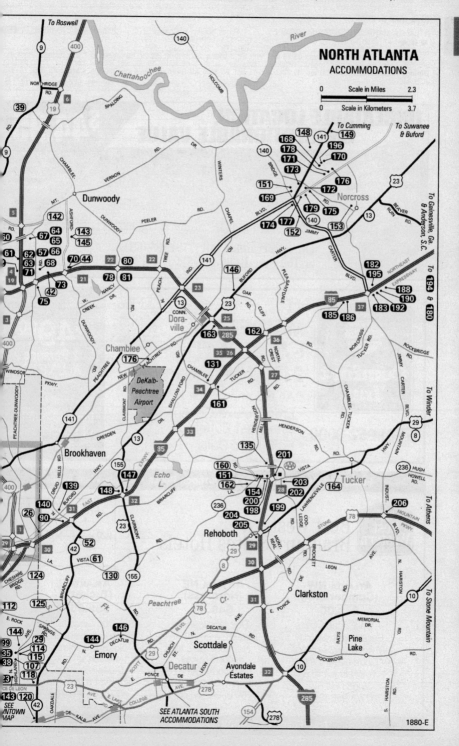

NORTH ATLANTA
ACCOMMODATIONS

(See map p. 202)

ATLANTA MARRIOTT SUITES MIDTOWN   Rates Subject to Change   **Phone:** 404/876-8888   122

◆◆◆   Sun-Thurs   1P: $159- 179   2P/1B: $159- 179
Suite Hotel   Fri & Sat   1P: $89- 179   2P/1B: $89- 179
Location: Midtown I-85/75 exit 14th St; 3 blks e. 35 14th St 30309. Fax: 404/876-7727. **Terms:** Check-in 4 pm; no pets. **Facility:** 254 rooms. Weekend rates for up to 5 persons; 19 stories; interior corridors. Fee: parking **Dining:** Restaurant; 6:30-10:30 am, 11:30-2 & 5-11 pm; $9-$15. **All Rooms:** free & pay movies. **Cards:** AE, CB, DI, DS, JCB, MC, VI.

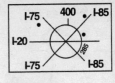

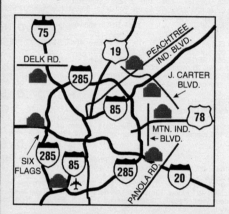

(See map p. 202)

BEST WESTERN BRADBURY SUITES   Rates Subject to Change   **Phone:** 770/956-9919   **38**
◆◆◆   All Year [BP]   1P: $55- 80   2P/1B: $60- 85   2P/2B: $60- 85   XP: $10   F6
Motel   **Location:** I-75, exit 110 (Windyhill Rd). 4500 Circle 75 Pkwy 30339. Fax: 770/955-3270. **Terms:** Sr. discount; no pets. **Facility:** 247 rooms. 3-5 stories; interior corridors. **All Rooms:** free & pay movies.
Cards: AE, CB, DI, DS, MC, VI. *(See ad p 204 & color ad p 182)*   ⬛ ⬛ CTV ⬛ ⬛ D

BEVERLY HILLS INN   Guaranteed Rates   **Phone:** 404/233-8520   **102**
◆◆   All Year [CP]   1P: $90- 120   2P/1B: $90- 140   2P/2B: $90- 140   XP: $10
Historic Bed   **Location:** Buckhead; from jct Piedmont & Peachtree rds, 1.1 mi s on Peachtree to Sheridan Dr, just e. 65
& Breakfast   Sheridan Dr NE 30305. Fax: 404/233-8659. **Terms:** Reserv deposit, 3 day notice; pets, $10 extra charge.
Facility: 18 rooms. 3 stories, no elevator; interior corridors. **All Rooms:** kitchens. **Cards:** AE, DI, DS, JCB,
MC, VI.   ⬛ CTV D

THE BUCKHEAD BED & BREAKFAST INN   Rates Subject to Change   **Phone:** 404/261-8284   **106**
◆◆◆   All Year [CP]   1P: $85- 105   2P/1B: $85- 105   2P/2B: $85- 105
Bed &   **Location:** I-85 exit 30 (southbound), exit 28 (northbound). 70 Lenox Pointe NE 30324. Fax: 404/237-9224.
Breakfast   **Terms:** No pets. **Facility:** 19 rooms. Rates for up to 3 persons; 3 stories; interior corridors; smoke free premises. **All Rooms:** free movies. **Cards:** AE, MC, VI.   Roll in showers.   CTV ⬛ D S

BUDGETEL INN-ATLANTA LENOX   Rates Subject to Change   **Phone:** 404/321-0999   **105**
◆◆   Fri & Sat [CP]   1P: $47- 60   2P/1B: $54- 67   2P/2B: $59
Motel   Sun-Thurs [CP]   1P: $42- 55   2P/1B: $49- 62   2P/2B: $54
Location: On e side of I-85 at southbound exit 30; northbound exit 28, 2 mi on Buford Hwy to Lenox Rd,
just e under highway to Chantilly Dr. 2535 Chantilly Dr NE 30324. Fax: 404/634-3384. **Terms:** Sr. discount; small pets only.
Facility: 102 rooms. Rates for up to 4 persons; 3 stories; interior corridors. **All Rooms:** free & pay movies. **Cards:** AE, CB,
DI, DS, MC, VI. *(See color ad p 188)*   ⬛ CTV ⬛ D S

COMFORT INN-SIX FLAGS   Rates Subject to Change   **Phone:** 404/696-2444   **51**
◆◆◆   All Year [CP]   1P: $69- 79   2P/1B: $69- 89   2P/2B: $69- 89   XP: $10   F12
Motel   **Location:** I-20 exit 14. 4330 Fulton Industrial Blvd 30336. Fax: 404/696-0333. **Terms:** Sr. discount; reserv
deposit, 10 day notice; no pets. **Facility:** 155 rooms. 7 stories; interior corridors. **All Rooms:** free movies.
Cards: AE, DI, DS, MC, VI.   ⬛ CTV ⬛ D S

COMFORT SUITES HOTEL PERIMETER CENTER   **Phone:** 770/828-0330   **71**
⬛⬛ ⬛   All Year [CP]   1P: $89- 104   2P/1B: $99- 114   2P/2B: $99- 114   XP: $10   F16
Location: I-285W, exit 20, 1 mi n; I-285E, exit 18 (Glenridge Dr), 0.5 mi n to Hammond Dr, 0.5 mi e to
◆◆◆   Peachtree Dunwoody Rd, just n. 6110 Peachtree Dunwoody Rd 30328. Fax: 770/604-9865.
Motor Inn   **Terms:** Weekend rates avail; no pets. **Facility:** 121 rooms. Large tastefully decorated rooms. Near business
park & shopping center. 12 two-room suites, $104; 7 stories; interior corridors; sauna. **Services:** Fee: coin
laundry. **All Rooms:** coffeemakers, microwaves, free & pay movies, refrigerators. **Cards:** AE, CB, DI, DS, MC, VI.   ⬛ ⬛ CTV ⬛ D

COUNTRY HEARTH INN   Rates Subject to Change   **Phone:** 770/393-2662   **131**
Motel   All Year [CP]   1P: $49- 64   2P/1B: $49- 64   2P/2B: $49- 64   XP: $5   F12
Too new to rate; **Location:** I-85 exit 34, just w. 2822 Chamblee-Tucker Rd 30341. **Terms:** Reserv deposit;
no pets. **Facility:** 52 rooms. Scheduled to open fall 1997; 2 stories; exterior corridors. **All Rooms:** free movies. **Cards:** AE,
DI, DS, MC, VI.   CTV D S

COURTYARD BY MARRIOTT-BUCKHEAD   Rates Subject to Change   **Phone:** 404/869-0818   **108**
⬛⬛   All Year   1P: $99- 109   2P/1B: $99- 109   2P/2B: $99- 109
Location: I-85 exit 30 (southbound), exit 28 (northbound), 3 mi n on Lenox Rd, then 0.8 mi sw. 3332
◆◆◆   Peachtree Rd NE 30326. Fax: 404/869-0939. **Terms:** Sr. discount; no pets. **Facility:** 181 rooms. 8 whirlpool
Motel   rms, extra charge; 11 stories; interior corridors. Fee: parking. **Dining:** Restaurant; 6:30 am-11 pm; $10-$23.
All Rooms: free & pay movies. **Cards:** AE, DI, DS, MC, VI. *(See color ad p 192)*   ⬛ ⬛ CTV ⬛ D S

COURTYARD BY MARRIOTT-CUMBERLAND CENTER   Rates Subject to Change   **Phone:** 770/952-2555   **55**
◆◆◆   All Year   1P: $92   2P/1B: $102   2P/2B: $102   XP: $10   F17
Motor Inn   **Location:** I-285N exit 13, I-285S exit 14; 0.5 mi s on US 41, just e. 3000 Cumberland Cir 30339.
Fax: 770/952-2409. **Terms:** Reserv deposit; no pets. **Facility:** 182 rooms. 8 stories; interior corridors.
Dining: Restaurant; 6:30 am-10:30 & 5:30-10:30 pm, Fri & Sat 7 am-noon, Sun 7 am-noon & 5:30-10:30 pm; $6-$10.
All Rooms: free & pay movies. **Cards:** AE, DI, DS, MC, VI. *(See color ad p 192)*   ⬛ ⬛ CTV ⬛ ⬛ D S

*T*his weekend,
take a vacation
from high rates.

$59-$69*

Fri., Sat. and Sun. Only

At the Wyndham Hotels & Resorts, we've paved the way for a relaxing visit. You'll enjoy a great rate and a great guest room filled with thoughtful amenities like a coffee maker and shower massager, plus an invigorating whirlpool, swimming pool and exercise room. For reservations, call the hotels direct, **800-WYNDHAM** or your travel planner.

WYNDHAM GARDEN BUCKHEAD–3340 Peachtree Rd. NE, 404-231-1234 . . . .$69
WYNDHAM GARDEN MIDTOWN–125 10th St., 404-873-4800 . . . .$69**
WYNDHAM GARDEN PERIMETER–800 Hammond Dr. NE, 404-252-3344 . . . .$59**
WYNDHAM GARDEN VININGS–2857 Paces Ferry Rd., 770-432-5555 . . . .$59***
WYNDHAM GARDEN NORTHWEST–1775 Parkway Place NW, 770-428-4400 . . . .$64

WYNDHAM HOTELS & RESORTS™
The Right Way. The Wyndham Way.

For reservations, call the hotels direct, **800-WYNDHAM** or your travel planner.

(See map p. 202)

COURTYARD BY MARRIOTT-MIDTOWN   Rates Subject to Change   **Phone:** 404/607-1112   121
◆◆◆   All Year   1P: $93   2P/1B: $103   2P/2B: $103   XP: $10   F18
Motor Inn   **Location:** I-75/85, exit 10th & 14th sts, just sw of 14th St. 1132 Techwood Dr 30318. Fax: 404/607-1020.
Terms: Reserv deposit; no pets. **Facility:** 168 rooms. Rates for up to 4 persons; suites, $118 for 2 persons; 8
stories; interior corridors. **Dining:** Restaurant; 6:30 am-10 & 5-10 pm, Sat & Sun 7 am-11 & 5-10 pm; $7-$9.
All Rooms: free & pay movies. **Cards:** AE, CB, DI, DS, MC, VI. *(See color ad p 192)*   🛥 ⊞ CTV ⊠ 🕭 D S

COURTYARD BY MARRIOTT-PEACHTREE
DUNWOODY-MEDICAL CENTER   Rates Subject to Change   **Phone:** 404/843-2300   75
◆◆◆   Sun-Thurs   1P: $94   2P/1B: $104   2P/2B: $104   XP: $10   F12
Motor Inn   Fri & Sat   1P: $59   2P/1B: $59   2P/2B: $59
Location: 0.8 mi s of jct I-285; westbound Peachtree-Dunwoody exit 20, eastbound Glenridge Dr exit 18, 0.5
mi e on Johnson Ferry Rd. 5601 Peachtree-Dunwoody Rd 30342. Fax: 404/851-1938. **Terms:** Sr. discount; check-in 4 pm;
no pets. **Facility:** 128 rooms. Weekend rates for up to 4 persons; 2 stories; interior corridors. **Dining:** 6:30-10:30 am, Sat &
Sun 7-11 am. **All Rooms:** free & pay movies. **Cards:** AE, CB, DI, DS, MC, VI. *(See color ad p 192)*

🛥 ⊞ CTV ⊠ 🕭 D S

COURTYARD BY MARRIOTT PERIMETER CENTER   Rates Subject to Change   **Phone:** 770/393-1000   62
◆◆◆   Sun-Thurs   1P: $89- 114   2P/1B: $89- 114   2P/2B: $89- 114   XP: $10   F18
Motor Inn   Fri & Sat   1P: $64   2P/1B: $74   2P/2B: $74
Location: I-285E exit 18 (Glenridge Dr), 1 mi n, 1 mi e on Hammond Dr to Peachtree-Dunwoody Rd, then
0.5 mi n; I-285W exit 20, 0.8 mi n. 6250 Peachtree-Dunwoody Rd 30328. Fax: 770/396-0762. **Terms:** Check-in 4 pm; no
pets. **Facility:** 145 rooms. 4 stories; interior corridors. **Dining:** 6:30 am-10:30 am, Sat & Sun 7am-noon. **All Rooms:** free &
pay movies. **Cards:** AE, CB, DI, DS, MC, VI. *(See color ad p 192)*   🛥 ⊞ CTV ⊠ 🕭 D S

COURTYARD BY MARRIOTT-WINDY HILL   Rates Subject to Change   **Phone:** 770/955-3838   35
◆◆◆   Sun-Thurs   1P: $92   2P/1B: $102   2P/2B: $102   XP: $10   F12
Motor Inn   Fri & Sat   1P: $69   2P/1B: $69   2P/2B: $69
Location: I-75, exit 110, Windy Hill Rd; 0.3 mi w to S Park Pl, just n. 2045 S Park Pl 30339.
Fax: 770/933-0394. **Terms:** Sr. discount; check-in 4 pm; reserv deposit; no pets. **Facility:** 127 rooms. 2 stories; interior corri-
dors. **Dining:** Coffee shop; 6:30 am-10:30 & 5-10 pm, Sat & Sun 7 am-noon (breakfast only). **All Rooms:** free & pay
movies. **Cards:** AE, DI, DS, MC, VI. *(See color ad p 192)*   🛥 ⊞ CTV ⊠ D S

CROWNE PLAZA RAVINIA   Rates Subject to Change   **Phone:** 770/395-7700   70
◆◆◆   Sun-Thurs   1P: $175   2P/1B: $175   2P/2B: $175   XP: $10   F18
Hotel   Fri & Sat   1P: $89- 109   2P/1B: $89- 109   2P/2B: $89- 109   XP: $10   F18
Location: I-285 exit 21, ne corner. 4355 Ashford-Dunwoody Rd 30346. Fax: 770/392-9503. **Terms:** Reserv
deposit; no pets. **Facility:** 495 rooms. 15 stories; interior corridors. **Dining:** Restaurant, deli; 6 am-10:30 pm; $11-$18; also,
La Grotta Ravinia Ristorante Italiano, see separate listing. **All Rooms:** free & pay movies. **Cards:** AE, CB, DI, DS, JCB,
MC, VI.   Roll in showers. 🛥 ⊞ CTV ⊠ 🕭 D S

(See map p. 202)

DAYS INN-CLAIRMONT RD

Phone: 404/633-8411   148

AAA SAVE   All Year [CP]   1P: $48   2P/1B: $58   2P/2B: $58   XP: $20   F12

Location: I-85 exit 32, sw corner. 2910 Clairmont Rd 30329. Fax: 404/633-1122. **Terms:** Reserv deposit; no pets. **Facility:** 236 rooms. 2 stories; exterior corridors. **Dining:** Restaurant nearby. **Services:** Fee: coin laundry. **All Rooms:** free movies. **Some Rooms:** microwaves, refrigerators, VCP's. **Cards:** AE, DS, MC, VI. **Special Amenities:** Free breakfast. *(See color ad p 208)*

Motel

DOUBLETREE GUEST SUITES

Rates Subject to Change   **Phone: 770/668-0808**   63

AAA   All Year   1P: $79- 143   2P/1B: $79- 143   2P/2B: $79- 143

Location: I-285W exit 20, 1 mi n; I-285E exit 18 (Glenridge Dr), 0.5 mi n to Hammond Dr, 0.5 mi e to Peachtree-Dunwoody Rd, just n. 6120 Peachtree-Dunwoody Rd 30328. Fax: 770/668-0008. **Terms:** No pets. **Facility:** 224 rooms. 6 stories; interior corridors. **Dining:** Restaurant; 6:30 am-10 pm; $11-$18. **All Rooms:** free & pay movies. **Cards:** AE, DI, DS, MC, VI.

Suite Hotel

DOUBLETREE GUEST SUITES ATLANTA-GALLERIA

Phone: 770/980-1900   42

AAA SAVE   All Year [BP]   1P: $165   2P/1B: $165   2P/2B: $165   XP: $20   D12

Location: I-285 exit 14 (westbound), exit 13 (eastbound), just n on Cobb Pkwy. 2780 Whitley Rd NW 30339. Fax: 770/980-1528. **Terms:** BP avail; package plans; no pets. **Facility:** 155 rooms. 1- & 2-bedroom suites with living room. 8 stories; interior corridors; small pool. **Dining & Entertainment:** Dining room, cafeteria; 6 am-11 pm; $12-$18; cocktails/lounge; entertainment. **Services:** valet laundry; area transportation, within 3 mi. **All Rooms:** coffeemakers, free & pay movies, refrigerators, combo or shower baths, whirlpools. **Some Rooms:** microwaves. Fee: VCP's. **Cards:** AE, CB, DI, DS, JCB, MC. **Special Amenities:** Early check-in/late check-out and preferred room (subject to availability with advanced reservations). *(See color ad below)*

Suite Hotel   Roll in showers.

EMBASSY SUITES HOTEL-GALLERIA

Rates Subject to Change   **Phone: 770/984-9300**   45

Sun-Thurs [BP]   1P: $154- 159   2P/1B: $164- 169   2P/2B: $174- 179   XP: $20   F12

Suite Hotel   Fri & Sat [BP]   1P: $99- 159   2P/1B: $99- 159   2P/2B: $99- 159   XP: $10   F12

Location: I-285 eastbound exit 13, westbound exit 14; 0.5 mi s; 0.3 mi e on Akers Mill Rd. 2815 Akers Mill Rd 30339. Fax: 770/955-4183. **Terms:** No pets. **Facility:** 261 rooms. Weekend rates for up to 4 persons; 9 stories; interior corridors. **Dining:** Restaurant; 11 am-10 pm; $10-$18. **All Rooms:** free & pay movies. **Cards:** AE, CB, DI, DS, JCB, MC, VI. *(See color ad p 210)*

EMBASSY SUITES HOTEL OF BUCKHEAD

Phone: 404/261-7733   95

AAA SAVE   6/1-10/31 [BP]   1P: $149   2P/1B: $149   2P/2B: $169

2/1-5/31 [BP]   1P: $139   2P/1B: $139   2P/2B: $159

Suite Hotel   12/1-1/31 & 11/1-11/30 [BP]   1P: $129   2P/1B: $129   2P/2B: $149

Location: 0.3 mi e of jct Piedmont Rd NE & Peachtree Rd NE. 3285 Peachtree Rd NE 30305. Fax: 404/262-0522. **Terms:** No pets. **Facility:** 317 rooms. Near Lenox Square Mall. 11 two-bedroom units. Rates for up to 4 persons; 16 stories; interior corridors; sauna, whirlpool. Fee: parking. **Dining & Entertainment:** Restaurant, deli; 11 am-10 pm, full cooked-to-order buffet breakfast; $13-$21; cocktails/lounge. **Services:** complimentary evening beverages; area transportation, within 1 mi. Fee: coin laundry. **All Rooms:** coffeemakers, microwaves, free & pay movies, refrigerators, safes. **Some Rooms:** Fee: whirlpools. **Cards:** AE, CB, DI, DS, MC, VI. **Special Amenities:** Free breakfast. *(See color ad p 210)*

EMBASSY SUITES HOTEL PERIMETER CENTER

Rates Subject to Change   **Phone: 770/394-5454**   65

Sun-Thurs [BP]   1P: $149   2P/1B: $169   2P/2B: $169   XP: $20   F17

Hotel   Fri & Sat [BP]   1P: $109- 139   2P/1B: $109- 139   2P/2B: $109- 139

Location: I-285, exit 21 (Ashford-Dunwoody Rd); n 0.5 mi, n to Perimeter Center W Rd, w 0.5 mi; opposite Perimeter Mall. 1030 Crown Pointe Pkwy NE 30338. Fax: 770/396-5167. **Terms:** Sr. discount; no pets. **Facility:** 241 rooms. Weekend rates for up to 4 persons; 10 stories; interior corridors. **Dining:** Restaurant; 11 am-11 pm; $8-$17. **All Rooms:** free pay movies. **Cards:** AE, CB, DI, DS, JCB, MC, VI. *(See color ad p 210)*

(See map p. 202)

EMORY INN
◆◆◆
Motor Inn
Rates Subject to Change
All Year   1P: $89- 99   2P/1B: $89- 99 2P/2B: $89- 99
Location: I-85 exit 31, 0.6 mi s on N Druid Hills Rd, 1.8 mi sw on Briarcliff Rd, then 0.8 mi s on Clifton Rd; adjacent to Emory University. 1641 Clifton Rd 30329. Fax: 404/712-6701. **Terms:** Pets, $25 extra charge.
Phone: 404/712-6700   `144`
Facility: 107 rooms. Weekend rates for up to 4 persons; 2-3 stories, no elevator; exterior corridors. **Dining:** Restaurant; 7-10 am, 11-2 & 5-10 pm, Sat 7 am-noon & 5-10 pm, Sun 7-10 am, 11:30-2 & 5-10 pm; $9-$20. **All Rooms:** free & pay movies. **Cards:** AE, DI, DS, MC, VI.

FAIRFIELD INN
◆◆◆
Motel
Rates Subject to Change
All Year [CP]   1P: $64- 74   2P/1B: $64- 74 2P/2B: $64- 74 XP: $10
Location: I-75/85, 14th St exit Peachtree St N. 1470 Spring St NW 30309. Fax: 404/874-3602. **Terms:** Sr. discount; check-in 4 pm; no pets. **Facility:** 182 rooms. Rates are for up to 4 persons; 4 stories; exterior corridors. **All Rooms:** free movies. **Cards:** AE, CB, DI, DS, MC, VI. *(See color ad p 211)*
Phone: 404/872-5821   `123`
F19
Roll in showers.

FAIRFIELD INN-ATLANTA/BUCKHEAD
Motel
Rates Subject to Change
All Year [CP]   1P: $69   2P/1B: $74   2P/2B: $74   XP: $5
Too new to rate; **Location:** From jct Piedmont Rd NE & Peachtree Rd NE, just s. 3092 Piedmont Dr 30305. Fax: 404/846-0900. **Terms:** Sr. discount; check-in 4 pm; reserv deposit; no pets. **Facility:** 116 rooms. Scheduled to open spring 1997; 5 stories; interior corridors. **All Rooms:** free movies. **Cards:** AE, DI, DS, MC, VI.
Phone: 404/846-0900   `98`
F16
Roll in showers.

FAIRFIELD INN ATLANTA/VININGS
◆◆◆
Motel
Rates Subject to Change
All Year [CP]   1P: $50- 75   2P/1B: $50- 75 2P/2B: $50- 75 XP: $5
Location: I-285 exit 12, just w. 2450 Paces Ferry Rd 30339. Fax: 770/438-0087. **Terms:** No pets. **Facility:** 145 rooms. 7 stories; interior corridors. **All Rooms:** free movies. **Cards:** AE, CB, DI, DS, JCB, MC, VI. *(See color ad p 211)*
Phone: 770/435-4500   `130`

FAIRFIELD INN BY MARRIOTT/DUNWOODY
Motel
Rates Subject to Change
All Year   1P: $65- 85   2P/1B: $65- 85 2P/2B: $65- 85
Too new to rate; **Location:** I-285 exit 18 eastbound, just n to Hammond Dr 0.8 mi e; I-285 exit 20 westbound, just n to Hammond Dr, just e. 1188 Hammond Dr 30346. **Terms:** No pets. **Facility:** 116 rooms. Scheduled to open summer 1997; 5 stories; interior corridors. **All Rooms:** free movies. **Cards:** AE, DI, DS, MC, VI.
Phone: 770/446-1500   `57`
Roll in showers.

FAIRFIELD INN BY MARRIOTT NORTHLAKE
◆◆◆
Motel
Rates Subject to Change
All Year [CP]   1P: $47- 60   2P/1B: $47- 62 2P/2B: $50- 70 XP: $6
Location: I-285 exit 28, w 0.4 mi. 2155 Ranchwood Dr 30345. Fax: 770/491-7444. **Terms:** Sr. discount; no pets. **Facility:** 133 rooms. 3 stories; interior/exterior corridors. **All Rooms:** free movies. **Cards:** AE, CB, DI, DS, MC, VI. *(See color ad p 211)*
Phone: 770/491-7444   `154`
F16

(See map p. 202)

FOUR POINTS HOTEL ATLANTA PERIMETER   Guaranteed Rates   **Phone:** 770/394-5000 ⑧⓪
◆◆◆   All Year   1P: $59- 159   2P/1B: $69- 159   2P/2B: $69- 159   XP: $10
Hotel   **Location:** I-285 exit 22, ne corner eastbound; I-285 westbound exit 22; 0.5 mi w. 1850 Cotillion Dr 30338.
          Fax: 770/551-0391. **Terms:** No pets. **Facility:** 393 rooms. 4 stories; interior corridors. **Dining:** Restaurant;
6:30 am-10 pm; $10-$17. **All Rooms:** free & pay movies. **Cards:** AE, CB, DI, DS, MC, VI. *(See ad below)*
                                                      Roll in showers. 🛄 ♿ CTV ✕ D S

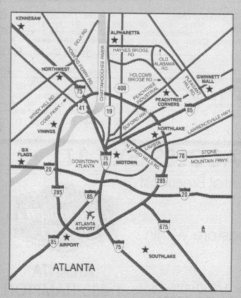

(See map p. 202)

FOUR SEASONS HOTEL ATLANTA Phone: 404/881-9898 **132**

12/1-12/31	1P: $179- 450	2P/1B: $209- 480	XP: $30	F18
1/1-4/30	1P: $210- 480	2P/1B: $240- 510	XP: $30	F18
5/1-11/30	1P: $220- 500	2P/1B: $250- 530	XP: $30	F18

(AAA) (SAVE) ◆◆◆◆ Hotel **Location:** Midtown I-75/85, exit 14th St, 3 blks e. 75 14th St 30309. Fax: 404/873-4692. **Terms:** Package plans; pets, $100 dep req. **Facility:** 244 rooms. In the art & business district. Dramatic red Spanish marble grand staircase under imported Baccaraat crystal chandelier. European style personal service. Elegant, lavishly appointed guest rooms, including suites. 1 three-bedroom unit, 3 two-bedroom units. 19 stories; interior corridors; sauna, steamrooms whirlpool; full service beauty salon. Fee: parking. **Dining & Entertainment:** Dining room, restaurant; $13-$25 cocktails/lounge; 24-hour room service; afternoon tea; also, Florencia, see separate listing; entertainment Services: childcare; valet laundry; area transportation, within 3 mi. Fee: massage; valet parking. **All Rooms:** honor bars safes. Fee: movies. **Some Rooms:** VCP's, whirlpools. **Cards:** AE, CB, DI, JCB, MC, VI. **Special Amenities:** Free newspaper.

THE GASLIGHT INN B&B   Guaranteed Rates   Phone: 404/875-1001 **143**
◆◆◆ Historic Bed & Breakfast   All Year [CP]   1P: $85- 125   2P/1B: $95- 125   2P/2B: $149- 195   XP: $12
Location: I-75/85 exit 96 (Freedom Pkwy) to Ponce de Leon, just e, just n on Frederic, then just e. 1001 S Charles Ave NE 30306. Fax: 404/876-1001. **Terms:** Reserv deposit, 7 day notice; no pets. **Facility:** 6 rooms 2 stories; interior corridors; smoke free premises. **Some Rooms:** kitchen. **Cards:** AE, DS, MC, VI.

GRANADA SUITE HOTEL   Rates Subject to Change   Phone: 404/876-6100 **120**
◆◆◆ Historic Hotel   All Year [BP]   1P: $71- 121   2P/1B: $71- 121   2P/2B: $71- 131   XP: $5
Location: I-75S exit 102 (14th St), just e on 14th, just n on W Peachtree to 16th St; I-75/85N exit 101, just e st to W Peachtree, n 0.6 mi. 1302 W Peachtree St 30309. Fax: 404/875-0502. **Terms:** Pets, $25 extra charge. **Facility:** 103 rooms. Apartments avail; 3 stories; interior corridors. Fee: parking. **All Rooms:** free movies **Some Rooms:** 45 kitchens. **Cards:** AE, CB, DI, DS, JCB, MC, VI. (See color ad p 195)

GRAND HYATT ATLANTA   Phone: 404/365-8100 **89**
Sun-Thurs	1P: $189	2P/1B: $189	XP: $20	F1
Fri & Sat	1P: $169	2P/1B: $169	XP: $20	F1

(AAA) (SAVE) ◆◆◆◆ Hotel **Location:** Buckhead; corner of Peachtree & Piedmont rds. 3300 Peachtree Rd 30305. Fax: 404/233-5686 **Terms:** Package plans; no pets. **Facility:** 439 rooms. Striking Georgian hi-rise on 40 acres with Japanese garden. 1 traditional Japanese Tatami suite. Suites from $435-$2500; 25 stories; interior corridors; luxury leve rooms; saunas, steamrooms. Fee: parking. **Dining & Entertainment:** 2 dining rooms; 6:30 am-11 pm; $14-$32; healt conscious menu; cocktails/lounge; 24-hour room service; afternoon tea; also, Kamogawa, see separate listing Services: valet laundry; area transportation, within 2 mi. Fee: massage; valet parking. **All Rooms:** honor bars coffeemakers, free & pay movies. **Some Rooms:** Fee: VCP's, whirlpools. **Cards:** AE, CB, DI, DS, JCB, MC, VI. (See color ad p 188)

HAMPTON INN ATLANTA BUCKHEAD   Rates Subject to Change   Phone: 404/233-5656 **8**
◆◆◆ Motel   All Year [CP]   1P: $85- 100   2P/1B: $88- 100   2P/2B: $95   XP: $7   F1
Location: Jct of Piedmont & Peachtree rds ne, just nw. 3398 Piedmont Rd 30305. Fax: 404/237-4688 **Terms:** No pets. **Facility:** 154 rooms. 6 stories; interior corridors. **All Rooms:** free & pay movies **Cards:** AE, CB, DI, DS, MC, VI.

HAMPTON INN CUMBERLAND   Rates Subject to Change   Phone: 770/333-6006 **4**
◆◆◆ Motel   All Year [CP]   1P: $62   2P/1B: $69- 79   2P/2B: $67- 77   XP: $10
Location: 0.5 mi sw of jct I-285 (exit 13) & US 41 behind Cumberland Mall. 2775 Cumberland Pkwy 30331 Fax: 770/333-7862. **Terms:** No pets. **Facility:** 129 rooms. 4 stories; interior corridors. **All Rooms:** free & pa movies. **Cards:** AE, CB, DI, DS, MC, VI.

HAMPTON INN-DRUID HILLS ROAD   Phone: 404/320-6600 **14**
(AAA) (SAVE) ◆◆◆ Motel   All Year [CP]   1P: $69- 99   2P/1B: $75- 99   2P/2B: $79- 99   XP: $10   F1
Location: I-85N exit 31, just w. 1975 N Druid Hills Rd 30329. Fax: 404/321-2994. **Terms:** No pet Facility: 111 rooms. Max rates for up to 4 persons; 5 stories; interior corridors; sauna. **Dining:** Restaura nearby. **Services:** valet laundry. **All Rooms:** coffeemakers, free movies. **Some Rooms:** microwave refrigerators. Fee: whirlpools. **Cards:** AE, CB, DI, DS, MC, VI. **Special Amenities:** Free breakfast and fre local telephone calls. (See color ad below)

(See map p. 202)

HAMPTON INN HOTEL
◆◆◆
Motel
Rates Subject to Change
All Year [CP] 1P: $60- 80 2P/1B: $62- 80 2P/2B: $64- 80 XP: $8
Phone: 770/493-1966 **151** F18
Location: Exit 28 off I-285; just w to Parklake Drive, 0.5 mi n. 3400 Northlake Pkwy 30345.
Fax: 770/723-0693. **Terms:** No pets. **Facility:** 130 rooms. 5 stories; interior corridors. **All Rooms:** free & pay movies. **Cards:** AE, CB, DI, DS, MC, VI.

HAMPTON INN-MIDTOWN
◆◆◆
Motel
Rates Subject to Change
All Year [CP] 1P: $79- 109 2P/1B: $89- 119 2P/2B: $99- 129
Phone: 404/872-3234 **141**
Location: I-75/85 exit 101 (northbound), exit 102 (southbound) just e. 1152 Spring St 30309.
Fax: 404/872-3234. **Terms:** Sr. discount; no pets. **Facility:** 218 rooms. 6 stories; exterior corridors.
All Rooms: free movies. **Cards:** AE, CB, DI, DS.
Roll in showers.

HAMPTON INN-PERIMETER CENTER
◆◆◆
Motel
Rates Subject to Change
Sun-Thurs [CP] 1P: $80 2P/1B: $88 2P/2B: $88
Fri & Sat [CP] 1P: $59 2P/1B: $59 2P/2B: $59
Phone: 404/303-0014 **61**
Location: I-285 exit 17, 0.5 mi n to Hammond Dr, 1.1 mi e. 769 Hammond Dr 30328. Fax: 404/303-1707.
Terms: Reserv deposit; no pets. **Facility:** 131 rooms. 8 stories; interior corridors. **All Rooms:** free & pay movies.
Cards: AE, DI, DS, MC, VI. *(See ad below)*
Roll in showers.

HAWTHORN SUITES-ATLANTA NW
AAA SAVE
◆◆◆
Apartment
Motel
All Year [BP] 1P: $79- 179 2P/1B: $79- 179 2P/2B: $79- 179 XP: $15
Phone: 770/952-9595 **37** F19
Location: I-75 exit 110, (Windy Hill) 0.5 mi e, 0.3 mi s on Powers Ferry Rd. 1500 Parkwood Cir 30339.
Fax: 770/984-2335. **Terms:** Check-in 4 pm; pets, $100 extra charge. **Facility:** 220 rooms. Well equipped residential style housekeeping units located in office park area. 122 two-bedroom units. Rates up to 4 persons. Handling fee imposed; 3 stories; exterior corridors; whirlpool; 2 lighted tennis courts; gas grills, basketball goal. **Services:** complimentary evening beverages, Mon-Thurs; area transportation, within 3 mi, 7 am-10 pm. **Fee:** coin laundry. **All Rooms:** coffeemakers, kitchens, microwaves, free & pay movies, refrigerators. **Cards:** AE, CB, DI, DS, MC, VI. **Special Amenities:** Free breakfast and preferred room (subject to availability with advanced reservations). *(See color ad below)*

HOLIDAY INN ATLANTA CENTRAL
AAA SAVE
◆◆◆
Motor Inn
All Year 1P: $69- 99 2P/1B: $69- 99 2P/2B: $69- 99 XP: $10
Phone: 404/873-4661 **118** F17
Location: I-85 northbound exit 28 to Monroe Dr, turn right to Armour Dr NE. 418 Armour Dr NE 30324.
Fax: 404/872-1292. **Terms:** Package plans; pets, $50 dep req. **Facility:** 341 rooms. Large property with courtyard. 9 two-bedroom units. 5 stories; exterior corridors; video game room. **Dining & Entertainment:** Restaurant; 6:30 am-2 & 5:30-10 pm; $8-$21; cocktails/lounge. **Services:** area transportation, within 5 mi. **Fee:** coin laundry. **All Rooms:** coffeemakers, free & pay movies, combo or shower baths. **Some Rooms:** refrigerators, whirlpools. **Cards:** AE, CB, DI, DS, JCB, MC, VI. **Special Amenities:** Preferred room (subject to availability with advanced reservations). *(See color ad p 194 & p 190)*
Roll in showers.

(See map p. 202)

HOLIDAY INN BUCKHEAD — Rates Subject to Change — Phone: 404/264-1111 ◆◆◆ 94
F19
Motor Inn
All Year — 1P: $99- 129 — 2P/1B: $109- 139 — 2P/2B: $109- 139 — XP: $10
Location: In Buckhead; I-85 exit 30, n on Lenox Rd to Peachtree Rd NE, 0.3 mi sw. 3377 Peachtree Rd NE 30326. Fax: 404/233-7061. **Terms:** Sr. discount; check-in 4 pm; no pets. **Facility:** 297 rooms. 11 stories; interior corridors. **Dining:** Restaurant; 6-11 am, 11:30-2 & 5-10 pm, breakfast & lunch buffets; $14-$22. **All Rooms:** free & pay movies. **Cards:** AE, CB, DI, DS, JCB, MC, VI. *(See ad below & color ad p 190)* 🛏 ➤ CTV ✕ 🅿 D S

HOLIDAY INN MIDTOWN NORTH — Rates Subject to Change — Phone: 404/351-3831 ◆◆◆ 115
Motor Inn
All Year — 1P: $52- 64 — 2P/1B: $52- 64 — 2P/2B: $64
Location: I-75 northbound exit 104B, southbound exit 104, sw corner. 1810 Howell Mill Rd 30318. Fax: 404/352-0125. **Terms:** Sr. discount; no pets. **Facility:** 201 rooms. 2-3 stories; exterior corridors. **Dining:** Restaurant; 6:30 am-10 pm; $8-$16. **All Rooms:** free movies. **Cards:** AE, CB, DI, DS, JCB, MC, VI. *(See color ad p 190)* Roll in showers. ➤ ➤ CTV ✕ D

HOLIDAY INN SELECT ATLANTA PERIMETER — Rates Subject to Change — Phone: 770/457-6363 ◆◆◆ 78
F18
Motor Inn
All Year — 1P: $95- 119 — 2P/1B: $95- 129 — 2P/2B: $95- 129 — XP: $10
Location: I-285, exit 22, eastbound sw corner; westbound follow access road 1.3 mi to Chamblee-Dunwoody Rd, just s; ne corner. 4386 Chamblee-Dunwoody Rd 30341. Fax: 770/936-9592. **Terms:** Sr. discount; small pets only, $25 extra charge, $125 dep req. **Facility:** 250 rooms. 5 stories; interior corridors. **Dining:** Restaurant; 6:30 am-2 & 5-10 pm, Sat & Sun from 7 am; $9-$16. **All Rooms:** free & pay movies. **Cards:** AE, CB, DI, DS, JCB, MC, VI. *(See color ad p 190)* Roll in showers. 🛏 ➤ ➤ CTV ✕ 🅿 D S

HOLIDAY INN SELECT - ATLANTA POWERS FERRY — Rates Subject to Change — Phone: 770/955-1700 ◆◆◆ 58
F18
Hotel
All Year — 1P: $79- 129 — 2P/1B: $89- 139 — 2P/2B: $89- 139 — XP: $10
Location: I-285 exit 15, se corner. 6345 Powers Ferry Rd NW 30339. Fax: 770/955-0853. **Terms:** Sr. discount; pets, $125 dep req. **Facility:** 296 rooms. 9 stories; interior corridors. **Dining:** Restaurant; 6:30 am-2 & 5-10 pm; $8-$18. **All Rooms:** Fee: movies. **Cards:** AE, DI, DS, MC, VI. Roll in showers. 🛏 ➤ ➤ ➤ CTV ✕ D S

HOMEWOOD SUITES-CUMBERLAND — Rates Subject to Change — Phone: 770/988-9449 ◆◆◆ 48
Suite Motel
Sun-Thurs [CP] — 1P: $96- 106 — 2P/1B: $105 — 2P/2B: $115
Fri & Sat [CP] — 1P: $89- 99 — 2P/1B: $89- 99 — 2P/2B: $99
Location: I-285, eastbound exit 13, westbound exit 14, 0.7 mi se on US 41 (Cobb Pkwy). 3200 Cobb Pkwy SW 30339. Fax: 770/933-9612. **Terms:** Sr. discount; pets, $75 extra charge. **Facility:** 124 rooms. Rates for up to 4 persons. Grocery shopping service; 3 stories; interior/exterior corridors. **Cards:** AE, DI, DS, MC, VI. 🛏 ➤ ➤ CTV ✕ 🅿 D S

J.W. MARRIOTT HOTEL AT LENOX — Rates Subject to Change — Phone: 404/262-3344 ◆◆◆◆ 97
Hotel
All Year — 1P: $144- 245 — 2P/1B: $144- 245 — 2P/2B: $144- 245
Location: Buckhead; I-85 exit 30 (southbound); exit 28 (northbound); 1.8 mi n. 3300 Lenox Rd NE 30326. Fax: 404/262-8689. **Terms:** Sr. discount; check-in 4 pm; no pets. **Facility:** 371 rooms. Rates for up to 4 persons; 25 stories; interior corridors. Fee: parking. **Dining:** Dining room; 6:30 am-10:30 pm; $12-$20. **All Rooms:** free & pay movies. **Cards:** AE, CB, DI, DS, JCB, MC, VI. ➤ ➤ CTV ✕ 🅿 D S

THE MARQUE OF ATLANTA HOTEL & SUITES — Phone: 770/396-6800 64
AAA SAVE
Mon-Thurs — 1P: $135- 179 — 2P/1B: $150- 194 — 2P/2B: $150- 194 — XP: $10 — F1
Fri-Sun 1/1-4/30 — 1P: $84- 104 — 2P/1B: $84- 114 — 2P/2B: $84- 114 — XP: $10 — F1
◆◆◆
Suite Hotel
Fri-Sun 12/1-12/31 & 5/1-11/30 — 1P: $89- 109 — 2P/1B: $89- 109 — 2P/2B: $89- 109 — XP: $10 — F1
Location: I-285 exit 21, (Ashford-Dunwoody), 0.5 mi n to Perimeter Center W, opposite Perimeter Mall. 111 Perimeter Center W 30346. Fax: 770/399-5514. **Terms:** No pets. **Facility:** 284 rooms. 12 stories; interior corridors; saunas; whirlpool. **Dining:** Restaurant; 6 am-10, noon-2 & 6-11 pm, Sat & Sun 7 am-10:30, noon-2 & 6-11 pm; $6-$17; cocktails. **Services:** area transportation, within 3 mi. Fee: coin laundry. **All Rooms:** free & pay movies. **Some Rooms:** coffeemakers; phones. **Cards:** AE, DI, DS, MC, VI. **Special Amenities:** Early check-in/late check-out and free room upgrade (subject to availability with advanced reservations). Roll in showers. ➤ 🦽 ➤ 🦽 CTV ✕ D S

(See map p. 202)

MASTERS ECONOMY INN SIX FLAGS
Phone: 404/696-4690   **111**

(AAA) SAVE ◆
Motor Inn

Fri & Sat 6/1-9/4	1P:	$60-	75	2P/1B:	$60-	75	2P/2B:	$60- 75 XP: $4	F16
Sun-Thurs 6/1-9/4	1P:	$40-	55	2P/1B:	$40-	55	2P/2B:	$45- 65 XP: $4	F16
12/1-5/31 & 9/5-11/30	1P:	$30-	50	2P/1B:	$30-	50	2P/2B:	$30- 50 XP: $4	F16

Location: I-20 exit 14, just n on SR 70. 4120 Fulton Industrial Blvd 30336. Fax: 404/696-8432. **Terms:** Small pets only. **Facility:** 169 rooms. Modest, unpretentious accommodations. 2-3 stories, no elevator; exterior corridors. **Dining:** Coffee shop; 24 hours; $4-$7. **All Rooms:** free movies. **Cards:** AE, CB, DI, DS, MC, VI. **Special Amenities:** Free local telephone calls. *(See color ad below)*

🛏️ 🏊 📶 CTV ✕ D

NORTHWEST ATLANTA HILTON
Phone: 770/953-9300   **36**

(AAA) SAVE ◆◆◆
Motor Inn

Mon-Thurs	1P:	$108-	132	2P/1B:	$118-	142	2P/2B:	$118- 142 XP: $10	F18
Fri-Sun	1P:	$89-	122	2P/1B:	$99-	132	2P/2B:	$99- 132 XP: $10	F18

Location: I-75 exit 110, Windy Hill Rd, just w to S Park Pl, just n. 2055 S Park Pl 30339. Fax: 770/953-9315. **Terms:** No pets. **Facility:** 222 rooms. Near corporate park area. 6 stories; interior corridors; luxury level rooms; whirlpool; small exercise room. **Dining & Entertainment:** Dining room, deli; 6:30 am-10:30 pm; $12-$18; cocktails/lounge. **Services:** valet laundry. **All Rooms:** coffeemakers, free & pay movies. **Some Rooms:** refrigerators. **Cards:** AE, CB, DI, DS, MC, VI. **Special Amenities:** Early check-in/late check-out and free newspaper. *(See color ad p 18)*

🏊 🏊 📶 ♿ CTV ✕ D S

RADISSON INN EXECUTIVE PARK-ATLANTA
Guaranteed Rates   **Phone: 404/321-4174**   **90**

◆◆◆
Motor Inn

All Year [CP]	1P:	$87-	125	2P/1B:	$87-	125	2P/2B:	$87- 125 XP: $10	F16

Location: I-85 exit 31, just w. 2061 N Druid Hills Rd NE 30329. Fax: 404/636-7264. **Terms:** Sr. discount; no pets. **Facility:** 208 rooms. 9 stories; interior corridors. **Dining:** Coffee shop; 6:30 am-10 & 5-11 pm; $5-$7. **All Rooms:** free & pay movies. **Cards:** AE, CB, DI, DS, MC, VI. *(See ad below)*

🏊 ♿ CTV ✕ 🎱 D S

RED ROOF INN-DRUID HILLS
Rates Subject to Change   **Phone: 404/321-1653**   **139**

◆◆
Motel

All Year	1P:	$40-	51	2P/1B:	$45-	61	2P/2B:	$49- 61 XP: $6	F18

Location: I-85N exit 31, just w. 1960 N Druid Hills Rd 30329. Fax: 404/248-9774. **Terms:** Small pets only. **Facility:** 115 rooms. 3 stories; exterior corridors. **All Rooms:** free & pay movies. **Cards:** AE, CB, DI, DS, MC, VI.

🛏️ CTV ✕ 🎱 D

RED ROOF INN-SIX FLAGS
Rates Subject to Change   **Phone: 404/696-4391**   **112**

◆◆
Motel

4/2-9/4	1P:	$40-	56	2P/1B:	$37-	56	2P/2B:	$53- 66 XP: $4	F18
12/1-4/1 & 9/5-11/30	1P:	$33-	56	2P/1B:	$37-	56	2P/2B:	$43- 65 XP: $4	F18

Location: 9 mi w on I-20 at Fulton Industrial Blvd exit 14, se corner. 4265 Shirley Dr SW 30336. Fax: 404/696-6372. **Terms:** Small pets only. **Facility:** 121 rooms. 3 stories; exterior corridors. **All Rooms:** free & pay movies. **Cards:** AE, CB, DI, DS, MC, VI.

🛏️ CTV ✕ D

(See map p. 202)

REGENCY SUITES HOTEL
Phone: 404/876-5003 **125**
All Year [CP]   1P: $85- 144   2P/1B: $85- 164   2P/2B: $95- 164   XP: $10   F16
Location: Midtown; I-75/85 10th St exit, just e. 975 W Peachtree St 30309. Fax: 404/817-7511.
Terms: Weekly/monthly rates; no pets. **Facility:** 96 rooms. European boutique style 1900's mid-rise apartment
building. 9 stories; interior corridors. Fee: parking. **Services:** Fee: coin laundry. **All Rooms:** coffeemakers,
efficiencies, microwaves, free movies, refrigerators. **Cards:** AE, CB, DI, DS, MC, VI. **Special Amenities:**
Free breakfast and free newspaper.

Apartment Motel

RENAISSANCE ATLANTA HOTEL DOWNTOWN   Rates Subject to Change   Phone: 404/881-6000 **128**
Mon-Thurs   1P: $165   2P/1B: $185   2P/2B: $185   XP: $20   F12
Fri-Sun   1P: $89   2P/1B: $89   2P/2B: $89   XP: $20   F12
Location: I-75 & I-85, exit 100, just e. 590 W Peachtree St NW 30308. Fax: 404/815-5350. **Terms:** Sr.
discount; check-in 4 pm; no pets. **Facility:** 504 rooms. Some rooms with private swimming pool, $350; 25 stories; interior cor-
ridors. Fee: parking. **Dining:** 2 restaurants; 6:30 am-midnight; $11-$25. **All Rooms:** free & pay movies. **Cards:** AE, CB, DI,
DS, JCB, MC, VI.

Hotel

RENAISSANCE WAVERLY HOTEL
Phone: 770/953-4500 **44**
All Year   1P: $174   2P/1B: $194   2P/2B: $194   XP: $20   F12
Location: I-285 w, exit 14 to Cobb Pkwy, just s on US 41; I-285 e, exit 13, just s on US 41. 2450 Galleria
Pkwy 30339. Fax: 770/953-0740. **Terms:** No pets. **Facility:** 521 rooms. Mid-rise connected to Galleria Mall &
Cobb Convention Center. Atrium draped with lush vines has a brass/glass elevator & suspended oversize hand
carved teak bells from Thailand. 14 stories; interior corridors; luxury level rooms; wading pool, sauna, steamroom, whirlpool, European spa treatments. Fee: racquetball courts. **Dining & Entertainment:** Dining room, restaurant; 6
am-11 pm; $14-$28; cocktails/lounge; Sun brunch 10:30 am-2:30 pm; 24-hour room service; entertainment. **Services:** valet
laundry; area transportation, within 1 mi. Fee: massage; valet parking. **All Rooms:** coffeemakers, free & pay movies.
Some Rooms: honor bars, refrigerators. Fee: VCP's. **Cards:** AE, CB, DI, DS, MC, VI.

Hotel

RESIDENCE INN BY MARRIOTT   Rates Subject to Change   Phone: 404/252-5066 **68**
All Year [CP]   1P: $119   2P/1B: $129   2P/2B: $129- 149   XP: $10   F18
Location: I-285E exit 18, 0.5 mi n on Glenridge to Hammond, 0.3 mi e to Barfield Rd; I-285W exit 20
Peachtree Dunwoody Rd, 0.5 mi n to Hammond Dr, just w to Barfield Rd. 6096 Barfield Rd 30328.
Fax: 404/851-1723. **Terms:** Pets, $100-$150 extra charge. **Facility:** 128 rooms. 2 stories; exterior corridors.
All Rooms: kitchens, free & pay movies. **Cards:** AE, DI, DS, MC, VI.

Apartment Motel

RESIDENCE INN BY MARRIOTT-BUCKHEAD   Rates Subject to Change   Phone: 404/239-0677 **104**
All Year [CP]   1P: $145   2P/1B: $145   2P/2B: $175
Location: I-85 exit 28, 1.5 mi n. 2960 Piedmont Rd NE 30305. Fax: 404/262-9638. **Terms:** Pets, $100 dep
req. **Facility:** 136 rooms. 2 stories; exterior corridors. **All Rooms:** kitchens, free movies. **Cards:** AE, DI, DS,
MC, VI.

Apartment Motel

RESIDENCE INN BY MARRIOTT MIDTOWN   Rates Subject to Change   Phone: 404/872-8885 **135**
All Year [CP]   1P: $124   2P/1B: $154   2P/2B: $154
Location: Midtown; I-75/I-85 10th St exit, just e to W Peachtree St, just n. 1041 W Peachtree St 30309.
Fax: 404/872-8885. **Terms:** Reserv deposit; pets, $100-$150 extra charge. **Facility:** 66 rooms. Rates for 2 to
5 persons; 7 stories; interior corridors. **All Rooms:** efficiencies, free movies. **Cards:** AE, CB, DI, DS, JCB,
MC, VI.

Apartment Motel

RESIDENCE INN BY MARRIOTT PERIMETER EAST   Rates Subject to Change   Phone: 404/455-4446 **81**
Sun-Thurs [CP]   1P: $89   2P/1B: $89   2P/2B: $107
Fri & Sat [CP]   1P: $69   2P/1B: $69   2P/2B: $99
Location: I-285N exit 22; just e on Savoy Drive. 1901 Savoy Dr 30341. Fax: 404/451-5183. **Terms:** Pets,
$82.50-$125 extra charge. **Facility:** 144 rooms. Rates for up to 4 persons; 2 stories; exterior corridors.
All Rooms: kitchens, free movies. **Cards:** AE, CB, DI, DS, JCB, MC, VI.

Apartment Motel

THE RITZ-CARLTON, BUCKHEAD
Phone: 404/237-2700 **92**
All Year   1P: $180- 300   2P/1B: $180- 300   2P/2B: $180- 300
Location: I-85 exit; 1.8 mi n of Cheshire Bridge-Lenox Rd, exit 28 off I-85; opposite Lenox Square Mall.
3434 Peachtree Rd NE 30326. Fax: 404/240-0078. **Terms:** Package plans; no pets. **Facility:** 553 rooms. Timeless Ritz elegance: mahogany paneling, crystal chandeliers, fine antiques, Old World gilt-framed oils, hand-
woven rugs, marble floors in extensive yet intimate public areas. Gracious & attentive service. 22 stories;
interior corridors; luxury level rooms; saunas, steamroom, whirlpool; health food bar. Fee: parking. **Dining &
Entertainment:** Dining room, restaurant, coffee shop; 6:30 am-11 pm; $9-$25; health conscious menu items;
cocktails/lounge; afternoon tea; also, The Dining Room, see separate listing; entertainment. **Services:** valet laundry; area transportation, within 3 mi. Fee: massage; valet parking. **All Rooms:** honor bars, free & pay
movies, safes. **Some Rooms:** refrigerators, VCP's. Fee: whirlpools. **Cards:** AE, CB, DI, DS, JCB, MC, VI. *(See ad p 197)*

Hotel

SHELLMONT BED & BREAKFAST LODGE   Guaranteed Rates   Phone: 404/872-9290 **138**
All Year [BP]   1P: $85- 120   2P/1B: $105- 120   2P/2B: $105- 150   XP: $23
Location: Midtown; I-75/85 northbound exit 99 (Piedmont Ave); southbound exit 100 (North Ave) e to
Piedmont Ave then n. 821 Piedmont Ave NE 30308. Fax: 404/872-5379. **Terms:** Age restrictions may apply;
reserv deposit, 7 day notice; 2 night min stay, weekends; no pets. **Facility:** 5 rooms. 2 stories; interior corri-
dors; designated smoking area. **Dining:** Fruit basket & soft drinks on arrival. **Some Rooms:** kitchen. **Cards:** AE, DI, JCB,
MC, VI.

Historic Bed & Breakfast

SHERATON COLONY SQUARE HOTEL   Rates Subject to Change   Phone: 404/892-6000 **133**
All Year   1P: $98   2P/1B: $98   2P/2B: $98   XP: $20   F
Location: Midtown; I-75/85 exit 14th St, 0.5 mi e. 188 14th St 30361. Fax: 404/872-9192. **Terms:** Sr.
discount; no pets. **Facility:** 467 rooms. 27 stories; interior corridors. Fee: parking. **Dining:** Restaurant, 6
am-11 pm, Fri & Sat-midnight; $9-$23. **All Rooms:** free & pay movies. **Some Rooms:** A/C. **Cards:** AE, DI, DS, JCB, MC.
Roll in showers.

Hotel

(See map p. 202)

SHERATON SUITES GALLERIA — Rates Subject to Change — Phone: 770/955-3900 🆎
◆◆◆ All Year [BP] 1P: $115 2P/1B: $115 2P/2B: $125 XP: $15 F17
Suite Hotel **Location:** I-285, exit 14 westbound; exit 13 eastbound; just s on US 41 (Cobb Pkwy). 2844 Cobb Pkwy SE 30339. Fax: 770/916-3165. **Terms:** No pets. **Facility:** 278 rooms. 17 stories; interior corridors.
Dining: Restaurant; 6:30 am-10:30 pm; $11-$25. **All Rooms:** free & pay movies. **Cards:** AE, CB, DI, DS, JCB, MC, VI.

🛏 🛏 ➕ CTV ✕ 🐾 D S

SUMMERFIELD SUITES HOTEL — Rates Subject to Change — Phone: 404/250-0110 🆖
◆◆◆ Sun-Thurs [BP] 1P: $129 2P/1B: $129 2P/2B: $159 XP: $15 F16
Suite Motel Fri & Sat [BP] 1P: $99 2P/1B: $99 2P/2B: $119 XP: $15 F16
Location: From I-285, exit 17; 1 mi n on Roswell Rd; & 1 mi e. 760 Mt Vernon Hwy NE 30328.
Fax: 404/250-9335. **Terms:** Sr. discount; reserv deposit; pets, $100-150 extra charge. **Facility:** 122 rooms. 2-3 stories; no elevator; interior/exterior corridors. **All Rooms:** free movies. **Cards:** AE, DI, DS, MC, VI.

🛏 🛏 ➕ CTV ✕ 🐾 D S

SUMMERFIELD SUITES HOTEL BUCKHEAD — Rates Subject to Change — Phone: 404/262-7880 🄌
◆◆◆ Sun-Thurs [BP] 1P: $159- 179 2P/1B: $159- 179 2P/2B: $189- 229 XP: $15 F12
Apartment Fri & Sat [BP] 1P: $109- 129 2P/1B: $109- 129 2P/2B: $129- 159 XP: $15 F12
Motel **Location:** Buckhead area; Pharr Rd & Maple Dr, just w of Piedmont. 505 Pharr Rd 30305.
Fax: 404/262-3734. **Terms:** Pets, fee varies. **Facility:** 88 rooms. 3 stories, no elevator; exterior corridors.
All Rooms: free movies. **Cards:** AE, DI, DS, MC, VI.

🛏 🛏 ➕ CTV ✕ 🐾 D S

SWISSOTEL — Phone: 404/365-0065 🄡
🅐🅐🅐 [SAVE] All Year 1P: $185- 210 2P/1B: $220- 270 2P/2B: $220- 270 XP: $25 F13
◆◆◆◆ **Location:** Buckhead; adjacent to Lenox Mall. 3391 Peachtree Rd NE 30326. Fax: 404/365-8787.
Hotel **Terms:** Reserv deposit; no pets. **Facility:** 349 rooms. White metal/glass high rise with elegant, intimate public areas. Excellent art collection of contemporary & post modern works throughout. Rich Biedermeier-style room furnishings. 22 stories; interior corridors; saunas, steamroom. Fee: parking; golf & tennis privileges. **Dining &**
Entertainment: Cocktail lounge; 24-hour room service; also, The Palm Restaurant, see separate listing. **Services:** valet laundry; area transportation, within 3 mi. Fee: massage; valet parking. **All Rooms:** honor bars, coffeemakers, free & pay movies. **Some Rooms:** 2 efficiencies, refrigerators, whirlpools. Fee: VCP's. **Cards:** AE, DI, DS, MC, VI. **Special Amenities:**
Free newspaper.

🛏 🍽 ➕ 🕂 CTV ✕ 🐾 D S

TERRACE GARDEN BUCKHEAD — Rates Subject to Change — Phone: 404/261-9250 🄥
◆◆◆ 7/4-8/18 1P: $105- 160 2P/1B: $125- 195 2P/2B: $125- 195 XP: $15 F18
Hotel 12/1-7/3 & 8/19-11/30 1P: $135- 190 2P/1B: $145- 190 2P/2B: $145- 190 XP: $15 F18
Location: I-85, exit 30 (southbound), exit 28 (northbound). 1.8 mi n. 3405 Lenox Rd NE 30326.
Fax: 404/848-7391. **Terms:** Sr. discount; reserv deposit; no pets. **Facility:** 360 rooms. Handling fee imposed; 10 stories; interior corridors. Fee: parking. **Dining:** Restaurant; 6:30 am-2 & 5-10 pm; $11-$24. **All Rooms:** free & pay movies. **Cards:** AE, CB, DI, DS, JCB, MC, VI.

🛏 🛏 ➕ CTV ✕ 🐾 D S

UNIVERSITY INN AT EMORY — Phone: 404/634-7327 🄦
🅐🅐🅐 [SAVE] All Year [CP] 1P: $64- 114 2P/1B: $64- 114 2P/2B: $94- 120 XP: $15 F12
◆◆ **Location:** I-85 exit 32, 3.8 mi s on Clairmont Rd to N Decatur Rd, then 0.8 mi w; opposite Emory University
Apartment Rd Hospital. 1767 N Decatur Rd 30307. Fax: 404/320-7023. **Terms:** Pets, $15 extra charge. **Facility:** 49
Motel rooms. Close to Emory University. Office hours 6:30 am-11 pm. Many spacious, tastefully appointed rooms. 2-3 stories, no elevator; interior/exterior corridors; designated smoking area; small pool. **Services:** area transportation, to campus. Fee: coin laundry. **All Rooms:** free movies, refrigerators, combo or shower baths. **Some Rooms:** coffeemakers, 8 efficiencies, 9 kitchens, microwaves. **Cards:** AE, CB, DI, DS, MC, VI. **Special Amenities:**
Free breakfast and free local telephone calls. Roll in showers. 🛏 🍽 ➕ CTV ✕ 🐾 D S

THE WESTIN ATLANTA NORTH — Rates Subject to Change — Phone: 770/395-3900 🄧
◆◆◆ Tue & Wed 1P: $129 2P/1B: $129 2P/2B: $129 XP: $10 F12
Hotel Thurs-Mon 1P: $95 2P/1B: $95 2P/2B: $95 XP: $10 F12
Location: I-285W, exit 20; I-285E, exit 18 (Glenridge Dr) just n to Hammond Dr, just e. 7 Concourse Pkwy 30328. Fax: 770/395-3935. **Terms:** Sr. discount; no pets. **Facility:** 369 rooms. Weekend rates for up to 4 persons; 1 suite with whirlpool & sauna. Handling fee imposed; 20 stories; interior corridors. **Dining:** Restaurant; 6:30 am-11 pm; $14-$23.
All Rooms: free & pay movies. **Cards:** AE, DS, MC, VI. *(See color ad below)* 🛏 ➕ CTV ✕ 🐾 D S

THE WOODRUFF BED & BREAKFAST INN — Guaranteed Rates — Phone: 404/875-9449 🄦
◆◆ All Year [BP] 1P: $89- 129 2P/1B: $99- 149 2P/2B: $109 XP: $10 F5
Historic Bed **Location:** I-75-85 exit 102 (southbound), exit 101 (northbound), 0.8 mi e on 10th Ave to Myrtle, 0.7 mi s.
& Breakfast 223 Ponce de Leon Ave 30308. Fax: 404/870-0042. **Terms:** Sr. discount; no pets. **Facility:** 9 rooms. 3 stories, no elevator; interior corridors; designated smoking area. **Cards:** AE, DS, MC, VI.

✕ D

(See map p. 202)

WYNDHAM GARDEN HOTEL AT VININGS   Rates Subject to Change   Phone: 770/432-5555   **50**
◆◆◆   Sun-Thurs [BP]   1P: $110   2P/1B: $120   2P/2B: $120   XP: $10   F18
Hotel   Fri & Sat [EP]   1P: $79   2P/1B: $89   2P/2B: $89   XP: $10   F18
Location: I-285 exit 12, 0.6 mi e. 2857 Paces Ferry Rd 30339. Fax: 770/436-5558. **Terms:** No pets.
Facility: 159 rooms. 4 stories; interior corridors. **Dining:** Restaurant; 6:30 am-2:30 & 5-10 pm, Sat & Sun 7 am-2 & 5-10
pm; $10-$19. **All Rooms:** Fee: movies. **Some Rooms:** 9 kitchens. **Cards:** AE, CB, DI, DS, JCB, MC, VI.
(See color ad p 207)   ⊶ ⊕ CTV ✕ 🖉 D S

WYNDHAM GARDEN HOTEL BUCKHEAD   Rates Subject to Change   Phone: 404/231-1234   **88**
◆◆◆   Sun-Thurs   1P: $119   2P/1B: $129   2P/2B: $129   XP: $10   F18
Hotel   Fri & Sat   1P: $79   2P/1B: $79   2P/2B: $79   XP: $10   F18
Location: I-85, exit 30, 3 mi n on Lenox Rd to Peachtree Rd NE, 0.8 mi sw. 3340 Peachtree Rd NE 30326.
Fax: 404/231-5236. **Terms:** No pets. **Facility:** 221 rooms. 6 stories; interior corridors. **Dining:** Restaurant; 6:30 am-10 pm,
Sat & Sun from 7 am; $10-$23. **All Rooms:** free movies. **Cards:** AE, CB, DI, DS, JCB, MC, VI. *(See color ad p 207)*
⊕ CTV ✕ 🖉 D S

WYNDHAM GARDEN HOTEL PERIMETER CENTER   Rates Subject to Change   Phone: 404/252-3344   **72**
◆◆◆   Sun-Thurs [BP]   1P: $108   2P/1B: $118   2P/2B: $118   XP: $10   F18
Motor Inn   Fri & Sat [EP]   1P: $64   2P/1B: $64   2P/2B: $64   XP: $10   F18
Location: I-285 westbound exit 20, just n on Peachtree-Dunwoody Rd, 0.5 mi w; eastbound exit 18; 0.5 n
on Glenridge Dr, just e. 800 Hammond Dr NE 30328. Fax: 404/843-1228. **Terms:** No pets. **Facility:** 143 rooms. 4 stories; in-
terior corridors. **Dining:** Restaurant; 6:30-11 am, 11-2 pm & 5-10 pm, Sat & Sun 6:30 am-2 & 5-10 pm; breakfast & lunch
buffet avail; $10-$20. **All Rooms:** Fee: movies. **Cards:** AE, CB, DI, DS, JCB, MC, VI. *(See color ad p 207)*
⊶ ⊶ ⊕ CTV ✕ 🖉 D S

WYNDHAM HOTEL MIDTOWN ATLANTA   Rates Subject to Change   Phone: 404/873-4800   **124**
◆◆◆   Sun-Thurs   1P: $107   2P/1B: $117   2P/2B: $117   XP: $10-20   F18
Hotel   Fri & Sat   1P: $79   2P/1B: $79   2P/2B: $79   XP: $10-20   F18
Location: I-75/85, exit 10th St, just e. 125 10th St 30309. Fax: 404/870-1530. **Terms:** No pets. **Facility:** 191
rooms. Rates for up to 4 persons; 11 stories; interior corridors. Fee: parking. **Dining:** Restaurant; 6:30 am-10 pm; $10-$23.
All Rooms: free & pay movies. **Cards:** AE, CB, DI, DS, JCB, MC, VI. *(See color ad p 207)*   ⊶ ⊕ CTV ✕ 🖉 D

RESTAURANTS

THE ABBEY   **Dinner:** $17-$28   Phone: 404/876-8831   **103**
◆◆◆   **Location:** Jct of Ponce de Leon Ave & Piedmont Rd; in midtown. 163 Ponce De Leon Ave 30308. **Hours:** 6
Regional   pm-10 pm. **Reservations:** suggested. **Features:** casual dress; cocktails & lounge; entertainment; valet
Continental   parking; a la carte. Converted Gothic church, served by monk robed waiters. **Cards:** AE, DI, DS, MC, VI.
✕

ACACIA   **Dinner:** $20-$28   Phone: 770/395-3900   **42**
◆◆◆   **Location:** I-285W exit 20; I-285E exit 18 (Glenridge Dr) just n to Hammond Dr, just e; in Doubletree Hotel at
American   Concourse. 7 Concourse Pkwy 30328. **Hours:** 6 pm-10 pm, Fri & Sat-11 pm. Closed major holidays & Sun.
Reservations: suggested. **Features:** cocktails; valet parking; a la carte. Small, candle-lit dining room with
elegant club-like ambience. Private dining room seating 12 avail. Jacket suggested. **Cards:** AE, DI, DS, MC, VI.   ✕

ANTHONY'S   **Dinner:** $18-$35   Phone: 404/262-7379   **83**
◆◆◆   **Location:** Just s of jct of Piedmont & Peachtree rds. 3109 Piedmont Rd 30305. **Hours:** 6 pm-10:30 pm.
South   Closed major holidays & Sun. **Reservations:** suggested. **Features:** dressy casual; cocktails & lounge; valet
American   parking; a la carte. Authentically restored plantation home. Traditional menu served in a charming
atmosphere. **Cards:** AE, DI, DS, MC, VI.   ✕

ATLANTA FISH MARKET   **Lunch:** $9-$28   **Dinner:** $14-$28   Phone: 404/262-3165   **80**
◆◆◆   **Location:** Jct Peachtree & Pharr rds, 2 blks e; in Buckhead. 265 Pharr Rd 30305. **Hours:** 11 am-2:30 &
Seafood   5:30-11 pm, Fri & Sat-midnight, Sun 4:30 pm-10 pm. Closed: 11/26 & 12/25. **Reservations:** suggested; for
dinner. **Features:** casual dress; carryout; cocktails & lounge; valet parking; a la carte. Bustling ambience of a
warm, casual, Savannah-style fish market. Wide variety of fresh fish entrees plus some pasta, chops, chicken & duck.
Excellent dessert. **Cards:** AE, CB, DI, DS, JCB, MC, VI.   ✕

AZIO   **Lunch:** $6-$10   **Dinner:** $11-$16   Phone: 404/233-7626   **46**
◆◆   **Location:** 8 mi n of downtown, just off Peachtree St; in the heart of "Buckhead". 220 Pharr Rd 30305.
Northern   **Hours:** 11 am-11 pm. **Reservations:** accepted. **Features:** casual dress; children's menu; health conscious
Italian   menu; carryout; cocktails & lounge; street parking & valet parking. Full service Italian cuisine with pasta,
pizza, veal, seafood & chicken also featured. Bistro atmosphere with handsome decor. **Cards:** AE, CB, DI,
DS, MC, VI.   ✕

BABETTE'S CAFE   **Dinner:** $9-$16   Phone: 404/523-9121   **120**
◆◆   **Location:** From jct Ponce de Leon & Highland Ave, 0.5 mi s. 471 N Highland Ave 30307. **Hours:** 6 pm-10
American   pm, Fri & Sat-11 pm, Sun 10:30 am-2:30 & 5-9 pm. Closed major holidays & Mon. **Features:** casual dress;
Sunday brunch; carryout; cocktails; a la carte. A friendly neighborhood bistro serving European provincial
cuisine. Cassoulet, paella, artichoke & olive ravioli are popular. Homemade chocolate bread pudding with banana ice cream.
Cards: AE, DI, DS, MC, VI.   ✕

BACCHANALIA   **Dinner:** $40-$54   Phone: 404/365-0410   **84**
◆◆◆   **Location:** In Buckhead; just s of jct Peachtree Rd & Piedmont Rd NE. 3125 Piedmont Rd 30305. **Hours:** 6
Northern   pm-10 pm. Closed: Sun & Mon. **Reservations:** suggested. **Features:** casual dress; health conscious menu
American   items; beer & wine only; prix fixe. Small Victorian cottage serving New American cuisine with Northern
California influence. Menu changes weekly. Excellent food preparation & presentation. Smoke free premises.
Cards: AE, DI, MC, VI.   ✕

BASIL'S MEDITERRANEAN CAFE   **Lunch:** $6-$10   **Dinner:** $12-$18   Phone: 404/233-9755   **24**
◆◆   **Location:** Off Pharr Rd, just s on Grandview Ave; in the heart of Buckhead. 2985 Grandview Ave 30305.
Ethnic   **Hours:** 11:30 am-2:30 & 6-10 pm, Fri & Sat-11 pm. Closed major holidays & Sun. **Reservations:** accepted.
Features: casual dress; health conscious menu; carryout; cocktails & lounge; a la carte. Appreciate the
atmosphere as much as the food in this quaint little cafe serving Mediterranean cuisine & great dessert. **Cards:** AE, CB, DI,
DS, MC, VI.   ✕

(See map p. 202)

THE BISTRO AT ANDREWS SQUARE   **Dinner:** $25-$40   **Phone:** 404/231-5733   56
◆◆◆   **Location:** Buckhead; from jct W Paces Ferry & Peach Tree rds, 2 blks w on Paces Ferry to E Andrews Dr
French   NW, then 2 blks n. 56 E Andrews Dr NW 30305. **Hours:** 6 pm-11 pm. Closed: Sun, Mon, 1/1 & 12/25.
        Reservations: suggested. **Features:** carryout; cocktails. Country French cuisine served in sophisticated
bistro. Patio dining. Well-chosen wine list. Espresso/cappuccino. **Cards:** DI, DS, MC, VI.   ✕

BLUE RIDGE GRILL   **Lunch:** $9-$16   **Dinner:** $16-$26   **Phone:** 404/233-5030   34
ⱲⱲⱲ   **Location:** I-75 exit 107, ne corner. 1261 W Paces Ferry Rd 30327. **Hours:** 11:30 am-2:30 & 5:30-11 pm, Sat
        from 5:30 pm. Closed major holidays. **Reservations:** accepted. **Features:** casual dress; Sunday brunch;
◆◆◆   cocktails & lounge; valet parking. Elegantly rustic Adirondack style atmosphere, featuring upscale southern
Regional   cuisine. Offers many fresh organic vegetables. **Cards:** AE, DI, DS, MC, VI.
American

BONE'S RESTAURANT   **Lunch:** $12-$21   **Dinner:** $20-$37   **Phone:** 404/237-2663   65
ⱲⱲⱲ   **Location:** In Buckhead; from jct Piedmont Rd NE & Peachtree Rd NE, just e. 3130 Piedmont Rd NE 30305.
        Hours: 11:30 am-2:30 & 5-11 pm, Sat & Sun from 6 pm. Closed major holidays. **Reservations:** suggested.
◆◆◆   **Features:** casual dress; cocktails & lounge; valet parking; a la carte. Featuring aged prime beef, fresh
American   seafood, lamb chops & veal. New York club with comfortable ambience. Private dining rooms avail.
        Cards: AE, CB, DI, DS, MC, VI.   ✕

BUCKHEAD DINER   **Lunch:** $4-$14   **Dinner:** $10-$17   **Phone:** 404/262-3336   86
◆◆◆   **Location:** In Buckhead; at corner of Piedmont Rd NE & East Paces Ferry Rd. 3073 Piedmont Rd NE 30305.
American   **Hours:** 11 am-midnight, Sun 10 am-10 pm. Closed: 1/1, 11/26 & 12/25. **Features:** casual dress; Sunday
        brunch; carryout; cocktails & lounge; valet parking; a la carte. Reproduction of luxury railroad dining car.
Bustling, energetic ambience. **Cards:** AE, DI, DS, MC, VI.   ✕

THE CABIN   **Lunch:** $8-$11   **Dinner:** $18-$28   **Phone:** 404/315-7676   26
◆◆   **Location:** I-85 exit 30 southbound, just w to Buford Hwy, 0.4 mi n; I-85 exit 28 northbound, 2.4 mi n. 2678
Steak and   Buford Hwy 30324. **Hours:** 11:30 am-2:30 & 5:30-10 pm, Fri & Sat-11 pm. Closed major holidays & Sun.
Seafood   **Reservations:** suggested. **Features:** dressy casual; cocktails & lounge; valet parking. A rustic & cozy
        atmosphere serving prime cuts of beef. **Cards:** AE, CB, DI, DS, MC, VI.   ✕

CAFE INTERMEZZO   **Lunch:** $7-$12   **Dinner:** $8-$18   **Phone:** 404/355-0411   27
◆◆   **Location:** 1845 Peachtree Rd 30309. **Hours:** 11:30 am-3 am, Fri-4 am, Sat 10:30 am-4 am, Sun 10:30
American   am-3 am. **Features:** casual dress; carryout; cocktails & lounge; a la carte. Sophisticated European coffe bar
        & restaurant. A wide range of dessert specialties. Saturday & Sunday brunch. **Cards:** AE, DI, DS, MC, VI.
        ✕

CAFE PREGO   **Lunch:** $5-$11   **Dinner:** $9-$16   **Phone:** 404/252-0032   50
ⱲⱲⱲ   **Location:** I-285, exit 17, 3 mi s on Roswell Rd in Chastain Sq. 4279 Roswell Rd 30342. **Hours:** 11:30 am-2
        & 5:30-11 pm, Mon & Sat from 5:30 pm. Closed: Sun, 1/1, 11/26 & 12/25. **Reservations:** suggested;
◆◆◆   weekends. **Features:** casual dress; carryout; cocktails; a la carte. Italian cuisine graciously served in
Italian   comfortable atmosphere. **Cards:** AE, DI, DS, MC, VI.

CAFE TU TU TANGO   **Lunch:** $7-$15   **Dinner:** $7-$15   **Phone:** 404/841-6222   28
◆◆   **Location:** N on Peachtree & E on Pharr Rd. 220 Pharr Rd 30305. **Hours:** 11:30 am-1 am, Sat-2 am, Sun-11
Ethnic   pm. Closed: 1/1 & 12/25. **Features:** casual dress; Sunday brunch; children's menu; carryout; cocktails &
        lounge; entertainment; fee for valet parking. Tapas style dining with food from all over the world & a truly
unique eatery. **Cards:** AE, DI, MC, VI.   ✕

CAMILLE'S   **Lunch:** $9-$20   **Phone:** 404/872-7203   29
◆◆   **Location:** 1186 N Highland Ave 30306. **Hours:** 5:30 pm-11 pm. Closed: 11/26. **Features:** casual dress;
Italian   carryout; cocktail lounge; beer & wine only. Featuring "Old World" cuisine of pasta, pizza, seafood, veal &
        chicken. Loud, bustling atmosphere. Outdoor dining avail. **Cards:** AE, DI, MC, VI.   ✕

(See map p. 202)

CANOE
◆◆◆
American
Lunch: $7-$13   **Dinner:** $16-$20   **Phone:** 404/432-2808   37
Location: I-285, exit 12, 1 mi se, then 1 mi e. 4199 Paces Ferry Rd NW 30339. **Hours:** 11:30 am-2:30 & 5-10:30 pm, Fri 11:30 am-2:30 & 5:30-11:30 pm, Sat 5:30 pm-11:30 pm, Sun 10:30 am-2: 30 & 5:30-11:30 pm. Closed major holidays. **Reservations:** suggested. **Features:** Sunday brunch; carryout; cocktails; valet parking; a la carte. Contemporary American cuisine. **Cards:** AE, DI, DS, MC, VI.   ✕

CHEFS' CAFE
◆◆◆
American
Lunch: $6-$9   **Dinner:** $8-$18   **Phone:** 404/872-2284   125
Location: Adjacent to Comfort Inn-Buckhead. 2115 Piedmont Rd NE 30324. **Hours:** 11:30 am-2 & 6-10 pm, Fri & Sat 6 pm-11 pm, Sun 11 am-2:30 & 6-10 pm, Sun-Thur 6 pm-7 pm prix fixe. Closed: 1/1, 11/26, 12/25. **Reservations:** suggested. **Features:** casual dress; Sunday brunch; health conscious menu items; carryout cocktails; a la carte, also prix fixe. Intimate atmosphere. Fresh cuisine with a California influence. **Cards:** AE, DI, DS, MC, VI.   ✕

CHOPS
◆◆◆
Steakhouse
Lunch: $7-$15   **Dinner:** $16-$30   **Phone:** 404/262-2675   60
Location: Buckhead; on W Paces Ferry Rd, just w of Peachtree Rd; in Buckhead Plaza. 70 W Paces Ferry Rd 30305. **Hours:** 11:30 am-2:30 & 5:30-11 pm, Fri-midnight, Sat 5:30 pm-midnight, Sun 5:30 pm-10 pm Closed major holidays. **Reservations:** suggested. **Features:** casual dress; cocktails & lounge; valet parking; a la carte. Cosmopolitan New York style steakhouse with exhibition kitchen. Extensive wine list. **Cards:** AE, CB, DI, DS, MC, VI.

CHOPSTIX RESTAURANT
◆◆◆
Chinese
Lunch: $5-$11   **Dinner:** $11-$23   **Phone:** 404/255-4868   51
Location: I-285, exit 17, 2.6 mi s; in Chastain Square. 4279 Roswell Rd 30342. **Hours:** 11:30 am-2:15 & 6-11 pm, Sat & Sun from 6 pm. Closed: 1/1, 11/26, 12/25. **Reservations:** suggested; weekends. **Features:** casual dress; health conscious menu items; carryout; cocktails & lounge; entertainment; minimum charge-$10 per person dinner, $4 per person lunch; a la carte. Unique blend of old & new cuisines using the freshest & best ingredients. Stir-fry lobster, venison with garlic brown sauce; alligator. Gracious service. **Cards:** AE, DI, DS, MC, VI.   ✕

CIBOULETTE
◆◆◆
French
Dinner: $18-$30   **Phone:** 404/874-7713   112
Location: Midtown; se corner of jct Monroe Dr & Piedmont Ave, NE. 1529 Piedmont Ave NE 30324. **Hours:** 6 pm-10 pm, Fri & Sat 5:30 pm-11 pm. Closed: Sun. **Reservations:** suggested. **Features:** semi-formal attire; cocktails & lounge; a la carte. Upscale bistro serving both classic & innovative cuisine. Excellent wine list. Smoke free premises. **Cards:** AE, CB, DI, DS, MC, VI.   ✕

THE COACH & SIX RESTAURANT
◆◆◆
Steakhouse
Dinner: $20-$30   **Phone:** 404/872-6666   96
Location: I-75/85, exit 101, 10th St to Peachtree St, 0.5 mi n. 1776 Peachtree St NW at 26th St 30309 **Hours:** 5:30 pm-10 pm, Fri & Sat-10:30 pm. Closed: Sun, 1/1 & 12/25. **Reservations:** suggested **Features:** cocktails & lounge; valet parking; a la carte. Long established. Elegant yet relaxed atmosphere & service. Business casual attire. **Cards:** AE, CB, DI, DS, MC, VI.

THE COUNTRY PLACE
◆◆
American
Phone: 404/881-0144   30
Location: I-75 & I-85, 10th & 14th St exit, located in Colony Square at Peachtree & 14th sts. 1197 Peachtree St 30361. **Hours:** 11:30 am-2:30 & 5:30-11 pm, Fri-midnight, Sat 5:30 pm-midnight, Sun 11 am-3 & 5:30-10 pm; Pianist entertainment Tue-Sat evenings. Closed: 11/26 & 12/25. **Reservations:** accepted **Features:** cocktails & lounge. **Cards:** AE, CB, DI, DS, MC, VI.

THE CRAB HOUSE SEAFOOD RESTAURANT
◆◆
Seafood
Lunch: $8-$11   **Dinner:** $13-$31   **Phone:** 404/872-0011   102
Location: 0.5 mi ne; in Rio Mall. 595 Piedmont Ave N 30308. **Hours:** 11:30 am-10 pm, Fri & Sat-11 pm, Sun brunch 11 am-3 pm. Closed: 11/26, 12/24 & 12/25. **Features:** casual dress; children's menu; carryout; salad bar; cocktails & lounge; a la carte. Market fresh seafood also some chicken & beef. **Cards:** AE, DI, DS, MC VI.

DANTE'S DOWN THE HATCH
AAA
◆◆
Ethnic
Dinner: $11-$25   **Phone:** 404/266-1600   136
Location: 3380 Peachtree Rd 30326. **Hours:** 4 pm-1 am, Sun 5 pm-11:30 pm. **Reservations:** suggested **Features:** casual dress; cocktails & lounge. Watch crocodiles swim in a moat surrounding an 18th century sailing vessel. Live stellar jazz trio. Cuisine consisting of various fondues including beef, pork chicken, shrimp, chinese dumplings, cheese & vegtable. **Cards:** AE, DI, DS, MC, VI.   ✕

THE DINING ROOM
AAA
◆◆◆◆◆
Nouvelle
American
Dinner: $70   **Phone:** 404/237-2700   67
Location: I-85 exit; 1.8 mi n of Cheshire Bridge-Lenox Rd, exit 28 off I-85; in The Ritz-Carlton, Buckhead 3434 Peachtree Rd NE 30326. **Hours:** 6 pm-9:30 pm. Closed: Sun, 1/1 & 12/25. **Reservations:** suggested **Features:** formal attire; cocktail lounge; entertainment; fee for parking; valet parking; prix fixe, a la carte. Silk upholstery, Old World oils on mahogany panelling, intimate lighting, exotic flowers & soft classical music Internationally renowned chef creates traditional European haute cuisine with American overtones. Smoke free premises. **Cards:** AE, DI, DS, JCB, MC, VI. *(See ad p 197)*   ✕

FLORENCIA
◆◆◆◆
Continental
Dinner: $23-$29   **Phone:** 404/881-9898   105
Location: Midtown; I-75/85, exit 14th St, 3 blks e, in the Four Seasons Hotel Atlanta. 75 14th St 30309 **Hours:** 6 pm-10:30 pm, Fri & Sat-11 pm. Closed: Sun & 1/1. **Reservations:** suggested. **Features:** dressy casual; cocktails & lounge; entertainment; valet parking; a la carte, also prix fixe. Elegant, formal service in a rich yet warm atmosphere. Highly unique & creative food preparation & presentation. Smoke free premises. **Cards:** AE, CB DI, DS, JCB, MC, VI.   ✕

GEORGIA GRILLE
◆◆
Southwest
American
Dinner: $9-$20   **Phone:** 404/352-3517   137
Location: Just s of Peachtree Rd & Peachtree Battle Ave; in Peachtree Sq. 2290 Peachtree Rd 30309 **Hours:** 6 pm-10 pm, Fri & Sat-11 pm. Closed major holidays. **Features:** casual dress; carryout; beer & wine only. Pleasant sunny bistro atmosphere, with visible kitchen. Patio dining avail. Features creative Southwestern cuisine. Eclectic wine selection. Smoke free premises. **Cards:** AE, MC, VI.   ✕

GRAND CHINA RESTAURANT
◆◆
Chinese
Lunch: $5-$7   **Dinner:** $7-$21   **Phone:** 404/231-8690   138
Location: Buckhead; from jct Peachtree Rd & W Paces Ferry, 3 blks s. 2975 Peachtree Rd 30305 **Hours:** 11:30 am-10:45 pm, Fri-11 pm, Sat noon-11 pm, Sun noon-10 pm. Closed: 11/26 **Reservations:** accepted. **Features:** casual dress; children's menu; carryout; cocktails & lounge; minimum charge-$5. Wide variety of Hunan, Cantonese, Szechuan & Mandarin entrees. Comfortable, casual ambience. **Cards:** AE CB, DS, MC, VI.   ✕

(See map p. 202)

THE HEDGEROSE HEIGHTS INN **Dinner:** $16-$25 **Phone:** 404/233-7673 78
◆◆◆ **Location:** In Buckhead; from jct Piedmont Rd & E Paces Ferry Rd NE, just w. 490 E Paces Ferry Rd NE
Continental 30305. **Hours:** 6 pm-10 pm. Closed major holidays, Sun & Mon. **Reservations:** suggested; weekends.
Features: semi-formal attire; cocktails & lounge; a la carte. Romantic, European, intimate dining. Excellent
wine list. Gracious service. Innovative touches on creative entrees. Smoking in lounge only. Smoke free premises.
Cards: AE, DI, MC, VI. ✕

HORSERADISH GRILL **Lunch:** $8-$16 **Dinner:** $16-$22 **Phone:** 404/255-7277 139
◆◆◆ **Location:** At the corner of Chastain Park & Powers Ferry rds. 4320 Powers Ferry Rd 30342. **Hours:** 11:30
Regional am-3:30-5:30-10 pm, Fri & Sat-11 pm, Sun 11 am-3 pm. Closed: 1/1 & 12/25. **Reservations:** suggested.
American **Features:** casual dress; Sunday brunch; children's menu; cocktails & lounge; valet parking; a la carte. This
restaurant offers a taste of the New South. A former old barn it is beautifully decorated in wood, natural
stone & modern paintings. Highly unique & creative regional cuisine. Smoke free premises. **Cards:** AE, CB, DI, DS, MC, VI. ✕

THE IMPERIAL FEZ **Phone:** 404/351-0870 140
◆◆ **Location:** 2285 Peachtree Rd 30341. **Hours:** 6 am-11 pm. **Reservations:** required. **Features:** semi-formal
Ethnic attire; children's menu; health conscious menu; cocktails & lounge. Enjoy a 5-course Moroccan
Mediterranean cusine in a beautifully decorated atmosphere. The walls & ceiling are padded with brilliant
fabrics. Bellydancers entertain as you surrender your shoes & dine in a nest of pillows & rugs. **Cards:** AE, CB, DI, DS, MC,
VI. ✕

INDIGO COASTAL GRILL **Dinner:** $15-$19 **Phone:** 404/876-0676 114
◆◆ **Location:** From jct Ponce de Leon Ave & Highland Ave, 1.5 mi n. 1397 N Highland Ave 30306. **Hours:** 5:30
Seafood pm-11 pm, Fri & Sat-11:30 pm, Sun 10 am-3 pm. Closed major holidays. **Features:** casual dress; Sunday
brunch; carryout; cocktails; street parking. A spicy little joint with seafood from Cape Cod to the Islands.
Cards: AE, DI, MC, VI. ✕

JAVA JIVE **Lunch:** $4-$6 **Dinner:** $4-$6 **Phone:** 404/876-6161 141
◆ **Location:** E on Ponce de Leon from Ponce & Peachtree. 790 Ponce de Leon Ave 30306. **Hours:** 8 am-2 &
American 6-11 pm, Fri-midnight, Sat 10 am-2:30 & 6-midnight, Sun 10 am-2:30 pm. Closed: Mon & 12/25.
Features: casual dress; Sunday brunch; health conscious menu; carryout. Take a nostalgic trip back in time
in this retro cafe/coffeehouse. Pleasant menu of sandwiches, salads & on-site baked desserts & ice cream. ✕

JOEY D'S OAK ROOM **Lunch:** $9-$20 **Dinner:** $9-$20 **Phone:** 770/512-7063 142
◆◆ **Location:** I-285 exit 21, 0.5 mi n, 0.5 mi w on Perimeter Center West. 1015 Crown Pointe Pkwy 30338.
Steak and **Hours:** 11 am-10 pm, Fri & Sat-11 pm. Closed major holidays. **Reservations:** accepted. **Features:** casual
Seafood dress; children's menu; cocktails & lounge. Informal dining room set on acres of oak parquet. **Cards:** AE,
CB, DI, DS, MC, VI. ✕

KAMOGAWA **Lunch:** $7-$20 **Dinner:** $17-$28 **Phone:** 404/841-0314 63
◆◆◆ **Location:** Buckhead; corner of Peachtree & Piedmont rds; in Grand Hyatt Hotel. 3300 Peachtree Rd 30305.
Ethnic **Hours:** 11:30 am-2 & 6-10 pm, Fri & Sat 6 pm-10:30 pm. **Reservations:** suggested. **Features:** semi-formal
attire; health conscious menu items; carryout; cocktails & lounge; valet parking. Authentic Japanese cuisine
creatively & artistically prepared. Tatami rooms avail. Sushi bar. Gracious service. Soft soothing decor. **Cards:** AE, DI, JCB,
MC, VI. ✕

KUDZU CAFE **Lunch:** $8-$17 **Dinner:** $9-$21 **Phone:** 404/262-0661 74
ⓐⓐ **Location:** In Buckhead; from jct Piedmont Rd NE & Peachtree Rd NE, just s. 3215 Peachtree Rd NE 30305.
Hours: 11 am-11 pm, Fri & Sat-midnight. Closed: 7/4, 11/26 & 12/25. **Features:** casual dress; carryout;
◆◆ cocktails & lounge; valet parking; a la carte. Lively friendly atmosphere. Contemporary southern cuisine,
Regional ample portions. Fried green tomotoes. Real mashed potatoes. Favorites are seared chicken pasta, grilled
American meatloaf & crawfish salad. Brunch served Sat & Sun 11 am-2:30 pm. **Cards:** AE, DS, MC, VI. ✕

LA BONNE CUISINE **Lunch:** $6-$8 **Dinner:** $11-$17 **Phone:** 770/414-6077 135
◆◆ **Location:** I-285, exit 28, just w in the Northlake Square. 4135 La Vista Rd, Suite 630 30084. **Hours:** 11:30
Continental am-2 & 5:30-10 pm. Closed: Sun, Mon, 1/1 & 12/25. **Features:** casual dress; beer & wine only; a la carte.
Small, intimate dining room. Creative entrees offered with French influence. Smoke free premises.
Cards: AE, DI, MC, VI. ✕

LA GROTTA RAVINIA RISTORANTE ITALIANO **Lunch:** $10-$15 **Dinner:** $14-$24 **Phone:** 404/395-7700 44
ⓐⓐ **Location:** I-285 exit 21, ne corner; in Crowne Plaza Ravinia. 4355 Ashford-Dunwoody Rd 30346.
Hours: 11:30 am-2 & 5:45-10 pm. Closed major holidays & Sun. **Reservations:** suggested.
◆◆◆◆ **Features:** casual dress; cocktails; valet parking; a la carte. Excellent Italian wine selections. **Cards:** AE, DI,
Northern DS, JCB, MC, VI. ✕
Italian

LA GROTTA RISTORANTE ITALIANO **Dinner:** $14-$27 **Phone:** 404/231-1368 88
ⓐⓐ **Location:** In Buckhead; I-85/75 northbound, exit 101, (0.5 mi e on 10th to Peachtree Rd) 3.5 mi n. 2637
Peachtree Rd 30305. **Hours:** 6 pm-10:30 pm. Closed major holidays & Sun. **Reservations:** suggested.
◆◆◆◆ **Features:** semi-formal attire; health conscious menu; cocktails; valet parking; a la carte. Relaxed formal
Northern atmosphere. Local favorite for fresh fish, veal, chicken & beef entrees. Homemade pasta specialties such as
Italian Ravioloni con Caprino. Tiramisu & other delectable desserts. Excellent wine list. Espresso/cappuccino.
Smoke free premises. **Cards:** AE, DI, DS, MC, VI. ✕

MAMBO RESTAURANTE CUBANO **Phone:** 404/876-2626 144
◆◆ **Location:** 1402 N Highland Ave 30306. **Hours:** 5:30 pm-10:30 pm, Fri & Sat-11:30 pm, Sun-10 pm. Closed:
Ethnic 1/1, 11/26 & 12/25. **Reservations:** accepted. **Features:** casual dress; beer & wine only. Traditional &
progressive cuban cuisine specializing in Chino-Latino (Chinese-Cuban). Enjoy marvelous food & friendly
service in this quaint little restaurant. **Cards:** AE, MC, VI. ✕

MCKENDRICK'S STEAK HOUSE **Lunch:** $9-$30 **Dinner:** $16-$30 **Phone:** 770/512-8888 143
◆◆◆ **Location:** I-285 exit 21, 0.5 mi n. 4505 Ashford Dunwoody Rd 30346. **Hours:** 11:30 am-2:30 & 5:30-10:30
Steak and pm, Fri & Sat 5:30 pm-11 pm, Sun 5:30 pm-10 pm. Closed major holidays. **Reservations:** suggested.
Seafood **Features:** children's menu; cocktails & lounge; valet parking; a la carte. Prime beef steak house also
featuring a varity of seafood items & extended wine list. Dressy casual attire. **Cards:** AE, DI, DS, MC, VI. ✕

(See map p. 202)

MCKINNON'S LOUISIANE RESTAURANT   **Dinner:** $16-$21   **Phone:** 404/237-1313   76
◆◆   **Location:** In Buckhead; from jct Piemont & Peachtree rds, just s on Peachtree to Maple Dr. 3209 Maple Dr
American   30305. **Hours:** 6 pm-10 pm, Fri & Sat-10:30 pm. Closed major holidays & Sun. **Reservations:** suggested;
weekends. **Features:** casual dress; children's menu; health conscious menu items; cocktails & lounge; a la
carte. French Creole & Cajun cuisine. **Cards:** AE, DI, DS, MC, VI.   ☒

MI SPIA   **Lunch:** $9-$12   **Dinner:** $13-$23   **Phone:** 770/393-1333   145
◆◆   **Location:** I-285 exit 21, 0.5 mi n; in Park Place Shopping Center. 4505 Ashford Dunwoody Rd 30346.
Northern   **Hours:** 11:30 am-2:30 pm, Fri & Sat 5 pm-11 pm, Sun 5 pm-10 pm. Closed major holidays.
Italian   **Reservations:** suggested. **Features:** casual dress; children's menu; carryout; cocktails & lounge; a la carte.
A suburban upscale trattoria. Smoke free premises. **Cards:** AE, CB, DI, DS, MC, VI.   ☒

NAVA   **Lunch:** $8-$14   **Dinner:** $15-$25   **Phone:** 404/240-1984   57
◆◆◆   **Location:** In Buckhead at jct Peachtree & W Paces Ferry rds. 3060 Peachtree Rd 30305. **Hours:** 11:30
Southwest   am-2:30 & 5:30-11 pm, Fri & Sat-midnight. **Reservations:** required. **Features:** dressy casual; cocktails &
American   lounge; valet parking; a la carte. Upscale Southwestern cuisine served in a sophisticated Santa Fe style
interior. Specialties include chili cured lamb rack & fire-roasted quail. Smoke free premises. **Cards:** AE, CB,
DI, DS, MC, VI.   ☒

NEW ORLEANS CAFE   **Lunch:** $7-$9   **Dinner:** $7-$15   **Phone:** 770/396-9665   39
◆◆   **Location:** I-285 exit 17, 4 mi n; in the Shoppes of Morgan Falls. 7887-A Roswell Rd 30350. **Hours:** 11 am-2
Ethnic   & 5:30-10 pm, Sat noon-3 & 5:30-10 pm. Closed major holidays & Sun. **Features:** casual dress; children's
menu; carryout; beer & wine only. Cajun & creole specialties. Crawfish etouffee, jambalaya, shrimp creole.
Acclaimed pecan pie. **Cards:** AE, DI, DS, MC, VI.   ☒

NICKIEMOTO'S   **Dinner:** $11-$20   **Phone:** 404/842-0334   43
◆◆   **Location:** E on Pharr Rd off of Peachtree Rd, just n on Buckhead Ave. 247 Buckhead Ave 30305. **Hours:** 5
Ethnic   pm-11 pm, Fri & Sat-midnight. Closed: 12/25. **Reservations:** accepted. **Features:** casual dress; carryout;
cocktails & lounge; valet parking; a la carte. Sophisticated Japanese-American restaurant. Menu changes
often. **Cards:** AE, DI, DS, MC, VI.   ☒

NICOLA'S   **Phone:** 404/325-2524   61
◆   **Location:** Between Briarcliff Rd & Cheshire Bridge Rd in northeast Atlanta. 1602 LaVista Rd 30329.
Ethnic   **Hours:** 5:30 pm-10:30 pm. Closed: 1/1, 11/26 & 12/25. **Reservations:** suggested. **Features:** casual dress;
carryout; beer & wine only. Lebanese/mideastern cuisine served by a cheery proprietor. **Cards:** AE, DI, MC,
VI.   ☒

O K CAFE   **Lunch:** $6-$9   **Dinner:** $8-$10   **Phone:** 404/233-2888   48
◆   **Location:** I-75 northbound exit 107, 0.3 mi n on US 41 to W Paces Ferry Rd, ne corner; I-75 southbound
American   exit 107, ne corner. 1284 W Paces Ferry Rd 30327. **Hours:** 24 hours. Closed major holidays.
Features: casual dress; Sunday brunch; carryout; beer & wine only; a la carte. Diner type well-lighted cafe.
Fast service. Fountain drinks. Fresh made comfort foods. Smoke free premises. **Cards:** AE, DI, DS, MC, VI.

103 WEST   **Dinner:** $17-$35   **Phone:** 404/233-5993   55
◆◆◆◆   **Location:** In Buckhead; from jct Peachtree & W Paces Ferry rds, 2 blks w. 103 W Paces Ferry Rd 30305.
Continental   **Hours:** 6 pm-11 pm. Closed major holidays & Sun. **Reservations:** suggested. **Features:** semi-formal attire;
health conscious menu; cocktails & lounge; valet parking; a la carte. Varied, innovative menu in elegant yet
relaxed atmosphere. Smoke free premises. **Cards:** AE, CB, DI, DS, JCB, MC, VI.   ☒

THE ORIENT AT VININGS   **Lunch:** $5-$8   **Dinner:** $15-$25   **Phone:** 404/438-8866   36
◆◆◆   **Location:** I-285, exit 12, 1.5 mi e. 4199 Paces Ferry Rd 30339. **Hours:** 11:30 am-10 pm, Fri-11 pm, Sat 6
Chinese   pm-11 pm. Closed major holidays. **Reservations:** suggested; weekends. **Features:** semi-formal attire;
Sunday brunch; carryout; cocktails; minimum charge-$8; a la carte. New Cantonese-style cuisine
emphasizing fresh ingredients & no preservatives. Located by the Chattahoochee River. **Cards:** AE, DI, MC, VI.

PALISADES   **Phone:** 404/350-6755   62
◆◆   **Location:** Corner of Palisades St, 0.5 mi n on Peachtree, 85 crosses underneath; just s of Piedmont
Continental   Hospital. 1829 Peachtree Rd 30341. **Hours:** 5:30 pm-10 pm, Sat-11 pm. **Reservations:** accepted.
Features: casual dress; health conscious menu; cocktails & lounge. Charming restaurant with European flair.
Decor of carefully chosen original artwork, pretty brick walls & classic French doors. **Cards:** AE, CB, DI, DS, MC, VI.   ☒

THE PALM RESTAURANT   **Lunch:** $10-$15   **Dinner:** $15-$30   **Phone:** 404/814-1955   70
◆◆◆   **Location:** Buckhead; adjacent to Lenox Mall; in Swissotel. 3391 Peachtree Rd 30326. **Hours:** 6:30
American   am-10:30 & 11:30-11 pm. **Reservations:** suggested. **Features:** dressy casual; Sunday brunch; children's
menu; cocktails & lounge; valet parking; a la carte. Huge portions. US prime steak & seafood specialties.
Cards: AE, CB, DI, MC, VI.   ☒

PANO'S & PAUL'S   **Dinner:** $17-$34   **Phone:** 404/261-3662   47
◆◆◆◆   **Location:** On US 41, just off I-75 W Paces Ferry Rd, exit 107; Northside Dr & W Paces Ferry Rd. 1232 W
Continental   Paces Ferry Rd NW 30327. **Hours:** 6 pm-10:30 pm, Sat 5:30 pm-11 pm. Closed major holidays & Sun.
Reservations: required. **Features:** semi-formal attire; health conscious menu items; cocktails & lounge; a la
carte. Ornate Old World elegance. Formal, yet warm atmosphere. Smoke free premises. **Cards:** AE, CB, DI, DS, JCB, MC,
VI.   ☒

PARTNERS, A MORNINGSIDE CAFE   **Dinner:** $15-$19   **Phone:** 404/876-8104   115
◆◆   **Location:** From jct Ponce de Leon & Highland aves, 1.5 mi n. 1397 N Highland Ave 30306. **Hours:** 6 pm-10
American   pm, Fri & Sat-11 pm. Closed major holidays. **Reservations:** suggested; Sun-Thurs. **Features:** casual dress;
carryout; cocktails; street parking. Cozy neighborhood bistro. Variety of beer & hand selected wines. Creative
blackboard specials. Espresso/cappuccino. **Cards:** AE, DI, MC, VI.   ☒

PEACHTREE CAFE   **Dinner:** $9-$21   **Phone:** 404/233-4402   66
◆◆   **Location:** Just e off Peachtree Rd; on the corner of E Paces Ferry Rd & Bolling Way. 268 E Paces Ferry Rd
American   30305. **Hours:** 11 am-midnight, Sun & Mon-10 pm. **Reservations:** suggested. **Features:** casual dress;
Sunday brunch; children's menu; health conscious menu; carryout; cocktails & lounge. Upbeat atmosphere
on two levels of dining. Delightful terrace shaded by large umbrellas also avail. **Cards:** AE, DI, DS, MC, VI.   ☒

(See map p. 202)

THE PEASANT RESTAURANT ON PIEDMONT   **Lunch:** $9-$14   **Dinner:** $13-$21   **Phone:** 404/231-8740 ⑨⑴
◆◆◆   **Location:** Just w of Peachtree Rd on Piedmont. 3402 Piedmont Rd 30350. **Hours:** 11:30 am-2:30 & 5:30-10
American   pm, Fri & Sat-11 pm. Closed major holidays. **Reservations:** accepted. **Features:** casual dress; Sunday
brunch; children's menu; health conscious menu items; carryout; cocktails & lounge; valet parking; a la carte.
Upscale contemporary dining. **Cards:** AE, CB, DI, DS, MC, VI. ✕

PETITE AUBERGE RESTAURANT FRANCAIS   **Lunch:** $6-$9   **Dinner:** $12-$18   **Phone:** 404/634-6268 ⒀⓪
◆◆   **Location:** I-85 exit 31, 1.5 mi se; Toco Hills Center. 2935 N Druid Hills Rd 30329. **Hours:** 11:30 am-2:30 &
Continental   6-10 pm, Sat from 6 pm. Closed major holidays & Sun. **Reservations:** suggested; evenings.
Features: semi-formal attire; carryout; cocktails. Intimate ambience. Additional authentic German menu avail
on Fri & Sat nights. **Cards:** AE, DI, DS, MC, VI. ✕

PLEASANT PEASANT   **Lunch:** $6-$10   **Dinner:** $10-$20   **Phone:** 404/874-3223 ⑴⓪⓪
◆◆◆   **Location:** From I-85 & I-75N exit 100, 3 blks e on Linden to Peachtree St, then just s. 555 Peachtree St NE
American   30308. **Hours:** 11:30 am-2:30 & 5:30-11 pm, Sat & Sun from 5:30 pm. Closed: 11/26 & 12/25.
Features: cocktails; valet parking; a la carte. Distinctive intimate decor. Eclectic menu of well-prepared
entrees. **Cards:** AE, DI, DS, MC, VI. ✕

PRICCI   **Lunch:** $10-$16   **Dinner:** $12-$22   **Phone:** 404/237-2941 ⑧⑴
◆◆◆   **Location:** In Buckhead; Pharr Rd & Maple Dr, just w of Piedmont. 500 Pharr Rd 30305. **Hours:** 11 am-11
Italian   pm, Fri & Sat-midnight, Sun 5 pm-10 pm. Closed: 1/1, 11/26 & 12/25. **Reservations:** suggested.
Features: casual dress; carryout; cocktails & lounge; valet parking; a la carte. Open kitchen with
wood-burning pizza ovens. Bustling atmosphere. **Cards:** AE, DI, DS, MC, VI. ✕

RAY'S ON THE RIVER   **Lunch:** $6-$10   **Dinner:** $10-$18   **Phone:** 770/955-1187 ㉝
◆◆◆   **Location:** I-285 exit 15, 0.8 mi sw, at Powers Ferry Landing. 6700 Powers Ferry Rd 30339. **Hours:** 11 am-3
Seafood   & 5:30-10:30 pm, Fri & Sat 5 pm-midnight, Sun 9:30 am-3:30 & 5-10 pm. Closed: 12/25.
Reservations: suggested. **Features:** casual dress; Sunday brunch; children's menu; health conscious menu
items; cocktails & lounge; entertainment; valet parking; a la carte. On the Chattahoochee River featuring fresh seafood &
oyster bar. Beef entrees also avail. Extensive wine list. **Cards:** AE, CB, DI, DS, MC, VI. ✕

ST. CHARLES DELI   **Lunch:** $6-$13   **Dinner:** $6-$13   **Phone:** 404/876-3354 ⑴⑴⑧
◆   **Location:** 2 mi ne via Ponce De Leon Ave to Highland Ave, just n. 752 N Highland Ave 30306. **Hours:** 7
American   am-10 pm. Closed: 11/26 & 12/25. **Features:** casual dress; children's menu; carryout; beer & wine only; a la
carte. Large portions of freshly prepared salads, sandwiches, omelettes & burgers. Sat & Sun brunch.
Cards: AE, DI, DS, MC, VI. ✕

SOUTH CITY KITCHEN   **Lunch:** $8-$12   **Dinner:** $10-$21   **Phone:** 404/873-7358 ㉙⑨
◆◆   **Location:** I-75, exit 14th St, 0.3 mi e to Crescent Ave, just s. 1144 Crescent Ave 30309. **Hours:** 11 am-11
American   pm, Fri & Sat-midnight. Closed major holidays. **Reservations:** suggested. **Features:** casual dress; Sunday
brunch; carryout; cocktails & lounge; street parking. Contemporary Southern cuisine served in an upscale
atmosphere. Good wine list. **Cards:** AE, DI, MC, VI. ✕

SUNDOWN CAFE   **Dinner:** $8-$13   **Phone:** 404/321-1118 ⑴㉔
◆◆   **Location:** Northbound I-85 exit 31, n exit ramp to re-enter I-85 going s to exit 30 (Cheshire Bridge Rd,
Mexican   Lenox Rd), 0.8 mi e. 2165 Cheshire Bridge Rd 30324. **Hours:** 5:30 pm-10 pm, Fri & Sat-11 pm. Closed
major holidays & Sun. **Features:** casual dress; children's menu; cocktails; a la carte. Also featuring creative
Southwestern cuisine. **Cards:** AE, DI, MC, VI. ✕

SUNTORY   **Dinner:** $21-$30   **Phone:** 404/261-3737 ⑴⓪⑥
◆◆   **Location:** I-285 exit 17, 3.5 mi inside 285 on Roswell Rd. 3847 Roswell Rd 30342. **Hours:** 11:30 am-2 &
Steak and   6-10 pm, Fri & Sat-10:30 pm. Closed major holidays & Sun. **Reservations:** accepted. **Features:** dressy
Seafood   casual; children's menu; health conscious menu items; carryout; cocktails & lounge. Built in the shape of a
"U" around a charming Japanese courtyard, three separate type dining areas including a sushi bar.
Cards: AE, CB, DI, DS, JCB, MC, VI. ✕

SURIN OF THAILAND   **Dinner:** $11-$20   **Phone:** 404/892-7789 ⑴⓪⑺
◆◆   **Location:** 2 blks n of Ponce de Leon Ave. 810 N Highland Ave 30306. **Hours:** 11:30 am-10:30 pm, Fri-11:30
Ethnic   pm, Sat noon-11:30 pm, Sun noon-10:30 pm. Closed: 11/26 & 12/25. **Features:** casual dress; carryout;
cocktails & lounge. Authentic Thai cuisine. **Cards:** AE, DS, MC, VI. ✕

SUSHI HUKU   **Dinner:** $11-$20   **Phone:** 770/956-9559 ⑨⑺
◆◆   **Location:** I-285 exit 15, inside shopping center, opposite Holiday Inn. 6300 Powers Ferry Rd 30339.
Ethnic   **Hours:** 5:30 pm-10:30 pm. Closed: 1/1 & 12/25. **Reservations:** suggested. **Features:** health conscious
menu; beer & wine only; a la carte. Specializing in sushi/tempura Japanese food. **Cards:** AE, MC, VI. ✕

THAI CHILLI   **Dinner:** $11-$20   **Phone:** 404/315-6750 ㊼
◆◆   **Location:** In Briarvista Shopping Ctr. 2169 Briarcliff Rd 30329. **Hours:** 11 am-2:30 & 5-10 pm, Sat 5 pm-11
Traditional   pm, Sun 5 pm-10 pm. Closed major holidays & Mon. **Reservations:** suggested. **Features:** casual dress;
Ethnic   carryout; beer & wine only. Family-owned & operated, the waitresses dress in traditional Thai attire.
Cards: AE, DS, MC, VI. ✕

TOM TOM, A BISTRO   **Lunch:** $9-$10   **Dinner:** $9-$15   **Phone:** 404/264-1163 ⑺⑴
◆◆◆   **Location:** Buckhead; in Lenox Square Mall. Plaza level by the Food Court, I-85 southbound exit 30,
American   northbound exit 28; 0.8 mi n. 3393 Peachtree Rd 30326. **Hours:** 11:30 am-10 pm, Fri & Sat-11 pm, Sun
noon-9 pm. Closed major holidays. **Features:** carryout; cocktails; a la carte. Upscale casual. Fusion cuisine
blending Asian, Italian, Southwestern & Southern foods using local fresh ingredients. Cellar wine selections.
Espresso/cappuccino. Dessert chef. **Cards:** AE, DI, DS, MC, VI. ✕

TOULOUSE   **Dinner:** $21-$30   **Phone:** 404/351-9533 ㊾
◆◆◆   **Location:** Just s of Peachtree Battle. 2293-B Peachtree Rd 30309. **Hours:** 6 pm-10 pm, Fri & Sat-11 pm.
American   Closed: Mon, 1/1 & 12/25. **Reservations:** accepted. **Features:** casual dress; cocktails & lounge. Menu
inspired by south of France cuisine. **Cards:** AE, DI, MC, VI. ✕

(See map p. 202)

VENI VIDI VICI   **Lunch:** $10-$13   **Dinner:** $12-$24   **Phone:** 404/875-8424   〔98〕
◆◆◆   **Location:** Midtown; I-75/85 exit 14th St; corner 14th & W Peachtree sts. 41 14th St 30309. **Hours:** 11:30
Italian   am–11 pm, Fri & Sat-midnight, Sun 5 pm-10 pm. Closed major holidays. **Reservations:** suggested.
     Features: dressy casual; health conscious menu; cocktails & lounge; valet parking. Classic, open design
with chic New York sophistication. Authentic, rustic Italian cuisine. Pre & post-theater specialties. Excellent Italian wine list.
Cards: AE, DI, DS, MC, VI.   ✗

WINFIELD'S   **Lunch:** $7-$10   **Dinner:** $10-$20   **Phone:** 404/955-5300   〔32〕
◆◆◆   **Location:** I-285 exit 14, ne corner; in Galleria Mall. 1 Galleria Pkwy 30339. **Hours:** 11:30 am-3 & 5:30-11
American   pm, Fri-11 pm, Sat 5:30 pm-11 pm, Sun 11:30 am-3 & 5:30-9 pm. Closed: 11/26 & 12/25. **Features:** casual
     dress; Sunday brunch; children's menu; health conscious menu items; carryout; cocktails & lounge;
entertainment; valet parking; a la carte. Casual elegance reminiscent of the great dining halls of Europe. **Cards:** AE, CB, DI,
DS, MC, VI.   ✗

ATLANTA SOUTH   (See map p. 225; index below)

Index of Establishments on the SOUTH ATLANTA ACCOMMODATIONS Spotting Map

LODGINGS

ATLANTA AIRPORT HILTON & TOWERS   Rates Subject to Change   **Phone:** 404/767-9000   〔215〕
ⓐ   All Year   1P: $79- 208   2P/1B: $79- 229   2P/2B: $79- 229   XP: $15
     Location: I-85, exit 19 (Virginia Ave), just e. 1031 Virginia Ave 30354. Fax: 404/768-0185. **Terms:** No pets.
◆◆◆◆   **Facility:** 503 rooms. 17 stories; interior corridors. **Dining:** 3 restaurants; 6 am-midnight; $8-$18.
Hotel   **All Rooms:** free & pay movies. **Cards:** AE, CB, DI, DS, JCB, MC, VI. *(See color ad p 18)*
                                                          🛥 🛥 ➕ CTV 🛁 ✗ 🌀 D S

CROWNE PLAZA ATLANTA AIRPORT   **Phone:** 404/768-6660   〔217〕
Hotel   Under construction; **Location:** I-85, exit 19 (Virginia Ave), nw corner. 1325 Virginia Ave 30344.
     Fax: 404/762-9675. **Terms:** Sr. discount; no pets. **Facility:** 377 rooms. Scheduled to open January 1998; 12
stories; interior corridors. **Dining:** Restaurant; $9-$11. **All Rooms:** Fee: movies. **Cards:** AE, CB, DI, DS, JCB, MC, VI.
                                   Roll in showers. 🛥 ➕ CTV ✗ 🌀 D S

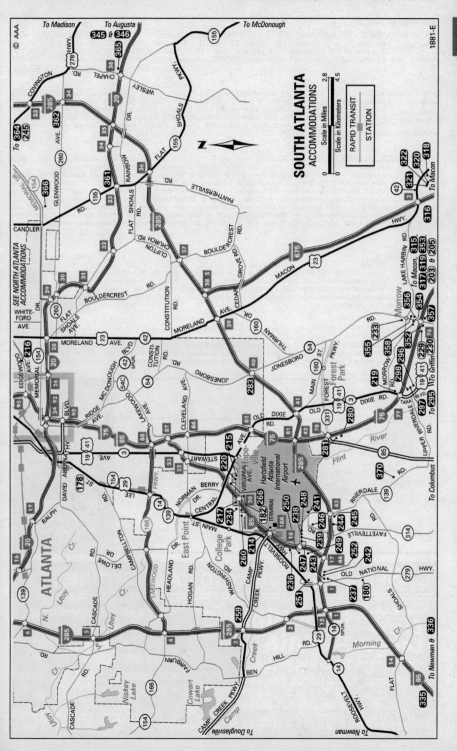

1881-E

To Madison   To Augusta   To McDonough

SOUTH ATLANTA
ACCOMMODATIONS

Scale in Miles

Scale in Kilometers

RAPID TRANSIT
STATION

(See map p. 225)

DRURY INN & SUITES ATLANTA AIRPORT   Rates Subject to Change   **Phone:** 404/761-4900   220
Motel   All Year   1P: $66- 79   2P/1B: $76- 89   2P/2B: $76- 89   XP: $10   F18
Too new to rate; **Location:** From I-85 exit 19, e. 1270 Virginia Ave 30344. Fax: 404/688-6034. **Terms:** Sr.
discount; pets. **Facility:** 155 rooms. Scheduled to open fall 1997; 6 stories; interior corridors. **Cards:** AE, CB, DI, DS, MC,
VI.   Roll in showers. 🛏 🛄 🛄 ✕ Ⓓ

OAKWOOD HOUSE   Guaranteed Rates   **Phone:** 404/521-9320   216
◆ ◆   All Year [CP]   1P: $75- 90   2P/1B: $79- 150   2P/2B: $79- 95
Historic Bed   **Location:** I-85/75, exit 96, following signs on SR 10/42 to Jimmy Carter Library & on to N Highland Ave, sw
& Breakfast   0.5 mi to Elizabeth St, 4 blks s to Edgewood Ave, just w. 951 Edgewood Ave 30307. Fax: 404/688-6034.
Terms: Check-in 4 pm; reserv deposit, 3 day notice; no pets. **Facility:** 4 rooms. 2 stories; interior corridors;
designated smoking area. **Cards:** AE, DS, MC, VI.   ✕ Ⓓ Ⓢ

RENAISSANCE ATLANTA HOTEL CONCOURSE   **Phone:** 404/209-9999   214
(AAA) (SAVE)   All Year   1P: $139- 185   2P/1B: $159- 205   2P/2B: $159- 205   XP: $20   F12
   Location: I-85 exit 19, Virginia Ave; just e to Toffie Ter, just s. One Hartsfield Centre Pkwy 30354.
◆ ◆ ◆ ◆   Fax: 404/209-8934. **Terms:** Package plans; weekend rates avail; no pets. **Facility:** 387 rooms. Some guest
Hotel   rooms have full view of adjacent runways. 14 two-bedroom units. 11 stories; interior corridors; luxury level
rooms; saunas, steamrooms, whirlpool. **Dining & Entertainment:** Restaurant; 7 am-11 pm; $7-$22;
cocktails/lounge; 24-hour room service; entertainment. **Services:** valet laundry; area transportation, within 5 mi.
Fee: childcare; massage; valet parking. **All Rooms:** honor bars, coffeemakers, free & pay movies, combo or shower baths.
Some Rooms: refrigerators, whirlpools. **Cards:** AE, CB, DI, DS, MC, VI. **Special Amenities:** Free newspaper.
Roll in showers. 🛄 🛄 🎖 🌐 🛜 CTV ✕ 🎴 Ⓓ Ⓢ

SUPER 8 MOTEL   **Phone:** 404/363-8811   219
(AAA) (SAVE)   All Year   1P: $46   2P/1B: $56   2P/2B: $56   XP: $10
   Location: I-75 exit 77, just e. 410 Old Dixie Way 30050. Fax: 404/361-1789. **Terms:** BP avail; small pets
◆ ◆   only. **Facility:** 54 rooms. Contemporary room appointments. 3 units with whirlpool, extra charge; 2 stories; ex-
Motel   terior corridors. **Dining:** Coffee shop nearby. **All Rooms:** free & pay movies, combo or shower baths.
Some Rooms: microwaves, refrigerators. **Cards:** AE, DI, DS, MC. **Special Amenities:** Early check-in/late
check-out and free breakfast.   Roll in showers. 🛏 🛄 CTV ✕ Ⓓ

RESTAURANT

PILGREEN'S   **Phone:** 404/758-4669   178
◆   **Location:** 3 mi sw on US 29; between Donnelly & Avon. 1081 Lee St 30310. **Hours:** 11:30 am-9:30 pm,
Steakhouse   Fri-10:30 pm, Sat 5 pm-10:30 pm. Closed major holidays. **Features:** casual dress; children's menu; carryout;
cocktails & lounge. Popular steak house; one of the oldest in Atlanta. **Cards:** AE, CB, DI, DS, MC, VI.   ✕

The Atlanta Vicinity

ACWORTH—4,500

LODGINGS

BEST WESTERN FRONTIER INN   Phone: 770/974-0116
(AAA) (SAVE)   All Year [CP]   1P: $40- 70 2P/1B: $40- 70 2P/2B: $40- 70 XP: $5   F12
◆◆   **Location:** I-75 exit 120, just nw. Hwy 92 30101 (PO Box 600). **Fax:** 770/917-0104. **Terms:** Reserv deposit;
Motel   pets, $5 extra charge. **Facility:** 120 rooms. 2 stories; exterior corridors; kiddie playground. **Dining &**
Entertainment: Cocktail lounge; restaurant nearby. **Services:** Fee: coin laundry. **All Rooms:** free movies.
Some Rooms: Fee: microwaves, refrigerators. **Cards:** AE, DI, DS, MC, VI. **Special Amenities: Free**
breakfast. *(See color ad p 182)*   (H) (➔) (CTV) (✕) (D)

DAYS INN   Phone: 770/974-1700
(AAA) (SAVE)   All Year [CP]   1P: $35- 75 2P/1B: $45- 80 2P/2B: $45- 80 XP: $10   F12
◆◆   **Location:** I-75 exit 120, just sw. 5035 Cowan Rd 30101. **Fax:** 770/974-1700. **Terms:** Pets, $5 extra charge.
Motel   **Facility:** 64 rooms. Contemporary room appointments. 2 stories; exterior corridors. **Dining:** Restaurant
nearby. **All Rooms:** free movies. **Some Rooms:** 4 efficiencies, no utensils. **Cards:** AE, DS, MC, VI.
Special Amenities: Free breakfast and preferred room (subject to availability with advanced
reservations).   (H) (➔) (🛇) (CTV) (✕) (D)

QUALITY INN   Phone: 770/974-1922
(AAA) (SAVE)   All Year [CP]   1P: $39- 45 2P/1B: $43- 49 2P/2B: $45- 55 XP: $5   F12
◆◆◆   **Location:** I-75 exit 120, just sw. 4980 Cowan Rd 30101. **Fax:** 770/975-9733. **Terms:** Pets, $10 extra charge.
Motel   **Facility:** 60 rooms. 2-3 stories; exterior corridors. **Dining:** Restaurant nearby. **Services:** valet laundry.
All Rooms: coffeemakers, free movies. **Some Rooms:** refrigerators. **Cards:** AE, CB, DI, DS, MC, VI.
Special Amenities: Free breakfast and free local telephone calls.   (H) (➔) (🛇) (CTV) (✕) (D)

RAMADA LIMITED   Rates Subject to Change   Phone: 770/975-9000
◆◆◆   3/1-7/17 & 8/6-8/31 [CP] 1P: $32- 52 2P/1B: $32- 52 2P/2B: $38- 62 XP: $4   F12
Motel   12/1-2/28, 7/18-8/5 &
9/1-11/30 [CP]   1P: $28- 48 2P/1B: $28- 48 2P/2B: $35- 58 XP: $4   F12
Location: I-75 exit 120, just ne. 164 N Point Way 30102. **Fax:** 770/975-1397. **Terms:** Reserv deposit; no pets. **Facility:** 40
rooms. 2 king study rooms; 2 stories; exterior corridors. **All Rooms:** free movies. **Cards:** AE, CB, DI, DS, MC, VI.
(➔K) (CTV) (✕) (🗗) (D)

SUPER 8 MOTEL   Phone: 770/966-9700
(AAA) (SAVE)   All Year [CP]   1P: $38- 55 2P/1B: $42- 60 2P/2B: $42- 65 XP: $5   F16
◆◆◆   **Location:** I-75 exit 120, just sw. 4970 Cowan Rd 30101. **Fax:** 770/974-7292. **Terms:** Pets, $10 dep req.
Motel   **Facility:** 49 rooms. 2-3 stories, no elevator; exterior corridors. **Dining:** Restaurant nearby. **All Rooms:** free
movies. **Cards:** AE, CB, DI, DS, JCB, MC, VI. **Special Amenities: Free breakfast and preferred room**
(subject to availability with advanced reservations).   (H) (➔) (CTV) (✕) (🗗) (D) (S)

TRAVELODGE   Phone: 770/974-5400
(AAA) (SAVE)   All Year   1P: $36   2P/1B: $40   2P/2B: $45   XP: $5   F17
◆◆   **Location:** I-75 exit 121; just sw. 5320 Bartow Rd 30101. **Fax:** 770/974-6718. **Terms:** Reserv deposit; small
Motel   pets only. **Facility:** 48 rooms. Attractive comfortable guest rooms. Suites for up to 4 persons, $60; 2 stories;
exterior corridors. **Dining:** Restaurant nearby. **All Rooms:** free movies. **Some Rooms:** refrigerators, VCP's.
Fee: whirlpools. **Cards:** AE, CB, DI, DS, JCB, MC, VI. **Special Amenities: Free breakfast and free local**
telephone calls.   (H) (➔) (CTV) (✕) (🗗) (D)

ALPHARETTA—13,000

LODGINGS

FAIRFIELD INN BY MARRIOTT   Rates Subject to Change   Phone: 770/663-4000
◆◆◆   All Year [CP]   1P: $63- 85 2P/1B: $70- 95 2P/2B: $70- 95 XP: $7   F18
Motel   **Location:** Hwy 400 exit 9, just w. 11385 Haynes Bridge Rd 30201. **Fax:** 770/663-4000. **Terms:** No pets.
Facility: 88 rooms. 3 stories; interior corridors. **All Rooms:** free movies. **Cards:** AE, DI, DS, MC, VI.
(See color ad p 211)   Roll in showers. (CTV) (✕) (🗗) (D) (S)

HOLIDAY INN EXPRESS   Guaranteed Rates   Phone: 770/664-6661
◆◆◆   Sun-Thurs [CP]   1P: $99   2P/1B: $99   2P/2B: $99
Motel   Fri & Sat [CP]   1P: $69   2P/1B: $69   2P/2B: $69
Location: SR 400 exit 11, 0.5 mi w. 5455 Windward Pkwy 30201. **Fax:** 770/664-4775. **Terms:** Sr. discount;
no pets. **Facility:** 65 rooms. 4 stories; interior corridors. **All Rooms:** free & pay movies. **Cards:** AE, CB, DI, DS, JCB, MC,
VI. *(See color ad p 190)*   Roll in showers. (CTV) (🛗) (✕) (D) (S)

RESIDENCE INN BY MARRIOTT   Rates Subject to Change   Phone: 770/664-0664
◆◆◆   All Year [CP]   1P: $78- 175 2P/1B: $78- 175 2P/2B: $78- 175
Apartment   **Location:** SR 400 exit 11; 0.6 mi w. 5465 Windward Pkwy W 30201. **Fax:** 770/664-7781. **Terms:** Sr.
Motel   discount; pets, $100-$200 fee. **Facility:** 103 rooms. Rates for 3 to 5 persons; 2-3 stories; interior/exterior cor-
ridors. **All Rooms:** kitchens, free movies. **Cards:** AE, CB, DI, DS, MC, VI.
(H) (➔) (➔K) (CTV) (✕) (🗗) (D) (S)

AUSTELL—4,200   (See map p. 202; index p. 199)

LODGINGS

DAYS INN SIX FLAGS   Phone: 770/941-1400   (210)
(AAA) (SAVE)   All Year [CP]   1P: $64- 79 2P/1B: $69- 85 2P/2B: $69- 85 XP: $5   F5
◆◆   **Location:** I-20, westbound exit 13C; eastbound exit 13, just s. 95 S Service Rd SW 30001.
Motel   **Fax:** 770/819-9988. **Terms:** Reserv deposit, 7 day notice; small pets only. **Facility:** 97 rooms. 6 rooms with 3
beds $69 for up to 6 persons; 2 stories; exterior corridors. **All Rooms:** free movies, safes. **Cards:** AE, DI,
DS, MC, VI. **Special Amenities: Free breakfast.**   (H) (➔) (🛇) (CTV) (✕) (D)

(See map p. 202)

KNIGHTS INN-ATLANTA WEST/SIX FLAGS　　　Rates Subject to Change　　　**Phone:** 770/944-0824　🔲212
◆　　　5/1-9/30　　　　　　　　1P: $52　　2P/1B: $57　　2P/2B: $59　　XP: $5　　F18
Motel　　12/1-4/30 & 10/1-11/30　1P: $42　　2P/1B: $47　　2P/2B: $49　　XP: $5　　F18
　　　　　Location: Just ne of I-20, exit 12. 1595 Blair Bridge Rd 30001. Fax: 770/819-9739. **Terms:** Sr. discount;
check-in 4 pm; pets, $10 extra charge. **Facility:** 95 rooms. 1 story; exterior corridors. **All Rooms:** free movies. **Cards:** AE,
DS, MC, VI.　　　　　　　　　　　　　　　　　　　　　　　　　　　　🛏️ 🅿️ 📺 ✖️ 🐾 🇩

LA QUINTA ATLANTA WEST-SIX FLAGS　　　　　　　　　　　　　　**Phone:** 770/944-2110　🔲211
🆎 SAVE　5/25-9/2 [CP]　　　　　1P: $86　　2P/1B: $86　　2P/2B: $86　　XP: $10　　F18
　　　　12/1-5/24 & 9/3-11/30 [CP]　1P: $65- 77　2P/1B: $65- 77　2P/2B: $65- 77　XP: $10　　F18
◆◆◆　**Location:** At I-20 exit 13B westbound, exit 13 eastbound. 7377 Six Flags Dr 30001. Fax: 770/739-1698.
Motel　　**Terms:** Check-in 4 pm; small pets only. **Facility:** 106 rooms. Hillside location. Spanish-style architecture. 3
　　　　stories; interior/exterior corridors. **Dining:** Restaurant nearby. **Services:** Fee: coin laundry.
All Rooms: coffeemakers, free & pay movies. **Some Rooms:** microwaves, refrigerators. **Cards:** AE, CB, DI, DS, MC, VI.
Special Amenities: Free breakfast and free local telephone calls. *(See color ad p 205)*
　　　　　　　　　　　　　　　　　　　　　　　　　　　　　　🛏️ 🅿️ 🍴 📺 ✖️ 🐾 🇩

RESTAURANT
WALLACE BARBECUE　　　**Lunch:** $4-$9　　　**Dinner:** $4-$9　　　**Phone:** 770/739-1686　🔲167
◆　　　**Location:** I-20 exit 12, 2.8 mi n on Thornton Rd, 0.8 mi e on US 78/US 278 (Bankhead Hwy). 3035
American　Bankhead Hwy 30001. **Hours:** 10:30 am-9 pm, Fri & Sat-10 pm. Closed major holidays, Sun & Mon.
　　　　　Features: casual dress; children's menu; carryout. Traditional Georgia hickory pit barbecue from family
recipes dating back to 1947.

CHAMBLEE—7,700　　(See map p. 202; index p. 199)
RESTAURANT
ORIENTAL PEARL RESTAURANT　　　　　　　　　　　　　　　　**Phone:** 770/986-9866　🔲176
◆◆　　**Location:** In Chinatown Square. 5399 New Peachtree Rd 30341. **Hours:** 11 am-3 & 5-10:30 pm, Fri-11 pm,
Chinese　Sat 11 am-11 pm, Sun 11 am-10:30 pm. **Reservations:** suggested. **Features:** casual dress; Sunday brunch;
　　　　　children's menu; beer & wine only. Decorated with handsome etched glass & strips of mirror fanned out in a
style reminiscent of Art Deco. **Cards:** AE, DS, MC, VI.　　　　　　　　　　　　　　　　✖️

COLLEGE PARK—20,500　　(See map p. 225; index p. 224)
LODGINGS
BUDGETEL INN-ATLANTA AIRPORT　　　　　　　　　　　　　　**Phone:** 404/766-0000　🔲237
🆎 SAVE　All Year [CP]　　　　　1P: $49　　2P/1B: $51　　2P/2B: $60　　XP: $7　　F18
　　　　　Location: I-85S, exit 16; I-285, exit 1; se corner behind Holiday Inn. 2480 Old National Pkwy 30349.
◆◆　　Fax: 404/763-9162. **Terms:** Small pets only. **Facility:** 100 rooms. 3 stories; interior corridors.
Motel　　**Dining:** Restaurant nearby. **Services:** valet laundry. **All Rooms:** coffeemakers, free & pay movies.
　　　　　Some Rooms: microwaves, refrigerators. **Cards:** AE, CB, DI, DS, MC, VI. **Special Amenities:** Free
breakfast and free local telephone calls. *(See color ad p 188)*　　　🛏️ 🍴 ♿ 📺 ✖️ 🐾 🇩 🇸

CLUB HOTEL BY DOUBLETREE　　　　Rates Subject to Change　　　**Phone:** 404/761-4000　🔲243
◆◆◆　Mon-Thurs　　　　　　　1P: $90　　2P/1B: $90　　2P/2B: $90　　XP: $10　　F18
Motor Inn　Fri-Sun　　　　　　　1P: $65　　2P/1B: $65　　2P/2B: $65　　XP: $10　　F18
　　　　　Location: I-85, exit 16 or I-285 exit 1, se corner. 5010 Old National Hwy 30349. Fax: 404/763-0181.
Terms: Sr. discount; pets, $20 extra charge. **Facility:** 232 rooms. 7 stories; interior corridors. **Dining:** Restaurant; 6 am-2 &
5-10 pm; $8-$17. **All Rooms:** Fee: movies. **Cards:** AE, CB, DI, DS, MC, VI.　　🛏️ 🅿️ 🍴 ♿ 📺 ✖️ 🇩 🇸

COMFORT INN ATLANTA AIRPORT　　　　　　　　　　　　　　**Phone:** 770/991-1099　🔲244
🆎 SAVE　All Year　　　　　　　1P: $79- 129　2P/1B: $79- 129　2P/2B: $79- 129　XP: $10　　F18
　　　　　Location: I-285 exit 43, just s on Riverdale Rd; 0.5 mi w on Phoenix Blvd. 1808 Phoenix Blvd 30349.
◆◆　　Fax: 770/991-1076. **Terms:** No pets. **Facility:** 194 rooms. 4 stories; interior corridors. **Dining &**
Motor Inn　**Entertainment:** Restaurant; 6 am-2 & 6-11 pm, Sat & Sun 7 am-11 & 6-11 pm; $7-$16; cocktails/lounge.
　　　　　Services: area transportation, within 3 mi. Fee: coin laundry. **All Rooms:** free & pay movies. **Cards:** AE,
CB, DI, DS, JCB, MC, VI. **Special Amenities:** Free breakfast and free local telephone calls. *(See ad below)*
　　　　　　　　　　　　　　　　　　　　　　　　　　　　　　🅿️ 🍴 ♿ 📺 ✖️ 🐾 🇩

(See map p. 225)

COMFORT SUITES-ATLANTA AIRPORT   Phone: 770/996-0000   241
All Year [CP]   1P: $65- 89 2P/1B: $65- 89 2P/2B: $65- 89 XP: $10-20   F18
Location: I-85 exit 18, 0.8 mi to Sullivan Rd; 0.8 mi sw; I-285 exit 43, 1 mi n to Sullivan Rd, 0.8 mi sw. 4820
Massachusetts Blvd 30337-6603. Fax: 770/996-9260. Terms: Check-in 4 pm; no pets. Facility: 70 rooms.
Suite Motel   Spacious rooms. 4 stories; interior corridors. Services: valet laundry; area transportation, within 2 mi.
All Rooms: coffeemakers, microwaves, free movies, refrigerators. Cards: AE, CB, DI, DS, JCB, MC, VI.
Special Amenities: Free breakfast and free local telephone calls.

COURTYARD BY MARRIOTT-AIRPORT SOUTH   Rates Subject to Change   Phone: 770/997-2220   247
Motor Inn   Sun-Thurs   1P: $99   2P/1B: $109   2P/2B: $109   XP: $10   F12
Fri & Sat   1P: $79   2P/1B: $79   2P/2B: $79
Location: I-85, Riverdale Rd exit 18, 0.8 mi e on Riverdale Rd, then 0.8 mi sw on Sullivan Rd. I-285 exit 43,
1 mi n to Sullivan Rd, then 0.8 mi sw. 2050 Sullivan Rd 30337. Fax: 770/994-9743. Terms: Sr. discount; check-in 4 pm; no
pets. Facility: 144 rooms. Weekend rates for up to 4 persons; 3 stories; interior/exterior corridors. Dining: Restaurant;
6:30-11 am, Sat & Sun 7 am-noon, dinner delivery avail. All Rooms: free & pay movies. Cards: AE, CB, DI, DS, MC, VI.
See color ad p 192)

DAYS INN AIRPORT SOUTH   Rates Subject to Change   Phone: 770/996-7300   245
Motel   All Year [CP]   1P: $59- 69 2P/1B: $67- 75 2P/2B: $67- 75 XP: $5   F13
Location: I-285 exit 43, just s. 1540 Phoenix Blvd 30349. Fax: 770/907-2101. Terms: Sr. discount; no pets.
Facility: 50 rooms. 2 stories; interior corridors. All Rooms: free movies. Cards: AE, DI, DS, MC, VI.
Roll in showers.

EMBASSY SUITES HOTEL AT ATLANTA AIRPORT   Guaranteed Rates   Phone: 404/767-1988   236
Suite Hotel   All Year [BP]   1P: $119   2P/1B: $119   2P/2B: $119   XP: $20   F18
Location: I-85S exit 18; 0.3 mi w on Riverdale Rd. 4700 Southport Rd 30337. Fax: 404/768-2080.
Terms: No pets. Facility: 233 rooms. 5 stories; interior corridors. Dining: Restaurant; 11 am-2 & 5:30-10
pm, Sat & Sun-11 pm; $10-$19. All Rooms: free & pay movies. Cards: AE, DI, DS, MC, VI. (See color ad p 210)

FAIRFIELD INN-BY MARRIOTT AIRPORT   Rates Subject to Change   Phone: 404/761-8371   252
Motel   All Year [CP]   1P: $50- 60 2P/1B: $60- 70 2P/2B: $60- 70 XP: $10   F18
Location: From I-85S, exit 16; I-285, exit 1; se corner behind Holiday Inn. 2451 Old National Pkwy 30349.
Fax: 404/761-8371. Terms: No pets. Facility: 132 rooms. 3 stories; interior/exterior corridors.
All Rooms: free & pay movies. Cards: AE, CB, DI, DS, MC, VI. (See color ad p 211)

HAMPTON INN-ATLANTA AIRPORT   Rates Subject to Change   Phone: 770/996-2220   239
Motel   All Year [CP]   1P: $70   2P/1B: $80   2P/2B: $80
Location: I-85 exit 18, 0.8 mi e on Riverdale Rd, 0.5 mi s on Sullivan Rd; I-285 exit 43, Riverdale Rd N, 1
mi to Sullivan Rd, 0.5 mi sw. 1888 Sullivan Rd 30337. Fax: 770/996-2488. Terms: Sr. discount; no pets.
Facility: 130 rooms. Rates for up to 4 persons; 4 stories; interior corridors. All Rooms: free & pay movies. Cards: AE, CB,
DI, DS, MC, VI.

LA QUINTA INN AIRPORT   Phone: 404/768-1241   251
All Year [CP]   1P: $59- 65 2P/1B: $65- 71 2P/2B: $65- 71 XP: $7   F18
Location: I-85 exit 16B, I-285 exit 1, ne corner. 4874 Old National Hwy 30337. Fax: 404/766-3642.
Terms: Small pets only. Facility: 122 rooms. Nicely done "gold medal" rooms. 2 stories; exterior corridors.
Motel   Dining: Restaurant nearby. Services: valet laundry; area transportation, 6 am-midnight.
All Rooms: coffeemakers, free & pay movies. Cards: AE, CB, DI, DS, MC, VI. Special Amenities: Free
breakfast and free local telephone calls. (See color ad p 205)

MARRIOTT ATLANTA AIRPORT   Rates Subject to Change   Phone: 404/766-7900   250
Hotel   Sun-Thurs   1P: $134   2P/1B: $134   2P/2B: $149
Fri & Sat   1P: $74   2P/1B: $74   2P/2B: $74
Location: I-85, exit 18; just w, se on access road to Best Rd, just s. 4711 Best Rd 30337.
Fax: 404/209-6808. Terms: Sr. discount; small pets only. Facility: 642 rooms. Handling fee imposed; 16 stories; interior cor-
ridors. Dining: Dining room, restaurant, coffee shop; 6:30 am-11 pm; $7-$24. All Rooms: free & pay movies. Cards: AE,
CB, DI, DS, JCB, MC, VI.   Roll in showers.

MICROTEL INN   Guaranteed Rates   Phone: 770/994-3003   248
Motel   All Year   1P: $41- 55 2P/1B: $41- 55 2P/2B: $41- 55
Too new to rate; Location: I-85 exit 18, 0.8 mi e on Riverdale Rd, 0.8 mi sw; I-285 exit 43, Riverdale Rd N,
1 mi to Sullivan Rd, 0.5 mi sw. Massachusetts Blvd 30349. Terms: Sr. discount; no pets. Facility: 103 rooms. Scheduled to
open August 1997; 3 stories; interior corridors. All Rooms: free movies. Cards: AE, CB, DI, DS, MC, VI.
See color ad p 245)   Roll in showers.

RADISSON HOTEL-ATLANTA AIRPORT   Rates Subject to Change   Phone: 404/768-7800   234
Motor Inn   All Year   1P: $85- 125 2P/1B: $95- 125 2P/2B: $95- 125 XP: $10   F16
Location: I-85, exit 19 (Virginia Ave), just w. 1419 Virginia Ave 30337. Fax: 404/767-5451. Terms: Sr.
discount; no pets. Facility: 245 rooms. 6 stories; interior corridors. Dining: Restaurant; 11 am-11 pm; food
court on site 6 am-1 am; $6-$16. All Rooms: free & pay movies. Cards: AE, DI, DS, MC, VI.

RED ROOF INN AIRPORT   Rates Subject to Change   Phone: 404/761-9701   242
5/1-9/30   1P: $56   2P/1B: $39- 63 2P/2B: $47- 72 XP: $7   F18
Motel   4/1-4/30   1P: $49   2P/1B: $56   2P/2B: $63   XP: $7   F18
12/1-3/31 & 10/1-11/30   1P: $44   2P/1B: $51   2P/2B: $58   XP: $7   F18
Location: I-85 exit 16; I-285 exit 1, just s. 2471 Old National Pkwy 30349. Fax: 404/761-9861. Terms: Small pets only.
Facility: 108 rooms. 2 stories; exterior corridors. All Rooms: free & pay movies. Cards: AE, CB, DI, DS, MC, VI.

(See map p. 225)

SHERATON GATEWAY HOTEL, ATLANTA AIRPORT   Rates Subject to Change   **Phone: 770/997-1100** 24
◆◆◆   Mon-Thurs   1P: $109- 154 2P/1B: $119- 164 2P/2B: $119- 164 XP: $10   F1
Hotel   Fri-Sun   1P: $77- 139 2P/1B: $77- 149 2P/2B: $77- 149 XP: $10   F1
   Location: I-85 exit 18, 0.8 mi e to Sullivan Rd, 0.8 mi sw; I-285, exit 43, 1 mi n to Sullivan Rd, 0.8 mi sw. 1900 Sullivan Rd 30337. Fax: 770/991-5906. **Terms:** No pets. **Facility:** 396 rooms. 12 stories; interior corridor. **Dining:** Restaurant; 6:30 am-10 pm; $16-$24. **All Rooms:** free & pay movies. **Cards:** AE, CB, DI, DS, JCB, MC, VI.

THE WESTIN HOTEL-ATLANTA AIRPORT   **Phone: 404/762-7676** 24
AAA SAVE   Mon-Thurs   1P: $109- 170 2P/1B: $109- 170 2P/2B: $129- 190 XP: $20   F1
   Fri-Sun 12/1-6/14 &
   9/16-11/30   1P: $79- 99 2P/1B: $79- 99 2P/2B: $79- 99 XP: $10   F1
◆◆◆   Fri-Sun 6/15-9/15   1P: $69- 99 2P/1B: $69- 99 2P/2B: $69- 99 XP: $10   F1
Hotel   **Location:** I-85 exit 18, just w, se on access road to Best Rd, just s. 4736 Best Rd 3033. Fax: 404/763-4199. **Terms:** Reserv deposit; no pets. **Facility:** 495 rooms. 10 stories; interior corridors. **Dining:** Restaurant 6:30 am-11 pm; $17-$28. **All Rooms:** free & pay movies. **Cards:** AE, CB, DI, DS, JCB, MC, VI. *(See ad below)*
   Roll in showers.

WINGATE INN ATLANTA AIRPORT   Guaranteed Rates   **Phone: 770/994-3666** 23
Motel   All Year   1P: $69- 89 2P/1B: $69- 89 2P/2B: $69- 89
   Too new to rate; **Location:** I-85 exit 18, 0.8 mi e on Riverdale Rd, I-285 exit 43, Riverdale Rd N, 1 mi Sullivan Rd, 0.5 mi sw. Sullivan Rd 30337. **Terms:** Sr. discount; check-in 4 pm; no pets. **Facility:** 125 rooms. Scheduled open August 1997; 4 stories; interior corridors. **All Rooms:** free movies. **Cards:** AE, CB, DI, DS, MC, VI.

RESTAURANT

CAJUN CRAB HOUSE   **Lunch: $6-$12**   **Dinner: $11-$20**   **Phone: 404/209-9432** 18
◆◆   **Location:** I-85 exit 16, I-285 exit 1; 1 mi s on Old National Hwy. 5495 Old National Hwy 30349. **Hours:** 1 am-10 pm, Fri-midnight, Sat 1 pm-midnight, Sun 1 pm-10 pm. Closed major holidays. **Features:** casu
Ethnic   dress; children's menu; senior's menu; carryout; cocktails & lounge. Good variety of Cajun & Creole seafoo dishes served in upscale atmosphere which reflects a touch of New Orleans. Jazz 5 nights a week. **Cards:** AE, DI, DS, MC VI.

CONLEY—5,500

LODGING

ECONO LODGE-CONLEY/ATLANTA   **Phone: 404/363-696**
AAA SAVE   All Year [CP]   1P: $39- 45 2P/1B: $45- 55 2P/2B: $50- 65 XP: $5   F1
   Location: I-285 exit 39. 3140 Moreland Ave 30027. Fax: 404/363-2799. **Terms:** No pets. **Facility:** 94 room
◆◆   Budget accommodations. 2 stories; exterior corridors. **Services:** Fee: coin laundry. **All Rooms:** free movie
Motel   **Cards:** AE, CB, DI, DS, JCB, MC, VI. **Special Amenities:** Free breakfast and free newspaper.

CRABAPPLE—300

RESTAURANT

MR JOHN B'S, A HISTORIC RESTAURANT Historical **Lunch: $6-$8**   **Dinner: $13-$17**   **Phone: 404/751-738**
◆◆   **Location:** Historic district; jct SR 372 & Mayfield Rd, just e. 780 Mayfield Rd 30201. **Hours:** 11:30 am-3 pr
American   Wed-Sat 11:30 am-3 & 5:30-9:30 pm. Closed: Sun, 1/1, 11/26 & 12/25. **Reservations:** suggeste
   Features: casual dress; health conscious menu items; carryout; beer & wine only. Historic farm house cir
1860 with period antiques. Fireplace in each cozy dining room. Smoke free premises. **Cards:** AE, DI, MC, VI.

DECATUR—17,300   (See map p. 225; index p. 224)

LODGINGS

ECONO LODGE I-20   **Phone: 404/243-4422** 36
AAA SAVE   All Year [CP]   2P/1B: $50 2P/2B: $65 XP: $5   F1
   Location: I-20 exit 33 ne corner; 1.5 mi w of I-285. 2574 Candler Rd 30032. Fax: 404/243-526
◆◆   **Terms:** Reserv deposit; no pets. **Facility:** 59 rooms. 2 stories; exterior corridors. **Dining:** Restaurant nearb
Motel   **All Rooms:** free movies. **Some Rooms:** coffeemakers, radios. Fee: whirlpools. **Cards:** AE, CB, DI, D
   JCB, MC, VI. **Special Amenities:** Free breakfast and preferred room (subject to availability wi
advanced reservations).

(See map p. 225)

GLENWOOD INN
Phone: 404/288-5504 · **362**
All Year 1P: $42 2P/1B: $48 2P/2B: $52 XP: $5 F7
[AAA] [SAVE]
◆ ◆
Motel
Location: I-285 exit 34, 0.3 mi w. 4460 Glenwood Rd 30032. **Terms:** No pets. **Facility:** 34 rooms. In neighborhood that is in transition. Rates for up to 4 persons; 2 stories; exterior corridors. **Dining:** Restaurant nearby. **All Rooms:** free movies. **Some Rooms:** Fee: VCP's. **Cards:** AE, DI, DS, MC, VI. **Special Amenities:** Free breakfast and free local telephone calls. [CTV] [D] [S]

HOLIDAY INN EXPRESS I-20 EAST
Phone: 770/981-5670 · **365**
All Year [CP] 1P: $53- 70 2P/1B: $60- 70 2P/2B: $60- 70 XP: $6 F18
[AAA] [SAVE]
◆ ◆ ◆
Motel
Location: I-20 exit 36; just ne. 4300 Snapfinger Woods Dr 30035. Fax: 770/322-9854. **Terms:** Pets, $25 dep req. **Facility:** 167 rooms. 2 stories; exterior corridors; wading pool. **Services:** valet laundry. **All Rooms:** combo or shower baths. Fee: movies. **Cards:** AE, CB, DI, DS, JCB, MC, VI. **Special Amenities:** Free breakfast and free newspaper. *(See color ad p 190)*
Roll in showers. [icons] [CTV] [X] [D]

HOLIDAY INN SELECT DECATUR CONFERENCE PLAZA
Phone: 404/371-0204 · **364**
All Year 1P: $99 2P/1B: $109 2P/2B: $109 XP: $10 F12
[AAA] [SAVE]
◆ ◆ ◆
Motor Inn
Location: I-85, exit 32; 4 mi se. 130 Clairemont Ave 30030. Fax: 404/377-2726. **Terms:** BP avail; no pets. **Facility:** 184 rooms. 1 blk from Marta. Stylish room decor. Atrium lobby. 3 king suites with refrigerator, wet bar & parlor; 5 stories; interior corridors; whirlpool. **Dining & Entertainment:** Restaurant; 6:30 am-11 pm; $11-$17; cocktails/lounge; lunch buffet Mon-Fri; Sun brunch. **Services:** valet laundry; area transportation, within 5 mi. **All Rooms:** coffeemakers, free & pay movies. **Some Rooms:** Fee: refrigerators. **Cards:** AE, CB, DI, DS, JCB, MC, VI. **Special Amenities:** Free local telephone calls and free newspaper. *(See color ad p 190)*
[icons] [CTV] [X] [D] [S]

RAMADA LIMITED
Phone: 404/288-8722 · **366**
All Year [CP] 1P: $55 2P/1B: $60- 75 2P/2B: $65- 75 XP: $10 F18
[AAA] [SAVE]
◆ ◆
Motel
Location: I-285, exit 32, 2.5 mi sw. 3403 Memorial Dr 30032. Fax: 404/286-2843. **Terms:** No pets. **Facility:** 80 rooms. Handling fee imposed; 2 stories; exterior corridors. **All Rooms:** free movies. **Some Rooms:** microwaves, refrigerators. **Some Rooms:** Fee: whirlpools. **Cards:** AE, CB, DI, DS, MC, VI. **Special Amenities:** Free breakfast and free room upgrade (subject to availability with advanced reservations). [icons] [CTV] [X] [D] [S]

RESTAURANT

TOP OF THE PLAZA
Lunch: $7-$10
Phone: 404/377-7371 · **245**
◆ ◆ ◆
Regional
American
Location: I-85 exit 32, 4 mi se on Clairmont Rd, just n. 250 E Ponce de Leon Ave 30030. **Hours:** 11:30 am-2 pm, Sun 11 am-2:30 pm. Closed major holidays & Sat. **Reservations:** suggested. **Features:** casual dress; Sunday brunch; carryout; cocktails. Enjoy a magnificent view of Atlanta with a clever menu of delicious lunches. Smoke free premises. **Cards:** AE, DS, MC, VI. [X]

DORAVILLE—7,600 (See map p. 202; index p. 199)

LODGINGS

COMFORT INN CONFERENCE CENTER
Phone: 770/455-3700 · **163**
All Year [BP] 1P: $59- 89 2P/1B: $59- 89 2P/2B: $59- 89 XP: $5 F18
[AAA] [SAVE]
◆ ◆ ◆
Motor Inn
Location: I-285 exit 25, se corner. 2001 Clearview Ave. Fax: 770/986-9977. **Terms:** No pets. **Facility:** 252 rooms. 4 stories; interior corridors. **Dining & Entertainment:** Restaurant; 6 am-2:30 & 4:30-8:30 pm, Fri & Sat-9:30 pm; cocktails/lounge. **Services:** area transportation, to rapid transit. Fee: coin laundry. **All Rooms:** free movies, combo or shower baths, VCP's. **Some Rooms:** microwaves, radios, refrigerators. **Cards:** AE, CB, DI, DS, MC, VI. **Special Amenities:** Free breakfast and free local telephone calls.
Roll in showers. [icons] [CTV] [X] [D] [S]

HOLIDAY INN EXPRESS I-85 NORTH
Rates Subject to Change
Phone: 770/448-7220 · **162**
All Year [CP] 1P: $57 2P/1B: $63 2P/2B: $63 XP: $6 F18
◆ ◆
Motel
Location: I-85 exit 36, just sw; 1.3 mi n of I-285; from 285E to I-85, exit Pleasantdale Rd. 4422 Northeast Expwy 30340. Fax: 770/416-6419. **Terms:** Sr. discount; no pets. **Facility:** 199 rooms. 2-4 stories; exterior corridors. **All Rooms:** Fee: movies. **Cards:** AE, CB, DI, DS, JCB, MC, VI. *(See color ad p 190)*
Roll in showers. [icons] [CTV] [X] [D]

MASTERS ECONOMY INN DORAVILLE
Phone: 770/454-8373 · **161**
All Year 1P: $35- 49 2P/1B: $38- 45 2P/2B: $41- 50 XP: $4 F18
[AAA] [SAVE]
◆
Motel
Location: I-85 exit 34, just e, n on Presidential Pkwy. 3092 Presidential Pkwy 30340. Fax: 770/451-4756. **Terms:** Pets, $10 extra charge. **Facility:** 88 rooms. 2 stories; exterior corridors. **All Rooms:** free movies. **Some Rooms:** microwaves, refrigerators. **Cards:** AE, CB, DI, DS, MC, VI. **Special Amenities:** Free local telephone calls. *(See color ad p 215)* [icons] [CTV] [X] [D]

RESTAURANT

SEOUL GARDEN RESTAURANT
Lunch: $6-$10 **Dinner:** $10-$21
Phone: 770/452-0123 · **146**
◆ ◆
Ethnic
Location: I-285 exit 25, 0.8 mi n. 5938 Buford Hwy 30340. **Hours:** 10:30 am-midnight. **Reservations:** accepted. **Features:** casual dress; carryout; beer & wine only. Featuring authentic Korean & Japanese dishes. Sushi bar. **Cards:** AE, MC, VI. [X]

DOUGLASVILLE—11,600

LODGING

QUALITY INN
Rates Subject to Change
Phone: 770/920-9228
◆ ◆ ◆
Motel
5/1-8/31 [CP] 1P: $64- 80 2P/1B: $69- 85 2P/2B: $69- 85 XP: $5 F18
12/1-4/30 & 9/1-11/30 [CP] 1P: $53- 75 2P/1B: $58- 80 2P/2B: $58- 80 XP: $5 F18
Location: I-20 exit 8. 7101 Concourse Pkwy 30134. Fax: 770/920-9482. **Terms:** No pets. **Facility:** 101 rooms. 5 stories; interior corridors. **All Rooms:** free movies. **Cards:** AE, CB, DI, DS, JCB, MC, VI.
Roll in showers. [icons] [CTV] [X] [D] [S]

RESTAURANT

GUMBEAUX'S, A CAJUN CAFE
Lunch: $3-$7 **Dinner:** $11-$20
Phone: 770/947-8288
◆
Ethnic
Location: I-20, exit 9, 2 mi n on Chapel Hill Rd, 0.3 mi w on Broad St. 6698 A Broad St 30134. **Hours:** 11 am-2 & 5-10 pm. Closed major holidays, Sun & Mon. **Features:** casual dress; children's menu; cocktails; a la carte. Cajun & New Orleans style food. Carry out service avail. **Cards:** AE, CB, DI, DS, MC, VI. [X]

DULUTH—9,000

LODGINGS

AMERISUITES/GWINNETT MALL   Phone: 770/623-6800
(AAA) (SAVE)   Sun-Thurs [CP]   1P: $99- 139   2P/1B: $109- 149 2P/2B: $109- 149   XP: $10   F17
              Fri & Sat [CP]   1P: $65- 95   2P/1B: $70- 100 2P/2B: $70- 100   XP: $5   F17
◆ ◆ ◆   **Location:** I-85 exit 40, just w to Venture Pkwy, just n. 3390 Venture Pkwy 30136. Fax: 770/623-0911.
Suite Motel   **Terms:** Weekly/monthly rates; pets, $10 extra charge. **Facility:** 114 rooms. Near Gwinnett Mall. 6 stories; in-
terior corridors. **Dining:** Restaurant nearby. **Services:** valet laundry. **All Rooms:** coffeemakers, microwaves,
free movies, refrigerators, VCP's. **Cards:** AE, CB, DI, DS, JCB, MC, VI. **Special Amenities:** Free breakfast and free local
telephone calls. (See color ad p 10)   🛏 🛍 🍽 ♿ CTV ♿ ✕ 🐾 D S

AMERISUITES-JOHN'S CREEK   Phone: 770/622-5858
(AAA) (SAVE)   All Year   1P: $79- 109   2P/1B: $79- 109 2P/2B: $79- 109   XP: $10   F18
              Too new to rate; **Location:** At corner of SR 141 (Medlock Bridge Rd) & Findley Rd. 11505 Medlock Bridge
Suite Motel   Rd 30155. Fax: 770/622-1113. **Terms:** Small pets only. **Facility:** 128 rooms. Scheduled to open summer 1997.
6 stories; interior corridors. **Services:** complimentary evening beverages, Wed; area transportation, within 4
mi. Fee: coin laundry. **All Rooms:** coffeemakers, microwaves, free movies, refrigerators, combo or shower baths, VCP's, no
A/C. **Cards:** AE, DI, DS, JCB, MC, VI. **Special Amenities:** Free breakfast and free local telephone calls.
(See color ad p 10)   Roll in showers.   🛏 🛍 🍽 ♿ CTV ✕ 🐾 D S

ATLANTA MARRIOTT GWINNETT PLACE   Rates Subject to Change   Phone: 770/923-1775
◆ ◆ ◆   Sun-Thurs   1P: $129- 179   2P/1B: $129- 179 2P/2B: $129- 179
Hotel   Fri & Sat   1P: $59- 99   2P/1B: $59- 99   2P/2B: $59- 99
              Location: I-85 exit 40, just e. 1775 Pleasant Hill Rd 30096. Fax: 770/923-0017. **Terms:** Sr. discount,
check-in 4 pm; small pets only. **Facility:** 426 rooms. Rates for up to 5 persons; 9-17 stories; interior corridors.
Dining: Restaurant, coffee shop; 6:30 am-10:30 pm, Sat & Sun from 7 am; $16-$25. **All Rooms:** free & pay movies.
Cards: AE, CB, DI, DS, JCB, MC, VI.   🛏 🛍 🛍 ✈ CTV ✕ 🐾 D S

COMFORT SUITES-ATLANTA DULUTH   Rates Subject to Change   Phone: 770/931-9299
◆ ◆ ◆   Mon-Thurs [CP]   2P/2B: $69   XP: $6   F18
Motel   Fri-Sun [CP]   2P/2B: $59
              Location: I-85 exit 40, 0.4 mi e. 3700 Shackleford Rd 30136. Fax: 770/564-8614. **Terms:** No pets.
Facility: 85 rooms. 2 stories; interior corridors. **All Rooms:** free & pay movies. **Cards:** AE, CB, DI, DS, JCB, MC, VI.
                                            Roll in showers.   🛍 🛍 CTV ✕ 🐾 D S

COURTYARD BY MARRIOTT-GWINNETT MALL   Rates Subject to Change   Phone: 770/476-4666
◆ ◆ ◆   Mon-Thurs   1P: $94   2P/1B: $104   2P/2B: $104   XP: $10   F18
Motor Inn   Fri-Sun   1P: $49- 59   2P/1B: $49- 59   2P/2B: $49- 59
              Location: I-85 exit 40; just w to Venture Pkwy, just n. 3550 Venture Pkwy 30136. Fax: 770/623-0198.
Terms: Check-in 4 pm; no pets. **Facility:** 146 rooms. 3 stories; interior corridors. **Dining:** 6:30-10 am, Sat & Sun 7-11 am,
breakfast buffet. **All Rooms:** free & pay movies. **Cards:** AE, DI, DS, MC, VI. (See color ad p 192)
                                                  🛍 ✈ CTV ✕ 🐾 D S

FAIRFIELD INN ATLANTA/GWINNETT MALL   Rates Subject to Change   Phone: 770/623-9300
◆ ◆ ◆   All Year [CP]   1P: $50   2P/1B: $60   2P/2B: $60
Motel   **Location:** I-85, exit 40; just w to Venture Pkwy; just n. 3500 Venture Pkwy 30136. Fax: 770/623-9300
              Terms: Sr. discount; no pets. **Facility:** 135 rooms. 3 stories; interior/exterior corridors. **All Rooms:** free &
pay movies. **Cards:** AE, CB, DI, DS, MC, VI. (See color ad p 211)   🛍 ✈ CTV ♿ ✕ 🐾 D S

HOLIDAY INN EXPRESS   Rates Subject to Change   Phone: 770/935-7171
◆ ◆ ◆   Mon-Thurs [CP]   2P/2B: $65
Motel   Fri-Sun [CP]   2P/2B: $55
              Location: I-85 exit 40, 0.4 mi e. 3670 Shackleford Rd 30136. Fax: 770/806-1691. **Terms:** Sr. discount; no
pets. **Facility:** 68 rooms. 3 stories; interior corridors. **All Rooms:** free & pay movies. **Cards:** AE, DI, DS, MC, VI.
                                                  🛍 CTV ✕ 🐾 D S

SUMNER SUITES- GWINNETT MALL   Phone: 770/623-9699
(AAA) (SAVE)   All Year [CP]   1P: $79- 109   2P/1B: $79- 109 2P/2B: $79- 109   XP: $10   F18
              Location: 3530 Venture Park Way 30136. Fax: 770/623-4643. **Terms:** Weekend rates avail; no pets.
◆ ◆ ◆   **Facility:** 125 rooms. 6 stories; interior corridors. **Dining & Entertainment:** Cocktail lounge; restaurant
Motel   nearby. **Services:** Fee: coin laundry. **All Rooms:** coffeemakers, microwaves, free movies, refrigerators.
              Some Rooms: Fee: VCP's. **Cards:** AE, CB, DI, DS, MC, VI. **Special Amenities:** Free breakfast and free
local telephone calls.   🛍 🍽 ♿ CTV 🐾 D S

RESTAURANTS

CORKY'S BAR B-Q   **Lunch:** $6-$14   **Dinner:** $6-$14   Phone: 770/564-8666
◆   **Location:** I-75, exit 40, 0.8 mi e. 1605 Pleasant Hill Rd 30136. **Hours:** 11 am-10 pm, Fri & Sat-11 pm
Regional   Closed: 11/26 & 12/25. **Features:** casual dress; Sunday brunch; children's menu; carryout; cocktails &
American   lounge. Casual with class. Inviting decor accented with touch of Memphis blues. Traditional Memphis-style
              slow cooked barbecue. **Cards:** AE, MC, VI.   ✕

KURT'S   **Lunch:** $7-$13   **Dinner:** $15-$26   Phone: 770/623-4128
(AAA)   **Location:** From jct Peachtree Industrial Blvd & Pleasant Hill Rd, 1 mi n. 4225 River Green Pkwy 30136
              Hours: 11:30 am-2:30 & 6-10 pm, Sat from 6 pm. Closed major holidays & Sun. **Reservations:** suggested
◆ ◆ ◆   **Features:** casual dress; carryout; cocktails & lounge. Fine dining in a quiet, rural setting. Upscale casual
Continental   dress. Gracious service. Very good wine list. Espresso/cappuccino. Flambe desserts. Veal, shrimp India &
              lamb chops are favorites. **Cards:** AE, DI, DS, JCB, MC, VI.   ✕

PROVINO'S ITALIAN RESTAURANT   **Dinner:** $7-$15   Phone: 770/497-8841
◆ ◆   **Location:** I-85, exit 40, 2 blks w in Mall Corners Shopping Center, behind Burger King. 3606 Satellite Blvd
Italian   30136. **Hours:** 4:30 pm-10 pm, Fri & Sat-11 pm. Closed: 1/1, 11/26, 12/24 & 12/25. **Features:** casual dress;
              children's menu; early bird specials; carryout; beer & wine only; a la carte. Family-oriented. **Cards:** AE, DS
MC, VI.   ✕

EAST POINT—34,400   (See map p. 225; index p. 224)

LODGINGS

HOLIDAY INN AIRPORT NORTH   Rates Subject to Change   **Phone:** 404/762-8411   **260**
◆◆◆   All Year   1P: $89   2P/1B: $101   2P/2B: $101   XP: $12   F18
Motor Inn   **Location:** I-85, southbound exit 19 sw corner; northbound exit 19B. 1380 Virginia Ave 30344.
Fax: 404/767-4963. **Terms:** Sr. discount; no pets. **Facility:** 493 rooms. 4-5 stories; interior/exterior corridors.
Dining: Restaurant; 6 am-2 & 5-11 pm; $8-$17. **All Rooms:** free & pay movies. **Cards:** AE, CB, DI, DS, JCB, MC, VI.
(See color ad p 190)   Roll in showers. 🛏 ✈ CTV ♿ ✕ 🐾 D

SHERATON INN ATLANTA AIRPORT   Rates Subject to Change   **Phone:** 404/762-5566   **259**
◆◆◆   All Year   1P: $89   2P/1B: $89   2P/2B: $89   XP: $10   F18
Motor Inn   **Location:** I-285 exit 3, just ne. 3601 N Desert Dr 30344. Fax: 404/768-1106. **Terms:** No pets. **Facility:** 189
rooms. 6 stories; interior corridors. **Dining:** Dining room; 6 am-2 & 6-10 pm; $15-$25. **All Rooms:** free & pay
movies. **Cards:** AE, CB, DI, DS, MC, VI.   🛏 🛏 ✈ CTV ✕ D S

RESTAURANT

MALONE'S GRILL & BAR-AIRPORT   **Lunch:** $8-$19   **Dinner:** $8-$19   **Phone:** 404/762-5577   **182**
◆   **Location:** I-85, exit 19, se corner. 1258 Virginia Ave 30344. **Hours:** 11 am-1 am, Sun from 11:30 am.
American   Closed: 11/26 & 12/25. **Features:** casual dress; children's menu; health conscious menu; carryout; cocktails
& lounge. Specialties include fajitas & steak. **Cards:** AE, DI, DS, MC, VI.
✕

FOREST PARK—16,900   (See map p. 225; index p. 224)

LODGINGS

COMFORT INN FOREST PARK   **Phone:** 404/361-1111   **283**
AAA SAVE   All Year [CP]   1P: $50- 100   2P/1B: $55- 110   2P/2B: $55- 120   XP: $5   F18
◆◆   **Location:** I-285 exit 40, just n. 3701 Jonesboro Rd 30354. Fax: 404/366-0294. **Terms:** Reserv deposit; no
Motel   pets. **Facility:** 73 rooms. Across from Atlanta Exposition Center. 1 suite avail $65-$125; 2 stories; exterior cor-
ridors. **Services:** Fee: coin laundry. **All Rooms:** free movies. **Some Rooms:** microwaves, refrigerators.
Cards: AE, CB, DI, DS, JCB, MC, VI. **Special Amenities: Free breakfast and free local telephone calls.**
🛏 🖐 CTV ✕ D

DAYS INN AIRPORT EAST   Rates Subject to Change   **Phone:** 404/768-6400   **281**
◆◆   5/1-9/15 [CP]   1P: $50- 60   2P/1B: $55- 80   2P/2B: $55- 80   XP: $5   F13
Motel   12/1-4/30 & 9/16-11/30 [CP]   1P: $45- 55   2P/1B: $50- 75   2P/2B: $50- 75   XP: $5   F13
Location: I-75 southbound exit 80; I-75 northbound exit 78; 0.5 mi w. 5116 Hwy 85 30297.
Fax: 404/767-5138. **Terms:** Sr. discount; no pets. **Facility:** 206 rooms. Safe key, $1.50; 4 stories; exterior corridors.
All Rooms: free & pay movies. **Cards:** AE, CB, DI, DS, MC, VI.   🛏 ✈ CTV ✕ D

RAMADA LIMITED SUITES   Rates Subject to Change   **Phone:** 404/768-7799   **280**
◆◆◆   5/1-9/15 [CP]   1P: $75- 95   2P/1B: $95- 105   2P/2B: $95- 105   XP: $5   F13
Motel   12/1-4/30 & 9/16-11/30 [CP]   1P: $65- 75   2P/1B: $75- 85   2P/2B: $75- 85   XP: $5   F13
Location: I-75 southbound exit 80; I-75 northbound exit 78, 0.5 mi w. 357 Lee St 30297. Fax: 404/768-5282.
Terms: Sr. discount; no pets. **Facility:** 79 rooms. 4 stories; interior corridors. **All Rooms:** free & pay movies. **Cards:** AE,
CB, DI, DS, MC.   Roll in showers. ✈ CTV ✕ D S

HAPEVILLE—5,500   (See map p. 225; index p. 224)

LODGING

COURTYARD BY MARRIOTT ATLANTA AIRPORT NORTH   Rates Subject to Change   **Phone:** 404/559-1043   **266**
◆◆◆   Sun-Thurs   1P: $89   2P/1B: $98   2P/2B: $98   XP: $10
Motor Inn   Fri & Sat   1P: $71   2P/1B: $71   2P/2B: $71
Location: I-85, exit 19 (Virginia Ave), 0.5 mi e to International Blvd 2 blks n. 3399 International Blvd 30354.
Fax: 404/559-1234. **Terms:** No pets. **Facility:** 151 rooms. Weekend rates for up to 4 persons; 4 stories; interior corridors.
Dining: Restaurant; 6:30 am-9 pm, Sat & Sun from 7 am; $7-$12. **All Rooms:** free & pay movies. **Cards:** AE, DI, DS, MC,
VI. *(See color ad p 192)*   🛏 ✈ CTV ✕ D S

JONESBORO—3,600   (See map p. 225; index p. 224)

LODGINGS

COMFORT INN ATLANTA-SOUTH   **Phone:** 770/961-6336   **296**
AAA SAVE   All Year [CP]   1P: $50- 60   2P/1B: $55- 70   2P/2B: $60- 70   XP: $5   F16
◆◆   **Location:** I-75 exit 77, just sw. 6370 Old Dixie Hwy 30236. Fax: 770/961-0946. **Terms:** No pets. **Facility:** 67
Motel   rooms. Tastefully appointed rooms. 2 stories; exterior corridors. **Dining:** Restaurant nearby.
All Rooms: microwaves, free movies, refrigerators. Fee: VCP. **Cards:** AE, CB, DI, DS, JCB, MC, VI.
Special Amenities: Free breakfast and free local telephone calls.   🛏 🖐 CTV ✕ 🐾 D

DAYS INN   Rates Subject to Change   **Phone:** 770/968-4700   **297**
◆◆   All Year [CP]   1P: $36- 50   2P/1B: $41- 85   2P/2B: $41- 85   XP: $5   F18
Motel   **Location:** I-75 exit 77; just sw. 6326 Old Dixie Hwy 30236. Fax: 770/968-6677. **Terms:** Sr. discount; no pets.
Facility: 156 rooms. 4 stories; exterior corridors. **All Rooms:** free movies. **Cards:** AE, CB, DI, DS, JCB, MC,
VI.   🛏 ✈ CTV ✕ D S

ECONOMY INN   Rates Subject to Change   **Phone:** 770/603-6700   **295**
◆◆   All Year   1P: $45- 50   2P/1B: $50- 60   2P/2B: $50- 65   XP: $5   F18
Motel   **Location:** I-75 exit 77, 4 mi sw. 8425 Tara Blvd 30236. **Terms:** Reserv deposit; no pets. **Facility:** 29 rooms.
Exterior corridors. **All Rooms:** free movies. **Cards:** AE, DS, MC, VI.   CTV ✕ D S

HOLIDAY INN-SOUTH   Rates Subject to Change   **Phone:** 770/968-4300   **298**
◆◆◆   All Year   1P: $74- 125   2P/1B: $84- 135   2P/2B: $84- 135   XP: $10   F18
Motor Inn   **Location:** I-75 exit 77, just sw. 6288 Old Dixie Hwy 30236. Fax: 770/968-3872. **Terms:** Sr. discount; pets,
$15 extra charge. **Facility:** 180 rooms. 6 stories; interior corridors. **Dining:** Restaurant; 6:30 am-2 & 5:30-10
pm, Sat & Sun from 7 am; $7-$17. **All Rooms:** Fee: movies. **Cards:** AE, DI, DS, MC, VI. *(See color ad p 190)*
🐾 🛏 CTV ✕ D

KENNESAW—8,900

LODGINGS

COMFORT INN
◆◆
Motel
Rates Subject to Change
All Year [CP]   1P: $60- 65   2P/1B: $70- 75   2P/2B: $70- 75   XP: $5   F12
Location: I-75, exit 116, just e. 750 Cobb Place Blvd 30144. Fax: 770/421-8535. **Terms:** Sr. discount; pets, $5 extra charge. **Facility:** 80 rooms. 2 stories; exterior corridors. **Cards:** AE, DI, DS, MC, VI.
Phone: 770/419-1530

COUNTRY INN & SUITES BY CARLSON
◆◆◆
Motel
Rates Subject to Change
All Year [CP]   1P: $69- 89   2P/1B: $69- 89   2P/2B: $69- 89   XP: $10   F18
Location: I-75 exit 117, just w to Barrett Lakes Blvd, just s. 3192 Barrett Lakes Blvd 30144. Fax: 770/420-1330. **Terms:** Sr. discount; no pets. **Facility:** 46 rooms. 2 stories; interior corridors.
All Rooms: free movies. **Cards:** AE, DI, DS, MC, VI.
Phone: 770/423-7105

ECONO LODGE TOWN CENTER
◆◆◆
Motel
Rates Subject to Change
All Year [CP]   1P: $49- 59   2P/1B: $55- 65   2P/2B: $55- 65   XP: $5   F18
Location: I-75 exit 116,adjacent to Town Center Mall. 2625 George Busbee Pkwy 30144. Fax: 770/426-0045. **Terms:** Sr. discount; no pets. **Facility:** 60 rooms. 4 stories; interior corridors.
All Rooms: free movies. **Cards:** AE, CB, DI, DS, MC, VI.   Roll in showers.
Phone: 770/426-0045

FAIRFIELD INN ATLANTA/KENNESAW
◆◆◆
Motel
All Year [CP]   1P: $54   2P/1B: $59   2P/2B: $59   XP: $3   F12
Location: I-75 exit 117, just e. 3425 George Busbee Pkwy. 30144. Fax: 770/427-9700. **Terms:** Sr. discount; no pets. **Facility:** 87 rooms. 3 stories; interior corridors. **All Rooms:** free movies. **Cards:** AE, CB, DI, DS, MC, VI. *(See color ad p 211)*   Roll in showers.
Phone: 770/427-9700

HAMPTON INN
◆◆◆
Motel
Rates Subject to Change
All Year [CP]   1P: $75- 79   2P/1B: $84- 86   2P/2B: $82
Location: I-75 exit 116, just w to Cobb Place Blvd, just n. 871 Cobb Place Blvd 30144. Fax: 770/426-0071. **Terms:** No pets. **Facility:** 60 rooms. Rates for up to 4 persons; 3 stories; interior corridors. **All Rooms:** free movies. **Cards:** AE, CB, DI, DS, MC, VI.   Roll in showers.
Phone: 770/426-0017

HOLIDAY INN EXPRESS-TOWN CENTER MALL
◆◆◆
Motel
Guaranteed Rates
All Year [CP]   1P: $62- 79   2P/1B: $65- 85   2P/2B: $65- 85   XP: $6   F18
Location: I-75, exit 116; ne corner; adjacent to Town Center Mall. 2485 George Busbee Pkwy NW 30144. Fax: 770/425-4211. **Terms:** No pets. **Facility:** 147 rooms. 6 stories; interior corridors. **All Rooms:** free movies. **Cards:** AE, CB, DI, DS, MC, VI. *(See color ad below)*
Phone: 770/427-5210

RED ROOF INN-TOWN CENTER MALL
◆◆
Motel
Rates Subject to Change
3/1-8/31   1P: $36- 46   2P/1B: $43- 53   2P/2B: $49- 59   XP: $7   F18
12/1-2/28 & 9/1-11/30   1P: $30- 40   2P/1B: $37- 47   2P/2B: $43- 53   XP: $7   F18
Location: I-75 exit 116; se corner. 520 Roberts Ct NW 30144. Fax: 770/429-0262. **Terms:** Small pets only.
Facility: 136 rooms. 3 stories; exterior corridors. **All Rooms:** free movies. **Cards:** AE, CB, DI, DS, MC, VI.
Phone: 770/429-0323

RODEWAY INN
ⒶⒶ SAVE
◆◆
Motel
All Year [CP]   1P: $39- 60   2P/1B: $39- 60   2P/2B: $45- 65   XP: $5   F15
Location: I-75 exit 118, just e. 1460 George Busbee Pkwy 30144. Fax: 770/425-0722. **Terms:** Reserv deposit; pets, $5 extra charge. **Facility:** 57 rooms. 2 stories; exterior corridors. **Dining:** Restaurant nearby. **All Rooms:** free movies. **Some Rooms:** coffeemakers, microwaves, refrigerators, whirlpools. **Cards:** AE, DS, MC, VI.
Phone: 770/590-0519

SHONEY'S INN
◆◆◆
Motel
Guaranteed Rates
All Year [CP]   1P: $58- 79   2P/1B: $64- 85   2P/2B: $64- 85   XP: $6   F18
Location: I-75 exit 116, adjacent to Holiday Inn Express & Town Center Mall. 2489 George Busbee Pkwy 30144. Fax: 770/499-7173. **Terms:** No pets. **Facility:** 61 rooms. 5 stories; interior corridors. **All Rooms:** free movies. **Cards:** AE, CB, DI, DS, MC, VI. *(See color ad p 208)*
Phone: 770/499-9200

WINDSOR INN
ⒶⒶ SAVE
◆◆
Motel
All Year [CP]   1P: $38- 42   2P/1B: $48- 55   2P/2B: $48   XP: $5   F5
Location: I-75 exit 117, 2.3 mi w, 0.8 mi n on US 41. 2655 Cobb Pkwy 30152. Fax: 770/419-8837. **Terms:** No pets. **Facility:** 32 rooms. 1 story; exterior corridors. **Services:** area transportation, within 3 mi. **All Rooms:** coffeemakers, free movies, combo or shower baths. **Some Rooms:** microwaves, refrigerators, whirlpools. Fee: VCP's. **Cards:** AE, DS, MC, VI.
Phone: 770/424-6330

RESTAURANTS

BELL'S BARBECUE & STEAKS   **Lunch:** $5-$11   **Dinner:** $5-$11   **Phone:** 770/419-2626
◆
Regional   **Location:** I-75, exit 118, 0.5 mi w. 3815 Cherokee St 30144. **Hours:** 10:30 am-9 pm, Fri & Sat-10 pm.
American   Closed major holidays, Sun & Mon. **Features:** casual dress; carryout. Beef, pork & chicken barbecue
entrees, Delmonico & NY Strip steak, Brunswick Stew. Casual family eatery.   ⊠

IPPOLITO'S   **Lunch:** $6-$8   **Dinner:** $7-$14   **Phone:** 770/514-8500
◆
Italian   **Location:** I-75 exit 116, 0.3 mi e. 425 Ernest Barret Pkwy 30144. **Hours:** 11:30 am-10 pm, Fri & Sat-11 pm.
Closed major holidays. **Features:** casual dress; children's menu; carryout; cocktail lounge; beer & wine only.
Bustling Italian style cafe featuring pizza, pasta, chicken & veal dishes. Very good desserts. **Cards:** AE, DI,
DS, MC, VI.   ⊠

MANDARIN VILLAGE   **Lunch:** $5-$10   **Dinner:** $7-$16   **Phone:** 770/499-9944
◆ ◆
Chinese   **Location:** I-75 exit 116, opposite Town Center Mall in the Esplanade. 2700 Town Center Dr, Suite 6 30144.
Hours: 11:30 am-3 & 4-10 pm; Fri & Sat - 11 pm; Sun noon-3 pm. Closed major holidays. **Features:** casual
dress; carryout; beer & wine only. Wide variety of Mandarin & Szechaun dishes in a casual setting.   ⊠

SKEETER'S GRILLE   **Dinner:** $9-$17   **Phone:** 770/499-0676
◆ ◆
   Location: I-75 exit 116, opposite Town Center Mall in the Esplanade. 2700 Town Center Dr 30144.
Hours: 11:15 am-10:30 pm, Fri-11:30 pm, Sat 4 pm-11:30 pm, Sun 4 pm-10 pm. Closed: 12/25.
Features: casual dress; children's menu; carryout; cocktails & lounge. Grilled steak, chicken, fish & pasta with ribs a house
specialty. **Cards:** AE, CB, DI, DS, JCB, MC, VI.

LAWRENCEVILLE—16,800

LODGINGS

THE APARTMENT INN-LAWRENCEVILLE   Rates Subject to Change   **Phone:** 770/962-5660
◆ ◆   All Year   1P: $41   2P/1B: $46-   52   2P/2B: $46-   52   XP: $5
Apartment   **Location:** 0.5 mi s on SR 120 from jct SR 316. 474 W Pike St 30245. **Fax:** 770/962-5660. **Terms:** No pets.
Motel   **Facility:** 126 rooms. 2 stories; exterior corridors. **All Rooms:** efficiencies, free movies. **Cards:** AE, DI, DS,
MC, VI.   CTV ⊠ Ⓓ Ⓢ

MICROTEL INN & SUITES   Rates Subject to Change   **Phone:** 770/237-5992
Ⓐ   All Year [CP]   1P: $45-   55   2P/1B: $49-   59   XP: $4   F16
◆ ◆   **Location:** I-85N exit 41, 4.5 mi e to Collins Hill Rd, just n to Collins Industrial Way, just w; I-85S exit 41, 6 mi
Motel   se on SR 22 to SR 316, 0.5 mi w. 215 Collins Industrial Way 30243. **Fax:** 770/237-5908. **Terms:** Sr.
discount; no pets. **Facility:** 92 rooms. 3 stories; interior corridors. **All Rooms:** free movies. **Cards:** AE, CB,
DI, DS, JCB, MC, VI.   Roll in showers.   ♿ ⓕ ⊠ Ⓩ Ⓓ Ⓢ

LILBURN—9,300

RESTAURANT

SAMMI'S CONTINENTAL CUISINE   **Dinner:** $12-$22   **Phone:** 770/564-2434
◆ ◆ ◆   **Location:** I-85 exit 38, 3 mi e. 605 Indiana Trail Rd 30247. **Hours:** 5:30 pm-10:30 pm, Sun brunch 11:30
Continental   am-3 pm. Closed: Mon. **Reservations:** suggested. **Features:** dressy casual; cocktails; a la carte. Specialties
include New Zealand lamb loin, Long Island duck breast chicken Sami. Very good wine list. **Cards:** AE, CB,
DI, DS, MC, VI.

LITHONIA—2,400   (See map p. 225; index p. 224)

LODGINGS

COURTYARD BY MARRIOTT   Rates Subject to Change   **Phone:** 770/988-8169   **345**
Motor Inn   All Year   1P: $81   2P/1B: $81   2P/2B: $81
Too new to rate; **Location:** I-20 exit 37, just n. 100 Hospitality Ln 30058. **Terms:** No pets. **Facility:** 78 rooms.
Scheduled to open summer 1997; 3 stories; interior corridors. **All Rooms:** free movies. **Cards:** AE, DI, DS, MC, VI.
Roll in showers.   ♿ CTV Ⓓ Ⓢ

LA QUINTA INN PANOLA ROAD   **Phone:** 770/981-6411   **346**
Ⓐ Ⓢ   Fri & Sat [CP]   1P: $68-   77   2P/1B: $68-   77   2P/2B: $68-   77   XP: $6   F18
   Sun-Thurs [CP]   1P: $59-   68   2P/1B: $64-   73   2P/2B: $64-   73   XP: $6   F18
◆ ◆ ◆   **Location:** I-20 exit 37 just n; 3.5 mi e of jct I-285. 2859 Panola Rd 30058-4837. **Fax:** 770/981-2094.
Motel   **Terms:** Small pets only. **Facility:** 130 rooms. Renovated Spanish-style architecture. 3 stories; interior/exterior
corridors. **Dining:** Restaurant nearby. **Services:** Fee: coin laundry. **All Rooms:** free & pay movies.
Fee: VCP. **Some Rooms:** microwaves. Fee: refrigerators. **Cards:** AE, CB, DI, DS, MC, VI. **Special Amenities:** Free
breakfast and free local telephone calls. *(See color ad p 205)*   🐕 🛏 🐾 🛁 CTV ⊠ Ⓩ Ⓓ

MARIETTA—44,100   (See map p. 202; index p. 199)

LODGINGS

ATLANTA TRAVELODGE NORTHWEST   **Phone:** 770/952-0052   **19**
Ⓐ Ⓢ   All Year [CP]   1P: $45   2P/1B: $45   2P/2B: $50
◆ ◆   **Location:** I-75 exit 110 (Windy Hill), just e, 0.3 mi n. 1940 Leland Dr 30067. **Fax:** 770/952-0501. **Terms:** No
Motel   pets. **Facility:** 108 rooms. On quiet street with quick access to nearby commercial area, rooms contemporarily
furnished. $20 telephone/key deposit; 3 stories; interior/exterior corridors. **Services:** Fee: coin laundry, area
transportation, within 3 mi. **All Rooms:** free movies. **Cards:** AE, CB, DI, DS, MC, VI. **Special Amenities:**
Free breakfast and free local telephone calls.   🐾 ♿ CTV ⊠ Ⓓ Ⓢ

BEST INNS OF AMERICA   **Phone:** 770/955-0004   **11**
Ⓐ Ⓢ   All Year [BP]   1P: $47-   53   2P/1B: $54-   63   2P/2B: $60   XP: $7-10   F17
◆ ◆   **Location:** I-75, exit 111; 0.3 mi w to jct Delk & Franklin rds; just s. 1255 Franklin Rd 30067.
Motel   **Fax:** 770/955-0004. **Terms:** Small pets only. **Facility:** 116 rooms. 3 stories; interior corridors.
Dining: Restaurant nearby. **All Rooms:** free movies. **Some Rooms:** whirlpools. Fee: microwaves,
refrigerators. **Cards:** AE, CB, DI, DS, MC, VI. **Special Amenities:** Free breakfast and free local telephone
calls.   🛏 🛏 🐾 CTV ⊠ Ⓩ Ⓓ Ⓢ

(See map p. 202)

BEST WESTERN-BON AIR MOTEL
Phone: 770/427-4676 ②
All Year [CP] 2P/1B: $58- 66 2P/2B: $66- 74 XP: $3 F12
Location: Southbound on I-75 from exit 112, 0.5 mi w on loop 120, 0.5 mi on US 41S; northbound on I-75 from exit 111, 0.8 mi w on SR 280, then 0.5 mi n on US 41N. 859 Cobb Pkwy SE 30062. Fax: 770/514-1327. Terms: Reserv deposit, 3 day notice, 30 day in season; no pets. Facility: 39 rooms. Cozy to large rooms. Mature property. 1 two-bedroom unit. 1 story; exterior corridors; playground. Dining: Restaurant nearby. All Rooms: free movies. Some Rooms: radios, refrigerators. Cards: AE, CB, DI, DS, MC, VI. Special Amenities: Free room upgrade and preferred room (each subject to availability with advanced reservations). *(See color ad p 182)*

COMFORT INN-MARIETTA
Phone: 770/952-3000 ⑧
All Year [CP] 1P: $69- 79 2P/1B: $69- 79 2P/2B: $79- 89 XP: $5 F19
Location: I-75 exit 111, 0.3 mi w to Delk & Franklin rds, just s. 2100 Northwest Pkwy 30067. Fax: 770/956-7394. Terms: Reserv deposit, 24 day notice; no pets. Facility: 185 rooms. Some small rooms. $1 daily for unlimited local phone calls; 5 stories; exterior corridors. Dining: Restaurant nearby. Services: valet laundry; area transportation, within 5 mi. All Rooms: coffeemakers, efficiencies, microwaves, free & pay movies, refrigerators. Cards: AE, CB, DI, DS, MC, VI. Special Amenities: Free breakfast and free local telephone calls. *(See color ad p 204)*

COURTYARD BY MARRIOTT-MARIETTA Rates Subject to Change Phone: 770/956-1188 ⑭
Mon-Thurs 1P: $109- 149 2P/1B: $119- 159 2P/2B: $119- 159 XP: $10 F15
Fri-Sun 1P: $89- 119 2P/1B: $99- 129 2P/2B: $99- 129 XP: $10 F15
Location: I-75 exit 111 (Delk Rd) 0.3 mi e. 2455 Delk Rd 30067. Fax: 770/933-0489. Terms: Sr. discount; check-in 4 pm; no pets. Facility: 146 rooms. 3 stories; interior corridors. Dining: 6:30-10 am, Sat & Sun 7 am-noon. All Rooms: free & pay movies. Cards: AE, CB, DI, DS, MC, VI. *(See color ad p 192)*

DRURY INN-ATLANTA NORTH Rates Subject to Change Phone: 770/612-0900 ⑰
All Year [CP] 1P: $70- 83 2P/1B: $80- 93 2P/2B: $80- 93 XP: $10 F18
Location: I-75, exit 111 (Delk Rd), just e. 1170 Powers Ferry Pl 30067. Fax: 770/612-0900. Terms: Sr. discount; small pets only. Facility: 143 rooms. 7 stories; interior corridors. All Rooms: free movies. Cards: AE, CB, DI, DS, MC, VI. *(See ad below)* Roll in showers.

FAIRFIELD INN BY MARRIOTT-NORTHWEST Rates Subject to Change Phone: 770/952-9863 ⑫
All Year [CP] 1P: $47- 65 2P/1B: $54- 66 2P/2B: $54- 66 XP: $7 F17
Location: I-75, exit 111, just w on Delk Rd to Franklin Rd, just s to Northwest Pkwy; just e. 2191 Northwest Pkwy 30067. Fax: 770/952-9863. Terms: Sr. discount; no pets. Facility: 130 rooms. 3 stories; interior/exterior corridors. All Rooms: free & pay movies. Cards: AE, DI, DS, MC, VI. *(See color ad p 211)*

(See map p. 202)

HAMPTON INN MARIETTA
Rates Subject to Change **Phone: 770/425-9977** **1**
◆◆◆ All Year [CP] 1P: $59- 79 2P/1B: $59- 89 2P/2B: $59- 89
Motel **Location:** I-75, exit 112; nw corner. 455 Franklin Rd 30067. **Fax:** 770/427-2545. **Terms:** Sr. discount; no pets. **Facility:** 140 rooms. Rates for up to 5 persons; 2-4 stories; interior/exterior corridors. **All Rooms:** free movies. **Cards:** AE, DI, DS, MC, VI. *(See ad below)* 🛋 CTV ✕ 🕸 D S

HOLIDAY INN & SUITES MARIETTA
⚠️ SAVE **Phone: 770/952-7581** **6**
All Year 1P: $89 2P/1B: $89 2P/2B: $89
◆◆◆ **Location:** On I-75, exit 111; 0.3 mi w. 2265 Kingston Ct 30067. **Fax:** 770/984-9518. **Terms:** BP avail;
Motor Inn package plans; no pets. **Facility:** 195 rooms. Rates for up to 4 persons, suite includes breakfast, $119; 7 stories; interior corridors. **Dining:** Restaurant; 6:30 am-2 & 5-10 pm; $7-$15; cocktails. **Services:** valet laundry; area transportation, within 5 mi. **All Rooms:** coffeemakers, free & pay movies. **Some Rooms:** refrigerators.
Cards: AE, DI, DS, MC, VI. **Special Amenities: Early check-in/late check-out and free room upgrade (subject to availability with advanced reservations).** *(See color ad p 190 & below)* 🛋 🍴 🎖 🕸 CTV ✕ D

HYATT REGENCY SUITES HOTEL
⚠️ SAVE **Phone: 770/956-1234** **16**
Mon-Thurs [EP] 1P: $165 2P/1B: $190 2P/2B: $190 XP: $25 F18
◆◆◆ Fri-Sun [BP] 1P: $109 2P/1B: $109 2P/2B: $109 XP: $25 F18
Suite Hotel **Location:** I-75 exit 110, 0.5 mi e on Windy Hill Rd at Powers Ferry Rd. 2999 Windy Hill Rd 30067.
Fax: 770/956-9479. **Terms:** No pets. **Facility:** 200 rooms. Up to 4 persons on weekends; 7 stories; interior corridors; sauna, whirlpool, heated pool open 4/1-9/30. **Dining & Entertainment:** Restaurant; 6:30 am-10:30 pm; $9-$20; health conscious menu items; cocktails/lounge. **Services:** valet laundry; area transportation, within 5 mi. **All Rooms:** coffeemakers, free & pay movies, refrigerators. **Some Rooms:** microwaves. **Cards:** AE, CB, DI, DS, JCB, MC, VI. *(See color ad p 188)* 🍴 🎖 🎖 CTV ✕ 🕸 D S

LA QUINTA INN MARIETTA
⚠️ SAVE **Phone: 770/951-0026** **10**
All Year [CP] 1P: $59- 74 2P/1B: $65- 80 2P/2B: $65- 80 XP: $7 F18
◆◆◆ **Location:** I-75; Lockheed-Dobbins AFB exit 111, 0.3 mi w. 2170 Delk Rd 30067-8761. **Fax:** 770/952-5372.
Motel **Terms:** Small pets only, in smoking rooms. **Facility:** 130 rooms. 3 stories; interior/exterior corridors. **Dining:** Restaurant nearby. **Services:** valet laundry. **All Rooms:** free & pay movies. **Some Rooms:** Fee: microwaves, refrigerators. **Cards:** AE, CB, DI, DS, MC, VI. **Special Amenities: Free breakfast and free local telephone calls.** *(See color ad p 205)* 🛏 🛋 🍴 🎖 CTV ✕ 🕸 D

MASTERS ECONOMY INN MARIETTA
⚠️ SAVE **Phone: 770/951-2005** **9**
All Year 1P: $35- 49 2P/1B: $38- 45 2P/2B: $41- 50 XP: $4 F18
◆ **Location:** I-75 exit 110, just w, Circle 75, just w. 2682 Windy Hill Rd 30067. **Fax:** 770/988-0144.
Motel **Terms:** Package plans; pets, $5 extra charge. **Facility:** 86 rooms. 2 stories; exterior corridors.
Dining: Restaurant nearby. **All Rooms:** free movies. **Some Rooms:** microwaves, refrigerators. **Cards:** AE, CB, DI, DS, MC, VI. **Special Amenities: Free local telephone calls.** *(See color ad p 215)* 🛏 CTV ✕ D

(See map p. 202)

MOTEL 6 - 749   Guaranteed Rates   **Phone:** 770/952-8161   **15**
AAA   All Year   1P: $35- 45   2P/1B: $42- 55   2P/2B: $42- 55   XP: $3   F17
◆ ◆   **Location:** I-75 exit 111. 2360 Delk Rd 30067. **Fax:** 770/984-2307. **Terms:** Sr. discount; small pets only.
Motel   **Facility:** 332 rooms. 5 stories; exterior corridors. **All Rooms:** free movies.
Roll in showers. 🛏 🐕 CTV ✕ D

RAMADA LIMITED SUITES   **Phone:** 770/919-7878   **7**
AAA SAVE   All Year [CP]   1P: $42- 90   2P/1B: $42- 90   2P/2B: $45- 90
◆ ◆ ◆   **Location:** I-75 exit 112, 0.3 mi to Franklin Rd, 0.3 mi s. 630 Franklin Rd 30067. **Fax:** 770/514-0824.
Motel   **Terms:** Reserv deposit; small pets only. **Facility:** 46 rooms. Large rooms. 2 stories; exterior corridors.
All Rooms: coffeemakers, microwaves, free movies, refrigerators, combo or shower baths. **Some Rooms:**
Fee: whirlpools. **Cards:** AE, CB, DI, DS, MC, VI. **Special Amenities:** Early check-in/late check-out and
free breakfast.   Roll in showers. 🛏 🐕 🛇 CTV ✕ D S

SLEEP INN   **Phone:** 770/952-9005   **18**
AAA SAVE   All Year [CP]   1P: $55- 75   2P/1B: $55- 75   2P/2B: $55- 75   XP: $5   F18
◆ ◆   **Location:** I-75 exit 111, ne corner. 1175 Powers Ferry Pl 30067. **Fax:** 770/612-9872. **Terms:** No pets.
Motel   **Facility:** 91 rooms. Nicely done, space maximizer rooms, contemporary, designed with the business traveler
in mind. 3 stories; interior corridors; whirlpool, small heated indoor pool. **Services:** Fee: coin laundry.
All Rooms: free & pay movies, combo or shower baths. **Cards:** AE, CB, DI, DS, JCB, MC, VI.
Special Amenities: Free breakfast and free local telephone calls.   Roll in showers. 🛏 🛇 🛇 CTV ✕ D S

SUPER 8 MOTEL   **Phone:** 770/919-2340   **5**
AAA SAVE   5/1-8/31 [CP]   1P: $55   2P/1B: $55   2P/2B: $65   XP: $25   F12
◆ ◆ ◆   9/1-11/30 [CP]   1P: $45   2P/1B: $50   2P/2B: $55   XP: $5   F12
Motel   12/1-4/30 [CP]   1P: $45   2P/1B: $45   2P/2B: $50   XP: $5   F12
Location: I-75, exit 112; 0.3 mi w to Franklin Rd; 0.3 mi s. 610 Franklin Rd 30067. **Fax:** 770/919-1111.
Terms: Reserv deposit; small pets only, $5 extra charge. **Facility:** 58 rooms. 2 stories; exterior corridors.
Dining: Restaurant nearby. **All Rooms:** free movies. **Some Rooms:** microwaves, refrigerators. **Cards:** AE, CB, DI, DS,
JCB, MC, VI. **Special Amenities:** Early check-in/late check-out and free breakfast. Super 8.
🛏 🐕 🛇 CTV ✕ D

THE WHITLOCK INN BED & BREAKFAST   Rates Subject to Change   **Phone:** 770/428-1495   **3**
◆ ◆ ◆   All Year [BP]   1P: $100- 125   2P/1B: $100- 125   2P/2B: $100- 125
Historic Bed   **Location:** I-75 exit 112, 2.7 mi w to Powder Springs Rd, 0.3 mi n to Whitlock, just w. 57 Whitlock Ave 30064.
& Breakfast   **Fax:** 770/919-9620. **Terms:** Age restrictions may apply; reserv deposit; no pets. **Facility:** 5 rooms. 2 stories;
interior corridors; designated smoking area. **All Rooms:** free movies. **Cards:** AE, DS, MC, VI.
CTV ✕ D S

WYNDHAM GARDEN HOTEL-ATLANTA NORTHWEST   Rates Subject to Change   **Phone:** 770/428-4400   **4**
◆ ◆ ◆   Mon-Thurs   1P: $98   2P/1B: $98   2P/2B: $98
Hotel   Fri-Sun   1P: $59   2P/1B: $59   2P/2B: $59
Location: I-75, exit 112, sw corner. 1775 Parkway Pl NW 30067. **Fax:** 770/424-5756. **Terms:** Sr. discount;
no pets. **Facility:** 219 rooms. 10 stories; interior corridors. **Dining:** Restaurant; 6:30 am-2 & 5-10 pm; $8-$18.
All Rooms: free & pay movies. **Cards:** AE, CB, DI, DS, JCB, MC, VI. *(See color ad p 207)* 🛇 🛇 CTV ✕ D S

RESTAURANTS

ANTONIETTA'S   **Lunch:** $5-$10   **Dinner:** $8-$14   **Phone:** 770/973-3368   **7**
◆   **Location:** At corner of Johnson Ferry Rd & Roswell Rd in East Cobb Crossing. 4285 Roswell Rd 30062.
Italian   **Hours:** 11 am-2:30 & 5-9 pm, Fri-10 pm, Sat 5 pm-10 pm. Closed major holidays & Sun. **Features:** casual
dress; children's menu; beer & wine only. Family style cafe with bakery, serving Northern Italian specialties
since 1978. **Cards:** AE, CB, DI, MC, VI.   ✕

BABY DOE'S   **Lunch:** $8-$15   **Dinner:** $15-$27   **Phone:** 404/612-8588   **3**
◆ ◆ ◆   **Location:** I-285, exit 15, follow New Northside Pkwy to Interstate N Pkwy, w 1.5 mi to Powers Ferry Rd.
American   2239 Powers Ferry Rd 30067. **Hours:** 11:30 am-2:30 & 4:30-10 pm, Fri-11 pm, Sat 4:30 pm-11 pm, Sun 10
am-3 & 4:30-10 pm. **Reservations:** suggested. **Features:** casual dress; Sunday brunch; cocktails & lounge;
a la carte. A rustic building on a hillside overlooking Chattahoochee River & wooded areas. Beer cheese soup, steak, fresh
seafood, some homemade desserts. Upscale casual. **Cards:** AE, DI, DS, MC, VI.   ✕

CAFE ST. MICHEL   **Lunch:** $6-$8   **Dinner:** $6-$15   **Phone:** 770/953-9009   **5**
◆   **Location:** I-75 exit 110 (Windy Hill), 0.5 mi e; in Terrace on Windy Hill Plaza. 3000 Windy Hill Rd 30067.
American   **Hours:** 7 am-10 pm, Fri & Sat-11 pm. **Features:** casual dress; wine only. Cozy European style cafe featuring
soup, salad, sandwiches & daily specials. Also offering Beanery gourmet coffee. Smoke free premises.
Cards: AE, DS, MC, VI.   ✕

CHEROKEE CATTLE COMPANY   **Lunch:** $7-$14   **Dinner:** $11-$19   **Phone:** 770/427-0490   **4**
◆   **Location:** I-75 exit 114 A, 2.5 mi ne. 2710 Canton Rd. 30066. **Hours:** 11 am-10 pm, Fri-11 pm, Sat 4 pm-11
Steakhouse   pm, Sun 4 pm-10 pm. Closed major holidays. **Features:** casual dress; children's menu; carryout; cocktails &
lounge. Rustic Texas style roadhouse featuring USDA Choice cut steak, prime rib, ribs & chicken dishes
also. **Cards:** AE, CB, DI, DS, MC, VI.   ✕

1848 HOUSE   **Dinner:** $16-$24   **Phone:** 770/428-1848   **1**
◆ ◆ ◆ ◆   **Location:** I-75 exit 111, 4 mi w. 780 S Cobb Dr 30060. **Hours:** 6 pm-9:30 pm, Sun 10:30 am-2:30 & 5:30-8
Regional   pm. Closed major holidays & Mon. **Reservations:** suggested. **Features:** dressy casual; cocktails & lounge;
American   valet parking; a la carte. National historic greek revival mansion set on lush acreage. Charleston she-crab
soup & sweet potato pecan pie are local favorites. Soft jazz at Sunday brunch. Upscale casual. **Cards:** AE,
DI, DS, MC, VI. *(See ad p 219)*   ✕

RIO MEXICO RESTAURANTE MEXICANO   **Lunch:** $4-$9   **Dinner:** $6-$11   **Phone:** 770/977-9480   **2**
◆   **Location:** 0.5 mi s of Rt 120 (Roswell Rd) on Johnson Ferry Rd in Woodlawn Square Plaza. 1205 Johnson
Mexican   Ferry Rd 30067. **Hours:** 11 am-2:15 & 5-10 pm, Sat & Sun from 5 pm. Closed major holidays.
Features: casual dress; children's menu; health conscious menu items; carryout; cocktails & lounge; a la
carte. **Cards:** AE, DS, MC, VI.   ✕

(See map p. 202)

WILLIAMSON BROS BAR-B-Q   **Lunch:** S5-$15   **Dinner:** $5-$15   **Phone:** 770/971-3201   ⑥
◆
Regional
American
   Location: I-75 exit 112 northbound, 0.5 mi w to US 41, 0.5 mi n to Roswell Rd, 0.5 mi e; exit 113 southbound, 0.3 mi e to US 41, 0.5 mi s. 1425 Roswell Rd 30062. **Hours:** 10 am-9 pm. Closed: Sun, 1/1 & 12/25. **Features:** casual dress; children's menu; carryout; beer & wine only. Specialties include barbecue ribs, pork & chicken. Rustic atmosphere/setting. **Cards:** AE, DI, DS, MC, VI.

MORROW—5,200   (See map p. 225; index p. 224)
LODGINGS

BEST WESTERN SOUTHLAKE INN   **Phone:** 770/961-6300   354
(AAA) (SAVE)
◆ ◆
Motel
  All Year [CP]   1P: $60   2P/1B: $60   2P/2B: $60
  Location: I-75 exit 76, just e. 6437 Jonesboro Rd 30260. Fax: 770/968-5933. **Terms:** Reserv deposit; small pets only. **Facility:** 114 rooms. 2 stories; exterior corridors. **Dining:** Restaurant nearby. **Services:** valet laundry. **Some Rooms:** microwaves, refrigerators. **Cards:** AE, CB, DI, DS, MC, VI. **Special Amenities:** Free breakfast and free local telephone calls. *(See color ad p 182)*

DRURY INN-ATLANTA SOUTH   Rates Subject to Change   **Phone:** 770/960-0500   355
◆ ◆ ◆   All Year [CP]   1P: $65- 78   2P/1B: $75- 88   2P/2B: $75- 88   XP: $10   F18
Motel
VI. *(See ad p 236)*
  Location: I-75 exit 76, just e. 6520 S Lee St 30260. Fax: 770/960-0500. **Terms:** Sr. discount; small pets only. **Facility:** 132 rooms. 7 stories; interior corridors. **All Rooms:** free movies. **Cards:** AE, CB, DI, DS, MC,

FAIRFIELD INN BY MARRIOTT SOUTHLAKE   Rates Subject to Change   **Phone:** 770/961-6044   356
◆ ◆ ◆   3/1-5/21 [CP]   1P: $45- 59   2P/1B: $48   2P/2B: $48- 59   XP: $7   F17
Motel   5/22-11/7 [CP]   1P: $45- 52   2P/1B: $59   2P/2B: $59   XP: $7   F17
  12/1-2/28 & 11/8-11/30 [CP]   1P: $42- 48   2P/1B: $44   2P/2B: $44- 51   XP: $7   F17
Location: I-75, exit 76; 0.3 mi ne. 1599 Adamson Pkwy 30260. Fax: 770/961-6044. **Terms:** No pets. **Facility:** 134 rooms. 3 stories; interior/exterior corridors. **All Rooms:** free & pay movies. **Cards:** AE, CB, DI, DS, MC, VI. *(See color ad p 211)*

HAMPTON INN SOUTHLAKE   Rates Subject to Change   **Phone:** 770/968-8990   357
◆ ◆ ◆   All Year [CP]   1P: $69   2P/1B: $77   2P/2B: $77
Motel
All Rooms: free movies. **Cards:** AE, CB, DI, DS, MC, VI.
  Location: I-75 exit 76, just w & just s on Mt Zion Rd. 1533 Southlake Pkwy 30260. Fax: 770/968-6730. **Terms:** Sr. discount; no pets. **Facility:** 124 rooms. Rates for up to 4 persons; 5 stories; interior corridors.

QUALITY INN   **Phone:** 770/960-1957   352
(AAA) (SAVE)
◆ ◆ ◆
Motel
  All Year [CP]   1P: $45- 59   2P/1B: $49- 69   2P/2B: $49- 69   XP: $5   F15
  Location: I-75 exit 76, just w. 6597 Hwy 54 30260. Fax: 770/960-9544. **Terms:** Reserv deposit, 7 day notice; no pets. **Facility:** 98 rooms. 3 stories; exterior corridors. **Dining:** Restaurant nearby. **Services:** Fee: coin laundry. **All Rooms:** coffeemakers, free movies. **Some Rooms:** refrigerators. **Cards:** AE, CB, DI, DS, MC, VI. **Special Amenities:** Free breakfast and free local telephone calls. *(See color ad below)*

RED ROOF INN-SOUTH   Rates Subject to Change   **Phone:** 770/968-1483   358
◆ ◆   All Year   1P: $35- 45   2P/1B: $40- 45   2P/2B: $46- 51   XP: $6   F18
Motel
VI.
  Location: I-75, exit 76; 0.5 mi n. 1348 South Lake Plaza Dr 30260. Fax: 770/968-4745. **Terms:** Small pets only. **Facility:** 108 rooms. 2 stories; exterior corridors. **All Rooms:** free movies. **Cards:** AE, CB, DI, DS, MC,

SLEEP INN   **Phone:** 770/472-9800   353
(AAA) (SAVE)
◆ ◆
Motel
  12/1-4/30 & 6/1-11/30 [CP]   1P: $55- 125   2P/1B: $55- 135   2P/2B: $65- 145   XP: $10   F12
  5/1-5/31 [CP]   1P: $45- 99   2P/1B: $45- 99   2P/2B: $45- 99   XP: $10   F12
  Location: I-75 exit 75A, just w & just s. 2185 Mt Zion Pkwy 30260. Fax: 770/472-9070. **Terms:** Reserv deposit, 3 day notice; pets, $50 dep req. **Facility:** 90 rooms. Contemporary room appointments. 3 stories; interior corridors. **Dining:** Restaurant nearby. **Services:** Fee: coin laundry. **Recreation:** small pool.
All Rooms: free movies, shower baths. **Some Rooms:** microwaves, refrigerators, whirlpools. **Cards:** AE, CB, DI, DS, JCB, MC, VI. **Special Amenities:** Free breakfast and free local telephone calls. *(See color ad p 240)*

(See map p. 225)

RESTAURANTS

AZTECA GRILL **Lunch:** $5-$6 **Dinner:** $7-$12 **Phone:** 770/968-0908 (230)
◆◆ **Location:** I-75 exit 76, 0.3 mi w to Morrow Industrial Blvd; 0.7 mi n. 1140 Morrow Industrial Blvd 30260.
Mexican **Hours:** 11 am-10 pm, Fri-11 pm, Sat noon-11 pm. Closed major holidays & Sun. **Features:** casual dress;
children's menu; carryout; cocktails & lounge; a la carte, a la carte. Tex-Mex Southwestern standbys.
Cards: AE, DI, MC, VI. ☒

CHINA CAFE **Lunch:** $4-$6 **Dinner:** $6-$10 **Phone:** 770/968-1100 (229)
(AAA) **Location:** I-75, exit 76; 0.3 mi w to Mount Zion Rd, just s. 1497 Mount Zion Rd 30260. **Hours:** 11 am-11
pm. Closed: 11/26. **Features:** casual dress; health conscious menu items; carryout; cocktails; a la carte.
◆◆ Traditional Chinese cuisine in a family atmosphere. **Cards:** AE, DI, DS, MC, VI. ☒
Chinese

PILGREEN'S SOUTH **Lunch:** $7-$10 **Dinner:** $7-$20 **Phone:** 770/961-1666 (233)
◆ **Location:** I-75 exit 76; 0.3 mi e. 6335 Jonesboro Rd 30260. **Hours:** 11:30 am-9:30 pm, Fri-10:30 pm, Sat 5
Steakhouse pm-10:30 pm, Sun noon-9 pm. Closed major holidays. **Features:** casual dress; children's menu; carryout;
cocktails & lounge. Family owned since 1932. **Cards:** AE, DI, MC, VI. ☒

NORCROSS—5,900 (See map p. 202; index p. 199)

LODGINGS

AMBERLEY SUITE HOTEL Rates Subject to Change **Phone:** 770/263-0515 (188)
◆◆◆ All Year 1P: $59- 89 2P/1B: $64- 94 2P/2B: $64- 94 XP: $5
Motor Inn **Location:** I-85, exit 37; 0.5 mi e to Live Oak Pkwy, 0.5 mi n & w. 5885 Oakbrook Pkwy 30093.
Fax: 770/263-0185. **Terms:** Pets, $50 dep req. **Facility:** 177 rooms. 3 stories; interior corridors.
Dining: Restaurant; 6:30-11:30 am; $6-$9. **All Rooms:** free & pay movies. **Some Rooms:** 40 efficiencies, 36 kitchens.
Cards: AE, CB, DI, DS, MC, VI. (See color ad p 206) 🛏 🕳 📺 ☒ 📶 D

AMERISUITES ATLANTA/PEACHTREE INDUSTRIAL **Phone:** 770/416-7655 (177)
(AAA) (SAVE) All Year [CP] 1P: $105- 115 2P/1B: $105- 115 2P/2B: $105- 115 XP: $10 F12
Location: I-285 exit 23, 4.5 mi n. 5600 Peachtree Pkwy 30092-2811. Fax: 770/416-8672. **Terms:** Weekend
◆◆◆ rates avail; small pets only. **Facility:** 128 rooms. Large, very well-equipped units & tastefully done. 6 stories;
Suite Motel interior corridors. **Services:** complimentary evening beverages, Wed; area transportation, within 4 mi.
Fee: coin laundry. **All Rooms:** coffeemakers, microwaves, free & pay movies, refrigerators, combo or
shower baths, VCP's. **Cards:** AE, DI, DS, MC, VI. **Special Amenities:** Free breakfast and free local telephone calls.
(See color ad p 10) Roll in showers. 🛏 🕳 📶 📺 🏧 ☒ 📶 D S

ATLANTA MARRIOTT NORCROSS Rates Subject to Change **Phone:** 770/263-8558 (170)
◆◆◆ Sun-Thurs 12/1-5/31,
Hotel 6/1-8/31 & Sun-Thurs
9/1-11/30 1P: $111- 120 2P/1B: $111- 120 2P/2B: $111- 120 XP: $10 F9
Fri & Sat 12/1-5/31 &
9/1-11/30 1P: $47 2P/1B: $47 2P/2B: $47
Location: I-85, exit 37, 4 mi w to Peachtree Industrial Blvd, west on Holcomb Bridge Road, then 0.8 mi n on Peachtree
Pkwy, (SR 141), right on Technology Pkwy 1 block. 475 Technology Pkwy 30092. Fax: 770/263-0766. **Terms:** Sr. discount;
check-in 4 pm; pets, $50 extra charge. **Facility:** 222 rooms. 6 stories; interior corridors. **Dining & Entertainment:**
Restaurant; 6:30 am-10 pm; lounge open to 2 am if busy; $8-$12. **All Rooms:** free & pay movies. **Cards:** AE, CB, DI, DS,
JCB, MC, VI. Roll in showers. 🛏 🕳 📶 📺 ☒ 📶 D S

BEST WESTERN BRADBURY INN Rates Subject to Change **Phone:** 770/662-8175 (192)
◆◆◆ All Year [BP] 1P: $50- 100 2P/1B: $60- 100 2P/2B: $66- 100 XP: $5 F12
Motel **Location:** I-85, exit 37 0.5 mi, e to Live Oak Pkwy, 0.8 mi n & w. 5985 Oakbrook Pkwy 30093.
Fax: 770/840-1183. **Terms:** Sr. discount; no pets. **Facility:** 121 rooms. 3 stories; interior corridors.
All Rooms: free & pay movies. **Cards:** AE, CB, DI, DS, MC, VI. (See ad p 204) 🕳 📶 📺 ☒ 📶 D

BEST WESTERN-PEACHTREE CORNERS Rates Subject to Change **Phone:** 770/409-0004 (169)
◆◆◆ All Year [CP] 1P: $60- 80 2P/1B: $60- 80 2P/2B: $60- 80 XP: $10 F12
Motel **Location:** I-85 exit 37, 4 mi w; I-285 exit 23B, 4 mi n. 7035 Jimmy Carter Blvd 30092. Fax: 770/409-1495.
Terms: No pets. **Facility:** 81 rooms. 3 stories; interior corridors. **All Rooms:** free movies. **Cards:** AE, CB,
DI, DS, MC, VI. Roll in showers. 📶 📺 ☒ 📶 D S

(See map p. 202)

BUDGETEL INN-ATLANTA PEACHTREE   Rates Subject to Change   **Phone: 770/446-2882**   **171**
◆◆   All Year [CP]   1P: $42- 55   2P/1B: $49- 62   2P/2B: $54
Motel   **Location:** I-285, exit 23, 5.5 mi n. 5395 Peachtree Industrial Blvd 30092. Fax: 770/242-6882. **Terms:** Sr. discount; small pets only. **Facility:** 139 rooms. 12 ambassador suites; 2-room suite with fully equipped kitchen & 2 full baths; 3 stories; interior corridors. **All Rooms:** free & pay movies. **Some Rooms:** 12 efficiencies. **Cards:** AE, CB, DI, DS, MC, VI. *(See color ad p 188)*

CLUBHOUSE INN & SUITES   Rates Subject to Change   **Phone: 770/368-9400**   **190**
◆◆◆   Sun-Thurs [BP]   1P: $75   2P/1B: $85   2P/2B: $85   XP: $10   F16
Motel   Fri & Sat [BP]   1P: $63   XP: $10   F16
Location: I-85 exit 37; 0.5 mi e to Live Oak Pkwy, 0.5 mi nw. 5945 Oakbrook Pkwy 30093.
Fax: 770/416-7370. **Terms:** No pets. **Facility:** 147 rooms. 3 stories; interior corridors. **All Rooms:** free movies. **Cards:** AE, CB, DI, DS, JCB, MC, VI. *(See color ad below)*

COMFORT INN-NORCROSS   **Phone: 770/368-0218**   **182**
ⒶⒶⒶ SAVE   All Year [CP]   1P: $40- 70   2P/1B: $45- 70   2P/2B: $45- 70   XP: $5   F18
◆◆   **Location:** I-85N, exit 37; 0.8 mi w on Jimmy Carter Blvd, just n on N Norcross Tucker Rd to Western Hills
Motel   Dr, 1 blk. 5990 Western Hills Dr 30071. Fax: 770/409-8360. **Terms:** No pets. **Facility:** 110 rooms. In light industrial/residential area. 2 stories; exterior corridors. **Dining:** Restaurant nearby. **Services:** Fee: coin laundry. **All Rooms:** free movies. **Some Rooms:** Fee: microwaves, refrigerators. **Cards:** AE, CB, DI, DS, MC, VI. **Special Amenities: Free breakfast and free local telephone calls.** *(See color ad p 204)*

COURTYARD BY MARRIOTT I-85 JIMMY CARTER   Rates Subject to Change   **Phone: 770/242-7172**   **185**
◆◆◆   Sun-Thurs   1P: $94   2P/1B: $104   2P/2B: $104   XP: $10   F12
Motor Inn   Fri & Sat   1P: $49- 90   2P/1B: $49- 99   2P/2B: $59- 99
Location: I-85 exit 37 just e to McDonough Dr, just s. 6235 McDonough Dr 30093. Fax: 770/840-8768.
Terms: Check-in 4 pm; no pets. **Facility:** 122 rooms. Weekend rates for up to 4 persons; 2 stories; interior corridors.
Dining: Coffee shop; 6:30-10 am, Sat & Sun 7-11 am, breakfast buffet. **All Rooms:** free & pay movies. **Cards:** AE, DI, DS, MC, VI. *(See color ad p 192)*

COURTYARD BY MARRIOTT-PEACHTREE CORNERS   Rates Subject to Change   **Phone: 770/446-3777**   **172**
◆◆◆   Sun-Thurs   1P: $92   2P/1B: $102   2P/2B: $102
Motel   Fri & Sat   1P: $59   2P/1B: $59   2P/2B: $59- 69
Location: I-285, exit 23, 4 mi n to Holcomb Bridge Rd, just w. 3209 Holcomb Bridge Rd 30092.
Fax: 770/246-9152. **Terms:** Sr. discount; no pets. **Facility:** 131 rooms. Weekend rates for up to 4 persons; 2-3 stories; interior corridors. **Dining:** Restaurant; 6:30-10 am, Sat & Sun 7 am-noon. **All Rooms:** free & pay movies. **Cards:** AE, DI, DS, MC, VI. *(See color ad p 192)*

DAYS INN   Rates Subject to Change   **Phone: 770/416-9021**   **178**
◆◆◆   All Year [CP]   1P: $60- 80   2P/1B: $60- 80   2P/2B: $60- 80
Motel   **Location:** I-285 exit 23, 5.5 mi n. 5385 Peachtree Industrial Blvd 30092. Fax: 770/416-9512. **Terms:** Sr. discount; no pets. **Facility:** 60 rooms. 2 whirlpool rms, extra charge; 2 stories; interior corridors.
All Rooms: free movies. **Cards:** AE, DI, DS, MC, VI.

DRURY INN-ATLANTA NORTHEAST   Rates Subject to Change   **Phone: 770/729-0060**   **195**
◆◆◆   All Year [CP]   1P: $70- 83   2P/1B: $80- 93   2P/2B: $80- 93   XP: $10   F18
Motel   **Location:** I-85 exit 37, just w. 5655 Jimmy Carter Blvd 30071. Fax: 770/729-0060. **Terms:** Sr. discount; small pets only. **Facility:** 136 rooms. 5 stories; interior corridors. **All Rooms:** free movies. **Cards:** AE, CB, DI, DS, MC, VI. *(See ad p 236)*   Roll in showers.

FAIRFIELD INN BY MARRIOTT PEACHTREE CORNERS   Rates Subject to Change   **Phone: 770/441-1999**   **174**
◆◆◆   All Year [CP]   1P: $50- 63   2P/1B: $66- 70   2P/2B: $66- 70   XP: $6   F18
Motel   **Location:** I-285, exit 23, 3 mi n on Peachtree Industrial Blvd to Jones Mill Rd. 6650 Bay Circle Dr 30071.
Fax: 770/441-1999. **Terms:** Sr. discount; no pets. **Facility:** 135 rooms. 3 stories; interior/exterior corridors.
All Rooms: free & pay movies. **Cards:** AE, DI, DS, MC, VI. *(See color ad p 211)*

HAMPTON INN   Rates Subject to Change   **Phone: 770/729-0015**   **196**
◆◆◆   Sun-Thurs [CP]   1P: $79- 89   2P/1B: $79   2P/2B: $89
Motel   Fri & Sat [CP]   1P: $55   2P/1B: $55   2P/2B: $55
Location: I-85 exit 37, 4 mi w to Peachtree Industrial Blvd, 0.8 mi n on Peachtree Pkwy (SR 141). 440 Technology Pkwy 30092. Fax: 770/300-0624. **Terms:** Sr. discount; no pets. **Facility:** 149 rooms. Rates for up to 4 persons; 5 stories; interior corridors. **All Rooms:** free movies. **Cards:** AE, CB, DI, DS, JCB, MC.   Roll in showers.

(See map p. 202)

HOLIDAY INN SELECT-PEACHTREE CORNERS   Rates Subject to Change   **Phone: 770/448-4400**   [175]
◆◆◆   Sun-Thurs   1P: $99- 149   2P/1B: $109- 159   2P/2B: $109- 159   XP: $10   F19
Hotel   Fri & Sat   1P: $59- 89   2P/1B: $59- 89   2P/2B: $59- 89   XP: $10   F19
Location: 4.5 mi ne of I-285, exit 23. 6050 Peachtree Industrial Blvd NW 30071. Fax: 770/840-7292.
Terms: Sr. discount; no pets. **Facility:** 246 rooms. 9 stories; interior corridors. **Dining:** Restaurant; 6:30 am-11 pm; $8-$18.
All Rooms: free & pay movies. **Cards:** AE, CB, DI, DS, JCB, MC, VI. *(See color ad p 190)*

🛥 🛥 🛏 CTV ✕ 🖉 D S

HOMEWOOD SUITES-NORCROSS   Rates Subject to Change   **Phone: 770/448-4663**   [168]
◆◆◆   All Year [CP]   1P: $110- 120   2P/1B: $110- 120   2P/2B: $125- 135
Apartment   **Location:** I-85N exit 37, 4 mi w to Peachtree Industrial Blvd, 0.4 mi n, w on Holcomb Bridge Rd, 2 blks n on
Motel   Peachtree Pkwy. 450 Technology Pkwy 30092. Fax: 770/242-6979. **Terms:** No pets. **Facility:** 92 rooms. 4 two-
DI, DS, MC, VI.   bedroom units $195; 3 stories; interior/exterior corridors. **All Rooms:** kitchens, free movies. **Cards:** AE, CB,

🛏 CTV ✕ 🖉 D S

LA QUINTA INN JIMMY CARTER   **Phone: 770/448-8686**   [186]
🄰🄰🄰 SAVE   All Year [CP]   1P: $61- 68   2P/1B: $67- 73   2P/2B: $67- 73   XP: $6   F18
   Location: I-85, exit 37, just e to McDonough Dr; just s. 6187 Dawson Blvd 30093-1224. Fax: 770/840-8924.
◆◆◆   **Terms:** Weekend rates avail; small pets only. **Facility:** 130 rooms. Located in office park/commercial area. 3
Motel   stories; exterior corridors. **Dining:** Restaurant nearby. **Services:** valet laundry. **All Rooms:** free & pay
   movies. **Some Rooms:** microwaves, refrigerators. **Cards:** AE, CB, DI, DS, MC, VI. **Special Amenities:** Free
breakfast and free local telephone calls. *(See color ad p 205)*

🐄 🛥 🐾 CTV ✕ D

LA QUINTA-PEACHTREE   **Phone: 770/449-5144**   [176]
🄰🄰🄰 SAVE   All Year [CP]   1P: $59   2P/1B: $59   2P/2B: $59   XP: $8   F18
   Location: I-285 exit 23, 5.5 mi n. 5375 Peachtree Industrial Blvd 30092. Fax: 770/840-8576. **Terms:** Pets.
◆◆◆   **Facility:** 130 rooms. Especially clean rooms. 3 to 4 persons, $72; 3 stories; exterior corridors.
Motel   **Dining:** Coffee shop nearby. **Services:** valet laundry. **All Rooms:** free & pay movies.
   Some Rooms: coffeemakers. Fee: microwaves, refrigerators. **Cards:** AE, CB, DI, DS, MC, VI.
Special Amenities: Free breakfast and free local telephone calls. *(See color ad p 205)*

🐾 🛥 🐾 🛏 CTV ✕ 🖉 D

NORTHEAST ATLANTA HILTON   **Phone: 770/447-4747**   [173]
🄰🄰🄰 SAVE   Mon-Thurs   1P: $144   2P/1B: $144   2P/2B: $144   XP: $10   F18
   Fri-Sun   1P: $75   2P/1B: $75   2P/2B: $75   XP: $10   F18
◆◆◆   **Location:** I-285 exit 23B, 4.5 mi w. 5993 Peachtree Industrial Blvd 30092. Fax: 770/448-8853. **Terms:** No
Hotel   pets. **Facility:** 272 rooms. 10 stories; interior corridors. **Dining:** Restaurant, coffee shop; 6:30 am-2:30 &
   5:30-10:30 pm; $7-$18. **All Rooms:** free & pay movies. **Cards:** AE, DI, DS, MC, VI. *(See color ad p 18)*

🛥 🛥 🛏 CTV ✕ 🖉 D S

QUALITY INN-NORCROSS   Guaranteed Rates   **Phone: 770/449-7322**   [183]
◆◆   All Year [CP]   1P: $49   2P/1B: $59   2P/2B: $69   XP: $6   F18
Motel   **Location:** I-85, exit 37, just e to Live Oak Pkwy, 1 mi w. 6045 Oakbrook Pkwy 30093. Fax: 770/368-1868.
   Terms: Sr. discount; small pets only. **Facility:** 109 rooms. 2 stories; interior/exterior corridors.
All Rooms: free movies. **Cards:** AE, CB, DI, DS, MC.

🐾 🛏 CTV ✕ D

RED ROOF INN-INDIAN TRAIL   Rates Subject to Change   **Phone: 770/448-8944**   [180]
◆◆   6/1-8/31   1P: $40   2P/1B: $47   2P/2B: $46   XP: $7   F18
Motel   3/1-5/31   1P: $38   2P/1B: $45   2P/2B: $44   XP: $7   F18
   9/1-11/30   1P: $36   2P/1B: $43   2P/2B: $42   XP: $7   F18
   12/1-2/28   1P: $34   2P/1B: $41   2P/2B: $41   XP: $7   F18
Location: I-85 exit 38, just w to Brook Hollow Pkwy, just s. 5171 Brook Hollow Pkwy 30071. Fax: 770/448-8955.
Terms: Small pets only. **Facility:** 115 rooms. 3 stories; exterior corridors. **All Rooms:** free movies. **Cards:** AE, CB, DI, DS,
MC, VI.

🐾 CTV ✕ D

SHONEY'S INN OF ATLANTA NORTHEAST   **Phone: 770/564-0492**   [194]
🄰🄰🄰 SAVE   All Year   1P: $50- 65   2P/1B: $65- 75   2P/2B: $65- 75   XP: $7   F18
   Location: I-85, exit 38, just e. 2050 Willow Trail Pkwy 30093. Fax: 770/564-0297. **Terms:** No pets.
◆◆◆   **Facility:** 144 rooms. Located in semi-rural, light commercial area. 3 stories; exterior corridors.
Motel   **Dining:** Restaurant nearby. **Services:** valet laundry. **All Rooms:** free & pay movies.
   Some Rooms: coffeemakers, microwaves, radios, refrigerators. **Cards:** AE, CB, DI, DS, MC, VI.
Special Amenities: Free local telephone calls and free newspaper.

🛥 🐾 CTV ✕ D

WINGATE INN   Rates Subject to Change   **Phone: 770/263-2020**   [179]
Motel   All Year [CP]   1P: $69- 135   2P/1B: $69- 135   2P/2B: $69- 135   XP: $10   D
   Too new to rate; **Location:** I-285 exit 23, 4.5 mi n. 5800 Peachtree Industrial Blvd 30071.
Fax: 770/263-2022. **Terms:** Sr. discount; reserv deposit; no pets. **Facility:** 118 rooms. Scheduled to open June 1997; 4 sto-
ries; interior corridors. **All Rooms:** free movies. **Cards:** AE, DI, DS, MC, VI.   Roll in showers. 🛥 CTV ✕ D S

RESTAURANTS

CAFE RENAISSANCE   Lunch: $6-$11   Dinner: $12-$19   **Phone: 770/441-0291**   [152]
◆◆   **Location:** I-85, exit 37, 3.5 mi w. 7050 Jimmy Carter Blvd 30092. **Hours:** 11:30 am-3 pm & 6-10 pm. Closed
Continental   major holidays & Sun. **Reservations:** suggested. **Features:** casual dress; carryout; cocktails; a la carte.
   Fusion cuisine; classical French & Italian with Korean touches. Comfortable upscale casual dress.
Cards: AE, DI, DS, MC, VI.   ✕

DOMINICK'S   Lunch: $7-$9   Dinner: $11-$25   **Phone: 770/449-1611**   [153]
◆◆   **Location:** Downtown at corner of Peachtree & Holcomb Bridge Rd. 95 S Peachtree St 30071. **Hours:** 11:30
Italian   am-3 & 5-10 pm, Sat 5 pm-11 pm, Sun 5 pm-9 pm. Closed major holidays. **Features:** casual dress;
   children's menu; carryout; cocktail lounge; beer & wine only; street parking. Enjoy this fun & friendly Italian
restaurant in the old town of Norcross. Bustling atmosphere. **Cards:** AE, DI, DS, MC, VI.   ✕

(See map p. 202)

FOGHORN GRILL   **Lunch: $6-$8**   **Dinner: $7-$15**   **Phone:** 770/246-0643   151
◆◆   **Location:** I-285, exit 23; 5.5 mi n to Medlock Bridge Rd, just w. 3230 Medlock Bridge Rd 30092. **Hours:** 11
American   am-10 pm, Fri & Sat-11 pm, Sun-9:30 pm. Closed major holidays. **Reservations:** Reservations accepted for parties of 6 or more. **Features:** casual dress; children's menu; carryout; cocktails & lounge. Casual, friendly neighborhood restaurant. Fresh fish specials & ribs are local favorites. Jack Daniels pecan pie. **Cards:** AE, DI, DS, MC, VI.

GW JANOUSEK'S   **Lunch: $8-$14**   **Dinner: $9-$21**   **Phone:** 770/449-8585   149
◆◆◆   **Location:** I-85 exit 37, 4 mi w to Peachtree Industrial Blvd, 0.4 mi n, just w on Holcomb Bridge Rd, 1.2 mi n.
Continental   5450 Peachtree Pkwy NW 30092. **Hours:** 11:30 am-2 & 6-11 pm, Mon from 6 pm. Closed major holidays & Sun. **Reservations:** accepted. **Features:** casual dress; children's menu; health conscious menu; cocktails. Wide selection of International dishes served in an intimate atmosphere. Very good wine list. Smoke free premises. **Cards:** AE, DI, DS, MC, VI.

RESTO NAX   **Dinner: $9-$20**   **Phone:** 770/416-9665   148
◆◆◆   **Location:** N of Holcomb Bridge on 141 or Peachtree Pkwy. 6025 Peachtree Pkwy 30092. **Hours:** 11:15
Continental   am-10 pm, Sat 5 pm-11 pm. Closed major holidays & Sun. **Reservations:** accepted. **Features:** casual dress; children's menu; cocktails & lounge; a la carte. European style dining featuring some very creative preparations & presentations.

RIVERDALE—9,400   (See map p. 225; index p. 224)

LODGING

SCOTTISH INN   Rates Subject to Change   **Phone:** 770/907-3838   370
◆◆   All Year [CP]   1P: $35- 45   2P/1B: $40- 60   2P/2B: $40- 60   XP: $5   F18
Motel   **Location:** I-285 exit 43, 3 mi s to King Rd, just e. 709 King Rd 30296. **Fax:** 770/907-3838. **Terms:** No pets. **Facility:** 40 rooms. 8 whirlpool rms, extra charge; 2 stories; exterior corridors. **All Rooms:** free movies.

ROSWELL—47,900   LODGINGS

BEST WESTERN ROSWELL SUITES   Guaranteed Rates   **Phone:** 770/552-5599
◆◆◆   All Year [CP]   1P: $69- 84   2P/1B: $69- 84   2P/2B: $69- 84
Motel   **Location:** SR 400 exit 7B, 1 mi w. 907 Holcomb Bridge Rd 30076. **Fax:** 770/552-8180. **Terms:** Sr. discount; check-in 4 pm; pets, $100 dep req. **Facility:** 167 rooms. Rates for up to 4 persons. 12 whirlpool rms, extra charge; 3 stories; interior corridors. **All Rooms:** free & pay movies. **Cards:** AE, CB, DI, DS, JCB, MC, VI.
(See color ad p 182)   Roll in showers.

BUDGETEL INN-ATLANTA ROSWELL   Rates Subject to Change   **Phone:** 770/552-0200
◆◆   All Year [CP]   1P: $50- 61   2P/1B: $57- 68   2P/2B: $62
Motel   **Location:** SR 400 exit 7B, just w. 575 Old Holcomb Bridge Rd 30076. **Fax:** 770/552-0110. **Terms:** Sr. discount; small pets only. **Facility:** 106 rooms. 4 stories; interior corridors. **All Rooms:** free & pay movies. **Cards:** AE, CB, DI, DS, MC, VI. *(See color ad p 188)*

COURTYARD BY MARRIOTT   Rates Subject to Change   **Phone:** 770/992-7200
◆◆◆   Sun-Thurs   1P: $99   2P/1B: $99   2P/2B: $109   XP: $10   F
Motor Inn   Fri & Sat   1P: $64   2P/1B: $74   2P/2B: $74   XP: $10   F
    Location: SR 400 exit 7A, just e. 1500 Market Blvd 30076. **Fax:** 770/993-7133. **Terms:** Check-in 4 pm; no pets. **Facility:** 154 rooms. 2-4 stories; interior corridors. **Dining:** Breakfast 6:30-11 am, Sat & Sun 7-11 am. **All Rooms:** free & pay movies. **Cards:** AE, DI, DS, MC, VI. *(See color ad p 192)*

HAMPTON INN   Rates Subject to Change   **Phone:** 770/587-5161
◆◆◆   All Year [CP]   1P: $59- 69   2P/1B: $67- 72   2P/2B: $72   XP: $8   F18
Motel   **Location:** SR 400 exit 7B; just w to Old Dogwood Rd; just n. 9995 Old Dogwood Rd 30076. **Fax:** 770/594-9566. **Terms:** Pets, $25 extra charge. **Facility:** 129 rooms. 3 stories; exterior corridors. **All Rooms:** free & pay movies. **Cards:** AE, DI, DS, JCB, MC, VI.

HOLIDAY INN ROSWELL/ATLANTA   **Phone:** 770/992-9600
◆◆◆   Sun-Thurs   1P: $109- 185   2P/1B: $129- 185   2P/2B: $129- 185   XP: $10   F12
Hotel   Fri & Sat   1P: $85- 185   2P/1B: $95- 185   2P/2B: $95- 185   XP: $10   F12
    Location: SR 400 exit 7B, just w. 1075 Holcomb Bridge Rd 30076. **Fax:** 770/992-6539. **Terms:** Package plans; no pets. **Facility:** 174 rooms. Imposing brick mid-rise with Colonial detail atop wooded hill overlooking commercial area. Spacious lobby with intimate seating areas. Rich, comfortable rooms. Up to 4 persons in room; 7 stories; interior corridors. **Dining & Entertainment:** Restaurant; 6:30 am-2 & 5:30-10:30 pm; $11-$15; cocktails/lounge; nightclub. **Services:** valet laundry. **All Rooms:** free movies. **Some Rooms:** coffeemakers, refrigerators. **Cards:** AE, DI, DS, MC, VI. **Special Amenities:** Early check-in/late check-out and free room upgrade (subject to availability with advanced reservations). *(See ad p 201 & color ad p 190)*

RESTAURANTS

BROOKWOOD GRILL   **Lunch: $6-$16**   **Dinner: $6-$16**   **Phone:** 770/587-0102
◆◆   **Location:** SR 400, exit 7B, 0.8 mi w. 880A Holcomb Bridge Rd 30076. **Hours:** 11 am-10:30 pm, Fri &
American   Sat-11:30 pm. Closed: 11/26 & 12/25. **Features:** casual dress; children's menu; cocktails & lounge; a la carte. Warm, casual neighborhood restaurant. Marinated Salmon & Jack Daniels Strip are favorites. Salad, pasta & dessert from scratch. **Cards:** AE, DI, DS, MC, VI.

CHICAGO'S RESTAURANT   **Dinner: $9-$16**   **Phone:** 770/993-7464
◆◆   **Location:** Jct Shallowford & Johnson's Ferry rds; in Shallowford Corners Shopping Center. 4401 Shallowford
American   Rd, Suite 106 30075. **Hours:** 5 pm-10 pm, Fri & Sat-11 pm. Closed major holidays. **Features:** casual dress; children's menu; health conscious menu items; carryout; cocktails & lounge; a la carte. A wide variety of high quality food in a casual neighborhood atmosphere. Sauteed shrimp & scallops, seafood mixed grill & stockyard steak are popular favorites. Fresh ground espresso & cappuccino. **Cards:** AE, DI, DS, MC, VI.

GREENWOOD'S ON GREEN STREET   **Dinner: $7-$17**   **Phone:** 770/992-5383
◆◆   **Location:** SR 400, exit 4, 1.5 mi w to Alpharetta St, 1 mi s to Woodstock St, 1.3 mi w to Green St; just s.
Regional   1087 Green St 30075. **Hours:** 5 pm-10 pm, Sun-9 pm. Closed major holidays, Mon & Tues.
American   **Features:** casual dress; carryout; beer & wine only; a la carte. All fresh ingredients. Catfish, chicken, duck & beef. 150 year-old eclectic interior house. Brick courtyard dining in season. Smoke free premises.

IPPOLITO'S **Lunch:** $6-$8 **Dinner:** $7-$14 **Phone:** 770/998-5683
♦ Italian
VI.
Location: SR 400 exit 7A, 0.3 mi e. **Hours:** 11:30 am-2:30 & 5-10 pm, Fri & Sat 5 pm-11 pm. Closed major holidays. **Features:** casual dress; children's menu; carryout; cocktail lounge; beer & wine only. Bustling Italian style cafe featuring pizza, pasta, chicken & veal dishes. Very good desserts. **Cards:** AE, DI, DS, MC, VI. ⊠

THE PUBLIC HOUSE Historical **Lunch:** $5-$11 **Dinner:** $11-$20 **Phone:** 770/992-4646
♦♦♦ American
Location: Downtown. 605 S Atlanta St 30075. **Hours:** 11:30 am-2:30 & 5:30-10 pm, Fri-11 pm, Sat 11:30 am-3 & 5:30-11 pm, Sun 11:30 am-3 & 5:30-10 pm. Closed major holidays. **Features:** casual dress; Sunday brunch; cocktails; a la carte. Charming historic restaurant located adjacent to the Roswell Visitor Center. Desserts made on premises. Lamb, steak au poivre & pasta. **Cards:** AE, DI, DS, MC, VI. ⊠

VAN GOGH'S RESTAURANT & BAR **Lunch:** $7-$13 **Dinner:** $13-$27 **Phone:** 770/993-1156
♦♦♦ Regional American
Location: SR 400, exit 7B, 2.7 mi w via Holcomb Bridge Rd to Crossville Rd (SR 92); jct Crabapple & Crossville rds. 70 W Crossville Rd 30075. **Hours:** 11:30 am-midnight. Closed major holidays & Sun. **Reservations:** suggested. **Features:** casual dress; children's menu; carryout; cocktails & lounge; valet parking; a la carte. Intimate ambience. Innovative pasta, stirfry, meat, fish & seafood. "Killer" dessert.
Cards: AE, DI, DS, MC, VI. ⚥ ⊠

VILLA D' ESTE RISTORANTE ITALIANO Historical **Dinner:** $9-$22 **Phone:** 770/998-0645
♦♦♦ Northern Italian
Location: SR 400, exit 4, 1.5 mi w to Alpharetta St; 2 mi s (Alpharetta changes to S Atlanta St). 647 Atlanta St 30075. **Hours:** 6 pm-10:30 pm, Sun 11 am-3 & 6-10:30 pm. Closed major holidays, Mon & 6/23-7/8. **Reservations:** suggested. **Features:** casual dress; Sunday brunch; cocktails; a la carte. Comfortable casual elegance of old home. Fresh & unusual entrees of veal, fish & chicken. Desserts baked on premises. Espresso/cappuccino. **Cards:** AE, DI, DS, MC, VI. ⊠

SANDY SPRINGS—67,800 (See map p. 202; index p. 199)

LODGING

COUNTRY HEARTH INN PERIMETER **Phone:** 404/252-6400 **213**
(AAA) [SAVE]
♦♦♦ Motel
All Year [CP] 2P/1B: $76- 78 2P/2B: $74 XP: $6 F
Location: I-285, exit 17, ne corner. 5793 Roswell Rd NE 30328. Fax: 404/851-9306. **Terms:** No pets. **Facility:** 82 rooms. 4 stories; interior corridors. **Dining:** Restaurant nearby. **Services:** valet laundry. **All Rooms:** coffeemakers, free movies. **Some Rooms:** microwaves, radios, refrigerators. **Cards:** AE, CB, DI, DS, MC, VI. **Special Amenities:** Free breakfast and free local telephone calls.
⊜ 🐕 ➕ 🛁 CTV ⊠ Ⓓ

RESTAURANTS

BILLY MCHALE'S **Lunch:** $10-$16 **Dinner:** $10-$16 **Phone:** 404/303-0177 **173**
♦♦ American
Location: From I-285, exit 17, 0.4 mi n. 5925 Roswell Rd NE 30328. **Hours:** 11:30 am-10 pm, Fri-11 pm, Sat noon-11 pm. Closed: 11/26 & 12/25. **Features:** casual dress; children's menu; early bird specials; senior's menu; carryout; cocktails & lounge. Lively bustling atmosphere with electic decor featuring a wide variety of steak, seafood, pasta & chicken dishes. Lighter fare items also avail. **Cards:** AE, DS, MC, VI. ⚥ ⊠

CAFE SUNFLOWER **Phone:** 404/256-1675 **172**
♦ Vegetarian
Location: At jct I-285 & Roswell Rd, 0.5 mi n on Roswell, turn right on Hammond Dr, then right into shopping center. 5975 Roswell Rd 30328. **Hours:** 11:30 am-2:30 & 5-9 pm, Fri-9:30 pm, Sat noon-2:30 & 5-9:30 pm. Closed: Sun, 11/26 & 12/25. **Reservations:** accepted. **Features:** casual dress; health conscious menu; carryout. Enjoy a playful & sophisticated atmosphere of sunflowers & colorful accessories in this vegetarian restaurant. The elaborate menu presentation is full of tasty dishes topped off with luscious desserts. **Cards:** AE, DS, MC, VI. ⊠

EMBERS **Phone:** 404/256-0977 **171**
♦♦ Seafood
Location: Off Roswell Rd at I-285. 234 Hilderbrand Dr 30328. **Hours:** 11:30 am-2:30 & 6-10:30 pm, Sat from 6 pm. Closed major holidays & Sun. **Reservations:** suggested. **Features:** casual dress; carryout; cocktails & lounge. **Cards:** AE, CB, DI, DS, MC, VI. ⊠

SMYRNA—31,000 (See map p. 202; index p. 199)

LODGINGS

AMERIHOST INN-SMYRNA **Phone:** 404/794-1600 **25**
(AAA) [SAVE]
♦♦♦ Motel
All Year [CP] 1P: $52- 62 2P/1B: $62- 72 2P/2B: $62- 72 XP: $10 F16
Location: I-285 exit 10; 0.3 mi n. 5130 S Cobb Dr 30082. Fax: 404/794-3600. **Terms:** Pets, $10 extra charge. **Facility:** 60 rooms. 2 whirlpool rms, extra charge; 2 stories; interior corridors; sauna, whirlpool. **Dining:** Restaurant nearby. **Services:** valet laundry. **All Rooms:** coffeemakers, free & pay movies, safes. **Some Rooms:** microwaves, refrigerators. **Cards:** AE, DI, DS, MC, VI. **Special Amenities:** Free breakfast and free newspaper. (See color ad p 191)
🐕 ⊜ 🐕 🛁 CTV ⊠ Ⓓ Ⓢ

HOLIDAY INN EXPRESS, CUMBERLAND/SMYRNA **Phone:** 770/333-9910 **24**
(AAA) [SAVE]
♦♦ Motel
All Year [CP] 1P: $59- 89 2P/1B: $64- 89 2P/2B: $64- 89 XP: $5 F19
Location: I-285W exit 11; just w. 1200 Winchester Pkwy 30080. Fax: 770/438-7462. **Terms:** No pets. **Facility:** 118 rooms. 5 stories; interior corridors; whirlpool. **Services:** complimentary evening beverages, Mon-Thurs. Fee: coin laundry. **All Rooms:** free & pay movies. **Some Rooms:** Fee: refrigerators. **Cards:** AE, CB, DI, DS, JCB, MC, VI. **Special Amenities:** Free breakfast and free local telephone calls.
⊜ 🐕 ➕ 🛁 CTV ⊠ Ⓓ

HOLIDAY INN EXPRESS GALLERIA CENTRE/COBB PARKWAY Rates Subject to Change **Phone:** 770/435-4990 **22**
♦♦♦ Motel
All Year [CP] 1P: $62 2P/1B: $69 2P/2B: $69 XP: $7 F18
Location: From jct I-285, exit 14 westbound; exit 13 eastbound; Just n on US 41 (Cobb Pkwy), just w on Spring St. 2855 Springhill Pkwy 30080. Fax: 770/434-2573. **Terms:** No pets. **Facility:** 144 rooms. 6 stories; interior corridors. **All Rooms:** free & pay movies. **Cards:** AE, DI, DS, JCB, MC, VI. (See color ad p 190)
Roll in showers. ⊜ CTV ⊠ Ⓓ Ⓢ

MICROTEL INN Guaranteed Rates **Phone:** 404/799-7000 **26**
(AAA)
Motel
All Year 1P: $38- 55 2P/1B: $38- 55 2P/2B: $38- 55
Too new to rate; **Location:** I-285 exit 10, just e. 5300 S Cobb Dr SE 20080. **Terms:** Sr. discount; no pets. **Facility:** 87 rooms. Scheduled to open July 1997; 3 stories; interior corridors. **All Rooms:** free movies. **Cards:** AE, CB, DI, DS, MC, VI.
Roll in showers. CTV ⊠ Ⓓ Ⓢ

(See map p. 202)

RED ROOF INN-NORTH
◆◆ Motel

| | | Rates Subject to Change | | | | | | Phone: 770/952-6966 | 20 |

	4/1-6/30	1P: $49- 61	2P/1B: $57- 69	2P/2B: $49- 63	XP: $8	F18
	1/1-3/31 & 7/1-8/31	1P: $44- 55	2P/1B: $52- 63	2P/2B: $50- 58	XP: $8	F18
	12/1-12/31 & 9/1-11/30	1P: $40- 50	2P/1B: $47- 57	2P/2B: $43- 50	XP: $7	F18

Location: I-75 exit 110, just w to Corporate Plaza, just s. 2200 Corporate Plaza 30080. Fax: 770/952-1348. **Terms:** Small pets only. **Facility:** 136 rooms. 2 stories; exterior corridors. **All Rooms:** free & pay movies. **Cards:** AE, CB, DI, DS, MC, VI.

SUMNER SUITES-ATLANTA CUMBERLAND
AAA SAVE
◆◆◆ Motel

| | | | | | | Phone: 770/384-0060 | 21 |

| | Sun-Thurs [CP] | 1P: $99 | 2P/1B: $109 | 2P/2B: $109 | XP: $10 | F18 |
| | Fri & Sat [CP] | 1P: $79- 99 | 2P/1B: $79- 99 | 2P/2B: $79- 99 | XP: $10 | F18 |

Location: I-285 exit 14 westbound, exit 13 eastbound, just n to Spring Rd, just w to Spring Hill Pkwy (from I-75 exit 109). 2876 Spring Hill Pkwy 30080. Fax: 770/384-0075. **Terms:** Package plans; no pets. **Facility:** 125 rooms. Very tastefully done lobby & rooms. 6 stories; interior corridors. **Dining:** Lobby bar 5 pm-11 pm; restaurant nearby. **Services:** Fee: coin laundry. **All Rooms:** coffeemakers, microwaves, refrigerators, combo or shower baths. **Cards:** AE, DI, DS, MC, VI. **Special Amenities:** Free breakfast and free local telephone calls.

RESTAURANTS

THE CRAB HOUSE
◆◆ Seafood

| **Lunch:** $6-$10 | **Dinner:** $10-$20 | **Phone:** 770/955-2722 | 10 |

Location: I-285, exit 14; 1.5 mi n on US 41. 2175 Cobb Pkwy 30080. **Hours:** 11:30 am-11 pm, Sun 1 pm-10 pm. Closed: 11/26, 12/24 & 12/25. **Features:** casual dress; children's menu; carryout; salad bar; cocktails & lounge; valet parking; a la carte. Dining in bustling nautical atmosphere. Oyster bar; seafood bar. **Cards:** AE, CB, DI, DS, MC, VI.

HAVELI INDIAN CUISINE
◆◆ Ethnic

| **Lunch:** $7 | **Dinner:** $7-$15 | **Phone:** 770/955-4525 | 13 |

Location: I-285 exit 14 westbound, exit 13 eastbound, 0.3 mi n. 2650 Cobb Pkwy NW 30080. **Hours:** 11:30 am-2:30 & 5:30-10:30 pm, Sat from noon, Sun 5:30 pm-10:30 pm. Closed: 1/1 & 12/25. **Reservations:** accepted; weekdays. **Features:** casual dress; carryout; cocktails; a la carte. Authentic Indian cuisine. Lunch buffet $7.25. **Cards:** AE, DI, DS, MC, VI.

HOUSE OF CHAN
AAA
◆◆ Chinese

| **Lunch:** $6-$8 | **Dinner:** $8-$15 | **Phone:** 770/955-9444 | 11 |

Location: I-285, exit 14 westbound, exit 13 eastbound, 1 mi n on US 41 (Cobb Pkwy). 2469 Cobb Pkwy SE 30080. **Hours:** 11:30 am-2:30 & 5-10 pm, Sat 5 pm-10:30 pm, Sun noon-3 & 5-10 pm. Closed major holidays. **Features:** casual dress; carryout; beer & wine only. Hong Kong style cuisine. No MSG used. Coconut shrimp, whole steamed/fried fish, authentic sweet & sour sauce. Art deco ambience. **Cards:** AE, MC, VI.

SCALINI'S
◆◆ Italian

| | **Dinner:** $7-$17 | **Phone:** 770/952-7222 | 12 |

Location: I-285, exit 14 westbound, exit 13 eastbound, 1 mi n on Cobb Pkwy, in Loehmann's Plaza. 2390 Cobb Pkwy SE 30080. **Hours:** 4:30 pm-11 pm, Fri & Sat-11:30 pm, Sun 4 pm-10 pm. Closed major holidays. **Features:** casual dress; children's menu; carryout; cocktails & lounge; a la carte. Warm, welcoming family atmosphere. Venetian special of veal, shrimp, chicken a local favorite. Large array of pasta dishes. Specialty coffee drinks. **Cards:** AE, CB, DI, DS, MC, VI.

STONE MOUNTAIN—6,500

LODGINGS

DAYS INN
AAA SAVE
◆◆◆ Motel

| | | | | | | Phone: 770/879-0800 | |

| | 5/1-10/31 [CP] | 1P: $50- 125 | 2P/1B: $60- 125 | 2P/2B: $60- 125 | XP: $7 | F10 |
| | 12/1-4/30 & 11/1-11/30 [CP] | 1P: $50- 90 | 2P/1B: $50- 90 | 2P/2B: $50- 90 | XP: $7 | F10 |

Location: On US 78; 1.3 mi e of entrance to Stone Mountain Park, behind Krystal Restaurant. 2006 Glen Club Dr 30087. Fax: 770/879-5674. **Terms:** Weekly rates; no pets. **Facility:** 81 rooms. View of Stone Mountain from 2nd level. 2 stories; exterior corridors. **Dining:** Restaurant nearby. **Services:** valet laundry. **All Rooms:** free movies. **Some Rooms:** coffeemakers, microwaves, radios, refrigerators. **Cards:** AE, CB, DI, DS, MC, VI.

EVERGREEN CONFERENCE CENTER & RESORT
Phone: 770/879-9900

(AAA) [SAVE]

◆◆◆◆
Resort Hotel

| | All Year | 1P: $120 | 2P/1B: $140 | 2P/2B: $140 | XP: $20 | F18 |

Location: In Stone Mountain Park; I-285 exit 30B. 1 Lakeview Dr 30086 (PO Box 1363). Fax: 770/879-6818. **Terms:** Check-in 4 pm; package plans; no pets. **Facility:** 249 rooms. Peaceful park setting overlooking lake. Balcony or patio. 5 stories; interior corridors; wading pool, whirlpool; 2 lighted tennis courts; park facilities. Fee: parking; 36 holes golf. **Dining & Entertainment:** Restaurant; 6:30 am-10 pm; $13-$21; cocktails/lounge; 24-hour room service. **Services:** valet laundry; area transportation, within the park; valet parking. **All Rooms:** coffeemakers, free & pay movies, refrigerators, combo or shower baths. **Some Rooms:** whirlpools. **Cards:** AE, CB, DI, DS, JCB, MC, VI. **Special Amenities:** Early check-in/late check-out and free newspaper.
Roll in showers. [icons]

HOLIDAY INN EXPRESS
Phone: 770/465-8847

◆◆◆
Motel

| | All Year [CP] | Rates Subject to Change | | | | |
| | | 1P: $62- 89 | 2P/1B: $62- 89 | 2P/2B: $62- 89 | XP: $6 |

Location: US 78 exit West Park Pl eastbound, Park Pl exit westbound, 0.3 mi n. 1790 East Park Place Blvd 30087. Fax: 770/465-9184. **Terms:** Sr. discount; no pets. **Facility:** 63 rooms. 6 whirlpool rms, extra charge. Rates are higher on weekends; 3 stories; interior corridors. **All Rooms:** free movies. **Cards:** AE, DS, MC, VI.
(See color ad p 190)
Roll in showers. [icons]

STONE MOUNTAIN PARK INN
Phone: 770/469-3311

(AAA)

◆◆◆
Motor Inn

	5/18-9/7	1P: $69- 125	2P/1B: $69- 125	2P/2B: $89- 109
	3/1-5/17 & 9/8-11/30	1P: $59- 115	2P/1B: $59- 115	2P/2B: $79- 99
	12/1-2/28	1P: $50- 70	2P/1B: $50- 70	2P/2B: $60- 65

Location: In Stone Mountain Park. Hwy 78E 30086 (PO Box 775). Fax: 770/498-5691. **Terms:** Check-in 4 pm; no pets. **Facility:** 92 rooms. Maximum rates for up to 4 persons; 2 stories; interior/exterior corridors. **Dining:** Restaurant; 6:30 am-10:30 & 11:30-9 pm. **All Rooms:** free movies. **Cards:** AE, DI, DS, JCB, MC, VI.
Roll in showers. [icons]

RESTAURANTS

MAGNOLIA TEA ROOM & RESTAURANT
Lunch: $7-$8   **Dinner:** $13-$20   **Phone:** 770/498-6304

◆◆
Regional
American

Location: Stone Mountain Village, from jct Main St & E Mountain St, 3 blks n. 5459 E Mountain St 30083. **Hours:** 11 am-2:30 & 5:30-9:30 pm, Fri & Sat from 5:30 pm, Sun brunch 11 am-2:30 pm. Closed major holidays & Mon. **Reservations:** suggested. **Features:** casual dress; children's menu; carryout; beer & wine only. Pre-Civil War structure. Freshly prepared food in historic atmosphere. Innovative pasta & seafood entrees. Banana cheesecake with warm praline sauce. Smoke free premises. [icon]

ROCKBRIDGE DINER
Lunch: $5-$7   **Dinner:** $12-$16   **Phone:** 404/414-6077

◆◆
Continental

Location: Southbound I-285 exit 32 (SR 10/Memorial Dr), 1 mi e on Memorial Dr to Rockbridge Rd; then 2.3 mi se to N Hairston Rd; nw corner shopping center. 414 N Hairston Rd 30083. **Hours:** 11:30 am-2 & 5:30-10 pm, Sat from 5:30 pm. Closed major holidays & Sun. **Reservations:** suggested; weekends. **Features:** casual dress; carryout; beer & wine only; a la carte. New York cafe style. Casual European atmosphere. All freshly made entrees of fish, veal, seafood & chicken. **Cards:** AE, DI, DS, MC, VI.

SUWANEE—2,400

LODGINGS

BEST WESTERN FALCON INN & CONFERENCE CENTER
Phone: 770/945-6751

(AAA) [SAVE]

◆◆◆
Motor Inn

| | All Year | 1P: $45- 55 | 2P/1B: $55- 60 | 2P/2B: $55- 60 | XP: $5 | F12 |

Location: I-85, exit 44. Two Falcon Pl 30174. Fax: 770/945-6751. **Terms:** No pets. **Facility:** 101 rooms. Training camp & practice field of the Atlanta Falcons. 2 stories; exterior corridors. Fee: 4 lighted tennis courts. **Dining & Entertainment:** Restaurant; 7 am-9:30 & 11-1:30 pm; cocktails/lounge; breakfast buffet avail; buffet lunch only. **Services:** valet laundry. Fee: childcare. **Recreation:** jogging. **All Rooms:** free movies. **Some Rooms:** refrigerators. **Cards:** AE, DI, DS, MC, VI. **Special Amenities:** Free local telephone calls and free newspaper. *(See color ad p 182)* [icons]

COMFORT INN SUWANEE
Phone: 770/945-1608

(AAA) [SAVE]

◆◆
Motel

| | All Year [CP] | 1P: $60 | 2P/1B: $65 | 2P/2B: $65 | XP: $6 | F18 |

Location: I-85, exit 44. 2945 Hwy 317 30174. Fax: 770/945-1608. **Terms:** No pets. **Facility:** 80 rooms. Tastefully furnished rooms. 2 stories; exterior corridors. **Dining:** Restaurant nearby. **Services:** valet laundry. Fee: childcare. **All Rooms:** free movies. **Cards:** AE, CB, DI, DS, MC, VI. [icons]

DAYS INN
Phone: 770/945-8372

◆◆
Motel

| | All Year | Rates Subject to Change | | | | |
| | | 1P: $48- 58 | 2P/1B: $58- 68 | 2P/2B: $58- 68 | XP: $10 | F18 |

Location: I-85 exit 44, nw corner. 3103 Hwy 317 30024. Fax: 770/932-2421. **Terms:** Sr. discount; no pets. **Facility:** 100 rooms. 2 stories; exterior corridors. **Cards:** AE, DI, DS, JCB, MC, VI. [icons]

HOLIDAY INN
Phone: 770/945-4921

(AAA) [SAVE]

◆◆◆
Motor Inn

| | 6/1-8/31 | 1P: $74 | 2P/1B: $82 | 2P/2B: $82 | XP: $6 |
| | 12/1-5/31 & 9/1-11/30 | 1P: $69 | 2P/1B: $77 | 2P/2B: $77 | XP: $6 |

Location: I-85 exit 44. 2955 Hwy 317 30174. Fax: 770/945-0440. **Terms:** Small pets only. **Facility:** 120 rooms. 2 stories; exterior corridors; putting green; wading pool. **Dining & Entertainment:** Restaurant; 6:30-11 am, 11:30 am-2 & 5-10 pm; $7-$15; cocktails/lounge. **Services:** Fee: coin laundry. **All Rooms:** free & pay movies. **Some Rooms:** safes, whirlpools. **Cards:** AE, DI, DS, MC, VI. **Special Amenities:** Early check-in/late check-out and free newspaper. [icons]

TUCKER—25,800   (See map p. 202; index p. 199)

LODGINGS

BEST WESTERN BRADBURY SUITES
Phone: 770/496-1070   [202]

◆◆◆
Motel

| | All Year [BP] | 1P: $79 | 2P/1B: $82 | 2P/2B: $82 | XP: $10 | F12 |

Location: I-285 exit 28, 0.5 mi se. 2060 Crescent Centre Blvd 30084. Fax: 770/939-9947. **Terms:** Check-in 4 pm; no pets. **Facility:** 113 rooms. Theme suites avail; 6 stories; interior corridors. **Dining:** Cafeteria; Breakfast buffet, 6-8:30 am, Sat & Sun 7-10:30 am. **All Rooms:** free & pay movies. **Cards:** AE, CB, DI, DS, MC, VI. *(See ad p 204 & color ad p 182)* [icons]

COUNTRY INN & SUITES BY CARLSON
Phone: 770/270-9009   [203]

Suite Motel

| | All Year [CP] | 1P: $69- 119 | 2P/1B: $69- 119 | 2P/2B: $69- 119 |

Too new to rate; **Location:** I-285 exit 28, 0.5 mi se. 2081 Northlake Parkway 30084. **Terms:** Sr. discount; reserv deposit; no pets. **Facility:** 49 rooms. Rates for up to 4 persons. 23 two-room suites avail $95-$149. 2 whirlpool rms, extra charge. Scheduled to open summer 1997; 5 stories; interior corridors. **Cards:** AE, CB, DI, DS, JCB, MC, VI.
Roll in showers.

(See map p. 202)

COURTYARD BY MARRIOTT-NORTH LAKE Rates Subject to Change **Phone:** 770/938-1200 **200**
◆◆◆   Sun-Thurs   1P: $99   2P/1B: $109   2P/2B: $109   XP: $10   F18
Motel Fri & Sat   1P: $72   2P/1B: $79   2P/2B: $79
       Location: I-285 exit 28, just w. 4083 La Vista Rd 30084. Fax: 770/934-6497. **Terms:** No pets. **Facility:** 128
rooms. Up to 4 persons on weekends; 2 stories; interior corridors. **Dining:** Restaurant; 6:30-10 am, Sat & Sun 7 am-noon.
All Rooms: free & pay movies. **Cards:** AE, CB, DI, DS, MC, VI. (See color ad p 192)   `🛰` `CTV` `X` `🏊` `D` `S`

HOLIDAY INN ATLANTA NORTHLAKE Rates Subject to Change **Phone:** 770/938-1026 **198**
◆◆◆   Mon-Thurs   1P: $99- 129   2P/1B: $109- 129 2P/2B: $109- 129 XP: $10   F18
Motel Fri-Sun   1P: $79- 106   2P/1B: $85- 116   2P/2B: $85- 116   XP: $10   F18
       Location: I-285 exit 28, nw corner. 4156 La Vista Rd 30084 (ATLANTA). Fax: 770/491-8113. **Terms:** No
pets. **Facility:** 182 rooms. Rates for up to 4 persons; 5 stories; interior corridors. **Dining:** Restaurant; 6:30 am-2 & 5-10 pm;
$11-$15. **All Rooms:** free & pay movies. **Cards:** AE, DI, DS, JCB, MC, VI.   `🛰` `🐾` `CTV` `X` `🏊` `D`

LA QUINTA ATLANTA STONE MOUNTAIN **Phone:** 770/496-1317 **206**
AAA `SAVE` All Year [CP]   1P: $56- 69   2P/1B: $61- 75   2P/2B: $61- 75   XP: $6   F18
       Location: I-285 exit 30B, 3.5 mi e to Mountain Industrial Blvd, ne corner. 1819 Mountain Industrial Blvd
◆◆◆   30084. Fax: 770/493-4785. **Terms:** Small pets only. **Facility:** 128 rooms. 3 stories; exterior corridors.
Motel   **Dining:** Restaurant nearby. **Services:** Fee: coin laundry. **All Rooms:** free & pay movies. **Some Rooms:**
       Fee: microwaves, refrigerators. **Cards:** AE, CB, DI, DS, MC, VI. **Special Amenities:** Free breakfast and
free local telephone calls. (See color ad p 205)   `🛏` `🛰` `🍴` `CTV` `X` `🏊` `D`

MASTERS ECONOMY INN TUCKER **Phone:** 770/938-3552 **205**
AAA `SAVE` All Year   1P: $35- 49   2P/1B: $38- 45   2P/2B: $41- 50   XP: $4   F18
       Location: I-285 exit 29, just w. 1435 Montreal Rd 30084. Fax: 770/934-4520. **Terms:** Weekly rates; pets,
◆ $10 extra charge. **Facility:** 107 rooms. 3 stories; exterior corridors; small pool. **Dining:** Coffee shop nearby.
Motel   **All Rooms:** free movies. **Some Rooms:** microwaves, refrigerators. **Cards:** AE, CB, DI, DS, MC, VI.
       Special Amenities: Free local telephone calls. (See color ad p 215)   `🛏` `CTV` `X` `D` `S`

RAMADA NORTHLAKE Rates Subject to Change **Phone:** 770/939-1000 **201**
AAA   All Year [CP]   1P: $49- 59   2P/1B: $59- 79   2P/2B: $59- 79   XP: $10   F12
       Location: I-285 exit 28, 0.3 mi e. 2180 Northlake Pkwy 30084. Fax: 770/939 7430. **Terms:** Sr. discount;
◆◆   pets, $20 dep req. **Facility:** 159 rooms. 3 stories; interior/exterior corridors. **All Rooms:** free & pay movies.
Motel   **Cards:** AE, DI, DS, MC, VI.   `🛏` `🛰` `🍴` `CTV` `X` `D`

RED ROOF INN-ATLANTA (TUCKER NE) Rates Subject to Change **Phone:** 770/496-1311 **204**
◆◆   All Year   1P: $33- 41   2P/1B: $40- 48   2P/2B: $46- 55   XP: $7   F18
Motel   **Location:** I-285 exit 29, just w. 2810 Lawrenceville Hwy 30084. Fax: 770/496-0077. **Terms:** Small pets only.
       Facility: 120 rooms. 3 stories; exterior corridors. **All Rooms:** free & pay movies. **Cards:** AE, CB, DI, DS,
MC, VI.   `🛏` `🍴` `CTV` `X` `🏊` `D`

SUPER 8 MOTEL **Phone:** 770/491-8778 **199**
AAA `SAVE` All Year   1P: $45   2P/2B: $50   2P/2B: $50   XP: $5   F18
       Location: I-285 exit 29, just e. 1600 Cresent Center Blvd 30084. Fax: 770/270-1423. **Terms:** Reserv
◆◆   deposit; no pets. **Facility:** 52 rooms. In commercial area. Unpretentious accommodations. Handling fee im-
Motel   posed; 3 stories; exterior corridors. **All Rooms:** free movies. **Cards:** AE, CB, DI, DS, MC, VI.
       Special Amenities: Free breakfast and free local telephone calls.   `X` `D`

RESTAURANTS

BLUE RIBBON GRILL **Lunch:** $4-$8   **Dinner:** $7-$16   **Phone:** 770/491-1570 **160**
◆   **Location:** I-285, exit 28, 0.3 mi w. 4006 La Vista Rd 30084. **Hours:** 11 am-10 pm. Closed: Sun, 11/26 &
American 12/25. **Features:** casual dress; children's menu; health conscious menu; carryout; cocktails & lounge. Local
       favorite serving comfort foods. Childern under 10 eat free. **Cards:** AE, DS, MC, VI.   `X`

EVELYN'S CAFE **Lunch:** $5-$12   **Dinner:** $5-$12   **Phone:** 770/496-0561 **164**
◆   **Location:** I-285, exit 29, 2.3 mi e; Brockett Sq. 3853-F Lawrenceville Hwy 30084. **Hours:** 11 am-3 & 5-10
Ethnic pm. Closed major holidays & Sun. **Features:** casual dress; children's menu; carryout; beer & wine only; a la
       carte. Greek-Italian-American cuisines. Casual popular local eatery serving excellent from scratch entrees.
Daily lunch specials. **Cards:** MC, VI.

ITALIAN OVEN **Lunch:** $5-$10   **Dinner:** $5-$10   **Phone:** 770/493-6836 **162**
◆   **Location:** I-285 exit 28, 0.8 mi w. 3925 La Vista Rd 30184. **Hours:** 11 am-10 pm, Fri & Sat-11 pm. Closed:
Italian 11/26 & 12/25. **Features:** children's menu; carryout; cocktails. Bright family eatery serving over 20 pasta
       dishes, wood-burning brick oven stromboli, calzone & pizza. Espresso/cappuccino. **Cards:** AE, DS, MC, VI.
       `X`

UNION CITY—8,400 (See map p. 225; index p. 224)

LODGINGS

DAYS INN SHANNON MALL Rates Subject to Change **Phone:** 770/964-3777 **335**
◆◆   All Year [CP]   1P: $49- 59   2P/1B: $57- 69   2P/2B: $57- 69   XP: $5   F18
Motel   **Location:** I-85 exit 13; 0.3 mi w to Shannon Pkwy; just s. 6840 Shannon Pkwy S 30291. Fax: 770/964-6631.
       Terms: Sr. discount; no pets. **Facility:** 100 rooms. 2 stories; exterior corridors. **All Rooms:** free movies.
Cards: AE, CB, DI, DS, MC, VI.   `🛰` `CTV` `X` `D` `S`

ECONO LODGE SOUTHWEST **Phone:** 770/964-9999 **336**
AAA `SAVE` All Year [CP]   1P: $75   2P/1B: $75   2P/2B: $85   XP: $6   F18
       Location: I-85 exit 13; just e. 7410 Oakley Rd 30291. Fax: 770/964-6867. **Terms:** Reserv deposit; no pets.
◆◆   **Facility:** 57 rooms. Unpretentious accommodations. 2 stories; exterior corridors. **Dining:** Coffee shop
Motel   nearby. **All Rooms:** free movies, refrigerators. **Cards:** AE, CB, DI, DS, JCB, MC, VI. **Special Amenities:**
       Early check-in/late check-out and free newspaper. (See color ad p 226)   `X` `D`

AUGUSTA—44,600

LODGINGS

AMERISUITES   Phone: 706/733-4656
(AAA) [SAVE]   All Year [CP]   1P: $53   2P/1B: $58   2P/2B: $58   XP: $5   F18
◆◆◆   **Location:** I-20, exit 65 (Washington Rd), just n to Stevens Creek Rd, 0.5 mi e. 1062 Claussen Rd 30907.
Motel   Fax: 706/736-1133. **Terms:** Small pets only, $5 extra charge. **Facility:** 111 rooms. Large rooms. 6 stories; in-
terior corridors; whirlpool; playground, basketball, volleyball, picnic tables. **Services:** Fee: coin laundry.
All Rooms: coffeemakers, microwaves, free movies, refrigerators, VCP's. **Some Rooms:** honor bars.
Cards: AE, CB, DI, DS, JCB, MC, VI. **Special Amenities:** Free breakfast and free local telephone calls.
(See color ad p 10)   Roll in showers. 🛏 ⛱ 🎱 CTV ⛷ ✕ 🐾 D S

COMFORT INN   Phone: 706/855-6060
(AAA) [SAVE]   All Year [CP]   1P: $70   2P/1B: $75   2P/2B: $75   XP: $5   F18
◆◆◆   **Location:** I-20, exit 64B, 0.3 mi n to Scott Nixon Memorial, w on Frontage Rd. 629 Frontage Rd NW 30907.
Motel   Fax: 706/855-8008. **Terms:** Package plans; no pets. **Facility:** 123 rooms. Close to interstate. 5 stories; interior
corridors; whirlpool; basketball, picnic table & grill. **Dining:** Restaurant nearby. **Services:** Fee: coin laundry.
All Rooms: coffeemakers, free movies. **Some Rooms:** microwaves, refrigerators, VCP's, whirlpools.
Cards: AE, CB, DI, DS, JCB, MC, VI. **Special Amenities:** Free breakfast and free newspaper.
⛱ 🎱 🌐 CTV ✕ D

COURTYARD BY MARRIOTT-AUGUSTA   Rates Subject to Change   Phone: 706/737-3737
◆◆◆   Sun-Thurs   1P: $66- 84   2P/1B: $76- 94 2P/2B: $76- 94 XP: $10   F18
Motor Inn   Fri & Sat   1P: $44- 71   2P/1B: $44- 71 2P/2B: $44- 71
Location: I-20, exit 65 (Washington Rd), just n to Stevens Creek Rd, 0.5 mi e. 1045 Stevens Creek Rd
30907. Fax: 706/738-7851. **Terms:** No pets. **Facility:** 130 rooms. Weekend rates for up to 4 persons; 2 stories; interior corri-
dors. **Dining:** Restaurant; 6-10 am, Sat 7 am-noon, Sun 7 am-1 pm. **All Rooms:** free & pay movies. **Cards:** AE, DI, DS,
MC, VI.   ⛱ CTV ⛷ ✕ 🐾 D S

DAYS INN   Rates Subject to Change   Phone: 706/793-9600
◆◆   All Year   1P: $30- 34   2P/1B: $30- 34 2P/2B: $34- 38 XP: $5
Motel   **Location:** I-520, exit 5A, 1 mi s. 3320 Dean's Bridge Rd 30906. Fax: 706/798-3352. **Terms:** Reserv deposit
3 day notice; no pets. **Facility:** 42 rooms. 2 stories; exterior corridors. **All Rooms:** free movies. **Cards:** AE,
CB, DI, DS, MC, VI.   CTV ✕ D

DAYS INN WHEELER RD   Phone: 706/868-8610
(AAA) [SAVE]   All Year [CP]   1P: $38- 48   2P/1B: $38- 48 2P/2B: $38- 48 XP: $5   F12
◆◆   **Location:** I-520, exit 2, 0.3 mi w. 3654 Wheeler Rd 30909. Fax: 706/868-8610. **Terms:** No pets. **Facility:** 55
Motel   rooms. 2 stories; exterior corridors. **Dining:** Restaurant nearby. **Services:** Fee: coin laundry.
All Rooms: free movies. Fee: safes. **Some Rooms:** Fee: microwaves, refrigerators. **Cards:** AE, DI, DS, MC,
VI. **Special Amenities:** Free breakfast and free newspaper.   🎱 CTV ✕ D

FAIRFIELD INN   Rates Subject to Change   Phone: 706/733-8200
◆◆   All Year [CP]   1P: $40- 46   2P/1B: $40- 46 2P/2B: $40- 46
Motel   **Location:** I-20, exit 65 (Washington Rd), 0.3 mi s to Boy Scout Rd, 0.5 mi w. 201 Boy Scout Rd 30909.
Fax: 706/733-8200. **Terms:** Sr. discount; no pets. **Facility:** 117 rooms. Handling fee imposed; 3 stories;
interior/exterior corridors. **All Rooms:** free movies. **Cards:** AE, CB, DI, DS, MC, VI.   ⛱ CTV ✕ D S

HAMPTON INN   Phone: 706/737-1122
(AAA) [SAVE]   All Year [CP]   1P: $53- 59   2P/1B: $59- 65 2P/2B: $62- 65 XP: $6   F16
◆◆◆   **Location:** On SR 28; 0.3 mi nw of jct I-20, exit 65. 3030 Washington Rd 30907. Fax: 706/738-9988.
Motel   **Terms:** No pets. **Facility:** 145 rooms. Busy commercial location, close to interstate. 2 stories; exterior corri-
dors; sauna. **Dining:** Restaurant nearby. **Services:** valet laundry. **All Rooms:** free movies.
Some Rooms: refrigerators, VCP's. **Cards:** AE, CB, DI, DS, MC, VI. **Special Amenities:** Free breakfast
and free local telephone calls. *(See color ad p 212 & below)*   ⛱ 🎱 🌐 CTV ✕ D

HOLIDAY INN EXPRESS   Rates Subject to Change   Phone: 706/724-5560
◆◆◆   All Year [CP]   1P: $54   2P/1B: $54   2P/2B: $54   XP: $5   F19
Motel   **Location:** J C Calhoun Exwy, 0.5 mi s; opposite Medical College of GA Hospital. 1103 15th St 30901.
Fax: 706/724-5560. **Terms:** Sr. discount; reserv deposit; no pets. **Facility:** 42 rooms. 2 stories; exterior corri-
dors. **All Rooms:** free movies. **Cards:** AE, CB, DI, DS, JCB, MC, VI.   CTV ✕ D

HOLIDAY INN GORDON HIGHWAY AT BOBBY JONES Guaranteed Rates **Phone:** 706/737-2300
◆◆◆ All Year 1P: $69- 74 2P/1B: $75- 80 2P/2B: $75- 80 XP: $6 F18
Motor Inn **Location:** On SR 78 & 278 at jct I-520E, exit 4A. 2155 Gordon Hwy 30909. Fax: 706/737-0418. **Terms:** Sr. discount; small pets only. **Facility:** 150 rooms. 2 stories; exterior corridors. **Dining:** Dining room; 6 am-2 & -10 pm, Sat & Sun from 7 pm; $5-$15. **All Rooms:** free movies. **Cards:** AE, CB, DI, DS, JCB, MC, VI. *See color ad below)*

HORNES MOTOR LODGE Rates Subject to Change **Phone:** 706/798-2230
◆ All Year 1P: $28 2P/1B: $33 2P/2B: $33 XP: $5 F7
Motor Inn **Location:** Hwy 1 & 25. 1520 Gordon Hwy 30906. Fax: 706/798-2230. **Terms:** Reserv deposit, 10 day notice; no pets. **Facility:** 118 rooms. 2 stories; exterior corridors. **Dining:** Mom's Country Kitchen, see separate sting. **All Rooms:** free movies. **Cards:** AE, DI, DS, MC, VI.

LA QUINTA INN **Phone:** 706/733-2660
AAA SAVE ◆◆◆ Hotel All Year [CP] 1P: $41- 48 2P/1B: $48- 54 2P/2B: $48- 54 XP: $7 F18
Location: I-20, exit 65 (Washington Rd), just n. 3020 Washington Rd 30907-3811. Fax: 706/738-3637. **Terms:** Small pets only. **Facility:** 129 rooms. Spanish-style exterior. 2-3 stories; interior/exterior corridors. **Dining:** Restaurant nearby. **Services:** valet laundry. **All Rooms:** free & pay movies. **Some Rooms:** Fee: microwaves, refrigerators. **Cards:** AE, CB, DI, DS, MC, VI. **Special Amenities: Free breakfast and ree local telephone calls.**

THE PARTRIDGE INN Rates Subject to Change **Phone:** 706/737-8888
◆◆◆ All Year [BP] 1P: $100- 135 2P/1B: $110- 145 2P/2B: $110- 145 XP: $10 F18
Historic Hotel **Location:** 1.3 mi w off 15th St. 2110 Walton Way 30904. Fax: 706/731-0826. **Terms:** Sr. discount; no pets. **Facility:** 155 rooms. Rates for up to 4 persons; 6 stories; interior corridors. **Dining:** Dining room, restaurant; am-10 pm, Sun-9 pm; $8-$22. **All Rooms:** Fee: movies. **Some Rooms:** 20 kitchens. **Cards:** AE, CB, DI, DS, MC, VI.

RADISSON RIVERFRONT HOTEL AUGUSTA **Phone:** 706/722-8900
AAA SAVE ◆◆◆ Hotel All Year 1P: $99- 134 2P/1B: $114- 134 2P/2B: $114- 134 XP: $15 F18
Location: Downtown, on River Walk at 10th & Reynolds. 2 10th St 30901. Fax: 706/823-6513. **Terms:** Check-in 4 pm; reserv deposit; package plans; small pets only. **Facility:** 234 rooms. Elegant public areas. Many rooms with excellent river view. 11 stories; interior corridors; saunas. **Dining & Entertainment:** Dining room; 6:30 am-10:30 pm; $10-$17; health conscious menu items; cocktails/lounge. **Services:** valet aundry. **All Rooms:** coffeemakers, free & pay movies. **Some Rooms:** refrigerators. **Cards:** AE, CB, DI, DS, MC, VI. **Special Amenities: Free local telephone calls and free newspaper.** *(See ad below)*

RADISSON SUITES INN   Phone: 706/868-180(
AAA SAVE   Mon-Thurs [BP]   1P: $69- 99   2P/1B: $79- 109 2P/2B: $79- 109 XP: $10   F1
           Fri-Sun [BP]   1P: $59- 99   2P/1B: $69- 109 2P/2B: $69- 109 XP: $10   F1
◆◆◆   **Location:** Washington Rd at I-20, exit 65, 0.3 mi n. 3038 Washington Rd 30907. Fax: 706/868-9300
Motor Inn **Terms:** Reserv deposit; package plans; small pets only, $25 dep req. **Facility:** 176 rooms. Older property. ·
stories; exterior corridors. **Dining & Entertainment:** Restaurant; 6 am-10, noon-2 & 5-10 pm, Sat 7 am-11
noon-2 & 5-10 pm, Sun 7 am-11 am; $7-$14; cocktails/lounge. **Services:** valet laundry. **All Rooms:** coffeemakers, free &
pay movies. **Some Rooms:** microwaves, refrigerators, whirlpools. Fee: VCP's. **Cards:** AE, CB, DI, DS, MC, V
Special Amenities: Free breakfast and free local telephone calls.   🛏 🛆 🍽 CTV ⊠ 🕼 D

RAMADA LIMITED   Rates Subject to Change   Phone: 706/733-811
◆   All Year [CP]   1P: $36- 40   2P/1B: $40- 50 2P/2B: $40- 50 XP: $5   F
Motel   **Location:** I-520, exit 4A, on SR 78 & 278. 2154 Gordon Hwy 30909. Fax: 706/733-8115. **Terms:** Reser
           deposit; pets, $25 dep req. **Facility:** 30 rooms. 2 stories; exterior corridors. **All Rooms:** free movies
Cards: AE, CB, DI, DS, MC, VI.   🛏 CTV ⊠ D

SHERATON AUGUSTA HOTEL   Guaranteed Rates   Phone: 706/855-810(
◆◆◆   All Year   1P: $110- 150   2P/1B: $120- 150 2P/2B: $120- 150 XP: $10   F1
Hotel   **Location:** Jct I-520, exit 2 & Wheeler Rd; entrance 0.3 mi w at Perimeter Pkwy. 2651 Perimeter Pkwy
           30909. Fax: 706/860-1720. **Terms:** Sr. discount; small pets only. **Facility:** 179 rooms. 30 suites, $139-$300;
stories; interior corridors. **Dining:** Restaurant; 6:30 am-10:30 pm; $8-$17. **All Rooms:** free & pay movies. **Cards:** AE, DS
MC, VI.   🛏 🛆 🛆 🕂 CTV 🕼 ⊠ 🕼 D S

WEST BANK INN   Phone: 706/733-1724
AAA SAVE   All Year [CP]   1P: $34- 37   2P/1B: $37   2P/2B: $37   XP: $4   D
           Location: I-20, exit 65; 0.3 mi s on Washington Rd. 2904 Washington Rd 30909. Fax: 706/733-1724
◆◆   **Terms:** Weekly/monthly rates; no pets. **Facility:** 47 rooms. Some large rooms, located in busy commercia
Motel   area. 2 stories; exterior corridors. **Dining:** Restaurant nearby. **Services:** Fee: coin laundry. **All Rooms:** free
           & pay movies. **Some Rooms:** microwaves, refrigerators. Fee: VCP's. **Cards:** AE, DI, DS, MC, VI.
Special Amenities: Early check-in/late check-out and free local telephone calls.   CTV ⊠ D

RESTAURANTS

THE BOLL WEEVIL - A CAFE & SWEETERY   **Lunch:** $4-$8   **Dinner:** $4-$12   Phone: 706/722-7772
◆   **Location:** End of Ninth St, next to Riverwalk & Radisson Riverfront Hotel. 10 Ninth St 30901. **Hours:** 1
American   am-midnight. Closed major holidays. **Features:** casual dress; health conscious menu; carryout; beer & wine
specials. Wide selection of desserts. Outdoor seating avail. Smoking permitted outdoors only. **Cards:** DS, MC, VI.   ⊠

CALVERT'S   **Dinner:** $12-$20   Phone: 706/738-451
◆◆   **Location:** 3 mi w in Surrey Center. 475 Highland Ave 30909. **Hours:** 5 pm-10 pm. Closed major holidays &
Continental Sun. **Reservations:** suggested; weekends. **Features:** semi-formal attire; early bird specials; health
           conscious menu; carryout; cocktails & lounge; buffet. Sophisticated atmosphere in cozy dining room
Cards: AE, DI, DS, MC, VI.   ⊠

FRENCH MARKET GRILLE   **Lunch:** $6-$9   **Dinner:** $11-$18   Phone: 706/737-4865
◆◆   **Location:** 3 mi w in Surrey Center. 425 Highland Ave 30909. **Hours:** 11 am-10 pm, Fri & Sat-11 pm. Close
Regional   major holidays & Sun. **Features:** casual dress; children's menu; health conscious menu; carryout; cocktails &
American   lounge. Cajun & Creole cuisine. Casual bustling atmosphere. Large selection of beer & ale. Exceptiona
           fresh-made desserts. Espresso. **Cards:** AE, DI, DS, MC, VI.

THE KING GEORGE   **Lunch:** $5-$8   **Dinner:** $9-$17   Phone: 706/724-475
◆◆   **Location:** Downtown on the Riverwalk. 2 Eighth St 30901. **Hours:** 11 am-3 & 5-10 pm, Fri-10:30 pm, Sat 1
American   am-4 & 5-10:30 pm, Sun 11:30 am-9 pm. Closed: 11/26 & 12/25. **Features:** casual dress; children's menu
           carryout; cocktails & lounge; a la carte. Authentic English pub designed & built in the United Kingdom
shipped to Augusta. Wide variety of draft bottled beers. **Cards:** AE, CB, DI, DS, MC, VI.   ⊠

LA MAISON ON TELFAIR   **Lunch:** $8-$13   **Dinner:** $18-$30   Phone: 706/722-480
◆◆◆   **Location:** 4 blks s; 2 blks e of US 1 (Gordon Hwy) in Olde Town. 404 Telfair St 30901. **Hours:** 6 pm-10:3
Continental pm, Thurs & Fri 11:30 am-2 & 6-10:30 pm. Closed major holidays & Sun. **Reservations:** suggested
           Features: semi-formal attire; health conscious menu; carryout; cocktails. Beautifully restored 1855 Victoria
home. Formal atmosphere. Modern French & Regional American cuisine. **Cards:** AE, CB, DI, DS, MC, VI.   ⊠

LE CAFE DUTEAU   **Dinner:** $12-$25   Phone: 706/733-350!
◆◆◆   **Location:** 0.5 mi w of 15th St. 1855 Central Ave 30904. **Hours:** 6 pm-10 pm, Fri-Sun to 10:30 pm. Closed
Continental Mon, 1/1, 7/4 & 12/25. **Reservations:** suggested; weekends. **Features:** semi-formal attire; health consciou
           menu; carryout; cocktails. Casual intimate decor. French & Cajun specialties. Jazz combo on Sun; jaz
pianist Thur-Sat. Well-chosen wine list. **Cards:** AE, CB, DI, DS, MC, VI.   ⊠

MICHAELS FINE FOOD & ENTERTAINMENT   **Dinner:** $12-$23   Phone: 706/733-286(
◆◆◆   **Location:** On Washington Rd, 0.3 mi s of I-20, exit 65. 2860 Washington Rd 30909. **Hours:** 6 pm-10 pm
Continental Closed: Mon after a Sun holiday. **Features:** casual dress; health conscious menu; cocktails. Intimat
           ambience. Nightly piano entertainment in lounge. **Cards:** AE, DI, DS, MC, VI.

MOM'S COUNTRY KITCHEN   **Lunch:** $5-$6   **Dinner:** $5-$6   Phone: 706/798-228
◆   **Location:** Hwy 1 & 25; in Hornes Motor Lodge. 1520 Gordon Hwy 30906. **Hours:** 6 am-9 pm, Sat-11 pm
American   Closed: 7/4, 11/26 & 12/25. **Features:** casual dress; carryout; salad bar; buffet. All-day buffet. **Cards:** DI, DS
MC, VI.

T-BONES STEAKHOUSE-GORDON HWY   **Lunch:** $4-$7   **Dinner:** $7-$17   Phone: 706/796-187!
◆   **Location:** At jct Gordon Hwy & Dean's Bridge Rd; from I-520, exit 5, then 2.5 mi e on US 1. 1654 Gordo
Steakhouse Hwy 30906. **Hours:** 11 am-11 pm. Closed: 11/26 & 12/25. **Features:** casual dress; children's menu; healt
           conscious menu items; carryout; cocktails; buffet. Casual dining. Southwest decor. **Cards:** AE, MC, VI.   ⊠

T-BONES STEAKHOUSE-WASHINGTON ROAD   **Lunch:** $5-$9   **Dinner:** $7-$18   Phone: 706/737-832!
◆   **Location:** I-20, exit 65, 0.3 mi s. 2856 Washington Rd 30909. **Hours:** 11 am-10:30 pm, Fri & Sat-11 pm
Steakhouse Sun noon-10 pm. Closed: 11/26 & 12/25. **Features:** casual dress; children's menu; health conscious menu
           carryout; cocktails & lounge; a la carte. Casual dining in lively atmosphere. **Cards:** AE, MC, VI.   ⊠

VILLA EUROPA　　　　**Lunch:** $4-$7　　　　**Dinner:** $11-$20　　　　**Phone:** 706/798-6211
🔷　　　　**Location:** 0.5 mi n from jct I-520 & Dean's Bridge Rd. 3044 Dean's Bridge Rd 30906. **Hours:** 11 am-3 &
　　　　5-10 pm, Fri-11 pm, Sat 5 pm-11 pm, Sun 5 pm-10 pm. Closed: 11/26, 12/24 & 12/25. **Features:** casual
◆◆　　　dress; children's menu; health conscious menu items; carryout; cocktails & lounge. Also featuring American &
German　　Italian foods; casual & cozy atmosphere. **Cards:** AE, CB, DI, DS, MC, VI.　　　　❌

WILLIAMS SEAFOOD RESTAURANT OF SAVANNAH　　**Lunch:** $5-$12　　**Dinner:** $6-$16　　**Phone:** 706/737-9415
◆　　　　**Location:** I-520, exit 3, 1.8 mi ne. 3160 Wrightsboro Rd 30909. **Hours:** 11 am-9:30 pm, Sun-9 pm. Closed:
Seafood　　11/26, 12/24 & 12/25. **Features:** casual dress; children's menu; carryout; beer & wine only. Family operated.
　　　　Also selections of beef & chicken. Casual atmosphere & decor. **Cards:** AE, DI, DS, MC, VI.　　❌

AUSTELL—*see Atlanta & Vicinity p. 227.*

BAXLEY—3,800

LODGING

BUDGET HOST INN　　　　　　　　　　　　　　　　　　　　　　**Phone:** 912/367-2200
🔷 SAVE　　All Year　　　　　　1P: $36　　2P/1B: $38　　2P/2B: $45　　XP: $5　　D14
　　　　Location: 1 mi e on US 341. 714 E Parker St 31513 (Rt 6, Box 4). Fax: 912/367-2200. **Terms:** Reserv
◆◆　　　deposit; no pets. **Facility:** 30 rooms. Cozy, comfortable rooms. 2 stories; exterior corridors. **All Rooms:** free
Motel　　movies. **Some Rooms:** refrigerators. **Cards:** AE, DI, DS, MC, VI. **Special Amenities:** Free local telephone
　　　　calls. *(See color ad p 183)*　　　　　　　　　　　　　　　　CTV ❌ D

RESTAURANT

CAPTAIN JOE'S SEAFOOD　　**Lunch:** $4-$11　　　　**Dinner:** $8-$11　　　　**Phone:** 912/367-7795
◆　　　　**Location:** 2 mi e on US 341 & SR 27. US 341 31513. **Hours:** 11 am-9 pm, Fri & Sat-10 pm. Closed major
Seafood　　holidays & 12/28. **Features:** casual dress; children's menu; carryout; salad bar. Friendly, nautical ambience.
　　　　Generous portions. **Cards:** AE, CB, DI, DS, MC, VI.　　　　　　　　　❌

BLAIRSVILLE—600

LODGINGS

BEST WESTERN MILTON INN　　　　　Rates Subject to Change　　　　　**Phone:** 706/745-6995
◆◆◆　　10/1-10/31 [CP]　　　　1P: $70　　2P/1B: $79　　2P/2B: $79　　XP: $5　　F12
Motel　　5/1-9/30 [CP]　　　　　1P: $55　　2P/1B: $60　　2P/2B: $60　　XP: $5　　F12
　　　　12/1-4/30 & 11/1-11/30 [CP]　1P: $45　　2P/1B: $45　　2P/2B: $45　　XP: $5　　F12
Location: Just e of jct SR 19/US 129 & SR 515/US 76. 222 Hwy 515 30512. Fax: 706/745-1048. **Terms:** Sr. discount; no
pets. **Facility:** 60 rooms. 2 stories; interior/exterior corridors. **All Rooms:** free movies. **Cards:** AE, CB, DI, DS, MC, VI.
　　　　　　　　　　　　　　　　　　　　　　　　🛌 CTV ❌ D

NOTTLEY DAM GUEST HOUSE　　　　　　　　　　　　　　**Phone:** 706/745-7939
🔷 SAVE　　9/1-11/30 [CP]　　　　　　2P/1B: $65　　2P/2B: $75　　XP: $5　　F18
　　　　12/1-8/31 [CP]　　　　　　2P/1B: $55　　2P/2B: $65　　XP: $5　　F18
◆◆　　　**Location:** 8 mi w on US 76/SR 515, 4 mi n on CR 325. 2266 Nottley Dam Rd 30512. Fax: 706/745-7560.
Bed &　　**Terms:** 2 night min stay; small pets only. **Facility:** 6 rooms. Contemporary country-style home located in gor-
Breakfast　geous rural setting. 2 stories; interior corridors; designated smoking area. **Recreation:** fishing.
　　　　Fee: horseback riding. **All Rooms:** no phones. **Special Amenities:** Early check-in/late check-out and free
breakfast.　　　　　　　　　　　　　　　　　　　🛏 ❌ D

BLUE RIDGE—1,300

RESTAURANT

FORGE MILL CROSSING RESTAURANT　　**Lunch:** $4-$7　　　**Dinner:** $6-$16　　**Phone:** 706/374-5771
◆◆　　　**Location:** 6 mi e on APD 515 & US 76. Appalachian Hwy at Forge Rd 30560. **Hours:** 11:30 am-2:30 & 5-9
Regional　　pm, Fri & Sat-10 pm, Sun 10 am-9 pm. Closed: Mon, 1/1-1/14 & 9/3-9/8. **Reservations:** suggested;
American　　weekends. **Features:** casual dress; Sunday brunch; children's menu; carryout. Rural, hilltop location.
　　　　Regional southern specialties. Smoke free premises. **Cards:** AE, DI, DS, MC, VI.　　❌

BRASELTON—400

LODGING

THE LODGE AT CHATEAU ELAN/DAYS INN　　Rates Subject to Change　　　**Phone:** 770/867-8100
◆◆◆　　All Year [CP]　　　　1P: $55- 65　2P/1B: $65- 75　2P/2B: $65- 75　XP: $10　　F18
Motel　　**Location:** I-85 exit 48, 0.3 mi w. 2069 Hwy 211 NW 30517. Fax: 770/867-3236. **Terms:** Reserv deposit; no
　　　　pets. **Facility:** 80 rooms. 2 stories; interior corridors. **All Rooms:** free movies. **Cards:** AE, DI, DS, MC, VI.
　　　　　　　　　　　　Roll in showers. ♿ CTV ❌ 🐾 D Ⓢ

BREMEN—4,400

LODGINGS

DAYS INN BREMEN　　　　　　　　　　　　　　　　　　**Phone:** 770/537-4646
🔷 SAVE　　6/1-9/30 [CP]　　1P: $69- 99　2P/1B: $79- 109　2P/2B: $79- 109　XP: $10　　F15
　　　　12/1-5/31 & 10/1-11/30 [CP]　1P: $49- 79　2P/1B: $59- 89　2P/2B: $59- 89　XP: $10　　F15
◆◆　　　**Location:** I-20 exit 3. 35 Price Creek Rd 30110. Fax: 770/537-1831. **Terms:** Small pets only, $5 extra
Motel　　charge. **Facility:** 62 rooms. Large,contemporary rooms. 2 stories; exterior corridors. **Services:** Fee: coin
　　　　laundry. **All Rooms:** free movies. **Some Rooms:** Fee: microwaves, refrigerators. **Cards:** AE, DI, DS, MC,
VI. **Special Amenities:** Free breakfast and free newspaper.　　　🛒 🛌 CTV ❌ D Ⓢ

DAYS INN OF BREMEN　　　　　　　Rates Subject to Change　　　　　**Phone:** 770/537-3833
◆　　　　3/1-9/30 [CP]　　　1P: $45- 90　2P/1B: $45- 90　2P/2B: $45- 90　XP: $6　　F12
Motor Inn　12/1-2/28 & 10/1-11/30 [CP]　1P: $38- 45　2P/1B: $42- 48　2P/2B: $42- 48　XP: $6　　F12
Terms: Small pets only, $7 extra charge. **Facility:** 78 rooms. 2 stories; exterior corridors. **Dining:** Restaurant; 7 am-2 & 6-9
pm, Sun-3 pm; $10-$14. **All Rooms:** free movies. **Cards:** AE, DS, MC, VI.　🛌 🛒 CTV ❌ D

BRUNSWICK—16,400

LODGINGS

BEST WESTERN BRUNSWICK INN   Phone: 912/264-0144
(AAA) [SAVE]   12/1-4/30, 6/1-8/31 &
              10/16-11/30 [CP]   1P: $43- 53   2P/1B: $47- 57   2P/2B: $47- 57   XP: $4   F12
◆◆   5/1-5/31 & 9/1-10/15 [CP] 1P: $37- 47   2P/1B: $43- 53   2P/2B: $43- 53   XP: $4   F12
Motel   **Location:** I-95, exit 7B & US 341 & 25. 5323 New Jesup Hwy 31525. Fax: 912/264-0144. **Terms:** Pets.
             Facility: 143 rooms. 2 stories; exterior corridors. **Cards:** AE, CB, DI, DS. *(See color ad p 182 & ad below)*

🛏️ 🍽️ CTV ✕ D

BUDGETEL INN   Rates Subject to Change   Phone: 912/265-7725
◆◆   All Year [CP]   1P: $39- 48   2P/1B: $44- 53   2P/2B: $47
Motel   **Location:** I-95 exit 7A, 0.3 mi se. 105 Tourist Dr 31520. Fax: 912/264-6151. **Terms:** Sr. discount; small pets
            only. **Facility:** 102 rooms. 3 stories; interior corridors. **All Rooms:** Fee: movies. **Cards:** AE, CB, DI, DS, MC,
VI. *(See color ad below)*

🛏️ 🍽️ CTV ✕ 🐾 D S

COMFORT INN   Phone: 912/264-6540
(AAA) [SAVE]   All Year [CP]   1P: $49- 89   2P/1B: $59- 89   2P/2B: $59- 89   XP: $6   F18
            Location: I-95, exit 7B, just w on US 25 & 341. 5308 New Jesup Hwy 31523. Fax: 912/264-9296.
◆◆◆   **Terms:** Weekly rates; package plans; pets. **Facility:** 118 rooms. 5 stories; interior corridors.
Motor Inn   **Dining:** Restaurant; 24 hours; $6-$8; wine/beer only. **Services:** valet laundry. **All Rooms:** combo or shower
            baths. **Some Rooms:** coffeemakers. Fee: microwaves, refrigerators, VCP's. **Cards:** AE, CB, DI, DS, JCB,
MC, VI. **Special Amenities: Free breakfast and free newspaper.** *(See color ad p 253)*
                                                    Roll in showers.   🛏️ 🍽️ 🛁 CTV ✕ 🐾 D

DAYS INN-DOWNTOWN   Phone: 912/265-8830
(AAA) [SAVE]   5/1-9/15   1P: $39- 47   2P/1B: $43- 50   2P/2B: $47- 55   XP: $5   F16
            12/1-4/30 & 9/16-11/30   1P: $35- 41   2P/1B: $39- 45   2P/2B: $39- 45   XP: $5   F16
◆   **Location:** At jct of US 17 & SR 25; from I-95 southbound, follow e on SR 25 spur to US 17S; from I-95
Motor Inn   northbound, follow 8 mi on US 17N. 2307 Gloucester St, Rt 25 31520. Fax: 912/264-5860.
            Terms: Weekly/monthly rates; small pets only, $5 extra charge. **Facility:** 98 rooms. In light
commercial/residential area. 2 stories; exterior corridors. **Dining & Entertainment:** Restaurant; 11 am-2 & 5-10 pm; $9-$12;
cocktails/lounge. **Services:** Fee: coin laundry. **All Rooms:** free movies. **Some Rooms:** microwaves, refrigerators.
Cards: AE, CB, DI, DS, JCB, MC, VI. **Special Amenities: Free local telephone calls and free room upgrade (subject to
availability with advanced reservations).**
                                                                       🛏️ 🍽️ 🛁 CTV ✕ D

DAYS INN-NEW JESUP HWY   Rates Subject to Change   Phone: 912/264-4330
◆◆   All Year   1P: $44- 54   2P/2B: $49- 59   XP: $5   F
Motor Inn   **Location:** On US 341; jct I-95, exit 7A. 5033 New Jesup Hwy 31525. Fax: 912/264-4330. **Terms:** Sr.
            discount; no pets. **Facility:** 154 rooms. 2 stories; exterior corridors. **Dining:** Restaurant; 6 am-midnight;
$7-$10. **All Rooms:** free movies. **Cards:** AE, CB, DI, DS, JCB, MC, VI.
                                                                       🍽️ CTV ✕ D

ECONO LODGE   Guaranteed Rates   **Phone:** 912/264-8666
◆◆◆   All Year [CP]   1P: $45- 55   2P/1B: $45- 55   2P/2B: $45- 55   XP: $5   F17
Motel   **Location:** I-95, exit 8; 0.5 mi sw. 630 Perry Lane Rd 31525. **Fax:** 912/264-6808. **Terms:** Sr. discount; no
      pets. **Facility:** 69 rooms. 1-2 stories; interior/exterior corridors. **All Rooms:** free movies. **Cards:** AE, DI, DS,
MC, VI.

EMBASSY SUITES   **Phone:** 912/264-6100
Ⓐ Ⓢ   All Year [BP]   1P: $79   2P/1B: $79   2P/2B: $79   XP: $10   F18
     Location: I-95, exit 8, 1.5 mi s on SR 25; in Glynn Place Mall. 500 Mall Blvd 31525. **Fax:** 912/267-1615.
◆◆◆   **Terms:** Package plans; small pets only. **Facility:** 130 rooms. Guest rooms overlook an enclosed spacious
Suite Hotel   atrium with cascading waterfalls, illuminated trees & a carousel theme. 3 two-bedroom units. 29 suites with
      whirlpool, $10 extra charge; 5 stories; interior corridors. **Services:** valet laundry. **All Rooms:** coffeemakers,
microwaves, free & pay movies, refrigerators. **Some Rooms:** whirlpools. **Cards:** AE, CB, DI, DS, JCB, MC, VI.
Special Amenities: Free breakfast and preferred room (subject to availability with advanced reservations).

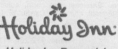

DIAMONDS tell the story—read The Ⓐ Diamonds.

HAMPTON INN
♦♦♦
Motel
Rates Subject to Change
All Year [CP]   1P: $62   2P/1B: $70   2P/2B: $70
Phone: 912/261-0002
Location: I-95, exit 7A, 0.3 mi se. 112 Tourist Dr 31520. Fax: 912/265-5599. **Terms:** Sr. discount; no pets. **Facility:** 127 rooms. Maximum of 4 adults per room; 3 stories; interior/exterior corridors. **All Rooms:** free movies. **Cards:** AE, CB, DI, DS, MC, VI.

HOLIDAY INN I-95
(AAA) [SAVE]
♦♦
Motor Inn
Phone: 912/264-4033
All Year [BP]   1P: $69- 79   2P/1B: $69- 79   2P/2B: $69- 79
Location: I-95, exit 7B, nw corner, on US 341. 5252 New Jesup Hwy 31525. Fax: 912/267-1314. **Terms:** Package plans; small pets only. **Facility:** 126 rooms. Located in commercial area with mature, attractive landscaping. Some units overlook a small scenic pond. 2 stories; exterior corridors; wading pool; playground. **Dining & Entertainment:** Restaurant; 6 am-2 & 5-9 pm; $11-$17; cocktails/lounge. **Services:** valet laundry. **Recreation:** fishing. **All Rooms:** free movies. **Some Rooms:** coffeemakers. **Cards:** AE, DI, DS, MC, VI. **Special Amenities: Free breakfast and free newspaper.** (See color ad p 253)
Roll in showers.

MOTEL 6 - 790
(AAA)
♦
Motel
Guaranteed Rates
All Year   1P: $35- 39   2P/1B: $39- 49   2P/2B: $39- 49   XP: $3   F17
Phone: 912/264-8582
Location: I-95 exit 7B, sw corner. 403 Butler Dr 31525. Fax: 912/264-6028. **Terms:** Sr. discount; small pets only. **Facility:** 122 rooms. 1 story; exterior corridors. **All Rooms:** free movies. **Cards:** AE, DI, DS, MC, VI.
Roll in showers.

QUALITY INN
(AAA) [SAVE]
♦♦♦
Motel
Phone: 912/265-4600
All Year [CP]   1P: $49- 59   2P/1B: $60- 70   2P/2B: $60- 70   XP: $6   F18
Location: I-95 exit 8, sw corner. 125 Venture Dr 31525. Fax: 912/265-8268. **Terms:** Package plans; no pets. **Facility:** 83 rooms. Traditionally-furnished, stylish guest rooms, spacious sunken lobby & contemporary design, all nested in quiet surroundings. 2 stories; interior/exterior corridors. **Services:** Fee: coin laundry. **All Rooms:** coffeemakers, free movies. **Some Rooms:** microwaves, refrigerators, whirlpools. **Cards:** AE, DI, DS, MC, VI. **Special Amenities: Free breakfast and free local telephone calls.**

QUALITY INN & SUITES
(AAA) [SAVE]
♦♦♦
Motel
Phone: 912/264-9111
4/14-9/9 [CP]   1P: $64- 84   2P/1B: $64- 84   2P/2B: $64- 84   XP: $5   F12
12/1-4/13 & 9/10-11/30 [CP]   1P: $48- 68   2P/1B: $48- 68   2P/2B: $48- 68   XP: $5   F12
Location: On Hwy 17. 3302 Glynn Ave 31525. Fax: 912/267-6474. **Terms:** Small pets only, $20 extra charge. **Facility:** 100 rooms. 2 stories; interior corridors. **Services:** Fee: coin laundry. **All Rooms:** coffeemakers, free movies. **Some Rooms:** microwaves, refrigerators. **Cards:** AE, CB, DI, DS, MC, VI.

RAMADA INN I-95
♦♦
Motor Inn
Rates Subject to Change
All Year   1P: $45   2P/1B: $52   2P/2B: $52   XP: $7   F18
Phone: 912/264-3621
Location: Jct I-95, exit 7A & US 341 & 25. 3040 Scarlet St 31520. Fax: 912/280-9154. **Terms:** Sr. discount; small pets only. **Facility:** 213 rooms. 2 stories; exterior corridors. **Dining:** Restaurant; 6 am-9 & 5-9 pm, Sat & Sun 7 am-11 & 5-9 pm, lunch buffet Mon-Fri 11:30 am-1:30 pm; $9-$16. **All Rooms:** free movies. **Cards:** AE, CB, DI, DS, MC, VI.

SLEEP INN I-95
(AAA) [SAVE]
♦♦
Motel
Phone: 912/261-0670
All Year [CP]   1P: $45- 85   2P/1B: $49- 89   2P/2B: $49- 89   XP: $6   F18
Location: I-95, exit 7B, just w on US 25 & 341. 5272 New Jesup Hwy 31523. Fax: 912/264-0441. **Terms:** Weekly rates; package plans; pets. **Facility:** 93 rooms. Cozy, contemporary guest rooms. Warm hospitality. Modern facilities & over-sized tiled showers. 2 stories; interior corridors. **Dining:** Restaurant nearby. **Services:** valet laundry. **All Rooms:** combo or shower baths. **Some Rooms:** whirlpools. Fee: VCP's. **Cards:** AE, CB, DI, DS, JCB, MC, VI. **Special Amenities: Free breakfast and free newspaper.** (See color ad p 253)
Roll in showers.

SUPER 8 MOTEL
♦♦
Motel
Rates Subject to Change
All Year   1P: $41- 46   2P/1B: $46   2P/2B: $51   XP: $5   F12
Phone: 912/264-8800
Location: I-95 exit 7B, just w. 5280 New Jesup Hwy 31520. Fax: 912/264-8800. **Terms:** Sr. discount; reserv deposit, 7 day notice; small pets only. **Facility:** 62 rooms. 3 stories, no elevator; interior corridors. **All Rooms:** free movies. **Cards:** AE, CB, DI, DS, MC, VI.

RESTAURANTS

GRAPEVINE CAFE
♦
American
Lunch: $4-$6
Phone: 912/265-0115
Location: Downtown, historic district; Hwy 341. 1519 Newcastle St 31520. **Hours:** 11:30 am-3:30 pm. Closed: Sun, 11/26 & 12/25. **Features:** casual dress; health conscious menu items; salad bar; beer & wine only; street parking; a la carte. Specializing in vegetarian, tuna steak, other seafood & homemade dessert. Smoke free premises.

JINRIGHT'S SEAFOOD HOUSE
(AAA)
♦
Seafood
Lunch: $5-$7   **Dinner:** $7-$21
Phone: 912/267-1590
Location: 1.2 mi n on SR 17 from jct SR 25 & US 17. 2815 Glynn Ave 31520. **Hours:** 11 am-10 pm. **Features:** casual dress; Sunday brunch; children's menu; senior's menu; beer & wine only. A family-owned seafood restaurant. **Cards:** DS, MC, VI.

MATTEO'S ITALIAN RESTAURANT
♦
Italian
Lunch: $5-$12   **Dinner:** $5-$12
Phone: 912/267-0248
Location: I-95 exit 7B US 341/US 25; 0.4 mi n. 5448 New Jesup Hwy 31525. **Hours:** 11 am-9:30 pm, Sat from 4:30 pm. Closed: Sun, 7/4, 9/1-9/14, 11/26 & 12/25. **Features:** casual dress; children's menu; beer & wine only. A family-owned restaurant with a large variety of Italian dishes & pizza. **Cards:** MC, VI.

BYRON—2,300

LODGINGS

BEST WESTERN INN AND SUITES
Motel
Phone: 912/956-3056
Under construction; **Location:** I-75, exit 46, se corner. 101 Dunbar Hwy 49 Rd 31008. **Terms:** Sr. discount; pets, $20 dep req. **Facility:** 71 rooms. Scheduled to open fall 1997; 2 stories; exterior corridors. **All Rooms:** free movies. **Cards:** AE, CB, DI, DS, JCB, MC, VI. (See color ad p 255) Roll in showers.

COMFORT INN

Phone: 912/956-1600

All Year [CP]   1P: $52   2P/1B: $58   2P/2B: $58   XP: $5   F12
Location: I-75 exit 46 nw corner. 607 Chapman Rd 31008. Fax: 912/956-2680. **Terms:** Reserv deposit; no pets. **Facility:** 60 rooms. Handling fee imposed; 2 stories; exterior corridors. **Dining:** Restaurant nearby.
All Rooms: free movies. **Some Rooms:** microwaves, refrigerators, VCP's, whirlpools. **Cards:** AE, CB, DI, DS, JCB, MC, VI. **Special Amenities: Free breakfast and preferred room (subject to availability with advanced reservations).**

Motel

[icons]

DAYS INN

Phone: 912/956-5100

All Year [CP]   1P: $30- 37   2P/1B: $32- 44   2P/2B: $32- 44   XP: $4
Location: I-75, exit 46, just w. 246 N Hwy 49 31008 (Rt 1, Box 35). Fax: 912/956-5033. **Terms:** Reserv deposit, 3 day notice; weekly rates; EP avail; no pets. **Facility:** 62 rooms. 2 stories; exterior corridors. **Dining:** Restaurant nearby. **Services:** Fee: coin laundry. **All Rooms:** free movies. **Some Rooms:** microwaves, refrigerators. **Cards:** AE, CB, DI, DS, JCB, MC, VI. **Special Amenities: Early check-in/late check-out and free local telephone calls.**

Motel

[icons]

Check out our **bold** listings!

ECONO LODGE
Phone: 912/956-5600
(AAA) [SAVE] 4/1-8/31 [CP] 1P: $36- 43 2P/1B: $39- 46 2P/2B: $39- 46 XP: $4 F12
12/1-3/31 & 9/1-11/30 [CP] 1P: $29- 34 2P/1B: $32- 38 2P/2B: $32- 38 XP: $4 F12
◆ **Location:** I-75 exit 46, just w. 106 Old Macon Rd 31008. Fax: 912/956-5600. **Terms:** Weekly rates; small
Motel pets only, $5 extra charge. **Facility:** 96 rooms. 2 whirlpool rms, extra charge; 2 stories; exterior corridors; playground. **Dining:** Restaurant nearby. **All Rooms:** free movies. **Some Rooms:** microwaves, refrigerators.
Cards: AE, DS, MC, VI. **Special Amenities:** Free breakfast and preferred room (subject to availability with advanced
reservations). [icons]

SUPER 8 MOTEL
Phone: 912/956-3311
(AAA) [SAVE] All Year [CP] 1P: $44 2P/1B: $47 2P/2B: $47 XP: $4 F12
◆◆◆ **Location:** I-75 exit 46, just e. 305 Hwy 49N 31008. Fax: 912/956-5885. **Terms:** No pets. **Facility:** 57 rooms.
Motel 2 stories; exterior corridors. **Dining:** Restaurant nearby. **Services:** guest laundry. **All Rooms:** microwaves,
free movies, refrigerators. **Some Rooms:** VCP's, whirlpools. **Cards:** AE, CB, DI, DS, MC, VI.
Special Amenities: Free breakfast and free local telephone calls. *(See color ad p 255)* [icons]

CAIRO—9,000

LODGING

BEST WESTERN EXECUTIVE INN
Phone: 912/377-8000
(AAA) [SAVE] All Year [CP] 1P: $42- 55 2P/1B: $47- 67 2P/2B: $47- 67 XP: $5 F12
◆◆◆ **Location:** 1 mi e on US 84. 2800 US 84E 31728. Fax: 912/377-8000. **Terms:** Reserv deposit; small pets
Motor Inn only, $5 extra charge. **Facility:** 50 rooms. 2 stories; exterior corridors; sauna. **Dining & Entertainment:**
Restaurant; 11 am-2:30 & 5:30-9 pm, Sun to 2 pm; $7-$11; cocktails/lounge. **Services:** valet laundry.
All Rooms: free movies. **Some Rooms:** whirlpools. **Cards:** AE, DI, DS, MC, VI. **Special Amenities:** Early
check-in/late check-out and free local telephone calls. *(See color ad p 182)* [icons]

CALHOUN—7,100

LODGINGS

BEST WESTERN OF CALHOUN
Phone: 706/629-4521
(AAA) [SAVE] All Year [CP] 1P: $36- 42 2P/1B: $36- 50 2P/2B: $36- 50 XP: $4 F12
◆◆ **Location:** I-75 exit 132, just e. 2261 US 41 NE 30701. Fax: 706/629-1650. **Terms:** Reserv deposit, 7 day
Motel notice; pets, $5 extra charge. **Facility:** 40 rooms. Compact, neat property set back from freeway pleasant
decor. 2 stories; exterior corridors; enclosed whirlpool open all year. **Dining:** Restaurant nearby.
All Rooms: free movies. **Cards:** AE, DI, DS, MC, VI. **Special Amenities:** Free breakfast and free local
telephone calls. *(See color ad p 182)* [icons]

BUDGET HOST SHEPHERD MOTEL
Phone: 706/629-8644
(AAA) [SAVE] All Year [CP] 1P: $30- 34 2P/1B: $34- 38 2P/2B: $37- 44 XP: $3 F12
◆◆ **Location:** I-75 exit 129, just e. 3900 Hwy 53 E Hwy SE 30703-2407 (PO Box 2407). **Terms:** Small pets
Motor Inn only. **Facility:** 73 rooms. Wide variety of rooms ranging from modestly furnished compact to good sized with
pleasant decor. Rooms are located in 2 buildings on either side of street. 1-2 stories; exterior corridors.
Dining: BJ's Restaurant, see separate listing. **Services:** Fee: coin laundry. **All Rooms:** free movies, combo
or shower baths. **Some Rooms:** microwaves, refrigerators, phones. **Cards:** AE, CB, DI, DS, MC, VI. **Special Amenities:**
Free breakfast and free local telephone calls. *(See color ad p 183)* Roll in showers. [icons]

CALHOUN RAMADA LTD
Phone: 706/629-9207
(AAA) [SAVE] All Year [CP] 1P: $35- 39 2P/1B: $39- 43 2P/2B: $40- 46 XP: $5 F18
◆◆ **Location:** I-75 exit 130, just w. 1204 Red Bud Rd NE 30701. Fax: 706/625-9862. **Terms:** Weekly rates; no
Motel pets. **Facility:** 49 rooms. 2 stories; exterior corridors. **Dining:** Restaurant nearby. **All Rooms:** free movies.
Some Rooms: refrigerators. **Cards:** AE, CB, DI, DS, JCB, MC, VI. **Special Amenities:** Free breakfast and
free local telephone calls. [icons]

DUFFY'S MOTEL NORTH
Phone: 706/629-4436
(AAA) [SAVE] All Year 1P: $20- 24 2P/1B: $22- 26 2P/2B: $24- 28 XP: $3
◆ **Location:** I-75 exit 132, just w. 1441 US 41N 30701. **Terms:** Small pets only. **Facility:** 37 rooms. 1-2 stories;
exterior corridors. **All Rooms:** free movies. **Cards:** AE, DS, MC, VI. **Special Amenities:** Free local
Motor Inn telephone calls. [icons]

ECONO LODGE
Phone: 706/625-5421
(AAA) [SAVE] All Year [CP] 1P: $22- 27 2P/1B: $28- 32 2P/2B: $30- 37 XP: $4 F18
◆ **Location:** I-75 exit 132, just w. 1438 US Hwy 41N 30701. Fax: 706/625-9309. **Terms:** No pets. **Facility:** 37
Motel rooms. Older property located in commercial area. 2 stories; exterior corridors; small pool. **All Rooms:** free
movies. **Cards:** AE, CB, DI, DS, MC, VI. [icons]

HAMPTON INN
Rates Subject to Change
Phone: 706/629-0999
◆◆◆ All Year [CP] 1P: $46- 52 2P/1B: $50 2P/2B: $56- 58
Motel **Location:** I-75 exit 129, just w. 115 Hampton Dr SE 30701. Fax: 706/629-1228. **Terms:** Sr. discount; no
pets. **Facility:** 59 rooms. Rates for up to 4 persons; 2 stories; exterior corridors. **All Rooms:** free movies.
Cards: AE, CB, DI, DS, MC, VI. [icons]

JAMESON INN
Guaranteed Rates
Phone: 706/629-8133
◆◆ All Year [CP] 1P: $52 2P/1B: $56 2P/2B: $56 XP: $1-4 F12
Motel **Location:** I-75 exit 129, just sw. 189 Jameson St 30701. Fax: 706/629-7985. **Terms:** Sr. discount; no pets.
Facility: 59 rooms. 2 stories; exterior corridors. **All Rooms:** free movies. **Cards:** AE, CB, DI, DS, MC, VI. [icons]

QUALITY INN-CALHOUN
Phone: 706/629-9501
(AAA) [SAVE] All Year [CP] 1P: $40- 50 2P/1B: $50- 60 2P/2B: $50- 60 XP: $5 F18
◆◆◆ **Location:** I-75 exit 129, just e on Hwy 53. 915 Hwy 53E SE 30701. Fax: 706/629-9501. **Terms:** Pets, $5
Motel extra charge. **Facility:** 100 rooms. RV & bus parking. Near Calhoun Outlet Center. 2 stories; exterior corridors.
Dining: Restaurant; 11 am-midnight; $11-$17; cocktails; sports bar, banquet room. **Services:** Fee: coin
laundry. **All Rooms:** coffeemakers, free & pay movies. **Some Rooms:** microwaves, refrigerators. **Cards:** AE,
CB, DI, DS, JCB, MC, VI. **Special Amenities:** Free breakfast and free local telephone calls. [icons]

SMITH MOTEL   Phone: 706/629-8427
(AAA) [SAVE]   All Year   1P: $21- 24 2P/1B: $25- 28 2P/2B: $27- 30 XP: $4
◆◆   Location: I-75, exit 132, 0.3 mi sw. 1437 US Hwy 41N 30701. Fax: 706/629-8427. Terms: Reserv deposit;
Motel   no pets. Facility: 40 rooms. Pleasant rooms located off main highway. 2 stories; exterior corridors.
                       All Rooms: free movies. Cards: AE, DS, MC, VI. Special Amenities: Free local telephone calls and
                       preferred room (subject to availability with advanced reservations).   [📶] [CTV] [✕] [D]

RESTAURANT
BJ'S RESTAURANT   Lunch: $5-$7   Dinner: $8-$15   Phone: 706/629-3461
◆◆   Location: I-75 exit 129, just e; in Budget Host Shepherd Motel. 940 Hwy 53E 30701. Hours: 11 am-9 pm,
Regional   Sun-2:30 pm. Closed major holidays. Features: casual dress; children's menu; health conscious menu
American   items; carryout; buffet. Where the local folks meet to eat. Fresh, home style vegetables. Touch of southern
                       hospitality. Cards: AE, DS, MC, VI.   [✕]

CARROLLTON—16,000

LODGINGS
DAYS INN OF CARROLLTON   Rates Subject to Change   Phone: 770/830-1000
◆◆   All Year [CP]   1P: $40- 45 2P/1B: $45- 49 2P/2B: $45- 49 XP: $5   F12
Motel   Location: Jct US 27 & SR 166. 180 Centennial Rd 30117. Fax: 770/830-1113. Terms: Pets, $10 dep req.
                       Facility: 58 rooms. 2 stories; exterior corridors. Cards: AE, CB, DI, DS, JCB, MC, VI.   [📶] [CTV] [✕] [D]

RAMADA INN   Rates Subject to Change   Phone: 770/834-7700
◆◆◆   All Year   1P: $55- 61 2P/1B: $62- 66 2P/2B: $62- 66 XP: $5   F18
Motor Inn   Location: Jct US 27 & SR 166. 1202 S Park St 30117. Fax: 770/834-1113. Terms: Pets, $10 dep req.
                       Facility: 104 rooms. 2 stories; exterior corridors. Dining: Restaurant, coffee shop; 6:30 am-11 pm, Sun-10
pm; $10-$15. All Rooms: free movies. Cards: AE, CB, DI, DS, JCB, MC, VI.   [📶] [CTV] [✕] [D]

RESTAURANT
DANYEL'S   Lunch: $5-$7   Dinner: $7-$25   Phone: 770/832-9620
◆◆   Location: On US 27, 0.3 mi n of SR 166. 911 S Park St 30117. Hours: 11 am-2 & 5-10 pm. Closed major
Continental   holidays, Sun & Mon. Features: casual dress; children's menu; salad bar; cocktails & lounge. Pleasant
                       dining room. Serving mainly American dishes for lunch & French, Italian & American dishes for dinner.
Cards: AE, DS, MC, VI.   [✕]

CARTERSVILLE—12,000

LODGINGS
BUDGET HOST INN   Phone: 770/386-0350
(AAA) [SAVE]   6/1-8/31   1P: $25- 39 2P/1B: $30- 59 2P/2B: $30- 59 XP: $5   D12
                  3/2-5/31   1P: $25- 35 2P/1B: $29- 45 2P/2B: $29- 55 XP: $5   D12
◆◆   12/1-12/31 & 9/1-11/30   1P: $22- 29 2P/1B: $29- 39 2P/2B: $29- 49 XP: $5   D12
Motor Inn   1/1-3/1   1P: $22- 29 2P/1B: $29- 40 2P/2B: $29- 40 XP: $5   D12
                  Location: I-75 exit 127, just w. 851 Cass-White Rd 30120. Fax: 770/386-0350. Terms: Pets, $3 extra
charge. Facility: 92 rooms. Soft, inviting room decor. Quiet rural location. 2 stories; exterior corridors. Dining: Restaurant; 6
am-2 & 5-9 pm; $5-$8. Cards: AE, DS, MC, VI. Special Amenities: Early check-in/late check-out and preferred room
(subject to availability with advanced reservations). *(See color ad p 183)*   [📶] [📶] [CTV] [✕] [D]

COMFORT INN   Phone: 770/387-1800
(AAA) [SAVE]   All Year [CP]   1P: $34- 48 2P/1B: $34- 48 2P/2B: $34- 55 XP: $5   F18
◆◆   Location: I-75 exit 125, 0.3 mi se. 28 Hwy 294 SE 30121. Fax: 770/387-1800. Terms: Reserv deposit, 3
Motel   day notice; pets, $5 extra charge, $10 dep req. Facility: 60 rooms. Contemporary style property from lobby to
                  rooms. 2 stories; exterior corridors. Dining: Restaurant nearby. Some Rooms: microwaves.
free newspaper.   Fee: refrigerators, whirlpools. Cards: AE, CB, DI, DS, JCB, MC. Special Amenities: Free breakfast and
                                                                                                  [📶] [📶] [CTV] [✕] [D]

CROWN INN   Phone: 770/382-7100
(AAA) [SAVE]   All Year   1P: $30   2P/2B: $35   XP: $5   F12
◆   Location: I-75 exit 125, 2 mi w on SR 20; 0.4 mi s of jct US 61 & 411. 1214 N Tennessee St 30120.
Motel   Terms: Reserv deposit, 7 day notice; weekly rates; no pets. Facility: 41 rooms. Handling fee imposed; 2 sto-
                  ries; exterior corridors. Cards: AE, CB, DI, DS, MC, VI. Special Amenities: Free local telephone calls and
                  preferred room (subject to availability with advanced reservations).   [CTV] [✕] [D]

DAYS INN-CARTERSVILLE   Phone: 770/382-1824
(AAA) [SAVE]   All Year [CP]   1P: $32- 88 2P/1B: $38- 88 2P/2B: $42- 88 XP: $2-3   F12
◆◆   Location: I-75 exit 125, just w. 5618 Hwy 20 SE 30120. Fax: 770/606-9312. Terms: Reserv deposit; pets,
Motel $4 extra charge. Facility: 52 rooms. 2 stories; exterior corridors; small pool. Dining: Restaurant nearby.
                  All Rooms: free movies. Some Rooms: refrigerators. Fee: whirlpools. Cards: AE, CB, DI, DS, MC, VI.
                  Special Amenities: Free breakfast and free local telephone calls.   [📶] [CTV] [✕] [D]

ECONO LODGE   Phone: 770/386-0700
(AAA) [SAVE]   All Year   1P: $25- 30 2P/1B: $25- 30 2P/2B: $30- 40 XP: $5   F12
◆◆   Location: I-75 exit 127, nw corner. 25 Carson Loop NW 30121. Fax: 770/386-6535. Terms: Pets.
Motor Inn   Facility: 64 rooms. 2 stories; exterior corridors; playground. Dining: Restaurant nearby. Services: Fee: coin
                  laundry. All Rooms: free movies. Some Rooms: coffeemakers. Fee: VCP's. Cards: AE, DI, DS, MC, VI.
                  Special Amenities: Free breakfast and free local telephone calls.   [📶] [CTV] [✕] [D]

HAMPTON INN   Rates Subject to Change   Phone: 770/382-8999
◆◆◆   All Year [CP]   1P: $54   2P/1B: $59   2P/2B: $59   XP: $5   F18
Motel   Location: I-75 exit 125, just w. 5600 Hwy 20 SE 30120. Fax: 770/383-3000. Terms: Sr. discount; no pets.
VI.   Facility: 66 rooms. 3 stories; interior corridors. All Rooms: free & pay movies. Cards: AE, CB, DI, DS, MC,
                                                  Roll in showers. [📶] [CTV] [✕] [🐾] [D] [S]

HOLIDAY INN   Rates Subject to Change   Phone: 770/386-0830
◆◆◆   All Year   1P: $65   2P/1B: $65   2P/2B: $65
Motor Inn   Location: I-75, exit 126, sw corner. 2336 Hwy 411 NE 30120 (PO Box 200306). Fax: 770/386-0867.
                  Terms: Sr. discount; small pets only. Facility: 150 rooms. 2 stories; interior corridors. Dining: Restaurant; 6
am-midnight; $6-$10. All Rooms: free movies. Cards: AE, DI, DS, MC, VI.   [📶] [📶] [CTV] [✕] [D]

KNIGHTS INN
                                                                        Phone: 770/386-7263
(AAA) [SAVE]   All Year [CP]   1P: $33- 85   2P/1B: $40- 90 2P/2B: $40- 90   XP: $6-10   F12
◆◆   **Location:** I-75 exit 124, 1.5 mi w. 420 E Church St 30121. Fax: 770/386-5635. **Terms:** Weekly rates; small
Motel   pets only. **Facility:** 70 rooms. 1 story; exterior corridors. **Dining:** Restaurant nearby. **All Rooms:** free
movies. **Some Rooms:** microwaves, refrigerators. Fee: VCP's. **Cards:** AE, CB, DI, DS, MC, VI.
Special Amenities: Free breakfast and free local telephone calls.   [📶] [CTV] [✕] [D]

MOTEL 6
◆◆   Rates Subject to Change   Phone: 770/386-1449
Motel   All Year   1P: $31- 50 2P/1B: $39- 90 2P/2B: $39- 90   XP: $6
Location: I-75 exit 125, 0.3 mi e. 5657 Hwy 20 NE 30120. Fax: 770/387-0651. **Terms:** Sr. discount; no pets.
Facility: 50 rooms. 2 stories; exterior corridors. **Cards:** AE, CB, DI, DS, MC, VI.   [CTV] [✕] [D]

QUALITY INN
                                                                        Phone: 770/386-0510
(AAA) [SAVE]   All Year [CP]   1P: $39- 50 2P/1B: $43- 53 2P/2B: $47- 57   XP: $5   F18
◆◆◆   **Location:** I-75 exit 124, 2.5 mi w. 235 Dixie Ave 30120 (PO Box 158). Fax: 770/386-1361. **Terms:** Reserv
Motor Inn deposit; no pets. **Facility:** 84 rooms. Located at edge of town. 2 stories; exterior corridors.
Dining: Restaurant; 6:30 am-8 pm; $6-$14; cocktails. **Services:** Fee: coin laundry.
All Rooms: coffeemakers, free movies. **Cards:** AE, DI, DS, JCB, MC, VI. **Special Amenities:** Free
breakfast and free local telephone calls.   [🛏] [🍴] [CTV] [✕] [D]

RAMADA LIMITED
                                                            Phone: 770/382-1515
(AAA) [SAVE]   All Year [CP]   1P: $35- 75 2P/1B: $45- 85 2P/2B: $50-105   XP: $5   F12
◆◆◆   **Location:** I-75 exit 125, 0.3 mi se. 45 Hwy 20 Spur SE 30121. Fax: 770/382-1515. **Terms:** Reserv deposit, 3
Motel   day notice; pets, $8 extra charge. **Facility:** 50 rooms. 2 stories; exterior corridors. **All Rooms:** free movies.
Some Rooms: microwaves, refrigerators. **Cards:** AE, CB, DI, DS, JCB, MC, VI.
         [🛏] [🍴] [CTV] [✕] [D]

RED CARPET INN-CARTERSVILLE
                                             Phone: 770/382-8000
(AAA) [SAVE]   6/1-8/31   1P: $22- 35 2P/1B: $30- 45 2P/2B: $30- 45   XP: $5   D12
◆◆   12/1-5/31 & 9/1-11/30   1P: $22- 26 2P/1B: $27- 35 2P/2B: $27- 35   XP: $5   D12
Motor Inn **Location:** I-75 exit 127, just w. 851 Cass-White Rd 30120. Fax: 770/382-8000. **Terms:** Weekly rates; pets,
$3 extra charge. **Facility:** 47 rooms. Rural location. 3 stories, no elevator; exterior corridors.
Dining: Restaurant; 6 am-10 & 5-9 pm; $5-$8. **Services:** Fee: coin laundry. **Cards:** AE, DS, MC, VI.
**Special Amenities: Early check-in/late check-out and preferred room (subject to availability with advanced
reservations).** (See ad below)   [🛏] [🍴] [CTV] [✕] [D]

RED TOP MOUNTAIN LODGE
◆◆◆   Rates Subject to Change   Phone: 770/975-0055
           All Year   1P: $55- 65 2P/1B: $55- 65 2P/2B: $55- 65   XP: $6   F12
Resort Motor **Location:** I-75 exit 123, 3 mi ne. 653 Red Top Mountain Rd, SE 30121. Fax: 770/975-4211. **Terms:** Sr.
Inn   discount; check-in 4 pm; reserv deposit, 3 day notice; no pets. **Facility:** 51 rooms. 2 stories; exterior corridors.
Dining: Restaurant; 7-10 am, 11:30-2 & 5-9 pm, closed Sun evening; $8-$13. **All Rooms:** free movies.
Cards: AE, DI, DS, MC, VI.   [🍴] [CTV] [✕] [D] [S]

SUPER 8 MOTEL
◆◆   Rates Subject to Change   Phone: 770/382-8881
Motel   All Year   1P: $38- 42 2P/1B: $42   2P/2B: $46   XP: $5   F12
Location: I-75 exit 125, 0.3 mi e. 41 SR 20 Spur SE 30121. Fax: 770/382-8881. **Terms:** Sr. discount; reserv
deposit, 7 day notice; small pets only. **Facility:** 62 rooms. 3 stories, no elevator; interior corridors.
All Rooms: free & pay movies. **Cards:** AE, CB, DI, DS, MC, VI.   [🛏] [♿] [CTV] [✕] [D]

RESTAURANTS

THE MEATING PLACE DELI & CAFE   **Lunch:** $4-$8   **Dinner:** $8-$14   Phone: 770/386-4563
◆   **Location:** I-75, exit 124, 1.5 mi w; in Main Street East Shopping Center. 485 E Main St 30120. **Hours:** 7
American am-9 pm, Mon & Sat-5 pm. Closed major holidays & Sun. **Features:** casual dress; children's menu; carryout;
a la carte. Cheery decor. Sandwiches, salads & grilled meat selections. **Cards:** AE, DS, MC, VI.   [✕]

WINSTON'S RESTAURANT   **Lunch:** $5-$10   **Dinner:** $7-$14   Phone: 770/387-9479
◆   **Location:** I-75, exit 124, 1.5 mi w; in Main Street East Shopping Center. 463 E Main St 30120. **Hours:** 11:30
American am-10 pm, Fri & Sat-midnight, Sunday noon-8 pm. Closed: 3/7, 11/26 & 12/25. **Features:** casual dress;
children's menu; carryout; cocktails & lounge; a la carte. Hand-cut steak, hand-formed burgers, sizzling
fajitas, baby-back ribs. Imported ale. **Cards:** AE, DI, DS, MC, VI.

CHAMBLEE—See Atlanta & Vicinity p. 228.

CHATSWORTH—2,900

LODGING

KEY WEST INN
◆◆
Motel
VI.
Rates Subject to Change
All Year   1P: $41- 52   2P/1B: $46- 57   2P/2B: $46- 57   XP: $5   F12
Location: Jct SR 52 & US 411. 501 Gl Maddox Pkwy 30705. Fax: 706/517-1510. **Terms:** Pets, $5 extra charge. **Facility:** 43 rooms. 2 stories; exterior corridors. **All Rooms:** free movies. **Cards:** AE, DI, DS, MC,
Phone: 706/517-1155

RESTAURANT

EDNA'S RESTAURANT   **Lunch:** $4-$8   **Dinner:** $4-$8   **Phone: 706/695-4951**
Ⓐ
◆
Regional
American
Location: 1 mi s on Hwy 411S. 1300 Hwy 411S 30705. **Hours:** 11 am-7:45 pm. Closed: Sun, Mon, first 2 weeks in July & last 2 weeks in Dec. **Features:** casual dress; carryout. Popular, long established eatery. Serving home-style Southern comfort foods. Heirloom recipe peanut butter coconut & chocolate pies, fried chicken, ham shanks & vegetables. Friendly service.

CHICKAMAUGA—2,100

LODGING

THE GORDON-LEE MANSION BED & BREAKFAST   Rates Subject to Change   **Phone: 706/375-4728**
◆◆◆
Historic Bed
& Breakfast
All Year [BP]   1P: $65- 80   2P/1B: $75- 110   2P/2B: $75- 110   XP: $10
Location: Just s on SR 341. 217 Cove Rd 30707. **Terms:** Sr. discount; age restrictions may apply; no pets. **Facility:** 5 rooms. 2 stories; interior corridors; smoke free premises. **Cards:** MC, VI.

RESTAURANT

QUARTER-MASTER'S STEAK & SEAFOOD   **Lunch:** $5-$15   **Dinner:** $6-$15   **Phone: 706/375-5555**
◆
Steak and
Seafood
Location: 0.5 mi n on US 27; 0.5 mi s of Chickamauga & Chattanooga Military Park. 1015 US Hwy 27 30707. **Hours:** 11:30 am-9 pm, Fri & Sat-10 pm, Sun 11:30 am-3 pm. **Features:** carryout; beer & wine only. Light fare avail. **Cards:** AE, DI, DS, MC, VI.

CLARKESVILLE—1,200

LODGING

BURNS-SUTTON INN   Rates Subject to Change   **Phone: 706/754-5565**
◆◆◆
Historic
Country Inn
All Year [BP]   1P: $65- 90   2P/1B: $65- 90   2P/2B: $70- 90   XP: $20
Location: 0.5 mi s on historic US 441. 855 S Washington St 30523. **Terms:** Sr. discount; reserv deposit; no pets. **Facility:** 7 rooms. 3 stories, no elevator; interior corridors; smoke free premises. **Dining:** Restaurant; 11 am-2:30 pm, Thurs-Sun also 6 pm-10 pm; $15-$24. **Cards:** MC, VI.

CLAYTON—1,600

LODGINGS

OLD CLAYTON INN   Rates Subject to Change   **Phone: 706/782-7722**
◆◆
Historic Lodge
All Year   1P: $45- 75   2P/1B: $50- 85   2P/2B: $55- 95   XP: $10   F5
Location: Downtown; just w of jct US 441 & 6W. S Main St 30525 (PO Box 907). Fax: 706/782-2511. **Terms:** No pets. **Facility:** 28 rooms. 4 suites $95-$150, for up to 2 persons; 2 stories; interior corridors; designated smoking area. **Cards:** AE, DS, MC, VI.

REGAL INN   Rates Subject to Change   **Phone: 706/782-4269**
Ⓐ
◆
Motel
All Year   1P: $32- 45   2P/1B: $34- 45   2P/2B: $36- 65   XP: $5
Location: 0.8 mi s on US 23 & 441. Hwy. 441 S 30525 (PO Box 1057). **Terms:** Reserv deposit; no pets. **Facility:** 19 rooms. 1 story; exterior corridors. **All Rooms:** free movies. **Cards:** AE, MC, VI.

SHONEY'S INN-STONEBROOK INN   **Phone: 706/782-2214**
Ⓐ SAVE
◆◆◆
Motel
8/1-8/31 & 10/1-11/15 [CP]   1P: $65- 70   2P/1B: $70- 89   2P/2B: $75- 89   XP: $10   F12
6/1-7/31 & 9/1-9/30 [CP]   1P: $60- 70   2P/1B: $65- 75   2P/2B: $65- 75   XP: $10   F12
12/1-4/15 & 11/16-11/30 [CP]   1P: $45- 50   2P/1B: $45- 50   2P/2B: $50- 60   XP: $10   F12
4/16-5/31 [CP]   1P: $45- 50   2P/1B: $50- 55   2P/2B: $50- 60   XP: $10   F12
Location: 1 mi s on US 441S. US 441 S 30525 (Rt 3, Box 300-17). Fax: 706/782-1093. **Terms:** No pets. **Facility:** 49 rooms. 1 two-bedroom unit. 2 stories; exterior corridors. **Dining:** Restaurant nearby. **All Rooms:** free movies. **Some Rooms:** microwaves, refrigerators. **Cards:** AE, DI, DS, MC, VI.

TUT'S MOUNTAIN CABINS   **Phone: 706/782-6218**
Ⓐ SAVE
◆◆◆
Cottage
7/1-10/31   2P/2B: $109- 198
4/1-6/30   2P/2B: $99- 179
12/1-3/31 & 11/1-11/30   2P/2B: $88- 161
Location: 2.5 mi s on US 441 to Seed Tick Rd. 30525 (PO Box 1470). Fax: 706/782-7911. **Terms:** Reserv deposit, 7 day notice; no pets. **Facility:** 5 rooms. 1 cabin $554-$588 for up to 14 persons in season; 1 story; exterior corridors. **All Rooms:** kitchens. **Cards:** AE, MC, VI.

RESTAURANTS

JULIA'S SOUTHERN NIGHTS   **Dinner:** $10-$23   **Phone: 706/782-2052**
◆◆
Steak and
Seafood
Location: 2 mi s on US 441S. 30525. **Hours:** 4 pm-9:30 pm. Closed major holidays & Sun. **Features:** casual dress; children's menu; early bird specials; carryout; cocktail lounge; beer & wine only. Cozy place with fresh seafood & great steak. **Cards:** DS, MC, VI.

STOCKTON HOUSE RESTAURANT   **Lunch:** $6-$7   **Dinner:** $9-$15   **Phone: 706/782-6175**
Ⓐ
◆◆
American
Location: 1 mi e on Warwoman Rd, from jct US 441. 30525. **Hours:** 11 am-2 & 5-9 pm. Closed: 4/7, 6/10 & 12/25. **Reservations:** suggested; in summer. **Features:** casual dress; Sunday brunch; children's menu; carryout; salad bar; beer & wine only. Charming country decor; pastoral setting. Smoke free premises. **Cards:** AE, DS, MC, VI.

STONEBROOK RESTAURANT   **Lunch:** $5-$9   **Dinner:** $6-$15   **Phone: 706/782-6789**
◆◆
American
Location: 1 mi s on US 441S. 30525. **Hours:** 11 am-9 pm; 12/1-4/30 11 am-2 pm, Fri & Sat-9 pm. Closed: 1/1 & 12/25. **Features:** casual dress; Sunday brunch; children's menu; carryout; salad bar; beer & wine only. Warm, inviting ambience. Daily lunch buffet. At dinner, seafood, steak, prime rib & mountain trout.
Cards: MC, VI.

COLLEGE PARK—*See Atlanta & Vicinity p. 228.*

COLQUITT—2,000

LODGING

TARRER INN Phone: 912/758-2888
ⒶⒶⒶ ⓈⒶⓋⒺ All Year [CP] 1P: $66 2P/1B: $66 2P/2B: $66
◆◆◆ **Location:** Center of town on square (Corner SR 91 & SR 27). 155 S Cuthbert St 31737. Fax: 912/758-2825.
Country Inn **Terms:** Reserv deposit; package plans; no pets. **Facility:** 12 rooms. Gracious lodging with southern hospitality. 1 bedroom suite avail; 2 stories; interior corridors; smoke free premises; city park nearby. **Dining:** Restaurant; 11:30 am-2 & 5:30-9:30 pm, Thurs-Sat from 5:30 pm; $12-$20.
All Rooms: coffeemakers, free movies. **Some Rooms:** VCP's. **Cards:** AE, DS, MC, VI. **Special Amenities: Free breakfast and preferred room (subject to availability with advanced reservations).** 🛏 ⒸⓉⓋ 👤 ✕ Ⓓ Ⓢ

COLUMBUS—179,300

Airport Accommodations

Listings for these establishments are found under the heading for the city in which they are located.

COLUMBUS METROPOLITAN

Budgetel Inn, 1.5 mi sw of airport terminal via I-185 S & SR 85/COLUMBUS
Courtyard by Marriott, 2.3 mi se of airport terminal via I-185 S & SR 85/COLUMBUS
Hampton Inn Airport, 1 mi nw of airport terminal via airport thruway road/COLUMBUS
Super 8 Motel of Columbus, 1.5 mi sw of airport/COLUMBUS

LODGINGS

BUDGETEL INN Rates Subject to Change Phone: 706/323-4344
◆◆◆ All Year [CP] 1P: $38- 53 2P/1B: $45- 60 2P/2B: $51 XP: $7 F18
Motel **Location:** I-185, southbound exit 5; northbound exit 5A. 2919 Warm Springs Rd 31909. Fax: 706/596-9622.
Terms: Sr. discount; small pets only. **Facility:** 102 rooms. 3 stories; interior corridors. **All Rooms:** free & pay movies. **Cards:** AE, CB, DI, DS, MC, VI. *(See color ad p 252)* 🛏 🚲 ⒸⓉⓋ ✕ 🐾 Ⓓ Ⓢ

COMFORT INN Phone: 706/568-3300
ⒶⒶⒶ ⓈⒶⓋⒺ All Year [CP] 1P: $55 2P/1B: $59 2P/2B: $56 XP: $6 F18
◆◆ **Location:** I-185 exit 4. 3443B Macon Rd 31907. Fax: 706/563-2388. **Terms:** Small pets only. **Facility:** 66 rooms. 4 stories; exterior corridors; whirlpool; exercise equipment. **Dining:** Restaurant nearby.
Motel **Services:** valet laundry. **All Rooms:** coffeemakers, free movies, refrigerators. **Some Rooms:** microwaves. Fee: whirlpools. **Cards:** AE, CB, DI, DS, JCB, MC, VI. 🛏 🚲 ⒸⓉⓋ ✕ Ⓓ

COURTYARD BY MARRIOTT Rates Subject to Change Phone: 706/323-2323
◆◆◆ Sun-Thurs 1P: $64 2P/1B: $74 2P/2B: $74
Motor Inn Fri & Sat 1P: $52 2P/1B: $52 2P/2B: $61
Location: On US 27, 80 & SR 85, Columbus-Manchester Expwy; 0.8 mi e of I-185, southbound exit 5; northbound exit 5A. 3501 Courtyard Way 31904. Fax: 706/327-6030. **Terms:** No pets. **Facility:** 139 rooms. Rates for up to 4 persons; 2 stories; interior corridors. **Dining:** Breakfast room only, 6:30-10 am, Sat & Sun 7 am-noon. **All Rooms:** free & pay movies. **Cards:** AE, CB, DI, DS, MC, VI. 🚲 ⒸⓉⓋ ✕ 🐾 Ⓓ Ⓢ

DAYS INN Rates Subject to Change Phone: 706/561-4400
◆◆◆ All Year [CP] 1P: $46- 48 2P/1B: $52- 54 2P/2B: $52- 54 XP: $7 F12
Motel **Location:** I-185 exit 4. 3452 Macon Rd 31907. Fax: 706/568-3075. **Terms:** Small pets only. **Facility:** 122 rooms. Max of 4 persons per room; 5 stories; exterior corridors. **All Rooms:** free & pay movies. **Cards:** AE, CB, DI, DS, MC, VI. 🛏 🚲 ⒸⓉⓋ ✕ Ⓓ

HAMPTON INN AIRPORT Rates Subject to Change Phone: 706/576-5303
◆◆◆ All Year [CP] 1P: $60 2P/1B: $70 2P/2B: $70
Motel **Location:** I-185 exit 6, 0.5 mi w on airport thruway road; behind Simons Plaza Mall. 5585 Whitesville Rd 31904. Fax: 706/596-8076. **Terms:** No pets. **Facility:** 119 rooms. Max of 6 persons per room; 2 stories; exterior corridors. **All Rooms:** free movies. **Cards:** AE, CB, DI, DS, MC, VI. 🚲 ♿ ⒸⓉⓋ ✕ Ⓓ

HISTORIC COLUMBUS HILTON
Phone: 706/324-1800

(AAA) [SAVE]

All Year   1P: $79- 129   2P/1B: $89- 139   2P/2B: $89- 139   XP: $10

◆◆◆   **Location:** Downtown at edge of historic district, jct of 9th St & Broadway. 800 Front Ave 31901.

Hotel   Fax: 706/576-4413. **Terms:** BP avail; no pets. **Facility:** 177 rooms. Exceptional southern-style hospitality in an elegantly-restored 19th-century grist mill blended with a contemporary brick tower. 3-6 stories; interior corridors; video game room. **Dining & Entertainment:** Restaurant; 6:30 am-10 pm, Sat & Sun from 7 am; $10-$18; cocktails/lounge. **Services:** valet laundry. **All Rooms:** honor bars, coffeemakers, free & pay movies. **Some Rooms:** Fee: refrigerators, VCP's, whirlpools. **Cards:** AE, DI, DS, MC, VI. **Special Amenities: Free newspaper and preferred room (subject to availability with advanced reservations).** *(See color ad p 18 & p 260)*

🛌 🏝 CTV ✕ D S

HOWARD JOHNSON EXPRESS
Rates Subject to Change   **Phone: 706/322-6641**

◆◆◆   All Year [CP]   1P: $45- 55   2P/1B: $45- 55   2P/2B: $45- 55   XP: $5   F18

Motel   **Location:** Downtown center. 1011 Veterans Pkwy 31901. Fax: 706/322-1999. **Terms:** Sr. discount; pets. **Facility:** 130 rooms. 2 stories; exterior corridors. **Dining:** Restaurant; 11 am-2 & 5-10 pm; $7-$20.

All Rooms: free movies. **Cards:** AE, CB, DI, DS, JCB, MC, VI. *(See color ad below)*

Roll in showers.   🛏 🏝 🛌 CTV ✕ D

LA QUINTA INN
Phone: 706/568-1740

(AAA) [SAVE]

All Year [CP]   1P: $48- 54   2P/1B: $48- 54   2P/2B: $48- 54   XP: $6   F18

◆◆◆   **Location:** On SR 22, at I-185, exit 4; adjoining Cross Country Shopping Plaza. 3201 Macon Rd 31906-1717.

Motel   Fax: 706/569-7434. **Terms:** Small pets only. **Facility:** 122 rooms. Very nicely done rooms which are well equipped. 2 stories; exterior corridors. **Dining:** Restaurant nearby. **Services:** Fee: coin laundry. **All Rooms:** coffeemakers, free & pay movies. **Some Rooms:** Fee: refrigerators. **Cards:** AE, CB, DI, DS, MC, VI. **Special Amenities: Free breakfast and free local telephone calls.**

🛏 🏝 🛌 CTV ✕ 🌀 D

ROTHSCHILD-POUND HOUSE BED & BREAKFAST
Rates Subject to Change   **Phone: 706/322-4075**

◆◆◆   All Year [BP]   1P: $85- 135   2P/1B: $85- 135   2P/2B: $85- 135   XP: $10   D12

Bed &   **Location:** I-185 exit 7, 4 mi 2nd Ave exit, on corner. 201 7th St 31901. Fax: 706/322-3772. **Terms:** Sr.

Breakfast   discount; age restrictions may apply; no pets. **Facility:** 7 rooms. 2 stories; interior/exterior corridors.

All Rooms: free movies. **Cards:** AE, MC, VI.

🛌 CTV ✕ D

SHERATON INN-COLUMBUS AIRPORT
Guaranteed Rates   **Phone: 706/327-6868**

◆◆◆   All Year   1P: $75- 85   2P/1B: $75- 85   2P/2B: $75- 85   XP: $6   F12

Motor Inn   **Location:** I-185, exit 6. 5351 Simons Blvd 31904. Fax: 706/327-0041. **Terms:** Sr. discount; no pets. **Facility:** 178 rooms. 5 stories; interior corridors. **Dining:** Restaurant; 6:30 am-2 & 5-10 pm; $10-$17.

All Rooms: free & pay movies. **Cards:** AE, DI, DS, MC, VI.

🏝 🛌 CTV ✕ D S

SUPER 8 MOTEL OF COLUMBUS
Rates Subject to Change   **Phone: 706/322-6580**

◆◆   All Year   1P: $41- 47   2P/1B: $43- 51   2P/2B: $47- 55   XP: $5   F12

Motel   **Location:** I-185, southbound exit 5; northbound exit 5A; just off US 27, 80 & SR 85. 2935 Warm Springs Rd 31909. Fax: 706/322-6580. **Terms:** Sr. discount; reserv deposit, 7 day notice; small pets only. **Facility:** 76 rooms. 3 stories, no elevator; interior corridors. **All Rooms:** free & pay movies. **Cards:** AE, CB, DI, DS, MC, VI.

🛏 CTV ✕ D

RESTAURANTS

BLUDAU'S AT THE 1839 GOETCHIUS HOUSE
Historical   Dinner: $14-$24   **Phone: 706/324-4863**

◆◆   **Location:** In the historic district. 405 Broadway 31901. **Hours:** 5 pm-9:45 pm, Fri & Sat-10:45 pm. Closed

Continental   major holidays & Sun. **Reservations:** suggested. **Features:** casual dress; cocktails & lounge. Relaxed gracious dining in a charming antebellum mansion. Varied menu served in 6 cozy Victorian dining rooms or back porch. **Cards:** AE, DI, DS, MC, VI.

✕

MIDTOWN GRILL & BAR
Lunch: $4-$9   Dinner: $4-$9   **Phone: 706/563-4488**

◆◆   **Location:** 0.3 mi w of I-185, exit 4; in upper level of Cross Country Plaza. 2042A Auburn Ave 31906.

American   **Hours:** 11:30 am-3 & 5:30-10 pm, Fri & Sat-11 pm. Closed major holidays & Sun. **Features:** casual dress; children's menu; health conscious menu; cocktails & lounge; a la carte. Friendly, lively setting. **Cards:** AE, DI, MC, VI.

✕

COMMERCE—4,100

LODGINGS

COMFORT INN
AAA SAVE
◆◆ Motel
Phone: 706/335-9001
All Year [CP]   1P: $39- 45   2P/1B: $45- 65   2P/2B: $45- 65   XP: $5-6   F18
Location: I-85, exit 53, 0.3 mi ne. 165 Eisenhower Dr 30529. **Fax:** 706/335-9001. **Terms:** No pets.
Facility: 62 rooms. 2 suites with refrigerator & microwave, $80-$100; 2 stories; exterior corridors; whirlpool.
Dining: Restaurant nearby. **All Rooms:** free movies. **Some Rooms:** microwaves, refrigerators, whirlpools.
Cards: AE, CB, DI, DS, JCB, MC, VI. **Special Amenities:** Free breakfast and free local telephone calls.

DAYS INN
◆◆ Motel
Phone: 706/335-2595
Rates Subject to Change
4/1-11/1 [CP]   1P: $85   2P/1B: $85   2P/2B: $85   XP: $7   F16
12/1-3/31 & 11/2-11/30 [CP]   1P: $45- 50   2P/1B: $48- 54   2P/2B: $48- 54   XP: $7   F16
Location: I-85 exit 53, 0.3 mi se. 30976 US Hwy 441 S 30529. **Fax:** 706/335-3901. **Terms:** Sr. discount; no
pets. **Facility:** 61 rooms. 2 stories; interior corridors. **All Rooms:** free movies. **Cards:** AE, DI, DS, JCB, MC, VI.

GUESTHOUSE INN-BANKS CROSSING
AAA SAVE
◆ Motel
Phone: 706/335-5147
All Year [CP]   1P: $36   2P/1B: $38   2P/2B: $40   XP: $3
Location: I-85 exit 53, 0.3 mi s. 30934 US 441S 30529 (PO Box 209). **Fax:** 706/335-7788. **Terms:** Small
pets only. **Facility:** 74 rooms. Very well kept property with some contemporary features. 1-2 stories; exterior
corridors. **Dining:** Restaurant nearby. **All Rooms:** free movies. **Cards:** AE, DI, DS, JCB, MC, VI.
Special Amenities: Free breakfast and free local telephone calls. *(See color ad below)*

HAMPTON INN
◆◆◆ Motel
Phone: 706/335-6161
Rates Subject to Change
All Year [CP]   1P: $55- 57   2P/1B: $59   2P/2B: $59
Location: I-75 exit 53, ne corner. 153 Hampton Ct 30529. **Fax:** 706/335-6555. **Terms:** Sr. discount; no pets.
Facility: 61 rooms. 2 whirlpool rms, extra charge; 3 stories; interior corridors. **All Rooms:** free & pay
movies. **Cards:** AE, CB, DI, DS, MC, VI.   Roll in showers.

HOLIDAY INN EXPRESS
AAA SAVE
◆◆ Motel
Phone: 706/335-5183
All Year [CP]   1P: $52   2P/1B: $58   2P/2B: $58   XP: $6   F18
Location: I-85 exit 53, just s. 30747 US 441S 30529 (PO Box 247). **Fax:** 706/335-6588. **Terms:** Small pets
only. **Facility:** 96 rooms. 2 stories; exterior corridors. **Dining:** Restaurant nearby. **Services:** Fee: coin
laundry. **All Rooms:** free movies. **Some Rooms:** microwaves, VCP's. Fee: refrigerators. **Cards:** AE, CB, DI,
DS, MC, VI. **Special Amenities:** Free breakfast and free local telephone calls.

THE PITTMAN HOUSE
◆◆◆ Historic Bed & Breakfast
Phone: 706/335-3823
Guaranteed Rates
All Year [BP]   1P: $50- 55   2P/1B: $60- 65   2P/2B: $60- 65   XP: $10   F10
Location: Jct I-85 exit 53, 1 mi s on 441, 2 mi s Business Rt 441. 81 Homer Rd 30529. **Terms:** No pets.
Facility: 4 rooms. 2 stories; interior corridors; designated smoking area. **Cards:** MC, VI.

CONLEY—*See Atlanta & Vicinity p. 230.*

CONYERS—7,400

LODGINGS

COMFORT INN
AAA SAVE
◆◆◆ Motel
Phone: 770/760-0300
All Year [CP]   1P: $70   2P/1B: $75   2P/2B: $75   XP: $5   F18
Location: I-20 exit 41. 1363 Klondike Rd 30207. **Fax:** 770/922-1034. **Terms:** Pets, $25 extra charge.
Facility: 83 rooms. 4-5 stories; interior corridors; sauna, whirlpool. **Dining:** Restaurant nearby. **Services:**
Fee: coin laundry. **All Rooms:** free movies. **Some Rooms:** microwaves, refrigerators, whirlpools. **Cards:** AE,
CB, DI, DS, MC, VI. **Special Amenities:** Free breakfast and free local telephone calls.
(See color ad p 226)

DAYS INN
◆◆ Motel
Phone: 770/922-3314
Rates Subject to Change
5/1-9/1 [CP]   1P: $53- 59   2P/1B: $59   2P/2B: $70   XP: $10   F12
12/1-4/30 & 9/2-11/30 [CP]   1P: $50   2P/1B: $53   2P/2B: $63   XP: $7   F12
Location: I-20 exit 42, just n to Frontage Rd. 1350 Dogwood Dr 30208. **Fax:** 770/760-1651. **Terms:** Sr.
discount; reserv deposit; no pets. **Facility:** 59 rooms. 2 whirlpool rms, extra charge; 2 stories; exterior corridors.
All Rooms: free & pay movies. **Cards:** AE, CB, DI, DS, MC.

RAMADA LIMITED

Phone: 770/760-0777

(AAA) SAVE	4/1-10/15 [CP]	1P:	$65- 125	2P/1B:	$75- 150	2P/2B:	$75- 150	XP: $15	F12
	12/31-3/31 [CP]	1P:	$60- 110	2P/1B:	$60- 110	2P/2B:	$60- 110	XP: $6	F12
◆◆	12/1-12/30 & 10/16-11/30								
Motel	[CP]	1P:	$49- 95	2P/1B:	$49- 95	2P/2B:	$49- 95	XP: $6	F12

Location: I-20 exit 42, just n Hwy 138, 0.5 mi w. 1070 Dogwood Dr 30207. Fax: 770/760-8434.
Terms: Reserv deposit; small pets only, $5 extra charge. **Facility:** 66 rooms. Handling fee imposed; 2 stories; exterior corridors. **All Rooms:** free movies. **Some Rooms:** microwaves, refrigerators. **Cards:** AE, CB, DI, DS, MC, VI.
Special Amenities: Free breakfast and free local telephone calls. 🐾 🛏 🎱 CTV ✕ D

RESTAURANT

SEVEN GABLES RESTAURANT

Dinner: $9-$16   **Phone:** 770/922-8824
◆◆◆   **Location:** I-20, exit 42, SR 20S, 1.5 mi s. 1897 GA Hwy 20S 30208. **Hours:** 5 pm-10 pm. Closed: Sun &
Continental   12/25. **Reservations:** suggested. **Features:** semi-formal attire; children's menu; health conscious menu;
cocktails & lounge. Romantic dining with European cuisine & seafood grill. **Cards:** AE, DI, MC, VI.   ✕

CORDELE—10,300

LODGINGS

COLONIAL INN

Phone: 912/273-5420

(AAA) SAVE	All Year [CP]	1P:	$42	2P/1B:	$45	2P/2B:	$45	XP: $5	F18

Location: I-75, exit 33, just w. 2016 16th Ave E 31015. Fax: 912/273-5501. **Terms:** Pets. **Facility:** 92 rooms.
◆◆◆   2 stories; interior/exterior corridors; playground. **Dining:** Restaurant nearby. **Services:** valet laundry.
Motel   **All Rooms:** free movies. **Some Rooms:** microwaves, refrigerators. **Cards:** DI, DS, MC, VI.
Special Amenities: Free breakfast and free local telephone calls.   🛏 CTV ✕ D

COMFORT INN

Guaranteed Rates   **Phone:** 912/273-2371

◆◆◆	All Year [CP]	1P:	$42- 60	2P/1B:	$45- 65	2P/2B:	$45- 65	XP: $5	F16

Motel   **Location:** I-75, exit 33; 0.3 mi w. 1601 16th Ave E 31015. Fax: 912/273-3251. **Terms:** Sr. discount; no pets.
Facility: 59 rooms. 2 stories; exterior corridors. **All Rooms:** free & pay movies. **Cards:** AE, CB, DI, DS,
JCB, MC, VI.   🛏 CTV ✕ 🐾 D

DAYS INN

Rates Subject to Change   **Phone:** 912/273-1123

◆◆	10/15-10/22	1P:	$50- 55	2P/1B:	$55- 65	2P/2B:	$55- 65		
Motel	12/1-12/31, 1/1-10/14 &								
	10/23-11/30	1P:	$35- 40	2P/1B:	$40- 48	2P/2B:	$40- 48	XP: $4	

Location: Jct I-75, exit 33 & US 280. 215 S 7th St 31015. Fax: 912/273-3545. **Terms:** Small pets only. **Facility:** 126 rooms.
2 stories; exterior corridors. **All Rooms:** free movies. **Cards:** AE, CB, DI, DS, MC, VI.   🐾 🛏 ➕ CTV ✕ D

ECONO LODGE

Phone: 912/273-2456

(AAA) SAVE	All Year	1P:	$32- 40	2P/1B:	$36- 45	2P/2B:	$36- 45	XP: $5	F12

Location: I-75, exit 33, 0.3 mi w. 1618 E 16th Ave 31015. Fax: 912/273-3251. **Terms:** Pets. **Facility:** 45
◆◆   rooms. Handling fee imposed; 2 stories; exterior corridors. **Dining:** Restaurant nearby. **All Rooms:** free
Motel   movies. **Cards:** AE, CB, DI, DS, JCB, MC, VI. **Special Amenities:** Early check-in/late check-out and free
breakfast.   🛏 CTV ✕ D

HOLIDAY INN

Phone: 912/273-4117

(AAA) SAVE	All Year	1P:	$50	2P/1B:	$50	2P/2B:	$50	XP: $6	F19

Location: Jct I-75, exit 33 & US 280. 1711 16th Ave E 31015 (PO Box 916). Fax: 912/273-1344.
◆◆◆   **Terms:** Package plans; pets. **Facility:** 187 rooms. Variety of carefully-kept room decors & furnishings. Outdoor
Motor Inn   snack bar in season. 2 stories; exterior corridors. **Dining:** Dixie Lee Restaurant & Lounge, see separate
listing. **All Rooms:** free movies. **Cards:** AE, CB, DI, DS, JCB, MC, VI. **Special Amenities:** Free room
upgrade and preferred room (each subject to availability with advanced reservations).   🐾 🛏 🎱 ➕ CTV ✕ D

RAMADA INN

Phone: 912/273-5000

(AAA) SAVE	All Year	1P:	$44	2P/1B:	$49	2P/2B:	$49	XP: $5	F18

Location: Jct I-75, exit 33 & US 280. 2016 16th Ave E 31015. Fax: 912/273-5501. **Terms:** BP avail;
◆◆◆   package plans; pets. **Facility:** 102 rooms. Vibrant room decors. 2 stories; exterior corridors.
Motor Inn   **Dining:** Restaurant; 6:30 am-2 & 5-9:30 pm; $5-$14; wine/beer only. **Services:** complimentary evening
beverages. **All Rooms:** free movies. **Some Rooms:** refrigerators, whirlpools. **Cards:** AE, CB, DI, DS, JCB,
MC, VI. **Special Amenities:** Free local telephone calls and preferred room (subject to availability with advanced
reservations). *(See color ad below)*   🐾 🛏 CTV ✕ D

RESTAURANTS

DAPHNE LODGE RESTAURANT   **Dinner:** $7-$18   **Phone:** 912/273-2596
◆◆
American   **Location:** 11 mi w of I-75 exit 33. Hwy 280 W 31015. **Hours:** 6 pm-10 pm. Closed major holidays, Sun & Mon. **Reservations:** suggested; weekends. **Features:** casual dress; beer & wine only. A cozy red cabin nestled in tall Georgia pines near Lake Blackshear. Family owned since 1952. Specializing in angus beef, steak, fried catfish & seafood, as well as regional dishes. **Cards:** AE, DS, MC, VI.   ⊠

DIXIE LEE RESTAURANT & LOUNGE   **Lunch:** $5-$6   **Dinner:** $8-$14   **Phone:** 912/273-4117
ⒶⒶⒶ   **Location:** Jct I-75, exit 33 & US 280; in Holiday Inn. 1711 16th Ave E 31015. **Hours:** 6 am-10 pm, Sun-9
◆◆   pm. **Features:** casual dress; children's menu; health conscious menu; carryout; salad bar; beer & wine only;
Regional   buffet. Family dining featuring traditional Southern-style cooking served in 3 different all-you-can-eat buffets.
American   Specialty is fried chicken; homemade peach cobbler (in season). Also, menu entrees. **Cards:** AE, CB, DI, DS, MC, VI.   ⊠

CORNELIA—3,200

LODGINGS

COMFORT INN   Rates Subject to Change   **Phone:** 706/778-9573
◆◆◆   10/1-10/31 [CP]   1P: $69- 89   2P/1B: $69- 89   2P/2B: $69- 89   XP: $5   F18
Motel   12/1-9/30 & 11/1-11/30 [CP]   1P: $45- 50   2P/1B: $50- 55   2P/2B: $50   XP: $5   F18
    Location: Jct SR 365 & US 441 business route, sw corner. 2965 J Warren Rd. 30531. **Fax:** 706/776-3329.
Terms: Sr. discount; no pets. **Facility:** 60 rooms. 2 stories; interior corridors. **All Rooms:** free movies. **Cards:** AE, CB, DI, DS, JCB, MC, VI.   ⒸⓉⓋ ⊠ Ⓓ

HOLIDAY INN EXPRESS   Rates Subject to Change   **Phone:** 706/778-3600
◆◆◆   All Year [CP]   1P: $65   2P/1B: $65   2P/2B: $65   XP: $5   F18
Motel   **Location:** Jct SR 365 & US 441, just e. 1105 Business 441 30531. **Fax:** 706/778-1299. **Terms:** Reserv
deposit; no pets. **Facility:** 60 rooms. 2 stories; interior corridors. **All Rooms:** free movies. **Cards:** AE, DI, DS, MC, VI.   Roll in showers.   ⊠ ⒸⓉⓋ ⊠ Ⓓ Ⓢ

COVINGTON—10,000

LODGINGS

BEST WESTERN WHITE COLUMNS INN   Rates Subject to Change   **Phone:** 770/786-5800
◆◆◆   All Year [CP]   1P: $40   2P/1B: $40   2P/2B: $46   XP: $10   F18
Motel   **Location:** I-20 exit 45A, just n. 10130 Alcovy Rd 30209. **Fax:** 770/786-5880. **Terms:** No pets. **Facility:** 94 rooms. 2 stories; exterior corridors. **All Rooms:** free movies. **Cards:** AE, CB, DI, DS, MC, VI.   ⊠ ⒸⓉⓋ ⊠ Ⓓ Ⓢ

HOLIDAY INN EXPRESS   Rates Subject to Change   **Phone:** 770/787-4900
◆◆◆   All Year [CP]   1P: $62   2P/1B: $62   2P/2B: $62   XP: $5   F18
Motel   **Location:** I-20 exit 45A. 10111 Alcovy Rd 30209. **Fax:** 770/385-9805. **Terms:** Sr. discount; small pets only, $25 extra charge. **Facility:** 50 rooms. 2 stories; exterior corridors. **All Rooms:** free movies. **Cards:** AE, CB, DI, DS, JCB, MC, VI.   Roll in showers.   🐾 ⊠ ⒸⓉⓋ ⊠ Ⓓ Ⓢ

2119-THE INN   Rates Subject to Change   **Phone:** 770/787-0037
◆◆   All Year [CP]   1P: $80   2P/1B: $85   2P/2B: $85
Historic Bed   **Location:** Downtown, just w of Town Square. 2119 N Emory St 30209. **Terms:** Age restrictions may apply;
& Breakfast   reserv deposit; no pets. **Facility:** 4 rooms. 2 stories; interior corridors; smoke free premises.   ⊠ Ⓓ

RESTAURANT

THE DEPOT AT COVINGTON   Historical   **Lunch:** $8-$14   **Dinner:** $11-$15   **Phone:** 770/784-1128
◆◆   **Location:** I-20 exit 45, 1.3 mi e on US 278 to Emory St, just n. 4122 N Emory St 30209. **Hours:** 11 am-10
American   pm, Sat 5 pm-11 pm. Closed: 11/26 & 12/25. **Features:** casual dress; children's menu; health conscious menu items; cocktails & lounge. Comfortable family dining in historic depot. Entree salad, prime rib, steak. **Cards:** AE, DS, MC, VI.   ♿ ⊠

CRABAPPLE—*See Atlanta & Vicinity p. 230.*

DAHLONEGA—3,100

LODGING

ECONO LODGE   **Phone:** 706/864-6191
ⒶⒶⒶ SAVE   All Year [CP]   1P: $35- 90   2P/1B: $39- 90   2P/2B: $39- 90   XP: $5   F18
    Location: 0.5 mi n on US 19. 619A N Grove St 30533. **Fax:** 706/864-6191. **Terms:** No pets. **Facility:** 40
◆◆   rooms. Contemporary room appointments. 4 stories; exterior corridors. **Dining:** Restaurant nearby.
Motel   **All Rooms:** free movies. **Some Rooms:** whirlpools. **Fee:** microwaves, refrigerators. **Cards:** AE, CB, DI, DS, MC, VI. **Special Amenities:** Free breakfast and free local telephone calls.   ⊠ ⒸⓉⓋ ⊠ Ⓓ

RESTAURANT

CARUSO'S RISTORANTE ITALIANO   **Lunch:** $4-$6   **Dinner:** $6-$12   **Phone:** 404/864-4664
◆   **Location:** Downtown by square. 113 Main St 30533. **Hours:** 11 am-2 & 4-9:30 pm, Sun noon-8 pm. Closed
Italian   major holidays & 12/19-12/25. **Features:** children's menu; carryout; beer & wine only. Many homemade pasta choices & desserts. Cappuccino/espresso. **Cards:** AE, MC, VI.   ⊠

DALTON—21,800

LODGINGS

BEST INNS OF AMERICA   **Phone:** 706/226-1100
ⒶⒶⒶ SAVE   All Year [BP]   1P: $46- 52   2P/1B: $53- 59   2P/2B: $56   XP: $7   F17
    Location: I-75 exit 136, se corner. 1529 W Walnut Ave 30720. **Fax:** 706/226-1100. **Terms:** Small pets only.
◆◆   **Facility:** 91 rooms. Well-maintained sparkling rooms. Near Dalton Factory Stores Mall. 2 stories; exterior cor-
Motel   ridors. **Dining:** Restaurant nearby. **All Rooms:** free movies. **Cards:** AE, CB, DI, DS, MC, VI. **Special Amenities:** Free breakfast and free local telephone calls.   🐾 ⊠ 🍴 ⒸⓉⓋ ⊠ Ⓓ Ⓢ

BEST WESTERN INN OF DALTON

Phone: 706/226-5022

	1P:	$65	2P/1B:	$70	2P/2B:	$70	XP:	$6	F12
7/1-8/31									
12/1-6/30 & 9/1-11/30	1P:	$44	2P/1B:	$49	2P/2B:	$49	XP:	$6	F12

Location: I-75 exit 137, just nw. 2106 Chattanooga Rd 30720. Fax: 706/226-5022. **Terms:** Small pets only. **Facility:** 99 rooms. 2 stories; exterior corridors; playground. **Dining:** Restaurant; 6 am-2 & 5-9:30 pm; $7-$12; cocktails. **Services:** Fee: coin laundry. **All Rooms:** free movies. **Cards:** AE, DS, MC, VI. **Special Amenities:** Free local telephone calls and free newspaper. *(See color ad p 182)*

COUNTRY HEARTH INN

Rates Subject to Change   **Phone:** 706/278-4300

All Year [CP]   1P: $55   2P/1B: $55   2P/2B: $55   XP: $5   F18

Location: I-75 exit 137, just e. 2007 Chattanooga Rd 30720. Fax: 706/279-3284. **Terms:** Sr. discount; no pets. **Facility:** 92 rooms. 2 stories; interior corridors. **All Rooms:** free movies. **Cards:** AE, CB, DI, DS, MC, VI.

DAYS INN

Phone: 706/278-0850

All Year [CP]   1P: $40- 45 2P/1B: $45- 50 2P/2B: $45- 60 XP: $7   F12

Location: I-75 exit 136, just e. 1518 W Walnut Ave 30720. Fax: 706/278-7212. **Terms:** Pets, $5 extra charge. **Facility:** 145 rooms. Mature property located in commercial area. Good sized rooms. 2 stories; exterior corridors. **Dining:** Restaurant nearby. **All Rooms:** coffeemakers, free movies, safes. **Some Rooms:** Fee: microwaves, refrigerators. **Cards:** AE, CB, DI, DS, MC, VI. **Special Amenities:** Early check-in/late check-out and free room upgrade (subject to availability with advanced reservations).

HAMPTON INN

Rates Subject to Change   **Phone:** 706/226-4333

All Year [CP]   1P: $58- 65 2P/1B: $66- 72 2P/2B: $72

Location: I-75 exit 136, just se. 1000 Market St 30720. Fax: 706/278-6443. **Terms:** Sr. discount; no pets. **Facility:** 125 rooms. Rates for up to 4 persons; 3 stories; exterior corridors. **Cards:** AE, CB, DI, DS, MC, VI.

HOLIDAY INN

Phone: 706/278-0500

All Year   1P: $70   2P/1B: $75   2P/2B: $75

Location: I-75 exit 136, nw corner. 515 Holiday Dr 30720. Fax: 706/226-0279. **Terms:** Pets, $10 dep req. **Facility:** 199 rooms. 2 stories; exterior corridors; wading pool. **Dining & Entertainment:** Restaurant; 6:30 am-1:30 & 5:30-10 pm; $9-$17; cocktails/lounge. **Services:** Fee: coin laundry. **All Rooms:** coffeemakers, free & pay movies. **Cards:** AE, CB, DI, DS, JCB, MC, VI. **Special Amenities:** Early check-in/late check-out and preferred room (subject to availability with advanced reservations). *(See ad below)*

RESTAURANTS

THE CELLAR RESTAURANT   Lunch: $7-$13   Dinner: $14-$27   Phone: 706/226-6029
(AAA)
◆◆◆   **Location:** I-75, exit 136, 0.5 mi e, in Dalton Shopping Center. 1331 W Walnut Ave 30720. **Hours:** 11 am-2 &
          6-10:30 pm, Sat from 6 pm. Closed major holidays & Sun. **Reservations:** accepted. **Features:** casual dress;
Continental   cocktails & lounge; a la carte. Gently elegant, relaxing atmosphere. Fresh seafood, rack of lamb, Black
          Angus beef. Extensive dessert menu including tableside preparation of bananas foster, cherries jubilee &
          Steak Diane. Dietary requests honored. **Cards:** AE, DI, DS, MC, VI.   [⊠]

FLAMMINI'S CAFE ITALIA   Dinner: $8-$17   Phone: 706/226-0667
◆◆   **Location:** I-75, exit 136, 0.8 mi e. 1205 W Walnut Ave 30720. **Hours:** 5 pm-10 pm, Thurs & Fri from 11 am.
Italian   Closed major holidays & Sun. **Features:** casual dress; children's menu; senior's menu; health conscious
          menu; carryout; beer & wine only. Authentic cuisine. Lasagne, red snapper francese, shrimp alfredo, steak.
Espresso/cappuccino. **Cards:** AE, DI, DS, MC, VI.   [⊠]

DARIEN—1,800

LODGINGS

HOLIDAY INN EXPRESS   Rates Subject to Change   Phone: 912/437-5373
◆◆◆   All Year [CP]   1P: $53- 58   2P/1B: $53- 58 2P/2B: $53- 58
Motel   **Location:** I-95, exit 10, just w. I-95 & SR 251 Magnolia Bluff 31305. **Fax:** 912/437-5374. **Terms:** Sr. discount;
          pets, $5 extra charge. **Facility:** 60 rooms. 2 stories; interior corridors. **All Rooms:** free movies. **Cards:** AE,
CB, DI, DS, JCB, MC, VI.   [🛏] [🏊] [CTV] [⊠] [🐾] [D]

SUPER 8 MOTEL   Phone: 912/437-6660
(AAA) [SAVE]   All Year   1P: $36- 40 2P/1B: $36   2P/2B: $40   XP: $4   F12
◆◆   **Location:** I-95, exit 10, just w. Hwy 251 & I-95 31305 (PO Box 556). **Fax:** 912/437-3676. **Terms:** Pets, $10
Motor Inn   extra charge. **Facility:** 60 rooms. Quiet setting off road. 2 stories; exterior corridors. **All Rooms:** free movies.
          Cards: AE, DS, MC, VI.   [🛏] [🏊] [CTV] [⊠] [D]

DAWSONVILLE—500

LODGINGS

AMICALOLA FALLS LODGE   Guaranteed Rates   Phone: 706/265-8888
◆◆◆   4/1-11/30   1P: $75- 150 2P/1B: $75- 150 2P/2B: $75- 150 XP: $6   F18
Lodge   12/1-3/31   1P: $65- 150 2P/1B: $65- 150 2P/2B: $65- 150 XP: $6   F18
          Location: Jct SR 53 & 183, 13 mi n on SR 183, just e on SR 52. 418 Amicalola Falls Lodge Dr 30534.
Fax: 706/265-1456. **Terms:** Sr. discount; check-in 4 pm; 2 night min stay, weekends 10/1-10/31; no pets. **Facility:** 57 rooms.
1-to 3- bedroom cabins with modern bath & kitchen avail in remote areas from lodge $70-$100; 4 stories; interior corridors.
Dining: Dining room; 7-10 am, 11:30-2 & 5-8 pm. **All Rooms:** free movies. **Some Rooms:** kitchen. **Cards:** AE, DI, DS, MC,
VI.   [CTV] [⊠] [🐾] [D]

THE VILLAGE AT GOLD CREEK   Rates Subject to Change   Phone: 706/265-2441
◆◆◆   All Year   1P: $109- 289
Resort Motor   **Location:** 2 mi e on Rt 9 to SR 136, 0.8 mi w. 1 Gold Creek Dr 30534. **Fax:** 706/265-1057. **Terms:** Check-in
Inn   4 pm; no pets. **Facility:** 72 rooms. 2 stories; interior corridors. **Dining:** Dining room, 2 cafeterias; 7 am-9 pm;
          $11-$25. **All Rooms:** free movies. **Cards:** AE, MC, VI.   Roll in showers.   [🏊] [♿] [CTV] [⊠] [D]

DECATUR—See Atlanta & Vicinity p. 230.

DILLARD—200

LODGING

THE DILLARD HOUSE   Rates Subject to Change   Phone: 706/746-5348
(AAA)   10/1-11/7   1P: $69- 109 2P/1B: $69- 109 2P/2B: $69- 109 XP: $5   F12
          6/1-8/31   1P: $59- 99 2P/1B: $59- 99 2P/2B: $59- 99 XP: $5   F12
◆◆◆   9/1-9/30 & 11/8-11/30   1P: $59- 79 2P/1B: $59- 79 2P/2B: $59- 79 XP: $5   F12
Motor Inn   12/1-5/31   1P: $45- 69 2P/1B: $45- 69 2P/2B: $45- 69 XP: $5   F12
          Location: US 441, 0.3 mi e via Old Dillard Rd. 30537 (PO Box 10). **Fax:** 706/746-3344. **Terms:** Reserv
deposit; pets, $5 extra charge. **Facility:** 66 rooms. 1-2 stories; exterior corridors. **Dining:** Restaurant; 6:30 am-10 &
11:30-8:30 pm; $12-$14. **All Rooms:** free movies. **Some Rooms:** 5 efficiencies, 3 kitchens. **Cards:** AE, CB, DI, DS, MC, VI.
          [🛏] [🏊] [CTV] [D]

DORAVILLE—See Atlanta & Vicinity p. 231.

DOUGLASVILLE—See Atlanta & Vicinity p. 231.

DUBLIN—16,300

LODGINGS

COMFORT INN   Phone: 912/274-8000
(AAA) [SAVE]   5/1-11/30 [CP]   1P: $60- 80 2P/1B: $60- 80 2P/2B: $60- 100
          12/1-4/30 [CP]   1P: $50- 60 2P/1B: $60- 70 2P/2B: $60- 70 XP: $5   F16
◆◆◆   **Location:** I-16, exit 14, 0.3 mi n. 2110 Hwy 441S 31021. **Fax:** 912/275-0009. **Terms:** No pets. **Facility:** 56
Motel   rooms. 2 stories; exterior corridors; small pool. **Dining:** Restaurant nearby. **All Rooms:** free movies,
          refrigerators. **Some Rooms:** whirlpools. Fee: VCP's. **Cards:** AE, DI, DS, MC, VI. **Special Amenities:** Free
breakfast and free local telephone calls.   [CTV] [♿] [⊠] [🐾] [D] [S]

HOLIDAY INN HOTEL & SUITES   Phone: 912/272-7862
(AAA) [SAVE]   All Year [BP]   1P: $54- 64 2P/1B: $59- 69 2P/2B: $64- 69 XP: $5   F19
          Location: I-16, exit 14, ne corner. Hwy 441 & I16 31040 (PO Box 768). **Fax:** 912/272-1077.
◆◆◆   **Terms:** Weekly/monthly rates; package plans; small pets only. **Facility:** 124 rooms. Recently completed reno-
Motor Inn   vation. Convenient to interstate. 12 two-bedroom units. 2 stories; exterior corridors. **Dining &**
          Entertainment: Restaurant; 6-9:30 am, Sat & Sun 7-10:30 am; $6-$13; cocktail lounge. **Services:** Fee: coin
laundry. **Recreation:** fishing; jogging. **All Rooms:** free & pay movies. **Some Rooms:** coffeemakers, microwaves,
refrigerators. **Cards:** AE, CB, DI, DS, JCB, MC, VI. **Special Amenities:** Free breakfast and free local telephone calls.
          [🛏] [🏊] [🛗] [♿] [🌊] [CTV] [♿] [⊠] [🐾] [D]

DULUTH—*See Atlanta & Vicinity p. 232.*

EASTMAN—5,200

LODGINGS

DAYS INN
◆
Motel
All Year [CP] — Rates Subject to Change — 1P: $50 — 2P/1B: $50 — 2P/2B: $55 — XP: $5 — F12
Location: 1.5 mi s on US 341 & 23. 1126 College St 31023. Fax: 912/374-1034. **Terms:** Reserv deposit; no pets. **Facility:** 30 rooms. Max of 4 persons per room; 2 stories; exterior corridors. **All Rooms:** free movies.
Cards: AE, CB, DI, DS, MC, VI.
Phone: 912/374-7000

THE JAMESON INN
◆ ◆
Motel
All Year [CP] — Rates Subject to Change — 1P: $38 — 2P/1B: $42 — 2P/2B: $42 — XP: $4 — F12
Location: 1 mi se on US 341 & 23. 103 Pine Ridge Rd 31023. Fax: 912/374-7790. **Terms:** No pets. **Facility:** 41 rooms. 2 stories; exterior corridors. **All Rooms:** free movies. **Cards:** AE, CB, DI, DS, MC, VI.
Phone: 912/374-7925

EAST POINT—*See Atlanta & Vicinity p. 233.*

ELBERTON—5,700

LODGING

DAYS INN
AAA SAVE
◆ ◆
Motel
All Year [CP] — 1P: $50 — 2P/1B: $57 — 2P/2B: $57 — XP: $10 — D10
Location: Hwy 17 & 72. 302 Elbert St 30635. Fax: 706/283-2500. **Terms:** Monthly rates; no pets. **Facility:** 35 rooms. 2 stories; exterior corridors. **Dining:** Restaurant nearby. **All Rooms:** free movies, refrigerators. **Some Rooms:** whirlpools. **Cards:** CB, DI, DS, JCB, MC, VI. **Special Amenities:** Free breakfast and free local telephone calls.
Phone: 706/283-2300

ELLIJAY—1,200

LODGING

BUDGET HOST INN
◆ ◆
Motel
All Year — Rates Subject to Change — 1P: $34- 60 — 2P/1B: $36- 70 — 2P/2B: $40- 80 — XP: $5
Location: 0.5 mi e on Hwy 52. 10 Jeff Dr 30540. Fax: 706/635-5313. **Terms:** No pets. **Facility:** 30 rooms. 2 stories; exterior corridors. **All Rooms:** free movies. **Cards:** AE, DS, MC, VI. *(See color ad p 183)*
Phone: 706/635-5311

FLOWERY BRANCH—1,300

LODGING

WHITWORTH INN
◆ ◆ ◆
Bed & Breakfast
All Year [BP] — Guaranteed Rates — 1P: $55- 65 — 2P/1B: $65- 75 — 2P/2B: $65- 75 — XP: $10 — F12
Location: I-985 exit 2, 1.9 mi w on SR 347N, 1.5 mi n. 6593 McEver Rd 30542. Fax: 770/967-2649. **Terms:** Sr. discount; reserv deposit, 3 day notice; no pets. **Facility:** 8 rooms. Rate includes 3-course home-cooked breakfast; 2 stories; interior corridors; designated smoking area. **Cards:** AE, MC, VI.
Phone: 770/967-2386

FOLKSTON—2,300

LODGING

DAYS INN
AAA SAVE
◆ ◆
Motor Inn
All Year [CP] — 1P: $35- 50 — 2P/1B: $42- 60 — 2P/2B: $42- 60 — XP: $6 — D12
Location: 0.8 mi s on US 1, 23 & 301. 1201 S 2nd St 31537. Fax: 914/496-2514. **Terms:** Reserv deposit; weekly rates; pets, $2 extra charge. **Facility:** 37 rooms. Handling fee imposed; 1 story; exterior corridors. **Dining:** Restaurant; 6 am-9 pm, Sun from 7 am; closed major holidays; $3-$9. **All Rooms:** free movies. **Cards:** AE, CB, DI, DS, JCB, MC, VI. **Special Amenities:** Free local telephone calls and free room upgrade (subject to availability with advanced reservations).
Phone: 912/496-2514

FOREST PARK—*See Atlanta & Vicinity p. 233.*

FORSYTH—4,300

LODGINGS

BEST WESTERN HILLTOP INN
AAA SAVE
◆ ◆
Motor Inn
All Year — 1P: $35- 45 — 2P/1B: $35- 45 — 2P/2B: $45- 60 — XP: $6 — F12
Location: On SR 42; e of I-75, exit 63. SR 42 & I-75 31029. Fax: 912/994-9260. **Terms:** Small pets only, $25 dep req. **Facility:** 120 rooms. 2 stories; exterior corridors; wading pool. **Dining:** Restaurant; 6:30 am-10:30 & 5-9:30 pm; $5-$10; wine/beer only. **All Rooms:** free movies. **Cards:** AE, CB, DI, DS, MC, VI. **Special Amenities:** Free local telephone calls. *(See color ad p 268 & p 182)*
Phone: 912/994-9260

COMFORT INN
AAA SAVE
◆ ◆ ◆
Motel
All Year — 1P: $45- 75 — 2P/1B: $45- 75 — 2P/2B: $45- 75 — XP: $5 — F14
Location: I-75 exit 60, sw corner. 333 Harold G Clark Pkwy 31029. Fax: 912/994-2003. **Terms:** Reserv deposit, 3 day notice; no pets. **Facility:** 59 rooms. Comfortable well-equipped rooms. Handling fee imposed; 2 stories; exterior corridors. **Services:** Fee: coin laundry. **All Rooms:** microwaves, free movies, refrigerators. **Cards:** AE, CB, DI, DS, MC, VI. **Special Amenities:** Free breakfast and free local telephone calls.
Phone: 912/994-3400

HAMPTON INN
◆ ◆ ◆
Motel
All Year [CP] — Rates Subject to Change — 1P: $46 — 2P/1B: $51 — 2P/2B: $51
Location: At I-75, exit 61, Tift College Dr & Juliette Rd. 520 Holiday Cir 31029. Fax: 912/994-3594. **Terms:** Pets. **Facility:** 125 rooms. 4 stories; interior corridors. **All Rooms:** free movies. **Cards:** AE, CB, DI, DS, MC, VI.
Phone: 912/994-9697

SUPER 8 MOTEL   **Phone: 912/994-9333**

    All Year   1P: $33- 40   2P/1B: $33- 40 2P/2B: $33- 50 XP: $5   F10

(AAA) (SAVE) **Location:** I-75, exit 63, just e. 990 Hwy 42 N 31029. **Fax:** 912/994-9333. **Terms:** Weekly rates; small pets

◆ ◆ only, $5 extra charge. **Facility:** 110 rooms. Large lawn & playground area. 2 stories; exterior corridors.

Motel **Dining:** Restaurant; 11 am-2 & 4-11 pm. **Services:** Fee: coin laundry. **Cards:** AE, DI, DS, MC, VI.

(See color ad below)   🐾 🛏 CTV ✖ D

RESTAURANT

MR LEUNG CHINESE RESTAURANT   **Lunch:** $4-$5   **Dinner:** $5-$11   **Phone:** 912/994-4418

(AAA) **Location:** I-75, exit 62, 3 blks w; in Wal-Mart Shopping Plaza on e side. 162 N Lee St 31029. **Hours:** 11:30

◆ am-3 & 5-10 pm; lunch buffet. Closed major holidays & Sun. **Features:** casual dress; children's menu;

Chinese carryout; beer & wine only; a la carte. Mandarin, Cantonese & Szechuan specialties. Smoke free premises.

    Cards: DS, MC, VI.   ✖

FORT GAINES—1,200

LODGING

LAKE WALTER F GEORGE LODGE   Rates Subject to Change   **Phone:** 912/768-2571

◆ ◆ ◆ 3/1-11/30   1P: $48   2P/1B: $48   2P/2B: $48   XP: $6   F12

Motor Inn 12/1-2/28   1P: $42   2P/1B: $42   2P/2B: $42   XP: $6   F12

    Location: On SR 39, 4 mi n of jct SR 37, then 1.8 mi w & s on park road; in George T Bagby State Park.

(Rt 1, Box 201, 31751). **Fax:** 912/768-3602. **Terms:** Check-in 4 pm; reserv deposit; 2 night min stay, in cabins; no pets.

Facility: 35 rooms. 5 cabins $65-$75; 1 story; exterior corridors. **Dining:** Restaurant; 11 am-2 & 5-9 pm, Tues-Thurs from

6:30 am, Fri-10 pm, Sat 6:30 am-10 pm, Sun 6:30 am-2:30 pm; $6-$12. **All Rooms:** free movies. **Cards:** AE, CB, DI, DS,

MC, VI.   🛏 CTV ✖ D S

FORT OGLETHORPE—5,900

LODGINGS

BEST WESTERN BATTLEFIELD INN   **Phone:** 706/866-0222

(AAA) (SAVE) 6/1-8/31 [CP]   1P: $49- 80 2P/1B: $69- 89 2P/2B: $59- 80 XP: $10   F12

    12/1-5/31 & 9/1-11/30 [CP] 1P: $49- 80 2P/1B: $59- 80 2P/2B: $59- 80 XP: $10   F12

◆ ◆ ◆ **Location:** Just n of jct US 27 & SR 2. 1715 Lafayette Rd (US 27) 30742. **Fax:** 706/866-4698.

Motel **Terms:** Reserv deposit, 3 day notice; no pets. **Facility:** 38 rooms. 1 suite with microwave, refrigerator & whirl-

pool; 8 super suites with whirlpool, $79-$109. Handling fee imposed; 1 story; exterior corridors.

All Rooms: free movies. **Some Rooms:** microwaves, refrigerators, whirlpools. **Cards:** AE, CB, DI, DS, MC, VI.

Special Amenities: Free newspaper and preferred room (subject to availability with advanced reservations).

(See color ad p 182)   🛏 🛏 🏋 CTV ✖ D

THE CAPTAINS QUARTERS BED & BREAKFAST INN   Phone: 706/858-0624

(AAA) (SAVE)   All Year [BP]   1P: $79- 119   2P/1B: $79- 119   XP: $15

Bed &   **Location:** 0.8 mi s jct SR 27/2, just w on Harker, just s. 13 Barnhardt Cir 30742. Fax: 706/861-4053.
Breakfast   **Terms:** Age restrictions may apply; reserv deposit, 3 day notice; no pets. **Facility:** 7 rooms. Easy walk to
Chickamauga National Park, former 6th Calvary Captain's quarters. Elegant guest "quarters". Handling fee imposed; 2 stories; interior corridors; designated smoking area. **Services:** complimentary evening beverages.
All Rooms: free movies, combo or shower baths, no phones. **Cards:** AE, DS, MC, VI. **Special Amenities:**
Free local telephone calls and free room upgrade (subject to availability with advanced reservations). (CTV) (X) (D)

FORT VALLEY—8,200

LODGING

THE EVANS-CANTRELL HOUSE   Guaranteed Rates   Phone: 912/825-0611

◆◆◆   All Year [BP]   1P: $65- 95   2P/1B: $65- 95 2P/2B: $65- 95 XP: $15
Historic Bed   **Location:** W of downtown, nw corner of College & Miller sts. 300 College St 31030. **Terms:** Age restrictions
& Breakfast   may apply; no pets. **Facility:** 5 rooms. 2 stories; interior corridors; smoke free premises. **All Rooms:** free
movies. **Cards:** AE, DS, MC, VI.   (CTV) (X) (D)

GAINESVILLE—17,900

LODGINGS

BEST WESTERN LANIER CENTRE HOTEL   Phone: 770/531-0907

(AAA) (SAVE)   12/1-3/31 & 11/1-11/30   1P: $69   2P/1B: $76   XP: $7   F18
4/1-10/31   1P: $77   2P/1B: $84   XP: $7   F18
Motor Inn   **Location:** Downtown; I-985, exit 6, 1 mi nw. 400 E E Butler Pkwy 30501. Fax: 770/531-0788. **Terms:** Reserv
deposit; package plans; no pets. **Facility:** 122 rooms. 4 stories; interior corridors. **Dining & Entertainment:**
Restaurant;   6:30 am-2 & 5-10 pm; $12-$19; cocktails/lounge. **Services:** valet laundry.
All Rooms: coffeemakers, free movies. **Some Rooms:** VCP's. Fee: refrigerators, whirlpools. **Cards:** AE, CB, DI, DS, MC,
VI. **Special Amenities: Free newspaper.** *(See color ad below)*   (symbols) (CTV) (X) (D) (S)

DUNLAP HOUSE BED AND BREAKFAST INN   Rates Subject to Change   Phone: 770/536-0200

◆◆◆   All Year [BP]   1P: $95- 155   2P/1B: $105- 160   XP: $15
Historic Bed   **Location:** I-985 exit 6, 2 mi nw on US 129. 635 Green St 30501. Fax: 770/503-7857. **Terms:** Sr. discount;
& Breakfast   reserv deposit, 3 day notice; no pets. **Facility:** 10 rooms. 2 stories; interior corridors; smoke free premises.
Cards: AE, CB, DI, DS, MC, VI.   (CTV) (X) (D)

SHONEY'S INN   Phone: 770/535-8100

(AAA) (SAVE)   All Year [CP]   1P: $55- 65   2P/1B: $59- 69 2P/2B: $59- 69 XP: $3   F18
◆◆◆   **Location:** I-985 exit 5, 1.8 mi nw on SR 60. 520 Queen City Pkwy SW 30501. Fax: 770/536-6089.
Motel   **Terms:** Check-in 4 pm; no pets. **Facility:** 99 rooms. 2 stories; exterior corridors. **Dining:** Restaurant nearby.
All Rooms: free movies. **Cards:** AE, DI, DS, MC, VI. **Special Amenities: Free breakfast and free local
telephone calls.**   (symbols) (CTV) (X) (D)

RESTAURANT

RUDOLPH'S ON GREEN STREET   Historical   **Lunch:** $4-$8   **Dinner:** $12-$20   Phone: 770/534-2226

◆◆◆   **Location:** 0.5 mi nw on US 129 & SR 60, or from I-985, exit 6, 2 mi nw on US 129 & SR 60. 700 Green St
American   30503. **Hours:** 5:30 pm-10 pm, Fri & Sat-11 pm, Sun brunch 11 am-2 pm. Closed major holidays & Sun for
dinner. **Reservations:** suggested; weekends. **Features:** casual dress; children's menu; early bird specials;
senior's menu; health conscious menu items; carryout; cocktails. In turn-of-the-century mansion. Prix fixe chef's dinners also
avail on Fri & Sat. **Cards:** AE, DS, MC, VI.   (X)

GARDEN CITY—7,400   (See map p. 297; index p. 296)

LODGING

MASTERS ECONOMY INN GARDEN CITY   Rates Subject to Change   Phone: 912/964-4344   (62)

◆◆   All Year   1P: $35- 40   2P/1B: $39- 44 2P/2B: $39- 44 XP: $4   F17
Motor Inn   **Location:** On SR 21N, 0.3 mi nw of terminus, I-516. 4200 Hwy 21N; Augusta Rd 31408. Fax: 912/964-4344.
Terms: Sr. discount; small pets only, $5 extra charge. **Facility:** 122 rooms. 2 stories; interior corridors.
Dining: Restaurant; 24 hours; $5-$10. **All Rooms:** free movies. **Cards:** AE, DI, DS, MC, VI.
(symbols) (CTV) (X) (D)

GLENNVILLE—3,700

LODGING

CHEERI-O MOTEL   Phone: 912/654-2176
All Year   1P: $32   2P/1B: $36   2P/2B: $38   XP: $4
Location: 0.8 mi s on US 25 & 301. (PO Box 393, 30427). **Terms:** Reserv deposit; small pets only.
Facility: 25 rooms. Spacious guest rooms with many amenities. 1 story; exterior corridors; Large tree shaded
lawn with picnic tables. **All Rooms:** free movies, combo or shower baths. **Some Rooms:** coffeemakers,
microwaves, refrigerators. **Cards:** AE, DS, MC, VI.

Motel

Golden Isles

JEKYLL ISLAND—600

$2.00 fee charged each time of entry to Jekyll Island

LODGINGS

CLARION RESORT BUCCANEER   Phone: 912/635-2261
5/15-8/17   1P: $119- 199   2P/1B: $119- 199   2P/2B: $119- 199   XP: $10   F18
2/16-5/14 & 8/18-11/15   1P: $89- 159   2P/1B: $89- 159   2P/2B: $89- 159   XP: $10   F18
12/1-2/15 & 11/16-11/30   1P: $79- 149   2P/1B: $79- 149   2P/2B: $79- 149   XP: $10   F18
Motor Inn   **Location:** 0.5 mi s from jct SR 520 (Ben Fortson Pkwy) & S Beachview Dr; from I-95, exit 6, follow 11 mi e
on US 17N & SR 520. 85 S Beachview Dr 31527. Fax: 912/635-3230. **Terms:** Check-in 4 pm; reserv
deposit, 3 day notice; weekly/monthly rates; package plans; pets, $10 extra charge. **Facility:** 206 rooms. Handicap-accessible
ramp leading to beach. 2-4 stories; interior/exterior corridors; oceanfront; luxury level rooms; beach, wading pool, whirlpool; 1
tennis court; playground, shuffleboard. **Dining & Entertainment:** Restaurant, deli; 7 am-10 pm; $5-$18; cocktails;
entertainment. **Services:** area transportation, on the island. Fee: coin laundry. **Recreation:** children's program in season;
swimming, high dunes block some room views from ocean. Silt-water beach. Fee: bicycles. **All Rooms:** coffeemakers.
Fee: movies. **Some Rooms:** 120 efficiencies, microwaves, refrigerators. **Cards:** AE, DI, DS, MC, VI. *(See color ad below)*

COMFORT INN ISLAND SUITES

Phone: 912/635-2211

(AAA) SAVE	5/15-8/17 [CP]	1P: $99- 175	2P/1B: $99- 175	2P/2B: $99- 175	XP: $10	F18
◆◆	2/16-5/14 & 8/18-11/30 [CP]	1P: $79- 135	2P/1B: $79- 135	2P/2B: $79- 135	XP: $10	F18
Motor Inn	12/1-2/15 [CP]	1P: $75- 105	2P/1B: $75- 105	2P/2B: $75- 105	XP: $10	F18

Location: 1.5 mi n from jct SR 520 (Ben Fortson Pkwy) & N Beachview Dr. 711 N Beachview Dr 31527. Fax: 912/635-2381. **Terms:** Check-in 4 pm; reserv deposit, 3 day notice; weekly/monthly rates; package plans; pets. **Facility:** 180 rooms. Many rooms with ocean view. 1 room with sauna; 2 stories; exterior corridors; beach, wading pool, whirlpools; playground. **Dining:** 2 restaurants; 6 am-midnight; Fri & Sat 24 hours; $5-$12; wine/beer only. **Services:** Fee: coin laundry. **Recreation:** swimming. Fee: bicycles. **All Rooms:** coffeemakers, free movies, refrigerators, combo or shower baths. **Some Rooms:** 78 efficiencies, microwaves, whirlpools. **Cards:** AE, DI, DS, MC, VI. *(See color ad p 270)*

Roll in showers. 🛏 🖵 📞 CTV ✕ D

HOLIDAY INN BEACH RESORT

Phone: 912/635-3311

(AAA) SAVE	5/2-9/15	1P: $119	2P/1B: $119	2P/2B: $119	XP: $10	F18
◆◆◆	2/16-5/1	1P: $99	2P/1B: $99	2P/2B: $99	XP: $10	F18
Motor Inn	12/1-12/31 & 9/16-11/30	1P: $71	2P/1B: $71	2P/2B: $71	XP: $10	F18
	1/1-2/15	1P: $64	2P/1B: $64	2P/2B: $64	XP: $10	F18

Location: 2 mi s of SR 520 (Ben Fortson Causeway). 200 S Beachview Dr 31527. Fax: 912/635-2901. **Terms:** Check-in 4 pm; reserv deposit, 3 day notice; weekly rates; small pets only, $7.50 extra charge. **Facility:** 205 rooms. Boardwalk, with gazebo, over tree-lined dunes to beach. 2-4 stories; interior corridors; beach, wading pool; 2 tennis courts; playground. **Dining & Entertainment:** Restaurant; 5 pm-9 pm, Fri & Sat 7 am-2 & 5:30-10 pm; $9-$20; cocktails/lounge. **Services:** Fee: area transportation, on Jekyll Island. **Recreation:** swimming; hiking trails, jogging. Fee: bicycles. **All Rooms:** coffeemakers, free movies. **Some Rooms:** microwaves, refrigerators. **Cards:** AE, CB, DI, DS, JCB, MC, VI. **Special Amenities:** Early check-in/late check-out and free local telephone calls. 🛏 🖵 📞 CTV 👤 ✕ 🏊 D

JEKYLL ISLAND CLUB HOTEL

Phone: 912/635-2600

(AAA) SAVE	3/6-9/3	1P: $129	2P/1B: $129	2P/2B: $129	XP: $20	F17
◆◆◆	9/4-11/30	1P: $115	2P/1B: $115	2P/2B: $115	XP: $20	F17
Historic Hotel	12/1-3/5	1P: $99	2P/1B: $99	2P/2B: $99	XP: $20	F17

Location: 0.5 mi n of SR 520 (Ben Fortson Pkwy); in historic district, following signs. 371 Riverview Dr 31527. Fax: 912/635-2818. **Terms:** Check-in 4 pm; reserv deposit, 3 day notice; weekly rates; AP, MAP avail; package plans; 2 night min stay, weekends 3/15-11/30; no pets. **Facility:** 134 rooms. Graciously restored turn-of-the-century hotel. Some smaller rooms. Sans Souci building does not have an elevator. Rates for 2 persons; 3-4 stories; interior corridors; putting green; beach access; croquet court, lending library, historic tour of hotel. Fee: 9 tennis courts (1 indoor, 5 lighted). **Dining & Entertainment:** Dining room, coffee shop; pool bar & grill in season; 7 am-10 pm; $5-$27; cocktails/lounge; afternoon tea; also, The Grand Dining Room, see separate listing; entertainment. **Services:** valet laundry; area transportation, on Jekyll Island; valet parking. Fee: massage. **Recreation:** children's program in season, social program. Fee: bicycles. **All Rooms:** VCP's. Fee: movies. **Some Rooms:** whirlpools. **Cards:** AE, CB, DI, DS, MC, VI. **Special Amenities:** Free newspaper and free room upgrade (subject to availability with advanced reservations). *(See ad below)* 🖵 📞 ✈ 🏋 CTV ✕ 🏊 D S

RAMADA INN

Rates Subject to Change

Phone: 912/635-2111

◆	5/22-9/6	1P: $95- 250	2P/1B: $95- 250	2P/2B: $95- 250	XP: $10
Motor Inn	3/1-5/21	1P: $75- 230	2P/1B: $75- 230	2P/2B: $75- 230	XP: $10
	12/1-2/28 & 9/7-11/30	1P: $65- 200	2P/1B: $65- 200	2P/2B: $65- 200	XP: $10

Location: From jct SR 520 (Ben Fortson Pkwy) & Beachview Dr, 0.8 mi s. 150 S Beachview Dr 31527. Fax: 912/635-2758. **Terms:** Sr. discount; check-in 4 pm; reserv deposit, checks not accepted; no pets. **Facility:** 110 rooms. Rates for up to 4 persons; 3 stories; interior corridors. **Dining:** Restaurant; 6:30-10 am, 11-2 & 5-10 pm; $8-$15. **Cards:** AE, CB, DI, DS, JCB, MC, VI. 🖵 CTV ✕ D

SEAFARER INN & SUITES

Rates Subject to Change

Phone: 912/635-2202

◆	4/15-9/6 [CP]	1P: $68- 88	2P/1B: $68- 88	2P/2B: $68- 88	XP: $8	F12
Motel	1/1-4/14 [CP]	1P: $62- 79	2P/1B: $62- 79	2P/2B: $62- 79	XP: $8	F12
	9/7-11/30 [CP]	1P: $48- 65	2P/1B: $48- 65	2P/2B: $48- 65	XP: $8	F12
	12/1-12/31 [CP]	1P: $46- 55	2P/1B: $46- 55	2P/2B: $46- 55	XP: $8	F12

Location: From jct SR 520 (Ben Fortson Pkwy) & Beachview Dr, 1.5 mi n. 700 N Beachview Dr 31527. Fax: 912/635-2927. **Terms:** Sr. discount; reserv deposit; pets, $10 dep req. **Facility:** 72 rooms. Rates for up to 4 persons; 2 stories; exterior corridors. **Some Rooms:** 5 efficiencies. **Cards:** AE, DI, DS, MC, VI. 🛏 🖵 CTV ✕ D

VILLAS BY THE SEA RESORT HOTEL (A CONDOMINIUM)   Phone: 912/635-2521

(AAA) (SAVE)   5/1-8/17   1P: $99- 154   2P/1B: $174- 189   2P/2B: $224- 239
   2/16-4/30 & 8/18-11/30   1P: $84- 124   2P/1B: $139- 154   2P/2B: $179- 194
◆◆◆   12/1-2/15   1P: $74- 114   2P/1B: $124- 134   2P/2B: $169- 179
Condo   **Location:** 3.5 mi n from jct SR 520 (Ben Fortston Pkwy) & N Beachview Dr. 1175 N Beachview Dr 31527.
Complex   Fax: 912/635-2569. **Terms:** Check-in 4 pm; reserv deposit, 14 day notice; weekly rates, monthly rates
11/1-3/31; package plans; pets, call for fee. **Facility:** 176 rooms. Meandering driveways through live oaks &
lush palmettos. Family-oriented. Individually-decorated units in 17 buildings. Daily maid service avail upon request when paying
daily rates. Short walk to beach over dunes. 85 two-bedroom units, 33 three-bedroom units. 3 stories, no elevator; exterior corridors; whirlpool; playground; badminton, basketball, horseshoe pits, shuffleboard, volleyball. **Dining & Entertainment:**
Restaurant; 7 am-2 & 5-9:30 pm; $6-$15; cocktails/lounge. **Services:** area transportation, on Jekyll Island. Fee: coin
laundry. **Recreation:** children's program in season; swimming, No beach at high tide. Silt water beach. Fee: bicycles.
All Rooms: coffeemakers, microwaves, refrigerators. **Some Rooms:** 164 kitchens, radios, VCP's. **Cards:** AE, CB, DI, DS,
MC, VI. **Special Amenities:** Free room upgrade and preferred room (each subject to availability with advanced
reservations). *(See ad below)*   🛏 🏊 📶 CTV ✕ D

RESTAURANTS

BLACKBEARDS RESTAURANT   **Lunch:** $4-$8   **Dinner:** $10-$19   Phone: 912/635-3522
◆   **Location:** 0.5 mi n on N Beachview Dr from jct Ben Fortson Cwsy. 200 N Beachview Dr 31527. **Hours:** 11
Seafood   am-10 pm. Closed: 12/10-1/3. **Features:** children's menu; cocktails & lounge. Casual dining in an
   unpretentious setting. Dining room & lounge offer wonderful ocean views. Features a variety of seafood,
steak & chicken dishes with an emphasis on sandwiches at lunch. **Cards:** AE, DS, MC, VI.   ✕

THE GRAND DINING ROOM   Historical   **Lunch:** $5-$12   **Dinner:** $18-$27   Phone: 912/635-2600
◆◆◆   **Location:** 0.5 mi n of SR 520 (Ben Fortson Pkwy); in historic district, following signs; in Jekyll Island Club
Continental   Hotel. 371 Riverview Dr 31527. **Hours:** 7 am-2 & 6-10 pm. **Reservations:** suggested. **Features:** Sunday
   brunch; children's menu; cocktails & lounge; entertainment; valet parking. Creative gourmet selections
offered in an elegant, sophisticated dining room. Relaxed, casual setting for breakfast & lunch. Jackets required at dinner.
Smoke free premises. **Cards:** AE, CB, DI, DS, MC, VI.   ✕

LATITUDE 31   **Dinner:** $10-$20   Phone: 912/635-3800
◆◆   **Location:** 1 mi n Jekyll Island Bridge. 1 Pier Rd 31527. **Hours:** 5:30 pm-9 pm; 10 pm or 11 pm in summer.
American   Closed major holidays. **Reservations:** suggested. **Features:** casual dress; children's menu; cocktails; a la
   carte. Indoor/outdoor dining on pier. Scrumptious seafood entrees. **Cards:** DS, MC, VI.   ✕

ST. SIMONS ISLAND—12,000

LODGINGS

QUEEN'S COURT   Rates Subject to Change   Phone: 912/638-8459
(AAA)   All Year   1P: $50   2P/1B: $56   2P/2B: $64- 72   XP: $4
   Location: Center of village. 437 Kings Way 31522. **Terms:** Reserv deposit, 3 day notice; no pets.
◆◆   **Facility:** 23 rooms. 9 two- & three-bedroom efficiencies, $64-$70 for up to 5 persons; 2 stories; exterior corri-
Motel   dors. **Cards:** MC, VI.   🏊 CTV D

SAINT SIMONS INN BY THE LIGHTHOUSE   Rates Subject to Change   Phone: 912/638-1101
◆◆   3/15-10/31 [CP]   1P: $79- 105   2P/1B: $89- 105   2P/2B: $89- 105   XP: $8   F11
Motel   12/1-3/14 & 11/1-11/30 [CP]   1P: $55- 75   2P/1B: $65- 75   2P/2B: $65- 75   XP: $8   F11
   Location: Center of village. 609 Beachview Dr 31522 (PO Box 20225). Fax: 912/638-0943. **Terms:** Sr.
discount; 2 night min stay, summer weekends; no pets. **Facility:** 34 rooms. 4 stories; interior corridors. **Cards:** AE, DI, DS,
MC, VI.   CTV ✕ D S

SEA GATE INN   Rates Subject to Change   Phone: 912/638-8661
◆◆   3/1-9/30   1P: $68- 280   2P/1B: $68- 280   2P/2B: $68- 280   XP: $7
Motel   12/1-2/28 & 10/1-11/30   1P: $50- 185   2P/1B: $50- 185   2P/2B: $50- 185   XP: $7
   Location: 1 mi e of village on Ocean Blvd. 1014 Ocean Blvd 31522. Fax: 912/638-4932. **Terms:** Reserv
deposit, 7 day notice; 3 night min stay, summer weekends; no pets. **Facility:** 48 rooms. Oceanfront suites, $120-$250. Handling fee imposed; 2-4 stories; exterior corridors. **Some Rooms:** 8 efficiencies, 6 kitchens. **Cards:** AE, MC, VI.   🏊 CTV D

RESTAURANTS

ALLEGRO RESTAURANT   **Dinner:** $15-$22   Phone: 912/638-7097
◆◆◆   **Location:** From toll plaza, 3.5 mi e on Demere Rd, in shops at Demere Shopping Center. 2465 Demere Rd
American   31522. **Hours:** 5:30 pm-10 pm, Fri & Sat-11 pm. Closed: Mon & 12/25. **Reservations:** suggested; after 7
   pm. **Features:** casual dress; health conscious menu items; cocktails; a la carte. Eclectic, innovative entrees
featuring pork, beef, poultry & seafood. Elegant, sophisticated ambience. Also, casual bistro cafe featuring homemade pasta
entrees & outdoor courtyard dining. Wines by the glass avail. **Cards:** AE, MC, VI.   ✕

BLANCHE'S COURTYARD SEAFOOD RESTAURANT   **Dinner:** $13-$18   **Phone:** 912/638-3030
◆◆   **Location:** Center of village, at jct of Kings Hwy & Ocean Blvd. 440 Ocean Blvd 31522. **Hours:** 5:30 pm-9
Seafood   pm, Sat-9:30 pm; to 10 pm in season. Closed: 11/26, 12/24 & 12/25. **Reservations:** suggested; in summer.
   Features: casual dress; children's menu; cocktails. An inviting Bayou Victorian ambience. Specializing in
broiled seafood, steak & chicken. A local favorite since 1974. Smoke free premises. **Cards:** AE, DI, MC, VI.   ⊠

THE FREDERICA HOUSE   **Dinner:** $9-$16   **Phone:** 912/638-6789
◆◆   **Location:** From toll plaza, 4 mi e on Demere Rd to Frederica Rd, 3.5 mi n. 3611 Frederica Rd 31522.
Steak and   **Hours:** 5:30 pm-9:30 pm, Fri & Sat-10 pm; 5/29-9/4 to 10:30 pm. Closed: 1/1, 1/29, 11/26, 12/24 & 12/25.
Seafood   **Reservations:** suggested; 6:30-8:30 pm. **Features:** casual dress; children's menu; early bird specials;
   carryout; cocktails. Very popular, cozy, family dining in a rustic setting with white cedar & cypress wood on 2
levels. Specializing in fresh local shrimp, grilled fish & hickory steak. **Cards:** AE, CB, DI, DS, MC, VI.   ⊠

GINO'S ITALIAN RESTAURANT   **Lunch:** $4-$6   **Dinner:** $8-$15   **Phone:** 912/634-9633
◆◆   **Location:** In Redfern Village on Frederica Rd, 0.3 mi n of jct Demere Rd. 228 Redfern Village 31522.
Italian   **Hours:** 11 am-2 & 5-10 pm, Sat from 5 pm. Closed: Sun, Mon, 1/1 & 12/24-12/28. **Reservations:** accepted.
   Features: casual dress; children's menu; carryout; cocktails & lounge. Cozy, candlelit dining amidst mirrored
walls. Homemade pasta & pastry. Grilled specailties & seafood nightly. Entrees cooked to order. A local favorite.
Family-operated. **Cards:** AE, DS, MC, VI.   ⊠

GREENSBORO—2,900

LODGING

MICROTEL INN   Rates Subject to Change   **Phone:** 706/453-7300
ⒶⒶ   All Year   1P: $39- 59   2P/1B: $39- 59   2P/2B: $39- 59
◆◆   **Location:** I-20 exit 53, just n. 2470 Old Eatonton Hwy 30642. Fax: 706/453-1417. **Terms:** Reserv deposit;
Motel   no pets. **Facility:** 48 rooms. 2 stories; interior corridors. **All Rooms:** free movies. **Cards:** AE, DI, DS, MC,
   VI.   Roll in showers.   CTV ♿ ⊠ D S

GRIFFIN—21,300

LODGINGS

HOLIDAY INN   Rates Subject to Change   **Phone:** 770/227-1516
◆◆◆   All Year   1P: $59   2P/1B: $67   2P/2B: $67   XP: $8   F12
Motel   **Location:** 2 mi n on US 41 & 19. 1690 N Expressway 30223. Fax: 770/227-2411. **Terms:** Sr. discount;
   reserv deposit; no pets. **Facility:** 101 rooms. 2 stories; exterior corridors. **Dining:** Dining room; 6:30 am-2 &
5-8 pm; $6-$12. **All Rooms:** free movies. **Cards:** AE, CB, DI, DS, JCB, MC, VI.   Roll in showers.   ☎ CTV ⊠ D

RAMADA LIMITED SUITES   Rates Subject to Change   **Phone:** 770/228-9799
◆◆◆   All Year [CP]   1P: $50- 60   2P/1B: $50- 60   2P/2B: $50- 60   XP: $10   F18
Motel   **Location:** 3 mi n Hwy 19/41. 1900 N Expressway 30223. Fax: 770/467-0366. **Terms:** Sr. discount; check-in
   4 pm; reserv deposit; no pets. **Facility:** 49 rooms. 2 stories; interior corridors. **All Rooms:** free movies.
Cards: AE, DI, DS, MC, VI.   ☎ CTV ⊠ D

HAMILTON—500

LODGING

MAGNOLIA HALL BED & BREAKFAST   Rates Subject to Change   **Phone:** 706/628-4566
◆◆◆   12/1-12/31 & 3/1-11/30 [BP]   1P: $85- 95   2P/1B: $85- 95   2P/2B: $85- 95   XP: $15
Bed &   1/1-2/28 [BP]   1P: $75- 85   2P/1B: $75- 85   2P/2B: $75- 85   XP: $15
Breakfast   **Location:** I-185 exit 11, 9 mi w on Hwy 116, n on US 27, just w on 1st St. 127 Barnes Mill Rd 31811 (PO
   Box 326). Fax: 706/628-5802. **Terms:** Check-in 4 pm; reserv deposit, 3 day notice; no pets. **Facility:** 5 rooms.
Handling fee imposed; 2 stories; interior corridors. **All Rooms:** free movies.   Roll in showers.   CTV ⊠ D

RESTAURANT

OAK TREE VICTORIAN RESTAURANT   Historical   **Dinner:** $8-$24   **Phone:** 706/628-4218
◆◆◆   **Location:** 0.5 mi s on US 27. 31811. **Hours:** 6 pm-9 pm. Closed major holidays & Sun.
Continental   **Reservations:** suggested. **Features:** casual dress; children's menu; cocktails. Old World dining in an 1871
   home. American, Franco & Italian dishes. Dinner specials offered nightly, $9.95-$16.95. **Cards:** AE, CB, DI,
DS, JCB, MC, VI.

HAPEVILLE—see Atlanta & Vicinity p. 233.

HARTWELL—4,600

LODGINGS

DAYS INN   Rates Subject to Change   **Phone:** 706/376-4707
◆◆   All Year [CP]   1P: $39- 59   2P/1B: $39- 59   2P/2B: $49- 69   XP: $5   D12
Motel   **Location:** 2 mi e on N US 29. 1679 Anderson Hwy 30643. Fax: 706/376-6687. **Terms:** Sr. discount; no pets.
   Facility: 32 rooms. 2 suites avail; 1 story; exterior corridors. **All Rooms:** free movies. **Some Rooms:** 2
kitchens. **Cards:** AE, DS, MC, VI.   CTV ⊠ D

THE JAMESON INN   Rates Subject to Change   **Phone:** 706/376-7298
◆◆   All Year [CP]   1P: $44   2P/1B: $48   XP: $4   F12
Motel   **Location:** 1.5 mi n on US 29. 1091 E Franklin St 30643. Fax: 706/376-7298. **Terms:** No pets. **Facility:** 40
   rooms. 2 stories; exterior corridors. **All Rooms:** free movies. **Cards:** AE, DI, DS, MC, VI.   ☎ CTV ⊠ D

HAWKINSVILLE—3,500

LODGING

BLACK SWAN INN   Rates Subject to Change   **Phone:** 912/783-4466
◆◆◆   All Year [CP]   1P: $55- 70   2P/1B: $55- 70   2P/2B: $65
Country Inn   **Location:** On US 341. 411 Progress Ave 31036. Fax: 912/892-9009. **Terms:** No pets. **Facility:** 6 rooms. 2 sto-
   ries; interior corridors. **Dining:** Dining room; 11:30 am-1:30 & 6-10 pm, Sat from 6 pm, closed Sun; $13-$20.
Cards: AE, DI, MC, VI.   CTV D

HAZLEHURST—4,200

LODGINGS

BEST WESTERN OF HAZLEHURST INN   Phone: 912/375-3400
AAA SAVE   All Year [CP]   1P: $39- 48 2P/1B: $42- 48 2P/2B: $44- 52 XP: $5   F16
            Location: On Hwy 341. 601 Rowland St 31539. Fax: 912/375-0542. **Terms:** Reserv deposit; no pets.
◆◆◆   **Facility:** 44 rooms. Handling fee imposed; 1 story; exterior corridors. **Services:** Fee: coin laundry.
Motel   **All Rooms:** free movies, refrigerators. **Some Rooms:** whirlpools. **Cards:** AE, CB, DI, DS, JCB, MC, VI.
            Special Amenities: Free breakfast and free local telephone calls.

THE VILLAGE INN   Phone: 912/375-4527
AAA SAVE   All Year   1P: $36- 42 2P/1B: $36- 46 2P/2B: $48- 52
            Location: US 341, center of city. 312 Coffee St 31539. Fax: 912/375-2053. **Terms:** Reserv deposit; small
◆◆   pets only. **Facility:** 74 rooms. 1 story; exterior corridors. **Services:** valet laundry. **All Rooms:** coffeemakers,
Motor Inn   free movies, combo or shower baths. **Some Rooms:** microwaves, refrigerators. **Cards:** AE, CB, DI, DS, MC,
            VI. **Special Amenities: Free local telephone calls.**

HELEN—300

LODGINGS

BEST WESTERN ALPINE HELEN   Phone: 706/878-2111
AAA SAVE   9/1-11/15 [CP]   1P: $65- 129 2P/1B: $65- 129 2P/2B: $65- 129 XP: $5   F18
            6/1-8/31 [CP]   1P: $75- 119 2P/1B: $75- 119 2P/2B: $75- 119 XP: $5   F18
◆◆   5/1-5/31 [CP]   1P: $45- 95   2P/1B: $45- 95   2P/2B: $45- 95   XP: $10 F18
Motel   12/1-4/30 & 11/16-11/30 [CP] 1P: $35- 75   2P/1B: $35- 75   2P/2B: $35- 75   XP: $5   F18
            Location: 0.5 mi s on SR 17 & 75. 8220 Hwy 75 N 30545 (PO Box 319). **Terms:** Package plans; no pets.
Facility: 42 rooms. Large rooms. 2 stories; exterior corridors. **Dining:** Restaurant nearby. **All Rooms:** free movies.
Some Rooms: whirlpools. **Cards:** AE, CB, DI, DS, MC, VI. **Special Amenities: Free breakfast and free local telephone
calls.** (See color ad p 182)

COMFORT INN   Phone: 706/878-8000
AAA SAVE   Fri & Sat 9/15-10/31 [CP]   1P: $65- 129 2P/1B: $65- 129 2P/2B: $65- 129 XP: $5 F18
            Sun-Thurs 9/15-10/31 [CP]   1P: $55- 119 2P/1B: $55- 119 2P/2B: $55- 119 XP: $5 F18
◆◆   5/1-9/14 [CP]   1P: $50- 119 2P/1B: $50- 119 2P/2B: $50- 119 XP: $5 F18
Motel   12/1-4/30 & 11/1-11/30 [CP]   1P: $39- 109 2P/1B: $39- 109 2P/2B: $39- 109 XP: $5 F18
            Location: 1 mi on SR 75. 101 Edelweiss Strasse 30545 (PO Box 305). Fax: 706/878-1231. **Terms:** No
pets. **Facility:** 60 rooms. Modern building with Bavarian touches. Near the hills in a semi-rural setting. 2 stories; exterior corridors; small pool. **All Rooms:** free movies. **Some Rooms:** refrigerators. Fee: whirlpools. **Cards:** AE, CB, DI, DS, JCB, MC,
VI. **Special Amenities: Early check-in/late check-out and free breakfast.**

THE HELENDORF RIVER INN & TOWERS   Rates Subject to Change   Phone: 706/878-2271
◆◆   6/1-8/31 & 9/1-10/31 [CP]   1P: $74- 99 2P/1B: $74- 99 2P/2B: $74- 99 XP: $5   F12
Motel   4/1-5/31 & 11/1-11/30 [CP]   1P: $54- 79 2P/1B: $54- 79 2P/2B: $54- 79 XP: $5   F12
            12/1-3/31 [CP]   1P: $44- 69 2P/1B: $44- 69 2P/2B: $44- 69 XP: $5   F12
Location: Center on SR 17 & 75. 33 Muniche Strasse 30545 (PO Box 305). Fax: 706/878-2271. **Terms:** Reserv deposit, 10
day notice, 3 day off season; pets, $10 extra charge. **Facility:** 97 rooms. 2-3 stories; interior/exterior corridors.
All Rooms: free movies. **Some Rooms:** 26 efficiencies, 6 kitchens. **Cards:** DI, MC, VI.

SUPER 8 MOTEL   Phone: 706/878-2191
AAA SAVE   Fri & Sat 9/1-10/31   2P/2B: $55- 115 XP: $10 F11
            Sun-Thurs 9/1-10/31   2P/2B: $49- 115 XP: $5   F11
◆◆   5/1-8/31   2P/2B: $39- 95   XP: $5   F11
Motel   12/1-4/30 & 11/1-11/30   2P/2B: $29- 85   XP: $5   F11
            Location: 0.3 mi s on SR 17 & 75. 8396 S Main St 30545 (PO Box 1085). Fax: 706/878-1597. **Terms:** No
pets. **Facility:** 46 rooms. 2 stories; exterior corridors. **Dining:** Restaurant nearby. **All Rooms:** free movies.
Some Rooms: refrigerators, whirlpools. **Special Amenities: Early check-in/late check-out and
free local telephone calls.**

TANGLEWOOD RESORT CABINS   Rates Subject to Change   Phone: 706/878-3286
AAA   All Year   1P: $75   2P/1B: $75   2P/2B: $75- 110
            Location: 1 mi n on SR 75, then 3 mi ne on SR 356. Hwy 356 30545 (PO Box 435). Fax: 706/878-2044.
◆◆   **Terms:** Check-in 4 pm; reserv deposit, 7 day notice; no pets. **Facility:** 55 rooms. 1- to 6- bedroom cabins for
Cottage   6-22 persons. 4 motel units, $45; 1/15-5/15 special rate avail; 1-2 stories; exterior corridors.
            Some Rooms: 51 kitchens. **Cards:** AE, DS, MC, VI.

RESTAURANTS

HOFBRAUHAUS INN   Dinner: $9-$20   Phone: 706/878-2248
AAA   **Location:** 0.3 mi n on SR 17 & 75. 1 Main St 30545. **Hours:** 5 pm-10 pm, Fri & Sat-10:30 pm, Sun 3 pm-9
            pm. Closed: 12/25. **Reservations:** suggested. **Features:** casual dress; children's menu; carryout; cocktails &
◆◆◆   lounge. American food also featured. Overlooking river. **Cards:** AE, DI, DS, MC, VI.
German

PAUL'S STEAKHOUSE   Dinner: $10-$19   Phone: 706/878-2468
◆   **Location:** Downtown by the river. Main St 30545. **Hours:** 4 pm-10 pm, Fri & Sat-11 pm. Closed: 11/26 &
Steakhouse 12/25. **Features:** casual dress; children's menu; carryout; cocktails & lounge; entertainment. Many seats with
            view of river & downtown. **Cards:** AE, DI, MC, VI.

TANGLEWOOD RESTAURANT   Lunch: $4-$13   Dinner: $4-$13   Phone: 706/878-1044
◆   **Location:** 1 mi n on SR 75 & 3 mi ne on SR 356. Hwy 356 30571. **Hours:** 8 am-8:30 pm. Closed: 1/1,
American   12/24 & 12/25. **Reservations:** required; groups. **Features:** casual dress; children's menu; carryout. Country
            cooking dining with scenic mountain view. Smoke free premises.

HIAWASSEE—500

LODGINGS

FIELDSTONE INN CONFERENCE CENTER, RESTAURANT AND MARINA　　　　**Phone: 706/896-2262**

| | 4/1-11/30 | 1P: $89- 109 | 2P/1B: $89- 109 | 2P/2B: $89- 109 | XP: $10 | F10 |
| | 12/1-3/31 | 1P: $59- 79 | 2P/1B: $59- 79 | 2P/2B: $59- 79 | XP: $10 | F10 |

◆◆◆　Resort Motor Inn
Location: US 76, 3 mi w. 30546 (PO Box 670). **Fax:** 706/896-4128. **Terms:** Check-in 4 pm; package plans; no pets. **Facility:** 66 rooms. All rooms with balcony; many with view of lake. Spacious guest rooms, warm up-scale country decor in public areas. 4 executive rooms, $115 mountainside; lakeside $125; 2 stories; interior corridors; whirlpool; 1 lighted tennis court; boat ramp, marina; playground, croquet court. **Dining:** Restaurant, see separate listing. **Recreation:** fishing. Fee: jet ski & pontoon boats. Rental: boats, canoeing, paddleboats. **All Rooms:** free movies, combo or shower baths. **Some Rooms:** coffeemakers, refrigerators, whirlpools. **Cards:** AE, CB, DI, DS, MC, VI.

LAKE CHATUGE LODGE　　　Rates Subject to Change　　　**Phone: 706/896-5253**

◆◆◆　Motor Inn
| | 5/1-10/31 | | 2P/1B: $89- 109 | 2P/2B: $89- 109 | XP: $10 | F12 |
| | 12/1-4/30 & 11/1-11/30 | | 2P/1B: $69- 99 | 2P/2B: $69- 99 | XP: $10 | F12 |

Location: 1 mi w on US Hwy 76. 653 US Hwy 76 30546 (PO Box 347). **Fax:** 706/896-2876. **Terms:** Sr. discount; reserv deposit, 3 day notice; no pets. **Facility:** 106 rooms. Presidential suite with full kitchen $400 for up to 4 persons; 3 stories; interior corridors. **Some Rooms:** kitchen. **Cards:** AE, DS, MC, VI.

RESTAURANT

THE FIELDSTONE INN RESTAURANT　　**Lunch:** $5-$9　　　**Dinner:** $7-$17　　**Phone:** 706/896-4141

◆◆　Regional American
Location: 3 mi w; in Fieldstone Inn Conference Center, Restaurant and Marina. Hwy 76 W 30546. **Hours:** 7 am-2 & 5-9 pm, Fri & Sat-10 pm, Sun 7 am-3 & 5-9 pm. Closed: 12/25. **Reservations:** suggested; weekends. **Features:** casual dress; Sunday brunch; children's menu; carryout; salad bar; beer & wine only. Casual family dining; lake & mountain views. **Cards:** DS, MC, VI.

HINESVILLE—21,600

LODGINGS

DAYS INN　　　　　　　　　**Phone: 912/368-4146**

◆◆　Motel
| | All Year [CP] | 1P: $38- 45 | 2P/1B: $39- 50 | 2P/2B: $39- 50 | XP: $4 | F8 |

Location: 0.8 mi ne on US 84. 738 Ogelthorpe Hwy 31313. **Fax:** 912/369-0094. **Terms:** No pets. **Facility:** 52 rooms. 1 story; exterior corridors. **Dining:** Restaurant nearby. **All Rooms:** free movies. **Some Rooms:** microwaves, refrigerators. **Cards:** AE, DI, DS, MC, VI. **Special Amenities:** Free breakfast and free newspaper.

HOLIDAY INN HINESVILLE/FT STEWART　　Rates Subject to Change　　**Phone: 912/368-2275**

◆◆　Motor Inn
| | All Year | 1P: $45- 50 | 2P/1B: $50- 55 | 2P/2B: $50- 55 | XP: $5 | F19 |

Location: 0.8 mi ne on US 84. 726 E Oglethorpe Hwy 31313 (PO Box 1248). **Fax:** 912/368-5894. **Terms:** Sr. discount; no pets. **Facility:** 120 rooms. 2 stories; exterior corridors. **Dining:** Restaurant; 6 am-2 pm; $4-$9. **All Rooms:** free movies. **Cards:** AE, CB, DI, DS, JCB, MC, VI.

HOGANSVILLE—3,000

LODGING

KEY WEST INN　　　　　　　　　**Phone: 706/637-9395**

◆◆　Motel
| | All Year | 1P: $45 | 2P/1B: $55 | 2P/2B: $50 | XP: $5 | F18 |

Location: I-85 exit 6, just w. 1888 E Main St 30230. **Fax:** 706/637-6363. **Terms:** Pets, $5 extra charge. **Facility:** 44 rooms. Contemporary room appointments. 2 stories; exterior corridors; small pool. **All Rooms:** free movies. **Some Rooms:** coffeemakers, microwaves, refrigerators. **Cards:** AE, CB, DI, DS, MC, VI. **Special Amenities:** Free local telephone calls.

RESTAURANT

HOGAN'S HEROES　　　**Lunch:** $4-$7　　　**Dinner:** $10-$26　　　**Phone:** 706/637-4953

◆◆　Italian
Location: 235 Hwy 29 S 30230. **Hours:** 11 am-2 & 5-9:30 pm, Fri 5 pm-10 pm, Sat noon-10 pm. Closed: Sun, Mon, 12/25 & last 2 weeks in July. **Reservations:** suggested. **Features:** children's menu; carryout; beer & wine only. Casual Italian restaurant filled with fantastic food & pleasant waiters. Enjoy loads of homemade bread & dessert.

JEKYLL ISLAND—*See Golden Isles p. 270.*

JESUP—9,000

LODGINGS

THE JAMESON INN　　　Rates Subject to Change　　　**Phone: 912/427-6800**

◆◆◆　Motel
| | All Year [CP] | 1P: $49 | 2P/1B: $53 | 2P/2B: $53 | XP: $4 | F16 |

Location: Just n of jct US 341. 205 N Hwy 301 31545. **Fax:** 912/427-3668. **Terms:** No pets. **Facility:** 61 rooms. 2 stories; exterior corridors. **All Rooms:** free movies. **Cards:** AE, CB, DI, DS, MC, VI.

WESTERN MOTEL　　　Rates Subject to Change　　　**Phone: 912/427-7600**

◆◆　Motel
| | All Year [CP] | 1P: $38 | 2P/1B: $38 | 2P/2B: $45 | XP: $5 | F16 |

Location: On US 301, just s of jct US 341. 194 Hwy 301 S 31545. **Fax:** 912/427-7600. **Terms:** Pets dep req. **Facility:** 30 rooms. 2 stories; exterior corridors. **All Rooms:** free movies. **Cards:** AE, DI, DS, MC, VI.

RESTAURANT

CAPTAIN JOE'S SEAFOOD　　**Lunch:** $5-$14　　　**Dinner:** $5-$14　　**Phone:** 912/427-7729

◆　Seafood
Location: On US 84/301, 1 mi n of jct US 341. 31545. **Hours:** 11 am-9 pm, Fri & Sat-10 pm. Closed: 11/26, 12/24 & 12/25. **Features:** casual dress; children's menu; carryout; salad bar. Friendly, nautical ambience. Generous portions. Featuring fried, local seafood. Family-operated. **Cards:** AE, CB, DI, DS, MC, VI.

JONESBORO—*See Atlanta & Vicinity p. 233.*

KENNESAW—See Atlanta & Vicinity p. 234.

KINGSLAND—4,700

LODGINGS

BEST WESTERN KINGS BAY INN   Phone: 912/729-7666
(AAA) (SAVE)   All Year [CP]   1P: $55   2P/1B: $55- 85 2P/2B: $55- 85
◆◆◆   **Location:** 0.3 mi e of I-95, exit 2. 1353 Hwy 40 E 31548 (PO Box 3029). Fax: 912/729-1499. **Terms:** Reserv
Motel   deposit, 3 day notice; small pets only, $25 dep req. **Facility:** 62 rooms. Contemporary units with traditional
               rosewood furnishings. Max of 4 persons per room; 2 stories; exterior corridors; playground.
               Dining: Restaurant nearby. **Services:** Fee: coin laundry. **All Rooms:** microwaves, free movies, refrigerators.
Some Rooms: whirlpools. **Cards:** AE, CB, DI, DS, MC, VI. **Special Amenities: Free breakfast and free local telephone
calls.** (See ad below & color ad p 182)   [icons]

COMFORT INN   Phone: 912/729-6979
(AAA) (SAVE)   All Year [CP]   1P: $39- 69 2P/1B: $49- 79 2P/2B: $49- 79 XP: $6   F18
◆◆◆   **Location:** I-95, exit 2, just e. 111 Edenfield Rd 31548. Fax: 912/729-7819. **Terms:** Small pets only.
Motel   **Facility:** 130 rooms. Attractive gazebo with barbeque grill. 2 stories; exterior corridors; sauna, whirlpool.
               Dining: Restaurant nearby. **Services:** Fee: coin laundry. **All Rooms:** combo or shower baths. Fee: movies.
               Some Rooms: coffeemakers, 32 efficiencies, no utensils, microwaves, refrigerators, whirlpools.
Cards: AE, DI, DS, MC, VI. **Special Amenities: Free breakfast and free local telephone calls.** (See color ad below)
                                                                Roll in showers. [icons]

DAYS INN KINGSLAND   Phone: 912/729-5454
(AAA) (SAVE)   All Year [CP]   1P: $37- 65 2P/1B: $37- 75 2P/2B: $37- 75 XP: $5   F13
◆◆◆   **Location:** On SR 40, at jct I-95, exit 2, ne corner. 1050 E King Ave 31548. Fax: 912/729-6148.
Motel   **Terms:** Weekly rates; small pets only, $5 extra charge. **Facility:** 120 rooms. 2 stories; exterior corridors.
               Dining: Restaurant nearby. **Services:** Fee: coin laundry. **All Rooms:** free movies.
               Some Rooms: coffeemakers, microwaves, radios, refrigerators. **Cards:** AE, CB, DI, JCB, MC, VI.
Special Amenities: Free breakfast.   [icons]

ECONO LODGE
◆◆
Motel
Rates Subject to Change
All Year [CP] 1P: $48- 65 2P/1B: $53- 65 2P/2B: $53- 65 XP: $6 F18
Phone: 912/673-7336
Location: I-95, exit 2. 1135 E King Ave 31548. Fax: 912/729-4152. **Terms:** Sr. discount; pets, $25 dep req. **Facility:** 52 rooms. 2 stories; exterior corridors. **All Rooms:** free movies. **Cards:** AE, DS, MC, VI.
Roll in showers.

HAMPTON INN
(AAA) (SAVE)
◆◆◆
Motel
Phone: 912/729-1900
All Year [CP] 1P: $55- 65 2P/1B: $60- 70 2P/2B: $60- 70
Location: 0.3 mi e of I-95, exit 2. 1363 SR 40 E 31548. Fax: 912/729-7532. **Terms:** No pets. **Facility:** 57 rooms. Inviting contemporary decors. Max of 5 adults per room; 2 stories; exterior corridors; whirlpool, small pool, heated in winter. **Dining:** Restaurant nearby. **All Rooms:** free movies, combo or shower baths. **Some Rooms:** microwaves, refrigerators, whirlpools. **Cards:** AE, CB, DI, DS, MC, VI.
Roll in showers.

HOLIDAY INN KINGSLAND
(AAA) (SAVE)
◆◆◆
Motor Inn
Phone: 912/729-3000
All Year 1P: $59- 89 2P/1B: $59- 89 2P/2B: $59- 89 XP: $6 F18
Location: I-95 exit 2, nw corner. 930 40E 31548 (PO Box 1869). Fax: 912/729-3981. **Terms:** Check-in 4 pm; weekly/monthly rates; BP avail; small pets only. **Facility:** 156 rooms. Large attractive lawn & pool area. 2 stories; exterior corridors; wading pool, whirlpool. **Dining & Entertainment:** Restaurant; 6 am-10 pm; $7-$16; cocktails/lounge. **Services:** Fee: coin laundry. **All Rooms:** free movies. **Some Rooms:** coffeemakers, 6 kitchens, no utensils, microwaves. Fee: refrigerators. **Cards:** AE, CB, DI, DS, MC, VI. **Special Amenities:** Free local telephone calls and free newspaper. (See ad below)

PEACHTREE INN
(AAA) (SAVE)
◆◆◆
Motel
Phone: 912/882-8200
All Year [CP] 1P: $50- 65 2P/1B: $50- 65 2P/2B: $50- 65
Location: Just e of Kingsland exit 2. 1375 Hospitality Ave 31548 (PO Box 3029). Fax: 912/882-8208. **Terms:** Reserv deposit, 3 day notice; $12 service charge; no pets. **Facility:** 54 rooms. Comfortably decorated rooms. 2 stories; interior corridors. **Dining:** Restaurant nearby. **Services:** Fee: coin laundry. **All Rooms:** free movies, shower baths. **Cards:** AE, CB, DI, DS, MC, VI. **Special Amenities:** Free breakfast and free local telephone calls. (See ad below)

QUALITY INN & SUITES
(AAA) (SAVE)
◆
Motel
Phone: 912/729-4363
All Year [CP] 1P: $35 2P/1B: $39 2P/2B: $39 XP: $5 F18
Location: Just w of I-95, exit 2. 985 Boone St 31548. Fax: 912/729-2291. **Terms:** Pets, $25 dep req. **Facility:** 112 rooms. Quiet location. 2 stories; exterior corridors. **All Rooms:** coffeemakers, free movies. **Some Rooms:** microwaves, refrigerators. **Cards:** AE, CB, DI, DS, MC, VI. **Special Amenities:** Free breakfast and free local telephone calls.

LAGRANGE—25,600

LODGINGS

AMERIHOST INN-LAGRANGE
Phone: 706/885-9002
AAA SAVE   All Year [CP]   1P: $66   2P/1B: $72   2P/2B: $62   XP: $6
◆◆◆   Location: I-85, exit 4; just sw. 107 Hoffman Dr 30240. Fax: 706/885-1977. **Terms:** Reserv deposit, 14 day
Motel   notice; no pets. **Facility:** 59 rooms. 2 stories; interior corridors; sauna, whirlpool. **Services:** valet laundry.
All Rooms: coffeemakers, free & pay movies, safes, combo or shower baths. **Some Rooms:** refrigerators,
whirlpools. **Cards:** AE, DI, DS, MC, VI. **Special Amenities: Free breakfast and free newspaper.**
(See color ad p 191)   Roll in showers. 🛏 🍽 🖥 CTV ⊠ D S

BEST WESTERN LA GRANGE INN
Phone: 706/882-9540
AAA SAVE   All Year [CP]   1P: $42- 46   2P/1B: $47- 51   2P/2B: $47- 51   XP: $5   F12
◆◆   Location: I-85 exit 4, just ne. 1601 Lafayette Pkwy 30240. Fax: 706/882-3929. **Terms:** No pets. **Facility:** 101
Motel   rooms. Close to interstate, with a wooded area behind the property. Standard rooms with contemporary fur-
nishings. 2 stories; exterior corridors. **Services:** valet laundry. **Cards:** AE, CB, DI, DS, JCB, MC, VI.
Special Amenities: Early check-in/late check-out and free local telephone calls. *(See color ad p 182)*
🛏 🍽 CTV ⊠ D

DAYS INN-LA GRANGE/CALLAWAY GARDENS   Guaranteed Rates   Phone: 706/882-8881
◆◆   All Year [BP]   1P: $45   2P/1B: $50   2P/2B: $50   XP: $5   F17
Motor Inn   Location: I-85 exit 2, just e. 2606 Whitesville Rd 30240. Fax: 706/882-0156. **Terms:** Sr. discount; reserv
deposit; pets, $5 extra charge. **Facility:** 118 rooms. 2 stories; exterior corridors. **Dining:** Restaurant; 6:30
am-2 & 6-9 pm, Sun-2 pm. **All Rooms:** free movies. **Cards:** AE, CB, DI, DS, JCB, MC, VI. *(See ad below)*
Roll in showers. 🛏 🚘 CTV ⊠ D

RAMADA INN   Rates Subject to Change   Phone: 706/884-6175
◆◆◆   All Year   1P: $56   2P/1B: $66   2P/2B: $66   XP: $8   F16
Motor Inn   Location: I85, exit 4; just nw. 1513 Lafayette Pkwy 30240. Fax: 706/884-1106. **Terms:** No pets. **Facility:** 146
rooms. 2 stories; exterior corridors. **Dining:** Restaurant; 6:30 am-2 & 5:30-10 pm; $9-$15. **Cards:** AE, CB,
DI, DS, JCB, MC, VI.   🚘 CTV ⊠ 🔌 D

LAKE LANIER ISLANDS—100

LODGINGS

LAKE LANIER ISLANDS HILTON RESORT   Rates Subject to Change   Phone: 770/945-8787
◆◆◆   4/1-10/31   1P: $139- 159   2P/1B: $139- 159   2P/2B: $139- 159   XP: $10
Resort Hotel   12/1-3/31 & 11/1-11/30   1P: $89- 139   2P/1B: $89- 139   2P/2B: $89- 139   XP: $10
Location: From I-985 exit 2, 5.5 mi w follow Lake Lanier Islands signs. 7000 Holiday Rd 30518.
Fax: 770/932-5471. **Terms:** No pets. **Facility:** 224 rooms. $5 entrance fee for Lake Lanier Island; 4 stories; interior corridors.
Dining: Dining room; 6 am-midnight; $13-$25. **All Rooms:** free & pay movies. **Cards:** AE, DI, DS, MC, VI.
(See color ad p 18)   🚘 🔜 CTV ⊠ D S

RENAISSANCE PINEISLE RESORT
Phone: 770/945-8921
AAA SAVE   3/21-11/20   1P: $156- 250   2P/1B: $176- 270   2P/2B: $176- 270   XP: $20   F12
12/1-3/20 & 11/21-11/30   1P: $116- 179   2P/1B: $136- 199   2P/2B: $136- 199   XP: $20   F12
◆◆◆◆   Location: I-985 exit 0.3 mi w following Lake Lanier Islands signs. 9000 Holiday Rd 30518.
Resort Hotel   Fax: 770/945-1024. **Terms:** AP, BP, MAP avail; package plans; no pets. **Facility:** 250 rooms. Lakefront resort
with fine recreational facilities. 5 two-bedroom units. Suites, $420-$785. $5 entrance fee for Lake Lanier Island;
5 stories; interior corridors; putting green; beach, wading pool, saunas, whirlpool; marina; complimentary sunset cruises in
season. Fee: 18 holes golf; 10 tennis courts (3 indoor, 7 lighted). **Dining & Entertainment:** Restaurant; 6:30 am-10 pm;
entertainment 3/1-11/30; $11-$25; cocktails/lounge; 24-hour room service; afternoon tea. **Services:** valet laundry; area
transportation, within 15 mi; valet parking. Fee: childcare; massage. **Recreation:** children's program, social program in
season; swimming, charter fishing. Fee: fishing, sailboats, houseboats, waterpark privileges; bicycles, horseback riding.
Rental: boats, canoeing, paddleboats. **All Rooms:** honor bars, free & pay movies, safes, combo or shower baths.
Some Rooms: whirlpools. **Cards:** AE, CB, DI, DS, MC, VI.   🚘 🍽 🔜 🖥 CTV ⊠ D S

LAKE PARK—500

LODGINGS

COUNTRY HEARTH INN LAKE PARK/VALDOSTA   Rates Subject to Change   Phone: 912/559-4939
◆◆   All Year [CP]   1P: $45   2P/1B: $45   2P/2B: $45   XP: $6   F
Motel   Location: I-75, exit 1. 7008 Bellville Rd 31636. Fax: 912/559-4944. **Terms:** Sr. discount; small pets only.
Facility: 60 rooms. 2 stories; exterior corridors. **All Rooms:** free movies. **Cards:** AE, CB, DI, DS, MC, VI.
🛏 🚘 CTV ⊠

DAYS INN   Phone: 912/559-0229
(AAA) [SAVE] All Year [CP]   1P: $36- 38 2P/1B: $38- 42 2P/2B: $38- 42 XP: $3   F12
◆◆   **Location:** I-75, exit 2. 4913 Timber Dr 31636. Fax: 912/559-0416. **Terms:** Pets. **Facility:** 94 rooms. Very at-
Motel   tractive, well-maintained property. 2 stories; exterior corridors. **Dining:** Restaurant nearby. **All Rooms:** free
movies. **Cards:** AE, CB, DI, DS, MC, VI. **Special Amenities: Free local telephone calls and free
newspaper.**   [🛏] [🛁] [CTV] [✕] [D]

HOLIDAY INN EXPRESS   Guaranteed Rates   Phone: 912/559-5181
◆◆   All Year [CP]   1P: $49   2P/1B: $55   2P/2B: $55
Motel   **Location:** I-75 exit 2. 1198 Lake Blvd 31636. Fax: 912/559-4152. **Terms:** Sr. discount; small pets only, $5
extra charge. **Facility:** 66 rooms. 2 stories; exterior corridors. **All Rooms:** free movies. **Cards:** AE, CB, DI,
DS, JCB, MC, VI.   [🛏] [🛁] [CTV] [✕] [D]

SHONEY'S INN OF LAKE PARK   Rates Subject to Change   Phone: 912/559-5660
◆◆   All Year   1P: $36   2P/1B: $38   2P/2B: $42   XP: $4   F18
Motor Inn   **Location:** Jct I-75 & hwy 376, exit 2. 1075 Lakes Blvd 31636. Fax: 912/559-6779. **Terms:** Sr. discount; small
pets only. **Facility:** 120 rooms. 2 stories; exterior corridors. **Dining:** Restaurant; 6 am-11 pm, Fri & Sat-1 am;
$6-$10. **Cards:** AE, DI, DS, MC, VI.   [🛏] [🛁] [✚] [CTV] [✕] [D]

TRAVELODGE   Phone: 912/559-0110
(AAA) [SAVE] All Year   1P: $36   2P/1B: $38   2P/2B: $38   XP: $4   F12
◆◆   **Location:** I-75 exit 2, just w, just n. 4912 Timber Dr 31636. Fax: 912/559-0045. **Terms:** Check-in 4 pm;
Motel   reserv deposit; CP avail; pets. **Facility:** 80 rooms. Beautifully appointed rooms, well maintained property. Well
lit, quiet parking. Rates for up to 4 persons. Breakfast at local restaurant; 2 stories; interior corridors.
Dining: Restaurant nearby. **Services:** Fee: coin laundry. **All Rooms:** free movies, combo or shower baths.
Some Rooms: microwaves, refrigerators. **Cards:** AE, DI, DS, MC, VI. **Special Amenities: Free breakfast and free
newspaper.**   [🛏] [🛁] [CTV] [✕] [D] [S]

LAVONIA—1,800

LODGING

SLEEP INN   Guaranteed Rates   Phone: 706/356-2268
◆◆   All Year [CP]   1P: $36- 40 2P/1B: $38- 42 2P/2B: $40- 44 XP: $5   F18
Motel   **Location:** On SR 17, 0.3 mi se of jct I-85, exit 58. 890 Ross Place (PO Box 438). Fax: 706/356-7740.
Terms: Sr. discount; no pets. **Facility:** 74 rooms. 2 stories; interior corridors. **All Rooms:** free movies.
Cards: AE, CB, DI, DS, JCB, MC, VI.   Roll in showers. [🛁] [CTV] [✕] [D] [S]

LAWRENCEVILLE—*See Atlanta & Vicinity p. 235.*

LILBURN—*See Atlanta & Vicinity p. 235.*

LITHONIA—*See Atlanta & Vicinity p. 235.*

LOCUST GROVE—1,700

LODGING

SUPER 8 MOTEL   Phone: 770/957-2936
(AAA) [SAVE] All Year [CP]   1P: $37   2P/1B: $41   2P/2B: $45   XP: $5   F18
◆◆   **Location:** I-75 exit 68, just w. 4605 Hampton Rd 30248 (PO Box 613). Fax: 770/957-7993. **Terms:** Reserv
Motel   deposit, 3 day notice; small pets only. **Facility:** 56 rooms. Near Atlanta Speedway. 2 stories; exterior corridors;
wading pool. **Dining:** Restaurant nearby. **All Rooms:** free movies. **Some Rooms:** microwaves, refrigerators.
Cards: AE, CB, DI, DS, MC, VI.   [🛏] [🛁] [CTV] [✕] [D]

LOUISVILLE—2,400

LODGING

LOUISVILLE MOTOR LODGE   Phone: 912/625-7168
(AAA) [SAVE] All Year   1P: $39   2P/1B: $44   2P/2B: $44   XP: $5
◆◆   **Location:** 1 mi ne on US 1 bypass. 308 Hwy 1 Bypass 30434. **Terms:** Reserv deposit, 5 day notice; small
Motel   pets only, $5 extra charge. **Facility:** 40 rooms. Large contemporary rooms. 2 stories; exterior corridors; Large
lawn with picnic tables. **Dining:** Coffee shop nearby. **All Rooms:** free movies. **Some Rooms:**
Fee: refrigerators. **Cards:** AE, DS, MC, VI. **Special Amenities: Early check-in/late check-out and
preferred room** (subject to availability with advanced reservations).   [🛏] [CTV] [✕] [D]

MACON—106,600

LODGINGS

BEST WESTERN INN & SUITES   Phone: 912/781-5300
(AAA) [SAVE] All Year [CP]   1P: $52   2P/1B: $56   2P/2B: $56   XP: $7   F17
◆◆◆   **Location:** I-475, exit 1, se corner. 4681 Chambers Rd 31206. Fax: 912/784-8111. **Terms:** Reserv deposit;
Motel   pets, $20 dep req. **Facility:** 56 rooms. 2 stories; exterior corridors; whirlpool. **Dining:** Restaurant nearby.
Services: Fee: coin laundry. **All Rooms:** microwaves, free & pay movies, refrigerators.
Some Rooms: coffeemakers, VCP's, whirlpools. **Cards:** AE, CB, DI, DS, JCB, MC, VI. **Special Amenities:
Free breakfast and free local telephone calls.** *(See color ad p 280)*   [🛏] [🛁] [✚] [CTV] [✕] [D]

BEST WESTERN-RIVERSIDE INN   Phone: 912/743-6311
(AAA) [SAVE] All Year [CP]   1P: $56   2P/1B: $56   2P/2B: $56   XP: $7   F12
◆◆◆   **Location:** I-75 exit 54 (Pierce Ave), s 0.3 mi. 2400 Riverside Dr 31204. Fax: 912/743-9420. **Terms:** Reserv
Motor Inn   deposit; package plans; no pets. **Facility:** 125 rooms. Large, elegant lobby with fireplace. Established property
◆◆◆   on commercial strip. 2 stories; interior corridors. **Dining:** The Summit Restaurant, see separate listing.
Motor Inn   **Services:** Fee: coin laundry. **All Rooms:** coffeemakers, free movies, refrigerators. **Some Rooms:** phones,
VCP's. **Cards:** AE, CB, DI, DS, JCB, MC, VI. **Special Amenities: Free local telephone calls and free newspaper.**
(See color ad p 182)   [🛁] [✚] [CTV] [✕] [D]

COMFORT INN-NORTH   Phone: 912/746-8855
(AAA) [SAVE] All Year [CP]   1P: $54- 69 2P/1B: $54- 69 2P/2B: $59- 74 XP: $7   F18
◆◆◆   **Location:** I-75, exit 54. 2690 Riverside Dr 31204. Fax: 912/746-8881. **Terms:** Pets, $50 dep req.
Motel   **Facility:** 120 rooms. Comfortable rooms overlook well landscaped courtyard. 2-3 stories, no elevator;
interior/exterior corridors. **Services:** valet laundry. **All Rooms:** free movies. **Some Rooms:** refrigerators.
Fee: microwaves. **Cards:** AE, CB, DI, DS, JCB, MC, VI.   [🛏] [🛁] [✚] [CTV] [♿] [✕] [⊘] [D]

COMFORT INN-WEST
Phone: 912/788-5500
AAA SAVE — All Year [CP]   1P: $51   2P/1B: $53   2P/2B: $53   XP: $5   F18
◆◆◆
Motel
Location: I-475, exit 1, 0.3 mi e. 4951 Eisenhower Pkwy 31206. **Fax:** 912/788-5500. **Terms:** No pets.
Facility: 59 rooms. 2 stories; exterior corridors. **Dining:** Restaurant nearby. **Services:** Fee: coin laundry.
All Rooms: microwaves, free movies, refrigerators. **Some Rooms:** VCP's. **Cards:** AE, CB, DI, DS, MC, VI.
Special Amenities: Free breakfast and free local telephone calls.

COURTYARD BY MARRIOTT   Rates Subject to Change   **Phone:** 912/477-8899
◆◆◆
Motel
Sun-Thurs   1P: $89   2P/1B: $99   2P/2B: $99
Fri & Sat   1P: $74   2P/1B: $74   2P/2B: $89
Location: I-75, exit 55A, 0.3 mi ne. 3990 Sheraton Dr 31210. **Fax:** 912/477-4684. **Terms:** Sr. discount;
check-in 4 pm; no pets. **Facility:** 108 rooms. Rates for up to 5 persons. 6 suites; 3 stories; interior corridors. **Dining:** Coffee
shop; 6:30-10 am, breakfast buffet only, Sat & Sun 7-11 am. **All Rooms:** free & pay movies. **Cards:** AE, CB, DI, DS, JCB,
MC, VI.

ECONO LODGE   **Phone:** 912/474-1661
AAA SAVE — All Year   1P: $32- 36   2P/1B: $36- 40   2P/2B: $36- 42   XP: $4   F12
◆
Motel
Location: I-475, exit 1 sw corner. 4951 Romeiser Dr 31206. **Fax:** 912/474-4340. **Terms:** Weekly rates; small
pets only, $5 extra charge, $10 dep req. **Facility:** 60 rooms. Modest furnishings. 2 stories; exterior corridors.
All Rooms: microwaves, free movies, refrigerators. **Cards:** AE, CB, DI, DS, JCB, MC, VI.
Special Amenities: Free breakfast and free local telephone calls.

1842 INN   Rates Subject to Change   **Phone:** 912/741-1842
AAA
◆◆◆◆
Historic Bed
& Breakfast
All Year [CP]   1P: $95- 145   2P/1B: $115- 160   2P/2B: $115- 160   XP: $10
Location: I-75 exit 52, 0.5 mi e to College St, just n. 353 College St 31201. **Fax:** 912/741-1842. **Terms:** Sr.
discount; age restrictions may apply; reserv deposit, 3 day notice; no pets. **Facility:** 21 rooms. 2 stories; inte-
rior corridors. **Dining:** 24 hour beverage service. **Cards:** AE, MC, VI. *(See ad below)*

HAMPTON INN
◆◆◆ All Year [CP]
Motel
Rates Subject to Change
1P: $55- 65 2P/1B: $58- 69 2P/2B: $58- 69
Phone: 912/471-0660
Location: I-75, exit 55A, sw corner. 3680 Riverside Dr 31210. Fax: 912/471-2528. **Terms:** Sr. discount; reserv deposit; small pets only, $I0 extra charge. **Facility:** 151 rooms. 2 stories; exterior corridors. **All Rooms:** free movies. **Cards:** AE, CB, DI, DS, MC, VI. 🐾 🚗 CTV 🗙 D

HOLIDAY INN
◆◆◆ All Year
Motor Inn
Rates Subject to Change
1P: $47- 51 2P/1B: $50- 65 2P/2B: $50- 65 XP: $5 F18
Phone: 912/788-0120
Location: I-475 exit 1, se corner. 4775 Chambers Rd 31206-5364. Fax: 912/788-0122. **Terms:** Reserv deposit; 2 night min stay; no pets. **Facility:** 180 rooms. 2 stories; exterior corridors. **Dining:** Restaurant; 6 am-2 & 5-10 pm; $10-$19. **All Rooms:** free & pay movies. **Cards:** AE, CB, DI, DS, JCB, MC, VI. 🚗 CTV 🗙 🐾 D

HOLIDAY INN EXPRESS
🔺🔺🔺 SAVE
◆◆◆ Motel
Rates Subject to Change
All Year [CP] 1P: $52 2P/1B: $52 2P/2B: $52
Phone: 912/743-1482
XP: $6 F16
Location: I-75, exit 54, just nw. 2720 Riverside Dr 31204. Fax: 912/745-3967. **Terms:** Reserv deposit; small pets only. **Facility:** 94 rooms. Mid-rise located in commercial area. 6 stories; interior corridors. **Dining:** Restaurant nearby. **Services:** valet laundry. **All Rooms:** free & pay movies. **Some Rooms:** coffeemakers, microwaves, refrigerators. **Cards:** AE, CB, DI, DS, JCB, MC, VI. **Special Amenities:** Free local telephone calls and free room upgrade (subject to availability with advanced reservations).
Roll in showers. 🐾 🚗 🐾 CTV 🗙 D

HOLIDAY INN MACON CONFERENCE CENTER
🔺🔺🔺 SAVE
◆◆◆ Motor Inn
All Year 1P: $74 2P/1B: $80 2P/2B: $80
Phone: 912/474-2610
XP: $6 F12
Location: I-75, exit 55A. 3590 Riverside Dr 31210. Fax: 912/471-0712. **Terms:** Small pets only. **Facility:** 200 rooms. 2 stories; exterior corridors; whirlpool. **Dining & Entertainment:** Restaurant; 6:30 am-2 & 5-10 pm; $9-$14; cocktails/lounge. **Services:** valet laundry. **All Rooms:** coffeemakers, free & pay movies. **Some Rooms:** microwaves, refrigerators. **Cards:** AE, CB, DI, DS, JCB, MC, VI. **Special Amenities:** Free local telephone calls and free room upgrade (subject to availability with advanced reservations). 🐾 🚗 🐾 CTV 🗙 D

KNIGHTS INN-MACON
🔺🔺🔺 SAVE
◆◆ Motel
All Year 1P: $29- 35 2P/1B: $32- 40 2P/2B: $35- 45 XP: $10 F12
Phone: 912/471-1230
Location: I-475, at jct US 80, exit 1. 4952 Romiser Rd 31206. Fax: 912/477-5125. **Terms:** Reserv deposit; weekly rates; small pets only, $5 extra charge. **Facility:** 109 rooms. 1 story; exterior corridors. **Dining:** Restaurant nearby. **Services:** Fee: coin laundry. **All Rooms:** free movies. **Some Rooms:** microwaves, refrigerators. Fee: VCP's. **Cards:** AE, CB, DI, DS, JCB, MC, VI. **Special Amenities:** Early check-in/late check-out and free local telephone calls. 🐾 🚗 🐾 CTV 🗙 🐾 D

LA QUINTA INN & SUITES
🔺🔺🔺 SAVE
◆◆◆ Motel
All Year [CP] 1P: $68- 78 2P/1B: $74- 78 2P/2B: $74- 78 XP: $6 F18
Phone: 912/475-0206
Location: I-75 exit 55A, near corner. 3944 River Place Dr 31210. Fax: 912/475-8577. **Terms:** Reserv deposit; pets. **Facility:** 141 rooms. 2 stories; interior corridors; whirlpool. **Dining:** Restaurant nearby. **Services:** Fee: coin laundry. **All Rooms:** coffeemakers, free & pay movies. **Some Rooms:** microwaves, refrigerators. **Cards:** AE, CB, DI, DS, MC, VI. **Special Amenities:** Free breakfast and free local telephone calls.
(See color ad below) 🐾 🚗 🐾 🐾 CTV 🖐 🗙 D

MASTERS ECONOMY INN
🔺🔺🔺 SAVE
◆◆ Motel
All Year [CP] 1P: $28- 32 2P/1B: $32- 37 2P/2B: $32- 37 XP: $4 F18
Phone: 912/788-8910
Location: 0.3 mi s on Pio Nono Ave; jct I-75S, exit 49A, I-75N, exit 49. 4295 Pio Nono Ave 31206. Fax: 912/781-9550. **Terms:** Weekly rates; pets, $5 extra charge. **Facility:** 123 rooms. 2 stories; exterior corridors. **All Rooms:** free movies. **Some Rooms:** Fee: microwaves, refrigerators. **Cards:** AE, CB, DI, DS, MC, VI. **Special Amenities:** Free breakfast and free newspaper. 🐾 🚗 🐾 CTV 🗙 D

QUALITY INN
◆◆◆ Motel
All Year [CP] 1P: $35 2P/1B: $42 2P/2B: $42 XP: $5 D18
Phone: 912/781-7000
Location: I-475 exit 1, just se. 4630 Chambers Rd 31206. Fax: 912/781-7000. **Terms:** Sr. discount; reserv deposit; pets. **Facility:** 105 rooms. 2 stories; exterior corridors. **All Rooms:** free movies. **Cards:** AE, CB, DI, DS, JCB, MC, VI. 🐾 🚗 CTV 🗙 D

QUALITY INN & SUITES
◆◆◆ Motel
All Year [CP] 1P: $60 2P/1B: $65 2P/2B: $70 XP: $8 F18
Phone: 912/474-4000
Rates Subject to Change
Location: I-75, exit 55A, just w. 115 Riverside Pkwy 31204. Fax: 912/474-1220. **Terms:** No pets. **Facility:** 90 rooms. 2 stories; exterior corridors. **All Rooms:** free movies. **Cards:** AE, CB, DI, DS, JCB, MC, VI. 🚗 CTV 🗙 D

RAMADA INN AND CONFERENCE CENTER
Phone: 912/474-0871
(AAA) (SAVE)
◆ ◆
Motor Inn
All Year   1P: $48- 56 2P/1B: $48- 56 2P/2B: $48- 56 XP: $6   F18
Location: I-475 & exit 1, nw corner. 5009 Harrison Rd 31206. **Fax:** 912/474-5763. **Terms:** BP avail; package plans; small pets only. **Facility:** 120 rooms. 2 stories; exterior corridors. **Dining & Entertainment:** Restaurant; 6 am-2 & 5-10 pm; $10-$14; cocktails/lounge. **Services:** valet laundry. **All Rooms:** free movies. **Some Rooms:** coffeemakers, microwaves, refrigerators. **Cards:** AE, CB, DI, DS, JCB, MC.
Special Amenities: Free breakfast and free local telephone calls.   🛏 🖼 🐾 CTV ✕ D

RODEWAY INN
Phone: 912/781-4343
(AAA) (SAVE)
◆ ◆ ◆
Motel
All Year [CP]   1P: $49   2P/1B: $49   2P/2B: $49   XP: $4   F18
Location: I-475, exit 1, 0.3 mi e on US 80. 4999 Eisenhower Pkwy 31206. **Fax:** 912/784-8140. **Terms:** Pets, $20 dep req. **Facility:** 56 rooms. 2 stories; exterior corridors. **Dining:** Restaurant nearby. **All Rooms:** microwaves, free movies, refrigerators. **Some Rooms:** coffeemakers, radios, VCP's. **Cards:** AE, CB, DI, DS, MC, VI. **Special Amenities: Free breakfast and free local telephone calls.**
(See color ad below)   🛏 🖼 CTV ✕ D

SLEEP INN
Phone: 912/757-8300
(AAA) (SAVE)
◆ ◆
Motel
All Year [CP]   1P: $51   2P/1B: $56   2P/2B: $56   XP: $6   F12
Location: I-75 exit 55A, ne corner. 3928 River Place Dr 31210-1724. **Fax:** 912/757-0991. **Terms:** No pets. **Facility:** 59 rooms. 2 stories; interior corridors; whirlpool. **Dining:** Restaurant nearby. **Services:** valet laundry. **All Rooms:** free movies, combo or shower baths. **Cards:** AE, DI, DS, JCB, MC, VI. **Special Amenities: Free breakfast and free local telephone calls.**
Roll in showers.   🖼 🐾 CTV ✕ D

SUPER 8 MOTEL
Phone: 912/788-8800
(AAA) (SAVE)
◆ ◆
Motel
All Year   1P: $36   2P/1B: $38- 41 2P/2B: $43   XP: $5   F12
Location: I-475, exit 1, just e on US 80. 6007 Harrison Rd 31206. **Fax:** 912/788-2327. **Terms:** Reserv deposit; no pets. **Facility:** 60 rooms. Comfortably furnished rooms. Handling fee imposed; 2 stories; exterior corridors. **Dining:** Restaurant nearby. **Services:** Fee: coin laundry. **All Rooms:** free movies. **Some Rooms:** microwaves, refrigerators. Fee: VCP's. **Cards:** AE, CB, DI, MC, VI. **Special Amenities: Free breakfast.**   🖼 CTV ♿ ✕ D

TRAVELODGE
Phone: 912/471-6116
(AAA) (SAVE)
◆ ◆ ◆
Motel
12/1-4/30, 6/1-8/31 &
10/1-11/30 [CP]   1P: $38- 45 2P/1B: $40- 45 2P/2B: $45- 50 XP: $2-5   F12
5/1-5/31 & 9/1-9/30 [CP]   1P: $31   2P/1B: $33   2P/2B: $37   XP: $2-5   F12
Location: I-475, exit 1; just e on US 80, then just n. 5000 Harrison Rd 31206. **Fax:** 912/474-5506. **Terms:** No pets. **Facility:** 59 rooms. 2 stories; interior/exterior corridors. **All Rooms:** free movies.
Cards: AE, DI, DS, MC, VI.   🖼 CTV ✕ D

WINGATE INN
Phone: 912/476-8100
◆ ◆ ◆
Motel
Rates Subject to Change
All Year [CP]   1P: $69   2P/1B: $75   2P/2B: $75   XP: $5   F18
Location: I-75, exit 55A. 100 Northcrest Blvd 31210. **Fax:** 912/477-8180. **Terms:** Sr. discount; reserv deposit; no pets. **Facility:** 80 rooms. 3 stories, no elevator; interior corridors. **All Rooms:** free movies.
Cards: AE, CB, DI, DS, JCB, MC, VI.   Roll in showers.   🖼 CTV ✕ D

RESTAURANTS

BEALL'S 1860   Historical   **Dinner:** $12-$20   Phone: 912/745-3663
◆ ◆
American
Location: I-75 exit 52, 0.5 mi e to College St, just n. 315 College St 31201. **Hours:** 5 pm-10 pm. Closed major holidays & Sun. **Reservations:** suggested. **Features:** casual dress; children's menu; salad bar; cocktails; a la carte, buffet. Restored Greek Revival mansion with soft classical music. Creative fish, seafood, beef & chicken entrees plus signature chocolate chip walnut pie. **Cards:** AE, MC, VI.   ✕

J.L.'S OPEN PIT BAR-B-Q **Lunch:** $3-$5 **Dinner:** $3-$13 **Phone:** 912/788-1989
◆ **Location:** I-475, exit 1, 0.3 mi e on US 80. 5100 Eisenhower Pkwy 31206. **Hours:** 11 am-11 pm. Closed
American major holidays. **Features:** casual dress; children's menu. Local's favorite. Feature ostrich burgers.
Cards: AE, MC, VI. 🚹 ✕

LEN BERG'S **Lunch:** $7 **Phone:** 912/742-9255
ⓐ **Location:** In alley behind Federal Courthouse, between Broadway & Third. Old Post Office Alley 31201.
◆ **Hours:** 11 am-2:30 pm. Closed major holidays & Sun. **Features:** casual dress; carryout. Menu changes
American daily. Homemade bread, dessert, corn bread sticks & macaroon pie. ✕

NATALIA'S **Dinner:** $15-$28 **Phone:** 912/741-1380
◆◆◆ **Location:** I-75 exit 54 (Pierce Ave), just n on Riverside. 2720 Riverside Plaza 31204. **Hours:** 6 pm-11 pm.
Continental Closed major holidays & Sun. **Reservations:** required. **Features:** semi-formal attire; carryout; cocktails &
lounge; a la carte. Subdued lighting; intimate atmosphere. Extensive wine list. Fish in parchment, Bowtie
Pasta Ricotta Salata, triple cut lamb chops. Espresso. **Cards:** AE, DI, MC, VI. ✕

S & S CAFETERIA **Phone:** 912/746-9406
◆ **Location:** 2 mi n of jct I-75 & I-16, at jct I-75 & exit 54 (Pierce Ave) & SR 247. 2626 Riverside Dr 31204.
American **Hours:** 11 am-2:15 & 5-8 pm, Fri & Sat-8:30 pm. **Features:** casual dress; children's menu; carryout. A
relaxing, enclosed Southern courtyard ambience. Tasty variety of simply prepared foods. Trays carried on
request. **Cards:** AE, MC, VI. ✕

THE SUMMIT RESTAURANT **Lunch:** $4-$7 **Dinner:** $8-$15 **Phone:** 912/743-6311
ⓐ **Location:** I-75, exit 54, s 0.3 mi; in Best Western-Riverside. 2400 Riverside Dr 31204. **Hours:** 6:30 am-9
pm, Sun-8 pm. Closed: 12/24 & 12/25. **Reservations:** accepted. **Features:** casual dress; children's menu;
◆◆ early bird specials; carryout; cocktails & lounge. Southern-style home cooking. Popular locally. Comfortable
American ambience, friendly service. **Cards:** AE, DI, DS, MC, VI. ✕

MADISON—3,500

LODGINGS

BRADY INN Rates Subject to Change **Phone:** 706/342-4400
◆◆ All Year [BP] 1P: $60 2P/1B: $75 2P/2B: $75 XP: $15
Bed & **Location:** Exit 51 on I-20, 3 mi n on US 441, just w on Thomason St, n on 2nd St. 250 N 2nd St 30650.
Breakfast **Fax:** 706/342-4400. **Terms:** Reserv deposit; no pets. **Facility:** 7 rooms. 1 story; interior/exterior corridors.
Dining: Home baked treats avail during day. Lunch & dinner provided for a fee upon advance request.
Cards: AE, DS, JCB, MC, VI. 🅲🆃🆅 🅳

DAYS INN **Phone:** 706/342-1839
ⓐ SAVE All Year 1P: $50- 60 2P/1B: $50- 60 2P/2B: $50- 60 XP: $5 F12
Location: I-20 exit 51.just n. 2001 Eatonton Hwy 30650. **Fax:** 706/342-1839. **Terms:** Pets, $10 extra charge.
◆◆ **Facility:** 77 rooms. 2 stories; exterior corridors. **Dining:** Cafeteria nearby. **Services:** Fee: coin laundry.
Motor Inn **All Rooms:** free movies. **Some Rooms:** microwaves, refrigerators. **Cards:** AE, CB, DI, DS, JCB, MC, VI.
Special Amenities: Free breakfast and free newspaper. 🐾 🛬 🅲🆃🆅 ✕ 🅳

RAMADA INN-ANTEBELLUM **Phone:** 706/342-2121
ⓐ SAVE 4/1-11/30 [CP] 1P: $39- 69 2P/1B: $45- 75 2P/2B: $45- 75 XP: $6 F18
3/1-3/31 [CP] 1P: $49- 59 2P/1B: $49- 59 2P/2B: $55- 65 XP: $6 F18
◆◆◆ 12/1-2/28 [CP] 1P: $39- 49 2P/1B: $45- 55 2P/2B: $49- 55 XP: $6 F18
Motel **Location:** I-20, exit 51, just s. I-20 & US 441 30650 (PO Box 611). **Fax:** 706/342-3738. **Terms:** Small pets
only. **Facility:** 120 rooms. 2 stories; exterior corridors. **Dining:** Coffee shop nearby. **Services:** valet laundry.
All Rooms: free movies. **Some Rooms:** coffeemakers, microwaves, refrigerators. **Cards:** AE, CB, DI, DS, JCB, MC, VI.
Special Amenities: Free breakfast and free local telephone calls. 🐾 🛬 🅲🅿🆆 🅷 🅲🆃🆅 ✕ 🅳

SUPER 8 MOTEL **Phone:** 706/342-7800
ⓐ SAVE 6/1-6/30 1P: $49 2P/1B: $54 2P/2B: $58 XP: $5 F16
4/1-4/30 1P: $45 2P/1B: $50 2P/2B: $55 XP: $3 F16
◆◆ 12/1-3/31, 5/1-5/31 &
Motel 7/1-11/30 1P: $38 2P/1B: $40 2P/2B: $45 XP: $3 F16
Location: I-20 exit 5, just s. 2091 Eatonton Rd 30650. **Fax:** 706/342-3795. **Terms:** Reserv deposit; no pets.
Facility: 60 rooms. Modern compact rooms. 2 stories; interior corridors. **Dining:** Restaurant nearby. **Services:** Fee: coin
laundry. **All Rooms:** free movies. **Some Rooms:** microwaves, refrigerators. **Cards:** AE, CB, DI, DS, MC, VI.
Special Amenities: Free local telephone calls and free newspaper. 🅲🆃🆅 ✕ 🅳 🆂

RESTAURANTS

HUG'S COUNTRY EDITION RESTAURANT Historical **Dinner:** $8-$14 **Phone:** 706/342-9730
◆◆ **Location:** On US 441, 0.8 mi s of jct I-20, exit 51. 2230 Eatonton Rd, Hwy 441 30650. **Hours:** 4:30 pm-10
Italian pm. Closed: Sun, Mon, 1/1 & 12/25. **Reservations:** suggested; Fri & Sat. **Features:** casual dress; children's
menu; carryout; beer & wine only. Inviting 1850's country antebellum home serving northern Italian dishes &
steak. **Cards:** DS, MC, VI. ✕

YE OLDE COLONIAL RESTAURANT **Phone:** 706/342-2211
◆ **Location:** Center, on historic Town Square; on US 441. 108 E Washington St 30650. **Hours:** 5:30 am-8:30
Regional pm. Closed: Sun, 7/4, 11/26 & 12/25. **Features:** casual dress; children's menu; carryout; street parking.
American 1800's bank building is setting for locally owned cafeteria bank vault is papered with Reconstruction money.
Southern cuisine. ✕

MARIETTA—See Atlanta & Vicinity p. 235.

MCDONOUGH—2,900

LODGINGS

THE BRITTANY MOTOR INN **Phone:** 770/957-5821
ⓐ SAVE All Year [CP] 1P: $38 2P/1B: $38 2P/2B: $38
Location: I-75 exit 70, se corner. 1171 Hwy 20 & 81 30253 (PO Box 477). **Fax:** 770/957-5825. **Terms:** Small
◆◆ pets only. **Facility:** 148 rooms. Rates for up to 4 persons; 2 stories; exterior corridors. **Dining:** Restaurant
Motel nearby. **Cards:** AE, DI, DS, MC, VI. **Special Amenities: Preferred room (subject to availability with**
advanced reservations). 🐾 🛬 🅲🆃🆅 ✕ 🅳

COMFORT INN
Phone: 770/954-9110
(AAA) (SAVE)
◆◆◆
Motel
All Year [CP]　　　　　　1P: $55- 85　2P/1B:　$65- 95　2P/2B:　$65- 95
Location: I-75, exit 70, just w. 80 Hwy 81 W 30253. Fax: 770/914-0406. **Terms:** Reserv deposit, 7 day notice; package plans; no pets. **Facility:** 59 rooms. 2 stories; exterior corridors; small pool. **Dining:** Coffee shop nearby. **Services:** Fee: coin laundry. **All Rooms:** microwaves, free movies, refrigerators. **Cards:** AE, CB, DI, DS, JCB, MC, VI. **Special Amenities: Free breakfast and free local telephone calls.**
⊞ CTV ✕ D

DAYS INN
Phone: 770/957-5261
(AAA) (SAVE)
◆◆
Motel
All Year [CP]　　　　　　1P: $41- 45　2P/1B:　$43- 45　2P/2B:　$51- 59　XP:　$5　　F12
Location: I-75 exit 69, just e. 744 SR 155S & I-75 30253. Fax: 770/957-6638. **Terms:** Reserv deposit; weekly rates; pets, $4 extra charge. **Facility:** 60 rooms. 2 stories; exterior corridors. **Dining:** Restaurant nearby. **All Rooms:** free movies. **Some Rooms:** microwaves, refrigerators. Fee: VCP's. **Cards:** AE, CB, DI, DS, MC, VI. **Special Amenities: Early check-in/late check-out and free local telephone calls.**
⊞ ⌫ CTV ✕ D

ECONO LODGE
Phone: 770/957-2651
(AAA) (SAVE)
◆◆
Motel
All Year　　　　　　　　1P: $30- 40　2P/1B:　$36- 46　2P/2B:　$36- 46　XP:　$6　　F17
Location: I-75 exit 70, just w. 1279 Hampton Rd 30253. Fax: 770/957-2651. **Terms:** Pets, $6 extra charge. **Facility:** 40 rooms. Handling fee imposed; 2 stories; exterior corridors. **Dining:** Coffee shop nearby. **All Rooms:** coffeemakers, free movies. **Some Rooms:** microwaves, refrigerators. **Cards:** AE, DI, DS, MC, VI. **Special Amenities: Free local telephone calls.**
⊞ ⌫ CTV ✕ D

HAMPTON INN
◆◆◆
Motel
Rates Subject to Change
Phone: 770/914-0077
All Year [CP]　　　　　1P: $62　　2P/1B:　$65　　　2P/2B:　$65
Location: I-75 exit 70, e to Industrial Blvd, just s. 855 Industrial Blvd 30253. Fax: 770/914-7057. **Terms:** Sr. discount; no pets. **Facility:** 74 rooms. 2 stories; exterior corridors. **All Rooms:** free movies. **Cards:** AE, CB, DI, DS, MC, VI.
Roll in showers. CTV ✕ D S

HOLIDAY INN MCDONOUGH
Phone: 770/957-5291
(AAA) (SAVE)
◆◆◆
Motor Inn
All Year　　　　　　　　1P: $64- 84　2P/1B:　$64- 84　2P/2B:　$64- 84
Location: I-75 exit 69, just w. 930 Hwy 155 S 30253. Fax: 770/957-4103. **Terms:** Pets, $5 extra charge. **Facility:** 100 rooms. 2 stories; exterior corridors. **Dining:** Dining room; 6:30 am-1:30 & 5:30 -9:30 pm; $6-$15; wine/beer only; lunch buffet daily except Sat. **Services:** Fee: coin laundry. **All Rooms:** free movies. **Cards:** AE, CB, DI, DS, MC, VI. *(See color ad below)*
⊞ ⌫ ⊞ CTV ✕ ⊘ D

RESTAURANT

O. B.'S B-B-Q
◆
Regional
American
Lunch: $4-$9　　　　**Dinner:** $8-$18　　　**Phone:** 770/954-1234
Location: I-75, exit 70, e to Industrial Blvd, just s. 725 Industrial Blvd 30253. **Hours:** 11 am-9 pm. Closed: Sun, 11/26 & 12/25. **Features:** casual dress; children's menu; carryout. Authentic slow-cooked, hickory pit barbecue, served in family atmosphere. **Cards:** MC, VI.
✕

MCRAE—3,000

LODGING

PETE PHILLIPS LODGE
◆◆◆
Motor Inn
Rates Subject to Change
Phone: 912/868-7474
3/1-5/31 & 9/1-10/31　　1P: $55- 62　2P/1B:　$55- 75　2P/2B:　$55- 75　XP:　$6　　F12
12/1-2/28, 6/1-8/31 &
11/1-11/30　　　　　　1P: $50- 55　2P/1B:　$50- 75　2P/2B:　$50- 75　XP:　$6　　F12
Location: 3 mi n on US 441; in Little Ocmulgee State Park. Hwy 441 31055 (PO Box 149). Fax: 912/868-7474. **Terms:** Sr. discount; check-in 4 pm; reserv deposit, 3 day notice, handling fee imposed; no pets. **Facility:** 30 rooms. Vehicle entrance fee, $2; 1 story; exterior corridors. **Dining:** Restaurant; 7-10 am, 11:30-2 & 5-9 pm, Sun-2 pm; $5-$10. **All Rooms:** free movies. **Cards:** AE, DI, DS, MC, VI.
⌫ CTV ✕ ⊘ D

METTER—3,700

LODGINGS

COMFORT INN
Phone: 912/685-4100
(AAA) (SAVE)
◆◆
Motel
All Year [CP]　　　　　1P: $44- 73　2P/1B:　$50- 79　2P/2B:　$50- 79　XP:　$6　　F18
Location: I-16, exit 23, just nw. 30439 (PO Box 208). Fax: 912/685-3740. **Terms:** No pets. **Facility:** 42 rooms. 2 stories; exterior corridors. **Dining:** Restaurant nearby. **All Rooms:** free movies. **Cards:** AE, DI, DS, MC, VI. **Special Amenities: Early check-in/late check-out and free breakfast.**
⌫ CTV ✕ D

HOLIDAY INN EXPRESS
◆◆◆
Motel

Rates Subject to Change
All Year [CP]   1P: $49- 79 2P/1B: $49- 79 2P/2B: $49- 79 XP: $5   F18
Location: Jct 16 & SR 121, exit 23. (PO Box 1100, 30439). Fax: 912/685-3141. **Terms:** No pets. **Facility:** 61
rooms. 2 stories, no elevator; exterior corridors. **All Rooms:** free movies. **Cards:** AE, DI, DS, MC, VI.

Phone: 912/685-3000

[CTV] [X] [D]

MILLEDGEVILLE—17,700

LODGING

HOLIDAY INN
◆◆◆
Motor Inn

Rates Subject to Change
All Year   1P: $64   2P/1B: $69   2P/2B: $69   XP: $5   F18
Location: 4 mi nw on US 441 & SR 24. 2627 N Columbia St 31061. Fax: 912/453-3591. **Terms:** No pets.
Facility: 170 rooms. 2 stories; exterior corridors. **Dining:** Restaurant; 6:30 am-2 & 5:30-10 pm; $6-$12.
All Rooms: free movies. **Cards:** AE, CB, DI, DS, JCB, MC, VI.

Phone: 912/452-3502

[CTV] [X] [D]

MORROW—*See Atlanta & Vicinity p. 239.*

MOULTRIE—14,900

LODGING

SHONEY'S INN
◆◆
Motor Inn

Rates Subject to Change
All Year   1P: $39- 43 2P/1B: $44- 48 2P/2B: $48   XP: $5   F12
Location: Just w of jct Hwy 37 & Hwy 319 bypass. 1713 1st Ave SE 31768. Fax: 912/985-2200. **Terms:** Sr.
discount; reserv deposit, 7 day notice; small pets only, $10 extra charge. **Facility:** 100 rooms. 2 stories; exterior corridors. **Dining:** Restaurant; 6 am-midnight, Fri & Sat-2 am; $5-$7. **All Rooms:** free movies. **Cards:** AE, CB, DI, DS, MC, VI.

Phone: 912/985-2200

[🐂] [CTV] [X] [D]

NASHVILLE—4,800

LODGING

NASHVILLE INN
◆◆
Motel

Guaranteed Rates
All Year   1P: $40   2P/1B: $42   2P/2B: $46   XP: $4   F12
Location: 600 S Jefferson St 31639. Fax: 912/686-3697. **Terms:** Sr. discount; no pets. **Facility:** 30 rooms. 2
stories; exterior corridors. **All Rooms:** free movies. **Cards:** AE, DS, MC, VI.

Phone: 912/686-9445

[CTV] [X] [D]

NEWNAN—12,500

LODGINGS

COMFORT INN
◆◆◆
Motel

Guaranteed Rates
All Year   1P: $55- 65 2P/1B: $60- 70 2P/2B: $60- 70 XP: $5   F18
Location: I-85, exit 8, just sw. 1455 US 29 S 30263. Fax: 770/304-2200. **Terms:** Sr. discount; reserv
deposit; no pets. **Facility:** 52 rooms. 2 stories; exterior corridors. **All Rooms:** free movies. **Cards:** AE, CB, DI, DS, JCB, MC, VI.

Phone: 770/254-0089

[▲] [CTV] [X] [D]

DAYS INN OF NEWNAN
(AAA) [SAVE]
◆◆
Motor Inn

4/1-9/30   1P: $42- 79 2P/1B: $48- 79 2P/2B: $52- 79 XP: $5   F18
12/1-3/31 & 10/1-11/30   1P: $40- 49 2P/1B: $45- 59 2P/2B: $45- 59 XP: $5   F18
Location: I-85, exit 8, just w. 1344 S US Hwy 29 30263 (PO Box 548, 30264). Fax: 770/251-5898.
Terms: Weekly rates; pets, $5 extra charge. **Facility:** 148 rooms. 2 stories; exterior corridors; wading pool.
Dining: Restaurant; 6 am-11 pm, Fri & Sat-midnight; $7-$10; health conscious menu items; wine/beer only.
Services: Fee: coin laundry. **All Rooms:** free movies. **Some Rooms:** microwaves, refrigerators. **Cards:** AE, DI, DS, MC, VI.
Special Amenities: Early check-in/late check-out and free local telephone calls. *(See color ad below)*

Phone: 770/253-8550

[🛏] [▲] [🍴] [CTV] [X] [🐕] [D]

HOLIDAY INN EXPRESS
(AAA) [SAVE]
◆◆
Motel

All Year [CP]   1P: $53- 65 2P/1B: $58- 65 2P/2B: $58- 65 XP: $5   F18
Location: I-85, exit 9, just nw. 6 Herring Rd 30265. Fax: 770/254-0662. **Terms:** No pets. **Facility:** 83 rooms.
2 stories; exterior corridors. **Services:** valet laundry. **All Rooms:** free & pay movies. **Cards:** AE, CB, DI, DS, JCB, MC, VI. **Special Amenities:** Free breakfast and free local telephone calls.

Phone: 770/251-2828

[▲] [🍴] [CTV] [X] [🐕] [D]

RESTAURANT

SPRAYBERRY'S BAR-B-QUE
◆
American

Lunch: $4-$11   **Dinner:** $4-$11   **Phone: 770/253-4421**
Location: Just e of jct SR 70 on US 29. 229 Jackson St 30263. **Hours:** 7 am-9 pm. Closed major holidays
& Sun. **Features:** casual dress; children's menu; carryout. Family owned since 1926. Smoke free premises.
Cards: MC, VI.

[X]

NORCROSS—See Atlanta & Vicinity p. 240.

OAKWOOD—1,500

LODGING

COMFORT INN   Phone: 770/287-1000
(AAA) (SAVE)   10/1-10/31 [CP]   1P: $65   2P/1B: $69   2P/2B: $69   XP: $5   F18
              12/1-9/30 & 11/1-11/30 [CP] 1P: $52   2P/1B: $55   2P/2B: $59   XP: $5   F18
◆◆◆   **Location:** I-985 exit 4, se corner. Mundy Mill Rd 30566 (PO Box 187). Fax: 770/287-0038. **Terms:** Reserv
Motel   deposit; no pets. **Facility:** 72 rooms. 5 whirlpool rms, extra charge; 2 stories; exterior corridors.
              Dining: Coffee shop nearby. **Services:** Fee: coin laundry. **All Rooms:** free & pay movies.
Some Rooms: microwaves, refrigerators. **Cards:** AE, CB, DI, DS, JCB, MC, VI. **Special Amenities: Free breakfast and**
free newspaper.   (symbols) CTV ✕ D

PEACHTREE CITY—19,000

LODGINGS

DAYS INN   Phone: 770/631-1111
(AAA) (SAVE)   All Year [CP]   1P: $49   2P/1B: $58   2P/2B: $58   XP: $8   F12
◆◆   **Location:** From jct SR 74 & SR 54, 0.8 mi w on SR 54. 2800 Hwy 54W 30269. Fax: 770/631-3891.
Motel   **Terms:** No pets. **Facility:** 60 rooms. Massage recliners in many rooms. Contemporary room appointments. 2
              stories; exterior corridors. **Services:** Fee: coin laundry. **All Rooms:** coffeemakers, free movies, safes.
              Some Rooms: microwaves. Fee: refrigerators, VCP's. **Cards:** AE, CB, DI, DS, JCB, MC, VI.
Special Amenities: Free breakfast and free local telephone calls.   (symbols) ✕ D S

HAMPTON INN   Rates Subject to Change   Phone: 770/486-8800
◆◆◆   All Year [CP]   1P: $65   2P/1B: $70   2P/2B: $70
Motel   **Location:** From jct 74 & SR 54, 0.3 mi n on SR 74. 300 Westpark Dr 30269. Fax: 770/486-8822. **Terms:** No
              pets. **Facility:** 61 rooms. 2 stories; interior corridors. **All Rooms:** free movies. **Cards:** AE, CB, DI, DS, MC,
VI.   Roll in showers. CTV ✕ D S

PEACHTREE EXECUTIVE CONFERENCE CENTER & RESORT   Guaranteed Rates   Phone: 770/487-2000
◆◆◆   All Year   1P: $125   2P/1B: $145   2P/2B: $145   XP: $20   F12
Hotel   **Location:** From jct 74 & SR 54, 1 mi e on SR 54. 2443 Hwy 54 W 30269. Fax: 770/487-4428. **Terms:** Sr.
              discount; reserv deposit; no pets. **Facility:** 250 rooms. Handling fee imposed; 4 stories; interior corridors.
              Dining: Dining room, restaurant; 7 am-2 & 6-10 pm; Sun 7-10 am, 11-2 & 6-10 pm; $19-$27. **All Rooms:** Fee: movies.
              Cards: AE, CB, DI, MC, VI.   (symbols) CTV ✕ D S

PERRY—9,500

LODGINGS

COMFORT INN   Phone: 912/987-7710
(AAA) (SAVE)   6/16-8/23 [CP]   1P: $44- 60   2P/1B: $48- 80   2P/2B: $48- 100
              12/1-6/15 & 8/24-11/30 [CP] 1P: $44- 60   2P/1B: $48- 60   2P/2B: $48- 65 XP: $5   F18
◆◆◆   **Location:** I-75, exit 43, just w. 1602 Sam Nunn Blvd 31069. Fax: 912/988-2624. **Terms:** AP avail; no pets.
Motel   **Facility:** 102 rooms. 2 stories; exterior corridors; sauna, whirlpool. **Dining & Entertainment:** Cocktail
              lounge; restaurant nearby. **Services:** Fee: coin laundry. **All Rooms:** microwaves, free movies, refrigerators.
Some Rooms: VCP's, whirlpools. **Cards:** AE, CB, DI, DS, JCB, MC, VI. **Special Amenities: Free local telephone calls**
and free room upgrade (subject to availability with advanced reservations).   (symbols) CTV ✕ D

DAYS INN OF PERRY   Guaranteed Rates   Phone: 912/987-2142
◆   All Year   1P: $36- 46   2P/1B: $43- 51   2P/2B: $46- 51 XP: $5   F18
Motel   **Location:** I-75, exit 43; sw corner. 800 Valley Dr 31069. Fax: 912/987-0468. **Terms:** Sr. discount; no pets.
              Facility: 80 rooms. No fee 4th person; 2 stories; interior corridors. **All Rooms:** free movies. **Cards:** AE, CB,
DI, DS, JCB, MC, VI.   (symbols) CTV ✕ D

FAIRFIELD INN BY MARRIOTT   Guaranteed Rates   Phone: 912/987-4454
◆◆◆   All Year [CP]   1P: $41- 45   2P/1B: $46- 50   2P/2B: $46- 50 XP: $5   F18
Motel   **Location:** I-75, exit 43; 2 blks e. 110 Perimeter Rd 31069. Fax: 912/987-7123. **Terms:** Sr. discount; reserv
              deposit; no pets. **Facility:** 79 rooms. 2 stories; exterior corridors. **All Rooms:** free movies. **Cards:** AE, CB,
DI, DS, MC, VI.   (symbols) CTV ✕ D

HOLIDAY INN
◆◆◆
Motor Inn

Guaranteed Rates
All Year   1P: $54   2P/1B: $54   2P/2B: $54

Phone: 912/987-3313

Location: I-75, exit 43, sw corner. 200 Valley Dr 31069. **Fax:** 912/988-8269. **Terms:** Sr. discount; no pets. **Facility:** 203 rooms. Rates for up to 4 persons; 2 stories; exterior corridors. **Dining:** Restaurant; 6:30-10 am, 11-2 & 5:30-10 pm; $8-$13. **All Rooms:** free movies. **Cards:** AE, CB, DI, DS, JCB, MC, VI.

[icons]

NEW PERRY HOTEL-MOTEL
(AAA)
◆◆
Motor Inn

Rates Subject to Change
All Year   1P: $29- 45   2P/1B: $39- 46   2P/2B: $39- 51   XP: $3

Phone: 912/987-1000

Location: On US 341, just off US 41; from I-75, exit 43 then 0.8 mi se. 800 Main St 31069. **Terms:** Pets. **Facility:** 47 rooms. 1-3 stories; no elevator; interior/exterior corridors. **Dining:** Restaurant, see separate listing. **Cards:** AE, MC, VI.

[icons]

QUALITY INN
(AAA) [SAVE]
◆◆◆
Motor Inn

All Year [CP]   1P: $45- 75   2P/1B: $50- 75   2P/2B: $50- 75   XP: $5   F18

Phone: 912/987-1345

Location: I-75, exit 43. 1504 Sam Nunn Blvd 31069 (PO Drawer 1012). **Fax:** 912/987-5875. **Terms:** Small pets only. **Facility:** 71 rooms. 15 acres of landscaped gardens with lighted walkways. 1 story; exterior corridors. **Dining:** Restaurant; 11 am-2:30 & 5-9:30 pm; closed Sun; $6-$17; cocktails. **All Rooms:** coffeemakers, free movies. **Some Rooms:** microwaves, radios, refrigerators. **Cards:** AE, CB, DI, DS, JCB, MC, VI. **Special Amenities:** Free local telephone calls and free newspaper.

[icons]

TRAVELODGE
(AAA) [SAVE]
◆◆
Motel

All Year [CP]   1P: $39   2P/1B: $39   2P/2B: $45   XP: $5   F13

Phone: 912/987-7355

Location: I-75, exit 42, just e. 100 Westview Ln 31069. **Fax:** 912/987-7250. **Terms:** No pets. **Facility:** 62 rooms. In light commercial area. Good value for the budget-oriented traveler. 2 stories; interior corridors; whirlpool, small pool. **Dining:** Restaurant nearby. **Services:** Fee: coin laundry. **All Rooms:** coffeemakers, free movies, combo or shower baths. **Some Rooms:** microwaves, refrigerators. **Cards:** AE, DI, DS, MC, VI. **Special Amenities:** Free breakfast and free local telephone calls. *(See ad p 286)*

[icons]

RESTAURANTS

ANGELINA'S ITALIAN GARDEN CAFE
◆◆
Italian

Dinner: $7-$15

Phone: 912/987-9494

Location: I-75 exit 43, just w. 1500 Sam Nunn Blvd 31069. **Hours:** 11:30 am-2 & 5-9:30 pm, Fri-10 pm, Sat 5 pm-10 pm. Closed major holidays & Sun. **Reservations:** suggested. **Features:** casual dress; children's menu; carryout; cocktails & lounge. A casual dining with menu offering standard & diverse assortment. **Cards:** AE, DI, DS, MC, VI.

[icon]

MANDARIN HOUSE
◆
Chinese

Lunch: $4-$7   **Dinner:** $5-$9

Phone: 912/987-9468

Location: I-75, exit 42, just e to General C Hodges Blvd, just n. 401 General C Hodges Blvd 31069. **Hours:** 11:30 am-10 pm, Mon from 4 pm. Closed major holidays. **Reservations:** suggested. **Features:** casual dress; children's menu; carryout; beer & wine only. Lunch buffet daily except Mon. Well-prepared entrees. Large portions. Pleasant, comfortable atmosphere. **Cards:** DS, MC, VI.

[icon]

NEW PERRY HOTEL RESTAURANT
◆◆
Regional
American

Lunch: $6-$7   **Dinner:** $10-$13

Phone: 912/987-1000

Location: On US 341, just off US 41; from I-75, exit 43, 0.8 mi se; in New Perry Hotel-Motel. 800 Main St 31069. **Hours:** 7-10 am, 11:30-2:30 & 5:30-9 pm. **Reservations:** accepted. **Features:** casual dress; children's menu; carryout. Regional down-home cooking; homemade pastry & dessert. Homey, genteel ambience. Gracious, efficient servers. Smoke free premises. **Cards:** AE, MC, VI.

[icon]

PINE MOUNTAIN—900

LODGINGS

CALLAWAY GARDENS RESORT
(AAA) [SAVE]
◆◆◆
Hotel

All Year   1P: $96- 106   2P/1B: $96- 106   2P/2B: $96- 106

Phone: 706/663-2281

Location: Hwy 27, 1.5 mi s. (PO Box 2000, 31822-2000). **Fax:** 706/663-8114. **Terms:** Check-in 4 pm; reserv deposit, 7 day notice; package plans; no pets. **Facility:** 350 rooms. Suites, cottages & villas avail; 3 stories; exterior corridors; 63 holes golf, miniature golf, putting green; whirlpool; 10 lighted tennis courts; boat dock; playground. Fee: racquetball courts. **Dining & Entertainment:** Dining room, 4 restaurants; 6:30 am-11 pm; $13-$19; cocktail lounge; 24-hour room service. **Recreation:** children's program, nature program; swimming, fishing; hiking trails, jogging. Fee: boating; bicycles. **All Rooms:** honor bars, refrigerators. **Some Rooms:** VCP's. **Cards:** AE, CB, DI, DS, MC, VI. **Special Amenities:** Free room upgrade and preferred room (each subject to availability with advanced reservations).

[icons]

FIRESIDE INN
(AAA) [SAVE]
◆◆
Motel

12/1-1/1 & 3/2-11/30   1P: $46   2P/1B: $50- 85   2P/2B: $55- 85   XP: $6   F12
1/2-3/1   1P: $36   2P/1B: $40- 65   2P/2B: $40- 65   XP: $6   F12

Phone: 706/663-4141

Location: On US 27, 0.3 mi n of downtown. 31822 (PO Box 1308). **Terms:** Package plans; no pets. **Facility:** 11 rooms. Spacious rooms. 2 stories; interior corridors. **Dining:** Restaurant nearby. **Some Rooms:** refrigerators. Fee: VCP's. **Cards:** AE, DS, MC, VI. **Special Amenities:** Early check-in/late check-out and free local telephone calls.

[icons]

THE VALLEY INN RESORT
◆◆
Motel

Rates Subject to Change
All Year   1P: $50- 82   2P/1B: $55- 89   2P/2B: $72- 89   XP: $8-12   F5

Phone: 706/628-4454

Location: 5 mi s on US 27; 3 mi s of Callaway Gardens. 14420 US 27 31811. **Fax:** 706/628-4234. **Terms:** Reserv deposit, 5 day notice; 2 night min stay, weekends; no pets. **Facility:** 24 rooms. 1 story; exterior corridors. **All Rooms:** free movies. **Some Rooms:** 4 kitchens. **Cards:** MC, VI.

[icons]

WHITE COLUMNS MOTEL
◆
Motel

Guaranteed Rates
12/1-12/31, 3/1-11/2 &
11/23-11/30   1P: $45   2P/1B: $45   2P/2B: $45   XP: $6
1/1-2/28 & 11/3-11/22   1P: $33   2P/1B: $33   2P/2B: $33   XP: $6

Phone: 706/663-2312

Location: 1 mi s on US 27. 19727 S US 27 31822 (PO Box 531). **Terms:** Sr. discount; reserv deposit, 3 day notice; pets, in designated rooms. **Facility:** 13 rooms. 2 stories; exterior corridors. **Cards:** AE, DS, MC, VI.

[icons]

RESTAURANTS

BON CUISINE
◆◆
Continental

Dinner: $16-$30

Phone: 706/663-2019

Location: Downtown. 113 Broad St 31822. **Hours:** 11 am-2 & 5:30-10 pm. Closed: Sun & Mon. **Reservations:** suggested. **Features:** casual dress; street parking; fee for area transportation. Eclectic, adult atmosphere with many conversation pieces & art work. The sourdough rolls are heavenly. **Cards:** MC, VI.

CRICKET'S
◆◆
American

Dinner: $8-$17   **Phone:** 706/663-8136
Location: 2 mi s on SR 18; from I-185 exit 13, 3.5 mi ne. 31822. **Hours:** 5:30 pm-9:30 pm, Sun 11:30 am-2:30 & 5:30-9:30 pm. Closed: Mon, 1/1, 12/24 & 12/25. **Reservations:** suggested; weekends. **Features:** casual dress; Sunday brunch; children's menu; carryout; beer & wine only. Rural setting with country decor. Creole & Cajun specialties. **Cards:** DS, MC, VI.   ⊠

PORT WENTWORTH—4,012

LODGINGS

HAMPTON INN SAVANNAH NORTH
◆◆◆
Motel

Rates Subject to Change   **Phone:** 912/966-2000
All Year [CP]   1P: $74- 89 2P/1B: $74- 89 2P/2B: $74- 89 XP: $5-5   F17
Location: I-95, exit 19, just e. 7050 Hwy 21 31407. Fax: 912/966-2001. **Terms:** Sr. discount; no pets.
Facility: 106 rooms. 3 stories; interior corridors. **All Rooms:** free movies.
Roll in showers. 🛏️ 🕂 CTV 🔥 ⊠ D

SLEEP INN
◆◆
Motel

Rates Subject to Change   **Phone:** 912/966-9800
All Year [CP]   1P: $43- 59 2P/1B: $47- 65 2P/2B: $53- 69 XP: $6   F18
Location: I-95 exit 19, just w. 7206 Hwy 21 31407. Fax: 912/966-9800. **Terms:** Sr. discount; no pets.
Facility: 85 rooms. 2 stories; interior corridors. **Cards:** AE, CB, DI, DS, JCB, MC, VI.
Roll in showers. 🛏️ CTV ⊠ 🌀 D

REGISTER—200

LODGING

RED CARPET INN
◆◆
Motel

Rates Subject to Change   **Phone:** 912/852-5200
All Year [CP]   1P: $39   2P/1B: $39   2P/2B: $47   XP: $5   F12
Location: 2875 US Hwy 301 S 30452. Fax: 912/852-5029. **Terms:** Sr. discount; pets. **Facility:** 40 rooms. 2 stories; exterior corridors. **All Rooms:** free movies. **Cards:** AE, CB, DI, DS, MC, VI. 🐾 🕂 CTV ⊠ D

RICHMOND HILL—2,900

LODGINGS

ECONO LODGE RICHMOND HILL
(AAA) [SAVE]
◆
Motel

Rates Subject to Change   **Phone:** 912/756-3312
All Year [CP]   1P: $30- 46 2P/1B: $30- 46 2P/2B: $30- 46 XP: $5   F18
Location: On US 17 at I-95, exit 14. (PO Box 47, 31324). Fax: 912/756-3835. **Terms:** CP avail; small pets only, $25 dep req. **Facility:** 48 rooms. 2 stories; exterior corridors. **All Rooms:** free movies. **Some Rooms:** coffeemakers, microwaves, refrigerators. **Cards:** AE, DS, MC, VI. **Special Amenities:** Free local telephone calls and free room upgrade (subject to availability with advanced reservations).
🛏️ CTV ⊠ D

HOLIDAY INN
◆◆◆
Motor Inn

Rates Subject to Change   **Phone:** 912/756-3351
All Year   1P: $61- 69 2P/1B: $61- 69 2P/2B: $61- 69
Location: On US 17 at I-95 exit 14. (PO Box 399, 31324). Fax: 912/756-3647. **Terms:** Sr. discount; no pets. **Facility:** 136 rooms. Rates up to 4 persons; 2 stories; exterior corridors. **Dining:** Dining room; 6:30 am-2 & 5:30-9 pm; $9-$14. **All Rooms:** free movies. **Cards:** AE, CB, DI, DS, JCB, MC, VI. 🛏️ CTV ⊠ D

SCOTTISH INNS Phone: 912/756-3861
🔺🔺 (AAA) (SAVE) All Year 1P: $25- 30 2P/1B: $27- 36 2P/2B: $30- 36 XP: $3
◆◆ **Location:** 3888 Rt 1, Box 43 31324. **Fax:** 912/756-5093. **Terms:** Reserv deposit; pets, in designated rooms.
Motel **Facility:** 39 rooms. 1 story; exterior corridors. **All Rooms:** free movies. **Cards:** AE, DS, MC, VI.
[CTV] [X] [D]

RESTAURANTS

COURTESY HOUSE RESTAURANT **Lunch:** $2-$6 **Dinner:** $5-$9 Phone: 912/756-3381
(AAA) **Location:** On US 17; just sw of I-95, exit 14. **Hours:** 24 hours. **Features:** casual dress; children's menu;
◆ senior's menu; carryout; salad bar; a la carte, buffet. Family dining with southern homestyle specialties.
American **Cards:** AE, DS, MC, VI. [X]

THE DINING ROOM AND LOUNGE **Lunch:** $3-$7 **Dinner:** $6-$14 Phone: 912/756-3351
◆◆ **Location:** On US 17 at I-95 exit 14; in Holiday Inn. **Hours:** 6:30 am-2 & 5:30-9 pm. Closed major holidays.
American **Features:** casual dress; children's menu; cocktails. Relaxing dining with attentive service. Smoke free
premises. **Cards:** AE, CB, DI, DS, JCB, MC, VI. [X]

RINGGOLD—1,700

LODGINGS

COMFORT INN Rates Subject to Change Phone: 706/935-4000
◆◆◆ All Year [CP] 1P: $60- 70 2P/1B: $60- 70 2P/2B: $70- 80 XP: $5 F12
Motel **Location:** I-75 exit 140, just w. 177 Industrial Blvd 30736. **Fax:** 706/935-3900. **Terms:** Sr. discount; no pets.
Facility: 63 rooms. 3 stories; interior corridors. **All Rooms:** free movies. **Cards:** AE, CB, DI, DS, JCB, MC,
VI.
[CTV] [D] [S]

HAMPTON INN Rates Subject to Change Phone: 706/965-4100
Motel All Year [CP] 1P: $55 2P/1B: $65 2P/2B: $65
Too new to rate; **Location:** I-75 exit 140, just e. 100 Vining Cir 30736. **Terms:** No pets. **Facility:** 59 rooms. 2
whirlpool rms, extra charge. Scheduled to open summer 1997; 3 stories; exterior corridors. **All Rooms:** free movies.
Cards: AE, DI, DS, MC, VI. Roll in showers. [🛌] [CTV] [X] [D] [S]

HOLIDAY INN EXPRESS Rates Subject to Change Phone: 706/965-6500
Motel All Year [CP] 1P: $50 2P/1B: $59 2P/2B: $59
Too new to rate; **Location:** I-75 exit 140, just e. 5437 Alabama Hwy 30736. **Fax:** 706/965-4816.
Terms: Pets, $100 dep req. **Facility:** 58 rooms. Scheduled to open summer 1997; 2 stories; exterior corridors.
All Rooms: free movies. **Cards:** AE, DI, DS, MC, VI. Roll in showers. [🛌] [🛏] [CTV] [X] [D] [S]

SUPER 8 MOTEL Phone: 706/965-7080
🔺🔺 (AAA) (SAVE) All Year [CP] 1P: $44 2P/1B: $44- 46 2P/2B: $48 XP: $3 D12
◆◆ **Location:** I-75 exit 140, just e. 5400 Alabama Hwy 30736. **Fax:** 706/965-7130. **Terms:** Reserv deposit; small
Motel pets only, $3 extra charge. **Facility:** 40 rooms. Located on commercial strip off interstate. 2 stories; exterior
corridors; small pool. **Dining:** Restaurant nearby. **Services:** winter plug-ins. **All Rooms:** free movies.
Some Rooms: microwaves, refrigerators, whirlpools. Fee: VCP's. **Cards:** AE, DI, DS, MC, VI.
Special Amenities: Free breakfast and preferred room (subject to availability with advanced reservations).
[🛌] [CTV] [X] [D]

RESTAURANT

COUNTRY BUMPKIN RESTAURANT **Lunch:** $6-$12 **Dinner:** $6-$12 Phone: 706/935-9747
◆ **Location:** I-75 exit 140, 0.3 mi e to Lafayette, 0.3 mi s. 129 Christian Rd 30736. **Hours:** 6:30 am-9 pm, Sun
Regional 6:30 am-4 pm. **Features:** casual dress; children's menu; salad bar. Homestyle, family dining. Lunch & dinner
American buffets daily. Breakfast buffet Saturday. **Cards:** AE, DS, MC, VI. [X]

RIVERDALE—*See Atlanta & Vicinity p. 243.*

ROME—30,300

LODGINGS

DAYS INN ROME Rates Subject to Change Phone: 706/295-0400
◆◆ All Year [CP] 1P: $46 2P/1B: $51 2P/2B: $51 XP: $5 F12
Motel **Location:** Downtown on SR 20 & US 27. 840 Turner McCall Blvd 30161. **Fax:** 706/295-0400. **Terms:** Sr.
discount; no pets. **Facility:** 107 rooms. 5 stories; interior/exterior corridors. **All Rooms:** free movies.
Cards: AE, DI, DS, MC, VI. [🛏] [CTV] [X] [D]

HAMPTON INN
Rates Subject to Change   **Phone:** 706/232-9551
◆◆◆   All Year [CP]   1P: $68   2P/1B: $72   2P/2B: $70
Motel   **Location:** 2 mi e on US 411. 21 Chateau Dr 30161. Fax: 706/232-5272. **Terms:** Sr. discount; no pets.
Facility: 64 rooms. 2 stories; interior corridors. **All Rooms:** free movies. **Cards:** AE, DI, DS, MC, VI.
Roll in showers. ⏚ 📺 ⊠ 🅰 Ⓓ Ⓢ

HOLIDAY INN-SKY TOP CENTER
Rates Subject to Change   **Phone:** 706/295-1100
◆◆◆   All Year   1P: $61- 65   2P/1B: $67- 71   2P/2B: $71   XP: $6   F18
Motor Inn   **Location:** 2 mi e on US 411. 20 US 411E 30161. Fax: 706/291-7128. **Terms:** Sr. discount; pets. **Facility:** 197
rooms. Suite, $111; 2 stories; exterior corridors. **Dining:** Restaurant; 6:30 am-1:30 & 5:30-10 pm; $8-$15.
All Rooms: free movies. **Cards:** AE, CB, DI, DS, JCB, MC, VI.   🛏 ⏚ ⏚ 📺 ⊠ Ⓢ

SUPER 8 MOTEL
Rates Subject to Change   **Phone:** 706/234-8182
◆◆   All Year   1P: $37- 41   2P/1B: $42   2P/2B: $46   XP: $5   F12
Motel   **Location:** 2 mi e on US 411. 1590 Dodd Blvd SE 30161. Fax: 706/234-8182. **Terms:** Sr. discount; reserv
deposit, 7 day notice; small pets only. **Facility:** 62 rooms. 3 stories; interior corridors. **All Rooms:** free & pay
movies. **Cards:** AE, CB, DI, DS, MC, VI.   🛏 📺 ⊠ 🅰 Ⓓ Ⓢ

RESTAURANT

THE COUNTRY GENTLEMAN RESTAURANT   **Lunch:** $5-$8   **Dinner:** $8-$18   **Phone:** 706/295-0205
◆◆   **Location:** 2 mi e on US 411, s on Chateau Dr. 26 Chateau DR 30161. **Hours:** 11:30 am-2:30 & 4-10:30 pm.
American   Closed major holidays & Sun. **Reservations:** suggested; weekends. **Features:** casual dress; children's
menu; senior's menu; carryout; cocktails. Good variety of seafood offerings. Steak, chicken & many Italian
specialties. Country decor. **Cards:** AE, DI, DS, MC, VI.   ⊠

ROSWELL—See Atlanta & Vicinity p. 243.

ST. MARYS—8,200

LODGINGS

GOODBREAD BED & BREAKFAST
Rates Subject to Change   **Phone:** 912/882-7490
◆   All Year [BP]   1P: $55- 65   2P/1B: $55- 65   XP: $15
Bed &   **Location:** I-95, exit 2; 9 mi e on SR 40. 209 Osborne St 31558. **Terms:** Age restrictions may apply; no pets,
Breakfast   pet on premises. **Facility:** 4 rooms. 2 stories; interior corridors; smoke free premises.   📺 ⊠ Ⓓ

SPENCER HOUSE INN BED & BREAKFAST
Rates Subject to Change   **Phone:** 912/882-1872
◆◆   All Year [BP]   1P: $65- 90   2P/1B: $65- 90   XP: $15
Bed &   **Location:** 9 mi e of I-95 exit 2, on SR 40; corner of Bryant & Osborne. 101 E Bryant St 31558.
Breakfast   Fax: 912/882-9427. **Terms:** Reserv deposit, 5 day notice; no pets. **Facility:** 14 rooms. 3 stories; interior corri-
dors; designated smoking area. **All Rooms:** free movies. **Cards:** AE, DS, MC, VI.   ✈ 📺 ⊠ Ⓓ

ST. SIMONS ISLAND—See Golden Isles p. 272.

SANDY SPRINGS—See Atlanta & Vicinity p. 244.

SAVANNAH—137,600   (See map p. 291; index below)

To help you more easily locate accommodations in the Greater Savannah area, the following two indexes and maps show lodgings and restaurants in multiple cities. Listings
for these establishments are found under the heading for the city in which they are located. The Savannah area map comprises: Garden City and Savannah.

Airport Accommodations

Listings for these establishments are found under the heading for the city in which they are located.

Savannah International

Days Inn-Airport, opposite the airport/SAVANNAH
Quality Inn-Airport, at the airport/SAVANNAH

Index of Establishments on the DOWNTOWN SAVANNAH ACCOMMODATIONS Spotting Map

LODGINGS

BALLASTONE INN
Rates Subject to Change   **Phone:** 912/236-1484   ❿
🔺🔺🔺   All Year [CP]   1P: $145- 275   2P/1B: $145- 275   2P/2B: $185- 275   XP: $20
🔺🔺🔺🔺   **Location:** Just e of Bull St. 14 E Oglethorpe Ave. Fax: 912/236-4626. **Terms:** Age restrictions may
Historic Bed   apply; reserv deposit, 5 day notice; small pets only, in garden level rooms. **Facility:** 17 rooms. Handling fee
& Breakfast   imposed; 4 stories; interior corridors. **All Rooms:** free movies. **Cards:** AE, MC, VI.   🛏 📺 Ⓓ Ⓢ

(See map below)

DAYS INN-DAYS SUITES HISTORIC RIVERFRONT

Phone: 912/236-4440 **2**

3/18-10/31   1P: $89- 120   2P/2B: $99- 120   XP: $10   F16
12/1-3/17 & 11/1-11/30   1P: $76- 112   2P/2B: $86- 112   XP: $10   F16

Location: Historic district, corner of Bay & Barnard sts. 201 W Bay St 31401. Fax: 912/232-2725.
Terms: Package plans; no pets. **Facility:** 253 rooms. Across from riverfront. 7 two-bedroom units. 7 stories, no elevator; interior corridors. **Services:** valet laundry. **All Rooms:** free movies. Fee: safes.
Some Rooms: coffeemakers, 57 kitchens. **Cards:** AE, CB, DI, DS, JCB, MC, VI. *(See color ad p 292)*

Motel ◆◆

EAST BAY INN

Phone: 912/238-1225 **5**

All Year [CP]   1P: $99- 129   2P/1B: $99- 129   2P/2B: $99- 129   XP: $10   F18

Location: Historic District, corner of Bay & Lincoln sts. 225 E Bay St 31401. Fax: 912/232-2709.
Terms: Package plans; small pets only, $25 extra charge. **Facility:** 28 rooms. An elegantly restored 1853 cotton warehouse with charming, individually decorated Georgian-style rooms & 18 foot ceilings. Many brass or four poster rice beds \ & reproduction antiques. Limited private parking. 3 stories; interior corridors.
Dining: Restaurant; 11 am-3 pm, Wed-Sat 6 pm-10 pm, closed Sun; $8-$19; wine/beer only.
Services: complimentary evening beverages; valet laundry. **All Rooms:** coffeemakers. **Cards:** AE, CB, DI, DS, JCB, MC, VI. **Special Amenities:** Free breakfast and free newspaper. *(See ad p 294)*

Historic Country Inn ◆◆◆

ELIZA THOMPSON HOUSE INN

Rates Subject to Change   Phone: 912/236-3620 **1**

All Year [BP]   1P: $89- 189   2P/1B: $89- 189   2P/2B: $89- 189   XP: $20   F12

Location: Just e of jct Jones & Whitaker sts. 5 W Jones 31401. Fax: 912/238-1920. **Terms:** Age restrictions may apply; no pets. **Facility:** 23 rooms. 3 stories; interior/exterior corridors; designated smoking area.
Cards: MC, VI.

Bed & Breakfast ◆◆◆

FOLEY HOUSE INN

Rates Subject to Change   Phone: 912/232-6622 **13**

All Year [CP]   1P: $115- 200   2P/1B: $115- 200   2P/2B: $115- 200   XP: $15   F12

Location: Historic District. 14 W Hull St on Chippewa Sq 31401. Fax: 912/231-1218. **Terms:** Sr. discount; no pets. **Facility:** 19 rooms. 2-4 stories, no elevator; interior/exterior corridors. Fee: parking. **Cards:** AE, DS, JCB, MC. *(See ad p 293)*

Historic Bed & Breakfast ◆◆◆

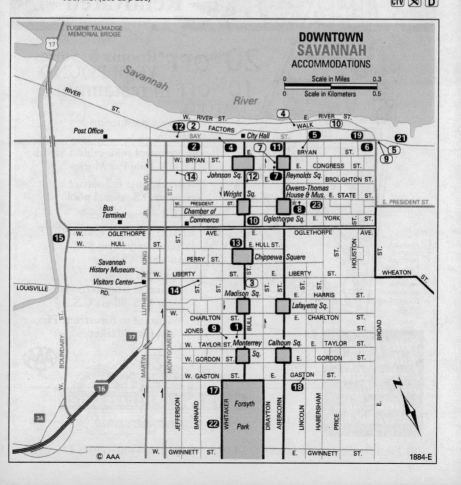

(See map p. 291)

THE FORSYTH PARK INN
◆◆◆
Historic Bed & Breakfast

Rates Subject to Change
All Year [CP]   1P: $100- 185   2P/1B: $125- 185   2P/2B: $185
Location: On Forsyth Park, between W Huntingdon & W Gwinnett. 102 W Hall St 31401. **Terms:** Reserv deposit, 7 day notice; no pets. **Facility:** 10 rooms. 3 stories, no elevator; interior corridors. **Cards:** AE, DS, MC, VI.
Phone: 912/233-6800   **22**
XP: $15
D S

THE GASTONIAN
AAA
◆◆◆◆
Historic Bed & Breakfast

Rates Subject to Change
All Year [BP]   1P: $165- 285   2P/1B: $165- 285   2P/2B: $165- 240
Location: E Gaston & Lincoln sts in historic district. 220 E Gaston St 31401. Fax: 912/232-0710.
Terms: Age restrictions may apply; reserv deposit, 5 day notice; no pets. **Facility:** 16 rooms. 2-4 stories, no elevator; interior/exterior corridors; designated smoking area. **Cards:** AE, MC, VI. *(See color ad p 293)*
Phone: 912/232-2869   **18**
CTV ✕ D S

HAMPTON INN-HISTORIC DISTRICT
◆◆◆
Motel

Rates Subject to Change
All Year [CP]   1P: $69- 109   2P/1B: $69- 109   2P/2B: $69- 109   XP: $10
Location: Center of historic district, corner of Bay & Abercorn. 201 E Bay St 31401. **Terms:** Check-in 4 pm; no pets. **Facility:** 144 rooms. Interior corridors. **Dining:** Cash Bar 4 pm-9 pm. **All Rooms:** free movies.
Cards: AE, DI, DS, JCB, MC, VI.
Phone: 912/231-9700   **11**
🏊 CTV ⓕ ✕ D

(See map p. 291)

HYATT REGENCY-SAVANNAH   Phone: 912/238-1234   [4]
 [AAA] [SAVE]   3/1-11/15   1P: $134- 159   2P/1B: $134- 159   2P/2B: $134- 159   XP: $25   F18
◆◆◆◆   12/1-2/28 & 11/16-11/30   1P: $124- 149   2P/1B: $124- 149   2P/2B: $124- 149   XP: $25   F18
Hotel   **Location:** Historic district, next to City Hall. 2 W Bay St 31401. Fax: 912/944-3678. **Terms:** AP, BP avail;
             package plans; no pets. **Facility:** 346 rooms. Car rental available. Riverfront rooms $25 extra charge; business
             rooms $15 extra charge; 7 stories; interior corridors. Fee: parking; boat dock. **Dining & Entertainment:**
Dining room; 6:30 am-11 pm, Fri & Sat-1 am; $10-$27; cocktails/lounge. **Services:** valet laundry. Fee: valet parking.
All Rooms: coffeemakers, free & pay movies, combo or shower baths. **Some Rooms:** Fee: refrigerators, VCP's.
Cards: AE, DI, DS, MC, VI. *(See color ad p 188)*   Roll in showers.   [icons]

JOAN'S ON JONES B & B   Guaranteed Rates   Phone: 912/234-3863   [9]
◆◆◆   All Year [CP]   1P: $115- 130   2P/1B: $115- 130   2P/2B: $115- 130   XP: $20   F5
Historic Bed **Location:** Se corner Jones & Whitaker sts. 17 W Jones St 31401. Fax: 912/234-1455. **Terms:** Reserv
& Breakfast   deposit, 7 day notice; pets, $50 dep req, dogs only in Suite B. **Facility:** 2 rooms. 2 stories; exterior corridors;
              smoke free premises. **All Rooms:** free movies. **Some Rooms:** efficiency, kitchen.   [icons]

(See map p. 291)

THE KEHOE HOUSE　　　　　　　　　　　　　　　　　　Phone: 912/232-1020 🈁
(AAA) SAVE　3/16-3/18 [BP]　　1P: $195- 325　2P/1B: $195- 325 2P/2B: $195- 325　XP: $35　F11
◆◆◆◆　12/1-3/15 & 3/19-11/30 [BP]　1P: $165- 250　2P/1B: $165- 250 2P/2B: $165- 250　XP: $35　F11
Historic Bed **Location:** In historic district on Columbia Square. 123 Habersham St 31401. Fax: 912/231-0208
& Breakfast **Terms:** Package plans; no pets. **Facility:** 15 rooms. European-style inn housed in magnificently restored dark
brick 1892 Victorian mansion with elevator. Gourmet breakfast. Separate townhouse avail, max of 10 persons;
2-4 stories; interior corridors; smoke free premises. **Dining:** Afternoon tea; restaurant nearby.
Services: complimentary evening beverages; valet laundry. **All Rooms:** combo or shower baths. **Some Rooms:** VCP's.
Cards: AE, CB, DI, DS, JCB, MC, VI. **Special Amenities:** Free breakfast and free local telephone calls.
(See ad p 293)　　　　　　　　　　　　　　　　　🆓 🈯 CTV ✖ D S

MAGNOLIA PLACE INN　　　　Rates Subject to Change　　　Phone: 912/236-7674 🈁
◆◆◆　All Year [CP]　　1P: $110- 215　2P/1B: $110- 215 2P/2B: $195　　XP: $15　F12
Historic Bed **Location:** On Forsyth Park, between Gaston W & Huntingdon W. 503 Whitaker St 31401
& Breakfast Fax: 912/236-1145. **Terms:** No pets. **Facility:** 13 rooms. 3 stories, no elevator; interior corridors; designated
smoking area. **Cards:** AE, MC, VI.　　　　　　　　　　　　CTV D S

THE MANOR HOUSE　　　　Rates Subject to Change　　　Phone: 912/233-9597 🈁
◆◆◆　All Year [CP]　　1P: $185- 225　2P/1B: $185- 225 2P/2B: $185- 225　XP: $10
Bed & **Location:** Corner Liberty & Barnard sts; in historic district. 201 W Liberty St 31401. **Terms:** Pets, in
Breakfast courtyard rooms. **Facility:** 5 rooms. 2 stories. **All Rooms:** free movies. **Some Rooms:** 2 kitchens
Cards: AE, MC, VI.　　　　　　　　　　　　　　　🛏 CTV D

THE MULBERRY-A HOLIDAY INN HOTEL　Rates Subject to Change　Phone: 912/238-1200 🈁
◆◆◆　All Year　　1P: $135- 185　2P/1B: $145- 195 2P/2B: $145- 195　XP: $10　F12
Hotel **Location:** On se corner of Washington Sq; in historic district. 601 E Bay St 31401. Fax: 912/236-2184
Terms: Reserv deposit; no pets. **Facility:** 122 rooms. 26 suites, $95-$125; 3 stories; interior/exterior corridors
Fee: parking. **Dining:** Dining room, coffee shop; 6:30-10:30 am, 11:30-2 & 6-9:30 pm; $11-$15. **All Rooms:** free & pay
movies. **Cards:** AE, DI, DS, JCB, MC, VI.　　　　　　　　　 🍴 CTV ✖ D

OLDE HARBOUR INN　　　　　　　　　　　　　　Phone: 912/234-4100 🈁
(AAA) SAVE　All Year [CP]　　1P: $115- 195　2P/1B: $115- 195 2P/2B: $115- 195　XP: $10　F11
◆◆◆　**Location:** Historical Riverfront District on Factors Walk; Lincoln St ramp off E Bay St. 508 E Factors Walk
Historic Bed 31401. Fax: 912/233-5979. **Terms:** Package plans; pets, $25 extra charge. **Facility:** 24 rooms. Excellent 1- &
& Breakfast 2-bedroom suites with living room & kitchen, most with river view. A lively location steps away from River Street
activities. Nightly turndown service, gracious hospitality. 3 stories, no elevator; exterior corridors; street parking
only. **Dining:** Restaurant nearby. **Services:** complimentary evening beverages; valet laundry.
All Rooms: coffeemakers, microwaves, free movies, refrigerators. **Cards:** AE, CB, DI, DS, JCB, MC, VI.
Special Amenities: Free breakfast and free newspaper. *(See ad below)*　🛏 CTV ✖ D

PLANTERS INN　　　　　Rates Subject to Change　　　Phone: 912/232-5678 🈁
◆◆◆　All Year [CP]　　1P: $99- 125　2P/1B: $99- 135 2P/2B: $99- 135　XP: $10　F12
Historic Bed **Location:** On Reynolds Square in historic district. 29 Abercorn St 31401. Fax: 912/232-8893. **Terms:** Sr
& Breakfast discount; check-in 4 pm; 2 night min stay, weekends 3/1-6/30; no pets. **Facility:** 56 rooms. 4 suites; 7 stories
interior corridors. Fee: parking. **Cards:** AE, DI, MC, VI.　　　　CTV ✖ D S

PRESIDENT'S QUARTERS　　　　　　　　　　　　　Phone: 912/233-1600 🈁
(AAA) SAVE　All Year [CP]　　1P: $137- 187　2P/1B: $137- 187 2P/2B: $137- 187　XP: $10　F11
◆◆◆◆　**Location:** In historic district at Ogelthorpe Square. 225 E President St 31401. Fax: 912/238-0849
Historic Bed **Terms:** Reserv deposit, 3 day notice; package plans; no pets. **Facility:** 16 rooms. Restored mansion with
& Breakfast walled garden. 4 stories; interior corridors; whirlpool. **Dining:** Afternoon tea. **Services:** complimentary
evening beverages; valet laundry. **All Rooms:** free movies, refrigerators, VCP's. **Some Rooms:** whirlpools
Cards: AE, DI, DS, MC, VI. **Special Amenities:** Free breakfast and free newspaper. *(See ad p 295)*
　　　　　　　　　　　　　　　　　　　　　　🆓 🈯 CTV ✖ D S

(See map p. 291)

QUALITY INN HEART OF SAVANNAH | | | | | | | Phone: 912/236-6321 | 🄵 12
AAA SAVE | 2/9-11/9 [CP] | 1P: $59- 89 | 2P/1B: $64- 89 | 2P/2B: $69- 99 | XP: $5 | | | F19
| Fri & Sat 12/1-2/8 & | | | | | | |
◆◆ | 11/10-11/30 [CP] | 1P: $49- 79 | 2P/1B: $54- 79 | 2P/2B: $59- 89 | XP: $5 | | | F19
Motel | Sun-Thurs 12/1-2/8 & | | | | | | |
| 11/10-11/30 [CP] | 1P: $44- 74 | 2P/1B: $49- 74 | 2P/2B: $54- 79 | XP: $5 | | | F19

Location: Downtown, between Montgomery & Jefferson sts. 300 W Bay St 31401. Fax: 912/234-5317. **Terms:** No pets. **Facility:** 53 rooms. Some larger, contemporary units. 2 stories; exterior corridors. **Dining:** Restaurant nearby. **Some Rooms:** radios. **Cards:** AE, CB, DI, DS, MC, VI. **Special Amenities:** Free breakfast and free local telephone calls. *(See color ad below)*

[CTV] [X] [🖧] [D]

SAVANNAH MARRIOTT RIVERFRONT | Rates Subject to Change | Phone: 912/233-7722 | 🄵 21
◆◆◆ | All Year | 1P: $139- 179 | 2P/1B: $139- 179 | 2P/2B: $139- 179 | XP: $20 | F18

Hotel | **Location:** Historic district; e end of Bay St area. 100 General McIntosh Blvd 31401. Fax: 912/233-3765. **Terms:** Sr. discount; check-in 4 pm; reserv deposit; no pets. **Facility:** 384 rooms. 8 stories; interior corridors. Fee: parking. **Dining:** Restaurant, coffee shop; breakfast buffet only 6:30-11 am, bistro menu 11 am-midnight; $6-$16. **All Rooms:** free & pay movies. **Cards:** AE, CB, DI, DS, JCB, MC, VI.

[⊃] [⊃] [📶] [CTV] [X] [D] [S]

TRAVELODGE HISTORIC DISTRICT | Rates Subject to Change | Phone: 912/236-1355 | 🄵 15
◆◆ | All Year | 1P: $42- 51 | 2P/1B: $47- 65 | 2P/2B: $55 | XP: $5 | F18

Motor Inn | **Location:** 5 blks sw of riverfront at end of US 17A. 121 W Boundary St 31401. Fax: 912/236-2853. **Terms:** Sr. discount; no pets. **Facility:** 202 rooms. Exterior corridors. **Dining:** Restaurant; 6:30 am-2 & 4:30-10 pm; Sat & Sun from 7:30 am; $7-$15. **All Rooms:** free & pay movies. **Some Rooms:** 45 efficiencies. **Cards:** AE, CB, DI, DS, MC, VI.

[⊃] [CTV] [X] [D]

RESTAURANTS

CHUTZPAH & PANACHE | Lunch: $7-$10 | Phone: 912/234-5007 | 🄵 3
◆ | **Location:** Historic district, corner of Bull & Liberty sts. 251 Bull St 31401. **Hours:** 11:30 am-3 pm. Closed:
American | Sun. **Features:** casual dress; beer & wine only. Scrumptious salad, wide selection of soup & variety of pastry. A relaxing dining experience around the corner from the crowd. Smoke free premises. **Cards:** MC, VI.

[X]

SHERMAN'S WHARF | Dinner: $12-$17 | Phone: 912/232-1565 | 🄵 10
◆ | **Location:** 4 blks e on historic riverfront. 411 E River St 31401. **Hours:** 5 pm-10 pm, Fri & Sat-10:30 pm.
Seafood | Closed: 1/1, 12/25 & Easter. **Features:** casual dress; children's menu; carryout; cocktails & lounge; fee for parking. Nautical ambience in a converted warehouse along Savannah River. Featuring local seafood, fresh oysters & raw bar. Also, sandwiches & beef entrees. **Cards:** AE, DI, DS, MC, VI.

[X]

(See map p. 291)

45 SOUTH   **Dinner:** $21-$28   **Phone:** 912/233-1881   ⑨
◆◆◆   **Location:** 20 E Broad & Bay sts 31401. **Hours:** 6 pm-9 pm, Fri & Sat-9:30 pm. Closed major holidays &
American   Sun. **Reservations:** suggested; weekends. **Features:** semi-formal attire; cocktails & lounge; valet parking;
              la carte. Distinguished contemporary cuisine. Tuna Carpaccio, rack of lamb with braised cabbage
Cards: AE, DI, DS, MC, VI.

GARIBALDI'S CAFE   **Dinner:** $20-$30   **Phone:** 912/232-7118   ⑭
◆◆   **Location:** In historic district, on se side of Franklin Square, between Montgomery & Jefferson sts. 315 W
Northern   Congress St 31401. **Hours:** 6 pm-11 pm, Fri & Sat 5:30 pm-midnight. **Reservations:** required.
Italian   **Features:** casual dress; carryout; cocktails; street parking; a la carte. A cozy, lively, candlelit cafe in
              restored 1871 Germania firehouse with original tin-pressed ceiling. A local favorite. Fresh local seafood
eclectic recipes, veal entrees & pasta. **Cards:** AE, MC, VI.   ⊠

IL PASTICCIO   **Dinner:** $13-$26   **Phone:** 912/231-8888   ①
◆◆◆   **Location:** Downtown; corner Broughton & Bull. 2 E Broughton 31401. **Hours:** 5:30 pm-10:30 pm, Fri
Italian   Sat-11 pm, Sun 5:30 pm-9:30 pm. **Reservations:** required. **Features:** casual dress; Sunday brunch
              cocktails & lounge; a la carte. Authentic cuisine of all Italy. Homemade pasta, dessert & gelati
Espresso/cappuccino. Award winning wine list. Bustling atmosphere. Daily specials. **Cards:** AE, DI, DS, MC, VI.   ⊠

THE OLDE PINK HOUSE   Historical   **Dinner:** $16-$28   **Phone:** 912/232-4286   ⑦
◆◆◆   **Location:** Facing Reynolds Square. 23 Abercorn St 31401. **Hours:** 6 pm-10:30 pm
Regional   **Reservations:** suggested; weekends. **Features:** casual dress; children's menu; carryout; cocktails & lounge
American   street parking; a la carte. In converted 18th-century mansion, downstairs tavern. Classical southern cuisine
              Crispy scored flounder with apricot shallot sauce, colonial apple pie & espresso/cappuccino. Smoke free
premises. **Cards:** AE, MC, VI.   ⊠

THE PIRATES' HOUSE   Historical   **Lunch:** $6-$10   **Dinner:** $13-$19   **Phone:** 912/233-5757   ⑤
◆◆   **Location:** In historic district at Trustees' Garden. 20 E Broad & Bay Sts 31401. **Hours:** 11:30 am-2:30
Seafood   5:30-9:30 pm, Sun 11 am-3 & 5:30-9:30 pm. Closed: 12/24 for dinner & 12/25. **Reservations:** suggested
              3/1-7/30. **Features:** casual dress; children's menu; health conscious menu; carryout; cocktails & lounge
Popular historic landmark. 16 dining rooms. **Cards:** AE, DI, DS, MC, VI.   ⊠

RIVER HOUSE   **Lunch:** $6-$11   **Dinner:** $10-$22   **Phone:** 912/234-1900   ②
(AAA)   **Location:** On historic waterfront. 125 W River St 31401. **Hours:** 8 am-10 pm, Fri & Sat-11 pm. Bake
              serves breakfast 8 am-noon every morning. Closed: 11/26 & 12/25. **Reservations:** suggested
◆◆   **Features:** casual dress; children's menu; early bird specials; carryout; cocktails; fee for parking. Nautica
Seafood   atmosphere. Fresh fish, seafood & prime rib. **Cards:** AE, DI, DS, MC, VI.   ⊠

THE SHRIMP FACTORY   **Lunch:** $9-$15   **Dinner:** $14-$24   **Phone:** 912/236-4229   ④
(AAA)   **Location:** 3 blks e on historic riverfront. 313 E River St 31401. **Hours:** 11 am-10 pm, Fri & Sat-11 pm, Su
              noon-10 pm. Closed: 11/26 & 12/25. **Features:** casual dress; carryout; cocktails & lounge; fee for parking
◆◆   Popular dining in a 1820's cotton warehouse with original heart-pine rafters & handmade gray bricks. Variet
Seafood   of shrimp entrees & regional seafood featuring pine bark stew. **Cards:** AE, CB, DI, DS, MC, VI.   ⊠

GREATER SAVANNAH   (See map p. 297; index below)

Index of Establishments on the SAVANNAH ACCOMMODATIONS Spotting Map

LODGINGS

BEST WESTERN CENTRAL   **Phone:** 912/355-1000   ④
(AAA) [SAVE]   3/14-3/17 [CP]   1P: $90   2P/1B: $115   2P/2B: $115   XP: $6-10   F1
                12/1-3/13 & 3/18-11/30 [CP]   1P: $50- 75   2P/1B: $53- 80   2P/2B: $53- 80   XP: $6-10   F1
◆◆   **Location:** 5.8 mi sw of historic district on SR 204; 2.8 mi sw jct US 80. 45 Eisenhower Dr 3140
Motor Inn   Fax: 912/352-1671. **Terms:** Small pets only, $10 extra charge. **Facility:** 128 rooms. Max of 4 adults per room
                2 stories; exterior corridors. **All Rooms:** free movies. **Cards:** AE, CB, DI, DS, JCB, MC, VI.
                                                                                     [🛏] [🖼] [CTV] [✕] [

Look for the (AAA) in our listings!

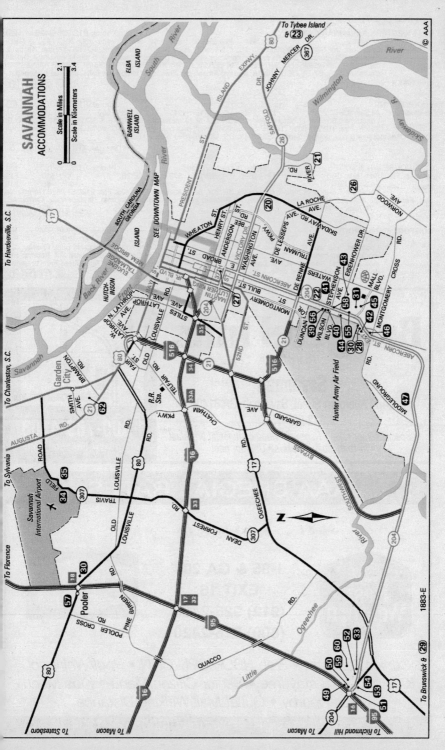

SAVANNAH
ACCOMMODATIONS

Scale in Miles
0   2.1
Scale in Kilometers
0   3.4

© AAA

1883-E

(See map p. 297)

BEST WESTERN SAVANNAH GATEWAY　　　　　　　　　　　　Phone: 912/925-2420　🏨
AAA SAVE　All Year　　1P: $44- 50　2P/1B: $54- 60　2P/2B: $54- 60　XP: $5　F18
◆◆　**Location:** Jct I-95 & SR 204, exit 16. 1 Gateway Blvd 31419. Fax: 912/925-7363. **Terms:** No pets.
Motor Inn　**Facility:** 122 rooms. 2 stories; exterior corridors; whirlpool. **Dining:** Restaurant; 5 am-11 pm, Fri & Sat 24
hrs; $7-$10; wine/beer only. **Services:** valet laundry. **All Rooms:** free movies. **Some Rooms:** refrigerators.
Cards: AE, CB, DI, DS, JCB, MC, VI. **Special Amenities:** Free local telephone calls and free newspaper.
(See color ad below & p 182)　　　　　　　　　　　　　　　　　🍽️ ☎️ ⊠ D

BUDGETEL INN　　　　　Rates Subject to Change　　　　　　Phone: 912/927-7660　🏨
◆◆◆　All Year [CP]　　1P: $40- 54　2P/1B: $45- 59　2P/2B: $50
Motel　**Location:** 6.3 mi sw of historic district on SR 204 or 12 mi ne of I-95, exit 16 & SR 204. 8484 Abercorn St
31406. Fax: 912/927-6392. **Terms:** Sr. discount; small pets only. **Facility:** 102 rooms. 3 stories; interior corridors. **All Rooms:** free & pay movies. **Cards:** AE, CB, DI, DS, MC, VI. *(See color ad below)*

🛏️ ☎️ ⊠ 🐾 D S

CLUBHOUSE INN & SUITES　　　Rates Subject to Change　　　Phone: 912/356-1234　🏨
◆◆◆　Sun-Thurs [BP]　　1P: $69　　2P/1B: $79　　2P/2B: $79　　XP: $10　F16
Motel　Fri & Sat [BP]　　1P: $66　　　　　　　　　　　　　　　XP: $5　F16
Location: 5.5 mi s of historic district, via SR 204. 6800 Abercorn St 31405. Fax: 912/352-2828. **Terms:** No
pets. **Facility:** 138 rooms. 2 stories; interior corridors. **All Rooms:** free movies. **Some Rooms:** 16 efficiencies. **Cards:** AE,
CB, DI, DS, MC, VI. *(See color ad p 299)*　　　　　　　　　　　☎️ ☎️ ⊠ 🐾 D

COMFORT INN-AIRPORT　　　　　　　　　　　　　　　　Phone: 912/748-5242　🏨
AAA SAVE　All Year [CP]　　1P: $45- 55　2P/1B: $50- 60　2P/2B: $50- 60　XP: $10　F18
◆◆　**Location:** I-95 exit 18, 0.3 mi e. 1016 Hwy 80 31408. Fax: 912/748-6858. **Terms:** No pets. **Facility:** 101
Motel　rooms. 1 two-bedroom unit. 3 stories; exterior corridors. **Dining:** Coffee shop nearby. **All Rooms:** free
movies. **Some Rooms:** VCP's. **Cards:** AE, CB, DI, DS, JCB, MC, VI. **Special Amenities:** Free breakfast
and free local telephone calls.　　　　　　　　　　　　　　　　　☎️ ☎️ ⊠ D

(See map p. 297)

COUNTRY INN AND SUITES
Motel
Phone: 912/352-2671   42
Under construction; **Location:** 5.6 mi sw of historic distric. Adjacent to mall. 7576 White Bluff 31405. **Facility:** 62 rooms. Scheduled to open fall 1997; 3 stories; interior corridors.

COURTYARD BY MARRIOTT   Rates Subject to Change   Phone: 912/354-7878   39
◆◆   Sun-Thurs   1P: $89- 92   2P/1B: $92   2P/2B: $92   XP: $10   F18
Motor Inn   Fri & Sat   1P: $72   2P/1B: $75   2P/2B: $75
Location: 5.5 mi sw of historic district on SR 204 (Abercorn St) or 12.5 mi ne of I-95, exit 16 & SR 204. 6703 Abercorn St 31405. Fax: 912/354-1432. **Terms:** Sr. discount; check-in 4 pm; reserv deposit; no pets. **Facility:** 144 rooms. Max of 5 persons per room; 3 stories; interior corridors. **Dining:** Restaurant; 6:30-10 am, Sat & Sun 7 am-12:30 pm. **All Rooms:** free & pay movies. **Cards:** AE, DI, DS, MC, VI.   📶 CTV 🚫 ✕ 🔗 D S

DAYS INN-AIRPORT   Guaranteed Rates   Phone: 912/966-5000   35
◆◆   All Year   1P: $65   2P/1B: $70   2P/2B: $70   XP: $5   F18
Motor Inn   **Location:** Opposite Savannah International Airport; on SR 307. 2500 Dean Forest Rd 31408. Fax: 912/966-5000. **Terms:** Sr. discount; reserv deposit; no pets. **Facility:** 121 rooms. 2 stories; exterior corridors. **Dining:** Restaurant; 6:30 am-10 pm; $7-$13. **All Rooms:** free & pay movies. **Cards:** AE, CB, DI, DS, MC, VI.   📶 ✈ CTV ✕ 🔗 D

DAYS INN-I-95/204   Guaranteed Rates   Phone: 912/925-3680   59
◆◆   All Year   1P: $43- 65   2P/1B: $46- 65   2P/2B: $43- 65   XP: $6   F17
Motel   **Location:** Jct I-95 & SR 204, exit 16. 31419 (Rt 4, Box 441C). Fax: 912/925-3680. **Terms:** Sr. discount; pets. **Facility:** 82 rooms. 3 stories; interior corridors. **All Rooms:** free movies. **Cards:** AE, CB, DI, DS, JCB, MC, VI. *(See color ad below)*   🍴 📶 CTV ✕ D

DAYS INN-OGLETHORPE MALL   Guaranteed Rates   Phone: 912/352-4455   45
◆   All Year   1P: $49- 79   2P/1B: $55- 85   2P/2B: $55- 85   XP: $6   F12
Motor Inn   **Location:** 5.8 mi sw just off SR 204; 2.8 mi sw of jct US 80. 114 Mall Blvd 31406. Fax: 912/352-0395. **Terms:** Sr. discount; no pets. **Facility:** 122 rooms. 2 stories; exterior corridors. **Dining:** Restaurant; 6 am-8:30 pm; $6-$11. **All Rooms:** free movies. **Cards:** AE, CB, DI, DS, MC, VI. *(See ad p 412)*   📶 CTV ✕ D

DAYS INN SOUTHSIDE   Rates Subject to Change   Phone: 912/927-7720   47
◆◆   3/16-3/18 [CP]   1P: $100- 125   2P/1B: $100- 125   2P/2B: $100- 125   XP: $5   F18
Motel   12/1-3/15 & 3/19-11/30 [CP]   1P: $60- 100   2P/1B: $60- 100   2P/2B: $60- 100   XP: $5   F18
Location: 10 mi sw of downtown on SR 204; 8 mi ne of jct I-95 & SR 204 (exit 16). 11750 Abercorn St 31419. Fax: 912/925-8424. **Terms:** Sr. discount; reserv deposit; no pets. **Facility:** 114 rooms. 2 stories; exterior corridors. **All Rooms:** free movies. **Cards:** AE, DI, DS, MC, VI. *(See color ad below)*   Roll in showers. CTV ✕ D

(See map p. 297)

ECONO LODGE   Rates Subject to Change   **Phone: 912/352-1657**
◆◆   All Year   1P: $34- 55   2P/1B: $38- 55   2P/2B: $48- 55   XP: $5   F
Motel   **Location:** 6 mi sw on SR 204 (Abercorn St); 3 mi sw of jct US 80 (Victory Dr). 7500 Abercorn St 314
Fax: 912/352-1657. **Terms:** Reserv deposit; no pets. **Facility:** 74 rooms. 2 stories; exterior corrido
All Rooms: free movies. **Cards:** AE, CB, DI, DS, MC, VI.   [CTV] [✕] [

ECONO LODGE - SAVANNAH POOLER   **Phone: 912/748-4124**
ⒶⒶⒶ SAVE   All Year [CP]   1P: $59- 79   2P/1B: $59- 79   2P/2B: $59- 79   XP: $6   F
◆◆   **Location:** I-95 exit 18, 0.3 mi w. 500 E Hwy 80 31322. Fax: 912/748-2377. **Terms:** Reserv deposit; no pe
Motel   **Facility:** 105 rooms. Large contemporary rooms. 1 story; exterior corridors. **Dining:** Restaurant near
Services: valet laundry. **All Rooms:** free movies. **Some Rooms:** microwaves, refrigerators, whirlpoo
Cards: AE, CB, DI, DS, JCB, MC, VI. **Special Amenities: Free breakfast and free local telephone calls**
[📷] [CTV] [✕] [

FAIRFIELD INN   Rates Subject to Change   **Phone: 912/353-7100**
◆◆◆   Fri & Sat [CP]   1P: $68   2P/1B: $68   2P/2B: $71   XP: $7-10   F
Motel   Sun-Thurs [CP]   1P: $42- 60   2P/1B: $48- 60   2P/2B: $50- 65   XP: $7-10   F
Location: 12.5 mi ne of I-95, exit 16 & SR 204 or 5.5 mi sw on SR 204; 2.5 mi sw of jct US 80E & SR 20
2 Lee Blvd 31405. Fax: 912/353-7100. **Terms:** Sr. discount; reserv deposit; no pets. **Facility:** 135 rooms. 3 storie
interior/exterior corridors. **All Rooms:** free movies. **Cards:** AE, DI, DS, MC, VI.   [📷] [CTV] [✕] [🍽] [D] [

HAMPTON INN-MIDTOWN   Rates Subject to Change   **Phone: 912/355-4100**
◆◆◆   All Year [CP]   1P: $57- 69   2P/1B: $62- 74   2P/2B: $62- 74
Motel   **Location:** 5 mi s on SR 204 Abercorn St, just e. 201 Stephenson Ave 31405. Fax: 912/356-5385. **Terms:**
pets. **Facility:** 129 rooms. Max of 4 adults per room; 2 stories; exterior corridors. **All Rooms:** free movie
Cards: AE, CB, DI, DS, MC, VI. *(See ad below)*   [📷] [CTV] [✕] [

HAMPTON INN-SAVANNAH I-95 GATEWAY   Rates Subject to Change   **Phone: 912/925-1212**
◆◆◆   All Year [CP]   1P: $58- 74   2P/1B: $66- 84   2P/2B: $69- 84
Motel   **Location:** I-95, exit 16, just e on SR 204. 17007 Abercorn St 31419. Fax: 912/925-1227. **Terms:**
discount; no pets. **Facility:** 60 rooms. Max of 5 adults per room; 2 stories; exterior corrido
All Rooms: free movies. **Cards:** AE, CB, DI, DS, MC, VI.   [📷] [CTV] [✕] [

HOLIDAY INN-MIDTOWN   Rates Subject to Change   **Phone: 912/352-7100**
◆◆◆   All Year   1P: $69   2P/1B: $75   2P/2B: $75   XP: $6   F
Motor Inn   **Location:** 5.8 mi sw on SR 204 from historic district. 7100 Abercorn St 31406. Fax: 912/355-64
Terms: Sr. discount; no pets. **Facility:** 174 rooms. 2 stories; exterior corridors. **Dining:** Dining room; 6:
am-2 & 5:30-10 pm; $10-$16. **All Rooms:** free & pay movies. **Cards:** AE, CB, DI, DS, JCB, MC, VI. [📷] [✈] [CTV] [✕] [

e map p. 297)

LIDAY INN SOUTH — Phone: 912/925-2770 — **54**
All Year — 1P: $55- 65 — 2P/1B: $55- 65 — 2P/2B: $55- 65 — XP: $5 — F18
Location: I-95, exit 16, se corner. (PO Box 441B Rte. 4, 31419). Fax: 912/925-2770.
Terms: Weekly/monthly rates; package plans; pets. **Facility:** 177 rooms. 2 stories; exterior corridors; wading pool. **Dining & Entertainment:** Restaurant; 6:30 am-10:30 & 5-10 pm; $9-$18; cocktail lounge; entertainment. **Services:** Fee: coin laundry. **All Rooms:** free movies. **Some Rooms:** coffeemakers, refrigerators. **Cards:** AE, CB, DI, DS, MC, VI. **Special Amenities:** Free local telephone calls and free newspaper.

ERIAL SUITES — Rates Subject to Change — Phone: 912/354-8560 — **43**
All Year — 1P: $75- 95 — 2P/1B: $75- 95 — 2P/2B: $75- 95 — XP: $10 — D15
Location: 5.8 mi sw of historic district on SR 204, 2 blks e on Eisenhower Dr. 7110 Hodgson Memorial Dr 31406. Fax: 912/356-1438. **Terms:** Sr. discount; age restrictions may apply; no pets. **Facility:** 52 rooms. 3 stories; interior corridors. **All Rooms:** free movies. **Cards:** AE, DS, MC. — Roll in showers.

QUINTA INN — Phone: 912/355-3004 — **40**
All Year [CP] — 1P: $51- 58 — 2P/1B: $58- 64 — 2P/2B: $58- 64 — XP: $7 — F18
Location: 5.5 mi sw of historic district, via SR 204. 6805 Abercorn St 31405-5822. Fax: 912/355-0143.
Terms: Small pets only. **Facility:** 154 rooms. 2 stories; exterior corridors. **Dining:** Restaurant nearby. **Services:** valet laundry. **All Rooms:** free & pay movies. **Some Rooms:** microwaves, refrigerators. **Cards:** AE, CB, DI, DS, MC, VI. **Special Amenities:** Free breakfast and free local telephone calls.
(e color ad below)

QUINTA INN-SAVANNAH I-95 — Phone: 912/925-9505 — **51**
All Year [CP] — 1P: $50- 75 — 2P/1B: $50- 75 — 2P/2B: $50- 75 — XP: $5 — F14
Location: I-95 exit 16, just e off SR 204. 6 Gateway Blvd S 31419. Fax: 912/925-3495. **Terms:** No pets.
Facility: 120 rooms. Upscale room furnishings. 2 stories; exterior corridors. **Dining:** Restaurant nearby. **All Rooms:** free movies. **Cards:** AE, DI, DS, MC, VI. **Special Amenities:** Free breakfast and free local telephone calls. *(See color ad below)*

ALITY INN-AIRPORT — Rates Subject to Change — Phone: 912/964-1421 — **34**
All Year — 1P: $54 — 2P/1B: $59 — 2P/2B: $59 — XP: $8 — F16
Location: On SR 307. 1130 Bob Harmon Rd 31408. Fax: 912/966-5646. **Terms:** Reserv deposit; pets, $10 extra charge. **Facility:** 171 rooms. Suites avail, $85; 2 stories; interior corridors. **Dining:** Dining room; 6:30-2 & 6-9 pm; lunch buffet Mon-Fri; $11-$23. **All Rooms:** free movies. **Cards:** AE, DI, DS, MC, VI.

ALITY INN & SUITES — Phone: 912/925-6666 — **49**
All Year — 1P: $80- 120 — 2P/1B: $80- 120 — 2P/2B: $80- 120 — XP: $5 — F18
Location: Jct I-95, Hwy 204 exit 16, ne corner. 6 Gateway Blvd E 31419. Fax: 912/927-3110.
Terms: Package plans; 2 night min stay; no pets. **Facility:** 107 rooms. Well decorated inviting rooms. 18 two-bedroom units. 1-bedroom suites, $110-$200. Handling fee imposed; 2 stories, no elevator; interior/exterior corridors; sauna, whirlpool. **Services:** Fee: coin laundry. **All Rooms:** coffeemakers, microwaves, free movies, refrigerators, combo or shower baths. **Some Rooms:** efficiency, whirlpools. **Cards:** AE, CB, DI, DS, JCB, MC, VI. **Special Amenities:** Free breakfast and free local telephone calls.
Roll in showers.

DNEY'S INN — Phone: 912/925-7050 — **33**
2/1-4/30 & 6/16-9/1 [CP] — 1P: $53 — 2P/1B: $58 — 2P/2B: $58- 62 — XP: $5 — F18
12/1-1/31, 5/1-6/15 &
9/2-11/30 [CP] — 1P: $48 — 2P/1B: $48- 53 — 2P/2B: $50- 55 — XP: $5 — F18
Location: I-95 exit 16, SR 204, ne corner. 17003 Abercorn St 31419. Fax: 912/925-3443. **Terms:** Reserv deposit, 14 day notice; pets, $20 dep req. **Facility:** 65 rooms. 2 stories; exterior corridors; small pool. **Some Rooms:** microwaves, refrigerators. **Cards:** AE, DI, DS, MC, VI.
(e color ad p 300)

EP INN — Rates Subject to Change — Phone: 912/921-1010 — **60**
All Year [CP] — 1P: $44- 75 — 2P/1B: $44- 79 — 2P/2B: $44- 89 — XP: $5 — F18
Location: I-95, exit 16, ne corner of frontage road. 17013 Abercorn St 31419. **Terms:** No pets. **Facility:** 51 rooms. 2 stories; interior corridors. **All Rooms:** free movies. **Cards:** AE, DI, DS, MC, VI.
Roll in showers.

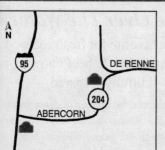

(See map p. 297)

TRAVELODGE SAVANNAH I-95   Phone: 912/927-2999

(AAA) (SAVE) All Year [CP]   1P: $40- 45 2P/1B: $45- 47 2P/2B: $55   XP: $5

◆◆ **Location:** I-95, exit 16, just e off SR 204. 390 Canebrake Rd 31419. Fax: 912/927-9830. **Terms:** Small
Motel only, $5 extra charge. **Facility:** 56 rooms. 2 stories; exterior corridors; small pool. **Dining:** Restau
nearby. **All Rooms:** coffeemakers, free movies. **Some Rooms:** Fee: VCP's. **Cards:** AE, CB, DI, DS, MC

🛏️ 📱 CTV ✕

RESTAURANTS

ELIZABETH ON 37TH   **Dinner:** $22-$30   Phone: 912/236-5547
◆◆◆ **Location:** Corner of Drayton & 37th. 105 E 37th St 31401. **Hours:** 6 pm-10 pm. Closed major holidays,
Regional & 2 weeks in Aug. **Reservations:** suggested. **Features:** semi-formal attire; cocktails; street parking. Man
American in Victorian district. Warm, candlelit ambience.Variety of creative, skillfully-prepared entrees by chef/ow
James Beard award for best chef in state. Smoke free premises. **Cards:** AE, DI, DS, MC, VI.

JOHNNY HARRIS RESTAURANT   **Lunch:** $7-$8   **Dinner:** $8-$22   Phone: 912/354-7810
(AAA) **Location:** 2.8 mi e on US 80 (Victory Dr). 1651 E Victory Dr 31404. **Hours:** 11:30 am-10:30 pm, F
Sat-midnight. Closed: Sun, 1/1 & 12/25. **Reservations:** suggested; weekends. **Features:** casual dr
◆◆ children's menu; carryout; cocktails & lounge; a la carte. Popular area landmark since 1924. Round di
American room has a domed blue ceiling with "stars". Mostly from-scratch cooking including famous hickory-smo
barbecue. Ballroom dancing on Sat, jackets required. **Cards:** AE, DI, DS, MC, VI.

KYOTO JAPANESE STEAK & SEAFOOD HOUSE   **Dinner:** $13-$22   Phone: 912/355-9800
◆◆ **Location:** At Chatham Plaza; 6 mi s of historic district via SR 204. 7805 Abercorn St 31406. **Hour**
Ethnic pm-10 pm, Fri & Sat-11 pm. Closed: 11/26, 12/25 & Super Bowl. **Reservations:** required; weeke
Features: casual dress; children's menu; early bird specials; cocktails; minimum charge-$5. Very pop
Hibachi-style cooking at tables of 8 by talented, entertaining chefs. Featuring steak, chicken & shrimp prepa
Japanese-style. Smoke free premises. **Cards:** AE, CB, DI, MC, VI.

LOVE'S SEAFOOD RESTAURANT   **Dinner:** $9-$20   Phone: 912/925-3616
◆◆ **Location:** On US 17, 2.5 mi s of jct SR 204; or I-95, exit 15, 1.5 mi e on SR 144, then 2.5 mi n on US
Steak and 6817 Basin Rd, Rt 17S 31419. **Hours:** 5 pm-10 pm, Sun noon-9 pm. Closed: Mon & 12
Seafood **Features:** casual dress; children's menu; carryout; beer & wine only. Friendly dining overlooking so
Ogeechee River. Family-operated since 1949. Specialty is golden-fried river catfish & local seafood. Orig
family recipes. A rustic ambience. Chef/owner. **Cards:** AE, CB, DI, DS, MC, VI.

THE MILL BREWERY, BAKERY & EATERY   **Lunch:** $5-$9   **Dinner:** $5-$13   Phone: 912/355-1625
◆ **Location:** At Chatham Plaza; 6 mi s of historic district via SR 204. 7805 Abercorn 31406. **Hours:**
American am-11 pm, Fri-11:30 pm, Sat 11 am-11:30 pm, Sun 11 am-10:30 pm. Closed major holid
Features: casual dress; children's menu; carryout; cocktails; a la carte. Friendly, rustic setting with too
artifacts of yesteryear. Aromas of baking breads from the open-air kitchen. **Cards:** AE, DS, MC, VI.

PEARL'S ELEGANT PELICAN   **Dinner:** $7-$17   Phone: 912/352-8221
◆◆ **Location:** 5.8 mi sw via SR 204 (Abercorn St) to Eisenhower Dr, 2.5 mi e to LaRoche Ave, then 2 bl
Seafood (Eisenhower becomes Nottingham Rd). 7000 LaRoche Ave 31406-4213. **Hours:** 5 pm-10 pm, F
Sat-10:30 pm. Closed: 11/26 & 12/25. **Features:** casual dress; children's menu; carryout; cocktails & lou
Bustling casual eatery on river. Strong nautical decor. Regional fish specials plus seafood boiled in lowcountry traditio
fried. **Cards:** AE, DI, DS, MC, VI.

THE RIVER'S END   **Dinner:** $11-$22   Phone: 912/354-2973
(AAA) (SAVE) **Location:** 5.5 mi e on US 80 (Victory Dr); 0.5 mi s. 3122 River Dr 31404. **Hours:** 5 pm-10 pm, Fri & Sa
pm. Closed: Sun, 11/26, 12/24 & 12/25. **Reservations:** suggested. **Features:** casual dress; children's m
◆◆ cocktails & lounge; entertainment. Overlooking placid Wilmington River. Also featuring steak, veal, poult
Seafood pasta entrees. **Cards:** AE, DI, DS, MC, VI. **Special Value: $1 off the price of a dinner entree.**
(See ad below)

S & S CAFETERIA   **Lunch:** $4-$5   **Dinner:** $4-$5   Phone: 912/355-0683
◆ **Location:** 3.5 mi s on SR 204 (Abercorn St); in Twelve Oaks Shopping Center. 5500 Abercorn St 31
American **Hours:** 11 am-2:15 & 4:30-8 pm, Fri-8:30 pm, Sat 11 am-8:30 pm, Sun 10:45 am-8 pm. Closed: 12
MC, VI. **Features:** casual dress; children's menu; health conscious menu; carryout. Family atmosphere. **Cards:**

e map p. 297)

APPERS   **Lunch:** $5-$8   **Dinner:** $7-$17   **Phone:** 912/897-6101   ㉓
afood   **Location:** 9 mi e on US 80, Victory Dr, just s. 104 Bryan Woods Rd 31410. **Hours:** 11 am-10 pm, Sun-9 pm. Closed: 11/26 & 12/25. **Features:** casual dress; children's menu; carryout; cocktails. Bustling family restaurant in marsh setting. Fresh local seafood. **Cards:** AE, DS, MC, VI.   ✗

MYRNA—See Atlanta & Vicinity p. 244.

PARKS—11,200

LODGING

B PLANTATION INN   Rates Subject to Change   **Phone:** 912/549-6552
untry Inn   All Year [BP]   1P: $49   2P/2B: $59   2P/2B: $59
Location: I-75 exit 11, just w. 101 Roundtree Branch Rd 31647 (PO Box 327). **Terms:** Reserv deposit; no pets. **Facility:** 19 rooms. 2 stories. **Dining:** Restaurant; Fri & Sat 6 am-10 & 6-10 pm, Sun 11 am-3 pm.
ds: AE, MC, VI.   ✗ D

STATESBORO—15,900

LODGINGS

DRED'S TRELLIS GARDEN INN   Rates Subject to Change   **Phone:** 912/489-8781
◆◆   All Year [CP]   1P: $50   2P/1B: $50   2P/2B: $50
tel   **Location:** 2 blks s on US 301 & 25; 1 mi n of Georgia Southern University. 107 S Main St 30458. Fax: 912/764-5461. **Terms:** Sr. discount; no pets. **Facility:** 39 rooms. 2 stories; exterior corridors. **Rooms:** free movies. **Some Rooms:** efficiency. **Cards:** AE, CB, DI, DS, MC, VI.   ☄ ✛ CTV ✗ D

MFORT INN   **Phone:** 912/489-2626
SAVE   All Year [BP]   1P: $45- 100 2P/1B: $45- 100 2P/2B: $45- 100 XP: $5   F
Location: 0.3 mi s on US 301. 316 S Main St 30458. Fax: 912/489-2626. **Terms:** No pets. **Facility:** 65 rooms.
tel   2 stories; exterior corridors; small pool. **Dining:** Restaurant nearby. **Services:** Fee: coin laundry. **All Rooms:** coffeemakers, microwaves, free movies, refrigerators, VCP's. **Some Rooms:** 24 efficiencies, utensil deposit, whirlpools. **Cards:** AE, DI, DS, MC, VI. **Special Amenities:** Free breakfast and free local phone calls.   🐾 CTV ✗ D

YS INN OF STATESBORO   **Phone:** 912/764-5666
SAVE   3/1-9/7 [CP]   1P: $40- 70 2P/1B: $40- 70 2P/2B: $45- 80 XP: $5   F16
◆   12/1-2/28 & 9/8-11/30 [CP] 1P: $36- 70 2P/1B: $36- 70 2P/2B: $40- 80 XP: $5   F16
tel   **Location:** 0.5 mi s on US 301/25. 461 S Main St 30458. Fax: 912/489-8193. **Terms:** Weekly rates; small pets only. **Facility:** 44 rooms. Moderate room decor. 1-2 stories; exterior corridors. **Dining:** Restaurant nearby. **All Rooms:** coffeemakers, free movies. **Some Rooms:** microwaves, refrigerators. **Cards:** AE, CB, DS, JCB, MC, VI. **Special Amenities:** Free breakfast and free newspaper.   🐾 ☄ CTV ✗ D

RFIELD INN   **Phone:** 912/871-2525
SAVE   All Year [CP]   1P: $44- 48 2P/1B: $44- 48 2P/2B: $46- 54 XP: $5   F18
◆◆   **Location:** Just s, 301 bypass. 225 Lanier Dr 30458 (PO Box 25, 30459). Fax: 912/871-3535. **Terms:** No pets. **Facility:** 63 rooms. 3 stories; interior corridors. **All Rooms:** free movies. **Cards:** AE, CB, DI, DS, MC, VI.   Roll in showers. ☄ CTV ⚅ ✗ 🎦 D S

MADA INN   Rates Subject to Change   **Phone:** 912/764-6121
◆   All Year [BP]   1P: $47   2P/1B: $52   2P/2B: $52   XP: $5   F18
or Inn   **Location:** 0.3 mi s on US 301 & 25. 230 S Main St 30458. Fax: 912/489-8742. **Terms:** Pets. **Facility:** 129 rooms. 2 stories; exterior corridors. **Dining:** Restaurant; 6:30 am-10 pm; $5-$15. **All Rooms:** free movies.
ds: AE, DI, DS, MC, VI.   🐾 ☄ CTV ✗ D

E JAMESON INN   Rates Subject to Change   **Phone:** 912/681-7900
◆◆   All Year [CP]   1P: $51   2P/1B: $56   2P/2B: $56   XP: $5   F13
el   **Location:** 1.5 mi s on US 301; opposite Georgia Southern University. 1 Jameson Ave 30458. Fax: 912/681-7905. **Terms:** Sr. discount; no pets. **Facility:** 39 rooms. 2 stories; exterior corridors. **Rooms:** free movies. **Cards:** AE, CB, DI, DS, JCB, MC, VI.   ☄ CTV ✗ D

ATESBORO INN & RESTAURANT   **Phone:** 912/489-8628
SAVE   All Year [BP]   1P: $85- 125 2P/1B: $85- 125 2P/2B: $85- 125 XP: $10
◆◆   **Location:** Downtown; just s of town center on US 301/25. 106 S Main St 30458. Fax: 912/489-4785.
toric   **Terms:** Small pets only. **Facility:** 19 rooms. 1904 late Victorian/Neoclassical home. Wraparound porch. Some
untry Inn   rooms with operable fireplace & private screened porch. On National Register of Historic Places. 2 stories; interior/exterior corridors. **Dining:** Restaurant, see separate listing. **Services:** childcare; guest laundry.
VI.   **All Rooms:** coffeemakers, free movies. **Some Rooms:** refrigerators, VCP's, whirlpools. **Cards:** AE, DI, DS, VI.   🐾 🐾 ✛ CTV ✗ D

RESTAURANTS

E BEAVER HOUSE   **Dinner:** $7-$13   **Phone:** 912/764-2821
erican   **Location:** Center of town, on Hwy 301. 121 S Main Street Box 189 30458. **Hours:** 11 am-2:30 & 5:30-9 pm, Sun 11 am-2:30 pm. Closed: 1/1 & 12/25. **Features:** casual dress; Sunday brunch; children's menu; carryout. Family style, homemade desserts. **Cards:** AE, MC, VI.   ✗

'S SEAFOOD & STEAKS   **Lunch:** $5-$12   **Dinner:** $5-$12   **Phone:** 912/489-8658
Location: 1 mi s of downtown on US 301. 434 S Main St. 30458. **Hours:** 11 am-10 pm, Fri & Sat-11 pm. Closed: 1/1, 7/4 & 12/25. **Features:** casual dress; Sunday brunch; children's menu; senior's menu; health conscious menu; carryout; salad bar; cafeteria. Cafeteria-style selections, accomodating friendly staff.
ak and   **Cards:** AE, MC, VI.   ✗
afood

E STATESBORO INN RESTAURANT Historical   **Dinner:** $14-$26   **Phone:** 912/489-8628
◆◆   **Location:** Downtown; just s of town center on US 301 & 25; in Statesboro Inn & Restaurant. 106 S Main St
ntinental   30458. **Hours:** 6 pm-9 pm. Closed: major holidays & Sun. **Reservations:** suggested. **Features:** casual dress; children's menu; health conscious menu items; carryout; beer & wine only. Casual but elegant dining
istoric inn. Local seafood plus veal, chicken, beef. Fresh made desserts & breads. Espresso/cappuccino. Varied wine list.
ds: AE, DI, DS, MC, VI.   ✗

STOCKBRIDGE—3,400   (See map p. 225; index p. 224)

LODGINGS

AMERIHOST INN - EAGLES LANDING
Phone: 770/507-6500
(AAA) (SAVE)   All Year [CP]   1P: $55- 60   2P/1B: $60   2P/2B: $55- 60   XP: $6
◆◆◆   **Location:** I-75, exit 73, ne corner. 100 North Park Ct 30281. Fax: 770/507-6300. **Terms:** Pets, $8 e
Motel   charge. **Facility:** 60 rooms. 2 stories; interior corridors; sauna, whirlpool. **Services:** valet laun
All Rooms: coffeemakers, free & pay movies, safes, combo or shower baths. **Some Rooms:** microwa
refrigerators, whirlpools. **Cards:** AE, CB, DI, DS, JCB, MC, VI. **Special Amenities: Free breakfast and**
newspaper. *(See color ad p 191)*   Roll in showers. 🛏 🚿 📶 📶 CTV ⊠ D

BEST WESTERN ATLANTA SOUTH
Phone: 770/474-8771
(AAA) (SAVE)   All Year   1P: $39   2P/1B: $49   2P/2B: $49   XP: $5
◆◆◆   **Location:** I-75 exit 75, just e; I-675 exit 1, just w. 3509 Hwy 138 30281. Fax: 770/474-24
Motor Inn   **Terms:** Package plans; pets. **Facility:** 116 rooms. Convenient to area shopping strip. 2 stories; exterior c
dors; wading pool. **Dining & Entertainment:** Restaurant; 6 am-10:30 & 5:30-9:30 pm; $10-$16; coc
lounge; wine/beer only. **Services:** valet laundry; area transportation, within 3 mi. **Some Rooms:** microwa
refrigerators. Fee: VCP's. **Cards:** AE, DI, DS, MC, VI. **Special Amenities: Early check-in/late check-out and free l**
telephone calls. *(See color ad p 182)*   🛏 🚿 📶 📶 CTV ⊠

COMFORT INN
Phone: 770/507-7911
(AAA) (SAVE)   Fri & Sat [EP]   1P: $45- 59   2P/1B: $49- 65   2P/2B: $49- 65
Sun-Thurs [CP]   1P: $45- 55   2P/1B: $49- 59   2P/2B: $49- 59   XP: $5
◆◆◆   **Location:** I-675 exit 1, ne corner. 7325 Davidson Pkwy N 30281. Fax: 770/507-7921. **Terms:** No p
Motel   **Facility:** 51 rooms. Well equipped rooms. Suites $69-99; 2 stories; exterior corridors. **Dining:** Restau
nearby. **Services:** Fee: coin laundry. **All Rooms:** microwaves, free movies, refrigerators, combo or sho
baths. **Some Rooms:** VCP's, whirlpools. **Cards:** AE, CB, DI, DS, JCB, MC, VI. **Special Amenities: Free local teleph**
calls and free newspaper.   Roll in showers. 🚿 CTV ⊠ D

DAYS INN
Phone: 770/507-4440
(AAA) (SAVE)   All Year [CP]   1P: $64   2P/1B: $69   2P/2B: $74   XP: $5
◆◆◆   **Location:** I-75 exit 75, 0.7 mi e; I-675 exit 1, just w. 7385 Hanover Pkwy N 30281. Fax: 770/507-44
Motel   **Terms:** No pets. **Facility:** 56 rooms. Rates for up to 4 persons. 6 whirlpool rms, extra charge; 2 stories;
terior corridors; small pool. **Dining:** Restaurant nearby. **All Rooms:** microwaves, free movies, refrigera
combo or shower baths. **Some Rooms:** radios. **Cards:** AE, CB, DI, DS, JCB, MC, VI. **Special Amenit**
Free breakfast and free local telephone calls.   Roll in showers. 📶 CTV ⊠ D

HOLIDAY INN EXPRESS
Phone: 770/474-0555
(AAA) (SAVE)   All Year [CP]   1P: $50- 60   2P/1B: $50- 60   2P/2B: $50- 60
◆◆◆   **Location:** I-675 exit, just e. 7395 Davidson Circle E 30281. Fax: 770/389-3839. **Terms:** No pets. **Facility**
Hotel   rooms. Tastefully appointed lobby & rooms. Rates for up to 4 persons; 2 stories; exterior corridors; small p
Services: valet laundry. **All Rooms:** free movies, combo or shower baths. **Some Rooms:** radios, pho
Cards: AE, CB, DI, DS, MC, VI. **Special Amenities: Free breakfast and free local telephone calls.**
Roll in showers. 📶 CTV ⊠ D

MOTEL 6 - 1117
Guaranteed Rates   **Phone:** 770/389-1142
(AAA)   All Year   1P: $35- 45   2P/1B: $39- 49   2P/2B: $39- 49   XP: $3
◆   **Location:** I-675 exit 1, ne corner. 7233 Davidson Pkwy 30281. Fax: 770/507-8385. **Terms:** Sr. disco
Motel   small pets only. **Facility:** 107 rooms. 1 story; exterior corridors. **All Rooms:** free movies. **Cards:** AE, DI,
MC, VI.   Roll in showers. 🛏 🚿 ⊠ 🐾

RAMADA LIMITED
Rates Subject to Change   **Phone:** 770/474-1700
◆◆◆   All Year [CP]   1P: $55   2P/1B: $65   2P/2B: $65   XP: $10
Motel   **Location:** I-675 exit 1, just e. 7265 Davidson Pkwy N 30281. Fax: 770/507-9393. **Terms:** Small pets c
Facility: 51 rooms. 1 whirlpool rm, extra charge; 2 stories; exterior corridors. **All Rooms:** free mov
Cards: AE, CB, DI, DS, MC, VI.   Roll in showers. 🛏 CTV ⊠ D

SUPER 8 MOTEL ATLANTA SOUTH
Phone: 770/474-5758
(AAA) (SAVE)   All Year [CP]   1P: $41- 56   2P/1B: $46- 61   2P/2B: $51- 66   XP: $6
◆◆   **Location:** I-75, exit 73, sw corner. 1451 Hudson Bridge Rd 30281. Fax: 770/474-1297. **Terms:** Small
Motel   only, $5 extra charge. **Facility:** 56 rooms. 3 upgraded executive singles with VCP; 2 stories; exterior corri
All Rooms: free movies. **Cards:** AE, CB, DI, DS, MC, VI.   🛏 🚿 CTV ⊠

RESTAURANTS

EMPEROR'S GOURMET
Lunch: $4-$6   **Dinner:** $6-$15   **Phone:** 770/389-6688
◆◆   **Location:** I-75, exit 75, just e; I-675 exit 1, just w. 3642 Hwy 138 30281. **Hours:** 11:30 am-10 pm, Fri-1
Chinese   pm, Sat noon-10:30 pm, Sun noon-10 pm. Closed: 1/1, 9/2 for lunch, 11/26 & 12/25. **Features:** casual dr
children's menu; early bird specials; health conscious menu; carryout; cocktails; a la carte. Authentic foo
contemporary decor. Large aquarium, relaxing atmosphere. Cantonese seafood, szechuan pork & beef dishes, bar
tempura. Oriental wines & imported beer. **Cards:** AE, DS, MC, VI.

FRONTERA TEX-MEX GRILL
Lunch: $4-$8   **Dinner:** $5-$12   **Phone:** 770/474-1540
◆◆   **Location:** I-75 exit 75 just e; I-675 exit 1 just w. 3607 Hwy 138 30284. **Hours:** 11 am-10:30 pm, Sat &
Mexican   from noon. **Features:** casual dress; carryout; cocktails; a la carte. Extensive offerings served in a bus
atmosphere. **Cards:** AE, CB, DI, DS, MC, VI.

STONE MOUNTAIN—*See Atlanta & Vicinity p. 245.*

SUWANEE—*See Atlanta & Vicinity p. 246.*

SWAINSBORO—7,400

LODGING

BRADFORD INN
Phone: 912/237-2
(AAA) (SAVE)   All Year   1P: $41   2P/1B: $46   2P/2B: $46   XP: $5
◆◆   **Location:** 2.2 mi s of jct US 80, SR 26 & US 1. 688 S Main St 30401. **Terms:** Reserv deposit, 5 day no
Motel   small pets only, $5 extra charge. **Facility:** 50 rooms. 2 stories; exterior corridors. **All Rooms:** free mov
Some Rooms: whirlpools. **Cards:** AE, DS, MC, VI. **Special Amenities: Early check-in/late check-out**
preferred room (subject to availability with advanced reservations).   🛏 CTV ⊠

YLVANIA—3,400

LODGING

AYS INN
◆
otel
S, MC, VI.

Rates Subject to Change
All Year   1P: $46   2P/1B: $46   2P/2B: $52   XP: $5   F12
Location: 2 mi s on Business Rts SR 21 & 73, just e. 404 W Ogeechee St 30467. Fax: 912/564-2490.
Terms: No pets. **Facility:** 34 rooms. 2 stories; exterior corridors. **All Rooms:** free movies. **Cards:** AE, DI,

Phone: 912/564-2490

[📻] [CTV] [✕] [D]

HOMASVILLE—17,500

LODGINGS

VANS HOUSE BED & BREAKFAST
storic Bed
Breakfast

Rates Subject to Change
All Year [BP]   1P: $70- 95   2P/1B: $75- 125
Location: 0.3 mi s of US 84 business route. 725 S Hansell St 31792. Fax: 912/226-0653. **Terms:** No pets.
Facility: 4 rooms. 2 stories; interior corridors; smoke free premises.

Phone: 912/226-1343
XP: $20
Roll in showers. [CTV] [✕] [D]

OLIDAY INN THOMASVILLE
[SAVE]
◆◆◆
otor Inn

Phone: 912/226-7111
All Year [CP]   1P: $54- 64   2P/1B: $59- 69 2P/2B: $59- 69 XP: $5   F17
Location: 0.3 mi s of US 319. 15138 US Hwy 19S 31757. Fax: 912/226-7257. **Terms:** Small pets only, on
leash. **Facility:** 147 rooms. Variety of rooms. 2 stories; exterior corridors; wading pool, whirlpool. **Dining &
Entertainment:** Restaurant; 6:30 am-2 & 5:30-9 pm, Fri & Sat-10 pm; $10-$16; cocktails/lounge. **Services:**
Fee: coin laundry. **All Rooms:** free & pay movies. **Some Rooms:** coffeemakers, refrigerators, safes.
ards: AE, DI, DS, JCB, MC, VI. **Special Amenities:** Free breakfast and free local telephone calls.

[🍽] [📻] [📶] [CTV] [♿] [✕] [🌀] [D]

RESTAURANTS

HE GRAND OLD HOUSE RESTAURANT Historical   **Lunch:** $6-$9   **Dinner:** $12-$23   **Phone:** 912/227-0108
◆◆◆   **Location:** Downtown. 502 S Broad St 31792. **Hours:** 11:30 am-2:30 & 6-9:30 pm. Closed major holidays &
ontinental   Sun. **Reservations:** suggested. **Features:** casual dress; cocktails & lounge. Elegant ambience & warm,
personable service. Creative cuisine. Espresso/cappuccino. Homemade desserts. Smoke free premises.
ards: AE, MC, VI.
[✕]

ELISSA'S   **Lunch:** $5-$10   **Dinner:** $8-$15   **Phone:** 912/228-9844
◆   **Location:** 134 S Madison St 31792. **Hours:** 11 am-10 pm. Closed major holidays & Sun. **Features:** casual
nerican   dress; health conscious menu; carryout; cocktails & lounge. Located in the historic Thomasville Laundry
Building overlooking an antique shop, featuring unique food selections. **Cards:** AE, DS, MC, VI.
[✕]

OM & DAD'S ITALIAN RESTAURANT   **Dinner:** $7-$15   **Phone:** 912/226-6265
◆   **Location:** 2.5 mi e on US 84E. 1800 Smith Ave 31792. **Hours:** 5 pm-10 pm. Closed major holidays, Sun,
alian   Mon & week of 7/4. **Features:** casual dress; carryout; beer & wine only; buffet. Authentic food & bread
cooked on premises; informal dining in family restaurant; pleasant Italian decor. **Cards:** AE, DI, DS, MC, VI.
[✕]

HOMSON—6,900

LODGINGS

EST WESTERN WHITE COLUMNS INN   Phone: 706/595-8000
[SAVE]   All Year   1P: $45- 49   2P/1B: $45- 49 2P/2B: $50- 59 XP: $5   F18
◆◆◆   **Location:** I-20, exit 59. 1890 Washington Rd 30824. Fax: 706/595-8822. **Terms:** Monthly rates, 6
otor Inn   one-bedroom suites; package plans; pets, Restricted rooms. **Facility:** 136 rooms. Tasteful room decor. Well-
cared for property with rooms that shine. 2 stories; exterior corridors. **Dining:** The Plantation Room, see
separate listing. **Services:** Fee: coin laundry. **All Rooms:** coffeemakers, free movies.
me Rooms: whirlpools. Fee: microwaves, refrigerators. **Cards:** AE, CB, DI, DS, MC, VI. **Special Amenities:** Free
eakfast and free local telephone calls. *(See color ad p 182)*
[🍽] [📻] [📶] [➕] [CTV] [✕] [D] [S]

AYS INN   Phone: 706/595-2262
[SAVE]   4/5-9/30 [CP]   1P: $42   2P/1B: $45   2P/2B: $45   XP: $5   F16
1/1-4/4 [CP]   1P: $39   2P/1B: $42   2P/2B: $42   XP: $5   F16
12/1-12/31 & 10/1-11/30 [CP] 1P: $36   2P/1B: $39   2P/2B: $39   XP: $5   F16
otel   **Location:** I-20 exit 60, ne corner. 2658 Cobb Ham Rd 30824. Fax: 706/595-2262. **Terms:** Reserv deposit;
small pets only, $6 extra charge. **Facility:** 40 rooms. Convenient to interstate. 1 story; exterior corridors.
ning: Restaurant nearby. **Services:** guest laundry. **All Rooms:** free & pay movies. **Some Rooms:** microwaves,
frigerators. Fee: VCP's. **Cards:** AE, CB, DI, DS, JCB, MC, VI. **Special Amenities:** Free breakfast and free local
lephone calls.
[🍽] [✕] [D]

CONO LODGE   Phone: 706/595-7144
[SAVE]   All Year   1P: $36- 40   2P/1B: $40- 42 2P/2B: $42- 46 XP: $5   F
◆◆   **Location:** I-20, exit 59, just s. 130 N Seymour Dr NW 30824. Fax: 706/595-7144. **Terms:** Reserv deposit,
otel   handling fee imposed; no pets. **Facility:** 47 rooms. 2 stories; exterior corridors. **Dining:** Restaurant nearby.
All Rooms: free movies. **Some Rooms:** microwaves, refrigerators. **Cards:** AE, CB, DI, DS, MC, VI.
[CTV] [✕] [D]

AMADA LTD   Phone: 706/595-8700
[SAVE]   All Year [CP]   1P: $37   2P/1B: $37   2P/2B: $40   XP: $5   F16
◆◆   **Location:** I-20, exit 59, just s. 1847 Washington Rd 30824. Fax: 706/595-9642. **Terms:** Reserv deposit, 3
otel   day notice; no pets. **Facility:** 59 rooms. Compact rooms. 2 stories; interior corridors. **Dining:** Restaurant
nearby. **Services:** Fee: coin laundry. **All Rooms:** free movies. **Some Rooms:** 3 efficiencies, no utensils,
microwaves, refrigerators. **Cards:** AE, CB, DI, DS, JCB, MC, VI. **Special Amenities:** Free breakfast and
e local telephone calls.
[📶] [CTV] [✕] [D] [S]

RESTAURANT

HE PLANTATION ROOM   **Lunch:** $5-$7   **Dinner:** $8-$18   **Phone:** 706/595-8000
◆   **Location:** I-20, exit 59, just s; in Best Western White Columns Inn. 1890 Washington Rd 30824.
nerican   **Hours:** 6:30 am-2 & 6-10 pm, Sat from 6 pm. Closed: Sun, 12/24 & 12/25. **Reservations:** accepted.
Features: casual dress; children's menu; early bird specials; carryout; cocktails & lounge. Formal dining
om featuring prime rib & seafood. Noon buffet. **Cards:** AE, DI, DS, MC, VI.

TIFTON—14,200

LODGINGS

BEST WESTERN OF TIFTON
◆◆
Motor Inn

	Rates Subject to Change			Phone: 912/386-21
10/15-10/22	1P: $65	2P/1B: $65	2P/2B: $65	XP: $5	F
12/1-10/14 & 10/23-11/30	1P: $41- 51	2P/1B: $51- 61	2P/2B: $51- 61	XP: $5	F

Location: Jct I-75, exit 19W 2nd St. 1103 King Rd 31794. Fax: 912/386-2100. **Terms:** Small pets only,
extra charge. **Facility:** 118 rooms. 2 stories; exterior corridors. **Dining:** Restaurant; 24 hours; $5-$12. **All Rooms:** fr
movies. **Some Rooms:** 2 efficiencies. **Cards:** AE, CB, DI, DS, MC, VI. *(See color ad p 182)*

COMFORT INN
◆◆◆
Motel

	Rates Subject to Change			Phone: 912/382-44
10/15-10/22 [CP]	1P: $75	2P/1B: $75	2P/2B: $75	XP: $5	F
12/1-10/14 & 10/23-11/30				
[CP]	1P: $49	2P/1B: $67	2P/2B: $67	XP: $5	F

Location: I-75, exit 19. 1104 King Rd 31794. Fax: 912/382-4410. **Terms:** Small pets only, $2 extra charge. **Facility:** 90 room
2 stories; exterior corridors. **All Rooms:** free movies. **Cards:** AE, CB, DI, DS, MC, VI.

COURTYARD BY MARRIOTT
🅰🅰🅰
◆◆◆
Motel

| | Rates Subject to Change | | Phone: 912/388-08 |
| All Year | 2P/1B: 69 | 2P/2B: $59- 69 | |

Location: I-75 & US 319 exit 18. 814 W 7th St 31794. Fax: 912/388-1795. **Terms:** Sr. discount; no pe
Facility: 90 rooms. 3 stories; interior corridors. **Dining:** Restaurant; 6:30-10 am, Sat & Sun 7-11 a
All Rooms: free movies. **Cards:** AE, CB, DI, DS, MC, VI. *(See color ad below)*
Roll in showers.

HAMPTON INN
◆◆◆
Motel

| | Rates Subject to Change | | | Phone: 912/382-88 |
| All Year [CP] | 1P: $55- 59 | 2P/1B: $59- 63 | 2P/2B: $59 | XP: $5 | F |

Location: On US 319 at jct I-75, exit 18. 720 Hwy 319S 31794. Fax: 912/382-0563. **Terms:** Sr. discou
small pets only. **Facility:** 82 rooms. Max 4 persons per room; 2 stories; exterior corridors. **All Rooms:** fr
movies. **Cards:** AE, CB, DI, DS, MC, VI.

HOLIDAY INN
◆◆◆
Motor Inn

| | Rates Subject to Change | | | Phone: 912/382-66 |
| All Year | 1P: $52 | 2P/1B: $52 | 2P/2B: $52 | |

Location: At jct I-75, US 82 & 319, exit 18. I-75 & US 82W 31793. Fax: 912/382-1533. **Terms:** Sr. discou
reserv deposit, 14 day notice; pets. **Facility:** 189 rooms. Rates for up to 4 persons; 2 stories; exterior co
dors. **Dining:** Restaurant, see separate listing. **All Rooms:** free & pay movies. **Cards:** AE, CB, DI, DS, MC, VI.

MASTERS ECONOMY INN-TIFTON
🅰🅰🅰 SAVE
◆◆
Motel

| | Rates Subject to Change | | | Phone: 912/382-81 |
| All Year | 1P: $30- 35 | 2P/1B: $34- 39 | 2P/2B: $34- 39 | XP: $4 | F |

Location: At jct I-75, US 82 & 319. (PO Box 1310, 31793). Fax: 912/382-5339. **Terms:** Pets, $5 ex
charge. **Facility:** 120 rooms. 2 stories; exterior corridors. **Dining:** Coffee shop nearby. **All Rooms:** fr
movies. **Some Rooms:** radios. **Cards:** AE, CB, DI, DS, MC, VI. **Special Amenities:** Free breakfast a
free local telephone calls.

SUPER 8 MOTEL
◆◆
Motel

| | Guaranteed Rates | | | Phone: 912/382-95 |
| All Year [CP] | 1P: $34 | 2P/1B: $39 | 2P/2B: $39 | XP: $2-4 | C |

Location: I-75 exit 19, se corner W 2nd St. (PO Box 47, 31793). Fax: 912/382-2922. **Terms:** Sr. discou
pets, $5 extra charge. **Facility:** 70 rooms. 2 stories; exterior corridors. **All Rooms:** free movies. **Cards:** A
CB, DI, DS, MC, VI.

RESTAURANT

HOLIDAY INN RESTAURANT
◆◆
American
VI.

Lunch: $5 **Dinner:** $5-$12 **Phone:** 912/382-66
Location: At jct I-75, US 82 & 319, exit 18; in Holiday Inn. 31793. **Hours:** 6:30 am-10 pm. **Features:** cas
dress; children's menu; carryout; salad bar; beer & wine only. Good selection on menu. Prime rib
homemade cinnamon rolls are nightly specialties. Daily breakfast & lunch buffets. **Cards:** AE, DI, DS, M

TUCKER—See Atlanta & Vicinity p. 246.

TYBEE ISLAND—2,800

LODGINGS

BEST WESTERN DUNES INN
◆◆
Motel

		Guaranteed Rates			Phone: 912/786-4591
5/1-9/6	1P: $79- 145	2P/1B: $79- 145	2P/2B: $79- 145	XP: $5	F12
12/1-4/30 & 9/7-11/30	1P: $59- 145	2P/1B: $59- 145	2P/2B: $59- 145	XP: $5	F12

Location: On US 80. 1409 Butler Ave 31328. Fax: 912/786-4593. **Terms:** Sr. discount; reserv deposit, 3 day notice; 2 night min stay, weekends 5/1-9/30; no pets. **Facility:** 32 rooms. Rates for up to 4 persons; 2 stories; exterior corridors. **Some Rooms:** 10 efficiencies, 2 kitchens. **Cards:** AE, DI, DS, MC, VI.

⊡ CTV ⊠ D

HOWARD JOHNSON
◆◆
Motel

		Rates Subject to Change			Phone: 912/786-0700
5/1-9/6	1P: $85- 125	2P/1B: $85- 125	2P/2B: $85- 125	XP: $5	F18
3/13-4/30	1P: $65- 85	2P/1B: $65- 85	2P/2B: $65- 85	XP: $5	F18
9/7-10/31	1P: $55- 65	2P/1B: $55- 65	2P/2B: $55- 65	XP: $5	F18
12/1-3/12 & 11/1-11/30	1P: $50- 60	2P/1B: $50- 60	2P/2B: $50- 60	XP: $5	F18

Location: On US 80; center. 1501 Butler Ave 31328 (PO Box 596). Fax: 912/786-0399. **Terms:** Sr. discount; reserv deposit; no pets. **Facility:** 41 rooms. 2 stories; interior corridors. **Cards:** AE, CB, DI, DS, JCB, MC, VI.

CTV ⌂ ⊠ D S

RESTAURANT

THE HUNTER HOUSE
◆◆
Regional
American

Dinner: $10-$15   Phone: 912/786-7515

Location: Corner of 17th St & Butler Ave; just s of jct US 80; just sw of Atlantic Ocean. 1701 Butler Ave 31328. **Hours:** 6 pm-9 pm, Fri & Sat-10 pm. Closed: Mon & 12/15-1/2. **Reservations:** suggested; weekends. **Features:** casual dress; carryout; cocktails & lounge. Cozy, charming dining rooms in a graciously-restored home circa 1910. Featuring southern recipes with local seafood & steak. **Cards:** AE, MC, VI.

⊠

UNADILLA—1,600

LODGINGS

SCOTTISH INN
AAA SAVE
◆
Motel

				Phone: 912/627-3228
All Year	1P: $26	2P/1B: $29	2P/2B: $32	XP: $3 D6

Location: I-75, exit 39. 31091 (Rt 2, Box 100). Fax: 912/627-3495. **Terms:** Reserv deposit; weekly rates; pets, $3 extra charge. **Facility:** 60 rooms. 1 story; exterior corridors; playground. **Dining:** Coffee shop nearby. **All Rooms:** free movies. **Cards:** AE, DS, MC, VI. **Special Amenities:** Early check-in/late check-out and free room upgrade (subject to availability with advanced reservations).

🐾 ⊡ CTV ⊠ D

SUGAR HILL B&B
◆◆◆
Bed &
Breakfast

		Guaranteed Rates		Phone: 912/627-3557
All Year [BP]	1P: $45- 75	2P/1B: $50- 75		XP: $15 F12

Location: I-75 exit 40, 1.9 mi e Hwy 230, 2.2 mi n to house on left at dead end. (PO Box 308, 31091). Fax: 912/627-3612. **Terms:** No pets. **Facility:** 4 rooms. Handling fee imposed; 2 stories; interior corridors. **All Rooms:** free movies. **Cards:** MC, VI.

⊡ CTV ⊠ D

UNION CITY—*See Atlanta & Vicinity p. 247.*

VALDOSTA—39,800

LODGINGS

BEST WESTERN KING OF THE ROAD
AAA SAVE
◆◆◆
Motor Inn

				Phone: 912/244-7600
All Year [CP]	1P: $38- 42	2P/1B: $42- 49	2P/2B: $42- 49	XP: $4 F12

Location: Jct I-75 & SR 94, exit 5. 1403 N St. Augustine Rd 31601. Fax: 912/245-1734. **Terms:** Pets. **Facility:** 137 rooms. 3 stories; exterior corridors. **Dining & Entertainment:** Restaurant; 6-10 am, 11:30-2:30 & 5-9 pm; $6-$14; cocktails/lounge; entertainment. **Services:** valet laundry. **All Rooms:** free movies. **Some Rooms:** refrigerators. **Cards:** AE, CB, DI, DS, MC, VI. **Special Amenities:** Free local telephone calls and free newspaper.

🐾 ⊡ 🍴 ✈ CTV ⊠ 🎱 D

CLUBHOUSE INN & SUITES
◆◆◆
Motel

		Rates Subject to Change		Phone: 912/247-7755
Sun-Thurs [BP]	1P: $63	2P/1B: $73	2P/2B: $73	XP: $10 F16
Fri & Sat [BP]	1P: $63	2P/1B: $63	2P/2B: $63	XP: $10 F16

Location: I-75 exit 5, 0.3 mi e. 1800 Clubhouse Dr 31601. Fax: 912/245-1359. **Terms:** No pets. **Facility:** 121 rooms. Suites avail; 2 stories; interior corridors. **All Rooms:** free movies. **Cards:** AE, CB, DI, DS, MC, VI.
(See color ad p 308)

⊡ CTV ⊠ 🎱 D

COMFORT INN
Phone: 912/242-1212
AAA SAVE   All Year [CP]   1P: $49- 53 2P/1B: $53- 57 2P/2B: $53- 57 XP: $4   F18
◆◆◆   Location: I-75, exit 4, sw corner. 2799 W Hill Ave 31602 (PO Box 1191). Fax: 912/242-2639. Terms: Small
Motor Inn   pets only. Facility: 138 rooms. Variety of rooms ranging from standard motel to deluxe rooms. 2 stories;
interior/exterior corridors; volleyball court, shuffleboard court. Dining & Entertainment: Restaurant; 11
am-10 pm; $7-$15; cocktail lounge. Services: valet laundry. All Rooms: coffeemakers, free movies.
Some Rooms: microwaves, refrigerators. Cards: AE, CB, DI, DS, JCB, MC, VI. Special Amenities: Free newspaper and
free room upgrade (subject to availability with advanced reservations).   🛏 🖼 🛠 🚭 🏋 CTV ✕ D S

DAYS INN I-75
Phone: 912/244-4460
◆◆   All Year   Rates Subject to Change   1P: $32- 37 2P/1B: $35- 40 2P/2B: $35- 40 XP: $5   F12
Motel   Location: I-75 exit 6, nw corner. 4598 N Valdosta Rd 31602. Fax: 912/244-4461. Terms: Sr. discount; small
pets only, $5 extra charge. Facility: 100 rooms. 2 stories; exterior corridors. All Rooms: free movies.
Cards: AE, CB, DI, DS, MC, VI.   🛏 🖼 CTV ✕ D

FAIRFIELD INN
Phone: 912/253-9300
AAA SAVE   All Year [CP]   1P: $51   2P/1B: $51   2P/2B: $51   XP: $5
◆◆◆   Location: I-75, exit 5. 1311 St. Augustine Rd 31603. Fax: 912/253-8600. Terms: No pets. Facility: 108 rooms.
Motel   2 stories; exterior corridors. Services: coin laundry. All Rooms: free movies, combo or shower baths.
Some Rooms: microwaves, refrigerators. Cards: AE, CB, DI, DS, JCB, MC, VI. Special Amenities: Free
breakfast and free local telephone calls. (See color ad below)   🖼 🛠 🏋 CTV ✕ D

HOLIDAY INN
Phone: 912/242-3881
AAA SAVE   All Year   1P: $51   2P/1B: $51   2P/2B: $51   XP: $5   D18
◆◆◆   Location: Jct I-75 & SR 94, exit 5. 1309 St. Augustine Rd 31603. Fax: 912/242-3881. Terms: Reserv
Motor Inn   deposit; pets. Facility: 168 rooms. 2 stories; exterior corridors. Dining & Entertainment: Dining room; 6
am-2 & 5-11 pm; $7-$15; cocktails/lounge; entertainment. Services: area transportation, within 10 mi.
Fee: coin laundry. All Rooms: coffeemakers, free & pay movies, combo or shower baths.
Some Rooms: microwaves, refrigerators. Cards: AE, DI, DS, MC, VI. Special Amenities: Early check-in/late check-out
and free room upgrade (subject to availability with advanced reservations). (See color ad p 309)   🛏 🖼 🛠 🚭 CTV ✕ D

QUALITY INN NORTH
Phone: 912/244-8510
AAA SAVE   All Year [CP]   1P: $59- 69 2P/1B: $59- 69 2P/2B: $59- 69 XP: $5
◆◆◆   Location: Jct I-75 & SR 94, exit 5. 1209 St. Augustine Rd 31601. Fax: 912/249-8215. Terms: Small pets
Motel   only. Facility: 124 rooms. 2 stories; exterior corridors; 1 lighted tennis court. Dining: Restaurant nearby.
Services: Fee: coin laundry. All Rooms: coffeemakers, free movies. Some Rooms: microwaves,
refrigerators. Cards: AE, CB, DI, DS, JCB, MC, VI. Special Amenities: Free breakfast and free local
telephone calls.   🛏 🖼 🛠 🏋 CTV ✕ D

QUALITY INN SOUTH
◆◆
Motel
All Year [CP]   Rates Subject to Change   Phone: 912/244-4520
1P: $36- 55 2P/1B: $38- 60 2P/2B: $38- 60 XP: $4   F17
Location: Jct I-75 & US 84, exit 4. 1902 W Hill Ave 31601. Fax: 912/244-4520. **Terms:** Sr. discount; pets.
Facility: 48 rooms. 2 stories; exterior corridors. **All Rooms;** free movies. **Cards:** AE, CB, DI, DS, MC, VI.

RAMADA LIMITED
◆◆◆
Motel
JCB, MC, VI.
All Year [CP]   Rates Subject to Change   Phone: 912/242-1225
1P: $44   2P/1B: $49   2P/2B: $49   XP: $5   F12
Location: I-75, exit 4, just e. 2008 W Hill Ave 31601. Fax: 912/247-2755. **Terms:** Sr. discount; small pets
only. **Facility:** 102 rooms. 2 stories; exterior corridors. **All Rooms:** free movies. **Cards:** AE, CB, DI, DS,

RODEWAY INN
(AAA) [SAVE]
◆◆
Motel
reservations). *(See color ad below)*
                                                        Phone: 912/241-1177
All Year   1P: $34- 44   2P/2B: $38- 48 XP: $6   F12
Location: I-75, exit 4, se corner. 2015 Westhill Ave 31601. Fax: 912/241-1177. **Terms:** Small pets only, $25
dep req. **Facility:** 84 rooms. 2 stories; exterior corridors. **All Rooms:** free movies.
Some Rooms: coffeemakers, microwaves, refrigerators. **Cards:** AE, CB, DI, DS, JCB, MC, VI.
Special Amenities: Free breakfast and free room upgrade (subject to availability with advanced

RESTAURANTS

ALIGATOU JAPANESE AND CHINESE CUISINE   **Lunch:** $4-$20   **Dinner:** $4-$20   **Phone:** 912/244-4784
◆
Chinese
Location: I-75 exit 4, just e. 1902 W Hill Ave 31602. **Hours:** 11 am-2 & 5-10 pm, Fri & Sat-11 pm. Closed:
11/26 & 12/25. **Features:** casual dress; cocktails. Traditional Japanese cooks prepare meal at your table.
Cards: AE, MC, VI.

FIDDLERS GREEN   **Dinner:** $10-$18   **Phone:** 912/247-0366
(AAA)
◆◆
American
Location: 0.3 mi e of jct I-75 & N Valdosta Rd, exit 6. 4479 N Valdosta Rd 31602. **Phone:** 912/247-0366
Closed major holidays & Sun. **Reservations:** suggested; weekends. **Features:** casual dress; children's
menu; carryout; cocktails & lounge; entertainment. Steak & seafood. Pleasantly rustic atmosphere in wooded
setting. **Cards:** AE, DI, DS, MC, VI.

J.P. MULLDOONS RESTAURANT   **Lunch:** $5-$7   **Dinner:** $8-$15   **Phone:** 912/247-6677
◆◆
American
Location: Exit 5, I-75; 0.4 mi e to Gornto Rd 1st light; then 1.5 mi n. 1405 Gornto Rd 31605. **Hours:** 11
am-10 pm, Fri & Sat-11 pm. Closed major holidays & Sun. **Reservations:** suggested; lunch & weekend.
Features: casual dress; early bird specials; health conscious menu; carryout; cocktails & lounge. Casual,
congenial atmosphere; serving salads, sandwiches & full dinners. **Cards:** AE, MC, VI.

MOM & DAD'S ITALIAN RESTAURANT   **Dinner:** $8-$16   **Phone:** 912/333-0848
◆◆
Italian
Location: 1.5 mi e of jct I-75 & N Valdosta Rd, exit 6. 4143 N Valdosta Rd 31602. **Hours:** 5 pm-10 pm.
Closed major holidays, Sun & Mon. **Features:** casual dress; children's menu; carryout; cocktails. Authentic
cuisine, including homemade bread, pasta & desserts. **Cards:** AE, CB, DI, DS, MC, VI.

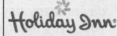

VIDALIA—11,100

LODGINGS

DAYS INN
△△△ [SAVE]
◆◆
Motel
Phone: 912/537-9251
All Year [CP]　　　　　　　　1P: $35- 50　2P/1B: $35- 55　2P/2B: $35- 55　XP: $5　F12
Location: 1 mi e on US 280. 1503 Lyons Hwy, 280E 30474 (PO Box 626). Fax: 912/537-9251. **Terms:** Reserv deposit; weekly rates; pets, $10 extra charge. **Facility:** 65 rooms. In town location. Tidy property with moderate room decor. 1-2 stories; exterior corridors. **Dining:** Restaurant nearby. **All Rooms:** free movies, refrigerators. **Cards:** AE, DI, DS, MC, VI. **Special Amenities: Free breakfast and free local telephone calls.**　🛏️ 🛎️ CTV ✖️ D

HOLIDAY INN EXPRESS
◆◆◆
Motel
VI.
Rates Subject to Change　　　　　　　　Phone: 912/537-9000
All Year [CP]　　　　　　1P: $41- 63　2P/1B: $41- 52　2P/2B: $41- 63
Location: 2.3 mi e on US 280. 2619 E First St 30474-3913. Fax: 912/537-9000. **Terms:** Sr. discount; small pets only. **Facility:** 65 rooms. 2 stories; exterior corridors. **All Rooms:** free movies. **Cards:** AE, DI, DS, MC,
🛏️ 🛎️ CTV ✖️ D

VILLA RICA—6,500

LODGING

COMFORT INN
◆◆
Motel
Rates Subject to Change　　　　　　　　Phone: 770/459-8000
5/15-9/15 [CP]　　　1P: $53- 80　2P/1B: $55- 85　2P/2B: $58- 85　XP: $6　F18
12/1-5/14 & 9/16-11/30 [CP]　1P: $45- 75　2P/1B: $50- 80　2P/2B: $53- 85　XP: $6　F18
Location: I-20, exit 5. 128 Hwy 61 30180. Fax: 770/459-8413. **Terms:** Sr. discount; no pets. **Facility:** 64 rooms. 2 stories; exterior corridors. **All Rooms:** free movies. **Cards:** AE, CB, DI, DS, JCB, MC, VI.　🛎️ CTV ✖️ D

WARNER ROBINS—43,700

LODGINGS

COMFORT INN
△△△ [SAVE]
◆◆◆
Motel
Phone: 912/922-7555
All Year [CP]　　　　　　1P: $49- 123　2P/1B: $54- 123　2P/2B: $54- 123　XP: $6　F18
Location: Jct US 129/SR 247 & Russell Pkwy on nw corner; I-75 exit 45 Rt 247 Connector 1.3 mi e to SR 247/US 129 then 1.3 mi s. 95 S Hwy 247 31088. Fax: 912/929-3404. **Terms:** Check-in 4 pm; no pets. **Facility:** 65 rooms. Large, well-furnished rooms. Some with fireplaces & whirlpools. Large selection of suites. Across street from Robins Air Force Base Museum of Aviation. 2 stories; interior corridors. **Dining:** Coffee shop nearby. **Services:** Fee: coin laundry. **Some Rooms:** coffeemakers, microwaves, refrigerators. **Cards:** AE, DI, DS, MC, VI. **Special Amenities: Free breakfast and free local telephone calls.**　🛎️ 🕭 CTV ✖️ 🌀 D S

SUPER 8 MOTEL
◆◆
Motel
Rates Subject to Change　　　　　　　　Phone: 912/923-8600
All Year　　　　　1P: $35- 39　2P/1B: $42　　2P/2B: $46　　XP: $5　F12
Location: From SR 129, 6 mi e (Watson Blvd) to Woodcrest Blvd. 105 Woodcrest Blvd 31013. Fax: 912/923-8600. **Terms:** Sr. discount; reserv deposit, 7 day notice; small pets only. **Facility:** 62 rooms. 3 stories, no elevator; interior corridors. **All Rooms:** free movies. **Cards:** AE, CB, DI, DS, MC, VI.　🛏️ CTV ✖️ D

RESTAURANT

RICHARDS
Ⓐ
◆◆
American
Location: From jct US 129 & SR 247, 2 mi w. 604 Russell Pkwy 31088. **Hours:** 11 am-2:30 & 5:30-9:30 pm; Fri-10 pm, Sat 5 pm-10 pm. Closed: Sun, 11/26 & 12/25. **Reservations:** suggested. **Features:** casual dress; children's menu; senior's menu; carryout; cocktails. Steak & seafood featured. **Cards:** AE, DI, MC, VI.
Lunch: $4-$10   **Dinner:** $7-$28   **Phone:** 912/922-1547 ☒

WASHINGTON—4,300

RESTAURANT

ANOTHER THYME CAFE Historical   **Lunch:** $4-$8   **Dinner:** $8-$16   **Phone:** 706/678-1672
Ⓐ
◆◆
American
Location: US 78; historic Town Square. 5 E Public Sq 30673. **Hours:** 11 am-2:30 & 6-9 pm. Closed: Sun, Mon for dinner, 11/26 & 12/25. **Reservations:** accepted. **Features:** casual dress; children's menu; health conscious menu; carryout; street parking. Variety of bread & dessert baked fresh daily. In historic 1890's building. Smoke free premises. **Cards:** MC, VI. ☒

WAYCROSS—16,400

LODGINGS

DAYS INN   **Phone:** 912/285-4700
Ⓐ SAVE
◆◆
Motel
All Year [CP]   1P: $32- 38 2P/1B: $36- 40 2P/2B: $40   XP: $5   D17
Location: 2 mi se on US 1 & 23. 2016 Memorial Dr 31501. Fax: 912/285-0971. **Terms:** Reserv deposit, 7 day notice; pets. **Facility:** 56 rooms. 2 stories; exterior corridors. **Dining:** Restaurant nearby. **All Rooms:** free movies. **Some Rooms:** microwaves, refrigerators. **Cards:** AE, CB, DI, DS, MC, VI.
🛏 🛋 🕂 📺 ☒ Ⓓ

HOLIDAY INN   **Phone:** 912/283-4490
Ⓐ SAVE
◆◆◆
Motor Inn
All Year [BP]   1P: $50- 55 2P/1B: $50- 55 2P/2B: $55- 60 XP: $5   F19
Location: 1.5 mi se on US 1 & 23 at jct US 82. 1725 Memorial Dr 31501 (PO Box 1357). Fax: 912/283-4490. **Terms:** Weekly rates; small pets only. **Facility:** 145 rooms. Some rooms with patio & balcony. 2 stories; exterior corridors; putting green. **Dining & Entertainment:** Restaurant; 6 am-2 & 5-9:30 pm; $7-$16; cocktails/lounge. **Services:** valet laundry. **All Rooms:** free movies. **Fee:** VCP. **Some Rooms:** refrigerators. **Cards:** AE, CB, DI, DS, MC, VI. **Special Amenities:** Free breakfast and free local telephone calls.
🛏 🛋 🐾 🕂 🛗 📺 ♿ ☒ ⚅ Ⓓ

JAMESON INN   **Phone:** 912/283-3800
◆◆◆
Motel
All Year [CP]   Rates Subject to Change
1P: $44- 49 2P/1B: $48- 53 2P/2B: $48- 53 XP: $4   F11
Location: Just e US 1. 950 City Blvd 31501. Fax: 912/283-9135. **Terms:** Sr. discount; pets, in designated rooms. **Facility:** 60 rooms. 1-2 stories; exterior corridors. **All Rooms:** free movies.
🛏 🛋 📺 🐾 ☒ Ⓓ

PINE CREST MOTEL   **Phone:** 912/283-3580
Ⓐ SAVE
◆
Motel
All Year [CP]   1P: $28- 30 2P/1B: $30- 32 2P/2B: $30- 32 XP: $3   F16
Location: 1.5 mi se on US 1 & 23; just s of jct US 82. 1761 Memorial Dr 31501. **Terms:** Small pets only. **Facility:** 30 rooms. Spacious units. 1 story; exterior corridors. **Dining:** Restaurant nearby. **All Rooms:** free movies, refrigerators. **Cards:** AE, DI, DS, MC, VI.
🛏 🛋 🕂 📺 ☒ Ⓓ

RESTAURANT

THE DINING ROOM   **Lunch:** $3-$7   **Dinner:** $10-$16   **Phone:** 912/283-4490
◆
American
Location: 1.5 mi se on US 1 & 23 at jct US 82; in Holiday Inn. 1725 Memorial Dr 31501. **Hours:** **Features:** casual dress; children's menu; a la carte. Casual dining offering local fare. **Cards:** AE, CB, DI, DS, MC, VI. ☒

WINDER—7,400

LODGING

THE JAMESON INN   **Phone:** 770/867-1880
◆◆
Motel
All Year [CP]   1P: $53   2P/1B: $57   2P/2B: $57   XP: $4   F12
Location: Center; jct SR 81, 11, 53 & 8. 9 Stafford St 30680. Fax: 770/867-1890. **Terms:** Sr. discount; no pets. **Facility:** 40 rooms. 2 stories; exterior corridors. **All Rooms:** free movies. **Cards:** AE, DI, DS, JCB, MC, VI.
🛋 📺 ☒ Ⓓ

YOUNG HARRIS—600

LODGING

BRASSTOWN VALLEY RESORT   Rates Subject to Change   **Phone:** 706/379-9900
◆◆◆
Resort Hotel
4/1-11/30   1P: $119- 159 2P/1B: $119- 159 2P/2B: $119- 159 XP: $10   F18
12/1-3/31   1P: $99- 139 2P/1B: $99- 139 2P/2B: $99- 139 XP: $10   F18
Location: 6321 US Hwy 76 30582. Fax: 706/379-9999. **Terms:** Check-in 4 pm; reserv deposit, 3 day notice; no pets. **Facility:** 134 rooms. 8 four-bedroom cottages, $99-$159 per bedroom per night; 5 stories; interior corridors. **Dining:** Restaurant, cafeteria; 7 am-10 pm; $8-$20. **All Rooms:** free & pay movies. **Cards:** AE, DI, DS, JCB, MC, VI.
Roll in showers. 🛋 🛋 📺 ☒ Ⓓ Ⓢ

NORTH CAROLINA

State law may restrict pets in hotel and motel rooms. Be sure to ask your lodging about this before you finalize your reservations.

ABERDEEN—2,700

LODGINGS

BEST WESTERN PINEHURST MOTOR INN   Rates Subject to Change   **Phone:** 910/944-2367
◆◆◆   All Year [CP]   1P: $50- 60   2P/1B: $60- 70   2P/2B: $60- 70   XP: $10   F12
Motel   **Location:** From jct of US 15-501 on US 1, 0.3 mi s. 1500 Sandhills Blvd 28315. Fax: 910/944-2730.
Terms: Pets, small dogs only, $10 extra charge. **Facility:** 50 rooms. 1-2 stories; exterior corridors.
All Rooms: free movies. **Cards:** AE, DI, DS, MC, VI.   🛒 🛏️ CTV ✕ 🏊 D

INN AT THE BRYANT HOUSE   Rates Subject to Change   **Phone:** 910/944-3300
◆◆   All Year [CP]   1P: $40- 70   2P/1B: $40- 70   2P/2B: $40- 70   XP: $10   F
Historic Bed   **Location:** From jct US 15/501 (from southern end), 0.3 mi n on US 1 to W Maple Ave then 1 blk. 214 N
& Breakfast   Poplar St 28315. Fax: 910/944-8898. **Terms:** Small pets only, cats on premises. **Facility:** 8 rooms. 2 stories;
interior corridors; smoke free premises. **All Rooms:** free movies. **Cards:** AE, CB, DS, MC, VI.
🛏️ CTV ✕ D

MOTEL 6 - 1234   Guaranteed Rates   **Phone:** 910/944-5633
Ⓐ   All Year   1P: $35- 45   2P/1B: $35- 45   2P/2B: $39- 49   XP: $3   F17
◆   **Location:** From jct US 15-501 on US 1; 0.3 mi s. 1408 Sandy Hills Blvd 28315. Fax: 910/944-1101.
Motel   **Terms:** Sr. discount; small pets only. **Facility:** 81 rooms. 1 story; exterior corridors. **All Rooms:** free movies.
Cards: AE, DI, DS, MC, VI.   🛒 ✕ D

ALBEMARLE—14,900

LODGINGS

COMFORT INN   **Phone:** 704/983-6990
Ⓐ Ⓢ   All Year [CP]   1P: $45- 49   2P/1B: $49- 53   2P/2B: $49   XP: $6   F18
◆◆◆   **Location:** 1.5 mi e of US 52S; on SR 24/27 bypass. 735 SR 24/27 bypass 28001. Fax: 704/983-5597.
Motel   **Terms:** No pets. **Facility:** 80 rooms. 2 stories; exterior corridors. **Dining:** Restaurant nearby. **Services:** valet
laundry. **All Rooms:** free movies. **Some Rooms:** 6 efficiencies, no utensils. **Cards:** AE, CB, DI, DS, JCB,
MC, VI. **Special Amenities:** Free local telephone calls and free newspaper.   🛁 🔧 CTV ✕ 🏊 D

HAMPTON INN   **Phone:** 704/985-1111
All Year [CP]   1P: $50- 54   2P/1B: $54- 60   2P/2B: $54- 60
Location: 3.5 mi n on US 52 (Bypass). 2300 US 52 N 28001. **Terms:** No pets.
Facility: 50 rooms. 2 stories; interior corridors; small pool. **Dining:** Restaurant nearby. **Services:** Fee: coin laundry. **All Rooms:** coffeemakers, free movies. **Some Rooms:** Fee: whirlpools. **Cards:** AE, CB, DI, DS, MC, VI. **Special Amenities:** Free breakfast and free newspaper. *(See color ad p 312)*
Roll in showers.

RODEWAY INN   Rates Subject to Change   **Phone:** 704/982-3939
All Year [CP]   1P: $45- 49   2P/1B: $53   2P/2B: $49   XP: $6   F18
Location: 1.5 mi e on SR 24 & 27 from jct US 52 bypass; behind Denny's. 200 Henson St 28001.
Fax: 704/983-5597. **Terms:** Sr. discount; pets, $50 dep req. **Facility:** 42 rooms. 2 stories; interior corridors.
All Rooms: free movies. **Cards:** AE, CB, DI, DS, JCB, MC, VI.

ANDREWS—2,600

LODGINGS

COUNTRY HEARTH INN   Rates Subject to Change   **Phone:** 704/321-2176
10/1-10/31 [CP]   1P: $73   2P/1B: $79   2P/2B: $85   XP: $6   F12
4/1-9/30 [CP]   1P: $62   2P/1B: $68   2P/2B: $74   XP: $6   F12
12/1-12/31 & 11/1-11/30 [CP] 1P: $54   2P/1B: $60   2P/2B: $66   XP: $6   F12
1/1-3/31 [CP]   1P: $41   2P/1B: $47   2P/2B: $53   XP: $6   F12
Location: Rest area exit, US 19,74,129. Beaver Creek Rd,US 19/74 28901 (PO Box 1629). Fax: 704/321-5453. **Terms:** No pets. **Facility:** 50 rooms. 2 stories; exterior corridors. **All Rooms:** free movies. **Cards:** AE, DS, MC, VI.

THE COVER HOUSE   Rates Subject to Change   **Phone:** 704/321-5302
All Year [BP]   1P: $50- 70   2P/1B: $70- 80   XP:$10-20
Bed & Breakfast
Location: Center. 34 Wilson St 28901. Fax: 704/321-2145. **Terms:** Age restrictions may apply; reserv deposit, 3 day notice; no pets. **Facility:** 6 rooms. 4 stories; interior corridors; smoke free premises. **Some Rooms:** kitchen.

HAWKESDENE HOUSE BED & BREAKFAST INN AND COTTAGES   **Phone:** 704/321-6027
All Year [BP]   1P: $65- 95   2P/1B: $65- 95   XP: $20
Bed & Breakfast
Location: From US 19 Business (Wachovia Bank), 3.2 mi on Cherry St & 0.5 mi n on Phillips Creek Rd. (PO Box 670, 28901). Fax: 704/321-5007. **Terms:** Age restrictions may apply; no pets. **Facility:** 4 rooms. English country architecture, many antique furnishings. Cascading stream through property; very well maintained grounds; charming rooms & public areas. Patio/observation deck. 2 two-bedroom cottages, $250 weekends, $450 weekly, up to 4 persons; 2 stories; interior corridors; smoke free premises; mountain view. Fee: llama treking. **Recreation:** hiking trails. **All Rooms:** free movies, combo or shower baths, no phones. **Some Rooms:** A/C, coffeemakers, kitchen, radios, refrigerators, VCP's. **Cards:** AE, DS, MC, VI. **Special Amenities:** Free local telephone calls.

ARCHDALE—6,800

LODGING

THE BOULDIN HOUSE B & B-HIGH POINT   Rates Subject to Change   **Phone:** 910/431-4909
All Year [BP]   1P: $85- 95   2P/1B: $85- 95   XP: $25
Historic Bed & Breakfast
Location: Exit 111, I-85 just n to Balfour Dr, 1 mi w on Balfour to Archdale Rd, just n. 4332 Archdale Rd 27263. Fax: 910/431-4914. **Terms:** Age restrictions may apply; check-in 5 pm; reserv deposit, 10 day notice; no pets, pets on premises. **Facility:** 4 rooms. 2 stories; interior corridors; smoke free premises. **Cards:** DS, MC, VI.

ARDEN—500   (See map p. 315; index p. 314)

LODGING

SHONEY'S INN   Rates Subject to Change   **Phone:** 704/684-6688   67
6/1-10/31 [CP]   1P: $59- 79   2P/1B: $69- 89   2P/2B: $69- 89   XP: $10   F18
12/1-5/31 & 11/1-11/30 [CP] 1P: $39- 49   2P/1B: $59- 69   2P/2B: $59- 69   XP: $10   F18
Location: I-26, exit 6. 1 Skyland Inn Dr 28704. Fax: 704/684-6688. **Terms:** Sr. discount; reserv deposit; no pets. **Facility:** 117 rooms. 4 stories; interior corridors. **All Rooms:** free movies. **Cards:** AE, DS, MC, VI.
Roll in showers.

ASHEBORO—16,400

LODGINGS

COMFORT INN   **Phone:** 910/626-4414
All Year [CP]   1P: $49- 80   2P/1B: $54- 95   2P/2B: $54- 95   XP: $6   F19
Location: 1 mi w on US 64. 825 W Dixie Dr 27203. Fax: 910/625-0056. **Terms:** Check-in 4 pm; no pets.
Facility: 90 rooms. Well-manicured grounds & pool area. Attractive public areas. 2 stories; interior corridors.
Dining: Restaurant nearby. **All Rooms:** free & pay movies. **Some Rooms:** Fee: microwaves, refrigerators.
Cards: AE, CB, DI, DS, JCB, MC, VI. **Special Amenities:** Free breakfast and free local telephone calls.

HAMPTON INN   Rates Subject to Change   **Phone:** 910/625-9000
All Year [CP]   1P: $56- 63   2P/1B: $69   2P/2B: $63
Location: 2 mi e on US 64, across from Lowe's. 1137 E Dixie Dr 27203. Fax: 910/625-9111. **Terms:** No pets. **Facility:** 68 rooms. 3 stories; interior corridors. **All Rooms:** free movies. **Cards:** AE, DI, DS, MC, VI.
Roll in showers.

RESTAURANT

BAMBOO GARDEN ORIENTAL RESTAURANT   **Lunch:** $4-$5   **Dinner:** $5-$9   **Phone:** 910/629-0203
Chinese
Location: On US 64, 0.8 mi e of jct US 220 bypass. 405 E Dixie Dr 27203. **Hours:** 11 am-2 & 5-9:30 pm, Sun noon-2 & 5-9 pm. **Closed:** Mon, 11/26 & 12/25. **Features:** senior's menu; carryout. Large, tastefully decorated dining room with Oriental ambience. Daily buffet. Lunch & dinner, $4.95-$7.50 drive-thru window.
Cards: MC, VI.

ASHEVILLE—61,600   (See map p. 315; index below)

To help you more easily locate accommodations in the Asheville area, the following index and map show lodgings and restaurants in multiple cities. Listings for these establishments are found under the heading for the city in which they are located. The Asheville area map comprises: Asheville, Arden, Candler, Enka, Fletcher, and Weaverville.

Airport Accommodations

Listings for these establishments are found under the heading for the city in which they are located.

Asheville International

Fairfield Inn by Marriott, across the road/FLETCHER
Holiday Inn Asheville-Airport, 0.3 mi e on Airport Rd/FLETCHER

Index of Establishments on the ASHEVILLE & VICINITY ACCOMMODATIONS Spotting Map

LODGINGS

ABINGTON GREEN BED & BREAKFAST INN   39
◆◆◆
Historic Bed & Breakfast
Rates Subject to Change   **Phone: 704/251-2454**
All Year [BP]   2P/1B: $95- 125   2P/2B: $150   XP: $40
Location: I-240 exit 4C, n to W Chestnut St, just e to Cumberland Ave, 0.3 mi n; in Montford Historic District. 46 Cumberland Cir 28801. Fax: 704/251-2872. **Terms:** Age restrictions may apply; reserv deposit, 5 day notice; no pets. **Facility:** 6 rooms. 3 stories, no elevator; interior corridors; smoke free premises.
All Rooms: free movies. **Some Rooms:** kitchen. **Cards:** AE, DS, MC, VI.   [CTV] [X] [D]

ALBEMARLE INN   40
(AAA)
◆◆◆
Historic Bed & Breakfast
Rates Subject to Change   **Phone: 704/255-0027**
All Year [BP]   1P: $95- 160   2P/1B: $95- 160   2P/2B: $110- 150   XP: $25
Location: Exit 5B I-240, 0.9 mi n on Charlotte & 0.3 mi e on Edgemont Rd. 86 Edgemont Rd 28801 **Terms:** Age restrictions may apply; reserv deposit, 7 day notice; 2 night min stay, weekends 4/1-12/31; no pets. **Facility:** 11 rooms. 3 stories, no elevator; interior corridors; smoke free premises. **Some Rooms:** A/C
Cards: DS, MC, VI.   [≈] [CTV] [X] [D]

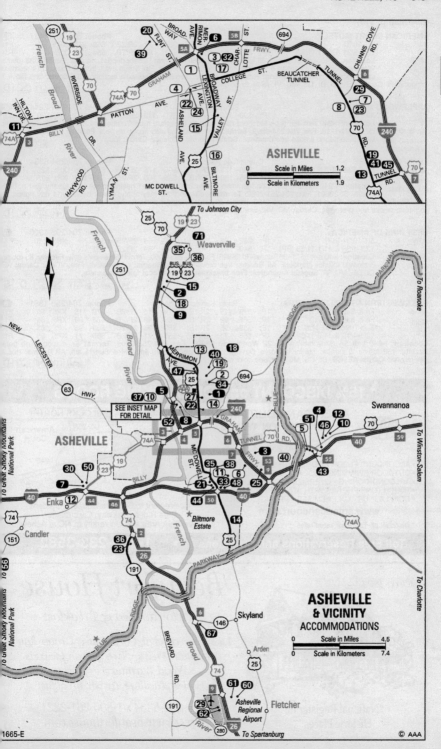

ASHEVILLE

| 0 | Scale in Miles | 1.2 |
| 0 | Scale in Kilometers | 1.9 |

ASHEVILLE
& VICINITY
ACCOMMODATIONS

| 0 | Scale in Miles | 4.5 |
| 0 | Scale in Kilometers | 7.4 |

1665-E

© AAA

(See map p. 315)

AMERICAN COURT MOTEL
Phone: 704/253-4427
AAA SAVE 6/1-10/31   1P: $57- 67 2P/1B: $64- 77 2P/2B: $69- 77 XP: $3   F18
◆◆   12/1-5/31 & 11/1-11/30   1P: $47- 54 2P/1B: $47- 65 2P/2B: $54- 65 XP: $3   F18
Motel   **Location:** I-240 exit 5A, just n. 85 Merrimon Ave 28801. **Terms:** Reserv deposit; no pets. **Facility:** 23 rooms.
          Well established. Very clean & well maintained. Guest oriented. Fax & iron avail. Ironing board in all rooms.
          story; exterior corridors. **Dining:** Restaurant nearby. **Services:** Fee: coin laundry. **All Rooms:** free movies
refrigerators. **Cards:** AE, CB, DI, DS, MC, VI. *(See ad below)*

APPLEWOOD MANOR INN   Rates Subject to Change   Phone: 704/254-2244   5
AAA   All Year [BP]   1P: $90- 110 2P/1B: $90- 110 2P/2B: $90- 110 XP: $20
◆◆◆   **Location:** I-240 exit 4C; n on Montford Ave, e on W Chestnut, n on Cumberland, then ne. 62 Cumberland
Historic Bed   Cir 28801-1718. Fax: 704/254-0899. **Terms:** Age restrictions may apply; no pets. **Facility:** 5 rooms. 2 stories
& Breakfast   interior corridors; smoke free premises. **Some Rooms:** efficiency. **Cards:** MC, VI.

BEAUFORT HOUSE   Guaranteed Rates   Phone: 704/254-8334   1
◆◆◆   Fri & Sat [BP]   1P: $95- 175 2P/1B: $95- 175 2P/2B: $95- 175 XP: $25
Historic Bed Sun-Thurs [BP]   1P: $65- 160 2P/1B: $65- 160 2P/2B: $65- 160 XP: $25
& Breakfast   **Location:** I-240 exit 5A, just n on Merrimon Ave to 2nd light, e on Chestnut close to N Liberty, just n. 61 N
          Liberty St 28801. Fax: 704/251-2082. **Terms:** Age restrictions may apply; reserv deposit, 14 day notice; no
pets. **Facility:** 11 rooms. 1 two-bedroom suite $195, double $240 for 3 or more persons; 3 stories, no elevator; interior/exterior
corridors; smoke free premises. **Cards:** MC, VI. *(See ad below)*

BEST INNS OF AMERICA   Phone: 704/298-4000   4
AAA SAVE 5/1-10/31 [BP]   1P: $52- 58 2P/1B: $59- 68 2P/2B: $65   XP: $7-10   F1
◆◆◆   12/1-4/30 & 11/1-11/30 [BP] 1P: $40- 47 2P/1B: $57- 64 2P/2B: $51
Motel   **Location:** I-40 exit 55. 1435 Tunnel Rd 28805. Fax: 704/298-4000. **Terms:** Small pets only. **Facility:** 85 rooms.
          3 stories; interior corridors. **All Rooms:** free movies. **Some Rooms:** refrigerators. Fee: VCP's. **Cards:** AE,
DI, DS, MC, VI. **Special Amenities: Free breakfast and free local telephone calls.**

BEST WESTERN ASHEVILLE CENTRAL   Rates Subject to Change   Phone: 704/253-1851   6
◆◆   Fri & Sat 6/13-11/8   1P: $79- 115 2P/1B: $79- 115 2P/2B: $79- 115 XP: $5   F1
Motel   Fri & Sat 4/11-6/12   1P: $65- 99   2P/1B: $65- 99   2P/2B: $65- 99   XP: $5   F1
          Sun-Thurs 4/11-11/8   1P: $59- 95   2P/1B: $59- 95   2P/2B: $59- 95   XP: $5   F1
          12/1-4/10 & 11/9-11/30   1P: $55- 71   2P/1B: $55- 71   2P/2B: $55- 71   XP: $5   F1
Location: I-240 exit 5A (Merrimon Ave). 22 Woodfin St 28801. Fax: 704/252-9205. **Terms:** Sr. discount; no pets.
Facility: 150 rooms. 5 stories; interior corridors. **Dining:** Coffee shop; 6:30-10 am, Sat & Sun-11 am. **All Rooms:** free
pay movies. **Cards:** AE, CB, DI, DS, MC, VI. *(See color ad p 317)*

(See map p. 315)

BEST WESTERN OF ASHEVILLE   Phone: 704/298-5562   **3**

5/29-9/6 & 9/25-10/31 [CP]	1P: $74		2P/2B: $74	XP: $4	F15
3/27-5/28 & 9/7-9/24 [CP]	1P: $62		2P/2B: $62	XP: $4	F15
12/1-3/26 & 11/1-11/30 [CP]	1P: $50		2P/2B: $50	XP: $4	F15

Motel   **Location:** I-240 exit 7, 0.5 mi e. 501 Tunnel Rd 28805. Fax: 704/298-5002. **Terms:** No pets. **Facility:** 89 rooms. 2 stories; exterior corridors. **Dining:** Restaurant nearby. **All Rooms:** free movies. **Some Rooms:** refrigerators. **Cards:** AE, CB, DI, DS, MC, VI. *(See color ad p 318)*

CAIRN BRAE   Rates Subject to Change   Phone: 704/252-9219   **18**

4/1-11/30 [BP]	1P: $85	2P/1B: $95- 110	2P/2B: $95- 110 XP: $20

Location: I-240 Charlotte exit s to College, just e to Town Mountain Rd; 2.5 mi n to Patton Mountain Rd; right 1 mi at water tank on unpaved road. 217 Patton Mountain Rd 28804. **Terms:** Open 4/1-11/30; age restrictions may apply; reserv deposit, 4 day notice; no pets. **Facility:** 3 rooms. 2-bedroom unit $150 for 4 persons; 2 stories; interior corridors; smoke free premises. **Cards:** DS, MC, VI.

Bed &
Breakfast

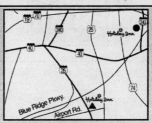

(See map p. 315)

CEDAR CREST VICTORIAN INN   Phone: 704/252-1389   38
(AAA) SAVE   All Year [BP]   2P/1B: $120- 185   2P/2B: $120- 185   XP: $20
◆◆◆◆   **Location:** I-40 exit 50, 1.1 mi n. 674 Biltmore Ave 28803. Fax: 704/253-7667. **Terms:** Age restrictions may
Historic Bed   apply; reserv deposit, 10 day notice; no pets. **Facility:** 11 rooms. Opulent Victorian mansion. Lavish woodwork
& Breakfast   in public areas. Rooms beautifully appointed. 3 stories, no elevator; interior corridors; smoke free premises.
   All Rooms: combo or shower baths. **Some Rooms:** VCP's, whirlpools. **Cards:** AE, DI, DS, MC, VI.

CTV ✕ D

THE COLBY HOUSE   Rates Subject to Change   Phone: 704/253-5644   8
◆◆◆   12/1-12/31 & 3/1-11/30 [BP]   1P: $80- 110   2P/1B: $80- 110
Historic Bed   **Location:** I-240 exit 4C (Montford Ave) 0.8 mi n to Wautauga, just w. 230 Pearson Dr 28801.
& Breakfast   Fax: 704/259-9479. **Terms:** Open 12/1-12/31 & 3/1-11/30; age restrictions may apply; 2 night min stay,
   weekends; no pets. **Facility:** 4 rooms. 2 stories; interior corridors; smoke free premises. **Cards:** AE, MC, VI.

✕ D

COMFORT INN   Rates Subject to Change   Phone: 704/298-9141   25
◆◆◆   6/1-10/31 [CP]   1P: $69- 159   2P/1B: $69- 159   2P/2B: $69- 159   XP: $8   F18
Motel   4/1-5/31 [CP]   1P: $69- 139   2P/1B: $69- 139   2P/2B: $69- 139   XP: $8   F18
   12/1-3/31 & 11/1-11/30 [CP]   1P: $69- 129   2P/1B: $69- 129   2P/2B: $69- 129   XP: $8   F18
Location: I-240 exit 8 at jct I-40 & US 74; above River Ridge Market Place. 800 Fairview Rd 28803. Fax: 704/298-6629.
Terms: Sr. discount; pets. **Facility:** 178 rooms. 3 stories, no elevator; interior corridors. **All Rooms:** free movies.
Some Rooms: 24 efficiencies. **Cards:** AE, CB, DI, DS, MC, VI.

🐄 🛥 CTV ✕ D

COMFORT INN-WEST   Rates Subject to Change   Phone: 704/665-6500   30
◆◆◆   6/1-10/31 [CP]   1P: $59- 109   2P/1B: $59- 109   2P/2B: $59- 109   XP: $6   F18
Motel   12/1-5/31 & 11/1-11/30 [CP]   1P: $49- 89   2P/1B: $49- 89   2P/2B: $49- 89   XP: $6   F18
   Location: I-40 exit 44, just n on 19/23, just w on Old Haywood Rd, then just s. 15 Crowell Rd 28806.
Fax: 704/665-6600. **Terms:** Sr. discount; reserv deposit, 14 day notice; no pets. **Facility:** 63 rooms. 4 whirlpool rms, extra
charge; 3 stories; interior corridors. **All Rooms:** free movies. **Cards:** AE, CB, DI, DS, JCB, MC, VI.
Roll in showers. 🛥 CTV 🔔 ✕ D S

COMFORT SUITES   Rates Subject to Change   Phone: 704/665-4000   23
◆◆◆   10/1-10/31 [CP]   1P: $69- 89   2P/1B: $79- 99   2P/2B: $79- 99   XP: $7   F18
Motel   5/1-9/30 [CP]   1P: $69- 79   2P/1B: $69- 89   2P/2B: $69- 89   XP: $7   F18
   12/1-4/30 & 11/1-11/30 [CP]   1P: $59- 79   2P/1B: $59- 79   2P/2B: $59- 79   XP: $7   F18
Location: I-26 exit 2. 890 Brevard Rd 28806. Fax: 704/665-9082. **Terms:** Sr. discount; pets, $20 extra charge. **Facility:** 125
rooms. 5 stories; interior corridors. **All Rooms:** free & pay movies. **Cards:** AE, CB, DI, DS, JCB, MC, VI.

🛏 🛥 🛗 CTV ✕ 🅿 D S

COURTYARD BY MARRIOTT   Rates Subject to Change   Phone: 704/281-0041   45
◆◆◆   All Year   1P: $69- 129   2P/1B: $69- 129   2P/2B: $69- 129
Motel   **Location:** I-240 exit 6, 0.5 mi e. 1 Buckstone Pl 28805. Fax: 704/281-1069. **Terms:** Sr. discount; check-in 4
pm; no pets. **Facility:** 78 rooms. 3 stories; interior corridors. **Dining:** 6:30-10:30 am, Sat & Sun 7-11 am,
$5.95. **All Rooms:** free movies. **Some Rooms:** 3 efficiencies. **Cards:** AE, DI, DS, MC, VI.
Roll in showers. CTV ✕ D S

(See map p. 315)

DAYS INN ASHEVILLE MALL
Phone: 704/254-4311 〔29〕

6/1-7/31 & 10/1-11/15	1P:	$75	2P/1B:	$75	2P/2B:	$75	XP: $5	F18
12/1-12/31, 1/1-5/31, 8/1-9/30 & 11/16-11/30	1P:	$50	2P/1B:	$50	2P/2B:	$50	XP: $5	F18

Motel **Location:** I-240 exit 6 eastbound, exit 7 westbound, 0.5 mi e on US 70. 199 Tunnel Rd 28805. Fax: 704/258-3970. **Terms:** Reserv deposit; weekly/monthly rates; no pets. **Facility:** 77 rooms. 5 stories; exterior corridors. **Dining:** Coffee & hot tea; restaurant nearby. **Services:** complimentary evening beverages. **All Rooms:** free movies. **Some Rooms:** VCP's. **Cards:** AE, CB, DI, DS, JCB, MC, VI. **Special Amenities:** Early check-in/late check-out.
(See ad below)
〔🚲〕〔CTV〕〔✕〕〔D〕

DAYS INN-EAST
Phone: 704/298-5140 〔10〕

6/1-10/31 [CP]	1P:	$58- 110		2P/2B:	$58- 110	XP: $5	F17
4/1-5/31 [CP]	1P:	$36		2P/2B:	$50	XP: $5	F17
12/1-3/31 & 11/1-11/30 [CP]	1P:	$31		2P/2B:	$37	XP: $5	F17

Motor Inn **Location:** I-40 exit 55. 1500 Tunnel Rd 28805. Fax: 704/298-8191. **Terms:** Pets, $4 extra charge. **Facility:** 125 rooms. 3 stories, no elevator; exterior corridors; playground. **Dining:** Restaurant; 11 am-10 pm; $6-$13. **All Rooms:** free movies, safes. **Some Rooms:** 15 efficiencies, refrigerators. **Cards:** AE, DI, DS, MC, VI. **Special Amenities:** Early check-in/late check-out and free breakfast.
〔🛏〕〔🚲〕〔CTV〕〔✕〕〔D〕

DAYS INN NORTH
Rates Subject to Change
Phone: 704/645-9191 〔9〕

All Year [CP]	1P:	$43- 89	2P/1B:	$48- 89	2P/2B:	$48- 99	XP: $5	F13

Motel **Location:** 4 mi n on US 19/23, New Bridge exit, Merriman/N Asheville exit southbound. 3 Reynolds Mountain Blvd 28804. Fax: 704/645-7180. **Terms:** Sr. discount; reserv deposit; no pets. **Facility:** 48 rooms. 2 whirlpool rms, extra charge; 2 stories; exterior corridors. **All Rooms:** free movies. **Cards:** AE, DI, DS, MC, VI.
Roll in showers. 〔CTV〕〔✕〕〔D〕

ECONO LODGE BILTMORE EAST
Phone: 704/298-5519 〔46〕

10/3-10/31 [CP]	1P:	$56	2P/1B:	$61		XP: $5	F18
6/2-10/2 [CP]	1P:	$51	2P/1B:	$56		XP: $5	F18
5/1-6/1 [CP]	1P:	$39	2P/1B:	$43		XP: $5	F18
12/1-4/30 & 11/1-11/30 [CP]	1P:	$39	2P/1B:	$39		XP: $5	F18

Motel **Location:** I-40 exit 55. 1430 Tunnel Rd 28815. Fax: 704/298-4739. **Terms:** No pets. **Facility:** 138 rooms. Weekend rates higher 10/1-10/31; 2 stories; exterior corridors. **All Rooms:** free movies. **Some Rooms:** microwaves, refrigerators. **Cards:** AE, CB, DI, DS, JCB, MC, VI. **Special Amenities:** Free breakfast and free local telephone calls.
〔🚲〕〔🏊〕〔CTV〕〔✕〕〔D〕

ECONO LODGE-TUNNEL ROAD
Phone: 704/254-9521 〔19〕

10/1-10/31	1P:	$65- 85	2P/1B:	$65- 85	2P/2B:	$65- 85	XP: $5	F18
6/3-9/30	1P:	$50- 65	2P/1B:	$55- 70	2P/2B:	$60- 75	XP: $5	F18
12/1-6/2 & 11/1-11/30	1P:	$45- 55	2P/1B:	$50- 60	2P/2B:	$50- 60	XP: $5	F18

Motel **Location:** I-240 exit 6, 0.5 mi e. 190 Tunnel Rd 28805. Fax: 704/254-9521. **Terms:** Small pets only. **Facility:** 53 rooms. Contemporary room appointments. 2 stories; exterior corridors. **Dining:** Restaurant nearby. **All Rooms:** free movies. **Some Rooms:** coffeemakers. Fee: microwaves, refrigerators, VCP's. **Cards:** AE, CB, DI, DS, JCB, MC, VI. **Special Amenities:** Free local telephone calls and preferred room (subject to availability with advanced reservations).
〔🛏〕〔CTV〕〔✕〕〔D〕

FLINT STREET INNS
Guaranteed Rates
Phone: 704/253-6723 〔20〕

All Year [BP]	1P:	$75	2P/1B:	$95	2P/2B:	$95	XP: $25

Historic Bed & Breakfast **Location:** I-240 eastbound Patton Ave exit 4 to Haywood, 0.5 mi n; westbound Charlotte St exit 5B, just s to College, 0.5 mi w to Haywood, then 0.5 mi n. 116 Flint St 28801. **Terms:** Age restrictions may apply; reserv deposit; 2 night min stay, some weekends; no pets. **Facility:** 8 rooms. 2 stories; interior corridors.
Cards: AE, DS, MC, VI.
〔✕〕〔D〕

FOREST MANOR INN
Rates Subject to Change
Phone: 704/274-3531 〔14〕

9/25-10/31 [CP]	2P/1B:	$79- 129	2P/2B:	$79- 129	XP: $10
6/19-9/6 [CP]	2P/1B:	$69- 119	2P/2B:	$69- 119	XP: $10
3/27-6/18 & 9/7-9/24 [CP]	2P/1B:	$59- 99	2P/2B:	$59- 99	XP: $10
12/1-3/26 & 11/1-11/30 [CP]	2P/1B:	$49- 89	2P/2B:	$49- 89	XP: $10

Motel **Location:** I-40 exit 50, 1 mi s on US 25. 866 Hendersonville Rd 28803. Fax: 704/274-3036. **Terms:** No pets. **Facility:** 21 rooms. 3 kitchen units $15 extra; 1 story; exterior corridors. **All Rooms:** free movies. **Cards:** AE, DS, MC, VI.
(See color ad p 320)
〔🚲〕〔CTV〕〔✕〕〔D〕

(See map p. 315)

FOUR SEASONS MOTOR INN Rates Subject to Change Phone: 704-254-5324

	6/1-10/31	1P:	$32	2P/1B:	$43	2P/2B:	$43	XP: $5	F1
	12/1-5/31 & 11/1-11/30	1P:	$26	2P/1B:	$30	2P/2B:	$30	XP: $5	F1

Motel
Location: I-240 exit 5A (Merrimon Ave), 2 mi n. 820 Merrimon Ave 28804. **Terms:** Reserv deposit; no pets. **Facility:** 20 rooms. 1 story; exterior corridors. **All Rooms:** free movies. **Cards:** AE, DS, MC, VI. (CTV) (D)

GREAT SMOKIES HOLIDAY INN SUNSPREE GOLF & TENNIS RESORT Phone: 704-254-3211

	10/1-10/31	1P:	$95- 125	2P/1B:	$95- 125	2P/2B:	$95- 125	XP: $10	F1
	9/18-9/30 & 11/1-11/14	1P:	$85- 99	2P/1B:	$85- 99	2P/2B:	$85- 99	XP: $10	F1
	4/24-9/17	1P:	$75- 89	2P/1B:	$75- 89	2P/2B:	$75- 89	XP: $10	F1
	12/1-4/23 & 11/15-11/30	1P:	$65- 79	2P/1B:	$65- 79	2P/2B:	$65- 79	XP: $10	F1

Resort Hotel
Location: I-240 exit 3B Holiday Inn Dr exit, just w. 1 Holiday Inn Dr 28806. Fax: 704/254-1603. **Terms:** Package plans; no pets. **Facility:** 280 rooms. Handsome location on 87-acre golf course, very attractive public areas 2-5 stories; interior corridors; mountain view; wading pool; tennis & golf pro shop; playground, basketball & volleyball courts game room. Fee: 18 holes golf, miniature golf, putting green; 8 tennis courts (4 indoor, 4 lighted). **Dining & Entertainment:** 2 restaurants; 6:30 am-10 pm; deli counter 6:30 am-midnight; $15-$25; cocktails/lounge; piano entertainment Thurs-Sun. **Services:** valet laundry. Fee: childcare. **Recreation:** children's program in season, children's activity center. **All Rooms:** coffeemakers, free & pay movies, refrigerators. **Cards:** AE, DS, MC, VI. **Special Amenities:** Free local telephone calls and free newspaper. (See color ad p 321)

THE GROVE PARK INN RESORT Rates Subject to Change Phone: 704-252-2711

	12/1-12/31 & 4/16-11/30		2P/1B:	$119- 325	2P/2B:	$119- 325	XP: $25	F1
	1/1-4/15		2P/1B:	$89- 265	2P/2B:	$89- 265	XP: $25	F1

Resort Hotel
Location: I-240 Charlotte St exit, 2 mi n on Macon Ave via Charlotte St, follow signs. 290 Macon Ave 28804. Fax: 704/253-7053. **Terms:** Sr. discount; check-in 4 pm; reserv deposit, 7 day notice, handling fee imposed; no pets. **Facility:** 510 rooms. 9 stories; interior corridors. **Dining:** Dining room, restaurant, cafeteria; 6:30 am-11 pm; $15-$35; also Horizons, see separate listing. **All Rooms:** free & pay movies. **Cards:** AE, DI, DS, MC, VI. (See color ad p 321)

ee map p. 315)

AMPTON INN Rates Subject to Change **Phone:** 704/667-2022 **36**
6/1-10/31 [CP] 1P: $59- 119 2P/1B: $59- 119 2P/2B: $59- 119
12/1-5/31 & 11/1-11/30 [CP] 1P: $59- 99 2P/1B: $59- 99 2P/2B: $59- 99
Location: I-26 exit 2. 1 Rocky Ridge Rd 28806. Fax: 704/665-9680. **Terms:** No pets. **Facility:** 121 rooms.
Handling fee imposed; 5 stories; interior corridors. **All Rooms:** free movies. **Cards:** AE, CB, DI, DS, MC, VI.
(See color ad below)

(See map p. 315)

HAMPTON INN TUNNEL ROAD   Rates Subject to Change   **Phone: 704/255-9220**
All Year [CP]   1P: $49- 119 2P/1B: $49- 119 2P/2B: $49- 119 XP: $10
Location: I-240 exit 6, 0.5 mi e. 204 Tunnel Rd 28805. Fax: 704/254-4303. **Terms:** No pets. **Facility:**
rooms. 5 stories; interior corridors. **All Rooms:** free movies. **Cards:** AE, CB, DI, DS, MC, VI.
Motel   (See color ad p 321)   Roll in showers.

HOLIDAY INN-ASHEVILLE MALL   **Phone: 704/252-4000**
7/1-11/5   1P: $69- 99   2P/1B: $79- 99 2P/2B: $79- 99 XP: $5
12/1-6/30 & 11/6-11/30   1P: $49- 69   2P/1B: $49- 69 2P/2B: $49- 69 XP: $5
Location: I-240 exit 6, 0.5 mi e. 201 Tunnel Rd 28805. Fax: 704/258-0359. **Terms:** Reserv deposit; sm
Motor Inn   pets only. **Facility:** 131 rooms. 2 stories; exterior corridors. **Dining & Entertainment:** Restaurant; 6 am-11
5-10 pm; $9-$14; cocktails/lounge. **Services:** valet laundry. **All Rooms:** free movies, combo or show
baths. **Some Rooms:** coffeemakers. Fee: refrigerators. **Cards:** AE, DS, MC, VI. **Special Amenities:** Early check-in/l
check-out and free newspaper. (See ad p 317)   Roll in showers.

HOLIDAY INN EAST/BLUE RIDGE PKWY   Rates Subject to Change   **Phone: 704/298-5611**
6/1-11/30   1P: $65- 90   2P/1B: $75- 95 2P/2B: $75- 95 XP: $5
Motor Inn   12/1-5/31   1P: $55- 75   2P/1B: $55- 75 2P/2B: $55- 75 XP: $5
Location: I-40 exit 55. 1450 Tunnel Rd 28805. Fax: 704/299-3308. **Terms:** Small pets only. **Facility:**
rooms. 4 stories; interior corridors. **Dining:** Restaurant; 7 am-10 & 5-9 pm, Sat & Sun 7 am-11 & 5-9 pm; $10-$
All Rooms: free movies. **Cards:** AE, CB, DI, DS, JCB, MC, VI.

HOLIDAY INN EXPRESS   Rates Subject to Change   **Phone: 704/274-0101**
Fri & Sat 7/1-7/31 &
Motel   10/1-10/31 [CP]   1P: $110   2P/1B: $110   2P/2B: $110   XP: $7
Fri & Sat 12/1-9/30, 8/1-9/30
& 11/1-11/30 [CP]   1P: $89   2P/1B: $89   2P/2B: $89   XP: $7
Sun-Thurs [CP]   1P: $69   2P/1B: $69   2P/2B: $69   XP: $7
Location: I-40 exit 50, just n. 234 Hendersonville Rd 28803. Fax: 704/277-9800. **Terms:** No pets. **Facility:** 72 rooms. 3 s
ries, no elevator; exterior corridors. **All Rooms:** free movies. **Cards:** AE, CB, DI, DS, JCB, MC, VI.

HOTEL WEST   Rates Subject to Change   **Phone: 704/667-4501**
6/1-10/31 [CP]   2P/1B: $75- 95 2P/2B: $75- 95 XP: $5
Motor Inn   12/1-5/31 & 11/1-11/30 [CP]   2P/1B: $55- 65 2P/2B: $55- 65 XP: $5
Location: I-40 exit 44; 0.3 mi e. 275 Smoky Park Hwy 28806. Fax: 704/665-4265. **Terms:** Check-in 4 p
no pets. **Facility:** 225 rooms. 2 stories; interior/exterior corridors. **All Rooms:** free movies. **Cards:** AE, CB, DS, MC, VI.

HOWARD JOHNSON BILTMORE   **Phone: 704/274-2300**
10/1-10/31   1P: $68- 139 2P/1B: $75- 139 2P/2B: $75- 139 XP: $8
4/1-9/30   1P: $58- 129 2P/1B: $66- 129 2P/2B: $69- 129 XP: $8
12/1-4/10 & 11/1-11/30   1P: $55- 73   2P/1B: $59- 80 2P/2B: $59- 89 XP: $8
Motor Inn   **Location:** I-40 exit 50, 0.3 mi n. on US 25. 190 Hendersonville Rd 28803. Fax: 704/274-23
Terms: Weekly/monthly rates; no pets. **Facility:** 68 rooms. 2 blocks from Biltmore Estate. Large rooms. 2 s
ries; interior corridors. **Dining:** Restaurant; 6:30 am-2 & 5:30-8:30 pm, Sat & Sun from 7 am; $6-$12; cockta
Services: valet laundry. **Some Rooms:** radios, refrigerators. **Cards:** AE, DI, DS, MC, VI. **Special Amenities:** Ea
check-in/late check-out and preferred room (subject to availability with advanced reservations).
(See color ad below)

THE LOG CABIN MOTOR COURT   Rates Subject to Change   **Phone: 704/645-6546**
10/1-11/1   1P: $34   2P/1B: $34- 66 2P/2B: $50- 81 XP: $5
12/1-9/30 & 11/2-11/30   1P: $31   2P/1B: $31- 61 2P/2B: $45- 76 XP: $5
Location: 4 mi n on US 19 & 23, New Bridge exit, then 1 mi n on Weaverville Hwy, Meriman & N Ashev
Cottage   exit southbound. 330 Weaverville Hwy 28804. **Terms:** Reserv deposit, 14 day notice; no pets. **Facility:**
rooms. 3 two-bedroom cottages with kitchen, $76 for 5 persons, 2 night min stay. Handling fee imposed
story; exterior corridors. **All Rooms:** free movies, no A/C. **Some Rooms:** 10 kitchens. **Cards:** DS, MC, VI.

MOTEL 6 - 1134   Guaranteed Rates   **Phone: 704/299-3040**
All Year   1P: $37- 42   2P/1B: $42- 49 2P/2B: $42- 49 XP: $2
Location: I-40 exit 55. 1415 Tunnel Rd 28805. Fax: 704/298-3158. **Terms:** Sr. discount; small pets o
Motel   **Facility:** 106 rooms. 1 story; exterior corridors. **All Rooms:** free movies. **Cards:** AE, DI, DS, MC, VI.
Roll in showers.

(See map p. 315)

THE PINES COTTAGES   Guaranteed Rates   Phone: 704/645-9661   **15**
All Year   2P/1B: $50- 75   2P/2B: $55- 95   XP: $10   F14
Location: 4 mi n on US 19 & 23, New Bridge exit, 1.1 mi n on Weaverville Hwy, Merriman/N Asheville exit
southbound. 346 Weaverville Hwy 28804. Fax: 704/645-6949. **Terms:** Reserv deposit, 14 day notice; no
pets. **Facility:** 15 rooms. 2 two-bedroom cottages, $115-$125 for up to 4 persons; 1 story; exterior corridors.
All Rooms: free movies, no A/C. **Some Rooms:** 14 kitchens. **Cards:** AE, CB, DI, DS, MC, VI.
Cottage
(See ad below)   (CTV) (D)

THE PLAZA MOTEL   Phone: 704/274-2050   **35**
5/1-10/31   1P: $43   2P/1B: $47   2P/2B: $51   XP: $2   F6
12/1-4/30 & 11/1-11/30   1P: $32   2P/1B: $36   2P/2B: $40   XP: $2   F6
Location: I-40 exit 50, 1 mi n, 2 blks s of Biltmore entrance. 111 Hendersonville Rd 28803. **Terms:** No pets.
Facility: 18 rooms. Well kept property. 1 two-bedroom unit. 2 stories; exterior corridors. **Dining:** Restaurant
Motel
nearby. **All Rooms:** free movies. **Cards:** DS, MC, VI.
(CTV) (D)

QUALITY INN BILTMORE   Rates Subject to Change   Phone: 704/274-1800   **21**
5/1-10/31   1P: $90- 135   2P/1B: $90- 145   2P/2B: $90- 145   XP: $8   F18
12/1-4/30 & 11/1-11/30   1P: $85- 130   2P/1B: $85- 130   2P/2B: $85- 130   XP: $8   F18
Motor Inn
Location: I-40 exit 50, 0.5 mi n on US 25. 115 Hendersonville Rd 28803. Fax: 704/274-5960. **Terms:** No
pets. **Facility:** 160 rooms. 20 suites, $130; 5 stories; interior corridors. **Dining:** Dining room, restaurant; 6:30 am-10 pm;
$11-$19. **All Rooms:** free movies. **Cards:** AE, CB, DI, DS, MC, VI.
(symbols) (CTV) (X) (symbol) (D) (S)

RADISSON HOTEL ASHEVILLE   Phone: 704/252-8211   **32**
12/1-12/15 & 4/1-11/30   1P: $99- 119   2P/1B: $109- 129   2P/2B: $109- 129   XP: $10   F18
12/16-3/31   1P: $79- 109   2P/1B: $89- 119   2P/2B: $89- 119   XP: $10   F18
Location: I-240 Merrimon exit, adjacent to Thomas Wolfe Memorial Home. 1 Thomas Wolfe Plaza 28801.
Fax: 704/254-1374. **Terms:** Reserv deposit; monthly rates; no pets. **Facility:** 281 rooms. 12 stories; interior
Hotel
corridors; luxury level rooms. **Dining:** Dining room, coffee shop; 6:30 am-10 pm. Full
service rooftop dining room & mall style food fair deli just off lobby; $9-$20; cocktails/lounge. **Services:** valet laundry.
All Rooms: honor bars, coffeemakers, free & pay movies. **Some Rooms:** VCP's. **Cards:** AE, CB, DI, DS, JCB, MC, VI.
(symbols) (symbols) (symbols) (symbols) (CTV) (X) (symbol) (D) (S)

RED ROOF INN-WEST   Rates Subject to Change   Phone: 704/667-9803   **7**
12/1-12/31 & 10/1-11/30   1P: $60   2P/1B: $68   2P/2B: $65   XP: $6   F18
6/1-7/31   1P: $52   2P/1B: $58   2P/2B: $63   XP: $6   F18
8/1-9/30   1P: $45   2P/1B: $51   2P/2B: $54   XP: $6   F18
1/1-5/31   1P: $39   2P/1B: $44   2P/2B: $47   XP: $5   F18
Motel
Location: I-40 exit 44, just n on US 19 & 23, just w on old Haywood Rd, just s. 16 Crowell Rd 28806. Fax: 704/667-9810.
Terms: Small pets only. **Facility:** 109 rooms. 3 stories; exterior corridors. **All Rooms:** free movies. **Cards:** AE, CB, DI, DS,
MC, VI.
(symbol) (CTV) (X) (D)

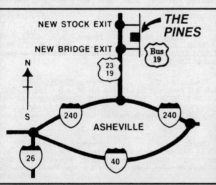

346 WEAVERVILLE HWY.
ASHEVILLE, NC 28804
(704) 645-9661
•Cottages & Cabins • Some Fireplaces
•Cable TV • Kitchens • Credit Cards

(See map p. 315)

RICHMOND HILL INN
Rates Subject to Change   Phone: 704/252-7313

Fri & Sat [BP]	1P: $190- 375	2P/1B: $190- 375	2P/2B: $190- 375	XP: $20	F
Sun-Thurs [BP]	1P: $145- 300	2P/1B: $145- 300	2P/2B: $145- 300	XP: $20	F

◆◆◆◆ **Location:** I-240, exit Weaverville US 19/23, exit SR 251, just w under overpass, 1st light s (Riverside Dr
Historic 0.5 mi to Pearson Br Rd, just w across bridge. 87 Richmond Hill Dr 28806. Fax: 704/252-872
Country Inn **Terms:** Reserv deposit, 3 day notice; no pets. **Facility:** 36 rooms. 28 rooms with gas fireplace. Handling fe
imposed; 3 stories, no elevator; interior/exterior corridors; smoke free premises. **Dining:** Restaurant; 11:3
am-2:30 & 5-9 pm, hours vary off season; $12-$19; also, Gabrielle's at Richmond Hill, see separate listing. **All Rooms:** fre
movies. **Cards:** AE, MC, VI. *(See color ad p 323)*

SLEEP INN BILTMORE
Rates Subject to Change   Phone: 704/277-1800

12/1-12/31 & 5/1-11/30 [CP]	1P: $69	2P/1B: $85	2P/2B: $85	XP: $6	F1
4/1-4/30 [CP]	1P: $67	2P/1B: $73	2P/2B: $73	XP: $6	F1
1/1-3/31 [CP]	1P: $45	2P/1B: $51	2P/2B: $51	XP: $6	F1

Motel
Location: I-40 exit 50, 0.3 mi n on US 25. 117 Hendersonville Rd 28803. Fax: 704/274-7101. **Terms:** Sr. discount; no pet
Facility: 64 rooms. 3 stories; interior corridors. **All Rooms:** free movies. **Cards:** AE, CB, DI, DS, MC, VI.
Roll in showers.

SUPER 8 EAST
Phone: 704/298-7952

6/12-8/15 & 10/1-10/31	1P: $54	2P/1B: $59	2P/2B: $59	XP: $5	F1
8/16-9/30 & 11/1-11/30	1P: $44	2P/1B: $49	2P/2B: $49	XP: $5	F1
3/27-6/11	1P: $42	2P/1B: $47	2P/2B: $47	XP: $5	F1
12/1-3/26	1P: $32	2P/1B: $37	2P/2B: $37	XP: $5	F1

◆◆◆ **Location:** I-40 exit 55, 0.3 mi w. 1329 Tunnel Rd 28805. Fax: 704/298-4447. **Terms:** Weekly rates; pets, $2
Motel dep req. **Facility:** 124 rooms. Tastefully appointed, contemporary rooms. 2 stories; exterior corridors; picnic area by creeksid
on rear of property. **Dining:** Restaurant nearby. **Services:** Fee: coin laundry. **Recreation:** fishing
Some Rooms: microwaves, refrigerators. **Cards:** AE, CB, DI, DS, MC, VI. **Special Amenities:** Free breakfast and fre
local telephone calls.

THE WRIGHT INN & CARRIAGE HOUSE
Rates Subject to Change   Phone: 704/251-0789

All Year [BP]	1P: $95- 145	2P/1B: $95- 145		XP: $25

Location: I-240 exit 4C (Montford Ave), 0.8 mi n to Wautauga, just w. 235 Pearson Dr 2880
◆◆◆ Fax: 704/251-0929. **Terms:** Age restrictions may apply; reserv deposit; 2 night min stay, weekends; no pets
Historic Bed **Facility:** 10 rooms. Reduced rates for extended stays; 3 stories; interior/exterior corridors; smoke free prem
& Breakfast ises. **All Rooms:** free movies. **Some Rooms:** kitchen. **Cards:** DS, MC, VI.

RESTAURANTS

BLUE MOON BAKERY   **Lunch:** $5-$7   **Dinner:** $11-$16   **Phone:** 704/252-6063
◆◆ **Location:** Downtown, corner Aston. 60 Biltmore Ave 28801. **Hours:** 7:30 am-6 pm, Wed-Sat to 10 pm
Nouvelle Sunday brunch 9 am-3 pm. Closed major holidays. **Features:** casual dress; beer & wine only; a la carte
American also prix fixe. Bakery/cafe offering excellent bread & pastry. Unique & creative dinners 4 nights a wee
Espresso/cappuccino. Smoke free premises. **Cards:** MC, VI.

CHARLOTTE STREET GRILL & PUB   **Lunch:** $4-$7   **Dinner:** $6-$10   **Phone:** 704/253-5348
◆◆ **Location:** I-240, exit 5B, 0.5 mi n. 159 Charlotte St 28801. **Hours:** 11:30 am-9 pm, Sat & Sun 2 pm-10 pm
Continental **Reservations:** suggested. **Features:** casual dress. Burgers, pasta, steak, milkshakes, cocktails & an Englis
pub. Casual upbeat dining on 2nd floor. **Cards:** AE, DS, MC, VI.

CHINA PALACE   **Lunch:** $4-$6   **Dinner:** $6-$12   **Phone:** 704/298-7098
◆◆ **Location:** On SR 74, opposite Asheville Mall, 200 yards s of jct SR 70 & SR 74. 4 S Tunnel Rd 2880
Chinese **Hours:** 11:30 am-2:30 & 5-10 pm, Sat noon-10:30 pm, Sun noon-9 pm. **Reservations:** accepted
Features: casual dress; Sunday brunch; children's menu; carryout; cocktails. Comfortable surroundings wit
tasteful Far East decor. Delivery service to local motels avail. All natural ingredients, no MSG. **Cards:** AE, DI, DS, MC, VI.

FINE FRIENDS   **Lunch:** $5-$9   **Dinner:** $8-$20   **Phone:** 704/253-6649
◆◆ **Location:** On US 25, 2.8 mi n of I-240, exit 5A (Merrimon Ave). 946 Merrimon Ave 28804. **Hours:** 11:3
American am-9 pm, Thurs-Sat to 10 pm. Closed major holidays. **Reservations:** suggested; weekend
Features: casual dress; Sunday brunch; children's menu; carryout; cocktails & lounge. Pasta, sandwiches
fish, chicken & beef. **Cards:** AE, CB, DI, DS, MC, VI.

(See map p. 315)

GABRIELLE'S AT RICHMOND HILL　　　**Dinner: $23-$30**　　　**Phone: 704/252-7313**　⑩
Location: I-240, exit Weaverville US 19/23, exit SR 251, just w under overpass, 1st light s (Riverside Dr), 0.5 mi to Pearson Br Rd, just w across bridge; in Richmond Hill Inn. 87 Richmond Hill Dr 28806. **Hours:** 6
Regional　pm-10 pm. Closed: Tues & Wed off season. **Reservations:** required. **Features:** semi-formal attire; cocktails; American　valet parking. Gracious service in Victorian dining room or glass enclosed veranda. Some unique southern variations done on many dishes. Smoke free premises. **Cards:** AE, MC, VI.　　　❌

GOODFELLAS　　　**Dinner: $7-$17**　　　**Phone: 704/658-3267**　⑱
Location: 4 mi n on US 19 & 23, New Bridge exit then 1.3 mi n. 330 Weaverville Hwy 28804. **Hours:** 5:30
◆◆ Italian　pm-9:30 pm. Closed: Mon & Tues. **Features:** casual dress; beer & wine only; a la carte. Chef owned &
operated. Rustic decor. Well prepared homemade cuisine.　　　❌

THE GREENERY RESTAURANT　　　**Dinner: $15-$20**　　　**Phone: 704/253-2809**　⑦
Location: I-240, exit 7, 0.5 mi w on US 70 & 74. 148 Tunnel Rd 28805. **Hours:** 5 pm-9 pm.
◆◆◆ Continental　**Reservations:** suggested. **Features:** casual dress; early bird specials; cocktails & lounge. Fresh seafood,
duck & Maryland crabcakes. Wine spectator award. **Cards:** AE, MC, VI.　　　❌

GROVEWOOD CAFE　　　**Lunch: $7-$10**　　　**Dinner: $11-$17**　　　**Phone: 704/258-8956**　⑲
Location: I-240 exit Charlotte St, 2 mi n via Charlotte St & Macon Ave, adjacent to Grove Park Inn. 111
◆◆◆ Continental　Grovewood Rd 28804. **Hours:** 11 am-10 pm. Closed: Sun. **Reservations:** accepted. **Features:** casual
dress; children's menu; cocktails; a la carte. Graceful setting with atmosphere of turn-of-the-century
Asheville. Innovative menu, very well prepared & presented cuisine. Smoke free premises. **Cards:** AE, DS, MC, VI.

HORIZONS　　　**Dinner: $21-$33**　　　**Phone: 704/252-2711**　②
Location: I-240 Charlotte St exit, 2 mi n on Macon Ave via Charlotte St, follow signs; in Grove Park Inn
◆◆◆◆ Regional　Resort. 290 Macon Ave 28804. **Hours:** 6 pm-10 pm. **Reservations:** required. **Features:** health
American　conscious menu; cocktails; entertainment; fee for valet parking; a la carte, also prix fixe. Elegant. Arts &
crafts style furnishings. Superior, innovative cuisine. Smoke free premises. **Cards:** AE, CB, DI, DS, MC, VI.　❌

J & S CAFETERIA　　　　　　**Phone: 704/298-0507**　⑫
Location: I-240, exit 8; in River Ridge Market Place. 800 Fairview Rd 28803. **Hours:** 6-10 am, 11-2:15 &
◆ American　4-8 pm, Sun 6 am-8:30 pm, 11 am-9 pm Fri-Sun in summer. Closed: 12/25. **Features:** health conscious
menu items.　　　❌

LA PAZ RESTAURANTE CANTINA　　　**Lunch: $6-$9**　　　**Dinner: $9-$13**　　　**Phone: 704/277-8779**　⑪
Location: I-40 exit 50, 0.3 mi n on US 25 to SR 81, just e on SR 81 to US 25A, just s on US 25A in
◆◆ Mexican　Biltmore Village. 10 Biltmore Plaza 28803. **Hours:** 11 am-10 pm, Fri & Sat-11 pm. Closed: 11/26 & 12/25.
Features: children's menu; carryout; cocktails; street parking; a la carte. Tex-Mex ambience. **Cards:** AE, CB,
DI, DS, MC, VI.

LAUGHING SEED CAFE　　　**Lunch: $5-$8**　　　**Dinner: $7-$10**　　　**Phone: 704/252-3445**　㉒
Location: 40 Wall St 28801. **Hours:** 11:30 am-9 pm, Sun-8 pm. Closed major holidays & 12/24.
◆◆ Vegetarian　**Features:** casual dress; children's menu; health conscious menu; carryout; beer & wine only; street parking.
Creative vegetarian cuisine, large & varied menu. Pleasant contemporary decor. Smoke free premises.
Cards: AE, DS, MC, VI.　　　❌

MAGNOLIA'S RAW BAR & GRILLE　　　**Lunch: $3-$9**　　　**Dinner: $10-$19**　　　**Phone: 704/251-5211**　③
Location: Downtown; Walnut & Market sts. 26 Walnut St 28801. **Hours:** 11:30 am-midnight, Fri-2 am, Sat 5
◆◆ American　pm-2 am, Sun 5 pm-9:30 pm. Closed: 11/26, 12/25 & Sun 9/5-5/30. **Reservations:** suggested.
Features: casual dress; children's menu; carryout; cocktails & lounge; street parking. International cuisine &
seafood with southern accents; casual raw bar. Light menu after 10 pm. **Cards:** AE, CB, DI, DS, MC, VI.　❌

THE MARKET PLACE　　　**Dinner: $12-$27**　　　**Phone: 704/252-4162**　④
Location: Downtown, just e of Federal Bldg. 20 Wall St 28801. **Hours:** 6 pm-9:30 pm. Closed major
◆◆◆ Nouvelle　holidays & Sun except 10/1-10/31. **Reservations:** suggested. **Features:** dressy casual; cocktails & lounge;
American　street parking; a la carte. Modernist, high-ceilinged dining room. Innovative market cuisine. Excellent
preparation & presentation. Smoke free premises. **Cards:** AE, DI, MC, VI.　　　❌

MCGUFFEY'S　　　**Lunch: $7-$9**　　　**Dinner: $10-$16**　　　**Phone: 704/252-0956**　㉓
Location: I-240 exit 6, s on Tunnel Rd. 13 Kenilworth Knoll 38805. **Hours:** 11 am-1 am. Closed: 11/26 &
◆◆ American　12/25. **Features:** casual dress; Sunday brunch; children's menu; senior's menu; health conscious menu;
carryout; cocktails & lounge; a la carte. Eclectic selection of freshly prepared dishes served in contemporary
atmosphere. **Cards:** AE, DS, MC, VI.　　　❌

POSEIDON STEAK AND SEAFOOD HOUSE　　　**Dinner: $10-$20**　　　**Phone: 704/298-4121**　⑤
Location: I-40 exit 55. 1327 Tunnel Rd 28805. **Hours:** 4 pm-10 pm, Fri & Sat-11 pm. Closed: 11/26 & 12/25.
Steak and　**Reservations:** suggested; weekends. **Features:** casual dress; children's menu; carryout; cocktails & lounge.
Seafood　Family dining. Some Greek specialties. **Cards:** AE, CB, DI, DS, MC, VI.　　　❌

POSSUM TROT GRILL　　　**Lunch: $4-$12**　　　**Dinner: $8-$15**　　　**Phone: 704/253-0062**　㉔
Location: 8 Wall St 28801. **Hours:** 11 am-2 & 5-9 pm. Closed: Sun, Mon & 1/15-2/14.
◆ Ethnic　**Reservations:** accepted. **Features:** casual dress; carryout; beer & wine only; street parking; a la carte.
Authentic New Orleans cuisine served in a simply decorated, informal dining room. Pleasant, knowledgable
service. Smoke free premises. **Cards:** MC, VI.　　　❌

SAVOY　　　**Lunch: $4-$8**　　　**Dinner: $7-$16**　　　**Phone: 704/253-1077**　㉗
Location: I-240 exit 5A, 1.8 mi n on Merrimon Ave. 641 Merrimon Ave 28804. **Hours:** 11 am-2:30 & 5-9 pm,
◆◆ Ethnic　Fri & Sat-10 pm. Closed: 11/26 & 12/25. **Reservations:** accepted. **Features:** casual dress; carryout; beer &
wine only; a la carte. Art deco decor. Creative fusion of Mediterranean, Oriental & Southwestern American
cuisine. Smoke free premises. **Cards:** AE, MC, VI.　　　❌

TREVI　　　**Lunch: $4-$9**　　　**Dinner: $8-$17**　　　**Phone: 704/281-1400**　⑯
Location: I-40 exit 50, 1 mi n on Biltmore Rd. 2 Hendersonville Rd 28803. **Hours:** 11:30 am-2:30 & 5-10
◆◆ Italian　pm, Sun 5 pm-9 pm. Closed: 12/25. **Reservations:** accepted. **Features:** casual dress; children's menu;
carryout; cocktails & lounge. Homemade pasta, fresh seafood & pizza. **Cards:** AE, DS, MC, VI.　　　❌

(See map p. 315)

23 PAGE AT HAYWOOD PARK **Dinner:** $13-$30 **Phone:** 704/252-3685 [1]
   Location: Center, in Haywood Park Promenade; in Haywood Park Hotel. 1 Battery Park 28801. **Hours:** 5:30
   pm-9:30 pm, Fri & Sat-10 pm. Closed major holidays. **Reservations:** suggested. **Features:** casual dress
   senior's menu; cocktails & lounge. American cooking with international influences. Local fresh mountain trout
American   Prix fix menu available. **Cards:** AE, DI, MC, VI.
   ☒

VICENZO'S **Dinner:** $11-$20 **Phone:** 704/254-4698 [17]
◆◆◆   **Location:** Center; Walnut at Market St. 10 N Market St 28801. **Hours:** 6 pm-10 pm, Sun-9 pm
Northern   **Reservations:** suggested. **Features:** dressy casual; children's menu; carryout; cocktails & lounge
Italian   entertainment; a la carte. Classic menu including veal, fish, chicken & pasta. Uncomplicated preparation with
   emphasis on taste. Austere 2nd floor dining room with interesting art deco features. Cigar bar in bistro
Smoke free premises. **Cards:** AE, DS, MC, VI.
   ☒

THE WINDMILL EUROPEAN GRILL-IL PESCATORE **Dinner:** $10-$19 **Phone:** 704/253-5285 [8]
◆◆◆   **Location:** I-240 exit 6; in Innsbruck Mall. 85 Tunnel Rd 28805. **Hours:** 5:30 pm-9:30 pm, Fri & Sat-10 pm
Ethnic   Closed major holidays, Sun & Mon. **Reservations:** suggested. **Features:** casual dress; children's menu
   carryout; cocktails & lounge; minimum charge-$9. Basement restaurant serving wide menu of international
dishes. Specializing in German, Indian & classical Italian. **Cards:** AE, DS, MC, VI.
   ☒

ATLANTIC BEACH—1,900

LODGINGS

A PLACE AT THE BEACH III Rates Subject to Change **Phone:** 919/247-2636
◆◆

6/14-8/24	2P/1B: $156	2P/2B: $209
Condo Motel 4/1-6/13 & 8/25-10/31	2P/1B: $128	2P/2B: $150
3/1-3/31 & 11/1-11/30	2P/1B: $85	2P/2B: $118
12/1-2/28	2P/1B: $75	2P/2B: $107

Location: 2 mi s on US 58 from Atlantic Beach Causeway. 1904 E Ft Macon Rd 28512 (PO Box 1090). **Fax:** 919/247-1067
Terms: Check-in 4 pm; reserv deposit; 7 night min stay, 5/27-9/4; no pets. **Facility:** 103 rooms. 5 three-bedroom units, $180
in season. Rates for up to 6 persons. Phone charge $.50 per call; 3 stories, no elevator; exterior corridors
All Rooms: kitchens, free movies. **Cards:** AE, DS, MC, VI.
   🛥 🛥 D

HOLIDAY INN OCEANFRONT Rates Subject to Change **Phone:** 919/726-2544
◆◆

5/26-9/4	1P: $89- 135	2P/1B: $89- 135	2P/2B: $89- 135	XP: $10	F19
Motor Inn 3/1-5/25 & 9/5-10/31	1P: $59- 130	2P/1B: $59- 130	2P/2B: $59- 130	XP: $10	F19
12/1-2/28 & 11/1-11/30	1P: $39- 69	2P/1B: $39- 69	2P/2B: $39- 69	XP: $10	F19

Location: 2.5 mi n on SR 58N. Salter Path Rd 28512 (PO Box 280). **Fax:** 919/726-6570. **Terms:** Sr. discount; reserv
deposit, 3 day notice, 4/15-10/15; no pets. **Facility:** 114 rooms. 5 stories; interior/exterior corridors. **Dining:** Dining room; 7
am-11 & 5:30-9:30 pm; $8-$13. **All Rooms:** free movies. **Cards:** AE, CB, DI, DS, JCB, MC.
   🛥 CTV ☒ 🛇 D

SEA HAWK MOTEL Rates Subject to Change **Phone:** 919/726-4146
🔺

6/1-9/5	2P/2B: $98- 108	XP: $10	F15
4/2-5/31 & 9/6-10/17	2P/2B: $73- 83	XP: $10	F15
12/1-4/1 & 10/18-11/30	2P/2B: $45- 50	XP: $10	F15

Motel   **Location:** 2.5 mi n on SR 58N. Salter Path Rd 28512 (PO Box 177). **Terms:** Reserv deposit, 7 day notice
handling fee imposed; no pets. **Facility:** 36 rooms. 2 three-bedroom townhouses, $1600 weekly, 2 bedroom
cottage $75-$130; 2 stories; exterior corridors. **Dining:** Coffee shop; 7 am-2 pm in season. **All Rooms:** free movies
Cards: MC, VI.
   🛥 CTV D

SHERATON ATLANTIC BEACH OCEANFRONT HOTEL & CONFERENCE CENTER **Phone:** 919/240-1155
🔺 SAVE

5/15-8/15	1P: $155- 189	2P/1B: $165- 189	2P/2B: $155- 189	XP: $15	F17
3/13-5/14 & 8/16-10/24	1P: $95- 125	2P/1B: $95- 125	2P/2B: $95- 125	XP: $15	F17
12/1-3/12 & 10/25-11/30	1P: $55- 65	2P/1B: $55- 65	2P/2B: $55- 65	XP: $15	F17

Hotel   **Location:** 2.3 mi n on SR 58N. 2717 W Fort Macon Rd 28512 (PO Box 3040). **Fax:** 919/240-1452
Terms: Check-in 4 pm; reserv deposit, 3 day notice; no pets. **Facility:** 200 rooms. 9 stories; interior corridors
Dining: Dining room; 6:30 am-10:30 pm; $8-$18. **All Rooms:** free & pay movies. **Cards:** AE, CB, DI, DS, MC, VI.
   🛥 🛥 ♦ CTV 🛈 ☒ 🛇 D S

SHOWBOAT MOTEL **Phone:** 919/726-6163
🔺 SAVE

Fri & Sat 5/22-9/8 [CP]	1P: $79- 99	2P/1B: $79- 99	2P/2B: $79- 99	XP: $5	F18
Sun-Thurs 5/22-9/8 [CP]	1P: $59- 79	2P/1B: $59- 79	2P/2B: $59- 79	XP: $5	F18
4/1-5/21 & 9/9-10/31 [CP]	1P: $44- 74	2P/1B: $44- 74	2P/2B: $44- 74	XP: $5	F18
12/1-3/31 & 11/1-11/30 [CP]	1P: $34- 54	2P/1B: $34- 54	2P/2B: $34- 54	XP: $5	F18

Motel   **Location:** Just over bridge from Morehead City. Atlantic Beach Cswy 28512 (PO Box 340)
Fax: 919/726-1587. **Terms:** Reserv deposit, 3 day notice; weekly rates; no pets. **Facility:** 42 rooms. Many rooms with water-
front view. 2 stories; exterior corridors; boat dock, boat ramp; grills & picnic area. **Dining:** Restaurant nearby
Recreation: fishing, scuba diving, fish cleaning table. Fee: scuba equipment. **All Rooms:** free movies, refrigerators
Cards: AE, MC, VI. **Special Amenities:** Free local telephone calls and preferred room (subject to availability with
advanced reservations).
   🛥 🛅 CTV ☒ D

RESTAURANT

TRATTORIA DA FRANCO'S **Dinner:** $8-$12 **Phone:** 919/240-3141
◆◆◆   **Location:** On SR 58W; town center. Ft Macon Rd & Kinston Ave 28512. **Hours:** 5 pm-10 pm, Fri & Sat-11
Italian   pm. Closed: 11/26, 12/25 & Tues. **Reservations:** suggested. **Features:** children's menu; carryout; cocktails
   Homemade pasta, bread, sauce & dessert; owner/chef. Seafood, chicken & beef entrees; Northern &
southern Italian cuisine. Very popular. **Cards:** DS, MC, VI.
   ☒

BALD HEAD ISLAND—100

LODGING

THEODOSIA'S BED & BREAKFAST Rates Subject to Change **Phone:** 910/457-6563
◆◆◆

3/1-11/30 [BP]	1P: $130- 175	2P/1B: $140- 190	2P/2B: $160	XP: $25	D15
12/1-2/28 [BP]	1P: $115- 155	2P/1B: $130- 170	2P/2B: $145	XP: $25	D15

Bed &
Breakfast   **Location:** Catch ferry at Indigo Plantation at Southport, from US 17, 17 mi e on SR 211. Located off marina
   in the Harbor Row area of the island. 91 Keelson Row 28461 (PO Box 3130). **Fax:** 910/457-6055
Terms: Age restrictions may apply; reserv deposit, 7 day notice; no pets, owner has cat. **Facility:** 10 rooms. Ferry transpor-
tation not included in room rates; 3 stories; interior corridors; smoke free premises. Fee: parking. **All Rooms:** free movies
Cards: DS, MC, VI.
   Roll in showers. CTV ☒ D S

BANNER ELK—900

LODGINGS

THE BANNER ELK INN BED & BREAKFAST — Rates Subject to Change — **Phone:** 704/898-6223
◆◆◆ All Year [BP]   1P: $70   2P/1B: $80- 110   XP: $10
Historic Bed **Location:** Hwy 194N. 407 Main St E 28604. **Terms:** Age restrictions may apply; reserv deposit, 30 day
& Breakfast notice; 2 night min stay, 5/1-10/31; pets. **Facility:** 4 rooms. Handling fee imposed; 2 stories; interior corridors;
designated smoking area. **All Rooms:** no A/C. **Cards:** MC, VI.

HOLIDAY INN/BANNER ELK-BEECH MTN — **Phone:** 704/898-4571
Ⓐ Ⓢᴬⱽᴱ   Fri & Sat   1P: $119   2P/1B: $119   2P/2B: $199   XP: $8   F12
     Sun-Thurs   1P: $55- 79   2P/1B: $55- 79   2P/2B: $55- 79   XP: $8   F12
◆◆◆ **Location:** 1 mi se on SR 184. Hwy 184 28604 (PO Box 1478). Fax: 704/898-8437. **Terms:** Reserv deposit,
Motor Inn   3 day notice; no pets. **Facility:** 101 rooms. Very attractive public areas. 2 stories; exterior corridors.
Dining: Restaurant; 7 am-2 & 5-10 pm, Fri & Sat-9 pm; lunch buffet Mon-Fri, $3.99; Fri night seafood buffet,
$8.99. Sun brunch, $6.99; $6-$12; wine/beer only. **All Rooms:** coffeemakers, free movies. **Some Rooms:** Fee: refrigerators.
Cards: AE, CB, DI, DS, MC, VI. **Special Amenities:** Early check-in/late check-out and free room upgrade (subject to
availability with advanced reservations).

BEAUFORT—3,800

LODGINGS

BEAUFORT INN — Rates Subject to Change — **Phone:** 919/728-2600
Ⓐ   5/1-9/30 [BP]   2P/1B: $109- 129   2P/2B: $109- 129   XP: $15
     3/1-4/30 & 10/1-11/30 [BP]   2P/1B: $79- 99   2P/2B: $79- 99   XP: $15
◆◆◆ 12/1-2/28 [BP]   2P/1B: $59- 79   2P/2B: $59- 79   XP: $15
Motel **Location:** US 70 to Moore St, s 2 blks then 1 blk w on Ann St. 101 Ann St 28516. Fax: 919/728-1864.
Terms: Reserv deposit, 4 day notice; 2 night min stay, summer weekends; no pets. **Facility:** 44 rooms. Handling fee imposed; 3 stories, no elevator; exterior corridors; designated smoking area. **All Rooms:** free movies. **Cards:** AE,
CB, DI, DS, MC, VI.

DELAMAR INN — Guaranteed Rates — **Phone:** 919/728-4300
◆◆◆ 5/1-9/30 [CP]   1P: $98- 102   2P/1B: $98- 102   XP: $12   D
Historic Bed 4/1-4/30 & 10/1-10/31 [CP]   1P: $78   2P/1B: $78- 84   XP: $12   D
& Breakfast 12/1-2/28 [CP]   1P: $68   2P/1B: $72   XP: $12   D
     3/1-3/31 & 11/1-11/30 [CP]   1P: $72   2P/1B: $78   XP: $12   D
Location: Center. 217 Turner St 28516. Fax: 919/728-1471. **Terms:** Sr. discount; age restrictions may apply; no pets.
Facility: 3 rooms. 2 stories; interior corridors; smoke free premises. **Cards:** MC, VI.

INLET INN — **Phone:** 919/728-3600
Ⓐ Ⓢᴬⱽᴱ   5/22-9/7 [CP]   2P/1B: $115- 135   2P/2B: $115- 135   XP: $15   F16
     4/3-5/21 & 9/8-10/31 [CP]   2P/1B: $95- 115   2P/2B: $95- 115   XP: $15   F16
◆◆ 3/1-4/2 & 11/1-11/28 [CP]   2P/1B: $85- 105   2P/2B: $85- 105   XP: $15   F16
Motel 12/1-2/28 & 11/29-11/30 [CP]   2P/1B: $60- 80   2P/2B: $60- 80   XP: $15   F16
     Location: Center, facing Beaufort waterfront on corner of Queen & Front. 601 Front St 28516.
Fax: 919/728-5833. **Terms:** No pets. **Facility:** 35 rooms. Many rooms with porch, most with waterfront view. Spacious well-
appointed rooms, some with fireplace. 3 stories; exterior corridors. **Dining:** Restaurant nearby. **All Rooms:** coffeemakers,
free movies, refrigerators. **Cards:** AE, DS, MC, VI. **Special Amenities:** Free breakfast and free newspaper.

PECAN TREE INN — Guaranteed Rates — **Phone:** 919/728-6733
Ⓐ   4/1-9/30 [CP]   1P: $75- 125   2P/1B: $85- 135   XP: $15
     12/1-3/31 & 10/1-11/30 [CP]   1P: $55- 105   2P/1B: $65- 115   XP: $15
◆◆◆ **Location:** In historic district. 116 Queen St 28516. **Terms:** Age restrictions may apply; reserv deposit, 10 day
Historic Bed notice; no pets. **Facility:** 7 rooms. 2 stories; interior corridors; smoke free premises. **Cards:** DS, MC, VI.
& Breakfast

RESTAURANT

THE SPOUTER INN RESTAURANT — **Lunch:** $5-$7 — **Dinner:** $14-$18 — **Phone:** 919/728-5190
◆◆ **Location:** Waterfront, opposite historic homes. 218 Front St 28516. **Hours:** 11:30 am-2:30 & 6-9:30 pm.
American   Closed: 11/26, 12/25 & Mon. **Features:** Sunday brunch; children's menu; carryout; cocktails. Seafood &
sandwiches; dining room with view of water. Patio dining on the dock weather permitting. Reservations
suggested for dinner in summer. **Cards:** MC, VI.

BELHAVEN—2,300

LODGING

RIVER FOREST MANOR — Guaranteed Rates — **Phone:** 919/943-2151
◆◆◆ All Year [CP]   1P: $65- 85   2P/1B: $65- 85   2P/2B: $65- 85   XP: $10   D
Historic **Location:** 6 blks e. 600 E Main St 27810. Fax: 919/943-6628. **Terms:** Reserv deposit; no pets. **Facility:** 6
Country Inn rooms. Interior corridors. **Dining:** Dining room; 5:30 pm-8:30 pm, famous for dinner smorgasborg & seasonal
oyster fritters; $13-$16; Sun brunch 11 am-2 pm, $6.95. **All Rooms:** free movies. **Cards:** AE, MC, VI.

BLACK MOUNTAIN—5,400

LODGINGS

APPLE BLOSSOM MOTEL — Rates Subject to Change — **Phone:** 704/669-7922
Ⓐ   5/25-11/30   2P/1B: $54- 64   2P/2B: $58- 74   XP: $5   F10
     12/1-5/24   1P: $24- 28   2P/1B: $28- 30   2P/2B: $30- 34   XP: $4   F10
◆ **Location:** I-40 exit 64, 0.5 mi n to US 70 (State St), 0.7 mi w. 602 W State St 28711. **Terms:** Sr. discount;
Motel reserv deposit, 30 day notice; no pets. **Facility:** 20 rooms. 1 story; exterior corridors. **Cards:** AE, DS, MC,
VI.

COMFORT INN — **Phone:** 704/669-9950
Ⓐ Ⓢᴬⱽᴱ   All Year [CP]   1P: $39- 125   2P/1B: $44- 149   2P/2B: $44- 149   XP: $5   F18
◆◆◆ **Location:** Just s on SR 9 off I-40, exit 64. 585 Hwy 9 28711. Fax: 704/669-1165. **Terms:** No pets.
Motel **Facility:** 57 rooms. 2 stories; exterior corridors; small pool. **Dining:** Restaurant nearby. **Services:** Fee: coin
laundry. **All Rooms:** free movies. **Some Rooms:** microwaves, refrigerators, VCP's. Fee: whirlpools.
Cards: AE, DI, DS, MC, VI. **Special Amenities:** Free breakfast and free local telephone calls.

BLOWING ROCK—1,300

LODGINGS

ALPEN ACRES MOTEL/ALPEN MOTOR COURT
Phone: 704/295-7981

6/5-11/1		2P/1B:	$50- 85	2P/2B:	$60- 99	XP:	$5	F
12/1-6/4 & 11/2-11/30		2P/1B:	$35- 69	2P/2B:	$59- 79	XP:	$5	F

AAA SAVE ◆◆ Motel **Location:** 1.3 mi n on US 221 & 321; 0.3 mi n of Blue Ridge Pkwy exit. 318 Old US Hwy 321 28605. **Fax:** 704/295-7900. **Terms:** Reserv deposit, 3 day notice; no pets. **Facility:** 19 rooms. Built on side of hill with scenic views. 1 two-bedroom unit with kitchen, $125-$185 for up to 10 persons; 1 story; exterior corridors; playground. **All Rooms:** free movies, combo or shower baths, no phones. **Cards:** AE, DS, MC, VI. **Special Amenities:** Early check-in/late check-out and free newspaper.   🛥 CTV ✕ D

ALPINE VILLAGE INN
Rates Subject to Change   **Phone: 704/295-7206**

12/22-2/28 & 6/6-11/1		2P/1B:	$46- 66	2P/2B:	$46- 66	XP: $5	D12
12/1-12/21, 3/1-6/5 & 11/2-11/30		2P/1B:	$39- 49	2P/2B:	$39- 49	XP: $5	D12

◆◆ Motel **Location:** Just e of Main St. 297 Sunset Dr 28605 (PO Box 429). **Terms:** Reserv deposit, 4 day notice; no pets. **Facility:** 15 rooms. Handling fee imposed; 1 story; exterior corridors. **All Rooms:** free movies. **Cards:** AE, DS, MC, VI.   CTV ✕ D

AZALEA GARDEN INN
Rates Subject to Change   **Phone: 704/295-3272**

7/1-10/31	2P/2B:	$89- 98	XP:	$25
6/1-6/30	2P/2B:	$79- 89	XP:	$25
5/1-5/31	2P/2B:	$69- 79	XP:	$25
4/1-4/30	2P/2B:	$59- 69	XP:	$25

◆◆◆ Motel **Location:** 3 blks n on US 221 & 321 business route. 793 N Main St 28605 (PO Box 165). **Terms:** Open 4/1-10/31; age restrictions may apply; no pets. **Facility:** 17 rooms. Log cabin with fireplace & kitchen, $125-$135; off season $95-$110 for 2 persons; 2 stories; exterior corridors; smoke free premises. **All Rooms:** free movies. **Cards:** AE, DS, MC, VI.   CTV ✕ D

BLOWING ROCK INN
Rates Subject to Change   **Phone: 704/295-7921**

7/1-10/26	2P/2B:	$59- 84	XP: $5	F12
6/1-6/30 & 10/27-11/28	2P/2B:	$49- 79	XP: $5	F12
5/1-5/31	2P/2B:	$49- 74	XP: $5	F12
4/1-4/30	2P/2B:	$44- 54	XP: $5	F12

◆◆◆ Motel **Location:** Just n on US 221 & 321 business route. 788 N Main St 28605 (PO Box 265). **Terms:** Open 4/1-11/28; reserv deposit, 3 day notice; no pets. **Facility:** 24 rooms. 4 villas with kitchen & fireplace, $59-$125; 1 story; exterior corridors. **All Rooms:** free movies. **Cards:** AE, DS, MC, VI.   🛥 CTV ✕ D

BOXWOOD LODGE
Rates Subject to Change   **Phone: 704/295-9984**

12/22-12/31 & 5/1-10/31		2P/1B:	$65- 110	2P/2B:	$65- 110	XP: $10	D16
12/1-12/21, 4/1-4/30 & 11/1-11/30		2P/1B:	$55- 65	2P/2B:	$55- 65	XP: $10	D16

◆◆◆ Motel **Location:** US 221 & 321 business route. 671 N Main St 28605 (PO Box 1509). **Terms:** Open 12/1-12/31 & 4/1-11/30; reserv deposit, 7 day notice; no pets. **Facility:** 22 rooms. 1 cabin with fireplace for up to 4 persons (non-smoking) $150; 2 stories; interior/exterior corridors; designated smoking area. **All Rooms:** free movies. **Cards:** MC, VI.   CTV ✕ D

BROOKSIDE INN
Rates Subject to Change   **Phone: 704/295-3380**

7/1-10/31 [CP]		2P/1B:	$89- 94	2P/2B:	$89- 94	XP: $15	
6/1-6/30 [CP]		2P/1B:	$69- 89	2P/2B:	$69- 89	XP: $15	
5/1-5/31 [CP]		2P/1B:	$59- 89	2P/2B:	$59- 89	XP: $15	
3/20-4/30 & 11/1-11/30 [CP]		2P/1B:	$49- 59	2P/2B:	$49- 59	XP: $15	

AAA ◆◆◆ Motel **Location:** On US 321 bypass, 2 blks e of city park. US 321 bypass 28605 (PO Box 372). **Terms:** Open 3/20-11/30; reserv deposit, 10 day notice; 2 night min stay, weekends in season; no pets. **Facility:** 22 rooms. 3 brookside villas, $105-$145. 4 suites $79-$109; 1 story; exterior corridors; smoke free premises. **All Rooms:** free movies. **Some Rooms:** 3 kitchens. **Cards:** DS, MC, VI.   CTV ✕ D

CHETOLA LODGE
Rates Subject to Change   **Phone: 704/295-5500**

5/1-10/31	2P/2B:	$110- 214	XP: $10	F12
12/1-4/30 & 11/1-11/30	2P/2B:	$80- 195	XP: $10	F12

◆◆◆ Resort Motor Inn **Location:** 1 mi e on Business Rt 321, or via signs off US 321 bypass; 0.5 mi n of Blue Ridge Pkwy via US 321. 28605 (PO Box 17). **Fax:** 704/295-5529. **Terms:** 2 night min stay; no pets. **Facility:** 42 rooms. 3 stories; interior corridors. **Dining:** Restaurant; 8-10 am, 11:30-2 & 5:30-9 pm, Sun 8-10:30 am, 11:30-2 & 5:30-9:30 pm; hours may vary seasonally; $10-$19. **All Rooms:** free movies. **Cards:** AE, DS, MC, VI.   🛥 CTV ✕ D

CLIFF DWELLERS INN
Rates Subject to Change   **Phone: 704/295-3121**

5/1-10/31	1P:	$95- 110	2P/1B:	$95- 110	2P/2B:	$95- 110	XP: $5	F12
12/1-4/30 & 11/1-11/30	1P:	$65- 95	2P/1B:	$65- 95	2P/2B:	$65- 95	XP: $5	F12

◆◆ Motel **Location:** 1 mi n; jct US 321 bypass & US 221, opposite Shoppes on the Parkway. 116 Lakeview Terr 28605. **Terms:** Reserv deposit, 3 day notice, handling fee imposed; 2 night min stay, weekends in season; no pets. **Facility:** 18 rooms. 1- & 2-bedroom suites, $140-$215. Open weekends only 11/1-4/30; rates $60-$90; 3 stories; exterior corridors. **All Rooms:** free movies. **Cards:** AE, CB, DI, MC, VI.   CTV ✕ D

DAYS INN
Rates Subject to Change   **Phone: 704/295-4422**

12/1-12/31 & 5/31-11/30	1P:	$70- 104	2P/1B:	$75- 109	2P/2B:	$75- 109	XP: $5	F18
1/1-5/30	1P:	$65- 75	2P/1B:	$65- 75	2P/2B:	$65- 75	XP: $5	F18

◆◆◆ Motel **Location:** On US 321 bypass at Ransom St. Hwy 321 Bypass at Ransome St 28605 (PO Box 2307). **Fax:** 704/295-0313. **Terms:** Sr. discount; check-in 4 pm; reserv deposit, 3 day notice; no pets. **Facility:** 118 rooms. 3 stories; interior corridors. **Dining:** Coffee shop; 7-10 am, Sat & Sun-11 am. **All Rooms:** free movies. **Cards:** AE, CB, DI, DS, MC, VI.   🛥 ✕ D S

HILLWINDS INN
Rates Subject to Change   **Phone: 704/295-7660**

5/26-10/31	2P/1B:	$62- 89	2P/2B:	$62- 89	XP: $8
12/1-12/15, 3/1-5/25 & 11/1-11/30	2P/1B:	$59- 75	2P/2B:	$59- 75	XP: $8

◆◆◆ Motel **Location:** Just e of Main St. Sunset Dr & Ransom St 28605 (PO Box 649). **Terms:** Open 12/1-12/15 & 3/1-11/30; reserv deposit, 7 day notice; 2 night min stay, 5/1-10/31; no pets. **Facility:** 19 rooms. 1-bedroom suite with fireplace, $90-$125; 1 story; exterior corridors. **All Rooms:** free movies. **Some Rooms:** 2 kitchens. **Cards:** DS, MC, VI.   CTV ✕ D

HOMESTEAD INN
Motel
◆◆

Guaranteed Rates

Phone: 704/295-9559

Fri & Sat 6/6-11/2	1P:	$52- 57	2P/1B:	$54- 59	2P/2B:	$59	XP:	$5	F12
Sun-Thurs 6/6-11/2	1P:	$40- 45	2P/1B:	$45- 49	2P/2B:	$49	XP:	$5	F12
Fri & Sat 12/1-6/5 & 11/3-11/30	1P:	$39- 44	2P/1B:	$39- 44	2P/2B:	$44	XP:	$5	F12
Sun-Thurs 12/1-6/5 & 11/3-11/30	1P:	$32- 37	2P/1B:	$34- 39	2P/2B:	$39	XP:	$5	F12

Location: Just s of US 321 business route; just e of town park. 153 Morris St 28605 (PO Box 1030). **Terms:** Reserv deposit, 4 day notice; no pets. **Facility:** 14 rooms. Handling fee imposed; 1 story; exterior corridors. **All Rooms:** free movies. **Cards:** DS, MC, VI.   (CTV) (X) (D)

MAPLE LODGE
(AAA)
◆◆◆
Bed & Breakfast

Rates Subject to Change

Phone: 704/295-3331

12/1-1/1 & 4/1-11/30 [BP]	1P:	$85	2P/1B:	$95- 135	2P/2B:	$95	XP:	$20

Location: Just s on Sunset Dr from town center park. 152 Sunset Dr 28605 (PO Box 1236). **Terms:** Open 12/1-1/1 & 4/1-11/30; age restrictions may apply; reserv deposit, 7 day notice; no pets. **Facility:** 11 rooms. 1 suite, $139. Handling fee imposed; 2 stories; interior/exterior corridors; smoke free premises. **All Rooms:** free movies. **Some Rooms:** A/C. **Cards:** AE, DI, DS, MC, VI.   (CTV) (X) (D)

MEADOWBROOK INN
◆◆◆
Motor Inn

Rates Subject to Change

Phone: 704/295-4300

4/1-11/30 [CP]	1P:	$109- 259	2P/1B:	$109- 259	2P/2B:	$109	XP:	$10	F12
12/1-3/31 [CP]	1P:	$89- 259	2P/1B:	$89- 259	2P/2B:	$89	XP:	$10	F12

Location: Just n on US 221 & 321 business route. 711 N Main St 28605 (PO Box 2005). **Fax:** 704/295-9341. **Terms:** Sr. discount; 2 night min stay, weekends in season; no pets. **Facility:** 61 rooms. 2 units with fireplace. 18 whirlpool rms, extra charge; 4 stories; interior corridors. **Dining:** Dining room; 7-10 am, 11-2 & 6-9 pm, lunch seasonal; $9-$18. **All Rooms:** free movies. **Cards:** AE, CB, DI, DS, MC, VI.   (➔) (CTV) (X) (D)

MOUNTAINAIRE INN & LOG CABINS
◆◆
Motel

Rates Subject to Change

Phone: 704/295-7991

12/1-2/23 & 5/9-10/31	2P/1B:	$52- 68	2P/2B:	$55- 82	XP:	$7
4/1-5/8 & 11/1-11/30	2P/1B:	$42- 55	2P/2B:	$48- 63	XP:	$7

Location: 3 blks n on US 221 & 321 business route. 827 N Main St 28605 (PO Box 407). **Terms:** Open 12/1-2/23 & 4/1-11/30; 2 night min stay, weekends in season; no pets. **Facility:** 16 rooms. 5 log cabins with fireplace, $110-$170. Handling fee imposed; 1 story; exterior corridors; smoke free premises. **All Rooms:** free movies. **Some Rooms:** 5 kitchens. **Cards:** DS, MC, VI.   (CTV) (X) (D)

RIDGEWAY INN
(AAA)
◆◆◆
Motel

Rates Subject to Change

Phone: 704/295-7321

Fri & Sat 5/15-11/4	2P/2B:	$69- 89	XP:	$5
Sun-Thurs 5/15-11/4	2P/2B:	$49- 79	XP:	$5
12/1-2/28, 4/1-5/14 & 11/5-11/30	2P/2B:	$49- 69	XP:	$5

Location: Just n of jct US 221 & 321 business route, on US 221 business route. 127 Yonahlossee 28605 (PO Box 1086). **Terms:** Open 12/1-2/28 & 4/1-11/30; reserv deposit, 3 day notice; 2 night min stay, weekends in season; no pets. **Facility:** 19 rooms. 2 cottages with fireplace, whirlpool bath & private deck, $125-$175. 4 whirlpool rms, extra charge; 2 stories; exterior corridors. **All Rooms:** free movies. **Some Rooms:** 3 kitchens. **Cards:** AE, DS, MC, VI.   (CTV) (X) (D)

RESTAURANTS

THE BEST CELLAR
◆◆
American

Dinner: $14-$18

Phone: 704/295-3466

Location: Off US 321 bypass; shared entry with Food Lion. Little Springs Rd 28605. **Hours:** 6 pm-9:30 pm. Closed: Sun; also Mon-Thurs 11/1-5/31. **Reservations:** suggested. **Features:** beer & wine only; valet parking. Authentic log cabin featuring seafood, prime rib, roast duck, veal & raw bar. Smoke free premises. **Cards:** AE, CB, DI, MC, VI.   (X)

BLOWING ROCK CAFE
◆◆
American

Lunch: $7-$9   Dinner: $7-$14

Phone: 704/295-9474

Location: 2 blks e of Sunset Dr; just w of Hwy 321. Sunset Dr 28605. **Hours:** 7 am-8 pm; 6/1-11/15 to 9 pm, Sun 7 am-11 & noon-8 pm; 7 am-2 pm off season. Closed: 12/25 & 3/1-3/31. **Features:** children's menu; carryout; beer & wine only. Cozy & comfortable atmosphere. Menu features homemade soup & dessert; fresh mountain trout. Famous for strawberry bran muffins. **Cards:** AE, MC, VI.   (X)

DOCKSIDE IRA'S
◆◆
American

Dinner: $15-$19

Phone: 704/295-4008

Location: From city park, just s on Main & 2 blks w on Laurel. 3148 Wonderland Tr 28605. **Hours:** 5 pm-9 pm. Closed: Mon & Tues 1/1-3/31, 7/4 & 12/25. **Features:** children's menu; carryout; cocktails & lounge. Good variety of fresh seafood, steak, ribs & chicken. Cozy dining room with nautical motif. Summer deck. **Cards:** AE, DI, DS, MC, VI.

ORIGINAL EMPORIUM RESTAURANT
◆◆
American

Lunch: $5-$8   Dinner: $6-$10

Phone: 704/295-7661

Location: 1.3 mi s on US 321. Hwy US 321S 28605. **Hours:** 11 am-9 pm, Fri & Sat-10 pm. Closed: 11/26, 12/24 & 12/25. **Features:** Sunday brunch; children's menu; health conscious menu; carryout; cocktails & lounge. Awesome mountain view & sunsets. Homemade soup & dessert; preservatives & chemicals strictly avoided. Eclectic menu with some Mexican specialties & gourmet sandwiches. **Cards:** AE, DS, MC, VI.   (X)

THE RIVERWOOD
(AAA)
◆◆◆
Nouvelle American

Dinner: $16-$20

Phone: 704/295-4162

Location: 0.5 mi s of Blue Ridge Pkwy. 7179 Valley Blvd 28605. **Hours:** 6 pm-9 pm, Sat 5:30 pm-10 pm, Sun 5:30 pm-9 pm. Closed: Tues 4/1-11/30 & 9/2. **Reservations:** suggested. **Features:** carryout; cocktails & lounge. Fine dining. Innovative culinary creations. Smoke free premises. **Cards:** DS, MC, VI.   (X)

WOODLANDS BBQ
(AAA)
◆
American

Lunch: $5-$10   Dinner: $5-$10

Phone: 704/295-3651

Location: 0.5 mi s on US 321 Bypass from Sunset Dr. US 321 Bypass 28605. **Hours:** 11 am-11 pm. Closed: 4/7,11/26 & 12/25; also Mon 11/1-6/1. **Features:** children's menu; carryout; cocktails; entertainment. Popular local barbecue in casual atmosphere. **Cards:** DS, MC, VI.

BOONE—12,900

LODGINGS

EAGLE'S RETREAT Rates Subject to Change Phone: 704/264-3007
◆◆◆ All Year [BP] 1P: $75- 95 2P/1B: $75- 95 XP: $20
Bed & **Location:** 2.7 mi s on US 321; 0.5 mi e on Fairway Dr, 0.3 mi s. 333 Eagle Dr 28607. Fax: 704/264-2202.
Breakfast **Terms:** No pets. **Facility:** 4 rooms. 2 stories; interior corridors; smoke free premises. **All Rooms:** free movies. **Some Rooms:** kitchen. **Cards:** MC, VI.

(CTV) (X) (D)

HAMPTON INN Rates Subject to Change Phone: 704/264-0077
◆◆◆ 6/1-8/24 & 10/1-10/31 [CP] 1P: $85- 109 2P/1B: $93- 117 2P/2B: $93- 117
Motel 12/1-12/25, 8/25-9/30 &
11/1-11/30 [EP] 1P: $59- 79 2P/1B: $67- 87 2P/2B: $67- 87
12/26-5/31 [CP] 1P: $54- 74 2P/1B: $62- 82 2P/2B: $62- 82
Location: On SR 105S; just sw of jct US 321. 1075 Hwy 105 28607. Fax: 704/264-4600. **Terms:** Sr. discount; no pets.
Facility: 95 rooms. 5 stories; interior corridors. **All Rooms:** free movies. **Cards:** AE, CB, DI, DS, JCB, MC, VI.

(CTV) (X) (🔊) (D) (S)

HOLIDAY INN EXPRESS Rates Subject to Change Phone: 704/264-2451
◆◆◆ Fri & Sat 6/15-10/31 [CP] 1P: $79- 110 2P/1B: $79- 110 2P/2B: $79- 110 XP: $8 F18
Motel Fri & Sat 12/26-3/15 [CP] 1P: $59- 80 2P/1B: $59- 80 2P/2B: $59- 80 XP: $8 F18
Sun-Thurs, Fri & Sat &
12/1-12/25, 3/16-6/14 &
11/1-11/30 [CP] 1P: $49- 70 2P/1B: $49- 79 2P/2B: $49- 79 XP: $8 F18
Location: 1.8 mi s on US 321. 1855 Blowing Rock Rd 28607. Fax: 704/265-3861. **Terms:** Sr. discount; no pets.
Facility: 138 rooms. 2 stories; interior/exterior corridors. **All Rooms:** free movies. **Cards:** AE, CB, DI, DS, JCB, MC, VI.

(🔊) (CTV) (X) (D)

LOVILL HOUSE INN Rates Subject to Change Phone: 704/264-4204
ⒶⒶⒶ All Year [BP] 1P: $95- 215 2P/1B: $95- 215 2P/2B: $95- 215 XP: $25
  Location: 1 mi n on SR 421/321; 0.5 mi e. 404 Old Bristol Rd 28607. **Terms:** Age restrictions may apply;
◆◆◆◆ reserv deposit, 14 day notice, handling fee imposed; no pets. **Facility:** 5 rooms. Closed 3/1-31 & 9/8-9/17; 2
Historic Bed stories; interior corridors; smoke free premises. **All Rooms:** free movies, no A/C. **Cards:** MC, VI.
& Breakfast

(CTV) (X) (D)

OAKWOOD INN Rates Subject to Change Phone: 704/262-1047
ⒶⒶⒶ 12/15-2/28 & 6/15-10/31 1P: $38- 44 2P/2B: $52- 74 XP: $4-8 F12
  12/1-12/14, 3/1-6/14 &
◆◆ 11/1-11/30 1P: $28- 32 2P/2B: $38- 44 XP: $4-8 F12
Motel **Location:** 2 mi s on US 321. 2015 Blowing Rock Rd 28607. Fax: 704/262-0818. **Terms:** Sr. discount; reserv
deposit, 3 day notice; no pets. **Facility:** 24 rooms. 1 story; exterior corridors. **All Rooms:** free movies.
Cards: AE, DI, DS, MC, VI.

(🔊) (CTV) (X) (D)

RESTAURANTS

CASA RUSTICA Dinner: $7-$14 Phone: 704/262-5128
◆◆ **Location:** 0.5 mi w on SR 105S; 0.3 mi s from jct US 321. Hwy 105S 28607. **Hours:** 5 pm-10 pm. Closed:
Italian 11/26, 12/24 & 12/25. **Reservations:** suggested. **Features:** children's menu; early bird specials; beer & wine
only. Also American cuisine served in rustic log cabin; relaxed atmosphere. **Cards:** AE, DI, DS, MC, VI.

MEL'S DINER Lunch: $5-$8 Dinner: $5-$8 Phone: 704/265-1344
◆◆ **Location:** 0.5 mi sw on SR 105S from jct US 321. 1286 Hwy 105 28607. **Hours:** 7 am-midnight, Thurs-Sat
American to 2 am. Closed: 12/25. **Features:** children's menu; carryout; beer only; a la carte. 1950's style diner;
chicken baskets, burgers, sandwiches, shakes & 50's memorabilia. **Cards:** AE, DI, DS, MC, VI. (X)

PICCADELI Lunch: $6-$8 Dinner: $9-$13 Phone: 704/262-3500
◆◆ **Location:** 2.3 mi s on US 321. 2161 Blowing Rock Rd 28607. **Hours:** 11 am-10 pm. Closed: 11/26 & 12/25.
American **Features:** children's menu; carryout; cocktail lounge; beer & wine only. Italian entrees, soup from scratch,
salad & homemade dessert. **Cards:** AE, DS, MC, VI. (X)

SAM & STU'S FRENCH & ITALIAN BISTRO Dinner: $11-$17 Phone: 704/265-0500
◆◆◆ **Location:** 1.2 mi s on US 421. 115 New Market Ctr 28607. **Hours:** 5:30 pm-9 pm, Fri & Sat-10 pm. Closed:
Italian Sun, 11/26 & 12/25. **Reservations:** suggested; weekends. **Features:** beer & wine only; a la carte. Some
French entrees; cosmopolitan, house made sauces, all entrees made to order. Changing art. Smoke free
premises. **Cards:** AE, DI, DS, MC, VI. (X)

BREVARD—5,400

LODGINGS

HAMPTON INN-BREVARD Rates Subject to Change Phone: 704/883-4800
◆◆◆ 9/1-10/31 [CP] 1P: $59 2P/1B: $65 2P/2B: $65
Motel 12/1-8/31 & 11/1-11/30 [CP] 1P: $49 2P/1B: $49 2P/2B: $49
Location: From downtown 3.8 mi e on US 64, just e on SR 280, adjoins east end of Forest Gate Shopping
Ctr. 800 Forest Gate Ctr 28712 (PO Box 2000). Fax: 704/877-5884. **Terms:** Sr. discount; small pets only. **Facility:** 81 rooms.
3 stories; interior corridors. **All Rooms:** free movies. **Cards:** AE, DS, MC, VI.
Roll in showers. (♿) (🔊) (CTV) (X) (🔊) (D) (S)

SUNSET MOTEL Phone: 704/884-9106
ⒶⒶ (SAVE) 6/1-11/30 1P: $55 2P/1B: $55 2P/2B: $70 XP: $5
  12/1-5/31 1P: $40 2P/1B: $40 2P/2B: $45 XP: $5
◆ **Location:** 4 blks s on US 64W. 415 S Broad St 28712. **Terms:** Pets, $5 extra charge. **Facility:** 18 rooms. 3
Motel kitchen units $70-$80, $45-$50 off season; 1 story; exterior corridors; free game of bowling per guest daily.
Dining: Restaurant nearby. **All Rooms:** refrigerators. **Cards:** AE, CB, DI, DS, JCB, MC, VI.

(♿) (CTV) (X) (D)

RESTAURANT

THE FALLS LANDING Lunch: $5-$7 Dinner: $11-$19 Phone: 704/884-2835
◆◆ **Location:** Center. 23 E Main St 28712. **Hours:** 11 am-10 pm, Sat & Sun 11:30 am-9 pm. Closed: Sun
American 2/1-5/15. **Reservations:** accepted. **Features:** casual dress; carryout; cocktails & lounge; street parking; a la
carte. Specializing in seafood with a Caribbean flair. **Cards:** MC, VI. (X)

BRYSON CITY—1,100

LODGING

HEMLOCK INN   Rates Subject to Change   **Phone:** 704/488-2885
◆◆◆   4/19-11/1 [MAP]   2P/1B: $130   2P/2B: $130- 180 XP: $20-39   F4
Country Inn   **Location:** 3 mi ne on US 19, 1 mi n at sign. 28713 (PO Drawer EE). **Terms:** Open 4/19-11/1; reserv
deposit, 14 day notice; no pets. **Facility:** 24 rooms. 4 housekeeping cottages, $140-$162; 1 story; exterior corridors. **Dining:** Restaurant; seatings at 8:30 am & 6 pm, Sun 8:30 am & 12:30 pm; $6-$13. **All Rooms:** no A/C.
Some Rooms: 2 efficiencies. **Cards:** DS, MC, VI.   Ⓓ

BURLINGTON—39,500

LODGINGS

COMFORT INN   Rates Subject to Change   **Phone:** 910/227-3681
◆◆   All Year [CP]   1P: $55   2P/1B: $59   2P/2B: $59   XP: $4   F19
Motel   **Location:** Exit 145 off I-85 & I-40, via service road. 978 Plantation Dr 27215. Fax: 910/570-0900.
Terms: Small pets only. **Facility:** 127 rooms. 2 stories; exterior corridors. **All Rooms:** free & pay movies.
Cards: AE, CB, DI, DS, JCB, MC, VI.   🛏 🈯 ⒸⓉⓋ ✕ Ⓓ

HOLIDAY INN   **Phone:** 910/229-5203
ⒶⒶ ⓈⒶⓋⒺ   All Year   1P: $69- 79 2P/1B: $75- 85 2P/2B: $75- 85 XP: $8   F19
Location: Exit 145 off I-85 & I-40. 2444 Maple Ave 27216. Fax: 910/570-0529. **Terms:** No pets. **Facility:** 132
◆◆◆   rooms. $1 daily fee for phone; 2 stories; interior corridors. **Dining:** Dining room; 6:30 am-2 & 5-9 pm;
Motor Inn $7-$13; cocktails. **Services:** valet laundry. **All Rooms:** coffeemakers, free & pay movies.
Some Rooms: microwaves, refrigerators. Fee: whirlpools. **Cards:** AE, CB, DI, DS, JCB, MC, VI.
Special Amenities: Early check-in/late check-out and preferred room (subject to availability with advanced
reservations).** *(See color ad below)*   🈯 🈴 ♿ ✕ 🈯 Ⓓ

MOTEL 6 - 1257   Guaranteed Rates   **Phone:** 910/226-1325
ⒶⒶ   All Year   1P: $35- 45 2P/1B: $39- 49 2P/2B: $39- 49 XP: $8   F17
Location: Exit 145 off I-85 & I-40, SR 49. 2155 Hanford Rd 27215. Fax: 910/570-9158. **Terms:** Sr. discount;
◆◆   small pets only. **Facility:** 112 rooms. 1 story; exterior corridors. **All Rooms:** free movies. **Cards:** AE, DI, DS,
Motel   MC, VI.   🛏 🈯 ✕ Ⓓ

RAMADA INN   Rates Subject to Change   **Phone:** 910/227-5541
◆◆   All Year [BP]   1P: $59   2P/1B: $59   2P/2B: $59   XP: $6   F18
Motor Inn   **Location:** Exit 143 off I-85 & I-40. 2703 Ramada Rd 27215. Fax: 910/570-2701. **Terms:** Sr. discount; no
pets. **Facility:** 138 rooms. 2 stories; interior/exterior corridors. **Dining:** Restaurant; 6 am-2 pm; $6-$12.
All Rooms: free movies. **Cards:** AE, CB, DI, DS, MC.   🈯 ✕ Ⓓ

RESTAURANT

THE CUTTING BOARD   **Lunch:** $6-$8   **Dinner:** $8-$12   **Phone:** 910/226-0291
◆◆   **Location:** Exit 143 off I-85 & I-40, 2 blks n on Hwy 62. 2619 Alamance Rd 27215. **Hours:** 11:30 am-2 & 5-9
American   pm, Fri & Sat 11:30 am-10 pm, Sun 11:30 am-9 pm. Closed: for lunch 1/1, 11/26, 12/24 for dinner & 12/25.
Features: children's menu; carryout; salad bar; cocktails. Casual dining in nautical decor or glass enclosed
patios. Also beef, fish & chicken grilled over live charcoal. Very popular. **Cards:** AE, MC, VI.   ✕

BUXTON—*See Outer Banks p. 396.*

CALABASH—1,200

RESTAURANT

ELLA'S OF CALABASH   **Dinner:** $5-$12   **Phone:** 910/579-6728
◆◆   **Location:** US 17 to NC 179 to Calabash, right at stoplight, 100 yds on right. River Rd. **Hours:** 11 am-9 pm.
Seafood   **Features:** casual dress; children's menu. **Cards:** MC, VI.

CANDLER—1,020   (See map p. 315; index p. 314)

LODGING

MOUNTAIN SPRINGS CABINS/CHALETS   Phone: 704/665-1004   **56**
    SAVE   All Year   2P/1B: $80- 145 2P/2B: $80- 145 XP: $10-20   D19
    Location: I-40 exit 44, 3 mi s on US 23, 19 & 74 to SR 151, 5 mi s at Emma's Cove Rd. 28715 (PO Box
Cottage 6922, ASHEVILLE, 28816). Fax: 704/667-1581. **Terms:** Reserv deposit, 15 day notice; weekly rates; no pets.
    Facility: 12 rooms. Rustic, yet modern cabins with fireplace. Porch, overlooking scenic mountain stream.
Picnic area on 100 acres of woods with 30 acres landscaped. 1 three-bedroom unit, 3 two-bedroom units. 12
kitchens, dep req. Handling fee imposed; 1 story; exterior corridors; mountain view; barbecue grills. Fee: hot air balloon
rides. **Recreation:** swimming, fishing, tubing; bicycles, hiking trails. **All Rooms:** coffeemakers, microwaves, refrigerators,
combo or shower baths, no A/C. **Cards:** MC, VI. **Special Amenities:** Free local telephone calls and preferred room
(subject to availability with advanced reservations). (See color ad p 317)   **CTV** **D**

CANTON—3,800

LODGINGS

COMFORT INN   Rates Subject to Change   Phone: 704/648-4881
◆◆   6/1-10/31 [CP] 1P: $55- 70 2P/1B: $70- 80 2P/2B: $70- 80 XP: $8   F16
Motel   12/1-5/31 & 11/1-11/30 [CP] 1P: $40- 45 2P/1B: $50- 55 2P/2B: $50- 55 XP: $8   F16
    Location: I-40 exit 31, just s. 737 Champion Dr 28716 (PO Box 866). Fax: 704/648-2477. **Terms:** Sr.
discount; no pets. **Facility:** 76 rooms. 2 stories; interior corridors. **All Rooms:** free movies. **Some Rooms:** 4 efficiencies.
Cards: AE, CB, DI, DS, JCB, MC, VI.   **CTV** **X** **D** **S**

ECONO LODGE-CANTON   Rates Subject to Change   Phone: 704/648-0300
◆◆   6/1-10/31 1P: $43- 48 2P/1B: $54- 68 2P/2B: $54- 68 XP: $5   F16
Motel   5/1-5/31 1P: $39- 42 2P/1B: $45- 58 2P/2B: $45- 58 XP: $5   F16
    12/1-4/30 & 11/1-11/30 1P: $36- 39 2P/1B: $45- 48 2P/2B: $45- 48 XP: $5   F16
Location: I-40 exit 31. 55 Buckeye Cove Rd 28716. Fax: 704/648-0322. **Terms:** Sr. discount; no pets. **Facility:** 40 rooms. 2
stories; exterior corridors. **All Rooms:** free movies. **Cards:** AE, CB, DI, DS, JCB, MC, VI.   **CTV** **X** **D**

CAPE CARTERET—1,000

LODGING

HARBORLIGHT GUEST HOUSE BED & BREAKFAST Rates Subject to Change   Phone: 919/393-6868
◆◆◆   All Year [BP] 1P: $60- 110 2P/1B: $75- 175   XP: $25
Bed &   Location: 1.5 e on SR 24 from jct SR 58, 0.5 mi s on Bayshore Dr; just e on Edgewater & just s. 332 Live
Breakfast Oak Dr 28584. Fax: 919/393-6868. **Terms:** Age restrictions may apply; reserv deposit; 2 night min stay,
weekends; no pets, dogs on premises. **Facility:** 9 rooms. 5 luxury suites $125-$175, 4 suites & rooms have
winter/summer rates $75-$125; 3 stories; exterior corridors; smoke free premises. **All Rooms:** free movies. **Cards:** AE, MC,
VI.   **CTV** **X** **D**

CAROLINA BEACH—3,600

RESTAURANT

MARINA'S EDGE   Lunch: $6-$16   Dinner: $6-$16   Phone: 910/458-6001
    Location: On US 421, jct of Carl Winner & Lake Park Blvd. 300 Lake Park Blvd 28428. **Hours:** 4 pm-11 pm, Sat
& Sun from 11 am. **Closed:** 11/26 & 12/25. **Reservations:** accepted. **Features:** casual dress; children's
◆◆   menu; early bird specials; carryout; cocktails & lounge. Serving a variety of food, including steak & fresh
Steak and seafood items. A softly lit dining room & friendly service. **Cards:** AE, DS, MC, VI.   **X**
Seafood

CARRBORO—11,600   (See map p. 358; index p. 357)

LODGING

THE INN AT BINGHAM SCHOOL   Guaranteed Rates   Phone: 919/563-5583   **55**
◆◆   All Year [BP] 1P: $65- 110 2P/1B: $75- 120 2P/2B: $75- 120 XP: $15   F5
Historic Bed Location: 12 mi w on SR 54 from US 15-501 in Chapel Hill; at corner of Mebane Oaks Rd & Historical
& Breakfast Marker. 6720 Mebane Oaks Rd 27302 (PO Box 267, CHAPEL HILL, 27514). Fax: 919/563-9826. **Terms:** Sr.
discount; reserv deposit, 7 day notice; no pets, pets on premises. **Facility:** 5 rooms. Handling fee imposed; 2
stories; exterior corridors. **All Rooms:** free movies. **Cards:** AE, DS, MC, VI.   **X** **D**

CARY—43,900   (See map p. 404; index p. 402)

LODGINGS

BEST WESTERN CARY INN   Phone: 919/481-1200   **32**
    SAVE   All Year [CP] 1P: $65- 95 2P/1B: $71- 101 2P/2B: $71- 101 XP: $6   F12
    Location: From I-40 exit 293, 0.3 mi sw on US 1 & US 64W; at Cary, Walnut St exit, then just w. 1722
◆◆◆   Walnut St 27511. Fax: 919/481-1200. **Terms:** No pets. **Facility:** 98 rooms. 2 stories; interior corridors.
Motel   **Dining & Entertainment:** Cocktail lounge; restaurant nearby. **All Rooms:** free movies. **Some Rooms:** 2
kitchens, microwaves, refrigerators. Fee: whirlpools. **Cards:** AE, CB, DI, DS, MC, VI. **Special Amenities:**
Free breakfast and free local telephone calls.   **CTV** **X** **D**

COURTYARD BY MARRIOTT-CARY   Rates Subject to Change   Phone: 919/481-9666   **30**
◆◆◆   Sun-Thurs 1P: $94 2P/1B: $104 2P/2B: $104
Motel   Fri & Sat 1P: $65- 69 2P/1B: $65- 69 2P/2B: $65- 69
    Location: Exit 128B off US 1 & 64; 0.3 mi w in MacGregor Park. 102 Edinburgh Dr 27511.
Fax: 919/460-0380. **Terms:** Sr. discount; no pets. **Facility:** 149 rooms. 3 stories; interior corridors. **Dining:** Dining room;
6:30-10 am, Sat & Sun 7 am-noon. **All Rooms:** free & pay movies. **Cards:** AE, CB, DI, DS, MC, VI. (See color ad p 406)
    CTV **X** **D** **S**

FAIRFIELD INN   Phone: 919/481-4011   **34**
    SAVE   All Year [CP] 1P: $54- 64 2P/1B: $59- 69 2P/2B: $59- 74 XP: $5   D18
    Location: From I-40, exit 293, 0.3 mi sw on US 1 & US 64W, Walnut St exit, just w. 1716 Walnut St 27511.
◆◆◆   Fax: 919/481-1200. **Terms:** No pets. **Facility:** 125 rooms. 2 stories; interior corridors. **Dining:** Restaurant
Motel   nearby. **All Rooms:** free movies. **Cards:** AE, DI, DS, JCB, MC, VI. **Special Amenities:** Free breakfast and
free local telephone calls.   **X** **D**

(See map p. 404)

HAMPTON INN Rates Subject to Change **Phone:** 919/859-5559 **35**
◆◆◆ All Year [CP] 1P: $69 2P/1B: $77 2P/2B: $77 XP: $8 F18
Motel **Location:** 0.8 mi e on Tryon Rd from US 1 & 64, exit 128A; in Ashley Village Medical Park. 201 Asheville Ave 27511. Fax: 919/859-0682. **Terms:** Sr. discount; no pets. **Facility:** 130 rooms. 5 stories; interior corridors.
All Rooms: free movies. **Cards:** AE, CB, DI, DS, MC, VI.  (icons)

HOMEWOOD SUITES Rates Subject to Change **Phone:** 919/467-4444 **36**
◆◆◆ All Year [CP] 1P: $109- 175 2P/1B: $109- 175 2P/2B: $109- 175
Suite Motel **Location:** Exit 128B off US 1 & 64; 0.3 mi w in MacGregor Park. 100 Mac Alyson Ct 27511. Fax: 919/467-3074. **Terms:** Sr. discount; no pets. **Facility:** 50 rooms. 4 stories; interior corridors.
All Rooms: kitchens, free movies. **Cards:** AE, CB, DI, DS, JCB, MC, VI. Roll in showers. (icons)

RED ROOF INN Rates Subject to Change **Phone:** 919/469-3400 **33**
◆◆ All Year 1P: $47- 59 2P/1B: $52- 69 2P/2B: $55- 69 XP: $6 F18
Motel **Location:** I-40 exit 293, 0.3 mi sw on US 1 & 64W; at Cary-Walnut St exit, just e. 1800 Walnut St 27511. Fax: 919/460-9027. **Terms:** No pets. **Facility:** 67 rooms. TDD phone 800-843-9999; 4 stories; interior corridors. **All Rooms:** free movies. **Some Rooms:** 4 efficiencies. **Cards:** AE, CB, DI, DS, MC, VI. (icons)

RESTAURANTS

FOX & HOUND RESTAURANT & PUB **Lunch:** $6-$9 **Dinner:** $9-$16 **Phone:** 919/380-0080 **18**
◆◆ **Location:** Exit 128B off US 1 & US 64, then 0.3 mi w on US 64 into MacGregor Park. **Hours:** 11:30 am-2 & 5:30-10 pm, Sun 5:30 pm-9 pm. Closed major holidays. **Reservations:** suggested; weekends.
Regional **Features:** children's menu; carryout; cocktails & lounge. Irish folk singer on Wed in authentic English pub.
Continental English entrees; very popular. Favorite is Yorkshire pudding & shepherd pie. Good selection of beer.
Cards: AE, CB, DI, DS, MC, VI. (icon)

SELDOM BLUES CAFE **Dinner:** $13-$21 **Phone:** 919/859-2583 **19**
◆◆ **Location:** Exit 128A off US 64 & US 1, 1 mi e to Waverly Place Shopping Center. 206 B Waverly Pl 27511.
American **Hours:** 5 pm-10 pm, Fri & Sat-10:30 pm. Closed: Mon, 11/26 & 12/25. **Reservations:** suggested.
Features: Sunday brunch; cocktails; entertainment. Uptown Miami ambience. **Cards:** AE, MC, VI. (icon)

CASHIERS—600

LODGINGS

HIGH HAMPTON INN **Phone:** 704/743-2411
AAA SAVE 7/1-10/31 [AP] 1P: $88- 98 2P/2B: $156- 188 XP: $48-60
◆◆◆ 4/12-6/30 & 11/1-11/30 [AP] 1P: $86- 95 2P/2B: $150- 178 XP: $44-57
Resort **Location:** 1.5 mi s on SR 107 from jct US 64. 28717 (PO Box 338). Fax: 704/743-5991. **Terms:** Open
Complex 4/12-11/30; reserv deposit, 14 day notice; weekly rates; package plans; pets, in kennels only. **Facility:** 125 rooms. Historic inn featuring rustic lodge rooms & cottages; most cottages with fireplace. Family owned & operated since 1933. 3 stories, no elevator; interior/exterior corridors; playground, exercise trail, fly fishing school, tennis & golf clinics. Fee: 18 holes golf; 6 tennis courts. **Dining & Entertainment:** Restaurant, cafeteria; 7 am-9:30, noon-2:15 & 6:30-8:15 pm; $15-$17; cocktail lounge; wine/beer only; evening dress code, includes coat & tie; afternoon tea; entertainment. **Services:** Fee: coin laundry; massage. **Recreation:** children's program in summer, nature program, recreation program, social program; swimming, fishing; hiking trails, jogging. Fee: sailboats, driving range, sailing; bicycles. Rental: boats, canoeing, paddleboats. **All Rooms:** no A/C, no phones. **Cards:** AE, DS, MC, VI. **Special Amenities:** Free newspaper. *(See color ad below)* (icons)

INNISFREE VICTORIAN INN Rates Subject to Change **Phone:** 704/743-2946
AAA 6/1-10/31 [BP] 1P: $150- 290 2P/1B: $150- 290
◆◆◆◆ 12/1-5/31 & 11/1-11/30 [BP] 1P: $125- 260 2P/1B: $125- 260
Bed & **Location:** 1 mi n on SR 107N following signs; 6 mi n on SR 107N from jct US 64 in Cashiers. 7 Lakeside
Breakfast Knoll 28736 (PO Box 469, GLENVILLE). **Terms:** Age restrictions may apply; reserv deposit, 14 day notice; 2 night min stay, weekends; no pets. **Facility:** 10 rooms. Handling fee imposed; 2 stories; interior/exterior corridors; smoke free premises. **All Rooms:** no A/C. **Cards:** AE, DS, MC, VI. (icons)

LAURELWOOD MOUNTAIN INN Rates Subject to Change **Phone:** 704/743-9939
◆◆ 5/15-11/5 2P/1B: $58- 145 2P/2B: $58- 145 XP: $5 F12
Motel 12/1-5/14 & 11/6-11/30 2P/1B: $48- 125 2P/2B: $48- 125 XP: $5 F12
Location: Just n on Hwy 107 from jct US 64. Hwy 107N 28717 (PO Box 188). Fax: 704/743-5300.
Terms: No pets. **Facility:** 22 rooms. 2 night min stay weekends 7/1-8/31 & 10/1-10/31. Log cabin suite in 1 or 2 bedrooms; $95-$125; 1-2 stories; exterior corridors. **All Rooms:** free movies. **Some Rooms:** A/C, efficiency, 3 kitchens. **Cards:** AE, CB, DI, DS, MC, VI. (icons)

RESTAURANT

HORACIO'S RESTAURANTE   **Lunch:** $6-$10   **Dinner:** $13-$20   **Phone:** 704/743-2792
◆◆   **Location:** Center; on US 64, just e of jct SR 107. 28717. **Hours:** 11 am-2 & 5:30-9:30 pm, Sat from 5:30
Italian   pm. Closed: Sun. **Features:** No A/C; casual dress; a la carte. Rustic dining room. Very well-prepared
          Southern & Northern Italian cuisines. BYOB permitted. Smoke free premises. **Cards:** MC, VI.   ⊠

CHAPEL HILL—38,700   (See map p. 358; index p. 357)

LODGINGS

BEST WESTERN UNIVERSITY INN   Rates Subject to Change   **Phone:** 919/932-3000   **44**
◆◆◆   All Year [CP]   1P: $65- 80   2P/1B: $70- 105 2P/2B: $80- 105
Motel   **Location:** 0.3 mi e of jct US 15 & 501 bypass on SR 54, or 2.5 mi w of I-40, exit 273. 1310 Hwy 54 E 27514
(PO Box 2118). Fax: 919/968-6513. **Terms:** Reserv deposit, 7 day notice; no pets. **Facility:** 84 rooms. 2 stories; exterior corridors. **All Rooms:** free movies. **Cards:** AE, CB, DI, DS, MC, VI.   ⊠ CTV ⊠ 🔊 D

CAROLINA INN   **Phone:** 919/933-2001   **42**
(AAA) (SAVE)   All Year   1P: $129- 144   2P/1B: $129- 144 2P/2B: $144   XP: $10   F18
◆◆◆◆   **Location:** 0.3 mi s on SR 86 from jct Franklin & Columbia sts; on UNC Campus. 211 Pittsboro St 27516.
Historic Hotel   Fax: 919/962-3400. **Terms:** No pets. **Facility:** 184 rooms. Few small rooms. Historic property opened in 1924.
          Elegant public areas & handsomely appointed rooms. 2 phone lines in all rooms. 2 two-bedroom units. Handling fee imposed; 3 stories; interior corridors; designated smoking area. Fee: parking. **Dining:** Carolina Crossroads, see separate listing. **Services:** Fee: coin laundry; valet parking. **All Rooms:** free & pay movies. **Some Rooms:** refrigerators. **Cards:** AE, CB, DI, DS, JCB, MC, VI. **Special Amenities:** Free newspaper and preferred room (subject to availability with advanced reservations).   Roll in showers. 📶 📶 🚻 ⊠ 🔊 D S

HAMPTON INN   Rates Subject to Change   **Phone:** 919/968-3000   **43**
◆◆◆   All Year [CP]   1P: $61- 69   2P/1B: $72- 76 2P/2B: $72- 76
Motel   **Location:** 3 mi n on US 15-501 bypass via service road; 1 mi s of exit 270 off I-40 on US 15-501. 1740 US
15-501 27514. Fax: 919/929-0322. **Terms:** Sr. discount; no pets. **Facility:** 122 rooms. 2 stories; exterior corridors. **All Rooms:** free & pay movies. **Cards:** AE, CB, DI, DS, MC, VI.   ⊠ 🏠 ⊠ 🔊 D

HOLIDAY INN   Rates Subject to Change   **Phone:** 919/929-2171   **45**
◆◆◆   All Year   1P: $69- 110   2P/1B: $75- 110 2P/2B: $79- 110 XP: $6   F16
Motor Inn   **Location:** 2.8 mi n on US 15-501 bypass; 2 mi s on US 15-501 bypass from I-40 exit 270. 1301 N Fordham
Blvd 27514. Fax: 919/929-5736. **Terms:** Sr. discount; no pets. **Facility:** 135 rooms. 2 stories; exterior corridors. **Dining:** Restaurant; 6:30 am-10 & 5-10 pm; $9-$14. **All Rooms:** free & pay movies. **Cards:** AE, CB, DI, DS, JCB, MC, VI.   ⊠ ⊠ 🔊 D

OMNI CHAPEL HILL   **Phone:** 919/968-4900   **40**
(AAA) (SAVE)   All Year   1P: $89- 139   2P/1B: $89- 139 2P/2B: $89- 139
◆◆◆   **Location:** 1 mi s on 15/501 from jct I-40. 1 Europa Dr 27514. Fax: 919/968-3520. **Terms:** No pets.
Hotel   **Facility:** 172 rooms. 4 stories; interior corridors. **Dining:** Dining room, restaurant; 6:30 am-10 pm; $10-$20.
          All Rooms: free & pay movies. **Cards:** AE, CB, DI, DS, JCB, MC, VI.   ⊠ CTV 🏠 ⊠ 🔊 D S

THE SIENA HOTEL   **Phone:** 919/929-4000   **41**
(AAA) (SAVE)   All Year [BP]   1P: $134   2P/1B: $134   2P/2B: $134   XP: $10   F17
◆◆◆◆   **Location:** 2 mi s on US 15/501 from I-40. 1505 E Franklin St 27514. Fax: 919/968-8527. **Terms:** Check-in 4
Motor Inn   pm; pets, $50 dep req. **Facility:** 80 rooms. Accented by reproductions from Italian Renaissance art & imported
          Italian furnishings. Offers guests a unique experience with many luxury services & amenities. Rooms range from spacious to larger 1-room suites. 4 stories; interior corridors. **Dining:** Il Palio Ristorante, see separate listing. **Services:** valet laundry; area transportation, to Chapel Hill. **All Rooms:** free movies. **Some Rooms:** refrigerators. **Cards:** AE, CB, DI, MC, VI. **Special Amenities:** Free breakfast and free newspaper.   🛒 🎱 🛬 CTV ⊠ 🔊 D

RESTAURANTS

AURORA RESTAURANT   **Lunch:** $7-$10   **Dinner:** $10-$18   **Phone:** 919/942-2400   (19)
◆◆◆   **Location:** 1 mi w on US 54 at jct Greensboro St; in Carr Mill Shops, Carrboro. 200 N Greensboro St 27510.
Northern   **Hours:** 11:30 am-2 & 6-10 pm, Sat & Sun from 6 pm. Closed major holidays. **Reservations:** suggested.
Italian   **Features:** senior's menu; carryout; cocktails & lounge; a la carte. Salad, pasta & seafood served in a
          restored textile mill. Dinner menu changes daily. Homemade Tuscan bread, dessert, pasta & sauce.
Cards: AE, MC, VI.   ⊠

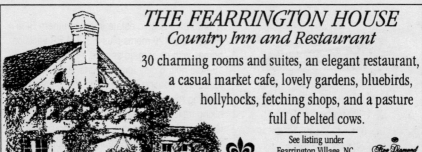

THE FEARRINGTON HOUSE
Country Inn and Restaurant

30 charming rooms and suites, an elegant restaurant,
a casual market cafe, lovely gardens, bluebirds,
hollyhocks, fetching shops, and a pasture
full of belted cows.

See listing under
Fearrington Village, NC.
919-542-2121
www.fearrington.com

RELAIS &
CHATEAUX

(See map p. 358)

CAROLINA CROSSROADS Historical   **Lunch:** $8-$12   **Dinner:** $14-$22   **Phone:** 919/933-2001   ③⓪
◆◆◆◆   **Location:** 0.3 mi s on SR 86 from jct Franklin & Columbia sts; on UNC Campus; in Carolina Inn. 211
Regional   Pittsboro St 27516. **Hours:** 6:30-10 am, 11-2 & 5-10 pm. **Reservations:** suggested. **Features:** Sunday
American   brunch; children's menu; health conscious menu; cocktails & lounge; fee for parking & valet parking; a la
               carte. Upscale intimate dining; southern regional cuisine; focused on fine American wines; superior entree &
dessert presentations. Smoke free premises. **Cards:** AE, CB, DI, DS, JCB, MC, VI.   ☒

CROOK'S CORNER   **Dinner:** $11-$17   **Phone:** 919/929-7643   ②⑦
◆◆   **Location:** At jct of Franklin St & Merritt Mill Rd. 610 W Franklin St 27516. **Hours:** 6 pm-10:30 pm, Sun
Regional   10:30 am-2 pm. Closed major holidays. **Reservations:** suggested. **Features:** Sunday brunch; carryout;
American   cocktails & lounge; a la carte. Casual with upscale decor & changing art by local artist every 6 weeks.
               Imaginative southern cuisine by accomplished chef. Smoke free premises. **Cards:** AE, MC, VI.   ☒

DIP'S TRADITIONAL COUNTRY   **Lunch:** $7-$9   **Dinner:** $8-$11   **Phone:** 919/942-5837   ②①
◆   **Location:** Center. 405 W Rosemary St 27516. **Hours:** 8 am-3 & 4-10 pm, Sun 8 am-9 pm. Closed major
American   holidays. **Features:** children's menu; senior's menu; carryout; beer & wine only; street parking. Excellent
               fried chicken, homemade dessert, bread & fresh vegetables. Also seafood, ribs, chitterlings & dumplings.
Cards: MC, VI.   ☒

411 WEST ITALIAN CAFE   **Lunch:** $6-$10   **Dinner:** $6-$15   **Phone:** 919/967-2782   ②⑨
◆   **Location:** 0.5 mi w of jct Columbia & Franklin sts. 411 W Franklin St 27514. **Hours:** 11:30 am-10 pm, Fri &
Italian   Sat-10:30 pm. Closed: 7/4, 11/26 & 12/25. **Features:** No A/C; children's menu; carryout; cocktails; a la carte.
               Wood burning ovens. Very popular. Homemade soup, sauce & pasta. Smoke free premises. **Cards:** AE, DI,
DS, MC, VI.   ☒

IL PALIO RISTORANTE   **Lunch:** $7-$11   **Dinner:** $16-$20   **Phone:** 919/918-2545   ②⑥
◆◆◆◆   **Location:** 2 mi s on US 15/501 from I-40; in The Siena Hotel. 1505 E Franklin St 27514. **Hours:** 6-10:30
Northern   am, 11:30-2:30 & 6-10:30 pm. **Reservations:** suggested. **Features:** children's menu; cocktails & lounge;
Italian   entertainment; a la carte. Cozy dining room with elegant appointments & upscale casual ambience. Varied
               selection of meat, seafood & poultry. Features wide selection of pasta, gnocchi, risotto & polenta. Smoke
free premises. **Cards:** AE, CB, DI, JCB, MC, VI.   ☒

LA REZ   **Dinner:** $20-$30   **Phone:** 919/967-2506   ②⓪
◆◆◆   **Location:** 2 blks off downtown area. 202 W Rosemary St 27514. **Hours:** 6 pm-9:30 pm, Sun-8:30 pm.
Continental   Closed: Mon, 1/1, 1/2, 12/24-12/26. **Reservations:** suggested. **Features:** cocktails & lounge; fee for parking;
               a la carte. Limited variation of eclectic European cuisine served in candlelit ambience. Garden patio dining
weather permitting. **Cards:** AE, CB, DI, MC, VI.   ☒

THE NEW ORLEANS COOKERY   **Lunch:** $7-$9   **Dinner:** $9-$18   **Phone:** 919/929-9162   ②⑤
◆◆   **Location:** 2 blks from downtown area. 220 W Rosemary St 27516. **Hours:** 11:30 am-2 & 5:30-9:30 pm, Sat
Ethnic   5:30 pm-10:30 pm. Closed: 1/1, 9/2 & 12/25. **Reservations:** suggested. **Features:** Sunday brunch;
               children's menu; carryout; cocktails. Creole & Cajun cuisine. All entrees prepared by owner/chef. Some
closely spaced tables. Patio dining weather permitting. Smoke free premises. **Cards:** CB, DI, DS, MC, VI.   ☒

ORIENTAL GARDEN CHINESE & THAI RESTAURANT **Lunch:** $5-$7 **Dinner:** $8-$11 **Phone:** 919/967-8818 ②④
◆◆   **Location:** 5 blks w from downtown area. 503 W Rosemary St 27514. **Hours:** 11:30 am-2 & 5-9:30 pm, Fri &
Chinese   Sat-10:30 pm. **Features:** carryout; beer & wine only. Authentic Chinese & Thai cuisine served in relaxing
               atrium atmosphere. Limited smoking area. Smoke free premises. **Cards:** AE, DS, MC, VI.   ☒

PYEWACKET RESTAURANT   **Lunch:** $7-$8   **Dinner:** $11-$17   **Phone:** 919/929-0297   ②③
ⒶⒶⒶ   **Location:** 0.5 mi w of jct Columbia & Franklin sts at The Courtyard. 431 W Franklin St at Roberson 27516.
               Hours: 11:30 am-2:30 & 5:30-9:30 pm, Fri & Sat-10 pm, Sun 5:30 pm-9 pm. Closed major holidays.
◆◆   **Reservations:** suggested. **Features:** casual dress; carryout; cocktails & lounge. Seafood & vegetarian
American   dishes served in fashionable surroundings. Patio dining, weather permitting. Seasonal eclectic menu.
               Cards: AE, DI, DS, MC, VI.   ☒

SQUID'S RESTAURANT, MARKET & OYSTER BAR   **Dinner:** $12-$18   **Phone:** 919/942-8757   ①⑧
◆◆   **Location:** On US 15-501 bypass; 0.5 mi n of jct US 54. 1201 N Fordham Blvd 27514. **Hours:** 5 pm-9:30
Seafood   pm, Fri & Sat-10 pm, Sun 5 pm-9 pm. Closed major holidays. **Features:** children's menu; carryout; cocktails
               & lounge. Mesquite grilled, broiled, fried & sauteed entrees served in contemporary surroundings. Smoke
free premises. **Cards:** AE, CB, DI, DS, MC, VI.   ☒

WEATHERVANE   **Lunch:** $6-$10   **Dinner:** $11-$20   **Phone:** 919/929-9466   ②⑧
◆◆◆   **Location:** 2.7 mi n on US 15-501 bypass, at Eastgate Shopping Center in "A Southern Season". Eastgate
American   Shopping Center 27514. **Hours:** 10 am-10 pm, Fri & Sat-11 pm, Sun noon-6 pm. Closed major holidays.
               Features: Sunday brunch; children's menu; carryout; cocktails; a la carte. Enclosed patio dining. Extensive
wine list; homemade soup & bread. Smoke free premises. **Cards:** AE, MC, VI.   ☒

CHARLOTTE—395,900   (See map p. 336; index below)

To help you more easily locate accommodations in the Greater Charlotte area, the following two indexes and maps show lodgings and restaurants in multiple cities. Listings
for these establishments are found under the heading for the city in which they are located. The Charlotte area map comprises: Charlotte and Matthews.

Index of Establishments on the DOWNTOWN CHARLOTTE ACCOMMODATIONS Spotting Map

(See map below)

LODGINGS

CHARLOTTE MARRIOTT CITY CENTER Rates Subject to Change **Phone: 704/333-9000** **2**
♦♦♦   Sun-Thurs [EP]   1P: $169   2P/1B: $179   2P/2B: $179
Hotel   Fri & Sat [BP]   1P: $69   2P/1B: $69   2P/2B: $69
    Location: At Trade & Tryon sts, Trade St exit, off I-77. 100 W Trade St 28202. Fax: 704/342-3419.
Terms: No pets. **Facility:** 434 rooms. 19 stories; interior corridors. Fee: parking. **Dining:** Dining room; 6:30 am-11 pm;
$10-$28. **All Rooms:** free & pay movies. **Cards:** AE, DI, DS, JCB, MC, VI.   🏊 ✕ 🎿 Ⓓ Ⓢ

DAYS INN CENTRAL   Rates Subject to Change   **Phone: 704/333-4733** **10**
♦♦   All Year [CP]   1P: $49- 69   2P/1B: $49- 69   2P/2B: $49- 69   XP: $5   F18
Motel   **Location:** 0.6 mi e from jct Trade & Tryon sts. 601 N Tryon St 28202. Fax: 704/372-9925. **Terms:** Sr.
    discount; pets. **Facility:** 100 rooms. Key deposit, $10. Phone, $.75 daily; 2 stories; exterior corridors.
All Rooms: free movies. **Cards:** AE, CB, DI, DS, MC, VI.   🛒 CTV ✕ Ⓓ

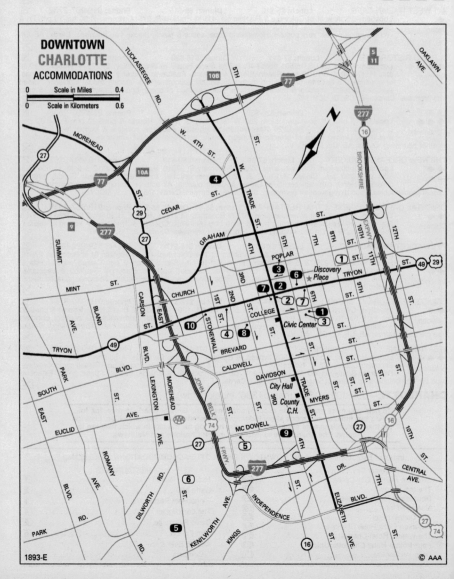

(See map p. 336)

DOUBLETREE HOTEL-CHARLOTTE
Phone: 704/347-0070 **4**

[AAA] [SAVE]	Sun-Thurs	1P:	$89	2P/1B:	$99	2P/2B:	$99	XP: $10	F12
◆◆◆	Fri & Sat	1P:	$65	2P/1B:	$65	2P/2B:	$65	XP: $10	F12

Motor Inn   **Location:** Exit 10B off I-77; then 0.5 mi se Trade St downtown. 895 W Trade St 28202. Fax: 704/347-0267.
Terms: Reserv deposit; BP avail; package plans; no pets. **Facility:** 187 rooms. Stylish rooms & public areas.
8 stories; interior corridors; sauna, whirlpool, small pool. **Dining & Entertainment:** Dining room; 6-10 am,
11:30-2 & 5-10 pm; closed Sun for lunch; $7-$18; cocktails/lounge. **Services:** valet laundry; area transportation, to uptown.
All Rooms: coffeemakers, free & pay movies. **Some Rooms:** refrigerators. **Cards:** AE, CB, DI, DS, JCB, MC, VI.
Special Amenities: Early check-in/late check-out and free newspaper. *(See ad below)*

🛏 ➕ 👤 CTV 🛋 ✕ 🏊 D S

THE DUNHILL HOTEL
Phone: 704/332-4141 **6**

◆◆◆	Mon-Thurs	1P: $149	2P/1B:	$149	2P/2B:	$149	XP: $10	F12
Historic Hotel	Fri-Sun	1P: $99	2P/1B:	$109	2P/2B:	$109	XP: $10	F12

Rates Subject to Change

Location: Diagonal from public library; Tryon St exit off Brookshire Frwy. 237 N Tryon St 28202.
Fax: 704/376-4117. **Terms:** Reserv deposit; no pets. **Facility:** 60 rooms. Handling fee imposed; 10 stories; interior corridors.
Dining: Dining room; 6:30 am-2 & 5:30-10 pm; $10-$20. **All Rooms:** free & pay movies. **Cards:** AE, DI, DS, MC, VI.

➕ CTV ✕ D S

FOUR POINTS HOTEL CHARLOTTE UPTOWN
Phone: 704/372-7550 **9**

[AAA] [SAVE]	All Year	1P: $129	2P/1B:	$129	2P/2B:	$129	XP: $10	F17

Location: S McDowell & 3rd sts. 201 S McDowell St 28204. Fax: 704/334-7284. **Terms:** No pets.
◆◆◆   **Facility:** 195 rooms. Many rooms with balcony. All rooms & public areas recently renovated. 11 stories; inte-
Hotel   rior corridors; luxury level rooms. **Dining & Entertainment:** Dining room; 6:30-10:30 am, 11-2 & 5-10 pm;
$8-$15; cocktails/lounge. **Services:** valet laundry; area transportation, within 2 mi. **All Rooms:** free & pay
movies. **Some Rooms:** coffeemakers, microwaves, refrigerators, safes. **Cards:** AE, CB, DI, DS, MC, VI. **Special Amenities:**
Free newspaper. *(See ad below)*

🏊 🛏 CTV ✕ 🏊 D

HOLIDAY INN CENTER CITY
Phone: 704/335-5400 **1**

◆◆	All Year	1P: $89- 129	2P/1B:	$99- 139	2P/2B:	$99- 139	XP: $10	F18

Rates Subject to Change

Motor Inn   **Location:** On College St between 5th & 6th sts; adjacent to Charlotte Apparel Center. 230 N College St
28202. Fax: 704/376-4921. **Terms:** No pets. **Facility:** 300 rooms. 14 stories; interior corridors.
Dining: Restaurant; 6:30 am-10 pm; $6-$18. **All Rooms:** free & pay movies. **Cards:** AE, CB, DI, DS, JCB, MC, VI.

🏊 CTV 🛋 ✕ 🏊 D S

(See map p. 336)

THE INN UPTOWN   Phone: 704/342-2800   **3**
AAA SAVE   All Year [BP]   1P: $99- 109   2P/1B: $119- 169   XP: $10
◆◆◆   **Location:** At corner of 5th & Poplar sts. 129 N Poplar St 28202. Fax: 704/342-2222. **Terms:** Age restrictions
Historic Bed   may apply; reserv deposit, 5 day notice; no pets. **Facility:** 7 rooms. A nostalgic chateausque home built in
& Breakfast   1890. Rooms nicely decorated & furnished. Many rooms with gas log fireplace, 1 with private porch. 3 stories;
               interior corridors; smoke free premises. **Dining:** Restaurant nearby. **Services:** complimentary evening
               beverages; valet laundry. **All Rooms:** free movies, combo or shower baths. **Some Rooms:** whirlpools.
               Cards: AE, CB, DI, DS, JCB, MC, VI. **Special Amenities:** Early check-in/late check-out and free breakfast.
               (See ad below)   📞 CTV ⊗ D S

MOREHEAD INN   Rates Subject to Change   Phone: 704/376-3357   **5**
◆◆◆   All Year [CP]   1P: $110- 160   2P/1B: $110- 160   2P/2B: $110- 160   XP: $10   F12
Historic Bed   **Location:** From I-277, exit Kenilworth Ave, 0.5 mi s, then w on Morehead St, at corner of Morehead &
& Breakfast   Berkeley Ave. 1122 E Morehead St 28204. Fax: 704/335-1110. **Terms:** No pets. **Facility:** 12 rooms. 1 two-
               bedroom apartment with full kitchen, $225; 2 stories; interior/exterior corridors; smoke free premises.
All Rooms: free movies. **Some Rooms:** A/C. **Cards:** AE, DI, DS, MC, VI.   ⊞ CTV ⊗ D

RADISSON PLAZA HOTEL CHARLOTTE   Rates Subject to Change   Phone: 704/377-0400   **7**
◆◆◆   Sun-Thurs   1P: $135- 219   2P/1B: $135- 219   2P/2B: $135- 219   XP: $10   F18
Hotel   Fri & Sat   1P: $99- 159   2P/1B: $99- 159   2P/2B: $99- 159   XP: $10   F18
               Location: At Trade & Tryon sts; downtown Trade St E exit off I-77, College St exit off I-277. 101 S Tryon St
28280. Fax: 704/347-0649. **Terms:** Sr. discount; no pets. **Facility:** 365 rooms. 15 stories; interior corridors. **Dining:** Dining
room; 6:30 am-11 pm; $6-$20. **All Rooms:** free & pay movies. **Cards:** AE, CB, DI, DS, MC, VI. *(See color ad below)*
                                                                      🏊 ⊞ CTV ⊗ 🎨 D S

THE WESTIN HOTEL-CHARLOTTE   Phone: 704/377-6664   **8**
AAA SAVE   Mon-Thurs   1P: $139   2P/1B: $139   2P/2B: $139
◆◆◆◆   Fri-Sun   1P: $99   2P/1B: $99   2P/2B: $99   XP: $10
Hotel   **Location:** Corner of College & E Third sts. 222 E Third St 28202. Fax: 704/377-4143. **Terms:** Check-in 4
               pm; package plans; no pets. **Facility:** 407 rooms. Rooms decorated with a warm color scheme & tastefully fur-
nished. 6 whirlpool rms, extra charge; 22 stories; interior corridors; luxury level rooms. Fee: parking; health
club privileges. **Dining & Entertainment:** Dining room; 6 am-11 pm, daily breakfast buffet, lunch buffet Mon-Fri; $9-$18;
health conscious menu items; cocktails/lounge. **Services:** valet laundry. Fee: valet parking. **All Rooms:** honor bars,
coffeemakers, free & pay movies. **Cards:** AE, CB, DI, DS, JCB, MC, VI. **Special Amenities:** Free newspaper and free
room upgrade (subject to availability with advanced reservations).   🏊 ⊞ CTV 🏋 ⊗ 🎨 D S

RESTAURANTS

ATLANTIC BEER & ICE COMPANY   **Lunch:** $7-$10   **Dinner:** $12-$21   **Phone:** 704/339-0566   ⑦
◆◆   **Location:** Downtown; just e of jct Trade & Tryon sts. 330 N Tryon St 28202. **Hours:** 11 am-10 pm, Fri &
Regional   Sat-11 pm, Sun-3 pm. Closed: 1/1, 11/26 & 12/25. **Features:** cocktails & lounge. Carribean & South Florida
American   influence on entrees. Ybor sandwich signature lunch item. **Cards:** AE, DI, MC, VI.   ⊗

(See map p. 336)

BISTRO 100 ◆◆◆ American
Lunch: $7-$11   **Dinner:** $9-$18   **Phone:** 704/344-0515   ②
Location: On corner of Tryon & College sts. Valet parking entrance off Trade St n of College St. In Founders Hall Bldg. 100 N Tryon 28202. **Hours:** 11:30 am-10 pm, Fri & Sat-11 pm, Sun 11 am-9 pm. Closed major holidays. **Features:** Sunday brunch; health conscious menu; carryout; cocktails & lounge; valet parking; a la carte. An upbeat bistro featuring American entrees with a French flare. Also entrees of wood oven-cooked specialty pizza, wood-roasted meat & pasta. A warm & cozy atmosphere. **Cards:** AE, DI, DS, MC, VI.
☒

BRAVO RISTORANTE ◆◆◆ Northern Italian
Dinner: $12-$39   **Phone:** 704/372-5440   ⑤
Location: On SR 27, between Stonewall & E 2nd sts. 555 S McDowell St 28204. **Hours:** 5:30 pm-10 pm, Fri & Sat-10:30 pm. **Reservations:** suggested. **Features:** semi-formal attire; cocktails & lounge; entertainment; a la carte. Service by professional singers performing show tunes, opera & operetta. **Cards:** AE, CB, DI, DS, MC, VI.
☒

GINGERROOT RESTAURANT ◆◆ Chinese
Lunch: $5-$6   **Dinner:** $7-$15   **Phone:** 704/377-9429   ③
Location: Corner 5th & College sts, in street level of the International Trade Center. 201 E 5th St 28202. **Hours:** 11:30 am-2:30 & 5-10 pm. Closed: 11/26 & 12/25. **Reservations:** suggested; for dinner. **Features:** casual dress; carryout; cocktails & lounge; fee for parking; a la carte. Szechuan cuisine served in a comfortable cosmopolitan atmosphere. **Cards:** AE, CB, DI, MC, VI.
☒

THE LAMPLIGHTER ◆◆◆ Continental
Dinner: $14-$28   **Phone:** 704/372-5343   ④
Location: From I-277, exit Kenilworth Ave, 0.5 mi s, then 0.3 mi w on Morehead St. 1065 E Morehead St 28204. **Hours:** 6 pm-10 pm, Fri & Sat-10:30 pm, Sun-9:30 pm. Closed major holidays. **Reservations:** suggested. **Features:** semi-formal attire; cocktails & lounge; valet parking; a la carte. Some American dishes, changing specials of duck, wild game & lamb. Intimate dining in restored home. Excellent wine list. **Cards:** AE, DI, MC, VI.
☒

MCNINCH HOUSE Historical ◆◆◆◆ Continental
Phone: 704/332-6159   ①
Location: Just w on N Church St from I-277 (Brookshire Blvd). 511 N Church St 28202. **Hours:** 6:30 pm-10 pm; by reservation only. Closed: Sun & Mon. **Features:** Reservations: required. **Features:** semi-formal attire; health conscious menu; cocktails; valet parking; prix fixe. 1892 Victorian house. Owner/chef. Intimate & simple elegance; personalized service. Candle-lit tables with beautiful bouquet of flowers & eclectic mix of antique china & crystal. Signature entree rack of lamb. Smoke free premises. **Cards:** AE, MC, VI.
☒

30TH EDITION ◆◆ Continental
Dinner: $14-$22   **Phone:** 704/372-7778   ⑥
Location: Center; S Tryon & 2nd sts. Two 1st Union Plaza, 301 28282. **Hours:** 6 pm-9:30 pm, Fri-10 pm, Sat-10:30 pm. Closed: 1/1, 11/26 & 12/25. **Reservations:** suggested. **Features:** semi-formal attire; health conscious menu items; carryout; cocktails; a la carte. Intimate atmosphere with panoramic view of Charlotte from 30th floor of 1st Union Bank. Choices of USDA prime steak & fresh seafood. **Cards:** AE, CB, DI, MC, VI.
☒

GREATER CHARLOTTE (See map p. 342; index below)

Index of Establishments on the CHARLOTTE ACCOMMODATIONS Spotting Map

(See map p. 342)

Days Inn Charlotte South/Carowinds	58
The Homeplace Bed & Breakfast	59
Hampton Inn Airport	60
Red Roof Inn-Airport	61
La Quinta Inn-Airport	62
Clarion Hotel	63
Fairfield Inn by Marriott-Airport	64
HoJo Inn	65
Summerfield Suites Hotel	66
Days Inn-Airport	67
Wyndham Garden Hotel	68
Holiday Inn at University Executive Park	69
Courtyard by Marriott-South Park	70
Residence Inn by Marriott-Tyvola Executive Park	71
Courtyard by Marriott-Airport	72
Charlotte Marriott-Executive Park	73
Days Inn Sunset Rd	74
Comfort Inn-Merchandise Mart	75
Sleep Inn	76
The Park Hotel	78
Holiday Inn Express	79
Quality Inn Central	80
Comfort Inn UNCC	81
Continental Inn	82
Hyatt Charlotte at South Park	85
Homewood Suites-University Research Park	87

Country Inn and Suites by Carlson	88
Sheraton Airport Plaza Hotel	89

RESTAURANTS

Texas Ranch Steakhouse & Saloon	14
Villa Antonio Fine Italian Ristorante	15
Dilworth Brewing Company	16
Morrocrofts	17
Ranch House	19
The Townhouse	20
The Silver Cricket	22
PJ McKenzies	23
Cajun Queen Restaurant	24
La Bibliotheque	25
Cotton Street Diner	26
The Epicurean	27
The Blue Marlin	29
The Fishmarket	30
Sonoma on Providence	31
Mama Ricotta's	32
Cino Grill	33

MATTHEWS

Comfort Inn Matthews	95
Best Western Luxbury Hotel	96
Hampton Inn-Charlotte Matthews	97

LODGINGS

AMERISUITES
Phone: 704/522-8400 49
All Year [CP]   1P: $79- 99   2P/1B: $89- 109   2P/2B: $89- 109   XP: $10   F1
Location: Southbound, just e of I-77, exit 3; northbound, just e of exit 2, I-77, follow Arrowood Rd signs
Suite Motel 7900 Forest Point Blvd 28273. Fax: 704/522-8489. **Terms:** Pets, $50 extra charge. **Facility:** 128 rooms. Ap
pealing public areas & handsomely appointed suites. 6 stories; interior corridors. **Dining:** Restaurant nearby
Services: area transportation, within 5 mi. Fee: coin laundry. **All Rooms:** coffeemakers, free & pay movies
combo or shower baths, VCP's. **Cards:** AE, CB, DI, DS, MC, VI. **Special Amenities:** Free breakfast and free loca
telephone calls. *(See color ad p 10)*   Roll in showers.   D S

(See map p. 342)

APARTMENT INN
◆◆
Apartment
Motel
Rates Subject to Change
1P: $55   2P/1B: $65   2P/2B: $65   XP: $5
Phone: 704/399-1600   [20]
F19
Location: I-85, exit 34B. 1700 I-85S Service Rd 28208. Fax: 704/399-1600. **Terms:** Sr. discount; no pets. **Facility:** 92 rooms. 2 stories; exterior corridors. **All Rooms:** kitchens, free movies. **Cards:** AE, DI, DS, MC, VI.

BEST WESTERN AIRPORT HOTEL & CONFERENCE CENTER
[logo] [SAVE]
◆◆◆
Fee: coin laundry.
Sun-Thurs   1P: $79- 89   2P/1B: $79- 89   2P/2B: $79- 89
Fri & Sat   1P: $73- 89   2P/1B: $73- 89   2P/2B: $73- 89
Phone: 704/394-4301   [57]
Location: Just e of I-85 exit 32, (Little Rock Rd). 2707 Little Rock Rd 28214. Fax: 704/394-1844. **Terms:** Weekly/monthly rates; no pets. **Facility:** 218 rooms. 4 stories; interior corridors; sauna, whirlpool. **Dining & Entertainment:** Dining room; 6 am-11 pm, Fri-Sun to 10 pm; $7-$14; cocktails/lounge. **Services:** All Rooms: free & pay movies. **Some Rooms:** microwaves, refrigerators. Fee: whirlpools. **Cards:** AE, CB, DI, DS, JCB, MC, VI. **Special Amenities:** Free local telephone calls.

BEST WESTERN LUXURY INN
[logo] [SAVE]
◆◆◆
Motel
All Year [CP]   1P: $50- 53   2P/1B: $56- 59   2P/2B: $59   XP: $6
Phone: 704/596-9229   [27]
F18
Location: I-85 & Sugar Creek Rd. 4904 I-85N Service Rd 28206. Fax: 704/598-6725. **Terms:** No pets. **Facility:** 98 rooms. Spacious rooms. 3 stories; interior corridors. **Services:** valet laundry. **All Rooms:** free movies. **Some Rooms:** Fee: refrigerators. **Cards:** AE, DI, DS, MC, VI. **Special Amenities:** Early check-in/late check-out and free room upgrade (subject to availability with advanced reservations).

BEST WESTERN MERCHANDISE MART
[logo]
◆◆
Motor Inn
am-2 & 5-10 pm; $6-$15.
All Year [CP]   1P: $51- 61   2P/1B: $57- 67   2P/2B: $57- 67   XP: $8
Phone: 704/358-3755   [23]
F16
Location: From I-277, 2 mi e on US 74, next to Merchandise Mart. 3024 E Independence Blvd 28205. Fax: 704/358-4718. **Terms:** Pets. **Facility:** 150 rooms. 8 stories; interior corridors. **Dining:** Restaurant; 10 **All Rooms:** free movies. **Cards:** AE, CB, DI, DS, MC, VI.

BROOKWOOD INN EXPRESS
[logo] [SAVE]
◆◆
Motel
3/30-10/31 [CP]   1P: $43- 79   2P/1B: $48- 84   2P/2B: $48- 84   XP: $5
12/1-3/29 & 11/1-11/30 [CP]   1P: $43- 73   2P/1B: $48- 79   2P/2B: $48- 79   XP: $5
Phone: 704/597-8500   [42]
F18
F18
Location: I-85, exit 41. 1200 W Sugar Creek Rd 28213. Fax: 704/598-1815. **Terms:** No pets. **Facility:** 132 rooms. 2 stories; exterior corridors. **Dining:** Restaurant nearby. **Services:** Fee: coin laundry. **All Rooms:** free movies. **Some Rooms:** microwaves, refrigerators. Fee: whirlpools. **Cards:** AE, DI, DS, MC, VI. **Special Amenities:** Early check-in/late check-out and free room upgrade (subject to availability with advanced reservations).

CHARLOTTE HILTON AT UNIVERSITY PLACE
◆◆◆
Hotel
am-2 & 6-10 pm; $10-$22.
Sun-Thurs   1P: $89- 169   2P/1B: $104- 184   2P/2B: $104- 184   XP: $15
Fri & Sat   1P: $89   2P/1B: $89   2P/2B: $89
Phone: 704/547-7444   [24]
F16
Location: I-85 exit 45A, Harris Blvd-UNCC, 0.3 mi e. 8629 J M Keynes Dr 28262. Fax: 704/549-9708. **Terms:** Sr. discount; small pets only, dep req. **Facility:** 243 rooms. 12 stories; interior corridors. **Dining:** Dining room; 6:30 **All Rooms:** free & pay movies. **Cards:** AE, CB, DI, DS, MC, VI. *(See color ad p 18)*

CHARLOTTE HILTON EXECUTIVE PARK
[logo] [SAVE]
◆◆◆
Hotel
Fri & Sat-11 pm; $10-$18;
Mon-Thurs   1P: $129- 164   2P/1B: $129- 164   2P/2B: $129- 164   XP: $10
Fri-Sun   1P: $99- 149   2P/1B: $99- 149   2P/2B: $99- 149   XP: $10
Phone: 704/527-8000   [54]
F
F
Location: I-77 & Tyvola Rd, exit 5, in Executive Park. 5624 Westpark Dr 28217. Fax: 704/527-4278. **Terms:** Reserv deposit; monthly rates; package plans; small pets only, $50 dep req. **Facility:** 178 rooms. Attractive public areas. 7 stories; interior corridors; indoor whirlpool. **Dining:** Restaurant; 6:30 am-2 & 6-10 pm, cocktails; lobby piano bar. **Services:** valet laundry; area transportation, within 5 mi. **All Rooms:** coffeemakers, free & pay movies. **Some Rooms:** microwaves, refrigerators. **Cards:** AE, CB, DI, DS, MC, VI. **Special Amenities:** Free breakfast and free newspaper. *(See color ad p 18 & ad p 344)*
Roll in showers.

CHARLOTTE MARRIOTT-EXECUTIVE PARK
◆◆◆
Hotel
om 7 am; $10-$20.
Sun-Thurs   1P: $139   2P/1B: $139   2P/2B: $139
Fri & Sat   1P: $89   2P/1B: $89   2P/2B: $89
Rates Subject to Change
Phone: 704/527-9650   [73]
Location: I-77 & Tyvola Rd exit 5. 5700 Westpark Dr 28217. Fax: 704/527-6918. **Terms:** Sr. discount; check-in 4 pm; no pets. **Facility:** 297 rooms. 19 stories; interior corridors. **Dining:** Restaurant; 6:30 am-11 pm, Sat & Sun **All Rooms:** free & pay movies. **Cards:** AE, DI, DS, MC, VI.

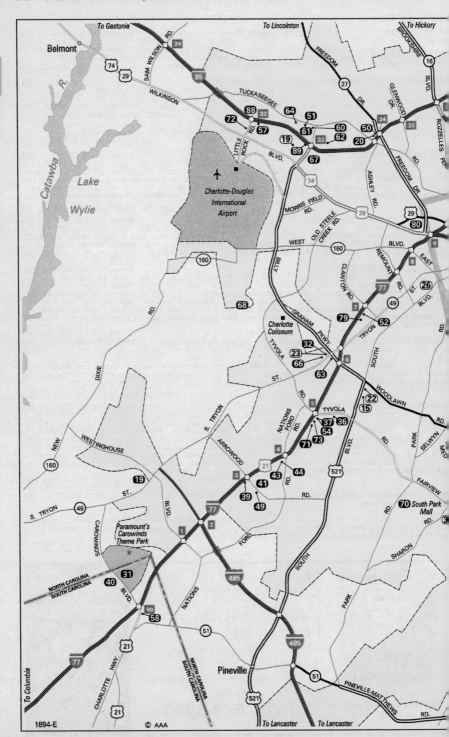

© AAA

CHARLOTTE
ACCOMMODATIONS

(See map p. 342)

CLARION HOTEL   Phone: 704/523-1400 [63]

		1P:	$80	2P/1B:	$80	2P/2B:	$90	XP:	$5	F12
(AAA) (SAVE) 4/1-5/31 & 9/1-11/30
Hotel   2/16-3/31 & 6/1-8/31   1P: $70   2P/1B: $70   2P/2B: $80   XP: $5   F12
12/1-2/15   1P: $60   2P/1B: $60   2P/2B: $70   XP: $5   F12
Too new to rate; **Location:** Just w of I-77, exit 6B. 321 W Woodlawn Rd 28217. Fax: 704/529-1448.
Terms: Reserv deposit, 3 day notice; pets. **Facility:** 174 rooms. Scheduled to open summer 1997. 6 stories; interior corridors; luxury level rooms; whirlpool, cabana bar at pool. **Dining & Entertainment:** Restaurant; cocktails/lounge. **Services:** complimentary evening beverages, Mon-Thurs; area transportation, within 5 mi. Fee: coin laundry. **All Rooms:** coffeemakers, free movies, combo or shower baths. **Some Rooms:** microwaves, refrigerators. **Cards:** AE, DI, DS, MC, VI. **Special Amenities: Free newspaper and preferred room (subject to availability with advanced reservations).** *(See color ad below)*   Roll in showers.   [icons]

COMFORT INN CAROWINDS   Phone: 803/548-5200 [31]

(AAA) (SAVE) 6/1-8/31 [CP]   1P: $59- 69   2P/1B: $75- 85   2P/2B: $75- 85   XP: $8   F19
◆◆◆   12/1-5/31 & 9/1-11/30 [CP]   1P: $59- 69   2P/1B: $69- 79   2P/2B: $69- 79   XP: $8   F19
Motel   **Location:** Off I-77, exit 90; at Carowinds. 3725 Avenue Of The Carolinas 29715. Fax: 803/548-6692.
Terms: Reserv deposit, 24 day notice; no pets. **Facility:** 103 rooms. Attractively decorated rooms, North Carolina phone 704-339-0574. 4 stories; interior corridors. **Dining:** Restaurant nearby. **Services:** valet laundry. **All Rooms:** free & pay movies. **Some Rooms:** microwaves, refrigerators, safes. Fee: whirlpools. **Cards:** AE, CB, DI, DS, MC, VI. **Special Amenities: Free breakfast and free local telephone calls.** *(See color ad p 341)*   [icons]

COMFORT INN-EXECUTIVE PARK   Phone: 704/525-2626 [37]

(AAA) (SAVE) All Year [CP]   1P: $59- 64   2P/1B: $69   2P/2B: $69   XP: $5   F18
◆◆◆   **Location:** I-77 exit 5, (Tyvola Rd). 5822 Westpark Dr 28217. Fax: 704/525-3372. **Terms:** Check-in 4 pm; no
Motel   pets. **Facility:** 150 rooms. Attractive public areas. 6 stories; interior corridors. **Dining:** Restaurant nearby. **Services:** complimentary evening beverages, Mon-Thurs. **All Rooms:** coffeemakers, free & pay movies. **Cards:** AE, CB, DI, DS, JCB, MC, VI. **Special Amenities: Free room upgrade (subject to availability with advanced reservations).** *(See color ad p 340)*   Roll in showers.   [icons]

COMFORT INN-MERCHANDISE MART   Phone: 704/375-8444 [75]

(AAA) (SAVE) All Year [CP]   1P: $49- 69   2P/1B: $55- 69   2P/2B: $69- 75   XP: $6   F18
◆◆◆   **Location:** 3.5 mi e on US 74, opposite Merchandise Mart. 2721 E Independence Blvd 28205.
Motel   Fax: 704/375-8444. **Terms:** No pets. **Facility:** 106 rooms. Phone charge, $.50 daily; 2 stories; exterior corridors. **Dining:** Restaurant nearby. **Services:** valet laundry. **All Rooms:** free movies. **Some Rooms:** coffeemakers, refrigerators. **Cards:** AE, CB, DI, DS, JCB, MC. **Special Amenities: Free breakfast and free newspaper.**   Roll in showers.   [icons]

(See map p. 342)

COMFORT INN UNCC   Phone: 704/598-0007   81
All Year [CP]   1P: $49- 69   2P/1B: $53- 79   2P/2B: $53- 79   XP: $6   F12
Location: I-85 & Sugar Creek Rd, exit 41. 5111 N I-85 Service Rd 28269. Fax: 704/598-0007.
Terms: Reserv deposit, 3 day notice; pets, $6 extra charge. **Facility:** 87 rooms. Handling fee imposed; 2 stories; interior corridors; whirlpool. **Dining:** Restaurant nearby. **Services:** valet laundry. **All Rooms:** free
movies. **Some Rooms:** coffeemakers. Fee: microwaves, refrigerators, whirlpools. **Cards:** AE, CB, DI, DS,
JCB, MC. **Special Amenities:** Early check-in/late check-out and free breakfast.

CONTINENTAL INN   Phone: 704/597-8100   82
All Year [CP]   1P: $38- 40   2P/1B: $42- 45   2P/2B: $48- 52   XP: $5
Location: I-85, exit 41. 1100 W Sugar Creek Rd 28213. **Terms:** Reserv deposit, 3 day notice; no pets.
Facility: 40 rooms. 2 stories; exterior corridors; designated smoking area. **All Rooms:** free movies.
Cards: AE, DS, MC, VI.

COUNTRY INN AND SUITES BY CARLSON   Phone: 704/394-2000   88
All Year [CP]   1P: $59- 99   2P/1B: $59- 109   2P/2B: $59- 110   XP: $5   F16
Location: 0.3 mi e of I-85, exit 32 (Little Rock Rd). 2541 Little Rock Rd 28214. Fax: 704/394-7467.
Terms: No pets. **Facility:** 119 rooms. Handsomely appointed public areas & rooms. 2 stories; interior corridors.
Dining: Restaurant nearby. **Services:** valet laundry. **All Rooms:** coffeemakers, free & pay movies.
Some Rooms: microwaves, refrigerators. **Cards:** AE, CB, DI, DS, MC, VI. **Special Amenities:** Free
breakfast and free local telephone calls. *(See color ad below)*

COURTYARD BY MARRIOTT-AIRPORT   Phone: 704/392-8899   72
All Year [BP]   1P: $70- 100   2P/1B: $70- 100   2P/2B: $70- 100   XP: $10   F18
Too new to rate; **Location:** Just e of I-85, exit 32 (Little Rock Rd). 2700 Little Rock Rd 28214. **Terms:** No
pets. **Facility:** 90 rooms. Scheduled to open spring 1997. 5 whirlpool rms, extra charge; 3 stories; interior corridors; whirlpool. **Dining & Entertainment:** Cocktail lounge. **Services:** Fee: coin laundry. **All Rooms:** free
movies, combo or shower baths. **Some Rooms:** microwaves, refrigerators. **Cards:** AE, CB, DI, DS, JCB, MC, VI.
(See color ad p 346)   Roll in showers.

COURTYARD BY MARRIOTT-ARROWOOD   Rates Subject to Change   Phone: 704/527-5055   41
Sun-Thurs   1P: $75- 85   2P/1B: $75- 85   2P/2B: $75- 85
Fri & Sat   1P: $61   2P/1B: $61   2P/2B: $61
Location: Southbound Arrowood exit 3 off I-77, 2 blks e; northbound exit 2, I-77 follow signs. 800 E
Arrowood Rd 28217. Fax: 704/525-5848. **Terms:** Sr. discount; no pets. **Facility:** 146 rooms. 3 stories; interior corridors.
Dining: Dining room; 6-10 am, Sat & Sun 7-11 am. **All Rooms:** free & pay movies. **Cards:** AE, CB, DI, DS, MC, VI.
(See color ad p 346)

COURTYARD BY MARRIOTT-SOUTH PARK   Rates Subject to Change   Phone: 704/552-7333   70
Sun-Thurs   1P: $109   2P/1B: $119   2P/2B: $119   XP: $10   F18
Fri & Sat   1P: $71   2P/1B: $71   2P/2B: $71
Location: Just sw of South Park Mall. 6023 Park South Dr 28210. Fax: 704/552-2056. **Terms:** No pets.
Facility: 149 rooms. 3 stories; interior corridors. **Dining:** Coffee shop; 6:30-10:30 am, Sat & Sun 7-11:30 am.
All Rooms: free & pay movies. **Cards:** AE, CB, DI, DS, MC, VI. *(See color ad p 346)*

COURTYARD BY MARRIOTT-UNIVERSITY PARK   Rates Subject to Change   Phone: 704/549-4888   21
All Year   1P: $94   2P/1B: $104   2P/2B: $104
Location: Harris Blvd exit off I-85, 0.3 mi e. 333 West W T Harris Blvd 28262. Fax: 704/549-4946.
Terms: Sr. discount; no pets. **Facility:** 152 rooms. 4 stories; interior corridors. **Dining:** Restaurant;
6:30-10:30 am, Sat & Sun 7-11 am. **All Rooms:** free & pay movies. **Cards:** AE, DI, DS, MC, VI. *(See color ad p 346)*

DAYS INN-AIRPORT   Phone: 704/394-3381   67
All Year [CP]   1P: $45- 49   2P/1B: $45- 49   2P/2B: $45- 49
Location: I-85 at Billy Graham Pkwy exit 33. 3101 I-85S Service Rd 28208. Fax: 704/394-3381. **Terms:** No
pets. **Facility:** 118 rooms. Handling fee imposed; 3 stories; interior corridors. **Dining:** Restaurant; 5 pm-11
pm, closed Sun; $5-$15; cocktails. **Services:** Fee: coin laundry. **All Rooms:** free movies. **Cards:** AE, DI,
DS, MC, VI.

(See map p. 342)

DAYS INN CHARLOTTE SOUTH/CAROWINDS   Rates Subject to Change   **Phone:** 803/548-8000   [58]
◆◆   All Year [CP]   1P: $40- 70   2P/1B: $45- 75   2P/2B: $45- 75   XP: $5   F18
Motel   **Location:** Exit 90, off I-77 (Carowinds Blvd). 3482 Carowinds Blvd 29715 (Po Box 397). Fax: 803/548-6058.
Terms: Pets, $5 extra charge. **Facility:** 119 rooms. 2 stories; exterior corridors. **All Rooms:** free movies.
Cards: AE, CB, DI, DS, MC, VI.

DAYS INN SUNSET RD   **Phone:** 704/598-7712   [74]
 All Year [CP]   1P: $53- 55   2P/1B: $39- 140   2P/2B: $44- 145   XP: $5   F18
Location: Just e of I-77N exit 16A. 4924 Sunset Rd 28269. Fax: 704/596-7173. **Terms:** No pets. **Facility:** 74
◆◆   rooms. 3 stories; exterior corridors; small indoor heated pool. **Dining:** Coffee shop nearby. **All Rooms:** free
Motel   movies. **Cards:** AE, CB, DI, DS, JCB, MC, VI. **Special Amenities: Free breakfast and free local
telephone calls.**

DRURY INN & SUITES   **Phone:** 704/593-0700   [22]
Motel   Under construction; **Location:** 0.3 mi e from I-85, exit 45. 415 W W T Harris Blvd 28262. **Terms:** Age
restrictions may apply; no pets. **Facility:** 144 rooms. Scheduled to open summer 1997; 5 stories.
All Rooms: free movies. *(See ad below)*

(See map p. 342)

ECONOLODGE I-85 SUGAR CREEK ROAD Phone: 704/597-0470 29
AAA SAVE All Year [CP] 1P: $39-125 2P/1B: $39-125 2P/2B: $39-125 XP: $6 F16
◆◆ **Location:** I-85 exit 41, w on Sugar Creek Rd to I-85 service road for 0.5 mi. 1415 Tom Hunter Rd 28213.
Motel Fax: 704/597-0470. **Terms:** Reserv deposit, 15 day notice; no pets. **Facility:** 97 rooms. 2 stories; exterior corridors. **Dining:** Restaurant nearby. **All Rooms:** free movies. **Some Rooms:** coffeemakers, microwaves, radios, refrigerators. **Cards:** AE, DI, DS, MC, VI. **Special Amenities: Free breakfast and free local telephone calls.**
🏊 CTV 🚫 📷 D

EMBASSY SUITES Rates Subject to Change Phone: 704/527-8400 32
◆◆◆ Sun-Thurs [BP] 1P: $159 2P/1B: $159 2P/2B: $159 XP: $10 F18
Suite Hotel Fri & Sat [BP] 1P: $119 2P/1B: $119 2P/2B: $119 XP: $10 F18
Location: Exit 6B, off I-77. 4800 S Tryon St 28217. Fax: 704/527-7035. **Terms:** Sr. discount; no pets. **Facility:** 274 rooms. Rates for up to 6 persons; 8 stories; interior corridors. **Dining:** PJ McKenzies, see separate listing. **All Rooms:** free & pay movies. **Cards:** AE, CB, DI, DS, JCB, MC, VI.
🏊 ✈ CTV 🛏 🚫 📷 D S

FAIRFIELD INN BY MARRIOTT-AIRPORT Rates Subject to Change Phone: 704/392-0600 64
◆◆◆ All Year [CP] 1P: $49-53 2P/1B: $49-53 2P/2B: $50-53 XP: $3 F18
Motel **Location:** Exit 33, Billy Graham Pkwy, off I-85. 3400 I-85S Service Rd 28208. Fax: 704/392-0600. **Terms:** No pets. **Facility:** 135 rooms. 3 stories; interior/exterior corridors. **All Rooms:** free & pay movies. **Cards:** AE, CB, DI, DS, MC. *(See color ad below)*
🏊 🛏 🚫 📷 D S

FAIRFIELD INN BY MARRIOTT-ARROWOOD 39
◆◆◆ All Year [CP] 1P: $49-69 XP: $18 F18
AAA SAVE Too new to rate; **Location:** Southbound just e of I-77 exit 3; northbound I-77 exit 2, follow signs. 7920
Motel Arrowridge Blvd 28273. **Terms:** No pets. **Facility:** 83 rooms. Scheduled to open summer 1997. 3 stories; interior corridors. **Dining:** Restaurant nearby. **All Rooms:** free movies, combo or shower baths. **Cards:** AE, CB, DI, DS, JCB, MC, VI. *(See color ad below)* Roll in showers. 🏊 ✈ CTV ♿ 🚫 📷 D S

FAIRFIELD INN BY MARRIOTT-NORTHEAST Rates Subject to Change Phone: 704/596-2999 30
◆◆◆ All Year [CP] 1P: $46-52 2P/1B: $51-57 2P/2B: $52-57 XP: $5 F18
Motel **Location:** At I-85 & Sugar Creek Rd, exit 41. 5415 I-85N Service Rd 28262. Fax: 704/596-2999. **Terms:** Sr. discount; no pets. **Facility:** 133 rooms. 3 stories; interior/exterior corridors. **All Rooms:** free & pay movies. **Cards:** AE, DI, DS, MC, VI. *(See color ad below)*
🏊 🛏 🚫 📷 D S

HAMPTON INN AIRPORT Rates Subject to Change Phone: 704/392-1600 60
◆◆◆ All Year [CP] 1P: $68-72 2P/1B: $72-80 2P/2B: $72-80 XP: $8 F18
Motel **Location:** Exit Billy Graham Pkwy off I-85, exit 33. 3127 Sloan Dr 28208. Fax: 704/392-7952. **Terms:** No pets. **Facility:** 122 rooms. 4 stories; interior corridors. **All Rooms:** free & pay movies. **Cards:** AE, CB, DI, DS, MC, VI.
🛏 🚫 📷 D S

HAMPTON INN-EXECUTIVE PARK Rates Subject to Change Phone: 704/525-0747 36
◆◆◆ All Year [CP] 1P: $64 2P/1B: $72 2P/2B: $74 XP: $8 F18
Motel **Location:** Off I-77, exit Tyvola Rd; in Executive Center. 440 Griffith Rd 28217. Fax: 704/522-0968. **Terms:** Sr. discount; no pets. **Facility:** 161 rooms. 4 stories; interior corridors. **All Rooms:** free & pay movies. **Cards:** AE, CB, DI, DS, MC, VI.
🏊 ✈ 🚫 📷 D S

HAMPTON INN UNIVERSITY PLACE Rates Subject to Change Phone: 704/548-0905 47
◆◆◆ All Year [CP] 1P: $72 2P/1B: $80 2P/2B: $80 XP: $8 F18
Motel **Location:** Harris Blvd exit 45A off I-85, 0.3 mi to US 29, then 2 blks e. 8419 N Tryon St 28262. Fax: 704/548-0971. **Terms:** Sr. discount; no pets. **Facility:** 125 rooms. 6 stories; interior corridors; designated smoking area. **All Rooms:** free movies. **Cards:** AE, CB, DI, DS, MC, VI.
🏊 ✈ CTV 🛏 🚫 📷 D S

(See map p. 342)

HOJO INN   Rates Subject to Change   Phone: 704/596-0042   **65**
◆◆   All Year   1P: $44   2P/1B: $47   2P/2B: $50   XP: $5
Motel   **Location:** I-85 exit 45A, 0.3 mi e on Harris Blvd, then 2.5 mi s on US 29. 6426 N Tryon St 28213.
Terms: Reserv deposit, 3 day notice; no pets. **Facility:** 42 rooms. 2 stories; exterior corridors; designated
smoking area. **All Rooms:** free movies. **Cards:** AE, CB, DI, DS, JCB, MC, VI.   CTV ⊗ D

HOLIDAY INN AT UNIVERSITY EXECUTIVE PARK   Phone: 704/547-0999   **69**
AAA SAVE   Sun-Thurs [BP]   1P: $104   2P/1B: $104   2P/2B: $104   XP: $10   F19
   Fri & Sat [BP]   1P: $79   2P/1B: $79   2P/2B: $79   XP: $10   F19
◆◆◆   **Location:** Harris Blvd exit off I-85, 0.3 mi e. 8520 University Executive Park Dr 28262. Fax: 704/549-4018.
Motor Inn   **Terms:** Weekly/monthly rates; pets, $10 extra charge. **Facility:** 175 rooms. Attractive public areas. 7 stories;
interior corridors; sauna, whirlpool. **Dining & Entertainment:** Restaurant; 6:30 am-10 pm, Sat & Sun from 7
am; $5-$15; health conscious menu items; cocktails/lounge. **Services:** valet laundry. **All Rooms:** free movies.
Some Rooms: coffeemakers, refrigerators. **Cards:** AE, CB, DI, DS, JCB, MC, VI. **Special Amenities: Free breakfast and
free local telephone calls.**   🛏 ⊃ 🐾 ⊕ 🖶 CTV 🔥 ⊗ 🎬 D S

HOLIDAY INN EXPRESS   Phone: 704/523-0633   **79**
AAA SAVE   All Year [CP]   1P: $59- 65   2P/1B: $65   2P/2B: $59
   Location: Just e of I-77, exit 7. 575 Clanton Rd 28217. Fax: 704/523-0633. **Terms:** No pets. **Facility:** 88
◆◆   rooms. 3 stories; interior corridors; designated smoking area. **Dining:** Restaurant nearby. **Services:** valet
Motel   laundry. **All Rooms:** free movies. **Some Rooms:** Fee: whirlpools. **Cards:** AE, CB, DI, DS, JCB, MC, VI
Special Amenities: Free breakfast and free newspaper.   ⊃ 🐾 ⊕ CTV ⊗ 🎬 D

HOLIDAY INN EXPRESS   Phone: 803/548-0100   **40**
AAA SAVE   5/1-10/11 [CP]   1P: $79- 99   2P/1B: $79- 99   2P/2B: $79- 99   XP: $6   F19
   12/1-4/30 & 10/12-11/30 [CP]   1P: $69- 89   2P/1B: $69- 89   2P/2B: $69- 89   XP: $6   F19
◆◆◆   **Location:** Off I-77, exit 90; at Carowinds. (3560 Lakemont Blvd, FORT MILL, 29715). Fax: 803/548-5305.
Motel   **Terms:** Check-in 4 pm; weekly/monthly rates; no pets. **Facility:** 68 rooms. 2 stories; interior corridors; small
pool. **Dining:** Restaurant nearby. **Services:** valet laundry. **All Rooms:** coffeemakers, free movies.
Some Rooms: microwaves, radios, refrigerators. Fee: whirlpools. **Cards:** AE, CB, DI, DS, JCB, MC, VI. **Special Amenities:
Free breakfast and free local telephone calls.** *(See color ad below)* Roll in showers. 🐾 🖶 CTV ⊗ ⊗

HOLIDAY INN EXPRESS SUGAR CREEK   Rates Subject to Change   Phone: 704/596-9390   **38**
◆◆◆   All Year [CP]   1P: $69   2P/1B: $74   2P/2B: $74   XP: $5   F18
Motel   **Location:** At I-85 & Sugar Creek Rd, exit 41. 5301 I-85N 28213. Fax: 704/596-9390. **Terms:** No pets.
Facility: 100 rooms. 2 stories; exterior corridors; smoke free premises. **All Rooms:** free & pay movies.
Cards: AE, CB, DI, DS, JCB, MC, VI.   ⊃ 🔥 ⊗ 🎬 D

HOLIDAY INN INDEPENDENCE   Phone: 704/537-1010   **48**
AAA SAVE   All Year   1P: $56   2P/1B: $56   2P/2B: $56   XP: $10   F18
◆◆◆   **Location:** On US 74, Independence Blvd, just se of city route 4, 0.3 mi s of Merchandise Mart. 3501 E
Motor Inn   Independence Blvd 28205. Fax: 704/531-2439. **Terms:** No pets. **Facility:** 176 rooms. 2-3 stories;
interior/exterior corridors. **Dining & Entertainment:** Restaurant; 6 am-2 & 5-9 pm; $6-$14; cocktails/lounge
Services: valet laundry. **All Rooms:** coffeemakers, free movies. **Some Rooms:** Fee: whirlpools. **Cards:** AE
DI, DS, MC, VI.   Roll in showers. ⊃ CTV & ⊗ 🎬 D

THE HOMEPLACE BED & BREAKFAST   Rates Subject to Change   Phone: 704/365-1936   **59**
◆◆◆   All Year [BP]   1P: $98   2P/1B: $98   XP: $20
Historic Bed   **Location:** From I-77 exit 5, 10 mi e; from US 74 Independence Blvd, 3 mi w. 5901 Sardis Rd 28270
& Breakfast   Fax: 704/366-2729. **Terms:** Age restrictions may apply; reserv deposit; no pets. **Facility:** 3 rooms. Suite, $125
for 2 persons; 2 stories; interior corridors; smoke free premises. **All Rooms:** free movies. **Cards:** AE, MC
VI.   CTV ⊗ D

HOMEWOOD SUITES-UNIVERSITY RESEARCH PARK   Rates Subject to Change   Phone: 704/549-8800   **87**
◆◆◆   All Year [MAP]   1P: $109- 119   2P/1B: $114- 124   2P/2B: $124
Suite Motel   **Location:** From I-85 exit 45A, 0.3 mi to US 29, just s. 8340 N Tryon St 28262. Fax: 704/510-0055
Terms: Sr. discount; no pets. **Facility:** 112 rooms. 2-4 stories; interior/exterior corridors
All Rooms: efficiencies. Fee: movies. **Cards:** AE, CB, DI, DS, MC, VI.   ⊃ ⊕ CTV 🔥 ⊗ 🎬 D

HOWARD JOHNSON LODGE   Rates Subject to Change   Phone: 704/393-9881   **50**
◆◆   All Year [CP]   1P: $30- 36   2P/1B: $32- 41   2P/2B: $40- 50   XP: $5   F12
Motel   **Location:** I-85 exit 34B. 4419 Tuckaseegee Rd 28208. Fax: 704/398-2421. **Terms:** Reserv deposit; no pets
Facility: 114 rooms. Handling fee imposed; 2 stories; exterior corridors. **All Rooms:** free movies. **Cards:** AE
CB, DI, DS, MC, VI.   ⊃ ⊕ ⊗ D

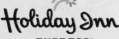

(See map p. 342)

HYATT CHARLOTTE AT SOUTH PARK
Phone: 704/554-1234 [85]

| | Sun-Thurs | 1P: $155 | 2P/1B: $180 | 2P/2B: $180 | XP: $25 | F18 |
| | Fri & Sat | 1P: $89- 125 | 2P/1B: $89- 125 | 2P/2B: $89- 125 | | |

(AAA) [SAVE]
◆◆◆
Hotel

Location: Exit 5 off I-77, Tyvola Rd to Fairview, just n on Barclay Downs; opposite South Park Mall. 5501 Carnegie Blvd 28209. Fax: 704/554-8319. **Terms:** Package plans; no pets. **Facility:** 262 rooms. Appealing guest room furnishings & decor. 7 stories; interior corridors; sauna. **Dining & Entertainment:** Dining room; 6 am-3 & 5-10 pm; $10-$20; health conscious menu items; cocktails/lounge. **Services:** valet laundry; area transportation, within 1 mi; valet parking. **All Rooms:** coffeemakers, free & pay movies. **Cards:** AE, CB, DI, DS, JCB, VI.

[icons]

LA QUINTA INN-AIRPORT
Phone: 704/393-5306 [62]

| | All Year [CP] | 1P: $55- 61 | 2P/1B: $68 | 2P/2B: $61 | XP: $6 | F18 |

(AAA) [SAVE]
◆◆◆
Motel

Location: I-85 & Billy Graham Pkwy, exit 33. 3100 I-85 S Service Rd 28208. Fax: 704/394-0550. **Terms:** Small pets only. **Facility:** 130 rooms. Well-maintained; excellent housekeeping; very attractive public areas & handsomely appointed & comfortable rooms. 2-3 stories; exterior corridors; small pool. **Dining:** Restaurant nearby. **Services:** valet laundry. **All Rooms:** free & pay movies. **Some Rooms:** Fee: microwaves, refrigerators. **Cards:** AE, CB, DI, DS, MC, VI. **Special Amenities:** Free breakfast and free local telephone calls. (See color ad below)

[icons]

LA QUINTA SOUTH
Phone: 704/522-7110 [44]

| | All Year [CP] | 1P: $55- 63 | 2P/1B: $70 | 2P/2B: $62 | XP: $7 | F18 |

(AAA) [SAVE]
◆◆◆
Motel

Location: Just e of I-77 & Nations Ford Rd, exit 4. 7900 Nations Ford Rd 28217. Fax: 704/521-9778. **Terms:** Small pets only. **Facility:** 118 rooms. Very well kept rooms. 3 stories; interior/exterior corridors. **Dining:** Restaurant nearby. **Services:** valet laundry. **All Rooms:** free & pay movies. **Some Rooms:** microwaves, refrigerators. **Cards:** AE, CB, DI, DS, MC, VI. **Special Amenities:** Free breakfast and free local telephone calls. (See color ad below)

[icons]

MICROTEL CHARLOTTE-AIRPORT
Rates Subject to Change **Phone: 704/398-9601** [51]

| | 3/30-11/30 | 1P: $45- 50 | 2P/1B: $50- 55 | 2P/2B: $55- 60 | XP: $5 | F16 |
| | 12/1-3/29 | 1P: $42- 46 | 2P/1B: $44- 49 | 2P/2B: $50- 55 | XP: $5 | F16 |

(AAA)
◆◆
Motel

Location: Just w on Mulberry Church Rd & just s on I-85 S Service Rd from I-85, exit 33 (Billy Graham Pkwy). 3412 S I-85 Service Rd 28208. Fax: 704/398-0850. **Terms:** Sr. discount; small pets only. **Facility:** 99 rooms. 3 stories; interior corridors. **All Rooms:** free & pay movies. **Cards:** AE, CB, DI, DS, MC, VI.

Roll in showers. [icons]

MICROTEL UNIVERSITY PLACE
Guaranteed Rates **Phone: 704/549-9900** [45]

| | 3/31-11/30 | 1P: $48- 58 | 2P/1B: $52- 62 | 2P/2B: $58- 68 | XP: $5 | F18 |
| | 12/1-3/30 | 1P: $43- 53 | 2P/1B: $47- 57 | 2P/2B: $53- 63 | XP: $5 | F18 |

(AAA)
◆◆
Motel

Location: Exit 45A, I-85, 0.5 mi e on W T Harris Blvd, 0.4 mi s on N Tryon, just e. 132 E McCullough Dr 28262. Fax: 704/549-4700. **Terms:** Sr. discount; no pets. **Facility:** 99 rooms. 3 stories; interior corridors. **All Rooms:** free & pay movies. **Cards:** AE, CB, DI, DS, MC, VI.

Roll in showers. [icons]

THE PARK HOTEL
Phone: 704/364-8220 [78]

| | Mon-Thurs | 1P: $190 | 2P/1B: $230 | 2P/2B: $210 | XP: $20 | F17 |
| | Fri-Sun | 1P: $109- 169 | 2P/1B: $109- 169 | 2P/2B: $109- 169 | XP: $20 | F17 |

(AAA) [SAVE]
◆◆◆◆
Hotel

Location: Opposite South Park Mall. 2200 Rexford Rd 28211. Fax: 704/365-4712. **Terms:** Reserv deposit, 3 day notice, handling fee imposed; BP avail; package plans; no pets. **Facility:** 194 rooms. Very appealing public areas & rooms offering warmth & charm of a boutique hotel. Fine English furnishings & original art throughout. 6 stories; interior corridors; steamroom, whirlpools. **Dining & Entertainment:** Cocktails/lounge; also, Morrocrofts, see separate listing. **Services:** valet laundry; valet parking. **All Rooms:** safes. Fee: movies. **Some Rooms:** refrigerators. **Cards:** AE, CB, DI, DS, MC, VI. A Preferred Hotel.

[icons]

QUALITY INN & SUITES-CROWN POINT
Phone: 704/845-2810 [35]

| | All Year [CP] | 1P: $49- 89 | 2P/1B: $49- 89 | 2P/2B: $49- 89 | XP: $5 | F16 |

(AAA) [SAVE]
◆◆◆
Motel

Location: 10.5 mi se of I-277 on US 74 E Independence Blvd; in the Crown Point Park. 2501 Sardis Rd N 28227. Fax: 704/845-1743. **Terms:** No pets. **Facility:** 100 rooms. In business park area. Large shopping complex nearby. 3 stories; interior corridors. **Dining:** Restaurant nearby. **Services:** valet laundry. **All Rooms:** coffeemakers, free & pay movies. **Some Rooms:** microwaves, refrigerators. **Cards:** AE, CB, DI, DS, MC, VI. **Special Amenities:** Early check-in/late check-out and free local telephone calls. (See color ad p 339)

[icons]

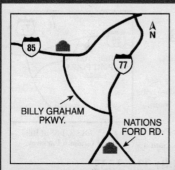

(See map p. 342)

QUALITY INN CENTRAL   Phone: 704/377-6961   80
All Year   1P: $55- 125   2P/1B: $60- 130   2P/2B: $65- 140   XP: $10   F18
Location: From I-77 exit 9 & US 74, 1 mi w. 2400 Wilkinson Blvd 28208. Fax: 704/332-8977. **Terms:** Reserv deposit; no pets. **Facility:** 114 rooms. 3 stories; interior corridors. **Dining & Entertainment:** Restaurant; 7:30 am-2 & 5:30-10 pm; $5-$8; cocktails/lounge. **Services:** Fee: coin laundry. **All Rooms:** free movies. **Some Rooms:** microwaves, refrigerators. **Cards:** AE, CB, DI, DS, JCB, MC, VI. **Special Amenities: Early check-in/late check-out and free newspaper.**
Motor Inn

RAMADA INN AIRPORT CENTRAL   Phone: 704/527-3000   52
All Year [BP]   1P: $59- 64   2P/1B: $59- 64   2P/2B: $64- 74   XP: $5   F18
Location: 2.5 mi sw on Clanton Rd, jct I-77 exit 7. 515 Clanton Rd 28217. Fax: 704/527-9476. **Terms:** No pets. **Facility:** 166 rooms. 6 stories; interior corridors; volleyball. **Dining & Entertainment:** Dining room; 6 am-2 & 5-10 pm; $7-$14; cocktails/lounge. **Services:** Fee: coin laundry. **All Rooms:** free & pay movies. **Some Rooms:** refrigerators. **Cards:** AE, CB, DI, DS, JCB, MC, VI. **Special Amenities: Free breakfast and free newspaper.**
Motor Inn

RED ROOF INN-AIRPORT   Rates Subject to Change   Phone: 704/392-2316   61
All Year   1P: $42- 55   2P/1B: $47- 60   2P/2B: $52- 60   XP: $7   F18
Location: I-85 at Billy Graham Pkwy, exit 33. 3300 I-85S Service Rd 28208. Fax: 704/392-7149. **Terms:** Small pets only. **Facility:** 84 rooms. 2 stories; exterior corridors. **All Rooms:** free movies. **Cards:** AE, CB, DI, DS, MC, VI.
Motel

RED ROOF INN COLISEUM   Rates Subject to Change   Phone: 704/529-1020   43
All Year   1P: $54   2P/1B: $59   2P/2B: $54   XP: $8   F18
Location: Just e of I-77 & Nations Ford Rd, exit 4. 131 Red Roof Dr 28217. Fax: 704/529-1054. **Terms:** Small pets only. **Facility:** 115 rooms. 3 stories; exterior corridors. **All Rooms:** free movies. **Cards:** AE, CB, DI, DS, MC, VI.
Motel

RED ROOF INN UNIVERSITY PLACE   Rates Subject to Change   Phone: 704/596-8222   28
4/15-9/30   1P: $40- 60   2P/1B: $46- 68   2P/2B: $50- 70   XP: $7   F18
10/1-11/30   1P: $39- 56   2P/1B: $45- 58   2P/2B: $46- 60   XP: $7   F18
12/1-4/14   1P: $38- 49   2P/1B: $42- 50   2P/2B: $44- 55   XP: $7   F18
Location: I-85 & Sugar Creek Rd, exit 41. 5116 I-85N 28206. Fax: 704/596-8298. **Terms:** Small pets only. **Facility:** 108 rooms. 2 stories; exterior corridors. **All Rooms:** free movies. **Cards:** AE, CB, DI, DS, MC, VI.
Motel

RESIDENCE INN BY MARRIOTT   Rates Subject to Change   Phone: 704/547-1122   46
3/1-5/13, 5/27-9/20 &
10/11-11/23 [CP]   2P/1B: $119   2P/2B: $139
12/1-2/28, 5/14-5/26,
9/21-10/10 & 11/24-11/30
[CP]   2P/1B: $99   2P/2B: $119
Location: Exit 45A, I-85; 0.3 mi e on Wt Harris Blvd & just s. 8503 N Tryon St 28262. Fax: 704/547-1122. **Terms:** Pets, $200 extra charge. **Facility:** 91 rooms. 2 stories; exterior corridors. **All Rooms:** kitchens, free movies. **Cards:** AE, CB, DI, DS, JCB, MC, VI.
Apartment Motel

RESIDENCE INN BY MARRIOTT-TYVOLA EXECUTIVE PARK   Rates Subject to Change   Phone: 704/527-8110   71
All Year [CP]   1P: $139   2P/1B: $139   2P/2B: $189   XP: $10   F16
Location: I-77 & Tyvola Rd, exit 5. 5800 Westpark Dr 28217. Fax: 704/521-8282. **Terms:** Sr. discount; pets, $100 dep, $5 extra charge. **Facility:** 80 rooms. 2 stories; exterior corridors. **All Rooms:** kitchens, free movies. **Cards:** AE, CB, DI, DS, JCB, MC, VI.
Apartment Motel

RODEWAY INN   Phone: 704/597-5074   33
All Year [CP]   1P: $40- 60   2P/1B: $45- 65   2P/2B: $45- 70   XP: $5   F16
Location: I-85 exit 41. 1416 W Sugar Creek Rd 28213. Fax: 704/597-5074. **Terms:** Reserv deposit; no pets. **Facility:** 56 rooms. Nicely decorated. 2 stories; exterior corridors. **Dining:** Restaurant nearby. **All Rooms:** free movies. **Some Rooms:** coffeemakers, radios. Fee: whirlpools. **Cards:** AE, CB, DI, DS, JCB, MC, VI. **Special Amenities: Free breakfast and free local telephone calls.**
Motel

(See map p. 342)

SHERATON AIRPORT PLAZA HOTEL   Guaranteed Rates   Phone: 704/392-1200   **89**
◆◆◆   All Year [BP]   1P: $89   2P/1B: $89   2P/2B: $89   XP: $10   F17
Hotel   **Location:** I-85 & Billy Graham Pkwy, exit 33. 3315 I-85S at Billy Graham Pkwy 28208. Fax: 704/393-2207.
            Terms: Sr. discount; reserv deposit; small pets only. **Facility:** 216 rooms. 8 stories; interior corridors.
Dining: Dining room; 6:30 am-10:30 pm; $8-$20. **All Rooms:** free & pay movies. **Cards:** AE, CB, DI, DS, JCB, MC, VI.
(See ad p 350)

SLEEP INN   Phone: 704/549-4544   **76**
(AAA) (SAVE)   All Year [CP]   1P: $79   2P/1B: $89   2P/2B: $89   F17
            Too new to rate; **Location:** Just s on US 29, from I-85 exit 45A. 8525 N Tryon St 26262. Fax: 704/549-4452.
Motel   **Terms:** Pets, $5 extra charge. **Facility:** 107 rooms. Scheduled to open summer 1997. Interior corridors.
            Dining: Restaurant nearby. **All Rooms:** free movies, combo or shower baths. **Cards:** AE, CB, DI, DS, JCB,
MC, VI. **Special Amenities:** Free breakfast and free local telephone calls. *(See color ad p 340)*

SOUTHPARK SUITE HOTEL   Phone: 704/364-2400   **34**
(AAA) (SAVE)   Sun-Thurs   1P: $169   2P/1B: $169   2P/2B: $169
            Fri & Sat   1P: $99   2P/1B: $99   2P/2B: $99
◆◆◆   **Location:** 2 mi se on Morrison Blvd at South Park Mall, Billy Graham Pkwy s off I-85, Woodlawn Rd e off
Suite Hotel I-77. 6300 Morrison Blvd 28211. Fax: 704/362-0203. **Terms:** Reserv deposit; weekly/monthly rates; package
plans; no pets. **Facility:** 208 rooms. 1- & 2-bedroom suites with kitchen. 4-6 stories; interior corridors; saunas,
whirlpool. **Dining & Entertainment:** Dining room; 6:30 am-11 pm; $10-$19; cocktails/lounge. **Services:** Fee: coin laundry.
All Rooms: coffeemakers, microwaves, free & pay movies, refrigerators. **Cards:** AE, CB, DI, DS, MC, VI. *(See ad below)*
                                                Roll in showers.

SUMMERFIELD SUITES HOTEL   Rates Subject to Change   Phone: 704/525-2600   **66**
◆◆◆   All Year [BP]   1P: $110   2P/1B: $110   2P/2B: $110
Suite Motel **Location:** Just w of I-77, exit 6B. 4920 S Tryon St 28217. Fax: 704/521-9932. **Terms:** Sr. discount; no pets.
            Facility: 135 rooms. 9 two-bedroom units, $139; 5 stories; interior corridors. **All Rooms:** kitchens, free
movies. **Cards:** AE, DI, DS, MC, VI.

WYNDHAM GARDEN HOTEL   Rates Subject to Change   Phone: 704/357-9100   **68**
◆◆◆   Sun-Thurs [BP]   1P: $109   2P/1B: $119   2P/2B: $119   XP: $10   F18
Motor Inn   Fri & Sat [EP]   1P: $64   2P/1B: $64   2P/2B: $64   XP: $10   F18
            Location: From Billy Graham Pkwy, Tyvola/Coliseum exit, 0.3 mi s. 2600 Yorkmont Rd 28208.
Fax: 704/357-9159. **Terms:** No pets. **Facility:** 173 rooms. 3 stories; interior corridors. **Cards:** AE, CB, DI, DS, JCB, MC, VI. *(See color ad below)*
11-2:30 & 5-10 pm; $9-$18. **All Rooms:** Fee: movies.

(See map p. 342)

YORKSHIRE INN   Phone: 704/588-3949   [19]
☆☆ [SAVE]   All Year   1P: $40- 45 2P/1B: $45- 59 2P/2B: $49- 56 XP: $5   F10
◆◆◆   **Location:** From I-77 exit 1 Westinghouse Blvd 1.5 mi; 0.5 mi s on SR 49. 9900 S Tryon St 28273.
Motel   Fax: 704/588-7380. **Terms:** Reserv deposit; no pets. **Facility:** 30 rooms. 2 stories; exterior corridors; desig-
nated smoking area. **All Rooms:** free movies. **Some Rooms:** refrigerators. Fee: whirlpools. **Cards:** AE, CB,
DI, DS, MC, VI.

[CTV] [ñ] [X] [D]

RESTAURANTS

THE BLUE MARLIN   **Dinner:** $9-$15   Phone: 704/334-3838   [29]
◆◆   **Location:** S Scott Ave on East Blvd. 1511 East Blvd 28203. **Hours:** 5 pm-11 pm, Sun-10 pm.
Steak and   **Features:** casual dress; children's menu; carryout; cocktails; a la carte. Fresh seafood as well as meat,
Seafood   pasta & some low country-style entrees. All served in a casual 40's-style diner atmosphere. **Cards:** AE, DI,
MC, VI.
[X]

CAJUN QUEEN RESTAURANT   **Dinner:** $10-$19   Phone: 704/377-9017   [24]
◆◆   **Location:** Exit 2B off Brookshire Frwy; 2 blks to Hawthorne Ln, then w to 7th St & 1.5 blks s. 1800 E 7th St
Ethnic   28204. **Reservations:** suggested; weekdays. **Features:** casual dress; cocktails & lounge; entertainment. Casual &
convivial with closely spaced tables. Also some American entrees, served in a restored home. **Cards:** AE, CB, DI, DS, MC,
VI.
[X]

CINO GRILL   **Lunch:** $6-$10   **Dinner:** $10-$20   Phone: 704/365-8226   [33]
◆◆   **Location:** Opposite South Park Mall in the shopping complex Specialty Shop on the Park. 6401 Morrison
Regional   Blvd 28211. **Hours:** 11:30 am-10 pm, Fri-11 pm, Sun 11 am-10 pm. Closed major holidays.
American   **Features:** Sunday brunch; children's menu; carryout; cocktails. A casual elegant atmosphere, featuring
distinctive Ssouthwest cuisine. Martini & cigar bar. **Cards:** AE, CB, DI, DS, MC, VI.
[X]

COTTON STREET DINER   **Lunch:** $7-$9   **Dinner:** $7-$15   Phone: 704/375-0000   [26]
◆◆   **Location:** 1.5 mi n on South Blvd from jct Woodlawn Rd. 2140 South Blvd 28203. **Hours:** 11 am-11 pm, Fri
Regional   & Sat-2 am. Closed: 12/25. **Features:** cocktails. Upscale 90's diner with southern flare on entrees. Some
American   counter seating avail. **Cards:** AE, DI, DS, MC, VI.
[X]

DILWORTH BREWING COMPANY   **Lunch:** $4-$6   **Dinner:** $6-$13   Phone: 704/377-2739   [16]
☆☆   **Location:** Corner of East Blvd & Kenilworth Ave; in Dilworth Area. 1301 East Blvd 28203. **Hours:** 11 am-10
pm, Fri & Sat-1 am. Closed major holidays. **Features:** casual dress; children's menu; carryout; cocktails &
◆◆   lounge; entertainment; a la carte. Featuring meat, pasta, fresh fish & specializing in hand crafted beer, all
American   served in a light & airy casual atmosphere. **Cards:** AE, DS, MC, VI.
[X]

THE EPICUREAN   **Dinner:** $16-$22   Phone: 704/377-4529   [27]
◆◆   **Location:** 1.3 mi e of Tryon St; in Dilworth residential area. 1324 East Blvd 28203. **Hours:** 6 pm-10 pm.
American   Closed major holidays, Sun & 7/1-7/14. **Reservations:** suggested. **Features:** semi-formal attire; carryout;
cocktails; minimum charge-$10. Beef, lamb, seafood & veal served in relaxed atmosphere. Extensive wine
selection. Well-established family operation. **Cards:** AE, CB, DI, MC, VI.

THE FISHMARKET   **Lunch:** $6-$11   **Dinner:** $14-$20   Phone: 704/365-0883   [30]
☆☆   **Location:** On Morrison Blvd in The Pavillion Shopping Complex, opposite South Park Mall. 6631 Morrison
Blvd 28211. **Hours:** 11:30 am-2 & 6-10 pm, Sun-9 pm. Closed major holidays. **Reservations:** suggested.
◆◆◆   **Features:** health conscious menu; carryout; cocktails & lounge; a la carte. Serving fresh seafood in an
Seafood   elegant atmosphere. **Cards:** AE, DI, MC, VI.
[X]

LA BIBLIOTHEQUE   **Lunch:** $9-$12   **Dinner:** $19-$29   Phone: 704/365-5000   [25]
☆☆   **Location:** On Roxborough Rd; at jct Roxborough Rd & Morrison Blvd, opposite South Park Mall; in the
Roxborough Building, 1st floor. 1901 Roxborough Rd 28211. **Hours:** 11:30 am-2:30 & 5:30-10:30 pm, Sat
◆◆◆◆   from 5:30 pm. Closed: Sun, 1/1, 11/26 & 12/25. **Reservations:** suggested. **Features:** cocktails; area
French   transportation. Classical French & American prepared entrees served in an elegant atmosphere. Extensive
wine list. Patio dining in season. **Cards:** AE, CB, DI, DS, MC, VI.
[X]

MAMA RICOTTA'S   **Lunch:** $6-$8   **Dinner:** $7-$18   Phone: 704/343-0148   [32]
◆◆   **Location:** Just n of Moorehead on S King Dr; in the King's Court Shopping Center. 901 S Kings Dr, Suite
Italian   115 28204. **Hours:** 11:30 am-2 & 5-10 pm, Fri & Sat-11 pm. Closed major holidays. **Features:** children's
menu; carryout; beer & wine only; a la carte. Comfortable casual atmosphere with well prepared entrees.
Cards: AE, DI, DS, MC, VI.
[X]

MORROCROFTS   **Lunch:** $4-$10   **Dinner:** $12-$20   Phone: 704/364-8220   [17]
◆◆◆   **Location:** Opposite South Park Mall; in The Park Hotel. 2200 Rexford Rd 28211. **Hours:** 6:30 am-11 pm.
American   **Reservations:** suggested. **Features:** Sunday brunch; children's menu; health conscious menu items;
cocktails & lounge; entertainment; valet parking; a la carte. Very well prepared entrees; daily changing menu
with seasonal meat & fish. Served in a soothing, light & charming informal atmosphere. **Cards:** AE, DI, DS, MC, VI.
[X]

PJ MCKENZIES   **Lunch:** $9-$13   **Dinner:** $11-$17   Phone: 704/529-1922   [23]
◆◆   **Location:** Exit 6B, off I-77; in Embassy Suites. 4800 S Tryon St 28217. **Hours:** 11 am-11 pm.
American   **Features:** children's menu; carryout; salad bar; cocktails & lounge. 6 dining rooms with different theme.
Featuring grilled steak, chicken & fish. Daily pasta bar. **Cards:** AE, DI, MC, VI.
[X]

RANCH HOUSE   **Dinner:** $13-$19   Phone: 704/399-5411   [19]
◆◆   **Location:** 5.5 mi w on US 74; between Mulberry & Little Rock rds. 5614 Wilkinson Blvd 28208. **Hours:** 5
Steakhouse   pm-11 pm. Closed major holidays, Sun & 7/1-7/15. **Features:** casual dress; children's menu; carryout;
cocktails. Very popular. Casual dining in rustic atmosphere, featuring steak & hot spicy shrimp cocktail.
Cards: AE, CB, DI, MC, VI.

THE SILVER CRICKET   **Dinner:** $11-$21   Phone: 704/525-0061   [22]
☆☆   **Location:** 0.8 mi e off I-77 from Woodlawn Rd exit, 0.3 blk s on South Blvd. 4705 South Blvd 28217.
Hours: 5 pm-10 pm. Closed major holidays. **Reservations:** suggested. **Features:** casual dress; cocktails;
◆◆◆   minimum charge-$8; a la carte. New Orleans French fine dining, intimate atmosphere, extensive wine list.
Regional   **Cards:** AE, CB, DI, DS, MC, VI.
American
[X]

(See map p. 342)

SONOMA ON PROVIDENCE   **Lunch:** $5-$8   **Dinner:** $14-$19   **Phone:** 704/377-1333   ③①
◆◆   **Location:** I-277 take 3rd & 4th St exit, then s 1.5 mi on SR 16 (Providence Rd). 801 Providence Rd 28207.
Regional   **Hours:** 11 am-2:30 & 5-10:30 pm, Sat from 5 pm; Sun brunch 11 am-2 pm. Closed major holidays.
American   **Reservations:** suggested. **Features:** health conscious menu; carryout; cocktails & lounge; a la carte. An
eclectic menu with a California Wine Country flavor. Wine list. All in a restored 1904 home with a casual
atmosphere. **Cards:** AE, DI, DS, MC, VI.   ✕

TEXAS RANCH STEAKHOUSE & SALOON   **Lunch:** $6-$8   **Dinner:** $13-$17   **Phone:** 704/598-2215   ⑭
◆◆   **Location:** Just w on Sugar Creek Rd off I-85, exit 41. 1310 W Sugar Creek Rd 28213. **Hours:** 11 am-11 pm,
Steakhouse   Sat from 4 pm, Sun 4 pm-10 pm. Closed major holidays. **Features:** children's menu; carryout; cocktails &
lounge. Baby back ribs & filet mignon signature entrees; close to many motel accommodations. Homemade
sauces, chili & soup. **Cards:** AE, CB, DI, DS, MC, VI.   ✕

THE TOWNHOUSE   **Dinner:** $17-$26   **Phone:** 704/335-1546   ②⓪
◆◆◆   **Location:** 1.5 mi s on 3rd St to jct of Providence & Queens rds. 1011 Providence Rd 28207. **Hours:** 6
American   pm-10 pm. Closed major holidays. **Reservations:** suggested. **Features:** carryout; cocktails & lounge; a la
carte. Landmark restaurant since 1939 specializing in beef, seafood & fowl. Elegant ambience. Modern
American with French accent. **Cards:** AE, CB, DI, DS, MC, VI.   ✕

VILLA ANTONIO FINE ITALIAN RISTORANTE   **Lunch:** $7-$9   **Dinner:** $12-$25   **Phone:** 704/523-1594   ⑮
◆◆   **Location:** From I-77 exit 6A (Woodlawn Rd) 0.8 mi e to South Blvd, then just s. 4707 South Blvd 28217.
Italian   **Hours:** 11 am-3 & 5-midnight, Sat from 5 pm, Sun-11 pm. **Closed:** 1/1, 11/26 & 12/25.
Reservations: suggested. **Features:** casual dress; Sunday brunch; health conscious menu items; cocktails;
a la carte. Featuring a wide variety of very well prepared Italian entrees with fine ambience. Lunch buffet Mon-Fri.
Cards: AE, DI, DS, MC, VI.   ✕

CHEROKEE—624

LODGINGS

BEST WESTERN GREAT SMOKIES INN   **Phone:** 704/497-2020
Ⓐ Ⓐ Ⓐ [SAVE]   5/26-11/30   1P: $95   2P/2B: $95   XP: $6   F12
    12/1-5/25   1P: $65   2P/2B: $65   XP: $6   F12
◆◆◆   **Location:** 2.5 mi n, just off 441N. Acquoni Rd 28719 (PO Box 1809). Fax: 704/497-3903. **Terms:** Reserv
Motor Inn   deposit; no pets. **Facility:** 152 rooms. Attractive, rustic style public areas. 2 stories; exterior corridors; wading
pool. **Dining:** Restaurant; 7 am-9 pm; $7-$12. **Services:** Fee: coin laundry. **All Rooms:** free movies.
Some Rooms: whirlpools. **Cards:** AE, CB, DI, DS, JCB, MC, VI. **Special Amenities: Free local telephone calls.**
🅿 🛎 [CTV] ✕ [D]

BUDGETEL INN   **Phone:** 704/497-2102
Ⓐ Ⓐ Ⓐ [SAVE]   5/22-9/6 & 10/2-10/31 [CP]   1P: $69- 95   2P/1B: $69- 95   2P/2B: $69- 95
    4/1-5/21 & 9/7-10/1 [CP]   1P: $45- 69   2P/1B: $45- 69   2P/2B: $45- 69
◆◆◆   11/1-11/15 [CP]   1P: $39- 65   2P/1B: $39- 65   2P/2B: $39- 65
Motel   **Location:** 2.5 mi n, just w off US 441 N. Acquoni Rd 28719 (PO Box 1865). Fax: 704/497-5242.
Terms: Open 4/1-11/15; reserv deposit; no pets. **Facility:** 3 stories; interior corridors; small pool.
Dining: Restaurant nearby. **Services:** Fee: coin laundry. **All Rooms:** coffeemakers, free movies, combo or shower baths.
Some Rooms: microwaves, refrigerators. **Cards:** AE, CB, DI, DS, MC, VI. **Special Amenities: Free breakfast and free
local telephone calls.** *(See color ad below)*   Roll in showers.   🛎 [CTV] ✕ [D] [S]

COMFORT INN   Rates Subject to Change   **Phone:** 704/497-2411
◆◆◆   5/23-11/1 [CP]   1P: $68   2P/1B: $88   2P/2B: $77   XP: $8   F18
Motel   3/15-5/22 & 11/2-11/30 [CP]   1P: $47   2P/1B: $65   2P/2B: $54   XP: $8   F18
    12/1-12/31 [CP]   1P: $43   2P/1B: $60   2P/2B: $49   XP: $8   F18
Location: Just w of jct US Hwys 19 & 441, on US 19S. 28719 (PO Box 132). Fax: 704/497-6555. **Terms:** Sr. discount;
Open 12/1-12/31 & 3/15-11/30; no pets. **Facility:** 87 rooms. 2 stories; exterior corridors. **All Rooms:** free movies.
Some Rooms: kitchen. **Cards:** AE, DI, DS, MC, VI.   🅿 [CTV] ✕ 🍽 [D]

COMFORT SUITES   Rates Subject to Change   **Phone:** 704/497-3500
Suite Motel   4/1-10/31   2P/1B: $125   2P/2B: $125   XP: $8   F12
    12/1-3/31 & 11/1-11/30   2P/1B: $80   2P/2B: $80   XP: $8   F12
Too new to rate; **Location:** 1 mi n on US 441. 35 Hwy 441 N 28719 (Box 35). Fax: 704/497-3500. **Terms:** Sr. discount; no
pets. **Facility:** 92 rooms. Scheduled to open July 1997; 3 stories; interior corridors. **All Rooms:** free movies. **Cards:** AE,
CB, DI, DS, JCB, MC, VI.   Roll in showers.   🅿 [CTV] ✕ [D] [S]

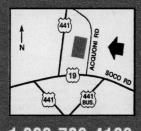

CRAIG'S MOTEL

(AAA) SAVE

◆◆ Motel

Phone: 704/497-3821

6/12-9/7 & 10/1-11/1		2P/1B:	$55-	60	2P/2B:	$65-	75	XP: $5	F12
5/1-6/11 & 9/8-9/30		2P/1B:	$45-	55	2P/2B:	$50-	60	XP: $5	F12

Location: 1.5 mi e on US 19N. 28719 (PO Box 1047). **Terms:** Open 5/1-11/1; reserv deposit; $1 service charge; no pets. **Facility:** 31 rooms. Some units near stream with picnic tables & grills. Walk to casino. 1 story; exterior corridors; wading pool; playground. **Dining:** Restaurant nearby. **Recreation:** fishing. **All Rooms:** free movies. **Cards:** AE, DS, MC, VI. **Special Amenities:** Free local telephone calls and free room upgrade (subject to availability with advanced reservations). 🖪 🛠 ✕ D

DAYS INN

(AAA) SAVE

◆◆◆ Motel

Phone: 704/497-9171

5/22-9/6 & 10/2-11/2	1P:	$60-	95		2P/2B:	$60-	95	XP: $3	F12
4/1-5/21 & 9/7-10/1	1P:	$39-	60		2P/2B:	$39-	60	XP: $3	F12

Location: 1.5 mi e on US 19N. 28719 (PO Box 1865). Fax: 704/497-3424. **Terms:** Open 4/1-11/2; reserv deposit; $1 service charge; no pets. **Facility:** 58 rooms. Landscaped grounds with stream in back. Most units ground level. Some rooms overlooking stream. 2 stories; exterior corridors; wading pool; playground. **Dining:** Restaurant nearby. **Recreation:** fishing. **All Rooms:** free movies. **Cards:** AE, CB, DI, DS, JCB, MC, VI. **Special Amenities:** Free local telephone calls. 🖪 CTV ✕ D

ELA MOTOR COURT

(AAA)

◆◆ Motel

Rates Subject to Change

Phone: 704/488-2284

6/15-9/5 & 10/1-11/1		2P/2B:	$50	XP: $3-5	F10
5/1-6/14 & 9/6-9/30		2P/2B:	$36	XP: $3-5	F10

Location: 5 mi w on US 19 S. 5280 Ela Rd (US 19) N 28713. **Terms:** Open 5/1-11/1; reserv deposit; no pets. **Facility:** 21 rooms. 1 three-bedroom housekeeping cottage, $110-$120 in season for up to 8 persons, 3 night minimum stay; 1 story; exterior corridors. **All Rooms:** free movies. **Cards:** MC, VI. 🖪 CTV D

HAMPTON INN

(AAA) SAVE

◆◆◆ Motel

Phone: 704/497-3115

10/1-10/25 [CP]	1P: $87	2P/1B: $87	2P/2B: $87
3/15-9/30 & 10/26-11/7 [CP]	1P: $74	2P/1B: $74	2P/2B: $74

Location: At US 441S & US 19S junction. 28719 (PO Box 1926). Fax: 704/497-3137. **Terms:** Open 3/15-11/7; reserv deposit, 3 day notice; small pets only, $ 25 dep req. **Facility:** 67 rooms. 2 stories; interior corridors. **All Rooms:** free movies. **Cards:** AE, DI, DS, MC, VI. 🐾 🖪 CTV ✕ D S

HOLIDAY INN

◆◆◆ Motor Inn

Rates Subject to Change

Phone: 704/497-9181

6/26-8/23	1P: $76-	99	2P/1B: $76-	99	2P/2B: $76-	99	XP: $6	F18
5/25-6/25, 8/24-8/29 & 10/2-10/31	1P: $59-	89	2P/1B: $59-	89	2P/2B: $59-	89	XP: $6	F18
12/1-5/24, 8/30-10/1 & 11/1-11/30	1P: $44-	89	2P/1B: $50-	89	2P/2B: $50-	89	XP: $6	F18

Location: 0.8 mi w on US 19S. 28719 (PO Box 1929). Fax: 704/497-5973. **Terms:** Sr. discount; no pets. **Facility:** 154 rooms. 2 stories; exterior corridors. **Dining:** Restaurant; 7 am-11 & 5-9 pm, Sun 7 am-9 pm; $8-$15. **All Rooms:** free movies. **Cards:** AE, CB, DI, DS, JCB, MC, VI. 🖪 🖪 CTV ✕ 🗲 D

PAGEANT HILLS MOTEL

(AAA)

◆◆ Motel

Rates Subject to Change

Phone: 704/497-5371

7/1-8/25	1P: $40-	75	2P/2B: $40-	75
10/14-11/1	1P: $34-	60	2P/2B: $34-	60
4/15-6/30 & 8/26-10/13	1P: $30-	38	2P/2B: $30-	38

Location: 1 mi n on US 441. (PO Box 172, 28719). **Terms:** Open 4/15-11/1; reserv deposit; no pets. **Facility:** 42 rooms. 2 stories; exterior corridors. **Cards:** DS, MC, VI. CTV ✕ D

PIONEER MOTEL

(AAA) SAVE

◆◆ Motel

Phone: 704/497-2435

6/15-10/31		2P/2B:	$48-	64	XP: $5	F12
4/1-6/14		2P/2B:	$28-	48	XP: $5	F12

Location: 0.8 mi w on US 19S. 28719 (PO Box 397). **Terms:** Open 4/1-10/31; reserv deposit, 3 day notice, 14 day for cabins; $1 service charge; weekly rates, in cabins; 2 night min stay, in cabins; small pets only, except in cabins. **Facility:** 21 rooms. 4 one-to three-bedroom cabins with kitchen; 2 riverside, $85-$170 for 6-8 persons; 1 story; exterior corridors; basketball court, horseshoes. **Dining:** Restaurant nearby. **Recreation:** fishing. **All Rooms:** free movies. **Cards:** AE, DS, MC, VI. **Special Amenities:** Early check-in/late check-out and free local telephone calls. 🐾 🖪 CTV ✕ D

QUALITY INN

(AAA) SAVE

◆◆◆ Motel

Phone: 704/497-4702

Fri & Sat 5/27-11/30 [CP]	1P: $99		2P/1B: $49-	99	2P/2B: $49-	99	XP: $5	F18
Sun-Thurs 5/27-11/30 [CP]	1P: $49-	69	2P/1B: $49-	89	2P/2B: $49-	89	XP: $5	F18
Fri & Sat 12/1-5/26 [CP]	1P: $69		2P/1B: $45-	79	2P/2B: $45-	79	XP: $5	F18
Sun-Thurs 12/1-5/26 [CP]	1P: $39-	59	2P/1B: $39-	59	2P/2B: $39-	59	XP: $5	F18

Location: 0.5 mi s on US 441 bypass from jct US 19. US 441 S bypass 28719 (PO Box 495). Fax: 704/497-5107. **Terms:** No pets. **Facility:** 63 rooms. Attractive public areas & well-appointed rooms. 2 stories; interior corridors. **Dining:** Restaurant nearby. **All Rooms:** free movies, combo or shower baths. **Some Rooms:** Fee: whirlpools. **Cards:** AE, CB, DI, DS, JCB, MC, VI. **Special Amenities:** Free breakfast and free local telephone calls.

Roll in showers. 🖪 🛠 CTV ✕ D

STARLIGHT MOTEL

(AAA) SAVE

◆◆ Motel

Phone: 704/497-5936

4/15-10/31	1P: $35-	65	2P/1B: $45-	65	2P/2B: $45-	75	XP: $5	F12
11/1-11/30	1P: $32-	50	2P/1B: $32-	50	2P/2B: $32-	50	XP: $5	F12

Location: US 441/74, 1 mi e of US 74, exit 74. (8682 US Hwy 74, WHITTIER, 28789). Fax: 704/497-3201. **Terms:** Open 4/15-11/30; reserv deposit; weekly rates; no pets. **Facility:** 13 rooms. Unpretentious accomodations. 1 two-bedroom unit. Kitchenettes $55-$75; 1 story; exterior corridors; horseshoe pits, small picnic area with grills. **All Rooms:** free movies, combo or shower baths. **Some Rooms:** coffeemakers, 4 kitchens, radios. **Cards:** AE, DS, MC, VI. **Special Amenities:** Early check-in/late check-out and free local telephone calls. CTV ✕ D

TE PEE VILLAGE INN ECONO LODGE

◆◆◆ Motel

Rates Subject to Change

Phone: 704/497-2226

4/1-11/30 [CP]	1P: $70	2P/2B: $75	XP: $5	F18
12/1-12/31 [CP]	1P: $50	2P/2B: $55	XP: $5	F18

Location: 2.5 mi n & just off US 441 N. 28719 (PO Box 2207). Fax: 704/497-3427. **Terms:** Sr. discount; Open 12/1-12/31 & 4/1-11/30; reserv deposit, 30 day notice; no pets. **Facility:** 66 rooms. 3 stories, no elevator; exterior corridors. **All Rooms:** free movies. **Cards:** AE, DI, DS, JCB, MC, VI. 🖪 CTV ✕ D

CHIMNEY ROCK—100

LODGINGS

CHIMNEY VIEW MOTEL   Guaranteed Rates   **Phone: 704/625-1429**
◆   12/1-12/31 & 3/1-11/30   1P: $40- 60   2P/1B: $40- 60   2P/2B: $40- 60
Motel   **Location:** Just e on US Hwys 64/74A. (PO Box 189, 28720). Fax: 704/625-1429. **Terms:** Open 12/1-12/31 &
3/1-11/30; reserv deposit, 7 day notice; no pets. **Facility:** 11 rooms. Apartment, cabin & cottage rates $55-$85;
$5 extra person. Reservation required 11/1-3/31; 1 story; exterior corridors. **All Rooms:** free movies. **Some Rooms:** 2
kitchens. **Cards:** AE, DS, MC, VI.
    (CTV) (X) (VI)

MOUNTAIN VILLAGE CHALETS   Guaranteed Rates   **Phone: 704/625-9783**
◆◆   All Year   1P: $60- 150   2P/1B: $60- 150   2P/2B: $60- 150
Complex   **Location:** Center; on US 74A. PO Box 68 28720-0068. Fax: 704/625-9783. **Terms:** Reserv deposit, 15 day
notice; no pets. **Facility:** 19 rooms. 2 stories; exterior corridors. **Some Rooms:** 14 kitchens. **Cards:** AE, DS,
MC, VI.
    (CTV) (D)

CLEMMONS—6,000

LODGING

RAMADA LIMITED   Rates Subject to Change   **Phone: 910/766-9121**
◆◆   All Year   1P: $56   2P/1B: $62   2P/2B: $62   XP: $6   F18
Motel   **Location:** Just s of I-40, exit 184. 6205 Ramada Dr 27012 (PO Box 926). Fax: 910/766-3269. **Terms:** No
pets. **Facility:** 148 rooms. 2 stories; interior corridors. **Dining & Entertainment:** Cocktail lounge serving light
fare, closed Sun. **All Rooms:** free & pay movies. **Cards:** AE, CB, DI, DS, JCB, MC, VI.
    Roll in showers. (wheelchair) (access) (X) (VI) (D)

CONCORD—27,300

LODGINGS

HAMPTON INN   Rates Subject to Change   **Phone: 704/793-9700**
◆◆◆   All Year [CP]   1P: $65   2P/1B: $71   2P/2B: $71   XP: $6   F18
Motel   **Location:** Just e from exit 60, I-85. 612 Dickens Pl NE 28025. Fax: 704/793-1765. **Terms:** No pets.
Facility: 102 rooms. 5 stories; interior corridors. **All Rooms:** free movies. **Cards:** AE, DI, DS, MC, VI.
    Roll in showers. (access) (CTV) (access) (X) (VI) (D) (S)

RODEWAY INN   **Phone: 704/788-8550**
(AAA) (SAVE)   All Year   1P: $42- 49   2P/1B: $45- 53   2P/2B: $50- 60   XP: $5   D16
◆◆   **Location:** Concord exit 58 off I-85, just e on US 29 to first traffic light. 2541 Kannapolis Hwy 28025.
Motel   Fax: 704/788-8583. **Terms:** No pets. **Facility:** 32 rooms. Contemporary room decor. 2 stories; exterior corri-
dors. **Dining:** Restaurant nearby. **All Rooms:** free movies, refrigerators. **Some Rooms:** coffeemakers.
Cards: AE, CB, DI, DS, MC, VI. **Special Amenities:** Free local telephone calls and free newspaper.
    (access) (CTV) (X) (VI) (D)

CONOVER—5,500

LODGING

BEST WESTERN OF HICKORY   Rates Subject to Change   **Phone: 704/465-2378**
◆◆◆   All Year [CP]   1P: $60- 63   2P/1B: $68   2P/2B: $65   XP: $5   F12
Motel   **Location:** 2 blks s from exit 128, I-40. 1710 Fairgrove Church Rd 28613. Fax: 704/465-6488. **Terms:** Sr.
discount; no pets. **Facility:** 59 rooms. 2 stories; exterior corridors. **All Rooms:** free movies. **Cards:** AE, CB,
DI, DS, MC, VI.
    (access) (CTV) (access) (X) (VI) (D)

CORNELIUS—2,600

LODGINGS

BEST WESTERN LAKE NORMAN   Rates Subject to Change   **Phone: 704/896-0660**
◆◆◆   All Year [CP]   1P: $75   2P/1B: $82   2P/2B: $82   XP: $7   F13
Motel   **Location:** I-77, exit 28. 19608 Liverpool Pkwy 28031 (PO Box 2037). Fax: 704/896-8633. **Terms:** Reserv
deposit; no pets. **Facility:** 76 rooms. Phone access $1 daily; 4 stories; interior corridors. **All Rooms:** free
movies. **Cards:** AE, CB, DI, DS, MC, VI.
    (access) (CTV) (access) (X) (VI) (D)

COMFORT INN LAKE NORMAN   Rates Subject to Change   **Phone: 704/892-3500**
◆◆◆   All Year [CP]   1P: $69   2P/1B: $69   2P/2B: $69
Motel   **Location:** Just nw of I-77, exit 28. 20740 Torrence Chapel Rd 28031. Fax: 704/892-6473. **Terms:** Sr.
discount; no pets. **Facility:** 90 rooms. Phone & safe, $2; 2-3 stories; exterior corridors. **All Rooms:** free
movies. **Cards:** AE, CB, DI, DS, JCB, MC, VI.
    (access) (CTV) (access) (X) (VI) (D)

HAMPTON INN LAKE NORMAN   Rates Subject to Change   **Phone: 704/892-9900**
◆◆◆   All Year [CP]   1P: $64- 84   2P/1B: $69- 89   2P/2B: $69- 89   XP: $5   F18
Motel   **Location:** Just se of I-77, exit 28. 19501 Statesville Rd 28031. Fax: 704/896-7488. **Terms:** Sr. discount;
small pets only, $35 extra charge. **Facility:** 117 rooms. 5 stories; interior corridors. **All Rooms:** free movies.
Cards: AE, CB, DI, DS, MC, VI.
    (pets) (access) (CTV) (access) (X) (VI) (D) (S)

HOLIDAY INN LAKE NORMAN   Rates Subject to Change   **Phone: 704/892-9120**
◆◆◆   All Year   1P: $79- 99   2P/1B: $84- 104   2P/2B: $84- 104   XP: $5   F17
Motor Inn   **Location:** Just e of I-77, exit 28. 19901 Holiday Ln 28031. Fax: 704/892-3854. **Terms:** Sr. discount; small
pets only, $35 extra charge. **Facility:** 119 rooms. 2 stories; exterior corridors. **Dining:** Restaurant; 6-10 am,
11:30-2 & 5:30-10 pm; $9-$19. **All Rooms:** free & pay movies. **Cards:** AE, CB, DI, DS, JCB, MC, VI.
    (pets) (access) (CTV) (access) (X) (VI) (D)

MICROTEL INN   Rates Subject to Change   **Phone: 704/895-1828**
(AAA)   7/1-10/31 [CP]   1P: $65- 73   2P/1B: $65- 73   2P/2B: $65- 73
   3/1-6/30 [CP]   1P: $49- 58   2P/1B: $49- 58   2P/2B: $49- 58
◆◆   12/1-2/28 & 11/1-11/30 [CP]   1P: $49- 53   2P/1B: $49- 53   2P/2B: $49- 53
Motel   **Location:** Just w of I-77, exit 28. 20820 Torrence Chapel Rd 28031. Fax: 704/895-1258. **Terms:** Sr.
discount; no pets. **Facility:** 60 rooms. 3 stories; interior corridors. **All Rooms:** free & pay movies.
Cards: AE, CB, DI, DS, MC, VI.   Roll in showers. (CTV) (access) (X) (VI) (D) (S)

CREEDMOOR—1,500

LODGINGS

COMFORT INN
◆◆◆
Motel
Rates Subject to Change
| | 1P: | 2P/1B: | 2P/2B: | XP: | |
5/1-10/31 [CP]   1P: $65   2P/1B: $65   2P/2B: $65   XP: $5   F18
12/1-4/30 & 11/1-11/30 [CP]   1P: $58   2P/1B: $58   2P/2B: $58   XP: $5   F18
Location: Just e on SR 56 from I-85, exit 191. 1585 SR 56 27522. Fax: 919/528-2904. **Terms:** Sr. discount;
no pets. **Facility:** 51 rooms. 4 whirlpool rms, extra charge; 2 stories; interior corridors. **All Rooms:** free movies. **Cards:** AE,
CB, DI, DS, JCB, MC, VI.
Phone: 919/528-9296

SUNSET INN
(AAA) (SAVE)
◆◆
Motel
All Year   1P: $32- 38   2P/1B: $35- 40   2P/2B: $39- 49   XP: $5   D
Location: Just w of exit 191, I-85. 2575 Lyon Station Rd 27522. Fax: 919/575-9003. **Terms:** Reserv deposit;
weekly rates; no pets. **Facility:** 70 rooms. 2 stories; exterior corridors. **Dining:** Restaurant nearby.
All Rooms: free movies. **Some Rooms:** refrigerators. **Cards:** AE, CB, DI, DS, MC, VI. **Special Amenities:**
Free breakfast and free local telephone calls.
Phone: 919/575-6565

CULLOWHEE—5,700

LODGING

UNIVERSITY INN
(AAA) (SAVE)
◆◆
Motel
All Year   1P: $69- 79   2P/1B: $69- 79   2P/2B: $59- 79   XP: $5   F
Location: On N Country Club Rd, 0.5 mi sw of SR 107. N Country Club Rd 28723 (PO Box 2745).
Fax: 704/293-5406. **Terms:** CP avail, weekends; no pets. **Facility:** 24 rooms. 3 stories; exterior corridors; 2
tennis courts. **All Rooms:** free movies. **Some Rooms:** kitchen, refrigerators. **Cards:** AE, DS, MC, VI.
**Special Amenities: Free local telephone calls and preferred room (subject to availability with
advanced reservations).**
Phone: 704/293-5442

DAVIDSON—4,000

LODGING

DAVIDSON VILLAGE INN
◆◆◆
Bed &
Breakfast
Rates Subject to Change
Fri & Sat [CP]   1P: $110- 150   2P/1B: $110- 150   2P/2B: $110- 150   XP: $10   F
Sun-Thurs [CP]   1P: $100- 115   2P/1B: $100- 115   2P/2B: $100- 115   XP: $10   F
Location: Just sw from Davidson College main entrance. 117 Depot St 28036 (PO Box 1463).
Fax: 704/892-8044. **Terms:** Sr. discount; no pets. **Facility:** 18 rooms. 3 stories; interior corridors.
All Rooms: free movies. **Cards:** AE, CB, DI, DS, MC, VI.
Phone: 704/892-8044

DILLSBORO—100

LODGING

APPLEGATE INN
(AAA) (SAVE)
◆◆
Bed &
Breakfast
4/1-4/30 [BP]   1P: $65   2P/1B: $85   2P/2B: $95   XP: $15   F9
12/1-3/31 & 5/1-11/30 [BP]   1P: $65   2P/1B: $75   2P/2B: $85   XP: $15   F9
Location: 2 blks s on Depot St from Haywood & 2 blks w on Hemlock. 163 Hemlock St 28725 (PO Box
567). **Terms:** Weekly rates; no pets. **Facility:** 7 rooms. Attractive & comfortable public area, grounds & fish
pond; scenic stream. 1 story; interior/exterior corridors; smoke free premises; creekside gazebo, picnic area.
Dining: Restaurant nearby. **Recreation:** fishing. **All Rooms:** free movies, combo or shower baths, no
phones. **Some Rooms:** coffeemakers, 3 efficiencies, microwaves. **Cards:** CB, DI, DS, MC, VI. **Special Amenities: Free
breakfast and preferred room (subject to availability with advanced reservations).**
Phone: 704/586-2397

DOBSON—1,200

LODGING

SURRY INN
(AAA) (SAVE)
◆◆
Motel
All Year   1P: $30- 33   2P/1B: $35- 39   2P/2B: $39- 43   XP: $4   F12
Location: Exit 93 off I-77, on CR 1001. 1166 Zephyr Rd 27017. **Terms:** No pets. **Facility:** 30 rooms. Friendly
guest-oriented staff, exceptional housekeeping. 2 stories; exterior corridors. **Dining:** Restaurant nearby.
All Rooms: free movies. **Cards:** AE, DS, MC, VI.
Phone: 910/366-3000

DORTCHES—800

LODGING

HOLIDAY INN DORTCHES
(AAA) (SAVE)
◆◆◆
Motor Inn
All Year   1P: $55- 70   2P/1B: $55- 73   2P/2B: $55- 73   XP: $6   F19
Location: I-95 exit 141, sw via service road. 5350 Dortches Blvd 27801 (PO Box 7215, ROCKY MOUNT,
27802-7215). Fax: 919/937-6312. **Terms:** Small pets only, $5 extra charge. **Facility:** 154 rooms. 2 stories; ex-
terior corridors. **Dining:** Restaurant; 6 am-1 & 5-10 pm; $9-$13; wine/beer only. **Services:** Fee: coin laundry.
All Rooms: coffeemakers, free movies. **Some Rooms:** microwaves, refrigerators. **Cards:** AE, DI, DS, MC,
VI. **Special Amenities: Free newspaper.** (See color ad p 411)
Phone: 919/937-6300

DUCK—See Outer Banks p. 396.

DUNN—8,300

LODGING

RAMADA INN
◆◆◆
Motor Inn
Rates Subject to Change
All Year   1P: $59   2P/1B: $69   2P/2B: $69   XP: $6   F17
Location: Exit 73 off I-95, just w on US 421. I-95 & US 421 28334 (PO Box 729). Fax: 910/892-2836.
Terms: Small pets only, in smoking rooms. **Facility:** 100 rooms. 2 stories; exterior corridors.
Dining: Restaurant; 6:30 am-2 & 5-9 pm, Sat 6:30 am-10:30 & 5-9 pm; $7-$11. **All Rooms:** free movies. **Cards:** AE, CB,
DI, DS, MC, VI.
Phone: 910/892-8101

RESTAURANT

BRASS LANTERN
(AAA)
◆◆
Steakhouse
Dinner: $10-$15
Location: Exit 72, I-95 (Pope Rd). 515 Springbranch Rd 28335. **Hours:** 5 pm-9:30 pm. Closed: Sun.
Features: children's menu; carryout; salad bar; beer & wine only. Featuring prime rib; also seafood entrees.
Cards: AE, DS, MC, VI.
Phone: 910/892-6309

DURHAM—136,600 (See map p. 358; index below)

To help you more easily locate accommodations in the Durham area, the following index and map show lodgings and restaurants in multiple cities. Listings for these establishments are found under the heading for the city in which they are located. The Durham area map comprises: Carrboro, Chapel Hill, Durham, Fearrington Village and Research Triangle Park.

Index of Establishments on the DURHAM/CHAPEL HILL ACCOMMODATIONS Spotting Map

LODGINGS

ARROWHEAD INN BED AND BREAKFAST   Rates Subject to Change   Phone: 919/477-8430   **16**
◆◆◆ All Year [BP]   1P: $90- 160   2P/1B: $95- 185   XP: $15
Historic Bed & Breakfast   **Location:** 7 mi n of I-85 on US 501 Roxboro Rd. 106 Mason Rd 27712. Fax: 919/471-9538. **Terms:** No pets. **Facility:** 8 rooms. 2 stories; interior/exterior corridors. **All Rooms:** free movies. **Cards:** AE, CB, DI, DS, MC, VI.
(CTV) (X) (D)

BEST WESTERN SKYLAND INN   Phone: 919/383-2508   **19**
All Year [CP]   1P: $48- 58   2P/1B: $50- 64   2P/2B: $64- 74   XP: $10   F12
Location: On US 70 at jct I-85 exit 170. 5400 Hillsborough Rd 27705 (Rt 2, Box 560). Fax: 919/383-7316. **Terms:** Reserv deposit, 14 day notice; weekly/monthly rates; pets. **Facility:** 31 rooms. Quiet rural setting. Handling fee imposed; 1 story; exterior corridors; small pool; playground. **Dining:** Restaurant nearby.
◆◆ Motor Inn   **All Rooms:** coffeemakers, free movies, refrigerators. **Cards:** AE, CB, DI, DS, JCB, MC, VI.
Special Amenities: Free local telephone calls and free newspaper. (icons)

BROOKWOOD INN & SUITES AT DUKE UNIVERSITY   Phone: 919/286-3111   **4**
All Year   1P: $60- 98   2P/1B: $65- 105   2P/2B: $65- 110   XP: $5   F18
Location: Duke University exit off I-40; just n of Duke Hospital; US 15-501, Duke Hospital exit. 2306 Elba St 27705. Fax: 919/286-5115. **Terms:** No pets. **Facility:** 118 rooms. Opposite Duke Medical facilities; handsomely appointed rooms. 5-8 stories; interior corridors. **Dining:** Coffee shop; 6 am-2:30 & 5-9:30 pm; $4-$6.
◆◆◆ Motel   **Services:** area transportation, to Duke Hospital & Clinic. Fee: coin laundry. **All Rooms:** free & pay movies. **Some Rooms:** Fee: microwaves, refrigerators. **Cards:** AE, DI, DS, MC, VI. **Special Amenities:** Free local telephone calls and free room upgrade (subject to availability with advanced reservations). (icons)

CAROLINA DUKE MOTOR INN   Phone: 919/286-0771   **14**
All Year   1P: $37- 43   2P/1B: $40   2P/2B: $43   XP: $3   F12
Location: Just s of jct I-85. 2517 Guess Rd 27705. Fax: 919/286-0771. **Terms:** Reserv deposit; pets, $3 extra charge. **Facility:** 181 rooms. 2 stories; exterior corridors. **All Rooms:** free movies. **Cards:** AE, DS, MC, VI.
◆◆ Motel (icons)

COMFORT INN UNIVERSITY   Rates Subject to Change   Phone: 919/490-4949   **1**
◆◆◆ All Year [CP]   1P: $69   2P/1B: $75   2P/2B: $78   XP: $6   F16
Motel   **Location:** Exit 270 off I-40, just n on US 15-501, just e. 3508 Mount Moriah Rd 27707. Fax: 919/419-0535. **Terms:** Sr. discount; no pets. **Facility:** 138 rooms. $1/day for unlimited telephone use; 4 stories; interior corridors. **All Rooms:** free movies. **Cards:** AE, DI, DS, JCB, MC, VI. (icons)

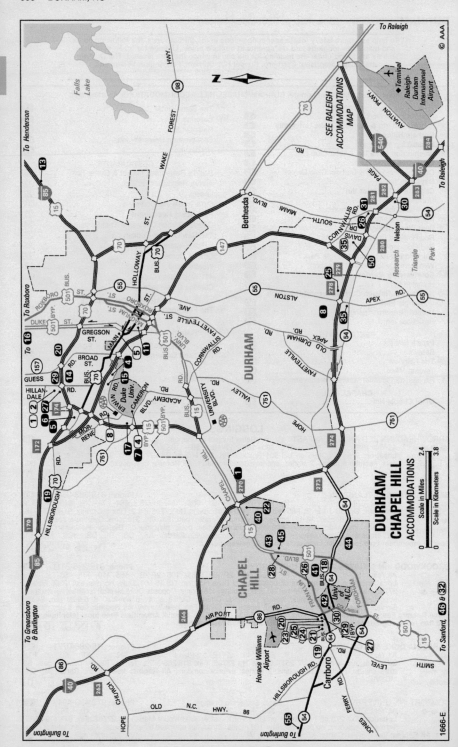

DURHAM/
CHAPEL HILL
ACCOMMODATIONS

© AAA

1666-E

(See map p. 358)

COURTYARD BY MARRIOTT   Phone: 919/309-1500   **27**

All Year   1P: $80- 100 2P/1B: $80- 100 2P/2B: $80- 100
Location: I-85, exit 174 (Hillendale Rd). 1815 Front St 27705. Fax: 919/383-8189. **Terms:** No pets.
◆◆◆   **Facility:** 151 rooms. 4 stories; interior corridors; whirlpool. **Dining & Entertainment:** Breakfast 6:30-10 am,
Motor Inn   Sat & Sun to noon; buffet $6.95; cocktail lounge; restaurant nearby. **Services:** Fee: coin laundry.
All Rooms: coffeemakers, free & pay movies. **Cards:** AE, CB, DI, DS, MC, VI. **Special Amenities:** Early
check-in/late check-out and preferred room (subject to availability with advanced reservations).
(See color ad below)   Roll in showers. 🖳 📶 📺 ♿ ✕ 🎬 D S

DAYS INN   Phone: 919/688-4338   **13**
All Year   1P: $45- 50 2P/1B: $50- 55 2P/2B: $50   XP: $5   F12
Location: Just w of I-85 exit 183. I-85 & Redwood Rd 27704. Fax: 919/688-3118. **Terms:** Reserv deposit,
15 day notice; small pets only, $10 extra charge. **Facility:** 119 rooms. 2 stories; exterior corridors; playground.
◆◆   **Dining:** Restaurant; 6 am-1 & 5-10 pm; $4-$8. **Services:** Fee: coin laundry. **All Rooms:** free movies.
Motor Inn **Some Rooms:** 5 efficiencies, utensils extra charge, refrigerators. **Cards:** AE, DI, DS, MC, VI.
Special Amenities: Early check-in/late check-out and free local telephone calls.   🐾 🖳 📶 CTV ✕ D

DOUBLETREE GUEST SUITES   Rates Subject to Change   Phone: 919/361-4660   **8**
◆◆◆   Sun-Thurs   1P: $144- 160 2P/1B: $164- 180 2P/2B: $164- 180 XP: $20 F17
Suite Hotel Fri & Sat   1P: $79- 89 2P/1B: $79- 89 2P/2B: $79- 89 XP: $10 F17
Location: I-40 exit 278, just n on SR 55. 2515 Meridian Pkwy 27713. Fax: 919/361-2256. **Terms:** Sr.
discount; no pets. **Facility:** 203 rooms. 2 two-bedroom suites avail; 7 stories; interior corridors. **Dining:** Dining room; 6:30
am-10 pm, Sat & Sun from 7 am; $8-$20. **All Rooms:** free & pay movies. **Cards:** AE, DI, DS, MC, VI.
🖳 🖳 📺 ✕ 🎬 D S

(See map p. 358)

DURHAM HILTON
Phone: 919/383-8033 **5**
(AAA) [SAVE]   All Year   1P: $99- 149   2P/1B: $109- 169   2P/2B: $109- 169   XP: $10   F18
◆◆◆   **Location:** At jct I-85 & US 70 business route, exit off I-85 southbound, exit 173 northbound, turn left on Cole
Hotel   Mill Rd. 3800 Hillsborough Rd 27705. Fax: 919/383-4287. **Terms:** Reserv deposit; no pets. **Facility:** 152
rooms. Tastefully furnished rooms; handsomely appointed public areas. 6 stories; interior corridors; sauna,
whirlpool. **Dining:** Dining room; 6 am-10 pm; Mon-Fri lunch buffet; Sun brunch 11 am-2 pm; $10-$18;
cocktails. **Services:** area transportation, to Duke Medical Center. **All Rooms:** coffeemakers, free & pay movies.
Some Rooms: refrigerators. **Cards:** AE, CB, DI, DS, JCB, MC, VI. **Special Amenities: Early check-in/late check-out and
preferred room (subject to availability with advanced reservations).** *(See color ad p 18 & p 359)*
🛆 ⊞ ⊞ ⊞ CTV ⋔ ✕ 🕭 D S

FAIRFIELD INN BY MARRIOTT   Rates Subject to Change   Phone: 919/382-3388 **6**
◆◆◆   All Year [CP]   1P: $54   2P/1B: $59   2P/2B: $59   XP: $6   F18
Motel   **Location:** On US 70; exit off I-85 southbound, exit 173 northbound; turn left on Cole Mill Rd. 3710
Hillsborough Rd 27705. Fax: 919/382-3388. **Terms:** Sr. discount; no pets. **Facility:** 135 rooms. 3 stories;
interior/exterior corridors. **All Rooms:** free movies. **Cards:** AE, DI, DS, MC, VI.
🛆 CTV ⋔ ✕ 🕭 D S

FAIRFIELD INN-RESEARCH TRIANGLE PARK   Phone: 919/361-2656 **25**
(AAA) [SAVE]   All Year [CP]   1P: $54- 70   2P/1B: $54- 75   2P/2B: $59- 85   XP: $5   F18
◆◆◆   **Location:** Exit 278, I-40 on SR 55. 4507 SR 55 27713. Fax: 919/544-0288. **Terms:** No pets. **Facility:** 96
Motel   rooms. 3 stories; interior/exterior corridors. **Dining:** Restaurant nearby. **Services:** valet laundry.
All Rooms: free & pay movies. **Some Rooms:** refrigerators. **Fee:** whirlpools. **Cards:** AE, CB, DI, DS, MC,
VI. **Special Amenities: Free breakfast and free local telephone calls.**
⊞ ⊞ ⋔ ✕ 🕭 D

HAMPTON INN   Rates Subject to Change   Phone: 919/471-6100 **29**
◆◆◆   All Year [CP]   1P: $54   2P/1B: $82- 89   2P/2B: $80- 89
Motel   **Location:** Exit 174A (Hillandale Rd), I-85. 1816 Hillandale Rd 27705. Fax: 919/479-7026. **Terms:** Sr.
discount; no pets. **Facility:** 137 rooms. 6 stories; interior corridors. **All Rooms:** free movies. **Cards:** AE, CB,
DI, DS, MC, VI.
🛆 ⊞ CTV ⋔ ✕ 🕭 D

HOLIDAY INN RALEIGH-DURHAM AIRPORT-RESEARCH TRIANGLE PARK   Phone: 919/941-6000 **30**
(AAA) [SAVE]   Mon-Thurs   1P: $144   2P/1B: $144   2P/2B: $144   XP: $10   F12
◆◆◆   Fri-Sun   1P: $99   2P/1B: $99   2P/2B: $99   XP: $10   F12
Motor Inn   **Location:** I-40, exit 282. 4810 Page Rd 27709 (PO Box 13816, RESEARCH TRIANGLE PARK).
Fax: 919/941-6030. **Terms:** Reserv deposit; package plans; no pets. **Facility:** 249 rooms. Uniquely designed
with a resort-like appearance. Rooms & public areas have an elegant country inn decor. 4-5 stories; interior
corridors; luxury level rooms; sauna. **Dining & Entertainment:** Dining room, restaurant; 6 am-11 pm; Mon-Fri lunch buffet;
$10-$20; cocktails/lounge. **Services:** area transportation, within Research Park area. **Fee:** coin laundry. **All Rooms:** free &
pay movies. **Some Rooms:** microwaves, refrigerators, whirlpools. **Cards:** AE, CB, DI, DS, JCB, MC, VI. **Special Amenities:**
Early check-in/late check-out and free newspaper. *(See ad p 403)*
Roll in showers. 🛆 ⊞ ⊞ ⊞ ⋔ ✕ 🕭 D S

MARRIOTT-RESEARCH TRIANGLE PARK   Rates Subject to Change   Phone: 919/941-6200 **31**
◆◆◆   Sun-Thurs   1P: $125- 130   2P/1B: $125- 130   2P/2B: $125- 130
Hotel   Fri & Sat   1P: $59- 130   2P/1B: $59- 130   2P/2B: $59- 130
Location: I-40 at Miami Blvd, exit 281. 4700 Guardian Dr 27703. Fax: 919/941-6229. **Terms:** Sr. discount;
check-in 4 pm; no pets. **Facility:** 224 rooms. 6 stories; interior corridors. **Dining:** Dining room; 6:30-10 am, 11:30-3 & 5-11
pm; $8-$14. **All Rooms:** free & pay movies. **Cards:** AE, CB, DI, DS, JCB, MC, VI.
Roll in showers. 🛆 ⊞ CTV ⚱ ✕ 🕭 D S

OMNI DURHAM HOTEL & DURHAM CIVIC CENTER   Rates Subject to Change   Phone: 919/683-6664 **11**
◆◆◆   All Year   1P: $99- 109   2P/1B: $109- 119   2P/2B: $109- 119   XP: $10   F18
Hotel   **Location:** Center, downtown exit off I-85 via Mangum St, then 2 blks w on Morgan. 201 Foster St 27701.
Fax: 919/683-2046. **Terms:** Sr. discount; no pets. **Facility:** 188 rooms. 9 stories; interior corridors.
Dining: Dining room; 6:30 am-2 & 6-10 pm. Breakfast & lunch buffet; $10-$16. **All Rooms:** free & pay movies. **Cards:** AE,
CB, DI, DS, MC, VI.
CTV ⋔ ✕ 🕭 D S

RED ROOF INN CHAPEL HILL   Rates Subject to Change   Phone: 919/489-9421 **22**
◆◆   All Year   1P: $50   2P/1B: $56   2P/2B: $58   XP: $6   F18
Motel   **Location:** Exit 270, off I-40; at jct US 15-501, just s of I-40 via service road. 5623 Chapel Hill Blvd 27707.
Fax: 919/489-8001. **Terms:** Small pets only. **Facility:** 114 rooms. 3 stories; exterior corridors.
All Rooms: free movies. **Cards:** AE, CB, DI, DS, MC, VI.
⚱ ⋔ ✕ 🕭 D

(See map p. 358)

RED ROOF INN DURHAM — Rates Subject to Change — Phone: 919/471-9882 ⬛20
◆◆ All Year — 1P: $48- 67 2P/1B: $53- 74 2P/2B: $58- 62 XP: $5-6 F18
Motel **Location:** Guess Rd exit off I-85 via service road at MM 175. 2000 I-85 service road 27705. Fax: 919/477-0512. **Terms:** Small pets only. **Facility:** 120 rooms. 3 stories; exterior corridors.
All Rooms: free movies. **Cards:** AE, CB, DI, DS, MC, VI. 🛏 ✕ 🎫 Ⓓ

REGAL UNIVERSITY HOTEL — Rates Subject to Change — Phone: 919/383-8575 ⬛17
〰〰〰 All Year [CP] — 1P: $89 2P/1B: $89 2P/2B: $89 XP: $15 F17
◆◆◆ **Location:** US 15-501 bypass & Morreene Rd, exit 108A; 5.5 mi n of I-40, exit 270. 2800 Campus Walk Ave
Hotel 27705. Fax: 919/383-8495. **Terms:** Sr. discount; no pets. **Facility:** 315 rooms. 4 stories; interior corridors.
Dining: Dining room; 6:30 am-2 & 5-10 pm; $12-$20. **All Rooms:** Fee: movies. **Some Rooms:** 10 efficiencies. **Cards:** AE, CB, DI, DS, JCB, MC, VI. *(See color ad p 360)* 🛬 ♿ ✕ 🎫 Ⓓ

RESIDENCE INN — Rates Subject to Change — Phone: 919/361-1266 ⬛35
◆◆◆ All Year [CP] — 1P: $109- 142 2P/1B: $109- 142 2P/2B: $109- 142
Suite Motel **Location:** Just s on SR 55 from I-40, exit 278. 1919 Hwy 54 E 27713. Fax: 919/361-1200. **Terms:** Pets, $200 extra charge. **Facility:** 122 rooms. 2 stories; exterior corridors. **All Rooms:** kitchens, free movies.
Cards: AE, CB, DI, DS, MC, VI. 🛏 🛬 🏠 ✕ 🎫 Ⓓ Ⓢ

UNIVERSITY INN — Rates Subject to Change — Phone: 919/286-4421 ⬛15
◆◆◆ All Year [CP] — 1P: $65- 75 2P/1B: $75- 85 2P/2B: $75- 85 XP: $5 F18
Motel **Location:** Elba St exit off SR 147; 0.3 mi s. 502 Elf St 27705. Fax: 919/286-3817. **Terms:** Sr. discount; no pets. **Facility:** 48 rooms. 4 stories; interior corridors. **All Rooms:** free movies. **Some Rooms:** 19 efficiencies. **Cards:** AE, DS, MC, VI. 📺 🏠 ✕ 🎫 Ⓓ

WASHINGTON DUKE INN & GOLF CLUB — Phone: 919/490-0999 ⬛7
〰〰 💾 3/13-6/11 — 1P: $210- 230 2P/1B: $210- 230 2P/2B: $210- 230 XP: $15 F17
9/3-11/30 — 1P: $180- 200 2P/1B: $180- 200 2P/2B: $180- 200 XP: $15 F17
◆◆◆◆ 6/12-9/2 — 1P: $160- 180 2P/1B: $160- 180 2P/2B: $160- 180 XP: $15 F17
Hotel 12/1-3/12 — 1P: $140- 160 2P/1B: $140- 160 2P/2B: $140- 160 XP: $15 F17
Location: On SR 751, 0.8 mi e of jct US 15/501. 3001 Cameron Blvd 27706. Fax: 919/688-0105. **Terms:** No
pets. **Facility:** 171 rooms. Quiet, wooded location. Public areas include memorabilia devoted to the memory of the Washington Duke family. Some rooms overlook golf course. 5 stories; interior corridors; pro shop. Fee: 18 holes golf; 6 lighted tennis courts. **Dining & Entertainment:** Cocktail lounge; afternoon tea; also, The Fairview, see separate listing. **Services:** valet laundry; area transportation, limited; valet parking. **Recreation:** jogging. **All Rooms:** honor bars, free movies, safes. **Some Rooms:** refrigerators. Fee: VCP's. **Cards:** AE, CB, DI, MC, VI. **Special Amenities:** Free newspaper and free room upgrade (subject to availability with advanced reservations). 🛬 ♿ 📺 ✕ Ⓓ Ⓢ

WYNDHAM GARDEN HOTEL-RTP AIRPORT — Rates Subject to Change — Phone: 919/941-6066 ⬛26
◆◆◆ Sun-Thurs [BP] — 1P: $119 2P/1B: $119 2P/2B: $119 XP: $10 F12
Motor Inn Fri & Sat [BP] — 1P: $69 2P/1B: $69 2P/2B: $69 XP: $10 F12
Location: Exit 281, off I-40; 0.3 mi n on Miami Blvd. 4620 S Miami Blvd 27703 (PO Box 13568, RESEARCH TRIANGLE PARK, 27709). Fax: 919/941-6363. **Terms:** No pets. **Facility:** 172 rooms. 7 stories; interior corridors.
Dining: Dining room; 6:30-10 am, 11:30-1 & 5-10 pm; $10-$14. **All Rooms:** free & pay movies. **Cards:** AE, CB, DI, DS, JCB, MC, VI. 🛬 ♿ 🏠 ✕ 🎫 Ⓓ Ⓢ

RESTAURANTS

THE FAIRVIEW — Lunch: $8-$10 — Dinner: $17-$27 — Phone: 919/490-0999 ④
〰〰 **Location:** On SR 751, 0.8 mi e of jct US 15-501 at Duke Golf Course; in Washington Duke Inn & Golf Club.
◆◆◆◆ 3001 Cameron Blvd 27706. **Hours:** 7 am-10 pm. **Reservations:** suggested. **Features:** cocktails & lounge;
Continental entertainment; valet parking; a la carte. Sedate elegance with resort casual ambience. Atmosphere gets energized prior to Duke University special events. Regional American cuisine incorporating French & Italian influences. **Cards:** AE, CB, DI, MC, VI. ✕

PAPAGAYO'S GOURMET MEXICAN RESTAURANT — Lunch: $4-$6 — Dinner: $8-$11 — Phone: 919/286-1910 ⑧
◆◆ **Location:** Fulton St exit off SR 147 to Erwin Rd, w 0.3 mi to Douglas St, just n. 501 Douglas St 27715-3129.
Mexican **Hours:** 11:30 am-10 pm, Sat & Sun from 5:30 pm. Closed: 11/26, 12/24 & 12/25. **Features:** children's menu; health conscious menu; carryout; cocktails. Attractive, comfortable, very popular dining room. Patio dining, weather permitting. **Cards:** AE, MC, VI. ✕

PAPA'S GRILL — Lunch: $7-$10 — Dinner: $13-$20 — Phone: 919/383-8502 ①
◆◆◆ **Location:** At ne I-85 & Hillandale Rd exit, in Loehmann's Plaza. 1821 Hillandale Rd 27705. **Hours:** 11:30
Regional am-2:30 & 5-10 pm, Fri & Sat-10:30 pm. Closed: Sun, 1/1, 11/26 & 12/25. **Reservations:** suggested;
Greek weekends. **Features:** carryout; cocktails & lounge. Greek & Mediterranean cuisines served in elegant & intimate atmosphere. Well-established. **Cards:** AE, CB, DI, DS, MC, VI. ✕

SASSY'S — Lunch: $6-$8 — Dinner: $8-$13 — Phone: 919/383-0244 ②
◆◆ **Location:** Hillandale exit off I-85; in Loehmann's Plaza. 1821 Hillandale Rd 27705. **Hours:** 11 am-9 pm.
American Closed major holidays & Sun. **Features:** children's menu; health conscious menu; carryout; cocktails. Varied selection of sandwiches, also beef & chicken dishes served in relaxed, oak paneled atmosphere. **Cards:** AE, MC, VI. ✕

TAVERNA NIKOS — Lunch: $5-$8 — Dinner: $9-$14 — Phone: 919/682-0043 ⑤
◆◆◆ **Location:** Downtown exit off I-85 via Mangum & Chapel Hill sts to Main St; in Brightleaf Sq, 21A. 905 W
Greek Main St 27701. **Hours:** 11 am-3 & 5-10 pm. Closed major holidays, Sun & 12/24 for dinner.
Reservations: suggested. **Features:** carryout; cocktails; a la carte. Salads, hearty dishes, sandwiches & appetizers served in large, bustling warehouse with mediterranean touches. Casual & popular. **Cards:** AE, DI, MC, VI. ✕

EDEN—15,200

LODGING

DAYS INN   Phone: 910/623-1500
(AAA) [SAVE]   All Year [CP]   1P: $44- 48 2P/1B: $48- 52 2P/2B: $48- 52 XP: $5   F12
◆◆   **Location:** SR 14 at Kings Hwy; 1.3 mi s of SR 87 (from VA line); opposite Morehead Memorial Hospital. 115
Motel   W Kings Hwy 27288. Fax: 919/623-5132. **Terms:** Reserv deposit; weekly/monthly rates; no pets. **Facility:** 57
        rooms. All rooms ground level. Well-maintained & landscaped grounds; attractive public areas. 6 efficiencies,
        $40-$60 for up to 2 persons. Handling fee imposed; 1 story; exterior corridors. **Dining:** Restaurant nearby.
All Rooms: free movies. **Cards:** AE, CB, DI, DS, MC, VI. **Special Amenities: Free breakfast and free local telephone
calls.**   [⊠] [❄] [CTV] [✕] [⊿] [D]

EDENTON—5,300

LODGINGS

GOVERNOR EDEN INN   Rates Subject to Change   Phone: 919/482-2072
◆◆   All Year [BP]   1P: $55   2P/1B: $77   2P/2B: $77
Historic Bed   **Location:** 3 blks n on N Broad St. 304 N Broad St 27932 (PO Box 1145). **Terms:** Age restrictions may
& Breakfast   apply; reserv deposit, 7 day notice; no pets. **Facility:** 4 rooms. 2 stories; interior corridors; designated smoking
        area. **All Rooms:** free movies.   [CTV] [✕] [D]

TRAVEL HOST INN   Phone: 919/482-2017
(AAA) [SAVE]   All Year [CP]   1P: $47- 51 2P/1B: $55- 59 2P/2B: $55   XP: $5   F12
        Location: At jct US 17 (Bypass) & SR 32. 501 Virginia Rd 27932. Fax: 919/482-3106. **Terms:** Reserv
◆◆   deposit; weekly rates; no pets. **Facility:** 66 rooms. 2 stories; exterior corridors. **Dining:** Restaurant nearby.
Motel   **All Rooms:** free movies. **Cards:** AE, MC, VI. **Special Amenities: Early check-in/late check-out.**
                                                                     [⊠] [CTV] [♠] [✕] [⊿] [D]

THE TRESTLE HOUSE INN   Rates Subject to Change   Phone: 919/482-2282
◆◆   12/1-12/31 & 3/1-11/30 [BP] 1P: $60   2P/1B: $80- 95 2P/2B: $80- 125 XP: $15
Bed &   1/1-2/28 [CP]   1P: $52   2P/1B: $60   2P/2B: $60   XP: $15
Breakfast   **Location:** Just n on S Broad St, to SR 32; 2 mi s; 2.8 mi w on Soundside Rd. 632 Soundside Rd 27932.
        Terms: Sr. discount; reserv deposit; no pets. **Facility:** 5 rooms. 3 stories; interior corridors; smoke free prem-
ises. **Cards:** AE, MC, VI.   [✕] [D]

RESTAURANT

WATERMAN'S GRILL   **Lunch:** $5-$7   **Dinner:** $10-$14   Phone: 919/482-7733
◆◆   **Location:** Town Center - in historic area. 427 S Broad St 27932. **Hours:** 11:30 am-10 pm; Mon-3 pm.
Seafood   Closed: Sun, 1/1, 11/26 & 12/25. **Features:** children's menu; cocktails; street parking. Homemade soup &
        dessert; crab cakes & cajun tuna featured. **Cards:** AE, DS, MC, VI.   [✕]

ELIZABETH CITY—14,300

LODGINGS

COMFORT INN   Rates Subject to Change   Phone: 919/338-8900
◆◆◆   All Year [CP]   1P: $63- 125 2P/1B: $71- 125 2P/2B: $71- 125 XP: $18
Motel   **Location:** 0.8 mi s on US 17 bypass. 306 S Hughes Blvd 27909. Fax: 919/338-6420. **Terms:** No pets.
        Facility: 80 rooms. 5 stories; interior corridors. **All Rooms:** free movies. **Cards:** AE, CB, DI, DS, MC, VI.
                                                               [⊠] [CTV] [♿] [✕] [⊿] [D] [S]

TRAVELERS MOTEL   Phone: 919/338-5451
(AAA) [SAVE]   All Year [CP]   1P: $40- 45 2P/1B: $48- 55 2P/2B: $55- 75 XP: $5
◆◆   **Location:** 3 mi n on SR 158 & US 17 bypass. 1211 N Road St 27909. Fax: 919/338-5451. **Terms:** Reserv
Motel   deposit; no pets. **Facility:** 25 rooms. 2 stories; exterior corridors. **Dining:** Restaurant nearby.
        All Rooms: free movies. **Some Rooms:** 5 efficiencies, no utensils, refrigerators. **Cards:** AE, DI, DS, MC, VI.
        Special Amenities: Free breakfast and free newspaper.   [CTV] [✕] [D]

RESTAURANTS

MARINA RESTAURANT   **Lunch:** $4-$7   **Dinner:** $7-$14   Phone: 919/335-7307
◆   **Location:** On US 158, just e of Camden Bridge. 27909. **Hours:** 5 pm-10 pm, Sun 11 am-9 pm. Closed:
Seafood   Mon, 11/26, 12/24 & 12/25. **Features:** children's menu; carryout; cocktails & lounge. Good variety of broiled
        & fried seafood, sandwiches & appetizers served in small, wood paneled dining rooms. On the Pasquotank
River. Seasonal deck dining. Oyster bar/raw bar open year round. **Cards:** MC, VI.   [✕]

MULLIGAN'S GRILLE   **Lunch:** $5-$8   **Dinner:** $12-$16   Phone: 919/331-2431
◆◆   **Location:** Downtown; in Water Works Bldg. 400 S Water St 27909. **Hours:** 11:30 am-10 pm, Fri & Sat-11
American   pm. Closed major holidays. **Features:** children's menu; carryout; cocktails. Warm, tavern-like ambience.
        Homemade dessert. Cozy & comfortable on the waterfront with panorama view of the Pasquotank River.
Patio dining, weather permitting. Owner/chef. **Cards:** AE, DI, DS, MC, VI.   [✕]

ELKIN—3,800

LODGING

ELK INN   Phone: 910/835-7780
(AAA) [SAVE]   All Year   1P: $34   2P/1B: $45   2P/2B: $45   XP: $10   F12
◆◆   **Location:** Exit 85 off I-77, then 2 mi to Business Rt 21 via signs. 1101 N Bridge St 28621. **Terms:** No pets.
Motel   **Facility:** 32 rooms. 2 stories; exterior corridors. **All Rooms:** free movies. **Cards:** AE, MC, VI.
                                                                     [CTV] [♠] [✕] [D]

EMERALD ISLE—2,400

LODGINGS

EMERALD ISLE INN & BED & BREAKFAST   Rates Subject to Change   Phone: 919/354-3222
◆◆   5/31-9/9 [BP]   1P: $115- 150 2P/1B: $115- 150 2P/2B: $115- 150 XP: $15   F6
Bed &   12/1-5/30 & 9/10-11/30 [BP] 1P: $75- 115 2P/1B: $75- 115 2P/2B: $75- 115 XP: $10   F6
Breakfast   **Location:** At Mile Marker 12.5; on SR 58 & 5th St. 502 Ocean Dr 28594. Fax: 919/354-3222. **Terms:** Sr.
        discount; reserv deposit, 10 day notice; 2 night min stay, weekends in season; no pets. **Facility:** 5 rooms. 2
stories; interior/exterior corridors; smoke free premises. **All Rooms:** free movies. **Some Rooms:** 2 kitchens. **Cards:** MC, VI.
                                                                     [CTV] [✕] [D]

THE ISLANDER

Phone: 919/354-3464

AAA SAVE	12/1-3/14 & 5/19-9/4	1P:	$68-	85	2P/1B:	$68-	85	2P/2B:	$68- 85	XP: $5	F12

AAA SAVE 12/1-3/14 & 5/19-9/4 1P: $68- 85 2P/1B: $68- 85 2P/2B: $68- 85 XP: $5 F12
◆◆ Fri & Sat 3/15-5/18 1P: $50- 80 2P/1B: $50- 80 2P/2B: $50- 80 XP: $5 F12
Motel Sun-Thurs 3/15-5/18 1P: $32- 52 2P/1B: $32- 52 2P/2B: $32- 52 XP: $5 F12
9/5-11/30 1P: $26- 52 2P/1B: $26- 52 2P/2B: $26- 52 XP: $5 F12

Location: In Boardwalk & Playland Plaza. 102 Islander Dr 28594 (PO Box 4444). Fax: 919/354-3528.
Terms: 2 night min stay, weekends in season; no pets. **Facility:** 81 rooms. 2 stories; exterior corridors. **All Rooms:** free movies. **Cards:** AE, DS, MC, VI.

RESTAURANT

MIKE'S PLACE **Lunch:** $4-$6 **Dinner:** $6-$10 **Phone: 919/354-5277**
◆ **Location:** Center at MP 19.5. 8302 Emerald Dr 28594. **Hours:** 7 am-9 pm, Sun-3 pm. Closed: 11/26 &
American 12/25. **Features:** children's menu; carryout; beer & wine only. Limited parking. Daily specials & hearty portions. Homemade soup, sauce & dessert. Pie is a favorite. **Cards:** AE, MC, VI.

ENKA—6,000   (See map p. 315; index p. 314)

RESTAURANT

K & S CAFETERIA **Phone: 704/665-1911** 40
◆ **Location:** 1.3 mi s on US 19 & 23 from I-40, exit 44; in Westridge Mall. 28728. **Hours:** 11 am-2:15 & 4-8:30
American pm, Fri & Sat-9 pm, Sun 11 am-8:30 pm. Closed: 12/25. **Features:** carryout. Popular with seniors & families. Trays carried on request.

FAYETTEVILLE—75,700

LODGINGS

COMFORT INN CROSS CREEK **Phone: 910/867-1777**
AAA SAVE All Year [CP] 1P: $50- 54 2P/1B: $56- 60 2P/2B: $56- 60 XP: $6 F16
Location: US 401 bypass, just s of jct with Morganton Rd. 1922 Skibo Rd 28314. Fax: 910/867-0325.
◆◆◆ **Terms:** Package plans; no pets. **Facility:** 176 rooms. Daily phone charge—$.75; 4 stories; interior corridors;
Motel small pool. **Dining:** Restaurant nearby. **Services:** Fee: coin laundry. **All Rooms:** free movies.
Some Rooms: coffeemakers, microwaves, refrigerators. **Cards:** AE, CB, DI, DS, JCB, MC, VI.
Special Amenities: Free breakfast and free room upgrade (subject to availability with advanced reservations).

COMFORT INN I-95 **Phone: 910/323-8333**
AAA SAVE All Year [BP] 1P: $53- 56 2P/1B: $58- 61 2P/2B: $58- 61 XP: $6 F18
Location: I-95 exit 49 at jct SR 210 & 53. 1957 Cedar Creek Rd 28301. Fax: 910/323-3946.
◆◆◆ **Terms:** Package plans; small pets only. **Facility:** 120 rooms. Very comfortable, modern, & attractively ap-
Motel pointed rooms & public areas. 2 stories; exterior corridors; small pool. **Dining:** Restaurant nearby. **Services:**
Fee: coin laundry. **All Rooms:** coffeemakers, microwaves, free movies, refrigerators. **Some Rooms:** radios.
Cards: AE, CB, DI, DS, JCB, MC, VI. **Special Amenities: Free breakfast and free local telephone calls.**
(See ad below)

COURTYARD BY MARRIOTT Rates Subject to Change **Phone:** 910/487-5557
◆◆◆ Fri & Sat 6/1-9/30 1P: $76 2P/1B: $86 2P/2B: $86 XP: $7 F18
Motel 12/1-5/31, Sun-Thurs
6/1-9/30 & 10/1-11/30 1P: $68 2P/1B: $78 2P/2B: $78 XP: $7 F18
Location: From All American Frwy, just e of Morgantown Rd exit. 4192 Sycamore Dairy Rd 28303. Fax: 910/487-1158
Terms: Sr. discount; no pets. **Facility:** 108 rooms. Suites $95-$120; 3 stories; interior corridors. **Dining:** Coffee shop; 6-10
am, Sat 7-11 am. **All Rooms:** free & pay movies. **Cards:** AE, CB, DI, DS, MC, VI. *(See color ad below)*

DAYS INN I-95 **Phone:** 910/483-6191
AAA SAVE All Year 1P: $44 2P/1B: $50 2P/2B: $50 XP: $7 F17
Under major renovation; **Location:** Just e on SR 53 & 210 from I-95, exit 49. 2065 Cedar Creek Rd 28301
Motor Inn Fax: 910/483-4113. **Terms:** No pets. **Facility:** 122 rooms. Scheduled to open summer 1997. 2 stories; interior
corridors. **Dining & Entertainment:** Dining room; 6:30 am-9:30 & 5-10 pm; $7-$13; cocktails/lounge
All Rooms: free movies. **Cards:** AE, CB, DI, DS, MC, VI. **Special Amenities: Free breakfast.** *(See ad below)*

ECONO LODGE I-95 **Phone:** 910/433-2100
AAA SAVE All Year [CP] 1P: $50- 70 2P/1B: $50- 70 2P/2B: $50- 70 XP: $5 F18
Location: Off I-95, exit 49; at jct Hwys 53 & 210. 1952 Cedar Creek Rd 28301 (PO Box 65177, 28306)
◆◆◆ Fax: 910/433-2009. **Terms:** Package plans; no pets. **Facility:** 150 rooms. Tastefully decorated public areas &
Motel rooms. 12 whirlpool rms $76.95-$99.95; 2 stories; exterior corridors. **Dining:** Restaurant nearby
All Rooms: free movies. **Cards:** AE, CB, DI, DS, JCB, MC, VI. **Special Amenities: Free breakfast and
free local telephone calls.** *(See color ad p 365)*

FAIRFIELD INN BY MARRIOTT Rates Subject to Change **Phone:** 910/487-1400
◆◆◆ 5/1-9/30 [CP] 1P: $52- 70 2P/1B: $60- 73 2P/2B: $60- 73 XP: $6 F13
Motel 12/1-4/30 & 10/1-11/30 [CP] 1P: $48- 56 2P/1B: $50- 66 2P/2B: $50- 66 XP: $6 F13
Location: All American Frwy at US 401 bypass; w side of Cross Creek Mall. 562 Cross Creek Mall 28303
Fax: 910/487-1400. **Terms:** No pets. **Facility:** 135 rooms. Handling fee imposed; 3 stories; interior/exterior corridors
All Rooms: free & pay movies. **Cards:** AE, DI, DS, MC, VI. *(See color ad below)*

FAIRFIELD INN-I-95
Motel Under construction; **Location:** Just w on SR 53 & 210 from exit 49, I-95. (PO Box 65177, 28301)
Terms: No pets. **Facility:** 63 rooms. Scheduled to open winter 1998; 3 stories; interior corridors
All Rooms: free movies. **Cards:** AE, CB, DI, DS, MC, VI. *(See color ad p 365)*

HAMPTON INN Rates Subject to Change **Phone:** 910/323-0011
◆◆◆ All Year [CP] 1P: $62 2P/1B: $68 2P/2B: $68
Motel **Location:** I-95 exit 49 at jct SR 210 & 53. 1922 Cedar Creek Rd 28301. Fax: 910/323-8764. **Terms:** Sr
discount; no pets. **Facility:** 122 rooms. 2 stories; exterior corridors. **All Rooms:** free movies. **Cards:** AE, CB
DI, DS, MC, VI.

HAMPTON INN
◆◆◆
Motel
Rates Subject to Change
Phone: 910/487-4006
All Year [CP]   1P: $54   2P/1B: $60   2P/2B: $60   XP: $6   F18
Location: US 401 bypass, 0.4 mi N of Morganton Rd; opposite Cross Creek Mall; enter thru Cross Creek Plaza entrance. 1700 Skibo Rd 28303. Fax: 910/487-5773. **Terms:** Sr. discount; no pets. **Facility:** 131 rooms. 4 stories; interior corridors. **All Rooms:** free movies. **Cards:** AE, DI, DS, MC, VI.
Roll in showers. 🛋 [CTV] 🔊 ✖ 🏊 [D] [S]

HOLIDAY INN BORDEAUX
◆◆◆
Motor Inn
Rates Subject to Change
Phone: 910/323-0111
All Year   1P: $78   2P/1B: $78   2P/2B: $78
Location: From jct I-95 business route & US 301, 2.3 mi w; from I-95 exit 40, southbound exit 56. 1707 Owen Dr 28304. Fax: 910/484-9444. **Terms:** Pets, $100 dep req. **Facility:** 289 rooms. 3-6 stories; interior/exterior corridors. **Dining:** Dining room; 6 am-2 & 5-10 pm, Fri & Sat open 24 hours; $9-$16. **All Rooms:** free & pay movies. **Cards:** AE, CB, DI, DS, JCB, MC, VI.
🛏 🛋 ➕ [CTV] 🔊 ✖ 🏊 [D] [S]

HOLIDAY INN I-95
(AAA) [SAVE]
◆◆◆
Motor Inn
Phone: 910/323-1600
3/1-9/1   1P: $84- 129   2P/1B: $84- 129   2P/2B: $84- 129
12/1-2/28 & 9/2-11/30   1P: $74- 99   2P/1B: $74- 99   2P/2B: $74- 99
Location: Exit 49 off I-95, at jct SR 210 & 53. 1944 Cedar Creek Rd 28301 (PO Box 2245, 28302). Fax: 910/323-0691. **Terms:** AP avail; package plans; no pets. **Facility:** 198 rooms. Nicely landscaped grounds. 2 stories; interior/exterior corridors; luxury level rooms; whirlpool. **Dining & Entertainment:** Dining room; Sun brunch 11 am-2 pm, $13.95; 6:30 am-2 & 5-10 pm; $10-$20; cocktails/lounge. **Services:** Fee: coin laundry. **All Rooms:** coffeemakers, free & pay movies. **Some Rooms:** microwaves, refrigerators. **Cards:** AE, CB, DI, DS, MC, VI. **Special Amenities: Free breakfast and free local telephone calls.** 🛋 🍴 ➕ 🏨 [CTV] 🔊 ✖ 🏊 [D]

HOWARD JOHNSON PLAZA HOTEL
(AAA) [SAVE]
◆◆◆
Motor Inn
Phone: 910/323-8282
All Year   1P: $65- 70   2P/1B: $71- 82   2P/2B: $71- 82   XP: $6   F18
Location: I-95 exit 49, jct SR 210 & 53. 1965 Cedar Creek Rd 28301 (PO Box 2086, 28302). Fax: 910/323-4039. **Terms:** Package plans; pets, $25 extra charge. **Facility:** 168 rooms. 4 stories; interior/exterior corridors; luxury level rooms; sauna, whirlpool. **Dining & Entertainment:** Dining room; 6 am-2 & 5-10 pm; $9-$14; cocktails/lounge. **Services:** valet laundry. **All Rooms:** free movies. **Some Rooms:** refrigerators. **Cards:** AE, CB, DI, DS, MC, VI. **Special Amenities: Free breakfast and free newspaper.**
(See ad below)   🛏 🛋 🛋 🍴 ➕ 🏨 [CTV] 🔊 ✖ 🏊 [D]

INNKEEPER
◆◆◆
Motel
Rates Subject to Change
Phone: 910/867-7659
All Year [CP]   1P: $48- 52   2P/1B: $53- 57   2P/2B: $57- 62   XP: $5   F18
Location: US 401 bypass, 0.4 mi n of jct Morganton Rd, opposite Cross Creek Mall, enter through Cross Creek Plaza entrance. 1720 Skibo Rd 28303. Fax: 910/867-7659. **Terms:** Sr. discount; no pets. **Facility:** 127 rooms. 2-3 stories; interior/exterior corridors. **All Rooms:** free movies. **Cards:** AE, CB, DI, DS, MC, VI.
[CTV] ✖ [D]

QUALITY INN AMBASSADOR
(AAA) [SAVE]
◆◆◆
Motor Inn
Phone: 910/485-8135
All Year   1P: $42- 50   2P/1B: $50- 65   2P/2B: $62   XP: $6   F18
Location: 2.3 mi s on US 301 & I-95 business route; from I-95 northbound exit 40, southbound exit 56. 2205 Gillespie St 28306 (PO Box 64166). Fax: 910/485-8682. **Terms:** Package plans; no pets. **Facility:** 62 rooms. 2 two-bedroom units. 1 story; exterior corridors. **Dining:** Restaurant; 6 am-9 pm; $6-$12. **Services:** valet laundry. **All Rooms:** coffeemakers, free movies. **Cards:** AE, CB, DI, DS, JCB, MC, VI. **Special Amenities: Early check-in/late check-out and free local telephone calls.** (See color ad p 365) 🛋 🍴 [CTV] ✖ 🏊 [D]

RADISSON PRINCE CHARLES HOTEL AND SUITES
◆◆◆
Historic Hotel
Rates Subject to Change
Phone: 919/433-4444
All Year   1P: $60- 80   2P/1B: $70- 90   2P/2B: $70- 90   XP: $10   F18
Location: From I-95 exit 49, 3.3 mi via Hwys 53 & 210 to 1st jct, then 2.3 mi w on Clinton & Person sts, Hay St blends in just n of downtown rotary. 450 Hay St 28301. Fax: 910/485-8269. **Terms:** Sr. discount; no pets. **Facility:** 83 rooms. 8 stories; interior corridors. **Dining:** Dining room; 6:30 am-10:30 pm; $9-$15. **All Rooms:** free & pay movies. **Cards:** AE, CB, DI, DS, JCB, MC, VI.
➕ [CTV] ✖ 🏊 [D] [S]

SLEEP INN FAYETTEVILLE
(AAA) [SAVE]
◆◆
Motel
Phone: 910/433-9090
All Year [CP]   1P: $60- 85   2P/1B: $60- 85   2P/2B: $60- 85   XP: $6   F18
Location: Off I-95, exit 49; at jct Hwys 53 & 210. 1915 Cedar Creek Rd 28301 (PO Box 65118, 28306). Fax: 910/433-9115. **Terms:** Package plans; no pets. **Facility:** 62 rooms. Very attractive & comfortable public areas; attentive service. 2 stories; interior corridors. **Dining:** Restaurant nearby. **Services:** complimentary evening beverages; valet laundry. **All Rooms:** free movies, combo or shower baths. **Cards:** AE, CB, DI, DS, JCB, MC, VI. **Special Amenities: Free breakfast and free newspaper.** (See color ad p 365)
Roll in showers. 🍴 [CTV] 🔊 ✖ [D] [S]

RESTAURANTS

DE LA FAYETTE RESTAURANT **Dinner:** $15-$30 **Phone:** 910/868-4600
Ⓐ
Location: From US 401 bypass Skibo Rd, 0.5 mi w on Cliffdale Rd. 6112 Cliffdale Rd 28314. **Hours:** 5
◆ ◆ pm-10 pm. Closed: Sun, Mon, 1/1, 11/26 & 12/25. **Reservations:** suggested. **Features:** dressy casual;
Continental carryout; cocktails & lounge. Some tables overlooking McFayden Pond. Featuring very nicely prepared &
presented entrees with emphasis on Creole & Cajun styles. **Cards:** AE, CB, DI, DS, MC, VI. ☒

HAYMONT GRILL & STEAKHOUSE **Lunch:** $4-$10 **Dinner:** $5-$12 **Phone:** 910/484-0261
Ⓐ
Location: From I-95S exit 46, Hwy 87N to Hays St exit, then 2 blks; at corner Morgan & Fort Bragg rds; on
◆ top of Haymont Hill. 1304 Morganton Rd 78305. **Hours:** 6 am-10 pm, Sun 7 am-9 pm. Closed: 11/26 &
12/25. **Reservations:** accepted. **Features:** casual dress; carryout; beer & wine only. Very popular with local
American following. Hearty portions, homemade soup & dessert; noted for daily specials & many Greek dishes. Fresh
seafood & some Italian entrees. **Cards:** MC, VI. ☒

FEARRINGTON VILLAGE—1,100 (See map p. 358; index p. 357)

LODGING

THE FEARRINGTON HOUSE INN Rates Subject to Change **Phone:** 919/542-2121 🔟
Ⓐ
All Year [BP] 1P: $165- 275 2P/1B: $165- 275 2P/2B: $165- 275
◆ ◆ ◆ ◆ ◆ **Location:** 13.2 mi s on US 15-501 from I-40 exit 270; town center. (2000 Fearrington Village Ctr,
Country Inn PITTSBORO, 27312). Fax: 919/542-4202. **Terms:** Age restrictions may apply; reserv deposit, 7 day notice;
no pets. **Facility:** 30 rooms. 2 stories; interior/exterior corridors; designated smoking area.
Dining: Restaurant, see separate listing. **All Rooms:** free movies. **Cards:** AE, MC, VI. *(See ad p 334)*

🛥 🕂 CTV 🏠 ☒ Ⓓ

RESTAURANT

THE FEARRINGTON HOUSE RESTAURANT Country Inn **Dinner:** $55 **Phone:** 919/542-2121 🔢
Ⓐ
Location: 13.2 mi s on US 15-501 from I-40 exit 270, town center; in The Fearrington House Inn. 2000
◆ ◆ ◆ ◆ Fearrington Village Ctr 27312. **Hours:** 6 pm-9 pm, Sun-8 pm. Closed: Mon. **Reservations:** suggested.
Regional **Features:** semi-formal attire; cocktails & lounge; minimum charge-$55; prix fixe. Fine intimate dining in
American restored farmhouse. Candlelit dining rooms overlook beautiful gardens & arbors. Southern cuisine with
contemporary & artistic interpretations. Sophisticated dessert presentations. Smoke free premises.
Cards: AE, MC, VI. ☒

FLETCHER—2,800 (See map p. 315; index p. 314)

LODGINGS

ECONO LODGE AIRPORT **Phone:** 704/684-1200 🔟
Ⓐ SAVE
| | 9/27-11/3 | 1P: $60- 86 | 2P/1B: $60- 91 | 2P/2B: $60- 91 | XP: $5 | F18 |
| | 6/14-9/26 | 1P: $50- 81 | 2P/1B: $55- 86 | 2P/2B: $55- 86 | XP: $5 | F18 |
◆ ◆ | 4/12-6/13 | 1P: $38- 60 | 2P/1B: $50- 60 | 2P/2B: $50- 60 | XP: $5 | F18 |
Motel | 12/1-4/11 & 11/4-11/30 | 1P: $33- 38 | 2P/1B: $37- 43 | 2P/2B: $37- 43 | XP: $5 | F18 |
Location: I-26 exit 9, on service road following signs. 196 Underwood Rd 28732. Fax: 704/687-7861.
Terms: No pets. **Facility:** 60 rooms. 2 stories; exterior corridors; wading pool. **Dining:** Coffee shop nearby. **All Rooms:** free
movies. **Some Rooms:** microwaves, refrigerators. **Cards:** AE, CB, DI, DS, JCB, MC, VI. **Special Amenities:** Free
breakfast and free local telephone calls. 🛥 CTV ☒ Ⓓ

FAIRFIELD INN BY MARRIOTT Rates Subject to Change **Phone:** 704/684-1144 🔢
◆ ◆ ◆
| | 7/1-10/31 | 1P: $69 | 2P/1B: $79 | 2P/2B: $79 | | |
Motel | 5/23-6/30 | 1P: $54 | 2P/1B: $62 | 2P/2B: $62 | XP: $7 | F18 |
| | 4/1-5/22 | 1P: $54 | 2P/1B: $60 | 2P/2B: $60 | XP: $7 | F18 |
| | 12/1-3/31 & 11/1-11/30 | 1P: $49 | 2P/1B: $49 | 2P/2B: $49 | | |
Location: I-26, exit 9, 0.3 mi w on Airport Rd. 31 Airport Park Rd 28732. Fax: 704/684-3377. **Terms:** No pets. **Facility:** 107
rooms. 3 stories; interior corridors. **All Rooms:** free movies. **Cards:** AE, CB, DI, DS, MC, VI. *(See color ad p 320)*
Roll in showers. 🛥 🕂 ☒ Ⓓ Ⓢ

HOLIDAY INN ASHEVILLE-AIRPORT **Phone:** 704/684-1213 🔢
Ⓐ SAVE
| | 10/1-10/25 | 1P: $95- 135 | 2P/1B: $100- 140 | 2P/2B: $100- 140 | XP: $7 | F18 |
| | 5/1-9/30 | 1P: $69- 89 | 2P/1B: $74- 94 | 2P/2B: $74- 94 | XP: $7 | F18 |
◆ ◆ ◆ | 12/1-4/30 & 10/26-11/30 | 1P: $59- 79 | 2P/1B: $64- 84 | 2P/2B: $64- 84 | XP: $7 | F18 |
Motor Inn **Location:** I-26 exit 9, just e. 550 Airport Rd 28732. Fax: 704/684-3778. **Terms:** No pets. **Facility:** 150 rooms.
Some rooms with mountain view. 2 stories; interior corridors; sauna. **Dining & Entertainment:** Restaurant;
6:30 am-2 & 5-10 pm; $11-$21; cocktails; nightclub. **Services:** valet laundry. **All Rooms:** coffeemakers, free & pay movies.
Some Rooms: microwaves, refrigerators. **Cards:** AE, CB, DI, DS, MC, VI. **Special Amenities:** Early check-in/late
check-out and free newspaper. *(See ad p 317)* 🛥 🛥 🍴 🕂 🕂 CTV ☒ Ⓓ

RESTAURANT

J & S CAFETERIA **Phone:** 704/684-3418 🔢
◆ ◆
Location: I-26, exit 9. 645 New Airport Rd 28732. **Hours:** 11 am-8 pm. Closed: 12/25. **Features:** children's
American menu; carryout. Hearty portions; homemade desserts. Smoke free premises. **Cards:** MC, VI. ☒

FOREST CITY—7,500

LODGING

DAYS INN Guaranteed Rates **Phone:** 704/248-3400
◆ ◆ ◆
All Year [CP] 1P: $50- 55 2P/1B: $55- 60 2P/2B: $55- 60 XP: $5 F13
Motel **Location:** On US 74A; opposite Tri-City Mall. 205 Commercial Dr 28043. Fax: 704/248-1183. **Terms:** Sr.
discount; no pets. **Facility:** 67 rooms. 2 stories; exterior corridors. **All Rooms:** free movies. **Cards:** AE, CB,
DI, DS, JCB, MC, VI. 🛥 CTV ☒ Ⓓ

FRANKLIN—2,900

LODGINGS

COLONIAL INN **Phone:** 704/524-6600
Ⓐ SAVE
All Year 1P: $40- 43 2P/1B: $42- 45 2P/2B: $47- 50 XP: $5 F15
Location: 3.5 mi s on US 441. 3157 Georgia Rd 28734. Fax: 704/524-6828. **Terms:** No pets. **Facility:** 42
◆ ◆ rooms. 1 story; exterior corridors; wading pool. **Dining:** Restaurant nearby. **Services:** Fee: coin laundry.
Motel **All Rooms:** coffeemakers, combo or shower baths. **Some Rooms:** refrigerators. **Cards:** AE, DS, MC, VI.
Special Amenities: Free local telephone calls and preferred room (subject to availability with
advanced reservations). Roll in showers. 🛥 CTV ☒ Ⓓ

COUNTRY INN TOWN-MOTEL
Phone: 704/524-4451

(AAA) — Motel — ◆◆

Rates Subject to Change

5/1-10/31	1P:	$34- 37	2P/1B:	$36- 38	2P/2B:	$42- 45	XP:	$5			F12
12/1-4/30 & 11/1-11/30	1P:	$30- 32	2P/1B:	$32- 34	2P/2B:	$34- 36	XP:	$5			F12

Location: On US 441S business route. 277 E Main St 28734. Fax: 704/524-0703. **Terms:** Reserv deposit, 3 day notice; no pets. **Facility:** 46 rooms. 1 story; exterior corridors. **Cards:** AE, DS, MC, VI. *(See color ad below)*

📡 CTV ✕ Ⓓ

DAYS INN-FRANKLIN
Phone: 704/524-6491

(AAA) SAVE — Motel — ◆◆◆

5/1-10/31 [CP]	1P:	$54- 64	2P/1B:	$54- 64	2P/2B:	$59- 85	XP:	$5			F12
12/1-4/30 & 11/1-11/30 [CP]	1P:	$34- 54	2P/1B:	$34- 54	2P/2B:	$44- 59	XP:	$5			F12

Location: 1 mi ne on US 23 & US 441 business route, at jct US 23 & 441 bypass. 1320 E Main St 28734. Fax: 704/369-9636. **Terms:** Reserv deposit, 3 day notice; no pets. **Facility:** 41 rooms. Spacious grounds with picnic area. 1 two-bedroom unit. Deluxe rooms avail; 1 story; exterior corridors. **Dining:** Restaurant nearby. **All Rooms:** combo or shower baths. **Some Rooms:** Fee: microwaves, refrigerators. **Cards:** AE, CB, DI, DS, MC, VI. **Special Amenities:** Free breakfast and free newspaper.

📡 🍴 CTV ✕ Ⓓ

FRANKLIN MOTEL
Phone: 704/524-4431

(AAA) SAVE — Motel — ◆◆

5/1-10/31	1P:	$38- 45	2P/1B:	$38- 45	2P/2B:	$45- 55	XP:	$2			F12
12/1-4/30 & 11/1-11/30	1P:	$32- 36	2P/1B:	$32- 36	2P/2B:	$36- 40	XP:	$2			F12

Location: 0.3 mi w at jct US 23, 64, 441 & SR 28. 17 W Palmer St 28734. Fax: 704/369-3614. **Terms:** No pets. **Facility:** 52 rooms. 2 stories; exterior corridors. **Cards:** AE, CB, DI, DS, MC, VI. *(See ad below)*

Roll in showers. 📡 ✕ Ⓓ

HAMPTON INN
Phone: 704/369-0600

◆◆◆ — Motel

Rates Subject to Change

9/16-11/1 [CP]	1P:	$89- 109	2P/1B:	$89- 109	2P/2B:	$89- 109	XP:	$10			F13
5/1-9/15 [CP]	1P:	$65- 89	2P/1B:	$75- 85	2P/2B:	$85- 105	XP:	$10			F13
12/1-4/30 & 11/2-11/30 [CP]	1P:	$55- 79	2P/1B:	$65- 75	2P/2B:	$75- 95	XP:	$10			F13

Location: US 441 bypass N. 244 Cunningham Rd 28734. Fax: 704/369-0700. **Terms:** No pets. **Facility:** 81 rooms. Rates for up to 4 persons; 3 stories; interior corridors. **All Rooms:** free movies. **Cards:** AE, CB, DI, DS, JCB, MC, VI.

Roll in showers. 📡 CTV ✕ Ⓓ Ⓢ

HERITAGE INN BED & BREAKFAST
Phone: 704/524-4150

◆◆ — Bed & Breakfast

Rates Subject to Change

4/1-11/30 [BP]	1P:	$55- 65	2P/1B:	$65- 75				
12/1-3/31 [BP]	1P:	$50- 59	2P/1B:	$59- 68				

Location: Off Business 441 (Porter St) in Heritage Shopping Village. 43 Heritage Hollow Dr 28734. **Terms:** Age restrictions may apply; reserv deposit, 7 day notice; 2 night min stay, weekends 10/1-10/31; no pets. **Facility:** 7 rooms. 1 apartment unit $95, $10 extra person; 2 stories; exterior corridors. **Some Rooms:** efficiency, 2 kitchens. **Cards:** MC, VI.

✕ Ⓓ

MOUNTAINSIDE VACATION LODGING Rates Subject to Change **Phone:** 704/524-6209
All Year 1P: $50- 65 2P/1B: $50- 65 2P/2B: $50- 65 XP: $5 F12
Location: 6 mi n on US 441 & 23. 8356 Sylva Rd 28734. **Terms:** Reserv deposit, 14 day notice; no pets.
Facility: 5 rooms. Rates for up to 4 persons. Handling fee imposed; 1 story; exterior corridors.
All Rooms: kitchens. **Cards:** DS, MC, VI. D

Apartment
Motel

RESTAURANTS

THE FROG & OWL KITCHEN **Lunch:** $7-$9 **Dinner:** $11-$19 **Phone:** 704/349-4112
Location: Downtown. 12 E Main St 28734. **Hours:** 11 am-2 pm & 5-9 pm, Mon-Wed to 2 pm, Sat 5 pm-9
pm. Closed: Sun. **Reservations:** accepted. **Features:** casual dress; wine only; street parking; a la carte.
Creative variations on duck, lamb, steak & chicken dishes. French influenced. Smoke free premises.
Cards: MC, VI. ✕

Regional
American

GAZEBO CREEKSIDE CAFE **Lunch:** $3-$6 **Phone:** 704/524-8783
Location: Off Business 441 (Porter St) in Heritage Shopping Village. 103 Heritage Hollow 28734. **Hours:** 11
am-2:30 pm. Closed: Sun & 11/1-3/31. **Features:** No A/C. Soup, salad & sandwiches served in an open air
gazebo. Creekside setting. ✕

American

HICKORY RANCH RESTAURANT **Lunch:** $5-$8 **Dinner:** $7-$10 **Phone:** 704/369-9909
Location: Downtown; on US 441N business route. 126 Palmer St 28734. **Hours:** 11 am-9 pm. Closed:
11/26 & 12/25. **Reservations:** suggested. **Features:** children's menu; carryout; wine only. Sandwiches, fresh
seafood, steak, rib & chicken served in casual dining rooms with antiques & model train. Also, homemade
bread, soup & dessert. Old time ice cream parlor & wine bar. Featuring certified Angus prime beef.
Cards: AE, MC, VI. ✕

American

GARNER—15,000 (See map p. 404; index p. 402)

LODGING

COMFORT INN-SOUTH RALEIGH **Phone:** 919/779-7888 52
All Year [CP] 1P: $59- 69 2P/1B: $59- 69 2P/2B: $69 XP: $5 F16
Location: At jct US 70/50 SE & US 401S; 1.5 mi e on US 70 from I-40, exit 298A just n. 1602 Mechanical
Blvd 27529. Fax: 919/779-4603. **Terms:** Reserv deposit; no pets. **Facility:** 60 rooms. Very attractive public
areas & comfortable rooms. Suite, $89; 2 stories; exterior corridors; sauna, whirlpool. **Dining:** Restaurant
nearby. **All Rooms:** free movies. **Some Rooms:** microwaves, refrigerators. Fee: VCP's, whirlpools.
Cards: AE, CB, DI, DS, JCB, MC, VI. **Special Amenities:** Early check-in/late check-out and free breakfast.

Motel

⛵ 🛁 🛗 CTV ✕ D

GASTONIA—54,700

LODGINGS

FAIRFIELD INN BY MARRIOTT **Phone:** 704/867-5073
All Year [CP] 1P: $55- 69 2P/1B: $60- 79 2P/2B: $60- 150 XP: $5 F16
Too new to rate; **Location:** I-85 & New Hope Rd, exit 20. 1860 Remount Rd 28054. **Terms:** No pets.
Facility: 89 rooms. Scheduled to open Spring 1997. 4 stories; interior corridors; whirlpool.
Dining: Restaurant nearby. **All Rooms:** free movies, combo or shower baths. **Cards:** AE, CB, DI, DS, MC,
VI. **Special Amenities: Free breakfast and free local telephone calls.** *(See color ad below)*

Motel

Roll in showers. ⛵ 🛁 🛗 CTV ♿ ✕ 🐾 D S

HAMPTON INN Rates Subject to Change **Phone:** 704/866-9090
All Year [CP] 1P: $64 2P/1B: $71 2P/2B: $71
Location: Just w of I-85, Exit 20 (New Hope Rd). 1859 Remount Rd 28054. Fax: 704/866-7070. **Terms:** No
pets. **Facility:** 109 rooms. 5 stories; interior corridors. **All Rooms:** free movies. **Cards:** AE, CB, DI, DS, MC,
VI.

Motel

⛵ CTV 🎣 ✕ 🐾 D S

HOLIDAY INN EXPRESS Rates Subject to Change **Phone:** 704/864-8744
All Year [CP] 1P: $54 2P/1B: $54 2P/2B: $54 XP: $5 F16
Location: 1.5 mi e on US 29/74 from jct US 321. 1400 E Franklin Blvd 28054. Fax: 704/864-8744.
Terms: Sr. discount; no pets. **Facility:** 60 rooms. 2 stories; exterior corridors. **All Rooms:** free movies.
Cards: AE, CB, DI, DS, JCB, MC, VI.

Motel

CTV ✕ 🐾 D

INNKEEPER MOTOR LODGE Rates Subject to Change **Phone:** 704/868-2000
All Year [CP] 1P: $52- 80 2P/1B: $52- 80 2P/2B: $57- 80 XP: $5 F18
Location: New Hope Rd, exit off I-85. 360 McNeil St 28054. Fax: 704/868-2000. **Terms:** Sr. discount; no
pets. **Facility:** 63 rooms. 3 stories, no elevator; interior/exterior corridors. **All Rooms:** free movies.
Cards: AE, CB, DI, DS, MC, VI.

Motel

CTV ✕ D

MOTEL 6 - 1281   Guaranteed Rates   **Phone:** 704/868-4900
(AAA)   All Year   1P: $35- 45 2P/1B: $39- 49 2P/2B: $39- 49 XP: $3   F17
          Location: I-85 & US 321 via Broadcast St, n of I-85 exit 17. 1721 Broadcast St 28052. Fax: 704/861-1603.
◆ ◆   **Terms:** Sr. discount; small pets only. **Facility:** 109 rooms. 1 story; exterior corridors. **All Rooms:** free
Motel   movies. **Cards:** AE, DI, DS, MC, VI.   Roll in showers. (symbols) (D)

RESTAURANT
HAYDEN'S   **Lunch:** $8-$10   **Dinner:** $10-$15   **Phone:** 704/867-1598
◆ ◆   **Location:** On US 29N (Franklin Blvd), 0.5 me ne of I-85, exit 21. 3078 E Franklin Blvd 28054. **Hours:** 11
American   am-11 pm, Fri & Sat-midnight, Sun-10 pm. Closed: 11/26 & 12/25. **Features:** children's menu; carryout;
          cocktails. Contemporary interior includes brick walls & unfinished ceiling. Menu includes blackened beef,
fresh seafood, salads & fajitas. **Cards:** AE, DI, DS, MC, VI.   (X)

GERTON—400
LODGING
MOUNTAIN MEADOWS MOTEL   Guaranteed Rates   **Phone:** 704/625-1025
◆   4/1-11/30   1P: $35- 40 2P/1B: $40- 50 2P/2B: $45- 55 XP: $5
Motel   12/1-3/31   1P: $28- 35 2P/1B: $30- 40 2P/2B: $35- 43 XP: $5
          Location: On Hwy 74A, 12.5 mi se of Ashville. 28735 (Rt 1 Box 8). **Terms:** Sr. discount; reserv deposit, 7
day notice; no pets. **Facility:** 9 rooms. Rates for up to 4 persons. Kitchenettes $10 extra charge, 2-night min stay. Reserva-
tions required 11/1-3/31; 1 story; exterior corridors. **All Rooms:** free movies, no A/C. **Cards:** DS, MC, VI.   (CTV) (D)

GLENDALE SPRINGS—200
LODGING
PARK VISTA MOTEL   **Phone:** 910/877-2750
(AAA) (SAVE) 5/8-11/1   2P/1B: $40- 45 2P/2B: $50- 55 XP: $5   F6
          3/27-5/7   2P/1B: $35- 39 2P/2B: $42- 46 XP: $4   F6
◆ ◆   **Location:** 10 mi s on Blue Ridge Pkwy, at milepost 268; at Benge Gap. (1907 Park Vista Rd, WEST
Motor Inn JEFFERSON, 28694). **Terms:** Open 3/27-11/1; weekly rates; no pets. **Facility:** 20 rooms. Serene mountain lo-
          cation. 3 efficiencies, $6 extra charge; 1 story; exterior corridors. **Dining:** Restaurant; 7 am-8 pm; $4-$7.
Recreation: nature trails. **All Rooms:** no phones. **Cards:** MC, VI. **Special Amenities:** Early check-in/late check-out and
preferred room (subject to availability with advanced reservations).   (X) (D)

GOLDSBORO—40,700
LODGINGS
BEST WESTERN GOLDSBORO INN   Rates Subject to Change   **Phone:** 919/735-7911
◆ ◆ ◆   All Year   1P: $46- 48 2P/1B: $51- 54 2P/2B: $54   **Phone:**
Motor Inn **Location:** 2 mi n on US 70E bypass Williams St exit; follow service road. 801 US 70E bypass 27534.
          Fax: 919/735-5030. **Terms:** Sr. discount; pets, $10 extra charge small dogs only. **Facility:** 112 rooms. 2 sto-
ries; exterior corridors. **Dining:** Restaurant; 6 am-9 pm; $8-$12. **All Rooms:** free movies. **Cards:** AE, CB, DI, DS, MC, VI.
                                                          (symbols) (X) (D)

COMFORT INN   Rates Subject to Change   **Phone:** 919/751-1999
◆ ◆ ◆   All Year [CP]   1P: $62- 65 2P/1B: $68- 73 2P/2B: $68- 73 XP: $6   F18
Motel   **Location:** Just n on Spence Ave exit from US 70E (Bypass). 909 N Spence Ave 27534. Fax: 919/751-1506.
          Terms: Reserv deposit; no pets. **Facility:** 122 rooms. 5 stories; interior corridors. **All Rooms:** free & pay
movies. **Cards:** AE, CB, DI, DS, MC, VI.   (symbols) (D) (S)

DAYS INN   Rates Subject to Change   **Phone:** 919/734-9471
◆ ◆   All Year   1P: $42- 46 2P/1B: $49   2P/2B: $46- 50 XP: $4   F17
Motor Inn **Location:** 2.3 mi n on US 70 bypass, Wayne Memorial Dr exit. 2000 Wayne Memorial Dr 27534.
          Fax: 919/736-2623. **Terms:** Sr. discount; pets, $5 extra charge. **Facility:** 120 rooms. 2 stories; exterior corri-
dors. **Dining:** Restaurant; Fri & Sat 24 hours, Mon-Thurs 6 am-9 pm, Sun-4 pm; $4-$8. **All Rooms:** free movies.
Cards: AE, CB, DI, DS, MC, VI.   (symbols) (X) (D)

HAMPTON INN   Rates Subject to Change   **Phone:** 919/778-1800
◆ ◆ ◆   All Year [CP]   1P: $57- 61 2P/1B: $63   2P/2B: $67
Motel   **Location:** Just n on Spence Ave exit from US 70E (bypass), Spence Ave exit. 905 N Spence Ave 27534.
          Fax: 919/778-5891. **Terms:** Sr. discount; no pets. **Facility:** 111 rooms. 4 stories; interior corridors.
All Rooms: free & pay movies. **Cards:** AE, CB, DI, DS, MC, VI.   Roll in showers. (symbols) (D) (S)

QUALITY INN & SUITES   Guaranteed Rates   **Phone:** 919/735-7901
◆ ◆   All Year [CP]   1P: $59   2P/1B: $66   2P/2B: $66   XP: $8   F18
Motor Inn **Location:** On service road, Williams St exit off US 70E. US Hwy 70 E Bypass 27533. Fax: 919/734-2946.
          Terms: Sr. discount; pets, $25 extra charge. **Facility:** 108 rooms. 2 stories; exterior corridors.
Dining: Restaurant; 6:30 am-9 & 6-9 pm; $8-$12. **All Rooms:** free movies. **Cards:** AE, CB, DI, JCB, MC, VI.
                                                          (symbols) (X) (D)

RESTAURANTS
MIMMO'S ITALIAN RESTAURANT   **Dinner:** $7-$11   **Phone:** 919/734-2228
◆ ◆   **Location:** 3.8 mi n on US 70E (bypass), 1.5 mi s on Spence Ave, 0.3 mi w on E Ash St. 2215 E Ash St
Italian   27530. **Hours:** 5 pm-10 pm, Fri & Sat-11 pm. **Features:** children's menu; carryout; cocktails. **Cards:** AE, DS,
          MC, VI.   (X)

WILBER'S BARBECUE   **Lunch:** $4-$5   **Dinner:** $4-$5   **Phone:** 919/778-5218
◆   **Location:** 4 mi e on US 70 bypass. 4172 US 70E 27534. **Hours:** 6 am-9 pm. Closed: 11/26 & 12/25.
Regional   **Features:** children's menu; carryout. Family oriented & popular. Pepper & vinegar based barbecue. Pork,
American   sandwiches, fried chicken & Brunswick stew. Knotty pine paneled dining rooms.

GREENSBORO—183,500

Airport Accommodations

Listings for these establishments are found under the heading for the city in which they are located.

Piedmont Triad International

Airport Marriott Hotel, 0.5 mi w on Marriott Dr/GREENSBORO
Embassy Suites, 2.5 mi s on SR 68/GREENSBORO
Homewood Suites, 2.5 mi s on SR 68/GREENSBORO

LODGINGS

AIRPORT MARRIOTT HOTEL ◆◆◆ Hotel
Rates Subject to Change   **Phone: 910/852-6450**
Sun-Thurs [EP]   1P: $114- 134   2P/1B: $114- 134   2P/2B: $114- 134
Fri & Sat [BP]   1P: $59- 89   2P/1B: $59- 89   2P/2B: $59- 89
Location: Exit 210, I-40, 2 mi n on Hwy 68, then 1.5 mi e. Marriott Dr, at Triad Int 27409.
Fax: 910/665-6522. **Terms:** No pets. **Facility:** 299 rooms. 5 stories; interior corridors. **Dining:** Dining room; 6 am-10 pm; $8-$22. **All Rooms:** free & pay movies. **Cards:** AE, CB, DI, DS, JCB, MC, VI.
Roll in showers.

AMERISUITES GREENSBORO/WENDOVER ⊕ ⃝SAVE ◆◆◆ Motel
Phone: 910/852-1443
All Year [CP]   1P: $69- 175   2P/1B: $79- 175   2P/2B: $79- 175   XP: $5   F16
Location: 0.3 me s on Wendover from I-40, exit 214. 1619 Stanley Rd 27403. Fax: 910/854-9339.
Terms: Weekly/monthly rates; no pets. **Facility:** 126 rooms. 6 stories; interior corridors. **Dining:** Restaurant nearby. **Services:** area transportation, within 10 mi. Fee: coin laundry. **All Rooms:** coffeemakers, microwaves, free movies, refrigerators. **Cards:** AE, CB, DI, DS, JCB, MC, VI. **Special Amenities:** Free breakfast and free local telephone calls. *(See color ad p 10)*
Roll in showers.

BATTLEGROUND INN ⊕ ⃝SAVE ◆◆◆ Motel
Phone: 910/272-4737
All Year [CP]   1P: $49- 65   2P/1B: $49- 70   2P/2B: $52
Location: 2.3 mi n on US 220 or Wendover exit off I-40, 3 mi to Westover Terr exit, 0.3 mi n. 1517 Westover Terr 27408. Fax: 910/274-6242. **Terms:** No pets. **Facility:** 48 rooms. Near shopping areas. 4 stories; interior corridors. **Dining:** Restaurant nearby. **All Rooms:** free movies. **Some Rooms:** microwaves, refrigerators. Fee: whirlpools. **Cards:** AE, CB, DI, DS, MC, VI.

BEST INNS OF AMERICA ⊕ ⃝SAVE ◆◆ Motel
Phone: 910/668-9400
All Year [CP]   1P: $42- 75   2P/1B: $49- 75   2P/2B: $59- 80   XP: $7   F17
Location: At jct I-40 & Old SR 68; I-40 exit 210. 6452 Burnt Poplar Rd 27409. Fax: 910/668-9331.
Terms: BP avail; no pets. **Facility:** 106 rooms. Average size modern rooms. 2 stories; exterior corridors.
Dining: Restaurant nearby. **Services:** Fee: coin laundry. **All Rooms:** free movies.
Some Rooms: coffeemakers. Fee: microwaves, refrigerators. **Cards:** AE, CB, DI, DS, MC, VI.
Special Amenities: Free breakfast and free local telephone calls.

BILTMORE GREENSBORO HOTEL ◆◆ Hotel
Rates Subject to Change   **Phone: 910/272-3474**
All Year [CP]   1P: $75- 110   2P/1B: $75- 110   2P/2B: $75- 110
Location: Town center. 111 W Washington St 27401. Fax: 910/275-2523. **Terms:** Sr. discount; no pets.
Facility: 25 rooms. 3 stories; interior corridors. Fee: parking. **All Rooms:** free movies. **Cards:** AE, DI, DS, MC, VI.

COMFORT INN ⊕ ⃝SAVE ◆◆◆ Motel
Phone: 910/294-6220
All Year [CP]   1P: $57   2P/1B: $65   2P/2B: $62   XP: $5   F12
Location: 0.3 mi s of I-40; on High Point Rd, exit 217 via Veasley St. 2001 Veasley St 27407.
Fax: 910/294-6220. **Terms:** No pets. **Facility:** 123 rooms. Spacious rooms near major mall. 2 stories; interior corridors. **Dining:** Restaurant nearby. **All Rooms:** free movies. **Some Rooms:** coffeemakers. **Cards:** AE, CB, DI, DS, MC, VI. **Special Amenities: Free breakfast and free local telephone calls.**

COURTYARD BY MARRIOTT-GREENSBORO ◆◆◆ Motel
Rates Subject to Change   **Phone: 910/294-3800**
Sun-Thurs   1P: $85- 89   2P/1B: $85- 89   2P/2B: $85- 89
Fri & Sat   1P: $69- 74   2P/1B: $69- 74   2P/2B: $64
Location: Just s off I-40, exit 214 (Wendover). 4400 W Wendover 27407. Fax: 910/294-9982.
Terms: Check-in 4 pm; no pets. **Facility:** 149 rooms. 3 stories; interior corridors. **Dining:** Dining room; 6:30-10 am, Sat & Sun 7-11 am. **All Rooms:** free & pay movies. **Cards:** AE, CB, DI, DS, MC, VI. *(See color ad below)*

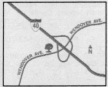

DAYS INN

Phone: 910/275-9571

AAA SAVE

◆◆
Motel

All Year [CP]   1P: $42- 48   2P/1B: $48- 54   2P/2B: $48- 58   XP: $6   F12
Location: Exit 125 off I-85 & 40 (S Elm St exit), just s & just e via Seneca Rd. 120 Seneca Rd 27406.
Fax: 910/275-9572. **Terms:** No pets. **Facility:** 122 rooms. Convenient access to interstate. 2 stories;
interior/exterior corridors; wading pool; playground. **Dining:** Restaurant nearby. **All Rooms:** free movies.
Cards: AE, CB, DI, DS, MC, VI.

DAYS INN-FOUR SEASONS

Rates Subject to Change   **Phone: 910/297-1996**

AAA

◆◆◆
Motel

All Year [CP]   1P: $52- 62   2P/1B: $58- 68   2P/2B: $58- 68   XP: $6   F12
Location: Just s on High Point Rd & just w on Veasley to Isler from I-40, exit 217. 3304 Isler St 27407.
Fax: 910/297-1136. **Terms:** No pets. **Facility:** 52 rooms. 2 stories; exterior corridors. **All Rooms:** free
movies. **Cards:** AE, DI, DS, JCB, MC, VI.   Roll in showers.

EMBASSY SUITES

Rates Subject to Change   **Phone: 910/668-4535**

◆◆◆
Suite Hotel

Sun-Thurs [BP]   1P: $139   2P/1B: $139   2P/2B: $139   XP: $10   F16
Fri & Sat [BP]   1P: $99   2P/1B: $99   2P/2B: $99   XP: $10   F16
Location: 12 mi w, at jct I-40 & airport exit 210, just n with entry on Centreport Dr. 204 Centreport Dr 27409.
Fax: 910/668-3901. **Terms:** No pets. **Facility:** 221 rooms. 7 stories; interior corridors. **Dining:** Dining room; 11 am-10 pm;
$7-$19. **All Rooms:** free & pay movies. **Cards:** AE, CB, DI, DS, JCB, MC, VI.

Roll in showers.

FAIRFIELD INN BY MARRIOTT

Rates Subject to Change   **Phone: 910/294-9922**

◆◆◆
Motel

All Year [CP]   1P: $48   2P/1B: $54   2P/2B: $54   XP: $3   F18
Location: Exit 217 off I-40, entry via Veasley St off High Point Rd. 2003 Athena Ct 27407.
Fax: 910/294-9922. **Terms:** No pets. **Facility:** 135 rooms. 3 stories; interior/exterior corridors.
All Rooms: free movies. **Cards:** AE, CB, DI, DS, MC, VI. *(See color ad p 371)*

GREENWOOD BED & BREAKFAST

Rates Subject to Change   **Phone: 910/274-6350**

◆◆
Historic Bed
& Breakfast

4/1-4/30 & 10/1-10/31 [BP]   1P: $85- 100   2P/1B: $95- 110   2P/2B: $95- 110   XP: $25   D16
12/1-3/31, 5/1-9/30 &
11/1-11/30 [BP]   1P: $75- 95   2P/1B: $90- 100   2P/2B: $90- 100   XP: $25   D16
Location: From town center, Market St, 0.8 mi n on N Elm to N Park. 205 N Park Dr 27401.
Fax: 910/274-9943. **Terms:** Age restrictions may apply; check-in 4 pm; reserv deposit, handling fee imposed; no pets.
Facility: 5 rooms. 2 stories; interior corridors; smoke free premises. **Cards:** AE, DS, MC, VI.

HAMPTON INN-AIRPORT

Rates Subject to Change   **Phone: 910/605-5500**

◆◆◆
Motel

All Year   1P: $69- 74   2P/1B: $79- 87   2P/2B: $79- 84
Terms: Sr. discount; no pets. **Facility:** 127 rooms. 5 stories; interior corridors. **All Rooms:** free movies.
Cards: AE, CB, DI, DS, MC, VI.   Roll in showers.

HAMPTON INN-FOUR SEASONS

Rates Subject to Change   **Phone: 910/854-8600**

◆◆◆
Motel

All Year [CP]   1P: $61- 69   2P/1B: $70- 78   2P/2B: $74
Location: I-40 exit 217. 2004 Veasley St 27407. **Fax:** 910/854-8741. **Terms:** No pets. **Facility:** 121 rooms. 2
stories; exterior corridors. **All Rooms:** free & pay movies. **Cards:** AE, CB, DI, DS, JCB, MC, VI.

HOLIDAY INN EXPRESS

Phone: 910/697-4000

AAA SAVE

◆◆◆
Motel

free breakfast.

All Year [CP]   1P: $40- 65   2P/1B: $45- 75   2P/2B: $45- 95   XP: $10   F18
Location: I-40/I-85, exit 128 (Lee St). 3114 Cedar Park Rd 27405. **Fax:** 910/697-0102. **Terms:** No pets.
Facility: 140 rooms. Beautifully decorated guest rooms. 2 stories; exterior corridors. Fee: 12 rooms with
steambath. **Services:** valet laundry. **All Rooms:** coffeemakers, free movies. **Some Rooms:** microwaves,
refrigerators. **Cards:** AE, CB, DI, DS, JCB, MC, VI. **Special Amenities:** Early check-in/late check-out and

HOMEWOOD SUITES

Rates Subject to Change   **Phone: 910/393-0088**

◆◆◆
Suite Motel

Sun-Thurs [CP]   1P: $119   2P/1B: $119   2P/2B: $119
Fri & Sat [CP]   1P: $89   2P/1B: $89   2P/2B: $89
Location: Exit 210 I-40, just n on SR 68 to Triad Center Dr with entry on Centreport Dr. 201 Centreport Dr
27409. **Fax:** 910/393-0070. **Terms:** Age restrictions may apply; no pets. **Facility:** 104 rooms. 3 stories; interior corridors.
All Rooms: kitchens, free & pay movies. **Cards:** AE, CB, DI, DS, MC, VI.

Roll in showers.

INNKEEPER MOTOR LODGE

Rates Subject to Change   **Phone: 910/854-0090**

◆◆
Motel

All Year [CP]   1P: $54- 90   2P/1B: $54- 90   2P/2B: $62- 90   XP: $5   F18
Location: Wendover exit 214 off I-40. 4305 Big Tree Way 27409. **Fax:** 910/854-4516. **Terms:** Sr. discount;
no pets. **Facility:** 123 rooms. 4 stories; interior corridors. **All Rooms:** free movies. **Cards:** AE, CB, DI, DS,
MC, VI.

JOURNEY'S END MOTEL

Rates Subject to Change   **Phone: 910/288-5611**

AAA

◆◆
Motel

All Year   1P: $40- 60   2P/1B: $40- 60   2P/2B: $50- 75   XP: $5-10   F18
Location: 3.3 mi n, on US 220. 2310 Battleground Ave 27408. **Terms:** Sr. discount; no pets. **Facility:** 36
rooms. 2 stories; exterior corridors. **All Rooms:** free movies. **Some Rooms:** 3 efficiencies. **Cards:** AE, MC,
VI.

MICROTEL INN

Rates Subject to Change   **Phone: 910/547-7007**

AAA

◆◆
Motel

All Year   1P: $45- 49   2P/1B: $48- 52   2P/2B: $54- 60   XP: $5   F18
Location: Just n off I-40, exit 214. 4304 Big Tree Way 27409. **Fax:** 910/547-0450. **Terms:** Sr. discount; no
pets. **Facility:** 122 rooms. 3 stories; interior corridors. **All Rooms:** free movies. **Cards:** AE, CB, DI, DS, JCB,
MC, VI.   Roll in showers.

RAMADA INN-AIRPORT

Rates Subject to Change   **Phone: 910/668-3900**

◆◆◆
Motor Inn

All Year [BP]   1P: $54- 83   2P/1B: $56- 85   2P/2B: $56- 85   XP: $4   F12
Location: 12 mi w at jct I-40 & SR 68, airport exit 210. 7067 Albert Pick Rd 27409. **Fax:** 910/668-7012. **Terms:** No
pets. **Facility:** 170 rooms. 2 stories; interior corridors. **Dining:** Dining room; 7 am-2:30 & 5-10 pm; $9-$17.
All Rooms: free & pay movies. **Cards:** AE, CB, DI, DS, MC, VI.

RED ROOF INN-COLISEUM | Rates Subject to Change | | | Phone: 910/852-6560
◆◆   4/1-11/30 | 1P: $48 | 2P/1B: $55 | 2P/2B: $62 | XP: $7 | F18
Motel   12/1-3/31 | 1P: $43 | 2P/1B: $50 | 2P/2B: $57 | XP: $7 | F18
Location: I-40, High Point Rd exit 217B. 2101 W Meadowview Rd 27403. Fax: 910/852-6673. **Terms:** Small pets only. **Facility:** 108 rooms. 2 stories; exterior corridors. **All Rooms:** free movies. **Cards:** AE, CB, DI, DS, MC, VI.

🛏 📶 ⊠ 🐾 Ⓓ

RED ROOF INN GREENSBORO-AIRPORT | Rates Subject to Change | | | Phone: 910/271-2636
◆◆   7/1-9/30 | 1P: $41- 82 | 2P/1B: $48- 82 | 2P/2B: $53- 82 | XP: $8 | F18
Motel   4/1-6/30 | 1P: $39- 82 | 2P/1B: $46- 82 | 2P/2B: $50- 82 | XP: $8 | F18
    12/1-3/31 | 1P: $36- 61 | 2P/1B: $44- 61 | 2P/2B: $48- 61 | XP: $8 | F18
    10/1-11/30 | 1P: $36- 43 | 2P/1B: $44- 49 | 2P/2B: $49- 53 | XP: $8 | F18
Location: I-40 exit 210, at jct SR 68 via service road. 615 Regional Rd S 27409. Fax: 910/884-8053. **Terms:** Small pets only. **Facility:** 112 rooms. 2 stories; exterior corridors. **All Rooms:** free movies. **Cards:** AE, CB, DI, DS, MC, VI.

🛏 📶 ⊠ 🐾 Ⓓ

RESIDENCE INN BY MARRIOTT | Rates Subject to Change | | Phone: 910/294-8600
◆◆◆   All Year [CP] | 1P: $96 | 2P/1B: $99 | 2P/2B: $124
Apartment   **Location:** Exit 217, off I-40; just s then just w. 2000 Veasley St 27407. Fax: 910/294-2201. **Terms:** Reserv
Motel   deposit; pets, $100 fee, $5 extra charge. **Facility:** 128 rooms. 2 stories; exterior corridors. **All Rooms:** kitchens, free movies. **Cards:** AE, CB, DI, DS, JCB, MC, VI.   🛏 🛋 CTV ⊠ 🐾 Ⓓ

SHONEY'S INN | | | Phone: 910/297-1055
ⒶⒶ SAVE   All Year [CP] | 1P: $66- 82 | 2P/1B: $72- 88 | 2P/2B: $66- 82 | XP: $6 | F18
Location: Just s on Wendover from I-40, exit 214. 1103 Lanada Dr 27407. Fax: 910/297-1904. **Facility:** 115
◆◆◆   rooms. Very attactive & handsomely appointed public areas. 5 stories; interior corridors. **Dining:** Restaurant
Motel   nearby. **Services:** Fee: coin laundry. **All Rooms:** free movies. **Some Rooms:** coffeemakers, microwaves, radios, refrigerators. **Cards:** AE, CB, DI, DS, MC, VI. **Special Amenities:** Free breakfast and free local
telephone calls.   Roll in showers. 🛋 🍴 ♿ ⊠ 🐾 Ⓓ Ⓢ

RESTAURANTS

ANTON'S RESTAURANT | **Lunch:** $7-$9 | **Dinner:** $8-$13 | Phone: 910/273-1386
◆◆   **Location:** 1.3 mi nw on Battleground Ave, just n of Wendover Ave. 1628 Battleground Ave 27408. **Hours:** 11
Italian   am-10 pm, Fri-10:30 pm, Sat 4:30 pm-10:30 pm. Closed major holidays & Sun. **Features:** children's menu; carryout; cocktails. Chicken, beef & fresh seafood. Loyal local following, serving Greensboro since 1960.
Also American dishes. **Cards:** AE, MC, VI.   ⊠

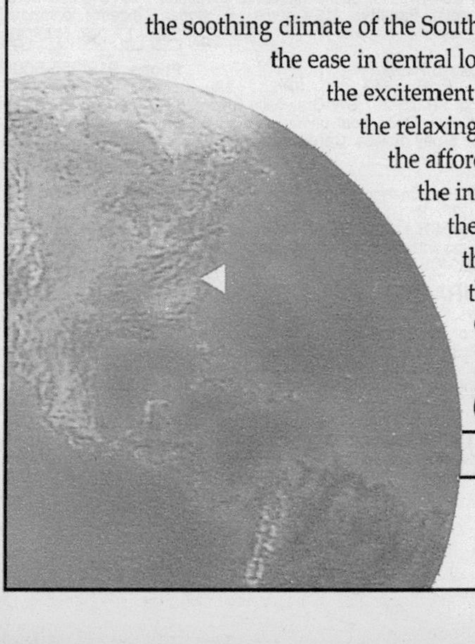

GATE CITY CHOP HOUSE | **Lunch:** $7-$10 | **Dinner:** $15-$29 | Phone: 910/294-9977
◆◆◆   **Location:** 1.8 mi ne of I-40, exit 214B to Holden Rd exit & 0.3 mi n. 106 S Holden Rd 27407. **Hours:** 11:30
American   am-10 pm, Fri & Sat-10:30 pm. Closed: Sun, 11/26 & 12/25. **Reservations:** suggested. **Features:** children's
MC, VI   menu; carryout; salad bar; cocktails. Certified Angus beef; upscale appetizer selections. **Cards:** AE, DI, DS, ♿ ⊠

KYOTO JAPANESE STEAKHOUSE   **Dinner:** $11-$17   **Phone:** 919/299-1003
◆◆   **Location:** Coliseum exit off I-40 & I-85; at jct of Holden Rd & Patterson St. 1200 S Holden Rd 27407.
Ethnic   **Hours:** 5 pm-10 pm, Fri & Sat-11 pm. Closed: 11/26, 12/24 & 12/25. **Reservations:** suggested; weekends.
Features: children's menu; cocktails & lounge. Hibachi steak, chicken, shrimp & vegetables prepared with flair at tables, communal seating in tasteful Japanese ambience. Sushi bar open Tue-Sun. **Cards:** AE, CB, DI, MC, VI. (X)

LA SPIEDO DI NOBLE   **Dinner:** $17-$20   **Phone:** 910/333-9833
◆◆◆   **Location:** 0.3 mi e on Battleground Ave from US 222N (Wendover Ave); in Irving Park Plaza. 1720
Italian   Battleground Ave 27408. **Hours:** 5:30 pm-10 pm, Fri & Sat-11 pm. Closed: Sun & Mon.
Reservations: suggested. **Features:** carryout; cocktails; entertainment; a la carte. Wood-burning oven, grill & rotisserie, northern Italian decor & entrees. Extensive wine list. Attentive service & homemade bread, soup & dessert. **Cards:** AE, DI, MC, VI.

LIBERTY OAK WINE & CHEESE   **Lunch:** $7-$9   **Dinner:** $9-$14   **Phone:** 910/273-7057
◆   **Location:** 2.5 mi nw on Battleground, just n of Wendover Ave; in Irving Park Plaza. 1722 Battleground
American   27408. **Hours:** 11:30 am-2:30 & 5:30-9:30 pm, Fri & Sat-10 pm. Closed major holidays & Sun.
Features: carryout; beer & wine only. Small neighborhood cafe & deli offering salads, croissants, pasta & entrees from fresh ingredients in a specialty foods shop. Menu changes daily. **Cards:** MC, VI. (X)

LUCKY 32   **Lunch:** $6-$9   **Dinner:** $8-$16   **Phone:** 910/370-0707
◆◆◆   **Location:** Just n of Wendover Ave & Westover Terr. 1421 Westover Terr 27408. **Hours:** 11:15 am-10:30 pm,
American   Fri & Sat-11 pm, Sun 10:45 am-10 pm; Sat & Sun brunch 11:15 am-3 pm. Closed: 11/26 & 12/25.
Reservations: suggested. **Features:** carryout; cocktails & lounge. Casually, elegant atmosphere. Imaginative entrees, gourmet pizza & home cooking capably served in large, high tech dining rooms. **Cards:** AE, DI, MC, VI. (X)

THE MADISON PARK RESTAURANT   **Dinner:** $23-$29   **Phone:** 910/294-6505
ⓐⓐⓐ   **Location:** Wendover E exit off I-40, 2 blks to Meadowood, then w 1 mi, go over Market St, then 1 mi on
         Dolley Madison Rd. 616 Dolley Madison Rd 27410. **Hours:** 6 pm-10 pm. Closed major holidays & Sun.
◆◆◆   **Reservations:** suggested. **Features:** cocktails. Also Northern Italian dishes served in wood paneled,
Provincial   comfortable dining room by professional & attentive staff. Extensive wine list. **Cards:** AE, DS, MC, VI. (X)
French

GREENVILLE—45,000

LODGINGS

DAYS INN   **Phone:** 919/752-0214
ⓐⓐⓐ [SAVE]   All Year [CP]   1P: $38- 39   2P/1B: $38- 39   2P/2B: $46   XP: $5   F12
         Location: 1.8 mi n on US 13 & SR 11 from jct US 264. 810 S Memorial Dr 27834. Fax: 919/752-4565.
◆◆   **Terms:** No pets. **Facility:** 47 rooms. All rooms with iron, ironing board & fax line. 2 stories; exterior corridors;
Motel   small pool. **Dining:** Restaurant nearby. **Services:** Fee: coin laundry. **All Rooms:** free movies, refrigerators.
         Cards: AE, CB, DI, DS, MC, VI. **Special Amenities:** Free breakfast.   (⊕) (CTV) (X) (D)

EAST CAROLINA INN   **Phone:** 919/752-2122
ⓐⓐⓐ [SAVE]   All Year [CP]   1P: $38- 43   2P/1B: $43   2P/2B: $41- 46
         Location: On US 264; 0.3 mi w of jct SR 11 & 13 (Memorial Dr). 2095 Stantonsburg Rd 27834.
◆◆◆   Fax: 919/752-2122. **Terms:** Weekly rates; no pets. **Facility:** 53 rooms. Tastefully appointed lobby & guest
Motel   rooms. Opposite medical center. 2 stories; exterior corridors. **Dining:** Restaurant nearby. **All Rooms:** free
         movies. **Some Rooms:** coffeemakers, 10 efficiencies, microwaves. Fee: refrigerators, whirlpools. **Cards:** AE,
CB, DI, DS, MC, VI.   (⊕) (CTV) (X) (D)

FAIRFIELD INN BY MARRIOTT   Rates Subject to Change   **Phone:** 919/758-5544
◆◆◆   All Year [CP]   1P: $43- 49   2P/1B: $49- 55   2P/2B: $49   XP: $4   F18
Motel   **Location:** On Hwys 11 & 13, just s of jct US 264 bypass. 821 S Memorial Dr 27834. Fax: 919/758-1416.
         Terms: Sr. discount; reserv deposit; no pets. **Facility:** 115 rooms. 2 stories; exterior corridors.
All Rooms: free movies. **Cards:** AE, CB, DI, DS, MC, VI.   (⊕) (⊕) (⅋) (X) (⌁) (D)

GREENVILLE HILTON INN   Guaranteed Rates   **Phone:** 919/355-5000
◆◆◆   All Year   1P: $89   2P/1B: $94   2P/2B: $99   XP: $10   F
Hotel   **Location:** On US 264 Alt & SR 43; 1 mi e of jct SR 11. 207 SW Greenville Blvd 27834. Fax: 919/355-5099.
         Terms: Sr. discount; no pets. **Facility:** 141 rooms. Daily local phone charge; 6 stories; interior corridors.
Dining: Restaurant; 6:30 am-10 pm; $14-$19. **All Rooms:** free & pay movies. **Cards:** AE, CB, DI, DS, MC, VI.
(See color ad p 18)   (⊕) (⊕) (CTV) (X) (⌁) (D) (S)

RAMADA PLAZA HOTEL   Rates Subject to Change   **Phone:** 919/355-8300
◆◆◆   All Year   1P: $79   2P/1B: $89   2P/2B: $89   XP: $6   F18
Motor Inn   **Location:** On US 264 Alt & SR 43; 1 mi e of jct SR 11. 203 W Greenville Blvd 27834. Fax: 919/355-3553.
         Terms: No pets. **Facility:** 192 rooms. 4 stories; interior corridors. **Dining:** Dining room; 6:30 am-10 pm;
$9-$18. **All Rooms:** free & pay movies. **Cards:** AE, CB, DI, DS, JCB, MC, VI.   (⊕) (CTV) (X) (⌁) (D) (S)

RESTAURANTS

CHICO'S MEXICAN RESTAURANT   **Lunch:** $5-$7   **Dinner:** $6-$11   **Phone:** 919/757-1666
◆◆   **Location:** Downtown; across from ECU at jct of 5th St & Cotanche St. 521 Cotanche St 27835. **Hours:** 11
Mexican   am-10 pm, Fri & Sat-11 pm. Closed major holidays. **Reservations:** suggested; weekends.
         Features: children's menu; carryout; cocktails & lounge. Popular East Carolina University dining spot, tastefuly decorated dining rooms. Good variety of Mexican dishes, delicious chicken soup. **Cards:** AE, DS, MC, VI. (X)

RAGAZZI'S-AN ITALIAN PLACE   **Lunch:** $6-$8   **Dinner:** $9-$13   **Phone:** 919/321-1976
◆◆   **Location:** On US 264A, 1 mi e from jct SR 11 & US 264A. 109 E Greenville Blvd 27834. **Hours:** 11 am-10
Italian   pm, Sat-11 pm. Closed: 11/26 & 12/25. **Features:** children's menu; carryout; cocktails. Fresh homemade
sauces, soup, dessert & bread. Wood burning oven for pizza & calzone. Charming Italian ambience.
Cards: AE, MC, VI.   (X)

HATTERAS—*See Outer Banks p. 397.*

HAVELOCK—20,300

LODGINGS

COMFORT INN — Rates Subject to Change — **Phone: 919/444-8444**
◆◆
Motel
3/31-9/30 [CP] — 1P: $60 — 2P/1B: $65 — 2P/2B: $65 — XP: $5 — F18
12/1-3/30 & 10/1-11/30 [CP] — 1P: $50 — 2P/1B: $55 — 2P/2B: $55 — XP: $5 — F18
Location: 1 mi e on US 70. 1013 E Main St 28532. Fax: 919/444-5546. **Terms:** No pets. **Facility:** 58 rooms. Interior corridors. **All Rooms:** free movies. **Cards:** AE, DI, DS, MC, VI. — Roll in showers. (CTV) (&) (X) (D)

HOLIDAY INN — Rates Subject to Change — **Phone: 919/444-1111**
◆◆◆
Motor Inn
All Year — 1P: $54 — 2P/1B: $56- 58 — 2P/2B: $60 — XP: $6 — F18
Location: 1.8 mi w on US 70. 400 Hwy 70 W 28532 (PO Box 870). Fax: 919/444-1510. **Terms:** Sr. discount; no pets. **Facility:** 104 rooms.; interior corridors. **Dining:** Dining room; 6 am-10:30 & 5:30-10 pm; $7-$12. **All Rooms:** free movies. **Cards:** AE, CB, DI, DS, MC, VI. (☎) (CTV) (X) (D)

HENDERSON—15,700

LODGINGS

BUDGET HOST INN — **Phone: 919/492-2013**
(AAA) (SAVE)
◆◆
Motel
All Year — 1P: $34- 37 — 2P/1B: $36- 40 — 2P/2B: $44- 50 — XP: $4 — F12
Location: I-85 at US 1 & 158E, exit 215. 1727 N Garnett St 27536. Fax: 919/492-7908. **Terms:** No pets. **Facility:** 26 rooms. 2 stories; exterior corridors. **All Rooms:** free movies. **Cards:** AE, CB, DI, DS, MC, VI. *(See color ad p 312)* (CTV) (X) (D)

HOWARD JOHNSON LODGE — **Phone: 919/492-7001**
(AAA) (SAVE)
◆◆
Motor Inn
All Year — 1P: $49- 60 — 2P/1B: $60- 65 — 2P/2B: $54- 64 — XP: $6 — F17
Location: Jct I-85 & Parham Rd, exit 215. 27536 (PO Drawer F). Fax: 919/438-2389. **Terms:** Small pets only. **Facility:** 98 rooms. All rooms with balcony or patio. 2 stories; interior corridors. **Dining:** Restaurant; 6 am-10 pm; $7-$12; wine/beer only. **All Rooms:** free movies. **Some Rooms:** microwaves, refrigerators. **Cards:** AE, CB, DI, DS, MC, VI. **Special Amenities: Free breakfast and free local telephone calls.** (🛏) (☎) (🍽) (CTV) (X) (D)

HENDERSONVILLE—7,300

LODGINGS

APPLE INN BED & BREAKFAST — Guaranteed Rates — **Phone: 704/693-0107**
◆◆◆
Bed &
Breakfast
All Year [BP] — 1P: $79- 89 — 2P/1B: $79- 89 — 2P/2B: $89 — XP: $10
Location: I-26 exit 18B, 4 mi w on US 64, just s on Daniel to White Pine Dr, just w. 1005 White Pine Dr 28739. **Terms:** Age restrictions may apply; reserv deposit, 3 day notice; no pets. **Facility:** 5 rooms. Cottage, $450 weekly; 2 stories; interior corridors; designated smoking area. **Cards:** MC, VI. (X) (D)

BRIARWOOD MOTEL — Rates Subject to Change — **Phone: 704/692-8284**
(AAA)
◆◆
Motel
6/1-10/31 [CP] — 2P/1B: $45- 55 — 2P/2B: $45- 55 — XP: $5 — F18
12/1-5/31 & 11/1-11/30 [CP] — 2P/1B: $30- 35 — 2P/2B: $30- 35 — XP: $5 — F18
Location: 2 mi s on US 25. 1510 Greenville Hwy 28792. **Terms:** Sr. discount; no pets. **Facility:** 20 rooms. 1 story; exterior corridors. **Some Rooms:** 3 kitchens. **Cards:** AE, DS, MC, VI. (☎) (CTV) (X) (D)

CLADDAGH INN — Rates Subject to Change — **Phone: 704/697-7778**
◆◆
Historic Bed
& Breakfast
12/1-12/31 & 5/21-11/30 [BP] — 1P: $75- 99 — 2P/1B: $85- 109 — 2P/2B: $89 — XP: $10 — F6
1/1-5/20 [BP] — 1P: $69- 85 — 2P/1B: $79- 99 — 2P/2B: $79 — XP: $10 — F6
Location: Exit 18B, 2 mi w on US 64 W, just n. 755 N Main St 28792. Fax: 704/697-8664. **Terms:** No pets. **Facility:** 14 rooms. 3 stories, no elevator; interior corridors; smoke free premises. **Cards:** AE, DI, DS, MC, VI. (X) (D)

COMFORT INN — **Phone: 704/693-8800**
(AAA) (SAVE)
◆◆◆
Motel
4/1-10/31 [CP] — 1P: $56- 84 — 2P/1B: $60- 95 — 2P/2B: $60- 95 — XP: $10 — F18
12/1-3/31 & 11/1-11/30 [CP] — 1P: $44 — 2P/1B: $50 — 2P/2B: $50 — XP: $10 — F18
Location: I-26 exit 18 B, just w. 206 Mitchell Dr 28792. Fax: 704/693-8800. **Terms:** Small pets only. **Facility:** 85 rooms. Light, tasteful decor & furnishings. 2 stories; exterior corridors; small heated pool. **Dining:** Restaurant nearby. **Services:** valet laundry. **All Rooms:** coffeemakers, free movies, VCP's. **Some Rooms:** microwaves, refrigerators. Fee: whirlpools. **Cards:** AE, CB, DI, DS, MC, VI. **Special Amenities: Free local telephone calls and free newspaper.** (🛏) (🍽) (CTV) (X) (D)

DAYS INN — **Phone: 704/697-5999**
(AAA) (SAVE)
◆◆
Motel
6/1-10/31 [CP] — 1P: $50- 89 — 2P/1B: $56- 95 — 2P/2B: $55- 95 — XP: $5 — F18
12/1-5/31 & 11/1-11/30 [CP] — 1P: $35- 55 — 2P/1B: $35- 55 — 2P/2B: $39- 59 — XP: $5 — F18
Location: I-26 exit 18B, just w. 102 Mitchell Dr 28792. Fax: 704/697-5999. **Terms:** No pets. **Facility:** 46 rooms. 2 stories; exterior corridors. **Dining:** Restaurant nearby. **All Rooms:** free movies. **Cards:** AE, CB, DS, JCB, MC, VI. (🍽) (CTV) (X) (D)

ECHO MOUNTAIN INN — Rates Subject to Change — **Phone: 704/693-9626**
◆◆
Historic
Country Inn
5/1-9/4 & 10/1-10/31 [CP] — 1P: $65- 135 — 2P/1B: $65- 135 — 2P/2B: $55- 160 — XP: $10 — F12
12/1-4/30, 9/5-9/30 & 11/1-11/30 [CP] — 1P: $55- 115 — 2P/1B: $55- 115 — 2P/2B: $55- 120 — XP: $10 — F12
Location: Exit 18B off I-26, Hwy 64W to US 25S, just s to 5th Ave W, 3 mi w on 5th Ave (Laurel Park Hwy). 2849 Laurel Park Hwy 28739. Fax: 704/697-2047. **Terms:** Sr. discount; no pets. **Facility:** 36 rooms. 2 stories; interior/exterior corridors; designated smoking area. **Dining:** Restaurant; 11:30 am-2 & 5-9 pm; Sun Brunch 11 am-2:30 pm; closed Mon; $15-$24. **Some Rooms:** A/C, 9 efficiencies. **Cards:** AE, MC, VI. (☎) (CTV) (X) (D)

HAMPTON INN
◆◆◆
Motel

Rates Subject to Change

Phone: 704/697-2333

		1P:		2P/1B:		2P/2B:	
Fri & Sat 7/1-8/31 & 10/1-10/31 [CP]		1P: $84-	92	2P/1B: $84-	92	2P/2B: $84-	92
6/1-6/30, Sun-Thurs 7/1-8/31, 9/1-9/30 & Sun-Thurs 10/1-10/31 [CP]		1P: $58-	69	2P/1B: $68-	79	2P/2B: $72	
4/1-5/31 [CP]		1P: $47-	60	2P/1B: $57-	70	2P/2B: $63	
12/1-3/31 & 11/1-11/30 [CP]		1P: $40-	52	2P/1B: $45-	62	2P/2B: $55	

Location: I-26, exit 18A just e to Sugarloaf Rd. 155 Sugarloaf Rd 28793 (PO Box 247). Fax: 704/693-5280. **Terms:** Sr. discount; no pets. **Facility:** 119 rooms. 4 stories; interior corridors. **All Rooms:** free movies. **Cards:** AE, DI, DS, MC, VI. *(See ad below)*

HOLIDAY INN EXPRESS-HENDERSONVILLE/FLATROCK   Rates Subject to Change   **Phone: 704/698-8899**
◆◆◆
Motel
All Year [CP]   1P: $60- 90   2P/1B: $65- 95   2P/2B: $65- 95 XP: $5   F19
Location: I-26 exit 22. 111 Commerical Blvd 28731. Fax: 704/698-8622. **Terms:** No pets. **Facility:** 54 rooms. 2 stories; interior corridors. **All Rooms:** free movies. **Cards:** AE, CB, DI, DS, JCB, MC, VI.
Roll in showers.

QUALITY INN & SUITES
(AAA) SAVE
◆◆◆
Motor Inn

Phone: 704/692-7231

		1P:		2P/1B:		2P/2B:		XP:	
6/1-6/27 & 8/24-10/31		1P: $69-	135	2P/1B: $69-	135	2P/2B: $69-	135	XP: $6	F16
6/28-8/23		1P: $59-	130	2P/1B: $59-	130	2P/2B: $59-	130	XP: $6	F16
12/1-3/31, 5/1-5/31 & 11/1-11/30		1P: $44-	84	2P/1B: $65-	84	2P/2B: $65-	84	XP: $6	F16
4/1-4/30		1P: $49-	84	2P/1B: $65-	84	2P/2B: $49-	84	XP: $6	F16

Location: I-26, exit 18A. 201 Sugar Loaf Rd 28792. Fax: 704/693-9905. **Terms:** Pets. **Facility:** 150 rooms. Attractive public areas. Food court. Well equipped rooms. 16 suites avail; 2 stories; interior/exterior corridors; sauna, whirlpool; game room. **Dining & Entertainment:** Restaurant; 6:30 am-10 & 5-9 pm; $11-$14; cocktails/lounge. **Services:** Fee: coin laundry. **All Rooms:** coffeemakers, free movies. **Some Rooms:** microwaves, refrigerators, whirlpools. **Cards:** AE, CB, DI, DS, JCB, MC, VI. **Special Amenities:** Free breakfast and free local telephone calls.

RAMADA LIMITED
(AAA) SAVE
◆◆◆
Motel

Phone: 704/697-0006

		1P:		2P/1B:		2P/2B:		XP:	
6/1-10/31 [CP]		1P: $55-	95	2P/1B: $59-	95	2P/2B: $62-	95	XP: $5	F13
12/1-5/31 & 11/1-11/30 [CP]		1P: $35-	49	2P/1B: $37-	49	2P/2B: $37-	49	XP: $5	F13

Location: I-26 exit 18A, just e to Sugarloaf Rd. 150 Sugarloaf Rd 28792. Fax: 704/697-0006. **Terms:** No pets. **Facility:** 53 rooms. Lobby well done & inviting. Good sized rooms. 2 stories; exterior corridors. **Dining:** Restaurant nearby. **All Rooms:** combo or shower baths, no phones. **Some Rooms:** whirlpools.
Cards: AE, CB, DI, DS, JCB, MC, VI.
Roll in showers.

THE WAVERLY INN
◆◆
Historic Bed
& Breakfast

Rates Subject to Change

Phone: 704/693-9193

		1P:	2P/1B:		2P/2B:	XP:	
5/26-11/30 [BP]		1P: $80	2P/1B: $109-	149	2P/2B: $149	XP: $15	F12
12/1-5/25 [BP]		1P: $80	2P/1B: $89-	129	2P/2B: $129	XP: $15	F12

Location: Exit 18B off I-26; 2 mi w on US 64, just n. 783 N Main 28792. Fax: 704/692-1010. **Terms:** Reserv deposit, 4 day notice; no pets. **Facility:** 14 rooms. 1 suite, $165-$195; 3 stories; no elevator; interior corridors; designated smoking area. **Cards:** AE, DS, MC, VI.

RESTAURANTS

EXPRESSIONS   Historical   **Dinner: $14-$24**   **Phone: 704/693-8516**
◆◆◆
American
Location: Opposite old courthouse. 114 N Main St 28792. **Hours:** 6 pm-9 pm. Closed major holidays, Sun & beginning mid Jan, call for availability. **Reservations:** suggested. **Features:** casual dress; cocktails & lounge; street parking. Refurbished 1900 storefront. Creative upscale dining featuring beef, fish, fowl, shellfish & pasta prepared with fresh ingredients, some tableside cooking. Intimate ambience. Award winning wine list. Smoke free premises. **Cards:** DI, MC, VI.

HAUS HEIDELBERG   **Lunch: $5-$8**   **Dinner: $9-$17**   **Phone: 704/693-8227**
◆◆
German
Location: Just s on US 25. 630 Greenville Hwy 28792. **Hours:** 11:30 am-2:30 & 5-9 pm, Sun noon-9 pm. Closed: Mon. **Reservations:** accepted. **Features:** casual dress; children's menu; beer & wine only. Popular dishes in casual atmosphere; wide variety of German beer. Also, deli, homemade soup, sauce & apple strudle; owner chef. Smoke free premises. **Cards:** DS, MC, VI.

THE POPLAR LODGE RESTAURANT   **Dinner: $15-$34**   **Phone: 704/692-9191**
◆◆
Steak and
Seafood
Location: I-26 exit 18B, Hwy 64 W to US 25 S, just s to 5th Ave; 3.3 mi w (Laurel Park Hwy). 2350 Hebron Rd 28731. **Hours:** 6 pm-10 pm. **Features:** casual dress; children's menu; carryout; salad bar; cocktails. Choice filet & ribeye steak. Chicken, seafood & pork also. In historic lodge/supper club site. **Cards:** AE, DI, DS, MC, VI.

THE SAMOVAR **Lunch:** $5-$6 Phone: 704/692-5981
◆
American **Location:** Downtown, on US 25S Church & Barnwell sts; in Heritage Square Mall. 121 Barnwell St 28739. **Hours:** 11 am-4 pm, Sun-3 pm. Closed major holidays. **Features:** children's menu; carryout; cocktails. Since 1977, variety of sandwiches & salads. Also quiche, crepes & bread baked daily. Casual plant bedecked dining rooms. Smoke free premises. ⊠

SINBAD MEDITERRANEAN RESTAURANT **Lunch:** $5-$7 **Dinner:** $11-$15 Phone: 704/696-2039
◆◆
Ethnic **Location:** Downtown, corner of 4th & King. 133 4th Ave E 28792. **Hours:** 11 am-2 & 5-9 pm. Closed major holidays, Sun, Mon & 1/1-1/31. **Reservations:** accepted. **Features:** No A/C; casual dress; carryout; cocktails. Greek, Lebanese, Indian & seafood offerings served in a casual Middle Eastern atmosphere. Smoke free premises. **Cards:** AE, DS, MC, VI. ⊠

HICKORY—28,300

LODGINGS

COMFORT SUITES Rates Subject to Change Phone: 704/323-1211
◆◆◆
Motel All Year [BP] 1P: $74- 125 2P/1B: $81- 132 2P/2B: $81- 132 XP: $7 F18
Location: Exit 125 off I-40, just s. 1125 13th Avenue Dr SE 28602. Fax: 704/322-4395. **Terms:** Sr. discount; no pets. **Facility:** 116 rooms. 2 stories; interior/exterior corridors. **All Rooms:** free movies.
Some Rooms: 12 efficiencies. **Cards:** AE, CB, DI, DS, JCB, MC, VI. 🛎 CTV 🛏 ⊠ 🍴 D

FAIRFIELD INN Rates Subject to Change Phone: 704/431-3000
◆◆◆
Motel All Year [CP] 1P: $69 2P/1B: $69 2P/2B: $69
Location: Just s of exit 125, I-40. 1950 13th Ave Dr SE 28602. Fax: 704/431-4714. **Terms:** Sr. discount; no pets. **Facility:** 108 rooms. 4 stories; interior corridors. **All Rooms:** free movies. **Cards:** AE, CB, DI, DS, MC, VI. Roll in showers. 🛎 CTV 🛁 ⊠ 🍴 D S

THE HICKORY BED & BREAKFAST Phone: 704/324-0548
AAA SAVE All Year [BP] 1P: $80 2P/1B: $85- 105 XP: $15
Location: I-40 exit 123 to SR 70E, e to 4th St SW, n to 7th Ave SW, just w. 464 7th St SW 28602.
Bed & Fax: 704/324-0443. **Terms:** Age restrictions may apply; check-in 4 pm; reserv deposit, 7 day notice; no pets.
Breakfast **Facility:** 4 rooms. 2 stories; interior corridors; smoke free premises. **Cards:** MC, VI. ⊠ D

HOLIDAY INN SELECT Rates Subject to Change Phone: 704/323-1000
◆◆◆
Motor Inn All Year 1P: $89- 99 2P/1B: $89- 99 2P/2B: $89- 99 XP: $6 D18
Location: I-40 exit 125, just s. 1385 Lenoir Rhyne Blvd SE 28602. Fax: 704/322-4275. **Terms:** Sr. discount; no pets. **Facility:** 200 rooms. 2 stories; interior/exterior corridors. **Dining:** Restaurant; 6 am-11 pm; $8-18.
All Rooms: free & pay movies. **Cards:** AE, CB, DI, DS, JCB, MC, VI. 🏈 CTV 🛏 ⊠ 🍴 D S

QUALITY INN & SUITES Rates Subject to Change Phone: 704/431-2100
◆◆◆
Motel All Year [BP] 1P: $64- 99 2P/1B: $79- 119 2P/2B: $74- 109 XP: $10 F18
Location: 2.8 mi n on US 321 from I-40, exit 123. 1725 13th Ave Dr NW 28601. Fax: 704/431-2109.
Terms: Sr. discount; no pets. **Facility:** 100 rooms. 26 whirlpool rms, extra charge; 3 stories; interior corridors.
All Rooms: free movies. **Cards:** AE, DI, DS, MC, VI. Roll in showers. CTV ⊠ 🍴 D S

RED ROOF INN HICKORY Rates Subject to Change Phone: 704/323-1500
◆◆
Motel 10/1-10/31 2P/1B: $48 2P/2B: $59 XP: $5 F18
6/1-9/30 2P/1B: $46 2P/2B: $54 XP: $5 F18
4/1-5/31 2P/1B: $44 2P/2B: $52 XP: $5 F18
12/1-3/31 & 11/1-11/30 2P/1B: $38 2P/2B: $47 XP: $5 F18
Location: Off I-40, exit 125. 1184 Lenoir Rhyne Blvd 28602. Fax: 704/323-1509. **Terms:** Small pets only. **Facility:** 108 rooms.
2 stories; exterior corridors. **All Rooms:** free & pay movies. **Cards:** AE, CB, DI, DS, MC, VI. 🐾 🛏 ⊠ 🍴 D

SLEEP INN Rates Subject to Change Phone: 704/323-1140
◆◆
Motel 12/1-4/30, 6/1-9/30 &
11/1-11/30 [CP] 1P: $51- 85 2P/1B: $58- 85 XP: $7 F18
5/1-5/31 & 10/1-10/31 [CP] 1P: $51- 125 2P/1B: $58- 125 XP: $7 F18
Location: Exit 125 off I-40, just s & just w; in Comfort Suite Park. 1179 13th Ave Dr SE 28602. Fax: 704/324-6203.
Terms: Sr. discount; no pets. **Facility:** 100 rooms. 3 stories; interior corridors. **All Rooms:** free movies. **Cards:** AE, CB, DI, DS, JCB, MC, VI. CTV ⊠ 🍴 D S

RESTAURANTS

1859 CAFE **Dinner:** $14-$21 Phone: 704/322-1859
AAA
◆◆◆ **Location:** I-40 exit 123, 0.5 mi e on US 70E, 0.5 mi n on 4th St SW, 0.3 mi w on 1st Ave SW, just s on 6th St SW, then just e on 2nd Ave SW. 443 2nd Ave SW 28602-2851. **Hours:** 5 pm-10 pm. Closed: 11/26
Continental & 12/25. **Reservations:** suggested. **Features:** cocktails & lounge. Intimate dining rooms in restored 1859 home provide an ambience of casual elegance. Deck dining avail in season. **Cards:** AE, CB, DI, DS, MC, VI. ⊠

J & S CAFETERIA Phone: 704/326-8926
◆◆
American **Location:** 0.5 mi e on service road from I-40, exit 125 on south side of interstate next to Hampton Inn. 1940 13th Ave Dr SE 28602. **Hours:** 6 am-8 pm. Closed: 12/25. **Features:** children's menu; carryout. Homemade bread & dessert. Hearty portions. No lard or pork used in veggie seasonings. Smoke free premises. ⊠

RAGAZZI'S **Lunch:** $5-$7 **Dinner:** $8-$12 Phone: 704/328-2558
◆◆
Italian **Location:** Exit 125, I-40; 2 blks s to US 70E & 2 blks e on US 70. 1770 US 70E 28602. **Hours:** 11 am-10 pm. Closed: 11/26 & 12/25. **Features:** children's menu; carryout; cocktails. Homemade soup & sauce. Very appealing Italian ambience. **Cards:** AE, MC, VI. ⊠

THE VINTAGE HOUSE RESTAURANT Historical **Dinner:** $18-$25 Phone: 704/324-1210
AAA
◆◆◆ **Location:** From I-40 exit 123, 0.5 mi e on Hwy 70 to 4th Street Dr SW, 1 mi n to Main Ave NW, just e, then 3 blks n on 3rd St NW. 271 3rd Ave NW 28601. **Hours:** 11:30 am-2 & 6-9 pm, Fri & Sat-11 pm. Closed
Continental major holidays, Sun & 7/3-7/5. **Reservations:** suggested. **Features:** carryout; cocktails & lounge. Fresh seafood & nightly specials served in a popular restored home; homemade dessert. Profiterole very popular. Grouper wrapped in lace potatoes signature entree. **Cards:** AE, MC, VI. ⊠

HIDDENITE—800

LODGING

HIDDEN CRYSTAL INN AND CONFERENCE CENTER   Rates Subject to Change   Phone: 704/632-0063
◆◆◆   All Year [MAP]   1P: $85- 90   2P/1B: $95- 160 2P/2B: $85   XP: $15   D14
Country Inn   **Location:** 1 mi n on Old Mountain Rd from US 64 (Bypass), exit 259. Sulphur Springs Rd 28636 (PO Box
58). Fax: 704/632-3562. **Terms:** Reserv deposit, 3 day notice; no pets. **Facility:** 13 rooms. 2 stories: interior
corridors; smoke free premises. **Dining:** Dining room; 11 am-2 & 5:30-9:30 pm; $15-$22. **All Rooms:** free movies.
Cards: AE, MC, VI.   🛏 CTV ✕ D

HIGHLANDS—900

LODGINGS

THE CHANDLER INN   Guaranteed Rates   Phone: 704/526-5992
◆◆◆   All Year [CP]   1P: $48- 72   2P/1B: $56- 140 2P/2B: $56- 105 XP: $12
Country Inn   **Location:** 0.5 mi e on US 64. US Hwy 64 28741 (PO Box 2156). **Terms:** Age restrictions may apply; reserv
deposit, 3 day notice; no pets. **Facility:** 15 rooms. 9 units with fireplace; 2 stories; exterior corridors.
All Rooms: free movies. **Some Rooms:** A/C, kitchen. **Cards:** MC, VI.   CTV ✕ D

HAMPTON INN   Rates Subject to Change   Phone: 704/526-5899
◆◆◆   5/1-10/31 [CP]   1P: $105   2P/1B: $125   2P/2B: $125
Motel   12/1-4/30 & 11/1-11/30 [CP]   1P: $79   2P/1B: $89   2P/2B: $89
Location: Just s from jct of SR 106/US 64. SR 106 & Spring St 28741 (PO Box 1060). Fax: 704/526-5979.
Terms: Check-in 4 pm; no pets. **Facility:** 58 rooms. 3 stories; interior/exterior corridors. **All Rooms:** free movies.
Cards: AE, CB, DI, DS, MC, VI.   CTV ✕ D

HIGHLANDS SUITE HOTEL   Phone: 704/526-4502
Ⓐ SAVE   6/20-8/31 & 9/26-11/1 [CP]   1P: $131- 181 2P/1B: $131- 181 2P/2B: $131- 181 XP: $10   F15
         5/16-6/19 & 9/1-9/25 [CP]   1P: $96- 146 2P/1B: $96- 146 2P/2B: $96- 146 XP: $10   F15
◆◆◆   4/18-5/15 [CP]   1P: $86- 137 2P/1B: $86- 137 2P/2B: $86- 137 XP: $10   F15
Suite Motel 12/1-4/17 & 11/2-11/30 [CP]   1P: $70- 130 2P/1B: $70- 130 2P/2B: $70- 130 XP: $10   F15
Location: Downtown. 205 Main St 28741 (PO Box 459). **Terms:** Check-in 3:30 pm; reserv deposit, 7 day
notice; no pets. **Facility:** 28 rooms. Well-equipped, 2-room suite units. 2 stories; exterior corridors. **Dining:** Restaurant
nearby. **All Rooms:** coffeemakers, microwaves, free movies, refrigerators, VCP's, whirlpools. **Cards:** AE, MC, VI.
Special Amenities: Free breakfast.   CTV ✕ D

MOUNTAIN HIGH MOTEL   Phone: 704/526-2790
Ⓐ SAVE   6/20-8/31 & 9/26-11/1   1P: $93- 175   2P/1B: $93- 175 2P/2B: $93- 175
         5/16-6/19 & 9/1-9/25   1P: $70- 145   2P/1B: $70- 145 2P/2B: $70- 145
◆◆   4/18-5/15   1P: $55- 130   2P/1B: $55- 130 2P/2B: $55- 130
Motel   12/1-4/17 & 11/2-11/30   1P: $50- 115   2P/1B: $50- 115 2P/2B: $50- 115
Location: Downtown. 200 Main St 28741 (PO Box 939). **Terms:** Check-in 3:30 pm; reserv deposit; small
pets only, in 2 rms. **Facility:** 55 rooms. 2 stories; exterior corridors. **Dining:** Restaurant nearby. **All Rooms:** free movies.
Some Rooms: coffeemakers, microwaves, refrigerators, whirlpools. **Cards:** AE, DS, MC, VI. **Special Amenities:** Free
breakfast.   🛏 🍴 CTV D

RESTAURANTS

THE CENTRAL HOUSE   Historical   **Lunch:** $7-$10   **Dinner:** $14-$18   Phone: 704/526-5036
◆◆   **Location:** Jct US 64 & 28; in the Old Edwards Inn. 4th & Main sts 28741. **Hours:** Open 4/1-11/30; 11:30
Seafood   am-2:30 & 5:30-9:30 pm, Sun from 5:30 pm. **Reservations:** required; for dinner. **Features:** casual dress;
             wine only; street parking. Tasteful country atmosphere in beautifully restored inn. Very popular. Smoke free
premises. **Cards:** AE, MC, VI.   ✕

PAOLETTI'S   **Lunch:** $6-$15   **Dinner:** $13-$26   Phone: 704/526-4906
Ⓐ   **Location:** Main St, next to Highlands Inn. 440 Main St 28741. **Hours:** noon-2:30 & 6-10 pm. Closed:
         1/1-1/31. **Reservations:** suggested. **Features:** dressy casual; carryout; wine only; street parking. Creative
◆◆◆   Italian dishes served in an Old World atmosphere. Excellent wine list. Smoke free premises. **Cards:** AE, MC,
Italian   VI.   ✕

HIGH POINT—69,500

LODGINGS

ATRIUM INN   Rates Subject to Change   Phone: 910/884-8838
◆◆   4/7-4/24 & 10/13-10/23   1P: $250   2P/1B: $250   2P/2B: $250   XP: $10   F17
Motel   12/1-4/6, 4/25-10/12 &
             10/24-11/30   1P: $69   2P/1B: $75- 79 2P/2B: $75- 79 XP: $10   F17
Location: On US 311; 1.5 mi n of Business Rt I-85, US 29 & 70, downtown exit off I-85. 425 S Main St 27260.
Fax: 910/885-4925. **Terms:** Sr. discount; reserv deposit; no pets. **Facility:** 38 rooms. 2 stories; exterior corridors.
All Rooms: free movies. **Cards:** AE, DI, DS, MC, VI.   ✕ D

HOLIDAY INN   Phone: 910/886-7011
Ⓐ SAVE   All Year   1P: $60- 150 2P/1B: $60- 150 2P/2B: $60- 150 XP: $10   F18
         Location: On US 311; 1.5 mi n of Business Rt I-85, US 29 & 70; downtown exit (311N) off I-85. 236 S Main
◆◆◆   St 27260. Fax: 910/886-5595. **Terms:** Pets. **Facility:** 165 rooms. Barber shop on property. $.75 for all local
Motor Inn   calls; 2-6 stories; interior corridors. **Dining:** Dining room; 7 am-1 & 5:30-9 pm; $6-$12; cocktails. **Services:**
             Fee: coin laundry. **All Rooms:** coffeemakers, free & pay movies. **Some Rooms:** microwaves, refrigerators.
Cards: AE, CB, DI, DS, JCB, MC. **Special Amenities: Free room upgrade (subject to availability with advanced
reservations).**   🛏 🛏 🍴 ✕ D

HOWARD JOHNSON   Phone: 910/886-4141
Ⓐ SAVE   All Year   1P: $47   2P/1B: $57   2P/2B: $57   XP: $6   F18
         Location: I-85 (Business) at Brentwood St. 2000 Brentwood St 27263. Fax: 910/886-5579. **Terms:** No pets.
◆◆   **Facility:** 104 rooms. Handling fee imposed; 2 stories; interior corridors. **Dining:** Restaurant; 6:30 am-1:30 &
Motor Inn   6-9 pm; wine/beer only. **All Rooms:** free movies. **Some Rooms:** microwaves, refrigerators. **Cards:** AE, CB
             DI, DS, MC, VI. **Special Amenities: Free room upgrade (subject to availability with advanced
reservations).**   🛏 ✕

SUPER 8 MOTEL

Phone: 910/882-4103

[AAA] [SAVE] All Year [CP]   1P: $45   2P/1B: $45   2P/2B: $50   XP: $5   D15

◆ ◆   **Location:** On US 311, 1.5 mi n of Business Rt I-85, US 29 & 70; downtown exit off I-85. 400 S Main St

Motel   27260. Fax: 910/882-7125. **Terms:** No pets. **Facility:** 44 rooms. Nicely appointed rooms. Handling fee imposed; 2 stories; exterior corridors. **Dining:** Restaurant nearby. **All Rooms:** free movies, refrigerators, VCP's. **Cards:** AE, DS, MC, VI. **Special Amenities:** Free breakfast and free local telephone calls.

(See color ad below)   [🛎] [✕] [📷] [D]

RESTAURANTS

ACT I RESTAURANT   **Lunch:** $6-$8   **Dinner:** $15-$20   Phone: 910/869-5614

◆ ◆   **Location:** From jct US 311 & SR 68, just n on Main, just e. 130 E Parris Ave 27262. **Hours:** 11:30 am-2 &

American   5-10 pm, Sat from 5 pm, Sun 11:30 am 2 & 5-9 pm. Closed major holidays. **Reservations:** suggested.

Features: senior's menu; carryout; cocktails & lounge. Seafood, poultry, veal, steaks & pasta served in casual ambience. **Cards:** AE, MC, VI.   [✕]

NOBLE'S RESTAURANT   **Dinner:** $23-$30   Phone: 919/889-3354

◆ ◆ ◆   **Location:** On US 311, downtown exit off I-85. 114 S Main St 27260. **Hours:** 6 pm-10 pm, Thurs-Sat to 11

Continental   pm. Closed major holidays & Sun. **Reservations:** suggested. **Features:** carryout; cocktails & lounge. Upscale French bistro with limited menu of fresh lamb, fowl, seafood, beef & veal. Jazz cellar & extensive wine list. Homemade bread, pastry & soup. Very popular. **Cards:** AE, CB, DI, MC, VI.

VILLAGE CAFE   **Lunch:** $5-$9   **Dinner:** $7-$12   Phone: 919/886-2233

◆ ◆   **Location:** Near Downtown; from Main St (SR 311) 1 mi e on E Lexington Ave. In college Village Shopping

Italian   Center. 1141 E Lexington Ave 27265. **Hours:** 11 am-9 pm, Fri-10 pm, Sat 5 pm-10 pm. Closed major holidays & Sun. **Features:** children's menu; carryout; beer & wine only. Casual dining. Favorite Italian & American dishes. Fresh seafood Thurs-Sat. **Cards:** AE, MC, VI.   [✕]

HILLSBOROUGH—4,300

LODGING

HILLSBOROUGH HOUSE INN   Rates Subject to Change   Phone: 919/644-1600

◆ ◆   All Year [CP]   1P: $95   2P/1B: $95- 105   XP: $25

Historic Bed   **Location:** I-40 exit 261, 3 mi n to E Tryon St; I-85 exit 164, 1.5 mi n to E Tryon St. 209 E Tryon St

& Breakfast   27278-0880 (PO Box 880). Fax: 919/644-1600. **Terms:** Age restrictions may apply; no pets. **Facility:** 6 rooms.

MC, VI.   Closed 12/20-1/5; 2 stories; interior corridors; smoke free premises. **All Rooms:** free movies. **Cards:** AE,

[🛏] [CTV] [✕] [D]

RESTAURANT

THE COLONIAL INN   Historical   **Lunch:** $5-$10   **Dinner:** $7-$14   Phone: 919/732-2461

◆ ◆   **Location:** Town Center; just w on W King St. 153 West King St 27278. **Hours:** 11:30 am-2 & 5-8:30 pm,

Regional   Sun-8 pm. Closed: Mon, 1/1, 7/4 & 12/24-12/26. **Reservations:** suggested. **Features:** children's menu;

American   carryout; beer & wine only; street parking. Built in 1759. 1 of 10 oldest inns in the nation. All southern dishes. **Cards:** MC, VI.

HUNTERSVILLE—3,000

LODGING

HOLIDAY INN EXPRESS   Phone: 704/875-1165

[AAA] [SAVE] 5/1-5/31 & 10/1-10/31 [CP]   1P: $100- 115   2P/1B: $105- 120   2P/2B: $105- 120   XP: $5   F16

12/1-4/30, 6/1-9/30 &

◆ ◆ ◆   11/1-11/30 [CP]   1P: $64- 69   2P/1B: $69- 74   2P/2B: $69- 74   XP: $5   F16

Motel   **Location:** I-77, exit 23. 14135 Statesville Rd 28070 (PO Box 1349). Fax: 704/875-1894. **Terms:** No pets.

Facility: 60 rooms. 2 stories; exterior corridors. **Dining:** Restaurant nearby. **All Rooms:** free movies. **Some Rooms:** microwaves, refrigerators. Fee: whirlpools. **Cards:** AE, CB, DI, DS, JCB, MC, VI. **Special Amenities:** Free breakfast and free newspaper.

[🛏] [🛎] [CTV] [🏋] [✕] [📷] [D]

JACKSONVILLE—30,000

LODGINGS

COMFORT SUITES   Rates Subject to Change   Phone: 910/346-8900

◆ ◆ ◆   All Year [CP]   1P: $70- 85   2P/1B: $70- 85   2P/2B: $70- 85   XP: $10   F18

Motel   **Location:** 2.8 mi n on US 17N. 130 Workshop Lane 28546. Fax: 910/455-0423. **Terms:** Sr. discount; small pets only, $10 dep req. **Facility:** 72 rooms. 3 stories; interior corridors. **All Rooms:** free & pay movies.

Cards: AE, CB, DI, DS, JCB, MC, VI.   Roll in showers.   [📞] [🛎] [CTV] [🏋] [✕] [📷] [D] [S]

HAMPTON INN
◆◆◆
Motel
Rates Subject to Change
All Year [CP]   1P: $58   2P/1B: $63   2P/2B: $63
Phone: 910/347-6500
Location: 2.5 mi n on US 17. 474 Western Blvd 28546. Fax: 910/347-6858. **Terms:** Sr. discount; no pets.
Facility: 120 rooms. 2 stories; exterior corridors. **All Rooms:** free movies. **Cards:** AE, CB, DI, DS, MC, VI.

HOLIDAY INN EXPRESS
◆◆
Motel
Rates Subject to Change
All Year [CP]   1P: $60   2P/1B: $65   2P/2B: $65   XP: $5   F16
Phone: 910/347-1900
Location: 2.8 mi n. 2115 Hwy 17N 28546. Fax: 910/347-7593. **Terms:** Sr. discount; no pets. **Facility:** 118
rooms. 4 stories; interior corridors. **All Rooms:** free & pay movies. **Cards:** AE, CB, DI, DS, JCB, MC, VI.
Roll in showers.

LIBERTY INN
ⒶⒶⒶ SAVE
◆◆◆
Motel
Phone: 910/353-3336
All Year [CP]   1P: $45- 60   2P/1B: $45- 60   2P/2B: $50- 60   XP: $8   F14
Location: On US 24, 2 mi e of jct US 17 or 2 mi w of Camp LeJeune. 1723 LeJeune Blvd 28540.
Fax: 919/353-3732. **Terms:** No pets. **Facility:** 80 rooms. Contemporary room decor attractive lobby & pool
area. 2 stories; interior corridors; whirlpool. Fee: tanning bed. **Dining:** Restaurant nearby. **Services:**
Fee: coin laundry. **All Rooms:** free movies. **Some Rooms:** Fee: whirlpools. **Cards:** AE, CB, DI, DS, MC, VI.

TRAVELODGE
ⒶⒶⒶ SAVE
◆◆
Motel
Phone: 910/347-5131
Fri-Sun [CP]   1P: $45   2P/1B: $50   2P/2B: $50   XP: $5   F18
Mon-Thurs [CP]   1P: $40   2P/1B: $45   2P/2B: $45   XP: $5   F18
Location: 1.5 mi n on US 17. 505 N Marine Blvd 28540. Fax: 910/347-5131. **Terms:** Reserv deposit; no
pets. **Facility:** 74 rooms. Attractive public areas. 1-2 stories; exterior corridors. **Dining:** Restaurant nearby.
All Rooms: free movies. **Some Rooms:** microwaves, refrigerators. **Cards:** AE, CB, DI, DS, JCB, MC, VI.
**Special Amenities: Free local telephone calls and free room upgrade (subject to availability with advanced
reservations).**

RESTAURANT

RAGAZZI'S
ⒶⒶⒶ
◆◆
Italian
Lunch: $6-$8   Dinner: $8-$14   **Phone: 910/577-2782**
Location: On US 24, 1.5 mi e of jct US 17; or 2.5 mi w of Camp Le Jeune. 1439 Le Jeune Blvd 28540.
Hours: 11 am-10 pm, Fri & Sat-11 pm. Closed: 11/26 & 12/25. **Features:** children's menu; carryout; cocktails
& lounge. Pasta, pizza, calzones, salad & sandwiches served by courteous staff in festive atmosphere; also
atrium dining area; kids 12 & under eat free on Sun 11 am-4 pm. **Cards:** AE, MC, VI.

JEFFERSON—1,300

LODGINGS

BEST WESTERN ELDRETH INN AT MOUNT JEFFERSON
ⒶⒶⒶ SAVE
◆◆◆
Motor Inn
Phone: 910/246-8845
Fri & Sat 5/24-10/26 [BP] 1P: $60- 66   2P/1B: $66- 74   2P/2B: $70- 74   XP: $6   F12
Sun-Thurs 5/24-10/26 &
10/27-11/30 [BP]   1P: $54- 58   2P/1B: $58- 64   2P/2B: $60- 64   XP: $6   F12
12/1-5/23 [BP]   1P: $52- 54   2P/1B: $56- 60   2P/2B: $58- 60   XP: $6   F12
Location: On US 221 & SR 88. 829 E Main St 28640 (PO Box 12). Fax: 910/246-9109. **Terms:** No pets.
Facility: 48 rooms. Scenic location; rural mountain setting. 2 night minimum stay weekends in season & 10/1-10/31; 1-2 stories; exterior corridors; sauna. **Dining:** Restaurant; 6 am-10 pm, Sun-3 pm; $6-$16. **All Rooms:** free movies.
Some Rooms: microwaves, refrigerators. **Cards:** AE, CB, DI, DS, MC, VI. **Special Amenities: Free local telephone calls
and free newspaper.**

JEFFERSON LANDING LODGE
◆◆◆
Motel
Rates Subject to Change
5/1-10/31 [CP]
12/1-4/30 & 11/1-11/30 [CP]
Phone: 910/982-4653
                                                      2P/2B: $85- 105 XP: $10   F18
                                                      2P/2B: $54   XP: $10   F18
Location: 1.5 mi se on SR 88 & 80 from jct US 221. SR 88 28640 (PO Box 110). Fax: 910/982-4965.
Terms: Reserv deposit; 2 night min stay, weekends, 5/1-10/31; no pets. **Facility:** 17 rooms. 2 stories; exterior corridors.
All Rooms: free movies. **Some Rooms:** kitchen. **Cards:** AE, DI, DS, MC, VI.

JONESVILLE—1,500

LODGINGS

COMFORT INN
ⒶⒶⒶ SAVE
◆◆◆
Motel
Phone: 910/835-9400
3/1-11/1 [CP]   1P: $47- 70   2P/1B: $55- 105 2P/2B: $55- 105 XP: $6   F18
12/1-2/28 & 11/2-11/30 [CP] 1P: $38- 50   2P/1B: $44- 65   2P/2B: $44- 75   XP: $6   F18
Location: Exit 82, off I-77. 1633 Winston Rd 28642 (PO Box 126). Fax: 910/835-9450. **Terms:** No pets.
Facility: 79 rooms. Stylishly attractive lobby & guest rooms. 2 stories; exterior corridors; whirlpool, small
heated indoor pool. **Dining:** Restaurant nearby. **Recreation:** sun deck. **All Rooms:** free movies.
Some Rooms: coffeemakers. Fee: VCP's. **Cards:** AE, CB, DI, DS, JCB, MC, VI. **Special Amenities: Free breakfast and
free local telephone calls.**

COUNTRY INN
ⒶⒶⒶ
◆◆
Motel
Rates Subject to Change
All Year   1P: $37- 51   2P/1B: $37- 57   2P/2B: $41- 66   XP: $4
Phone: 910/835-2261
Location: Just w off I-77 exit 79, entry between gas station & restaurant. 5702 US 21 S 28642. **Terms:** Sr
discount; no pets. **Facility:** 35 rooms. 2 stories; exterior corridors. **All Rooms:** free movies. **Cards:** AE, DS
MC, VI.

DAYS INN JONESVILLE-ELKIN
ⒶⒶⒶ SAVE
◆◆
Motel
Phone: 910/526-6777
Thurs-Sat 3/1-10/31   1P: $59- 89   2P/1B: $59- 89   2P/2B: $59- 89   XP: $5   F17
Sun-Wed 3/1-10/31   1P: $45- 69   2P/1B: $50- 69   2P/2B: $50- 69   XP: $5   F17
12/1-2/28 & 11/1-11/30   1P: $35- 40   2P/1B: $40- 45   2P/2B: $42- 47   XP: $5   F17
Location: Exit 82 off I-77, then 0.3 mi w. 1540 NC 67 Hwy 28642. Fax: 910/526-8950. **Terms:** No pets
Facility: 50 rooms. Budget furnished rooms. 2 stories; exterior corridors. **Dining:** Restaurant nearby.
All Rooms: free movies. **Cards:** AE, CB, DI, DS, MC, VI. **Special Amenities: Free local telephone calls and free room
upgrade (subject to availability with advanced reservations).**

HAMPTON INN
ⒶⒶⒶ SAVE
◆◆◆
Motel
Phone: 910/835-1994
All Year [CP]   1P: $59- 87   2P/1B: $67- 74   2P/2B: $67- 74
Location: Just w on SR 67 from I-77, exit 82. 1632 NC 67 Hwy 28642. Fax: 910/835-1568. **Terms:** No pets
Facility: 64 rooms. 3 stories; interior corridors. **Dining:** Restaurant nearby. **All Rooms:** free movies
Some Rooms: microwaves, refrigerators, VCP's. **Cards:** AE, CB, DI, DS, MC, VI. **Special Amenities: Free
breakfast and free newspaper.**

HOLIDAY INN OF JONESVILLE/ELKIN Rates Subject to Change **Phone:** 910/835-6000
◆◆ All Year 1P: $45- 79 2P/1B: $45- 79 2P/2B: $45- 79 XP: $5 F19
Motor Inn **Location:** I-77 exit 82 at jct SR 67. 1713 NC 67 Hwy 28642 (PO Box 66). Fax: 910/835-1771. **Terms:** Sr. discount; no pets. **Facility:** 116 rooms. 2 stories; interior corridors. **Dining:** Dining room; 6:30 am-2 & 5-9 pm; lunch buffet Mon-Fri, $5.50; $6-$14. **All Rooms:** free & pay movies. **Cards:** AE, CB, DI, DS, JCB, MC, VI.

KANNAPOLIS—29,700

LODGING

KANNAPOLIS FAIRFIELD INN **Phone:** 704/795-4888
AAA SAVE All Year [CP] 1P: $54- 60 2P/1B: $60- 66 2P/2B: $60- 66 XP: $6 F18
◆◆◆ **Location:** Just w of exit 58, I-85. 3033 Clover Leaf Pkwy 28083. Fax: 704/795-4888. **Terms:** No pets.
Motel **Facility:** 84 rooms. Very attractive public areas; handsomely appointed rooms. 4 stories; interior corridors. **Dining:** Restaurant nearby. **All Rooms:** free movies. **Some Rooms:** Fee: whirlpools. **Cards:** AE, CB, DI, DS, MC, VI. *(See color ad below)* Roll in showers.

KENLY—1,500

LODGINGS

BEST WESTERN INN **Phone:** 919/284-3800
AAA SAVE All Year [CP] 1P: $44- 64 2P/1B: $44- 64 2P/2B: $44- 64 XP: $5 F12
◆◆◆ **Location:** Exit 106 off I-95, Truck Stop Rd. 27542 (PO Box 520). Fax: 919/284-5669. **Terms:** Reserv
Motel deposit; no pets. **Facility:** 81 rooms. 2 stories; exterior corridors. **Dining:** Restaurant nearby. **All Rooms:** free movies. **Some Rooms:** Fee: VCP's, whirlpools. **Cards:** AE, CB, DI, DS, MC, VI. **Special Amenities:** Free breakfast and free local telephone calls. *(See color ad below)*

DAYS INN **Phone:** 919/284-3400
AAA SAVE All Year [CP] 1P: $42- 48 2P/1B: $47- 52 2P/2B: $47- 54 XP: $5 F17
◆◆ **Location:** I-95, exit 106. 923 Johnston Pkwy 27542. Fax: 919/284-5056. **Terms:** No pets. **Facility:** 79 rooms.
Motel Truck stop nearby. 2 stories; exterior corridors. **Dining:** Restaurant nearby. **All Rooms:** free movies. **Some Rooms:** Fee: VCP's. **Cards:** AE, DI, DS, MC, VI.

ECONO LODGE **Phone:** 919/284-1000
AAA SAVE 6/1-9/30 [CP] 1P: $40 2P/1B: $45 2P/2B: $55 XP: $5 F18
 12/1-5/31 [CP] 1P: $38 2P/1B: $42 2P/2B: $52 XP: $5 F18
◆◆ 10/1-11/30 [CP] 1P: $36 2P/1B: $40 2P/2B: $50 XP: $5 F18
Motel **Location:** Exit 107, I-95 on US 301N. 405 S Church St 27542 (PO Box 577). Fax: 919/284-4852. **Terms:** Small pets only. **Facility:** 60 rooms. 2 stories; exterior corridors; small pool. **Dining:** Restaurant nearby. **All Rooms:** free movies. **Cards:** AE, DS, MC, VI. **Special Amenities:** Free breakfast and free local telephone calls.

KERNERSVILLE—10,800

LODGING

QUALITY INN   Phone: 910/996-3501

(AAA) [SAVE]   All Year [CP]   1P: $44   2P/1B: $44   2P/2B: $44

◆ ◆   **Location:** Just s from exit 15, I-40 (business) & SR 66S; from I-40 bypass exit 203, 1.8 mi n. 707 Hwy 66S
Motor Inn   27284. Fax: 910/996-9701. **Terms:** No pets. **Facility:** 98 rooms. Centrally located between Greensboro &
Winston-Salem. 2 stories; exterior corridors. **Dining:** Restaurant; Mexican menu only; 11 am-2 & 4-9 pm,
Sun 7-10:30 am; $5-$13; cocktails. **All Rooms:** free movies. **Cards:** AE, CB, DI, DS, JCB, MC, VI.
Special Amenities: Free breakfast and free local telephone calls.   [⊞] [✈] [CTV] [✕] [D]

KILL DEVIL HILLS—See Outer Banks p. 397.

KING—4,100

LODGING

ECONO LODGE   Phone: 910/983-5600

(AAA) [SAVE]   4/20-5/1 & 10/10-10/31 [CP] 1P: $49   2P/1B: $54   2P/2B: S60   XP: $5   F18
12/1-4/19, 5/2-10/9 &
◆ ◆   11/1-11/30 [CP]   1P: $40   2P/1B: $45   2P/2B: $49   XP: $5   F18
Motel   **Location:** US 52, King/Tobaccoville exit 123. Vesta St 27021 (PO Box 1064). Fax: 910/983-6989. **Terms:** No
pets. **Facility:** 60 rooms. Spacious modern rooms. 2 stories; exterior corridors. **Dining:** Restaurant nearby.
All Rooms: free movies. **Some Rooms:** coffeemakers, microwaves, refrigerators. Fee: whirlpools. **Cards:** AE, DI, DS, MC,
VI. **Special Amenities:** Free breakfast and free local telephone calls.   [⊞] [✦] [CTV] [✕] [D]

KINGS MOUNTAIN—8,800

LODGING

COMFORT INN   Phone: 704/739-7070

(AAA) [SAVE]   All Year [CP]   1P: $43- 46   2P/1B: $46- 50 2P/2B: $56   XP: $5   F18
Location: I-85, exit 8. 720 A-York Rd 28086 (PO Box 996). Fax: 704/739-7070. **Terms:** Reserv deposit; no
◆ ◆   pets. **Facility:** 73 rooms. 2 stories; exterior corridors. **Dining:** Restaurant nearby. **Services:** Fee: coin
Motel   laundry. **All Rooms:** free movies. **Some Rooms:** microwaves, refrigerators. Fee: whirlpools. **Cards:** AE, CB,
DI, DS, MC, VI. **Special Amenities:** Free breakfast and free newspaper.   [⊞] [✦] [CTV] [✕] [D]

KINSTON—25,300

LODGINGS

COMFORT INN   Phone: 919/527-3200

(AAA) [SAVE]   All Year [CP]   1P: $49- 65   2P/1B: $49- 65 2P/2B: $49- 65 XP: $5   F12
Location: 5 mi e on US 70 bypass. 200 W NewBern Rd 28501. Fax: 919/527-3200. **Terms:** No pets.
◆ ◆ ◆ **Facility:** 60 rooms. Very attractive public areas with high quality room furnishings. 2 stories; exterior corridors.
Motel   wading pool, sauna. **Dining:** Restaurant nearby. **All Rooms:** microwaves, free movies, refrigerators.
Some Rooms: VCP's. Fee: whirlpools. **Cards:** AE, CB, DI, DS, JCB, MC, VI. **Special Amenities:** Free
breakfast and free newspaper.   [⊞] [✦] [CTV] [✕] [D]

DAYS INN   Phone: 919/527-6064

(AAA) [SAVE]   All Year [CP]   1P: $40   2P/1B: $45   2P/2B: $48   XP: $5
Location: On US 70 bypass, 0.5 mi e of US 258. 410 E New Bern Rd 28501. Fax: 919/527-6064.
◆   **Terms:** Reserv deposit; no pets. **Facility:** 60 rooms. 1 story; exterior corridors. **Dining:** Restaurant nearby.
Motel   **All Rooms:** microwaves, free movies, refrigerators. **Some Rooms:** 6 efficiencies, no utensils. **Cards:** AE,
DI, DS, MC, VI.   [✦] [CTV] [✕] [D]

SUPER 8 MOTEL   Rates Subject to Change   Phone: 919/523-8146

◆ ◆   All Year [CP]   1P: $45   2P/1B: $45   2P/2B: $45   XP: $5   F12
Motel   **Location:** On US 70 (Bypass) just e of US 258. 212 E New Bern Rd 28501. Fax: 919/523-8146. **Terms:** Sr.
discount; no pets. **Facility:** 48 rooms. 2 stories; exterior corridors. **All Rooms:** free movies. **Cards:** AE, CB,
DI, DS, MC, VI.   [CTV] [✕] [D]

KITTY HAWK—See Outer Banks p. 399.

KURE BEACH—600

LODGINGS

THE DOCKSIDER INN-OCEANFRONT   Phone: 910/458-4200

(AAA) [SAVE]   5/23-9/3   1P: $110- 149 2P/1B: $110- 149 2P/2B: $110- 149 XP: $5   F
4/25-5/22 & 9/4-10/4 1P: $75- 125 2P/1B: $75- 125 2P/2B: $75- 125 XP: $5   F
◆ ◆   12/1-4/24 & 10/5-11/30 1P: $55- 110 2P/1B: $55- 110 2P/2B: $55- 110 XP: $5   F
Motel   **Location:** On US 421, on corner of L Ave & N Fort Fisher Blvd; just n of fishing pier. 202 N Fort Fisher Blvd
28449 (PO Box 373). Fax: 910/458-6468. **Terms:** Reserv deposit; weekly rates; weekend rates avail; no
pets. **Facility:** 34 rooms. Many rooms with oceanfront balcony, rest with oceanview. Attractive property. Rates for up to 4 persons; 3 stories, no elevator; exterior corridors; oceanfront; beach. **Dining:** Restaurant nearby. **Recreation:** swimming, surf
fishing. **All Rooms:** refrigerators, combo or shower baths, no phones. **Some Rooms:** 13 kitchens, microwaves, VCP's.
Cards: CB, DI, DS, MC, VI. **Special Amenities:** Early check-in/late check-out and preferred room (subject to
availability with advanced reservations).   [⊞] [CTV] [D]

OCEAN PRINCESS INN   Phone: 910/458-6712

(AAA) [SAVE]   4/1-9/30 [BP]   1P: $69- 129 2P/1B: $89- 150 2P/2B: $139
12/1-3/31 & 10/1-11/30 [BP] 1P: $49- 89 2P/1B: $69- 109 2P/2B: $109
◆ ◆   **Location:** 0.8 mi s on US 421. 824 Fort Fisher Blvd S 28449. Fax: 910/458-7788. **Terms:** Age restrictions
Bed &   may apply; reserv deposit, 14 day notice; weekly rates; 2 night min stay, weekends in season; no pets.
Breakfast **Facility:** 9 rooms. Contemporary lodging near beach & between Atlantic Ocean & Cape Fear River inlet. 2 sto-
ries; interior/exterior corridors; smoke free premises; whirlpool. **Recreation:** bicycles.
All Rooms: coffeemakers, microwaves, free movies, refrigerators, combo or shower baths. **Some Rooms:** whirlpools.
Cards: AE, DS, MC, VI. **Special Amenities:** Free breakfast and free local telephone calls.   [⊞] [✦] [CTV] [✕] [D]

LAKE LURE—700

LODGING

THE LODGE ON LAKE LURE Rates Subject to Change **Phone:** 704/625-2789
4/1-11/15 [BP] 1P: $96- 135 2P/1B: $96- 135 2P/2B: $96- 135 XP: $15
12/1-3/31 & 11/16-11/30 [BP] 2P/1B: $86- 125 2P/2B: $86- 135 XP: $15
Location: 4 mi e on SR 64 & 74, 0.5 mi on Charlotte Dr; opposite golf course, entry at volunteer fire
Historic Bed department. Charlotte Dr 28746 (PO Box 519). Fax: 704/625-2421. **Terms:** Reserv deposit, 7 day notice; 2
& Breakfast night min stay, weekends; no pets. **Facility:** 12 rooms. 2 stories; interior corridors; designated smoking area.
All Rooms: free movies. **Cards:** AE, DS, MC, VI.
CTV ⊗ D

RESTAURANTS

JIMMY'S ORIGINAL SEAFOOD & STEAK & BAY TAVERN **Lunch:** $6-$8 **Dinner:** $11-$23 **Phone:** 704/625-4075
Location: 3.3 mi e on SR 64/74. 28746. **Hours:** 11:30 am-8:30 pm, Fri & Sat-9:30 pm. Closed: 11/26, 12/25
Regional & 12/31-2/1. **Features:** casual dress; children's menu; senior's menu; carryout; cocktails & lounge. Regional
American applications of steak & seafood along with good wine selections. Situated on Lake Lure with scenic mountain
view. On Mon in the the tavern/lounge, only food service is avail.
⊗

POINT OF VIEW RESTAURANT **Lunch:** $4-$14 **Dinner:** $14-$22 **Phone:** 704/625-4380
Location: 4.3 mi e on US 64/74. Hwys 64/74 28746. **Hours:** 11 am-2 & 5-10 pm, winter hrs vary. Closed:
Regional 11/26 & 12/25. **Reservations:** suggested. **Features:** casual dress; children's menu; cocktails. Fowl, veal, fish
American & beef preparations. Scenic mountain & lake setting. **Cards:** DI, DS, MC, VI.
⊗

LAKE TOXAWAY—360

LODGING

THE GREYSTONE INN Rates Subject to Change **Phone:** 704/966-4700
Fri & Sat 5/1-10/31 [MAP] 2P/1B: $330- 415 2P/2B: $350- 415 XP: $75-85 D
Sun-Thurs 5/1-10/31 [MAP] 2P/1B: $290- 380 2P/2B: $310- 380 XP: $45-85 D
12/1-4/30 & 11/1-11/30 [MAP] 2P/1B: $265- 340 2P/2B: $285- 340 XP: $45-85 D
Historic **Location:** 3.5 mi off US 64; from gate. Greystone Ln 28747. Fax: 704/862-5689. **Terms:** Reserv deposit, 15
Country Inn day notice; 15% service charge; 2 night min stay, weekends; no pets. **Facility:** 33 rooms. Many rooms with
fireplace, private balcony & lake view; 3 stories, no elevator; interior/exterior corridors. **Dining:** Dining room;
8 am-10 & 6:30-9 pm, guests only. **All Rooms:** free movies. **Cards:** MC, VI.
🏊 ♿ CTV ⊗ D

LAUREL SPRINGS—100

LODGING

BLUFF'S LODGE Rates Subject to Change **Phone:** 910/372-4499
5/1-10/31 1P: $70- 73 2P/1B: $73- 76 2P/2B: $73- 76 XP: $8 F12
Lodge **Location:** Off Blue Ridge Pkwy, milepost 241; 7 mi n on parkway from jct SR 18. 45356 Blue Ridge Pkwy
28644. Fax: 910/372-4499. **Terms:** Open 5/1-10/31; reserv deposit; no pets. **Facility:** 24 rooms. 2 stories; exterior corridors. **Dining:** Restaurant; 7:30 am-7:30 pm; $7-$12. **All Rooms:** no A/C. **Cards:** AE, CB, DI, DS, MC, VI.
⊗ D

LAURINBURG—11,600

LODGINGS

COMFORT INN Rates Subject to Change **Phone:** 910/277-7788
All Year [CP] 1P: $59- 95 2P/1B: $67- 95 2P/2B: $67- 95 XP: $8 F18
Motel **Location:** US 15 & 401 bypass, on service road. 1705 401 bypass S 28352. Fax: 910/277-7229. **Terms:** Sr.
discount; no pets. **Facility:** 80 rooms. 3 stories; interior corridors. **All Rooms:** free movies. **Cards:** AE, DI,
DS, MC, VI.
CTV ⊗ 🛗 D

HAMPTON INN Rates Subject to Change **Phone:** 910/277-1516
All Year [CP] 1P: $58- 64 2P/1B: $70 2P/2B: $64
Motel **Location:** At jct US 15 & 401 bypass. 115 Hampton Cir 28352. Fax: 910/277-1514. **Terms:** Pets. **Facility:** 50
rooms. 3 stories; interior corridors. **All Rooms:** free movies. **Cards:** AE, CB, DI, DS, MC, VI.
Roll in showers. 🛏 ⊗ 🛗 D S

RESTAURANT

WOOLY MCDUFF'S NEIGHBORHOOD GRILLE **Lunch:** $6-$8 **Dinner:** $13-$18 **Phone:** 910/276-6632
Location: US 15 & 401 bypass on service road in front of Comfort Inn. 1709 Hwy 401 & Bypass 28352.
American **Hours:** 11:30 am-11 pm. **Features:** salad bar; cocktails. Sports type grille & lounge. **Cards:** MC, VI.
⊗

LENOIR—14,200

LODGINGS

DAYS INN Rates Subject to Change **Phone:** 704/754-0731
All Year [CP] 1P: $44- 48 2P/1B: $48 2P/2B: $48- 58 XP: $4 F12
Motel **Location:** Just n on US 321 from jct US 64 & SR 18. 206 Blowing Rock Blvd 28645. Fax: 704/754-1078.
Terms: No pets. **Facility:** 78 rooms. 2 stories; exterior corridors. **All Rooms:** free movies. **Cards:** AE, CB,
DI, DS, MC, VI.
CTV 📶 ⊗ D

HOLIDAY INN EXPRESS Rates Subject to Change **Phone:** 704/758-4403
All Year [CP] 1P: $60- 65 2P/1B: $60- 65 2P/2B: $60- 65 XP: $10 D18
Motel **Location:** 1.3 mi e at jct SR 18 & US 321. 142 Wilkesboro Blvd SE 28645. Fax: 704/758-4403. **Terms:** Sr.
discount; no pets. **Facility:** 100 rooms. 2 stories; exterior corridors. **All Rooms:** free movies. **Cards:** AE, CB,
DI, DS, JCB, MC, VI.
🏊 CTV ⊗ D

LEXINGTON—16,600

LODGINGS

COMFORT SUITES OF LEXINGTON Rates Subject to Change **Phone:** 910/357-2333
All Year [BP] 1P: $69- 120 2P/1B: $76- 120 2P/2B: $76- 120 XP: $7 F16
Motel **Location:** Just s on SR 8 from I-85, exit 91. 1620 Cotton Grove Rd 27292. Fax: 910/357-2359. **Terms:** Sr.
discount; check-in 4 pm; no pets. **Facility:** 120 rooms. 2 stories; interior/exterior corridors. **All Rooms:** free
movies. **Some Rooms:** 5 efficiencies. **Cards:** AE, CB, DI, DS, JCB, MC, VI.
🏊 ⊗ D

SUPER 8 MOTEL

Phone: 910/357-6444

(AAA) [SAVE]   All Year [CP]   1P: $39- 49 2P/1B: $45- 55 2P/2B: $48- 58 XP: $3-5   F11
◆◆   **Location:** Just s on SR 8 from I-85, exit 91. 1631 Cotton Grove Rd 27292. Fax: 910/357-6444. **Terms:** N
Motel   pets. **Facility:** 42 rooms. 2 stories; exterior corridors; small pool. **Dining:** Restaurant nearby
             All Rooms: free movies. **Some Rooms:** microwaves, refrigerators. Fee: whirlpools. **Cards:** AE, DI, DS, MC
             VI. **Special Amenities:** Early check-in/late check-out and free breakfast.   [◉] [CTV] [X] [D

RESTAURANT

LEXINGTON BARBECUE 1   **Lunch:** $4-$7   **Dinner:** $4-$7   Phone: 910/249-9814
◆   **Location:** On Business Rt 85, at jct US 64W. 10 Hwy 29-70 S 27295. **Hours:** 10 am-9:30 pm. Closed majo
American   holidays & Sun. **Features:** children's menu; carryout. 1950's roadside-style diner.   [X]

LINCOLNTON—6,800

LODGING

COMFORT INN   Guaranteed Rates   Phone: 704/732-0011
◆◆◆   All Year [BP]   1P: $89   2P/1B: $99   2P/2B: $99   XP: $7   F18
Motel   **Location:** Just w of US 321, ex exit 24. 1550 E Main St 28092 (PO Box 814). Fax: 704/732-4872. **Terms:** S
             discount; no pets. **Facility:** 77 rooms. 3 stories; interior/exterior corridors. **All Rooms:** free movies
Some Rooms: 4 efficiencies. **Cards:** AE, CB, DI, DS, JCB, MC, VI.   [CTV] [X] [D

LITTLE SWITZERLAND—200

LODGINGS

BIG LYNN LODGE   Guaranteed Rates   Phone: 704/765-4257
(AAA)   4/16-11/1 [MAP]   1P: $73   2P/1B: $82- 120 2P/2B: $82- 100 XP: $23   F
◆◆   **Location:** 1.5 mi n on SR 226A; 1.5 mi w of jct SR 226 & Blue Ridge Pkwy; Mineral Museum exit. Hw
Country Inn 226A 28749 (PO Box 459). Fax: 704/765-0301. **Terms:** Open 4/16-11/1; reserv deposit, 7 day notice; n
             pets. **Facility:** 42 rooms. Suites avail Nov-March, $75. Handling fee imposed; 2 stories; exterior corridors
             Dining: Restaurant; 7:30 am-9 & 6-7:30 pm; $12. **Some Rooms:** A/C. **Cards:** MC, VI. *(See ad below)*
                                                                              [CTV] [X] [D

SWITZERLAND INN   Phone: 704/765-2153
(AAA) [SAVE]   4/28-11/5 [BP]   1P: $65- 85 2P/1B: $75- 120 2P/2B: $75- 120 XP: $15   D1
◆◆◆   **Location:** Jct SR 226A & Blue Ridge Pkwy; 1 mi se on SR 226A. 28749 (PO Box 399). Fax: 704/765-0049
Country Inn **Terms:** Open 4/28-11/5; reserv deposit, 7 day notice; no pets. **Facility:** 56 rooms. Property on top of a moun
             tain with awesome view. Attractive public areas. 5 two-bedroom units. Cabins for up to 4 persons, $100-$140
             Handling fee imposed; 2 stories; interior/exterior corridors; 2 tennis courts; horseback riding nearby, shuffle
board. **Dining:** Dining room; 7:30-9:30 am, 11:30-2 & 5:30-9 pm; $10-$18; wine/beer only. **Recreation:** hiking trails
All Rooms: combo or shower baths. **Some Rooms:** A/C. **Cards:** AE, MC, VI. **Special Amenities:** Free breakfast and fre
local telephone calls.   [≈] [◉] [CTV] [X] [D

LUMBERTON—18,600

LODGINGS

BEST WESTERN LUMBERTON   Phone: 910/618-979
(AAA) [SAVE]   All Year [CP]   1P: $55- 65 2P/1B: $65   2P/2B: $55   XP: $10   F1
◆◆◆   **Location:** I-95 & SR 301, exit 22. 201 Jackson Ct 28358. Fax: 910/618-9057. **Terms:** Small pets only
Motel   **Facility:** 63 rooms. Attractive public areas. Spacious, nicely furnished & decorated guest rooms. 2 stories; ex
             terior corridors. **Dining:** Restaurant nearby. **Services:** valet laundry. **All Rooms:** microwaves, free movies
             refrigerators, combo or shower baths. **Some Rooms:** Fee: whirlpools. **Cards:** AE, CB, DI, DS, JCB, MC, V
Special Amenities: Free breakfast and free local telephone calls.
                                      Roll in showers. [🛏] [≈] [◉] [CTV] [♿] [X] [D] [S

COMFORT INN   Phone: 910/739-480
(AAA) [SAVE]   All Year [CP]   1P: $55- 59 2P/1B: $55- 59 2P/2B: $55- 59 XP: $5   F1
◆◆◆   **Location:** I-95, exit 20. 3070 Roberts Ave 28359. Fax: 910/738-5299. **Terms:** No pets. **Facility:** 59 rooms
Motel   Handling fee imposed; 2 stories; exterior corridors; sauna, whirlpool. **Dining:** Restaurant nearby
             Services: valet laundry. **All Rooms:** coffeemakers, microwaves, free movies, refrigerators. **Some Rooms**
             Fee: VCP's, whirlpools. **Cards:** AE, CB, DI, DS, JCB, MC, VI. **Special Amenities:** Free breakfast and fre
local telephone calls. *(See color ad p 385)*   [≈] [◉] [📶] [CTV] [X] [🌙] [D

COMFORT SUITES   Rates Subject to Change   **Phone:** 910/739-8800
◆◆◆   All Year [CP]   1P: $60- 80 2P/1B: $60- 80 2P/2B: $60- 80 XP: $5   F18
Suite Motel   **Location:** I-95, exit 22 & US 301. 215 Wintergreen Dr 28358. Fax: 910/739-0027. **Terms:** Sr. discount; pets, $50 dep req. **Facility:** 93 rooms. 4 stories; interior corridors. **All Rooms:** free movies. **Cards:** AE, CB, DI, DS, JCB, MC, VI. *(See ad p 385)*
🛏 🖨 CTV ✕ D S

ECONO LODGE   **Phone:** 910/738-7121
(AAA) SAVE   All Year [CP]   1P: $45- 49 2P/1B: $55- 56 2P/2B: $45- 66 XP: $4   F12
◆   **Location:** I-95 at SR 211. 3591 Lackey St 28358 (PO Box 693, 28359). Fax: 910/739-4351. **Terms:** Reserv deposit; no pets. **Facility:** 103 rooms. 2 stories; exterior corridors. **Dining:** Restaurant nearby.
Motel   **All Rooms:** free movies. **Some Rooms:** Fee: microwaves, refrigerators. **Cards:** AE, CB, DI, DS, JCB, MC, VI. **Special Amenities:** Free breakfast and free local telephone calls. *(See ad p 385)*
🖨 CTV ✕ D

FAIRFIELD INN BY MARRIOTT   Rates Subject to Change   **Phone:** 910/739-8444
◆◆◆   All Year [CP]   1P: $50   2P/1B: $50   2P/2B: $50
Motel   **Location:** From jct I-95 exit 20 & SR 211, 0.5 mi s on Lackey St. 3361 Lackey St 28358. Fax: 910/739-8466. **Terms:** Sr. discount; no pets. **Facility:** 105 rooms. 3 stories; interior/exterior corridors. **All Rooms:** free movies. **Cards:** AE, CB, DI, DS, MC, VI. *(See color ad below)*   Roll in showers. 🖨 CTV ♿ ✕ 🐾 D S

HAMPTON INN

Phone: 910/738-3332

(AAA) SAVE
◆◆◆
Motel

All Year [CP]   1P: $60- 66   2P/1B: $65- 69   2P/2B: $65- 69
Location: I-95, exit 22. 201 Wintergreen Dr 28358. Fax: 910/739-8671. **Terms:** No pets. **Facility:** 68 rooms. Very attractive & comfortable public areas & rooms. All rooms with hair dryer, iron & ironing board. 2 stories; interior/exterior corridors; sauna, whirlpool. **Dining:** Restaurant nearby. **Services:** Fee: coin laundry. **All Rooms:** coffeemakers, microwaves, free movies, refrigerators. **Some Rooms:** VCP's. Fee: whirlpools.
Cards: AE, CB, DI, DS, MC, VI. **Special Amenities:** Free breakfast and free local telephone calls.
(See color ad below)

HOLIDAY INN

Phone: 910/671-1166

(AAA) SAVE
◆◆◆
Motor Inn

All Year   1P: $63- 69   2P/1B: $63- 69   2P/2B: $63- 69 XP: $6   F17
Location: I-95 exit 22. 5201 Fayetteville Rd 28358. Fax: 910/671-1166. **Terms:** No pets. **Facility:** 108 rooms. 2 stories; interior corridors. **Dining & Entertainment:** Restaurant; 24 hours; $6-$16; cocktail lounge; wine/beer only. **Services:** valet laundry. **All Rooms:** free movies. **Some Rooms:** Fee: refrigerators.
Cards: AE, CB, DI, DS, MC, VI. **Special Amenities:** Early check-in/late check-out and free room upgrade (subject to availability with advanced reservations).

QUALITY INN AND SUITES

Phone: 910/738-8261

(AAA) SAVE
◆◆◆
Motor Inn

All Year   1P: $55- 65   2P/1B: $61- 71   2P/2B: $61- 71 XP: $6
Location: I-95, exit 20. 3608 Kahn Dr 28358. Fax: 910/671-9075. **Terms:** Package plans; pets, $20 extra charge. **Facility:** 120 rooms. Very attractive & comfortable public areas. 2 stories; interior/exterior corridors; wading pool; gas grill & picnic tables in large outdoor pool area. **Dining & Entertainment:** Cafeteria; 6 am-2 & 5-9 pm; $7-$11; cocktail lounge; wine/beer only. **Services:** valet laundry. **All Rooms:** free & pay movies. **Some Rooms:** Fee: microwaves, refrigerators. **Cards:** AE, DI, DS, MC, VI. **Special Amenities:** Free breakfast and preferred room (subject to availability with advanced reservations). *(See color ad p 385)*

RAMADA LIMITED

Rates Subject to Change   **Phone:** 910/738-4261

◆◆
Motel

All Year [CP]   1P: $40   2P/1B: $44   2P/2B: $44
Location: I-95, exit 20 via se on service road. 3510 Capuano Rd 28358. Fax: 910/738-4261. **Terms:** No pets. **Facility:** 133 rooms. 2 stories; exterior corridors. **Dining:** Restaurant; 6 am-2 & 5:30-10 pm; $5-$13.
All Rooms: free movies. **Cards:** AE, CB, DI, DS, MC, VI.

SUPER 8 MOTEL

Phone: 910/671-4444

(AAA) SAVE
◆◆◆
Motel

All Year [CP]   1P: $45- 75   2P/1B: $45- 85   2P/2B: $45- 85 XP: $5   F12
Location: I-95 exit 22. 150 Jackson Ct 28358. Fax: 910/671-4444. **Terms:** Small pets only. **Facility:** 59 rooms. 2 stories; exterior corridors; small pool. **Dining:** Restaurant nearby. **All Rooms:** free movies, combo or shower baths. **Cards:** AE, CB, DI, DS, MC, VI. **Special Amenities:** Free local telephone calls.

RESTAURANT

JOHNS RESTAURANT

Dinner: $12-$22   **Phone:** 910/738-4709

(AAA)
◆◆
American

Location: From I-95 exit 22, 0.5 mi s on Kahn Dr. 4880 Kahn Dr 28358. **Hours:** 5:30 pm-10 pm. Closed: Sun, Mon & 7/1-7/10. **Reservations:** suggested. **Features:** dressy casual; children's menu; carryout; beer & wine only. Nicely presented entrees served in a comfortable atmosphere. **Cards:** AE, DI, DS, MC, VI.

MAGGIE VALLEY—200

LODGINGS

BEST WESTERN MOUNTAINBROOK INN

Phone: 704/926-3962

(AAA) SAVE
◆◆◆
Motel

Fri & Sat 5/22-9/1 & 10/2-10/31 [CP]	1P: $75- 89			2P/2B: $75- 99	XP: $8	F12
Sun-Thurs 5/22-9/1 & 10/2-10/31 [CP]	1P: $69- 89			2P/2B: $69- 89	XP: $8	F12
Fri & Sat 12/1-5/21, 9/2-10/1 & 11/1-11/30 [CP]	1P: $49- 69			2P/2B: $49- 69	XP: $8	F12
Sun-Thurs 12/1-5/21, 9/2-10/1 & 11/1-11/30 [CP]	1P: $29- 59			2P/2B: $39- 59	XP: $8	F12

Location: On US 19, 4 mi w of US 276. 3811 Soco Rd, Hwy 19 28751 (PO Box 565). Fax: 704/926-2947. **Terms:** Package plans; no pets. **Facility:** 48 rooms. In scenic mountain setting. Voice mail. Very attractive & well-maintained grounds & spa areas. Enclosed hot tub; 2 stories; exterior corridors; mountain view; whirlpool; picnic area with barbecue grills. Fee: miniature golf. **Dining:** Restaurant nearby. **All Rooms:** coffeemakers, microwaves, free movies, refrigerators.
Cards: AE, CB, DI, DS, MC. **Special Amenities:** Free local telephone calls and free newspaper. *(See color ad p 388)*

Roll in showers.

BLUE MOUNTAIN INN   Rates Subject to Change   **Phone:** 704/926-3385
◆   4/1-10/31   2P/1B: $31-   60
Motel   **Location:** On US 19, 4 mi w of US 276. 1005 Soco Rd, Hwy 19 28751 (PO Box 193). **Terms:** Open 4/1-10/31; small pets only. **Facility:** 19 rooms. 1 story; exterior corridors. **All Rooms:** free movies.
Some Rooms: 2 kitchens. **Cards:** DS, MC, VI.

COMFORT INN   **Phone:** 704/926-9106

5/29-10/31 [CP]	1P:	$49-	79	2P/2B:	$59-	99	XP: $10	F18
4/1-5/28 [CP]	1P:	$49-	69	2P/2B:	$49-	89	XP: $10	F18
12/1-3/31 & 11/1-11/30 [CP]	1P:	$39-	60	2P/2B:	$39-	79	XP: $10	F18

Motel   **Location:** On US 19; 3.5 mi w of jct US 276. 3282 Soco Rd, Hwy 19 28751. Fax: 704/926-9106. **Terms:** No pets. **Facility:** 68 rooms. 2 stories; interior corridors; mountain view; whirlpool; playground.
Dining: Restaurant nearby. **All Rooms:** free movies. **Some Rooms:** coffeemakers, efficiency, microwaves, refrigerators. Fee: whirlpools. **Cards:** AE, CB, DI, DS, JCB, MC, VI. **Special Amenities:** Free local telephone calls and free newspaper.

JONATHAN CREEK INN   **Phone:** 704/926-1232

Fri & Sat 5/22-9/6 & 10/2-10/31	1P:	$69-	89	2P/1B:	$79-	99	2P/2B:	$79- 99	XP: $8	F16
Sun-Thurs 5/22-9/6 & 10/2-10/31	1P:	$49-	89	2P/1B:	$59-	99	2P/2B:	$59- 99	XP: $8	F16
Fri & Sat 12/1-5/21, 9/7-10/1 & 11/1-11/30	1P:	$39-	69	2P/1B:	$49-	69	2P/2B:	$49- 69	XP: $8	F16
Sun-Thurs 12/1-5/21, 9/7-10/1 & 11/1-11/30	1P:	$29-	59	2P/1B:	$39-	59	2P/2B:	$39- 59		

Location: 4.5 mi w of US 276. 4224 Soco Rd, US 19 28751 (PO Box 66). Fax: 704/926-9751. **Terms:** Weekly rates; no pets. **Facility:** 42 rooms. Offers balconies overlooking mountain streams, mountain view from porch rocking chair & grill at stream side with deck. 3-bedroom house $300-$375 weekends with hot tub & wood burning fireplace; 2 stories; exterior corridors; small heated pool; basketball court. **Dining:** Restaurant nearby. **Recreation:** children's program; fishing. **All Rooms:** coffeemakers, free movies, refrigerators. **Some Rooms:** microwaves. Fee: whirlpools. **Cards:** AE, MC, VI. **Special Amenities:** Free local telephone calls and preferred room (subject to availability with advanced reservations).

LAUREL PARK INN

Phone: 704/926-1700

AAA SAVE

| | | 1P: | $40- | 95 | 2P/1B: | $40- | 75 | 2P/2B: | $45- | 80 | XP: | $5 | F12 |
5/20-10/31
| | | 1P: | $35- | 50 | 2P/1B: | $35- | 50 | 2P/2B: | $40- | 55 | XP: | $5 | F12 |
4/1-5/19

◆ ◆
Motel

Location: On US 19; 2 blks w of US 276. 257 Soco Rd (Hwy 19) 28751. **Terms:** Open 4/1-10/31; reserv deposit, 7 day notice, handling fee imposed; weekly rates; no pets. **Facility:** 18 rooms. For the budget traveler. Scenic area. 1 story; exterior corridors. **Dining:** Restaurant nearby. **All Rooms:** free movies. **Some Rooms:** refrigerators. **Cards:** AE, DS, MC, VI. **Special Amenities:** Free local telephone calls.
(See color ad p 388)

(symbols)

MICROTEL INN & SUITES

Rates Subject to Change

Phone: 704/926-8554

AAA

Fri & Sat 5/22-9/1 &
10/2-10/31 | 1P: | $70- | 90 | | | 2P/2B: | $70- | 90 | XP: | $5 | F16

◆ ◆ ◆
Motel

Sun-Thurs 5/22-9/1 &
10/2-10/31 | 1P: | $66- | 86 | | | 2P/2B: | $66- | 90 | XP: | $5 | F16
Fri & Sat 12/1-5/21, 9/2-10/1
& 11/1-11/30 | 1P: | $40- | 50 | | | 2P/2B: | $40- | 60 | XP: | $5 | F16
Sun-Thurs 12/1-5/21,
9/2-10/1 & 11/1-11/30 | 1P: | $30- | 50 | | | 2P/2B: | $30- | 56 | XP: | $5 | F16

Location: On US 19, 4 mi w of US 276. 377 Soco Rd, Hwy 19 28751 (PO Box 86). **Fax:** 704/926-1752. **Terms:** Sr. discount; no pets. **Facility:** 58 rooms. 1 whirlpool rm, $79.95-$129.95; 2 stories; interior corridors. **All Rooms:** free movies. **Cards:** AE, CB, DI, DS, MC. *(See color ad p 388)*   Roll in showers. (symbols)

MOUNT VALLEY LODGE

Phone: 704/926-9244

AAA SAVE

6/1-9/1 & 9/30-10/31 [CP] | 1P: | $45- | 75 | 2P/1B: | $52- | 98 | 2P/2B: | $86- | 110 | XP: | $5 | D12
9/2-9/29 [CP] | 1P: | $40- | 52 | 2P/1B: | $39- | 52 | 2P/2B: | $75- | 98 | XP: | $5 | D12

◆

12/1-2/28 [EP] | 1P: | $40- | 52 | 2P/1B: | $39- | 65 | 2P/2B: | $75- | 86 | XP: | $5 | D12
Country Inn

3/1-5/31 & 11/1-11/30 [EP] | 1P: | $29- | 39 | 2P/1B: | $35- | 39 | 2P/2B: | $55- | 65 | XP: | $5 | D12

Location: US 19, 2.8 mi w of jct US 276. 620 Soco Rd 28751. **Fax:** 704/926-9244. **Terms:** Age restrictions may apply; reserv deposit, 7 day notice; 2 night min stay, 10/1-10/31; no pets. **Facility:** 32 rooms. Mix styles of rooms, many with wood burning fireplace. 2 stories; interior/exterior corridors; mountain view; miniature golf; game room. **Dining:** Restaurant nearby. **Services:** Fee: coin laundry. **Some Rooms:** refrigerators. **Cards:** MC, VI. **Special Amenities:** Free local telephone calls and preferred room (subject to availability with advanced reservations). (symbols)

QUALITY INN

Rates Subject to Change

Phone: 704/926-0201

◆ ◆ ◆
Motel

5/30-10/31 [CP] | 1P: | $45- | 125 | 2P/1B: | $45- | 125 | 2P/2B: | $45- | 125 | XP: | $5 | F18
12/1-5/29 & 11/1-11/30 [CP] | 1P: | $35- | 55 | 2P/1B: | $35- | 55 | 2P/2B: | $35- | 55 | XP: | $5 | F18

Location: At jct US 276N & US 19. 70 Soco Rd 28751. **Fax:** 704/926-1461. **Terms:** Sr. discount; no pets. **Facility:** 102 rooms. 4 stories; interior corridors. **All Rooms:** free movies. **Cards:** AE, CB, DI, DS, JCB, MC, VI.

RIVERLET MOTEL

Phone: 704/926-1900

AAA SAVE

5/23-9/1 | 1P: | $39- | 99 | | | 2P/2B: | $39- | 99 | XP: | $7 | F12
10/5-11/8 | 1P: | $39- | 89 | | | 2P/2B: | $39- | 89 | XP: | $7 | F12

◆

9/2-10/4 | 1P: | $39- | 69 | | | 2P/2B: | $39- | 69 | XP: | $7 | F12
Motel

4/24-5/22 | 1P: | $55 | | | | 2P/2B: | $25- | 55 | XP: | $7 | F12

Location: On US 19, 4.5 mi w from jct US 276. 4102 Soco Rd, Hwy 19 28751. **Terms:** Open 4/24-11/8; reserv deposit; no pets. **Facility:** 21 rooms. Picnic deck over stream. 1-2 stories; exterior corridors. **Dining:** 7-11 am; breakfast only; coffee shop nearby. **Recreation:** fishing. **All Rooms:** free movies. **Some Rooms:** microwaves. Fee: refrigerators. **Cards:** DS, MC, VI. **Special Amenities:** Early check-in/late check-out and free local telephone calls.

(symbols)

SCOTTISH INN

Phone: 704/926-9137

AAA SAVE

5/20-10/31 | 1P: | $35- | 85 | 2P/1B: | $35- | 85 | 2P/2B: | $35- | 85 | XP: | $7 | F5
12/1-5/19 & 11/1-11/30 | 1P: | $25- | 35 | 2P/1B: | $25- | 35 | 2P/2B: | $25- | 35 | XP: | $7 | F5

◆ ◆
Motel

Location: On US 19, 2 blks w of jct US 276. 178 Soco Rd 28751. **Fax:** 704/926-9139. **Terms:** Reserv deposit, 3 day notice; no pets. **Facility:** 21 rooms. 1 story; exterior corridors. **All Rooms:** free movies. **Cards:** AE, DS, MC, VI.

(symbols)

RESTAURANTS

ARF'S RESTAURANT

Dinner: $9-$13

Phone: 704/926-1566

◆ ◆
American

Location: On US 19 4.5 mi w of US 276. 1316 Soco Rd 28751. **Hours:** 4:30 pm-9:30 pm, Fri & Sat-10 pm, Sun-9 pm. Closed: 11/26, 12/24 & 12/25; Mon & Tues 11/1-3/31 & 3/1-3/14. **Features:** carryout; salad bar; cocktails. Baby back ribs; many seafood entrees. Covered creekside outside dining weather permitting. **Cards:** AE, DS, MC, VI.

(symbol)

J. ARTHUR'S RESTAURANT

Dinner: $9-$15

Phone: 704/926-1817

◆ ◆ ◆
Steak and
Seafood

Location: On US 19, 3 mi w of jct US 276. 801 Soco Rd 28751. **Hours:** 5 pm-9:30 pm; 11/1-4/30 to 9 pm. Closed: 11/26, 12/25 & Sun-Tues 11/1-4/30. **Reservations:** accepted; for 10 or more. **Features:** children's menu; carryout; cocktails & lounge. Prime rib, fresh trout & gorgonaola cheese salads also served in 2-story, pine panelled dining room with fireplaces & country decor. Family oriented. **Cards:** AE, DI, MC, VI.

(symbol)

MOUNTAINEER BUFFET

Phone: 704/926-1730

AAA

◆
American

Location: 1.5 mi w of Ghost Town on US 19. 28751. **Hours:** Open 5/15-10/31; 8 am-8 pm; Mon-Fri from 4 pm 5/1-5/31 & 9/1-10/31. **Features:** casual dress; carryout; salad bar; buffet. Home style cooking. Homemade soup, biscuits & cornbread. **Cards:** AE, DS, MC, VI.

MAGNOLIA—700

LODGING

THE MAGNOLIA INN

Rates Subject to Change

Phone: 910/289-4050

◆ ◆
Historic Bed
& Breakfast

All Year [BP] | 1P: | $49- | 79 | 2P/1B: | $49- | 79 | | | | | XP: | $10 | D14

Location: Just s of jct SR 903 & US 117 to E Bleeker St, just w. 101 E Bleeker St 28453 (PO Box 580). **Terms:** Reserv deposit; no pets. **Facility:** 4 rooms. Handling fee imposed; 2 stories; interior corridors. **Cards:** AE, DS, MC, VI.

(symbols)

MANTEO—See Outer Banks p. 399.

MARION—4,800

LODGING

COMFORT INN   Phone: 704/652-4888
AAA SAVE
    10/2-10/31 [CP]   1P: $109   2P/1B: $109   2P/2B: $109   XP: $5   F18
    7/3-10/1 [CP]   1P: $64- 69   2P/1B: $64- 69   2P/2B: $64- 69   XP: $5   F18
◆◆◆   12/1-7/2 & 11/1-11/30 [CP]   1P: $59- 64   2P/1B: $59- 64   2P/2B: $59- 64   XP: $5   F18
Motel   **Location:** I-40 exit 86, 5 mi n, jct of N 221 bypass & US 70. Bypass 221 & US 70 28782 (PO Drawer 129, 28752). Fax: 704/652-3787. **Terms:** Reserv deposit; no pets. **Facility:** 56 rooms. 6 whirlpool rms, extra charge; 2 stories; interior corridors; whirlpool. **Dining:** Restaurant nearby. **Services:** Fee: coin laundry. **All Rooms:** free movies, combo or shower baths. **Some Rooms:** microwaves, refrigerators. **Cards:** AE, DI, MC, VI. **Special Amenities: Free breakfast and free local telephone calls.** Roll in showers. [icons]

MARS HILL—1,600

LODGING

WOLF LAUREL RESORT   Rates Subject to Change   Phone: 704/689-9777
◆◆◆   5/1-10/31   1P: $135   2P/1B: $175   2P/2B: $175   XP: $10   F13
Resort Motel   12/1-4/30 & 11/1-11/30   1P: $115   2P/1B: $115   2P/2B: $135   XP: $10   F13
    Location: 5 mi n on US 23, 4.5 mi ne following Wolf Laurel signage. Rt 3 28754. Fax: 704/689-9670. **Terms:** Reserv deposit, 14 day notice; no pets. **Facility:** 35 rooms. 10 three- to five-bedroom units, $175. Handling fee imposed; 2 stories; exterior corridors. **Dining:** Restaurant; 7:30 am-9 pm, 5/1-10/31; $10-$15. **All Rooms:** kitchens, no A/C. **Cards:** DS, MC, VI. [icons]

MATTHEWS—13,700   (See map p. 342; index p. 339)

LODGINGS

BEST WESTERN LUXBURY HOTEL   Phone: 704/845-5911 **96**
AAA SAVE   All Year [CP]   1P: $72   2P/1B: $78   2P/2B: $78   XP: $6   F18
    Location: 0.8 mi nw on US 74 from jct SR 51; in Windsor Square. 9701 E Independence Blvd 28105.
◆◆◆   Fax: 704/845-5536. **Terms:** No pets. **Facility:** 97 rooms. Spacious rooms. Suites, $79-$106; 3 stories; interior
Motel   corridors. **Dining:** Restaurant nearby. **Services:** valet laundry. **All Rooms:** free movies. **Some Rooms:** coffeemakers, refrigerators. Fee: whirlpools. **Cards:** AE, DI, DS, MC, VI. **Special Amenities: Early check-in/late check-out and free room upgrade (subject to availability with advanced reservations).** [icons]

COMFORT INN MATTHEWS   Rates Subject to Change   Phone: 704/847-5252 **95**
◆◆   All Year [CP]   1P: $63   2P/1B: $63   2P/2B: $63
Motel   **Location:** 0.7 mi se on US 74 from jct SR 51. 1938 Moore St 28105. Fax: 704/847-0140. **Terms:** Sr. discount; no pets. **Facility:** 65 rooms. Daily phone charge $1; 2 stories; exterior corridors. **All Rooms:** free movies. **Cards:** AE, DI, DS, MC, VI. [icons]

HAMPTON INN-CHARLOTTE MATTHEWS   Rates Subject to Change   Phone: 704/841-1155 **97**
◆◆◆   All Year [CP]   1P: $71- 95   2P/1B: $77- 101   2P/2B: $77- 101
Motel   **Location:** On US 74, 0.5 mi n from SR 51. 9615 Independence Point Pkwy 28105. Fax: 704/841-4992.
    Terms: No pets. **Facility:** 92 rooms. 5 stories; interior corridors. **All Rooms:** free movies. **Cards:** AE, CB, DI, DS, JCB, MC, VI. Roll in showers. [icons]

MOCKSVILLE—3,400

LODGING

COMFORT INN   Rates Subject to Change   Phone: 704/634-7310
◆◆◆   All Year [CP]   1P: $55- 95   2P/1B: $60- 105   2P/2B: $60- 105   XP: $5   F18
Motel   **Location:** Exit 170 off I-40, 0.3 mi s on US 601. 1500 Yadkinville Rd 27028. Fax: 704/634-7329. **Terms:** Sr. discount; no pets. **Facility:** 82 rooms. 2 stories; exterior corridors. **All Rooms:** free movies. **Cards:** AE, CB, DI, DS, MC, VI. [icons]

MONROE—16,100

LODGINGS

COMFORT INN   Rates Subject to Change   Phone: 704/283-9600
◆◆◆   All Year [CP]   1P: $59- 61   2P/1B: $59- 61   2P/2B: $59- 61
Motel   **Location:** 2 mi w on US 74. 2351 W Roosevelt Blvd 28110. Fax: 704/289-1118. **Terms:** No pets. **Facility:** 67 rooms. 2 stories; exterior corridors. **All Rooms:** free movies. **Some Rooms:** kitchen. **Cards:** AE, CB, DI, DS, JCB, MC, VI. [icons]

KNIGHTS INN-CHARLOTTE/MONROE   Phone: 704/289-9111
AAA SAVE   All Year   1P: $38- 62   2P/1B: $43- 68   2P/2B: $41- 68   XP: $6   F18
    Location: At jct of US 74 & 601; entry on Venus St. 350 Venus St 28112. Fax: 704/289-9111.
◆◆   **Terms:** Check-in 4 pm; weekly/monthly rates; no pets. **Facility:** 110 rooms. 1 story; exterior corridors; small
Motel   pool. **Some Rooms:** 11 efficiencies, radios. Fee: microwaves, refrigerators. **Cards:** AE, CB, DI, DS, MC, VI. **Special Amenities: Free room upgrade and preferred room (each subject to availability with advanced reservations).** [icons]

MOORESVILLE—9,300

LODGINGS

SPRING RUN BED & BREAKFAST   Guaranteed Rates   Phone: 704/664-6686
◆◆◆   All Year [BP]   1P: $95   2P/1B: $95   XP: $20
Bed &   **Location:** 5 mi sw of I-77, exit 33. 172 Spring Run 28115. Fax: 704/664-9282. **Terms:** Reserv deposit, 7 day
Breakfast   notice; no pets. **Facility:** 2 rooms. 3 stories; interior corridors. **All Rooms:** free movies. **Cards:** MC, VI. [icons]

SUPER 8   Rates Subject to Change   Phone: 704/662-6188
◆◆   Fri & Sat [CP]   1P: $65   2P/1B: $65   2P/2B: $75   XP: $3
Motel   Sun-Thurs [CP]   1P: $55   2P/1B: $55   2P/2B: $61   XP: $3
    Location: 0.3 mi w on SR 150 from I-77, exit 36. 484 River Hwy 28115. Fax: 704/662-6188. **Terms:** Sr. discount; reserv deposit, 3 day notice; no pets. **Facility:** 58 rooms. Surcharge on phone bill. Handling fee imposed; 2 stories; exterior corridors. **All Rooms:** free movies. **Cards:** AE, CB, DS, MC, VI. Roll in showers. [icons]

MOREHEAD CITY—6,000

LODGINGS

BEST WESTERN BUCCANEER INN   Phone: 919/726-3115

AAA SAVE
♦♦♦
Motor Inn

Fri & Sat 5/23-9/1	1P:	$85-	92	2P/1B:	$89-	92	2P/2B: $89-	92	XP: $5	F18
4/1-5/22 & 9/2-10/31	1P:	$50-	75	2P/1B:	$57-	75	2P/2B: $55-	71	XP: $5	F18
Sun-Thurs 5/23-9/1	1P:	$63-	70	2P/1B:	$67-	70	2P/2B: $67		XP: $5	F18
12/1-3/31 & 11/1-11/30	1P:	$36-	43	2P/1B:	$40-	43	2P/2B: $40		XP: $5	F18

Location: 1.8 mi w on US 70. 2806 Arendell St 28557. Fax: 919/726-3864. **Terms:** Weekly rates; AP, BP avail; package plans; no pets. **Facility:** 91 rooms. Contemporary room decor; attractive public areas. 2-3 stories; interior/exterior corridors. Fee: golf privileges. **Dining:** Anchor Inn Restaurant & Lounge, see separate listing. **All Rooms:** free movies, refrigerators. **Some Rooms:** Fee: whirlpools. **Cards:** AE, CB, DI, DS, JCB, MC, VI. **Special Amenities:** Free breakfast and free local telephone calls. *(See ad below)*   📶 ⊞ CTV ⓕ ☒ Ⓓ

COMFORT INN   Phone: 919/247-3434

♦♦
Motel

	Rates Subject to Change						
Fri & Sat 5/12-9/3 [CP]	1P: $75-	90	2P/1B:	$75-	90	2P/2B: $75-	90	XP: $5	F18
4/1-5/11 & 9/4-11/4 [CP]	1P: $58-	85	2P/1B:	$58-	85	2P/2B: $58-	85	XP: $5	F18
Sun-Thurs 5/12-9/3 [CP]	1P: $58-	71	2P/1B:	$58-	71	2P/2B: $58-	71	XP: $5	F18
12/1-3/31 & 11/5-11/30 [CP]	1P: $45-	70	2P/1B:	$45-	70	2P/2B: $45-	70	XP: $5	F18

Location: 2 mi w on US 70. 3100 Arendell St 28557. Fax: 919/247-4411. **Terms:** Sr. discount; reserv deposit; no pets. **Facility:** 100 rooms. 2 stories; exterior corridors. **All Rooms:** free movies. **Cards:** AE, CB, DI, DS, JCB, MC, VI.

📶 CTV ☒ Ⓓ

ECONO LODGE CRYSTAL COAST   Phone: 919/247-2940

♦♦
Motel

	Rates Subject to Change				
Fri & Sat 5/26-9/4 [CP]	1P: $69	2P/1B: $69	2P/2B: $69	XP: $5	F18
Fri & Sat 4/2-5/25, Sun-Thurs 5/26-9/4 & Fri & Sat 9/5-10/31 [CP]	1P: $49	2P/1B: $54	2P/2B: $54	XP: $5	F18
Sun-Thurs 4/2-5/25 & 9/5-10/31 [CP]	1P: $39	2P/1B: $44	2P/2B: $44	XP: $5	F18
12/1-4/1 & 11/1-11/30 [CP]	1P: $28	2P/1B: $33	2P/2B: $33	XP: $5	F18

Location: 2.5 mi w on US 70, just n on 35th St; opposite National Guard Armory. 3410 Bridges St 28557 (PO Box 1229). Fax: 919/247-0746. **Terms:** Sr. discount; 2 night min stay, weekends in season; no pets. **Facility:** 56 rooms. 2 stories; exterior corridors. **All Rooms:** free movies. **Cards:** AE, DI, DS, MC, VI.   📶 CTV ☒ Ⓓ Ⓢ

HAMPTON INN   Phone: 919/240-2300

♦♦♦
Motel

	Rates Subject to Change				
Fri & Sat 3/29-9/9 [CP]	1P: $80-	95	2P/1B: $85-	95	2P/2B: $85-	95
Sun-Thurs 3/29-9/9 [CP]	1P: $70-	85	2P/1B: $75-	85	2P/2B: $75-	80
12/1-12/26 & 9/10-11/3 [CP]	1P: $50-	70	2P/1B: $60-	75	2P/2B: $60-	70
12/27-3/28 & 11/4-11/30 [CP]	1P: $45	2P/1B: $45-	50	2P/2B: $45-	50

Location: 3 mi w on US 70. 4035 Arendell St 28557. Fax: 919/240-2311. **Terms:** Check-in 4 pm; no pets. **Facility:** 120 rooms. 4 stories; interior corridors. **All Rooms:** free movies. **Cards:** AE, DI, DS, MC, VI.   📶 CTV ⓕ ☒ 🅰 Ⓓ Ⓢ

RESTAURANTS

ANCHOR INN RESTAURANT & LOUNGE   **Dinner:** $10-$18   Phone: 919/726-2156

AAA
♦♦
Steak and
Seafood

Location: 1.8 mi w on US 70; in Best Western Buccaneer Motor Inn. 2806 Arendell St 28557. **Hours:** 6 am-noon & 5-10 pm, Fri & Sat-11 pm, Sun 6 am-1 & 5-10 pm. **Features:** children's menu; carryout; cocktails & lounge. Local favorite for down east clam chowder; fresh local seafood. Black Angus steak & prime rib; chicken & pasta entrees also. **Cards:** AE, DS, MC, VI. *(See ad below)*   ☒

MRS. WILLIS' RESTAURANT & LOUNGE   **Lunch:** $5-$7   **Dinner:** $6-$13   Phone: 919/726-3741

♦♦
American

Location: 2.3 mi w off US 70; behind Morehead Plaza. 3002 Bridges St 28557. **Hours:** 11:30 am-9 pm; 5/1-10/31 to 10 pm. Closed: 12/24-12/31. **Features:** children's menu; carryout; cocktails & lounge; minimum charge-$10. Since 1956, popular local establishment featuring fresh fish, charcoal steak, vegetables & barbecue. Homemade soup & dessert. Rustic dining rooms. **Cards:** DS, MC, VI.   ☒

SANITARY FISH MARKET & RESTAURANT   **Lunch:** $5-$14   **Dinner:** $9-$19   Phone: 919/247-3111

AAA
♦♦
Seafood

Location: Just s off US 70 on Bogue Sound, on Evans St between 5th & S 6th sts. 501 Evans St 28557. **Hours:** Open 2/5-11/30; 11 am-8:30 pm; 5/1-10/31 to 9 pm. **Features:** children's menu; carryout. Family oriented. Family owned & operated since 1938. Overlooking Bogue Sound. Steak & chicken entrees; live lobster tank; very popular, hearty portions. **Cards:** DS, MC, VI.   ☒

MORGANTON—15,100

LODGINGS

DAYS INN
AAA SAVE ◆◆ Motel
All Year [CP]   1P: $30- 50   2P/1B: $40- 60   2P/2B: $40- 60   XP: $5   D17
Location: Just s on SR 18 from I-40, exit 105. 2402 S Sterling St 28655. Fax: 704/437-0985. **Terms:** No pets. **Facility:** 115 rooms. 2 stories; exterior corridors. **Dining:** Restaurant nearby. **All Rooms:** free movies. **Cards:** AE, CB, DI, DS, MC, VI. *(See ad below)*
Phone: 704/433-0011

HOLIDAY INN
◆◆◆ Motor Inn
All Year   Rates Subject to Change
1P: $69- 89   2P/1B: $69- 89   2P/2B: $69- 89   XP: $5   F19
Location: SR 18 at I-40 exit 105. 2400 S Sterling St 28655. Fax: 704/437-0171. **Terms:** Sr. discount; no pets. **Facility:** 135 rooms. 2 stories; exterior corridors. **Dining:** Restaurant; 6 am-2 & 5-10 pm, Sat & Sun from 7 am; $7-$17. **All Rooms:** free movies. **Cards:** AE, CB, DI, DS, JCB, MC, VI.
Roll in showers.
Phone: 704/437-0171

SLEEP INN
◆◆ Motel
6/1-10/31   Rates Subject to Change
1P: $49- 69   2P/1B: $49- 69   2P/2B: $49- 69   XP: $5   F18
12/1-5/31 & 11/1-11/30   1P: $45- 49   2P/1B: $49- 55   2P/2B: $49- 55   XP: $5   F18
Location: Just n on SR 18 from I-40, exit 105. 2400A S Sterling St 28655. Fax: 704/433-9000. **Terms:** No pets. **Facility:** 61 rooms. 2 stories; interior corridors. **All Rooms:** free movies. **Cards:** AE, CB, DI, DS, JCB, MC, VI.
Phone: 704/433-9000

MORRISVILLE—1,000   (See map p. 404; index p. 402)

LODGINGS

BUDGETEL INN-RALEIGH
◆◆◆ Motel
All Year [CP]   Rates Subject to Change
1P: $45- 58   2P/1B: $52- 65   2P/2B: $56
Location: Exit 284 off I-40, 2 blks s; in Aerial Center Park. 1001 Aerial Center Pkwy 27560. Fax: 919/460-1584. **Terms:** Sr. discount; small pets only. **Facility:** 121 rooms. 4 stories; interior corridors. **All Rooms:** free & pay movies. **Cards:** AE, CB, DI, DS, MC, VI. *(See color ad p 403)*
Phone: 919/481-3600   45

COURTYARD BY MARRIOTT-AIRPORT
◆◆◆ Motor Inn
Sun-Thurs   Rates Subject to Change
1P: $107   2P/1B: $117   2P/2B: $117   XP: $10   F18
Fri & Sat   1P: $69   2P/1B: $69   2P/2B: $69
Location: Exit 284 off I-40, 2 blks s. 2001 Hospitality Ct 27560. Fax: 919/467-9332. **Terms:** No pets. **Facility:** 152 rooms. 4 stories; interior corridors. **Dining:** Dining room; 6:30 am-10 & 5-10 pm; $9-$12. **All Rooms:** free & pay movies. **Cards:** AE, CB, DI, DS, MC. *(See color ad p 406)*
Phone: 919/467-9444   44

DAYS INN AIRPORT/RTP
◆◆ Motel
All Year [CP]   Rates Subject to Change
1P: $79- 109   2P/1B: $89- 119   2P/2B: $89- 119   XP: $10   F18
Location: I-40 exit 284, 0.3 mi se. 1000 Airport Blvd 27560 (PO Box 13525, RESEARCH TRIANGLE PARK, 27709). Fax: 919/460-0811. **Terms:** No pets. **Facility:** 110 rooms. 3 stories; interior/exterior corridors. **Dining:** 8-10 pm. **All Rooms:** free movies. **Cards:** AE, CB, DI, DS, MC, VI.
Phone: 919/469-8688   47

LA QUINTA INN & SUITES-AIRPORT
◆◆◆ Motel
All Year [CP]   Rates Subject to Change
1P: $75- 89   2P/1B: $92- 99   2P/2B: $82- 89   XP: $7   F18
Location: Just s off I-40, exit 284; in Aerial Center Park. 1001 Hospitality Ct 27560. Fax: 919/461-1721. **Terms:** Small pets only. **Facility:** 135 rooms. 3-4 stories; interior corridors. **All Rooms:** free & pay movies. **Cards:** AE, CB, DI, DS, MC, VI. *(See color ad p 407)*   Roll in showers.
Phone: 919/461-1771   41

MICROTEL RALEIGH DURHAM AIRPORT
AAA ◆◆ Motel
12/1-1/31   1P: $44- 49   2P/1B: $49- 52   2P/2B: $54- 58   XP: $5   F18
2/1-11/30   1P: $45- 52   2P/1B: $45- 52   2P/2B: $45- 52   XP: $5   F18
Location: Just s of I-40 exit 284; in Concourse Shopping Ctr. 104 Factory Shops Rd 24560. Fax: 919/462-0373. **Terms:** No pets. **Facility:** 99 rooms. 3 stories; interior corridors. **All Rooms:** free & pay movies. **Cards:** AE, CB, DI, DS, JCB, MC, VI.   Roll in showers.
Phone: 919/462-0061   42

RESTAURANT

THE ANGUS BARN
◆◆◆ American
Dinner: $24-$31   **Phone: 919/787-3505**   24
Location: On US 70; 5 mi n from I-40, exit 284 to US 70, just e. US 70 27628. **Hours:** 5 pm-11 pm, Sun-10 pm. Closed: 1/1, 11/26, 12/24 & 12/25. **Reservations:** suggested. **Features:** children's menu; carryout; cocktails & lounge. Rustic atmosphere of 19th-century barn. Extensive wine list. Well-established & very popular. Impressive antique gun collection. Homemade soup, bread & dessert, some pasta entrees, fresh seafood daily & fresh lobster. **Cards:** AE, CB, DI, MC, VI.

MOUNTAIN HOME—1,900

LODGINGS

MOUNTAIN HOME BED & BREAKFAST   Rates Subject to Change   **Phone:** 704/697-9090
All Year [BP]   1P: $85- 129   2P/1B: $85- 129   XP: $20
Location: 2 mi s on US 25 from I-26, exit 13 & just w at post office on Courtland Blvd. 10 Courtland Blvd
28758 (PO Box 234). Fax: 704/698-2477. **Terms:** Sr. discount; age restrictions may apply; reserv deposit, 3
Bed &
Breakfast
day notice; no pets. **Facility:** 7 rooms. 2 night min stay Fri & Sat 10/1-10/31. Lower rates off season; 3 stories,
no elevator; interior/exterior corridors; designated smoking area. **Cards:** AE, MC, VI.   (CTV) (X) (D)

RANCH MOTEL   Rates Subject to Change   **Phone:** 704/693-4345
♦   6/1-10/31   2P/1B: $42- 44   2P/2B: $44- 46 XP: $2   D6
Motel   12/1-5/31 & 11/1-11/30   2P/1B: $34- 36   2P/2B: $38- 40 XP: $2   D6
Location: I-26 exit 13, 2.3 mi s on US 25. Asheville Hwy 28758 (PO Box 216). **Terms:** Reserv deposit, 3
day notice; no pets. **Facility:** 8 rooms. 1 story; exterior corridors. **Some Rooms:** 3 efficiencies.   (CTV) (D)

MOUNT AIRY—7,200

LODGINGS

BEST WESTERN BRYSON INN   **Phone:** 910/352-3400
12/1-12/31 & 4/1-11/30   1P: $36   2P/1B: $43   2P/2B: $42   XP: $6   F18
1/1-3/31   1P: $33   2P/1B: $40   2P/2B: $39   XP: $6   F18
Location: Just e of I-77, exit 100. 3630 W Pine St 27030. **Terms:** No pets. **Facility:** 60 rooms. Near outlet
Motel   shopping. 2 stories; exterior corridors. **Dining:** Restaurant nearby. **Some Rooms:** refrigerators. **Cards:** AE,
CB, DI, DS, MC, VI. **Special Amenities:** Free local telephone calls.   (a) (b) (X) (D)

COMFORT INN   Rates Subject to Change   **Phone:** 910/789-2000
All Year [CP]   1P: $55- 60   2P/1B: $61- 65   2P/2B: $61   XP: $5   F18
Motel   **Location:** On US 601, 0.8 mi s of jct US 52. 2136 Rockford St 27030. Fax: 910/789-7917. **Terms:** Sr.
discount; no pets. **Facility:** 99 rooms. 2 stories; exterior corridors. **All Rooms:** free movies. **Cards:** AE, CB,
DI, DS, JCB, MC, VI.   (a) (CTV) (X) (D)

THE MAYBERRY MOTOR INN   Rates Subject to Change   **Phone:** 910/786-4109
2/1-11/14 [CP]   1P: $44   2P/1B: $46- 48   2P/2B: $46- 48 XP: $5
12/1-1/31 & 11/15-11/30 [CP] 1P: $38   2P/1B: $44   2P/2B: $44   XP: $5
Location: On US 52N, 0.5 mi n of jct SR 89 Mayberry Mall. US 52 bypass 27030. **Terms:** No pets.
Motel   **Facility:** 27 rooms. 1 story; exterior corridors. **All Rooms:** free movies. **Cards:** AE, CB, DI, DS, MC, VI.
(a) (CTV) (X) (D)

PINE RIDGE INN   Guaranteed Rates   **Phone:** 910/789-5034
All Year [BP]   1P: $60- 100 2P/1B: $60- 100 2P/2B: $60- 100 XP: $10
Country Inn **Location:** 2.5 mi e on SR 89 from I-77, exit 100. 2893 W Pine St 27030. Fax: 910/786-9039. **Terms:** Sr.
discount; reserv deposit; no pets. **Facility:** 6 rooms. 1 whirlpool rm, extra charge; 2 stories; interior corridors;
designated smoking area. **Dining:** Dining room; 6 pm-9 pm, Sun brunch 11 am-2 pm smoke free; $10-$18. **All Rooms:** free
movies. **Cards:** AE, DS, MC, VI.   (a) (CTV) (X) (D)

MOUNT GILEAD—1,300

LODGING

THE PINES PLANTATION INN   Guaranteed Rates   **Phone:** 910/439-1894
All Year [BP]   1P: $55- 70   2P/1B: $55- 70   XP: $10
Historic Bed **Location:** 1 mi s on SR 73 from jct SR 24 & 27 from e side of Lake Tillery Bridge, 3.4 mi w on Lilly's Bridge
& Breakfast Rd. 1570 Lilly's Bridge Rd 27306. Fax: 910/439-1894. **Terms:** Check-in 4 pm; reserv deposit, 7 day notice;
no pets. **Facility:** 5 rooms. Interior corridors; smoke free premises. **Cards:** MC, VI.   (X) (D)

MOUNT PLEASANT—1,000

LODGING

CAROLINA COUNTRY INN   Guaranteed Rates   **Phone:** 704/436-9616
All Year   1P: $38- 50   2P/1B: $38- 50   2P/2B: $40- 50 XP: $5   F12
Location: SR 49; 1 mi n of SR 73. 8514 Hwy 49 28124. Fax: 704/436-9668. **Terms:** Reserv deposit; no
♦ ♦   pets. **Facility:** 25 rooms. 2 stories; exterior corridors. **All Rooms:** free movies. **Some Rooms:** kitchen.
Motel   **Cards:** AE, DS, MC, VI.   (CTV) (X) (D)

MURPHY—1,600

LODGINGS

BEST WESTERN OF MURPHY   **Phone:** 704/837-3060
5/1-10/31 [CP]   1P: $53- 89   2P/1B: $56- 89   2P/2B: $63- 89 XP: $5   F12
12/1-4/30 & 11/1-11/30 [CP] 1P: $46- 56 2P/1B: $51- 61   2P/2B: $51   XP: $5   F12
Location: US 74, US 19 & SR 129, exit Andrews Rd. 588 Andrews Rd. 28906 (PO Box 1099).
Motel   Fax: 704/837-9326. **Terms:** Check-in 4 pm; no pets. **Facility:** 54 rooms. 2 stories; exterior corridors.
Dining: Restaurant nearby. **All Rooms:** free movies. **Some Rooms:** VCP's. **Cards:** AE, CB, DI, DS, MC, VI.
Special Amenities: Free breakfast and free local telephone calls.   (a) (b) (CTV) (X) (D)

COMFORT INN   Rates Subject to Change   **Phone:** 704/837-8030
10/1-10/31 [CP]   1P: $89   2P/1B: $89   2P/2B: $89   XP: $5   F18
5/27-9/30 [CP]   1P: $75- 85   2P/1B: $75- 85   2P/2B: $75- 85 XP: $5   F18
11/1-5/26 & 11/1-11/30 [CP] 1P: $49- 50 2P/1B: $49- 55   2P/2B: $49- 55 XP: $5   F18
Location: On US 64W, US 19S, US 74W & US 129S. 114 US 64W 28906. Fax: 704/837-9669. **Terms:** Sr. discount; pets,
$30 dep req. **Facility:** 55 rooms. 2 stories; exterior corridors. **All Rooms:** free movies. **Cards:** AE, DI, DS, MC, VI.
(h) (a) (CTV) (X) (D)

ECONO-LODGE   **Phone:** 704/837-8880
5/1-10/31   1P: $40- 89   2P/1B: $46- 89   2P/2B: $46- 89 XP: $6   F18
12/1-4/30 & 11/1-11/30   1P: $30- 50   2P/1B: $36- 66   2P/2B: $36- 66 XP: $6   F18
Location: Jct Hwys 64 & 19/129. 100 Terrace St 28906 (PO Box 756). Fax: 704/837-0847. **Terms:** No pets.
Motor Inn   **Facility:** 40 rooms. 2 stories; interior/exterior corridors. **Dining:** Restaurant; 6 am-8 pm; $5-$13.
All Rooms: free movies. **Some Rooms:** refrigerators. **Cards:** AE, DI, DS, MC, VI.   (b) (CTV) (X) (D)

HOOVER HOUSE
◆◆
Bed &
Breakfast
Rates Subject to Change   Phone: 704/837-8734
12/1-12/31 & 2/1-11/30 [BP]   2P/1B: $60- 75   XP: $10
Location: 0.5 mi s on Business Rt 19 off US 74/19 s entry opposite shopping center. 306 Natural Springs Dr 28906. **Terms:** Open 12/1-12/31 & 2/1-11/30; age restrictions may apply; reserv deposit, 7 day notice; no pets. **Facility:** 4 rooms. 2 stories; interior corridors; smoke free premises. **All Rooms:** free movies.
Cards: MC, VI.   [CTV] [X] [D]

HUNTINGTON HALL BED & BREAKFAST   Phone: 704/837-9567
(AAA) [SAVE]
Historic Bed
& Breakfast
| | | | | | |
4/1-11/30 [BP]   1P: $65   2P/1B: $85   2P/2B: $85   XP: $20   F16
12/1-3/31 [BP]   1P: $49   2P/1B: $65   2P/2B: $65   XP: $10   F16
Location: On US 19 business, just n of US 64. 500 Valley River Ave 28906. Fax: 704/837-2527. **Terms:** Check-in 3:30 pm; reserv deposit; package plans; no pets. **Facility:** 5 rooms. Individually decorated rooms with wood floors, tall windows. Murder mystery weekends. 2 stories; interior corridors; smoke free premises. **All Rooms:** free movies, combo or shower baths, no phones. **Cards:** AE, CB, DI, DS, MC, VI.
Special Amenities: Free local telephone calls and free room upgrade (subject to availability with advanced reservations).   [CTV] [X] [D]

RESTAURANTS

JAMASON'S FINE DINING   Dinner: $11-$16   Phone: 704/837-2562
◆◆
American
Location: 3 mi e on Harshaw Rd, from Hwy 19 turn right into Cherokee Hills Country Club. Rt 4, Box 305A 28906. **Hours:** 5:30 pm-9:30 pm. Closed: Sun-Tues & 4/1-12/31. **Features:** Overlooking golf course; Fri, all-you-can eat seafood buffet $12.95, 5:30 pm-9:30 pm. Homemade soup; rack of lamb signature entree.
Cards: DS, MC, VI.

THE OAK BARREL RESTAURANT   Dinner: $10-$20   Phone: 704/837-7803
◆◆
Steak and
Seafood
Location: Hwy 64 to 19 business route, 2 mi n. 104 County Home Rd 28906. **Hours:** 5 pm-9:30 pm. Closed: Sun, Mon & 12/25. **Reservations:** suggested. **Features:** casual dress; children's menu; carryout; wine only. Aged beef & seafood entrees served in friendly, relaxed atmosphere. Screened porch dining spring & summer. **Cards:** DS, MC, VI.   [X]

NAGS HEAD—See Outer Banks p. 399.

NEW BERN—17,400

LODGINGS

THE AERIE   Phone: 919/636-5553
(AAA) [SAVE]
Historic Bed
& Breakfast
All Year [BP]   1P: $60   2P/1B: $79- 95 2P/2B: $79- 95 XP: $20   F12
Location: Downtown in Historic District; just e of Tryon Palace. 509 Pollock St 28562. Fax: 919/636-5553. **Terms:** Reserv deposit, 3 day notice; no pets. **Facility:** 7 rooms. Converted Victorian frame house. 2 stories; interior corridors; smoke free premises. **Dining:** Tea room, 2-5 pm Wed-Sat serving scones & pastry. **Services:** complimentary evening beverages. **All Rooms:** free movies, combo or shower baths. **Cards:** AE, DS, MC, VI. **Special Amenities:** Early check-in/late check-out and free breakfast.   [_] [CTV] [X] [D]

COMFORT SUITES & MARINA   Phone: 919/636-0022
◆◆◆
Motel
All Year [CP]   1P: $60- 125 2P/1B: $68- 125 2P/2B: $68- 125 XP: $7   F17
Location: On US 70 just e of US 17 jct (Lawson Bridge) & US 70 bypass (E Front St Exit) 1 mi w on US 70. 218 E Front St 28560. Fax: 919/636-0051. **Terms:** Sr. discount; no pets. **Facility:** 100 rooms. 4 stories; interior corridors. **All Rooms:** free movies. **Cards:** AE, CB, DI, DS, JCB, MC, VI.   [_] [CTV] [_] [X] [_] [D] [S]

HAMPTON INN   Phone: 919/637-2111
◆◆◆
Motel
All Year [CP]   1P: $56- 70 2P/1B: $59- 75 2P/2B: $59- 75
Location: Just n on US 17N from US 70 Bypass (US 17 & Jacksonville exit) across from Berne Square. US Hwys 17 & 70 Bypass 28562. Fax: 919/637-2000. **Terms:** No pets. **Facility:** 101 rooms. 4 stories; interior corridors. **All Rooms:** free movies. **Cards:** AE, DI, DS, MC, VI.   Roll in showers. [_] [CTV] [_] [X] [_] [D] [S]

HARMONY HOUSE INN   Phone: 919/636-3810
(AAA)
Historic Bed
& Breakfast
All Year [BP]   1P: $70   2P/1B: $89- 99 2P/2B: $89- 99 XP: $20
Location: Downtown in historic district; 5 blks e of Tryon Palace. 215 Pollock St 28560. Fax: 919/636-3810. **Terms:** Reserv deposit, 3 day notice; no pets. **Facility:** 10 rooms. 1 one-bedroom suite, $130; 2 stories; interior corridors; smoke free premises. **All Rooms:** free movies. **Cards:** DS, MC, VI.   [CTV] [X] [D]

HOLIDAY INN EXPRESS   Phone: 919/638-8266
◆◆◆
Motel
All Year [CP]   1P: $67- 77 2P/1B: $67- 77 2P/2B: $67- 77 XP: $5   D15
Location: 0.5 mi s on US 17 from US 70 (bypass). 3455 Clarendon Blvd 28562. Fax: 919/638-8257. **Terms:** Reserv deposit, 5 day notice; no pets. **Facility:** 60 rooms. 2 stories; interior corridors.
All Rooms: free movies. **Cards:** AE, CB, DI, DS, MC, VI.   Roll in showers. [_] [CTV] [_] [X] [_] [D] [S]

KING'S ARMS INN   Phone: 919/638-4409
(AAA) [SAVE]
Historic Bed
& Breakfast
All Year [CP]   1P: $60   2P/1B: $90   2P/2B: $90   XP: $10   D10
Location: Downtown in historic area; 5 blks e of Tryon Palace. 212 Pollock St 28560. Fax: 919/638-2191. **Terms:** Package plans; no pets. **Facility:** 8 rooms. Restored inn. Suite, $130; 3 stories, no elevator; interior corridors; designated smoking area. **Dining:** Restaurant nearby. **Services:** complimentary evening beverages. **All Rooms:** free movies. **Cards:** AE, CB, MC, VI. **Special Amenities:** Free room upgrade and preferred room (each subject to availability with advanced reservations).   [CTV] [X] [D]

NEW BERNE HOUSE INN   Phone: 919/636-2250
◆◆
Historic Bed
& Breakfast
All Year [BP]   1P: $68   2P/1B: $88
Location: Just n of Tryon Palace on US 17 & 70 business route. 709 Broad St 28560. **Terms:** Sr. discount age restrictions may apply; reserv deposit; no pets. **Facility:** 7 rooms. 3 stories, no elevator; interior corridors smoke free premises. **Cards:** AE, MC, VI.   [X] [D]

SHERATON GRAND HOTEL   Phone: 919/638-3585
◆◆◆
Hotel
| | | | | | |
4/1-11/30   1P: $110   2P/1B: $120   2P/2B: $120   XP: $10   F17
12/1-3/31   1P: $80   2P/1B: $90   2P/2B: $90   XP: $10   F17
Location: 3 mi e of US 17 & 70 Bypass; 0.5 mi n of E Front St exit off US 70 Bypass. 1 Bicentennial Park 28562. Fax: 919/638-8112. **Terms:** Pets, $10 extra charge. **Facility:** 172 rooms. 4 stories; interior corridors. **Dining:** 2 restaurants; 6:30 am-10 pm; deck dining-weather permitting; lunch buffet, $7.95; Fri night buffet, $15.95; Sun Brunch $11.95; $13-$16. **All Rooms:** free & pay movies. **Cards:** AE, CB, DI, DS, JCB, MC, VI.   [_] [_] [_] [_] [X] [_] [D] [S]

RESTAURANTS

THE HARVEY MANSION HISTORIC INN   Historical   **Lunch:** $7-$9   **Dinner:** $17-$22   **Phone:** 919/638-3205
AAA
♦♦♦
Continental
Location: In historic district; 3 blks e of Tryon Palace. 221 Tryon Palace Dr 28560. **Hours:** 5 pm-11 pm.
Reservations: suggested. **Features:** cocktails. Menu changes seasonally with international entrees.
Restored 1797 structure listed on the National Regiester of Historic Places. Cellar pub. Nightly fresh fish.
Swiss owner/chef. **Cards:** AE, CB, DI, DS, MC, VI.

HENDERSON HOUSE   Historical   **Dinner:** $18-$35   **Phone:** 919/637-4784
♦♦♦
Continental
Location: In historic district; 4.5 blks e of Tryon Palace. 216 Pollock St 28560. **Hours:** 6 pm-9 pm. Closed:
Mon & Tues. **Reservations:** suggested. **Features:** cocktails; minimum charge-$30; also prix fixe. In a
chef-owned 18th-century Federal home. Smoke free premises. **Cards:** AE, DS, MC, VI.

POLLOCK STREET DELICATESSEN   **Lunch:** $3-$6   **Dinner:** $4-$10   **Phone:** 919/637-2480
♦
American
Location: Downtown; in historic district, 5 blks e of Tryon Palace. 208 Pollock St 28560. **Hours:** 7 am-8 pm,
Fri & Sat 8 am-10 pm, Sun 11 am-4 pm, Mon 7 am-4 pm. Closed: 1/1, 11/26 & 12/25. **Features:** children's
menu; carryout; beer & wine only. Restored 1880's home.

NORTH TOPSAIL BEACH—900

LODGING

VILLA CAPRIANI   Rates Subject to Change   **Phone:** 910/328-1900
♦♦♦
Condo Motel

6/7-8/22 Weekly	2P/2B: $805-1195
5/23-6/6 & 8/23-9/5 Weekly	2P/2B: $685-1030
3/27-5/22 & 9/6-10/31 Weekly	2P/2B: $550- 855
12/1-3/26 & 11/1-11/30 Weekly	2P/2B: $400- 650

Location: 1.5 mi n on New River Inlet Rd from SR 210. 790 New River Inlet Rd 28460. Fax: 910/328-1900.
Terms: Check-in 4 pm; reserv deposit, 30 day notice; **Facility:** 45 rooms. Handling fee imposed; 4 stories; exterior corridors.
All Rooms: kitchens. **Cards:** MC, VI.

NORTH WILKESBORO—3,400—See also WILKESBORO.

RESTAURANT

ROSELLI'S MAIN STREET   **Lunch:** $5-$8   **Dinner:** $9-$14   **Phone:** 910/838-7070
♦
Italian
Location: Center. 910 Main St 28659. **Hours:** 11 am-2 & 5-10:30 pm. Closed: Sun, Mon, 11/26, 12/24 &
12/25. **Features:** children's menu; carryout; cocktails & lounge. Some American dishes. **Cards:** AE, CB, DI,
DS, MC, VI.

OCEAN ISLE BEACH—500

LODGINGS

BRICK LANDING PLANTATION   Rates Subject to Change   **Phone:** 910/754-4373
♦♦♦
Resort
Complex

5/1-9/3	2P/2B: $110- 135
3/1-4/30 & 9/4-11/30	2P/2B: $90- 100
12/1-2/28	2P/2B: $70- 80

Location: From US 17; 4 mi e to jct SR 904 & SR 179, then 2 mi n on SR 179. 1900 Goose Creek Rd SW
28469. Fax: 910/754-5612. **Terms:** Reserv deposit, 7 day notice; no pets. **Facility:** 42 rooms. 19 three-bedroom villas, $125-
$150, $80-$90 in winter. Rates for up to 6 persons. Handling fee imposed; 2-3 stories, no elevator; exterior corridors.
Dining: Restaurant; $10-$18. **All Rooms:** free movies. **Cards:** AE, MC, VI.

OCEAN ISLE INN   Rates Subject to Change   **Phone:** 910/579-0750
AAA
♦♦♦
Motel

5/8-9/5 [CP]	2P/1B: $104- 129	2P/2B: $104- 129
3/1-5/7 & 9/6-11/28 [CP]	2P/1B: $64- 99	2P/2B: $64- 99
12/1-2/28 & 11/29-11/30 [CP]	2P/1B: $49- 59	2P/2B: $49- 59

Location: 1.5 mi n of SR 904. 37 W First St 28469. Fax: 910/579-1319. **Terms:** Sr. discount; no pets.
Facility: 70 rooms. Rates for up to 4 persons; 3 stories; exterior corridors. **Cards:** MC, VI.

THE WINDS CLARION INN & SUITES   Phone: 910/579-6275

AAA SAVE   6/13-8/21 [CP]   1P: $109- 176   2P/1B: $109- 176   2P/2B: $131- 224   XP: $15   F18
             3/20-6/12 [CP]   1P: $81- 130   2P/1B: $81- 130   2P/2B: $94- 165   XP: $15   F18
◆◆◆   8/22-10/15 [CP]   1P: $79- 125   2P/1B: $79- 125   2P/2B: $97- 157   XP: $15   F18
Resort Motel 12/1-3/19 & 10/16-11/30 [CP] 1P: $53- 85   2P/1B: $53- 85   2P/2B: $64- 106   XP: $15   F18
Location: 1.5 mi n of SR 904. 310 E First St 28469. Fax: 910/579-2884. **Terms:** Check-in 4 pm; reserv deposit, Handling fee imposed; weekly rates; package plans; no pets. **Facility:** 72 rooms. Most units oceanfront with balcony, some with whirlpool. 3-7 day minimum stay may be required during peak season. 18 two-bedroom units. 2- & 3-bedroom suites, $86-$359 for up to 4 persons; 4-bedroom spa houses, from $218 for up to 8 persons. Penthouse, $134-$269 for up to 4 persons; 3-4 stories, no elevator; exterior corridors; free golf privileges in summer; beach, sauna, whirlpools; beach bocci, beach volleyball. Fee: beach chairs & umbrellas. **Services:** Fee: coin laundry. **Recreation:** swimming. Fee: sailboats, windsurfing; bicycles. Rental: canoeing. **All Rooms:** coffeemakers, microwaves, refrigerators. **Some Rooms:** 12 efficiencies, 35 kitchens. **Cards:** AE, CB, DI, DS, JCB, MC, VI. **Special Amenities: Free breakfast and free newspaper.**
(See color ad p 487 & ad p 395)

OCRACOKE—*See Outer Banks p. 401.*

ORIENTAL—800

LODGING

THE TAR HEEL INN B & B   Rates Subject to Change   Phone: 919/249-1078
◆◆◆   3/1-10/31 [BP]   1P: $60- 80   2P/1B: $70- 90   XP: $10
Bed &   12/1-2/28 & 11/1-11/30 [BP]   1P: $50   2P/1B: $60   XP: $10
Breakfast   **Location:** Town Center; corner of Broad & Church sts. 508 Church St 28571 (PO Box 176). **Terms:** Check-in 4 pm; reserv deposit, 3 day notice; no pets. **Facility:** 8 rooms. 2 stories; interior corridors; smoke free premises. **Cards:** DS, MC, VI.

Outer Banks

BUXTON—1,300

LODGINGS

CAPE HATTERAS BED & BREAKFAST   Phone: 919/995-6004

AAA SAVE   6/12-8/31 [BP]   2P/1B: $80- 90   2P/2B: $80- 90   XP: $15   F12
             12/1-12/14, 5/1-6/11 &
◆◆   9/1-11/30 [BP]   2P/1B: $60- 70   2P/2B: $60- 70   XP: $15   F12
Bed &   3/12-4/30 [BP]   2P/1B: $50- 60   2P/2B: $50- 60   XP: $10   F12
Breakfast   **Location:** Town center. Old Light House Rd 27920 (PO Box 490). **Terms:** Open 12/1-12/14 & 3/12-11/30; reserv deposit, 14 day notice; no pets. **Facility:** 6 rooms. 3 night min stay efficiency unit, $10 extra per night. Handling fee imposed; 2 stories; exterior corridors; smoke free premises. **All Rooms:** free movies. **Cards:** MC, VI.

COMFORT INN   Rates Subject to Change   Phone: 919/995-6100
◆◆◆   6/12-9/1 [CP]   2P/1B: $109   2P/2B: $109   XP: $5   F18
Motel   3/29-6/11 & 9/2-11/30 [CP]   2P/1B: $79   2P/2B: $79   XP: $5   F18
             12/1-3/28 [CP]   2P/1B: $49   2P/2B: $49   XP: $5   F18
Location: SR 12 & Old Lighthouse. 27920 (PO Box 1089). Fax: 919/995-5444. **Terms:** Sr. discount; reserv deposit; no pets. **Facility:** 60 rooms. Rates higher on weekends; 2 stories; exterior corridors. **All Rooms:** free movies. **Cards:** AE, DI, DS, JCB, MC, VI.

LIGHTHOUSE VIEW MOTEL   Rates Subject to Change   Phone: 919/995-5680
AAA   6/5-9/6   2P/1B: $88- 108   2P/2B: $88- 108   XP: $7
             5/15-6/4 & 9/7-9/19   2P/1B: $68- 83   2P/2B: $68- 83   XP: $6
◆◆   3/26-5/14 & 9/20-11/30   2P/1B: $58- 69   2P/2B: $58- 69   XP: $5
Complex   12/1-3/25   2P/1B: $46- 55   2P/2B: $46- 55   XP: $5
             Location: 0.5 mi n of Cape Hatteras lighthouse. Rt 12 27920 (PO Box 39). Fax: 919/995-5945. **Terms:** Reserv deposit, 30 day notice, handling fee imposed; 3 night min stay. **Facility:** 73 rooms. 8 efficiencies, $310-$550 weekly; 2 two-bedroom apts $310-$720 weekly; 22 one- & two-bedroom villas, $340-$1000 weekly; 19 cottages $380-$2100 weekly; 2 stories, no elevator; exterior corridors. **All Rooms:** free movies. **Cards:** AE, MC, VI.

OUTER BANKS MOTEL   Phone: 919/995-5601
AAA SAVE   All Year   2P/2B: $74- 92   XP: $4
             Location: 1.3 mi ne on SR 12. 27920 (PO Box 428). Fax: 919/995-5082. **Terms:** Reserv deposit, 42 day
◆◆   notice; weekly rates; no pets. **Facility:** 25 rooms. 12 two-bedroom units, 2 three-bedroom units. $1 per person
Motel   weekly additional linen charge in summer. Additional charge for credit card payment. Cottages, $240-$1090 weekly; 1-3 stories, no elevator; exterior corridors; oceanfront; beach, whirlpool. **Services:** Fee: coin laundry.
Recreation: swimming, boating, fishing. **All Rooms:** coffeemakers, microwaves, free movies, refrigerators. **Cards:** MC, VI.

DUCK—200

LODGING

SANDERLING INN RESORT & CONFERENCE CENTER   Rates Subject to Change   Phone: 919/261-4111
◆◆◆   5/16-9/28 [CP]   1P: $194- 414   2P/1B: $194- 414   2P/2B: $194- 414   XP: $35   F
Resort Hotel 12/1-5/15 & 9/29-11/30 [CP] 1P: $122- 319   2P/1B: $122- 319   2P/2B: $122- 319   XP: $35   F
             Location: 5 mi n on Hwy 12. 1461 Duck Rd (SR12) 27949. Fax: 919/261-1638. **Terms:** Check-in 4 pm; reserv deposit, 30 day notice; no pets. **Facility:** 88 rooms. Suites, $280-$375; $205-$275 off season. Handling fee imposed; 3 stories; interior corridors. **Dining:** Restaurant; 8 am-10 pm, off season to 9 pm; $16-$26. **All Rooms:** free movies. **Some Rooms:** 26 efficiencies, 28 kitchens. **Cards:** AE, MC, VI.

RESTAURANTS

THE BLUE POINT BAR & GRILL　　　**Lunch:** $7-$9　　　　**Dinner:** $16-$20　　　　**Phone:** 919/261-8090
◆◆◆　　**Location:** 1 mi n on SR 12 in waterfront shops on north end. 1240 Duck Rd 27949. **Hours:** 11:30 am-2:30 &
Regional　　5-10 pm. **Closed:** 11/26, 12/25 & Mon & Tues 12/1-3/24. **Reservations:** required; for dinner.
American　　**Features:** cocktails. 1950's diner ambience & popular. Wine spectator award of excellence since 1994.
Fiesta ware china, housemade bread, dessert, dressing & soup. Crab cake sandwich signature lunch item &
dinner entree. **Cards:** AE, MC, VI.　　　　　　　　　　　　　　　　　　　　　　　　　　　　　　　　⊠

ELIZABETH'S CAFE　　　**Lunch:** $9-$11　　　　**Dinner:** $23-$28　　　　**Phone:** 919-261-6145
◆◆◆　　**Location:** Town center in Scarborough Faire Shoppes. Duck Rd 27949. **Hours:** 11:30 am-2:30 & 6-8:30 pm,
French　　call for hours off season. **Closed:** 1/1 & 12/25. **Reservations:** required. **Features:** cocktails; a la carte.
Nouvelle & Country French entrees; prix fixe, 7-course wine dinner, $80. Best of Award of Excellence from
wine spectator; excellent, extensive wine selection. Menu changes daily. Smoke free premises. **Cards:** MC, VI.　　⊠

HATTERAS—2,600

LODGINGS

HOLIDAY INN EXPRESS & SUITES　　Rates Subject to Change　　　　　　　**Phone:** 919/986-1110
◆◆◆　　6/13-9/7 [CP]　　　　1P: $109- 129　2P/1B: $109- 129　2P/2B: $109- 129　XP: $10　　F18
Motel　　1/16-6/12 & 9/8-11/30 [CP]　1P: $69- 109　2P/1B: $89- 109　2P/2B: $89- 109　XP: $10　　F18
　　12/1-1/15 [CP]　　　　1P: $69- 89　2P/1B: $69- 89　2P/2B: $69- 89　XP: $10　　F18
Location: On SR 12 at Ocracoke Ferry. 58822 Hwy 12 27943 (PO Box 690). Fax: 919/986-1131. **Terms:** Sr. discount;
reserv deposit; no pets. **Facility:** 72 rooms. 2 stories; exterior corridors. **All Rooms:** free movies. **Cards:** AE, CB, DI, DS,
JCB, MC, VI.　　　　　　　　　　　　　　　　　　　　　　　　　　　　　⊠ CTV ⊠ D S

SEA GULL MOTEL　　　Rates Subject to Change　　　　　　　　　**Phone:** 919/986-2550
(AAA)　　5/16-9/15　　　　　　2P/1B: $65　　　2P/2B: $70- 80　XP: $5　　　F5
　　3/1-5/15 & 9/16-11/30　　　2P/1B: $45　　　2P/2B: $50- 60　XP: $5　　　F5
◆◆　　**Location:** 1.5 mi n on SR12 from Ocracoke Ferry. Hwy 12 27943 (PO Box 280). Fax: 919/986-2525.
Motel　　**Terms:** Open 3/1-11/30; reserv deposit, 15 day notice, for apartments & efficiencies; 3 night min stay, in
kitchen units; no pets. **Facility:** 45 rooms. 5 two-bedroom apartments $75-$100 for up to 4 persons, 1 one-
bedroom apartment & 5 efficiencies for up to 2 persons, $55-$80; 2 stories; exterior corridors. **All Rooms:** free movies.
Cards: DS, MC, VI.　　　　　　　　　　　　　　　　　　　　　　　⊠ CTV ⊠ D

RESTAURANTS

GARY'S RESTAURANT　　　**Lunch:** $4-$6　　　**Dinner:** $11-$16　　　**Phone:** 919/986-2349
◆◆　　**Location:** 1.5 mi n on SR 12 from Ocracoke Ferry. 461 Oden Ct 27943. **Hours:** 7 am-3 & 5:30-9:30 pm.
American　　**Closed:** Tues & 12/18-1/3. **Features:** children's menu; carryout; beer & wine only. Prime rib signature entree;
fresh local seafood entrees. **Cards:** AE, DS, MC, VI.　　　　　　　　　　　　　　　　⊠

THE GREAT SALT MARSH RESTAURANT　　**Lunch:** $6-$8　　　**Dinner:** $11-$19　　**Phone:** 919/995-6200
(AAA)　　**Location:** At Ocracoke Ferry-at Hatteras Landing on Hwy 12. 27943. **Hours:** 6 am-10 pm, Sun 11 am-3 pm.
　　Closed: 12/23-12/28. **Reservations:** suggested. **Features:** Sunday brunch; children's menu; senior's menu;
◆◆◆　　cocktail lounge; beer & wine only; a la carte. Local seafood, salads, pasta, prime rib. Light, bright, modern
Regional　　dining room. Cheerful atmosphere. Owner/chef. Smoke free premises. **Cards:** AE, DI, DS, MC, VI.　　⊠
American

KILL DEVIL HILLS—4,200

LODGINGS

BEST WESTERN OCEAN REEF SUITES　　Rates Subject to Change　　　　　　**Phone:** 919/441-1611
(AAA)　　5/22-9/6　　　　1P: $150- 185　2P/1B: $150- 185　2P/2B: $150- 185　XP: $10　　F17
　　3/27-5/21 & 9/7-10/31　1P: $86- 125　2P/1B: $86- 125　2P/2B: $86- 125　XP: $10　　F17
◆◆◆　　12/1-3/26 & 11/1-11/30　1P: $59- 70　2P/1B: $59- 70　2P/2B: $59- 70　XP: $10　　F17
Suite Motel　　**Location:** On SR 12, at milepost 8.5. 107 Virginia Dare Tr 27948 (PO Box 1440). Fax: 919/441-1482.
Terms: Sr. discount; check-in 4 pm; reserv deposit, 3 day notice; no pets. **Facility:** 70 rooms. 5 stories; ex-
terior corridors. **Dining:** Deli. **All Rooms:** kitchens, free movies. **Cards:** AE, CB, DI, DS, JCB, MC, VI.
　　　　　　　　　　　　　　　　　　　　　　　　　　　　⊠ CTV ⊠ ◿ D

COMFORT INN　　　　Rates Subject to Change　　　　　　　　　**Phone:** 919/480-2600
◆◆　　6/12-8/15 & Fri & Sat
Motel　　8/16-9/5 [CP]　　　2P/1B: $100- 155　2P/2B: $100- 155　XP: $5　　　F18
　　Sun-Thurs 8/16-9/5 [CP]　2P/1B: $75- 115　2P/2B: $75- 115　XP: $5　　　F18
　　9/6-9/30 [CP]　　　　2P/1B: $55- 100　2P/2B: $55- 100　XP: $5　　　F18
　　12/1-6/11 & 10/1-11/30 [CP]　2P/1B: $35- 100　2P/2B: $35- 100　XP: $5　　　F18
Location: On NC 12; at milepost 8.2. 401 Virginia Dare Tr 27948 (PO Box 3427). Fax: 919/480-2873. **Terms:** Sr. discount;
check-in 4 pm; no pets. **Facility:** 120 rooms. 3 stories; exterior corridors. **All Rooms:** free movies. **Cards:** AE, DI, DS, MC,
VI.　　　　　　　　　　　　　　　　　　　　　　　　　　　　　CTV ⊠ ◿ D

DAYS INN OCEANFRONT-WILBUR & ORVILLE WRIGHT　　　　　**Phone:** 919/441-7211
(AAA) SAVE　　6/8-9/2 [CP]　　1P: $70- 100　2P/1B: $70- 100　2P/2B: $80- 150　XP: $5　　F12
　　3/30-6/7 & 9/3-9/29 [CP]　1P: $45- 95　2P/1B: $45- 95　2P/2B: $50- 95　XP: $5　　F12
◆◆◆　　12/1-12/15, 1/10-3/29 &
Motel　　9/30-11/30 [CP]　　1P: $35- 70　2P/1B: $35- 70　2P/2B: $35- 70　XP: $5　　F12
　　Location: On NC 12 at milepost 8.3. 101 N Virginia Dare Tr 27948 (PO Box 3189). Fax: 919/441-8080.
Terms: Open 12/1-12/15 & 1/10-11/30; check-in 4 pm; reserv deposit, 3 day notice, in season; weekly rates; no pets.
Facility: 54 rooms. 16 efficiency units, $140-$150 in season; 2 stories; interior/exterior corridors; oceanfront; beach.
Dining: Seasonal afternoon refreshments. **Recreation:** swimming, fishing. **All Rooms:** free movies, refrigerators, combo or
shower baths. Fee: safes. **Some Rooms:** microwaves. **Cards:** AE, DI, DS, JCB, MC, VI.　　⊠ CTV ⊠ ◿ D

HOLIDAY INN　　　　Rates Subject to Change　　　　　　　　　**Phone:** 919/441-6333
◆◆　　5/21-9/18　　　1P: $129- 169　2P/1B: $129- 169　2P/2B: $129- 169　XP: $10　　F12
Motor Inn　　4/1-5/20 & 9/19-10/31　1P: $75- 109　2P/1B: $75- 109　2P/2B: $75- 109　XP: $10　　F12
　　12/1-3/31 & 11/1-11/30　1P: $45- 75　2P/1B: $45- 75　2P/2B: $45- 75　XP: $10　　F12
Location: On NC 12 Beach Rd at milepost 9.5. 1601 Virginia Dare Tr 27948 (PO Box 308). Fax: 919/441-7779.
Terms: Check-in 4 pm; reserv deposit, 3 day notice; no pets. **Facility:** 105 rooms. 4 stories; interior corridors.
Dining: Restaurant; 7 am-11 & 5:30-9 pm, hours may vary seasonally; $11-$17. **All Rooms:** free movies. **Cards:** AE, CB,
DI, DS, JCB, MC, VI.　　　　　　　　　　　　　　　　　　　⊠ CTV ⊠ ◿ D

NAGS HEAD BEACH HOTEL   Rates Subject to Change   **Phone:** 919/441-0411

◆◆◆   Fri & Sat 6/19-9/3 [CP]   1P: $95   2P/2B: $95

Motel   12/1-5/27, Sun-Thurs

     6/19-9/3 & 9/4-11/30 [CP]   1P: $65- 85   2P/1B: $75- 95   2P/2B: $85

     5/28-6/18 [CP]   1P: $49- 69   2P/1B: $59- 79   2P/2B: $69

Location: On SR 12 at milepost 8.1. 804 N Virginia Dare Tr 27948 (PO Box 1349). Fax: 919/441-7811. **Terms:** Check-in 4 pm; pets, $5 extra charge. **Facility:** 96 rooms. Rates are for up to 4 persons; 4 stories; interior/exterior corridors. **All Rooms:** free movies. **Cards:** AE, DI, DS, MC, VI.

QUALITY INN-JOHN YANCEY   Rates Subject to Change   **Phone:** 919/441-7141

◆◆   6/14-9/1   2P/2B: $89- 169   XP: $10   F12

Motel   5/24-6/13 & 9/2-9/29   2P/2B: $54- 129   XP: $10   F12

     4/5-5/23 & 9/30-11/2   2P/2B: $44- 109   XP: $10   F12

     12/1-4/4 & 11/3-11/30   2P/2B: $34- 99   XP: $10   F12

Location: On NC 12 beach road, at milepost 10.3. 2009 Virginia Dare Tr 27948 (PO Box 422). Fax: 919/441-4277. **Terms:** Check-in 4 pm; no pets. **Facility:** 107 rooms. 2-4 stories; exterior corridors. **All Rooms:** free movies. **Some Rooms:** 20 efficiencies. **Cards:** AE, CB, DI, DS, JCB, MC, VI.

RAMADA INN AT NAGS HEAD BEACH   **Phone:** 919/441-2151

(AAA) (SAVE)   5/22-8/31   1P: $129- 174   2P/1B: $129- 174   2P/2B: $129- 174   XP: $10   F18

     9/1-11/26   1P: $79- 129   2P/1B: $79- 129   2P/2B: $79- 129   XP: $10   F18

◆◆   2/14-5/21   1P: $54- 124   2P/1B: $54- 124   2P/2B: $54- 124   XP: $10   F18

Motor Inn   12/1-2/13 & 11/27-11/30   1P: $54- 84   2P/1B: $54- 84   2P/2B: $54- 84   XP: $10   F18

Location: On NC 12 Beach Rd at milepost 9.5. 1701 S Virginia Dare Trail 27948 (PO Box 2716). Fax: 919/441-1830. **Terms:** Check-in 4 pm; pets. **Facility:** 172 rooms. Many rooms with oceanfront or oceanview. All rooms with balcony. 5 stories; interior corridors; beach, whirlpool, shuffleboard, volleyball. Fee: golf privileges. **Dining:** Restaurant; 7 am-11:30 & 5-9:30 pm, in season 7 am-2 & 5-9:30 pm; $10-$14; cocktails. **Recreation:** swimming, fishing. **All Rooms:** coffeemakers, microwaves, refrigerators. Fee: movies. **Some Rooms:** Fee: VCP's. **Cards:** AE, CB, DI, DS, MC, VI. **Special Amenities:** Free local telephone calls and free newspaper. *(See color ad below)*

RESTAURANTS

COLINGTON CAFE   **Dinner:** $12-$17   **Phone:** 919/480-1123

◆◆◆   **Location:** 1 mi w of jct SR 12 on Colington Rd. 1029 Colington Rd 27848. **Hours:** 5 pm-10 pm. Closed: Continental   1/1-2/14 & Mon-Wed 12/1-12/25 & 2/15-3/15. **Reservations:** required; 3 day advance. **Features:** children's menu; beer & wine only; a la carte. Wide variety of French dishes, steak & local seafood. Homemade desserts. Smoke free premises. **Cards:** DI, MC, VI.

FLYING FISH CAFE   **Lunch:** $6-$8   **Dinner:** $12-$18   **Phone:** 919/441-6894

◆◆   **Location:** On US 158 (Bypass) at MP 10. 2003 Croatan Hwy 27948. **Hours:** 11:30 am-10 pm. Closed: American   12/24-12/26. **Features:** children's menu; early bird specials; carryout; cocktails. Some mediterranean entrees; homemade bread, dressing & dessert. Pot pie signature dish with daily change of meat. Patio dining, weather permitting. **Cards:** AE, DS, MC, VI.

MILLIE'S DINER   **Lunch:** $5-$7   **Dinner:** $14-$18   **Phone:** 919/480-3463

◆◆   **Location:** On SR 12 (Beach Dr) at MP 10. 2008 S Virginia Dare Tr 27948. **Hours:** Open 12/1-12/31 & American   2/1-11/30; 11 am-2:30 & 5-10 pm, Fri & Sat from 9 am. Closed: 12/25. **Features:** Sunday brunch; children's menu; carryout; cocktails. 1939 Kullman Diner from New Jersey. Eclectic American/European entrees. **Cards:** AE, DS, MC, VI.

PORT-O-CALL RESTAURANT   **Dinner:** $14-$20   **Phone:** 919/441-7484

◆◆   **Location:** On NC 12 beach road at milepost 8.8. 504 S Virginia Dare Tr 27948. **Hours:** 5 pm-10 pm, Sun Seafood   9:30 am-1:30 & 5-10 pm. Closed: 2/1-3/14. **Features:** Sunday brunch; children's menu; early bird specials; carryout; cocktails & lounge. In Victorian style art gallery. Also beef, veal, poultry & pasta dishes. **Cards:** AE, DS, MC, VI.

THE THAI ROOM   **Lunch:** $5-$6   **Dinner:** $8-$16   **Phone:** 919/441-1180

◆   **Location:** On SR 12 (beach road) at milepost 8.9. 27948. **Hours:** Open 12/1-12/31 & 3/1-11/30; 11:30 Ethnic   am-2:30 pm & 5-10 pm, Sun from 5 pm. Closed major holidays & Mon 9/5-5/31. **Reservations:** accepted; for 5 or more. **Features:** children's menu; carryout; cocktails & lounge. Chinese, Thai & American food. A true family operation with loyal local following. Dinner buffet in season. **Cards:** AE, MC, VI.

ZANZIBAR   **Dinner:** $12-$16   **Phone:** 919/480-3116

◆◆   **Location:** 1.3 mi w on Colington Rd from US 158, mile post 8.5. 1085 Colington Rd 27948. **Hours:** 5 pm-10 American   pm. Closed: Mon-Wed, 3/1-4/30 & 11/1-12/31. **Features:** beer & wine only. Table-top cooking, fondue style. **Cards:** CB, DI, DS, MC, VI.

KITTY HAWK—1,900

LODGINGS

BEACH HAVEN
Phone: 919/261-4785

		2P/1B			2P/2B		XP	
(AAA) SAVE	6/12-9/26	2P/1B:	$80-	91	2P/2B:	$101- 112	XP:	$6
	4/17-6/11	2P/1B:	$52-	69	2P/2B:	$59-	80	XP:	$6
◆◆◆	3/27-4/16 & 9/27-11/15	2P/1B:	$43-	54	2P/2B:	$52-	64	XP:	$6

Motel   **Location:** On SR 12 at milepost 3.9. 4104 Virginia Dare Tr 27949 (PO Box 916). **Terms:** Open 3/27-11/15; no pets. **Facility:** 5 rooms. Small immaculate motel across from beach with manicured lawn. Picnic area with gas grill. Comfortable rooms. 1 story; exterior corridors; beach. Fee: beach equipment. **Dining:** Restaurant nearby. **Recreation:** swimming. Fee: snorkeling equipment; bicycles. **All Rooms:** coffeemakers, microwaves, free movies, refrigerators, combo or shower baths. **Cards:** AE, MC, VI. **Special Amenities: Early check-in/late check-out and free local telephone calls.** [CTV] [D]

HOLIDAY INN EXPRESS
Phone: 919/261-4888

		2P/1B			2P/2B		XP	
(AAA) SAVE	5/27-9/4 [CP]	2P/1B:	$82- 105	2P/2B:	$82- 105	XP:	$5	F18
◆◆	12/1-5/26 & 9/5-11/30 [CP]	2P/1B:	$45-	69	2P/2B:	$45-	69	XP:	$5	F18

Motel   **Location:** On Rt 158 bypass (Four Mile Post). 3919 N Croatan Hwy 27949 (PO Box 1096). Fax: 919/261-3387. **Terms:** Check-in 4 pm; reserv deposit; no pets. **Facility:** 98 rooms. 2 stories; interior corridors. **Dining:** Restaurant nearby. **All Rooms:** free movies, refrigerators. **Some Rooms:** microwaves. **Cards:** AE, CB, DI, DS, JCB, MC, VI. **Special Amenities: Free breakfast and free local telephone calls.** [⌂] [♦] [CTV] [X] [D] [S]

RESTAURANT

OCEAN BOULEVARD
Dinner: $18-$22   **Phone: 919/261-2546**
◆◆◆   **Location:** On SR 12 at MP 2. 4700 Virginia Dare Tr 27948. **Hours:** 5 pm-11 pm; to 10 pm off season.
Regional   Closed: 12/24-12/26 & Sun off season. **Features:** cocktails. Homemade bread dessert, sauce & dressing.
American   Pastry chef. Menu changes seasonally. Cosmopolitan ambience with open kitchen. **Cards:** AE, MC, VI. [X]

MANTEO—1,000

LODGINGS

DUKE OF DARE MOTOR LODGE
Rates Subject to Change   **Phone: 919/473-2175**

		1P		2P/1B		2P/2B		XP	
◆	5/22-9/7	1P:	$43	2P/1B:	$49	2P/2B:	$55	XP:	$6
Motel	12/1-5/21 & 9/8-11/30	1P:	$33	2P/1B:	$38	2P/2B:	$44	XP:	$6

Location: On Roanoke Island, 2 blks s on US 64 & 264. 100 S Virginia Dare Rd 27954 (PO Box 746). **Terms:** Reserv deposit; no pets. **Facility:** 57 rooms. 2 stories; exterior corridors. **All Rooms:** free movies. **Cards:** MC, VI. [⌂] [CTV] [D]

THE TRANQUIL HOUSE INN
Rates Subject to Change   **Phone: 919/473-1404**

		1P		2P/1B		2P/2B		XP	
◆◆◆	5/15-10/2 [CP]	1P:	$119- 159	2P/1B:	$119- 159	2P/2B:	$119- 159	XP:	$10	F15
Country Inn	12/1-5/14 & 10/3-11/30 [CP]	1P:	$79- 139	2P/1B:	$79- 139	2P/2B:	$79- 139	XP:	$10	F15

Location: Center, opposite courthouse & Elizabeth II. 405 Queen Elizabeth St 27954 (PO Box 2045). Fax: 919/473-1526. **Terms:** Sr. discount; reserv deposit, 14 day notice; 2 night min stay, weekends in season; no pets. **Facility:** 25 rooms. 3 stories, no elevator; interior/exterior corridors. **Dining:** Dining room; 5 pm-10 pm; $17-$20. **All Rooms:** free movies. **Cards:** AE, DS, MC, VI. [CTV] [X] [D]

RESTAURANTS

CLARA'S SEAFOOD GRILL
Lunch: $5-$7   **Dinner: $9-$15**   **Phone: 919/473-1727**
◆◆   **Location:** On the waterfront in historic district via 400E. Queen Elizabeth Ave 27954. **Hours:** Open
Seafood   12/1-12/31 & 3/1-11/30; 11:30 am-9 pm, Sat, Sun & in summer-9:30 pm. Closed: 11/26, 12/24 & 12/25. **Features:** children's menu; carryout; beer & wine only. Fresh local seafood & regional cuisine served in a casual relaxing atmosphere. View of harbor & Elizabeth II. **Cards:** AE, DS, MC, VI. [X]

1587 RESTAURANT
Dinner: $17-$22   **Phone: 919/473-1587**
◆◆◆   **Location:** In Tranquil House Inn. 405 Queen Elizabeth St 27954. **Hours:** Open 2/14-11/29; 5 pm-10 pm.
Regional   Closed: Sun & Mon 2/1-3/31 & 10/1-11/30. **Features:** children's menu; health conscious menu; carryout;
American   beer & wine only. Certified Angus beef; home-grown herbs; global influence on all entrees; casual elegance. **Cards:** AE, DS, MC, VI. [X]

THE WEEPING RADISH BREWERY &
BAVARIAN RESTAURANT
Lunch: $7-$17   **Dinner: $7-$17**   **Phone: 919/473-1157**
◆◆◆   **Location:** 1 mi e on US 64. **Hours:** Open 12/1-12/31 & 2/14-11/30; 11:30 am-9 pm. Closed: 11/26 & 12/5.
German   **Features:** children's menu; carryout; cocktail lounge; beer & wine only. Also American entrees. German ambience. Micro-brewery, brewery tours. Playground. **Cards:** DS, MC, VI. [X]

NAGS HEAD—900

LODGINGS

BEACON MOTOR LODGE
Rates Subject to Change   **Phone: 919/441-5501**

		2P/1B			2P/2B		XP	
(AAA)	5/22-5/25 & 6/5-9/7	2P/1B:	$80- 105	2P/2B:	$80- 105	XP:	$10	F
◆◆	5/26-6/4 & 9/8-9/26	2P/1B:	$55-	85	2P/2B:	$55-	85	XP:	$5	F
Motel	5/1-5/21 & 9/27-10/12	2P/1B:	$40-	70	2P/2B:	$40-	70	XP:	$5	F
	4/3-4/30 & 10/13-10/25	2P/1B:	$35-	60	2P/2B:	$35-	60	XP:	$5	F

Location: On NC 12, beach road at milepost 11. 2617 S Virginia Dare Tr 27959 (PO Box 729). Fax: 919/441-2178. **Terms:** Open 4/3-10/25; check-in 4 pm; reserv deposit, 14 day notice, efficiencies 30 day, apartments 60 day; 3 night min stay, in season; no pets. **Facility:** 47 rooms. 2 two-room housekeeping units & 1 two-bedroom hskpg cottage, $675-$1000 weekly; 14 efficiencies, $620 in season. Rates for up to 4 persons; 2 stories; exterior corridors. **All Rooms:** free movies. **Some Rooms:** 6 kitchens. **Cards:** AE, CB, DI, DS, MC, VI. [⌂] [CTV] [X] [D]

BLUE HERON MOTEL
Rates Subject to Change   **Phone: 919/441-7447**

		2P/1B		2P/2B		XP	
◆◆	6/12-9/8	2P/1B:	$95	2P/2B:	$90- 95	XP:	$5
Motel	4/3-6/11 & 9/9-10/15	2P/1B:	$68	2P/2B:	$59- 68	XP:	$5
	12/1-4/2 & 10/16-11/30	2P/1B:	$48	2P/2B:	$43- 50	XP:	$5

Location: On NC 12 beach road, at Milepost 16. 6811 Virginia Dare Tr 27959. **Terms:** Check-in 4 pm; reserv deposit, 3 day notice; no pets. **Facility:** 30 rooms. Efficiencies $7 extra; 3 stories, no elevator; exterior corridors. **All Rooms:** free movies. **Cards:** DS, MC, VI. [⌂] [⌂] [CTV] [D]

COMFORT INN OCEANFRONT SOUTH   Rates Subject to Change   Phone: 919/441-6315

◆◆

Motel

5/24-9/3 [CP]		2P/1B:	$85- 155	2P/2B:	$90- 155	XP: $10	F17
4/1-5/23 & 9/4-11/3 [CP]	1P: $45- 135			2P/2B:	$45- 135	XP: $10	F17
12/1-3/31 & 11/4-11/30 [CP]	1P: $35- 86	2P/1B:	$55- 86	2P/2B:	$35- 86	XP: $10	F17

Location: Milepost 17 on beach road; in South Nags Head. 8031 Old Oregon Rd 27959 (PO Box 307). Fax: 919/441-6315.
Terms: Sr. discount; check-in 4 pm; reserv deposit; no pets. **Facility:** 105 rooms. 7 stories; interior corridors.
All Rooms: free movies. **Cards:** AE, DI, DS, MC, VI.   (symbols)

FIRST COLONY INN   Rates Subject to Change   Phone: 919/441-2343

(AAA)

◆◆◆◆
Historic Bed
& Breakfast

5/22-9/6 [BP]	1P: $150- 260	2P/1B:	$150- 260	2P/2B:	$150- 260	XP: $30
4/3-5/21 & 9/7-10/31 [BP]	1P: $120- 195	2P/1B:	$120- 195	2P/2B:	$120- 195	XP: $30
12/1-4/2 [BP]	1P: $75- 180	2P/1B:	$75- 180	2P/2B:	$75- 180	XP: $30
11/1-11/30 [BP]	1P: $80- 160	2P/1B:	$80- 160	2P/2B:	$80- 160	XP: $30

Location: US 158, milepost 16, in South Nags Head. 6720 S Virginia Dare Tr 27959. Fax: 919/441-9234.
Terms: Reserv deposit, 8 day notice; 2 night min stay, weekends; no pets. **Facility:** 26 rooms. $20 extra on
weekends from 3/28-10/26, $15 extra on weekends from 10/27-3/27; 3 stories, no elevator; exterior corridors; smoke free
premises. **All Rooms:** free movies. **Some Rooms:** 4 efficiencies. **Cards:** AE, DS, MC, VI.   (symbols)

THE ISLANDER   Rates Subject to Change   Phone: 919/441-6229

◆◆

Motel

6/12-9/30		2P/1B:	$98	2P/2B:	$98	XP: $10	F5
4/1-6/11 & 10/1-10/14		2P/1B:	$55- 68	2P/2B:	$55- 68	XP: $10	F5

Location: On NC 12 beach road, at milepost 16.5. 7001 Virginia Dare Tr 27959 (PO Box 605).
Terms: Open 4/1-10/14; reserv deposit, 3 day notice; no pets. **Facility:** 24 rooms. 3 stories, no elevator; exterior corridors.
All Rooms: free movies. **Some Rooms:** 6 efficiencies. **Cards:** AE, MC, VI.   (symbols)

NAGS HEAD INN   Rates Subject to Change   Phone: 919/441-0454

(AAA)

◆◆◆
Motel

5/22-9/7	2P/2B:	$99- 175	XP: $10	F11
5/1-5/21 & 9/8-9/26	2P/2B:	$69- 135	XP: $5	F11
3/6-4/30 & 9/27-11/30	2P/2B:	$59- 89	XP: $5	F11
12/1-3/5	2P/2B:	$49- 69	XP: $5	F11

Location: On NC 12 at milepost 13.8. 4701 S Virginia Dare Tr 27959 (PO Box 1599). Fax: 919/441-0454.
Terms: Check-in 4 pm; reserv deposit, 3 day notice; no pets. **Facility:** 100 rooms. 5 stories; interior corridors.
All Rooms: free movies. **Cards:** AE, DS, MC, VI.   (symbols)

QUALITY INN SEA OATEL   Phone: 919/441-7191

(AAA) (SAVE)

◆◆◆
Motel

6/1-9/8	1P: $92- 140	2P/1B:	$92- 140	2P/2B:	$92- 140	XP: $10	F18
4/1-5/31	1P: $42- 115	2P/1B:	$42- 115	2P/2B:	$42- 115	XP: $10	F18
12/1-12/31 & 9/9-11/30	1P: $40- 110	2P/1B:	$40- 110	2P/2B:	$40- 110	XP: $10	F18
1/1-3/31	1P: $41- 65	2P/1B:	$41- 65	2P/2B:	$41- 65	XP: $10	F18

Location: On SR 12 at MM 16.5, in South Nags Head. 7123 S Virginia Dare Tr 27959 (PO Box 489).
Fax: 919/441-1961. **Terms:** Check-in 4 pm; package plans; no pets. **Facility:** 111 rooms. Some smaller rooms. Many rooms
with oceanfront balcony. 1-3 stories; exterior corridors; beach, wading pool. **Dining:** Restaurant nearby. **Services:** Fee: coin
laundry. **Recreation:** swimming, fishing. **All Rooms:** coffeemakers, microwaves, free movies, refrigerators, combo or shower
baths. **Some Rooms:** Fee: VCP's. **Cards:** AE, CB, DI, DS, JCB, MC, VI.   (symbols)

SEA FOAM MOTEL   Guaranteed Rates   Phone: 919/441-7320

(AAA)

◆◆
Motel

5/23-9/7	2P/2B:	$74- 90	XP: $5	F12
12/1-12/15, 3/1-5/22 &			
9/8-11/30	2P/2B:	$42- 57	XP: $5	F12

Location: On NC 12, at milepost 16.5. 7111 S Virginia Dare Tr 27959. Fax: 919/441-7324. **Terms:** Open
12/1-12/15 & 3/1-11/30; reserv deposit, 14 day notice, handling fee imposed; no pets. **Facility:** 51 rooms. 2
two-bedroom cottages with kitchen, weekly rental only-in season, $695. 18 efficiencies, $510-$605; 1 deluxe apartment, $660;
2 stories; exterior corridors. **All Rooms:** free movies. **Cards:** AE, MC, VI.   (symbols)

THE SURF SIDE MOTEL   Phone: 919/441-2105

(AAA) (SAVE)

◆◆◆
Motel

6/12-9/6 [CP]	2P/2B:	$99- 189	XP: $5-10	F13
5/8-6/11 & 9/7-9/30 [CP]	2P/2B:	$67- 159	XP: $5-10	F13
3/27-5/7 & 10/1-10/31 [CP]	2P/2B:	$59- 139	XP: $5-10	F13
12/1-3/26 & 11/1-11/30 [CP]	2P/2B:	$39- 119	XP: $5-10	F13

Location: ON NC 12 beach road at milepost 16. 6701 S Virginia Dare Tr 27959 (PO Box 400).
Fax: 919/441-2456. **Terms:** Reserv deposit, 14 day notice, 4/1-9/30; no pets. **Facility:** 76 rooms. 4 suites. 7 loft suites $139-
$149 in season; 3-5 stories, no elevator; interior corridors. **Some Rooms:** 6 efficiencies. **Cards:** AE, DS, MC, VI.   (symbols)

TAR HEEL MOTEL   Rates Subject to Change   Phone: 919/441-6150

◆◆
Motel

5/28-9/6	1P: $51- 75	2P/1B:	$51- 55	2P/2B:	$57- 75	XP: $5-7	F5
4/1-5/27 & 9/7-10/31	1P: $36- 45	2P/1B:	$36- 38	2P/2B:	$39- 45	XP: $5	F5

Location: On NC 12 beach road, milepost 16. 7010 S Virginia Dare Tr 27959 (PO Box 242). **Terms:** Open
4/1-10/31; reserv deposit, 5 day notice; no pets. **Facility:** 33 rooms. 1 story; exterior corridors. **All Rooms:** free movies.
Some Rooms: 4 efficiencies. **Cards:** AE, MC, VI.   (symbols)

THE VACATIONER MOTEL   Rates Subject to Change   Phone: 919/441-7487

◆
Motel

6/20-8/25	1P: $60	2P/1B:	$60- 65	2P/2B:	$75- 95	XP: $5
5/28-6/19	1P: $47	2P/1B:	$49- 53	2P/2B:	$60- 70	XP: $5
8/26-10/9	1P: $40	2P/1B:	$40- 43	2P/2B:	$47- 65	XP: $5
4/1-5/27 & 10/10-11/30	1P: $30	2P/1B:	$30- 36	2P/2B:	$36- 47	XP: $5

Location: On NC 12 beach road, at milepost 16. 6923 Virginia Dare Tr 27959. **Terms:** Open 4/1-11/30; reserv deposit, 14
day notice, 60 day for cottages; 3 night min stay; no pets. **Facility:** 29 rooms. 2- & 4-bedroom cottages, $405-$675 weekly
5/24-9/6. 7 night min stay in cottages in season. Handling fee imposed; 3 stories, no elevator; exterior corridors.
Some Rooms: 12 efficiencies. **Cards:** MC, VI.   (symbols)

VIVIANNA MOTEL   Rates Subject to Change   Phone: 919/441-7409

◆
Motel

6/24-8/27 & 9/2-9/4	2P/2B:	$71- 86	XP: $5
6/11-6/23 & 8/28-9/1	2P/2B:	$53- 66	XP: $5
5/5-6/10 & 9/5-10/1	1P: $42	2P/2B:	$43- 59	XP: $5
3/1-5/4 & 10/2-11/30	1P: $36	2P/2B:	$37- 51	XP: $5

Location: On NC 12 beach road, at milepost 16.4. 6905 Virginia Dare Tr 27959 (PO Box 5). **Terms:** Open 3/1-11/30;
check-in 4 pm; reserv deposit, 3 day notice; no pets. **Facility:** 15 rooms. 1 one-bedroom apartment, $700 weekly; $575 mid
season, $450 off season; 1 story; exterior corridors. **Cards:** MC, VI.   (symbols)

RESTAURANTS

KELLY'S OUTER BANKS RESTAURANT & TAVERN **Dinner:** $12-$18 **Phone:** 919/441-4116
(AAA) **Location:** On SR 158, MM 10.5. 2316 S Croatan Hwy 27959. **Hours:** 5 pm-10 pm. Closed: 12/24 & 12/25.
◆◆ **Features:** children's menu; early bird specials; health conscious menu; cocktails & lounge; entertainment.
Seafood Local seafood, steak & Iowa prime-rib. Multiple level dining rooms with nautical decor. Warm atmosphere.
Homemade dessert, bread, soup & salad dressing. **Cards:** AE, DI, DS, MC, VI. ⊠

THE LONE CEDAR CAFE **Lunch:** $7-$9 **Dinner:** $15-$19 **Phone:** 919/441-5405
◆◆ **Location:** 0.8 mi w on US 64 from jct SR 12 & US 158. 7623 S Virginia Trail Dr 27959. **Hours:** Open
Seafood 2/15-11/30; 11:30 am-9 pm. **Features:** children's menu; carryout; cocktails. Excellent views of Roanoke
Sound; some pasta & steak entrees; deck bar, weather permitting. **Cards:** MC, VI. ⊠

OWENS' RESTAURANT **Dinner:** $13-$20 **Phone:** 919/441-7309
(AAA) **Location:** On NC 12 at milepost 16.5. 7114 S Virginia Dare Tr 27959. **Hours:** Open 12/1-1/1 & 2/14-11/30; 5
pm-10 pm. **Features:** children's menu; carryout; cocktails & lounge. Comfortable, nautical setting. Family
◆◆◆ owned & operated since 1946. **Cards:** AE, DI, DS, MC, VI. ⊠
Steak and
Seafood

PENGUIN ISLE **Dinner:** $10-$20 **Phone:** 919/441-2637
(AAA) **Location:** On US 158 bypass at milepost 16. 6708 S Croatan Hwy 27959. **Hours:** Open 12/1-12/31 &
3/1-11/30; 5 pm-10 pm. Closed: 12/24-12/26 & 1/1-3/1. **Features:** children's menu; early bird specials;
◆◆◆ carryout; cocktails & lounge. Creative cuisine & grilled seafood served in spacious warm dining room. Sunset
Northern view of Roanoke Sound. Expresso/Cappuccino. Own desserts & Angus beef. Wine spectator award of
American excellence. **Cards:** AE, DI, DS, MC, VI.

OCRACOKE—700

LODGINGS

THE ANCHORAGE INN Rates Subject to Change **Phone:** 919/928-1101
(AAA) Fri & Sat 5/1-5/31, 6/1-9/30 &
◆◆ Fri & Sat 10/1-10/31 [CP] 2P/2B: $79- 99 XP: $10
Motel Sun-Thurs 5/1-5/31 &
10/1-10/31 [CP] 2P/2B: $59- 89 XP: $10
4/1-4/30 [CP] 2P/2B: $59- 79 XP: $10
12/1-3/31 & 11/1-11/30 [CP] 2P/2B: $49- 69 XP: $10
Location: Just n on SR 12 from Cedar Island Ferry, on south end of island. 177 Nichols Lakeland Dr 27960. **Terms:** Reserv
deposit, 3 day notice; small pets only. **Facility:** 35 rooms. 2-4 stories; exterior corridors. **All Rooms:** free movies.
Cards: DS, MC, VI. 🛏 🛍 CTV ⊠ D

BLUFF SHOAL MOTEL Guaranteed Rates **Phone:** 919/928-4301
◆◆ 4/1-10/31 1P: $55- 75 2P/2B: $55- 75 XP: $8 F12
Motel 12/1-3/31 & 11/1-11/30 1P: $40- 55 2P/2B: $40- 55 XP: $8 F12
Location: 0.5 mi n of Cedar Island Ferry on SR 12. 27960 (PO Box 217). **Terms:** Reserv deposit, 3 day
notice; no pets. **Facility:** 7 rooms. 1 story; exterior corridors. **All Rooms:** free movies. **Cards:** DS, MC, VI. CTV D

HARBORSIDE MOTEL **Phone:** 919/928-3111
(AAA) (SAVE) 5/22-9/6 [CP] 2P/1B: $65 2P/2B: $75 XP: $10
5/1-5/21 & 9/7-10/31 [CP] 2P/1B: $55 2P/2B: $65 XP: $10
◆◆ 4/8-4/30 & 11/1-11/15 [CP] 2P/1B: $45 2P/2B: $55 XP: $10
Motel **Location:** 1.5 blks from ferry terminal. 27960 (PO Box 116). **Terms:** Open 4/8-11/15; reserv deposit, 7 day
notice, 14 day for efficiencies; no pets. **Facility:** 18 rooms. 6-night minimum stay for 4 efficiencies, $10 extra
charge; 2 stories; exterior corridors; boat dock, boat ramp; outdoor deck overlooking harbor. **Recreation:** fishing.
All Rooms: free movies, refrigerators. **Cards:** AE, DS, MC, VI. **Special Amenities: Free breakfast and free local
telephone calls.** CTV ⊠ D

RESTAURANTS

BACK PORCH **Dinner:** $14-$19 **Phone:** 919/928-6401
(AAA) **Location:** 0.5 mi n of ferry terminal, just w. SR 1324 27960. **Hours:** Open 4/15-10/15; 5 pm-9:30 pm.
Closed: 7/4. **Features:** children's menu; beer & wine only. Served in comfortable juniper panelled ambience
◆◆◆ with screened in porch dining. Very popular. Half portions available. **Cards:** DS, MC, VI. ⊠
Seafood

CAPTAIN BEN'S RESTAURANT **Lunch:** $4-$8 **Dinner:** $6-$20 **Phone:** 919/928-4741
◆◆ **Location:** 0.5 mi n of ferry terminal on US 12. US 12 27960. **Hours:** Open 4/1-10/31; 11:30 am-9 pm.
Seafood **Reservations:** accepted. **Features:** casual dress; children's menu; carryout; beer & wine only. Fresh
seafood, prime rib, chicken & pasta in rustic, nautical decor. Gourmet & traditional cuisine. **Cards:** AE, DS,
MC, VI. ⊠

HOWARD'S PUB & RAW BAR RESTAURANT **Lunch:** $6-$8 **Dinner:** $10-$13 **Phone:** 919/928-4441
(AAA) **Location:** 1 mi n on SR 12 from Cedar Island Ferry; on n end of village. **Hours:** 11 am-2 am.
Features: children's menu; carryout; beer & wine only. Open air ocean view upper deck; kid friendly; daily
◆◆ fresh fish entrees; screened porch dining; house-cut fresh french fries; fresh hand-weighed gourmet
American hamburgers signature dish; over 200 beer selections; pizza. **Cards:** DS, MC, VI.

THE ISLAND INN DINING ROOM **Dinner:** $11-$15 **Phone:** 919/928-4351
(AAA) **Location:** 0.5 mi n on SR 12 from Cedar Island Ferry. 100 Lighthouse Rd 27960. **Hours:** Open 2/15-11/25;
7 am-11 & 5-9 pm. Closed: 7/4 for dinner. **Features:** children's menu; carryout; beer & wine only. Southern
◆◆ regional entrees; homemade soup, bread & dessert. **Cards:** DS, MC, VI. ⊠
American

PONY ISLAND RESTAURANT **Dinner:** $10-$16 **Phone:** 919/928-5701
◆ **Location:** 0.5 mi n of Cedar Island Ferry; off Hwy 12. 27960. **Hours:** Open 4/1-11/8; 7 am-11 & 5-9 pm.
American **Features:** children's menu; carryout; beer & wine only. Casual family-style, specializing in seafood. Senior
meals available. **Cards:** DS, MC, VI.

WANCHESE—1,400

RESTAURANT

QUEEN ANNE'S REVENGE
◆◆
Steak and
Seafood

Dinner: $14-$20   **Phone:** 919/473-5466
Location: 3 mi w on US 64, 3 mi s on SR 345, then 1 mi w via signs, in the Wanchese Woods. 27981.
Hours: 5 pm-9:30 pm, in winter to 9 pm. Closed: Tues 10/1-5/31 & 12/20-1/2. **Features:** children's menu;
health conscious menu; carryout; beer & wine only. Featuring local seafood broiled & fried; served in
comfortable juniper panelled ambience. **Cards:** AE, CB, DI, DS, MC, VI.   ⊠

OXFORD—7,900

RESTAURANT

RENA'S RESTAURANT
◆
American

Dinner: $7-$12   **Phone:** 919/603-5747
Location: Just n on SR 96 from I-85, exit 204; 1 mi w on E Industry Dr. 202 E Industry Dr 27565. **Hours:** 11
am-9 pm, Fri-10 pm, Sat 4 pm-10 pm, Sun 11am-3 pm. Closed major holidays. **Reservations:** accepted.
Features: children's menu; carryout; beer & wine only.   ⊠

PINEHURST—5,100

LODGINGS

HOLLY INN
🆎 SAVE
◆◆◆
Historic Hotel

Phone: 910/295-2300
All Year   1P: $139   2P/1B: $139   2P/2B: $139   XP: $10   F12
Location: 1 mi s & w from Pinehurst traffic circle via Midland (Rt 2) & Cherokee rds. 2300 Cherokee Rd
28374 (PO Box 2300). Fax: 910/295-0988. **Terms:** BP, MAP avail; package plans; no pets. **Facility:** 76 rooms.
Victorian style. Established in 1895; fully renovated. 5 stories; interior corridors. Fee: golf privileges.
Dining & Entertainment: Dining room; 7 am-10 & 6:30-10 pm; $13-$19; cocktails/lounge.
Recreation: bicycles. **All Rooms:** free movies. **Cards:** AE, DI, MC, VI. **Special Amenities:** Free breakfast and free local
telephone calls.   ⊠⊠ CTV D S

THE MANOR INN
◆◆◆
Historic Motel

Rates Subject to Change   **Phone:** 910/295-8472
3/9-6/5 & 9/7-11/13 [MAP]   1P: $224   2P/1B: $288   2P/2B: $288   XP: $38   F12
6/6-9/6 [MAP]   1P: $158   2P/1B: $222   2P/2B: $222   XP: $38   F12
12/1-3/8 & 11/14-11/30 [MAP] 1P: $134   2P/1B: $188   2P/2B: $188   XP: $38   F12
Location: From jct US 15 & 501; 0.5 mi n on Dundee Rd. 5 Community Rd 28374 (PO Box 4000).
Fax: 910/295-8595. **Terms:** Check-in 4 pm; reserv deposit, 21 day notice; $15 service charge; no pets. **Facility:** 45 rooms. 4
stories; interior corridors. **All Rooms:** free movies. **Cards:** AE, CB, DI, MC, VI.   ➥ CTV ⊠ D S

PINEHURST RESORT & COUNTRY CLUB
🆎
◆◆◆
Resort
Complex

Rates Subject to Change   **Phone:** 910/295-8553
3/6-6/10 & 9/3-11/19 [MAP]   1P: $314   2P/1B: $388   2P/2B: $386   XP: $194   F12
6/11-9/2 [MAP]   1P: $264   2P/1B: $318   2P/2B: $318   XP: $159   F12
12/1-3/5 & 11/20-11/30 [MAP] 1P: $220   2P/1B: $294   2P/2B: $294   XP: $147   F12
Location: On SR 2; also accessible via US 15 & 501. Carolina Vista Dr 28374 (PO Box 4000).
Fax: 910/295-8503. **Terms:** Check-in 4 pm; reserv deposit, 21 day notice; $15 service charge; 2 night min
stay, some weekends; no pets. **Facility:** 299 rooms. 4 stories; interior corridors. **Dining:** 5 dining rooms;
6:30-10 am & 5-10 pm; $15-$40; also, Carolina Dining Room, see separate listing. **All Rooms:** free & pay movies.
Cards: AE, CB, DI, MC, VI.   ➥ ➥ CTV ⊠ D S

RESTAURANTS

CAROLINA DINING ROOM
◆◆◆
American

Lunch: $8-$12   **Phone:** 910/295-6811
Location: In Pinehurst Resort & Country Club. **Hours:** 6:30 am-10, noon-2 & 6:30-9:30 pm.
Reservations: required. **Features:** formal attire; health conscious menu; cocktails; entertainment; valet
parking. A 5-course prix fixe meal. A changing menu. Extensive wine list. **Cards:** AE, DI, DS, MC, VI.   ⊠

GREENHOUSE RESTAURANT
◆
American

Lunch: $5-$7   **Phone:** 919/295-1761
Location: From World Golf Hall of Fame, SR 2, 0.3 mi n on SR 5, 1.5 mi w on Linden Rd. 905
Linden Rd 28374. **Hours:** 11:30 am-3 pm. Closed major holidays & 1/15-1/28. **Features:** casual dress;
children's menu; health conscious menu; carryout; cocktails. Varied light offerings in greenhouse
atmosphere. Entry through gift shop. **Cards:** DS, MC, VI.   ⊠

RALEIGH—208,000   (See map p. 404; index below)

To help you more easily locate accommodations in the Raleigh area, the following index
and map show lodgings and restaurants in multiple cities. Listings for these establishments are found under the heading for the city in which they are located. The Raleigh
area map comprises: Cary, Garner, Morrisville and Raleigh.

Airport Accommodations

Listings for these establishments are found under the heading for the city in which they are located.

Raleigh-Durham International

Budgetel Inn-Raleigh, 2 mi se of entrance/MORRISVILLE
Courtyard by Marriott-Airport, 2 mi se of airport/MORRISVILLE
Days Inn Airport/RTP, 2 mi se of entrance/MORRISVILLE
🆎 **Holiday Inn Raleigh-Durham Airport-Research Triang, 3 mi sw of airport/DURHAM**

(See map p. 404)

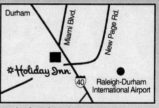 Quality Suites Hotel	....	15
The Plantation Inn Resort.	....	16
Holiday Inn State Capital	....	17
Raleigh Marriott Hotel-Crabtree Valley.	....	18
Best Western Hospitality Inn		19
The Oakwood Inn Bed & Breakfast	....	20
Holiday Inn-North	....	21
Country Inn by Carlson	....	22
William Thomas House Bed & Breakfast	....	24
Courtyard by Marriott-Raleigh Wake Forest	......	25

RESTAURANTS

The Falls Cooker	....	1
Irregardless	....	2
Wellspring Grocery	....	3
The Rathskeller	....	4
42nd St. Oyster Bar & Seafood Grill	....	5
Simpsons Beef & Seafood	....	7
Carvers Creek	....	8
K & S Cafeteria	....	11
Jean-Claude's French Cafe.	....	12
Lucky 32	....	17

CARY

Courtyard by Marriott-Cary.	....	30
Best Western Cary Inn	....	32
Red Roof Inn.	....	33
Fairfield Inn	....	34
Hampton Inn	....	35
Homewood Suites	....	36

RESTAURANTS

Fox & Hound Restaurant & Pub	....	18
Seldom Blues Cafe	....	19

MORRISVILLE

La Quinta Inn & Suites-Airport.	....	41
Microtel Raleigh Durham Airport	....	42
Courtyard by Marriott-Airport.	....	44
Budgetel Inn-Raleigh.	....	45
Days Inn Airport/RTP.	....	47

RESTAURANT

The Angus Barn	....	24

GARNER

Comfort Inn-South Raleigh	....	52

LODGINGS

BEST WESTERN HOSPITALITY INN   **Phone:** 919/872-8600   19
All Year [CP]   1P: $55- 62 2P/1B: $62- 65 2P/2B: $62- 65 XP: $6   F18
Location: 0.5 mi n on US 1N; off I-440 beltline, exit 11B. 2800 Brentwood Rd 27604. Fax: 919/872-5273.
Terms: No pets. **Facility:** 119 rooms. Very stylish room decor & furnishings. 3 stories; interior/exterior corridors. **Dining:** Restaurant nearby. **All Rooms:** free movies. **Some Rooms:** Fee: microwaves, refrigerators, whirlpools. **Cards:** AE, DI, DS, MC, VI. **Special Amenities: Free breakfast and free local telephone calls.**

Choose an establishment with the ⟨AAA⟩ next to its listing!

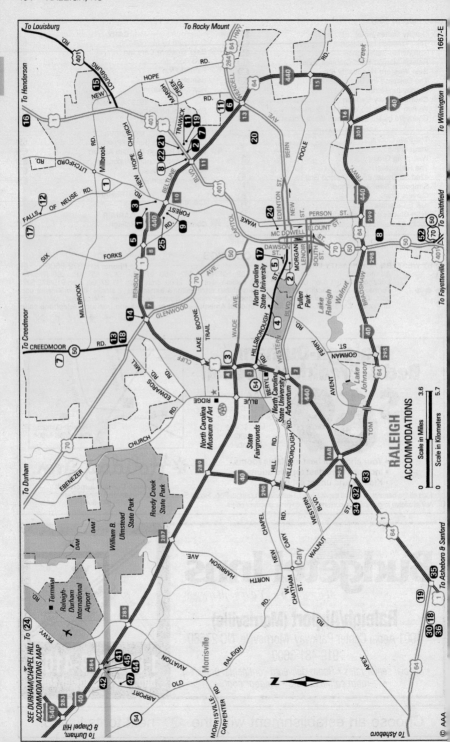

RALEIGH
ACCOMMODATIONS

(See map p. 404)

COMFORT INN SIX FORKS ROAD   Phone: 919/787-2300   **5**

	5/8-5/25 [CP]	1P: $72	2P/1B: $76	2P/2B: $76	XP: $4	F18
	10/1-10/31 [CP]	1P: $65	2P/1B: $70	2P/2B: $70	XP: $4	F18
	12/1-5/7, 5/26-9/30 &					
Motel	11/1-11/30 [CP]	1P: $49	2P/1B: $53	2P/2B: $53	XP: $4	F18

Location: Just n off I-440, exit 8. 4220 Six Forks Rd 27609. Fax: 919/787-2300. **Terms:** No pets. **Facility:** 84 rooms. Complimentary pizza Wed 6-7 pm. 3 stories; interior corridors. **Dining:** Restaurant nearby. **All Rooms:** free movies. Fee: VCP. **Cards:** AE, CB, DI, DS, MC, VI.

COMFORT INN-US 1 NORTH   Rates Subject to Change   Phone: 919/878-9550   **11**
◆◆◆   All Year [BP]   1P: $55- 63 2P/1B: $55- 63 2P/2B: $55- 63 XP: $5   F18
Motel   **Location:** 0.5 mi n on US 1N off I-440. 2910 Capital Blvd 27604. Fax: 919/876-5457. **Terms:** Sr. discount; no pets. **Facility:** 149 rooms. 2-4 stories; interior/exterior corridors. **All Rooms:** free movies. **Cards:** AE, CB, DI, DS, MC, VI.

(See map p. 404)

COUNTRY INN BY CARLSON Phone: 919/872-5000 **22**
AAA SAVE All Year [CP] 1P: $62- 75 2P/1B: $68- 81 2P/2B: $68- 81 XP: $6 F12
◆◆◆ **Location:** 0.3 mi n on US 1 from I-440, exit 11. 2715 Capital Blvd 27604. Fax: 919/790-7741.
Motel **Terms:** Reserv deposit; 2 night min stay, Mon & Tues; no pets. **Facility:** 157 rooms. Very upscale public areas; rooms handsomely appointed. 3 stories; interior corridors. **Dining & Entertainment:** Cocktail lounge; restaurant nearby. **Services:** Fee: coin laundry. **All Rooms:** coffeemakers, free movies. **Some Rooms:** microwaves, refrigerators. **Cards:** AE, CB, DI, DS, MC, VI. **Special Amenities:** Free breakfast and free local telephone calls. *(See color ad p 405)*

COURTYARD BY MARRIOTT-RALEIGH WAKE FOREST Rates Subject to Change Phone: 919/821-3400 **25**
◆◆◆ Sun-Thurs 1P: $74 2P/1B: $84 2P/2B: $84 XP: $10 F18
Motel Fri & Sat 1P: $52- 62 2P/1B: $52- 62 2P/2B: $52- 62
Location: Old Wake Forest Rd exit off I-440 north beltline, just s. 1041 Wake Towne Dr 27609. Fax: 919/821-1209. **Terms:** Check-in 4 pm; no pets. **Facility:** 153 rooms. 2-3 stories; interior corridors. **Dining:** Dining room; 6:30-10 am, Sat & Sun 7 am-noon. **All Rooms:** free & pay movies. **Cards:** AE, CB, DI, DS, MC, VI. *(See color ad below)*

EMBASSY SUITES HOTEL Rates Subject to Change Phone: 919/881-0000 **13**
◆◆◆ Sun-Thurs [BP] 1P: $169 2P/1B: $189 2P/2B: $189 XP: $20 F12
Suite Hotel Fri & Sat [BP] 1P: $109- 139 2P/1B: $109- 139 2P/2B: $109- 139 XP: $20 F12
Location: 0.5 mi w of jct US 1 & 64, at jct of US 70 & Creedmoor Rd, diagonally from Crabtree Valley Mall. 4700 Creedmoor Rd 27612. Fax: 919/782-7225. **Terms:** Sr. discount; no pets. **Facility:** 225 rooms. 5 cycle suites, $159-$174; 9 stories; interior corridors. **Dining:** Dining room; 6 am-9 & 11-11 pm, Sat & Sun 7 am-10:30 & 11-11 pm; Sun brunch, $14.95; $9-$16. **All Rooms:** free & pay movies. **Cards:** AE, CB, DI, DS, JCB, MC, VI.

FAIRFIELD INN BY MARRIOTT Rates Subject to Change Phone: 919/856-9800 **2**
◆◆◆ All Year [CP] 1P: $55 2P/1B: $60 2P/2B: $58 XP: $5 F
Motel **Location:** US 1N exit off I-440 north beltline, exit 11B. 2641 Appliance Ct 27604. Fax: 919/856-9800. **Terms:** Sr. discount; no pets. **Facility:** 132 rooms. 3 stories; interior/exterior corridors. **All Rooms:** free & pay movies. **Cards:** AE, DI, DS, MC. *(See color ad below)*

(See map p. 404)

HAMPTON INN-NORTH RALEIGH Rates Subject to Change **Phone:** 919/828-1813 **9**
◆◆◆ Sun-Thurs [CP] 1P: $62- 67 2P/1B: $67- 72 2P/2B: $67 XP: $5 F18
Motel Fri & Sat [CP] 1P: $59 2P/1B: $59 2P/2B: $59
Location: Old Wake Forest Rd, exit off I-440 north beltline, just s & just w. 1001 Wake Towne Dr 27609.
Fax: 919/834-2672. **Terms:** No pets. **Facility:** 131 rooms. 5 stories; interior corridors. **All Rooms:** free & pay movies.
Cards: AE, CB, DI, DS, MC, VI.

HOLIDAY INN-CRABTREE Rates Subject to Change **Phone:** 919/782-8600 **14**
◆◆◆ All Year 1P: $85 2P/1B: $91 2P/2B: $91 XP: $6 F19
Motor Inn **Location:** Exit 7B, I-440 beltline. 4100 Glenwood Ave 27612. Fax: 919/781-6077. **Terms:** Sr. discount;
reserv deposit, 3 day notice; no pets. **Facility:** 174 rooms. Handling fee imposed; 12 stories; interior corridors.
Dining: Restaurant; 6:30 am-2 & 5-10 pm, Lunch Buffet Mon-Fri, $6.95; $9-$15. **All Rooms:** free movies. **Cards:** AE, CB,
DI, DS, JCB, MC, VI.

HOLIDAY INN-NORTH Rates Subject to Change **Phone:** 919/872-7666 **21**
◆◆◆ 12/1-12/31 & 3/1-11/30 1P: $69 2P/1B: $69 2P/2B: $69
Motor Inn 1/1-2/28 1P: $49 2P/1B: $49 2P/2B: $49
Location: On US 1 & 401; 0.5 mi n of I-440 beltline, exit 11. 2815 Capital Blvd 27604. Fax: 919/872-3915.
Terms: Sr. discount; no pets. **Facility:** 200 rooms. 2-5 stories; interior/exterior corridors. **Dining:** Restaurant; 6:30 am-2 &
5:30-10 pm, Sat & Sun from 7 am; $9-$15. **All Rooms:** free movies. **Cards:** AE, CB, DI, DS, JCB, MC, VI.

HOLIDAY INN STATE CAPITAL Rates Subject to Change **Phone:** 919/832-0501 **17**
◆◆◆ All Year 1P: $84- 104 2P/1B: $84- 104 2P/2B: $84- 104 XP: $10 F18
Hotel **Location:** 0.3 mi n at Dawson & Hillsborough sts; Saunders St exit off I-40. 320 Hillsborough St 27603.
Fax: 919/833-1631. **Terms:** Sr. discount; pets. **Facility:** 202 rooms. 20 stories; interior corridors.
Dining: Dining room; 6:30 am-2 & 5:30-10 pm, Fri & Sat from 7 am, Sun brunch 11:30 am-2 pm; $8-$17. **All Rooms:** free &
pay movies. **Cards:** AE, CB, DI, DS, JCB, MC, VI. Roll in showers.

INNKEEPER SOUTH Rates Subject to Change **Phone:** 919/821-0521 **8**
◆◆ All Year [CP] 1P: $48- 80 2P/1B: $48- 80 2P/2B: $53- 80 XP: $5 F18
Motel **Location:** Exit (298A) off I-40, just s. 2501 S Saunders St 27603. Fax: 919/821-0521. **Terms:** Sr. discount;
no pets. **Facility:** 69 rooms. 2 stories; exterior corridors. **All Rooms:** free movies. **Cards:** AE, CB, DI, DS,
MC, VI.

NORTH RALEIGH HILTON Rates Subject to Change **Phone:** 919/872-2323 **3**
◆◆◆ All Year 1P: $115 2P/1B: $115 2P/2B: $115 XP: $10 F18
Hotel **Location:** 0.3 mi n on US 1 from I-440 exit 10 (Wake Forest Rd). 3415 Wake Forest Rd 27609.
Fax: 919/876-0890. **Terms:** No pets. **Facility:** 339 rooms. 6 stories; interior corridors. **Dining:** Dining room;
6:30 am-11 pm, Sun brunch 11 am-2 pm, $13.95; $10-$17. **All Rooms:** free & pay movies. **Cards:** AE, CB, DI, DS, MC, VI.
(See color ad p 18)

THE OAKWOOD INN BED & BREAKFAST Rates Subject to Change **Phone:** 919/832-9712 **20**
◆◆◆ All Year [BP] 1P: $75- 110 2P/1B: $85- 130 XP: $15
Historic Bed **Location:** In Oakwood Historic District. 411 N Bloodworth St 27604-1223. Fax: 919/836-9263. **Terms:** Sr.
& Breakfast discount; reserv deposit; no pets. **Facility:** 6 rooms. 2 stories; interior corridors; smoke free premises.
All Rooms: free movies. **Cards:** AE, DI, DS, MC, VI.

THE PLANTATION INN RESORT Guaranteed Rates **Phone:** 919/876-1411 **16**
◆◆ All Year 1P: $58- 105 2P/1B: $58- 105 2P/2B: $58- 105 XP: $5 F18
Motor Inn **Location:** 5 mi n on US 1 from I-440, exit 11B. 6401 Capital Blvd 27616. Fax: 919/790-7093. **Terms:** Sr.
discount; no pets. **Facility:** 101 rooms. 2 stories; interior/exterior corridors. **Dining:** 2 restaurants; 7-10:30
am, 11:30-2:30 & 5:30-10:30 pm, Sat 7:30 am-10:30 & 5:30-10:30 pm; $9-$14. **All Rooms:** free movies. **Cards:** AE, CB, DI,
MC, VI.

QUALITY SUITES HOTEL **Phone:** 919/876-2211 **15**
Ⓐ Ⓢ Sun-Thurs [BP] 1P: $99 2P/1B: $108 2P/2B: $108 XP: $10 F18
◆◆◆ Fri & Sat [BP] 1P: $76 2P/1B: $86 2P/2B: $86 XP: $10 F18
Suite Motel **Location:** 2 mi n of US 1 & 64 beltline (I-440); on US 1, or jct of US 1 & 401N. 4400 Capital Blvd 27604.
Fax: 919/790-1352. **Terms:** Monthly rates; 2 night min stay, Tues & Wed; no pets. **Facility:** 114 rooms. Iron &
ironing board in all rooms. 3 stories; interior corridors. **Services:** complimentary evening beverages; valet
laundry. **All Rooms:** coffeemakers, microwaves, free movies, refrigerators, VCP's. **Cards:** AE, CB, DI, DS, JCB, MC, VI.
Special Amenities: Free breakfast. *(See color ad p 405)*

(See map p. 404)

RALEIGH MARRIOTT HOTEL-CRABTREE VALLEY   Rates Subject to Change   **Phone: 919/781-7000** 🔞
◆◆◆   Sun-Thurs   1P: $119   2P/1B: $119   2P/2B: $119
Motor Inn   Fri & Sat   1P: $75   2P/1B: $75   2P/2B: $75
Location: On US 70, 0.5 mi w of jct I-440, Glenwood exit off beltline; opposite Crabtree Valley Mall. 4500 Marriott Dr 27612. Fax: 919/781-3059. **Terms:** No pets. **Facility:** 375 rooms. 6 stories; interior corridors. **Dining:** Dining room, restaurant; 6:30 am-11 pm; $9-$20. **All Rooms:** free & pay movies. **Cards:** AE, CB, DI, DS, JCB, MC, VI.

RED ROOF INN RALEIGH   Rates Subject to Change   **Phone: 919/231-0200** 6
◆◆   3/16-8/31   1P: $49   2P/1B: $55   2P/2B: $59   XP: $6   F18
Motel   9/1-11/30   1P: $47   2P/1B: $53   2P/2B: $57   XP: $6   F18
    12/1-3/15   1P: $44   2P/1B: $50   2P/2B: $54   XP: $6   F18
Location: US 64E & I-440, exit 13B; opposite Tower Shopping Plaza. 3520 Maitland Dr 27610. Fax: 919/231-0228. **Terms:** Small pets only. **Facility:** 115 rooms. 3 stories; exterior corridors. **All Rooms:** free movies. **Cards:** AE, CB, DI, DS, MC, VI.

RESIDENCE INN BY MARRIOTT   Rates Subject to Change   **Phone: 919/878-6100** 1
◆◆◆   Mon-Thurs [CP]   1P: $120- 144   2P/1B: $120- 144   2P/2B: $120- 144
Apartment   Fri-Sun [CP]   1P: $69- 129   2P/1B: $69- 129   2P/2B: $69- 129
Motel   **Location:** Old Wake Forest Rd n exit off beltline, just n, then 2 blks sw on Navaho Dr. 1000 Navaho Dr 27609. Fax: 919/876-4117. **Terms:** Sr. discount; reserv deposit; pets, $200 extra charge. **Facility:** 144 rooms. 2 stories; exterior corridors. **All Rooms:** kitchens, free movies. **Cards:** AE, CB, DI, DS, JCB, MC, VI.

SLEEP INN   **Phone: 919/755-6005** 7
AAA SAVE   All Year [CP]   1P: $59   2P/1B: $69   2P/2B: $69   XP: $6   F17
    Location: Just n on US 1N from I-440, exit 11B. 2617 Appliance Ct 27604. Fax: 919/755-9007. **Terms:** No
◆◆   pets. **Facility:** 107 rooms. 3 stories; interior corridors; small pool. **Dining:** Restaurant nearby.
Motel   **All Rooms:** free movies, shower baths. **Cards:** AE, CB, DI, DS, JCB, MC, VI. **Special Amenities: Free breakfast and free local telephone calls.**   Roll in showers.

WILLIAM THOMAS HOUSE BED & BREAKFAST   Rates Subject to Change   **Phone: 919/755-9400** 24
◆◆◆   All Year [BP]   1P: $102- 135   2P/1B: $102- 135   2P/2B: $102- 135   XP: $10
Historic Bed   **Location:** In Historic District. 530 N Blount St 27604. Fax: 919/755-3966. **Terms:** No pets, pets on premises.
& Breakfast   **Facility:** 4 rooms. 2 stories; interior corridors; smoke free premises. **All Rooms:** free movies. **Cards:** AE, MC, VI.

RESTAURANTS

CARVERS CREEK   **Lunch:** $8-$10   **Dinner:** $15-$20   **Phone:** 919/872-2300 8
◆◆   **Location:** Just off I-440 exit 11B, on US 1N, entry via Country Inn by Carlson. 2711 Capital Blvd 27604.
Steakhouse   **Hours:** 11:30 am-2 & 5-10 pm, Sat from 5 pm. Closed: 12/25. **Features:** children's menu; cocktails & lounge. Featuring prime rib, fresh seafood & specialty steak served in comfortable rustic surroundings.
Cards: AE, DI, MC, VI.

THE FALLS COOKER   **Lunch:** $6-$13   **Dinner:** $6-$13   **Phone:** 919/981-7400 1
◆◆   **Location:** 1.3 mi n on Wake Forest Rd/Falls of Neuse Rd from I-440, exit 10; in the Falls Centre Shopping
American   Center. 4516 Falls of Neuse Rd 27609. **Hours:** 11 am-10:30 pm, Fri & Sat-11:30 pm. Closed: 11/26 & 12/25. **Features:** children's menu; health conscious menu; carryout; cocktails. Regional American specialties from meatloaf to barbecue ribs. Popular following; busy lunch hour & expect 10-20 minute wait for seating. **Cards:** AE, CB, DI, DS, MC, VI.

42ND ST. OYSTER BAR & SEAFOOD GRILL   Historical **Lunch:** $6-$9 **Dinner:** $11-$18 **Phone:** 919/831-2811 5
◆◆   **Location:** 4 blks w & 2 blks n of State Capital. 508 W Jones St 27603. **Hours:** 11:30 am-11 pm, Sat from 5
Seafood   pm, Sun 5 pm-10 pm. Closed: 1/1, 11/26, 12/24 & 12/25. **Reservations:** suggested; for dinner. **Features:** children's menu; carryout; cocktails & lounge; a la carte. Restored 1931 warehouse, popular, lively & spacious. Fresh oysters, fish & lobster with fried or steamed platters, beef & fowl. Extensive wine & beer list; live lobster tank. **Cards:** AE, DI, MC, VI.

IRREGARDLESS   **Lunch:** $4-$6   **Dinner:** $11-$14   **Phone:** 919/833-8898 2
◆◆   **Location:** 1 mi w on Hillsborough from Capitol & just s on Morgan St. 901 W Morgan St 27603. **Hours:** 11:30 am-2:30 & 5:30-10 pm, Sun 10 am-2 pm. Closed: 1/1, 11/26 & 12/25. **Features:** No A/C;
American   casual dress; Sunday brunch; health conscious menu items; carryout; cocktails; entertainment. Health conscious environment well-known for vegan, a non-dairy vegetarian entree. Low fat & no pork or beef products. Fresh seafood & fowl. Well-established, unpretentious bistro. Smoke free premises. **Cards:** AE, DS, MC, VI.

JEAN-CLAUDE'S FRENCH CAFE   **Lunch:** $7-$9   **Dinner:** $10-$20   **Phone:** 919/872-6224 12
AAA   **Location:** 3 mi n of I-440 beltline, exit Old Wake Forest Rd; in North Ridge Shopping Center. 6112 Falls of Neuse Ave 27609. **Hours:** 11 am-2 & 5:30-9 pm, Fri & Sat-10 pm. Closed major holidays & Sun.
◆◆   **Features:** carryout; beer & wine only; a la carte. Casual cafe. Country French cuisine with fresh ingredients.
French   Salmon & puff pastry a favorite. Smoke free premises. **Cards:** AE, MC, VI.

K & S CAFETERIA   **Phone:** 919/231-8040 11
◆◆   **Location:** Jct I-440 beltline & Hwy 64E; in Tower Shopping Center, w end. 3620 Bastion Ln 27604.
American   **Hours:** 10:45 am-8:30 pm. Closed: 12/25. **Features:** early bird specials; carryout. Family & budget oriented, tastefully decorated dining rooms.

LUCKY 32   **Lunch:** $6-$10   **Dinner:** $8-$14   **Phone:** 919/876-9932 17
◆◆◆   **Location:** 3 mi n on Wake Forest Rd/ Falls of the Neuse from I-440 exit 10, just w on Spring Forest Rd. 832
Regional   Spring Forest Rd 27609. **Hours:** 11:15 am-10:30 pm, Fri & Sat-11 pm, Sun 10:45 am-10 pm, Sat & Sun
American   brunch. Closed: 11/26 & 12/25. **Reservations:** suggested. **Features:** health conscious menu; cocktails & lounge. Public areas with heavy mahogany trim & wool covered booth seats. Popular local following. Homemade soup & dessert. Regional & seasonal menu changes monthly. **Cards:** AE, DI, MC, VI.

(See map p. 404)

THE RATHSKELLER   **Lunch:** $6-$7   **Dinner:** $12-$16   **Phone:** 919/821-5342   ④
◆◆   **Location:** 1 mi e on Hillsborough St from I-440, exit 3; across from NCSU. 2412 Hillsborough St 27607.
American   **Hours:** 11:30 am-10:30 pm, Sat & Sun noon-10:30 pm. Closed: 7/4, 11/26, 12/24 & 12/25. **Features:** health
conscious menu; carryout; cocktails; street parking. Eclectic menu offering vegetarian, seafood, beef &
poultry entrees & sandwiches; metered street parking. **Cards:** AE, MC, VI.   ✖

SIMPSONS BEEF & SEAFOOD   **Lunch:** $8-$10   **Dinner:** $14-$25   **Phone:** 919/783-8818   ⑦
Ⓐ   **Location:** US 70W, Glenwood exit off Beltline I-440 exit 7, 0.8 mi w, then 0.8 mi n on Creedmoor Rd, in
Creedmoor Crossings. 5625 Creedmoor Rd 27612. **Hours:** 11 am-2:30 & 5-10 pm, Fri-11 pm, Sat 5 pm-11
◆◆◆   pm, Sun 5 pm-10 pm. Closed major holidays. **Reservations:** suggested. **Features:** dressy casual; carryout;
Steak and   cocktails & lounge. Aged western beef & fresh seafood courteously served in subdued elegance. **Cards:** AE,
Seafood   CB, DI, DS, MC, VI.   ✖

WELLSPRING GROCERY   **Phone:** 919/828-5805   ③
◆   **Location:** 0.3 mi e of I-440, exit 4; in Ridgewood Shopping Center. 3540 Wade Ave 27607. **Hours:** 9 am-9
American   pm. Closed: 11/26 & 12/25. **Features:** health conscious menu; carryout; beer only; cafeteria. Health
conscience & vegetarian dishes; deli & bakery using organic foods & grains; grocery with full line of
organically grown fresh fruits & vegetables. Overhead sidewalk dining, weather permitting. Smoke free premises.
Cards: MC, VI.   ✖

REIDSVILLE—12,200

LODGING

COMFORT INN   Rates Subject to Change   **Phone:** 910/634-0111
◆◆   4/10-4/30 & 10/1-10/31 [CP]   1P: $70- 80   2P/1B: $70- 80   2P/2B: $80- 95   XP: $5   F18
Motel   12/1-4/9, 5/1-9/30 &
11/1-11/30 [CP]   1P: $50   2P/1B: $55   2P/2B: $55   XP: $5   F18
Location: 2.5 mi s on SR 87 at jct US 29. 2203 Barnes St 27320. Fax: 910/349-2318. **Terms:** No pets. **Facility:** 51 rooms. 2
stories; exterior corridors. **All Rooms:** free movies. **Cards:** AE, DS, MC, VI.   🛄 CTV 👤 ✖ Ⓓ

RESEARCH TRIANGLE PARK   (See map p. 358; index p. 357)

LODGING

RADISSON GOVERNORS INN   **Phone:** 919/549-8631   🔟
Ⓐ Ⓢⓐⓥⓔ   All Year   1P: $134- 139   2P/1B: $134- 139   2P/2B: $134- 139   XP: $10   F18
     Location: Just n of I-40; exit 280 (Davis Dr). PO Box 12168 27709. Fax: 919/547-3510. **Terms:** Pets, $25
◆◆◆   extra charge. **Facility:** 193 rooms. Many rooms with upscale furnishings. 132 hypo-allergenic rooms. Exercise
Motor Inn   equipment avail for room use. 2 stories; interior corridors; 2 lighted tennis courts; basketball court, volleyball
court. **Dining:** The Galeria, see separate listing. **Services:** valet laundry; area transportation, within the park.
Recreation: jogging. **All Rooms:** coffeemakers, free movies, VCP's. **Some Rooms:** microwaves, refrigerators. **Cards:** AE,
CB, DI, DS, MC, VI. **Special Amenities: Free room upgrade and preferred room (each subject to availability with
advanced reservations).**   🐾 🛄 👷 🕂 ✖ Ⓓ

RESTAURANT

THE GALERIA   **Lunch:** $8-$10   **Dinner:** $11-$25   **Phone:** 919/549-8631   ㉟
Ⓐ   **Location:** Just n of I-40; exit 280 (Davis Dr); in Radisson Governors Inn. PO Box 12168 27709. **Hours:** 6:30
am-2 & 5:30-10 pm, Sat 7 am-noon & 5:30-10 pm, Sun-9 pm. Closed: 12/25. **Reservations:** suggested;
◆◆◆   Lunch. **Features:** children's menu; health conscious menu; cocktails & lounge. Fresh seafood & popular
American   luncheon buffet in subdued lighting, foliage & skylight. Smart-casual attire expected. **Cards:** AE, CB, DI, DS,
JCB, MC, VI.   ✖

ROANOKE RAPIDS—15,700

LODGINGS

COMFORT INN-NORTH   **Phone:** 919/537-1011
Ⓐ Ⓢⓐⓥⓔ   All Year [CP]   1P: $48   2P/1B: $54- 60   2P/2B: $54- 60   XP: $5   F18
     Location: Just w on SR 46 from I-95, exit 176. 27870 (PO Box 716). Fax: 919/537-9258. **Terms:** No pets.
◆◆◆   **Facility:** 100 rooms. 2 stories; exterior corridors. **Dining:** Restaurant nearby. **All Rooms:** free movies.
Motel   **Cards:** AE, CB, DI, DS, MC, VI. **Special Amenities: Free breakfast and free local telephone calls.**
(See color ad below)   🛄 👷 CTV 🖨 Ⓓ

FAIRFAX MOTEL   Phone: 919/537-3567
(AAA) [SAVE]   All Year   1P: $24- 28 2P/1B: $28- 32 2P/2B: $32- 35 XP: $4   F12
◆   **Location:** 1 mi w on US 158 from I-95, exit 173, 1 mi n on 10th St. 1135 E 10th St 27870.
Motel   **Fax:** 919/537-3567. **Terms:** Reserv deposit; no pets. **Facility:** 25 rooms. 1 story; exterior corridors.
               All Rooms: free movies. **Cards:** AE, DI, DS, MC, VI.   [CTV] [X] [D]

HAMPTON INN   Rates Subject to Change   Phone: 919/537-7555
◆◆◆   All Year [CP]   1P: $53- 65 2P/1B: $59- 65 2P/2B: $59- 65
Motel   **Location:** Exit 173 off I-95 at jct US 158. 1914 Weldon Rd 27870. **Fax:** 919/537-9852. **Terms:** Sr. discount;
DI, DS, MC, VI. no pets. **Facility:** 124 rooms. 2 stories; exterior corridors. **All Rooms:** free & pay movies. **Cards:** AE, CB,
                                                                              [≃] [CTV] [X] [D]

MOTEL 6 - 1278   Guaranteed Rates   Phone: 919/537-5252
(AAA)   All Year   1P: $35- 45 2P/1B: $39- 49 2P/2B: $39- 49 XP: $3   F17
◆◆   **Location:** US 158 & I-95, exit 173; just w on US 158. 1911 Weldon Rd 27870. **Fax:** 919/537-9469.
Motel   **Terms:** Sr. discount; small pets only. **Facility:** 94 rooms. 2 stories; interior corridors. **All Rooms:** free
               movies. **Cards:** AE, DI, DS, MC, VI.   [🐾] [CTV] [X] [D]

SLEEP INN   Rates Subject to Change   Phone: 919/537-3141
◆◆   All Year [CP]   1P: $48- 60 2P/1B: $48- 60 2P/2B: $48- 60 XP: $5   F18
Motel   **Location:** Just w off I-95, exit 173. 101 Sleep Inn Dr 27870. **Fax:** 919/537-3165. **Terms:** No pets.
               Facility: 117 rooms. 3 stories; interior corridors. **All Rooms:** free movies. **Cards:** AE, CB, DI, DS, MC, VI.
                                                                              [CTV] [X] [D] [S]

ROCKINGHAM—9,400   LODGING

DAYS INN   Phone: 910/895-1144
(AAA) [SAVE]   All Year [CP]   1P: $45   2P/1B: $45- 48 2P/2B: $48- 54 XP: $5   F12
◆◆   **Location:** 0.4 mi w of US 1; on US 74, jct of US 220. 408 W Broad Ave 28379. **Fax:** 910/895-8848.
Motel   **Terms:** Reserv deposit; no pets. **Facility:** 50 rooms. 2 stories; exterior corridors; Small pool.
               Dining: Restaurant nearby. **Services:** valet laundry. **All Rooms:** free movies, refrigerators.
               Some Rooms: microwaves. Fee: whirlpools. **Cards:** AE, CB, DI, DS, MC, VI.   [CTV] [X] [D]

ROCKY MOUNT—49,000   LODGINGS

BEST WESTERN INN I-95 GOLD ROCK   Phone: 919/985-1450
(AAA) [SAVE]   4/1-8/31   1P: $68   2P/1B: $72   2P/2B: $74   XP: $4   F18
◆◆◆   12/1-3/31 & 9/1-11/30 1P: $48   2P/1B: $57   2P/2B: $62   XP: $4   F18
Motel   **Location:** Exit 145 off I-95. 7095 NC 4 27809. **Fax:** 919/985-2236. **Terms:** No pets. **Facility:** 82 rooms. Attrac-
               tive, well maintained grounds. 2 stories; exterior corridors; small pool. **Dining:** Restaurant nearby.
               All Rooms: free movies. **Some Rooms:** radios. **Cards:** AE, CB, DI, DS, JCB, MC, VI. **Special Amenities:**
Free local telephone calls.   [CTV] [X] [D]

BEST WESTERN ROCKY MOUNT INN   Phone: 919/442-8101
(AAA) [SAVE]   All Year [CP]   1P: $42- 52 2P/1B: $52- 62 2P/2B: $52- 62 XP: $5   F12
◆◆   **Location:** 3 mi n on US 301 (bypass). 1921 N Wesleyan Blvd 27804. **Fax:** 919/442-1048. **Terms:** Weekly
Motel   rates; no pets. **Facility:** 72 rooms. 2 stories; exterior corridors. Fee: bowling. **Dining:** Coffee shop; 6-10 am.
               All Rooms: free movies. **Cards:** AE, CB, DI, DS, JCB, MC, VI. **Special Amenities:** Free local telephone
               calls and free room upgrade (subject to availability with advanced reservations). [≃] [🏊] [CTV] [X] [D]

CARLETON HOUSE INN   Phone: 919/977-0410
(AAA) [SAVE]   All Year [BP]   1P: $42- 49 2P/1B: $49- 56 2P/2B: $49- 56
◆◆◆   **Location:** From I-95 exit 138, 4.5 mi e on US 64, 0.5 mi s on N Church St, 0.5 mi s on Franklin St, just e on
Motor Inn   Sunset Ave, just n on N Church St. 215 N Church St 27804 (PO Box 1246, 27802-1246). **Fax:** 919/985-2115.
               Terms: No pets. **Facility:** 42 rooms. Stylishly furnished rooms, some theme units. 2 stories; exterior corridors;
               small pool. **Dining & Entertainment:** Cocktail lounge; restaurant, see separate listing.
All Rooms: coffeemakers, free movies. **Some Rooms:** refrigerators. Fee: whirlpools. **Cards:** AE, MC, VI.
Special Amenities: Free breakfast and free local telephone calls. (See ad p 411)   [🏊] [CTV] [X] [D]

COMFORT INN   Rates Subject to Change   Phone: 919/972-9426
◆◆   Fri & Sat 5/1-9/5 [CP] 1P: $50- 65 2P/1B: $55- 70 2P/2B: $75   XP: $5   F18
Motel   12/1-4/30, Sun-Thurs 5/1-9/5
               & 9/6-11/30 [CP]   1P: $50- 65 2P/1B: $55- 70 2P/2B: $55- 75 XP: $5   F18
Location: Exit 145, off I-95. 27809 (Rt 1, Box 153C, BATTLEBORO). **Fax:** 919/972-9426. **Terms:** Sr. discount; pets.
Facility: 50 rooms. 2 stories; exterior corridors. **All Rooms:** free movies. **Cards:** AE, CB, DI, DS, MC, VI.   [🐾] [CTV] [X] [D]

DAYS INN-GOLDEN EAST
◆◆◆   All Year [CP]
Motel
Guaranteed Rates
1P: $54- 60 2P/1B: $60- 66 2P/2B: $60- 66 XP: $6   F18
Phone: 919/977-7766
Location: 1.3 mi n on 301N from US 64 (bypass) US 301 Wilson-Battleboro exit. 1340 N Wesleyan Blvd 27804. Fax: 919/977-1802. **Terms:** Sr. discount; no pets. **Facility:** 110 rooms. 2 stories; interior/exterior corridors. **All Rooms:** free movies. **Cards:** AE, CB, DI, DS, MC, VI.

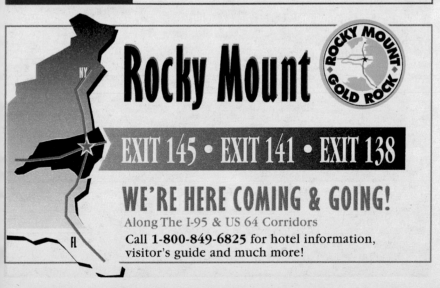

DAYS INN/ROCKY MOUNT-GOLD ROCK
◆◆   All Year [CP]   1P: $40- 60   2P/1B: $46- 66   2P/2B: $46- 66   XP: $6   F12
Motel   **Location:** Exit 145 off I-95 at jct SR 48. 6970 NC 4 27809. Fax: 919/977-1059. **Terms:** Sr. discount; pets, $6
          extra charge. **Facility:** 119 rooms. 2 stories; exterior corridors. **All Rooms:** free movies. **Cards:** AE, CB, DI,
DS, MC, VI. *(See ad below)*   **Phone:** 919/446-0621

⬚ ⬚ ⬚ ⬚ ⬚

FAIRFIELD INN   Rates Subject to Change   **Phone:** 919/972-9400
◆◆◆   All Year [CP]   1P: $40- 55   2P/1B: $40- 55   2P/2B: $40- 55
Motel   **Location:** At jct US 301 (Bypass) & SR 43. 1200 Benvenue Rd 27804. Fax: 919/972-9400. **Terms:** No pets.
          Facility: 104 rooms. 3 stories; interior/exterior corridors. **All Rooms:** free & pay movies. **Cards:** AE, CB, DI,
DS, MC, VI. *(See color ad below)*

⬚ ⬚ ⬚ ⬚

HAMPTON INN   Guaranteed Rates   **Phone:** 919/937-6333
◆◆◆   All Year [CP]   1P: $63   2P/1B: $69   2P/2B: $69
Motel   **Location:** Exit 138, I-95, 8 mi e on US 64 (Winstead Ave exit), just s. 530 N Winstead Ave 27804.
          Fax: 919/937-4333. **Terms:** Sr. discount; no pets. **Facility:** 124 rooms. 4 stories; interior corridors.
All Rooms: free movies. **Cards:** AE, DI, DS, MC, VI.

⬚ ⬚ ⬚ ⬚ ⬚

HOLIDAY INN ROCKY MOUNT　　　　　　　　　　　　　　　**Phone:** 919/937-6888
(AAA) [SAVE]　　All Year　　　　　　　　1P: $75- 95　2P/1B:　$81- 101　2P/2B:　$81- 101　XP:　$7　　F12
　　　　　　Location: Exit 138 off I-95, 1 mi e on US 64, Winstead Ave extension exit, adjacent to Gateway Convention
◆◆◆　　Center. 651 Winstead Ave 27804 (PO Box 7577). Fax: 919/937-4788. **Terms:** Package plans; **Facility:** 171
Motor Inn　rooms. Tastefully furnished rooms & public areas. 4 stories; interior corridors. **Dining & Entertainment:**
　　　　　　Dining room; 6:30 am-10 pm; $9-$18; cocktails/lounge. **All Rooms:** free & pay movies.
Some Rooms: microwaves, refrigerators. Fee: VCP's. **Cards:** AE, CB, DI, DS, JCB, MC, VI. **Special Amenities: Free local
telephone calls and free newspaper.**　　　　　　　　　　　　　[⊘] [🐾] [CTV] [✕] [D] [S]

HOWARD JOHNSON LODGE　　　　　　　　　　　　　　　**Phone:** 919/977-9595
(AAA) [SAVE]　　All Year　　　　　　　　1P: $30- 65　2P/1B:　$30- 85　2P/2B:　$30- 85　XP:　$4　　F12
　　　　　　Location: Exit 145 off I-95. 27809 (Rt 1, Box 161D, BATTLEBORO). Fax: 919/977-9457. **Terms:** Pets.
◆◆　　　**Facility:** 84 rooms. 2 stories; interior corridors. **Dining & Entertainment:** Restaurant; 6 am-10:30 pm; $5-$9;
Motor Inn　cocktail lounge; wine/beer only. **All Rooms:** free movies. **Some Rooms:** refrigerators. **Cards:** AE, CB, DI,
DS, JCB, MC, VI. **Special Amenities: Free local telephone calls and preferred room (subject to
availability with advanced reservations).** *(See color ad below)*　　　　　[🐾] [⊘] [🐾] [CTV] [✕] [D]

QUALITY INN & SUITES　　　　　　　　Guaranteed Rates　　　　　　　**Phone:** 919/977-0101
Motel　　　All Year　　　　　　　　1P: $52- 60　2P/1B:　$52- 60　2P/2B:　$52- 60　XP:　$5　　F18
　　　　　　Too new to rate; Location: Just e of I-95, exit 145. 7688 NC 48 27809. Fax: 919/977-0101. **Terms:** Sr.
discount; pets, $10 extra charge. **Facility:** 117 rooms. Scheduled to open summer 1997; 2 stories; interior corridors.
All Rooms: free movies. **Cards:** AE, DI, DS, MC, VI.　　　　　　　　　　[🐾] [⊘] [✕] [D]

SHONEY'S INN　　　　　　　　　　　　　　　　　　　**Phone:** 919/407-8100
(AAA) [SAVE]　　All Year [CP]　　　　　　1P: $34- 55　2P/1B:　$34- 60　2P/2B:　$36- 65　XP:　$5　　F13
　　　　　　Location: Just e from I-95, exit 145. Rt 1, Box 157 27809 (PO Box 1049, BATTLEBORO).
◆◆◆　　Fax: 919/407-8051. **Terms:** No pets. **Facility:** 59 rooms. 2 stories; exterior corridors. **All Rooms:** free
Motel　　movies. **Cards:** AE, DS, MC, VI.　　　　　　　　　　　　[⊘] [CTV] [✕] [D]

SUNSET INN BED AND BREAKFAST　　　　　　　　　　　　**Phone:** 919/446-9524
(AAA) [SAVE]　　All Year [BP]　　　　　　1P: $65　　2P/1B:　$65- 100　2P/2B:　$75- 125　XP:　$10
　　　　　　Location: 0.5 mi w on US 64E (Business) from town center; 3 mi e on US 64 to Sunset Ave US
◆◆◆　　64(Business) from I-95, exit 138, 2.5 mi e. 1210 Sunset Ave 27804. **Terms:** Pets, $5 extra charge, kennel
Historic Bed　provided. **Facility:** 4 rooms. Georgian architecture with Victorian ambience; art gallery on property featuring
& Breakfast　antique prints, first edition Audubons, Goulds, Botanical & 19th-century fashion prints. 2 stories; interior corri-
　　　　　　dors; smoke free premises. **Services:** complimentary evening beverages. **All Rooms:** free movies, shower
or tub baths, no phones. **Some Rooms:** refrigerators. **Cards:** AE, DS, MC, VI. **Special Amenities: Free breakfast and free
local telephone calls.**　　　　　　　　　　　　　　　　　[🐾] [CTV] [✕] [D]

RESTAURANTS

CARLETON HOUSE RESTAURANT **Lunch:** $4-$8 **Dinner:** $6-$20 Phone: 919/977-6576
AAA SAVE **Location:** From I-95 exit 138, 4.5 mi e on US 64, 0.5 mi s on N Church St, 0.5 mi s on Franklin St, just e on
♦♦ Sunset Ave, then just n N Church St; at Carleton House Inn. 213 N Church St 27802. **Hours:** 6:30 am-9 pm,
American Fri-10 pm, Sat 7:30 am-noon & 5-10 pm, Sun 7:30 am-2 & 5-8 pm. Closed major holidays.
Reservations: accepted. **Features:** casual dress; Sunday brunch; carryout; salad bar; cocktails & lounge;
buffet. Variety of continental cuisine in contemporary ambience; good selection of low calorie items. Lunch &
dinner buffet. Pianist Sat nights. Tues special, grilled pork chops with a reputation. Also certified Angus Beef. **Cards:** AE,
MC, VI. **Special Value:** $1 off the price of a dinner entree. *(See ad p 411)*

CHICO'S MEXICAN RESTAURANT **Lunch:** $4-$6 **Dinner:** $6-$15 Phone: 919/446-8600
♦♦ **Location:** 2 blks e of jct US 301 Business Rt & Sunset Ave, on US 64 Business Rt; in the Power Plant.
Mexican 1701 Sunset Ave 27804. **Hours:** 11 am-10 pm, Fri & Sat-11 pm. Closed: 1/1, 11/26 & 12/25.
Features: children's menu; carryout; cocktails & lounge. Variety of mesquite grilled items, combinations &
specialties offered in colorful dining rooms; also atrium & patio dining in former power plant overlooking Tar River.
Cards: AE, DS, MC, VI.

JUST WHAT THE DOCTOR ORDERED **Lunch:** $4-$10 **Dinner:** $4-$10 Phone: 919/937-4688
♦ **Location:** On US 64 business route; in Westridge Shopping Center. 3639 Sunset Ave 27804. **Hours:** 11
American am-2 & 5-8 pm, Sat 11:30 am-2:30 pm. Closed major holidays, Sat 5/30-9/2 & Sun. **Features:** health
conscious menu items; carryout; beer & wine only; a la carte. Extensive variety of sandwiches, soups &
several teas, served by hospital attired staff in ice cream parlor type atmosphere. Heart healthy items avail. 8 ft projection
TV, freshly squeezed orangeade & lemonade. **Cards:** AE, MC, VI.

ROWLAND—1,100
LODGINGS

DAYS INN Phone: 910/422-3366
AAA SAVE 12/1-4/30 & 6/16-9/9 [CP] 1P: $28- 61 2P/2B: $32- 65 XP: $4 F12
5/1-6/15 & 9/10-11/30 [CP] 1P: $28- 36 2P/2B: $32- 45 XP: $4 F12
♦♦ **Location:** I-95, exit 1A. (Rt 2, Box 187, 28383). Fax: 910/422-3366. **Terms:** Reserv deposit; no pets.
Motor Inn **Facility:** 122 rooms. 2 stories; exterior corridors; playground. **Dining:** Restaurant; 5 am-11 pm, Fri & Sat 24
hours; $5-$9. **All Rooms:** free movies. **Cards:** AE, CB, DI, DS, MC, VI. **Special Amenities:** Early
check-in/late check-out and free breakfast. *(See color ad below)*

HOLIDAY INN EXPRESS Phone: 910/422-3377
AAA SAVE All Year [CP] 1P: $45- 60 2P/1B: $49- 65 2P/2B: $49- 65 XP: $5 F12
♦♦♦ **Location:** I-95, exit 1A. (Rt 2 Box 187, 28383). Fax: 803/422-3377. **Terms:** Reserv deposit; no pets.
Motel **Facility:** 50 rooms. Very attractive & comfortable public areas & rooms. 2 stories; exterior corridors.
Dining: Restaurant nearby. **All Rooms:** free movies, combo or shower baths. **Some Rooms:** microwaves,
refrigerators, whirlpools. **Cards:** AE, CB, DI, DS, MC, VI. **Special Amenities:** Free breakfast and free local
telephone calls. *(See color ad below)* Roll in showers.

ROXBORO—7,300

LODGING

INNKEEPER
◆ ◆
Motel
Rates Subject to Change
All Year [CP]   1P: $53- 80   2P/1B: $59- 80   2P/2B: $58- 80   XP: $5   F18
Location: On US 501, 0.3 mi n of jct US 158E. 906 Durham Rd 27573. Fax: 910/599-3800. **Terms:** Sr. discount; no pets. **Facility:** 77 rooms. 2 stories; interior/exterior corridors. **All Rooms:** free movies.
Cards: AE, CB, DI, DS, MC, VI.
Phone: 910/599-3800

SALISBURY—23,100

LODGINGS

DAYS INN
(AAA) [SAVE]
◆
Motor Inn
All Year [CP]   1P: $35- 55   2P/1B: $38- 60   2P/2B: $46   XP: $6   F12
Location: On I-85 at Jake Alexander Blvd, exit 75. 1810 Lutheran Synod Dr 28144. Fax: 704/633-4211.
Terms: Weekly/monthly rates; pets, $6 extra charge. **Facility:** 147 rooms. Most rooms ground level. 2 stories; exterior corridors. **Dining & Entertainment:** Cocktail lounge; restaurant nearby. **All Rooms:** free & pay movies. **Some Rooms:** 3 efficiencies. Fee: microwaves, refrigerators. **Cards:** AE, CB, DI, DS, JCB, MC, VI.
Special Amenities: Free breakfast and free local telephone calls.
Phone: 704/633-4211

HAMPTON INN
◆ ◆ ◆
Motel

MC, VI.
Rates Subject to Change
All Year [CP]   1P: $58   2P/1B: $65   2P/2B: $65   XP: $6
Location: Exit 75 off I-85, Jake Alexander Blvd. 1001 Klumac Rd 28144. Fax: 704/639-9995. **Terms:** Small pets only. **Facility:** 121 rooms. 4 stories; interior corridors. **All Rooms:** free movies. **Cards:** AE, CB, DI, DS,
Phone: 704/637-8000

HOLIDAY INN
(AAA) [SAVE]

◆ ◆ ◆
Motor Inn
All Year   1P: $61- 65   2P/1B: $67- 71   2P/2B: $67   XP: $6   F18
Location: Exit 75 (Jake Alexander Blvd) off, 0.5 mi n. 530 Jake Alexander Blvd 28147. Fax: 704/637-9152.
Terms: Pets, $10 extra charge. **Facility:** 181 rooms. Near shopping plaza. 2-3 stories; interior/exterior corridors; whirlpool. **Dining:** Dining room; 7 am-2 & 5:30-9 pm; Fri & Sat-10 pm, Sun 7 am-2 pm, Sun brunch $8.50.; $9-$16; cocktails. **All Rooms:** coffeemakers, free movies. **Some Rooms:** Fee: microwaves, refrigerators. **Cards:** AE, CB, DI, DS, JCB, MC, VI. **Special Amenities: Free local telephone calls and free room upgrade (subject to availability with advanced reservations).**
Phone: 704/637-3100

ROWAN OAK HOUSE
◆ ◆ ◆
Historic Bed
& Breakfast
Rates Subject to Change
All Year [BP]   1P: $85- 125   2P/1B: $85- 125   XP: $20
Location: Exit 76B off I-85, 1 mi on E Innes St to Fulton, 2 blks s. 208 S Fulton 28144. **Terms:** Age restrictions may apply; check-in 4 pm; reserv deposit, 10 day notice; no pets. **Facility:** 4 rooms. TV in common room; 1 unit with whirlpool bath & gas fireplace. Two-person marbled shower in the Garden Room. Handling fee imposed; 2 stories; interior corridors; designated smoking area. **Cards:** AE, DS, MC, VI.
Phone: 704/633-2086

RESTAURANT

LAS PALMAS
◆
Mexican
Dinner: $9-$14
Location: I-85 exit 76B, 0.8 mi w on Innes St; then 2 blks w on Lee St to Fisher St. 122 E Fisher St 28144.
Hours: 5 pm-9:30 pm, Fri & Sat-10:30 pm. Closed major holidays & Mon. **Features:** children's menu; carryout; cocktails & lounge. Good variety of specials, combinations, burritos & enchiladas served in an open saloon setting. **Cards:** AE, CB, DI, MC, VI.
Phone: 704/636-9475

SALUDA—500

LODGING

THE OAKS BED & BREAKFAST
◆ ◆
Historic Bed
& Breakfast
Rates Subject to Change
All Year [BP]   1P: $85- 125   2P/1B: $85- 125   2P/2B: $85- 125   XP: $15   F5
Location: 0.5 mi s on Greenville St from Main St. 10 Greenville St 28773 (Rt 1 Box 10). Fax: 704/749-9613.
Terms: Reserv deposit, 7 day notice; no pets. **Facility:** 5 rooms. 2 stories; interior corridors; designated smoking area. **All Rooms:** no A/C. **Cards:** DS, MC, VI.
Phone: 704/749-9613

SANFORD—14,500

LODGINGS

COMFORT INN
(AAA) [SAVE]
◆ ◆ ◆
Motel

Cards: AE, CB, DI, DS, MC.
All Year [CP]   1P: $50   2P/1B: $52   2P/2B: $52   XP: $5   F18
Location: 0.5 mi n of jct US 421 & US 1, 15 & 501 bypass. 1403 N Horner Blvd (Hwy 421) 27330.
Fax: 919/774-7018. **Terms:** Weekly rates; package plans; no pets. **Facility:** 122 rooms. Tastefully decorated rooms. 2 stories; exterior corridors; sauna. **Dining & Entertainment:** Cocktail lounge; restaurant nearby. **Services:** Fee: coin laundry. **All Rooms:** free movies. **Some Rooms:** Fee: microwaves, refrigerators.
Phone: 919/774-6411

DAYS INN
◆ ◆ ◆
Motel
Rates Subject to Change
All Year [CP]   1P: $55- 60   2P/1B: $60   2P/2B: $60   XP: $5   F12
Location: Just n on US 421 from jct US 1 & 501. 1217 N Horner Blvd 27330. Fax: 919/776-8813.
Terms: Sr. discount; no pets. **Facility:** 44 rooms. 2 whirlpool rms, extra charge; 2 stories; exterior corridors.
All Rooms: free movies. **Cards:** AE, DS, MC, VI.   Roll in showers.
Phone: 919/776-3150

PALOMINO MOTEL
(AAA) [SAVE]
◆ ◆
Motel
All Year   1P: $34   2P/1B: $40   2P/2B: $40   XP: $3-4
Location: 2.5 mi s on US 1, 15 & 501 bypass. 27330 (PO Box 777, 27331-0777). Fax: 919/776-9670.
Terms: Weekly/monthly rates; package plans; pets. **Facility:** 92 rooms. Nicely manicured grounds. 1 story; exterior corridors; putting green; sauna, whirlpool; playground. Fee: golf privileges, indoor golf simulator.
Dining: Restaurant nearby. **Recreation:** fishing. **All Rooms:** free movies. **Some Rooms:** Fee: microwaves, refrigerators. **Cards:** AE, CB, DI, DS, MC, VI. **Special Amenities: Early check-in/late check-out and preferred room (subject to availability with advanced reservations).**
Phone: 919/776-7531

RESTAURANT

GUS' CAFE
◆ ◆
American
Lunch: $5-$7   Dinner: $7-$14
Location: Just n of jct US 421, 1, 15 & 501 bypass. 1204 N Horner Blvd 27330. **Hours:** 11 am-3 & 5-10 pm, Sat from 5 pm. Closed: Sun & 12/25. **Features:** children's menu; health conscious menu; carryout; cocktails. Homemade soup, bread & dessert. Fresh fish & some Italian & French entrees. **Cards:** AE, DI, MC, VI.
Phone: 919/776-4172

SEALEVEL—500

LODGING

SEA LEVEL INN

Phone: 919/225-3651

(AAA) SAVE

4/1-11/30	1P: $45	2P/1B: $55	2P/2B: $50	XP: $5
12/1-3/31	1P: $40	2P/1B: $45	2P/2B: $45	XP: $5

◆
Motor Inn

Location: 1 mi on US 70E from jct SR 12. (PO Box 97, 28577). **Terms:** AP, BP avail; no pets. **Facility:** 16 rooms. On Nelson Bay. Very well kept rooms. 1 story; exterior corridors; boat dock. **Dining:** Restaurant; 7-10 am, 11-2 & 5-9 pm; $5-$11; wine/beer only. **Services:** Fee: coin laundry. **Recreation:** fishing pier.
All Rooms: free movies, no phones. **Cards:** MC, VI.

[CTV] [D]

SELMA—4,600

LODGINGS

COMFORT INN SELMA-SMITHFIELD

Phone: 919/965-5200

(AAA) SAVE

All Year [CP]   1P: $49- 85 2P/1B: $49- 85 2P/2B: $53- 85 XP: $5   F16

◆◆◆
Motel

Location: I-95 exit 97; just s of US 70W via Industrial Park Dr. 1705 Industrial Park Dr 27576. Fax: 919/965-5200. **Terms:** Reserv deposit; no pets. **Facility:** 80 rooms. Handling fee imposed; 2 stories; exterior corridors; designated smoking area; whirlpool. **Dining:** Restaurant nearby. **All Rooms:** free movies. **Some Rooms:** whirlpools. Fee: microwaves, refrigerators, VCP's. **Cards:** AE, DI, DS, MC, VI.

(See color ad below)

[icons] [CTV] [X] [D]

HOLIDAY INN EXPRESS

Phone: 919/965-4000

(AAA) SAVE

All Year [CP]   1P: $61- 65 2P/1B: $61- 65 2P/2B: $61- 65 XP: $6   F19

◆◆◆
Motel

Location: Just e from I-95, exit 97. 115 US 70A 27576. Fax: 919/965-9999. **Facility:** 60 rooms. 2 stories; interior corridors. **Dining:** Restaurant nearby. **All Rooms:** free movies. **Some Rooms:** coffeemakers, microwaves, refrigerators. Fee: whirlpools. **Cards:** AE, CB, DI, DS, JCB, MC, VI. **Special Amenities:** Free breakfast and free local telephone calls.

[icons] [CTV] [X] [D] [S]

SHELBY—14,700

LODGINGS

DAYS INN

Phone: 704/482-6721

(AAA) SAVE

All Year   1P: $48   2P/1B: $52   2P/2B: $52   XP: $5   F17

◆◆
Motor Inn

Location: Jct 74 bypass & 74 business route at west end of town. Hwy 74 at Neisler St 28150. Fax: 704/480-1423. **Terms:** Reserv deposit; no pets. **Facility:** 97 rooms. In a commercial area. Some rooms with at-door parking. 1 kitchenette suite $125; 2 stories; exterior corridors. **Dining & Entertainment:** Restaurant; 6 am-2 & 5-10 pm, Sat 7 am-11 & 5-10 pm, Sun 7 am-10 & 11:30-2 pm; Sun country style buffet $6.95; $5-$12; cocktail lounge. **Services:** Fee: coin laundry. **All Rooms:** free movies. **Some Rooms:** refrigerators. **Cards:** AE, CB, DI, DS, JCB, MC, VI.

[icons] [CTV] [X] [D]

THE INN AT WEBBLEY
◆◆◆◆ All Year [BP]
Rates Subject to Change
Phone: 704/481-1403
1P: $165- 195   2P/1B: $165- 195   2P/2B: $165- 195
Historic Bed & Breakfast **Location:** 0.8 mi n on SR 18 (Dekalb St), from US 74 (Bypass). 403 S Washington St 28150 (PO Box 1000, 28151). Fax: 704/487-0619. **Terms:** Age restrictions may apply; 2 night min stay, weekends; no pets, pets on premises. **Facility:** 5 rooms. Limit of 2 persons per room; 2 stories; interior corridors; smoke free premises.
All Rooms: free movies. **Cards:** DS, MC, VI.
CTV ⊠ D

SUPER 8 MOTEL
Phone: 704/484-2101
AAA SAVE All Year [CP]
1P: $36- 43   2P/1B: $40   2P/2B: $40   XP: $4   F18
◆◆ **Location:** On US 74 (Bypass), 1 mi w of Cleveland Mall. 1716 E Dixon Blvd 28152. Fax: 704/484-2101.
Motel **Terms:** No pets. **Facility:** 59 rooms. 2 stories; exterior corridors. **Dining:** Restaurant nearby.
All Rooms: coffeemakers, free movies. **Cards:** AE, DI, DS, MC, VI. **Special Amenities:** Free breakfast and free local telephone calls.
CTV ⊠ D

RESTAURANT

SATTERFIELDS
Lunch: $4-$8
Dinner: $8-$19
Phone: 704/734-0400
AAA **Location:** On US 74, 1.5 mi e of Cleveland Mall. 4702 E Dixon 28150. **Hours:** 11 am-2 & 5-9:30 pm, Fri & Sat 5 pm-10 pm. Closed: Sun, 7/4 & 12/25. **Features:** children's menu; carryout; cocktails; entertainment.
Steak and Seafood Rural setting featuring broiled, grilled & blackened entrees served in casual, candlelit ambience. Also pasta & lite fare menu. **Cards:** AE, CB, DI, DS, MC, VI.
⊠

SMITHFIELD—7,500

LODGING

LOG CABIN MOTEL
Phone: 919/934-1534
AAA SAVE All Year
1P: $47- 49   2P/1B: $56   2P/2B: $54   XP: $5
◆◆ **Location:** 0.5 mi on US 70E; I-95 exit 95. 2491 US 70E business route 27577. Fax: 919/934-7399.
Motor Inn **Terms:** Pets, $5 extra charge. **Facility:** 61 rooms. 2 stories; exterior corridors. **Dining:** Restaurant, see separate listing. **All Rooms:** free movies. **Cards:** AE, DS, MC, VI.
🐾 🏊 CTV ⊠ D

RESTAURANT

BECKY'S LOG CABIN RESTAURANT
Lunch: $6-$8
Dinner: $8-$15
Phone: 919/934-3323
AAA **Location:** At Log Cabin Motel. 2491 US 70 (Business E) 27577. **Hours:** 11 am-2 & 5-10 pm, Fri & Sat 5 pm-10:30 pm. Closed: 11/26, 12/24 & 12/25. **Features:** children's menu; carryout; salad bar; cocktail lounge;
◆◆ beer & wine only. Featuring western aged beef, fresh flounder & oyster served in comfortable log cabin
Steakhouse setting. Also grilled fish. **Cards:** AE, MC, VI.
⊠

SOUTHERN PINES—9,100

LODGINGS

HAMPTON INN
Rates Subject to Change
Phone: 910/692-9266
◆◆◆ 3/1-11/30 [CP]
1P: $69   2P/1B: $77   2P/2B: $77
Motel 12/1-2/28 [CP]
1P: $49   2P/1B: $54   2P/2B: $54
Location: 1 mi s on US 1. 1675 Hwy 1S 28387. Fax: 910/692-9298. **Terms:** Sr. discount; no pets.
Facility: 126 rooms. 2 stories; exterior corridors. **All Rooms:** free movies. **Cards:** AE, CB, DI, DS, MC, VI.
🏊 CTV ⊠ 🎾 D

HOLIDAY INN SOUTHERN PINES
Guaranteed Rates
Phone: 910/692-8585
◆◆◆ All Year
1P: $75   2P/1B: $75   2P/2B: $75
Motor Inn **Location:** Just n on US 1, exit w on Morganton Rd. US Hwy 1 28387 (PO Box 1467, 28388).
Fax: 910/692-5213. **Terms:** Sr. discount; no pets. **Facility:** 160 rooms. 2 stories; interior/exterior corridors.
Dining: Restaurant; 6:30-10:30 am, 11-3 & 5:30-9:30 pm; $9-$14. **All Rooms:** free movies. **Cards:** AE, CB, DI, DS, JCB, MC, VI.
🏊 🔆 CTV ⊠ D

RESTAURANTS

THE LOB STEER INN
Dinner: $14-$19
Phone: 910/692-3503
◆◆ **Location:** Morganton Rd exit off US 1. US 1N 28387. **Hours:** 5 pm-10:30 pm. Closed: 11/26 & 12/25.
Steakhouse **Features:** casual dress; children's menu; early bird specials; carryout; salad bar; cocktails & lounge.
Featuring certified Angus Beef & outstanding salad bar. Very popular. **Cards:** AE, DI, DS, MC, VI.
⊠

SLEDDON'S RESTAURANT
Dinner: $18-$22
Phone: 910/692-4480
◆◆ **Location:** Off W Broad St, corner Massachusetts Ave & S Bennett St. 275 S Bennett St 28387. **Hours:** 6
American pm-9 pm. Closed: Sun, Mon & 8/1-8/30. **Reservations:** suggested. **Features:** casual dress; cocktails & lounge. A converted private home that serves a limited menu with a variety of meat, seafood & poultry.
Cards: MC, VI.

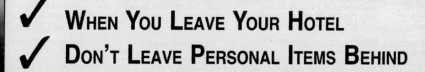

THE SQUIRE'S PUB   **Lunch:** $4-$8   **Dinner:** $7-$16   **Phone:** 910/695-1161
◆◆   **Location:** 1.1 mi s on US 1. 1720 US 1S 28387. **Hours:** 11 am-10 pm, Fri & Sat-11 pm. Closed: Sun, 11/26
Ethnic   & 12/24-12/25. **Features:** casual dress; children's menu; carryout; cocktails & lounge; a la carte. Featuring
traditional British fare as well as American. 43 different varieties of imported beers, mostly British.
Cards: DS, MC, VI.   ⊠

SPINDALE—400

LODGING

SUPER 8 SPINDALE   **Phone:** 704/286-3681
(AAA) [SAVE]   All Year   1P: $32- 36   2P/1B: $35- 37 2P/2B: $37   XP: $3   F8
     Location: On US 74A, exit Oak St & downtown. 210 Reservation Dr 28160. Fax: 704/286-8221.
◆◆   **Terms:** Reserv deposit, 3 day notice; no pets. **Facility:** 62 rooms. 2 stories; exterior corridors.
Motel   **Dining:** Restaurant nearby. **All Rooms:** free movies. **Some Rooms:** microwaves, refrigerators. **Cards:** AE,
DI, DS, MC, VI. **Special Amenities:** Free local telephone calls.   [⊇][CTV][⊠][D]

SPRING LAKE—7,500

LODGINGS

HOLIDAY INN EXPRESS   **Phone:** 910/436-1900
(AAA) [SAVE]   All Year [CP]   1P: $52   2P/1B: $58   2P/2B: $52   XP: $10   F10
     Location: 1 mi n on SR 87. 103 Brook Ln 28390. Fax: 910/436-9483. **Terms:** Package plans; no pets.
◆◆◆   **Facility:** 60 rooms. New, very attractive public areas & handsomely appointed rooms. Handling fee imposed;
Motel   2 stories; interior corridors. **Dining:** Restaurant nearby. **Services:** valet laundry. **All Rooms:** microwaves,
free movies, refrigerators. **Some Rooms:** Fee: whirlpools. **Cards:** AE, CB, DI, DS, JCB, MC, VI.
Special Amenities: Free breakfast and free local telephone calls.
                                   Roll in showers. [⊇][⊛][CTV][⅄][⊠][⊘][D][S]

SLEEP INN   **Phone:** 910/436-6700
(AAA) [SAVE]   All Year [CP]   1P: $51- 53   2P/1B: $56- 58 2P/2B: $56- 58 XP: $5   F18
     Location: 1 mi n on SR 87, near Walmart Plaza. 102 Sleepy Dr 28390. Fax: 910/436-6777. **Terms:** No pets.
◆◆   **Facility:** 107 rooms. Handling fee imposed; 2 stories; interior corridors. **Dining:** Restaurant nearby.
Motel   **Services:** Fee: coin laundry. **All Rooms:** free movies, combo or shower baths. **Cards:** AE, CB, DI, DS, JCB,
MC, VI. **Special Amenities:** Free breakfast and free local telephone calls.
                                                   [⊇][⊛][⊛][CTV][⊠][D][S]

SPRUCE PINE—2,000

LODGINGS

PINEBRIDGE INN   **Phone:** 704/765-5543
(AAA) [SAVE]   All Year [CP]   1P: $43- 125 2P/1B: $43- 125 2P/2B: $63- 125 XP: $6   F12
     Fax: 704/765-5544. **Terms:** Reserv deposit; weekly rates; package plans; no pets. **Facility:** 45 rooms. Circa
◆◆◆   1920's tastefully decorated & exceptionally large rooms in renovated school. Banquet facilities avail. 1 three-
Historic Motel   bedroom unit. 1 fully-furnished cottage & 2-bedroom apartment, $125. Handling fee imposed; 3 stories; interior
corridors; playground. **Services:** area transportation. **Recreation:** Fee: ice skating. **All Rooms:** free movies.
Some Rooms: coffeemakers, microwaves, refrigerators. **Cards:** AE, DS, MC, VI. **Special Amenities:** Free breakfast and
free newspaper.   [⊛][⊕][CTV][⊠][D]

PINE VALLEY MOTEL & EFFICIENCIES   Guaranteed Rates   **Phone:** 704/765-6276
(AAA)   All Year   1P: $40- 50   2P/1B: $45- 55 2P/2B: $50- 60 XP: $5
     Location: 1 mi s on SR 226S. 905 Hwy 226 S 28777. Fax: 704/766-9148. **Terms:** Reserv deposit; no pets.
◆◆   **Facility:** 28 rooms. 4 two-bedroom units, $80-$95; 1 story; interior/exterior corridors. **All Rooms:** free
Motel   movies. **Some Rooms:** 4 kitchens. **Cards:** AE, DS, MC, VI.   [CTV][⊠][D]

RICHMOND INN   **Phone:** 704/765-6993
(AAA) [SAVE]   12/1-12/31 & 4/1-11/30 [BP] 1P: $45- 65   2P/1B: $55- 70 2P/2B: $55- 70 XP: $10   F10
     1/1-3/31 [BP]   1P: $45- 60   2P/1B: $45- 60 2P/2B: $45- 60 XP: $10   F10
◆◆◆   **Location:** Downtown exit off US 19E & 226 to Oak Ave, 2 blks n on Walnut Ave following signs. 101 Pine
Bed &   Ave 28777. **Terms:** Check-in 4 pm; reserv deposit; no pets. **Facility:** 7 rooms. Circa 1939, large rambling home
Breakfast   overlooking town, shaded by towering pines. Some large rooms with antiques & reproductions. 2 stories; inte-
rior corridors; designated smoking area. **All Rooms:** combo or shower baths, no A/C, no phones.
Cards: DS, MC, VI. **Special Amenities:** Free breakfast and free local telephone calls.   [CTV][⊠][D]

RESTAURANT

CEDARCREST RESTAURANT   **Lunch:** $3-$5   **Dinner:** $6-$14   **Phone:** 704/765-6124
◆   **Location:** Downtown exit off US 19E & 226 bypass, Oak St to Locust Ave, just w; opposite train station. 311
American   Locust Ave 28777. **Hours:** 6 am-9 pm; 1/1-4/30 to 8 pm, Fri & Sat-9 pm. Closed major holidays, Sun & Mon.
     Features: children's menu; carryout; salad bar. Steak, seafood, chicken, sandwiches & Italian dishes.
Split-level, cedar panelled casual dining. **Cards:** AE, DS, MC, VI.   ⊠

STATESVILLE—17,600

LODGINGS

BEST WESTERN STATESVILLE INN   **Phone:** 704/881-0111
(AAA) [SAVE]   All Year [CP]   1P: $46- 60   2P/1B: $50- 60 2P/2B: $50- 65 XP: $5   F12
     Location: Just e on US 70 from I-77, exit 49A. 1121 Morland Dr 28677. Fax: 704/872-5056. **Terms:** No
◆◆◆   pets. **Facility:** 69 rooms. 2 stories; interior/exterior corridors. **All Rooms:** free movies. **Cards:** AE, DI, DS,
Motel   JCB, MC, VI.   [⊇][CTV][⊠][D]

CEDAR HILL FARM BED & BREAKFAST   Guaranteed Rates   **Phone:** 704/873-4332
◆◆◆   All Year [BP]   1P: $70- 95   2P/1B: $70- 95 2P/2B: $70- 95 XP: $5-10
Historic Bed   **Location:** 1.5 mi n on Elmwood Rd from US 70E, 6 mi e from I-77; exit 49A. 778 Elmwood Rd 28677
& Breakfast   **Terms:** Reserv deposit, 3 day notice; no pets. **Facility:** 3 rooms. 1 cottage with kitchen, $95; 2 stories;
interior/exterior corridors; smoke free premises. **All Rooms:** free movies. **Cards:** AE, MC, VI.
                                                                       [⊇][CTV][⊠][D]

FAIRFIELD INN BY MARRIOTT
Phone: 704/878-2091
All Year [CP]   1P: $49- 70   2P/1B: $49- 70 2P/2B: $49- 70 XP: $5   F18
Location: I-77 exit 50, just e. 1505 E Broad St 28677. **Fax:** 704/873-1368. **Terms:** No pets. **Facility:** 118
rooms. In shopping area. Well-appointed rooms. 2 stories; exterior corridors. **Dining:** Restaurant nearby.
All Rooms: free & pay movies. **Some Rooms:** microwaves, refrigerators. **Cards:** AE, CB, DI, DS, MC, VI.
Special Amenities: Free breakfast and free local telephone calls.

HISTORIC VANCE HOTEL
Phone: 704/872-3232
All Year [CP]   1P: $53- 79   2P/1B: $89   2P/2B: $59
Location: Town center; corner of E Front & S Center sts. 226 S Center St 28677-5807. **Fax:** 704/872-0823.
Terms: Weekly/monthly rates; no pets. **Facility:** 90 rooms. 5 stories; interior corridors; smoke free premises.
Dining & Entertainment: Dining room; 11 am-2 & 4-9 pm; $10-$15; cocktail lounge. **Services:** guest
laundry. **All Rooms:** free movies, combo or shower baths. **Cards:** AE, MC, VI. **Special Amenities: Early
check-in/late check-out and preferred room (subject to availability with advanced reservations).**

HOLIDAY INN
Rates Subject to Change
Phone: 704/878-9691
All Year   1P: $75   2P/1B: $75   2P/2B: $75   XP: $10   F19
Location: On Hwy 70E; from I-77, exit 49A. 1215 Garner Bagnal Blvd 28677. **Fax:** 704/873-6927.
Terms: Sr. discount; no pets. **Facility:** 134 rooms. 2 stories; interior corridors. **Dining:** Dining room; 6:30
am-2 & 5-9 pm; in summer-10 pm; $8-$13. **All Rooms:** free movies. **Cards:** AE, CB, DI, DS, JCB, MC, VI.
(See color ad below)

HOLIDAY INN EXPRESS HOTEL & SUITES
Guaranteed Rates
Phone: 704/872-4101
All Year [CP]   1P: $59- 69   2P/1B: $59- 69 2P/2B: $59- 69 XP: $10   F18
Location: Exit 151, off I-40. 740 Sullivan Rd 28677. **Fax:** 704/878-6014. **Terms:** Sr. discount; no pets.
Facility: 130 rooms. Weekend rates higher, 6/1-11/1; 2 stories; exterior corridors. **All Rooms:** free & pay
movies. **Cards:** AE, CB, DI, DS, JCB, MC, VI. *(See color ad below)*

MASTERS ECONOMY INN
Phone: 704/873-5252
All Year [CP]   1P: $29- 35   2P/1B: $33- 35 2P/2B: $33- 39 XP: $4   F18
Location: Just s on US 21 from I-40, exit 151. 702 Sullivan Rd 28677. **Terms:** No pets.
Facility: 119 rooms. 2 stories; exterior corridors. **Dining:** Restaurant nearby. **All Rooms:** free movies.
Some Rooms: microwaves, refrigerators. **Cards:** AE, CB, DI, DS, JCB, MC, VI. **Special Amenities: Free
breakfast and free local telephone calls.**

RED ROOF INN
Rates Subject to Change
Phone: 704/878-2051
All Year   1P: $39- 47   2P/1B: $47- 54 2P/2B: $54- 63 XP: $8   F18
Location: I-77 at Broad St, exit 50. 1508 E Broad St 28677. **Fax:** 704/872-3885. **Terms:** Small pets only.
Facility: 115 rooms. 3 stories; exterior corridors. **All Rooms:** free movies. **Cards:** AE, CB, DI, DS, MC, VI.

SUPER 8 MOTEL
Phone: 704/878-9888
(AAA) [SAVE]   All Year   1P: $39- 75 2P/1B: $39- 75 2P/2B: $42- 75 XP: $4
   Location: Exit 49A, I-77. 1125 Greenland Dr 28677. Fax: 704/871-2090. **Terms:** Small pets only, $5 extra
◆◆   charge. **Facility:** 41 rooms. 2 stories; interior/exterior corridors. **All Rooms:** free movies. **Cards:** AE, CB, DI,
Motel   DS, MC, VI.   [🐾] [CTV] [✕] [D]

RESTAURANTS

DRAGON GOLDEN   **Lunch:** $6-$7   **Dinner:** $7-$14   Phone: 704/872-1081
◆   **Location:** I-77 at Broad St, exit 50; in Newtowne Plaza, ne corner. 1529 E Broad St 28677. **Hours:** 11
Regional   am-10 pm, Sun from noon. Closed: 11/26. **Features:** children's menu; carryout; cocktails; a la carte. Also,
Chinese   American food served in Oriental ambience. Daily buffet 11 am-2:30 pm, family oriented. **Cards:** AE, MC, VI.

SAGEBUSH STEAK HOUSE & SALOON   **Lunch:** $6-$8   **Dinner:** $7-$18   Phone: 704/873-2466
◆◆   **Location:** I-40 & Hwy 21, exit 151. 117 Turnersburg Rd 28677. **Hours:** 11 am-10 pm, Fri & Sat-11 pm.
American   Closed: 12/25. **Features:** children's menu; carryout; cocktails & lounge. Airy, fun atmosphere. Miniature
   electric train at entrance. Flags suspended from ceiling. License plates, team pennants & classic pictures on
walls. **Cards:** AE, DI, DS, MC, VI.   [✕]

SUNSET BEACH—300   (See map p. 542; index p. 540)

LODGINGS

THE COLONY AT OYSTER BAY
Phone: 910/579-7181   [3]
(AAA) [SAVE]   All Year   2P/2B: $150
   Location: From US 17, 4 mi e to jct SR 904 & 179, 3 mi e on SR 179. 818 Colony Pl 28468.
◆◆◆   Fax: 910/579-1028. **Terms:** Check-in 4 pm; reserv deposit, 30 day notice; weekly rates; package plans; no
Resort   pets. **Facility:** 140 rooms. 2-bedroom villas on golf course; tastefully furnished & decorated. Rates for 4-6 per-
Complex   sons. Handling fee imposed; 3 stories, no elevator; exterior corridors; putting green; whirlpools; 2 lighted tennis
   courts. Fee: 18 holes golf, driving range, golf instruction. **Services:** guest laundry. **All Rooms:** coffeemakers,
kitchens, microwaves, refrigerators. **Some Rooms:** radios, whirlpools. Fee: VCP's. **Cards:** MC, VI. **Special Amenities: Free
local telephone calls and free room upgrade (subject to availability with advanced reservations).**
[🛥] [🛥] [🏊] [CTV] [✕] [D]

SEA TRAIL PLANTATION & GOLF RESORT
Phone: 910/287-1100   [1]
(AAA) [SAVE]   3/5-11/7   1P: $79   2P/1B: $79- 150 2P/2B: $79- 150
   12/1-3/4 & 11/8-11/30 1P: $55- 114 2P/1B: $55- 114 2P/2B: $55- 114
◆◆◆   **Location:** From US 17; 4 mi e to jct SR 904 & SR 179, then 1.5 mi s on SR 179. 211 Clubhouse Rd 28468.
Resort   Fax: 910/287-1104. **Terms:** Check-in 4 pm; reserv deposit; weekly/monthly rates; AP, BP, MAP avail;
Complex   package plans; no pets. **Facility:** 365 rooms. Nicely appointed villas with screened patio or balcony, on golf
   course. 1- to 4-bedroom villas, $130-$300; $80-$225 12/1-3/3. Handling fee imposed; 3 stories, no elevator;
exterior corridors; putting green, driving range; sauna, whirlpools; 2 lighted tennis courts. Fee: 54 holes golf, golf instruction.
Dining & Entertainment: Dining room, restaurant; 6 am-9 pm; $8-$20; cocktails/lounge. **Services:** guest laundry. Rental: bicycles. **Some Rooms:** coffeemakers, 173 efficiencies, 190 kitchens, microwaves, refrigerators, VCP's. **Cards:** AE, DI, DS,
MC, VI. **Special Amenities:** Free local telephone calls. (See color ad p 499)   [🛥] [🛥] [🏊] [♨] [CTV] [✕] [D]

SWANSBORO—1,200

RESTAURANT

YANA'S YE OLDE DRUGSTORE RESTAURANT   **Lunch:** $4-$6   Phone: 919/326-5501
◆   **Location:** Town Center just s on Front St from SR 24. 119 Front St 28584. **Hours:** 5 am-4 pm.
American   **Features:** children's menu; health conscious menu; carryout; street parking. Back to the "50's" with juke box;
   signature breakfast omelets & pancakes. Pictures adorn walls with Marilyn Monroe, James Dean, etc.
Homemade "hot" chili, pie & dessert; soda fountain. Smoke free premises.   [✕]

SYLVA—1,800

LODGINGS

COMFORT INN
Phone: 704/586-3315
(AAA) [SAVE]   6/1-10/31 [CP] 1P: $59- 85 2P/1B: $69- 99 2P/2B: $69- 99 XP: $6   F18
   12/1-5/31 [CP] 1P: $49- 79 2P/1B: $59- 99 2P/2B: $59- 99 XP: $6   F18
◆◆◆   11/1-11/30 [CP] 1P: $49- 55 2P/1B: $49- 55 2P/2B: $49- 55 XP: $6   F18
Motel   **Location:** 1 mi ne on US Hwys 23 & 74. (PO Box 2100, 28779). Fax: 704/586-5304. **Terms:** Package plans;
   no pets. **Facility:** 70 rooms. In tranquil mountain area. Many rooms with mountain view. 4 stories; interior corridors; small pool; recreation room. **All Rooms:** free movies, combo or shower baths. **Some Rooms:** VCP's. **Cards:** AE,
CB, DI, DS, JCB, MC, VI. **Special Amenities: Free local telephone calls and free room upgrade (subject to availability
with advanced reservations).**   [♨] [CTV] [✕] [🐾] [D]

MOUNTAIN BROOK COTTAGES
Phone: 704/586-4329
(AAA)   All Year   2P/1B: $80- 160 2P/2B: $90- 100 XP: $8   F18
   Location: 9 mi s of Dillsboro on US Hwys 23 & 441; Franklin-Atlanta, exit 81 off Hwys 19 & 23. 208
◆◆   Mountain Brook Rd 28779. **Terms:** Reserv deposit, 30 day notice; no pets. **Facility:** 13 rooms. Handling fee
Historic   imposed; 1 story; exterior corridors. **All Rooms:** kitchens. **Some Rooms:** A/C.   [D]
Cottage

TABOR CITY—2,300

LODGING

FOUR ROOSTER INN   Guaranteed Rates   Phone: 910/653-387?
◆◆◆   All Year [BP]   1P: $45- 65 2P/1B: $55- 75   XP: $15
Bed &   **Location:** From US 701 bypass 0.4 mi w on SR 904. 403 Pireway Rd/ Rt 904 28463. Fax: 910/653-3878.
Breakfast   **Terms:** Age restrictions may apply; no pets. **Facility:** 4 rooms. 2 stories; interior corridors; designated smokin
   area. **Cards:** AE, DI, DS, MC, VI.   [✕] [D]

TRYON—1,700

LODGING

PINE CREST INN   Rates Subject to Change   Phone: 704/859-913?
(AAA)   All Year [CP]   2P/1B: $135- 180 2P/2B: $135- 180 XP: $35   F1
   Location: I-26 exit Hwy 108, 4 mi s following signs. 200 Pine Crest Ln 28782. Fax: 704/859-9135.
◆◆◆◆   **Terms:** Reserv deposit; no pets. **Facility:** 37 rooms. 2 stories; interior/exterior corridors. **Dining:** Restaurant,
Country Inn   see separate listing. **All Rooms:** free movies. **Cards:** AE, DS, MC, VI.   [CTV] [✕] [D]

RESTAURANT

PINE CREST INN DINING ROOM   **Dinner:** $17-$25   **Phone:** 704/859-9135
◆◆◆   **Location:** I-26 exit Hwy 108, 4 mi s following signs; in Pine Crest Inn. 200 Pine Crest Ln 28782. **Hours:** 8
Regional   am-9:30 & 6-8:30 pm, Fri & Sat to 9:15 pm. Closed: Sun for dinner. **Reservations:** suggested.
American   **Features:** cocktails. Fresh regional southern cuisine featuring pan seared corn meal, crusted catfish & pan
roasted rack of lamb. Smoke free premises. **Cards:** AE, DS, MC, VI.   ☒

UNION GROVE

LODGING

MADELYN'S-IN THE GROVE-A BED & BREAKFAST   Rates Subject to Change   **Phone:** 704/539-4151
  All Year [BP]   2P/1B: $75- 100   2P/2B: $95- 135
Bed &   **Location:** 1.8 mi n on SR 901 from I-77, exit 65. 1836 W Memorial Hwy 28689-0298 (PO Box 298).
Breakfast   Fax: 704/539-4080. **Terms:** Sr. discount; reserv deposit, 7 day notice; no pets. **Facility:** 5 rooms. 2 stories;
  interior/exterior corridors; smoke free premises. **All Rooms:** free movies. **Some Rooms:** kitchen. **Cards:** AE,
MC, VI.   ☒ D

VILAS—160

LODGING

THE COTTAGES OF GLOWING HEARTH   Rates Subject to Change   **Phone:** 704/963-8800
◆◆◆   **Location:** From Boone, 4 mi sw on SR 105 from jct 321 & 1.3 mi w on Baird's Creek Rd. (171 Glowing
Cottage   Hearth Ln, 28692). Fax: 704/963-6822. **Terms:** Reserv deposit, 14 day notice; no pets. **Facility:** 5 rooms.
Rates for up to 4 persons; 1 story; exterior corridors; smoke free premises. **All Rooms:** kitchens, free movies. **Cards:** AE,
MC, VI.   CTV ☒ D

All Year   1P: $225   2P/2B: $225

WADE—200

LODGING

DAYS INN FAYETTEVILLE-NORTH   Rates Subject to Change   **Phone:** 910/323-1255
  All Year [BP]   1P: $42- 54   2P/1B: $48- 60   2P/2B: $48- 60   XP: $6   F12
Motor Inn   **Location:** I-95 & US 13; I-95 exit 58. 28395 (Rt 1, Box 216BB). Fax: 910/323-3925. **Terms:** Sr. discount;
  pets, $6 extra charge. **Facility:** 120 rooms. 2 stories; exterior corridors. **Dining:** Restaurant; 6 am-10 & 4-9
pm; $6-$9. **All Rooms:** free movies. **Cards:** AE, CB, DI, DS, MC, VI. *(See ad p 412)*   🐾 🛎 CTV ☒ 🌀 D

WADESBORO—3,600

LODGING

ANSON INN   **Phone:** 704/694-4616
[AAA] [SAVE]   All Year   1P: $39- 45   2P/1B: $35   2P/2B: $40   XP: $5   F16
◆◆   **Location:** On US 74; at US 52S. 1201 E Caswell 28170. Fax: 704/694-4616. **Terms:** No pets. **Facility:** 33
Motel   rooms. 2 stories; exterior corridors. **Dining:** Restaurant nearby. **All Rooms:** free movies.
  Some Rooms: coffeemakers, refrigerators. Fee: whirlpools. **Cards:** AE, CB, DI, DS, JCB, MC, VI.
  **Special Amenities: Free local telephone calls and preferred room (subject to availability with
advanced reservations).**   🐾 CTV ☒ D

WAKE FOREST—5,800

LODGING

HAMPTON INN   Rates Subject to Change   **Phone:** 919/354-0222
◆◆◆   All Year [CP]   1P: $63- 94   2P/1B: $69- 100   2P/2B: $69- 100   XP: $6   F18
Motel   **Location:** Exit Wake Union Church Rd off US 1 (behind Food Lion in Market Place Shopping Center). 12318
  Wake Union Church Rd 27587. Fax: 919/554-1499. **Terms:** Sr. discount; no pets. **Facility:** 114 rooms. 3 sto-
ries; interior corridors. **All Rooms:** free movies. **Cards:** AE, CB, DI, DS, MC, VI.
     Roll in showers. 🛎 CTV 🦽 ☒ 🌀 D

WANCHESE—*see Outer Banks p. 402.*

WARSAW—2,900

LODGING

THE VINTAGE INN   **Phone:** 910/296-1831
[AAA] [SAVE]   All Year [CP]   1P: $58   2P/2B: $65   XP: $15   F12
  Location: 7.8 mi e on SR 24, From I-40, exit 364. 28398 (748 NC 24 & 50). Fax: 910/296-1431.
  Terms: Weekly/monthly rates; no pets. **Facility:** 12 rooms. 2-bedroom cottage; 1 story; exterior corridors.
Motor Inn   Fee: golf privileges. **Dining:** Restaurant; 11:30 am-2 & 5:30-10 pm, Fri-11 pm, Sat 5:30 pm-11 pm; $8-$23;
  cocktails. **Some Rooms:** coffeemakers, refrigerators. **Cards:** AE, CB, DI, MC, VI. **Special Amenities: Free
breakfast and free local telephone calls.**   🐾 ☒ D

WASHINGTON—9,100

LODGING

ECONO LODGE   **Phone:** 919/946-7781
[AAA] [SAVE]   All Year   1P: $35- 38   2P/1B: $38- 46   2P/2B: $38- 46   XP: $5   D14
◆◆   **Location:** 1.3 mi n on US 17 at jct US 264. 1220 W 15th 27889. Fax: 919/946-7050. **Terms:** Weekly rates;
Motel   small pets only. **Facility:** 45 rooms. 2 stories; exterior corridors. **Dining:** Restaurant nearby. **Services:**
  Fee: coin laundry. **All Rooms:** free movies. **Some Rooms:** kitchen, no utensils, microwaves, refrigerators.
  Cards: AE, DI, DS, MC, VI. **Special Amenities: Early check-in/late check-out and free breakfast.**
     🐾 CTV ☒ 🌀 D

WAYNESVILLE—6,800

LODGINGS

BEST WESTERN SMOKY MOUNTAIN INN   Phone: 704/456-4402
(AAA) [SAVE]   7/1-7/31 & 10/10-10/31 [CP] 1P: $62- 99   2P/2B: $72- 99 XP: $10   F12
             5/22-6/30 & 8/1-10/9 [CP]   1P: $52- 75   2P/2B: $62- 85 XP: $10   F12
◆◆◆   12/1-5/21 & 11/1-11/30 [CP] 1P: $37- 45   2P/2B: $42- 55 XP: $10   F12
Motel   **Location:** W Waynesville exit off US 23 & 74, exit 98. 330 Hyatt Rd 28786. Fax: 704/456-4885.
Terms: Reserv deposit; no pets. **Facility:** 58 rooms. 1 suite, $120 in season; 2 stories; exterior corridors.
All Rooms: free movies. **Some Rooms:** efficiency. **Cards:** AE, CB, DI, DS, MC, VI.   [CTV] [X] [D]

ECONO LODGE   Rates Subject to Change   Phone: 704/452-0353
◆◆◆   6/1-10/31 [CP]   1P: $55   2P/1B: $75   2P/2B: $75   XP: $7   F18
Motel 5/1-5/31 [CP]   1P: $47   2P/1B: $50   2P/2B: $50   XP: $7   F18
       12/1-4/30 & 11/1-11/30 [CP] 1P: $37   2P/1B: $42   2P/2B: $42   XP: $7   F18
Location: Waynesville exit off US 74 bypass, exit 102. 909 Russ Ave 28786. Fax: 704/452-3329. **Terms:** Sr. discount; no
pets. **Facility:** 40 rooms. 2 stories; exterior corridors. **All Rooms:** free movies. **Cards:** AE, CB, DI, DS, MC, VI.
                                                                                          [CTV] [X] [D]

OAK PARK INN   Phone: 704/456-5328
(AAA) [SAVE]   5/1-10/31   2P/2B: $44- 61 XP: $4   F16
             12/1-4/30 & 11/1-11/30   2P/2B: $35- 50 XP: $4   F16
◆◆   **Location:** 0.3 mi s on US 23 business route. 314 S Main St 28786. Fax: 704/456-8126. **Terms:** Reserv
Motel deposit, 3 day notice; weekly/monthly rates, in winter; no pets. **Facility:** 39 rooms. Efficiency units $60 for 2
persons; weekly rates 11/1-4/30. 3-bedroom units avail; 1 story; exterior corridors. **Dining:** Restaurant
nearby. **Some Rooms:** 5 kitchens, radios. **Cards:** AE, DS, MC, VI. **Special Amenities: Early check-in/late check-out and
free local telephone calls.**   [CTV] [X] [D]

PARKWAY INN   Phone: 704/926-1841
(AAA) [SAVE]   5/20-10/31   2P/2B: $48- 95 XP: $5   F12
             12/1-1/2/28, 3/1-5/19 &
◆   11/1-11/30   2P/2B: $36- 48 XP: $5   F12
Motel **Location:** On US 19, 1.6 mi e of jct 276. 2093 Dellwood Rd 28786. **Terms:** Reserv deposit, 7 day notice;
weekly rates; no pets. **Facility:** 30 rooms. Very well kept property with some modern decor enhancements. 2
whirlpool rms, extra charge; 1 story; exterior corridors. **All Rooms:** combo or shower baths. **Some Rooms:** microwaves,
refrigerators. **Cards:** AE, DS, MC, VI. **Special Amenities: Early check-in/late check-out and preferred room (subject to
availability with advanced reservations).**   [CTV] [X] [D]

WAYNESVILLE COUNTRY CLUB INN   Rates Subject to Change   Phone: 704/456-3551
◆◆◆   5/1-10/31 [MAP]   1P: $109- 168   2P/2B: $144- 256 XP: $50   D18
Resort Lodge 12/1-4/30 & 11/1-11/30 [BP] 1P: $53- 103   2P/2B: $80- 176 XP: $21   D18
Location: 1.5 mi s on US 23 (business), 0.3 mi e. 176 Country Club Dr 28786 (PO Box 390).
Fax: 704/456-3555. **Terms:** Reserv deposit, 15 day notice; 3 night min stay, in villas; no pets. **Facility:** 94 rooms. 3 stories;
interior/exterior corridors. **Dining:** Dining room, restaurant, coffee shop; 7 am-9 pm; $11-$20. **All Rooms:** free & pay
movies. **Cards:** MC, VI.   [≜] [CTV] [D]

RESTAURANT

PISGAH INN RESTAURANT   **Lunch:** $6-$9   **Dinner:** $8-$15   Phone: 704/235-8228
◆   **Location:** On Blue Ridge Pkwy at mile marker 408.6; 28 miles s of Asheville. **Hours:** Open
American   4/5-11/20; 7:30 am-9 pm. **Features:** No A/C; children's menu; carryout; beer & wine only. Atop Mt Pisgah
           Most tables with mountain view. Smoke free premises. **Cards:** MC, VI.   [X]

WEAVERVILLE—2,100   (See map p. 315; index p. 314)

LODGING

WEAVERVILLE FEATHERBED & BREAKFAST   Rates Subject to Change   Phone: 704/645-7594   [71]
◆◆◆   12/1-12/31 & 4/1-11/30 [BP] 1P: $115- 150 2P/1B: $115- 150 2P/2B: $115- 150 XP: $20   F18
Historic Bed 1/1-3/31 [BP]   1P: $105- 150 2P/1B: $105- 150 2P/2B: $105- 150 XP: $20   F18
& Breakfast   **Location:** Weaverville exit off US 19, 23, 25 & 70; 0.8 mi e on Weaver/Williams St & just n. 3 Le Perrion Dr
28787. Fax: 704/658-3905. **Terms:** Reserv deposit, 7 day notice; no pets. **Facility:** 5 rooms. Suite, $125-$195
Handling fee imposed; 3 stories, no elevator; interior corridors; smoke free premises. **Cards:** AE, DS, MC, VI. [X] [D]

RESTAURANTS

THE FOUR CENT COTTON CAFE   **Lunch:** $5-$9   **Dinner:** $8-$16   Phone: 704/658-2660   [35]
(AAA)   **Location:** Center. 18 N Main St 28787. **Hours:** 11:30 am-9 pm, Sun-3 pm; later hours in summer. Closed
           major holidays & Mon. **Reservations:** suggested. **Features:** casual dress; Sunday brunch; children's menu
◆◆   carryout; beer & wine only. In Historic Main Street General Store. Entertainment Wed evening. Organic local
American   produce; free range veal. Smoke free premises. **Cards:** AE, MC, VI.   [X]

WEAVERVILLE MILLING COMPANY   **Dinner:** $9-$16   Phone: 704/645-4700   [36]
(AAA) [SAVE] **Location:** From US 23 & 19, New Stock Rd exit, follow Vance Birthplace signs on Reems Creek Rd, 1s
           right after Reems Creek Bridge. **Hours:** 5 pm-9 pm, Fri & Sat-9:30 pm. Closed: Wed, 12/24, 12/25,
◆◆   1/1-1/22, also Mon & Tues 2/1-3/1. **Reservations:** suggested. **Features:** No A/C; casual dress; children's
American   menu; carryout; beer & wine only. Unique dining in converted grain mill on Reems Creek. Mountain trout
featured. Displays of local crafts. **Cards:** MC, VI. **Special Value: $1 off the price of a dinner entree.**
(See ad p 324)   [X]

WELDON—1,400

LODGINGS

DAYS INN   Phone: 919/536-4867
(AAA) [SAVE] All Year [CP]   1P: $40   2P/1B: $40   2P/2B: $45   XP: $5   F1:
           Location: I-95 & US 158, exit 173. 1611 Roanoke Rapids Rd 27890. Fax: 919/536-2023. **Terms:** Pets, $
◆◆   extra charge. **Facility:** 97 rooms. 2 stories; exterior corridors; small pool. **Dining:** Restaurant nearby.
Motel   **All Rooms:** free movies. **Some Rooms:** microwaves, refrigerators. **Cards:** AE, DS, MC, VI.
           (See color ad p 410)   [♨] [♨] [CTV] [X] [D]

WELDON PLACE INN
Phone: 919/536-4582

AAA **SAVE**   All Year [BP]   1P: $65   2P/1B: $72   2P/2B: $72   XP: $5   F12

◆◆◆   **Location:** Town center. 500 Washington Ave 27890. **Terms:** Reserv deposit, 3 day notice; no pets.

Historic Bed   **Facility:** 4 rooms. 2 stories; interior corridors; smoke free premises. **All Rooms:** free movies.

& Breakfast   **Some Rooms:** phones, whirlpools. **Cards:** AE, DI, MC, VI. **Special Amenities:** Free breakfast and free local telephone calls.

[CTV] [X] [D]

WHITEVILLE—5,100

LODGING

BEST WESTERN PREMIERE INN
Phone: 910/642-2378

AAA **SAVE**   All Year   1P: $40- 45   2P/1B: $49- 52   2P/2B: $49- 52   XP: $7   F18

◆◆◆   **Location:** On US 701 bypass, 1 mi s of jct US 74 & 76. 503 N J K Powell Blvd 28472-0396 (PO Box 396).

Motel   Fax: 910/642-6214. **Terms:** No pets. **Facility:** 91 rooms. Traditional motel design & decor in commercial location. 2 stories; exterior corridors. **Dining:** Restaurant nearby. **Services:** valet laundry. **All Rooms:** free movies. **Some Rooms:** refrigerators, whirlpools. **Cards:** AE, CB, DI, DS, MC, VI. **Special Amenities:** Free local telephone calls and free newspaper.

[≈] [✦] [CTV] [X] [D]

WILKESBORO—2,600—See also NORTH WILKESBORO.

LODGINGS

ADDISON MOTOR INN   Rates Subject to Change   **Phone: 910/838-1000**

◆◆◆   All Year [CP]   1P: $52- 100   2P/1B: $56- 105   2P/2B: $56- 105   XP: $5   F17

Motel   **Location:** 2 mi n on US 421, 0.5 mi w of US 421 business route. Hwy 421N 28697 (PO Box 410). Fax: 910/667-7458. **Terms:** Sr. discount; no pets. **Facility:** 115 rooms. 2 stories; exterior corridors. **All Rooms:** free movies. **Cards:** AE, CB, DI, DS, MC, VI.

[CTV] [♠] [X] [♫] [D]

HOLIDAY INN EXPRESS   Rates Subject to Change   **Phone: 910/838-1800**

◆◆◆   All Year [CP]   1P: $64   2P/1B: $70   2P/2B: $70   XP: $6   F18

Motel   **Location:** 2 mi n on US 421 & SR 16. 1700 Winkler St 28697. Fax: 910/838-1800. **Terms:** No pets. **Facility:** 101 rooms. 4 stories; interior corridors. **All Rooms:** free movies. **Cards:** AE, DI, DS, MC, VI.

[≈] [CTV] [♠] [X] [♫] [D] [S]

QUALITY INN   Rates Subject to Change   **Phone: 910/667-2176**

◆◆   All Year [CP]   1P: $45- 57   2P/1B: $50- 62   2P/2B: $50- 62   XP: $5   F18

Motel   **Location:** Just w on SR 268 from US 421. 1206 River St 28697. Fax: 910/838-9103. **Terms:** Sr. discount; no pets. **Facility:** 100 rooms. 2 stories; exterior corridors. **All Rooms:** free movies. **Cards:** AE, CB, DI, DS, JCB, MC, VI.

[≈] [CTV] [X] [D]

RESTAURANT

THE CAROUSEL CAFE   **Lunch:** $4-$6   **Dinner:** $6-$12   **Phone: 910/838-9141**

◆   **Location:** 1.8 mi n on US 421 at jct US 421 business route, at w entrance of Wilkes Mall. 1605 Curtis

American   Bridge Rd 28697. **Hours:** 11 am-9 pm. Closed: Sun, 11/26 & 12/25. **Features:** children's menu; senior's menu; carryout; salad bar. Family & budget traveler oriented. Chicken, shrimp, steak & sandwiches. Casual dining room appointed with woven baskets. Homemade biscuits & cornbread. Daily lunch & dinner buffet. **Cards:** MC, VI.

[X]

WILLIAMSTON—5,500

LODGINGS

COMFORT INN   Rates Subject to Change   **Phone: 919/792-8400**

◆◆◆   All Year [CP]   1P: $43- 54   2P/1B: $47- 54   2P/2B: $47- 54   XP: $5   F18

Motel   **Location:** At jct US 64 & 17 bypass. 100 E Blvd 27892 (PO Box 663). Fax: 919/809-4800. **Terms:** Sr. discount; pets. **Facility:** 59 rooms. 2 stories; interior corridors. **All Rooms:** free & pay movies. **Cards:** AE, CB, DI, DS, JCB, MC, VI.

[🛏] [♠] [X] [♫] [D] [S]

HOLIDAY INN   Rates Subject to Change   **Phone: 919/792-3184**

◆◆◆   All Year   1P: $45- 59   2P/1B: $46- 59   2P/2B: $44- 59   XP: $4   F18

Motor Inn   **Location:** Jct Hwys 64 & 17. 101 E Blvd 27892 (PO Box 711). Fax: 919/792-9003. **Terms:** Sr. discount; pets. **Facility:** 100 rooms. 2 stories; interior/exterior corridors. **Dining:** Restaurant, coffee shop; 6 am-9:30 pm; $8-$11. **All Rooms:** free & pay movies. **Cards:** AE, CB, DI, DS, JCB, MC, VI.

[🛏] [≈] [X] [♫] [D]

WILMINGTON—55,500

LODGINGS

BEST WESTERN CAROLINIAN   Rates Subject to Change   **Phone: 910/763-4653**

AAA   Fri & Sat 4/5-10/20 [CP]   1P: $68- 74   2P/1B: $69- 76   2P/2B: $69- 76   XP: $8

Sun-Thurs 4/5-10/20 [CP]   1P: $55- 68   2P/1B: $55- 68   2P/2B: $55- 68   XP: $8

◆◆◆   12/1-4/4 & 10/21-11/30 [CP]   1P: $48- 58   2P/1B: $48- 58   2P/2B: $48- 60   XP: $8

Motel   **Location:** 2 mi n on US 17 & 74. 2916 Market St 28403. Fax: 910/763-0486. **Terms:** Reserv deposit, 14 day notice; no pets. **Facility:** 61 rooms. 1-2 stories; interior/exterior corridors. **All Rooms:** free movies. **Some Rooms:** efficiency. **Cards:** AE, DI, DS, JCB, MC, VI.

[≈] [CTV] [X] [D]

COMFORT INN EXECUTIVE CENTER   Rates Subject to Change   **Phone: 910/791-4841**

◆◆◆   5/28-9/5 [CP]   1P: $99   2P/1B: $99   2P/2B: $99   XP: $5   F18

Motel   3/1-5/27 [CP]   1P: $75   2P/1B: $75   2P/2B: $75   XP: $5   F18

12/1-2/28 & 9/6-11/30 [CP]   1P: $55   2P/1B: $60   2P/2B: $60   XP: $5   F18

Location: Just s on SR 132 from jct US 17. 151 S College Rd 28403. Fax: 910/790-9100. **Terms:** Sr. discount; no pets. **Facility:** 146 rooms. 6 stories; interior corridors. **All Rooms:** free movies. **Cards:** AE, CB, DI, DS, MC, VI.

[≈] [CTV] [X] [♫] [D]

THE CURRAN HOUSE
◆◆◆
Historic Bed
& Breakfast

Rates Subject to Change

Phone: 910/763-6603

Fri & Sat 3/1-9/30 [BP]	1P: 95- 100	2P/1B:	$95- 100	
Fri & Sat 12/1-2/28 & 10/1-11/30 [BP]	1P: $80- 85	2P/1B:	$80- 85	
Sun-Thurs 3/1-9/30 [BP]	1P: $75- 85	2P/1B:	$75- 85	
Sun-Thurs 12/1-2/28 & 10/1-11/30 [BP]	1P: $70- 80	2P/1B:	$70- 80	

Location: 0.3 mi s of Market St. 312 S 3rd St 28401. Fax: 910/763-5116. **Terms:** Age restrictions may apply; reserv deposit, 3 day notice; 2 night min stay, weekends in season; no pets. **Facility:** 3 rooms. Handling fee imposed; 2 stories; interior corridors; smoke free premises. **All Rooms:** free movies. **Cards:** MC, VI.   [CTV] [X] [D]

DAYS INN
◆◆◆
Motor Inn

Rates Subject to Change

Phone: 910/799-6300

4/1-9/30	1P: $48- 80	2P/1B: $54- 80	2P/2B: $54- 80	XP: $7	F13
12/1-3/31 & 10/1-11/30	1P: $40- 64	2P/1B: $46- 64	2P/2B: $46- 64	XP: $7	F13

Location: 3.5 mi n on US 17 & 74. 5040 Market St 28405. Fax: 910/791-7414. **Terms:** Sr. discount; reserv deposit; no pets. **Facility:** 122 rooms. 2 stories; exterior corridors. **Dining:** Restaurant; 6 am-8:45 pm; $5-$9. **All Rooms:** free movies. **Cards:** AE, CB, DI, DS, JCB, MC, VI.   [AAA] [CTV] [X] [🌙] [D]

FAIRFIELD INN BY MARRIOTT
(AAA) [SAVE]
◆◆◆
Motel

Phone: 910/791-8850

Mon-Thurs 5/1-9/27 [CP]	1P: $69- 79	2P/1B: $74- 89	2P/2B: $74- 94	XP: $5	F18
Fri-Sun 5/1-9/27 [CP]	1P: $79- 94	2P/1B: $84- 94	2P/2B: $84- 94	XP: $5	F18
9/28-11/30 [CP]	1P: $55- 69	2P/1B: $59- 74	2P/2B: $59- 74	XP: $5	F18
12/1-4/30 [CP]	1P: $49- 64	2P/1B: $59- 74	2P/2B: $59- 74	XP: $5	F18

Location: 3.4 mi n; on US 17 & 74. 4926 Market St 28405. Fax: 910/791-8858. **Terms:** No pets. **Facility:** 120 rooms. Basic motel construction; contemporary room decor. 2 stories; exterior corridors. **Dining:** Restaurant nearby. **Services:** valet laundry. **All Rooms:** free & pay movies. **Cards:** AE, DI, DS, MC, VI. **Special Amenities:** Free breakfast and free local telephone calls.   [🌙] [🍴] [CTV] [X] [🌙] [D]

FAIRFIELD INN BY MARRIOTT
◆◆◆
Motel

Rates Subject to Change

Phone: 910/392-6767

Fri & Sat 4/1-9/30 [CP]	1P: $93	2P/1B: $99	2P/2B: $99	XP: $6	F18
Sun-Thurs 4/1-9/30 [CP]	1P: $66	2P/1B: $72	2P/2B: $72	XP: $6	F18
12/1-3/31 & 10/1-11/30 [CP]	1P: $46	2P/1B: $52	2P/2B: $52	XP: $6-9	F18

Location: 0.3 mi s on SR 132 from jct US 17. 306 S College Rd 28403. Fax: 910/392-6767. **Terms:** Sr. discount; no pets. **Facility:** 134 rooms. 3 stories; interior/exterior corridors. **All Rooms:** free & pay movies. **Cards:** AE, CB, DI, DS, MC, VI. *(See color ad below)*   [🌙] [CTV] [X] [D] [S]

HAMPTON INN
◆◆◆
Motel

Rates Subject to Change

Phone: 910/395-5045

Fri & Sat 4/5-10/26 [CP]	1P: $89- 99	2P/1B: $89- 99	2P/2B: $89- 99	
Sun-Thurs 4/5-10/26 [CP]	1P: $65- 79	2P/1B: $71- 85	2P/2B: $71- 85	
12/1-4/4 & 10/27-11/30 [CP]	1P: $59- 73	2P/1B: $65- 79	2P/2B: $65- 79	

Location: 3.6 mi n on US 17 & 74. 5107 Market St 28403. Fax: 910/799-1974. **Terms:** Sr. discount; no pets. **Facility:** 118 rooms. 2 stories; exterior corridors. **All Rooms:** free movies. **Cards:** AE, CB, DI, DS, MC, VI.   [🌙] [CTV] [X] [🌙] [D]

HOJO INN
(AAA) [SAVE]
◆◆
Motel

Phone: 910/343-1727

4/1-9/30	1P: $56	2P/1B: $69- 95	2P/2B: $69- 95	XP: $8	F13
Fri & Sat 12/1-3/31 & 10/1-11/30	1P: $39	2P/1B: $45- 95	2P/2B: $45- 95	XP: $8	F13
Sun-Thurs 12/1-3/31 & 10/1-11/30	1P: $36	2P/1B: $39	2P/2B: $39	XP: $8	F13

Location: 2.3 mi n; on US 17 & 74. 3901 Market St 28403. Fax: 910/343-1727. **Terms:** CP avail; no pets. **Facility:** 80 rooms. Modest & traditional motel construction & decor. 1 story; exterior corridors. **Dining:** Restaurant nearby. **All Rooms:** free movies. **Some Rooms:** 8 efficiencies, microwaves, refrigerators. **Cards:** AE, DI, DS, MC, VI. **Special Amenities:** Free room upgrade and preferred room (each subject to availability with advanced reservations).   [CTV] [X] [D]

HOLIDAY INN EXPRESS HOTEL & SUITES
◆◆◆
Motel

Rates Subject to Change

Phone: 910/392-3227

Fri & Sat 3/28-10/5 [CP]	1P: $99	2P/1B: $99	2P/2B: $99	XP: $10	F18
Sun-Thurs 3/28-10/5 [CP]	1P: $81	2P/1B: $81	2P/2B: $81	XP: $10	F18
12/1-3/27 & 10/6-11/30 [CP]	1P: $71	2P/1B: $71	2P/2B: $71	XP: $10	F18

Location: 0.3 mi e from US 17 on SRs 132; just s on Imperial Dr. 160 Van Campen Blvd 28403. Fax: 910/395-9907 **Terms:** Sr. discount; no pets. **Facility:** 131 rooms. 5 stories; interior corridors. **All Rooms:** free & pay movies. **Cards:** AE, CB, DI, DS, MC, VI.
Roll in showers.   [🌙] [CTV] [♿] [X] [🌙] [D] [S]

HOLIDAY INN OF WILMINGTON

◆◆◆

Motor Inn

	Rates Subject to Change					
Fri & Sat 4/1-10/8 [BP]	1P:	$99	2P/1B:	$99	2P/2B:	$99
Sun-Thurs 4/1-10/8 [BP]	1P:	$75	2P/1B:	$75	2P/2B:	$75
12/1-3/31 & 10/9-11/30 [BP]	1P:	$65	2P/1B:	$65	2P/2B:	$65

Phone: 910/799-1440

Location: 3.3 mi n on US 17 & 74. 4903 Market St 28405. **Fax:** 910/799-2683. **Terms:** Sr. discount; no pets. **Facility:** 232 rooms. 24 whirlpool rms, extra charge; 2 stories; exterior corridors. **Dining:** Restaurant; 6 am-10 & 5-10 pm, Sat & Sun 6 am-11 & 5-10 pm; $8-$16. **All Rooms:** free & pay movies. **Cards:** AE, CB, DI, DS, MC, VI.

HOWARD JOHNSON PLAZA HOTEL

◆◆◆

Motor Inn

	Rates Subject to Change							
6/16-9/7	1P:	$119- 129	2P/1B:	$119- 129	2P/2B:	$119- 129	XP: $10	F18
4/1-6/15	1P:	$109	2P/1B:	$109	2P/2B:	$109	XP: $10	F18
12/1-3/31 & 9/8-11/30	1P:	$99	2P/1B:	$99	2P/2B:	$99	XP: $10	F18

Phone: 910/392-1101

Location: 3.5 mi n on US 17 & 74. 5032 Market St 28405. **Fax:** 910/392-1101. **Terms:** Sr. discount; reserv deposit; no pets. **Facility:** 124 rooms. 1 penthouse $250. 4 king deluxe $150; 5 stories; interior corridors. **Dining:** Dining room; 6 am-10 pm; $7-$16. **All Rooms:** free movies. **Cards:** AE, CB, DI, DS, MC, VI.

RODEWAY INN INTOWN

◆◆

Motel

	Rates Subject to Change							
3/1-9/7 [CP]	1P:	$45- 60	2P/1B:	$45- 60	2P/2B:	$60- 70	XP: $6	F18
9/8-10/31 [CP]	1P:	$35- 45	2P/1B:	$45- 50	2P/2B:	$50- 60	XP: $6	F18
12/1-2/28 & 11/1-11/30 [CP]	1P:	$35- 40	2P/1B:	$35- 40	2P/2B:	$45- 50	XP: $6	F18

Phone: 910/763-3318

Location: 2 mi n on US 17 & 74. 2929 Market St 28403. **Fax:** 910/763-3318. **Terms:** No pets. **Facility:** 48 rooms. Modest, traditional motel architecture & decor. Efficiency $60-$120. Handling fee imposed; 1 story; exterior corridors. **Dining:** Restaurant nearby. **Services:** valet laundry. **All Rooms:** no utensils, free movies, combo or shower baths. **Some Rooms:** coffeemakers, radios. **Cards:** AE, DI, DS, JCB, MC, VI. **Special Amenities: Free breakfast and free local telephone calls.**

ROSEHILL INN

◆◆◆

Historic Bed
& Breakfast

12/1-3/14 [BP]	1P:	$75- 115	2P/1B:	$75- 115	XP: $35
Sun-Thurs 3/15-11/30 [BP]	1P:	$85- 125	2P/1B:	$85- 125	XP: $35
Fri & Sat 3/15-11/30 [BP]	1P:	$125- 165	2P/1B:	$125- 165	XP: $35

Phone: 910/815-0250

Location: Just s from Business US 17. 114 S Third St 28401. **Fax:** 910/815-0350. **Terms:** Age restrictions may apply; check-in 4 pm; reserv deposit, 7 day notice; no pets. **Facility:** 6 rooms. 1848 neo-classic revival home in historic district near Cape Fear River. Handling fee imposed; 2 stories; interior corridors; smoke free premises. **All Rooms:** combo or shower baths. **Some Rooms:** VCP's. **Cards:** AE, DS. **Special Amenities: Free breakfast and free local telephone calls.**

TAYLOR HOUSE INN

◆◆◆

Historic Bed
& Breakfast

	Rates Subject to Change						
All Year [BP]	1P:	$95- 110	2P/1B:	$95- 110	2P/2B:	$95- 110	XP: $25

Phone: 910/763-7581

Location: Just n; corner Market st. 14 N 7th St 28401. **Terms:** Check-in 4 pm; reserv deposit, 7 day notice; no pets. **Facility:** 5 rooms. 2 stories; interior corridors; smoke free premises. **Cards:** AE, MC, VI.

TRAVEL INN
Motel

		1P:	2P/1B:	2P/2B:	XP:	
Fri & Sat 4/1-9/30		$49	$49	$65	$5	F12
Sun-Thurs 4/1-9/30		$45	$49	$49	$5	F12
10/1-11/30		$39	$39	$49	$5	F12
12/1-3/31		$35	$39	$45	$5	F12

Rates Subject to Change   Phone: 910/763-8217

Location: 3 mi n on US 74 & 17. 4401 Market St 28403. **Fax:** 910/763-8217. **Terms:** Reserv deposit; no pets. **Facility:** 30 rooms. Handling fee imposed; 1 story; exterior corridors. **All Rooms:** free movies. **Cards:** AE, CB, DI, DS, MC, VI.

WILMINGTON HILTON ◆◆◆
Hotel

Rates Subject to Change   Phone: 910/763-5900

All Year   1P: $99- 129   2P/1B: $109- 159   XP: $10   F18

Location: On Cape Fear River waterfront. 301 N Water St 28401. **Fax:** 910/763-0038. **Terms:** Sr. discount; check-in 4 pm; reserv deposit; no pets. **Facility:** 178 rooms. 3 suites $225-$300, 6 executive double rooms $149; 9 stories; interior corridors. **Dining:** Dining room; 6:30 am-10:30 pm; $8-$15. **All Rooms:** free & pay movies. **Cards:** AE, CB, DI, DS, MC, VI. *(See color ad p 18)*

THE WORTH HOUSE ◆◆◆
Historic Bed & Breakfast

Rates Subject to Change   Phone: 910/762-8562

		1P:	2P/1B:	2P/2B:	XP:
2/28-11/1 [BP]		$80- 115	$85- 120	$85- 120	$20
12/1-2/27 & 11/2-11/30 [BP]		$70- 105	$75- 110	$75- 110	$20

Location: 0.4 mi s of Market St. 412 S 3rd St 28401. **Fax:** 910/763-2173. **Terms:** Sr. discount; age restrictions may apply; check-in 4 pm; no pets. **Facility:** 7 rooms. 3 stories, no elevator; interior corridors; smoke free premises. **Cards:** AE, MC, VI.

RESTAURANTS

CANDLELIGHT CAFE ◆◆
Italian

Lunch: $5-$6   **Dinner:** $9-$13   **Phone:** 910/392-5541

Location: 0.5 mi s of jct US 17 & SR 132 in University Landing Shopping Center on SR 132. 417 S College Rd, Unit 24 28403. **Hours:** 11 am-2 & 5-9 pm. Closed: Sun, 1/1, 11/26 & 12/25. **Reservations:** suggested; weekends. **Features:** casual dress; health conscious menu items; carryout; cocktails; a la carte. Unique pasta specialties, variety of salads & sandwiches for lunch. Veal, steak & chicken specialties for dinner. **Cards:** DS, MC, VI.

ELIJAH'S
Seafood

Lunch: $6-$10   **Dinner:** $10-$22   **Phone:** 910/343-1448

Location: In Chandler's Wharf, overlooking Cape Fear River. 2 Ann St 28401. **Hours:** 11:30 am-3 & 5-10 pm, Fri & Sat-11 pm. Closed: 1/1, 11/26 & 12/25. **Features:** casual dress; children's menu; carryout; cocktails & lounge. Classic American cuisine. Lighter menu in oyster bar to midnight. Outdoor dining avail. **Cards:** AE, DS, MC, VI.

FRANKO'S CAFFE & TRATTORIA ◆◆
Provincial Italian

Lunch: $6-$8   **Dinner:** $12-$25   **Phone:** 910/763-8100

Location: Center. 10 Market St 28401. **Hours:** Open 12/1-12/31 & 2/10-11/30; 11:30 am-3:30 & 6:30-10:30 pm, Fri & Sat 11:30 am-3:30 & 6-10:30 pm. Closed: Sun, Mon & 12/25. **Reservations:** suggested. **Features:** casual dress; carryout; cocktails; street parking. Cuisine represents all the provinces & states of Italy. Fine all-Italian wine list. Outdoor sidewalk dining avail. **Cards:** AE, DS, MC, VI.

THE PILOT HOUSE ◆◆
Regional American

Lunch: $5-$8   **Dinner:** $10-$22   **Phone:** 910/343-0200

Location: In Chandler's Wharf. 2 Ann St 28401. **Hours:** 11:30 am-3 & 5-10 pm, Fri & Sat-11 pm. Closed: 1/1, 12/24, 12/25, Sun off season. **Reservations:** accepted. **Features:** casual dress; Sunday brunch; children's menu; carryout; cocktails; a la carte. Overlooking Cape Fear River. Outdoor dining avail. Innovations on Southern Regional cooking. **Cards:** AE, DS, MC, VI.

TRAILS END STEAKS ETC ◆◆
Steakhouse

Dinner: $12-$35   **Phone:** 910/791-2034

Location: From jct Cr 132 & US 76, just e on US 76, 1.9 mi se on Pine Grove Dr, 1.6 mi s on Masonboro Loop, 0.5 mi s. 613 Trails End Rd 38409. **Hours:** 6 pm-midnight. Closed major holidays & Sun. **Reservations:** accepted. **Features:** casual dress; children's menu; carryout; salad bar; cocktails & lounge. Charbroiled steak; cooked over hard wood charcoal. Really is at the end of the trail. **Cards:** AE, CB, DI, DS, MC, VI.

WILSON—36,900

LODGINGS

BEST WESTERN LA SAMMANA
Motel

Phone: 919/237-8700

All Year [CP]   1P: $56- 76   2P/1B: $56- 76   2P/2B: $56- 76   XP: $5   F12

Location: Exit 121, I-95, 5 mi e on US 264. 400 Ward Blvd SW 27893. **Fax:** 919/237-8092. **Terms:** Reserv deposit; no pets. **Facility:** 82 rooms. Very upscale public areas. Attractive grounds & pool area. 2 stories; exterior corridors. **Dining:** Restaurant nearby. **All Rooms:** free movies. **Some Rooms:** coffeemakers, microwaves, refrigerators. Fee: whirlpools. **Cards:** AE, CB, DI, DS, MC, VI. **Special Amenities:** Free breakfast and free newspaper.

HAMPTON INN ◆◆◆
Motel

Rates Subject to Change   Phone: 919/291-2323

All Year [CP]   1P: $52- 56   2P/1B: $57- 61   2P/2B: $57- 61

Location: 0.5 mi w on SR 42 (Tarboro St) from jct US 264; 6 mi e of I-95, exit 121. 1801 S Tarboro St 27893. **Fax:** 919/291-7696. **Terms:** Sr. discount; no pets. **Facility:** 100 rooms. 2 stories; exterior corridors. **All Rooms:** free movies. **Cards:** AE, CB, DI, DS, MC, VI.

HOLIDAY INN ◆◆◆
Motor Inn

Rates Subject to Change   Phone: 919/243-5111

All Year   1P: $54- 62   2P/1B: $57- 65   2P/2B: $57   XP: $5   F16

Location: 2 mi s on US 301. 1815 US 301 S 27893. **Fax:** 919/291-9697. **Terms:** Small pets only. **Facility:** 100 rooms. 2 stories; exterior corridors. **Dining:** Restaurant; 6 am-2 & 5-10 pm; $8-$12. **All Rooms:** free movies. **Cards:** AE, CB, DI, DS, JCB, MC, VI.

MISS BETTY'S BED & BREAKFAST INN ◆◆◆
Historic Bed & Breakfast

Rates Subject to Change   Phone: 919/243-4447

All Year [BP]   1P: $50- 60   2P/1B: $60- 75

Location: Town center 0.5 mi n on Nash St. 600 W Nash St 27893-3045. **Fax:** 919/243-4447. **Terms:** Age restrictions may apply; reserv deposit; no pets. **Facility:** 10 rooms. 2 stories; interior corridors. **All Rooms:** free movies. **Cards:** AE, CB, DI, DS, MC, VI.

QUALITY INN SOUTH
◆◆◆   All Year [CP]   Rates Subject to Change   **Phone:** 919/243-5165
Motor Inn   1P: $55- 75   2P/1B: $55- 75   2P/2B: $55   XP: $5   F18
Location: From I-95S exit 107, 15 mi n on US 301N; from I-95N exit 121, 8 mi e on US 264, then 0.5 mi s on US 301. 2901 US 301 S 27893. Fax: 919/243-5109. **Terms:** Sr. discount; small pets only, $5 extra charge. **Facility:** 100 rooms. 2 stories; exterior corridors. **Dining:** 2 restaurants; 5 am-11 pm; $8-$18. **All Rooms:** free movies. **Cards:** AE, CB, DI, DS, JCB, MC, VI.   🛏 🖚 CTV ⊠ D

RESTAURANT

PARKER'S BARBECUE   **Lunch:** $4-$6   **Dinner:** $4-$6   **Phone:** 919/237-0972
◆   **Location:** 2.5 mi s on US 301 & I-95 business loop. 27895. **Hours:** 9 am-9 pm. Closed: 11/26, 6/19-6/25,
American   12/24 & 12/25. **Features:** children's menu; carryout. Since 1946, well-known for NC barbecue. Limited menu of pork & chicken barbecue, shrimp & brunswick stew. Unpretentious dining rooms. Very popular.   ⊠

WINSTON-SALEM—143,500

LODGINGS

ADAM'S MARK WINSTON PLAZA   Rates Subject to Change   **Phone:** 910/725-3500
◆◆◆   All Year   1P: $99- 150   2P/1B: $99- 150   2P/2B: $99- 150
Hotel   **Location:** Cherry St exit off I-40 business route; downtown. 425 N Cherry St 27101. Fax: 910/721-2240.
Terms: Reserv deposit; no pets. **Facility:** 315 rooms. 17 stories; interior corridors. Fee: parking.
Dining: Dining room; 6:30 am-11 pm; $9-$18. **All Rooms:** free & pay movies. **Cards:** AE, CB, DI, DS, MC, VI.
(See color ad below)   ⊠ 🎞 D S

AUGUSTUS T ZEVELY INN   Rates Subject to Change   **Phone:** 910/748-9299
◆◆◆   All Year [CP]   1P: $80- 205   2P/1B: $80- 205   2P/2B: $100- 115   XP: $15
Historic Bed   **Location:** In Old Salem Historical District. 803 S Main 27101. Fax: 910/721-2211. **Terms:** Age restrictions
& Breakfast   may apply; small pets only, $5 extra charge. **Facility:** 12 rooms. 2 steambath rooms $115; 3 stories, no elevator; interior/exterior corridors; smoke free premises. **All Rooms:** free movies. **Cards:** AE, MC, VI.
🛏 CTV ⊠ D S

BROOKSTOWN INN   **Phone:** 910/725-1120
AAA SAVE   All Year [CP]   1P: $95- 115   2P/1B: $115- 130   2P/2B: $115- 130   XP: $20   F12
Location: Just s of I-40 business route, Cherry St exit. 200 Brookstown Ave 27101. Fax: 910/773-0147.
◆◆◆   **Terms:** Reserv deposit; BP avail; no pets. **Facility:** 71 rooms. In restored textile mill, circa 1837. Early
Historic Bed   American decor, poster bed & handmade quilts. Large rooms & attractive public areas, 15 garden tub rooms.
& Breakfast   4 stories; interior corridors. **Dining:** Homemade cookies & milk 8 pm; restaurant nearby.
Services: complimentary evening beverages; valet laundry. **All Rooms:** free movies.
Some Rooms: microwaves, refrigerators. **Cards:** AE, DI, MC, VI. **Special Amenities:** Free breakfast and free newspaper.
🐦 CTV ⊠ 🎞 D S

COMFORT INN CLOVERDALE PLACE   Rates Subject to Change   **Phone:** 910/721-0220
◆◆◆   All Year [CP]   1P: $56- 61   2P/1B: $63- 70   2P/2B: $69   XP: $10   F18
Motel   **Location:** Cloverdale exit off I-40 business route, 1 1/2 blks to Miller St, just n. 110 Miller St 27103.
Fax: 910/723-2117. **Terms:** Reserv deposit; no pets. **Facility:** 122 rooms. 5 stories; interior corridors.
All Rooms: free movies. **Cards:** AE, CB, DI, DS, MC, VI.   🖚 CTV ⊠ D

COMFORT INN COLISEUM   Rates Subject to Change   **Phone:** 910/767-8240
◆◆   4/23-5/1 & 10/15-10/23 [CP]   1P: $89   2P/1B: $89   2P/2B: $89   XP: $6   F18
Motel   12/1-4/22, 5/2-10/14 &
10/24-11/30 [CP]   1P: $52- 62   2P/1B: $58- 68   2P/2B: $58- 68   XP: $6   F18
Location: Exit 112, US 52 & Akron Dr. 531 Akron Dr 27105. Fax: 910/661-9513. **Terms:** Sr. discount; pets, $30 extra charge. **Facility:** 150 rooms. 8 stories; interior corridors. **All Rooms:** free movies. **Cards:** AE, CB, DI, DS, MC, VI.
🛏 🖚 CTV ⊠ 🎞 D

COURTYARD BY MARRIOTT   Rates Subject to Change   **Phone:** 910/727-1277
◆◆◆   All Year   1P: $69   2P/1B: $69   2P/2B: $69
Motel   **Location:** 3 mi n on University Pkwy from I-40 (business route) Cherry St exit; just n of coliseum. 3111
University Pkwy 27105. Fax: 910/722-8219. **Terms:** No pets. **Facility:** 123 rooms. 2 stories; interior corridors.
Dining: Restaurant; breakfast only 6:30-10 am, Sat & Sun 7-11 am. **All Rooms:** free movies. **Cards:** AE, CB, DI, DS, MC, VI. *(See color ad p 428)*   🖚 CTV ⊠ 🎞 D

DAYS INN-NORTH   **Phone:** 910/744-5755
AAA SAVE   All Year [CP]   1P: $44- 49   2P/1B: $44- 49   2P/2B: $48- 53   XP: $5   F17
Location: Just e off US 52, exit 114. 5218 Germanton Rd 27105. Fax: 910/744-5755. **Terms:** No pets.
◆◆   **Facility:** 60 rooms. 2 stories; exterior corridors. **All Rooms:** free movies. **Some Rooms:** Fee: refrigerators,
Motel   whirlpools. **Cards:** AE, DI, DS, MC, VI. **Special Amenities:** Free local telephone calls.   ⊠ 🎞 D

HAMPTON INN
◆◆◆
Motel

Rates Subject to Change
All Year [CP]   1P: $69   2P/1B: $76   2P/2B: $76   XP: $7   F18
Location: Exit 189, I-40. 1990 Hampton Inn Ct 27103. Fax: 910/768-9168. **Terms:** Sr. discount; no pets.
Facility: 131 rooms. 5 stories; interior corridors. **All Rooms:** free movies. **Cards:** AE, CB, DI, DS, MC, VI.
Roll in showers.

Phone: 910/760-1660

THE HENRY F SHAFFNER B & B INN
◆◆◆
Historic Bed
& Breakfast

Rates Subject to Change
All Year [BP]   1P: $99- 189   2P/1B: $99- 189 2P/2B: $129   XP: $15   F12
Location: Cherry St exit, I-40 Business Rt westbound to 1st St, just w on 1st St, 3 blks s on Marshall St,
eastbound Cherry St exit, just e. 150 S Marshall St 27101. Fax: 910/777-1188. **Terms:** Sr. discount; reserv
deposit, 3 day notice; no pets. **Facility:** 8 rooms. 3 stories, no elevator; interior corridors; smoke free premises. **All Rooms:** free movies. **Cards:** AE, MC, VI.

Phone: 910/777-0052

HOLIDAY INN-COLISEUM
◆◆◆
Motor Inn

Rates Subject to Change
All Year   1P: $69- 120   2P/1B: $69- 120 2P/2B: $69- 120
Location: 3 mi n of Memorial Coliseum, Cherry St exit off I-40 business route. 3050 University Pkwy 27105.
Fax: 910/777-1003. **Terms:** Reserv deposit; small pets only, $25 dep req. **Facility:** 193 rooms. 4 stories; inte-
rior corridors. **Dining:** Dining room; 6:30 am-2 & 5-10 pm, Sat & Sun from 7 am; $9-$15. **All Rooms:** free & pay movies.
Cards: AE, CB, DI, DS, JCB, MC, VI.

Phone: 910/723-2911

HOLIDAY INN SELECT
◆◆◆
Motor Inn

4/1-4/30 & 10/1-10/31   1P: $129   2P/1B: $139   2P/2B: $139   XP: $10   F16
12/1-3/31, 5/1-9/30 &
11/1-11/30   1P: $86   2P/1B: $96   2P/2B: $96   XP: $10   F16
Location: University Pkwy S exit 115B off US 52. 5790 University Pkwy 27105. Fax: 910/744-1888.
Terms: No pets. **Facility:** 150 rooms. Near shopping area. 7 stories; interior corridors; golf privileges.
Dining: Dining room; 6:30 am-10 pm; $10-$18; cocktails. **All Rooms:** coffeemakers, free & pay movies.
Some Rooms: refrigerators. **Cards:** AE, DI, DS, MC, VI. **Special Amenities:** Early check-in/late check-out and free local
telephone calls.

Phone: 910/767-9595

HOLIDAY INN-WEST
◆◆
Motor Inn

Rates Subject to Change
All Year   1P: $67- 100   2P/1B: $72- 105 2P/2B: $72- 105 XP: $5   F18
Location: Silas Creek Pkwy S off I-40 business route, e on Hawthorne via signs. 2008 S Hawthorne 27103.
Fax: 910/659-0436. **Terms:** No pets. **Facility:** 160 rooms. 2-3 stories; exterior corridors. **Dining:** Restaurant;
6:30 am-2 & 5:30-10 pm, Sat & Sun from 7 am; $8-$10. **All Rooms:** free movies. **Cards:** AE, CB, DI, DS, JCB, MC, VI.
(See ad below)

Phone: 910/765-6670

HYLEHURST BED & BREAKFAST INN
◆◆
Historic Bed
& Breakfast

Rates Subject to Change
All Year [BP]   1P: $65- 125   2P/1B: $65- 125
Location: Just s from I-40 (Business), Cherry St exit. 224 S Cherry St 27101. **Terms:** Age restrictions may
apply; reserv deposit, 14 day notice; no pets. **Facility:** 4 rooms. 2 stories; interior corridors; smoke free premises. **All Rooms:** free movies. **Cards:** MC, VI.

Phone: 910/722-7873

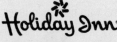

INNKEEPER
◆◆
Motel
Rates Subject to Change
All Year [CP]   1P: $45- 80 2P/1B: $45- 80 2P/2B: $50- 80 XP: $5   F18
Phone: 910/721-0062
Location: Peters Creek exit off I-40 business route, 1.3 mi s. 2115 Peters Creek Pkwy 27127.
Fax: 910/721-0062. **Terms:** Sr. discount; no pets. **Facility:** 126 rooms. 2 stories; exterior corridors.
All Rooms: free movies. **Cards:** AE, CB, DI, DS, MC, VI.

LADY ANNE'S VICTORIAN BED & BREAKFAST
◆◆
Historic Bed
& Breakfast
Rates Subject to Change
Sun-Thurs [BP]   2P/1B: $55- 95   XP: $15
Fri & Sat [BP]   2P/1B: $55- 160   XP: $15
Phone: 910/724-1074
Location: 0.8 mi n on Broad St from I-40 (business), Broad St exit to 6th St; just w on 6th St, then just n.
612 Summit St 27101. **Terms:** Age restrictions may apply; check-in 4:30 pm; reserv deposit, 7 day notice; no
pets, dogs on premises. **Facility:** 4 rooms. Handling fee imposed; 2 stories; interior/exterior corridors; designated smoking
area. **All Rooms:** free movies. **Cards:** AE, MC, VI.

MICKLE HOUSE BED & BREAKFAST
◆◆◆
Bed &
Breakfast
Rates Subject to Change
Fri & Sat [BP]   1P: $90   2P/1B: $90   2P/2B: $90   XP: $20
Sun-Thurs [BP]   1P: $80   2P/1B: $80   2P/2B: $80   XP: $20
Phone: 910/722-9045
Location: 1 mi w in West End Historical District. 927 W 5th St 27101. **Terms:** Age restrictions may apply;
check-in 4 pm; no pets, resident cat. **Facility:** 2 rooms. 1 story; interior corridors; smoke free premises.
All Rooms: free movies. **Cards:** MC, VI.

RADISSON MARQUE HOTEL
◆◆◆
Hotel
Rates Subject to Change
Mon-Thurs   1P: $125   2P/1B: $125   2P/2B: $125   XP: $15   F18
Fri-Sun   1P: $79- 89   2P/1B: $79- 89   2P/2B: $79- 89   XP: $15   F18
Phone: 910/725-1234
Location: Between Cherry & Marshall sts, Cherry St exit off I-40 business route. 460 N Cherry St 27101.
Fax: 910/722-9182. **Terms:** Check-in 4 pm; no pets. **Facility:** 293 rooms. 9 stories; interior corridors. Fee: parking. **Dining &
Entertainment:** Dining room; 6:30 am-midnight, entertainment Fri & Sat; $7-$18. **All Rooms:** free & pay movies.
Cards: AE, CB, DI, DS, JCB, MC, VI.

RESIDENCE INN BY MARRIOTT
◆◆◆
Apartment
Motel
Rates Subject to Change
All Year [CP]   1P: $99- 122   2P/1B: $99- 122 2P/2B: $99- 122
Phone: 910/759-0777
Location: US 52N exit off I-40 business route, 7 mi n to University Pkwy exit, 2 mi to N Point Blvd, just e.
7835 N Point Blvd 27106. Fax: 910/759-9671. **Terms:** Reserv deposit; small pets only, $100-$150 extra
charge. **Facility:** 88 rooms. 2 stories; exterior corridors. **All Rooms:** kitchens, free movies. **Cards:** AE, CB,
DI, DS, JCB, MC, VI.

SALEM INN
◆◆
Motel
Rates Subject to Change
All Year [CP]   1P: $52- 57 2P/1B: $58- 63 2P/2B: $58- 63 XP: $6   F18
Phone: 910/725-8561
Location: Just s from I-40 (business), Cherry St exit. 127 S Cherry St 27101. Fax: 910/725-2318.
Terms: Sr. discount; reserv deposit, 3 day notice; 4 night min stay; pets, $25 extra charge. **Facility:** 129 rooms.
2 stories; exterior corridors. **All Rooms:** free & pay movies. **Cards:** AE, CB, DI, DS, MC, VI.

RESTAURANTS

LEON'S CAFE
◆◆
Nouvelle
American
Dinner: $14-$19
Phone: 910/725-9593
Location: 0.8 mi s of I-40, Cherry St exit; just w & just s of Old Salem. 924 S Marshall 27101. **Hours:** 6
pm-10 pm. Closed major holidays. **Features:** cocktails. Unpretentious little neighborhood bistro with
innovative menu. **Cards:** AE, DS, MC, VI.

LUCKY 32
◆◆◆
Regional
American
Lunch: $6-$10   Dinner: $8-$14
Phone: 910/777-0032
Location: Just n in Stratford Place Shopping Center off I-40 (business) exit. 109 S Stratford 27106.
Hours: 11:15 am-10:30 pm, Fri & Sat-11 pm, Sun 10:45 am-10 pm. Closed: 11/26 & 12/25. **Features:** health
conscious menu; cocktails & lounge. Art Deco dining room; grill room & bar. Casual & upscale. Regional &
seasonal menu changes monthly. **Cards:** AE, DI, MC, VI.

MARCELLA'S
◆◆
Italian
Lunch: $8-$15   Dinner: $8-$15
Phone: 910/759-9553
Location: 0.3 mi e on North Point Blvd from jct University Pkwy. 7843 North Point Blvd 27106. **Hours:** 11
am-2 & 5-9:30 pm, Sat 5 pm-10 pm. Closed major holidays & Sun. **Features:** children's menu; carryout;
cocktails. Homemade sauces, pasta & dessert with interesting soup of the day. Very popular with attentive
service. **Cards:** AE, CB, DI, MC, VI.

MICHAEL'S   Historical
◆◆◆
Continental
Dinner: $22-$26
Phone: 910/777-0000
Location: Broad St exit off I-40; 0.5 mi n to 5th then just w. 848 W 5th St 27101. **Hours:** 5:30 pm-11 pm.
Closed: Sun, 11/26 & 12/25. **Reservations:** suggested. **Features:** cocktails & lounge; entertainment; a la
carte. Chef's specials with creative flair served in a relaxed atmosphere. Beautifully restored Georgian
mansion built in 1909, also patio dining. French American entrees. **Cards:** AE, DI, MC, VI.

NOBLE'S GRILLE
◆◆◆
Continental
Lunch: $7-$12   Dinner: $19-$30
Phone: 910/777-8477
Location: Just s on Knollwood from I-40 (business), exit 3A; in the Nations Bank building. 380 Knollwood St
27103. **Hours:** 11:30 am-2:30 & 5:30-10 pm, Fri & Sat-11 pm. Closed major holidays & Sun.
Features: carryout; cocktails; a la carte. French-Mediterranean flavors with California style grilling in open
oak-hickory wood fire ovens. Home made soup, dessert, bread & sauces. Menu changes daily. Live jazz band Mon night.
Cards: AE, DI, MC, VI.

PAUL'S FINE ITALIAN DINING
◆◆◆
Italian
Lunch: $6-$10   Dinner: $10-$18
Phone: 910/768-2645
Location: Silas Creek Pkwy N, exit off I-40 business route, 2.8 mi to Robinhood Rd, then 1 mi nw; in
Robinhood Center. 3443-B Robinhood Rd 27106. **Hours:** 11:30 am-2 & 5-10 pm, Fri-11 pm, Sat 5 pm-11
pm, Sun 4:30 pm-9:30 pm. Closed: 1/1, 11/26, 12/24, 12/25 & 7/1-7/14. **Reservations:** suggested.
Features: carryout; cocktails; a la carte. In small, intimate & relaxing dining room. Homemade pasta, soup, sauces &
dessert. Very popular. **Cards:** AE, CB, DI, MC, VI.

RYAN'S RESTAURANT
◆◆◆
Continental
Dinner: $18-$25
Phone: 910/724-6132
Location: Cherry St-Downtown exit off I-40 business route, 2.3 mi n, then 2 blks w on Coliseum Dr. 719
Coliseum Dr 27106. **Hours:** 5 pm-10 pm, Fri & Sat-10:30 pm. Closed major holidays & Sun except during
special events. **Reservations:** suggested. **Features:** cocktails & lounge. Fine dining in rustic & comfortable
ambience overlooking wooded stream. Well-established & popular. Extensive wine selection. Live lobster tank. **Cards:** AE,
CB, DI, MC, VI.

SALEM TAVERN DINING ROOM Historical **Lunch:** $5-$8   **Dinner:** $11-$22   **Phone:** 910/748-8585
◆◆ **Location:** In Old Salem; follow signs off I-40 business route or US 52. 736 S Main St 27101. **Hours:** 11:30
American am-2 & 5-9 pm, Fri-9:30 pm, Sat 11:30 am-2:30 & 5-9:30 pm, Sun 11:30 am-2 pm. Closed: 12/25, 1/1-1/9 &
Sun in Jan & Feb. **Reservations:** suggested; for dinner. **Features:** early bird specials; cocktails. Service in
Moravian-style dining rooms by costumed staff. Outdoor arbor dining 4/1-10/31. 15% service charge. **Cards:** AE, MC, VI.
[X]

THE VINEYARDS RESTAURANT   **Lunch:** $7-$9   **Dinner:** $14-$19   **Phone:** 919/748-0269
◆◆◆ **Location:** Silas Creek Pkwy exit n off I-40, 3.5 mi to Reynolda Village, then just e; in Reynolda Village below art
American gallery. 120 Reynolda Village 27106. **Hours:** 11 am-10 pm. Closed major holidays & Sun.
Reservations: suggested. **Features:** children's menu; carryout; cocktails. Patio dining weather permitting.
Homemade soup, sauce, dressing & dessert. **Cards:** AE, MC, VI.
[X]

ZEVELY HOUSE Historical   **Dinner:** $18-$24   **Phone:** 919/725-6666
(AAA) **Location:** Broad St exit off I-40, n to 4th, then 2 blks w. 901 W 4th St 27101. **Hours:** 5:30 pm-9 pm, Sun 11
am-2 pm. Closed major holidays. **Reservations:** suggested. **Features:** carryout; cocktails & lounge.
◆◆ Restored early 19th-century house, also garden dining weather permitting. **Cards:** AE, DI, MC, VI. [X]
American

WRIGHTSVILLE BEACH—2,900

LODGINGS

BLOCKADE RUNNER HOTEL & CONFERENCE CENTER   **Phone:** 910/256-2251
(AAA) [SAVE] 6/12-8/15 [BP]   2P/1B: $211- 299 2P/2B: $201- 289 XP: $25   F12
5/8-6/11 & 8/16-9/19 [BP] 2P/1B: $201- 273 2P/2B: $191- 263 XP: $25   F12
◆◆◆ 3/27-5/7 & 9/20-10/17 [BP] 2P/1B: $147- 208 2P/2B: $137- 198 XP: $25   F12
Hotel 12/1-3/26 & 10/18-11/30 [BP] 2P/1B: $100- 147 2P/2B: $90- 137 XP: $25   F12
Location: 1 mi s on US 76; 0.5 mi s on S Lumina Ave. 275 Waynick Blvd 28480 (PO Box 555)
Fax: 910/256-5502. **Terms:** Reserv deposit, 3 day notice; weekly/monthly rates; package plans; 3 night min stay, weekends
in season; no pets. **Facility:** 150 rooms. Rooms with oceanfront or harbor view, some with oceanfront balcony. 2-7 stories; in
terior corridors; beach, sauna, whirlpool. Fee: golf privileges; boat dock. **Dining & Entertainment:** Restaurant; 6:30 am-10
pm; $10-$18; cocktails/lounge. **Services:** valet laundry; area transportation, on island; valet parking. **Recreation:** children's
program in season; swimming. Fee: sailboats, sailboards, surf fishing, tourboat; bicycles. **All Rooms:** free & pay movies,
refrigerators. **Some Rooms:** coffeemakers. **Cards:** AE, CB, DI, DS, MC, VI. **Special Amenities: Free breakfast and free
local telephone calls.** (See color ad p 425)   [icons]

SUMMER SANDS MOTEL   Rates Subject to Change   **Phone:** 910/256-4175
◆◆ Fri & Sat 5/24-9/1   2P/1B: $170   2P/2B: $170   XP: $10   F18
Fri & Sat 3/29-5/23,
Apartment Sun-Thurs 5/24-9/1 & Fri &
Motel Sat 9/2-11/3   2P/1B: $130   2P/2B: $130   XP: $10   F18
Fri & Sat 12/1-3/28,
Sun-Thurs 3/29-5/23,
9/2-11/3 & 11/4-11/30   2P/1B: $105   2P/2B: $105   XP: $10   F18
Sun-Thurs 12/1-3/28 &
11/4-11/30   2P/1B: $90   2P/2B: $90   XP: $10   F18
Location: Just e of US 76, across bridge. 104 S Lumina Ave 28480 (PO Box 544). Fax: 910/256-8691. **Terms:** Reserv
deposit; no pets. **Facility:** 32 rooms. 4 stories; exterior corridors. **All Rooms:** kitchens, free movies. **Cards:** AE, DI, MC, VI.
[icons]

THE SURF SUITES   **Phone:** 910/256-2271
(AAA) [SAVE] 5/26-9/3   1P: $150- 175 2P/1B: $150- 175   XP: $10
3/15-5/25 & 9/4-11/30 1P: $105- 140 2P/1B: $105- 140   XP: $10
◆◆ 12/1-3/14   1P: $60- 70 2P/1B: $60- 70   XP: $10
Condo Motel **Location:** 2 mi s on US 76. 711 S Lumina Ave 28480. Fax: 910/256-1206. **Terms:** Reserv deposit, 3 day
notice; 2 night min stay, weekends in season; no pets. **Facility:** 46 rooms. 4 stories; exterior corridors.
All Rooms: kitchens. **Cards:** AE, CB, DI, DS, MC, VI.   [icons]

WATERWAY LODGE   **Phone:** 910/256-3771
(AAA) [SAVE] 5/16-9/30   1P: $100- 130 2P/1B: $100- 130 2P/2B: $100- 130 XP: $5   F11
4/1-5/15   1P: $90- 110 2P/1B: $90- 110 2P/2B: $90- 110 XP: $5   F11
◆◆ 12/1-3/31 & 10/1-11/30 1P: $60- 80 2P/1B: $60- 80 2P/2B: $60- 80 XP: $5   F11
Motel **Location:** From SR 132 & US 76, 4.7 mi e. (7246 Wrightsville Ave, WILMINGTON, 28403)
Fax: 910/256-6916. **Terms:** Weekly/monthly rates; 2 night min stay, weekends; weekend rates avail; pets,
$15 extra charge, in selected rooms. **Facility:** 40 rooms. Adjacent to Intracoastal Waterway, a variety of room decor. Weekend
rates higher; 2-4 stories; exterior corridors. **Dining:** Dining room nearby. **All Rooms:** microwaves, free movies, refrigerators.
Some Rooms: coffeemakers, 15 efficiencies, radios. **Cards:** AE, DS, MC, VI. **Special Amenities: Free local telephone
calls.**   [icons]

RESTAURANT

THE BRIDGE TENDER   **Lunch:** $6-$8   **Dinner:** $16-$24   **Phone:** 910/256-4519
◆◆ **Location:** Just s of US 76 & drawbridge on Inland Waterway. Airlie Rd on the sound 28480. **Hours:** 11:30
Seafood am-2 & 5:30-10 pm, Fri-11 pm, Sat 5:30 pm-11 pm, Sun 5:30 pm-10 pm. Closed: 1/1, 11/26 & 12/25.
Features: casual dress; cocktails & lounge. Casual dining. Overlooking the Intracoastal Waterway. Large
educational wine selection. **Cards:** AE, DI, DS, MC, VI.   [X]

YADKINVILLE—2,500

LODGING

SLEEP INN   Rates Subject to Change   **Phone:** 910/679-5000
◆◆ 2/1-2/28, 4/1-4/30, 6/1-8/31 &
Motel 10/1-10/31 [CP]   1P: $75 2P/1B: $75 2P/2B: $75 XP: $5   F18
12/1-1/31, 3/1-3/31, 5/1-5/31,
9/1-9/30 & 11/1-11/30 [CP] 1P: $45 2P/1B: $49 2P/2B: $49 XP: $5   F18
Location: Intersection of US 601 & 421. 220 Sharon Dr 27055 (PO Box 1175). Fax: 910/679-5008. **Terms:** Sr. discount; no
pets. **Facility:** 48 rooms. 2 stories; interior corridors. **All Rooms:** free movies. **Cards:** AE, CB, DI, DS, MC, VI.
Roll in showers.   [icons]

SOUTH CAROLINA

AREA CODE CHANGE - The Coastal and Pee Dee regions will change their area code from 803 to 843 effective March 22, 1998, when permissive dialing goes into effect. After September 27, 1998 only the 843 area code will be effective for these regions. Towns that will be located in the new area code will include Beaufort, Charleston, Darlington, Dillon, Florence, Georgetown, Hartsville, Hilton Head, McBee, McClellanville, McColl, Moncks Corner, Mount Pleasant, Murrells Inlet, Myrtle Beach, Pawleys Island, Sullivans Island, Summerville and West Myrtle Beach.

ABBEVILLE—5,800

RESTAURANT

TIMOTHY'S
◆◆
Continental

Lunch: $5-$7   **Dinner:** $12-$17   **Phone:** 864/459-9625
Location: Center, corner S Main St; in The Belmont Inn. 106 E Pickens St 29620. **Hours:** 11:30 am-2 & 5:30-9 pm. Closed major holidays & Sun. **Reservations:** suggested. **Features:** dressy casual; cocktails & lounge; a la carte. Serving regional southern cuisine in fine surroundings. Lunch & dinner served on veranda, weather permitting. Smoke free premises. **Cards:** AE, DI, DS, MC, VI.
⊠

AIKEN—19,900

LODGINGS

BEST WESTERN EXECUTIVE INN
◆◆
Motel

	Rates Subject to Change			**Phone:** 803/649-3968
4/1-4/16 [CP]	1P: $125	2P/1B: $125	2P/2B: $125	
12/1-3/31 & 4/17-11/30 [CP]	1P: $42	2P/1B: $44	2P/2B: $48	XP: $4 F17

Location: 2 mi w on US 1 & 78. 3560 Richland Ave W 29801. Fax: 803/649-3968. **Terms:** Sr. discount; no pets. **Facility:** 60 rooms. 2 stories; exterior corridors. **All Rooms:** free movies. **Cards:** AE, CB, DI, DS, MC, VI.
📶 CTV ⊠ D

COMFORT INN & SUITES
🆑 SAVE
◆◆◆
Motel

				Phone: 803/641-1100
All Year [CP]	1P: $44	2P/1B: $49	2P/2B: $54	XP: $5 F18

Location: 2.3 mi w on US 1 & 78. 3608 Richland Ave W 29801. Fax: 803/641-1100. **Terms:** Package plans; small pets only, $5 extra charge. **Facility:** 68 rooms. Large meeting space, bright contemporary decor. 2 stories; exterior corridors; whirlpool. **Dining:** Restaurant nearby. **Services:** valet laundry. **All Rooms:** coffeemakers, microwaves, free movies, refrigerators, VCP's. **Some Rooms:** 2 efficiencies, whirlpools. **Cards:** AE, DI, DS, JCB, MC, VI. **Special Amenities: Free breakfast and free local telephone calls.**
🛏 🖥 🍴 🖨 CTV ⊠ 🌀 D S

DAYS INN
◆◆
Motel
MC, VI.

	Rates Subject to Change			**Phone:** 803/642-5692
All Year [CP]	1P: $38	2P/1B: $42	2P/2B: $42	XP: $4 F18

Location: Jct I-20, exit 22 & US 1. 2654 Columbia Hwy 29801. Fax: 803/642-5692. **Terms:** Sr. discount; no pets. **Facility:** 78 rooms. 2 stories; exterior corridors. **All Rooms:** free movies. **Cards:** AE, CB, DI, DS, JCB,
CTV ⊠ D

DAYS INN-DOWNTOWN
🆑 SAVE
◆◆
Motel

				Phone: 803/649-5524
All Year [CP]	1P: $32- 34	2P/1B: $36- 38	2P/2B: $36- 38	XP: $4 F17

Location: 0.5 mi w on US 1 & 78. 1204 Richland Ave W 29801. Fax: 803/649-5524. **Terms:** Reserv deposit; weekly/monthly rates; small pets only, $5 extra charge. **Facility:** 42 rooms. 2 attractive buildings on a cozy lot. Variety of room decor & furnishings. Many units with 2 double beds. 2 stories; exterior corridors. **All Rooms:** microwaves, free movies, refrigerators. **Cards:** AE, CB, DI, DS, MC, VI. **Special Amenities: Free breakfast and free newspaper.**
🛏 🖥 🍴 CTV ⊠ D

HOLIDAY INN EXPRESS
◆◆◆
Motel

	Rates Subject to Change			**Phone:** 803/648-0999
All Year [CP]	1P: $59	2P/1B: $59	2P/2B: $59	XP: $5 F18

Location: From US 78 & US 1, 2 mi s on SR 19 off Whiskey/SR 19. 155 Colony Pkwy 29803. Fax: 803/648-9799. **Terms:** Sr. discount; no pets. **Facility:** 100 rooms. 2 stories; exterior corridors. **All Rooms:** free movies. **Cards:** AE, CB, DI, DS, MC, VI.
Roll in showers. 🖥 CTV ⊠ D S

HOLIDAY INN EXPRESS
◆◆◆
Motel

	Rates Subject to Change			**Phone:** 803/502-0900
All Year [CP]	1P: $55	2P/1B: $60	2P/2B: $60	XP: $5 F18

Location: Jct I-20, exit 22 & US 1. 110 E Frontage Rd 29801. Fax: 803/502-0903. **Terms:** No pets. **Facility:** 60 rooms. 2 stories; exterior corridors. **All Rooms:** free movies. **Cards:** AE, DI, DS, MC, VI.
Roll in showers. 🖥 CTV ⊠ D S

RAMADA LIMITED
🆑 SAVE
◆◆
Motel

				Phone: 803/648-6821
All Year [CP]	1P: $30- 34	2P/1B: $36- 40	2P/2B: $36- 40	XP: $5 F12

Location: 0.8 mi w on US 1. 1850 Richland Ave 29801. Fax: 803/643-8546. **Terms:** Reserv deposit, 3 day notice, handling fee imposed; weekly/monthly rates; pets, $4 extra charge. **Facility:** 80 rooms. Family-oriented property. 2 stories; exterior corridors. **Dining:** Restaurant nearby. **All Rooms:** free movies. **Some Rooms:** whirlpools. **Fee:** microwaves, refrigerators, VCP's. **Cards:** AE, DI, DS, MC, VI. **Special Amenities: Free breakfast and free local telephone calls.**
🛏 🖥 🍴 CTV ⊠ D

THE WILLCOX INN
🆑
◆◆◆
Historic
Country Inn

	Rates Subject to Change			**Phone:** 803/649-1377
12/1-5/31 & 9/15-11/30	1P: $95- 115	2P/1B: $105- 135	2P/2B: $105- 135	XP: $15 F12
Mon-Thurs 6/1-9/14	1P: $90- 115	2P/1B: $92- 117	2P/2B: $92- 117	XP: $15 F12
Fri-Sun 6/1-9/14	1P: $85- 110	2P/1B: $85- 110	2P/2B: $85- 110	XP: $15 F12

Location: Downtown, at corner of Colleton Ave & Whiskey Rd, SR 19; 2 blks s of US 78, Richland Ave. 100 Colleton Ave SW 29801. Fax: 803/643-0971. **Terms:** Small pets only. **Facility:** 30 rooms. 3 stories; interior corridors. **Dining:** Dining room; 7 am-2 & 5-9:30 pm, Sat 8 am-10 & 5-9:30 pm, Sun 8 am-2 pm; $10-$25. **Cards:** AE, DI, DS, MC, VI.
🛏 CTV ⊠ D

RESTAURANT

THE WEST SIDE BOWERY   **Lunch:** $5-$9   **Dinner:** $7-$15   **Phone:** 803/648-2900
◆◆   **Location:** Off Park Ave in Aiken's historic "downtown alley area". 151 Bee Ln 29801. **Hours:** 11:15 am-10
American   pm. Closed: Sun, 1/1, 7/4 & 12/25. **Reservations:** suggested. **Features:** No A/C; casual dress; children's
menu; early bird specials; carryout; cocktails & lounge; street parking. A comfortable atmosphere with wide
variety of food; including meat, pasta & fresh fish entrees. **Cards:** AE, CB, DI, DS, MC, VI.   ⊠

ALLENDALE—4,400

LODGING

VILLAGER LODGE   **Phone:** 803/584-2184
ⒶⒶⒶ [SAVE]   All Year   1P: $30   2P/1B: $35   XP: $5   F12
◆◆   **Location:** On US 301. 671 N Main St 29810. **Fax:** 803/584-4899. **Terms:** Reserv deposit; small pets only,
Motel $10 extra charge. **Facility:** 30 rooms. 1 story; exterior corridors. **All Rooms:** free movies.
Some Rooms: microwaves, refrigerators. **Cards:** AE, DS, MC, VI. **Special Amenities:** Free breakfast and
preferred room (subject to availability with advanced reservations).   🐾 ⓒⓉⓋ ⊠ Ⓓ

ANDERSON—26,200

LODGINGS

CAPE COD INN   **Phone:** 864/224-4464
ⒶⒶⒶ [SAVE]   All Year [CP]   1P: $35- 43   2P/1B: $40   2P/2B: $46   XP: $3   F12
◆◆   **Location:** 0.5 mi s of I-85, exit 19A; on US 76, SR 28 & US 178. 4020 Clemson Blvd 29621.
Motel   **Fax:** 864/224-4464. **Terms:** No pets. **Facility:** 40 rooms. 2 stories; exterior corridors. **Services:** valet laundry.
All Rooms: free movies. **Some Rooms:** whirlpools. **Cards:** AE, CB, DI, DS, MC, VI.   ⓒⓉⓋ ⊠ Ⓓ

DAYS INN   Rates Subject to Change   **Phone:** 864/375-0375
◆◆   All Year [CP]   1P: $57- 82   2P/1B: $65- 89   2P/2B: $65- 89   XP: $7   F18
Motel   **Location:** I-85 exit 19A, US 76, se corner. 1007 Smith Mill Rd 29625. **Fax:** 864/225-0010. **Terms:** Small pets
only. **Facility:** 54 rooms. Whirlpool rms, $89-$95 for 2 persons; 2 stories; exterior corridors. **All Rooms:** free
movies. **Cards:** AE, CB, DI, DS, JCB, MC, VI.   🐾 🛆 ⓒⓉⓋ Ⓛ ⊠ Ⓓ

HOLIDAY INN   **Phone:** 864/226-6051
ⒶⒶⒶ [SAVE]   All Year   1P: $59- 89   2P/1B: $65- 95   2P/2B: $65- 95   XP: $6   F18
◆◆◆   **Location:** 2 mi n on US 76, SR 28 & US 178; 3.5 mi s of I-85, exit 19A. 3025 N Main St 29621.
Motor Inn   **Fax:** 864/964-9145. **Terms:** Monthly rates; package plans; small pets only. **Facility:** 130 rooms. Variety of room
decors, some deluxe units. 2 stories; exterior corridors. **Dining & Entertainment:** Dining room; 6:30 am-2 &
5:30-10 pm; $8-$15; cocktails/lounge. **Services:** valet laundry. **All Rooms:** coffeemakers, free & pay movies.
Some Rooms: microwaves, refrigerators. **Cards:** AE, CB, DI, DS, MC, VI. **Special Amenities:** Early check-in/late
check-out and free room upgrade (subject to availability with advanced reservations). *(See color ad below)*
🐾 🛆 🄴 ⓒⓉⓋ ⊠ 🄳 Ⓓ

HOLIDAY INN EXPRESS

(AAA) [SAVE]	All Year [BP]	1P: $59 2P/1B: $59 2P/2B: $59 XP: $6 F18

Phone: 864/231-0231

Location: I-85 & SR 81, exit 27. 103 Anderson Business Park 29621. **Fax:** 864/231-8799. **Terms:** Small pets only. **Facility:** 64 rooms. 13 whirlpool rms, $79-$99; 3 stories; interior corridors. **Dining:** Coffee shop nearby.
◆◆◆ **All Rooms:** free movies, combo or shower baths. **Cards:** AE, CB, DI, DS, JCB, MC, VI. **Special Amenities:**
Motel Free breakfast and free local telephone calls. *(See color ad p 432)*

[symbols]

THE JAMESON INN   Rates Subject to Change   **Phone:** 864/375-9800
◆◆ All Year [CP]   1P: $50   2P/1B: $54   2P/2B: $54   XP: $4   F12
Motel **Location:** I-85 exit 19B, just nw. 128 Interstate Blvd 29621. **Fax:** 864/375-0329. **Terms:** No pets. **Facility:** 60 rooms. 1 bedroom suite $95 for up to 4 persons; 2 stories; exterior corridors. **All Rooms:** free movies.
Cards: AE, CB, DI, DS, MC, VI.

[symbols]

LA QUINTA INN   **Phone:** 864/225-3721
(AAA) [SAVE] All Year [CP]   1P: $49- 55   2P/1B: $54- 60   2P/2B: $54- 60   XP: $6   F18
Location: 2.5 mi s I-85, exit 19A. 3430 Clemson Blvd 29621. **Fax:** 864/225-7789. **Terms:** Small pets only.
◆◆◆ **Facility:** 100 rooms. Large courtyard. Comfortable guest rooms with contemporary decor. 2 stories; exterior
Motel corridors. **Dining:** Restaurant nearby. **Services:** valet laundry. **All Rooms:** free movies, combo or shower baths. **Some Rooms:** Fee: microwaves, refrigerators. **Cards:** AE, CB, DI, DS, MC, VI. **Special Amenities:**
Free breakfast and free local telephone calls.   Roll in showers. [symbols]

QUALITY INN   **Phone:** 864/226-1000
(AAA) [SAVE] All Year [CP]   1P: $49   2P/1B: $49   2P/2B: $49   XP: $7   F18
◆ **Location:** 2 mi s I-85, exit 19A. 3509 Clemson Blvd 29621. **Fax:** 864/261-9246. **Terms:** Pets, $10 dep req.
◆◆◆ **Facility:** 121 rooms. 4 stories; interior corridors; sauna. **Dining:** Restaurant nearby. **Services:** valet laundry.
Motel **All Rooms:** coffeemakers, free & pay movies. **Some Rooms:** microwaves, refrigerators, whirlpools.
Fee: VCP's. **Cards:** AE, CB, DI, DS, JCB, MC, VI. **Special Amenities:** Free breakfast and free local
telephone calls. *(See color ad below)*

[symbols]

ROYAL AMERICAN MOTOR INN   Rates Subject to Change   **Phone:** 864/226-7236
(AAA) All Year   1P: $33   2P/1B: $36   2P/2B: $38   XP: $4   F12
Location: I-85 exit 19A, US 76. 4515 Clemson Blvd 29621. **Terms:** Pets. **Facility:** 52 rooms. 1 suite with refrigerator & microwave; 3 stories, no elevator; exterior corridors. **All Rooms:** free movies. **Cards:** AE, MC, VI.
Motel

[symbols]

SUPER 8 MOTEL   Rates Subject to Change   **Phone:** 864/225-8384
◆◆ All Year   1P: $39- 45   2P/1B: $45- 49   2P/2B: $49- 53   XP: $5   F12
Motel **Location:** From I-85 exit 19A, 2 mi s on Clemson Rd. 3302 Cinema Ave 29621. **Fax:** 864/225-8384.
Terms: Sr. discount; reserv deposit, 7 day notice; small pets only. **Facility:** 62 rooms. 3 stories, no elevator;
interior corridors. **All Rooms:** free & pay movies. **Cards:** AE, CB, DI, DS, MC, VI.

[symbols]

RESTAURANT

1109 SOUTH MAIN RESTAURANT   Historical   **Dinner:** $13-$18   **Phone:** 864/225-1109
◆◆◆ **Location:** On SR 28, corner E Hampton; in Evergreen Inn. 1109 S Main St 29621. **Hours:** 6 pm-10 pm.
Continental Closed major holidays, Sun & Mon. **Reservations:** suggested. **Features:** cocktails & lounge; a la carte.
Gourmet entrees prepared by skilled Swiss chef/owner & served in elegant restored 1906 Greek Revival
mansion. Separate dining rooms for semi-formal or casual dining. **Cards:** AE, DI, DS, MC, VI.   [symbol]

BARNWELL—5,300

LODGING

DAYS INN   Rates Subject to Change   **Phone:** 803/541-5000
◆◆◆ All Year [CP]   1P: $49   2P/1B: $55   2P/2B: $55   XP: $5   F18
Motel **Location:** On 64, 0.5 mi w of jct SR 64 & 278. 1020 Dunbarton Blvd 29812. **Fax:** 803/541-5000. **Terms:** No pets. **Facility:** 31 rooms. 2 stories; exterior corridors. **All Rooms:** free movies. **Cards:** AE, DI, DS, MC, VI.
Roll in showers. [symbols]

BATESBURG-LEESVILLE—6,100

LODGING

THE ABLE HOUSE INN   Rates Subject to Change   **Phone:** 803/532-2763
◆◆◆ All Year [CP]   1P: $60   2P/1B: $65   2P/2B: $65   XP: $10   D12
Bed & **Location:** On Leesville side; 1.6 mi e of jct US 178. 244 E Columbia Ave 29070. **Terms:** Age restrictions
Breakfast may apply; check-in 4 pm; reserv deposit, 14 day notice; no pets. **Facility:** 5 rooms. 2 stories; interior corridors; designated smoking area. **Cards:** MC, VI.   [symbols]

BEAUFORT—9,600

LODGINGS

BATTERY CREEK INN
Phone: 803/521-1441
(AAA) (SAVE) All Year   1P: $70   2P/1B: $70   XP: $8   F13
◆◆   **Location:** From US 21, 6 mi on SR 280, follow signs to Paris Island, opposite main gate. 19 Marina Village
Suite Motel   Ln 29902. Fax: 803/524-7380. **Terms:** Reserv deposit, 3 day notice; weekly/monthly rates; pets, $50 extra charge. **Facility:** 20 rooms. All units with view of tidal creek. Located in quiet area. 2 stories; exterior corridors. Fee: marina. **Services:** valet laundry. **All Rooms:** coffeemakers, kitchens, free movies, refrigerators. **Cards:** AE, DI, DS, MC, VI. **Special Amenities: Early check-in/late check-out and preferred room (subject to availability with advanced reservations).**   🛏️ CTV ✕ D

BEAUFORT INN
Phone: 803/521-9000
(AAA) (SAVE) All Year [BP]   2P/1B: $125- 195   XP: $20
◆◆◆◆   **Location:** From US 21/Carteret St, just s. 809 Port Republic St 29902. Fax: 803/521-9500. **Terms:** Age
Historic Bed   restrictions may apply; weekly rates; package plans; no pets. **Facility:** 13 rooms. Warm & inviting rooms with
& Breakfast   the aura of a grand plantation home. The rooms are all differently furnished & tastefully decorated. Closed 12/24 & 12/25; 3 stories; interior corridors; designated smoking area. **Dining:** Restaurant; afternoon tea; also, Beaufort Inn Restaurant, see separate listing. **Services:** complimentary evening beverages; valet laundry. **Recreation:** jogging. Fee: bicycles. **All Rooms:** honor bars, coffeemakers, combo or shower baths, VCP's. **Some Rooms:** whirlpools. **Cards:** AE, DS, MC, VI. **Special Amenities: Free breakfast and free newspaper.**   🛏️ CTV 🛋️ ✕ D S

BEAUFORT LODGE
Phone: 803/524-5600
(AAA) (SAVE) Thurs. [CP]   1P: $65   2P/1B: $65   2P/2B: $65
     Wed. [CP]   1P: $50   2P/1B: $50   2P/2B: $50
     Fri-Tues [CP]   1P: $45   2P/1B: $45   2P/2B: $45
Motel   **Location:** On SR 281, 3.8 mi s on US 21. 1630 Ribaut Rd 29935. Fax: 803/524-5688. **Terms:** Reserv deposit; weekly rates; no pets. **Facility:** 12 rooms. Small cozy rooms that are nicely decorated. 1 story; exterior corridors. **Dining:** Restaurant nearby. **All Rooms:** combo or shower baths. **Some Rooms:** microwaves, refrigerators. **Cards:** AE, DS, MC, VI. **Special Amenities: Free breakfast and free local telephone calls.**   🏊 CTV ✕ D

BEST WESTERN SEA ISLAND INN
Phone: 803/522-2090
(AAA) (SAVE) 3/1-11/30 [CP]   2P/1B: $79- 99   XP: $10   F12
     12/1-2/28 [CP]   2P/1B: $71- 89   XP: $10   F12
◆◆◆   **Location:** Bay & New Castle sts. 1015 Bay St 29902. Fax: 803/521-4858. **Terms:** Reserv deposit; no pets.
Motel   **Facility:** 43 rooms. Enjoy breakfast in "The room by the Bay". 2 stories; exterior corridors. **Dining:** Restaurant nearby. **Recreation:** jogging. Rental: bicycles. **All Rooms:** free movies. **Some Rooms** Fee: refrigerators. **Cards:** AE, CB, DI, DS, MC, VI.   🏊 🛏️ 🏋️ CTV ✕ 🐾 D

COMFORT INN
Phone: 803/525-9360
(AAA) (SAVE) All Year [CP]   1P: $65   2P/1B: $75   2P/2B: $75   XP: $5   F18
◆◆   **Location:** 3 mi n on US 21, 0.5 mi s of SR 170. 2227 Hwy 21 29902. Fax: 803/525-1529. **Terms:** Reserv
Motel   deposit, 3 day notice; no pets. **Facility:** 79 rooms. 2 stories; exterior corridors; sauna, whirlpool, share facilities with motel next door. **Dining & Entertainment:** Cocktail lounge. **All Rooms:** microwaves, free movies, refrigerators. **Cards:** AE, CB, DI, DS, JCB, MC, VI. **Special Amenities: Free breakfast and free local telephone calls.**   🏊 🛏️ CTV ✕ 🐾 D

CUTHBERT HOUSE INN
Phone: 803/521-1315
(AAA) (SAVE) All Year [BP]   1P: $135- 155   2P/1B: $155- 175   2P/2B: $165- 175   XP: $25
◆◆◆   **Location:** Town center. 1203 Bay St 29902-5401. Fax: 803/521-1314. **Terms:** Check-in 4 pm; reserv
Bed &   deposit, 7 day notice; no pets. **Facility:** 5 rooms. A historic waterfront bed & breakfast built in 1790 with period
Breakfast   furniture. Enjoy the sunset refreshments. Handling fee imposed; 3 stories; interior corridors; smoke free premises. **Dining:** Restaurant nearby. **Services:** complimentary evening beverages. **Recreation:** jogging. Fee: bicycles. **All Rooms:** free movies, refrigerators, combo or shower baths. **Cards:** AE, DS, MC, VI. **Special Amenities: Free local telephone calls and free room upgrade (subject to availability with advanced reservations).**   CTV ✕ D

DAYS INN-PORT ROYAL   Rates Subject to Change   Phone: 803/524-1551
◆◆   Wed & Thurs [CP]   1P: $82   2P/1B: $82   2P/2B: $82   XP: $5   F1
Motel   Sun-Tues & Fri & Sat [CP]   1P: $52   2P/1B: $60   2P/2B: $60   XP: $5   F1
     Location: On SR 281, 4 mi s of US 21. 1660 S Ribaut 29935. Fax: 803/524-1551. **Terms:** Sr. discount; pets, $20 extra charge. **Facility:** 150 rooms. 2 stories; exterior corridors. **All Rooms:** free movies. **Cards:** AE, CB, DI, DS, JCB, MC, VI.   🛏️ 🏊 CTV ✕ D

HOLIDAY INN OF BEAUFORT   Rates Subject to Change   Phone: 803/524-2144
◆◆◆   All Year   1P: $69   2P/1B: $69   2P/2B: $69   XP: $8   F1
Motor Inn   **Location:** 2.5 mi nw on US 21 at Lovejoy St. 2001 Boundary St 29902 (PO Box 1008). Fax: 803/524-2144. **Terms:** Pets, $20 extra charge. **Facility:** 152 rooms. Rates higher Wed & Thurs; 4 stories; exterior corridors. **Dining:** Restaurant; 6 am-2 & 5-10 pm; $6-$16. **All Rooms:** free movies. **Cards:** AE, CB, DI, DS, JCB, MC, VI.   🛏️ 🏊 CTV ✕ D

HOWARD JOHNSON EXPRESS INN
Phone: 803/524-6025
(AAA) (SAVE) All Year [CP]   1P: $55- 60   2P/1B: $65   2P/2B: $65   XP: $7   F1
     Location: On US 21, 1.3 mi n of SR 170. 3651 Trask 29902. Fax: 803/524-2027. **Terms:** Weekly rates;
◆◆◆   small pets only. **Facility:** 63 rooms. Some rooms with tidal creek views. 2 stories; interior/exterior corridors.
Motel   **All Rooms:** free movies. **Some Rooms:** microwaves, refrigerators. Fee: VCP's. **Cards:** AE, CB, DI, DS, JCB, MC, VI. **Special Amenities: Free breakfast and free local telephone calls.**   🛏️ 🏊 CTV ✕ D

LORD CARTERET MOTEL
Phone: 803/521-1122
(AAA) (SAVE) All Year   1P: $35- 45   2P/1B: $40- 45   2P/2B: $45- 50
     Location: On Business US 21. 301 Carteret St 29902. **Terms:** Reserv deposit; no pets. **Facility:** 25 rooms.
◆   efficiencies, $10 extra charge; 2 stories; exterior corridors. **All Rooms:** free movies. **Cards:** AE, MC, VI.
Motel   CTV ✕ D

RAMADA LIMITED   Phone: 803/524-3322
🔺 SAVE   All Year   1P: $50- 55 2P/1B: $55- 65 2P/2B: $55- 65 XP: $7   F18
◆◆◆   **Location:** 3.5 mi n on US 21, or 0.3 mi n of SR 170 & US 21. 2448 Boundary St 29903 (PO Box 4236).
Motel   Fax: 803/524-7264. **Terms:** Reserv deposit; weekly/monthly rates; weekend rates avail; no pets. **Facility:** 62
rooms. 2 stories; exterior corridors. **Dining:** Restaurant nearby. **All Rooms:** free movies. **Some Rooms:**
Fee: whirlpools. **Cards:** AE, CB, DI, DS, MC, VI. **Special Amenities:** Free local telephone calls and
preferred room (subject to availability with advanced reservations).   📶 🛎 CTV ✖ D

THE RHETT HOUSE INN   Guaranteed Rates   Phone: 803/524-9030
◆◆◆◆   All Year [BP]   1P: $125- 225 2P/1B: $125- 225 2P/2B: $125- 225 XP: $25
Historic   **Location:** Corner of Craven & New Castle sts. 1009 Craven St 29902. Fax: 803/524-1310. **Terms:** Age
Country Inn restrictions may apply; reserv deposit, 10 day notice; no pets. **Facility:** 17 rooms. 11 whirlpool rms, extra
charge. Handling fee imposed; 3 stories; exterior corridors; smoke free premises. **Dining:** Restaurant; also,
Caroline's on Craven, see separate listing. **All Rooms:** free movies. **Cards:** AE, MC, VI.   CTV ✖ D

TWOSUNS INN BED & BREAKFAST   Rates Subject to Change   Phone: 803/522-1122
◆◆◆   12/17-12/31 & 2/25-11/30
Historic Bed [BP]   1P: $105- 120 2P/1B: $120- 135 2P/2B: $120- 135 XP: $22
& Breakfast   12/1-12/16 & 1/1-2/24 [BP] 1P: $85- 95 2P/1B: $95- 105 2P/2B: $95- 105 XP: $22
Location: Between Hamar & Adventure sts. 1705 Bay St 29902. Fax: 803/522-1122. **Terms:** Sr. discount;
age restrictions may apply; reserv deposit; no pets. **Facility:** 5 rooms. 2 stories; interior corridors; smoke free premises.
Cards: AE, DI, DS, MC, VI.   CTV ✖ D

RESTAURANTS

THE ANCHORAGE Historical   **Lunch:** $8-$14   **Dinner:** $18-$28   Phone: 803/524-9392
◆◆   **Location:** Center. 1103 Bay St 29902. **Hours:** 11 am-2:30 & 5:30-9 pm, Sun noon-3 pm seasonal. Closed:
Continental 1/1, 9/2 & 12/25 call first. **Reservations:** suggested. **Features:** casual dress; carryout; cocktails & lounge.
Cuisine served in historic ambience. A variety of meat & fish, very well prepared; also Lowcountry
specialties. **Cards:** AE, DS, MC, VI.   ✖

BEAUFORT INN RESTAURANT Historical   **Dinner:** $14-$24   Phone: 803/521-9000
◆◆◆◆   **Location:** From US 21/Carteret St, just s; in Beaufort Inn. 809 Port Republic St 29902. **Hours:** 8 am-10 &
Regional   6-9 pm, Sun-1 pm. **Reservations:** accepted. **Features:** casual dress; Sunday brunch; cocktails; a la carte.
American   New Southern Cuisine style prepared entrees. Featuring fresh local seafood, herbs & produce. The menu
changes with the seasons. It's all served in a cozy warm elegant atmosphere. Smoke free premises.
Cards: AE, DS, MC, VI.   ♿ ✖

CAROLINE'S ON CRAVEN Historical   **Dinner:** $12-$18   Phone: 803/524-9030
◆◆◆   **Location:** Corner of Craven & New Castle sts; in The Rhett House Inn. 1009 Craven St 29902. **Hours:** 6
Regional   pm-9:30 pm, Sun brunch noon-2 pm. Closed: Mon & Tues. **Reservations:** suggested. **Features:** casual
American   dress; cocktails; street parking; a la carte. Southern Regional cuisine featuring local seafood & produce, all
served in a soft & cozy dining room. Smoke free premises. **Cards:** AE, MC, VI.   ✖

THE GADSBY   **Lunch:** $3-$9   **Dinner:** $6-$20   Phone: 803/525-1800
◆◆   **Location:** Downtown. 822 Bay St 29902. **Hours:** 11:30 am-10 pm, Sun-9 pm. Closed: 12/25.
Seafood   **Reservations:** suggested. **Features:** casual dress; children's menu; carryout; cocktails & lounge; street
parking. A cozy atmosphere on the water. Also steaks & sandwiches. **Cards:** AE, DS, MC, VI.   ✖

BENNETTSVILLE—9,300

LODGINGS

THE BREEDEN INN & CARRIAGE HOUSE   Guaranteed Rates   Phone: 803/479-3665
◆◆◆   All Year [BP]   1P: $56   2P/1B: $66   2P/2B: $66   XP: $10
Historic Bed **Location:** 0.3 mi e of square. 404 E Main St 29512. Fax: 803/479-1040. **Terms:** Age restrictions may apply;
& Breakfast   no pets. **Facility:** 6 rooms. 2 stories; interior corridors; designated smoking area. **All Rooms:** free movies.
Cards: MC, VI.   📶 CTV ✖ D

HOLIDAY INN EXPRESS   Phone: 803/479-1700
🔺 SAVE   All Year [CP]   1P: $55- 89 2P/1B: $55- 89 2P/2B: $55- 89 XP: $6   F19
◆◆◆   **Location:** On US 15 & 401 bypass. 213 US Hwy 15 29512. Fax: 803/479-1700. **Terms:** No pets. **Facility:** 52
Motel   rooms. 2 stories; exterior corridors. **Dining:** Restaurant nearby. **Services:** valet laundry. **All Rooms:** free
movies, refrigerators, combo or shower baths. **Some Rooms:** Fee: whirlpools. **Cards:** AE, CB, DI, DS, MC,
VI. **Special Amenities:** Free breakfast and free local telephone calls. *(See color ad below)*
Roll in showers. 📶 🛎 CTV ♿ D

MARLBORO INN/MASTER HOSTS INNS
Phone: 803/479-4051
AAA SAVE
All Year [CP] 1P: $36 2P/1B: $36 2P/2B: $44 XP: $5 F5
Location: 3 blks s; on US 15 & 401 bypass. US 15 & 401 bypass 29512. Fax: 803/479-2275. **Terms:** No
◆◆ pets. **Facility:** 55 rooms. Bed & breakfast-style decor in many rooms. 2 stories; exterior corridors.
Motel **All Rooms:** free movies. **Cards:** AE, DI, DS, MC, VI. **Special Amenities:** Free local telephone calls.

[CTV] [X] [D]

BISHOPVILLE—3,600

LODGING

ECONO LODGE
Phone: 803/428-3200
AAA SAVE
All Year 1P: $32- 95 2P/1B: $36- 95 2P/2B: $42- 95 XP: $5 F18
Location: I-20, exit 116. 1153 S Main St 29010. **Terms:** Weekly rates; small pets only, $5 extra charge.
◆◆ **Facility:** 48 rooms. 2 stories; exterior corridors. **Dining:** Restaurant nearby. **All Rooms:** free movies.
Motel **Some Rooms:** coffeemakers. **Cards:** AE, CB, DI, DS, JCB, MC, VI. **Special Amenities:** Free breakfast
and free local telephone calls. *(See color ad p 575)*

[🛏] [CTV] [X] [D]

CAMDEN—6,700

LODGINGS

COLONY INN
Phone: 803/432-5508
AAA SAVE
All Year 1P: $41- 52 2P/1B: $45- 49 2P/2B: $50- 55 XP: $3 D12
◆◆◆ **Location:** 1 mi w on US 1 & 601. 2020 W DeKalb St 29020 (PO Box 131). Fax: 803/432-0920.
Terms: Reserv deposit; small pets only, $10 extra charge. **Facility:** 53 rooms. 2 stories; exterior corridors.
Motel **Dining:** Coffee shop; 5:30 pm-10:30 pm, Sun-11:30 pm. **Services:** valet laundry. **All Rooms:** free movies.
Cards: AE, CB, DI, DS, MC, VI. **Special Amenities:** Free local telephone calls. [🛏] [🖼] [CTV] [X] [D]

HOLIDAY INN OF CAMDEN
Phone: 803/438-9441
AAA SAVE
All Year [BP] 1P: $59- 95 2P/1B: $64- 100 2P/2B: $64- 100 XP: $5 F18
◆◆◆ **Location:** 4 mi sw on US 1 & 601. Hwy 1 South 29078 (PO Box 96, LUGOFF). Fax: 803/438-9441.
Terms: Package plans; small pets only. **Facility:** 117 rooms. 12 whirlpool rms, extra charge; 2 stories; exterior
Motor Inn corridors; wading pool. **Dining & Entertainment:** Dining room; 6:30 am-2 & 5:30-10 pm; $8-$15;
cocktails/lounge. **Services:** Fee: coin laundry. **All Rooms:** coffeemakers, free & pay movies. **Cards:** AE, CB,
DI, DS, JCB, MC, VI. **Special Amenities:** Free breakfast and free local telephone calls.

[🛏] [🖼] [🏊] [♿] [CTV] [X] [D]

Charleston & Vicinity

CHARLESTON—80,400   (See map p. 438; index below)

To help you more easily locate accommodations in the Greater Charleston area, the following two indexes and maps show lodgings and restaurants in multiple cities. Listings
for these establishments are found under the heading for the city in which they are located. The Charleston area map comprises: Charleston, Mount Pleasant and North
Charleston.

Airport Accommodations
Listings for these establishments are found under the heading for the city in which they are located.

Charleston AFB International
AAA Charleston Hilton Hotel, 4 mi via Montague Ave of entrance/NORTH CHARLESTON
AAA Comfort Inn-Airport, 3.8 mi via Montague Ave of entrance/NORTH CHARLESTON
Days Inn-Airport/Coliseum, 3.3 mi via Montague Ave of entrance/NORTH CHARLESTON
Hampton Inn Airport/Coliseum, 3.5 mi via Montague Ave/NORTH CHARLESTON
Quality Suites, 4 mi via Montague Ave of entrance/NORTH CHARLESTON

Index of Establishments on the DOWNTOWN CHARLESTON ACCOMMODATIONS Spotting Map

(See map p. 438)

LODGINGS

THE ANCHORAGE INN 🔺🔺🔺 (AAA) SAVE **Phone: 803/723-8300** 19

Historic Bed & Breakfast

	1P	2P/1B	2P/2B	XP
2/15-6/14 & 9/1-11/24 [CP] 12/1-2/14, 6/15-8/31 &	$135- 225	$135- 225	$135- 225	$10
11/25-11/30 [CP]	$105- 175	$105- 175	$105- 175	

Location: Off E Bay St. 26 Vendue Range 29401. Fax: 803/723-9543. **Terms:** No pets. **Facility:** 19 rooms. All rooms decorated with 17th-century English antiques & reproductions. Handling fee imposed; 2 stories; interior corridors; smoke free premises. Fee: parking. **Some Rooms:** Fee: whirlpools. **Cards:** AE, MC, VI.
Special Amenities: Free breakfast and free local telephone calls. *(See ad below)* 🐕 ✕ D S

ANDREW PINCKNEY INN 🔺🔺🔺 Rates Subject to Change **Phone: 803/937-8800** 28

Bed & Breakfast

	1P	2P/1B	2P/2B	XP	
Fri & Sat 2/1-11/15 [CP]	$129	$129	$129	$10	F12
Sun-Thurs 2/1-11/15 [CP]	$109	$109	$109	$10	F12
Fri & Sat 12/1-1/31 & 11/16-11/30 [CP]	$89	$89	$89	$10	F12
Sun-Thurs 12/1-1/31 & 11/16-11/30 [CP]	$79	$79	$79	$10	F12

Location: Corner Pinckney St. 199 Church St 29401. Fax: 803/937-8810. **Terms:** Sr. discount; no pets. **Facility:** 32 rooms. 4 stories; interior corridors. **All Rooms:** free movies. **Cards:** AE, MC, VI. ✈ CTV ✕ D S

ANSONBOROUGH INN 🔺🔺🔺 Rates Subject to Change **Phone: 803/723-1655** 12

Bed & Breakfast

	2P/1B	2P/2B	XP	
2/14-6/8 & 9/1-11/30 [CP]	$89- 179	$89- 179	$15	F12
12/1-2/13 & 6/9-8/31 [CP]	$89- 139	$89- 139	$15	F12

Location: Corner E Bay & Hasell sts. 21 Hasell St 29401. Fax: 803/577-6888. **Terms:** Reserv deposit; 2 night min stay, in season; no pets. **Facility:** 38 rooms. 3 stories; interior corridors. **Some Rooms:** 37 kitchens. **Cards:** AE, DS, MC, VI. *(See color ad p 444)* CTV ✕ D S

(See map below)

ASHLEY INN BED & BREAKFAST   Rates Subject to Change   Phone: 803/723-1848   **1**
◆◆◆   3/1-11/30 [BP]   1P: $95- 135   2P/1B: $95- 135   2P/2B: $95- 135   XP: $25
Historic Bed   12/1-2/28 [BP]   1P: $79- 110   2P/1B: $79- 110   2P/2B: $79- 110   XP: $20
& Breakfast   **Location:** Corner of Bee St & Ashley Ave. 201 Ashley Ave 29403. Fax: 803/768-1230. **Terms:** Age restrictions may apply; reserv deposit, 7 day notice; no pets. **Facility:** 8 rooms. Carriage house $175-$225, off season $125-$175; 3 stories; interior corridors; smoke free premises. **Some Rooms:** kitchen. **Cards:** AE, DS, MC, VI.   CTV ✕ D

BATTERY CARRIAGE HOUSE INN (1843)   Phone: 803/727-3100   **26**
AAA SAVE   3/1-6/15 & 9/15-11/15 [CP]   1P: $159- 225   2P/1B: $159- 225   XP: $15
◆◆◆   12/1-3/14, 6/16-9/14 &
Historic Bed   11/16-11/30 [CP]   1P: $139- 189   2P/1B: $139- 189   XP: $15
& Breakfast   **Location:** 20 South Battery 29401. Fax: 803/727-3130. **Terms:** Age restrictions may apply; reserv deposit, 30 day notice; 2 night min stay, weekends in season; no pets. **Facility:** 11 rooms. Rooms tastefully decorated. Silver tray breakfast daily in garden or room. 2 stories; interior corridors; smoke free premises; street parking only. **Services:** complimentary evening beverages. **All Rooms:** coffeemakers, combo or shower baths. **Some Rooms:** Fee: whirlpools. **Cards:** AE, DS, MC, VI. **Special Amenities:** Free breakfast and free local telephone calls. CTV ✕ D

BELVEDERE BED & BREAKFAST   Rates Subject to Change   Phone: 803/722-0973   **27**
◆◆◆   All Year [CP]   1P: $125   2P/1B: $125   XP: $15
Historic Bed   **Location:** 40 Rutledge Ave 29401. **Terms:** Age restrictions may apply; check-in 4 pm; reserv deposit, 14 day
& Breakfast   notice, handling fee imposed; no pets. **Facility:** 3 rooms. 2 stories; interior corridors; smoke free premises.   ✕ D

BEST WESTERN KING CHARLES INN   Rates Subject to Change   Phone: 803/723-7451   **5**
◆◆◆   3/13-6/30 & 10/1-11/30   1P: $99- 189   2P/1B: $99- 189   2P/2B: $99- 189   XP: $10   D14
Motel   7/1-9/30   1P: $89- 169   2P/1B: $89- 179   2P/2B: $89- 179   XP: $10   D14
    12/1-3/12   1P: $79- 159   2P/1B: $79- 159   2P/2B: $79- 159   XP: $10   D14
Location: Between Wentworth & Beaufain sts. 237 Meeting St 29401. Fax: 803/723-2041. **Terms:** Reserv deposit; no pets. **Facility:** 91 rooms. 4 stories; interior corridors. **Dining:** Coffee shop; 6:30-10:30 am, Sat & Sun 7-11 am. **Cards:** AE, CB, DI, DS, MC, VI.   ✈ CTV ✕ 🏊 D

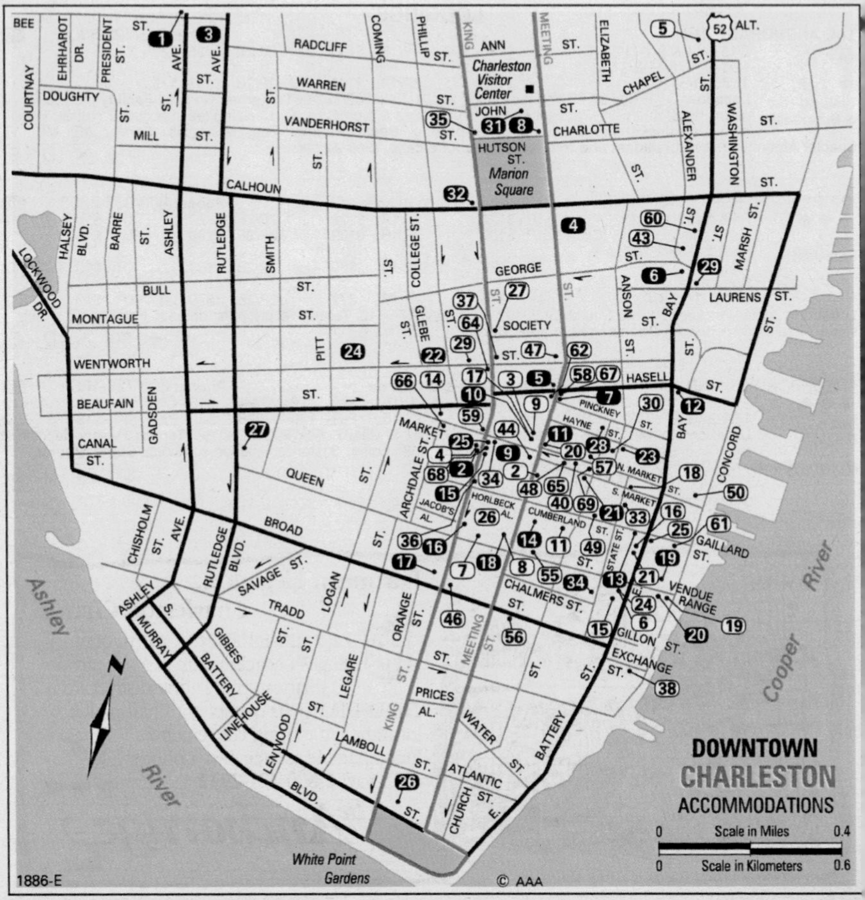

DOWNTOWN CHARLESTON ACCOMMODATIONS

	Scale in Miles	
0		0.4

	Scale in Kilometers	
0		0.6

1886-E

White Point Gardens

© AAA

(See map p. 438)

BRASINGTON HOUSE BED & BREAKFAST
◆◆◆
Historic Bed
& Breakfast

	Rates Subject to Change		Phone: 803/722-1274	29
2/20-6/5 [BP]	2P/1B: $134	2P/2B: $134	XP: $35	
6/6-11/30 [BP]	2P/1B: $115	2P/2B: $115	XP: $35	
12/1-2/19 [BP]	2P/1B: $98	2P/2B: $98	XP: $35	

Location: At corner of East Bay & George sts. 328 E Bay St 29401. **Terms:** Age restrictions may apply; reserv deposit, 7 day notice; 2 night min stay, weekends; no pets. **Facility:** 4 rooms. Also included: wine, liqueurs, coffee/tea in room; 3 stories; interior/exterior corridors; smoke free premises. **Cards:** MC, VI.

CTV ☒ D

CANNONBORO INN BED & BREAKFAST
◆◆◆
Historic Bed
& Breakfast

	Rates Subject to Change		Phone: 803/723-8572	3
3/1-11/30 [BP]	1P: $95- 145	2P/1B: $95- 145	2P/2B: $95- 145	XP: $25
12/1-2/28 [BP]	1P: $79- 110	2P/1B: $79- 110	2P/2B: $79- 110	XP: $20

Location: 184 Ashley Ave 29403. **Terms:** Age restrictions may apply; reserv deposit, 7 day notice; no pets. **Facility:** 8 rooms. 3 room suite with kitchen, $110-$155, off season $95-$125; 3 stories; interior corridors; smoke free premises. **Cards:** AE, DS, MC, VI.

CTV ☒ D

CHARLESTON PLACE
(AAA) (SAVE)
◆◆◆◆
Hotel

		Phone: 803/722-4900	10
3/1-6/30 & 9/1-11/30	1P: $189	2P/1B: $189	2P/2B: $189	XP: $20	F12
12/1-2/28 & 7/1-8/31	1P: $149	2P/1B: $149	2P/2B: $149	XP: $20	F12

Location: Between King & Meeting sts. 130 Market St 29401. Fax: 803/722-0728. **Terms:** Check-in 4 pm; reserv deposit, 3 day notice; weekly rates; AP, BP, MAP avail; package plans; no pets. **Facility:** 440 rooms. Lovely guest rooms with quality furnishings & decor. Boutique promenade. 8 stories; interior corridors; luxury level rooms; saunas, steamroom, whirlpool. Fee: parking. **Dining & Entertainment:** Dining room; 6 am-11 pm; $8-$22; cocktails; afternoon tea; also, Charleston Grill, see separate listing; entertainment. **Services:** valet laundry. Fee: massage; valet parking. **All Rooms:** free & pay movies. **Some Rooms:** Fee: VCP's. **Cards:** AE, CB, DI, DS, MC, VI. **Special Amenities:** Free newspaper and preferred room (subject to availability with advanced reservations).

⊇ ⊇ ⌘ ⊞ ⋒ CTV ☒ ⌖ D S

CHARLESTON'S VENDUE INN
(AAA) (SAVE)
◆◆◆◆
Historic
Country Inn

		Phone: 803/577-7970	20
3/12-6/14 & 9/17-11/30 [BP]	1P: $135- 210	2P/1B: $160- 235	2P/2B: $165- 235	XP: $15
12/1-3/11 & 6/15-9/16 [BP]	1P: $105- 175	2P/1B: $120- 205	2P/2B: $125- 205	XP: $15

Location: In historic area off E Bay St, just e of Market Area. 19 Vendue Range 29401. Fax: 803/577-2913. **Terms:** Reserv deposit, 7 day notice; no pets. **Facility:** 45 rooms. Tastefully appointed rooms & suites in restored 1858 building; some with fireplace. 5 one-bedroom suites, $165-$235; off season $150-$185; 3 stories; interior corridors. **Dining:** Restaurant; 11 am-2:30 & 6-10 pm, closed Sun; $11-$20; cocktails; also, The Library at Vendue, see separate listing. **Services:** valet laundry; valet parking. **All Rooms:** free movies. **Some Rooms:** refrigerators. Fee: whirlpools. **Cards:** AE, DI, DS, MC, VI. **Special Amenities:** Free breakfast and free newspaper. *(See ad p 441)*

⌘ ⋒ CTV ☒ D

(See map p. 438)

CHURCH STREET INN Rates Subject to Change Phone: 803/722-3420 **21**
◆◆◆ All Year [CP] 2P/1B: $119- 145 2P/2B: $119- 145 XP: $20 F12
Suite Motel **Location:** Corner S Market St. 177 Church St 29401. Fax: 803/853-7306. **Terms:** Reserv deposit; no pets. **Facility:** 31 rooms. 3 two-bedroom suites, $185; 2 stories; interior corridors. Fee: parking. **All Rooms:** free movies. **Some Rooms:** 28 efficiencies, 3 kitchens. **Cards:** AE, MC, VI. CTV ⊠ D S

DAYS INN HISTORIC DISTRICT Guaranteed Rates Phone: 803/722-8411 **14**
◆◆ All Year 1P: $70- 120 2P/1B: $80- 130 2P/2B: $80- 130 XP: $10 F12
Motor Inn **Location:** 155 Meeting St 29401. Fax: 803/723-5361. **Terms:** Sr. discount; no pets. **Facility:** 124 rooms. 2 stories; exterior corridors. **Dining:** Coffee shop; 6:30 am-2:30 pm; $5-$10. **All Rooms:** free movies. **Cards:** AE, CB, DI, DS, MC, VI. *(See ad p 412)* ⋥ CTV ⊠ ⊿ D

1837 BED & BREAKFAST Guaranteed Rates Phone: 803/723-7166 **24**
AAA 2/20-11/30 [BP] 1P: $69- 129 2P/1B: $69- 129 2P/2B: $69- 129 XP: $20
◆◆◆ 12/1-2/19 [BP] 1P: $54- 109 2P/1B: $54- 109 2P/2B: $54- 109 XP: $20
Historic Bed **Location:** Between Coming & Pitt sts. 126 Wentworth St 29401. **Terms:** Age restrictions may apply; reserv
& Breakfast deposit, 5 day notice; no pets. **Facility:** 8 rooms. 3 stories; exterior corridors; smoke free premises. **Cards:** AE, MC, VI. ⊠ D S

THE ELLIOTT HOUSE INN Rates Subject to Change Phone: 803/723-1855 **16**
◆◆◆ 3/15-7/4 & 10/1-11/1 [CP] 1P: $116- 137 2P/1B: $116- 137
Historic Bed 12/1-3/14, 7/5-9/30 &
& Breakfast 11/2-11/30 [CP] 1P: $94- 105 2P/1B: $94- 105
Location: Between King & Meeting sts. 78 Queen St 29401. Fax: 803/722-1567. **Terms:** Reserv deposit, 3 day notice; no pets. **Facility:** 26 rooms. 2-3 stories; exterior corridors. Fee: parking. **Cards:** AE, DS, MC, VI. CTV ⊠ D

EMBASSY SUITES HISTORIC CHARLESTON Rates Subject to Change Phone: 803/723-6900 **8**
◆◆◆ Thurs-Sat 12/1-4/28 &
Suite Motel 7/1-9/28 [BP] 1P: $219 2P/1B: $239 2P/2B: $239 XP: $20 F12
Sun-Wed 12/1-4/28 &
7/1-9/28 [BP] 1P: $189 2P/1B: $209 2P/2B: $209 XP: $20 F12
Thurs-Sat 4/29-6/30 &
9/29-11/30 [BP] 1P: $179 2P/1B: $189 2P/2B: $189 XP: $20 F12
Sun-Wed 4/29-6/30 &
9/29-11/30 [BP] 1P: $149 2P/1B: $149 2P/2B: $149 XP: $20 F12
Location: 337 Meeting St 29403. Fax: 803/723-6938. **Terms:** 2 night min stay, weekends; no pets. **Facility:** 153 rooms. 5 stories; interior corridors. Fee: parking. **All Rooms:** free movies. **Cards:** AE, CB, DI, DS, MC, VI. *(See color ad below)* ⋥ CTV ⊠ D S

(See map p. 438)

FRANCIS MARION HOTEL
◆◆◆
Historic Hotel

	Guaranteed Rates				Phone: 803/722-0600	32
Fri & Sat 2/14-11/16	1P: $119- 179	2P/1B: $119- 179	2P/2B: $119- 179	XP: $10		F12
Sun-Thurs 2/14-11/16	1P: $99- 159	2P/1B: $99- 159	2P/2B: $99- 159	XP: $10		F12
Fri & Sat 12/1-2/13 & 11/17-11/30	1P: $109- 159	2P/1B: $109- 159	2P/2B: $109- 159	XP: $10		F12
Sun-Thurs 12/1-2/13 & 11/17-11/30	1P: $79- 139	2P/1B: $79- 139	2P/2B: $79- 139	XP: $10		F12

Location: Corner Calhoun St. 387 King St 29403. Fax: 803/723-4633. **Terms:** Sr. discount; no pets. **Facility:** 226 rooms. 12 stories; interior corridors. Fee: parking. **Dining:** Restaurant, coffee shop; 7-10 am, 11-2 & 5:30-11 pm; $13-$19. **Cards:** AE, DI, DS, MC, VI. *(See color ad below)*
Roll in showers. ♿ CTV ✕ D S

FULTON LANE INN
AAA SAVE
◆◆◆◆
Historic Bed
& Breakfast

				Phone: 803/720-2600	2
3/6-6/7 & 9/18-11/30 [CP]	1P: $135- 155	2P/1B: $155- 220	2P/2B: $175	XP: $20	F12
12/1-3/5 & 6/8-9/17 [CP]	1P: $90- 100	2P/1B: $110- 180	2P/2B: $120	XP: $20	F12

Location: On King St, just s of Market St. 202 King St 29401. Fax: 803/720-2940. **Terms:** Reserv deposit; package plans; no pets. **Facility:** 27 rooms. Large rooms, some with working fireplace. The rooms are uniquely decorated & furnished. 5 suites, some with fireplace $180-$255; 3 stories; interior corridors; smoke free premises. **Dining:** Restaurant nearby. **Services:** valet laundry. **All Rooms:** refrigerators. **Some Rooms:** 2 kitchens. Fee: whirlpools. **Cards:** DI, DS, MC, VI. **Special Amenities:** Free local telephone calls and free newspaper. *(See ad p 440)*
🛎 CTV ♿ ✕ 🐾 D S

HAMPTON INN HISTORIC DISTRICT
AAA SAVE
◆◆◆
Historic Motel

				Phone: 803/723-4000	31
3/15-10/31 [CP]	1P: $89- 129	2P/1B: $99- 139	2P/2B: $99- 139	XP: $10	F18
11/1-11/30 [CP]	1P: $75- 129	2P/1B: $85- 139	2P/2B: $85- 139	XP: $10	F18
12/1-3/14 [CP]	1P: $69- 129	2P/1B: $69- 139	2P/2B: $69- 139	XP: $10	F18

Location: Corner of Meeting & John sts; next to Charleston Visitor Center. 345 Meeting St 29403. Fax: 803/722-3725. **Terms:** Check-in 4 pm; no pets. **Facility:** 171 rooms. Located in the historic district. Lovely courtyard. Rooms are tastefully furnished; 5 stories; interior corridors. Fee: parking. **Dining:** Restaurant nearby. **Services:** valet laundry. **All Rooms:** free movies, combo or shower baths. **Some Rooms:** coffeemakers. Fee: microwaves, refrigerators, VCP's, whirlpools. **Cards:** AE, DI, DS, MC, VI. **Special Amenities:** Free breakfast and free local telephone calls. *(See ad p 443)*
🛏 🛎 CTV ✕ 🐾 D S

HAWTHORN SUITES AT THE MARKET
◆◆◆
Suite Motel

	Guaranteed Rates			Phone: 803/577-2644	23
2/14-6/28 & 9/5-11/30 [BP]	1P: $125- 189	2P/1B: $125- 189	2P/2B: $125- 189		
6/29-9/4 [BP]	1P: $109- 149	2P/1B: $109- 149	2P/2B: $109- 149		
12/1-2/13 [BP]	1P: $89- 119	2P/1B: $89- 119	2P/2B: $89- 119		

Location: At N Market & Church sts. 181 Church St 29401. Fax: 803/577-2697. **Terms:** Small pets only, $125 fee, $10 extra charge. **Facility:** 182 rooms. 5 stories; interior corridors. **All Rooms:** Fee: movies. **Some Rooms:** 165 efficiencies. **Cards:** AE, CB, DI, DS, JCB, MC, VI.
Roll in showers. 🐾 ♿ CTV ✕ D S

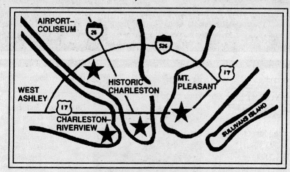
IT COULD HAPPEN.
Some lodgings require advance payment when you check in,
and if your trip is cut short a refund may be impossible.

(See map p. 438)

HOLIDAY INN - MILLS HOUSE   Phone: 803/577-2400   [18]
[AAA] [SAVE]   All Year   1P: $170- 250   2P/1B: $170- 250 2P/2B: $170- 250
◆◆◆◆   **Location:** 115 Meeting St 29401. Fax: 803/722-0623. **Terms:** Reserv deposit; package plans; no pets.
Hotel   **Facility:** 215 rooms. Historic hotel in Old Charleston. 7 stories; interior corridors; luxury level rooms.
Fee: parking. **Dining & Entertainment:** Restaurant; $12-$20; cocktails/lounge; also, Barbadoes Restaurant,
see separate listing; entertainment. **Services:** valet laundry. Fee: valet parking. **All Rooms:** coffeemakers,
free & pay movies. **Some Rooms:** refrigerators. **Cards:** AE, CB, DI, DS, JCB, MC, VI. **Special Amenities: Free
newspaper and free room upgrade (subject to availability with advanced reservations).** *(See ad below)*

INDIGO INN   Rates Subject to Change   Phone: 803/577-5900   [7]
◆◆◆   3/15-6/15 & 9/15-11/30 [CP] 1P: $145   2P/1B: $160   2P/2B: $160   XP: $10   D12
Historic Bed   12/24-1/1 [CP]   1P: $130   2P/1B: $145   2P/2B: $145   XP: $10   D12
& Breakfast   2/1-3/14 & 6/16-9/14 [CP] 1P: $115   2P/1B: $130   2P/2B: $130   XP: $10   D12
12/1-12/23 & 1/2-1/31 [CP] 1P: $95   2P/1B: $110   2P/2B: $110   XP: $10   D12
Location: Corner Meeting & Pinckney sts. 1 Maiden Ln 29401. Fax: 803/577-0378. **Terms:** Reserv deposit; 2 night min
stay, most weekends; pets, $10 extra charge. **Facility:** 40 rooms. 3 stories; exterior corridors. **All Rooms:** free movies.
Cards: AE, DI, DS, MC, VI. *(See color ad below)*

(See map p. 438)

JOHN RUTLEDGE HOUSE INN
(AAA) (SAVE)
♦♦♦♦
Historic Bed & Breakfast

Phone: 803/723-7999   **17**

Fri & Sat, Sun-Thurs 3/6-6/7 & 9/18-11/30 [CP]	1P: $195- 225	2P/1B: $215- 245	2P/2B: $215- 245	XP: $20 F12
Sun-Thurs 12/1-3/5 & 6/8-9/17 [CP]	1P: $135- 170	2P/1B: $155- 190	2P/2B: $155- 190	XP: $20 F12

Location: Corner of Broad & King sts. 116 Broad St 29401. Fax: 803/720-2615. **Terms:** Reserv deposit, 3 day notice; no pets. **Facility:** 19 rooms. A restored home from 1763, belonging to a signer of the Constitution. Decorated with period reproduction antiques. 1 bedroom suites $255-$310; 2-4 stories; interior/exterior corridors. **Dining:** Restaurant nearby. **Services:** valet laundry. **All Rooms:** honor bars, refrigerators. **Some Rooms:** Fee: whirlpools. **Cards:** AE, DI, DS, MC, VI. **Special Amenities:** Free local telephone calls and free newspaper. *(See ad p 440)*

🛎 ⊕ CTV ✕ D S

KINGS COURTYARD INN
(AAA) (SAVE)
♦♦♦♦
Historic Bed & Breakfast

Phone: 803/723-7000   **15**

3/6-6/7 & 9/18-11/30 [CP]	1P: $145- 165	2P/1B: $165- 185	2P/2B: $185	XP: $20 F12
12/1-3/5 & 6/8-9/17 [CP]	1P: $95- 115	2P/1B: $115- 135	2P/2B: $135	XP: $20 F12

Location: 198 King St 29401. Fax: 803/720-2608. **Terms:** Reserv deposit; no pets. **Facility:** 41 rooms. Renovated 1853 structure. Some rooms with fireplace. 1 bedroom suites $180-230, 2 bedroom suites $330-425; 3 stories; interior/exterior corridors; whirlpool. **Dining & Entertainment:** Breakfast room; 7-10 am, Sat & Sun-11 am; cocktail lounge. **Services:** valet laundry. **All Rooms:** refrigerators. **Some Rooms:** Fee: whirlpools. **Cards:** AE, DI, DS, MC, VI. **Special Amenities:** Free local telephone calls and free newspaper. *(See ad p 440)*

🛎 ⊕ CTV ✕ D S

THE LODGE ALLEY INN
(AAA)
♦♦♦
Historic Hotel

Rates Subject to Change   **Phone:** 803/722-1611   **13**

3/7-6/5 & 9/10-11/30	2P/1B: $149- 229	2P/2B: $149- 229	XP: $15 F12
12/1-3/6 & 6/6-9/9	2P/1B: $135- 225	2P/2B: $135- 225	XP: $15 F12

Location: At E Bay & Cumberland sts. 195 E Bay St 29401. Fax: 803/722-1611. **Terms:** Check-in 4 pm; reserv deposit; no pets. **Facility:** 95 rooms. 12 two-bedroom units, $229, $220 off season for 2 persons; 2-3 stories; interior/exterior corridors. **Dining:** Dining room; 7-10:30 am, 11-2:30 & 6- 9:30 pm; $13-$25. **All Rooms:** free movies. **Some Rooms:** 53 kitchens. **Cards:** AE, MC, VI.

CTV D

MAISON DUPRE'
♦♦♦
Historic Bed & Breakfast

Rates Subject to Change   **Phone:** 803/723-8691   **6**

All Year [CP]	2P/1B: $98- 200	2P/2B: $98- 200

Location: Corner George & E Bay sts. 317 E Bay St 29401. Fax: 803/723-3722. **Terms:** Reserv deposit, 7 day notice; no pets. **Facility:** 15 rooms. 3 suites, $160-$200; off season $145-$200. Handling fee imposed; 3 stories; interior/exterior corridors; designated smoking area. **Some Rooms:** kitchen. **Cards:** DS, MC, VI.

CTV ✕ D

THE MEETING STREET INN
♦♦♦
Historic Bed & Breakfast

Rates Subject to Change   **Phone:** 803/723-1882   **9**

12/1-3/19, 6/7-9/5 & 11/8-11/30 [CP]	1P: $91- 213	2P/1B: $91- 213	2P/2B: $91- 213	XP: $10 F12
3/20-6/6 & 9/6-11/7 [CP]	1P: $71- 190	2P/1B: $71- 190	2P/2B: $71- 190	XP: $10 F12

Location: 173 Meeting St 29401. Fax: 803/577-0851. **Terms:** No pets. **Facility:** 56 rooms. Weekend rates higher; 4 stories; exterior corridors. Fee: parking. **Cards:** AE, DI, DS, MC, VI. *(See color ad p 444)*

CTV ✕ 🏊 D S

PLANTERS INN
(AAA)
♦♦♦♦
Historic Bed & Breakfast

Rates Subject to Change   **Phone:** 803/722-2345   **11**

3/13-6/6 & 9/18-11/30	1P: $140- 199	2P/1B: $140- 199	2P/2B: $150- 195	XP: $15 F17
12/1-3/12 & 6/7-9/17	1P: $105- 160	2P/1B: $105- 175	2P/2B: $115- 170	XP: $15 F17

Location: Corner Meeting St. 112 N Market St 29401. Fax: 803/577-2125. **Terms:** Sr. discount; no pets. **Facility:** 62 rooms. Suites $225-$275, $200-$250 off season; 4 stories; interior corridors. **Dining:** Peninsula Grill, see separate listing. **All Rooms:** free movies. **Cards:** AE, CB, DI, DS, MC, VI. *(See color ad below)*

🛏 ⊕ CTV ✕ D S

(See map p. 438)

QUALITY INN-HEART OF CHARLESTON

Phone: 803/722-3391 **4**

4/1-5/31	1P:	$89- 99	2P/2B:	$99- 109	XP: $6	F18
2/1-3/31 & 6/1-11/30	1P:	$69- 89	2P/2B:	$79- 99	XP: $6	F18
12/1-1/31	1P:	$59- 79	2P/2B:	$69- 89	XP: $6	F18

Motor Inn

Location: 125 Calhoun St 29401. **Fax:** 803/577-0361. **Terms:** Check-in 4 pm; no pets. **Facility:** 126 rooms. Some rooms with balcony. 6 stories; interior corridors. **Dining:** Restaurant; 7 am-2 & 5-9 pm, Sun-noon; $6-$14; cocktails. **Services:** area transportation, in downtown area. Fee: coin laundry. **All Rooms:** coffeemakers. **Some Rooms:** refrigerators. **Cards:** AE, CB, DI, DS, JCB, MC, VI. **Special Amenities:** Free local telephone calls.

27 STATE STREET BED & BREAKFAST

Rates Subject to Change   Phone: 803/723-4243 **34**

3/1-11/30 [CP]	2P/1B: $130	XP: $20
12/1-2/28 [CP]	2P/1B: $110	XP: $20

Historic Bed & Breakfast

Location: On State St between Queen & Chalmers sts. 27 State St 29401. **Terms:** Reserv deposit, 4 day notice; no pets. **Facility:** 2 rooms. Handling fee imposed; 2 stories; exterior corridors; smoke free premises. **Some Rooms:** kitchen.

THE VICTORIA HOUSE INN

Phone: 803/720-2944 **25**

3/6-6/7 & 9/18-11/30 [CP]	1P: $155- 165	2P/1B: $175- 185	2P/2B: $185	XP: $20	F12
12/1-3/5 & 6/8-9/17 [CP]	1P: $100- 110	2P/1B: $120- 130	2P/2B: $130	XP: $20	F12

Historic Bed & Breakfast

Location: Just s of Market St on King St. 208 King St 29401. **Fax:** 803/720-2930. **Terms:** Reserv deposit; no pets. **Facility:** 18 rooms. Located in the heart of the historic district, an 1889 structure decorated with Victorian period reproductions. 4 rooms with fireplace & whirlpool, $225; off season $175 for 2 persons; 3 stories; interior corridors. Fee: parking. **Dining:** Restaurant nearby. **Services:** valet laundry. **All Rooms:** refrigerators. **Cards:** DI, DS, MC, VI. **Special Amenities:** Free local telephone calls and free newspaper. *(See ad p 440)*

WENTWORTH MANSION

Phone: 803/853-1886 **22**

Bed & Breakfast

Under construction; **Location:** E of King St. 149 Wentworth St 29401. **Fax:** 803/722-8634. **Terms:** Check-in 4 pm; reserv deposit, 7 day notice; no pets. **Facility:** 21 rooms. Scheduled to open February 1998; 4 stories; interior corridors; designated smoking area. **Dining:** Dining room; 5 pm-10 pm; $20-$35. **Cards:** AE, DI, DS, MC, VI. *(See ad below)*

RESTAURANTS

AARON'S DELI

Lunch: $3-$7   Dinner: $5-$14   Phone: 803/723-6000 **3**

American

Location: Just w of Market & the Omni Hotel at Charleston Place. 213 Meeting St 29401. **Hours:** 7 am-11 pm. Closed: 11/26, 12/25 & Jewish holidays. **Features:** casual dress; children's menu; health conscious menu; carryout; cocktails; fee for parking. Popular with locals. Casual dining serving traditional kosher deli items & a variety of fresh seafood. **Cards:** AE, DS, MC, VI.

ANDOLINI'S

Dinner: $2-$18   Phone: 803/722-7437 **29**

Italian

Location: Just s of King St. 82 Wentworth St 29401. **Hours:** 11:30 am-11 pm, Fri & Sat-midnight. Closed: 11/26 & 12/25-1/5. **Features:** casual dress; carryout; beer & wine only; a la carte. An old-style pizza parlor in a whimsical setting, with a no-frills menu inspiring confidence. Calzone, salad & gigantic pizza with all kinds of topping.

ANSON

Dinner: $8-$20   Phone: 803/577-0551 **30**

Regional American

Location: Just w of N Market St. 12 Anson St 29401. **Hours:** 5:30 pm-11 pm, Fri & Sat-midnight. **Reservations:** suggested. **Features:** carryout; cocktails & lounge; street parking; a la carte. Featuring Charleston regional-style preparation of fresh seafood entrees, as well as creative entrees of fresh pasta & prime meat. The dining room offers a soft & elegant upscale casual atmosphere with some New Orleans influence. **Cards:** AE, CB, DI, DS, MC, VI.

ARIZONA BAR & GRILL

Lunch: $4-$7   Dinner: $5-$15   Phone: 803/577-5090 **5**

American

Location: Corner of Chapel & E Bay sts. 14 Chapel St 29403. **Hours:** 11:30 am-3 & 5:30-10 pm, Fri & Sat-11 pm, Sun 1 pm-10 pm. Closed: 1/1, 11/26, 12/24 & 12/25. **Reservations:** suggested. **Features:** casual dress; carryout; cocktails & lounge. Featuring Southwestern cuisine, Native American Indian with accents on Mexican entrees. Casual atmosphere with decor from the Southwest. **Cards:** AE, DI, DS, MC, VI.

(See map p. 438)

A.W. SHUCKS   Lunch: $4-$8   Dinner: $6-$15   Phone: 803/723-1151   33
◆◆   **Location:** On Market & State sts, just off of East Bay & Market sts. 35 Market St. **Hours:** 11:30 am-11 pm,
Seafood   Fri & Sat-noon. Closed: 12/25. **Reservations:** accepted; large groups. **Features:** casual dress; children's
            menu; health conscious menu; salad bar; cocktails & lounge. A large seafood menu ranging from the basics
to the more refined, plus an array of Cajun-inspired dishes, a creative pasta selection, fried & un-fried seafood platters, &
chicken & beef. Attractively casual atmosphere. Raw bar. **Cards:** AE, DS, MC, VI.   ✖

THE BAKERS CAFE   Historical   Lunch: $4-$10   Phone: 803/577-2694   34
◆◆   **Location:** Just n of Market St. 214 King St 29401. **Hours:** 8 am-2:30 pm, Sat & Sun from 9 am. Closed
American   major holidays except Easter. **Reservations:** required; 6 or more. **Features:** casual dress; Sunday brunch;
            carryout; cocktails; street parking. Scones, croissants, Danish, muffins & homemade preserves served in this
popular meeting place. Offers many variations on the familiar Eggs Benedict, such as with Madiers sauce on Holland rusks.
Also pasta du jour. **Cards:** DI, MC, VI.

BARBADOES RESTAURANT   Lunch: $5-$9   Dinner: $12-$20   Phone: 803/577-2400   8
◆◆◆   **Location:** In Mills House Hotel. 115 Meeting St 29401. **Hours:** 7 am-3 & 5:30-10 pm.
Steak and   **Reservations:** suggested. **Features:** casual dress; Sunday brunch; children's menu; health conscious menu;
Seafood   cocktails & lounge; fee for parking; a la carte. Elegant & formal dining room overlooking fountain courtyard.
            Cards: AE, CB, DI, DS, MC, VI.   ✖

BLOSSOM CAFE   Lunch: $5-$8   Dinner: $5-$17   Phone: 803/722-9200   21
◆◆◆   **Location:** 171 E Bay St 29401. **Hours:** 11:30 am-midnight. Closed: 11/26, 12/25 & 1/1.
Ethnic   **Reservations:** suggested. **Features:** casual dress; Sunday brunch; children's menu; carryout; cocktails &
            lounge; a la carte. A bright & bustling atmosphere featuring innovative Mediterranean-style cuisine with fresh
local seafood & regional produce. Entrees also including freshly made pasta & bread, all very nicely prepared. **Cards:** AE,
MC, VI.

THE BOOKSTORE CAFE   Lunch: $5-$8   Dinner: $8-$15   Phone: 803/720-8843   35
◆◆   **Location:** Corner of King & Hutson sts. 412 King St 29403. **Hours:** 9 am-2:30 & 5:30-9 pm, Fri & Sat-10
South   pm, Sun-2 pm. Closed major holidays. **Features:** casual dress; Sunday brunch; health conscious menu;
Continental carryout; beer & wine only. Small menu, full of variety, offers "small" & "large" plates. Root Vegetable salad
            & a side are a "gracious plenty"; delicious is the oyster Hangtown Fry, with a wedge of sauteed grits, &
comforting pumpkin bread pudding. **Cards:** MC, VI.   ✖

CAFE CAFE   Historical   Phone: 803/723-3622   36
◆◆   **Location:** 190 King St 29401. **Hours:** 8 am-10 pm, Sun-5 pm. **Features:** beer & wine only. A sleek
American   coffee-house with a European tone. Small elegant menu offers a continental breakfast, while a lunch choice
            may be roasted tenderloin with brie on an onion roll dressed with horseradish sauce. Also splits of
champagne.

CAFE RAINBOW   Phone: 803/965-5000   37
◆   **Location:** 282 King St 29401. **Hours:** 7 am-11 pm, Sat from 8 am, Sun from 9 am. **Features:** Quiche,
American   salads, soups, muffins, baguettes, croissants & delicious coffee in this coffee-house patterned after those in
            Vienna.

CAROLINA'S   Dinner: $6-$26   Phone: 803/724-3800   38
◆◆◆   **Location:** East Bay & Brad Street. 10 Exchange St 29401. **Hours:** 5:30 pm-10:30 pm, Fri & Sat-11:30 pm,
Regional   Sun-9:30 pm. Closed: 11/26 & Super Bowl Sun. **Reservations:** suggested. **Features:** casual dress; health
American   conscious menu; carryout; cocktails & lounge; a la carte. Chic, attractive & interesting, with the menu running
            the gamut in imagination from a hamburger to a fine veal chop, with lots of options in between; mostly does
itself proud with the grilled meat. **Cards:** AE, DI, DS, MC, VI.   ✖

CELIA'S PORTA VIA   Lunch: $4-$14   Dinner: $3-$14   Phone: 803/722-9003   14
◆◆   **Location:** At corner of Archdale, Market & Beaufain sts; just w of Charleston Place Hotel. 49 Archdale St
Italian   29401. **Hours:** 10 am-2:30 & 5:30-10 pm, Fri-11 pm, Sat 5:30 pm-11 pm. Closed major holidays. An intimate
            Reservations: suggested. **Features:** dressy casual; carryout; cocktails & lounge; a la carte. An intimate
neighborhood restaurant serving very well prepared home-style pasta, freshly made bread & fresh seafood entrees in a
romantic setting. Extensive wine list, prepared foods & picnics to go. **Cards:** AE, DI, DS, MC, VI.

CHARLESTON GRILL   Dinner: $16-$21   Phone: 803/577-4522   17
◆◆◆   **Location:** Between King & Meeting sts; in Charleston Place. 224 King St 29401. **Hours:** 4:30 pm-11 pm.
Regional   **Reservations:** suggested. **Features:** dressy casual; health conscious menu; cocktails & lounge; fee for
American   parking & valet parking; a la carte. Featuring traditional Low Country appetizers & entrees. Live jazz nightly.
            Extensive wine list. **Cards:** AE, DI, DS, MC, VI.   ✖

THE CHEF & CLEF   Dinner: $9-$18   Phone: 803/722-0732   40
◆◆   **Location:** 102 N Market St 29401. **Hours:** 6 pm-1 am, Sun 11 am-2:30 pm. **Features:** Sunday brunch;
Ethnic   carryout; cocktails; entertainment. Delivers both food & live jazz in a slightly Bohemian atmosphere
            reminiscent of the '60s. Unexpected or unusual creations in every category on the menu, with several
choices of flambe desserts. **Cards:** AE, DI, DS, MC, VI.

DOE'S PITA PLUS   Dinner: $2-$5   Phone: 803/577-3179   43
◆   **Location:** 334 E Bay St 29401. **Hours:** 8 am-8:30 pm, Sat-5 pm, Sun 11 am-5 pm. **Features:** health
Vegetarian conscious menu items; carryout. Healthy & fresh food, with an emphasis on Middle-Eastern; a few meat &
            chicken dishes offered. Counter service only, a few tables inside & a couple out on the sidewalk. Peanut
butter & sliced banana pita pockets for the kids.

82 QUEEN RESTAURANT   Historical   Lunch: $6-$8   Dinner: $12-$19   Phone: 803/723-7591   7
◆◆   **Location:** Between Meeting & King sts. 82 Queen St 29401. **Hours:** 11:30 am-2 & 5:30-10 pm, Fri & Sat
American   5:30 pm-10:30 pm. **Reservations:** suggested; for dinner. **Features:** casual dress; children's menu; health
            conscious menu items; cocktails & lounge; street parking; a la carte. Charming dining rooms in an old
Charleston home. Fresh seafood specialties. Courtyard seating avail. **Cards:** AE, DI, MC, VI.   ✖

(See map p. 438)

11 LLAMAS Historical   **Lunch:** $4-$10   **Phone:** 803/723-7400 56
◆   **Location:** Broad & Church sts. 58 Broad St 29401. **Hours:** 8 am-6 pm. Closed: 12/25.
American   **Reservations:** accepted. **Features:** casual dress; health conscious menu; carryout; cocktail lounge. This
coffee-house has an elegant, refined look which is also cozy & comfortable; books, magazines, live music
(Thurs) & desserts. Also some sandwiches, a couple of quiches, & salads. Try a chocolate-dipped biscotti. Smoke free
premises. **Cards:** AE, DI, DS, MC, VI.   ⊠

FULFORD & EAGAN Historical   **Lunch:** $3-$5   **Dinner:** $3-$6   **Phone:** 803/723-4374 44
◆   **Location:** Meeting St at Hassell St. 231 Meeting St 29401. **Hours:** 8 am-10 pm. **Features:** casual dress;
American   entertainment; street parking. One of Charleston's first new-era coffee houses, it serves only coffee, tea,
pastry & bread, in a very attractive space with tile floors, exposed brick walls & high beamed ceilings. ⊠

FULTON FIVE   **Dinner:** $7-$19   **Phone:** 803/853-5555 4
◆◆◆   **Location:** On Fulton St, just off King St & s of Market St. 5 Fulton St 29401. **Hours:** 5:30 pm-10:30 pm, Fri
Italian   & Sat-midnight. Closed: Mid Aug-9/2. **Reservations:** suggested. **Features:** cocktails; street parking; a la
carte. Very well prepared Northern Italian entrees. All served in a cozy comfortable dining rooms. **Cards:** AE,
DI, MC, VI.

GARIBALDI'S   **Dinner:** $9-$19   **Phone:** 803/723-7153 18
◆◆   **Location:** On S Market between Church & State sts. 49 S Market St 29401. **Hours:** 6 pm-10:30 pm, Fri &
Italian   Sat-11 pm. **Reservations:** required. **Features:** casual dress; children's menu; carryout; cocktails; street
parking; a la carte. Featuring very well prepared entrees with northern Italian flare, served in a cozy soft lit
dining room or patio. **Cards:** AE, MC, VI.

GAULART & MALICLET   **Lunch:** $5-$8   **Dinner:** $5-$15   **Phone:** 803/577-9797 46
◆◆   **Location:** Located between Meeting & King sts. 98 Broad St 29401. **Hours:** 8:30 am-10 pm, Mon-Fri
French   & Sat-10:30 pm. Closed: Sun. **Reservations:** accepted; evenings. **Features:** casual dress; health conscious
menu; carryout; beer & wine only; a la carte. Also known as "Fast & French", is an attractive, cozy place
consisting entirely of counters & high stools. Salads of unusual combinations & delicious snacks for a late afternoon perk;
also vegetarian dinners. **Cards:** AE, DS, MC, VI.   ⊠

HYMAN'S SEAFOOD COMPANY   **Lunch:** $3-$13   **Dinner:** $3-$13   **Phone:** 803/723-6000 9
〔AAA〕〔SAVE〕   **Location:** Just w of Market & the Omni Hotel at Charleston Place. 215 Meeting St 29401. **Hours:** 7 am-11
◆   pm. Closed: 11/26, 12/25 & Jewish holidays. **Features:** casual dress; children's menu; health conscious
Seafood   menu items; carryout; cocktails & lounge; fee for parking. Casual dining with 10-20 fresh fish daily. Popular
with locals. **Cards:** AE, DS, MC, VI. **Special Value: Free item with each meal purchased.**
(See color ad below)   ⊠

JESTINE'S KITCHEN Historical   **Lunch:** $3-$10   **Dinner:** $3-$10   **Phone:** 803/722-7224 47
◆   **Location:** Corner of Meeting & Wentworth in downtown. 251 Meeting St 29401. **Hours:** 11 am-9:30 pm, Fri
Regional   & Sat-10 pm. Closed: Mon, 12/25, Rosh Hashanna & Yom Kippur. **Features:** casual dress; carryout; beer &
American   wine only; street parking. Enduring Southern favorites such as freshly made soup, salad made with "what
got picked this morning", local seafood & Coca Cola cake. Old-fashioned fixtures in an informal '50s
atmosphere. **Cards:** MC, VI.

KAMINSKY'S Historical   **Dinner:** $1-$5   **Phone:** 803/853-8270 48
◆   **Location:** In the market area, just n of Meeting St. 78 N Market St 29401. **Hours:** noon-2 am.
American   **Reservations:** accepted. **Features:** casual dress; carryout; cocktails & lounge. A small & cozy space with an
attractive, intimate atmosphere, where the dessert menu changes several times a day. Specialties are
buttercake, cobbler, pie, as well as coffees, coffee specialty drinks & sundaes. **Cards:** AE, MC, VI.

THE LIBRARY AT VENDUE   **Dinner:** $14-$21   **Phone:** 803/723-0485 19
〔AAA〕   **Location:** In historic area off E Bay St, just e of Market Area; in Charleston's Vendue Inn. 23 Vendue Range
29401. **Hours:** 11 am-2:30 & 6-9:30 pm, Fri 5:30 pm-10 pm. Closed: Sun & 12/25.
◆◆◆   **Reservations:** suggested. **Features:** cocktails; entertainment; fee for parking; a la carte. Very well prepared
American   & presented entrees, a progressive American style presentation. The menu changes with the seasons with
fresh meat, pasta & seafood items. Rooftop bar. Smoke free premises. **Cards:** AE, DI, DS, MC, VI. ⊠

LITE AFFAIR CAFE   **Dinner:** $4-$6   **Phone:** 803/722-0023 49
◆   **Location:** Just off the "market area". 30 Cumberland St 29401. **Hours:** 9 am-midnight. Closed major
American   holidays. **Features:** casual dress; carryout; cocktails. A good stop for lunch or light supper, with its emphasis
on homemade soup, salad & creative sandwiches. Stacks of reading material inside; umbrella-covered tables
in the adjoining courtyard outside. **Cards:** AE, MC, VI.

(See map p. 438)

MAGNOLIAS UPTOWN/DOWN SOUTH Historical **Lunch:** $4-$10 **Dinner:** $10-$17 **Phone:** 803/577-7771 ⑯
◆◆◆ American
Location: 185 E Bay St 29401. **Hours:** 11:30 am-11 pm, Fri & Sat-midnight. **Reservations:** suggested. **Features:** casual dress; cocktails & lounge; a la carte. The original Customs House circa 1739. Entrees very well prepared with a Low Country flair using fresh ingredients. Extensive wine list. A stimulating environment. **Cards:** AE, MC, VI. ☒

MARKET EAST BISTRO Historical **Lunch:** $5-$9 **Dinner:** $7-$15 **Phone:** 803/577-5080 ㊿
◆◆ Continental
Location: 14 N Market St 29401. **Hours:** 11:30 am-10 pm, Fri & Sat-11 pm. Closed: 1/1, 1/2 & Superbowl Sun. **Reservations:** accepted. **Features:** Sunday brunch; carryout; cocktail lounge; wine only; a la carte. Savory & satisying, fine bistro cooking, making use of earthy ingredients & many spices, in a small & unpretentious space with beautiful interior ironwork. Homemade pasta; espresso/cappuccino. **Cards:** AE, MC, VI. ☒

MCCRADY'S Historical **Lunch:** $4-$19 **Dinner:** $4-$19 **Phone:** 803/577-0025 ㉔
◆◆◆ American
Location: In small alley between 149 & 151 E Bay St. 2 Unit Alley 29401. **Hours:** 11:30 am-3 & 5:30-11 pm, Fri & Sat 5:30 pm-midnight. Closed major holidays & Sun. **Features:** casual dress; carryout; cocktails & lounge; fee for parking; a la carte. Located in 1 of America's oldest taverns, circa 1778. Very well prepared & presented entrees in a casual atmosphere. A variety of meat & fresh seafood entrees avail with regular & appetizer portions avail. **Cards:** AE, DI, DS, MC, VI.

MINT JULEPS Historical **Dinner:** $9-$19 **Phone:** 803/853-6468 (55)
◆◆◆ Regional American
Location: On Queen St between Church & Meeting sts, across from The Mills House Hotel. 68 Queen St 29401. **Hours:** 5:30 pm-10:30 pm, Fri & Sat-11:30 pm. Closed: 1/1. **Reservations:** suggested. **Features:** carryout; cocktails & lounge. Menu leans toward Southern with a lot of "California consciousness" added, & the plates arrive beautifully composed & decorated. In a typical Charleston dwelling modified with Victorian touches. Smoke free premises. **Cards:** AE, CB, DI, DS, MC, VI. ☒

MISTRAL **Lunch:** $5-$9 **Dinner:** $8-$19 **Phone:** 803/722-5708 ②
◆◆ French
Location: At corner of S Market & Meeting sts. 99 S Market St 29401. **Hours:** 11 am-10 pm, Fri & Sat-midnight. Closed: 12/25. **Reservations:** suggested. **Features:** casual dress; children's menu; carryout; cocktails & lounge; entertainment; street parking; a la carte. Featuring entrees prepared with French influences including fresh fish, various meat & some pasta. Extensive wine list. Jazz band weekends. **Cards:** AE, DI, DS, MC, VI. ☒

THE OYSTER FACTORY **Lunch:** $5-$9 **Dinner:** $9-$18 **Phone:** 803/722-5877 ⑪
◆ Seafood
Location: On S Market St between Church & Meeting sts. 85 S Market St 29401. **Hours:** 11 am-4 & 4:30-10:30 pm. Closed: 12/24 for dinner. **Features:** casual dress; children's menu; carryout; cocktails & lounge; street parking; a la carte. An atmosphere of a fishing village. Featuring fresh seafood entrees & various meat. **Cards:** AE, MC, VI. ☒

PAPILLON CONTEMPORY MEDITERRANEAN
CAFE & BAKERY Historical **Lunch:** $6-$7 **Dinner:** $7-$12 **Phone:** 803/723-6510 (57)
◆◆ Nouvelle Italian
Location: At corner of N Market & East Bay sts. 32 N Market St 29401. **Hours:** 11 am-11 pm, Fri & Sat-midnight, Sun-10 pm. **Reservations:** accepted. **Features:** casual dress; children's menu; carryout; cocktails & lounge. The menu is large & offers many appetizers, salads, "oven-baked specials", seafood & meat as well as pasta & pizza from wood-burning stoves, all served in generous portions from fresh ingredients. **Cards:** AE, CB, DI, DS, MC, VI. ☒

PENINSULA GRILL **Dinner:** $15-$23 **Phone:** 803/723-0700 ⑳
◆◆◆ Regional American
Location: In Planters Inn. 112 N Market St 29401. **Hours:** 5:30 pm-10:30 pm, Fri & Sat-11 pm. **Reservations:** suggested. **Features:** dressy casual; cocktails & lounge; a la carte. Exciting newcomer to city's dining scene. Decor is a pleasant mix of the contemporary & the traditional. Cuisine is fabulously creative & wine list features a wide selection of wines by the glass. Smoking is permitted in the lounge only. **Cards:** AE, DI, DS, MC, VI.

PINCKNEY CAFE & ESPRESSO Historical **Lunch:** $4-$7 **Dinner:** $7-$14 **Phone:** 803/577-0961 (58)
◆◆ American
Location: 18 Pinckney St 29401. **Hours:** 11:30 am-2:30 & 6-10 pm. Closed: Sun & Mon. **Features:** Sophisticated beer & wine selections, ambitious specials & naughty desserts; lunch is ordered through the window, waiters serve at night. Bouillabaisse & rich pasta fritters, also chicken fajita. Espresso/cappuccino. Smoke free premises. ☒

POOGAN'S PORCH Historical **Lunch:** $3-$6 **Dinner:** $10-$18 **Phone:** 803/577-2337 ㉖
(AAA) ◆◆ **American**
Location: 72 Queen St 29401. **Hours:** 11:30 am-2:30 & 5:30-10 pm, Fri & Sat-10:30 pm. **Reservations:** suggested; for dinner. **Features:** casual dress; children's menu; carryout; cocktails & lounge. Featuring fresh seafood & Low Country cuisine in an old Charleston home. **Cards:** AE, MC, VI. ☒

PORTSIDE CAFE **Dinner:** $3-$6 **Phone:** 803/722-0409 (59)
◆ American
Location: In the rear of the Birds & Ivy shop, across from Charleston Place. 235 King St 29401. **Hours:** 11 am-9 pm. **Features:** carryout. Many daily specials are ample enough for "dinner at lunch" in the old Charleston tradition. Imaginative sandwiches & selections from the grill, black bean & jack cheese soup, & crabcake with cilantro cocktail sauce.

RESTAURANT MILLION Historical **Dinner:** $30-$70 **Phone:** 803/577-3141 ⑥
◆◆◆◆ French
Location: Historic district, in small alley between 149 & 151 E Bay St. 2 Unity Alley 29401. **Hours:** 6:30 pm-10 pm. Closed: Sun, Mon & 1/1-1/31. **Reservations:** required. **Features:** cocktails; a la carte. Outstanding cuisine served in restored 1788 structure. Excellent service. Prix fixe menu available. Extensive wine list. **Cards:** AE, DI, MC, VI.

SAFFRON **Dinner:** $5-$7 **Phone:** 803/722-5588 (60)
◆ Continental
Location: Just e of Calhoun St. 333 E Bay St 29401. **Hours:** 7 am-9 pm, Sun 8 am-8 pm. **Features:** casual dress; Sunday brunch; health conscious menu items; carryout; beer & wine only. Offers everything from food with a Middle-Eastern tilt to franks & fries, with lots of interesting choices in between. Cakes & other dessert, as well as freshly baked bread, cheese, meat & take-out items in a deli atmosphere. **Cards:** AE, DI, MC, VI. ☒

(See map p. 438)

SARACEN RESTAURANT Historical **Dinner:** $14-$19 **Phone:** 803/723-6242 ⑮
◆◆◆ **Location:** Just w of Broad St. 141 E Bay St 29401. **Hours:** 6 pm-10 pm. Closed: Sun, Mon, 11/26 & 12/25.
Continental **Reservations:** suggested. **Features:** casual dress; carryout; cocktails & lounge; fee for parking; a la carte. Former location of Farmers & Exchange Bank. Very well prepared entrees; menu changes monthly featuring fresh meat & seafood. **Cards:** AE, CB, DI, MC, VI. ⊠

SLIGHTLY NORTH OF BROAD **Lunch:** $4-$8 **Dinner:** $4-$15 **Phone:** 803/723-3424 ㉕
◆◆◆ **Location:** Corner E Bay & Cumberland sts. 192 E Bay St 29401. **Hours:** 11:30 am-3 & 5:30-10 pm, Fri & Sat-11 pm. Closed major holidays. **Features:** health conscious menu; carryout; cocktails & lounge; street
Regional parking; a la carte. Very well prepared & presented entrees of a variety of meat & fresh fish entrees. All
American served in a bustling & soft light atmosphere & featuring a Maverick southern kitchen. **Cards:** AE, DI, DS,
MC, VI. ⊠

SQUEAKY'S **Lunch:** $4-$11 **Dinner:** $7-$11 **Phone:** 803/722-1541 ㉑
◆ **Location:** Just off E Bay St. 5 Cumberland St 29401. **Hours:** 11 am-10 pm, Fri & Sat-11 pm. Closed: Sun,
American 1/1, 11/26 & 12/25. **Features:** casual dress; children's menu; carryout; cocktails. Lowcountry cooking in an old brick building. Lunch is appetizers, sandwiches & soups, at dinner the emphasis is on grilled or sauteed seafood & the tried-&-true fried dishes. **Cards:** AE, DS, MC, VI. ⊠

STICKY FINGERS RESTAURANT & BAR **Lunch:** $3-$10 **Dinner:** $6-$13 **Phone:** 803/853-7427 ㉒
◆◆ **Location:** 235 Meeting St 29401. **Hours:** 11 am-11 pm, Sun-10 pm. Closed: 1/1, 11/26 & 12/25.
American **Features:** casual dress; children's menu; health conscious menu; carryout; cocktails & lounge; fee for parking. Featuring Memphis & Texas wet & dry ribs & Carolina sweet ribs. ⊠

SUSHI HIRO OF KYOTO **Dinner:** $10-$16 **Phone:** 803/723-3628 ㉗
◆◆ **Location:** On King St between Liberty & Society sts. 298 King St 29401. **Hours:** 5:30 pm-10:30 pm, Fri &
Ethnic Sat-11 pm; fall & winter 5 pm-10 pm, Fri & Sat-11 pm. Closed: Sun, 11/26 & 12/25. **Reservations:** accepted. **Features:** casual dress; carryout; beer & wine only; street parking; a la carte. Japanese-style restaurant featuring sushi as well as tempura entree items. **Cards:** AE, MC, VI. ⊠

TASTE OF INDIA **Dinner:** $5-$11 **Phone:** 803/723-8132 ㉔
◆◆ **Location:** Corner of King & Wentworth sts. 273 King St 29401. **Hours:** 11:30 am-3 & 5-10:30 pm, Sun
Ethnic noon-3 pm. **Reservations:** accepted; 4 or more. **Features:** Sunday brunch; children's menu; health conscious menu; carryout; beer & wine only; street parking; a la carte. Mostly Northern Indian cuisine in a simple but welcoming restaurant. Indian beers & the refreshing sweet or salted lassi, the grilled bread naan, a combination platter of appetizers, vegetable dishes & mango ice cream. **Cards:** AE, DS, MC, VI. ⊠

T BONZ GILL & GRILL **Lunch:** $4-$15 **Dinner:** $4-$15 **Phone:** 803/577-2511 ㉕
◆◆ **Location:** In the market area, just n of Meeting St. 80 N Market St. **Hours:** 11 am-1:30 am.
Steakhouse **Reservations:** accepted. **Features:** casual dress; children's menu; carryout; cocktails. Features many cuts & weights of beef, all choice & aged; also as many seafood, chicken & vegetarian selections. Atmosphere is inviting, with exposed brick walls, great wooden beams, & humorous art. **Cards:** AE, MC, VI. ⊠

VICKERY'S BAR & GRILL **Lunch:** $5-$13 **Dinner:** $5-$13 **Phone:** 803/577-5300 ㉖
◆◆ **Location:** Between Archdale & King sts. 15 Beaufain St 29401. **Hours:** 11:30 am-1 am. Closed: 7/4 &
American 12/25. **Reservations:** accepted; 6 or more. **Features:** casual dress; carryout; cocktails & lounge; a la carte. Low-country cuisine with a Cuban tilt. Menu offers all types of salads & light fare, & many interesting sandwiches. Try scallops in a bag, scallops steamed in parchment with lime, white wine, cilantro red peppers & onions. Bar & very pleasa. **Cards:** AE, DS, MC, VI. ⊠

VINCENZO'S RISTORANTE **Lunch:** $4-$9 **Dinner:** $5-$14 **Phone:** 803/577-7953 ㉗
◆◆ **Location:** Corner of Meeting & Hasel sts. 232 Meeting St 29401. **Hours:** 11:30 am-10 pm, Fri & Sat-11 pm.
Italian Closed major holidays Sun & 1/1-1/15. **Features:** dressy casual; children's menu; carryout; cocktails. Family-operated, all recipes have over 50 years of tradition behind them. **Cards:** AE, DS, MC, VI. ⊠

VIVA MEXICO **Lunch:** $4-$8 **Phone:** 803/853-1888 ㉘
◆◆ **Location:** Just e of N Market St. 193A King St 29401. **Hours:** 11 am-3 pm. Closed major holidays & Sun.
Mexican **Features:** casual dress; carryout; street parking. Authentic food served at only limited tables indoors & in the courtyard outdoors. Menu has about 5 entrees for lunch, along with 3 or 4 daily desserts & Latin coffees. Smoke free premises. **Cards:** AE, DS, MC, VI. ⊠

WILD WING **Dinner:** $4-$7 **Phone:** 803/722-9464 ㉙
◆ **Location:** Just n of East Bay St. 36 N Market St 29401. **Hours:** 11 am-2 am. **Features:** casual dress;
American children's menu; carryout; cocktails. Try a sampler of 25 hot wings, including the Chernobyl & the China Syndrome. Fun & cozy ambience in a sports bar-type setting. **Cards:** AE, DS, MC, VI.

GREATER CHARLESTON (See map p. 452; index below)

Index of Establishments on the CHARLESTON ACCOMMODATIONS Spotting Map

(See map p. 452)

LODGINGS

BEST WESTERN INN   Rates Subject to Change   **Phone:** 803/571-6100   52
◆◆◆   3/1-7/5 [CP]   1P: $79   2P/1B: $89- 99   2P/2B: $89- 110   XP: $10   F14
Motel   7/6-8/31 & 10/1-10/31 [CP]   1P: $59   2P/1B: $69- 89   2P/2B: $69- 99   XP: $10   F14
12/1-2/28, 9/1-9/30 &
11/1-11/30 [CP]   1P: $49   2P/1B: $49- 79   2P/2B: $49- 89   XP: $10   F14
Location: 5 mi w on US 17. 1540 Savannah Hwy 29407. Fax: 803/766-6261. **Terms:** Reserv deposit; small pets only.
Facility: 87 rooms. 2 stories; exterior corridors. **All Rooms:** free movies. **Cards:** AE, CB, DI, DS, MC, VI.
(See color ad below)   🛏 🛆 CTV ✕ 🐾 D

CHARLESTON SUPER 8 MOTEL   Rates Subject to Change   **Phone:** 803/572-2228   48
◆◆   All Year [CP]   1P: $42   2P/1B: $46   2P/2B: $48   XP: $4   F13
Motel   **Location:** I-26 exit 209. 2311 Ashley-Phosphate Rd 29406. Fax: 803/553-7849. **Terms:** Sr. discount; reserv
deposit; small pets only. **Facility:** 89 rooms. 2 stories; exterior corridors. **All Rooms:** free movies.
Cards: AE, CB, DI, DS, JCB, MC, VI.   🛏 🛆 CTV ✕ 🐾 D

COMFORT INN RIVERVIEW   Rates Subject to Change   **Phone:** 803/577-2224   40
◆◆◆   3/8-6/7 [CP]   1P: $69- 129   2P/1B: $69- 129   2P/2B: $69- 129   XP: $10   F18
Motel   6/8-11/20 [CP]   1P: $49- 99   2P/1B: $69- 109   2P/2B: $69- 109   XP: $10   F18
12/1-3/7 & 11/21-11/30 [CP]   1P: $49- 89   2P/1B: $49- 99   2P/2B: $49- 99   XP: $10   F18
Location: Off US 17. 144 Bee St 29401. Fax: 803/577-9001. **Terms:** No pets. **Facility:** 128 rooms. 7 stories; interior corridors. **All Rooms:** free movies. **Cards:** AE, CB, DI, DS, JCB, MC, VI.   🛆 CTV ✕ D S

DAYS INN-AIRPORT/COLISEUM   Guaranteed Rates   **Phone:** 803/747-4101   45
◆◆   All Year   1P: $45- 73   2P/1B: $51- 79   2P/2B: $51- 79   XP: $6   F12
Motor Inn   **Location:** At jct I-26 & W Montague Ave, exit 213; from airport 3.3 mi via Montague Ave. 2998 W Montague
Ave 29418. Fax: 803/566-0378. **Terms:** Sr. discount; small pets only, $6 extra charge. **Facility:** 147 rooms. 2
stories; exterior corridors. **Dining:** Coffee shop; 6 am-9 pm; $5-$10. **All Rooms:** free movies. **Cards:** AE, CB, DI, DS, MC,
VI. *(See ad p 412)*   🛏 🛆 ♿ CTV ✕ 🐾 D

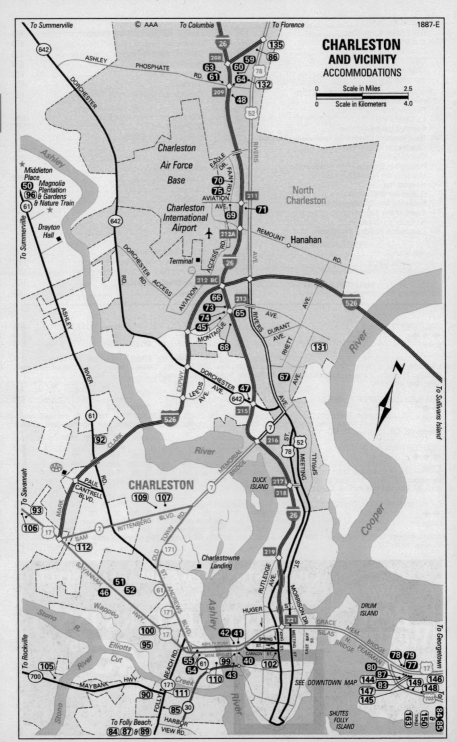

(See map p. 452)

DOWNTOWN/RIVERVIEW COURTYARD BY MARRIOTT   Rates Subject to Change   **Phone:** 803/722-7229   **43**
Motel   2/1-11/30   1P: $109- 129
               12/1-1/31   1P: $69- 109
Too new to rate; **Location:** Just off US 17. 35 Lockwood Dr 29401. Fax: 803/722-2080. **Terms:** No pets. **Facility:** 179 rooms.
Scheduled to open June 1997; 4 stories; interior corridors. **Dining:** Restaurant; 6-11 am. **All Rooms:** free & pay movies.
Cards: AE, DS, MC, VI. *(See color ad below)*   🛬 CTV ✕ D S

ECONO LODGE   Rates Subject to Change   **Phone:** 803/747-0961   **47**
◆◆   All Year   1P: $32- 55 2P/1B: $32- 55 2P/2B: $40- 65 XP: $5   F16
Motor Inn   **Location:** At jct I-26 & SR 642, Dorchester Rd exit 215 off I-26. 3668 Dorchester Rd 29405.
               Fax: 803/747-3230. **Terms:** Sr. discount; small pets only, $10 extra charge, $25 dep req. **Facility:** 199 rooms.
38 one-bedroom kitchen units, $52 for 2 persons; 7 two-bedroom kitchen units, $65 for 2 persons; 2 stories; exterior corridors.
Dining: Dining room, coffee shop; 5:30 am-9 pm; $5-$12. **All Rooms:** free movies. **Cards:** AE, CB, DI, DS, MC, VI.

🐾 🛬 CTV ✕ D

(See map p. 452)

| HAMPTON INN-RIVERVIEW | Rates Subject to Change | Phone: 803/556-5200 | 54 |

◆◆◆ All Year [CP]   1P: $65- 115 2P/1B: $65- 115 2P/2B: $65- 115 XP: $10   F18
Motel   **Location:** From US 17S, exit Albermarle Rd, 0.3 mi to Ashley Point Dr; from US 17N to SR 61 connector, left at 17S then 0.3 mi to Ashley Point Dr. 11 Ashley Point Dr 29407. Fax: 803/556-5200. **Terms:** Sr. discount; check-in 4 pm; no pets. **Facility:** 177 rooms. 3-4 stories; interior/exterior corridors. **All Rooms:** free & pay movies. **Cards:** AE, DI, DS, MC, VI. *(See ad p 443)*

HOLIDAY INN EXPRESS   Rates Subject to Change   **Phone:** 803/402-8300   46
◆◆◆ 3/1-7/5 [CP]   1P: $89   2P/1B: $99   2P/2B: $99   XP: $10   F18
Motel   7/6-8/31 & 10/1-10/31 [CP] 1P: $79   2P/1B: $89   2P/2B: $89   XP: $10   F18
12/1-2/28, 9/1-9/30 &
11/1-11/30 [CP]   1P: $69   2P/1B: $79   2P/2B: $79   XP: $10   F18
Location: On US 179, 3.5 mi w of Ashley River Bridge, just n of jct I-526 & US 17S. 1943 Savannah Hwy 29407. Fax: 803/763-6412. **Terms:** Reserv deposit; no pets. **Facility:** 80 rooms. 3 stories; interior corridors. **Cards:** AE, CB, DI, DS, JCB, MC, VI. *(See color ad p 455)*

(See map p. 452)

HOLIDAY INN-RIVERVIEW

Phone: 803/556-7100 [55]

3/15-9/1	1P:	$89- 99	2P/1B:	$89- 99	2P/2B:	$89- 99
2/10-3/14 & 9/2-11/30	1P:	$69- 79	2P/1B:	$69- 79	2P/2B:	$69- 79
12/1-2/9	1P:	$59- 69	2P/1B:	$59- 69	2P/2B:	$59- 69

Location: 1.8 mi w on US 17, s of bridge. 301 Savannah Hwy 29407. Fax: 803/556-6176. **Terms:** Reserv deposit; pets. **Facility:** 181 rooms. Many rooms with view of Ashley River. 14 stories; interior corridors. **Dining & Entertainment:** Dining room; 6:30 am-2 & 5-10 pm; $9-$14; cocktails/lounge. **Services:** Fee: coin laundry. **All Rooms:** free & pay movies. **Some Rooms:** coffeemakers, refrigerators. **Cards:** AE, CB, DI, DS, JCB, MC, VI.
(See color ad p 443)

HOWARD JOHNSON RIVERFRONT

Rates Subject to Change   Phone: 803/722-4000 [41]

3/1-7/5	1P:	$69- 79	2P/1B:	$89- 99	2P/2B:	$89- 109	XP: $10	F18
7/6-10/31	1P:	$59	2P/1B:	$59- 79	2P/2B:	$69- 89	XP: $10	F18
12/1-2/28 & 11/1-11/30	1P:	$49	2P/1B:	$49- 59	2P/2B:	$49- 69	XP: $10	F18

Location: 1 mi n on US 17S. 250 Spring St 29403. Fax: 803/723-2573. **Terms:** Reserv deposit; no pets. **Facility:** 150 rooms. 8 stories; interior corridors. **Dining:** Restaurant; 6:30 am-10 pm; $6-$14. **All Rooms:** free movies. **Cards:** AE, CB, DI, DS, MC, VI. *(See color ad below)*

MIDDLETON INN AT MIDDLETON PLACE

Phone: 803/556-0500 [50]

3/1-6/14 & 9/1-11/30 [CP]	1P: $119		2P/1B: $119		2P/2B: $129		XP: $20	F11
12/1-2/28, 6/15-6/30 &								
Fri-Sun 7/1-8/31 [CP]	1P: $109		2P/1B: $109		2P/2B: $119		XP: $20	F11
Mon-Thurs 7/1-8/31 [CP]	1P: $99		2P/1B: $99		2P/2B: $109		XP: $20	F11

Location: From SR 7, 9.5 mi nw on SR 61. 4290 Ashley River Rd 29414. Fax: 803/556-0500. **Terms:** Weekly rates; small pets only, $15 extra charge. **Facility:** 52 rooms. All rooms with fireplace. Nordic decor. Rural location with most rooms overlooking Ashley River. 2 stories; exterior corridors; 2 tennis courts; admission to Middleton Gardens. Fee: golf privileges. **Dining:** Breakfast 7:30-9:30 am, Sat & Sun-10:30 am; restaurant nearby. **Recreation:** nature program. Fee: river canoe trips; bicycles. Rental: canoeing. **All Rooms:** coffeemakers, refrigerators. **Cards:** AE, MC, VI. **Special Amenities:** Free breakfast. *(See ad p 456)*

SHERATON CHARLESTON HOTEL

Phone: 803/723-3000 [42]

3/1-6/15 & 9/1-11/30	1P:	$95- 110	2P/1B:	$105- 120	2P/2B:	$105- 120	XP: $15	F18
12/1-2/28 & 6/16-8/31	1P:	$69- 99	2P/1B:	$79- 99	2P/2B:	$79- 99	XP: $15	F18

Location: 1 mi n on US 17S. 170 Lockwood Dr 29403. Fax: 803/720-0844. **Terms:** Reserv deposit, 3 day notice; weekly/monthly rates; no pets. **Facility:** 333 rooms. 13 stories; interior corridors; luxury level rooms. **Dining & Entertainment:** Dining room; 6:30 am-10:30 pm; $9-$16; cocktails/lounge. **Services:** Fee: coin laundry. **All Rooms:** coffeemakers. Fee: movies. **Some Rooms:** refrigerators. **Cards:** AE, CB, DI, DS, MC, VI. **Special Amenities:** Free newspaper and preferred room (subject to availability with advanced reservations).

(See map p. 452)

TOWN & COUNTRY INN & CONFERENCE CENTER   Rates Subject to Change   **Phone:** 803/571-1000   🔟
◆◆◆   3/1-11/30   1P: $69- 99   2P/1B: $69- 99 2P/2B: $69- 99 XP: $7   F18
Motor Inn   12/1-2/28   1P: $59- 89   2P/1B: $59- 89 2P/2B: $59- 89 XP: $7   F18
              Location: On US 17; 3.5 mi w of Ashley River Bridge. 2008 Savannah Hwy 29407. Fax: 803/766-9444.
Terms: Pets. **Facility:** 122 rooms. 20 efficiencies, $10 extra charge; 2 stories; exterior corridors. **Dining:** Restaurant; 6:30
am-2 & 5:30-10 pm; $6-$19. **All Rooms:** free movies. **Some Rooms:** 2 kitchens. **Cards:** AE, CB, DI, DS, MC, VI.

🛏 🛋 🛋 🚭 CTV ✖ D

RESTAURANTS

ANGLE FISH   **Dinner:** $7-$14   **Phone:** 803/762-4722   85
◆◆   **Location:** 520 Folly Rd 29412. **Hours:** 11:30 am-3 & 6-9:30 pm, Fri & Sat 6 pm-10 pm. Closed: Sun.
Vegetarian   **Features:** Numerous seafood choices & other creative dishes are offered in this interesting & comfortable,
family-friendly restaurant. **Cards:** AE, DS, MC, VI.

BINH MINH   **Lunch:** $6-$13   **Dinner:** $7-$19   **Phone:** 803/569-2844   86
◆◆   **Location:** Near Northwoods Mall on Northwood Blvd, exit 209 on I-26W, straight at light, 0.3 mi on left. 7685
Ethnic   Northwood Blvd 29406. **Hours:** 11 am-3 & 5-10 pm, Sat from noon. Closed: Sun, Mon, 7/4, 11/26 & 12/25;
closed 2 weeks in Dec & July. **Reservations:** suggested. **Features:** casual dress; health conscious menu;
carryout; beer & wine only. Few of the Vietnamese dishes are fried & lots of fresh lettuces & varieties of mint are used.
Coriander appears in many dishes, as do bean sprouts, lemon grass & scallions. Food can be hot or mild, earthy or elegant.
Cards: DS, MC, VI.   ✖

BOWEN'S ISLAND   **Dinner:** $6-$15   **Phone:** 803/795-2757   87
◆   **Location:** 5.5 mi e of exit from James Island Bridge. 1870 Bowen's Island Rd 29412. **Hours:** 5 pm-10 pm.
Seafood   **Features:** casual dress. Great Low country cooking with "local color", fun & grubby building divided into 3
types of dining; the door of 1 primitive room stating "oyster eaters only" & serving all-you-can-eat roasted
oysters.

CALIFORNIA DREAMING   **Lunch:** $5-$11   **Dinner:** $5-$17   **Phone:** 803/766-1644   110
◆◆   **Location:** From US 17, exit Albermarle Rd; 0.3 mi to Ashley Point, at end of road. 1 Ashley Point Dr 29407.
American   **Hours:** 11 am-10 pm, Sat-11 pm. Closed: 11/26 & 12/25. **Features:** casual dress; children's menu; carryout
cocktails & lounge. A fort like structure overlooking Ashley River. **Cards:** AE, MC, VI.   ✖

CAPPY'S SEAFOOD RESTAURANT   **Lunch:** $5-$10   **Dinner:** $11-$17   **Phone:** 803/559-3552   105
◆   **Location:** From US 17, 1.5 mi s on SR 171/Folly Beach Rd. Turn right on Maybank Hwy/SR 700 for 2.5 mi
Seafood   on right just after bridge. Buzzard's Roost Marina 29412. **Hours:** 11:30 am-4 & 5-10 pm. Closed: 12/25
Features: casual dress; children's menu; carryout; cocktails & lounge. Located on the Stone River. A nautical
atmosphere with entrees of fresh seafood, various meat & pasta. **Cards:** AE, MC, VI.

CHARLESTON CRAB HOUSE   **Lunch:** $4-$8   **Dinner:** $8-$16   **Phone:** 803/795-1963   111
◆◆   **Location:** From US 17, 1.5 mi s on Westly/SR 171. Turn right on Maybank/SR 700, then right onto Wappoo
Seafood   Creek Dr. 145 Wappoo Creek Dr 29412. **Hours:** 11:30 am-3 & 3:30-10 pm, Fri & Sat-10:30 pm, Sun noon-3
& 3:30-9:30 pm. Closed: 1/1, 11/26 & 12/25. **Features:** casual dress; children's menu; carryout; cocktails &
lounge. On Intracoastal Waterway. Dock space & dock side dining avail. **Cards:** AE, DI, DS, MC, VI.

CISCO'S   **Lunch:** $4-$8   **Dinner:** $6-$9   **Phone:** 803/571-6441   109
◆   **Location:** 1 mi sw of Northbridge on SR 7. 1114 Sam Rittenberg Blvd 29407. **Hours:** 11:30 am-10:30 pm,
Mexican   Fri & Sat-11 pm, Sun-10 pm. Closed: 7/4, 11/26 & 12/25. **Features:** casual dress; children's menu; carryout
cocktails & lounge; a la carte. Casual family restaurant. **Cards:** AE, DS, MC, VI.   ✖

CRAWDADDY'S   **Dinner:** $6-$14   **Phone:** 803/762-4336   89
◆◆   **Location:** Off Folly Road. 1600 Pea's Island Rd 29412. **Hours:** 5 pm-10 pm. Closed: Mon. **Features:** Part
South Seafood traditional Lowcountry seafood & part crawfish & Cajun, the menu in this family restaurant nestled under
several large oaks offers an interesting variety of choices. **Cards:** AE, DI, MC, VI.

EASTERBY'S FAMILY GRILLE   **Lunch:** $3-$7   **Dinner:** $4-$15   **Phone:** 803/556-5707   92
◆   **Location:** From SR 7, 2 mi w. 2388 W Ashley River Rd 29414. **Hours:** 11 am-10 pm. Closed major holidays
American   & Sun. **Reservations:** accepted. **Features:** casual dress; children's menu; senior's menu; carryout; cocktails
& lounge. Featuring fresh local seafood & variety of meat items. **Cards:** AE, DI, DS, MC, VI.   ✖

(See map p. 452)

EASTERBY'S FAMILY GRILLE   **Lunch:** $3-$7   **Dinner:** $7-$16   **Phone:** 803/762-4890   **90**
◆   **Location:** From US 17, 1.5 mi s on Westly/SR 171, right on to Maybank Hwy/SR 700, then 0.8 mi. 1977
American   Maybank Hwy 29412. **Hours:** 11 am-10 pm. Closed: Sun, 11/26 & 12/25. **Reservations:** accepted.
Features: casual dress; children's menu; early bird specials; carryout; cocktails & lounge. Featuring steak,
barbecue & fresh seafood items. **Cards:** AE, CB, DI, DS, MC, VI.   ⊠

GILLIGAN'S STEAMER & RAW BAR   **Lunch:** $4-$6   **Dinner:** $8-$18   **Phone:** 803/766-2244   **93**
◆   **Location:** From US 17, 0.3 mi e. 160 Main Rd 29455. **Hours:** 11:30 am-10 pm, Sun-9 pm. Closed: 11/26 &
Seafood   12/25. **Reservations:** accepted. **Features:** casual dress; children's menu; carryout; cocktails. Casual
atmosphere featuring fresh seafood entrees as well as other meat & pasta. **Cards:** AE, DS, MC, VI.   ⊠

GILLI'S STEAK & RIB SHACK   **Dinner:** $8-$20   **Phone:** 803/763-1213   **106**
◆   **Location:** US 17, 0.3 mi e. 160 Main Rd 29455. **Hours:** 5 pm-10 pm, Sun-9 pm. Closed: 11/26, 12/25, Mon
Steakhouse   & Tues. **Features:** casual dress; children's menu; carryout; salad bar; cocktails. A casual atmosphere with a
Texas Roadhouse look. **Cards:** AE, DS, MC, VI.   ⊠

MED DELI   **Lunch:** $4-$6   **Dinner:** $6-$13   **Phone:** 803/766-0323   **95**
◆◆   **Location:** South Windermere Shopping Center at jct SR 171 & 700. 90 Folly Rd 29407. **Hours:** 11 am-10
American   pm. Closed major holidays & Sun. **Features:** casual dress; children's menu; carryout; beer & wine only.
Comfortable & cozy deli serving such wide variety of entrees. Large wine selection. **Cards:** AE, DS, MC, VI.

THE MIDDLETON PLACE RESTAURANT   Historical   **Lunch:** $5-$12   **Dinner:** $16-$18   **Phone:** 803/556-6020   **96**
◆◆◆   **Location:** 14 mi nw of jct US 17 & SR 61. Rt 4 Ashley River Rd 29414. **Hours:** 11 am-3 pm, Fri & Sat also
South   6 pm-9 pm. **Features:** casual dress; cocktail lounge; beer & wine only. In one of the many old buildings
American   gracing a lovely plantation. The menu is brief but interesting; she-crab soup, panned quail garnished with a
julienne of country ham & spoon bread. **Cards:** MC, VI.   ⊠

PUSSER'S LANDING OF CHARLESTON   **Dinner:** $6-$10   **Phone:** 803/853-1000   **99**
▲▲▲   **Location:** From US 17, just e on Lockwood Dr; in the Rice Mill Building next to the city marina. 17
                   Lockwood Dr 29404. **Hours:** 11 am-10 pm; Thurs-Sat to 11 pm. **Reservations:** suggested. **Features:** casual
◆◆◆   dress; children's menu; health conscious menu; carryout; cocktails & lounge; a la carte. A variety of meat,
Ethnic   pasta & fresh local fish prepared with influences from the West Indies & Britannia. Some tables with views of
the Ashley River. **Cards:** AE, DI, DS, MC, VI.   ⊠

S & S CAFETERIA   **Phone:** 803/556-9420   **107**
▲▲▲   **Location:** 1 mi sw of Northbridge on SR 7. 1104 Sam Rittenberg Blvd 29406. **Hours:** 11 am-2:15 & 4:30-8
                   pm, Sun 11 am-8 pm. Closed: 12/25. **Features:** casual dress; children's menu; health conscious menu;
◆   carryout. Trays carried on request. **Cards:** MC, VI.   ⊠
American

SEA ISLAND CAFE   **Lunch:** $3-$7   **Dinner:** $3-$11   **Phone:** 803/795-7700   **84**
◆◆   **Location:** 1006 Folly Rd 29412. **Hours:** 11 am-4 pm, Fri & Sat-9 pm. Closed major holidays & Sun.
American   **Reservations:** accepted. **Features:** casual dress; carryout; beer & wine only. A cordial & well-trained staff
serves familiar sandwiches & salads, as well as pasta & a soup of the day. The food is fresh & well made,
as in the artichoke & basil hero with a spread of pesto sauce, sliced tomato & shavings of cheese. **Cards:** MC, VI.   ⊠

SEASONS   **Lunch:** $4-$7   **Dinner:** $7-$17   **Phone:** 803/763-0487   **100**
▲▲▲   **Location:** On US 17S/Savannah Hwy. 851 Savannah Hwy 29407. **Hours:** 11 am-3:30 & 5-9:30 pm, Fri &
                   Sat-10 pm. Closed major holidays. **Reservations:** suggested. **Features:** casual dress; carryout; cocktails &
◆◆   lounge. Influences from all over the world can be detected on the menu, yet they have been made
Regional   thoroughly American, producing an interesting selection that nearly everyone can relate to. Attentive &
American   well-paced service, intimate setting. **Cards:** AE, CB, DI, MC, VI.   ⊠

SERMET'S GRILL   **Lunch:** $4-$8   **Dinner:** $6-$16   **Phone:** 803/769-4433   **112**
◆◆   **Location:** Just n of I-526 on Savannah Hwy/US 17 in the Quadrangle Shopping Center. 630 Skylark Rd
Ethnic   29407. **Hours:** 11 am-3 pm, also Tues-Sat 5 pm-10 pm, Sun 10 am-2 pm. Closed major holidays.
                   Reservations: accepted. **Features:** casual dress; children's menu; carryout; a la carte. Authentic
Mediterranean cuisine. **Cards:** AE, DS, MC, VI.   ⊠

TASTE OF NEW ORLEANS   Historical   **Dinner:** $10-$15   **Phone:** 803/723-3222   **102**
◆◆   **Location:** At Coming Street. 43-A Cannon St 29403. **Hours:** 11 am-3 & 6-10 pm, Sat from 6 pm. Closed:
South   Sun & Mon. **Reservations:** accepted. **Features:** casual dress; children's menu; carryout; beer & wine only.
American   Generous portions of down-home Southern cooking with New Orleans flavor, served in a colorfully decorated
                   place. Lunches are more strictly regional Southern, nights are dedicated to the cooking of Louisiana.
Cards: DS, MC, VI.

The Charleston Vicinity

EDISTO ISLAND—1,300

LODGING

CASSINA POINT PLANTATION   Guaranteed Rates   **Phone:** 803/869-2535
◆◆◆   All Year [BP]   1P: $90   2P/1B: $115   2P/2B: $115   XP: $25
Historic Bed   **Location:** From SR 174, ne on Indigo Hill Rd for 1.3 mi, left on Clark Rd for 0.5 mi then proceed 1.3 mi on
& Breakfast   dirt road to entrance. 1642 Clark Road 29438 (PO Box 535). Fax: 803/869-2535. **Terms:** Age restrictions
               may apply; reserv deposit, 7 day notice, handling fee imposed; no pets. **Facility:** 4 rooms. 3 stories; interior
corridors; smoke free premises.   ⊠ D

RESTAURANT

THE OLD POST OFFICE   **Dinner:** $18-$22   **Phone:** 803/869-2339
◆◆   **Location:** Hwy 174, Peters Point Rd, 4 mi from Edisto Beach. 1442 Hwy 174 29438. **Hours:** 6 pm-10 pm.
South   Closed major holidays, Sun & 1/2-1/16. **Reservations:** suggested. **Features:** casual dress; health conscious
American   menu; cocktails & lounge. A place where the heritage of Lowcountry & Southern cuisine has been kept alive.
               A fine presentation of local seafoods & the house specialty of "speckled" grits & other meat items. All in a
contemporary setting. **Cards:** MC, VI.   ⊠

FOLLY BEACH—1,400

LODGING

CHARLESTON ON THE BEACH-HOLIDAY INN   Rates Subject to Change   **Phone:** 803/588-6464

◆◆◆   6/1-8/31   1P: $146   2P/1B: $146   2P/2B: $146
Motor Inn   4/1-5/31 & 9/1-10/31   1P: $126   2P/1B: $126   2P/2B: $126
                   12/1-3/31 & 11/1-11/30   1P: $89   2P/1B: $89   2P/2B: $89
Location: At jct SR 171 & Center St. 1 Center St 29439 (PO Box 68). Fax: 803/588-2500. **Terms:** Reserv deposit, 3 day notice; no pets. **Facility:** 132 rooms. 9 stories; exterior corridors. **Dining:** Restaurant; 7 am-2 & 5:30-10 pm; $8-$15. **All Rooms:** free & pay movies. **Cards:** AE, DI, DS, MC, VI.   🛏 CTV ✕ 🎲 D

RESTAURANT

CAFE SUZANNE   **Dinner:** $9-$15   **Phone:** 803/588-2101
◆◆   **Location:** 4 Center St 29439. **Hours:** 5:30 pm-9:30 pm, Fri & Sat-10 pm, Sun brunch 10 am-2 pm. Closed:
American   11/26, 12/25 & Mon off season. **Reservations:** suggested. **Features:** casual dress; health conscious menu; carryout; beer & wine only; a la carte. Very well prepared & presented entrees specializing in fresh seafood, pasta & the use of fresh herbs as well as a variety of meat items. Freshly made pasta, bread & pastries. All in a cozy atmosphere & a screened patio. **Cards:** MC, VI.   ✕

GOOSE CREEK—24,700

LODGING

HOLIDAY INN EXPRESS   Rates Subject to Change   **Phone:** 803/572-9500
◆◆   All Year [CP]   1P: $49- 55   2P/1B: $59- 69 2P/2B: $59- 69 XP: $5   F19
Motel   **Location:** US 52 & 176. 103 Red Bank Rd 29445. Fax: 803/553-2827. **Terms:** Sr. discount; no pets.
                   Facility: 60 rooms. 2 stories; exterior corridors. **All Rooms:** free movies. **Cards:** AE, DI, DS, JCB, MC, VI.   CTV ✕ D

HOLLYWOOD—2,100

RESTAURANT

DEAN WALKER & FAMILY SEAFOOD RESTAURANT   **Lunch:** $3-$6   **Dinner:** $6-$12   **Phone:** 803/889-2413
ⓐⓐⓐ   **Location:** From US 17S, 0.3 mi s on SR 165; just w of jct SR 162. 6281 SR 162 29449. **Hours:** 11:30 am-3
◆   pm, Thurs-Sat to 9:30 pm. Closed major holidays, 12/24, Sun & Mon. **Features:** children's menu; senior's
Seafood   menu; carryout; cocktails. Casual dining. **Cards:** MC, VI.

ISLE OF PALMS—3,700

LODGINGS

THE BOARDWALK INN AT WILD DUNES   **Phone:** 803/886-6000
Resort Hotel   Under construction; **Location:** Jct SR 517 & 703, 2 mi n on SR 703, 0.3 mi. 5757 Palm Blvd 29451.
Fax: 803/886-2916. **Terms:** Check-in 4 pm; reserv deposit; no pets. **Facility:** 93 rooms. Scheduled to open October 1997; 5 stories; interior corridors. **Dining:** Restaurant; 7 am-10 pm; $10-$19. **All Rooms:** free movies. **Some Rooms:** 4 efficiencies. *(See ad p 454)*   🛏 ♿ CTV ✕ D S

SEA CABIN ON THE OCEAN   Rates Subject to Change   **Phone:** 803/886-8144
ⓐⓐⓐ   6/5-8/20   2P/1B: $100- 142
                  4/1-6/4 & 8/21-10/15   2P/1B: $80- 115
◆◆   12/1-3/31 & 10/16-11/30   2P/1B: $60- 85
Apartment   **Location:** Office located at jct of SR 517 & SR 703, Palm Blvd. 1304 Palm Blvd 29451. Fax: 803/886-5131.
Motel   **Terms:** Check-in 4 pm; reserv deposit, 14 day notice, handling fee imposed; no pets. **Facility:** 138 rooms.
                  Rates for up to 4 persons; 3 stories; exterior corridors. **All Rooms:** kitchens. **Cards:** AE, MC, VI.
(See ad p 454)   🛏 CTV ✕ D

WILD DUNES RESORT   Rates Subject to Change   **Phone:** 803/886-6000
◆◆◆   6/13-8/15   1P: $109- 199 2P/1B: $109- 199 2P/2B: $119- 279
Resort   3/19-6/12 & 8/16-11/19   1P: $109- 209 2P/1B: $109- 209 2P/2B: $109- 219
Complex   12/1-3/18 & 11/20-11/30   1P: $89- 149 2P/1B: $89- 149 2P/2B: $89- 199
                  Location: Jct SR 517 & 703; 2 mi n on SR 703, 0.3 mi on Palm Blvd. 5757 Palm Blvd 29451 (PO Box
20575, CHARLESTON, 29413). Fax: 803/886-2916. **Terms:** Check-in 4 pm; reserv deposit, 7 night min stay, 6/15-8/21; no pets. **Facility:** 300 rooms. 2- to 4-bedroom villas for 4-6 persons, $180-$400; $115-$275 off season; 5 stories; exterior corridors. **Dining:** 2 restaurants, cafeteria; 7 am-11 pm, snack shops; $7-$20. **All Rooms:** kitchens, free movies. **Cards:** AE, DI, DS, MC, VI. *(See ad p 454)*   🛏 🛏 ♿ CTV ✕ D

RESTAURANTS

ANGELO'S ITALIAN RESTAURANT & ISLAND SUSHI   **Dinner:** $8-$15   **Phone:** 803/886-5133
◆◆   **Location:** 0.5 mi s of causeway. 1010 A Ocean Blvd 29451. **Hours:** 5 pm-10 pm. Closed: Sun off season.
Italian   **Reservations:** accepted. **Features:** casual dress; carryout; cocktails & lounge; street parking. The other half of Island Sushi, this restaurant serves very good Italian in a beach atmosphere of casualness & camaraderie. Garlic- & rosemary-flavored oil presented with the crusty loaf of bread. A good wine list. **Cards:** AE, DI, DS, MC, VI.   ✕

LONG ISLAND CAFE   **Lunch:** $5-$8   **Dinner:** $5-$15   **Phone:** 803/886-8809
◆◆   **Location:** Island Shopping Center. Palm Blvd 29451. **Hours:** 11:30 am-2:30 & 5:30-9:30 pm, Sun 11 am-2 &
American   5:30-9:30 pm; may close Sun off season. Closed: 11/26 & 12/25. **Reservations:** accepted. **Features:** No A/C; casual dress; Sunday brunch; children's menu; carryout; cocktails. Many of the appetizers in this pleasant, unpretentious cafe, if coupled with a salad, would be enough for those who want to enjoy a small meal. Friendly & efficient service. **Cards:** AE, DS, MC, VI.   ✕

ONE EYED PARROT   **Dinner:** $7-$17   **Phone:** 803/886-4360
ⓐⓐⓐ   **Location:** 0.8 mi s of Isle of Palm Connector & Palm Blvd. 1130 Ocean Blvd 29451. **Hours:** 5 pm-10:30 pm,
◆   Fri & Sat-11 pm. Closed: 11/26 & 12/25. **Features:** casual dress; children's menu; carryout; cocktails; street
Seafood   parking. Located on the beach, featuring Floridean-style preparation of fresh seafood, pasta & meat. A blend of Caribbean, Florida & Mexican-style cooking. **Cards:** AE, CB, DI, DS, MC, VI.   ✕

SEA BISCUIT CAFE   **Lunch:** $3-$7   **Phone:** 803/886-4079
◆◆   **Location:** 0.3 mi s off causeway. 21 JC Long Blvd 29451. **Hours:** 6:30 am-2:30 pm, Sat & Sun 7:30 am-1
American   pm. Closed: Mon. **Features:** casual dress; Sunday brunch. In a wooden building which looks like a beach
house with a small front porch, the menu offers all kinds of biscuits, eggs with various breakfast meat, &
other breakfast fare. Also banana bread & grits with salmon cakes.

TRADEWINDS ISLAND CUISINE   **Dinner:** $6-$16   **Phone:** 803/886-5678
◆   **Location:** At Intracoastal Waterway. 41st Ave 29451. **Hours:** 5:30 pm-9 pm, Fri & Sat-10 pm. Closed: Sun
American   off season. **Features:** casual dress; children's menu; cocktails & lounge. Step right off your yacht into this
casual, airy restaurant for familiar, but creative, seafood; also beef, chicken & pasta, or a dinner of first
courses. Family-friendly, with friendly & efficient service. **Cards:** AE, DI, DS, MC, VI.

JOHNS ISLAND—7,600

RESTAURANTS

THE PRIVATEER SEAFOOD RESTAURANT   **Dinner:** $14-$18   **Phone:** 803/768-1290
◆◆   **Location:** In Bohicket Marina Village. 1882 Andell Bluff Blvd 29455. **Hours:** 5:30 pm-9 pm; 4/19-9/7 to 10
Seafood   pm. **Reservations:** suggested. **Features:** casual dress; children's menu; carryout; cocktails & lounge.
Contemporary dining room overlooking Bohicket Marina. Fresh seafood specialties. **Cards:** AE, DI, MC, VI.

ROSEBANK FARMS CAFE   **Lunch:** $8-$15   **Dinner:** $16-$25   **Phone:** 803/768-1807
◆◆   **Location:** At Bohicket Village Center & Market in the Bohicket Marina. 1886 Andell Bluff Rd 29455.
South   **Hours:** 11 am-2:30 & 6-9 pm. Closed: 1/1, 11/26, 12/24 & 12/25. **Features:** casual dress; children's menu;
American   carryout; cocktails & lounge; entertainment. Southern cooking modernized to suit contemporary tastes, using
vegetables grown at Rosebank Farms. Seafood sausage, southern caesar salad (fried grits instead of
croutons) & pulled, braised rabbit with butterbean succotash. **Cards:** AE, DS, MC, VI.

ST. JOHNS ISLAND CAFE   **Lunch:** $3-$12   **Dinner:** $6-$13   **Phone:** 803/559-9090
◆◆   **Location:** Maybank Hwy between River & Main/Bohicket. 3140 Maybank Hwy. **Hours:** 7 am-9 pm, Sun 9:30
American   am-2 pm. Closed: 1/1 & 12/25. **Features:** casual dress; Sunday brunch; children's menu; beer & wine only.
Gorgeous desserts, real breakfasts replete with steak & sausage biscuits with gravy, hot & cold sandwiches,
& a large range of choices of all kinds of cakes, pies & breads, which can be made to order. **Cards:** DS, MC, VI.

KIAWAH ISLAND—700

LODGINGS

KIAWAH ISLAND HOMES & VILLAS   Rates Subject to Change   **Phone:** 803/768-2121
◆◆◆   6/11-8/23   1P: $185- 475   2P/2B: $185- 475
Resort   3/5-6/10 & 8/24-11/30   1P: $125- 355   2P/2B: $125- 355
Cottage   12/1-3/4   1P: $99- 229   2P/2B: $99- 229
Location: From main gate follow the Parkway for 2.1 mi, follow signs to East Beach Village, turn right to
Town Center. 1 Town Center 29455 (12 Kiawah Beach Dr). Fax: 803/768-6058. **Terms:** Check-in 4 pm; reserv deposit, 30
day notice; no pets. **Facility:** 368 rooms. 3- & 4-bedroom villas & homes $273-$541 in season. Rates for 2 to 8 persons; 3
stories; exterior corridors. **Dining:** 2 dining rooms, 4 restaurants, cafeteria; 6:30 am-11 pm; in winter to 10 pm food court;
$6-$25. **All Rooms:** kitchens, free movies. **Cards:** AE, CB, DI, DS, JCB, MC, VI. *(See color ad below)*

KIAWAH ISLAND RESORT   Rates Subject to Change   **Phone:** 803/768-2121
◆◆◆◆   6/11-8/23   1P: $185- 475   2P/1B: $185- 475   2P/2B: $185- 475   XP: $25   F18
Resort Motor   3/5-6/10 & 8/24-11/30   1P: $125- 355   2P/1B: $125- 355   2P/2B: $125- 355   XP: $25   F18
Inn   12/1-3/4   1P: $99- 229   2P/1B: $99- 229   2P/2B: $99- 229   XP: $25   F18
Location: From US 17, 17 mi e on SR 20. 12 Kiawah Beach Dr 29455. Fax: 803/768-6099. **Terms:** Sr.
discount; check-in 4 pm; reserv deposit, 14 day notice; 4% service charge; no pets. **Facility:** 150 rooms. 3 stories; exterior
corridors. **Dining:** Dining room, 4 restaurants, cafeteria; 6:30 am-11 pm; $6-$25. **All Rooms:** free movies. **Cards:** AE, CB,
DI, DS, JCB, MC, VI.

RESTAURANTS

THE JASMINE PORCH   **Lunch:** $8-$20   **Dinner:** $26-$38   **Phone:** 803/768-2121
◆◆◆   **Location:** From US 17, 17 mi e on SR 20; in Kiawah Island Resort. 12 Kiawah Beach Dr 29455. **Hours:** 11
Steak and   am-10:30 pm. **Reservations:** accepted. **Features:** casual dress; cocktails & lounge. Seafood fresh from the
Seafood   docks of South Carolina low country. Dry aged steak & southern inspired dishes. **Cards:** AE, CB, DI, DS,
MC, VI.

SWEETGRASS ON KIAWAH ISLAND   **Lunch:** $6-$11   **Dinner:** $7-$17   **Phone:** 803/768-0500
◆◆   **Location:** On West Beach in the Straw Market. 12 Kiawah Beach Dr 29455. **Hours:** 11 am-2:30 & 5:30-9:30
Nouvelle   pm. **Features:** casual dress; carryout; beer & wine only. Very attractive with a sophisticated, casual look & 2
American   floors for dining, with outdoor space avail on both levels. The menu has enough interesting variations to
                       please almost any palate. Smoke free premises. **Cards:** AE, MC, VI.   ⊠

LADSON—10,300

LODGING

DAYS INN   Guaranteed Rates   **Phone:** 803/797-1214
◆◆◆   All Year [CP]   1P: $45- 70 2P/1B: $45- 70 2P/2B: $45- 70 XP: $7
Motel   **Location:** Off I-26, exit 203. 119 Gateway Dr 29456. **Fax:** 803/797-3538. **Terms:** Sr. discount; no pets.
             Facility: 63 rooms. 2 stories; exterior corridors. **All Rooms:** free movies. **Cards:** AE, DI, DS, MC, VI.
(See color ad p 439)   ⊠ CTV ⊠ ⊠ D

MCCLELLANVILLE—300

LODGING

LAUREL HILL PLANTATION   Rates Subject to Change   **Phone:** 803/888-3708
◆◆◆   All Year [BP]   1P: $85   2P/1B: $95   2P/2B: $95   XP: $15
Bed &   **Location:** 0.6 mi e from US 17; 4.3 mi s of SR 45; entrance opposite St. James Santee School & adjacent
Breakfast   to fire station. 8913 N Hwy 17 29458 (PO Box 190). **Terms:** Age restrictions may apply; check-in 4 pm;
             reserv deposit, 3 day notice; no pets. **Facility:** 4 rooms. 2 stories; interior corridors; smoke free premises.
Cards: AE, DI, DS, MC, VI.   ⊠ D

MOUNT PLEASANT—30,100   (See map p. 452; index p. 450)

LODGINGS

COMFORT INN EAST   Guaranteed Rates   **Phone:** 803/884-5853   **79**
◆◆◆   3/1-10/31 [CP]   1P: $59- 109 2P/1B: $59- 109 2P/2B: $59- 109 XP: $10   F18
Motel   12/1-2/28 & 11/1-11/30 [CP] 1P: $59- 99 2P/1B: $59- 99 2P/2B: $59- 99 XP: $10   F18
         Location: On US 17; just e of Cooper River Bridge. 310 Hwy 17 bypass 29464. **Fax:** 803/881-6279.
Terms: Sr. discount; pets, $10 extra charge. **Facility:** 122 rooms. 2 stories; exterior corridors. **All Rooms:** free movies.
Cards: AE, CB, DI, DS, MC, VI.   ⊠ ⊠ CTV ⊠ D

DAYS INN PATRIOT'S POINT   Guaranteed Rates   **Phone:** 803/881-1800   **80**
◆◆   All Year   1P: $49- 90 2P/1B: $55- 96 2P/2B: $55- 96 XP: $6   F12
Motor Inn   **Location:** On US 17, just e of Cooper River Bridge. 261 Hwy 17 bypass, Johnnie Dodds Blvd 29464.
             Fax: 803/881-3769. **Terms:** Sr. discount; small pets only, $6 extra charge. **Facility:** 131 rooms. 3 stories; ex-
terior corridors. **Dining:** Coffee shop; 24 hours; $4-$8. **All Rooms:** Fee: movies. **Cards:** AE, CB, DI, DS, MC, VI.
(See ad p 412)   ⊠ ⊠ CTV ⊠ ⊠ D

GUILDS INN   Rates Subject to Change   **Phone:** 803/881-0510   **85**
◆◆◆   All Year [CP]   2P/1B: $85- 135   XP: $15   F15
Historic Bed   **Location:** 6 mi n off US 17 business route, exit Coleman Blvd via Whilden St; center of historic area, corner
& Breakfast   Pitt & Venning sts. 101 Pitt St 29464. **Fax:** 803/884-5020. **Terms:** Reserv deposit, 3 day notice; pets, with
             prior notification. **Facility:** 6 rooms. 3 stories; interior corridors; smoke free premises. **Dining:** Restaurant;
11:30 am-2:30 & 6-10 pm, Sun brunch 10 am-2 pm; closed Mon; $15-$20. **Cards:** AE, MC, VI.   ⊠ ⊠ D

HAMPTON INN CHARLESTON/MT. PLEASANT   Rates Subject to Change   **Phone:** 803/881-3300   **87**
◆◆◆   2/14-11/30 [CP]   1P: $71- 95 2P/1B: $79- 95 2P/2B: $87- 95 XP: $8   F17
Motel   12/1-2/13 [CP]   1P: $63- 90 2P/1B: $71- 90 2P/2B: $79- 90 XP: $8   F17
         Location: Just n of Cooper River Bridge off US 17N. 255 Johnnie Dodds Blvd 29464. **Fax:** 803/881-6288.
Terms: Sr. discount; check-in 4 pm; 2 night min stay; no pets. **Facility:** 121 rooms. 4 stories; interior corridors.
All Rooms: free movies. **Cards:** AE, CB, DI, DS, MC. *(See ad p 443)*   ⊠ CTV ⊠ D S

HOLIDAY INN CHARLESTON/MT. PLEASANT   Rates Subject to Change   **Phone:** 803/884-6000   **78**
◆◆◆   3/1-10/31   1P: $89- 119 2P/1B: $99- 119 2P/2B: $99- 119 XP: $6   F19
Motor Inn   12/1-2/28 & 11/1-11/30 1P: $62- 76 2P/1B: $68- 82 2P/2B: $68- 82 XP: $6   F19
         Location: On US 17; just e of Cooper River Bridge. 250 Hwy 17 bypass 29464. **Fax:** 803/881-1786.
Terms: Sr. discount; reserv deposit; no pets. **Facility:** 158 rooms. 5 stories; interior corridors. **Dining:** Dining room; 5 am-10
pm; $8-$16. **All Rooms:** free & pay movies. **Cards:** AE, DI, DS, MC, VI. *(See ad below)*   ⊠ CTV ⊠ D

(See map p. 452)

MASTERS ECONOMY INN
Phone: 803/884-2814 [77]
(AAA) (SAVE)
♦♦
Motel
All Year [CP]   1P: $36- 46   2P/1B: $37- 50   2P/2B: $38- 57   XP: $6   F18
Location: On US 17; n of Cooper River Bridge, w on Magrath Darby, just n. 300 Wingo Way 29464.
Fax: 803/884-2958. **Terms:** Pets, $6 dep req. **Facility:** 120 rooms. 26 efficiencies, $44-$52; 2 stories; exterior corridors. **Dining:** Restaurant nearby. **Services:** Fee: coin laundry. **All Rooms:** free movies. **Some Rooms:** refrigerators. **Cards:** AE, CB, DI, DS, MC, VI. **Special Amenities: Free breakfast and free local telephone calls.**
[icons] (CTV) (X) (D)

RED ROOF INN
Phone: 803/884-1411 [83]
♦♦
Motel

	Rates Subject to Change						
3/1-4/30	1P: $81	2P/1B:	$91	2P/2B: $101	XP:	$7	F18
5/1-9/30	1P: $71	2P/1B:	$81	2P/2B: $91	XP:	$7	F18
12/1-12/31 & 10/1-11/30	1P: $61	2P/1B:	$71	2P/2B: $81	XP:	$7	F18
1/1-2/28	1P: $51	2P/1B:	$61	2P/2B: $71	XP:	$7	F18

Location: On US 17; just e of Cooper River Bridge. 301 Johnnie Dodds Blvd 29464. **Fax:** 803/884-1411. **Terms:** Small pets only. **Facility:** 124 rooms. 2 stories; exterior corridors. **All Rooms:** Fee: movies. **Cards:** AE, CB, DI, DS, MC, VI.
[icons] (CTV) (X) (D)

SHEM CREEK INN
Phone: 803/881-1000 [84]
♦♦♦
Motor Inn

	Rates Subject to Change				
3/1-7/31 [CP]	1P: $99- 125	2P/1B:	$110- 135	2P/2B: $110- 135	
8/1-9/30 [CP]	1P: $79- 99	2P/1B:	$89- 110	2P/2B: $99- 145	
12/1-2/28 [CP]	1P: $69- 89	2P/1B:	$79- 110	2P/2B: $79- 125	
10/1-11/30 [CP]	1P: $89- 99	2P/1B:	$99- 125	2P/2B: $99- 125	

Location: 6 mi n off US 17 business route, exit Coleman Blvd, 1 mi e. 1401 Shrimp Boat Ln 29464. **Fax:** 803/849-6969. **Terms:** Reserv deposit; no pets. **Facility:** 50 rooms. 3 stories; interior corridors. **Dining:** Restaurant; 4:30 pm-10:30 pm, Sun noon-9 pm; $12-$16. **Cards:** AE, DI, MC, VI. *(See color ad below)*
[icons] (CTV) (X) (D)

RESTAURANTS

ALLIGATOR JACK'S
Lunch: $4-$11   **Dinner:** $8-$16   **Phone: 803/884-7599** [149]
♦♦
Ethnic
Location: 414 Coleman Blvd 29464. **Hours:** 11:30 am-10 pm. **Features:** carryout. A simple, casual place serving good food in a fun atmosphere, with the focus on Cajun cooking; mainly seafood specialties, with a few choices of meat or chicken. The portions are large & filling, as many dishes are roux-based. **Cards:** AE, DI, DS, MC, VI.

CAPRICCIO
Dinner: $9-$15   **Phone: 803/881-5550** [151]
♦♦
Regional
Italian
Location: Hwy 526 to Mt Pleasant, turns into Chuck Dawley Blvd, 0.5 blk from Coleman Blvd on Chuck Dawley. 1034 Chuck Dawley Blvd 29464. **Hours:** 5 pm-10 pm. **Closed:** Sun & week of 7/4. **Reservations:** suggested. **Features:** casual dress; health conscious menu; carryout; beer & wine only. A popular place, the simple dishes are lovingly prepared & served in a warm, inviting atmosphere. The antipasto plate is enough for a main course. Try Cioppino "Livornese", red snapper, shrimp & mussels in a flavorful, subtle sauce. **Cards:** AE, CB, DI, DS, MC, VI.
(X)

CAPTAIN GUILD'S CAFE
Dinner: $8-$12   **Phone: 803/884-7009** [150]
♦♦
Seafood
Location: Attached to Guild's Inn. 101 Pitt St 29464. **Hours:** 11:30 am-2:30 & 6-10 pm, Sun 10 am-2 pm. **Closed:** Mon. **Features:** Sunday brunch. Interesting & well-prepared food such as baked potato stuffed with tomatoes & artichoke hearts & topped with a creamy basil sauce. Posted chalk-board changes daily. Open kitchen. All desserts made on premises. **Cards:** AE, MC, VI.

CATCH'N COW
Dinner: $9-$20   **Phone: 803/884-8103** [161]
♦♦♦
Steak and
Seafood
Location: Off US 17 business route exit Coleman Blvd, 1.5 mi to Mill St. 508 Mill St 29464. **Hours:** 5 pm-10 pm. **Closed:** Sun, 11/26 & 12/25. **Reservations:** suggested. **Features:** casual dress; children's menu; carryout; cocktails & lounge; a la carte. Located on Shem Creek, many views of the marsh & tidal creek. A comfortable setting featuring USDA prime aged steak, lamb & veal. Fresh seafood entrees very nicely prepared & presented. Extensive wine list. **Cards:** AE, DI, DS, MC, VI.
(X)

CHILI PEPPERS
Lunch: $3-$5   **Dinner:** $6-$8   **Phone: 803/884-5779** [148]
♦
Mexican
Location: Off US 17 business route, exit Coleman Blvd; 1 mi e. 426 Coleman Blvd 29464. **Hours:** 11 am-10 pm. **Closed:** Sun. **Features:** casual dress; children's menu; carryout; beer & wine only. The menu consists of the familiar basics, with some interesting specialties which feature thinly sliced beef. All ingredients are fresh & of high quality. **Cards:** DS, MC, VI.

(See map p. 452)

COCO'S CAFE & DELI   **Lunch:** $3-$5   **Dinner:** $8-$15   **Phone:** 803/884-7579   147
◆   **Location:** On US 17; in the Patriots Plaza. 863 Houston Northcutt Blvd 29464. **Hours:** 11 am-3 pm, Tues &
Continental   Sat also 6 pm-10 pm. Closed major holidays & Sun. **Features:** carryout; cocktails. During the day a deli, but
2 nights a week is transformed with diverse dishes ranging from a starter of Caribbean jerk tenders to
Flounder Alain, Filet au Poivre & Duck a l'Orange. **Cards:** AE, DS, MC, VI.

EASTSIDE BAKERY & CAFE   **Lunch:** $5-$7   **Phone:** 803/881-1260   146
◆ ◆   **Location:** Crickentree Village. 1055 Johnnie Dodds Blvd 29464. **Hours:** 11 am-3 pm, Thurs-Sat also 5:30
Nouvelle   pm-9:30 pm. Closed: Sun, Mon & 12/25-1/1. **Reservations:** accepted; for 6 or more. **Features:** health
American   conscious menu items; carryout; beer & wine only. Healthy food, homemade bread & dessert in a casual &
cheerful atmosphere. Menu basically consists of sandwiches & salads, with a fish or chicken dish offered
daily for a heartier meal. Gourmet coffees & teas. Smoke free premises. **Cards:** MC, VI.   ⊠

FONDUELY YOURS   **Dinner:** $10-$18   **Phone:** 803/849-6859   157
◆ ◆   **Location:** Off US 17 business route, Coleman Blvd, 2 mi e. 853 Coleman Blvd 29464. **Hours:** 5:30
Ethnic   pm, Fri & Sat-11 pm. Closed major holidays, 9/2-9/5 & 12/24. **Reservations:** accepted. **Features:** casual
dress; children's menu; cocktails & lounge. Foods cooked fondue style, a variety of meat & seafood items
with different sauces avail. A casual, cozy atmosphere to dine in. **Cards:** AE, DI, DS, MC, VI.

GOURMET BLEND   **Lunch:** $1-$4   **Phone:** 803/849-8949   145
◆ ◆   **Location:** 354 W Coleman Blvd 29464. **Hours:** 6 am-5 pm, Sat 7 am-4 pm, Sun 8 am-3 pm.
American   **Features:** carryout. Healthy, substantial sandwiches prepared with creativity & served either in the small
dining room, on the oak-shaded deck, or through the drive-in window. Also a "create your own" option. Large
selection of superior coffees. Smoke free premises.   ⊠

J. BISTRO   **Dinner:** $7-$16   **Phone:** 803/971-7778   152
◆ ◆ ◆   **Location:** 819 Coleman Blvd. **Hours:** 5 pm-10 pm, Fri & Sat-11 pm, Sun 10:30 am-2:30 & 5-10 pm. Closed
Regional   major holidays, 12/24 & Mon. **Reservations:** suggested; 8 or more. **Features:** casual dress; Sunday brunch;
American   health conscious menu; cocktails & lounge; a la carte. An interesting menu ranging from very traditional to
such offerings as pearl clams in a garlic broth served in a bowl with prosciutto & tarragon rice. Cozy tables
are lined up close together bistro-style. **Cards:** AE, MC, VI.   ⊠

R B'S SEAFOOD RESTAURANT   **Lunch:** $5-$7   **Dinner:** $10-$17   **Phone:** 803/881-0466   158
◆   **Location:** Off US 17 business route, exit Coleman Blvd; 1.5 mi turn right onto Church St, follow signs. 97
Seafood   Church St 29464. **Hours:** 11:30 am-10:30 pm. Closed: 12/25. **Reservations:** accepted; for 8 or more.
Features: casual dress; children's menu; carryout; cocktails. Fresh seafood entrees, pasta, & meat. All
served in a nautical theme dining room. Tables avail weather permitting overlooking Shem Creek. **Cards:** AE, MC, VI.

REAGAN'S   **Lunch:** $4-$13   **Dinner:** $6-$14   **Phone:** 803/881-8671   163
◆   **Location:** From US 17 business route, exit Coleman Blvd; 1 mi to Shrimpboat Ln. 1313 Shrimpboat Ln
American   29464. **Hours:** 11:30 am-10:30 pm. Closed: 12/24 & 12/25. **Reservations:** accepted. **Features:** casual
dress; children's menu; carryout; cocktails & lounge. A full range of entrees with pasta, chicken, meat &
specializing in fresh local seafood. A great view of Shem Creek. **Cards:** AE, DI, MC, VI.   ⊠

RONNIES SEAFOOD RESTAURANT   **Dinner:** $11-$17   **Phone:** 803/884-4074   159
◆ ◆   **Location:** Off US 17 business route, exit Coleman Blvd, 1 mi e. 1 Shrimpboat Ln 29464. **Hours:** 5 pm-10:30
Seafood   pm, Sun 11:30 am-9 pm. Closed: 12/24 & 12/25. **Reservations:** required; 8 or more. **Features:** casual
dress; Sunday brunch; children's menu; carryout; cocktails. Located on Shem Creek, featuring fresh fish
entrees, aged meat & pasta entrees. Live entertainment on patio deck in summer. **Cards:** AE, MC, VI.   ⊠

SHEM CREEK BAR & GRILL   **Lunch:** $4-$8   **Dinner:** $8-$18   **Phone:** 803/884-8102   162
ⓐⓐⓐ   **Location:** Off US 17 business route, exit Coleman Blvd, for 1.5 mi then left on Mill St. 508 Mill St 29464.
Hours: 11:30 am-10:30 pm, Fri-11 pm, Sat 11 am-11 pm, Sun 11 am-10:30 pm. Closed: 11/26 & 12/25.
◆ ◆   **Features:** casual dress; Sunday brunch; health conscious menu; carryout; cocktails & lounge. Located on
Steak and   Shem Creek, views of the creek & the marsh. Patio & screened in dining rooms & a oyster bar. Featuring
Seafood   fresh seafood, pasta entrees & some Lowcountry prepared entrees. **Cards:** AE, DI, DS, MC, VI.   ⊠

SLIGHTLY UP THE CREEK   **Dinner:** $12-$18   **Phone:** 803/884-5005   153
◆ ◆   **Location:** On Shem Creek from US 17, exit Coleman Blvd, 1.5 mi then turn right on Mill St. 130 Mill St
Regional   29464. **Hours:** 5:30 pm-10 pm. Closed: 1/1, 11/26 & 12/25. **Reservations:** accepted. **Features:** dressy
American   casual; children's menu; carryout; cocktails & lounge. Very rich Lowcountry food prepared with a
sophisticated edge. Featuring Maverick Southern cooking. Fresh seafood entrees as well as pasta & meat
served. Beautiful views from 2 levels of the restaurant. **Cards:** AE, DI, DS, MC, VI.   ⊠

STICKY FINGERS RESTAURANT & BAR   **Lunch:** $4-$11   **Dinner:** $5-$15   **Phone:** 803/856-9840   144
◆ ◆   **Location:** Just n of Cooper River off US 17. 341 Johnnie Dodds Blvd 29464. **Hours:** 11 am-10 pm, Fri &
American   Sat-10:30, Sun-9:30 pm. Closed: 11/26, 12/24 & 12/25. **Features:** casual dress; children's menu; health
conscious menu items; carryout; cocktails & lounge. Featuring Memphis & Texas wet & dry ribs & Carolina
sweet ribs. **Cards:** AE, DI, MC, VI.   ⊠

SUPPER AT STACKS   Historical   **Phone:** 803/884-7009   154
◆ ◆ ◆   **Location:** 6 mi n off US 17 business route, exit Coleman Blvd via Whilden St; center of historic area, corner
American   Pitt & Venning sts. 101 Pitt St 29464. **Hours:** 6:30 pm-10 pm. Closed: Sun & Mon. **Reservations:** required.
Features: casual dress; wine only; street parking; prix fixe. A cozy & intimate ambience, not unlike dining in
a private home; working fireplace, red walls, high ceilings. 4 courses including soup served from a large tureen; offerings
depend on the marketplace. Smoke free premises. **Cards:** AE, MC, VI.   ⊠

TOUCAN'S BAR & GRILL   **Lunch:** $4-$8   **Dinner:** $6-$12   **Phone:** 803/881-2770   155
◆ ◆   **Location:** Off US 17 business route, exit Coleman Blvd, 2 mi e. 730-G Coleman Blvd 29464. **Hours:** 11
Mexican   am-2 am. **Features:** casual dress; Sunday brunch; carryout; cocktails & lounge. While there is a definite
Tex-Mex influence, there are many fresh seafood dishes, various sandwiches & salads, as well as a few
pizzas. Also serves on an outdoor porch. **Cards:** AE, CB, DI, DS, MC, VI.   ⊠

NORTH CHARLESTON—69,100   (See map p. 452; index p. 450)

LODGINGS

BEST WESTERN CHARLESTON INTERNATIONAL AIRPORT
Phone: 803/572-2200 64

3/1-5/31 & 10/1-10/31 [BP]	1P:	$81	2P/1B:	$91	2P/2B:	$91	XP: $5	F18
6/1-9/30 [BP]	1P:	$76	2P/1B:	$86	2P/2B:	$86	XP: $5	F18
12/1-2/28 & 11/1-11/30 [BP]	1P:	$67	2P/1B:	$77	2P/2B:	$77	XP: $5	F18

Location: Nw on I-26, exit 209. 7401 Northwoods Blvd 29406. Fax: 803/863-8316. **Terms:** No pets. **Facility:** 197 rooms. 4 stories; interior/exterior corridors; sauna, whirlpool. **Dining & Entertainment:** Dining room; 6 am-1 & 5-10 pm; $7-$20; cocktails/lounge. **Services:** Fee: coin laundry. **All Rooms:** coffeemakers, free movies. **Some Rooms:** microwaves, refrigerators. **Cards:** AE, CB, DI, DS, MC, VI. **Special Amenities:** Free breakfast.

BUDGET INN OF CHARLESTON
Rates Subject to Change   **Phone: 803/747-7691**   70

All Year [CP]	1P:	$28	2P/1B:	$38	2P/2B:	$38	XP: $4	F12

Location: On I-26, Aviation Ave W, exit 211A. 6155 Fain St 29406. Fax: 803/747-7691. **Terms:** Reserv deposit, 7 day notice; no pets. **Facility:** 100 rooms. 2 stories; exterior corridors. **Dining:** Cafeteria; 4 pm-10 pm; $4-$12. **All Rooms:** free movies. **Cards:** AE, MC, VI.

CHARLESTON HILTON HOTEL
Phone: 803/747-1900   65

4/1-6/15 & 9/16-11/15	1P:	$99- 149	2P/1B:	$114- 164	2P/2B:	$114- 164	XP: $15	F18
6/16-9/15	1P:	$89- 139	2P/1B:	$104- 154	2P/2B:	$104- 154	XP: $15	F18
12/1-3/31 & 11/16-11/30	1P:	$79- 129	2P/1B:	$94- 144	2P/2B:	$94- 144	XP: $15	F18

Location: At jct Montague Ave & I-26, exit 213B. 4770 Goer Dr 29406-6543. Fax: 803/744-2530. **Terms:** Check-in 4 pm; no pets. **Facility:** 196 rooms. 9 stories; interior corridors. **Dining:** Dining room; 6:30 am-2 & 5-10 pm; $10-$17. **All Rooms:** free & pay movies. **Cards:** AE, CB, DI, DS, JCB, MC, VI. *(See color ad p 18 & ad p 453)*

CHARLESTON HOLIDAY INN AIRPORT
Phone: 803/744-1621   75

All Year	1P:	$69- 95	2P/1B:	$69- 95	2P/2B: $69- 95

Location: On I-26; Aviation Ave, exit 211A. 6099 Fain St 29406. Fax: 803/744-0942. **Terms:** Check-in 4 pm; no pets. **Facility:** 260 rooms. 2-3 stories; exterior corridors; 2 lighted tennis courts; playground. **Dining & Entertainment:** Dining room; 6 am-2 & 5:30-10 pm, Sat & Sun from 6:30 am; $6-$15; cocktails/lounge; entertainment. **Services:** Fee: coin laundry. **All Rooms:** free & pay movies. **Some Rooms:** coffeemakers, refrigerators. **Cards:** AE, CB, DI, DS, MC, VI. *(See color ad p 453)*

COMFORT INN-AIRPORT
Phone: 803/554-6485   73

All Year [CP]	1P:	$35- 65	2P/1B:	$42- 75	2P/2B:	$45- 85	XP: $6	F18

Location: Jct I-26 & Montague Ave, exit 213, 3.8 mi from airport via Montague Ave. 5055 N Arco Ln 29418. Fax: 803/566-9466. **Terms:** Pets, $5 extra charge. **Facility:** 122 rooms. 2 stories; exterior corridors. **Dining:** Restaurant nearby. **Services:** Fee: coin laundry. **All Rooms:** free movies. **Some Rooms:** coffeemakers, refrigerators. Fee: whirlpools. **Cards:** AE, CB, DI, DS, JCB, MC, VI. **Special Amenities:** Free breakfast and free local telephone calls. *(See color ad p 439)*

AIRFIELD INN BY MARRIOTT
Phone: 803/572-6677   63

Fri & Sat 2/1-11/30 [CP]	1P:	$62	2P/1B:	$67	2P/2B:	$72	XP: $5	F18
12/1-1/31 & Sun-Thurs 2/1-11/30 [CP]	1P:	$57	2P/1B:	$62	2P/2B:	$67	XP: $5	F18

Location: I-26 exit 209. 7415 Northside Dr 29420. Fax: 803/764-3790. **Terms:** No pets. **Facility:** 119 rooms. 2 stories; exterior corridors. **Dining:** Restaurant nearby. **Services:** valet laundry. **All Rooms:** free movies. **Cards:** AE, DI, DS, MC, VI. **Special Amenities:** Free breakfast and free local telephone calls.

HAMPTON INN AIRPORT/COLISEUM
Rates Subject to Change   **Phone: 803/554-7154**   68

All Year [CP]	1P:	$57- 87	2P/1B:	$64- 85	2P/2B:	$64- 85	XP: $8	F18

Location: At jct I-26 & W Montague Ave, exit 213. 4701 Saul White Blvd 29418. Fax: 803/566-9299. **Terms:** No pets. **Facility:** 125 rooms. 4 stories; interior corridors. **All Rooms:** free & pay movies. **Cards:** AE, DI, DS, MC, VI. *(See ad p 443)*

(See map p. 452)

HOLIDAY INN EXPRESS NORTH CHARLESTON　　Rates Subject to Change　　**Phone: 803/554-1600**　G7
◆◆◆　　All Year [CP]　　　　1P: $49　　2P/1B: $54　　2P/2B: $54　　　XP: $5　　F1
Motel　　**Location:** From I-26, exit 215 Dorchester Rd, 0.5 mi n to Rivers Ave, 0.3 mi w on Rivers Ave opposite Nava
Hospital. 2070 McMillan Ave 29405. Fax: 803/554-1600. **Terms:** Small pets only, $10 extra charge
Facility: 97 rooms. 2 stories; exterior corridors. **All Rooms:** free & pay movies. **Cards:** AE, CB, DI, DS, JCB, MC, VI.
(See color ad p 463)　　　　　　　　　　　　　　　　　　　　　　　　　　　　　　　　🛏 �foodⓉ Ⓣ ⓉⓉ Ⓣ Ⓣ Ⓣ Ⓣ

KNIGHTS INN　　　　　　　　　　　　　　　　　　　　　　　　　**Phone: 803/744-4900**　69
ⒶⒶⒶ SAVE　　All Year [CP]　　　1P: $28- 31　2P/1B: $32- 43　2P/2B: $38　　XP: $2-5　F1
　　　　Location: Off I-26 at W Aviation Ave, exit 211A. 2355 W Aviation 29418. Fax: 803/745-0668. **Terms:** N
◆◆　　pets. **Facility:** 246 rooms. 31 efficiencies, $48-$53, 14 two-room units $60-$63; 2 stories; exterior corridors
Motel　　**All Rooms:** free movies. **Cards:** AE, CB, DI, DS, MC, VI.　　�Ⓣ 🟳 Ⓣ Ⓣ Ⓣ

LA QUINTA INN　　　　　　　　　　　　　　　　　　　　　　　**Phone: 803/797-8181**　6
ⒶⒶⒶ SAVE　　Sun-Thurs [CP]　　1P: $49- 55　2P/1B: $58- 64　2P/2B: $58- 64　XP: $10　F1
　　　　Fri & Sat [CP]　　　　1P: $46- 52　2P/1B: $55- 61　2P/2B: $55- 61　XP: $10　F1
◆◆◆　　**Location:** Nw on I-26, exit 209. 2499 La Quinta Ln 29420. Fax: 803/569-1608. **Terms:** Small pets onl
Motel　　**Facility:** 122 rooms. Attractively decorated public areas. 2 stories; exterior corridors. **Dining:** Restaura
nearby. **Services:** valet laundry. **All Rooms:** free & pay movies. **Some Rooms:** Fee: microwave
refrigerators. **Cards:** AE, CB, DI, DS, MC, VI. **Special Amenities: Free breakfast and free local telephone calls.**
　　　　　　　　　　　　　　　　　　　　　　　　　　　　　　　　　🛏 🚓 🟳 Ⓣ Ⓣ Ⓣ Ⓣ

QUALITY SUITES　　　　Rates Subject to Change　　**Phone: 803/747-7300**　6
◆◆◆　　All Year [BP]　　　1P: $79　　2P/1B: $89　　2P/2B: $89　　XP: $10
Suite Motel　　**Location:** I-26 & Montague Ave, exit 213; 3.8 mi from airport via Montague Ave. 5225 N Arco Ln 2941
Fax: 803/747-6324. **Terms:** No pets. **Facility:** 168 rooms. 7 suites with dual whirlpool $175; 5 stories; interio
corridors. **All Rooms:** Fee: movies. **Cards:** AE, CB, DI, DS, MC, VI.　🚓 🟳 Ⓣ Ⓣ Ⓣ Ⓢ

RADISSON INN, CHARLESTON AIRPORT　　　　　　　　**Phone: 803/744-2501**　7
ⒶⒶⒶ SAVE　　All Year　　　　　1P: $85- 110　2P/1B: $95- 120　2P/2B: $95- 120　XP: $10　F1
　　　　Location: On I-26; Aviation Ave, exit 211B. 5991 Rivers Ave 29406. Fax: 803/744-2501. **Terms:** No pets
◆◆◆　　**Facility:** 158 rooms. 8 stories; interior corridors; sauna, whirlpool. **Dining & Entertainment:** Dining roor
Hotel　　6:30 am-10:30 pm; $7-$15; cocktails/lounge; lunch buffet Sun-Fri; entertainment. **Services:** valet laundr
All Rooms: Fee: movies. **Some Rooms:** refrigerators. **Cards:** AE, CB, DI, DS, JCB, MC
Special Amenities: Free newspaper and free room upgrade (subject to availability with advanced reservations).
(See color ad below)　　　　　　　　　　　　　　　　　　　　🚓 🟳 🟳 Ⓣ Ⓣ Ⓣ Ⓢ

RAMADA INN-COLISEUM　　　Rates Subject to Change　　**Phone: 803/744-8281**　7
◆◆◆　　3/13-6/7　　　　　1P: $59- 79　2P/1B: $69- 89　2P/2B: $69- 89　XP: $10　F1
Motor Inn　　12/1-3/12 & 6/8-11/30　1P: $49- 59　2P/1B: $59- 79　2P/2B: $59- 79　XP: $10　F1
　　　　Location: I-26 exit 213A, Montague Ave. 2934 W Montague Ave 29418. Fax: 803/744-6230. **Terms:** N
pets. **Facility:** 155 rooms. 2 stories; exterior corridors. **Dining:** Restaurant; 6-10:30 am, 11-2 & 5-10 pm; $9-$1
All Rooms: Fee: movies. **Cards:** AE, CB, DI, DS, MC, VI.　　🚓 🟳 Ⓣ Ⓣ Ⓣ Ⓣ

RED ROOF INN　　　　　Rates Subject to Change　　　　**Phone: 803/572-9100**　6
◆◆　　2/12-10/3　　　　1P: $46- 54　2P/1B: $53- 63　2P/2B: $56　　XP: $7-9　F1
Motel　　10/4-11/30　　　　1P: $43- 51　2P/1B: $50- 60　2P/2B: $53　　XP: $7-9　F1
　　　　12/1-2/11　　　　　1P: $40- 48　2P/1B: $47- 57　2P/2B: $50　　XP: $7-9　F1
Location: Nw on I-26, exit 209. 7480 Northwoods Blvd 29406. Fax: 803/572-0061. **Terms:** Small pets only. **Facility:** 10
rooms. 2 stories; exterior corridors. **All Rooms:** free movies. **Cards:** AE, CB, DI, DS, MC, VI.　🛏 Ⓣ Ⓣ Ⓣ Ⓣ

RESIDENCE INN BY MARRIOTT　　　Rates Subject to Change　　**Phone: 803/572-5757**　6
◆◆◆　　All Year [CP]　　　1P: $95- 130　2P/1B: $95- 130　2P/2B: $100- 150　XP: $10
Suite Motel　　**Location:** Jct I-26 & Ashley-Phosphate Rd, exit 209. 7645 Northwoods Blvd 29406. Fax: 803/797-852
Terms: Sr. discount; reserv deposit; pets, $50-$75 dep req. **Facility:** 96 rooms. 2 stories; exterior corridor
All Rooms: kitchens, free movies. **Cards:** AE, CB, DI, DS, MC.　　🛏 🚓 🟳 Ⓣ Ⓣ Ⓣ

RESTAURANTS

IDLE HOUR　　　　　**Lunch:** $1-$4　　　　　　**Phone: 803/747-3280**　13
◆　　**Location:** 1065 E Montague Ave 29405. **Hours:** 9:30 am-4 pm, Sat 9 am-3 pm. **Closed:** Su
American　　**Features:** carryout. Stripped down, basic atmosphere takes the guest back to the '50s. No menu; specia
du jour on a board. 3-napkin chili burgers on a green plastic school lunchroom plate, chips in the bag
Coke in a bottle. Very popular locally.

(See map p. 452)

THE NOISY OYSTER　　　　**Lunch:** $4-$9　　　　**Dinner:** $7-$18　　　　**Phone:** 803/824-1000　　[132]
◆　　　　**Location:** From I-26 exit 209, Ashley Phosphate Rd, 0.5 mi n, w on Rivers Ave/US 52. 7571 Rivers Ave
Seafood　　29418. **Hours:** 11 am-10 pm, Fri & Sat-10:30 pm. Closed: 12/25. **Features:** casual dress; children's menu;
salad bar; cocktails. A nautical atmosphere as well as a rustic fish camp look. Featuring fresh seafood
entrees & a variety of other meat entrees. **Cards:** AE, MC, VI.　　　　　　　　　　　　　　　　　　　　[X]

NORTH TOWNE GREEK RESTAURANT　　　**Lunch:** $4-$7　　　**Dinner:** $4-$13　　　**Phone:** 803/863-1001　　[135]
◆ ◆　　　　**Location:** From I-26 exit 209, Ashley-Phosphate Rd, 0.5 mi n, w on Rivers Ave/US 52; opposite Northwoods
Greek　　Mall. 2093 Eagle Landing Blvd 29418. **Hours:** 11 am-10 pm, Fri & Sat-11 pm. Closed: 12/25.
Reservations: suggested. **Features:** casual dress; children's menu; health conscious menu items; carryout;
cocktails & lounge. Features authentic Greek entrees as well as American favorites. **Cards:** AE, DI, DS, MC, VI.　[X]

ST. GEORGE—2,100

LODGINGS

BEST WESTERN-ST. GEORGE　　　　　　　　　　　　　　　　　　　　　　　**Phone:** 803/563-2277
[AAA] [SAVE]　　All Year [CP]　　　　　1P: $49- 59　2P/1B: $49- 59　2P/2B: $59- 69　XP: $5　　　F18
◆ ◆ ◆　　**Location:** Jct I-95 & US 78, exit 77. 29477 (PO Box 386). Fax: 803/563-2277. **Terms:** Small pets only, $5
Motel　　extra charge. **Facility:** 68 rooms. 1 story; exterior corridors. **Cards:** AE, CB, DI, DS, MC, VI.
　　　　　　　　　　　　　　　　　　　　　　　　　　　　　　　　[🛏] [🏊] [CTV] [X] [D]

COMFORT INN　　　　　　　　　　　Rates Subject to Change　　　　　　　**Phone:** 803/563-4180
◆ ◆　　　　All Year [CP]　　　　　1P: $43- 48　2P/1B: $45- 55　2P/2B: $48- 58　XP: $10　　F12
Motel　　**Location:** Jct I-95 & US 78, exit 77. 139 Motel Dr 29477 (PO Box 654). Fax: 803/563-6817. **Terms:** No pets.
Facility: 104 rooms. 2 stories; exterior corridors. **All Rooms:** free movies. **Cards:** AE, CB, DI, DS, JCB, MC,
VI.　　　　　　　　　　　　　　　　　　　　　　　　　　　　　　[CTV] [X] [D]

ECONOMY INN OF AMERICA　　　　　　　　　　　　　　　　　　　　　　**Phone:** 803/563-4195
[AAA] [SAVE]　　All Year　　　　　　1P: $21- 30　2P/1B: $25- 38　2P/2B: $26- 41　XP: $4　　　F5
◆　　　　**Location:** On US 78 at jct I-95, exit 77. 5971 W Jim Bilton Blvd 29477. Fax: 803/563-4981. **Terms:** Reserv
Motel　　deposit; weekly rates; pets, $2 extra charge. **Facility:** 68 rooms. 2 stories; exterior corridors.
Dining: Restaurant nearby. **All Rooms:** free movies. **Cards:** AE, DS, MC, VI.　[🛏] [🏊] [CTV] [X] [D]

HOLIDAY INN-ST GEORGE　　　　　　Guaranteed Rates　　　　　　**Phone:** 803/563-4581
◆ ◆ ◆　　All Year [BP]　　　　　1P: $59- 85　2P/1B: $59- 85　2P/2B: $59- 85　XP: $10　　F18
Motor Inn　　**Location:** At jct I-95 & US 78, exit 77. 6014 W Jim Bilton Blvd 29477 (PO Box 798). Fax: 803/563-5576.
Terms: Sr. discount; small pets only. **Facility:** 122 rooms. 2 stories; exterior corridors. **Dining:** Dining room;
6:30 am-2 & 5:30-10 pm; $7-$12. **All Rooms:** free & pay movies. **Cards:** AE, CB, DI, DS, JCB, MC, VI.
　　　　　　　　　　　　　　　　Roll in showers.　[🛏] [🏊] [CTV] [X] [D]

ST. GEORGE ECONOMY MOTEL　　　　　　　　　　　　　　　　　　　**Phone:** 803/563-2360
[AAA] [SAVE]　　All Year　　　　　　1P: $27- 40　2P/1B: $30- 40　2P/2B: $32- 40　XP: $5　　D16
◆　　　　**Location:** On US 78 at jct I-95, exit 77. 125 Motel Dr 29477. **Terms:** Weekly rates; small pets only.
Motel　　**Facility:** 34 rooms. 2 stories; exterior corridors. **Dining:** Restaurant nearby. **Cards:** AE, DS, MC, VI.
Special Amenities: Early check-in/late check-out and preferred room (subject to availability with
advanced reservations).　　　　　　　　　　　　　　　　[🛏] [🏊] [CTV] [X] [D]

ST. GEORGE MOTOR INN　　　　　　　　　　　　　　　　　　　　　　**Phone:** 803/563-3029
[AAA] [SAVE]　　All Year　　　　　　1P: $16　　　2P/1B: $19　　　2P/2B: $21　　XP: $3　　F12
◆　　　　**Location:** Off I-95, exit 77, 2 mi e on US 78, 0.3 mi s on US 15. 215 S Parler Ave 29477. **Terms:** Reserv
Motel　　deposit; weekly rates; pets, $2 extra charge. **Facility:** 16 rooms. Handling fee imposed; 2 stories; exterior cor-
ridors. **All Rooms:** free movies, combo or shower baths. **Cards:** AE, DS, MC, VI. **Special Amenities:** Early
check-in/late check-out and free local telephone calls.　　　　　　　　　　[🛏] [CTV] [X] [D]

SUPER 8 MOTEL　　　　　　　　　　　　　　　　　　　　　　　**Phone:** 803/563-5551
[AAA] [SAVE]　　All Year　　　　　　1P: $32- 57　2P/1B: $34- 57　2P/2B: $37- 57　XP: $5
◆ ◆　　　　**Location:** On US 78 at jct 95, exit 77. 114 Winningham Rd 29477 (Rt 3, Box 760, WALTERBORO, 29488).
Motel　　Fax: 803/563-5551. **Terms:** Small pets only. **Facility:** 59 rooms. 2 stories; exterior corridors.
Dining: Restaurant nearby. **All Rooms:** free movies. **Cards:** AE, DS, MC, VI. **Special Amenities:** Free
breakfast and free local telephone calls.　　　　　　　　　　　　　[🛏] [🏊] [CTV] [X] [D]

SULLIVANS ISLAND—1,600

RESTAURANTS

GIBSON'S GOURMET　　　　　　　　　　**Dinner:** $3-$5　　　　　　　**Phone:** 803/883-3536
◆ ◆　　　　**Location:** 2213 Middle St 29482. **Hours:** 8 am-7 pm, Sat 10 am-4 pm. Closed: Sun. **Features:** With only a
American　　few tables, it offers mostly gourmet take-out items for those busy on vacation. Menus & items change daily,
but the freshness & quality are constant. All sandwiches & main course items come with 2 sides. Smoke free
premises. **Cards:** MC, VI.　　　　　　　　　　　　　　　　　　　　　　　　[X]

STATION 22　　　　　　　　　　　**Dinner:** $6-$17　　　　　　　**Phone:** 803/883-3355
◆ ◆　　　　**Location:** 0.3 mi s of causeway. 2205 Middle St 29482. **Hours:** 5:30 pm-10 pm, Fri & Sat-10:30 pm. Closed
Seafood　　major holidays. **Features:** casual dress; children's menu; carryout; cocktails & lounge. In a welcoming &
comfortable atmosphere, with old framed local photos lining the walls, creative orders are served: Island Boy
Bread, soft shell crabs & pan-roasted local grouper flavored with a fricassee of apple-smoked bacon. **Cards:** AE, DS, MC,
VI.　　　　　　　　　　　　　　　　　　　　　　　　　　　　　　　　[X]

SUMMERVILLE—22,500

LODGINGS

COMFORT INN　　　　　　　　　　Rates Subject to Change　　　　　　**Phone:** 803/851-2333
◆ ◆ ◆　　All Year [CP]　　　　　1P: $49- 75　2P/1B: $52- 130　2P/2B: $52- 75　XP: $5　　F18
Motel　　**Location:** I-26 at jct US 17A, exit 199A. 1005 Jockey Ct 29483. Fax: 803/851-2333. **Terms:** Sr. discount; no
pets. **Facility:** 66 rooms. 2 stories; exterior corridors. **All Rooms:** free movies. **Cards:** AE, CB, DI, DS, MC,
VI.　　　　　　　　　　　　　　　　　　　　　　　[🏊] [CTV] [X] [🦮] [D]

ECONO LODGE
◆◆   Rates Subject to Change   **Phone:** 803/875-3022
Motel   All Year   1P: $45- 65 2P/1B: $45- 65 2P/2B: $45- 65 XP: $5   F17
            Location: Jct I-26 & US 17A exit 199A. 110 Holiday Dr 29483. Fax: 803/851-3120. **Terms:** Sr. discount;
            check-in 4 pm; small pets only, $15 extra charge. **Facility:** 98 rooms. Key deposit, $10; 3 stories; exterior cor-
ridors. **All Rooms:** free movies. **Cards:** AE, DS, MC, VI.

HOLIDAY INN EXPRESS-CHARLESTON/SUMMERVILLE   **Phone:** 803/875-3300
(AAA) [SAVE] All Year [CP]   1P: $60   2P/1B: $60   2P/2B: $60
◆◆   **Location:** I-26 at jct US 17A, exit 199A. 120 Holiday Inn Dr 29483. Fax: 803/851-9702. **Terms:** Reserv
Motel   deposit, 30 day notice; small pets only. **Facility:** 123 rooms. 5 stories; interior corridors. **Services:** valet
            laundry. **All Rooms:** free & pay movies. **Some Rooms:** refrigerators. **Cards:** AE, DS, MC.
            Special Amenities: Free breakfast and free local telephone calls.

WOODLANDS RESORT & INN   **Phone:** 803/875-2600
(AAA) [SAVE] 3/22-6/13 & 8/30-11/30   2P/1B: $295- 350 2P/2B: $295- 350 XP: $50
            6/14-8/29   2P/1B: $275- 325 2P/2B: $275- 325 XP: $50
◆◆◆◆◆   12/1-3/21   2P/1B: $225- 300 2P/2B: $225- 300 XP: $50
Historic   **Location:** 2 mi s on US 17A from jct I-26, exit 199A; 1.5 mi w on W Richardson Ave (SR 165), just s. 125
Country Inn Parsons Rd 29483. Fax: 803/875-2603. **Terms:** Age restrictions may apply; reserv deposit; CP avail
            package plans; no pets. **Facility:** 20 rooms. A classic Greek Revival mansion built in 1906 & nestled on 42
            acres of beautifully-tended grounds. Rooms are lavishly-decorated & furnished & public areas are fabulous. 3 stories; interior
            corridors; smoke free premises; 2 lighted tennis courts; lawn croquet, yoga classes, variety of facial & body treatments
            Dining & Entertainment: Cocktail lounge; afternoon tea; also, The Dining Room at Woodlands, see separate listing
            Services: valet laundry; valet parking. Fee: massage, area transportation, to airport & downtown. **Recreation:** bicycles
            jogging. **All Rooms:** free movies, safes, VCP's. **Some Rooms:** whirlpools. **Cards:** AE, CB, DI, DS, MC, VI.

RESTAURANTS

THE DINING ROOM AT WOODLANDS   **Lunch:** $5-$15   **Dinner:** $44-$56   **Phone:** 803/875-2600
(AAA)   **Location:** 2 mi s on US 17A from jct I-26, exit 199A; 1.5 mi w on W Richardson Ave (SR 165), just s; in
◆◆◆◆◆   Woodlands Resort & Inn. 125 Parsons Rd 29483. **Hours:** 6:30-10:30 am, 11:30-2:30 & 6-10 pm
Regional   **Reservations:** suggested. **Features:** semi-formal attire; health conscious menu; cocktails & lounge
American   entertainment; valet parking; prix fixe. Outstandingly-creative, market-sensitive cuisine with extensive use o
            local products. Menu changes daily & chef offers an exciting new tasting menu every night. Smoke free
            premises. **Cards:** AE, DI, DS, MC, VI.

MCNEILLS, THE RESTAURANT   **Lunch:** $5-$7   **Dinner:** $8-$15   **Phone:** 803/832-0912
◆◆   **Location:** From US 17-A, Main St just w on W Doty; in the Village Square Shops. 105 S Cedar St 29483
Regional   **Hours:** 11 am-2:30 & 5:30-9 pm, Fri & Sat 5:30 pm-10 pm. Closed major holidays, Sun & Mon
American   **Reservations:** required. **Features:** children's menu; carryout; cocktails. A nice variety in the small menu, a
            sort of combination of New American, Lowcountry & British Isles cooking. Simple but comforting decor
Cards: MC, VI.

STICKY FINGERS RESTAURANT & BAR   **Lunch:** $4-$7   **Dinner:** $5-$15   **Phone:** 803/875-7969
◆◆   **Location:** From I-26 exit 199A, 0.8 mi s on US 17A. 1200 N Main St 29483. **Hours:** 11 am-10 pm. Closed
American   11/26 & 12/25. **Features:** casual dress; children's menu; senior's menu; health conscious menu; carryout
            cocktails. Featuring Memphis & Texas wet & dry ribs & Carolina sweet ribs. **Cards:** AE, DI, DS, MC, VI.

CHERAW—5,500

LODGINGS

DAYS INN   **Phone:** 803/537-5554
(AAA) [SAVE] All Year [CP]   1P: $36- 60   2P/2B: $60- 70 XP: $5   F17
◆◆   **Location:** Jct US 9 & 52. 820 Market St 29520. Fax: 803/537-4110. **Terms:** Reserv deposit; small pets only
Motel $5 extra charge. **Facility:** 50 rooms. 2 stories; exterior corridors. **Services:** valet laundry. **All Rooms:** free
            movies, refrigerators. **Some Rooms:** microwaves, whirlpools. **Cards:** AE, CB, DI, DS, MC, VI
            Special Amenities: Free breakfast and free local telephone calls.

INN CHERAW   **Phone:** 803/537-2011
(AAA) [SAVE] All Year [CP]   1P: $40- 65 2P/1B: $45- 65 2P/2B: $45- 65 XP: $5   F
◆◆   **Location:** Downtown on US 1/52 & SR 9. 321 Second St 29520. Fax: 803/537-1398. **Terms:** Reserv
Motel   deposit; weekly/monthly rates; pets, $5 dep req. **Facility:** 50 rooms. Friendly, family-operated motel with com
            fortable, carefully-kept guest rooms. 2 stories; exterior corridors. **Dining:** Restaurant nearby. **Services:** vale
            laundry. **All Rooms:** coffeemakers, free & pay movies. Fee: refrigerators. **Some Rooms:** 2 efficiencies
Fee: microwaves, VCP's. **Cards:** AE, CB, DI, DS, MC, VI. **Special Amenities:** Free local telephone calls and preferre
room (subject to availability with advanced reservations).

CLEMSON—11,100

LODGINGS

COMFORT INN-CLEMSON   **Phone:** 864/653-3601
(AAA) [SAVE] All Year [CP]   1P: $59- 85 2P/1B: $69- 85 2P/2B: $69- 85 XP: $6   F11
◆◆   **Location:** At jct US 76 & SR 123. 1305 Tiger Blvd 29631 (PO Box 1496, 29633). Fax: 864/654-3123
Motel   **Terms:** Check-in 4 pm; reserv deposit; pets, $100 dep req. **Facility:** 122 rooms. Nicely appointed rooms
            Suites have data port. Suites, $90-$125 for up to 2 persons; 4 stories; interior corridors; sauna, whirlpool
            Dining: Restaurant nearby. **Services:** valet laundry. **All Rooms:** free movies. **Some Rooms:** coffeemakers
microwaves, refrigerators. Fee: VCP's, whirlpools. **Cards:** AE, CB, DI, DS, JCB, MC, VI. **Special Amenities:** Fre
breakfast and free local telephone calls. (See color ad p 467)

DAYS INN-CLEMSON   Rates Subject to Change   **Phone:** 864/653-441
◆◆   All Year [CP]   1P: $40- 46 2P/1B: $46- 50 2P/2B: $46- 50 XP: $5   F1
Motel   **Location:** On US 123, 0.4 mi s of jct 123 & US 76 & SR 28. 1387 Tiger Blvd 29631. Fax: 864/653-4411
            Terms: No pets. **Facility:** 46 rooms. 2 stories; exterior corridors. **All Rooms:** free movies. **Cards:** AE, CB
DI, DS, MC, VI.

HOLIDAY INN
◆◆
Motor Inn

Guaranteed Rates

Phone: 864/654-4450

All Year
1P: $54- 100 2P/1B: $54- 100 2P/2B: $54- 100 XP: $5 F12

Location: 1 mi e on US 76, 123 & SR 28. 894 Tiger Blvd 29631 (PO Box 512, 29633-0512). **Fax:** 864/654-8451. **Terms:** Sr. discount; pets. **Facility:** 219 rooms. 2 stories; exterior corridors. **Dining:** Restaurant; 6:30 am-2 & 5:30-9:30 pm; $8-$12. **All Rooms:** free movies. **Cards:** AE, DI, DS, JCB, MC, VI.

🛏 🏊 ♿ CTV ✕ Ⓓ

CLINTON—8,000

LODGINGS

COMFORT INN
ⒶⒶⒶ SAVE
◆◆
Motel

Phone: 864/833-5558

4/1-11/30 [CP]
1P: $48 2P/1B: $55 2P/2B: $58 XP: $6 F18

12/1-3/31 [CP]
1P: $45 2P/1B: $48 2P/2B: $52 XP: $6 F18

Location: N of I-26, exit 52. I-26 & US 56 29325 (Rt 5, Box 478). **Fax:** 864/833-5558. **Terms:** Weekly rates; small pets only, $10 extra charge. **Facility:** 81 rooms. Guestrooms with modern decor. Handling fee imposed; 2 stories; exterior corridors. **Dining:** Restaurant nearby. **Services:** Fee: coin laundry. **All Rooms:** free & pay movies. **Some Rooms:** coffeemakers, microwaves, radios, refrigerators. **Cards:** AE, CB, DI, DS, JCB, MC, VI. **Special Amenities: Free breakfast and preferred room (subject to availability with advanced reservations).**

🛏 🏊 🍴 CTV ✕ 🖉 Ⓓ

DAYS INN
ⒶⒶⒶ SAVE
◆◆
Motel

Phone: 864/833-6600

3/1-10/31 [CP]
1P: $44- 51 2P/1B: $49- 56 2P/2B: $51- 58 XP: $5 F16

12/1-2/28 & 11/1-11/30 [CP]
1P: $42- 49 2P/1B: $47- 54 2P/2B: $49- 56 XP: $5 F16

Location: S of I-26, exit 52. I-26 & SR 56 29325 (Rt 5 Box 410). **Fax:** 864/833-6600. **Terms:** Weekly rates; small pets only, $5 extra charge. **Facility:** 57 rooms. Rooms range in size from compact to more spacious & offer contemporary appointments. Suites $52-$70; 2 stories; exterior corridors; sauna, small pool. **Dining:** Restaurant nearby. **Services:** Fee: coin laundry. **All Rooms:** free movies. **Some Rooms:** kitchen, microwaves, refrigerators. Fee: whirlpools. **Cards:** AE, CB, DI, DS, MC, VI.

🛏 🍴 ♿ CTV ✕ Ⓓ

HOLIDAY INN
ⒶⒶⒶ SAVE
◆◆
Motor Inn

Phone: 864/833-4900

5/1-11/30 [CP]
1P: $65 2P/1B: $65 2P/2B: $65

12/1-4/30 [CP]
1P: $54 2P/1B: $54 2P/2B: $54

Location: I-26 & SR 56, exit 52. (PO Box 926, 29325). **Fax:** 864/833-4916. **Terms:** Small pets only, $10 extra charge. **Facility:** 102 rooms. 2 stories; exterior corridors. **Dining & Entertainment:** Restaurant; 6:30-10 am, 11-2 & 5-10 pm; $9-$14; cocktails/lounge. **All Rooms:** free & pay movies. **Some Rooms:** microwaves, refrigerators. **Cards:** AE, CB, DI, DS, JCB, MC. **Special Amenities: Free local telephone calls and free newspaper.**

🛏 🏊 🍴 ♿ CTV ✕ Ⓓ

COLUMBIA—98,100 (See map p. 468; index below)

To help you more easily locate accommodations in the Columbia area, the following index and map show lodgings and restaurants in multiple cities. Listings for these establishments are found under the heading for the city in which they are located. The Columbia area map comprises: Columbia and West Columbia.

(See map below)

Hampton Inn-Southeast	36
Comfort Inn Capital City	37
Holiday Inn Express-Ft Jackson	39
Knights Inn-Northwest	43

RESTAURANTS

Garibaldi's	1
Key West Grill & Raw Bar	2
Elite Epicurean	5
Al's Upstairs Italian Restaurant	6
Ava D's Wine & Gourmet Cafe	8
Yesterdays Restaurant & Tavern	9
S & S Cafeteria	10
Mangia Mangia	11
Richard's Fine Southern Cuisine	12
Annabelle's	13
California Dreaming	14

WEST COLUMBIA

Hampton Inn Airport	55
Holiday Inn Columbia Airport	56
Best Western Columbia West	57
Comfort Inn-Airport	58
Ramada Inn West	61

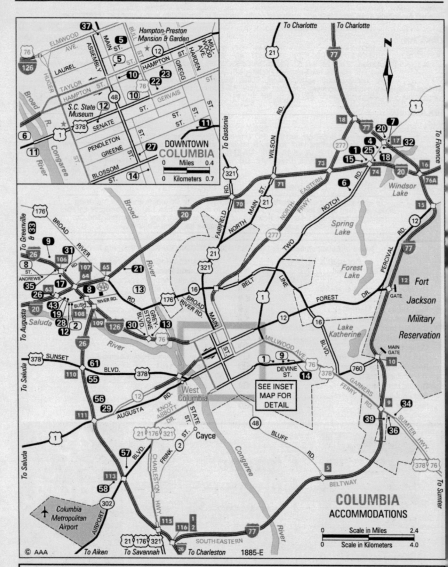

DOWNTOWN COLUMBIA

COLUMBIA
ACCOMMODATIONS

© AAA   1885-E

CLASSIFICATION explanations are found in <u>About Lodgings & Restaurants</u>.

(See map p. 468)

LODGINGS

ADAMS MARK HOTEL   Rates Subject to Change   Phone: 803/771-7000   **10**
◆◆◆   Sun-Thurs   1P: $109   2P/1B: $124   2P/2B: $124   XP: $10   F18
Hotel   Fri & Sat   1P: $69- 99   2P/1B: $69- 99   2P/2B: $69- 99   XP: $10   F18
          Location: Downtown on US 21; corner Main & Hampton sts. 1200 Hampton St 29201. Fax: 803/254-8307.
Terms: Reserv deposit; small pets only, $50 extra charge. **Facility:** 301 rooms. 15 stories; interior corridors. **Dining:** Dining
room; 6:30-10 am, 11-2, 5-10 pm; $4-$19. **All Rooms:** Fee: movies. **Cards:** AE, CB, DI, DS, MC, VI.
(See color ad below)   🛏 🎣 🔁 CTV ✕ 🖊 D S

AMERISUITES   Phone: 803/736-6666   **4**
(AAA) (SAVE)   2/1-9/30 [CP]   1P: $79- 89   2P/1B: $79- 89   2P/2B: $79- 89   XP: $5   F18
       12/1-1/31 & 10/1-11/30 [CP]   1P: $69- 79   2P/1B: $69- 79   2P/2B: $69- 79   XP: $5   F18
◆◆◆   **Location:** US 1 at jct I-20, exit 74 (Two Notch Rd). 7525 Two Notch Rd 29223. Fax: 803/788-6011.
Suite Motel   **Terms:** Weekly rates, for 10 days or more; small pets only. **Facility:** 112 rooms. 6 stories; interior corridors;
         whirlpool; limited exercise equipment. Fee: health club priviliges. **Dining:** Restaurant nearby. **Services:**
Fee: coin laundry. **All Rooms:** coffeemakers, microwaves, free movies, refrigerators, combo or shower baths, VCP's.
Cards: AE, CB, DI, DS, MC, VI. **Special Amenities: Free breakfast and free local telephone calls.** *(See color ad p 10)*
                               Roll in showers. 🛏 🎣 🔁 CTV ✕ 🖊 D S

BUDGETEL INN-COLUMBIA EAST   Rates Subject to Change   Phone: 803/736-6400   **1**
◆◆   All Year [CP]   1P: $38- 51   2P/1B: $45- 58   2P/2B: $49
Motel   **Location:** On US 1 (Two Notch Rd) at jct I-20, exit 74. 1538 Horseshoe Dr 29223. Fax: 803/788-7875.
         Terms: Sr. discount; small pets only. **Facility:** 102 rooms. Max rates for up to 4 persons; 3 stories; interior cor-
ridors. **All Rooms:** free & pay movies. **Cards:** AE, CB, DI, DS, MC, VI. *(See color ad below)*   🛏 CTV ✕ D S

BUDGETEL INN-COLUMBIA WEST   Rates Subject to Change   Phone: 803/798-3222   **12**
◆◆◆   All Year [CP]   1P: $37- 48   2P/1B: $42- 53   2P/2B: $44
Motel   **Location:** Jct I-26 & Bush River Rd. 911 Bush River Rd 29210. Fax: 803/731-5554. **Terms:** Sr. discount;
         small pets only. **Facility:** 103 rooms. 2 stories; interior corridors. **All Rooms:** free & pay movies. **Cards:** AE,
CB, DI, DS, MC, VI. *(See color ad below)*   🛏 🎣 CTV ✕ 🖊 D S

CHESTNUT COTTAGE BED & BREAKFAST   Guaranteed Rates   Phone: 803/256-1718   **23**
◆◆◆   All Year [CP]   1P: $75- 150   2P/1B: $85- 160   XP: $15
Historic Bed   **Location:** At corners of Hampton & Barnell sts. 1718 Hampton St 29201. Fax: 803/256-1718. **Terms:** Age
& Breakfast   restrictions may apply; check-in 4 pm; no pets. **Facility:** 5 rooms. 3 whirlpool rms, extra charge. Handling fee
         imposed; 2 stories; interior corridors; smoke free premises. **Some Rooms:** efficiency. **Cards:** AE, DI, DS,
MC, VI.   ✕ D

(See map p. 468)

CLARION TOWN HOUSE
Rates Subject to Change
♦♦♦ All Year 1P: $72- 95 2P/1B: $78- 110 2P/2B: $78- 110 XP: $6 F18
Phone: 803/771-8711 🔢
Motor Inn **Location:** 1615 Gervais St 29201. Fax: 803/252-9347. **Terms:** No pets. **Facility:** 142 rooms. 6 stories; interior/exterior corridors. **Dining:** Restaurant; 6:30 am-2 & 5-10 pm; $8-$14. **All Rooms:** Fee: movies.
Cards: AE, CB, DI, DS, MC, VI.
🛎 ⊞ CTV ✕ D

CLAUSSEN'S INN
Phone: 803/765-0440 🔢
AAA SAVE All Year [CP] 1P: $100- 115 2P/1B: $115- 130 2P/2B: $118 XP: $15 F12
♦♦♦♦ **Location:** 2 mi se; in Five Points Section. 2003 Greene St 29205. Fax: 803/799-7924. **Terms:** No pets.
Historic Bed **Facility:** 29 rooms. Tastefully appointed rooms in converted bakery. 2 stories; interior corridors; whirlpool.
& Breakfast **Dining:** Cocktails; restaurant nearby. **Services:** complimentary evening beverages; valet laundry.
All Rooms: Fee: VCP. **Some Rooms:** refrigerators. **Cards:** AE, DI, DS, MC, VI. **Special Amenities:** Free local telephone calls and free newspaper. (See ad below)
🐾 CTV ✕ D S

COMFORT INN
Phone: 803/798-0500 🔢
AAA SAVE 3/1-8/31 [CP] 1P: $49 2P/1B: $70 2P/2B: $70 XP: $5 F18
12/1-2/28 & 9/1-11/30 [CP] 1P: $39 2P/1B: $66 2P/2B: $66 XP: $5 F18
♦♦♦ **Location:** Jct I-26 & Piney Grove Rd, exit 104. 499 Piney Grove Rd 29210. Fax: 803/772-9556. **Terms:** No
Motel pets. **Facility:** 102 rooms. Spacious units with attractive traditional decor. 2-3 stories; exterior corridors.
Dining: Restaurant nearby. **Services:** valet laundry. **All Rooms:** free movies. **Some Rooms:** microwaves, refrigerators. Fee: whirlpools. **Cards:** AE, CB, DI, DS, JCB, MC, VI. **Special Amenities:** Free breakfast and free local telephone calls. (See color ad below)
🛎 ⊞ CTV ✕ D

COMFORT INN CAPITAL CITY
Phone: 803/252-6321 🔢
AAA SAVE All Year [CP] 1P: $49- 54 2P/1B: $54- 64 2P/2B: $54- 64 XP: $5 F18
♦♦♦ **Terms:** Small pets only. **Facility:** 148 rooms. Handling fee imposed; 2 stories; interior
Motel corridors. **Location:** Downtown on US 76; at corner of Elmwood & Main sts. 2025 Main St 29201. Fax: 803/252-6321.
Dining: Restaurant nearby. **Services:** complimentary evening beverages, Mon-Thurs; valet laundry.
All Rooms: free movies. **Some Rooms:** coffeemakers, kitchen, microwaves, refrigerators, phones.
Fee: VCP's, whirlpools. **Cards:** AE, CB, DI, DS, JCB, MC, VI.
🐾 🛎 ⊞ 📶 CTV ✕ D

COMFORT INN NORTHEAST
Phone: 803/788-5544 🔢
AAA SAVE All Year [CP] 1P: $46- 50 2P/1B: $50- 56 2P/2B: $50- 56 XP: $6 F18
♦♦ **Location:** On US 1 at jct I-20, exit 74 (Two Notch Rd); 0.3 mi n. 7700 Two Notch Rd 29223.
Motel Fax: 803/788-5544. **Terms:** Reserv deposit, 3 day notice; no pets. **Facility:** 96 rooms. Located near train
tracks. Comfortable rooms with attractive decor. Handling fee imposed; 3 stories; interior corridors; small pool.
Dining: Restaurant nearby. **All Rooms:** free movies. **Some Rooms:** coffeemakers. Fee: microwaves, refrigerators, whirlpools. **Cards:** AE, CB, DI, DS, JCB, MC, VI. **Special Amenities:** Free breakfast and free newspaper.
🐾 CTV ✕ 🎵 D

(See map p. 468)

COURTYARD BY MARRIOTT-COLUMBIA   Rates Subject to Change   **Phone: 803/731-2300**   🎱
◆◆◆   Sun-Thurs   1P: $75   2P/1B: $75   2P/2B: $75
Motel   Fri & Sat   1P: $39   2P/1B: $49   2P/2B: $49
     Location: Jct I-26 & Bush River Rd exit 108; just w on Bush River Rd. 347 Zimalcrest Dr 29210.
Fax: 803/772-6965. **Terms:** Sr. discount; check-in 4 pm; no pets. **Facility:** 149 rooms. 12 suites, $89-$99; 3 stories; interior
corridors. **Dining:** Coffee shop; 6:30-10 am, Sat & Sun 7-11 am. **All Rooms:** free & pay movies. **Cards:** AE, CB, DI, DS,
MC, VI. *(See color ad below)*   🛰 📺 ✖ 🌀 🅳 🆂

DAYS INN-NORTHEAST   Rates Subject to Change   **Phone: 803/736-0000**   🎲
◆   All Year [BP]   1P: $44   2P/1B: $44   2P/2B: $44   XP: $5   F12
Motel   **Location:** I-20 exit 74 (Two Notch Rd), 0.8 mi sw to Parklane Rd. 7128 Parklane Rd 29223.
     Fax: 803/736-9328. **Terms:** No pets. **Facility:** 136 rooms. 3 stories; exterior corridors. **Dining:** Coffee shop;
6-10 am. **All Rooms:** free movies. **Cards:** AE, CB, DI, DS, MC, VI.   🛰 ✖ 🅳

DAYS INN-SOUTHEAST   Rates Subject to Change   **Phone: 803/783-5500**   🎲
◆◆◆   All Year [CP]   1P: $49- 64   2P/1B: $54- 69   2P/2B: $54- 69   XP: $6   F12
Suite Motel   **Location:** From I-77 exit 9A, e on US 76 & 378. 7300 Garner's Ferry Rd 29209. Fax: 803/776-1391.
     Terms: Sr. discount; no pets. **Facility:** 120 rooms. 5 stories; interior corridors. **All Rooms:** free movies.
Cards: AE, CB, DI, DS, MC, VI.   🛰 📺 ✖ 🌀 🅳

EMBASSY SUITES HOTEL COLUMBIA   Rates Subject to Change   **Phone: 803/252-8700**   🎲
◆◆◆   Sun-Thurs [BP]   1P: $119   2P/1B: $119   2P/2B: $119   XP: $10   F18
Suite Hotel   Fri & Sat [BP]   1P: $99   2P/1B: $99   2P/2B: $99   XP: $10   F18
     Location: Just nw of I-126, exit Greystone Blvd. 200 Stoneridge Dr 29210. Fax: 803/256-8749. **Terms:** No
pets. **Facility:** 214 rooms. 7 stories; interior corridors. **Dining:** Restaurant; 11 am-2 & 5-10 pm, Fri & Sat-11 pm; $10-$23.
All Rooms: free & pay movies. **Cards:** AE, CB, DI, DS, MC, VI.   Roll in showers.   🛰 ✈ 📺 ♿ ✖ 🌀 🅳 🆂

FAIRFIELD INN BY MARRIOTT   **Phone: 803/736-0822**   🎯
(AAA) (SAVE)   All Year [CP]   1P: $49- 59   2P/1B: $54- 64   2P/2B: $54- 64   XP: $5   F17
     Location: From jct I-77 & Two Notch Rd (US 1) 0.4 mi n, from I-20 & US 1 exit 74, 0.5 mi n. 8104 Two
◆◆◆   Notch Rd 29223. Fax: 803/699-6058. **Terms:** No pets. **Facility:** 129 rooms. Near train tracks. 2 stories; exterior
Motel   corridors. **Dining:** Restaurant nearby. **Services:** valet laundry. **All Rooms:** free movies. **Cards:** AE, DI, DS,
MC, VI. **Special Amenities: Free breakfast and free local telephone calls.**
   🛰 ✈ 📺 ♿ ✖ 🌀 🅳

HAMPTON INN HARBISON   Rates Subject to Change   **Phone: 803/749-6999**   🎲
◆◆◆   All Year [CP]   1P: $61- 68   2P/1B: $67- 75   2P/2B: $65- 73   XP: $7   F12
Motel   **Location:** I-26 exit 103 (Harbison Blvd). 101 Woodcross Dr 29212. Fax: 803/749-9398. **Terms:** Sr. discount;
no pets. **Facility:** 112 rooms. 15 whirlpool suites $79-$99 for up to 4 persons; 6 stories; interior corridors.
All Rooms: free movies. **Cards:** AE, CB, DI, DS, MC, VI.   Roll in showers.   🛰 📺 🏠 ✖ 🅳 🆂

(See map p. 468)

HAMPTON INN-SOUTHEAST   Phone: 803/783-5410   **36**
All Year [CP]   1P: $59- 64   2P/1B: $64- 68   2P/2B: $64- 68   XP: $8   F16
Location: From I-77 exit 9A, e on US 378 & 76. 7333 Garner's Ferry Rd 29209. Fax: 803/783-8102.
Terms: No pets. **Facility:** 121 rooms. 5 stories; interior corridors. **Dining:** Restaurant nearby.
Services: valet laundry. **All Rooms:** coffeemakers, free movies. **Some Rooms:** microwaves, refrigerators.
Cards: AE, CB, DI, DS, MC, VI. **Special Amenities:** Free breakfast and free local telephone calls.
(See color ad p 471)

Motel

HOLIDAY INN-COLISEUM AT USC   Phone: 803/799-7800   **27**
All Year   1P: $98   2P/1B: $105   2P/2B: $112   XP: $7   F19
Location: 0.5 mi s on US 21, 176, 321 & SR 215. 630 Assembly St 29201. Fax: 803/252-5909.
Terms: Weekly/monthly rates; pets. **Facility:** 175 rooms. 1 whirlpool suite $150 for 2 persons; 9 stories; interior corridors. **Dining & Entertainment:** Dining room; 6:30 am-2 & 5:30-10 pm; $8-$16; cocktails/lounge.
Services: valet laundry. **All Rooms:** free & pay movies. **Some Rooms:** coffeemakers, microwaves, refrigerators. **Cards:** AE, CB, DI, DS, MC, VI. **Special Amenities:** Early check-in/late check-out and preferred room (subject to availability with advanced reservations). *(See color ad below)*

Hotel

(See map p. 468)

HOLIDAY INN EXPRESS
AAA SAVE
◆ ◆ ◆
Motel
All Year [CP]   1P: $49- 59   2P/1B: $49- 59   Phone: 803/772-7275 **35**
XP: $10   F18
Location: US 26, exit 106B, just w. 773 St Andrews Rd 29210. Fax: 803/750-1877. **Terms:** Reserv deposit; no pets. **Facility:** 100 rooms. 2 stories; exterior corridors. **Dining:** Restaurant nearby. **Services:** valet laundry. **All Rooms:** free movies. **Some Rooms:** coffeemakers. Fee: microwaves, refrigerators. **Cards:** AE, CB, DI, DS, MC, VI. **Special Amenities: Free breakfast and free local telephone calls.**
(See color ad p 472)

HOLIDAY INN EXPRESS-FT JACKSON
AAA SAVE
◆ ◆ ◆
Motel
All Year [CP]   1P: $74   2P/1B: $74   2P/2B: $74   Phone: 803/695-1111 **39**
XP: $6   F18
Location: I-77 exit 9A, e on US 378 & 76. 7251 Garner's Ferry Rd 29209. Fax: 803/695-0008. **Terms:** Reserv deposit; BP avail; no pets. **Facility:** 65 rooms. Tastefully decorated & furnished rooms. Attractive lobby area. 3 stories; exterior corridors. **Dining:** Restaurant nearby. **Services:** valet laundry. **All Rooms:** free movies, combo or shower baths. **Cards:** AE, CB, DI, DS, JCB, MC, VI. **Special Amenities: free breakfast and free local telephone calls.** (See color ad below)

HOLIDAY INN-NORTHEAST
AAA
Motor Inn
All Year   Rates Subject to Change   1P: $72- 98   2P/1B: $72- 98   2P/2B: $72- 82   Phone: 803/736-3000 **25**
XP: $6   F18
Location: On US 1 (Two Notch Rd) at jct I-20, exit 74. 7510 Two Notch Rd 29223. Fax: 803/736-6399. **Terms:** Sr. discount; reserv deposit; pets. **Facility:** 253 rooms. 2 stories; interior corridors. **Dining:** Dining room; 6:30 am-2 & 5-10:30 pm; $9-$15. **All Rooms:** free & pay movies. **Cards:** AE, CB, DI, DS, JCB, MC, VI.

HOWARD JOHNSON INN
AAA SAVE
◆
Motel
All Year [CP]   1P: $40- 50   2P/1B: $45- 55   2P/2B: $50- 60   Phone: 803/772-7200 **28**
XP: $5   F16
Location: Jct I-26 & Bush River Rd exit 108; just w on Bush River Rd. 200 Zimalcrest Dr 29210. Fax: 803/772-6484. **Terms:** No pets. **Facility:** 70 rooms. 2 stories; interior/exterior corridors. **All Rooms:** free movies. **Cards:** AE, CB, DI, DS, JCB, MC, VI.

KNIGHTS INN-NORTHWEST
AAA SAVE
Motel
All Year   1P: $30   2P/1B: $30   2P/2B: $35   Phone: 803/772-0022 **43**
XP: $5   D12
Location: Jct I-20 & Bush River Rd, exit 63. 1803 Bush River Rd 29210. Fax: 803/772-0022. **Terms:** Reserv deposit; 10 day notice; weekly/monthly rates; no pets. **Facility:** 105 rooms. 1 story; exterior corridors; small pool. **Dining:** Restaurant nearby. **All Rooms:** free movies. **Cards:** AE, CB, DS, JCB, MC. **Special Amenities: Free room upgrade and preferred room (each subject to availability with advanced reservations).**

LA QUINTA INN
AAA
◆ ◆ ◆
Motel
All Year [CP]   Rates Subject to Change   1P: $43- 50   2P/1B: $49- 55   2P/2B: $49- 55   Phone: 803/798-9590 **21**
XP: $6   F18
Location: Jct I-20 & US 176, exit 65. 1335 Garner Ln 29210. Fax: 803/731-5574. **Terms:** Small pets only. **Facility:** 120 rooms. 2-3 stories, no elevator; exterior corridors. **All Rooms:** free movies. **Cards:** AE, CB, DI, DS, MC, VI.

MOTEL 6 - 1404
AAA
Motel
All Year   Rates Subject to Change   1P: $32   2P/1B: $39   2P/2B: $39   Phone: 803/798-9210 **31**
XP: $4   F12
Location: I-26 exit 106 & St Andrews Rd. 1776 Burning Tree Rd 29210. Fax: 803/772-6580. **Terms:** Small pets only. **Facility:** 97 rooms. 3 stories; exterior corridors. **Cards:** AE, MC, VI.

QUALITY INN-NORTHEAST
AAA SAVE
◆ ◆
Motor Inn
All Year [BP]   1P: $54- 75   2P/1B: $54- 75   2P/2B: $54- 75   Phone: 803/736-1600 **15**
XP: $5   F18
Location: On US 1 at jct I-20 exit 74, (Two Notch Rd). 1539 Horseshoe Dr 29223. Fax: 803/736-1600. **Terms:** Monthly rates; no pets. **Facility:** 192 rooms. 5 stories; interior/exterior corridors; whirlpool. **Dining & Entertainment:** Dining room; 6 am-10 & 5-10 pm, Sat 7 am-11 & 5-10 pm, Sun 7-11 am; $7-$14; cocktails/lounge. **Services:** valet laundry. **All Rooms:** coffeemakers, free movies. **Some Rooms:** microwaves, radios, refrigerators, whirlpools. **Cards:** AE, CB, DI, DS, JCB, MC, VI.

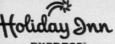

(See map p. 468)

RAMADA PLAZA HOTEL
Phone: 803/736-5600

(AAA) (SAVE)

Hotel

All Year   1P: $79   2P/1B: $79   2P/2B: $79   XP: $6   F1
Location: On US 1 (Two Notch Rd) 0.5 mi n jct I-20, exit 74. 8105 Two Notch Rd 2922:
Fax: 803/736-1241. **Terms:** Small pets only. **Facility:** 187 rooms. 6 stories; interior corridors; sauna, whirlpoc
Dining: 2 dining rooms; 6:30 am-2 & 6-10 pm; $8-$20; cocktails. **Services:** valet laundr
All Rooms: coffeemakers, free & pay movies. **Some Rooms:** microwaves, refrigerators, safes, whirlpool:
Cards: AE, CB, DI, DS, MC, VI. **Special Amenities:** Free local telephone calls and free newspaper.

RED ROOF INN-EAST
Rates Subject to Change   Phone: 803/736-0850

Motel

All Year   1P: $43- 63   2P/1B: $51- 71   2P/2B: $57- 77   XP: $9   F1
Location: On US 1 (Two Notch Rd) at jct I-20, exit 74. 7580 Two Notch Rd 29223. Fax: 803/736-4270
Terms: Small pets only. **Facility:** 108 rooms. 2 stories; exterior corridors. **All Rooms:** free movies
Cards: AE, CB, DI, DS, MC, VI.

RED ROOF INN-WEST
Rates Subject to Change   Phone: 803/798-9220

Motel

6/1-9/30	1P: $46	2P/1B: $53	2P/2B: $59 XP: $8 F1
3/1-5/31	1P: $44	2P/1B: $51	2P/2B: $57 XP: $7 F1
10/1-11/30	1P: $42	2P/1B: $49	2P/2B: $55 XP: $7 F1
12/1-2/28	1P: $40	2P/1B: $47	2P/2B: $53

Location: I-26 & St Andrews Rd, westbound exit 106A; eastbound exit 106. 10 Berryhill Rd 29210. Fax: 803/798-906:
Terms: Small pets only. **Facility:** 108 rooms. 2 stories; exterior corridors. **All Rooms:** free movies. **Cards:** AE, CB, DI, DS
MC, VI.

RESIDENCE INN BY MARRIOTT
Rates Subject to Change   Phone: 803/779-7000

Apartment
Motel

All Year   1P: $99- 119   2P/1B: $119- 129   2P/2B: $129- 136
Location: 1.5 mi ne of I-126, exit Greystone Blvd. 150 Stoneridge Dr 29210. Fax: 803/779-0408. **Terms:** S
discount; reserv deposit; 5% service charge; pets, $200 extra charge. **Facility:** 128 rooms. 2 stories; exterio
corridors. **All Rooms:** kitchens. **Fee:** movies. **Cards:** AE, CB, DI, DS, JCB, MC, VI.

RICHLAND STREET BED & BREAKFAST
Rates Subject to Change   Phone: 803/779-7001

Bed &
Breakfast

All Year [CP]   1P: $79- 89   2P/1B: $79- 135   2P/2B: $79- 135   XP: $10
Location: In the historic downtown district, just w of Bull St/US 76. 1425 Richland St 2920
Fax: 803/256-3725. **Terms:** Age restrictions may apply; check-in 4 pm; reserv deposit, 7 day notice; no pet
Facility: 8 rooms. Suite, $135. Handling fee imposed; 2 stories; interior corridors; smoke free premise:
Cards: AE, MC, VI.   Roll in showers.

SHERATON HOTEL & CONFERENCE CENTER
Phone: 803/731-0300

(AAA) (SAVE)

Hotel

Mon-Thurs   1P: $79   2P/1B: $89   2P/2B: $89   XP: $10   F1
Fri-Sun   1P: $72   2P/1B: $72   2P/2B: $72   XP: $10   F1
Location: Jct I-20 & Bush River Rd, exit 63. 2100 Bush River Rd 29210-5600. Fax: 803/731-283:
Terms: Weekly rates; no pets. **Facility:** 237 rooms. 5 stories; interior corridors; luxury level rooms; saun
whirlpool. **Dining & Entertainment:** Dining room, coffee shop; 6:30 am-10:30 pm; $5-$15; cocktail
nightclub. **Services:** valet laundry. **All Rooms:** coffeemakers, free & pay movies. **Some Rooms:** refrigerators, safe
Fee: whirlpools. **Cards:** AE, DI, DS, MC, VI. **Special Amenities:** Free newspaper and free room upgrade (subject
availability with advanced reservations).

SUPER 8 MOTEL
Rates Subject to Change   Phone: 803/796-4833

Motel

All Year   1P: $37   2P/1B: $37   2P/2B: $45   XP: $4   F1
Location: Jct I-26 & US 1, exit 111B. 2516 Augusta Rd 29169. Fax: 803/796-4833. **Terms:** Sr. discour
reserv deposit; small pets only, $5 extra charge. **Facility:** 88 rooms. 2 stories; interior/exterior corridor
All Rooms: free movies. **Some Rooms:** efficiency. **Cards:** AE, CB, DI, DS, MC, VI.

TRAVELODGE COLUMBIA WEST
Rates Subject to Change   Phone: 803/798-9665

Motel

All Year   1P: $44   2P/1B: $49   2P/2B: $49   XP: $5   F1
Location: At jct I-20, exit 63. 2210 Bush River Rd 29210. Fax: 803/798-9665. **Terms:** Sr. discount; rese
deposit, 7 day notice; small pets only. **Facility:** 107 rooms. 3 stories; interior/exterior corridor
All Rooms: free movies. **Cards:** AE, CB, DI, DS, MC, VI.

THE WHITNEY HOTEL
Guaranteed Rates   Phone: 803/252-0845

Apartment
Motel

All Year [CP]   1P: $129   2P/1B: $129   2P/2B: $149
Location: 2.5 mi se in Five Points Section, corner Devine & Woodrow sts. 700 Woodrow St 2920
Fax: 803/771-0495. **Terms:** Sr. discount; no pets. **Facility:** 74 rooms. 7 whirlpool rms, extra charge; 7 storie
interior corridors. **All Rooms:** free movies. **Cards:** AE, DI, DS, MC, VI.

RESTAURANTS

AL'S UPSTAIRS ITALIAN RESTAURANT
Dinner: $12-$18   Phone: 803/794-7404

Italian

Location: At jct US 1 & 378; just w of Gervais St Bridge. 304 Meeting St 29169. **Hours:** 5 pm-10 pr
Closed major holidays & Sun. **Reservations:** suggested. **Features:** dressy casual; cocktails; a la car
Intimate 2nd floor dining rooms. Some tables overlook the Columbia skyline. Upscale casual atmospher
Assorted veal, seafood & steak dishes offered with fettucini or linguini. **Cards:** AE, CB, DI, MC, VI.

ANNABELLE'S
Lunch: $4-$13   Dinner: $6-$15   Phone: 803/772-5586

(AAA)

American

Location: I-26 exit 108, 0.8 mi e on Bush River Rd. Dutch Square Mall 29210. **Hours:** 11:30 am-11 pm, F
& Sat-midnight, Sun noon-10 pm. Closed: 11/26 & 12/25. **Reservations:** suggested; evening
Features: casual dress; children's menu; carryout; salad bar; cocktails & lounge. Very popular, live
restaurant with wide ranging menu. **Cards:** AE, CB, DI, DS, MC, VI.

AVA D'S WINE & GOURMET CAFE
Lunch: $4-$7   Dinner: $8-$19   Phone: 803/772-0093

American

Location: Off I-26 exit 106A; in Ashland Park Shopping Plaza. 612 St Andrews Rd 29210. **Hours:** 11 am
& 5:30-10 pm, Mon & Tues-3 pm. Closed major holidays & Sun. **Features:** casual dress; carryout; casual bistro setting. Extensive selection of wines th
Featuring fresh seafood, pasta & meat entrees, in a casual bistro setting. Extensive selection of wines th
are chosen from a display rack. Entertainment on patio in summer. **Cards:** AE, MC, VI.

(See map p. 468)

CALIFORNIA DREAMING   Historical   **Lunch:** $5-$11   **Dinner:** $5-$15   **Phone:** 803/254-6767   ⑭
◆ ◆
American
Location: Center, 2 blks s of Blossom St. 401 S Main St 29208. **Hours:** 11 am-10 pm, Fri & Sat-11 pm. Closed: 11/26 & 12/25. **Features:** casual dress; children's menu; carryout; cocktails & lounge. Lively, popular eatery in restored Union train station, circa 1900. Prime rib & steak featured at dinner. Reservations taken before 4 pm, with phone ahead wait listing avail after 4 pm. **Cards:** AE, DI, DS, MC, VI.   ☒

ELITE EPICUREAN   **Lunch:** $4-$6   **Dinner:** $9-$19   **Phone:** 803/765-2325   ⑤
◆ ◆
American
Location: Center; opposite city hall. 1736 Main St 29201. Closed major holidays & Sun. **Reservations:** suggested; for dinner. **Features:** casual dress; children's menu; carryout; cocktails; street parking. Downtown coffee shop popular for light, fast lunches since 1932 transforms into fine dining at dinner featuring Greek specialties. **Cards:** AE, MC, VI.   ☒

GARIBALDI'S   **Dinner:** $8-$21   **Phone:** 803/771-8888   ①
◆ ◆ ◆
Italian
Location: Corner of Greene & Harden sts; in Five Points Section. 2013 Greene St 29205. **Hours:** 5:30 pm-10:30 pm, Fri & Sat-11 pm. **Reservations:** suggested. **Features:** cocktails & lounge; a la carte. Specializing in fine fresh seafood entrees, veal, poultry & gourmet pizzas. Lively atmosphere. Parking in rear. **Cards:** AE, MC, VI.

KEY WEST GRILL & RAW BAR   **Lunch:** $4-$7   **Dinner:** $6-$17   **Phone:** 803/772-0000   ②
◆ ◆
Steak and
Seafood
Location: I-20 exit 63 Bush River Rd, or I-26 exit 108 Bush River Rd, 1 mi nw. 1736 Bush River Rd 29210. **Hours:** 11 am-10:30 pm, Fri-11 pm, Sat 4 pm-11 pm, Sun 4 pm-9:30 pm. Closed: 11/26 & 12/25. **Reservations:** suggested. **Features:** casual dress; children's menu; early bird specials; carryout; cocktails & lounge. Also featuring poultry & pasta. Cheerful tropical decor. **Cards:** AE, DS, MC, VI.   ☒

MANGIA MANGIA   **Dinner:** $7-$20   **Phone:** 803/791-3443   ⑪
◆ ◆ ◆
Italian
Location: At jct US 1 & 378, w of Gervais St Bridge. 100 State St 29169. **Hours:** 5 pm-10 pm, Fri & Sat-11 pm. Closed: Sun. **Reservations:** suggested. **Features:** casual dress; children's menu; health conscious menu; carryout; cocktails & lounge; valet parking; a la carte. Featuring Northern Italian & Tuscan style entrees, specializing in meat, pasta & fresh seafood items. A unique decor with original art work. Smoking permitted in the bar area. Smoke free premises. **Cards:** AE, DI, MC, VI.   ☒

RICHARD'S FINE SOUTHERN CUISINE   **Dinner:** $13-$20   **Phone:** 803/212-7217   ⑫
◆ ◆ ◆
Regional
American
Location: In Columbia's Historic Vista area. At corner of Gervais & Lincoln sts, just w of Assembly St. 1109 Lincoln St 29201. **Hours:** 4:30 pm-11 pm. Closed: Sun. **Reservations:** suggested. **Features:** health conscious menu; carryout; cocktails; valet parking; a la carte. A unique combination of cooking techniques from the French to the Southern flairs. Fine entrees of fresh local seafood, pasta & a variety of meat. 3 rooms to choose from, all with local art work & soft lighting. Fine wine list. **Cards:** AE, MC, VI.   ☒

S & S CAFETERIA   **Phone:** 803/799-9477   ⑩
◆
American
Location: 3 blks e of Capitol Bldg. 1411 Gervais St 29201. **Hours:** 11 am-2:15 & 4:45-8 pm. Closed: 12/25. **Features:** casual dress; children's menu; carryout; salad bar. Trays carried to table. Handles large lunch crowds efficiently. **Cards:** MC, VI.   ☒

YESTERDAYS RESTAURANT & TAVERN   **Lunch:** $4-$7   **Dinner:** $6-$9   **Phone:** 803/799-0196   ⑨
◆
American
Location: 2 mi se in Five Points Section, corner Devine & Harden sts. 2030 Devine St 29205. **Hours:** 11:30 am-11 pm, Sat & Sun 11 am-10 pm. Closed: 11/26 & 12/25. **Features:** casual dress; Sunday brunch; children's menu; health conscious menu; carryout; cocktails & lounge. Very popular, casual dining in a lively tavern. Varied menu. Featuring Lowcountry style cooking. **Cards:** AE, DS, MC, VI.

CONWAY—*see The Grand Strand p. 481.*

DARLINGTON—7,300

LODGING

CROFT MAGNOLIA INN   Rates Subject to Change   **Phone:** 803/393-1908
◆
Historic Bed
& Breakfast

3/15-9/15 [BP]	1P: $70	2P/1B: $77	2P/2B: $90	XP: $5	F12
12/1-3/14 & 9/16-11/30 [BP]	1P: $65	2P/1B: $70	2P/2B: $77	XP: $5	F12

Location: 0.3 mi e of jct SR 34 & US 52 (Business). 306 Cashua St 29532. **Terms:** Sr. discount; reserv deposit, 7 day notice; no pets. **Facility:** 4 rooms. 3 stories; interior corridors; designated smoking area.   ☒ Ⓓ

DILLON—6,800

LODGINGS

COMFORT INN   **Phone:** 803/774-4137
AAA SAVE
◆ ◆ ◆
Motel
All Year [CP]   1P: $50- 60   2P/1B: $53- 65   2P/2B: $53- 65   XP: $4   F18
Location: On SR 9; at jct I-95, exit 193. 810 Radford Blvd 29536. Fax: 803/841-2425. **Terms:** Small pets only. **Facility:** 65 rooms. Pleasant variety of room decors & furniture styles; some deluxe units. Covered walkways. 1 story; exterior corridors. **Dining:** Restaurant nearby. **Services:** valet laundry. **All Rooms:** microwaves, free movies, refrigerators, VCP's. **Some Rooms:** Fee: whirlpools. **Cards:** AE, CB, DI, DS, MC, VI. **Special Amenities:** Free breakfast and free local telephone calls. (See color ad p 476)   🛏 �foto 🍴 CTV ☒ 🎿 Ⓓ

DAYS INN   **Phone:** 803/774-6041
AAA SAVE
◆ ◆
Motel
All Year [CP]   1P: $35- 49   2P/2B: $36- 59   XP: $5   F12
Location: On SR 9; at jct I-95, exit 193. 818 Radford Blvd 29536. Fax: 803/774-0683. **Terms:** Pets, $5 extra charge. **Facility:** 121 rooms. Simply furnished guest rooms, all with 2 standard double beds. 2 stories; exterior corridors; playground. **All Rooms:** free movies. **Cards:** AE, DI, DS, MC, VI. **Special Amenities:** Free breakfast and free local telephone calls.   🛏 �foto CTV ☒ Ⓓ

HAMPTON INN   Rates Subject to Change   **Phone:** 803/774-0222
◆ ◆ ◆
Motel
All Year [CP]   1P: $53- 59   2P/1B: $59- 65   2P/2B: $59- 65
Location: From I-95 exit 193, s on SR 9, 0.5 mi. 817 Radford Blvd 29536. Fax: 803/774-6711. **Terms:** Reserv deposit; no pets. **Facility:** 50 rooms. 2 stories; exterior corridors. **All Rooms:** free movies. **Cards:** AE, CB, DI, DS, MC, VI.   CTV ☒ 🎿 Ⓓ

HOLIDAY INN EXPRESS
◆◆◆
Motel
Rates Subject to Change
Phone: 803/774-5111
All Year [CP]　　　　1P: $35- 45　2P/1B: $35- 55　2P/2B: $42- 90　XP: $4　　F18
Location: On SR 9; at jct I-95, exit 193. 904 Radford Blvd 29536. Fax: 803/774-5111. **Terms:** Small pets only. **Facility:** 80 rooms. 2 stories; interior/exterior corridors. **All Rooms:** free movies. **Cards:** AE, CB, DI, DS, JCB, MC, VI.
🐾 📶 CTV ✕ D

SUPER 8 MOTEL
AAA SAVE
◆◆
Motel
Phone: 803/774-4161
All Year　　　　1P: $35- 42　2P/1B: $40- 42　2P/2B: $40- 46　XP: $5　　F10
Location: I-95 exit 193 & SR 9. 1203 Radford Blvd 29536. Fax: 803/774-4161. **Terms:** Small pets only. **Facility:** 99 rooms. Popular local lounge. 2 stories; exterior corridors; wading pool. **Dining & Entertainment:** Cocktail lounge; coffee shop nearby. **All Rooms:** free movies. **Cards:** AE, DI, DS, JCB, MC, VI. **Special Amenities:** Free breakfast and free local telephone calls. *(See color ad below)*
🐾 📶 ♨ CTV ✕ D

DUNCAN—2,200

LODGINGS

COMFORT INN-SOUTH
◆◆
Motel
Guaranteed Rates
Phone: 864/433-1333
All Year [CP]　　　　1P: $60- 70　2P/1B: $65- 75　2P/2B: $65- 75　XP: $5　　F16
Location: 0.3 mi n of jct I-85, exit 63 & SR 290. 1391 E Main St 29334. Fax: 864/433-1342. **Terms:** Sr. discount; no pets. **Facility:** 81 rooms. 2 stories; exterior corridors. **All Rooms:** free movies. **Cards:** AE, CB, DI, DS, MC, VI.
📶 CTV ✕ D

DAYS INN AIRPORT
◆◆◆
Motel
Rates Subject to Change
Phone: 864/433-1122
All Year [CP]　　　　1P: $45- 50　2P/1B: $50- 80　2P/2B: $55- 60　XP: $5　　F16
Location: 0.3 mi n of jct I-85, exit 63 & SR 290. 1386 E Main St 29334. Fax: 864/433-0049. **Terms:** No pets. **Facility:** 80 rooms. 2-3 stories, no elevator; exterior corridors. **All Rooms:** free & pay movies. **Cards:** AE, CB, DI, DS, MC, VI.
CTV ✕ D

EASLEY—15,200

LODGINGS

COMFORT INN OF EASLEY
◆ ◆
Motel
Rates Subject to Change
All Year [CP]   1P: $44   2P/1B: $49   2P/2B: $49   XP: $5   F16
Phone: 864/859-7520
Location: On US 123 at jct of SR 93. 5539 Calhoun Memorial Hwy 29640. Fax: 864/859-7520. **Terms:** Sr. discount; no pets. **Facility:** 93 rooms. 2 stories; exterior corridors. **All Rooms:** free movies. **Some Rooms:** 4 efficiencies. **Cards:** AE, CB, DI, DS, MC, VI.

DAYS INN
(AAA) SAVE
◆ ◆
Motel
All Year [CP]   1P: $44- 60   2P/1B: $49- 80   2P/2B: $51- 80   XP: $5   F16
Phone: 864/859-9902
Location: On US 123 bypass; 0.5 mi e of jct Sr 93. 121 Days Inn Dr 29640. Fax: 864/859-9902. **Terms:** Pets, $10 extra charge. **Facility:** 73 rooms. Rooms range in size from compact to spacious. 7 efficiencies, $55-$75; 2 stories; exterior corridors; sauna, small pool. **Dining:** Restaurant nearby. **Services:** valet laundry. **All Rooms:** free & pay movies, combo or shower baths. **Some Rooms:** microwaves, refrigerators. Fee: coffeemakers. **Cards:** AE, CB, DI, DS, MC, VI.

EDGEFIELD—2,600

LODGING

THE INN ON MAIN
◆
Historic Bed & Breakfast
Rates Subject to Change
All Year   1P: $35   2P/1B: $35   2P/2B: $45   XP: $5   F
Phone: 803/637-9915
Location: On US 25; in center of town. 303 Main St 29824. **Terms:** Reserv deposit; no pets. **Facility:** 6 rooms. 2 stories; interior corridors. **Cards:** MC, VI.

EDISTO ISLAND—*See Charleston & Vicinity p. 457.*

EHRHARDT—400

LODGING

EHRHARDT HALL
◆ ◆ ◆
Historic Bed & Breakfast
Rates Subject to Change
All Year [CP]   1P: $55   2P/1B: $65   2P/2B: $65   XP: $15
Phone: 803/267-2020
Location: On US 601, 0.5 mi s of jct SR 64 & US 601. 400 S Broadway St 29081. Fax: 803/267-2020. **Terms:** Age restrictions may apply; reserv deposit, 7 day notice; no pets. **Facility:** 5 rooms. Handling fee imposed; 2 stories; interior corridors; smoke free premises. **Cards:** AE, MC, VI.

ESTILL—2,400

LODGING

PALMETTO INN
(AAA) SAVE
◆ ◆
Motel
Fri & Sat   1P: $35   2P/1B: $38   2P/2B: $42   XP: $4   F10
Sun-Thurs   1P: $32- 35   2P/1B: $35   2P/2B: $36   XP: $4   F10
Phone: 803/625-4322
Location: 0.3 mi n of jct SR 3 & US 321, off US 321. 64 Wyman Blvd 29918. **Terms:** Reserv deposit; no pets. **Facility:** 28 rooms. Handling fee imposed; 2 stories; exterior corridors. **All Rooms:** free movies. **Some Rooms:** microwaves, refrigerators. **Cards:** AE, DS, MC, VI. **Special Amenities:** Free local telephone calls and preferred room (subject to availability with advanced reservations).

FLORENCE—29,800

LODGINGS

BEST WESTERN INN
(AAA) SAVE
◆ ◆ ◆
Motel
All Year [CP]   1P: $60- 69   2P/1B: $60- 69   2P/2B: $60- 69   XP: $5   F18
Phone: 803/678-9292
Location: On US 52; jct I-95 exit 164. 1808 W Lucas St 29501. Fax: 803/678-9990. **Terms:** No pets. **Facility:** 76 rooms. 2 stories; exterior corridors. **Dining:** Restaurant nearby. **Services:** valet laundry. **All Rooms:** coffeemakers, microwaves, free movies, refrigerators. Fee: VCP's. **Some Rooms:** Fee: whirlpools. **Cards:** AE, CB, DI, DS, MC, VI. **Special Amenities:** Free local telephone calls.

COMFORT INN
(AAA) SAVE
◆ ◆ ◆
Motel
All Year [CP]   1P: $45- 55   2P/1B: $45- 60   2P/2B: $45- 60   XP: $5   F18
Phone: 803/665-4558
Location: Jct US 52 & I-95, exit 164. 29502 (PO Box 5688). Fax: 803/665-4558. **Terms:** Small pets only. **Facility:** 165 rooms. 2 stories; interior/exterior corridors; whirlpool. **Dining:** Restaurant nearby. **Services:** valet laundry. **All Rooms:** free movies. **Some Rooms:** coffeemakers, microwaves, refrigerators, whirlpools. **Cards:** AE, CB, DI, DS, JCB, MC, VI. **Special Amenities:** Free breakfast and free local telephone calls. *(See ad p 478)*

DAYS INN SOUTH
(AAA) SAVE
◆ ◆
Motor Inn
All Year   1P: $29- 45   2P/2B: $33- 49   XP: $4   F12
Phone: 803/665-8550
Location: I-95, exit 157 & US 76. (PO Box 3806, 29502). Fax: 803/665-8550. **Terms:** Weekly/monthly rates; pets, $4 extra charge. **Facility:** 181 rooms. Truck parking. 2 stories; exterior corridors; whirlpool; playground. **Dining:** Restaurant; 6 am-9 pm; $5-$12; wine/beer only. **All Rooms:** free movies. Fee: safes. **Some Rooms:** 2 efficiencies. **Cards:** AE, DI, DS, MC, VI. **Special Amenities:** Free room upgrade and preferred room (each subject to availability with advanced reservations).

ECONO LODGE
(AAA) SAVE
◆ ◆
Motel
All Year [CP]   1P: $32- 40   2P/1B: $37- 45   2P/2B: $37- 57   XP: $4   F18
Phone: 803/665-8558
Location: On US 52; 2 blks s of jct I-95, exit 164. 2251 W Lucas St 29502 (PO Box 5688). Fax: 803/665-8558. **Terms:** Weekly/monthly rates; pets. **Facility:** 120 rooms. Nicely decorated rooms. 2 stories; exterior corridors; indoor whirlpool. **Dining:** Restaurant nearby. **All Rooms:** free movies. **Some Rooms:** coffeemakers, microwaves, refrigerators. **Cards:** AE, CB, DI, DS, JCB, MC, VI.
(See ad p 478)

FAIRFIELD INN BY MARRIOTT
◆ ◆ ◆
Motel
Rates Subject to Change
All Year [CP]   1P: $49- 69   2P/1B: $49- 69   2P/2B: $49- 69   XP: $7   F18
Phone: 803/669-1666
Location: I-95, exit 160A, 0.3 mi e on Business Rt 20. 140 Dunbarton Dr 29501. Fax: 803/669-0942. **Terms:** Sr. discount; no pets. **Facility:** 135 rooms. 3 stories; interior/exterior corridors. **All Rooms:** free movies. **Cards:** AE, CB, DI, DS, MC, VI. *(See color ad p 478)*

HAMPTON INN
◆ ◆ ◆
Motel
Rates Subject to Change
All Year [CP]   1P: $69   2P/1B: $69   2P/2B: $69
Phone: 803/662-7000
Location: On US 52; jct I-95, exit 164. 1826 W Lucas St 29501. Fax: 803/661-5150. **Terms:** Pets. **Facility:** 122 rooms. Weekend rates are higher; 2 stories; exterior corridors. **All Rooms:** free movies. **Cards:** AE, CB, DI, DS, MC, VI.

HAMPTON INN & SUITES
◆◆◆ Motel
Rates Subject to Change
Phone: 803/629-9900
All Year [CP] 1P: $79 2P/1B: $84 XP: $5 F18
Location: I-95, exit 160A; 0.3 mi e on Business Rt 20, adjacent to Florence Civic Center. 3000 Radio Dr 29501. Fax: 803/629-8907. **Facility:** 82 rooms. 3 stories; interior corridors. **All Rooms:** free movies. Roll in showers. **Cards:** AE, CB, DI, DS, MC, VI.

HOLIDAY INN EXPRESS CIVIC CENTER
◆◆◆ Motel
Guaranteed Rates
Phone: 803/664-2400
All Year [CP] 1P: $79 2P/1B: $79 2P/2B: $79
Location: I-95 exit 160A, 0.3 mi e on Business Rt 20 to Dunbarton Dr. 150 Dunbarton Dr 29501. Fax: 803/669-7510. **Terms:** Sr. discount; no pets. **Facility:** 80 rooms. 2 stories; exterior corridors. **All Rooms:** free movies. **Cards:** AE, CB, DI, DS, JCB, MC, VI. Roll in showers.

HOLIDAY INN HOTEL & SUITES
(AAA) (SAVE)
◆◆◆ Motor Inn
Phone: 803/665-4555
All Year 1P: $59- 65 2P/1B: $59- 65 2P/2B: $59- 65 XP: $6 F18
Location: On US 52 at jct I-95, exit 164. 1819 W Lucas St 29501. Fax: 803/665-4577. **Terms:** No pets. **Facility:** 204 rooms. Attractive pool area. Rooms tastefully decorated. 2 stories; exterior corridors; wading pool. **Dining & Entertainment:** Dining room; 6:30 am-2 & 5-10 pm; $8-$14; cocktails/lounge. **Services:** guest laundry. **All Rooms:** coffeemakers. Fee: movies. **Some Rooms:** microwaves, refrigerators. Fee: whirlpools. **Cards:** AE, DI, DS, MC, VI. **Special Amenities:** Free local telephone calls and free newspaper.

HOWARD JOHNSON

Phone: 803/664-9494

All Year   1P: $48- 53   2P/1B: $55- 65   2P/2B: $55- 78   XP: $5   F14

Location: I-95 exit 157 & US 76. 3821 Bancroft Rd 29501. Fax: 803/665-9125. **Terms:** CP avail; small pets only, $10 extra charge, $15 dep req. **Facility:** 51 rooms. Handling fee imposed; 2 stories; exterior corridors; small pool. **Dining:** Restaurant nearby. **All Rooms:** free movies, combo or shower baths. **Some Rooms:** whirlpools. **Cards:** AE, CB, DI, DS, MC, VI. **Special Amenities: Free breakfast and free local telephone calls.**

THE INN DOWNTOWN

Phone: 803/662-6341

All Year   Rates Subject to Change

1P: $34   2P/1B: $38   2P/2B: $38   XP: $4   F18

Location: On US 76 & 301 at jct US 52. 121 W Palmetto St 29501 (PO Drawer 2297, 29503). Fax: 803/662-6341. **Terms:** Reserv deposit; no pets. **Facility:** 81 rooms. 2 stories; exterior corridors. **Dining:** Dining room; 6:30 am-2 pm, closed Sat; $6-$12. **All Rooms:** free movies. **Cards:** AE, DS, MC, VI.

MOTEL 6 - 1250

Phone: 803/667-6100

All Year   Guaranteed Rates

1P: $35- 45   2P/1B: $39- 49   2P/2B: $39- 49   XP: $3   F17

Location: On US 52 at jct I-95, exit 164. 1834 W Lucas St 29501. Fax: 803/673-9555. **Terms:** Sr. discount; small pets only, 1 per room. **Facility:** 109 rooms. 1 story; exterior corridors. **All Rooms:** free movies. **Cards:** AE, DI, DS, MC, VI.

PARK INN INTERNATIONAL

Phone: 803/662-9421

All Year [BP]   1P: $37   2P/2B: $42   XP: $5   F16

Location: 1.3 mi s on US 301 & 52. 831 S Irby St 29501. Fax: 803/662-9421. **Terms:** Small pets only. **Facility:** 106 rooms. 2 stories; exterior corridors. **Dining & Entertainment:** Dining room, restaurant; 6 am-10 pm; $6-$16; cocktails/lounge. **Services:** Fee: coin laundry. **All Rooms:** free movies. **Some Rooms:** refrigerators. **Cards:** AE, CB, DI, DS, JCB, MC. **Special Amenities: Free breakfast and free local telephone calls.**

QUALITY INN/I-95

Phone: 803/669-1715

All Year [CP]   1P: $45   2P/1B: $50   2P/2B: $50   XP: $5   F17

Location: I-95 exit 169. 3024 TV Rd 29501. Fax: 803/669-1715. **Terms:** Pets, $5 extra charge. **Facility:** 96 rooms. 2 stories; exterior corridors; wading pool; 2 lighted tennis courts; playground. **Dining & Entertainment:** Cocktail lounge. **Services:** Fee: coin laundry. **All Rooms:** free movies. **Some Rooms:** coffeemakers. **Cards:** AE, DI, DS, MC, VI. **Special Amenities: Free breakfast and free local telephone calls.**

RADISSON INN

Phone: 803/317-6616

All Year [CP]   Rates Subject to Change

1P: $89   2P/1B: $89   2P/2B: $89   XP: $10   F18

Location: I-95, exit 164 & US 52. 1739 Mandeville Rd 29501. Fax: 803/317-9864. **Terms:** Sr. discount; reserv deposit, 3 day notice; no pets. **Facility:** 80 rooms. 3 stories; interior corridors. **All Rooms:** free movies. **Cards:** AE, CB, DI, DS, JCB, MC, VI.   Roll in showers.

RAMADA INN

Phone: 803/669-4241

All Year [MAP]   1P: $61   2P/1B: $67   2P/2B: $67   XP: $6   F18

Location: On US 52; at jct I-95, exit 164. 2038 W Lucas St 29501-1235. Fax: 803/665-8883. **Terms:** Weekly/monthly rates; BP avail; small pets only. **Facility:** 179 rooms. Nicely decorated rooms. 2 stories; interior/exterior corridors; sauna, whirlpool. **Dining & Entertainment:** Dining room; 6 am-2 & 5-10 pm, Sat & Sun 6 am-11 & 5-10 pm; $8-$15; cocktails/lounge; entertainment. **Services:** valet laundry. **All Rooms:** free & pay movies. **Some Rooms:** coffeemakers, microwaves, refrigerators. Fee: whirlpools. **Cards:** AE, DI, DS, MC, VI. **Special Amenities: Free breakfast and free newspaper.**

RED ROOF INN

Phone: 803/678-9000

All Year   Rates Subject to Change

1P: $38   2P/1B: $45   2P/2B: $45   XP: $7   F18

Location: I-95, exit 160A; 0.3 mi e on Business Rt 20. 2690 David McLeod Blvd 29501. Fax: 803/667-1267. **Terms:** Small pets only. **Facility:** 112 rooms. 2 stories; exterior corridors. **All Rooms:** free movies. **Cards:** AE, CB, DI, DS, MC, VI.

SLEEP INN

Phone: 803/662-8558

All Year [CP]   1P: $40- 60   2P/1B: $45- 60   2P/2B: $45- 65   XP: $5   F18

Location: On US 52, jct I-95 exit 164, just w of exit. I-95 & US 52 29502 (PO Box 5688). Fax: 803/662-8558. **Terms:** Weekly/monthly rates; no pets. **Facility:** 66 rooms. 2 stories; interior corridors. **Dining:** Restaurant nearby. **All Rooms:** free movies, combo or shower baths. **Some Rooms:** coffeemakers, microwaves, refrigerators. **Cards:** AE, CB, DI, DS, JCB, MC, VI. **Special Amenities: Free breakfast and free newspaper.** *(See ad p 478)*   Roll in showers.

SUPER 8 MOTEL   Guaranteed Rates   Phone: 803/661-7267
◆◆   All Year [CP]   1P: $44   2P/1B: $51   2P/2B: $51   XP: $6   F18
Motel   **Location:** Off US 52, s of I-95 exit 164. 1832 W Lucas St 29501. **Fax:** 803/661-7267. **Terms:** Sr. discount;
        small pets only. **Facility:** 67 rooms. 2 stories; exterior corridors. **All Rooms:** free movies. **Cards:** AE, CB, DI,
DS, MC, VI.   🛏 CTV ⊠ D S

THUNDERBIRD MOTOR INN   Phone: 803/669-1611
Ⓐ SAVE All Year [BP]   1P: $38   2P/1B: $43   2P/2B: $39- 42 XP: $5   F16
        Location: On US 52 at jct I-95, exit 164. (PO Box 3909, 29502). **Fax:** 803/669-1611. **Terms:** Package plans;
◆◆   small pets only. **Facility:** 134 rooms. 2 stories; exterior corridors. **Dining & Entertainment:** Dining room; 6
Motor Inn am-10:30 & 11-9:30 pm; $6-$11; cocktails/lounge. **Services:** Fee: coin laundry. **All Rooms:** free movies.
        Some Rooms: microwaves, refrigerators. **Cards:** AE, CB, DI, DS, MC, VI. **Special Amenities:** Free
breakfast and free local telephone calls. *(See color ad p 479)*   🛏 🖼 📶 CTV ⊠ D

TRAVELERS INN EXECUTIVE CENTER   Phone: 803/665-2575
Ⓐ SAVE All Year [BP]   1P: $35- 40 2P/1B: $40- 46 2P/2B: $45- 50 XP: $7   F18
        Location: I-95 & US 52, exit 164. 1914 W Lucas St 29502 (PO Box 4540). **Fax:** 803/661-0700. **Terms:** No
◆◆◆   pets. **Facility:** 168 rooms. Mini suites, $48.95; 2 stories; exterior corridors; wading pool, whirlpools. **Dining &**
Motel   **Entertainment:** Restaurant; 24 hours; $5-$8; cocktail lounge. **All Rooms:** free movies.
        Some Rooms: microwaves, refrigerators. Fee: whirlpools. **Cards:** AE, CB, DI, DS, MC, VI.
Special Amenities: Early check-in/late check-out and free breakfast. *(See color ad below)* 🖼 📶 📶 CTV ⊠ D

YOUNG'S PLANTATION INN   Phone: 803/669-4171
Ⓐ SAVE All Year   1P: $25   2P/1B: $30   2P/2B: $30   XP: $5   F12
        Location: Jct I-95 exit 157 & US 76W. US 76 & I-95 29502 (PO Box 3806). **Fax:** 803/669-4171.
◆◆   **Terms:** Package plans; pets, $4 extra charge. **Facility:** 120 rooms. 2 stories; exterior corridors; wading pool,
Motor Inn whirlpool. Fee: golf privileges. **Dining & Entertainment:** Restaurant; 6-11 am, 11:30-2 & 5:30-9:30 pm;
        $5-$14; cocktails/lounge. **All Rooms:** free movies. Fee: safes. **Cards:** AE, CB, DI, DS, MC, VI.
                                                                              🛏 🖼 📶 CTV ⊠ D

RESTAURANTS

BONNEAU'S Historical   **Dinner:** $12-$19   Phone: 803/665-2409
◆◆   **Location:** Downtown; on US 52. 231 S Irby St 29501. **Hours:** 5:30 pm-10 pm. Closed major holidays & Sun.
Steak and **Reservations:** suggested. **Features:** casual dress; cocktails. Restored southern mansion. **Cards:** AE, DI,
Seafood DS, MC, VI.   ⊠

P & M RESTAURANT DOWNTOWN   **Dinner:** $10-$15   Phone: 803/662-6311
◆◆   **Location:** 1.3 mi s on US 301 & 52; in Park Inn International. 829 S Irby St 29501. **Hours:** 5 pm-10 pm.
American Closed major holidays & Sun. **Reservations:** accepted. **Features:** casual dress; children's menu; cocktails &
        lounge. Pleasant dining room. Wide variety of well prepared meat & seafood. **Cards:** AE, CB, DI, DS, JCB,
MC, VI.   ⊠

P. A.'S RESTAURANT   **Lunch:** $4-$10   **Dinner:** $12-$20   Phone: 803/665-0846
◆◆   **Location:** 2 mi s on US 301 & 52 at jct SR 51; in Southpark Shopping Center. 1534 S Irby St 29504.
American **Hours:** 11:30 am-2 & 6-10 pm, Sat from 6 pm. Closed major holidays ,12/24 & Sun. **Reservations:** required.
        Features: semi-formal attire; cocktails. Very well prepared & presented entrees served in a cozy
atmosphere. **Cards:** AE, DS, MC, VI.   ⊠

PERCY & WILLIE'S FOOD AND SPIRITS   **Lunch:** $5-$7   **Dinner:** $6-$16 Phone: 803/669-1620
◆◆   **Location:** I-95 exit 160A, 0.8 mi e on Business Rt 20, left at light. 2401 David H McLeod Blvd 29501.
American **Hours:** 11 am-10 pm, Fri & Sat-11 pm. Closed: 11/26, 12/25 & 12/24 for lunch. **Features:** casual dress;
        children's menu; cocktails. A casual bustling atmosphere with a variety of food, meat, chops & pasta.
Cards: AE, MC, VI.   ⊠

FOLLY BEACH—*See Charleston & Vicinity p. 458.*

GAFFNEY—13,100

LODGINGS

COMFORT INN
Phone: 864/487-4200
⚠ SAVE
All Year [CP]   1P: $57   2P/1B: $62   2P/2B: $62   XP: $5   F18
♦♦ Motel
Location: Jct I-85 & SR 11, exit 92. 143 Corona Dr 29341. Fax: 864/487-4637. **Terms:** Weekly rates; pets, $5 extra charge. **Facility:** 83 rooms. 2 stories; exterior corridors. **Dining:** Restaurant nearby. **All Rooms:** microwaves, free movies, refrigerators. **Some Rooms:** whirlpools. **Cards:** AE, CB, DI, DS, MC, VI. **Special Amenities:** Free breakfast and free newspaper.

HOLIDAY INN EXPRESS
Phone: 864/489-1699
⚠ SAVE
All Year [CP]   1P: $50   2P/1B: $55   2P/2B: $55   XP: $5   F18
♦♦ Motel
Location: I-85 & SR 11 exit 92, 0.8 mi s on SR/Floyd Baker Blvd. 100 Ellis Ferry Ave 29341. Fax: 864/489-1699. **Terms:** No pets. **Facility:** 58 rooms. 2 stories; exterior corridors. **Dining:** Restaurant nearby. **All Rooms:** free movies. **Some Rooms:** microwaves, refrigerators. **Cards:** AE, CB, DI, DS, MC, VI. **Special Amenities:** Free breakfast and free local telephone calls.

GARDEN CITY BEACH—*See The Grand Strand on this page.*

GEORGETOWN—*See The Grand Strand p. 482.*

GOOSE CREEK—*See Charleston & Vicinity p. 458.*

The Grand Strand

CONWAY—9,800

LODGING

THE CYPRESS INN   Rates Subject to Change   Phone: 803/248-8199
♦♦♦ Bed & Breakfast
All Year [BP]   2P/1B: $105- 140
Location: Just s of jct US 905 & Business 501. 16 Elm St 29526 (PO Box 495). Fax: 803/248-0329. **Terms:** Age restrictions may apply; check-in 4 pm; reserv deposit, 5 day notice; 2 night min stay, weekends in summer; no pets. **Facility:** 12 rooms. 3 stories; interior corridors; smoke free premises. **Cards:** MC, VI.

RESTAURANTS

EL CERRO GRANDE   Dinner: $5-$8   Phone: 803/248-2533
♦♦ Mexican
Location: 621 Church St 29526. **Hours:** 11 am-3 & 5-10 pm. **Reservations:** suggested; groups only. **Features:** casual dress; cocktails. Good, basic & very authentic food. Dinners are filling & arrive quickly at your table. **Cards:** DI, MC, VI.

THE TRESTLE BAKERY & CAFE   Dinner: $2-$11   Phone: 803/248-9896
♦♦ American
Location: 308 Main St 29526. **Hours:** 6 am-6 pm, Sat 7 am-3 pm. Closed: Sun. **Reservations:** accepted. **Features:** casual dress. Good, mostly made-on-premises salad, soup, cake, cookies & bread in this squeaky clean, charming cafe with fresh daisies gracing the tables. The kid's meal is grilled cheese, pickle & cookie, $2.25. **Cards:** MC, VI.

GARDEN CITY BEACH—6,300   (See map p. 542; index p. 540)

LODGING

WATER'S EDGE RESORT   Phone: 803/651-0002 53
⚠ SAVE
6/6-8/9   2P/2B: $128- 266
♦♦♦
3/28-6/5   2P/2B: $106- 222
Apartment Motel
8/10-10/17   2P/2B: $116- 217
12/1-3/27 & 10/18-11/30   2P/2B: $62- 146
Location: From US 17 to Atlantic Ave, 0.5 mi n. 1012 N Waccamaw Dr 29576. Fax: 803/651-7970. **Terms:** Check-in 4 pm; reserv deposit, 14 day notice; weekly/monthly rates; package plans; no pets. **Facility:** 150 rooms. All units with balcony. 25 two-bedroom units. Rates for up to 6 persons. 3-bedroom units $95-$258. Handling fee imposed; 15 stories; exterior corridors; oceanfront; beach, whirlpools. Fee: golf privileges. **Dining & Entertainment:** Coffee shop; 7 am-7 pm 4/1-9/30; $4-$7; cocktail lounge. **Services:** guest laundry. **Recreation:** swimming, fishing. **All Rooms:** kitchens, microwaves, refrigerators. Fee: movies. **Some Rooms:** radios. **Cards:** AE, CB, DI, DS, MC, VI. *(See color ad below)*

(See map p. 542)

RESTAURANTS

GARDEN GATE CAFETERIA   **Phone:** 803/651-0600   59
◆   **Location:** 2700 Hwy 17 S 29115. **Hours:** 11 am-8:30 pm. **Features:** casual dress; beer & wine only. Choice
American   of fresh, healthy food or good, old-fashioned country cooking. Trays carried on request. **Cards:** MC, VI.

GULFSTREAM CAFE   **Dinner:** $13-$20   **Phone:** 803/651-8808   60
◆◆   **Location:** 2.3 mi s of Main St. 1536 S Waccamaw 29576. **Hours:** 5 pm-10 pm, Fri & Sat-10:30 pm. Closed:
Steak and   11/26 & 12/25. **Reservations:** suggested. **Features:** casual dress; children's menu; cocktails & lounge.
Seafood   Between waters of Atlantic Ocean & Murrell's Inlet. Some tables overlooking inlet. **Cards:** AE, DI, MC, VI.

GEORGETOWN—9,500

LODGINGS

ASHFIELD MANOR   Guaranteed Rates   **Phone:** 803/546-0464
◆◆◆   3/25-9/7 [CP]   1P: $50   2P/1B: $55   XP: $5
Bed &   12/1-3/24 & 9/8-11/30 [CP] 1P: $45   2P/1B: $50   XP: $5
Breakfast **Location:** 2 mi s from jct US 17 & US 17A; 2 mi se. 3030 S Island Rd 29440. **Terms:** Check-in 4 pm; no
           pets. **Facility:** 4 rooms. 2 stories; exterior corridors; smoke free premises. **Cards:** DS, MC, VI. [CTV] [X] [D]

CAROLINIAN INN-A CLARION HOUSE INN   **Phone:** 803/546-5191
(AAA) [SAVE]   All Year [CP]   1P: $48- 75   2P/1B: $55- 75 2P/2B: $55- 75 XP: $10   F18
              Location: 0.5 mi ne on US 17. 706 Church St 29440. Fax: 803/546-1514. **Terms:** No pets. **Facility:** 89 rooms
◆◆   2 locations; exterior corridors. **Dining:** Hook Line & Sinker, see separate listing. **Recreation:** fishing
Motor Inn   **All Rooms:** free movies. **Cards:** AE, CB, DI, DS, JCB, MC, VI. **Special Amenities:** Free local telephone
              calls.   [≈] [🛠] [CTV] [X] [D]

DAYS INN   **Phone:** 803/546-8441
(AAA) [SAVE]   4/1-6/29 & 7/6-8/31   1P: $49- 65   2P/1B: $54- 68 2P/2B: $56- 76 XP: $6   F12
              9/1-10/4   1P: $45- 68   2P/1B: $56- 72 2P/2B: $56- 72 XP: $6   F12
◆◆   6/30-7/5   1P: $45- 74   2P/1B: $49- 72 2P/2B: $56- 72 XP: $6   F12
Motel   12/1-3/31 & 10/5-11/30   1P: $43- 48   2P/1B: $48- 55 2P/2B: $52   XP: $6   F12
              Location: On US 17N. 210 N Church St 29440. Fax: 803/546-2265. **Terms:** No pets. **Facility:** 118 rooms
Some rooms with marsh & river view. 2 stories; exterior corridors. **Dining:** Restaurant nearby. **Services:** Fee: coin laundry
All Rooms: free movies. Fee: safes. **Some Rooms:** Fee: VCP's. **Cards:** AE, CB, DI, DS, JCB, MC, VI. **Special Amenities:**
Free newspaper and free room upgrade (subject to availability with advanced reservations). [≈] [🛠] [CTV] [X] [D]

DU PRE HOUSE   Rates Subject to Change   **Phone:** 803/546-0298
◆◆◆   All Year [BP]   2P/1B: $75- 115   XP: $25   F12
Historic Bed **Location:** 0.3 mi s of jct US 17 & SR 701 to Prince St, then 0.5 mi, just n of King St. 921 Prince St 29440
& Breakfast   (PO Box 1487, 29442). Fax: 803/546-0298. **Terms:** Sr. discount; reserv deposit, 7 day notice; no pets.
              Facility: 5 rooms. Handling fee imposed; 3 stories; interior corridors; smoke free premises. **Cards:** MC, VI.
                                                                              [X] [D]

ECONO LODGE   Rates Subject to Change   **Phone:** 803/546-5111
◆◆   4/1-8/31   1P: $40- 65   2P/1B: $40- 65 2P/2B: $60   XP: $6   F18
Motel   12/1-3/31 & 9/1-11/30   1P: $35- 50   2P/1B: $35- 50 2P/2B: $50   XP: $6   F18
              Location: 0.5 mi n from US 17 & US 17 alternate. 600 Church St 29440. Fax: 803/527-6400. **Terms:** Sr.
discount; reserv deposit; no pets. **Facility:** 56 rooms. Handling fee imposed; 1-2 stories; exterior corridors. **All Rooms:** free
movies. **Cards:** AE, DI, DS, MC, VI.   [≈] [CTV] [X] [D]

KING'S INN AT GEORGETOWN   Guaranteed Rates   **Phone:** 803/527-6937
◆◆◆   12/1-12/31 & 3/1-11/30 [BP]   2P/1B: $85- 125   XP: $20
Historic Bed 1/1-2/28 [BP]   2P/1B: $75- 99   XP: $20
& Breakfast   **Location:** From US 17, 0.3 mi e on Broad St, at corner of Broad & Highmarket sts. 230 Broad St 29440
Fax: 803/527-6937. **Terms:** Sr. discount; reserv deposit, 7 day notice; no pets. **Facility:** 7 rooms. 2 stories; in-
terior corridors; smoke free premises. **Cards:** AE, MC, VI.   [≈] [X] [D]

1790 HOUSE   Rates Subject to Change   **Phone:** 803/546-4821
◆◆◆   All Year [BP]   2P/1B: $75- 125 2P/2B: $75- 125 XP: $15
Historic Bed **Location:** From jct US 17 & US 17 bypass, 0.8 mi n to Screven St then 2 blks to Highmarket St, on corner.
& Breakfast   630 Highmarket St 29440. **Terms:** Sr. discount; reserv deposit, 7 day notice; no pets. **Facility:** 6 rooms. 2 sto-
ries; interior corridors; smoke free premises. **Cards:** AE, DS, MC, VI.   [CTV] [X] [D]

THE SHAW HOUSE   Guaranteed Rates   **Phone:** 803/546-9663
◆◆◆   All Year [BP]   1P: $55- 60   2P/1B: $65- 70 2P/2B: $70   XP: $10   D2
Bed &   **Location:** From US 17 & US 17 bypass, 0.8 mi n to Orange St, left to Palmeto then to Cypress, last house
Breakfast   on left. 613 Cypress St 29440. **Terms:** Sr. discount; reserv deposit, 3 day notice; no pets. **Facility:** 3 rooms.
              2 stories; interior corridors; smoke free premises.   [CTV] [X] [D]

SHIPWRIGHT'S BED & BREAKFAST   Guaranteed Rates   **Phone:** 803/527-4475
◆◆   All Year [BP]   2P/1B: $60   XP: $10
Bed &   **Location:** 0.3 mi n from jct US 17 & US 17 alternate, just w on Wood, just n on Palmetto, just w. 60
Breakfast   Cypress Ct 29440. **Terms:** Sr. discount; reserv deposit, 15 day notice; no pets. **Facility:** 2 rooms. Interior cor-
ridors; smoke free premises.   [X] [D]

RESTAURANT

HOOK LINE & SINKER   **Dinner:** $7-$15   **Phone:** 803/546-5191
◆◆   **Location:** 0.5 mi ne on US 17; in Carolinian Inn-A Clarion House Inn. 706 Church St 29440. **Hours:** 4:30
American   pm-9 pm. Closed: Sun. **Reservations:** suggested; for 5 or more. **Features:** casual dress; early bird specials;
             carryout; cocktails & lounge. **Cards:** AE, CB, DI, DS, JCB, MC, VI.   [X]

LITCHFIELD BEACH—600   (See map p. 542; index p. 540)

LODGING

LITCHFIELD BEACH & GOLF RESORT   Phone: 803/237-3000   **61**
AAA SAVE

6/7-8/24	1P:	$99- 129	2P/1B:	$99- 129	2P/2B:	$99- 345
5/24-6/6 & 8/25-9/21	1P:	$89- 119	2P/1B:	$89- 119	2P/2B:	$89- 295
3/3-5/23 & 9/22-11/2	1P:	$79- 109	2P/1B:	$79- 109	2P/2B:	$79- 245
12/1-3/2 & 11/3-11/30	1P:	$59- 89	2P/1B:	$59- 89	2P/2B:	$59- 185

♦♦♦
Resort
Complex
Location: US 17, opposite Litchfield Exchange. (PO Drawer 320, PAWLEYS ISLAND, 29585). Fax: 803/237-4282. **Terms:** Check-in 4 pm; reserv deposit, 30 day notice; weekly rates; BP avail; package plans; no pets. **Facility:** 365 rooms. Spacious suites & villas overlooking the ocean, salt marsh, fresh water lakes or golf fairways; all located on beautifully landscaped acres. 112 two-bedroom units, 72 three-bedroom units. 2 & 4-bedroom villas $945-$2590 in season; 1-5 stories; exterior corridors; putting green; beach, wading pool, sauna, whirlpools; 7 lighted tennis courts (Fee: 2 indoor); basketball, bike paths. Fee: 54 holes golf, golf instructions; 17 clay tennis courts, tennis instruction, racquetball. **Dining & Entertainment:** 2 restaurants, 3 cafeterias; 6:30 am-10 pm; $6-$20; cocktails/lounge; entertainment. **Services:** area transportation, beach shuttle in summer. Fee: coin laundry; massage. **Recreation:** children's program in summer; swimming, fishing. Rental: bicycles. **All Rooms:** coffeemakers, microwaves, refrigerators. Fee: movies. **Some Rooms:** 240 kitchens. Fee: VCP's, whirlpools. **Cards:** AE, DS, MC, VI. **Special Amenities: Preferred room (subject to availability with advanced reservations).** (See color ad p 544)

LITTLE RIVER—3,500   (See map p. 542; index p. 540)

LODGING

HARBOR INN   Phone: 803/249-3535   **7**
AAA

Guaranteed Rates

5/15-10/25	1P:	$48- 80	2P/1B:	$48- 80	2P/2B:	$48- 80	XP:	$5	F12
2/28-5/14	1P:	$42- 65	2P/1B:	$42- 65	2P/2B:	$42- 65	XP:	$5	F12
12/1-2/27 & 10/26-11/30	1P:	$40- 55	2P/1B:	$40- 55	2P/2B:	$40- 55	XP:	$5	F12

♦♦♦
Motel
Location: US 17 & Ellis Ave. 1564 US 17 Hwy N 29566 (PO Box 548). Fax: 803/249-0318. **Terms:** Reserv deposit; small pets only, $10 extra charge. **Facility:** 50 rooms. 13 efficiencies, $10 extra charge; 2 stories; exterior corridors. **Cards:** AE, MC, VI.

RESTAURANTS

NINO'S ITALIAN RESTAURANT   Dinner: $9-$17   Phone: 803/249-7666   **6**
AAA
Location: 0.5 mi s of center, on US 17. 1470 Hwy 17 29566. **Hours:** 5 pm-9 pm. Closed: Sun & 1/1-1/31. **Reservations:** accepted. **Features:** casual dress; children's menu; early bird specials; carryout; cocktails & lounge. A variety of Italian styles of preparation. Fresh seafood, pasta & meat dishes avail. **Cards:** AE, DS, MC, VI.
♦♦
Italian

THE PIER AT LITTLE RIVER   Dinner: $13-$20   Phone: 803/249-1220   **2**
♦♦
American
Location: Hwy 17N to Mineola Ave, turn right towards waterway. 4495 Mineola Ave 29566. **Hours:** 5 pm-10 pm. Closed: Sun. **Reservations:** accepted. **Features:** casual dress; children's menu; early bird specials; cocktails & lounge. Serving fresh local seafood & other meat items. **Cards:** DS, MC, VI.

TOBY'S RESTAURANT & RAW BAR   Dinner: $10-$19   Phone: 803/249-2624   **4**
♦♦
Seafood
Location: US 17S. 1359 Hwy 17 29566. **Hours:** 4 pm-midnight; happy hour 4 pm-7 pm. Closed: 12/12-12/26. **Reservations:** suggested. **Features:** casual dress; children's menu; health conscious menu; carryout; cocktails & lounge. Overlooking Turtle Lake. **Cards:** AE, CB, DI, DS, MC, VI.

UMBERTO'S CAFE   Dinner: $11-$25   Phone: 803/249-5552   **3**
♦♦
Italian
Location: Coquina Harbor on US 17. 1705 Hwy 17 N 29566. **Hours:** 5:30 pm-9:30 pm. **Reservations:** accepted. **Features:** casual dress; cocktails. On the water with a great view overlooking the marina. Pittsburg Italian trattoria featuring osso buco, Zuppa de Mare, prime steak, Provimi veal & lamb chops, served in a friendly atmosphere. **Cards:** AE, DI, MC, VI.

MURRELLS INLET—3,300   (See map p. 542; index p. 540)

LODGING

BROOKWOOD INN   Phone: 803/651-2550   **57**
AAA SAVE

5/20-8/20	2P/2B:	$45- 65	XP:	$5
3/15-5/19 & 8/21-10/31	2P/2B:	$35- 45	XP:	$5
12/1-3/14 & 11/1-11/30	2P/2B:	$30- 35	XP:	$5

Motel
Location: On US 17 business route. 5098 Business Hwy 17 29576 (PO Box 544). **Terms:** Reserv deposit, 10 day notice; no pets. **Facility:** 20 rooms. King whirlpool rms $55-$85, 3-room apartment $65-$95; 1 story; exterior corridors. **Cards:** MC, VI.

RESTAURANTS

ANCHOR INN   Dinner: $13-$19   Phone: 803/651-2295   **70**
♦♦
Seafood
Location: 3993 US 17 business route 29576. **Hours:** 5-9:30 pm. **Reservations:** suggested; in summer. **Features:** casual dress; children's menu; early bird specials. **Cards:** AE, MC, VI.

ANCHOVIES   Dinner: $9-$17   Phone: 803/651-0664   **73**
♦
Seafood
Location: On US Business 17, 0.6 mi s from SR 707. 4079 Hwy 17 Business 29576. **Hours:** 11:30 am-10 pm, Sun noon-9 pm. Closed: 11/26 & 12/25. **Features:** casual dress; children's menu; carryout; cocktails & lounge. Casual seafood restaurant overlooking tidal marsh. Outdoor dining in season. **Cards:** AE, DI, MC, VI.

BOVINES   Dinner: $14-$20   Phone: 803/651-2888   **67**
♦♦
American
Location: On Business Rt 17. 3779 Hwy 17 business route 29756. **Hours:** 5 pm-10 pm. Closed: 12/24 & 12/25. **Features:** casual dress; Sunday brunch; children's menu; cocktails & lounge. Serving a variety of meat & seafood entrees some with a southwestern flare, also serving brick oven pizza. **Cards:** AE, DI, DS, MC, VI.

CAPTAIN DAVES DOCKSIDE RESTAURANT   Dinner: $10-$18   Phone: 803/651-5850   **68**
AAA
♦♦
Seafood
Location: On Business Rt 17. 4037A Hwy 17 business route 29576. **Hours:** Open 2/14-11/30; 5 pm-10 pm. **Features:** casual dress; children's menu; senior's menu; carryout; cocktails & lounge. Located on the inlet, many tables with view. Service on the deck overlooking inlet in season. **Cards:** AE, DS, MC, VI.

(See map p. 542)

THE CAPTAIN'S RESTAURANT   Lunch: $4-$11   Dinner: $8-$16   Phone: 803/651-2416   64
◆◆   **Location:** On Business Rt 17. 3655 Business US 17 29576. **Hours:** 11:30 am-2:30 & 5-10 pm. Closed
Seafood   major holidays & Mon. **Reservations:** suggested. **Features:** casual dress; children's menu; carryout; cocktails. Well-established, locally popular seafood restaurant which uses subtle creativity in cuisine. Almost an institution. **Cards:** DS, MC, VI.   ⊠

DRUNKE'N JACK'S RESTAURANT   Dinner: $10-$20   Phone: 803/651-2044   65
◆◆   **Location:** On Business Rt 17. 4031 Hwy 17 business route 29576. **Hours:** 4:30 pm-10:30 pm; off season 5
Seafood   pm-9:30 pm. **Closed:** 1/1-1/13 & 11/26-12/25. **Features:** casual dress; children's menu; salad bar; cocktails & lounge. Located on the inlet, many tables with a view of the inlet. Entertainment in summer. **Cards:** AE, MC, VI.

HAPPY JACK'S GAZEBO BAR & GRILL   Dinner: $15-$23   Phone: 803/357-2110   71
◆◆   **Location:** 4911 US 17 29576. **Hours:** 11:30 am-3 & 5-10 pm. **Closed:** Sun. **Reservations:** accepted; for
Continental   dinner. **Features:** cocktails & lounge. **Cards:** AE, DI, MC, VI.

ROSA LINDA'S   Dinner: $5-$13   Phone: 803/651-2400   78
◆◆   **Location:** 3.4 mi s from SR 707. US 17 Bypass 29576. **Hours:** Open 12/1-12/31 & 2/1-11/30; 4
Ethnic   pm-midnight. **Closed:** 11/26, 12/24, 12/25 & 1/1-1/31. **Reservations:** suggested. **Features:** casual dress; children's menu; early bird specials; carryout; cocktails & lounge; a la carte. Mexican, Italian & casual American selections served in the relaxed setting of informal dining rooms. **Cards:** AE, DI, DS, MC, VI.   ⊠

SEAFARE SEAFOOD RESTAURANT   Dinner: $13-$23   Phone: 803/651-7666   79
◆◆   **Location:** Business Rt 17 & SR 707. **Hours:** 4-10 pm. **Reservations:** accepted; for 12 or more.
Seafood   **Features:** casual dress; buffet. **Cards:** AE, MC, VI.

MYRTLE BEACH—24,800   (See map p. 486; index below)

(See map p. 486; index below)

To help you more easily locate accommodations in the Greater Myrtle Beach area, the following two indexes and maps show lodgings and restaurant in multiple cities. Listings for these establishments are found under the heading for the city in which they are located. The Myrtle Beach area map comprises: Garden City Beach, Myrtle Beach, Litchfield Beach, Little River, Murrells Inlet, North Myrtle Beach, Surfside Beach and Sunset Beach, NC.

Index of Establishments on the DOWNTOWN MYRTLE BEACH ACCOMMODATIONS Spotting Map

(See map p. 486)

	Wave Rider Resort	88
	Waterside Inn	89
⚑	**The Tradewinds Motel**	90
⚑	**St. John's Inn**	91
⚑	**Poindexter Resort**	92
⚑	**Court Capri Motel**	93
⚑	**The Reef Resort**	94
⚑	**Sea Dip Motel**	95
	Embassy Suites at Kingston Plantation	97
⚑	**La Quinta Inn & Suites**	98
⚑	**The Beachcomber Motel**	99
⚑	**Beach Dunes Motel**	100
	Hampton Inn at Broadway	101
⚑	**Holiday South Motel**	102
	Fairfield Inn-Broadway At The Beach	103
⚑	**The Ocean Front Viking Motel**	105
⚑	**Sand Castle Family Resort**	106

RESTAURANTS

	Villa Romana	1
	Collectors Cafe	2
	Fullys A Restaurant	4
	Akel's House of Pancakes	5
⚑	**Aunt Maude's Seafood & Beef**	7
	The Library	9
⚑	**Sea Captain's House**	11
	Flamingo Seafood Grill	12
⚑	**Angelo's Steak & Pasta**	13
	Littles at the Beach Restaurant	14
	J Edward's Great Ribs & More	15

⚑	**Fusco's**	16
	Mancuso's Italian Restaurant	21
	Bagel Factory	22
	The Bistro	25
	Carolina Roadhouse Restaurant	26
	Chung Wah Restaurant	28
	The Crab House	29
	Gilley's	30
	Key West Grill	37
	Kyoto Japanese Steak House	39
	Latif's Bakery & Cafe	40
	Liberty Steakhouse & Brewery	41
	The Longhorn Steak House	42
	Midway Deli	44
⚑	**Mr Fish Seafood Market, Grill & Raw Bar**	45
	New York Prime, A Steakhouse	46
	Original Benjamin's	47
	Ding Ho Chinese Restaurant	48
	River City Cafe	49
	Sea Island	51
	Shamrock's	52
	Skeeter's	53
	TBonz Gill & Grill	54
⚑	**Thorny's Steak House & Saloon**	55
	Nascar Cafe	58
	Tripps	59
	Villa Mare Restaurant	61
	Vintage House Cafe	62
	Yamato	63

LODGINGS

ANDERSON INN   Rates Subject to Change   Phone: 803/448-1535   54

⚑
◆
Motel

6/2-8/26	2P/1B:	$45-	119	2P/2B:	$55-	114	XP:	$7	F13
4/14-6/1 & 8/27-9/3	2P/1B:	$35-	76	2P/2B:	$45-	71	XP:	$7	F13
3/10-4/13 & 9/4-10/14	2P/1B:	$29-	64	2P/2B:	$36-	61	XP:	$7	F13
12/1-3/9 & 10/15-11/30	2P/1B:	$20-	42	2P/2B:	$26-	39	XP:	$7	F13

Location: 26 Ave N & N Ocean Blvd. 2600 N Ocean Blvd 29577. Fax: 803/626-1929. **Terms:** Reserv deposit, 14 day notice; no pets. **Facility:** 112 rooms. Handling fee imposed; 4-6 stories; interior/exterior corridors. **Dining:** Coffee shop; 6 am-2:30 pm. **Some Rooms:** 12 efficiencies, 58 kitchens. **Cards:** AE, DS, MC, VI.
(See color ad below)   ⊠ ⊠ ⊞ CTV D

ATLANTIC PARADISE INN   Rates Subject to Change   Phone: 803/444-0346   6

⚑
◆◆
Motel

5/30-8/16	1P:	$68-	72	2P/1B:	$68-	72	2P/2B:	$77- 110	XP:	$7	F12
5/9-5/29 & 8/17-8/23	1P:	$34-	48	2P/1B:	$34-	48	2P/2B:	$36- 79	XP:	$6-7	F12
3/28-5/8 & 8/24-9/13	1P:	$27-	36	2P/1B:	$27-	36	2P/2B:	$31- 62	XP:	$5-6	F12
12/1-3/27 & 9/14-11/30	1P:	$18-	31	2P/1B:	$18-	31	2P/2B:	$19- 57	XP:	$3-6	F12

Location: 14th Ave S & S Ocean Blvd. 1401 S Ocean Blvd 29577. Fax: 803/444-0708. **Terms:** Reserv deposit, 14 day notice; no pets. **Facility:** 74 rooms. Handling fee imposed; 3 stories; exterior corridors. **Some Rooms:** 34 efficiencies. **Cards:** AE, DI, DS, MC, VI. *(See ad p 487)*   ⊠ CTV D

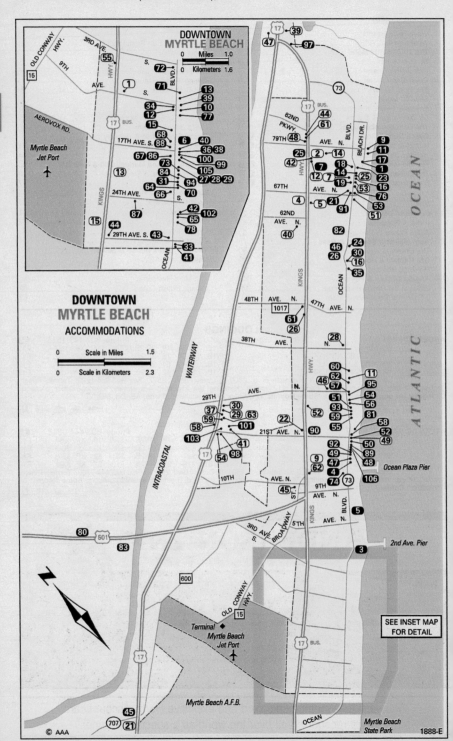

(See map p. 486)

BAR HARBOR MOTOR INN   Phone: 803/626-3200 **3**

AAA SAVE	6/1-8/16	1P:	$89- 140	2P/1B:	$89- 140	2P/2B:	$89- 140	XP: $7	F16
◆ ◆	5/11-5/31 & 8/17-9/13	1P:	$55- 98	2P/1B:	$55- 98	2P/2B:	$55- 98	XP: $7	F16
Motel	3/28-5/10 & 9/14-9/27	1P:	$49- 87	2P/1B:	$49- 87	2P/2B:	$49- 87	XP: $7	F16
	12/1-3/27 & 9/28-11/30	1P:	$29- 69	2P/1B:	$29- 69	2P/2B:	$29- 69	XP: $7	F16

Location: 1st Ave N & N Ocean Blvd. 100 N Ocean Blvd 29577 (PO Box 2390, 29578). Fax: 803/626-3205.
Terms: Reserv deposit, 10 day notice; weekly/monthly rates; package plans; no pets. **Facility:** 101 rooms. Most rooms with balcony & oceanfront view. 15 two-bedroom units. Handling fee imposed; 5-8 stories; exterior corridors; beach, wading pool. **Fee:** golf privileges. **Dining:** Restaurant nearby. **Services:** Fee: coin laundry. **Recreation:** children's program, social program in summer; swimming. **All Rooms:** free movies. **Some Rooms:** 88 efficiencies, microwaves, refrigerators, whirlpools. **Cards:** AE, DS, MC, VI. **Special Amenities:** Free room upgrade and preferred room (each subject to availability with advanced reservations). ⊃ ⊃ CTV D

TAXES—state, city and local—are extra.
Allow for them; our listed rates do not.

(See map p. 486)

BEACH COLONY RESORT

AAA [SAVE]
◆◆◆
Condo Hotel

6/6-8/21	2P/2B:	$109- 162	XP: $8	F17
5/9-6/5 & 8/22-9/18	2P/2B:	$74- 111	XP: $8	F17
3/7-5/8 & 9/19-10/16	2P/2B:	$60- 87	XP: $8	F17
12/1-3/6 & 10/17-11/30	2P/2B:	$40- 59	XP: $8	F17

Phone: 803/449-4010 [30]

Location: 3.3 mi n; 53rd Ave N & N Ocean Blvd. 5308 N Ocean Blvd 29577. Fax: 803/449-2810. **Terms:** Age restrictions may apply; reserv deposit, 14 day notice; no pets. **Facility:** 223 rooms. 14 three-bedroom units $1638-$1876 weekly in season; 6 four-bedroom units in season from $1918-$2163. Handling fee imposed; 12-22 stories; exterior corridors. **Dining:** Fusco's, see separate listing. **Cards:** MC, VI. *(See color ad inside front cover & p 488)*

🛴 🛴 ➕ CTV ✕ 🅿 Ⓓ Ⓢ

THE BEACHCOMBER MOTEL

AAA [SAVE]
◆◆
Apartment Motel

6/1-8/19	2P/2B:	$60- 95	XP: $5	F18
5/1-5/31 & 8/20-9/14	2P/2B:	$36- 70	XP: $5	F18
4/1-4/30 & 9/15-10/13	2P/2B:	$28- 60	XP: $5	F18
12/1-3/31 & 10/14-11/30	2P/2B:	$23- 33	XP: $5	F18

Phone: 803/448-4345 [99]

Location: 17 Ave S & S Ocean Blvd. 1705 S Ocean Blvd 29577. Fax: 803/626-8155. **Terms:** Age restrictions may apply; reserv deposit, 14 day notice; weekly/monthly rates; package plans; no pets. **Facility:** 45 rooms. 8 two-bedroom apartments, $37-115. Handling fee imposed; 4 stories; exterior corridors; oceanfront; beach, wading pool. Fee: golf privileges. **Dining:** Restaurant nearby. **Services:** Fee: coin laundry. **Recreation:** swimming, surf fishing. **All Rooms:** microwaves, free movies, refrigerators. Fee: safes. **Some Rooms:** 32 efficiencies. **Cards:** AE, DS, MC, VI. **Special Amenities: Free room upgrade (subject to availability with advanced reservations).** 🛴 CTV Ⓓ

BEACH DUNES MOTEL

AAA [SAVE]
◆◆
Motel

6/1-8/19	2P/2B:	$60- 111	XP: $5	F18
5/1-5/31 & 8/20-9/14	2P/2B:	$36- 74	XP: $5	F18
4/1-4/30 & 9/15-10/13	2P/2B:	$28- 61	XP: $5	F18
12/1-3/31 & 10/14-11/30	2P/2B:	$23- 36	XP: $5	F18

Phone: 803/626-3653 [100]

Location: 18th Ave S & S Ocean Blvd. 1807 S Ocean Blvd 29577. Fax: 803/946-6443. **Terms:** Age restrictions may apply; reserv deposit, 14 day notice; weekly/monthly rates; package plans; no pets. **Facility:** 72 rooms. 10 two-room efficiency apartments for up to 6 persons, penthouse avail. Handling fee imposed; 6 stories; interior/exterior corridors; oceanfront; beach, 2 wading pools, whirlpool. Fee: golf privileges. **Dining:** Restaurant nearby. **Services:** Fee: coin laundry. **Recreation:** swimming. **All Rooms:** microwaves, refrigerators. Fee: safes. **Some Rooms:** 52 kitchens. **Cards:** AE, DS, MC, VI. **Special Amenities: Free room upgrade (subject to availability with advanced reservations).** 🛴 🛴 CTV Ⓓ

(See map p. 486)

BEST WESTERN DAYTON HOUSE
Rates Subject to Change

Phone: 803/448-2441

5/29-8/22	2P/2B:	$76- 160	XP: $10
5/3-5/28 & 8/23-9/26	2P/2B:	$69- 129	XP: $10
4/3-5/2 & 9/27-10/31	2P/2B:	$49- 95	XP: $10
12/1-4/2 & 11/1-11/30	2P/2B:	$40- 80	XP: $10

Apartment Motel
Location: 1 mi n; 24th Ave N & N Ocean Blvd. 2400 N Ocean Blvd 29577 (PO Box 2113, 2957 **Terms:** Age restrictions may apply; reserv deposit, 14 day notice; no pets. **Facility:** 328 rooms. 16 stories; i terior corridors. **All Rooms:** free movies. **Some Rooms:** 323 efficiencies. **Cards:** AE, CB, DI, MC, VI.
(See color ad p 489)
Roll in showers. CTV

BLUEWATER RESORT
Phone: 803/626-8345

6/6-8/21	2P/2B:	$81- 154	XP: $5
5/9-6/5 & 8/22-9/11	2P/2B:	$60- 111	XP: $5
3/7-5/8 & 9/12-10/16	2P/2B:	$38- 87	XP: $5
12/1-3/6 & 10/17-11/30	2P/2B:	$29- 54	XP: $5

Apartment Motor Inn
Location: 2 mi s; 20th Ave S & S Ocean Blvd. 2001 S Ocean Blvd 29577 (PO Box 3000, 2957 Fax: 803/448-2310. **Terms:** Reserv deposit, 14 day notice; no pets. **Facility:** 224 rooms. 2-bedroom unit $224 in season. Handling fee imposed; 4-15 stories; exterior corridors. **Dining:** Coffee shop; 7-11 am; closed 11/1-2/2 **Cards:** AE, MC, VI. *(See color ad inside front cover & p 493)*
CTV

THE BREAKERS NORTH TOWER
Phone: 803/626-5000

6/2-8/19	2P/2B:	$100- 246	XP: $8
3/18-6/1 & 8/20-9/23	2P/2B:	$60- 140	XP: $8
2/11-3/17 & 9/24-11/18	2P/2B:	$35- 90	XP: $8
12/1-2/10 & 11/19-11/30	2P/2B:	$30- 80	XP: $8

Apartment Motor Inn
Location: 27th Ave N & N Ocean Blvd. 2701 N Ocean Blvd 29577 (PO Box 485 AAA, 2957 Fax: 803/626-5001. **Terms:** Reserv deposit, 14 day notice; no pets. **Facility:** 141 rooms. 19 stories; interior corridors. **Dining:** Dining room; 6 am-11 & 5:30-9 pm; $7-$17. **All Rooms:** Fee: movies. **Some Rooms:** 63 kitchen **Cards:** AE, CB, DI, DS, MC, VI. *(See color ad p 494)*
CTV D

THE BREAKERS RESORT HOTEL
Phone: 803/626-5000

5/31-9/1	1P:	$100- 308	2P/1B:	$100- 308	2P/2B:	$100- 308 XP: $8
3/8-5/30 & 9/2-10/19	1P:	$60- 152	2P/1B:	$60- 152	2P/2B:	$60- 152 XP: $8
2/9-3/7 & 10/20-11/16	1P:	$35- 129	2P/1B:	$35- 129	2P/2B:	$35- 129 XP: $8
12/1-2/8 & 11/17-11/30	1P:	$30- 85	2P/1B:	$30- 85	2P/2B:	$30- 85 XP: $8

Apartment Motor Inn
Location: 0.8 mi n; 21st Ave N & N Ocean Blvd. 2006 N Ocean Blvd 29577 (PO Box 485, 2957 Fax: 803/626-5001. **Terms:** Reserv deposit, 14 day notice; no pets. **Facility:** 245 rooms. Handling fee i posed; 3-14 stories; interior/exterior corridors. **Dining:** Dining room; 6:30 am-11 & 6-9:30 pm; in summer 7 am-11 p $6-$18. **All Rooms:** Fee: movies. **Some Rooms:** 231 efficiencies. **Cards:** AE, CB, DI, DS, MC, VI. *(See color ad p 494)*
CTV

BREAKWATER INN
Rates Subject to Change

Phone: 803/448-8591

5/27-8/20	1P:	$89- 135	2P/1B:	$89- 135	2P/2B:	$89- 135 XP: $5
4/1-5/5 & 9/12-10/1	1P:	$59- 120	2P/1B:	$59- 120	2P/2B:	$59- 120 XP: $5
5/6-5/26 & 8/21-9/11	1P:	$52- 120	2P/1B:	$52- 120	2P/2B:	$52- 120 XP: $5
12/1-3/31 & 10/2-11/30	1P:	$28- 85	2P/1B:	$28- 85	2P/2B:	$28- 85 XP: $5

Motel
Location: 14th Ave N & N Ocean Blvd. 1402 N Ocean Blvd 29577. **Terms:** Reserv deposit, 14 day notic no pets. **Facility:** 84 rooms. Handling fee imposed; 2-4 stories, no elevator; exterior corridors. **All Rooms:** free movie **Some Rooms:** 12 efficiencies, 11 kitchens. **Cards:** DS, MC, VI.
CTV

BRUSTMAN HOUSE
Rates Subject to Change

Phone: 803/448-7699

5/22-9/3 [BP]	1P:	$55- 60	2P/1B:	$65- 95	2P/2B: $75 XP: $15-20
3/6-5/21 & 9/4-10/15 [BP]	1P:	$50	2P/1B:	$55- 85	2P/2B: $65 XP: $15-20
12/1-3/5 & 10/16-11/30 [BP]	1P:	$40	2P/1B:	$45- 66	2P/2B: $55 XP: $10-15

Bed & Breakfast
Location: Between Kings Hwy (US 17) & S Ocean Blvd. 400 25th Ave S 29577. Fax: 803/626-247 **Terms:** Age restrictions may apply; reserv deposit, 14 day notice; no pets. **Facility:** 5 rooms. 2-bedroom suite with kitchen fro $120, from $110 off season, for 3-5 persons; 2 stories; interior corridors; smoke free premises.
CTV

CAPTAIN'S QUARTERS RESORT
Phone: 803/448-1404

6/6-8/21	2P/1B:	$107- 126	2P/2B:	$112- 131	XP: $5
5/9-6/5 & 8/22-9/18	2P/1B:	$70- 102	2P/2B:	$75- 102	XP: $5
3/7-5/8 & 9/19-10/9	2P/1B:	$51- 74	2P/2B:	$59- 74	XP: $5
12/1-3/6 & 10/10-11/30	2P/1B:	$59	2P/2B:	$32- 59	XP: $5

Motor Inn
Location: Between 9th Ave S & 10th Ave S. 901 S Ocean Blvd 29577. **Terms:** Reserv deposit, 14 d notice; no pets. **Facility:** 328 rooms. Handling fee imposed; 9-15 stories; exterior corridors. **Dining:** Dining room; 6 am-11 & 5-9:30 pm, closed Mon; $5-$13. **Some Rooms:** 279 efficiencies. **Cards:** AE, MC, VI.
(See color ad inside front cover & p 495)
Roll in showers. CTV

THE CARAVELLE RESORT
Rates Subject to Change

Phone: 803/449-3331

5/8-8/30	1P:	$74- 260	2P/1B:	$74- 260	2P/2B:	$74- 260 XP: $5
8/31-10/24	1P:	$68- 175	2P/1B:	$68- 175	2P/2B:	$68- 175 XP: $5
3/6-5/7	1P:	$54- 175	2P/1B:	$54- 175	2P/2B:	$54- 175 XP: $5
12/1-3/5 & 10/25-11/30	1P:	$32- 128	2P/1B:	$32- 128	2P/2B:	$32- 128 XP: $5

Motor Inn
Location: Corner 69th Ave N. 6900 N Ocean Blvd 29572. Fax: 803/449-0643. **Terms:** Reserv deposit, 7 notice; no pets. **Facility:** 575 rooms. Handling fee imposed; 1-15 stories; interior/exterior corridors. **Dining:** Dining room am-10 & 5-9 pm, poolside grill; $8-$15. **Some Rooms:** 135 efficiencies, 422 kitchens. **Cards:** AE, DS, MC, VI.
(See color ad inside front cover & p 496)
CTV

THE CARIBBEAN RESORT & VILLAS
Phone: 803/448-7181

6/5-8/22	2P/2B:	$83- 160	XP: $6
5/8-6/4 & 8/23-8/29	2P/2B:	$59- 132	XP: $6
3/6-5/7 & 8/30-10/10	2P/2B:	$39- 105	XP: $6
12/1-3/5 & 10/11-11/30	2P/2B:	$32- 68	XP: $6

Motel
Location: 1.5 mi n; 30th Ave & N Ocean Blvd. 3000 N Ocean Blvd 29577. Fax: 803/448-32 **Terms:** Reserv deposit, 14 day notice; no pets. **Facility:** 312 rooms. Handling fee imposed; 14 stories; exterior corrid **Some Rooms:** 39 efficiencies, 229 kitchens. **Cards:** DS, MC, VI. *(See color ad inside front cover & p 497)*
Roll in showers. CTV

MYRTLE BEACH'S

BlueWater
R E S O R T

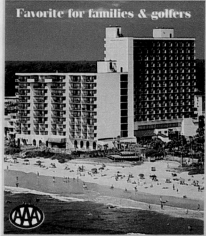

Favorite for families & golfers

Lazy River Ride   70-foot indoor pool   Five hot-water whirlpools   Four outdoor pools   Kiddie Pool   Free racquetball on site   Billiard room   Exercise Room & Saunas   Free Tennis Nearby   Quiet Rooftop Lounge   Video Arcade   Golf Packages   Restaurant on Site   Guest Laundry   Efficiency Apartments   Executive Suites   Two-bedroom Condos   Great Entertainment packages to some of the hottest shows including The Alabama Theatre, The Gatlin Brothers Theatre and more.

1998 RATES		W/AAA DISCOUNT
Jan. 1 - Feb. 5 Nov. 21 - Dec. 31	29.00 - 40.00	26.10 - 36.00
Feb. 6 - Mar. 6 Oct. 17 - Nov. 20	29.00 - 44.00	26.10 - 39.60
Oct. 10 - Oct. 16	38.00 - 52.00	34.20 - 46.80
Oct. 3 - Oct. 9	43.00 - 58.00	38.70 - 52.20
Mar. 7 - Mar. 20 Sept. 19 - Oct. 2	49.00 - 64.00	44.10 - 57.60
Mar. 21 - May 8 Sept. 12 - Sept. 18	56.00 - 74.00	50.40 - 66.60
May 9 - May 29 Aug. 29 - Sept. 11	60.00 - 79.00	54.00 - 71.10
May 30 - June 5 Aug. 22 - Aug. 28	71.00 - 94.00	63.90 - 84.60
June 6 - June 12 Aug. 15 - Aug. 21	81.00 - 111.00	72.90 - 99.90
June 13 - June 26	94.00 - 120.00	84.60 - 108.00
June 27 - Aug. 14	104.00 - 134.00	93.60 - 120.60

Rates listed are for Oceanview Eff. Apt. (Villa) & Angle Oceanview Ex. Suites w/ 2 adults & 2 children under 18. Only one discount per stay. Golf & Entertainment Pkgs. not subject to discount. A surcharge will apply to weekend reservations, some holidays & special events.

Call Toll Free For Reservations or Free Color Brochure.

1-800-845-6994

2001 S. Ocean Blvd. P.O. Box 3000
Myrtle Beach, SC 29578-3000
(803) 626-8345

(See map p. 486)

CAROLINA WINDS

AAA [SAVE]
◆◆◆
Apartment
Motor Inn

Phone: 803/449-2477   **11**

6/19-8/15		2P/2B:	$130- 262	XP: $5	F17
4/10-6/18 & 8/16-9/17		2P/2B:	$86- 247	XP: $5	F17
2/6-4/9 & 9/18-11/30		2P/2B:	$54- 156	XP: $5	F17
12/1-2/5		2P/2B:	$42- 92	XP: $5	F17

Location: 5.3 mi n. 200 76th Ave N 29572 (PO Drawer 7518, 29577). Fax: 803/449-7410. **Terms:** Age restrictions may apply; reserv deposit, 7 day notice, handling fee imposed; no pets. **Facility:** 138 rooms. 9-12 stories; interior/exterior corridors. **Dining:** Coffee shop; 7-10:30 am. **All Rooms:** kitchens. **Cards:** MC, VI.
(See color ad inside front cover & p 498)
🛥️ 🛥️ [CTV] [D]

CATOE VILLA

AAA
◆◆
Motel

Rates Subject to Change   Phone: 803/448-5706   **5**

6/1-8/21		2P/2B:	$69- 105	XP: $5-8	
5/1-5/31 & 8/22-9/6		2P/2B:	$52- 75	XP: $5	
4/1-4/30 & 9/7-9/30		2P/2B:	$39- 62	XP: $5	
3/4-3/31 & 10/1-10/31		2P/2B:	$29- 52	XP: $5	

Location: 2 blks s; 5th Ave N & N Ocean Blvd. 506 N Ocean Blvd 29577 (PO Box 1017, 29578).
Terms: Open 3/4-10/31; reserv deposit, 14 day notice; no pets. **Facility:** 24 rooms. Handling fee imposed; 3 stories; exterior corridors. **All Rooms:** free movies. **Some Rooms:** 16 efficiencies. **Cards:** DS, MC, VI.
🛥️ [CTV] [D]

CORAL BEACH RESORT

AAA [SAVE]
◆◆◆
Apartment
Hotel

Phone: 803/448-8421   **13**

6/5-8/23	2P/1B:	$110- 185	2P/2B:	$110- 185	XP: $10	F16
3/27-6/4 & 8/24-9/20	2P/1B:	$75- 150	2P/2B:	$75- 150	XP: $10	F16
3/6-3/26 & 9/21-10/18	2P/1B:	$63- 110	2P/2B:	$63- 110	XP: $10	F16
12/1-3/5 & 10/19-11/30	2P/1B:	$43- 75	2P/2B:	$43- 75	XP: $10	F16

Location: Oceanfront at 11th Ave S. 1105 S Ocean Blvd 29577. Fax: 803/626-0156. **Terms:** Reserv deposit, 7 day notice; weekly/monthly rates; package plans; no pets. **Facility:** 301 rooms. Spacious & expansive property with numerous recreational facilities. Handling fee imposed; 12 stories; exterior corridors; beach, 2 wading pools, saunas, whirlpools. Fee: golf privileges; bowling. **Dining & Entertainment:** Restaurant; 6:30 am-11 & 5:30-9 pm; $8-$14; cocktails/lounge; pool bar in season. **Services:** Fee: coin laundry. **Recreation:** children's program in season; swimming, water ride. **All Rooms:** coffeemakers, free & pay movies, refrigerators. Fee: safes. **Some Rooms:** 263 efficiencies, microwaves. **Cards:** AE, CB, DI, DS, JCB, MC, VI. **Special Amenities:** Free local telephone calls. *(See color ad p 500)*
🛥️ 🛥️ 🛟 [CTV] 🏊 [D]

COURT CAPRI MOTEL

AAA
◆◆
Motel

Rates Subject to Change   Phone: 803/448-6119   **93**

6/5-8/15	1P: $75		2P/2B:	$78- 109	XP: $10	F12
4/10-6/4 & 8/16-9/6	1P: $45- 59	2P/2B: $45- 59	2P/2B:	$39- 85	XP: $10	F12
3/7-4/9 & 9/7-10/17	1P: $32- 42	2P/2B: $32- 42	2P/2B:	$29- 68	XP: $10	F12
12/1-3/6 & 10/18-11/30	1P: $25- 29	2P/2B: $25- 29	2P/2B:	$25- 45	XP: $10	F12

Location: N Ocean Blvd; 26th Ave N. 2610 N Ocean Blvd 29577. Fax: 803/626-9259. **Terms:** Reserv deposit, 14 day notice; no pets. **Facility:** 100 rooms. Oceanview suites, $172 in season. Handling fee imposed; 4-10 stories; interior/exterior corridors. **Dining:** Coffee shop; 6:30 am-1 pm in season; $2-$5. **All Rooms:** free movies. **Some Rooms:** 80 efficiencies. **Cards:** AE, DS, MC, VI. *(See color ad p 501)*
🛥️ 🛥️ [CTV] [D]

CROWN REEF RESORT

AAA [SAVE]
◆◆◆
Apartment
Motor Inn

Phone: 803/626-8077   **41**

6/2-8/17	2P/1B:	$115- 162	2P/2B:	$105- 180	XP: $6	F12
5/12-6/1 & 8/18-9/21	2P/1B:	$105- 130	2P/2B:	$100- 120	XP: $6	F12
3/10-5/11 & 9/22-10/19	2P/1B:	$70- 105	2P/2B:	$70- 108	XP: $6	F12
12/1-3/9 & 10/20-11/30	2P/1B:	$46- 72	2P/2B:	$44- 70	XP: $6	F12

Location: 29th Ave S & S Ocean Blvd. 2913 S Ocean Blvd 29577. Fax: 803/626-7230. **Terms:** Age restrictions may apply; reserv deposit, 14 day notice; no pets. **Facility:** 204 rooms. Handling fee imposed; 14 stories; exterior corridors. **Dining:** Restaurant; 6 am-9 pm; $3-$12. **All Rooms:** free movies. **Some Rooms:** 111 efficiencies, 71 kitchens. **Cards:** AE, DS, MC, VI. *(See color ad p 502)*
🛥️ 🛥️ [CTV] 🚫 🏊 [D] [S]

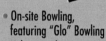

(See map p. 486)

DAYS INN MYRTLE BEACH OCEANFRONT

				Phone: 803/449-7431	**9**
	5/31-8/17	1P: $120- 150	2P/2B: $120- 150	XP: $10	F18
	3/29-5/30 & 8/18-9/21	1P: $70- 100	2P/2B: $70- 100	XP: $10	F18
◆◆	3/8-3/28 & 9/22-11/30	1P: $65- 95	2P/2B: $65- 95	XP: $10	F18
Motel	12/1-3/7	1P: $45- 75	2P/2B: $45- 75	XP: $10	F18

Location: 5.5 mi n; 77th Ave N & N Ocean Blvd. 205 77th Ave N 29577 (PO Box 7218). Fax: 803/449-7438. **Terms:** Reserv deposit, 3 day notice; package plans; no pets. **Facility:** 99 rooms. 5 two-bedroom units. 6 stories; exterior corridors; oceanfront; beach, wading pool. Fee: golf privileges. **Dining & Entertainment:** Coffee shop; 6-11 am; $2-$7; cocktails/lounge. **Services:** Fee: coin laundry. **Recreation:** swimming. **All Rooms:** free movies, refrigerators. **Some Rooms:** 39 efficiencies, 4 kitchens. **Cards:** AE, DI, DS, MC, VI. **Special Amenities:** Free local telephone calls and free room upgrade (subject to availability with advanced reservations).

FIGHT NOISE POLLUTION!

If there's too much bump in the night at your lodging, phone the 24-hour attendant.

(See map p. 486)

DAYS INN ON THE OCEAN

AAA SAVE	6/7-8/17 [CP]		2P/2B:	$96- 125	XP: $5	F12
	3/11-6/6 & 8/18-9/22 [CP]		2P/2B:	$55- 89	XP: $5	F12
◆◆◆	9/23-10/27 [CP]		2P/2B:	$53- 79	XP: $5	F12
Motel	12/1-3/10 & 10/28-11/30 [CP]		2P/2B:	$35- 65	XP: $5	F12

Phone: 803/448-1776   🄴

Location: At 21st Ave N & Ocean Blvd. 2104 N Ocean Blvd 29577. Fax: 803/448-4900. **Terms:** Age restrictions may apply; reserv deposit, 3 day notice; monthly rates; package plans; no pets. **Facility:** 49 rooms. Some oceanfront rooms. 5 two-bedroom units. 8 stories; exterior corridors; beach, wading pool, whirlpool; 1 tennis court. Fee: golf privileges. **Dining:** Restaurant nearby. **Services:** Fee: coin laundry. **Recreation:** swimming, surf fishing. **All Rooms:** free movies, refrigerators. Fee: safes. **Some Rooms:** 34 efficiencies, microwaves. **Cards:** AE, CB, DI, DS, MC, VI.
(See color ad p 501)

🛰 CTV 🗙 D

THE DRIFTWOOD ON THE OCEANFRONT

AAA SAVE	6/5-8/15		2P/1B:	$74- 79	2P/2B:	$79- 102	XP: $6	F12
	5/8-6/4 & 8/16-9/6		2P/1B:	$55- 74	2P/2B:	$60- 92	XP: $6	F12
◆◆	3/6-5/7 & 9/7-10/10		2P/1B:	$35- 45	2P/2B:	$38- 59	XP: $6	F12
Motel	12/1-3/5 & 10/11-11/30		2P/1B:	$22- 25	2P/2B:	$28- 36	XP: $6	F12

Phone: 803/448-1544   🄵

Location: At 16th Ave N. 1600 N Ocean Blvd 29577 (PO Box 275, 29578). Fax: 803/448-2917. **Terms:** Reserv deposit, 14 day notice, Handling fee imposed; no pets. **Facility:** 90 rooms. 52 efficiencies, $3-$7 extra charge; 3-5 stories; exterior corridors. **Cards:** AE, DS, MC, VI. *(See color ad below)*

🛰 CTV D

DUNES VILLAGE RESORT

AAA SAVE	6/6-8/22		2P/2B:	$115	XP: $8	F14
	8/23-9/26		2P/2B:	$74- 88	XP: $8	F14
◆◆◆	12/1-6/5 & 11/15-11/30		2P/2B:	$43- 84	XP: $8	F14
Motor Inn	9/27-11/14		2P/2B:	$49- 58	XP: $8	F14

Phone: 803/449-5275   🄵

Location: At 52nd Ave N. 5200 N Ocean Blvd 29577. Fax: 803/449-5275. **Terms:** Age restrictions may apply; reserv deposit, 7 day notice; weekly rates; package plans; no pets. **Facility:** 93 rooms. Quiet, lovely oceanfront setting with wonderful views from majority of rooms. Handling fee imposed; 8 stories; exterior corridors; beach, wading pool, sauna, whirlpool, heated lazy river; 3 tennis courts. Fee: golf privileges. **Dining:** Coffee shop; 7 am-10 pm, Sat & Sun-11 pm. **Services:** Fee: coin laundry. **Recreation:** swimming. **Some Rooms:** 86 efficiencies, 2 kitchens, refrigerators. Fee: VCP's. **Cards:** DS, MC, VI. **Special Amenities:** Free local telephone calls and free newspaper.

🛰 🛰 🅟 CTV D S

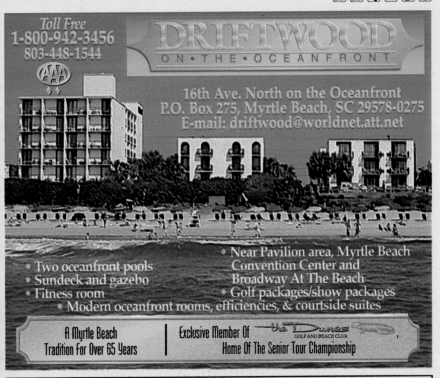
Relax over good food: Follow the recommendations in the Lodgings & Restaurants listings.

(See map p. 486)

EL DORADO MOTEL
Phone: 803/626-3559 **43**

(AAA) (SAVE)

		1P:	$52	2P/1B:	$52	2P/2B:	$59- 79	XP:	$5	F16
	6/13-8/16	1P:	$52	2P/1B:	$52	2P/2B:	$59- 79	XP:	$5	F16
	3/23-6/12 & 8/17-9/20	1P:	$33	2P/1B:	$33	2P/2B:	$37- 39	XP:	$5	F16
	3/3-3/22	1P:	$25	2P/1B:	$25	2P/2B:	$27- 37	XP:	$5	F16
Motel	12/1-3/2 & 9/21-11/30	1P:	$23	2P/1B:	$23	2P/2B:	$25- 31	XP:	$5	F16

◆◆

Location: 28th Ave S & S Ocean Blvd. 2800 S Ocean Blvd 29577. Fax: 803/448-8484. **Terms:** Reserv deposit, 21 day notice; weekly/monthly rates; pets, small dogs, $5 extra charge. **Facility:** 41 rooms. Unpretentious accommodation across street from beach. 2 two-bedroom units, $62-$118. Handling fee imposed; 2-3 stories; exterior corridors; sauna, whirlpool; barbecue grills. **Dining:** Restaurant nearby. **Services:** Fee: coin laundry. **All Rooms:** free movies, refrigerators, combo or shower baths. **Some Rooms:** coffeemakers, 35 kitchens, microwaves, radios. **Cards:** DS, MC, VI.

🛏 🖻 🖘 (CTV) (D)

EMBASSY SUITES AT KINGSTON PLANTATION
Rates Subject to Change   Phone: 803/449-0006 **97**

◆◆◆

		1P:	$179- 339	2P/1B:	$179- 339	2P/2B:	$179- 339	XP:	$20	F17
Resort	5/23-9/4	1P:	$179- 339	2P/1B:	$179- 339	2P/2B:	$179- 339	XP:	$20	F17
Complex	4/4-5/22 & 9/5-11/30	1P:	$114- 249	2P/1B:	$114- 249	2P/2B:	$114- 249	XP:	$20	F17
	3/14-4/3	1P:	$104- 204	2P/1B:	$104- 204	2P/2B:	$104- 204	XP:	$20	F17
	12/1-3/13	1P:	$84- 174	2P/1B:	$84- 174	2P/2B:	$84- 174	XP:	$20	F17

Location: 1.1 mi n from jct US 17N & Business 17N, then 1.3 mi e on Lake Arrowhead Rd. 9800 Lake Dr 29572. Fax: 803/497-7910. **Terms:** Check-in 4 pm; no pets. **Facility:** 750 rooms. 1- to 3-bedroom villas, $179-$339 in season; 1-20 stories; interior/exterior corridors. **Dining:** Dining room, restaurant; 6:30 am-11 pm; $8-$18. **All Rooms:** free movies. **Some Rooms:** 255 efficiencies, 480 kitchens. **Cards:** AE, DI, DS, MC, VI. *(See color ad below)*

🖻 🖘 🕂 (CTV) ✖ 🌙 (D) (S)

FAIRFIELD INN-BROADWAY AT THE BEACH
Rates Subject to Change   Phone: 803/444-8097 **103**

◆◆◆

		1P:	$50- 86	2P/1B:	$57- 93	2P/2B:	$57- 93	XP:	$8	F17
Motel	All Year [CP]	1P:	$50- 86	2P/1B:	$57- 93	2P/2B:	$57- 93	XP:	$8	F17

Location: Jct US 17 & 21st Ave. 1350 Paradise Circle 29577. Fax: 803/444-8394. **Terms:** Reserv deposit; no pets. **Facility:** 111 rooms. 4 stories; interior corridors. **All Rooms:** free movies. **Cards:** AE, CB, DI, DS, MC, VI.   Roll in showers.

🖘 (CTV) 🕭 ✖ 🌙 (D) (S)

FIREBIRD MOTOR INN
Phone: 803/448-7032 **73**

(AAA) (SAVE)

					2P/1B:	$56- 80	2P/2B:	$78- 109	XP:	$6
	6/4-8/14				2P/1B:	$56- 80	2P/2B:	$78- 109	XP:	$6
	3/26-6/3 & 8/15-9/18				2P/1B:	$35- 67	2P/2B:	$37- 109	XP:	$6
Motel	12/1-2/25 & 10/20-11/30				2P/1B:	$23- 45	2P/2B:	$32- 90	XP:	$6
	2/26-3/25 & 9/19-10/19				2P/1B:	$23- 67	2P/2B:	$30- 90	XP:	$6

◆◆

Location: 21st Ave S & S Ocean Blvd. 2007 S Ocean Blvd 29577. Fax: 803/448-9281. **Terms:** Reserv deposit, 14 day notice, handling fee imposed; monthly rates; package plans; no pets. **Facility:** 114 rooms. 28 two-bedroom units. 4 stories; exterior corridors; oceanfront; beach, water ride. Fee: golf privileges. **Dining:** Restaurant nearby. **Services:** Fee: coin laundry. **Recreation:** swimming, charter fishing. **All Rooms:** microwaves, free movies, refrigerators. Fee: safes. **Some Rooms:** A/C, coffeemakers, 53 efficiencies, VCP's. **Cards:** AE, DS, MC, VI. *(See color ad p 505)*

🖘 🕂 (CTV) (D)

(See map p. 486)

FOREST DUNES RESORT

Phone: 803/449-0864 [46]

AAA [SAVE]

◆◆◆

Apartment
Motor Inn

6/6-8/21	2P/2B:	$113- 148	XP:	$5	F17
5/9-6/5 & 8/22-9/18	2P/2B:	$80- 107	XP:	$5	F17
3/7-5/8 & 9/19-10/16	2P/2B:	$61- 90	XP:	$5	F17
12/1-3/6 & 10/17-11/30	2P/2B:	$44- 73	XP:	$5	F17

Location: Between 52nd Ave N & 62nd Ave N. 5511 N Ocean Blvd 29577. **Fax:** 803/449-8404. **Terms:** Reserv deposit, 14 day notice, handling fee imposed; no pets. **Facility:** 117 rooms. 17 stories; exterior corridors. **Dining:** Coffee shop. **All Rooms:** kitchens. **Cards:** MC, VI. *(See color ad p 506)* [icons] [CTV] [D] [S]

THE FRED RICK MOTEL

Phone: 803/448-6435 [12]

AAA [SAVE]

◆◆

Motel

5/27-8/14	2P/2B:	$42- 110	XP:	$5	D
8/15-9/1	2P/2B:	$32- 99	XP:	$5	D
3/1-5/26 & 9/2-9/30	2P/2B:	$22- 69	XP:	$5	D
12/1-2/28 & 10/1-11/30	2P/2B:	$18- 69			

Location: 9th Ave S & S Ocean Blvd. 900 S Ocean Blvd 29577. **Terms:** Reserv deposit, 14 day notice; weekly rates; no pets. **Facility:** 36 rooms. Coffeemaker avail upon request. Handling fee imposed; 3 stories; exterior corridors. **Dining:** Restaurant nearby. **Services:** Fee: coin laundry. **All Rooms:** refrigerators. **Some Rooms:** 17 efficiencies. **Cards:** AE, DS, MC, VI. **Special Amenities:** Free room upgrade and preferred room (each subject to availability with advanced reservations). [icons] [CTV] [D]

GASLITE INN

Phone: 803/449-5152 [23]

AAA [SAVE]

◆◆

Motel

6/2-9/1	2P/1B:	$52	2P/2B:	$57- 109	XP:	$5
3/15-6/1	2P/1B:	$33- 39	2P/2B:	$42- 75	XP:	$5
9/2-10/15	2P/1B:	$33- 43	2P/2B:	$43- 75	XP:	$5
12/1-3/14 & 10/16-11/30	2P/1B:	$28- 30	2P/2B:	$32- 65	XP:	$5

Location: N Ocean Blvd & 74 Ave N. 7302 N Ocean Blvd 29572. **Fax:** 803/692-8000. **Terms:** Age restrictions may apply; reserv deposit, 14 day notice, handling fee imposed; weekly/monthly rates; no pets. **Facility:** 17 rooms. 2 stories; exterior corridors; shuffleboard. **Dining:** Restaurant nearby. **Services:** Fee: coin laundry. **All Rooms:** coffeemakers, microwaves, refrigerators. **Some Rooms:** 12 efficiencies. **Cards:** AE, DS, MC, VI. **Special Amenities:** Early check-in/late check-out and free local telephone calls. [icons] [CTV] [X] [D]

GAZEBO INN

Rates Subject to Change   Phone: 803/448-9435 [84]

AAA

◆◆

Motel

5/22-8/8	2P/1B:	$55- 75	2P/2B:	$56- 100	XP:	$5	F12
5/8-5/21 & 8/9-8/30	2P/1B:	$41- 60	2P/2B:	$46- 85	XP:	$5	F12
3/6-5/7 & 8/31-9/19	2P/1B:	$35- 45	2P/2B:	$38- 75	XP:	$5	F12
12/1-3/5 & 9/20-11/30	2P/1B:	$25- 35	2P/2B:	$30- 50	XP:	$5	F12

Location: 16 Ave S & S Ocean Blvd. 1607 S Ocean Blvd 29577. **Terms:** Reserv deposit, 14 day notice; no pets. **Facility:** 60 rooms. Handling fee imposed; 5 stories; interior corridors. **Some Rooms:** 30 efficiencies. **Cards:** MC, VI. *(See color ad p 510)* [icons] [CTV] [X] [D]

GRAND STRAND MOTEL

Phone: 803/448-1461 [86]

AAA [SAVE]

◆◆

Motel

5/31-8/10	2P/1B:	$59- 88	2P/2B:	$78- 112	XP:	$6	D12
5/10-5/30 & 8/11-9/14	2P/1B:	$44- 59	2P/2B:	$55- 84	XP:	$6	D12
3/15-5/9 & 9/15-9/28	2P/1B:	$35- 51	2P/2B:	$44- 66	XP:	$6	D12
12/1-3/14 & 9/29-11/30	2P/1B:	$25- 38	2P/2B:	$29- 57	XP:	$6	D12

Location: 18 Ave S & S Ocean Blvd. 1804 S Ocean Blvd 29577-4695. **Fax:** 803/626-2242. **Terms:** Reserv deposit, 14 day notice; no pets. **Facility:** 92 rooms. Handling fee imposed; 3-4 stories; exterior corridors. **Some Rooms:** 50 efficiencies. **Cards:** AE, DS, MC, VI. *(See color ad p 507)* [icons] [CTV] [D]

HAMPTON INN AT BROADWAY

Phone: 803/916-0600 [101]

Motel
Under construction; **Location:** From US 17 bypass e on 21st N, just e to Central Pkwy; in the east end of Broadway at the Beach. 1140 Celebrity Cir 29578. **Terms:** No pets. **Facility:** 141 rooms. Scheduled to open January, 1998; 8 stories; interior corridors. **All Rooms:** free & pay movies. **Cards:** AE, CB, DI, DS, MC, VI. *(See color ad p 508)*   Roll in showers. [icons] [CTV] [X] [D] [S]

HAMPTON INN-48TH AVE NO.

Rates Subject to Change   Phone: 803/449-5231 [61]

◆◆◆

Motel

5/22-9/7 [CP]	1P:	$95- 119	2P/1B:	$105- 130	2P/2B: $105- 130
12/1-5/21 & 9/8-11/30 [CP]	1P:	$65- 89	2P/1B:	$72- 99	2P/2B: $72- 99

Location: 3 mi n on US 17 business route; 48th Ave N & Kings Hwy. 4709 N Kings Hwy 29577 (PO Box 7138). **Fax:** 803/449-1528. **Terms:** Sr. discount; no pets. **Facility:** 152 rooms. 4 stories; interior corridors. **All Rooms:** free movies. **Cards:** AE, CB, DI, DS, MC, VI. *(See color ad p 508)* [icons] [CTV] [X] [D] [S]

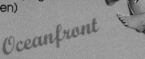

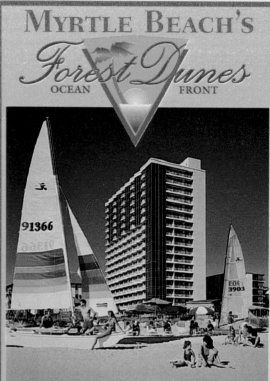

(See map p. 486)

HAMPTON INN-NORTHWOOD Rates Subject to Change Phone: 803/497-0077 **25**
◆◆◆   5/26-9/3 [CP]   1P: $79- 94   2P/1B: $85- 99   2P/2B: $85- 99
Motel   3/4-5/25 & 9/4-10/31 [CP]   1P: $52- 66   2P/1B: $59- 73   2P/2B: $59- 73
   12/1-3/3 & 11/1-11/30 [CP]   1P: $46- 49   2P/1B: $51- 54   2P/2B: $51- 54
Location: 75th Ave N & N Kings Hwy/Business Rt 17. 620 75th Ave N 29572 (PO Box 6950, 29577). Fax: 803/497-8845.
Terms: No pets. **Facility:** 122 rooms. 5 stories; interior corridors. **All Rooms:** free movies. **Cards:** AE, CB, DI, DS, MC, VI.
(See color ad p 508)   🛥 CTV ✕ Ⓓ

HARTS VILLA AN INN AT THE BEACH   Rates Subject to Change   Phone: 803/448-8541 **58**
Motel   5/9-9/1   2P/1B: $39- 58   2P/2B: $47- 99   XP: $5   F12
   4/4-5/8 & 9/2-9/28   2P/1B: $34   2P/2B: $47- 65   XP: $5   F12
   2/28-4/3   2P/1B: $26- 27   2P/2B: $35- 53   XP: $5   F12
   12/1-2/27 & 9/29-11/30   2P/1B: $23- 25   2P/2B: $27- 35   XP: $5   F12
Under major renovation; **Location:** 21st Ave & N Ocean Blvd. 2106 N Ocean Blvd 29577. Fax: 803/448-4900. **Terms:** Sr.
discount; reserv deposit, 34 day notice; no pets. **Facility:** 26 rooms. 3 stories; interior/exterior corridors. **All Rooms:** free
movies. **Some Rooms:** 19 efficiencies. **Cards:** AE, CB, DI, DS, MC, VI.   🛥 CTV ✕

THE HERITAGE   Rates Subject to Change   Phone: 803/449-3834 **18**
◆◆   6/9-8/24   1P: $54- 59   2P/2B: $54- 59   XP: $5
Apartment   3/17-6/8 & 8/25-10/12   1P: $37- 42   2P/2B: $37- 42   XP: $5
Motel   12/1-3/16 & 10/13-11/30   1P: $32- 37   2P/2B: $32- 37   XP: $5
   Location: 74 Ave N & N Ocean Blvd. 7401 N Ocean Blvd 29572. **Terms:** Reserv deposit, 14 day notice; no
pets. **Facility:** 18 rooms. 3 stories, no elevator; exterior corridors. **Some Rooms:** 12 efficiencies.   🛥 🅷 CTV ✕ Ⓓ

The best reservation is a *confirmed* reservation.

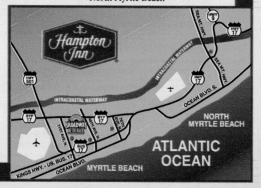

(See map p. 486)

HOLIDAY INN WEST ON THE WATERWAY   Phone: 803/236-1000   [83]
(AAA) [SAVE]

6/6-9/6	1P:	$99- 149	2P/1B:	$99- 149	2P/2B:	$99- 149	XP: $10		F19
3/25-6/5 & 9/7-11/27	1P:	$49- 99	2P/1B:	$49- 99	2P/2B:	$49- 99	XP: $10		F19
12/1-3/24 & 11/28-11/30	1P:	$44- 69	2P/1B:	$44- 69	2P/2B:	$44- 69	XP: $10		F19

◆◆◆
Motor Inn   **Location:** 2 mi w on US 501; w end of Intracoastal Waterway Bridge, adjacent to Outlet Mall & Fantasy Harbour. 101 Outlet Blvd 29577. Fax: 803/236-1012. **Terms:** Reserv deposit, 3 day notice; package plans; no pets. **Facility:** 151 rooms. On Intracoastal Waterway. 6 stories; sauna, whirlpool; boat dock. Fee: golf privileges. **Dining & Entertainment:** Dining room; 6 am-2 & 5-10 pm; $6-$16; cocktails/lounge. **Services:** Fee: coin laundry. **All Rooms:** free & pay movies. **Some Rooms:** refrigerators. **Cards:** AE, CB, DI, DS, JCB, MC, VI. *(See color ad p 507)*

🏊 🏊 🛉 🔌 🚭 CTV ✕ 🐕 D

HOLIDAY SOUTH MOTEL   Rates Subject to Change   Phone: 803/448-5542   [102]
(AAA)

5/22-8/15	2P/2B:	$68- 88	XP: $5	F12
3/27-5/21 & 8/16-8/22	2P/2B:	$45- 65	XP: $5	F12
2/27-3/26 & 8/23-10/3	2P/2B:	$34- 55	XP: $5	F12
12/1-2/26 & 10/4-11/30	2P/2B:	$27- 32	XP: $5	F12

◆◆
Apartment
Motel   **Location:** Just n of 26th Ave S & S Ocean Blvd. 2605 S Ocean Blvd 29577. Fax: 803/946-7535. **Terms:** Reserv deposit, 14 day notice, handling fee imposed; no pets. **Facility:** 66 rooms. 6 stories; exterior corridors. **All Rooms:** free movies. **Some Rooms:** 50 efficiencies. **Cards:** AE, DS, MC, VI.

CTV D

HOWARD JOHNSON MYRTLE BEACH RESORT   Rates Subject to Change   Phone: 803/626-4656   [34]
◆◆

6/2-9/4 [CP]	2P/1B:	$80- 98	2P/2B:	$90- 108	XP: $10		F16
5/1-6/1 [CP]	2P/1B:	$50- 60	2P/2B:	$55- 75	XP: $10		F16
3/5-4/30 & 9/5-10/1 [CP]	2P/1B:	$40- 49	2P/2B:	$43- 63	XP: $10		F16
12/1-3/4 & 10/2-11/30 [CP]	2P/1B:	$31- 40	2P/2B:	$35- 49	XP: $10		F16

Motel   **Location:** 10th Ave S & S Ocean Blvd. 1004 S Ocean Blvd 29577. Fax: 803/946-9477. **Terms:** Sr. discount; reserv deposit, 3 day notice; no pets. **Facility:** 63 rooms. Phone calls, $.50; 8 stories; exterior corridors. **All Rooms:** free movies. **Some Rooms:** 30 efficiencies. **Cards:** AE, DI, DS, MC, VI.

🏊 🏊 CTV ✕ D

HURL ROCK MOTEL   Rates Subject to Change   Phone: 803/626-3531   [67]
(AAA)

5/22-8/8	2P/1B:	$50- 70	2P/2B:	$57- 100	XP: $5		F12
5/8-5/21 & 8/9-8/30	2P/1B:	$34- 55	2P/2B:	$40- 60	XP: $5		F12
3/6-5/7 & 8/31-9/19	2P/1B:	$26- 40	2P/2B:	$33- 49	XP: $5		F12
12/1-3/5 & 9/20-11/30	2P/1B:	$23- 30	2P/2B:	$26- 40	XP: $5		F12

◆◆
Motel   **Location:** 2.5 mi s; 21st Ave S & S Ocean Blvd. 2010 S Ocean Blvd 29577. Fax: 803/626-3534. **Terms:** Age restrictions may apply; reserv deposit, 14 day notice; no pets. **Facility:** 55 rooms. Handling fee imposed; 5 stories; exterior corridors. **All Rooms:** free movies. **Some Rooms:** 48 efficiencies. **Cards:** MC, VI. *(See color ad below)*

🏊 🔌 CTV ✕ D

INDIGO INN   Rates Subject to Change   Phone: 803/448-5101   [64]
(AAA)

5/29-8/22	2P/2B:	$99- 131	XP: $7	F15
5/1-5/28 & 8/23-9/19	2P/2B:	$66- 97	XP: $7	F15
2/14-4/30 & 9/20-10/17	2P/2B:	$46- 65	XP: $7	F15
12/1-2/13 & 10/18-11/30	2P/2B:	$36- 52	XP: $7	F15

◆◆◆
Motel   **Location:** 2.3 mi s; 23rd Ave S & S Ocean Blvd. 2209 S Ocean Blvd 29577. **Terms:** Reserv deposit, 14 day notice, handling fee imposed; no pets. **Facility:** 53 rooms. 8 kitchen apartments, $126 for up to 4 persons in season; 9 stories; exterior corridors. **Some Rooms:** 18 efficiencies. **Cards:** AE, DS, MC, VI. *(See color ad p 511)*

🏊 🔌 CTV D

(See map p. 486)

JAMAICAN MOTOR INN   Rates Subject to Change   Phone: 803/448-4321   60

		2P/2B:	$72- 105	XP:	$5
6/5-8/22					
5/1-6/4 & 8/23-9/26		2P/2B:	$52- 73	XP:	$5
1/30-4/30 & 9/27-10/24		2P/2B:	$33- 67	XP:	$5
12/1-1/29 & 10/25-11/30		2P/2B:	$25- 42	XP:	$5

Motel   **Location:** 1.5 mi n; 31st Ave N & N Ocean Blvd. 3006 N Ocean Blvd 29577 (PO Box 1267, 29578). Fax: 803/448-4324. **Terms:** Age restrictions may apply; reserv deposit, 7 day notice, handling fee imposed; no pets. **Facility:** 44 rooms. 4 stories; exterior corridors. **All Rooms:** free movies. **Some Rooms:** 21 efficiencies. **Cards:** AE, DS, MC, VI.

KNIGHTS INN   Rates Subject to Change   Phone: 803/236-7400   80

	1P:	$46- 65	2P/1B:	$55- 79	XP:	$10	F18
3/3-9/4	1P:	$40- 55	2P/1B:				
12/1-3/2 & 9/5-11/30	1P:	$33- 36	2P/1B:	$37- 40	2P/2B:	$40- 46	XP: $10	F18

Motel   **Location:** On US 501; 1 mi e of jct US 17, opposite Outlet Mall. 3622 Hwy 501 29577. Fax: 803/236-2541. **Terms:** Reserv deposit, 7 day notice; no pets. **Facility:** 108 rooms. 1 story; exterior corridors. **All Rooms:** free movies. **Cards:** AE, CB, DI, DS, MC, VI.

(See map p. 486)

LANDMARK RESORT
⬥AAA⬥ SAVE

◆◆◆
Motor Inn

Phone: 803/448-9441   **40**

6/6-8/21		2P/1B:	$84-	219	2P/2B:	$84-	219	XP: $10	F17
5/9-9/6/5 & 8/22-9/18		2P/1B:	$64-	170	2P/2B:	$64-	170	XP: $10	F17
3/7-5/8 & 9/19-10/23		2P/1B:	$44-	135	2P/2B:	$44-	135	XP: $10	F17
12/1-3/6 & 10/24-11/30		2P/1B:	$29-	75	2P/2B:	$29-	75	XP: $10	F17

Location: 15th Ave S & S Ocean Blvd. 1501 S Ocean Blvd 29578-2310. Fax: 803/448-6701. **Terms:** Reserv deposit, 14 day notice; no pets. **Facility:** 574 rooms. Handling fee imposed; 15 stories; interior/exterior corridors. **Dining:** Dining room; 6 am-10 pm; $8-$15. **Some Rooms:** 13 efficiencies, 257 kitchens. **Cards:** AE, DI, DS, MC, VI. *(See color ad inside front cover & p 311)*

LA QUINTA INN & SUITES
⬥AAA⬥ SAVE

◆◆◆
Motel

Phone: 803/916-8801   **98**

6/13-11/30 [CP]	1P: $105-	115	2P/1B:	$110-	120	2P/2B:	$110	XP: $5	F18
5/23-6/12 [CP]	1P: $93-	103	2P/1B:	$98-	108	2P/2B:	$98	XP: $5	F18
2/21-5/22 [CP]	1P: $68-	78	2P/1B:	$85-	95	2P/2B:	$85	XP: $7	F18
12/1-2/20 [CP]	1P: $52-	62	2P/1B:	$59-	69	2P/2B:	$59	XP: $7	F18

Location: Just e of US Bypass 17, 1.4 mi n of US 501. 1561 21st Ave N 29577. Fax: 803/916-8701. **Terms:** Package plans; weekend rates avail; pets. **Facility:** 128 rooms. Spacious rooms with contemporary decor, fresh appearance. Commercial location. 4 stories; interior corridors; whirlpool. **Dining:** Restaurant nearby. **Services:** winter plug-ins. Fee: coin laundry. **All Rooms:** coffeemakers, free & pay movies, combo or shower baths. **Some Rooms:** microwaves, refrigerators. **Cards:** AE, CB, DI, DS, MC, VI. **Special Amenities:** Free breakfast and free local telephone calls. *(See color ad below)*   Roll in showers.

THE LONG BAY RESORT
⬥AAA⬥ SAVE

Apartment
Motor Inn

Phone: 803/449-3361   **14**

5/29-8/22		2P/2B:	$96-	165	XP: $6	F18
3/6-5/28		2P/2B:	$54-	109	XP: $6	F18
8/23-11/30		2P/2B:	$38-	94	XP: $6	F18
12/1-3/5		2P/2B:	$25-	44	XP: $6	F18

Too new to rate; **Location:** 5 mi n. 7200 N Ocean Blvd 29572. Fax: 803/449-8297. **Terms:** Reserv deposit, 14 day notice; no pets. **Facility:** 288 rooms. 104 three-bedroom units, $179-$249 in season. Handling fee imposed. Scheduled to open July 1997; 15 stories; exterior corridors. **Dining:** Dining room; 6 am-10 & 6-10 pm; $9-$17. **Some Rooms:** 108 efficiencies, 103 kitchens. **Cards:** DI, MC, VI. *(See color ad p 513)*

THE MARINER
⬥AAA⬥ SAVE

◆
Apartment
Motel

Phone: 803/449-5281   **21**

6/8-8/23	1P: $65-	94	2P/2B:	$65-	94	XP: $5
3/9-6/7 & 8/24-10/18	1P: $49-	72	2P/2B:	$49-	72	XP: $5
12/1-3/8 & 10/19-11/30	1P: $31-	50	2P/2B:	$31-	50	XP: $5

Location: 5 mi n; 71st Ave N & N Ocean Blvd. 7003 N Ocean Blvd 29572. **Terms:** Reserv deposit, 14 day notice, handling fee imposed; weekly/monthly rates; pets, in winter. **Facility:** 32 rooms. Across from ocean. Rooms have a nautical theme. Weekly rental only for 10 two-bedroom kitchen units 6/8-8/19, $555. 16 one-bedroom kitchen units, $495; 1-2 stories; exterior corridors; wading pool. **Dining:** Restaurant nearby. **Recreation:** fishing poles, paddle tennis, shuffleboard; bicycles. **All Rooms:** coffeemakers, refrigerators. **Some Rooms:** 12 efficiencies. **Cards:** AE, DS, MC, VI.

THE MERIDIAN PLAZA RESORT
⬥AAA⬥ SAVE

◆◆◆
Suite Motel

Phone: 803/626-4734   **65**

6/6-8/21		2P/2B:	$104-	150	XP: $5	F17
5/9-9/6/5 & 8/22-9/6		2P/2B:	$83-	98	XP: $5	F17
3/7-5/8 & 9/7-9/25		2P/2B:	$66-	78	XP: $5	F17
12/1-3/6 & 9/26-11/30		2P/2B:	$42-	66	XP: $5	F17

Location: Oceanfront 23rd Ave N & N Ocean Blvd. 2310 N Ocean Blvd 29577. Fax: 803/448-4569. **Terms:** Age restrictions may apply; reserv deposit, 14 day notice; no pets. **Facility:** 94 rooms. Handling fee imposed; 15 stories; exterior corridors. **Cards:** AE, MC, VI. *(See color ad p 514)*

MYRTLE BEACH MARTINIQUE RESORT HOTEL
◆◆◆
Hotel

Rates Subject to Change   Phone: 803/449-4441   **16**

5/27-9/4	2P/2B:	$115-	150	XP: $10	F17
3/25-5/26	2P/2B:	$95-	120	XP: $10	F17
9/5-10/27	2P/2B:	$90-	115	XP: $10	F17
12/1-3/24 & 10/28-11/30	2P/2B:	$52-	94	XP: $10	F17

Location: 5 mi n. 7100 N Ocean Blvd 29572 (PO Box 331, 29578). Fax: 803/497-3041. **Terms:** Sr. discount; reserv deposit, 3 day notice; no pets. **Facility:** 203 rooms. Handling fee imposed; 17 stories; interior/exterior corridors. **Dining:** Dining room; 7 am-2 & 5-9 pm; $9-$18. **All Rooms:** Fee: movies. **Some Rooms:** 85 efficiencies. **Cards:** AE, DI, DS, MC, VI. *(See color ad p 515)*

(See map p. 486)

MYRTLE SHORES MOTEL Rates Subject to Change **Phone:** 803/448-1434 **48**
AAA
5/22-8/15   2P/2B: $70- 90 XP: $5
4/10-5/21 & 8/16-9/19   2P/2B: $42- 60 XP: $5
◆ ◆ 3/15-4/9 & 9/20-10/17   2P/2B: $37- 52 XP: $5
Apartment 12/1-3/14 & 10/18-11/30 2P/2B: $34- 50 XP: $5
Motel **Location:** 0.8 mi n; 19th Ave N & N Ocean Blvd. 1902 N Ocean Blvd 29577 (PO Box 335, 29578).
Fax: 803/946-9426. **Terms:** Reserv deposit, 14 day notice; no pets. **Facility:** 41 rooms. Handling fee imposed;
3-4 stories, no elevator; exterior corridors. **Some Rooms:** 26 efficiencies. **Cards:** MC, VI. [🛏] [CTV] [D]

MYSTIC SEA MOTOR INN Rates Subject to Change **Phone:** 803/448-8446 **29**
AAA
6/25-8/22   2P/1B: $60-   80 2P/2B: $66- 114 XP: $6 F10
4/3-6/24 & 8/23-9/19 2P/1B: $33- 72 2P/2B: $38- 102 XP: $6 F10
◆ ◆ 3/6-4/2 & 9/20-10/17 2P/1B: $25- 36 2P/2B: $31- 60 XP: $6 F10
Motel 12/1-3/5 & 10/18-11/30 2P/1B: $18- 32 2P/2B: $20- 55 XP: $6 F10
Location: 2.3 mi s; 21st Ave S & S Ocean Blvd. 2105 S Ocean Blvd 29577 (PO Box 2463A, 29578).
Fax: 803/448-8447. **Terms:** Reserv deposit, 14 day notice, handling fee imposed; no pets. **Facility:** 82 rooms. 3 stories; exterior corridors. **Some Rooms:** A/C, 22 efficiencies, 17 kitchens. **Cards:** MC, VI. *(See color ad below)* [CTV] [D]

(See map p. 486)

OCEAN DUNES RESORT & VILLAS
Phone: 803/449-7441 🔟

(AAA) SAVE	6/12-8/22	2P/2B: $122- 154	XP: $10	F18
	4/26-6/11 & 8/23-9/6	2P/2B: $96- 134	XP: $10	F18
◆◆◆	3/6-4/25 & 9/7-10/31	2P/2B: $68- 105	XP: $10	F18
Apartment	12/1-3/5 & 11/1-11/30	2P/2B: $50- 68	XP: $10	F18

Apartment Hotel **Location:** 5.3 mi n between 74th & 75th aves N. 201 75th Ave N 29577 (PO Box 2035, 29578). Fax: 803/449-0558. **Terms:** Reserv deposit, 4 day notice; package plans; no pets. **Facility:** 400 rooms. Balconies. 45 two-bedroom units, 9 three-bedroom units. Villas $163-$215, off season $84-$194 for up to 4 persons. Handling fee imposed; 7 stories; interior/exterior corridors; oceanfront; beach, wading pool, saunas, steamrooms, whirlpools. Fee: golf privileges. **Dining & Entertainment:** Dining room; 6:30 am-10 pm, off season 6 am-10 & 6-10 pm; $9-$18; cocktails/lounge; entertainment. **Services:** Fee: coin laundry. **Recreation:** children's program in summer; swimming, Lazy River water ride, surf fishing. **All Rooms:** refrigerators. Fee: movies, safes. **Some Rooms:** 24 efficiencies, 211 kitchens, microwaves. **Cards:** AE, CB, DI, DS, MC, VI. *(See color ad p 490)*

OCEAN FOREST PLAZA
Phone: 803/497-0044 🏨

(AAA) SAVE	6/6-8/21	2P/2B: $94- 124	XP: $5	F17
	5/9-6/5 & 8/22-9/11	2P/2B: $77- 94	XP: $5	F17
◆◆◆	3/7-5/8 & 9/12-10/16	2P/2B: $52- 79	XP: $5	F17
Suite Hotel	12/1-3/6 & 10/17-11/30	2P/2B: $39- 51	XP: $5	F17

Suite Hotel **Location:** 4 mi n. 5523 N Ocean Blvd 29577. Fax: 803/497-3051. **Terms:** Check-in 4 pm; reserv deposit, 14 day notice; handling fee imposed; no pets. **Facility:** 172 rooms. 2-bedroom units $225 for up to 6 persons in season; 23 stories; exterior corridors. **Dining:** Coffee shop; 7-11 am. **All Rooms:** kitchens. **Cards:** AE, MC, VI. *(See color ad inside front cover & p 518)*

OCEAN FOREST VILLA RESORT
Phone: 803/449-9661 🏨

(AAA) SAVE	6/13-8/16	2P/2B: $160- 200	XP: $10	F18
	3/21-6/12 & 8/17-10/11	2P/2B: $110- 135	XP: $10	F18
◆◆	2/14-3/20 & 10/12-11/15	2P/2B: $80- 120	XP: $10	F18
Motel	12/1-2/13 & 11/16-11/30	2P/2B: $55- 75	XP: $10	F18

Motel **Location:** 4 mi n. 5601 N Ocean Blvd 29577. Fax: 803/449-9207. **Terms:** Reserv deposit, 4 day notice; monthly rates; package plans; no pets. **Facility:** 150 rooms. Attractive 2-bedroom units across from ocean; all with balcony. Rates for up to 4 persons. Handling fee imposed; 3 stories; interior corridors; beach, wading pool, whirlpools. Fee: golf privileges. **Services:** Fee: coin laundry. **Recreation:** children's program in summer; swimming. **All Rooms:** kitchens, microwaves, free movies, refrigerators. **Some Rooms:** Fee: VCP's. **Cards:** AE, CB, DI, DS, MC, VI.

THE OCEAN FRONT VIKING MOTEL
Phone: 803/448-4355 🔢

		Rates Subject to Change					
(AAA)	5/26-8/16	1P: $41- 79	2P/1B: $41- 79	2P/2B: $44-121	XP: $4-7	F12
	5/9-5/25 & 8/17-9/13	1P: $49- 65	2P/1B: $49- 65	2P/2B: $52-101	XP: $5-7	F12
◆◆	12/1-3/27 & 9/14-11/30	1P: $19- 41	2P/1B: $19- 41	2P/2B: $21- 63	XP: $3-5	F12
Motel	3/28-5/8	1P: $37- 41	2P/1B: $37- 41	2P/2B: $42- 59	XP: $4	F12

Motel **Location:** 18th Ave S & S Ocean Blvd. 1811 S Ocean Blvd 29577. Fax: 803/448-6174. **Terms:** Age restrictions may apply; reserv deposit, 14 day notice; no pets. **Facility:** 75 rooms. Handling fee imposed; 5 stories; exterior corridors. **Some Rooms:** 66 efficiencies. **Cards:** DI, DS, MC, VI. *(See ad below)*

OCEAN PARK RESORT
Phone: 803/448-1915 🏨

(AAA) SAVE	6/6-8/21	2P/2B: $93- 158	XP: $5	F17
	5/9-6/5 & 8/22-9/6	2P/2B: $71- 121	XP: $5	F17
◆◆◆	3/7-5/8 & 9/7-10/9	2P/2B: $59- 90	XP: $5	F17
Apartment	12/1-3/6 & 10/10-11/30	2P/2B: $39- 61	XP: $5	F17

Apartment Motel **Location:** 2 mi s; 19th Ave S & S Ocean Blvd. 1905 S Ocean Blvd 29577 (PO Drawer 3967, 29578). Fax: 803/626-2966. **Terms:** Age restrictions may apply; reserv deposit, 14 day notice; no pets. **Facility:** 128 rooms. Handling fee imposed; 12 stories; interior/exterior corridors. **Some Rooms:** 106 efficiencies. **Cards:** AE, MC, VI. *(See color ad p 519)*

THE PALACE SUITE RESORT
Phone: 803/448-4300 🏨

(AAA) SAVE	6/6-8/14	2P/2B: $84- 125	XP: $5	F17
	8/15-9/6	2P/2B: $79- 111	XP: $5	F17
◆◆◆	3/7-6/5 & 9/7-10/9	2P/2B: $54- 80	XP: $5	F17
Apartment	12/1-3/6 & 10/10-11/30	2P/2B: $39- 61	XP: $5	F17

Apartment Motor Inn **Location:** 16th Ave S & S Ocean Blvd. 1605 S Ocean Blvd 29577. Fax: 803/448-6300. **Terms:** Reserv deposit, 14 day notice; no pets. **Facility:** 161 rooms. Rates for 4 to 6 persons; 23 stories; interior corridors. **Dining:** Restaurant; 6 am-11 pm; 9/6-5/31, 7 am-2 & 5-9 pm; $7-$15. **All Rooms:** kitchens. **Cards:** AE, MC, VI. *(See color ad p 520)*

The Palace™

1605 S. Ocean Blvd.
P.O. Box 487, Myrtle Beach, SC 29578
1-800-334-1397 • 1-803-448-4300

This all-suite hotel features studio suites, one-bedroom condos, and two bedroom condos. Additional guest-pleasing amenities are:

- Two Pools (one enclosed Oct. 1-May 15) • Sauna
- Steam Room • Oceanfront Restaurant and Lounge • Exercise Room • Five Whirlpools •
- Guest Laundry • Free On-site Covered Parking •
- Video Game Room • Complete Banquet Facilities
- Golf and Entertainment Packages
- Fully Equipped Kitchens in all Units

20% Discount for three nights or longer stays Jan. 1-Feb. 12 and Oct. 24-Dec. 20, 1998. And for five nights or longer stays Feb. 13-Mar. 6; CAN-AM SPECIAL-stay seven nights or longer Mar. 6 - 21 and receive 20% off. Also for arriving on Sun. and staying five nights or longer Mar. 15-27, May 24-June 5, 1998. (Jan. 16-18 and Thanksgiving holidays Nov. 25-28, 1998 are excluded.) Only one discount per stay. Golf and Entertainment Packages not subject to discount. A surcharge will apply on weekend reservations, some holidays and special events DISCOUNTS ARE OFF RACK RATES.

SPECIAL RATES		1998 RATES (Rates apply to two adults and two children.)					
Jan 1 - Feb. 5 Nov. 29 - Dec. 31	Feb. 6 - Mar. 6 Oct. 17 - Nov. 28	Mar. 7 - May 29	May 30- June 12	June 13 -Aug. 7	Aug. 8 -Aug. 21	Aug. 22 -Sept. 25	Sept. 26 -Oct. 16
39.00 60.00	44.00 70.00	54.00 94.00	64.00 149.00	94.00 169.00	89.00 161.00	61.00 136.00	51.00 89.00

10% Discount for AAA, Senior Citizens, weekly stays and five or six night vacations, arriving on Sunday (excluding June 13 - Aug. 7).

RESORT

2500 North Ocean Blvd. • P.O. Box 3937,
Myrtle Beach, SC 29578 • 1-803-626-8334

- Outdoor Pool • Indoor Pool
- Two Indoor Whirlpools • Outdoor Whirlpool • Oceanfront Grass Lawn
- Indoor Kiddie Pool • Exercise Room
- Guest Laundry • A variety of executive suites, three bedroom condos and two, three and four bedroom penthouses available
- Two Remote Control Color TVs • Golf Packages on over 90 championship courses
- Great entertainment packages at the Alabama Theatre, Dollywood's Dixie Stampede, Gatlin Brothers Theatre, Magic On Ice and more

Toll Free **1-800-528-0451**

SPECIAL RATES	1998 RATES
Jan. 1 - Feb. 5 Nov. 29- Dec. 31	$47.00-109.00
Feb. 6 - Mar. 6 Oct. 24 - Nov. 28	52.00-128.00
Oct. 10 - Oct. 16	62.00-157.00
Oct. 17 - Oct. 23	56.00-139.00
Sept. 26- Oct. 9	67.00-169.00
Mar. 7 - Mar. 27 Sept. 19 - Sept. 25	73.00-189.00
Mar. 28 - May 8 Sept. 7 - Sept. 18	81.00-228.00
May 9 - May 29 Aug. 22 - Sept. 6	89.00-260.00
May 30 - June 5	101.00-276.00
June 6 - June 26	124.00-301.00
June 27 - Aug. 7	143.00-326.00
Aug. 8 - Aug. 14	138.00-316.00
Aug. 15 - Aug. 21	109.00-286.00

Rates apply to two adults and four children.

10% DISCOUNT FOR AAA , SENIOR CITIZENS, WEEKLY STAYS AND FIVE OR SIX NIGHT VACATIONS ARRIVING ON SUNDAY. (Excluding June 6 - August 7.)

20% DISCOUNT FOR THREE NIGHTS OR LONGER STAYS JANUARY 1 - FEBRUARY 12 AND OCTOBER 24 - DECEMBER 20, 1998. And for five nights or longer stays, Feb. 13-March 6; CAN-AM SPECIAL stay seven nights or longer March 6-21 and receive 20% off. Also for arriving on Sunday and staying five nights or longer March 15-27 and May 24-June 5, 1998. (Jan. 16-18 and Thanksgiving holidays Nov. 25-28, 1998 are excluded.) Only one discount per stay. Golf and Entertainment Packages not subject to discount. A surcharge will apply on weekend reservations, some holidays, and special events. Discount off rack rates.

(See map p. 486)

PALMS RESORT

Phone: 803/626-8334 **59**

AAA [SAVE]

6/6-8/21		2P/2B: $109- 152	XP: $5	F17
5/9-6/5 & 8/22-9/6		2P/2B: $89- 105	XP: $5	F17
3/7-5/8 & 9/7-9/25		2P/2B: $73- 85	XP: $5	F17
12/1-3/6 & 9/26-11/30		2P/2B: $47- 71	XP: $5	F17

◆◆◆

Apartment Motel

Location: 1 mi n; 24th Ave N & N Ocean Blvd. 2500 N Ocean Blvd 29577 (PO Box 3937, 29576). **Terms:** Age restrictions may apply; reserv deposit, 14 day notice; no pets. **Facility:** 83 rooms. Max rates for up to 6 persons. Handling fee imposed; 16 stories; exterior corridors. **All Rooms:** efficiencies. **Cards:** MC, VI. *(See color ad p 521)*

[icons] CTV D

THE PATRICIA GRAND

Phone: 803/448-8453 **57**

AAA [SAVE]

6/1-8/23	2P/1B: $86- 135	2P/2B: $81- 185	XP: $5	F17
3/30-5/31 & 8/24-9/20	2P/1B: $56- 116	2P/2B: $74- 146	XP: $5	F17
3/9-3/29 & 9/21-10/25	2P/1B: $49- 68	2P/2B: $64- 97	XP: $5	F17
12/1-3/8 & 10/26-11/30	2P/1B: $32- 55	2P/2B: $35- 75	XP: $5	F17

◆◆◆

Motor Inn

Location: 27th Ave N. 2710 N Ocean Blvd 29577 (PO Box 1855, 29578). Fax: 803/448-3080. **Terms:** Age restrictions may apply; reserv deposit, 7 day notice; no pets. **Facility:** 308 rooms. Handling fee imposed; 18 stories; exterior corridors. **Dining:** Restaurant; 7 am-11 & 5-10 pm; $5-$19. **Some Rooms:** 245 efficiencies. **Cards:** AE, DS, MC, VI. *(See color ad p 523)*

[icons] CTV D S

THE PATRICIA NORTH HOTEL SUITES

Phone: 803/449-4833 **53**

AAA [SAVE]

5/31-8/24	2P/1B: $98- 164	2P/2B: $98- 164	XP: $5	F
3/9-5/30 & 8/25-9/28	2P/1B: $78- 141	2P/2B: $78- 141	XP: $5	F
9/29-10/19	2P/1B: $57- 67	2P/2B: $59- 67	XP: $5	F
12/1-3/8 & 10/20-11/30	2P/1B: $40- 64	2P/2B: $37- 64	XP: $5	F

◆◆◆

Apartment Motel

Location: 68 Ave N & N Ocean Blvd. 6804 N Ocean Blvd 29572 (PO Box 1829, 29578). Fax: 803/449-8192. **Terms:** Age restrictions may apply; reserv deposit, 7 day notice; no pets. **Facility:** 194 rooms. Handling fee imposed; 16 stories; exterior corridors. **Dining:** Coffee shop; 6:30 am-2 pm. **All Rooms:** efficiencies. **Fee:** movies. **Cards:** AE, DS, MC, VI. *(See color ad p 523)* Roll in showers.

[icons] CTV D S

POINDEXTER RESORT

Rates Subject to Change Phone: 803/448-8327 **92**

AAA

6/5-8/15	1P: $65	2P/1B: $65	2P/2B: $75- 111	XP: $10	F12
5/8-6/4 & 8/16-9/5	1P: $49	2P/1B: $49	2P/2B: $59- 79	XP: $10	F12
3/6-5/7 & 9/6-10/31	1P: $41	2P/1B: $41	2P/2B: $47- 59	XP: $10	F12
12/1-3/5 & 11/1-11/30	1P: $29	2P/1B: $29	2P/2B: $29- 34	XP: $10	F12

◆◆

Motor Inn

Location: 17th Ave N & N Ocean Blvd. 1702 N Ocean Blvd 29577. Fax: 803/448-0043. **Terms:** Reserv deposit, 14 day notice; no pets. **Facility:** 228 rooms. Handling fee imposed; 5-10 stories; interior/exterior corridors. **Dining:** Cafeteria; 6 am-2 pm. **Some Rooms:** 137 efficiencies. **Cards:** AE, DS, MC, VI. *(See color ad p 501)*

[icons] CTV D

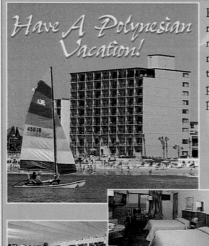

(See map p. 486)

POLYNESIAN BEACH & GOLF RESORT   Phone: 803/448-1781   **77**

◊◊◊ SAVE

5/24-9/3			2P/2B:	$65- 100	XP: $10		F12
3/1-5/23 & 9/4-10/31			2P/2B:	$35- 70	XP: $10		F12
12/1-2/28 & 11/1-11/30			2P/2B:	$25- 35	XP: $10		F12

◊◊

Apartment
Motel

Location: 1.3 mi s; 10th Ave S & S Ocean Blvd. 1001 S Ocean Blvd 29577. Fax: 803/626-7145. **Terms:** Reserv deposit; 7 day notice; weekly/monthly rates; package plans; no pets. **Facility:** 175 rooms. Modest traditional motel decor in mid-rise & high-rise concrete structures. 36 two-bedroom units. Handling fee imposed; 5-9 stories; exterior corridors; oceanfront; beach, 2 wading pools, whirlpools. Fee: golf privileges. **Dining:** Restaurant nearby. **Services:** Fee: coin laundry. **Recreation:** swimming, surf fishing. **All Rooms:** free movies, refrigerators. **Some Rooms:** coffeemakers, 146 efficiencies, microwaves. **Cards:** DS, MC, VI. *(See color ad p 522)*

(⇔) (⇔) (CTV) (D)

QUALITY INN BY THE SHORE   Phone: 803/626-8566   **74**

◊◊◊ SAVE

6/11-8/21 [CP]	1P: $90- 140	2P/1B: $90- 140	2P/2B: $90- 140	XP: $10	F18
5/28-6/10 & 8/22-9/5 [CP]	1P: $70- 130	2P/1B: $70- 130	2P/2B: $70- 130	XP: $10	F18
4/2-5/27 & 9/6-10/2 [CP]	1P: $55- 130	2P/1B: $55- 130	2P/2B: $55- 130	XP: $10	F18
12/1-4/1 & 10/3-11/30 [CP]	1P: $45- 85	2P/1B: $45- 85	2P/2B: $45- 85	XP: $10	F18

◊◊◊

Motel

Location: 13th Ave N & US 17, Kings Hwy; between Ocean Blvd N & Kings Hwy. 1301 N Withers Dr 29577. Fax: 803/626-8280. **Terms:** Reserv deposit; weekly/monthly rates; package plans; no pets. **Facility:** 60 rooms. Attractive public areas. Handling fee imposed; 11 stories; interior corridors; whirlpool. Fee: golf privileges. **Dining:** Restaurant nearby. **Services:** Fee: coin laundry. **All Rooms:** coffeemakers, microwaves, free movies, refrigerators. **Cards:** AE, CB, DI, DS, JCB, MC, VI. **Special Amenities:** Free breakfast and free local telephone calls. *(See color ad below)*

(⇔) (⇔) (⊞) (CTV) (✕) (🌫) (D)

RED ROOF INN   Rates Subject to Change   Phone: 803/626-4444   **44**

◊◊◊

Motel

5/15-9/5	1P: $71- 161	2P/1B: $78- 161	2P/2B: $85- 161	XP: $7	F18
9/6-11/30	1P: $38- 96	2P/1B: $45- 96	2P/2B: $49- 96	XP: $7	F18
3/2-5/14	1P: $36- 91	2P/1B: $43- 91	2P/2B: $45- 91	XP: $7	F18
12/1-3/1	1P: $36- 55	2P/1B: $43- 55	2P/2B: $50- 55	XP: $7	F18

Location: 4 mi s on US 17 business route. 2801 S Kings Hwy 29577. Fax: 803/626-0753. **Terms:** Small pets only. **Facility:** 153 rooms. 4 stories; interior corridors. **All Rooms:** free movies. **Some Rooms:** 14 efficiencies. **Cards:** AE, CB, DI, DS, MC, VI.

(🐾) (⇔) (CTV) (✕) (🌫) (D)

THE REEF RESORT   Phone: 803/448-1765   **94**

◊◊◊ SAVE

6/3-8/26		2P/1B: $90- 140	2P/2B: $103- 147	XP: $5	F17
5/20-6/2 & 8/27-9/22		2P/1B: $86- 89	2P/2B: $89- 103	XP: $5	F17
3/11-5/19 & 9/23-10/22		2P/1B: $73- 86	2P/2B: $75- 87	XP: $5	F17
12/1-3/10 & 10/23-11/30		2P/1B: $50- 63	2P/2B: $65- 73	XP: $5	F17

◊◊◊

Apartment
Motor Inn

Location: S Ocean Blvd & 21 Ave S. 2101 S Ocean Blvd 29577. Fax: 803/448-3288. **Terms:** Reserv deposit, 14 day notice; monthly rates, seasonal; package plans; no pets. **Facility:** 122 rooms. All rooms with oceanfront view & balcony. 57 two-bedroom units. Handling fee imposed; 12 stories; interior/exterior corridors; beach, wading pool, sauna, steamroom, whirlpools; game room. Fee: golf privileges. **Dining & Entertainment:** Restaurant; 6 am-10 pm; $7-$14; cocktails/lounge. **Services:** Fee: coin laundry. **Recreation:** children's program, social program; swimming, charter fishing. **All Rooms:** free & pay movies. Fee: safes. **Some Rooms:** 112 efficiencies, microwaves, refrigerators. **Cards:** AE, DI, DS.

(⇔) (⇔) (🌫) (⊞) (CTV) (D)

THE ROXANNE   Rates Subject to Change   Phone: 803/448-9486   **49**

◊◊◊

6/5-8/22		2P/2B: $63- 101	XP: $5	
5/1-6/4 & 8/23-9/26		2P/2B: $40- 72	XP: $5	
1/30-4/30 & 9/27-10/24		2P/2B: $30- 64	XP: $5	
12/1-1/29 & 10/25-11/30		2P/2B: $26- 40	XP: $5	

◊◊◊

Apartment
Motel

Location: 0.5 mi n; 16th Ave N & N Ocean Blvd. 1604 N Ocean Blvd 29577 (PO Box 1274, 29578). Fax: 803/448-8394. **Terms:** Age restrictions may apply; reserv deposit, 7 day notice; no pets. **Facility:** 69 rooms. Handling fee imposed; 2-3 stories, no elevator; exterior corridors. **All Rooms:** free movies. **Some Rooms:** 53 efficiencies. **Cards:** AE, DS, MC, VI.

(⇔) (CTV) (D)

(See map p. 486)

ST. JOHN'S INN — Rates Subject to Change — Phone: 803/449-5251 **91**

AAA / Motel

	6/13-8/16				2P/2B:	$79-	87	XP:	$5	F12
	5/2-6/12 & 8/17-9/1	2P/1B:	$69-	79	2P/2B:	$69-	79	XP:	$5	F12
◆◆	3/14-5/1 & 9/2-10/25	2P/1B:	$52-	69	2P/2B:	$52-	69	XP:	$5	F12
	12/1-3/13 & 10/26-11/30	2P/1B:	$39-	54	2P/2B:	$39-	54	XP:	$5	F12

Location: 68th Ave N & N Ocean Blvd. 6803 N Ocean Blvd 29572. Fax: 803/449-3306. **Terms:** Reserv deposit, 7 day notice; small pets only, $5 extra charge, $50 dep req. **Facility:** 90 rooms. Handling fee imposed; 3 stories; exterior corridors. **Dining:** Coffee shop; 7-11 am, Sat-9 pm, Sun 11 am-2 pm. **Some Rooms:** 28 efficiencies. **Cards:** AE, DS, MC, VI. *(See color ad below)*

SAND CASTLE FAMILY RESORT — Phone: 803/448-7101 **105**

AAA SAVE / Apartment Motel

5/29-8/8	2P/2B:	$99-	159	XP:	$7	D16
5/8-5/28 & 8/9-9/6	2P/2B:	$74-	154	XP:	$7	D16
3/6-5/7 & 9/7-10/24	2P/2B:	$39-	99	XP:	$7	D16
12/1-3/5 & 10/25-11/30	2P/2B:	$34-	69	XP:	$7	D16

Location: 18th Ave N & N Ocean Blvd. 1802 N Ocean Blvd 29577. Fax: 803/448-6023. **Terms:** Reserv deposit, 14 day notice; package plans; no pets. **Facility:** 241 rooms. Variety of room decor from traditional motel furnishings to contemporary design. Handling fee imposed; 8-9 stories; interior corridors; oceanfront; beach, wading pool, whirlpool. Fee: golf privileges. **Dining:** Coffee shop; 6 am-2 pm. **Services:** Fee: coin laundry. **Recreation:** swimming, water ride. **All Rooms:** microwaves, refrigerators, combo or shower baths. **Some Rooms:** coffeemakers, 64 efficiencies, 51 kitchens. **Cards:** AE, MC, VI. *(See color ad p 526)* — Roll in showers.

SANDCASTLE RESORT SOUTH — Phone: 803/448-4316 **70**

Motor Inn — Under construction; **Location:** 2.3 mi s, 22nd Ave S & S Ocean Blvd. 2207 S Ocean Blvd 29577 (PO Box 957). Fax: 803/448-5536. **Terms:** Reserv deposit, 14 day notice, Handling fee imposed; no pets. **Facility:** 240 rooms. Scheduled to open February 1998; 14 stories; exterior corridors. **Dining:** Restaurant; 6 am-2 pm. **Some Rooms:** 24 efficiencies, 96 kitchens. **Cards:** AE, MC, VI. — Roll in showers.

SAND DUNES RESORT HOTEL — Phone: 803/449-7441 **1**

AAA SAVE / Hotel

6/12-8/22	2P/2B:	$132-	176	XP:	$10	F18
4/26-6/11 & 8/23-9/6	2P/2B:	$107-	159	XP:	$10	F18
3/6-4/25 & 9/7-10/31	2P/2B:	$72-	130	XP:	$10	F18
12/1-3/5 & 11/1-11/30	2P/2B:	$55-	89	XP:	$10	F18

Location: 74th Ave N & N Ocean Blvd. 201 74th Ave N 29578 (PO Box 2035). Fax: 803/449-5036. **Terms:** Reserv deposit, 4 day notice; weekly rates; package plans; no pets. **Facility:** 312 rooms. All rooms with balcony. Rates for up to 4 persons. Tower III, $245, $150 off season. Handling fee imposed; 14 stories; interior/exterior corridors; oceanfront; beach, wading pool, sauna, whirlpools. Fee: golf & tennis privileges. **Dining & Entertainment:** Dining room; 6 am-10 pm, off season 6 am-10 & 6-10 pm; pizza parlor 2 pm-2 am; $9-$18; cocktails/lounge. **Services:** Fee: coin laundry. **Recreation:** swimming, surf fishing, Lazy River water ride, recreation facilities from Ocean Dunes avail. **All Rooms:** refrigerators. Fee: movies, safes. **Some Rooms:** 56 efficiencies, 104 kitchens, microwaves. **Cards:** AE, CB, DI, DS, MC, VI. *(See color ad p 490)*

SEA BANKS MOTOR INN — Rates Subject to Change — Phone: 803/448-2434 **66**

AAA / Motel

5/22-8/15	2P/1B:	$52	2P/2B:	$72-	86	XP:	$6	F16
8/16-9/6	2P/1B:	$45	2P/2B:	$59-	73	XP:	$6	F16
3/20-5/21 & 9/7-9/23	2P/1B:	$35	2P/2B:	$52-	69	XP:	$6	F16
12/1-3/19 & 9/24-11/30	2P/1B:	$23	2P/2B:	$32-	42	XP:	$6	F16

Location: 2.3 mi s; 22nd Ave S & S Ocean Blvd. 2200 S Ocean Blvd 29577. Fax: 803/448-0502. **Terms:** Sr. discount; reserv deposit, 14 day notice, handling fee imposed; no pets. **Facility:** 67 rooms. Rates for up to 4 persons; 3 stories; exterior corridors. **Some Rooms:** 39 efficiencies. **Cards:** AE, DS, MC, VI.

SEACREST RESORT — Phone: 803/626-3515 **39**

AAA SAVE / Motor Inn

6/26-8/15	2P/2B:	$90-	165	XP:	$6	F16
6/5-6/25 & 8/16-8/22	2P/2B:	$73-	160	XP:	$6	F16
3/6-6/4 & 8/23-10/10	2P/2B:	$42-	130	XP:	$6	F16
12/1-3/5 & 10/11-11/30	2P/2B:	$30-	65	XP:	$6	F16

Location: Oceanfront at 8th Ave S. 803 S Ocean Blvd 29577. Fax: 803/448-2966. **Terms:** Reserv deposit, 14 day notice; no pets. **Facility:** 357 rooms. Handling fee imposed; 2-14 stories; exterior corridors. **Dining:** Restaurant; 6 am-2 & 4:30-midnight; $7-$13. **All Rooms:** free movies. **Some Rooms:** 275 efficiencies. **Cards:** AE, DS, MC, VI. *(See color ad p 527)*

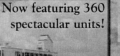

(See map p. 486)

SEA DIP MOTEL · Rates Subject to Change · Phone: 803/448-7971 · 95
(AAA)
	5/29-8/29	2P/1B:	$65	2P/2B:	$75- 110	XP: $10	F12
◆ ◆	5/8-5/28 & 8/30-9/19	2P/1B:	$40	2P/2B:	$50- 85	XP: $10	F12
Motel	3/13-5/7 & 9/20-10/17	2P/1B:	$35	2P/2B:	$45- 60	XP: $10	F12
	12/1-3/12 & 10/18-11/30	2P/1B:	$20	2P/2B:	$23- 34	XP: $10	F12

Location: 26th Ave N & N Ocean Blvd. 2608 N Ocean Blvd 29577. Fax: 803/626-8069. **Terms:** Reserv deposit, 14 day notice; no pets. **Facility:** 78 rooms. 2-8 stories; interior/exterior corridors. **All Rooms:** free movies. **Some Rooms:** 72 efficiencies. **Cards:** AE, DS, MC, VI. *(See color ad below)* (CTV) (D)

SEA ISLAND-AN INN ON THE BEACH · Rates Subject to Change · Phone: 803/449-6406 · 24
(AAA)
	6/8-8/16	2P/2B:	$108- 134	XP: $10	F11
◆ ◆ ◆	4/10-6/5 & 8/17-10/18	2P/2B:	$80- 114	XP: $10	F11
Apartment	2/6-4/9 & 10/19-11/30	2P/2B:	$52- 81	XP: $10	F11
Motor Inn	12/1-2/5	2P/2B:	$36- 52	XP: $10	F11

Location: 5 mi n. 6000 N Ocean Blvd 29577. Fax: 803/449-4102. **Terms:** Reserv deposit, 3 day notice; no pets. **Facility:** 113 rooms. 5 stories; exterior corridors. **Dining:** Dining room; 7:30 am-10 & 5:30-8 pm; $25; also, Sea Island, see separate listing. **All Rooms:** free movies. **Some Rooms:** 44 efficiencies. **Cards:** AE, DS, MC, VI. *(See color ad p 529)* (CTV)

THE SEA MIST RESORT · Rates Subject to Change · Phone: 803/448-1551 · 15
(AAA)
	5/24-9/16	1P: $60- 80	2P/1B: $60- 80	2P/2B: $75- 145	XP: $6-8	F15
◆ ◆	2/16-5/23 & 9/17-11/25	1P: $40- 60	2P/1B: $40- 60	2P/2B: $50- 100	XP: $6	F15
Motor Inn	12/1-2/15 & 11/26-11/30	1P: $29- 35	2P/1B: $29- 35	2P/2B: $30- 48	XP: $6	F15

Location: 1.5 mi s; 12th Ave S & S Ocean Blvd. 1200 S Ocean Blvd 29577 (PO Box 2548, 29578). Fax: 803/448-5858. **Terms:** Reserv deposit, 7 day notice, Handling fee imposed; pets, $20 extra charge. **Facility:** 827 rooms. Guest house & villa units, $70.50-$269. Suites, $48-$378; 2-16 stories; interior/exterior corridors. **Dining:** Restaurant, cafeteria, deli; 7-10 am; 6/1-9/30 to 11 pm; $8-$12. **All Rooms:** free movies. **Cards:** AE, CB, DI, DS, MC, VI. *(See color ad p 530)* (CTV) (X) (D)

SERENDIPITY, AN INN · Rates Subject to Change · Phone: 803/449-5268 · 7
◆ ◆ ◆
	5/10-9/23 [CP]	1P: $77	2P/1B: $77- 99	2P/2B: $89- 129	XP: $10	F5
Bed &	3/17-5/9 & 9/24-11/30 [CP]	1P: $59	2P/1B: $59- 79	2P/2B: $74- 89	XP: $10	F5
Breakfast	12/1-3/16 [CP]	1P: $45	2P/1B: $45- 63	2P/2B: $58- 73	XP: $10	F5

Location: 5 mi n. 407 71st Ave N 29572. **Terms:** Reserv deposit, 7 day notice; no pets. **Facility:** 14 rooms. 2 stories; exterior corridors. **Some Rooms:** 6 efficiencies. **Cards:** MC, VI. (CTV) (X) (D)

SHERATON MYRTLE BEACH HOTEL · Rates Subject to Change · Phone: 803/448-2518 · 78
◆ ◆ ◆
	5/23-8/31	1P: $120- 199	2P/1B: $120- 199	2P/2B: $120- 199	XP: $10	F18
Hotel	3/28-5/22 & 9/1-10/11	1P: $82- 149	2P/1B: $82- 149	2P/2B: $82- 149	XP: $10	F18
	2/16-3/27 & 10/12-11/8	1P: $54- 89	2P/1B: $54- 89	2P/2B: $54- 89	XP: $10	F18
	12/1-2/15 & 11/9-11/30	1P: $45- 75	2P/1B: $45- 75	2P/2B: $45- 75	XP: $10	F18

Location: 27th Ave S & S Ocean Blvd. 2701 S Ocean Blvd 29577. Fax: 803/448-1506. **Terms:** Sr. discount; reserv deposit, 4 day notice; no pets. **Facility:** 219 rooms. 16 stories; interior corridors. **Dining:** Restaurant; 7 am-10 pm; $8-$16. **All Rooms:** free & pay movies. **Some Rooms:** 46 efficiencies, 9 kitchens. **Cards:** AE, CB, DI, DS, MC, VI. *(See color ad p 531)* (CTV) (X) (D) (S)

SUPER 8 MOTEL · Rates Subject to Change · Phone: 803/293-6100 · 45
◆ ◆
	4/1-9/5 [CP]	1P: $95	2P/1B: $95	2P/2B: $95	XP: $10	F18
Motel	3/1-3/31 & 9/6-11/30 [CP]	1P: $63	2P/1B: $63	2P/2B: $63	XP: $10	F18
	12/1-2/28 [CP]	1P: $39	2P/1B: $39	2P/2B: $39	XP: $10	F18

Location: 1.5 mi s of US 501. 3450 Hwy 17S bypass 29577. Fax: 803/293-6100. **Terms:** Sr. discount; reserv deposit; pets, $10 extra charge. **Facility:** 92 rooms. 5 stories; interior corridors. **Cards:** AE, CB, DI, DS, MC, VI. (CTV) (X) (D)

Service Charges - See Using lodging listings.

(See map p. 486)

SURF AND DUNES

Phone: 803/448-1755 [31]

(AAA) SAVE	6/13-8/21	2P/1B:	$60-	70	2P/2B:	$66- 117	XP: $5	F16
♦♦	5/13-6/12 & 8/22-9/6	2P/1B:	$43-	51	2P/2B:	$56- 88	XP: $5	F16
Motel	4/4-5/12 & 9/7-9/26	2P/1B:	$37-	45	2P/2B:	$45- 75	XP: $5	F16
	12/1-4/3 & 9/27-11/30	2P/1B:	$28-	48	2P/2B:	$27- 52	XP: $5	F16

Location: 2.3 mi s; 22nd Ave S & S Ocean Blvd. 2201 S Ocean Blvd 29577 (PO Drawer 2487, 29578). Fax: 803/444-9360. **Terms:** Age restrictions may apply; reserv deposit, 14 day notice; weekly/monthly rates; package plans; no pets. **Facility:** 128 rooms. Rooms tastefully decorated & furnished. Many rooms with oceanfront view & balcony. 20 two-bedroom units. Handling fee imposed; 7 stories; exterior corridors; beach, wading pool, sauna, whirlpools; 1 lighted tennis court; playground. Fee: golf privileges. **Dining:** Snackbar 7 am-3 pm, 3/15-10/15. **Services:** Fee: coin laundry. **Recreation:** swimming, surf fishing. **All Rooms:** microwaves, free movies, refrigerators. Fee: safes. **Some Rooms:** 80 efficiencies. **Cards:** AE, CB, DI, DS, MC, VI. **Special Amenities:** Early check-in/late check-out and free room upgrade **(subject to availability with advanced reservations).** *(See color ad below)*

[icons] CTV D

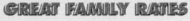

(See map p. 486)

SURF RIDER	Rates Subject to Change						Phone: 803/448-2394	81

ⒶⒶⒶ

5/24-9/7 — 2P/2B: $75- 120 XP: $6 F12
5/3-5/23 & 9/8-9/21 — 2P/2B: $62- 94 XP: $6 F12
◆◆ 3/22-5/2 & 9/22-10/12 — 2P/2B: $46- 70 XP: $6 F12
Apartment 12/1-3/21 & 10/13-11/30 — 2P/2B: $30- 58 XP: $6 F12
Motel **Location:** 1.3 mi n. 2304 N Ocean Blvd 29578 (PO Box 446, 29577). Fax: 803/626-8772. **Terms:** Sr. discount; reserv deposit, 14 day notice; no pets. **Facility:** 149 rooms. Townhouse, $300 in season. Handling fee imposed; 3-9 stories; interior corridors. **Dining:** Coffee shop; 7 am-2 pm; 5/1-9/1. **Some Rooms:** 71 efficiencies. **Cards:** AE, DS, MC, VI. *(See color ad below)* ⊇ ⊇ CTV D

SWAMP FOX OCEAN RESORTS							Phone: 803/448-8373	42

ⒶⒶⒶ [SAVE]

5/22-8/15 — 2P/2B: $79- 270 XP: $8 F14
8/16-9/24 — 2P/2B: $64- 240 XP: $8 F14
◆◆◆ 3/7-5/21 — 2P/2B: $54- 230 XP: $8 F14
Apartment 12/1-3/6 & 9/25-11/30 — 2P/2B: $39- 210 XP: $8 F14
Motor Inn **Location:** 2.5 mi s at 23rd Ave S & S Ocean Blvd. 2311 S Ocean Blvd 29577 (PO Box 1307, 29578). Fax: 803/448-5444. **Terms:** Reserv deposit, 3 day notice; weekly/monthly rates; package plans; no pets. **Facility:** 377 rooms. Balcony or patio. 54 two-bedroom units. 2-15 stories; exterior corridors; oceanfront; beach, 2 wading pools, saunas, whirlpools. Fee: golf & tennis privileges. **Dining:** Restaurant; 6 am-9 pm; in summer from 7 am; $4-$10; cocktails. **Services:** Fee: coin laundry. **Recreation:** swimming, surf fishing. **All Rooms:** refrigerators. Fee: movies, safes. **Some Rooms:** 288 efficiencies, microwaves. **Cards:** AE, CB, DI, DS, JCB, MC, VI. **Special Amenities:** Free room upgrade and preferred room (each subject to availability with advanced reservations). *(See color ad p 533)* ⊇ ⊇ 👍 🏋 👍 CTV D

TEAKWOOD MOTEL	Guaranteed Rates						Phone: 803/449-5653	19

ⒶⒶⒶ

5/30-8/14 — 2P/2B: $59- 63 XP: $3-5
4/25-5/29 & 8/15-9/11 — 2P/2B: $46- 50 XP: $3-5
◆◆ 3/7-4/24 & 9/12-10/2 — 2P/2B: $42- 46 XP: $3-5
Motel 2/13-3/6 & 10/3-11/15 — 2P/2B: $34- 36 XP: $3-5
Location: 5 mi n; 72nd Ave N & N Ocean Blvd. 7201 N Ocean Blvd 29572. **Terms:** Open 2/13-11/15; reserv deposit, 14 day notice; no pets. **Facility:** 25 rooms. Handling fee imposed; 2-3 stories, no elevator; exterior corridors. **Some Rooms:** 12 efficiencies. ⊇ ✈ CTV D

Change of plans? Listings indicate when more than a 48-hour cancellation notice is necessary for a deposit refund.

(See map p. 486)

THE TRADEWINDS MOTEL

Phone: 803/448-5441 (90)

AAA SAVE

◆ Motel

6/5-8/15	2P/2B:	$58-	65	XP:	$4	F6
5/8-6/4 & 8/16-9/6	2P/2B:	$40-	48	XP:	$4	F6
3/1-5/7 & 9/7-9/19	2P/2B:	$30-	40	XP:	$4	F6
12/1-2/28 & 9/20-11/30	2P/2B:	$26-	31	XP:	$4	F6

Location: Between Kings Hwy & Ocean Blvd. 23rd Ave N & 2201 Withers Dr 29577. Fax: 803/448-5441. **Terms:** Reserv deposit, 14 day notice; weekly rates; package plans; no pets. **Facility:** 40 rooms. Just a block from beach. 6 two-bedroom units. 6 units with 3 beds, $58-$64 in season. Handling fee imposed; 2 stories; exterior corridors. Fee: golf privileges. **Dining:** Restaurant nearby. **Services:** Fee: coin laundry. **All Rooms:** refrigerators, combo or shower baths. **Some Rooms:** 35 efficiencies. **Cards:** MC, VI. **Special Amenities:** Preferred room (subject to availability with advanced reservations). 🖼 CTV D

DON'T WAIT FOR THE BIG CHILL.

Check the blanket supply in your room when you arrive;
you might not be able to get extras during the night.

(See map p. 486)

TROPICAL SEAS   Phone: 803/448-1171   [33]
(AAA) [SAVE]   5/14-8/21   2P/1B: $43- 65   2P/2B: $85- 165   XP: $6   F12
              8/22-9/11   2P/2B: $72- 140   XP: $6   F12
◆◆   3/1-5/13 & 9/12-10/23   2P/2B: $53- 109   XP: $6   F12
Motel   12/1-2/28 & 10/24-11/30   2P/2B: $41- 97   XP: $6   F12
              Location: 3 mi s; 28th Ave S & S Ocean Blvd. 2807 S Ocean Blvd 29577. Fax: 803/448-0253.
Terms: Reserv deposit, 14 day notice; no pets. **Facility:** 91 rooms. 22 two-bedroom units, $110-$140 in season. Handling fee
imposed; 9 stories; interior corridors. **Dining:** Coffee shop; 7 am-2 pm, in season 4/1-10/31. **All Rooms:** free movies.
Some Rooms: 59 efficiencies. **Cards:** AE, DS, MC, VI. *(See color ad p 534)*   [CTV] [X] [📶] [D]

TROPICAL SEAS NORTH   Phone: 803/626-3610   [71]
(AAA) [SAVE]   5/26-8/17   2P/1B: $98- 112   2P/2B: $98- 158   XP: $6   F16
              5/12-5/25 & 8/18-9/14   2P/1B: $60- 70   2P/2B: $60- 112   XP: $6   F16
◆◆◆   3/10-5/11 & 9/15-10/12   2P/1B: $50- 59   2P/2B: $50- 95   XP: $6   F16
Motel   12/1-3/9 & 10/13-11/30   2P/1B: $27- 38   2P/2B: $29- 50   XP: $6   F16
              Location: 7th Ave S & S Ocean Blvd. 703 S Ocean Blvd 29577. Fax: 803/626-9830. **Terms:** Reserv deposit,
14 day notice, handling fee imposed; no pets. **Facility:** 122 rooms. 6 stories; interior corridors. **Dining:** Coffee shop; 7 am-2
pm, 3/1-10/31. **Some Rooms:** 83 efficiencies. **Cards:** AE, DS, MC, VI. *(See color ad p 534)*   [📶] [📶] [CTV] [📶] [D]

TROPICAL WINDS RESORT   Phone: 803/448-4304   [38]
(AAA) [SAVE]   6/6-8/21   2P/2B: $101- 131   XP: $5   F17
              5/9-6/5 & 8/22-9/6   2P/2B: $70- 97   XP: $5   F17
◆◆◆   3/7-5/8 & 9/7-10/9   2P/2B: $59- 74   XP: $5   F17
Apartment   12/1-3/6 & 10/10-11/30   2P/2B: $32- 59   XP: $5   F17
Motel   **Location:** 1 mi s; 7th Ave S & S Ocean Blvd. 705 S Ocean Blvd 29577 (PO Box 2529, 29578-2529).
Fax: 803/448-0015. **Terms:** Age restrictions may apply; reserv deposit, 14 day notice; no pets. **Facility:** 230
rooms. Handling fee imposed; 14 stories; interior/exterior corridors. **Some Rooms:** 184 efficiencies. **Cards:** AE, MC, VI.
(See color ad inside front cover & p 536)   [📶] [📶] [CTV] [D]

WAIKIKI VILLAGE   Rates Subject to Change   Phone: 803/448-8431   [68]
◆◆   6/9-8/10   2P/1B: $50- 65   2P/2B: $65- 79   XP: $5   D12
Apartment   5/24-6/8 & 8/11-9/1   2P/1B: $38- 50   2P/2B: $50- 65   XP: $5   D12
Motel   3/9-5/23 & 9/2-9/27   2P/1B: $30- 45   2P/2B: $38- 52   XP: $5   D12
              12/1-3/8 & 9/28-11/30   2P/1B: $25- 40   2P/2B: $30- 45   XP: $5   D12
Location: 15th Ave S & S Ocean Blvd. 1500 S Ocean Blvd 29577. **Terms:** Age restrictions may apply; reserv deposit, 14
day notice; no pets. **Facility:** 43 rooms. Handling fee imposed; 2 stories; exterior corridors. **All Rooms:** free movies.
Cards: MC, VI.   [📶] [CTV] [D]

WATERSIDE INN   Rates Subject to Change   Phone: 803/448-5935   [89]
◆◆   5/23-9/1   2P/2B: $92- 149   XP: $7   F16
Motel   3/28-5/22   2P/2B: $61- 114   XP: $7   F16
              9/2-9/18   2P/2B: $61- 87   XP: $7   F16
              12/1-3/27 & 9/19-11/30   2P/2B: $34- 64   XP: $7   F16
Location: 20th Ave N & N Ocean Blvd. 2000 N Ocean Blvd 29577. Fax: 803/448-3577. **Terms:** Small pets only, $7 extra
charge, $60 dep req. **Facility:** 47 rooms. 3 stories; interior/exterior corridors. **All Rooms:** free movies. **Some Rooms:** 32
efficiencies. **Cards:** AE, DS, MC, VI.   [🐾] [📶] [CTV] [D]

WAVE RIDER RESORT   Rates Subject to Change   Phone: 803/448-1591   [88]
◆◆◆   6/13-8/10   1P: $62- 79   2P/1B: $62- 79   2P/2B: $79   XP: $5
Condo Motel   5/3-6/12 & 8/11-9/7 1P: $42- 44   2P/1B: $42- 44   2P/2B: $44   XP: $5
              3/22-5/2 & 9/8-10/23 1P: $34- 36   2P/1B: $34- 36   2P/2B: $36   XP: $5
              12/1-3/21 & 10/24-11/30 1P: $24- 26 2P/1B: $24- 26   2P/2B: $26   XP: $5
Location: 16 Ave S & S Ocean Blvd. 1600 S Ocean Blvd 29577. Fax: 803/916-4154. **Terms:** Reserv deposit, 14 day notice;
no pets. **Facility:** 73 rooms. Rates for up to 4 persons. 2 room suites, extra charge. Handling fee imposed; 3 stories; exterior
corridors. **All Rooms:** free movies. **Some Rooms:** 62 efficiencies. **Cards:** AE, DS, MC, VI.   [📶] [📶] [CTV] [D]

(See map p. 486)

WAYFARER MOTEL
Phone: 803/448-5941 [72]

(AAA) [SAVE]	5/26-8/19	2P/1B:	$57	2P/2B:	$73	XP: $10
	8/20-8/31	2P/1B:	$38	2P/2B:	$53	XP: $10
◆	4/30-5/25 & 9/1-9/24	2P/1B:	$35	2P/2B:	$47	XP: $10
Motel	12/1-4/29 & 9/25-11/30	2P/1B:	$25	2P/2B:	$31	XP: $10

Location: 4th Ave N & N Ocean Blvd. 311 N Ocean Blvd 29577. **Terms:** Reserv deposit, 14 day notice, handling fee imposed; weekly/monthly rates; package plans; no pets. **Facility:** 34 rooms. Across from ocean. Thurs-Sat rates are higher; 2 stories; exterior corridors. Fee: golf privileges. **Dining:** Restaurant nearby. **Services:** Fee: coin laundry. **All Rooms:** free movies, refrigerators, combo or shower baths. **Some Rooms:** 30 efficiencies, microwaves. **Cards:** MC, VI.

WAYWARD WINDS OCEANFRONT INN
Phone: 803/448-5121 [65]

(AAA) [SAVE]	5/3-8/22	1P:	$66-	103	2P/1B:	$66-	83	2P/2B:	$66- 103	XP: $6	F16
	3/22-5/2 & 8/23-9/19	1P:	$44-	68	2P/1B:	$44-	67	2P/2B:	$44- 68	XP: $6	F16
◆ ◆	3/1-3/21 & 9/20-10/10	1P:	$36-	50	2P/1B:	$36-	44	2P/2B:	$36- 50	XP: $6	F16
Motel	12/1-2/28 & 10/11-11/30	1P:	$30-	36	2P/1B:	$30-	38	2P/2B:	$30- 38	XP: $6	F16

Location: 2.8 mi s; 27th Ave S & S Ocean Blvd. 2609 S Ocean Blvd 29577. Fax: 803/448-3416. **Terms:** Age restrictions may apply; reserv deposit, 14 day notice, handling fee imposed; no pets. **Facility:** 73 rooms. 8 two-bedroom apartments for up to 8 persons; 5 stories; exterior corridors. **Dining:** Coffee shop; 7 am-2 pm, 4/1-10/1. **All Rooms:** free movies. **Some Rooms:** 33 efficiencies. **Cards:** AE, DS, MC. *(See color ad p 535)*

RESTAURANTS

AKEL'S HOUSE OF PANCAKES **Lunch:** $3-$10 **Dinner:** $3-$10 Phone: 803/449-4815 [5]
◆
American **Location:** US 17/N Kings Hwy & 65 Ave N. 6409 N Kings Hwy 29572. **Hours:** 10 pm-2 pm. Closed: 12/24 & 12/25. **Features:** casual dress; children's menu; carryout. Great omelets & pancakes. **Cards:** AE, DI, DS, MC, VI.

ANGELO'S STEAK & PASTA **Dinner:** $6-$17 Phone: 803/626-2800 [13]
(AAA)
◆ ◆
Italian **Location:** US 17 (Kings Hwy) & 20 Ave S. 2011 S Kings Hwy 29577. **Hours:** 4 pm-9:30 pm, summer to 10 pm. Closed: 1/2-1/20 & 12/10-12/26. **Features:** casual dress; children's menu; early bird specials; carryout; cocktails & lounge; buffet. A casual atmosphere with entrees specializing in Italian food & seasoned ribeye. **Cards:** DI, DS, MC, VI.

AUNT MAUDE'S SEAFOOD & BEEF **Dinner:** $12-$14 Phone: 803/449-1434 [7]
(AAA)
◆ ◆
Steak and Seafood **Location:** 7001 Kings Hwy N 29572. **Hours:** 5 pm-9 pm. Closed: Sun & after 11/26 to early Spring. **Reservations:** accepted. **Features:** casual dress; children's menu; early bird specials; senior's menu; carryout; salad bar; cocktails & lounge; entertainment. Lowcountry cooking in a casual setting. Hushpuppies, orange blossom butter, crab casserole & steak cooked on a charcoal hearth, all served up in a country-style building with wrap-around porch. **Cards:** AE, DS, MC, VI.

BAGEL FACTORY **Lunch:** $2-$5 Phone: 803/626-6445 [22]
◆
American **Location:** 21st Ave N & Business Rt 17 (Kings Hwy). 2012 N Kings Hwy 29572. **Hours:** 6:30 am-3 pm, Sun-2 pm. Closed: 1/1, 12/25, Yom Kippur & Easter. **Features:** casual dress; health conscious menu; carryout. New York deli-style restaurant with on-premises bakery, specializing in bagels every which way. Also eggs, sandwich platters, Reubens, burgers & stir-fry.

THE BISTRO **Lunch:** $4-$11 **Dinner:** $12-$25 Phone: 803/449-0465 [25]
◆ ◆
Regional American **Location:** Kings Hwy n, e on 73rd Ave, n on Ocean Blvd. 208 73rd Ave 29572. **Hours:** noon-2:30 & 6-midnight, Sat from 6 pm. Closed: Sun, 1/1, 11/26 & 12/25. **Features:** casual dress; children's menu; senior's menu; health conscious menu; cocktails. Quaint setting folded into a small beach motel; seats about 40, also patio dining. Specialties include Schnitzel Munchen, lobster tails, steak au poivre, seafood pasta dishes & more. **Cards:** AE, CB, DI, DS, MC, VI.

CAROLINA ROADHOUSE RESTAURANT **Lunch:** $5-$10 **Dinner:** $8-$17 Phone: 803/497-9941 [26]
◆ ◆
American **Location:** On US 17/Kings Hwy, between 46th & 48th Aves N. 4617 N Kings Hwy 29577. **Hours:** 11 am-10 pm, Fri & Sat-11 pm. Closed: 11/26 & 12/25. **Reservations:** accepted. **Features:** casual dress; children's menu; carryout; cocktails & lounge. A contemporary dining room atmosphere. Variety of food; ribs, fresh seafood & meat. **Cards:** AE, DS, MC, VI.

CHUNG WAH RESTAURANT **Lunch:** $6-$14 **Dinner:** $6-$14 Phone: 803/448-9877 [28]
◆
Chinese **Location:** In the Village Square Shopping Ctr. 3901 N Kings Hwy, Ste 16 & 17 29577. **Hours:** 11:30 am-10 pm. Closed: 11/26. **Reservations:** accepted. **Features:** casual dress; health conscious menu; carryout; salad bar; cocktails & lounge. Many traditional dishes from pu pu platter to Phoenix & Dragon & hot & spicy dishes; also buffet. **Cards:** AE, CB, DI, DS, MC, VI.

COLLECTORS CAFE **Dinner:** $9-$19 Phone: 803/449-9370 [2]
◆ ◆ ◆
Ethnic **Location:** On US 17 & Kings Hwy & 79th Ave N. 7726 N Kings Hwy 29572. **Hours:** noon-midnight. Closed: Sun. **Reservations:** accepted. **Features:** casual dress; cocktails. A nice casual atmosphere decorated with art. The Mediterranean cuisine is very good, has a wide variety of meat, pasta & seafood creations. Also serving a wide variety of pastry & coffee. **Cards:** AE, MC, VI.

THE CRAB HOUSE **Lunch:** $2-$9 **Dinner:** $3-$20 Phone: 803/444-2717 [29]
◆ ◆
Seafood **Location:** Broadway at the Beach, US 17 Bypass near 21st Ave N. 1313 Celebrity Cir 29577. **Hours:** 11:30 am-10 pm, Fri & Sat-11 pm. **Reservations:** accepted; dinner. **Features:** casual dress; salad bar. Crab is prepared every imaginable way; trademark is blue crabs prepared South Florida-style with garlic & butter. All-you-can-eat salad & raw bar avail as an entree or along with a meal. Lively atmosphere; expect a wait. **Cards:** AE, DI, MC, VI.

DING HO CHINESE RESTAURANT **Lunch:** $5-$7 **Dinner:** $7-$10 Phone: 803/449-9005 [48]
◆
Chinese **Location:** 7817 N Kings Hwy 29577. **Hours:** 11 am-10 pm, Sun from noon. **Features:** casual dress; health conscious menu; carryout; a la carte. Excellent Chinese cuisine in a no-frills setting.

FLAMINGO SEAFOOD GRILL **Dinner:** $11-$15 Phone: 803/449-5388 [12]
◆ ◆
Steak and Seafood **Location:** On US 17 (Kings Hwy) & 71st Ave N. 29578. **Hours:** 5 pm-11 pm. Closed: Sun, 11/26 & 12/18-12/27. **Reservations:** suggested. **Features:** casual dress; children's menu; carryout; cocktails & lounge. Art Deco interior theme. Featuring grilled steak, seafood & poultry; also veal entrees & pasta. **Cards:** AE, DS, MC, VI.

(See map p. 486)

FULLYS A RESTAURANT   Dinner: $12-$17   Phone: 803/449-9596   ④
◆ ◆ ◆
Steak and
Seafood
Location: 4 mi n on US 17. 6507 N Kings Hwy 29577. **Hours:** 5 pm-10 pm. **Closed:** 12/24 & 12/25. **Reservations:** suggested. **Features:** casual dress; children's menu; early bird specials; cocktails & lounge. Very well prepared entrees. Also featuring veal, poultry & catfish entrees. **Cards:** AE, MC, VI.   ✕

FUSCO'S   Dinner: $8-$15   Phone: 803/497-0440   ⑯
Ⓐ Ⓢ
◆ ◆
Italian
Location: 3.3 mi n; 53rd Ave N & N Ocean Blvd; in Beach Colony Resort. 5308 N Ocean Blvd 29577. **Hours:** 6-11 am & 5-10 pm. **Reservations:** suggested. **Features:** casual dress; Sunday brunch; children's menu; carryout; cocktails & lounge. Oceanfront dining. Very well prepared entrees. **Cards:** AE, DI, DS, MC, VI. **Special Value: 10% discount on the price of any entree, excluding beverages, tax and gratuity.**

GILLEY'S   Lunch: $5-$11   Dinner: $6-$19   Phone: 803/448-3378   ㉚
◆ ◆
East American
Location: Broadway at the Beach, US 17 Bypass & 21st Ave. 1304 Celebrity Cir 29577. **Hours:** 11 am-11 pm, to 10 pm in winter. **Reservations:** accepted; large groups. **Features:** casual dress; children's menu; carryout; cocktails & lounge. Tex Mex with enchiladas, fajitas, burritos, chili with or without beans, barbecue, burgers, steak & lots of fun stuff to look at, especially for airplane buffs. Also deck dining. **Cards:** AE, DI, MC, VI.   ✕

J EDWARD'S GREAT RIBS & MORE   Dinner: $6-$18   Phone: 803/626-9986   ⑮
◆ ◆
American
Location: 23rd Ave S & US 17 (Kings Hwy). 2300 S Kings Hwy 29577. **Hours:** 4 pm-10:30 pm. **Reservations:** suggested. **Features:** casual dress; children's menu; early bird specials; carryout; cocktails & lounge. Casual atmosphere featuring barbecue ribs, steak, prime rib, chicken, pork & seafood. **Cards:** AE, DS, MC, VI.

KEY WEST GRILL   Dinner: $4-$25   Phone: 803/444-3663   ㊲
◆ ◆
Ethnic
Location: Broadway at the Beach. 1214 Celebrity Cir 29578. **Hours:** 11 am-10:30 pm. **Reservations:** accepted. **Features:** casual dress; children's menu; cocktails & lounge. Food is spicy in the style of Cuban, Spanish & Calusa Indian influences; conch fritters, calamari, escargot, catch-of-the-day, sandwiches & burgers, seafood, blackened frog legs. Also outdoor seating on the porch. **Cards:** AE, DI, MC, VI.

KYOTO JAPANESE STEAK HOUSE   Dinner: $13-$22   Phone: 803/449-9294   ㊴
◆ ◆
Ethnic
Location: Restaurant Row. 9732 Hwy 19 N 29577. **Hours:** 4:30 pm-10:30 pm. **Features:** The Japanese tradition of hibachi cooking is brought to your table. All entrees served with salad & a delicate onion soup. **Cards:** AE, MC, VI.

LATIF'S BAKERY & CAFE   Lunch: $6-$9   Dinner: $8-$15   Phone: 803/449-1716   ㊵
◆ ◆ ◆
American
Location: Just w of Kings Hwy (US 17). 503 61st Ave N 29577. **Hours:** 8 am-10 pm, Sun 10 am-3 pm. **Closed:** 11/26 & 12/25. **Reservations:** accepted. **Features:** dressy casual; carryout; cocktails; a la carte. Eclectic American cuisine served in trendy, classy dining room or on the terrace. Enjoy creative dishes such as chinese chicken salad or linguine with sesame seeds & shrimp. Dessert & pastry are homemade & they're fabulous. **Cards:** AE, DS, MC, VI.   ✕

LIBERTY STEAKHOUSE & BREWERY   Lunch: $5-$7   Dinner: $6-$16   Phone: 803/626-4677   ㊶
◆ ◆
Steakhouse
Location: Broadway at the Beach, US 17 Bypass between 21st & 29th aves N. 1321 Celebrity Cir 29577. **Hours:** 11 am-11 pm in summer; to 10 pm in winter. **Closed:** 11/26 & 12/25. **Features:** casual dress; children's menu; carryout; cocktails & lounge. 8 types of beer made are also used as ingredients in many recipes. Food choices range from fish & chips & pizza to steak & chicken. Also outdoor tables. Expect a wait, especially in summer. **Cards:** AE, MC, VI.

THE LIBRARY   Dinner: $16-$28   Phone: 803/448-4527   ⑨
◆ ◆ ◆
Continental
Location: On US 17 business route, between 12th Ave N & 13th Ave N. 1212 N Kings Hwy 29577. **Hours:** 5:30 pm-10:30 pm. **Closed:** Sun. **Reservations:** suggested. **Features:** dressy casual; cocktails & lounge; a la carte. Elegant candlelight dining. French continental menu features excellently prepared seafood, beef, veal, lamb & poultry dishes. Servers are well versed in tableside prepartions. Extensive wine list. **Cards:** AE, CB, DI, DS, MC, VI.   ✕

LITTLES AT THE BEACH RESTAURANT   Dinner: $9-$17   Phone: 803/449-3678   ⑭
◆ ◆
Steak and
Seafood
Location: Off US 17 Kings Hwy. 411 79th Ave N 29577. **Hours:** 5 pm-10 pm. **Closed:** Sun & 12/10-12/28. **Reservations:** suggested. **Features:** casual dress; children's menu; early bird specials; senior's menu; carryout; cocktails. Also features poultry entrees. **Cards:** AE, DI, DS, MC, VI.   ✕

THE LONGHORN STEAK HOUSE   Dinner: $9-$19   Phone: 803/449-7013   ㊷
◆ ◆
Seafood
Location: Corner 77th Ave N & N Kings Hwy, across from Wal-Mart. 7604 N Kings Hwy 29572. **Hours:** 5 pm-10 pm, Fri & Sat-10:30 pm, Sun-9:30 pm. **Closed:** 1/1, 11/26, 12/24 & 12/25. **Reservations:** accepted; 6 or more. **Features:** casual dress; children's menu; early bird specials; health conscious menu items; carryout; salad bar; cocktails & lounge. Family-owned restaurant not part of the chain by the same name. Red meat is the meal of choice; also chicken breast skinned & broiled over open charcoal, grouper & flounder broiled in herbs & spices sans butter. **Cards:** AE, CB, DI, DS, MC, VI.   ✕

MANCUSO'S ITALIAN RESTAURANT   Dinner: $8-$16   Phone: 803/293-3193   ㉑
◆ ◆
Regional
Italian
Location: 0.5 mi s of SR 707, 3.5 mi s of US 501. 4700 Bypass 17S 29577. **Hours:** 5 pm-10 pm. **Closed:** Sun, 11/26 & 12/25. **Reservations:** accepted. **Features:** casual dress; children's menu; early bird specials; health conscious menu; cocktails & lounge. Very well prepared entrees with Southern Italian influences. Fresh seafood entrees & pasta with other meat selections. Served in a cozy dining room. **Cards:** DS, MC, VI.   ✕

MIDWAY DELI   Dinner: $2-$10   Phone: 803/449-9138   ㊹
◆ ◆
American
Location: 7827 N Kings Hwy 29577. **Hours:** 6 am-10 pm. **Closed:** Sun. **Features:** casual dress; children's menu; carryout; beer only. A New York-style deli, where you can also take out items, which sell by the pound, like chicken in white wine sauce with garlic, black pepper linguini & jumbo shrimp & mussels on the half shell. Also subs & sandwiches. **Cards:** AE, DI, MC, VI.

MR FISH SEAFOOD MARKET, GRILL & RAW BAR   Lunch: $3-$12   Dinner: $3-$12   Phone: 803/946-6869   ㊺
Ⓐ
American
Location: 919 Broadway 29577. **Hours:** 10:30 am-3:30 & 5:30-9:30 pm, Sun-Wed to 3:30 pm. **Reservations:** accepted. **Features:** casual dress. Fresh catch-of-the-day fish & seafood platters, gumbo, & all-you-can-eat oyster roast for dinner. Some cooking in front of the guest, who points at the choice. Evening entertainment is watching tapes of people catching fish. **Cards:** MC, VI.

(See map p. 486)

NASCAR CAFE   Lunch: $6-$21   Dinner: $6-$21   Phone: 803/946-7223   58
◆◆   **Location:** At US 17 bypass & 21st Ave N, opposite Broadway at the Beach. 1808 21st Ave N 29577.
American   **Hours:** 11 am-10 pm, Fri & Sat-11 pm, in summer to midnight, Fri & Sat-1 am. **Closed:** 12/25.
Features: children's menu; cocktails. The room is like the infield on a racetrack with booths being like pit areas. Lots of racing artifacts & a small racing hall of fame area. **Cards:** AE, DI, DS, MC, VI.

NEW YORK PRIME, A STEAKHOUSE   Dinner: $18-$28   Phone: 803/448-8081   46
◆◆◆   **Location:** Between N Ocean Blvd & Kings Hwy. 405 28th Ave N 29577. **Hours:** 5 pm-11 pm. **Closed:** Sun,
Steakhouse   11/26 & 12/25. **Reservations:** suggested. **Features:** casual dress; carryout; cocktails & lounge; a la carte.
Large steak & lobster, informal atmosphere, attentive service. **Cards:** AE, CB, DI, DS, JCB, MC, VI.

ORIGINAL BENJAMIN'S   Phone: 803/626-9354   47
◆◆   **Location:** On Restaurant Row near McDonald's. 9301 N Kings Hwy 29572. **Hours:** 4 pm-9:30 pm.
Seafood   **Features:** early bird specials; buffet. Buffet includes fried, boiled & broiled shrimp, fried scallops, Alaskan
crab legs, stuffed flounder & more; for non-seafood lovers, even lasagna & spaghetti, corn-on-the-cob,
barbecued ribs & more. **Cards:** AE, DI, DS, MC, VI.

RIVER CITY CAFE   Lunch: $3-$6   Dinner: $3-$6   Phone: 803/448-1990   49
◆   **Location:** Between King Hwy & N Ocean Blvd. 404 21st Ave N 29577. **Hours:** 11 am-10 pm.
American   **Features:** casual dress; children's menu; carryout; cocktails; a la carte. Known for its great & huge burgers
fixed every which way, from chili burger to jalapeno burger to blackened burger. Other favorites like fried
bologna sandwich, grouper fingers & blooming onion.

SEA CAPTAIN'S HOUSE   Lunch: $7-$14   Dinner: $8-$18   Phone: 803/448-8082   11
(AAA)   **Location:** 1.5 mi n. 3002 N Ocean Blvd 29577. **Hours:** 6-10:30 am, 11:30-2:30 & 5-10 pm. **Closed:** 9/2,
11/26 & 12/24-12/26. **Features:** casual dress; children's menu; carryout; cocktails. Casual dining overlooking
◆◆   ocean. **Cards:** AE, DS, MC, VI. *(See color ad below & p 497)*
Seafood

SEA ISLAND   Phone: 803/449-6406   51
◆◆◆   **Location:** 5 mi n; in Sea Island-An Inn on the Beach. 6000 N Ocean Blvd 29577. **Hours:** 7:30 am-10 &
Continental   5:30-8 pm. **Reservations:** required; for dinner. **Features:** semi-formal attire; cocktails; prix fixe. Also offering
a "passing dish" that is passed among the diners, all is fresh & wonderfully prepared cuisine. In a beautiful,
romantic & intimate dining room with a sweeping ocean view. Men must wear jackets. Smoke free premises. **Cards:** AE, DI,
MC, VI.

SHAMROCK'S   Dinner: $9-$19   Phone: 803/448-2532   52
◆◆   **Location:** Across from Myrtle Square Mall. 2510 N Kings Hwy 29577. **Hours:** 11:30 am-1 am. **Closed:**
American   12/25. **Reservations:** accepted. **Features:** casual dress; children's menu; senior's menu; carryout; cocktails
& lounge. Friendly, unpretentious sports bar with dining; pub atmosphere with a simple menu. **Cards:** MC,
VI.

SKEETER'S   Lunch: $2-$7   Phone: 803/497-4781   53
◆   **Location:** Corner of 70th Avenue N & Kings Hwy. 410 70th Ave N 29572. **Hours:** 6:30 am-2 pm. **Closed:**
American   12/25. **Features:** casual dress. A local institution best known for waffles & pancakes, but there are the usual
egg offerings & grilled sandwiches as well.

TBONZ GILL & GRILL   Lunch: $3-$8   Dinner: $5-$17   Phone: 803/946-7111   54
◆◆   **Location:** US 17 Bypass & 21st Ave N. 1169 Seaboard 29577. **Hours:** 11 am-10 pm, Fri & Sat-10:30 pm.
Steak and   **Closed:** 11/26 & 12/25. **Reservations:** accepted; in off season for large groups. **Features:** casual dress;
Seafood   children's menu; carryout; cocktails & lounge. In a pleasant setting with high ceilings, ceiling fans, wood &
plants. Fresh seafood, low country dishes, burgers & lite snacks. **Cards:** AE, MC, VI.

(See map p. 486)

THORNY'S STEAK HOUSE & SALOON   Dinner: $8-$19   Phone: 803/448-8454   **55**
Location: At 5th Ave S, on US 17/S Kings Hwy. 512 S Kings Hwy 29577. **Hours:** 4 pm-11 pm. Closed: 12/24. **Features:** casual dress; children's menu; early bird specials; carryout; cocktails & lounge. A family atmosphere with an eclectic decor. Serving a variety of meat & seafood. **Cards:** AE, DI, DS, MC, VI.
Steakhouse

TRIPPS   Lunch: $4-$10   Dinner: $7-$16   Phone: 803/444-5693   **59**
Location: At Broadway at the Beach complex, Hwy 17 bypass at 21st Ave N. 1311 Celebrity Cir 29577. **Hours:** 11 am-11 pm, Fri & Sat-midnight. Closed: 11/26 & 12/25. **Reservations:** accepted. **Features:** casual dress; Sunday brunch; children's menu; health conscious menu; cocktails & lounge; entertainment. Baby back ribs, chicken Cordon Bleu, red roasted grouper served in a restaurant with lots of wood, plants & interesting things to look at. Also outdoor patio with live music. **Cards:** AE, MC, VI.
Steak and Seafood

VILLA MARE RESTAURANT   Lunch: $4-$6   Dinner: $7-$14   Phone: 803/449-8654   **61**
Location: In the Northwood Plaza at 29th N & N Kings Hwy. 7819 N Kings Hwy 29572. **Hours:** 11 am-10 pm. Closed: Sun, 1/1, 11/26, 12/25 & Easter. **Reservations:** suggested. **Features:** casual dress; children's menu; early bird specials; carryout; beer & wine only. Homemade food, all made on the premises, & served in an unpretentious dinery. Hoagies & calzones, salads & pizzas for lunch; several veal house specialties & Italian fare for dinner. **Cards:** DS, MC, VI.
Italian

VILLA ROMANA   Dinner: $9-$16   Phone: 803/448-4990   **1**
Location: Between 7th & 8th aves s on Kings Hwy (US 17). 707 S Kings Hwy 29577. **Hours:** 5 pm-10 pm. Closed: Sun & 12/15-1/15. **Reservations:** suggested. **Features:** casual dress; children's menu; carryout; cocktails. Featuring veal, chicken & seafood entrees. Fresh pasta & bread in a garden setting. **Cards:** AE, DI, DS, MC, VI.
Italian

VINTAGE HOUSE CAFE   Lunch: $4-$9   Dinner: $15-$20   Phone: 803/626-3918   **62**
Location: Business US 17 at 12th Ave N. 1210 N Kings Hwy 29577. **Hours:** 11 am-3 & 6-9 pm, Mon-3 pm. Closed: Sun, 5/26, 11/26 & 12/25. **Reservations:** suggested. **Features:** casual dress; health conscious menu; cocktails; street parking. Gourmet dining in a charming, romantic atmosphere. Menu offers specialties like pan-sauteed pasta cakes with roasted vegetables & local grouper dusted in Japanese bread crumbs. Complimenting wine list. **Cards:** DS, MC, VI.
Steak and Seafood

YAMATO   Dinner: $9-$24   Phone: 803/448-1959   **63**
Location: Broadway at the Beach; US 17 bypass & 21st Ave N. 1213 Celebrity Cir 29577. **Hours:** 4:30 pm-9:30 pm, to 10 pm in summer; Fri & Sat-10:30 pm. Closed: 11/26 & 12/25. **Reservations:** accepted. **Features:** casual dress; children's menu; early bird specials; cocktails & lounge. Teppan chefs prepare delicious entrees tableside, a dazzling show. Master sushi chefs create beautiful rolls, pieces & decorations from an 86-item sushi menu. Other entrees from sea scallops to filet mignon. Outside cocktail deck. **Cards:** AE, DI, DS, MC, VI.
Ethnic

GREATER MYRTLE BEACH   (See map p. 542; index below)

Index of Establishments on the MYRTLE BEACH ACCOMMODATIONS Spotting Map

(See map p. 542)

LODGINGS

BEACH COVE RESORT

Rates Subject to Change

Phone: 803/272-4044 33

5/8-8/30	1P:	$98- 148		2P/2B:	$150- 280	XP: $10	F17
3/6-5/7 & 8/31-10/17	1P:	$75- 91		2P/2B:	$110- 175	XP: $10	F17
12/1-3/5 & 10/18-11/30	1P:	$49- 62		2P/2B:	$79- 119	XP: $10	F17

Apartment Hotel

Location: In Windy Hill Section. 4800 S Ocean Blvd 29582. Fax: 803/272-2294. **Terms:** Sr. discount; age restrictions may apply; reserv deposit, 14 day notice; no pets. **Facility:** 317 rooms. Rates for up to 2 persons. Handling fee imposed; 2-16 stories; exterior corridors. **Dining:** Dining room, coffee shop; 7 am-10, noon-2 & 5-10 pm; $6-$18. **All Rooms:** efficiencies, free & pay movies. **Cards:** AE, DS, MC, VI.
(See color ad inside front cover & p 543)

🏊 🏊 CTV ✕ D S

FAIRFIELD INN BY MARRIOTT MYRTLE BEACH-BRIARCLIFF

Rates Subject to Change
Phone: 803/361-8100 32

6/6-9/1 [CP]	1P:	$99	2P/1B:	$119	2P/2B:	$119	XP: $5	F6
4/1-6/5 & 9/2-10/31 [CP]	1P:	$79	2P/1B:	$99	2P/2B:	$99	XP: $5	F6
12/1-3/31 [CP]	1P:	$69	2P/1B:	$79	2P/2B:	$79	XP: $5	F6
11/1-11/30 [CP]	1P:	$59	2P/1B:	$79	2P/2B:	$79	XP: $5	F6

Motel

Location: US 17 n at Briarcliff Mall. 10231 N Kings Hwy 29572. Fax: 803/361-9551. **Terms:** Reserv deposit; no pets. **Facility:** 86 rooms. 4 stories; interior corridors. **All Rooms:** free movies. **Cards:** AE, CB, DI, DS, MC, VI.

Roll in showers. 🏊 CTV 🚹 ✕ D S

HOLIDAY INN EXPRESS RESTAURANT ROW

Phone: 803/449-5348 36

5/27-8/20 [CP]			2P/1B:	$79- 99	2P/2B:	$79- 99	XP: $10	F18
9/6-9/30 [CP]			2P/1B:	$69- 72	2P/2B:	$72	XP: $10	F18
3/1-5/26 & 8/21-9/5 [CP]			2P/1B:	$69- 74	2P/2B:	$64- 69	XP: $10	F18
12/1-2/28 & 10/1-11/30 [CP]			2P/1B:	$54- 69	2P/2B:	$54- 69	XP: $10	F18

Motel

Location: Just n of jct US 17 bypass & US 17, opposite Galleria Shopping Center. 9551 Hwy 17N 29572. Fax: 803/449-5348. **Terms:** Package plans; no pets. **Facility:** 90 rooms. Nicely appointed rooms. 3 stories; interior corridors. **Fee:** golf privileges. **Dining:** Restaurant nearby. **Services:** Fee: coin laundry. **All Rooms:** combo or shower baths. **Fee:** movies. **Some Rooms:** microwaves, refrigerators. Fee: whirlpools. **Cards:** AE, CB, DI, DS, JCB, MC, VI.

Roll in showers. 🏊 🚐 🚹 CTV ✕ 🖨 D S

MYRTLE BEACH HILTON OCEANFRONT GOLF RESORT

Phone: 803/449-5000 35

5/14-9/6	1P: $129- 219	2P/1B:	$129- 219	2P/2B:	$129- 219	XP: $15	F18
3/27-5/13 & 9/7-11/14	1P: $94- 184	2P/1B:	$94- 184	2P/2B:	$94- 184	XP: $15	F18
12/1-3/26 & 11/15-11/30	1P: $59- 124	2P/1B:	$59- 124	2P/2B:	$59- 124	XP: $15	F18

Resort Hotel

Location: 9 mi n in Arcadian Shores & Golf Resort. 10000 Beach Club Dr 29572-5304. Fax: 803/497-0295. **Terms:** Check-in 4 pm; reserv deposit, 3 day notice; weekly rates; BP, CP avail; package plans; no pets. **Facility:** 381 rooms. All rooms with balcony. 11 suites, $99-$389; 15 stories; interior/exterior corridors; oceanfront; beach, wading pool; 4 lighted tennis courts; volleyball. Fee: 18 holes golf. **Dining & Entertainment:** Dining room; outdoor cafe in season; 6 am-10 pm; $15-$25; cocktails/lounge; poolside entertainment 5/22-9/6. **Services:** valet laundry. **Recreation:** children's program; swimming, surf fishing. Fee: bicycles. **All Rooms:** free & pay movies. **Cards:** AE, DI, DS, MC, VI. *(See color ad p 18 & p 511)*

🏊 🚐 🚹 CTV ✕ D S

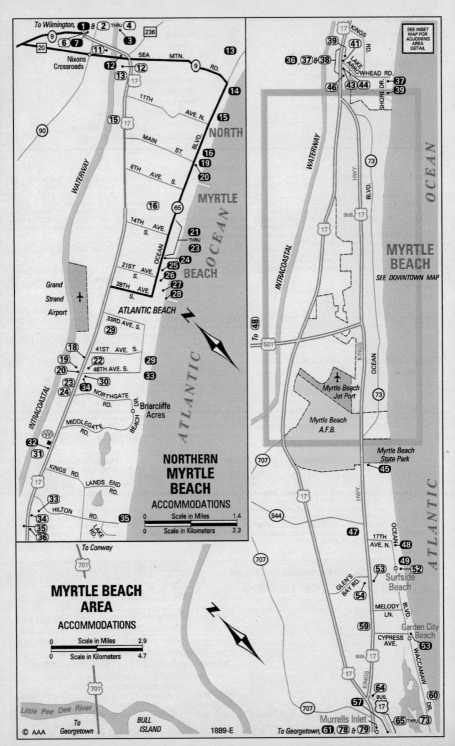

(See map p. 542)

OCEAN CREEK PLANTATION RESORT & CONFERENCE CENTER

Rates Subject to Change
Phone: 803/272-7724 **34**

(AAA)

6/5-8/22	2P/1B:	$83- 190	2P/2B:	$175- 260	XP:	$4
3/20-6/4 & 8/23-8/31	2P/1B:	$63- 150	2P/2B:	$120- 220	XP:	$4
3/6-3/19 & 9/1-10/18	2P/1B:	$55- 105	2P/2B:	$110- 130	XP:	$4
12/1-3/5 & 10/19-11/30	2P/1B:	$37- 95	2P/2B:	$75- 120	XP:	$4

Resort
Complex

Location: On US 17N, opposite Barefoot Landing. 10600 N Kings Hwy 29572. Fax: 803/272-9627. **Terms:** Reserv deposit, 14 day notice, handling fee imposed; no pets. **Facility:** 400 rooms. 64 three-bedroom villas, $260 in season; 3 stories; interior corridors. **Dining:** Restaurant; 6:30 am-11 & 5:30-10 pm; $10-$20. **All Rooms:** free movies. **Some Rooms:** 166 efficiencies, 234 kitchens. **Cards:** AE, DI, DS, MC, VI.
(See color ad inside front cover & p 546)

SANDS BEACH CLUB ALL SUITE RESORT HOTEL

Phone: 803/449-1531 **39**

(AAA) (SAVE)

6/12-8/22		2P/2B:	$160- 215	XP: $10	F18
4/26-6/11 & 8/23-9/6		2P/2B:	$110- 175	XP: $10	F18
3/6-4/25 & 9/7-10/31		2P/2B:	$85- 130	XP: $10	F18
12/1-3/5 & 11/1-11/30		2P/2B:	$55- 85	XP: $10	F18

Suite Hotel

Location: 8 mi n, Arcadian Shores section; Arrowhead Rd off US 17 to beach. 9400 Shore Dr 29572. Fax: 803/449-1879. **Terms:** Reserv deposit, 4 day notice; package plans; no pets. **Facility:** 125 rooms. All rooms with balcony. 95 two-bedroom units. Handling fee imposed; 5-11 stories; interior/exterior corridors; oceanfront; beach, wading pool, whirlpool; 2 lighted tennis courts. Fee: golf privileges. **Dining & Entertainment:** Dining room; 6 am-10 & 6-9 pm; 11 am-3 pm, 6/1-9/1; $8-$16; cocktails/lounge. **Services:** Fee: coin laundry. **Recreation:** children's program in season; swimming. **All Rooms:** kitchens, microwaves, free movies, refrigerators. Fee: safes. **Some Rooms:** Fee: VCP's. **Cards:** AE, CB, DI, DS, MC, VI.

SANDS OCEAN CLUB RESORT

Phone: 803/449-6461 **37**

(AAA) (SAVE)

6/12-8/22	1P: $105- 185	2P/1B: $105- 185	2P/2B: $105- 185	XP: $10	F18
4/26-6/11 & 8/23-9/6	1P: $80- 150	2P/1B: $80- 150	2P/2B: $80- 150	XP: $10	F18
3/6-4/25 & 9/7-10/31	1P: $55- 115	2P/1B: $55- 115	2P/2B: $55- 115	XP: $10	F18
12/1-3/5 & 11/1-11/30	1P: $40- 100	2P/1B: $40- 100	2P/2B: $40- 100	XP: $10	F18

Motor Inn

Location: 8 mi n in Arcadian Shores section; Arrowhead Rd off US 17 to beach. 9550 Shore Dr 29572. Fax: 803/449-1837. **Terms:** Reserv deposit, 4 day notice; package plans; no pets. **Facility:** 460 rooms. Balconies. 79 two-bedroom units. 2- & 3-bedroom suites. Handling fee imposed; 19 stories; interior corridors; oceanfront; beach, sauna, whirlpools; Lazy River water ride. Fee: golf privileges; tennis privileges. **Dining & Entertainment:** Dining room, deli; 6 am-10 pm; $8-$17; cocktails/lounge; entertainment. **Services:** Fee: coin laundry. **Recreation:** children's program in summer; swimming, surf fishing. **All Rooms:** microwaves, refrigerators. Fee: movies, safes. **Some Rooms:** 330 efficiencies, 130 kitchens. **Cards:** AE, CB, DI, DS, MC, VI.

RESTAURANTS

BARON'S STEAKS & CHOPS

Dinner: $16-$25   Phone: 803/497-8970 **44**

Steakhouse

Location: Off US 17N, restaurant row; in the Galleria Shopping Center. 9650 N Kings Hwy 29572. **Hours:** 5:30 pm-11 pm. Closed: Sun, 1/1, 11/26 & 12/25. **Reservations:** accepted. **Features:** casual dress; cocktail lounge; beer & wine only. An atmosphere of turn-of-the-century New York-style steakhouse; antique lithographs & jazz in a dimly lit atmosphere. Roast prime rib, several styles of steak & chops. **Cards:** AE, DI, MC, VI.

CAGNEY'S OLD PLACE

Dinner: $10-$16   Phone: 803/449-3824 **35**

Steak and
Seafood

Location: 8.5 mi n on US 17. 9911 N Kings Hwy 29577. **Hours:** 5 pm-11 pm. Closed: Sun, 11/26 & 12/16-2/9. **Reservations:** suggested. **Features:** casual dress; children's menu; cocktails & lounge. Unique decor. **Cards:** AE, DS, MC, VI.

CAPTAIN BENNETT'S CALABASH SEAFOOD #2

Lunch: $15-$19   Dinner: $15-$19   Phone: 803/449-7865 **38**

Regional Steak
and Seafood

Location: 7 mi from center of town, 17N, at jct US 17N & Lake Arrowhead Rd. 9701 N Kings Hwy 29577. **Hours:** 4 pm-10 pm, Sat & Sun from noon. Closed: 12/25. **Features:** casual dress; children's menu; early bird specials; salad bar; cocktails; buffet. Featuring Calabash-style seafood entrees. A large dining room decorated with a nautical theme. **Cards:** MC, VI.

CHESAPEAKE HOUSE

Dinner: $9-$17   Phone: 803/449-3231 **34**

Seafood

Location: On US 17 in restaurant section. 9918 N Kings Hwy 29572. **Hours:** 4:30 pm-10 pm. Closed: 11/26, 12/24 & 12/25. **Reservations:** accepted. **Features:** casual dress; children's menu; carryout; cocktails & lounge. Casual atmosphere. Some tables with marsh view. Early bird specials in fall & winter. **Cards:** AE, DS, MC, VI.

CHESTNUT HILL

Dinner: $10-$20   Phone: 803/449-3984 **33**

Seafood

Location: 8.5 mi n on US 17, restaurant row. 9922 N Kings Hwy 29572. **Hours:** 5 pm-10 pm, Fri & Sat-11 pm. Closed: 11/26, 12/24 & 12/25. **Reservations:** suggested. **Features:** casual dress; Sunday brunch; children's menu; carryout; cocktails & lounge. Featuring very well prepared prime rib, fresh catch & veal. **Cards:** AE, DI, MC, VI.

CHUCK'S STEAK HOUSE

Dinner: $5-$18   Phone: 803/449-7611 **37**

Steakhouse

Location: On US 17N, on restaurant row; at jct US 17 & Lake Arrowhead Rd; opposite the Galleria. 9695 N Kings Hwy 29577. **Hours:** 5 pm-11 pm, Sun-10 pm. Closed: 11/26 & 12/25. **Reservations:** suggested. **Features:** casual dress; children's menu; carryout; salad bar; cocktails & lounge. Also featuring some fresh seafood entrees; also Mexican & pasta entrees. **Cards:** AE, MC, VI. **Special Value: 10% discount on the price of any entree, excluding beverages, tax and gratuity.**

EL CERRO GRANDE

Lunch: $5-$8   Dinner: $5-$8   Phone: 803/946-9562 **48**

Mexican

Location: 2nd Ave S & US S 17. 108 S Kings Hwy 29577. **Hours:** 11 am-2:30 & 5-10 pm. Closed: 1/1, 11/26 & 12/25. **Reservations:** suggested; for groups. **Features:** casual dress; carryout; cocktails. Good, basic & very authentic food. Dinner is filling & arrives quickly at your table. **Cards:** DI, MC, VI.

HORST GASTHAUS

Dinner: $9-$15   Phone: 803/272-3351 **29**

German

Location: In Windy Hill Section, just off US 17N. 802 37th Ave S 29582. **Hours:** 5 pm-9 pm; 3/1-10/31 to 10 pm. Closed: Sun 11/1-1/31. **Reservations:** suggested. **Features:** casual dress; children's menu; early bird specials; senior's menu; carryout; cocktails & lounge; entertainment. Authentic food served in a cozy Bavarian atmosphere. Nightly German & American sing alongs. **Cards:** AE, DS, MC, VI.

Myrtle Beach's 57-Acre Oceanfront Resort

Ocean Creek
RESORT

10600 North Kings Hwy.
Myrtle Beach, SC 29572
(803) 272-7724
Fax (803) 272-9627
http://www.oceancreek.com
Call Toll Free
1-800-845-0353

- Luxurious accommodations in six separate complexes with daily maid service.
- All guests enjoy the indoor pool, whirlpool and large outdoor pools in the Lodge area.
- Oceanfront Beach Club with large outdoor pool, sundecks, kiddie pool, pool-side bar with grill and playground.
- Enjoy our Four Seasons Restaurant
- Golf Packages at over 90 courses
- On-site tennis courts (lights available for night play).
- Located across the street is Barefoot Landing offering over 113 shops and restaurants plus the famed Alabama Theatre.
- Nearby are five major shopping complexes including Waccamaw Pottery and Outlet Malls.
- Great Entertainment Packages available.

1998 RATES	Lodges (Studio,1BR,2BR)	Villas (1BR, 2BR,3BR)	Towers (2BR, 3BR)
1/1-2/4 11/29-12/31	42-64	51-77	77-97
2/5-2/18 10/18-11/28	47-70	59-87	90-117
2/19-3/18 9/20-10/17	52-78	65-95	100-122
3/19-6/3 9/7-9/19	65-112	90-135	122-182
6/4-8/21	85-142	112-192	175-270
8/22-9/6	80-117	102-152	182-222

Rates are for accommodating two adults and two children under 18.

10% OFF for AAA Members, Senior Citizens, Weekly Stays or 5 and 6 night vacations arriving on Sunday. (Excluding Oceanfront accommodations June 13-Aug. 21,1998.)

20% Discount available during certain dates. Minimum stay required. Call for details. Only one discount per stay. Golf, Entertainment and Conference packages not subject to discounts. A surcharge will apply on weekend reservations, some holidays and special events. Discounts are off rack rates.

©1998-Ocean Creek Resort

(See map p. 542)

NAKATO AT GALLERIA   **Dinner:** $10-$20   **Phone:** 803/449-4433 43
◆◆   **Location:** 8 mi n on US 17; in Galleria Shopping Center at Lake Arrowhead Rd & US 17, restaurant row.
Ethnic   9600 N Kings Hwy 29577. **Hours:** 5 pm-10 pm. Closed: 12/24 & 12/25. **Reservations:** suggested.
          Features: casual dress; children's menu; carryout; cocktails & lounge. Hibachi-style cooking at communal
tables. Steak, chicken & shrimp prepared Japanese-style. Sushi bar. **Cards:** AE, CB, DI, MC, VI.

NAKATO JAPANESE STEAK HOUSE   **Dinner:** $11-$20   **Phone:** 803/449-3344 36
🔺🔺🔺   **Location:** 8.5 mi n on US 17 on restaurant row. 9912 N Kings Hwy 29577. **Hours:** 5 pm-10 pm. Closed:
         12/24 & 12/25. **Reservations:** suggested. **Features:** casual dress; children's menu; cocktails & lounge.
◆◆   Hibachi-style cooking at communal tables. Steak, chicken, shrimp & selected seafood prepared. Sushi bar &
Ethnic   Robata Grill avail. **Cards:** AE, CB, DI, DS, MC, VI.

THE OLD PRO'S TABLE RESTAURANT & GOLF MUSEUM   **Dinner:** $10-$21   **Phone:** 803/272-6060 30
◆◆   **Location:** On US 17N; in Windy Hill area. 29598. **Hours:** 5:30 pm-10 pm. Closed: Sun & Mon in winter.
Steak and   **Reservations:** suggested. **Features:** casual dress; children's menu; carryout; salad bar; cocktails & lounge.
Seafood   Featuring fresh cut prime rib & fresh fish nightly. Dining rooms with golf related memorabilia. **Cards:** AE, MC,
         VI.   ❌

ROSSI'S ITALIAN RESTAURANT   **Dinner:** $9-$28   **Phone:** 803/449-0481 46
◆◆   **Location:** US 17N; restaurant row in Galleria Plaza. 9636 N Kings Hwy 29572. **Hours:** 4:30 pm-11 pm.
Italian   Closed: Sun & 12/15-12/30. **Reservations:** suggested. **Features:** casual dress; children's menu; carryout;
         cocktails & lounge. Featuring pasta, veal, seafood & beef. **Cards:** AE, CB, DI, DS, MC, VI.

SAM SNEAD'S TAVERN   **Dinner:** $6-$21   **Phone:** 803/497-0580 41
◆◆   **Location:** On US 17 N; in restaurant row. 9708 N Kings Hwy 29572. **Hours:** 4 pm-11 pm. Closed: 12/24 &
Steak and   12/25. **Reservations:** accepted. **Features:** casual dress; children's menu; carryout; cocktails & lounge.
Seafood   Casual elegance from soft lights to polished wood. From deep-fried niblicks (delicate pastry filled with puree
     of smoked chicken & peppers) to hand-rubbed, oak-smoked ribs served with homemade bourbon barbecue
sauce. **Cards:** AE, DS, MC, VI.   ❌

SHENANIGAN'S   **Dinner:** $6-$16   **Phone:** 803/272-1171 31
🔺🔺🔺   **Location:** On US 17, just s of Briarcliffe Mall. 10131 N Kings Hwy 29572. **Hours:** 4 pm-10:30 pm, Fri &
         Sat-11 pm, Sun-10 pm. Closed: 12/24 & 12/25. **Features:** casual dress; children's menu; cocktails & lounge.
◆◆   Featuring USDA prime & certified Angus beef, slow roasted prime rib & baby back ribs. Also fresh pasta &
Steak and   seafood. **Cards:** AE, DI, DS, MC, VI.
Seafood   ❌

THOROUGHBREDS   **Dinner:** $10-$18   **Phone:** 803/497-2636 39
🔺🔺🔺   **Location:** On US 17N; on restaurant row, between Magnolia Plaza & the Galleria. 9706 N Kings Hwy 29572.
         Hours: 5 pm-midnight. Closed: 1/1, 12/24 & 12/25. **Reservations:** suggested. **Features:** casual dress;
◆◆◆   children's menu; early bird specials; cocktails & lounge. Featuring very well prepared seafood, steak, veal &
Continental poultry. Some tableside preparation of food. Extensive wine list. **Cards:** AE, DI, DS, MC, VI.   ❌

NORTH MYRTLE BEACH—8,600 (See map p. 542; index p. 540)
LODGINGS

BAYWATCH INN   Rates Subject to Change   **Phone:** 803/272-5156 27

◆◆	6/7-8/17	2P/1B:	$99	2P/2B:	$99- 139	XP: $5	F12
Motel	4/11-6/6 & 8/18-9/22	2P/1B:	$39	2P/2B:	$79- 99	XP: $5	F12
	3/8-4/10 & 9/23-10/19	2P/1B:	$30	2P/2B:	$69- 79	XP: $5	F12
	12/1-3/7 & 10/20-11/30	2P/1B:	$29	2P/2B:	$49- 59	XP: $5	F12

Location: S Ocean Blvd & 27th Ave S. 2701 S Ocean Blvd 29582. Fax: 803/272-9987. **Terms:** Reserv deposit, 14 day notice, handling fee imposed; 4 night min stay, 6/1-8/30; no pets. **Facility:** 44 rooms. 3 stories; exterior corridors. **Some Rooms:** 19 efficiencies. **Cards:** AE, DS, MC, VI.   🛰 CTV D

BEL-AIRE MOTEL   Rates Subject to Change   **Phone:** 803/249-1434 19

🔺🔺🔺	6/14-8/17				
	5/17-6/13				
◆◆	3/29-5/16 & 8/18-9/30	2P/2B:	$67- 105	XP: $7	F12
Motel	12/1-3/28 & 10/1-11/30	2P/2B:	$55- 84	XP: $7	F12
		2P/2B:	$45- 72	XP: $6	F12
		2P/2B:	$26- 45	XP: $7	F12

Location: 2 blks n. 102 N Ocean Blvd 29582. Fax: 803/249-5617. **Terms:** Reserv deposit, 14 day notice; no pets. **Facility:** 74 rooms. Handling fee imposed; 2 stories; exterior corridors. **Some Rooms:** 49 efficiencies, 10 kitchens. **Cards:** AE, MC, VI.   🛰 CTV D

BLOCKADE RUNNER MOTOR INN   Rates Subject to Change   **Phone:** 803/249-3561 14

🔺🔺🔺	6/1-8/17	2P/2B:	$82- 85	XP: $4	
	4/1-5/31 & 8/18-10/11	2P/2B:	$57- 59	XP: $4	
◆◆	3/1-3/31 & 10/12-11/8	2P/2B:	$47- 49	XP: $4	
Motel	12/1-2/28 & 11/9-11/30	2P/2B:	$38- 41	XP: $4	

Location: 1.5 mi n on SR 65. 1910 N Ocean Blvd 29582. Fax: 803/249-2643. **Terms:** Reserv deposit, 4 day notice; no pets. **Facility:** 72 rooms. Handling fee imposed; 5 stories; exterior corridors. **Dining:** Coffee shop; 6 am-2:30 pm; $8-$14. **All Rooms:** free movies. **Some Rooms:** 50 efficiencies. **Cards:** AE, MC, VI. 🛰 CTV ❌ D

BLUE WATER INN   Rates Subject to Change   **Phone:** 803/272-5151 25

🔺🔺🔺	6/14-8/18	2P/2B:	$69- 119	XP: $6	D12
	5/17-6/13 & 8/19-9/1	2P/2B:	$59- 99	XP: $6	D12
◆◆	3/30-5/16 & 9/2-10/1	2P/2B:	$54- 79	XP: $6	D12
Motel	12/1-3/29 & 10/2-11/30	2P/2B:	$35- 52	XP: $6	D12

Location: 20th Ave S & S Ocean Blvd. 2001 S Ocean Blvd 29582. Fax: 803/272-7897. **Terms:** Reserv deposit, 14 day notice, handling fee imposed; no pets. **Facility:** 38 rooms. 3 stories; exterior corridors. **Some Rooms:** 27 efficiencies. **Cards:** AE, MC, VI.   🛰 CTV D

(See map p. 542)

BY THE SEA MOTEL — Rates Subject to Change — Phone: 803/272-5512 — 24
◆◆◆

	6/1-8/20	1P: $83			2P/2B: $89	XP: $5-10	F10
Motel	4/1-5/31 & 8/21-9/17		2P/1B:	$64		XP: $5-10	F10
	2/28-3/31		2P/1B:	$39		XP: $5-10	F10
	9/18-10/31		2P/1B:	$49		XP: $5-10	F10

Location: S Ocean Blvd & 17th Ave S. 1717 S Ocean Blvd 29282. Fax: 803/272-6101. **Terms:** Open 2/28-10/31; reserv deposit, 21 day notice; no pets. **Facility:** 26 rooms. Handling fee imposed; 3 stories, no elevator; exterior corridors. **All Rooms:** efficiencies. **Cards:** AE, MC, VI. (CTV) (D)

CHERRY GROVE MANOR & CAROLINA RESORTS CONDOS — Phone: 803/249-2731 — 15
(AAA) (SAVE)

	5/23-9/1	1P: $55- 95	2P/1B:	$65- 105	2P/2B: $85- 155	XP: $5	F12
	5/1-5/22 & 9/2-9/30	1P: $43- 75	2P/1B:	$55- 85	2P/2B: $65- 105	XP: $5	F12
◆ ◆	12/1-4/30 & 10/1-11/30	1P: $39- 65	2P/1B:	$45- 75	2P/2B: $55- 95	XP: $5	F12

Apartment
Motel — **Location:** In Cherry Grove section. 2104 N Ocean Blvd 29582 (PO Box 3359). Fax: 803/249-6699. **Terms:** Reserv deposit, 14 day notice, handling fee imposed; package plans; no pets. **Facility:** 80 rooms. Family oriented motel units, cottages & condos. Some oceanfront. 14 two-bedroom units, 32 three-bedroom units. 40 whirlpool rms, extra charge; 2 stories; interior/exterior corridors; beach, wading pool; playground. Fee: golf privileges. **Dining:** Restaurant nearby. **Services:** Fee: coin laundry. **Recreation:** swimming, surf fishing. **All Rooms:** coffeemakers, free movies, refrigerators, combo or shower baths. Fee: VCP. **Some Rooms:** 33 efficiencies, 40 kitchens, microwaves, radios. **Cards:** AE, DS, MC, VI. **Special Amenities: Free local telephone calls and free room upgrade (subject to availability with advanced reservations).** (CTV) (X) (D)

HAMPTON INN HARBORGATE — Rates Subject to Change — Phone: 803/249-1997 — 12
◆◆◆ — All Year [CP] — 1P: $110- 180 — 2P/1B: $110- 180 — 2P/2B: $110- 180

Motel — **Location:** From US 17 & Cherry Grove exit & SR 9 at corner of SR 9 & Little Neck Rd. 2120 Sea Mountain Hwy 29597 (PO Box 4330, 29582). Fax: 803/249-1998. **Terms:** Reserv deposit; no pets. **Facility:** 101 rooms. 5 stories; interior corridors. **All Rooms:** free & pay movies. **Cards:** AE, CB, DI, DS, MC, VI. *(See color ad p 508)*

Roll in showers. (CTV) (X) (D) (S)

HELMS VISTA OCEANFRONT MOTEL — Rates Subject to Change — Phone: 803/249-2521 — 16
(AAA)

	6/6-8/31	1P: $42- 66	2P/1B: $42- 66	2P/2B: $48- 109	XP: $6-8	F12
	5/2-6/5	1P: $46- 50	2P/1B: $45- 50	2P/2B: $52- 80	XP: $6-7	F12
◆ ◆	1/24-5/1 & 9/1-10/11	1P: $21- 38	2P/1B: $21- 38	2P/2B: $26- 57	XP: $4-6	F12
Motel	12/1-1/23 & 10/12-11/30	1P: $19- 34	2P/1B: $19- 34	2P/2B: $20- 49	XP: $3-5	F12

Location: 0.3 mi n from Main St; 3rd Ave N & N Ocean Blvd. 300 N Ocean Blvd 29582. Fax: 803/249-6354. **Terms:** Reserv deposit, 14 day notice; no pets. **Facility:** 73 rooms. Handling fee imposed; 2 stories; exterior corridors. **Some Rooms:** 55 efficiencies. **Cards:** AE, DI, DS, MC, VI. *(See ad p 541)* (CTV) (D)

HOLIDAY INN-NORTH — Phone: 803/272-6153 — 28
(AAA) (SAVE)

	5/1-8/16	1P: $129- 159	2P/1B: $129- 199	2P/2B: $139- 199	XP: $10	F18
	4/1-4/30 & 8/17-10/25	1P: $99	2P/1B: $99	2P/2B: $99	XP: $10	F18
◆◆◆	3/1-3/31 & 10/26-11/30	1P: $89	2P/1B: $89	2P/2B: $89	XP: $10	F18
Motor Inn	12/1-2/28	1P: $49	2P/1B: $49	2P/2B: $49	XP: $10	F18

Location: From US 17, 0.3 mi e, 27th Ave S & S Ocean Blvd. 2713 S Ocean Blvd 29582. Fax: 803/272-4963. **Terms:** Package plans; no pets. **Facility:** 134 rooms. Some rooms overlooking the ocean. 2 stories; interior corridors; beach. Fee: golf privileges. **Dining & Entertainment:** Dining room; 6:30-11 am & 5:30-9 pm; $9-$15; cocktails/lounge; entertainment. **Services:** Fee: coin laundry. **Recreation:** swimming, surf fishing. **Some Rooms:** microwaves, refrigerators. **Cards:** AE, CB, DI, DS, JCB, MC, VI. (CTV) (X) (D)

INLET MOTEL — Phone: 803/249-1853 — 13
(AAA) (SAVE)

	6/14-8/31		2P/1B:	$53- 69	2P/2B: $49- 59	XP: $6	F12
	5/16-6/13		2P/1B:	$42- 58	2P/2B: $39- 49	XP: $6	F12
◆ ◆	3/21-5/15 & 9/1-9/30		2P/1B:	$35- 45		XP: $6	F12
Motel	12/1-3/20 & 10/1-11/30		2P/1B:	$20- 33		XP: $6	F12

Location: From US 17, e on SR 9/Sea Mtn Hwy, 1.8 mi n. 5409 N Ocean Blvd 29582. Fax: 803/249-8661. **Terms:** Reserv deposit, 14 day notice; no pets. **Facility:** 28 rooms. 8 two-room units, $74-$84 in season. Handling fee imposed; 2 stories; exterior corridors. **All Rooms:** free movies. **Some Rooms:** 24 efficiencies. **Cards:** AE, MC, VI. (CTV) (D)

THE MARION EARL MOTEL — Rates Subject to Change — Phone: 803/272-5181 — 21
(AAA)

	6/14-8/17		2P/2B: $97- 105	XP: $6	
	5/17-6/13 & 8/18-9/2		2P/2B: $80- 86	XP: $6	
◆ ◆	3/29-5/16 & 9/3-9/30		2P/2B: $62- 72	XP: $6	
Motel	12/1-3/28 & 10/1-11/30		2P/2B: $42- 46	XP: $6	

Location: 14th Ave S & S Ocean Blvd. 1401 S Ocean Blvd 29582. Fax: 803/361-0097. **Terms:** Reserv deposit, 14 day notice; no pets. **Facility:** 51 rooms. Handling fee imposed; 3 stories; exterior corridors. **Some Rooms:** 43 efficiencies. **Cards:** AE, MC, VI. (CTV) (D)

OCEAN DRIVE BEACH & GOLF RESORT — Rates Subject to Change — Phone: 803/249-1436 — 20
(AAA)

	6/20-8/16	1P: $108- 139	2P/1B: $108- 139	2P/2B: $108- 139	XP: $8	F16
	5/9-6/19 & 8/17-8/31	1P: $103- 132	2P/1B: $103- 132	2P/2B: $103- 132	XP: $8	F16
Hotel	3/7-5/8 & 9/1-10/18	1P: $65- 82	2P/1B: $65- 82	2P/2B: $65- 82	XP: $8	F16
	12/1-3/6 & 10/19-11/30	1P: $36- 58	2P/1B: $36- 58	2P/2B: $36- 58	XP: $8	F16

Too new to rate; **Location:** N Ocean Blvd & Main St. 98 N Ocean Blvd 29597 (PO Box 296). Fax: 803/249-1437. **Terms:** Sr. discount; reserv deposit, 7 day notice, handling fee imposed; no pets. **Facility:** 177 rooms. Scheduled to open June 1997; 12 stories; interior/exterior corridors. **Dining:** 2 restaurants; 7 am-10 pm. **Some Rooms:** 90 efficiencies, 87 kitchens. **Cards:** AE, DI, DS, MC, VI. *(See color ad p 549)*

Roll in showers. (CTV) (X) (D) (S)

(See map p. 542)

OCEAN SANDS RESORT
AAA SAVE
◆◆◆
Motel

	Phone: 803/272-6101	23
6/1-8/22 [CP]	2P/2B: $109- 139 XP: $5	
4/10-5/31 & 8/23-9/19 [CP]	2P/2B: $75- 100 XP: $5	
3/3-4/9 & 9/20-10/21 [CP]	2P/2B: $60- 79 XP: $5	
12/1-3/2 & 10/22-11/30 [CP]	2P/2B: $37- 54 XP: $5	

Location: S Ocean Blvd & 16th Ave S. 1525 S Ocean Blvd 29582. Fax: 803/272-7908. **Terms:** Reserv deposit, 21 day notice; 4 night min stay, in season; no pets. **Facility:** 95 rooms. Handling fee imposed; 4-10 stories; exterior corridors; oceanfront; beach, wading pool, whirlpool; Lazy River ride, sand volleyball, video arcade. **Services:** Fee: coin laundry. **Recreation:** swimming. **All Rooms:** coffeemakers, microwaves, refrigerators, combo or shower baths. **Some Rooms:** 92 efficiencies. **Cards:** AE, DS, MC, VI. **Special Amenities:** Free breakfast and free newspaper. *(See color ad below)*

RED TREE INN
AAA
◆
Motel

	Rates Subject to Change	Phone: 803/272-5353	22
6/1-8/31		2P/2B: $74- 99 XP: $5	D10
4/1-5/31 & 9/1-9/30		2P/2B: $49- 69 XP: $5	D10
2/1-3/31 & 10/1-11/15		2P/2B: $37- 49 XP: $5	D10

Location: 1.3 mi s from Main St; 14th Ave S & S Ocean Blvd. 1415 S Ocean Blvd 29582. **Terms:** Open 2/1-11/15; reserv deposit, 7 day notice, handling fee imposed; no pets. **Facility:** 50 rooms. 5 stories; exterior corridors. **Some Rooms:** 24 efficiencies. **Cards:** AE, CB, DI, DS, MC, VI.

THE SEASIDE INN-OCEANFRONT
AAA
◆◆
Motel

		Rates Subject to Change			Phone: 803/272-5166	26
5/30-8/23	1P: $46- 89	2P/1B: $46- 89	2P/2B: $57- 109	XP: $7-8	F12
3/14-5/29 & 8/24-8/31	1P: $44- 61	2P/1B: $44- 61	2P/2B: $51- 75	XP: $5-7	F12
2/28-3/13 & 9/1-10/11	1P: $35- 52	2P/1B: $35- 52	2P/2B: $46- 66	XP: $5	F12
12/1-2/27 & 10/12-11/30	1P: $19- 45	2P/1B: $19- 45	2P/2B: $24- 58	XP: $3-5	F12

Location: In Cresent Beach section, 23rd Ave S & S Ocean Blvd. 2301 S Ocean Blvd 29582. Fax: 803/272-3786. **Terms:** Reserv deposit, 14 day notice; no pets. **Facility:** 48 rooms. Handling fee imposed; 3 stories; exterior corridors. **All Rooms:** efficiencies, free movies. **Cards:** AE, DI, DS, MC, VI. *(See ad below)*

TRICIA-LYN & CARRIAGE HOUSE MOTELS
AAA SAVE
◆
Motel

	Phone: 803/272-6570	29
6/10-8/19	2P/2B: $75- 125 XP: $40	F16
5/12-6/9 & 8/20-9/3	2P/2B: $60- 105 XP: $6	F16
4/1-5/11 & 9/4-9/30	2P/2B: $45- 89 XP: $6	F16
12/1-3/31 & 10/1-11/30	2P/2B: $39- 69 XP: $6	F16

Location: 46th Ave S & S Ocean Blvd. 4601 S Ocean Blvd 29582 (PO Box 2219, 29598). Fax: 803/272-6570. **Terms:** Reserv deposit, 14 day notice; weekly/monthly rates; package plans; no pets. **Facility:** 40 rooms. Modest traditional motel accommodation in 2 adjacent motels; 1 beach front & 1 across the street from beach. 4 two-bedroom units. Handling fee imposed; 2 stories; exterior corridors; beach. Fee: golf privileges. **Services:** Fee: coin laundry. **Recreation:** swimming. **All Rooms:** refrigerators. **Some Rooms:** coffeemakers, 26 kitchens, microwaves. **Cards:** MC, VI.

(See map p. 542)

RESTAURANTS

ALABAMA GRILL   **Lunch:** $4-$14   **Dinner:** $4-$14   **Phone:** 803/361-2262   20
◆◆   **Location:** In Barefoot Landing. 4390 Hwy 17 S 29582. **Hours:** 11 am-10 pm. Closed: 1/1 & 12/25.
American   **Features:** casual dress; children's menu; health conscious menu; carryout; cocktails & lounge. On the Intracoastal Waterway with a beautiful view, the interior chock full of memorabilia from the band Alabama & other music artists. **Cards:** AE, DI, MC, VI.   ✕

HEMINGWAY'S   **Dinner:** $11-$19   **Phone:** 803/272-6118   19
◆◆   **Location:** In Barefoot Landing. 4726 S Hwy 17 29872. **Hours:** 5-10 pm. Closed: 1/1 & 12/25.
Steak and   **Reservations:** accepted. **Features:** dressy casual; children's menu; carryout; cocktails & lounge. **Cards:** AE, CB, DI, DS, MC, VI.
Seafood

JOE'S BAR & GRILL   **Dinner:** $14-$17   **Phone:** 803/272-4666   22
◆◆   **Location:** Just off of US 17S across from Barefoot Landing. 810 Conway St 29582. **Hours:** 5 pm-10 pm.
Continental   Closed: 11/26 & 12/24-12/26. **Reservations:** suggested. **Features:** children's menu; early bird specials; carryout; cocktails & lounge. In an attractive old home with a deck overlooking the marsh. Specialties include shrimp & scallops Alfredo, steak au poivre, scallopes meuniere. **Cards:** AE, DS, MC, VI.

MAD BOAR BREWHOUSE   **Lunch:** $6-$9   **Dinner:** $5-$16   **Phone:** 803/272-7000   23
◆◆   **Location:** 4706 S Hwy 17 29582. **Hours:** 11 am-11 pm. **Reservations:** accepted; for dinner.
American   **Features:** casual dress; beer only. **Cards:** AE, DI, MC, VI.

MARINA RAW BAR   **Lunch:** $4-$8   **Dinner:** $8-$17   **Phone:** 803/249-3972   13
AAA   **Location:** Off US 17 at 11th Ave N, just behind Chase's Place. 1203 N Hwy 17 29582. **Hours:** 11:30 am-10
◆   pm. Closed: 11/26 & 12/25. **Features:** casual dress; children's menu; senior's menu; carryout; cocktails & lounge. Off Intracoastal Waterway. Fresh shell fish & steak. **Cards:** AE, MC, VI.
Seafood

MARKER 350   **Dinner:** $14-$18   **Phone:** 803/249-3888   11
◆◆   **Location:** Just w of US 17 via Cherry Grove exit; in Harbour Gate Marina. 4 Harbour Pl 29587. **Hours:** 5
Seafood   pm-10 pm. Closed: 1/1, 12/24 & 12/25. **Reservations:** suggested. **Features:** casual dress; children's menu; cocktails; a la carte. Dishes like grouper with pine nuts, shrimp in olive oil with black olives, plus capers & tomatoes on angel hair pasta, served in pleasant setting overlooking marina. Drinks can be enjoyed on wrap-around porches. **Cards:** AE, MC, VI.   ✕

OAK HARBOUR RESTAURANT   **Dinner:** $11-$19   **Phone:** 803/249-4737   12
AAA   **Location:** From US 17N, 0.3 mi n on 13th Ave. 1407 13th Ave N 29582. **Hours:** 5 pm-9 pm, -10 pm in
◆◆   season. Closed: 11/26, 12/16-12/28 & Sun 12/1-2/28. **Reservations:** suggested. **Features:** casual dress;
American   children's menu; early bird specials; carryout; cocktails. Very well prepared entrees featuring various meat & fresh seafood. Served in a cozy setting, some seating on the patio, weather permitting, overlooking a harbour area. **Cards:** AE, DI, DS, MC, VI.

"THE ORIGINAL" UMBERTO'S AT BAREFOOT LANDING   **Dinner:** $13-$19   **Phone:** 803/272-1176   24
◆◆   **Location:** US Hwy 17S. Barefoot Landing 29582. **Hours:** 5:30 pm-10 pm. **Reservations:** suggested.
Italian   **Features:** casual dress; children's menu; cocktails. Featuring veal, lamb & pork chops as well as some seafood & pasta entrees with an Italian flair. **Cards:** AE, MC, VI.

OUTRIGGER SEAFOOD HOUSE   **Dinner:** $7-$17   **Phone:** 803/272-8032   16
◆◆   **Location:** US 17 S & 14th Ave S. 1434 US 17 S 29582. **Hours:** 5 pm-10 pm. Closed: 12/1-1/31 & Sun
Seafood   11/1-11/30. **Reservations:** accepted; for large groups. **Features:** casual dress; children's menu; early bird specials; cocktails & lounge. A large seafood house catering to the fried seafood crowd. 2-item or 4-item combination platters. A tip: the steamed spice shrimp with secret sauce, also the mustard sauce served with hushpuppies. Popular, so expect a wait. **Cards:** AE, DI, DS, MC, VI.

SANTA FE STATION   **Dinner:** $6-$19   **Phone:** 803/249-3463   15
◆◆   **Location:** At US 17 N & 11th Ave N. 1101 US 17 N 29582. **Hours:** 4 pm-11 pm. Closed: 12/24-12/30.
American   **Reservations:** accepted; off season. **Features:** children's menu; early bird specials; carryout; cocktails & lounge. A fun casual place with an eclectic interior built around an old railroad. Entrees range from healthy salad & fresh seafood to large sandwiches, steak, burgers, chicken & ribs. **Cards:** AE, MC, VI.   ✕

TBONZ GILL & GRILL   **Lunch:** $5-$8   **Dinner:** $5-$17   **Phone:** 803/272-7111   18
◆◆   **Location:** Barefoot Landing, on US 17 S. 4732 Hwy 17 S 29582. **Hours:** 11 am-10 pm, Fri & Sat-10:30 pm.
Steak and   Closed: 11/26,12/25. **Reservations:** accepted; for large groups. **Features:** casual dress; children's menu;
Seafood   early bird specials; carryout; cocktails & lounge. In a pleasant setting with high ceilings, ceiling fans, wood & plants. Fresh seafood, low country dishes, burgers, lite snacks. **Cards:** AE, MC, VI.   ✕

PAWLEYS ISLAND—200

LODGINGS

PAWLEYS PLANTATION COUNTRY CLUB VILLAS   **Phone:** 803/237-6100

AAA SAVE	3/20-5/30	2P/2B:	$90- 210	XP: $10	F18
	9/7-11/7	2P/2B:	$80- 195	XP: $10	F18
◆◆◆	3/6-3/19	2P/2B:	$80- 190	XP: $10	F18
Resort Motor	12/1-3/5, 5/31-9/6 &				
Inn	11/8-11/30	2P/2B:	$70- 175	XP: $10	F18

Location: US 17 29585 (PO Box 2070). Fax: 803/237-0418. **Terms:** Reserv deposit, 4 day notice; weekly rates; package plans; no pets. **Facility:** 109 rooms. Villas located on 1st & 9th fairways, luxuriously decorated & furnished. Most units with fireplace, screened porch & open patio. 101 two-bedroom units, 7 three-bedroom units, $230; $170 off season. Rates for up to 6 persons. Handling fee imposed; 1 story; exterior corridors; putting green. Fee: 18 holes golf, golf instruction; 2 lighted tennis courts. **Dining:** Dining room; 6 am-9:30, noon-3:30 & 6-9 pm; dinner served Tues & Thurs evenings only; $10-$16; cocktails. **Services:** guest laundry; area transportation. **All Rooms:** coffeemakers, kitchens, microwaves, free movies. **Some Rooms:** Fee: whirlpools. **Cards:** AE, CB, DI, DS, MC, VI.   🛰 🛖 ✈ CTV 🌀 D

RAMADA INN
◆◆
Motor Inn

Rates Subject to Change

5/24-9/3	1P:	$74- 94	2P/1B:	$84- 104	2P/2B:	$84- 104	XP: $10	F18
3/1-5/23 & 9/4-10/31	1P:	$54- 74	2P/1B:	$64- 84	2P/2B:	$64- 84	XP: $10	F18
12/1-2/28 & 11/1-11/30	1P:	$44- 64	2P/1B:	$54- 74	2P/2B:	$54- 74	XP: $10	F18

Phone: 803/237-4261

Location: 1 mi s on US 17. 29585 (PO Box 2217). Fax: 803/237-9703. **Terms:** Sr. discount; no pets. **Facility:** 98 rooms. 2 stories; exterior corridors. **Dining:** Dining room; 6 am-10:30 & 6-10 pm; $7-$10. **All Rooms:** free & pay movies. **Cards:** AE, CB, DI, DS, JCB, MC, VI.   🛏 CTV ✕ D

RESTAURANTS

FRANK'S
◆◆◆
American

Dinner: $20-$35   Phone: 803/237-3030

Location: On US 17 just s from N Causeway Rd. 50 Ocean Hwy 29585. **Hours:** 6 pm-10 pm. Closed: Sun, 1/1, 11/26 & 12/25. **Reservations:** suggested. **Features:** casual dress; children's menu; health conscious menu; carryout; cocktails & lounge. Casual outback is a little cottage tucked away behind more upscale Frank's. Gourmet food, mostly seafood dishes, prepared in unique & exciting ways. Also outside dining under oak trees. **Cards:** DS, MC, VI.

ISLAND CAFE & DELI
◆◆
Regional
American

Lunch: $3-$10   Dinner: $8-$15   Phone: 803/237-9527

Location: In the Island Shops shopping center. US 17 S 29585. **Hours:** 11:30 am-10 pm. Closed: 11/26 & 12/25. **Reservations:** suggested. **Features:** casual dress; children's menu; early bird specials; carryout; cocktails. Locally popular casual cafe featuring seafood & comfort foods; outdoor dining avail in season. **Cards:** MC, VI.   ✕

THE LITCHFIELD MAYOR'S HOUSE
◆◆◆
Continental

Lunch: $4-$10   Dinner: $12-$19   Phone: 803/237-9082

Location: In the Litchfield Village Shops. 2614 Hwy 17 S 29585. **Hours:** 11:45 am-2:30 & 6-10 pm; Sat from 6 pm. Closed: Sun. **Reservations:** accepted. **Features:** casual dress; children's menu; carryout; cocktails & lounge. Very nicely presented entrees, some French influence as well as local touches. **Cards:** AE, CB, DI, DS, MC, VI.   ✕

OCEAN DRAGON
◆
Chinese

Dinner: $4-$11   Phone: 803/237-9988

Location: Food Lion Shopping Center. 9380 Ocean Hwy 29585. **Hours:** 11 am-10 pm, Thurs & Fri-10:30 pm. Closed: Sun. **Features:** Try the Happy Family, which is sliced beef, chicken, jumbo shrimp, roast pork & scallops sauteed with mushrooms, baby corn, bamboo shoots & snow peas. Take-out or eat-in.

OUTBACK AT FRANK'S
◆◆
Regional
Continental

Lunch: $7-$12   Dinner: $8-$19   Phone: 803/237-1777

Location: On US 17, just s from N Causeway Rd. 50 Ocean Hwy 29585. **Hours:** 11:30 am-3 & 6-10 pm, Mon-Sat. Closed major holidays & Sun. **Reservations:** suggested. **Features:** casual dress; children's menu; health conscious menu; carryout; cocktails & lounge; entertainment. Small cottage tucked behind more upscale restaurant. Quite casual atmosphere. **Cards:** DS, MC, VI.   ✕

SURFSIDE BEACH—3,800   (See map p. 542; index p. 540)

LODGINGS

DAYS INN SURFSIDE PIER RESORT
AAA SAVE
◆◆
Motor Inn

Phone: 803/238-4444   49

6/1-9/5	1P: $105- 145	2P/1B:	$115- 155	2P/2B:	$115- 155	XP: $10	F12
5/1-5/31	1P: $95- 125	2P/1B:	$105- 135	2P/2B:	$105- 135	XP: $10	F12
2/1-4/30 & 9/6-10/31	1P: $65- 85	2P/1B:	$75- 95	2P/2B:	$75- 95	XP: $10	F12
12/1-1/31 & 11/1-11/30	1P: $35- 45	2P/1B:	$45- 55	2P/2B:	$45- 55	XP: $10	F12

Location: Surfside Dr & S Ocean Blvd. 15 S Ocean Blvd 29575. Fax: 803/238-4264. **Terms:** Reserv deposit; weekly/monthly rates; package plans; no pets. **Facility:** 157 rooms. All rooms with ocean view, some with balcony. 8 stories; interior corridors; oceanfront; beach, whirlpools. Fee: golf privileges. **Dining & Entertainment:** Restaurant; 6 am-9 pm; $5-$9; cocktails/lounge. **Services:** valet laundry. **Recreation:** swimming. **All Rooms:** Fee: movies, safes. **Cards:** AE, CB, DI, DS, MC, VI.   🛏 🐕 CTV ✕ D

(See map p. 542)

HOLIDAY INN SUNSPREE

△△△ ◆◆◆ Motor Inn

	Rates Subject to Change			Phone: 803/238-5601	48
5/27-8/31	1P: $99- 159	2P/1B: $99- 159	2P/2B: $99- 159	XP: $10	F19
9/1-9/28	1P: $59- 99	2P/1B: $59- 99	2P/2B: $59- 99	XP: $10	F19
4/1-5/26	1P: $45- 99	2P/1B: $45- 99	2P/2B: $45- 99	XP: $10	F19
12/1-3/31 & 9/29-11/30	1P: $39- 69	2P/1B: $39- 69	2P/2B: $39- 69	XP: $10	F19

Location: At 16th Ave & N Ocean Blvd. 1601 N Ocean Blvd 29575. Fax: 803/238-4758. **Terms:** No pets. **Facility:** 133 rooms. 6 stories; interior corridors. **Dining:** Restaurant; 7 am-2 & 5:30-10 pm; $7-$15. **All Rooms:** Fee: movies. **Cards:** AE, CB, DI, DS, JCB, MC, VI. *(See color ad p 552)* 🛏 [CTV] [X] [D]

MYRTLE BEACH RESORT VACATION RENTALS, INC

△△△ [SAVE] ◆◆◆ Resort Cottage

			Phone: 803/238-4994	45
6/10-8/20		2P/2B: $110- 195	XP: $8	F12
5/20-6/9 & 8/21-9/28		2P/2B: $90- 150	XP: $8	F12
3/1-5/19 & 9/29-10/20		2P/2B: $65- 120	XP: $8	F12
12/1-2/28 & 10/21-11/30		2P/2B: $40- 75	XP: $8	F12

Location: On US Business 17, 1 mi s of SR 73. (PO Box 806, MYRTLE BEACH, 29576). Fax: 803/238-3208. **Terms:** Reserv deposit, 14 day notice, handling fee imposed; weekly/monthly rates; package plans; no pets. **Facility:** 110 rooms. Selected guest units in a complex of bldgs located at 5905 Hwy 17S. Registration/check-in located off site at 5833 Hwy 17S. 3-story midrise bldgs do not have elevator. 68 two-bedroom units. Rates for 2 to 4 persons; 3-21 stories; interior/exterior corridors; putting green; beach, saunas, whirlpools; 6 lighted tennis courts; basketball courts, bocci courts, shuffleboard. Fee: golf privileges. **Dining:** Restaurant nearby. **Services:** Fee: coin laundry. **Recreation:** swimming. **All Rooms:** kitchens, free movies, refrigerators. **Some Rooms:** microwaves. **Cards:** AE, DS, MC, VI. 🛏 🛏 🍴 [CTV] [X] [D]

PLANTATION RESORT OF MYRTLE BEACH

△△△ ◆◆◆ Resort Complex

	Rates Subject to Change			Phone: 803/913-5000	47
6/12-8/22	1P: $115	2P/1B: $115	2P/2B: $115- 138		
5/8-6/11 & 8/23-9/12	1P: $91- 100	2P/1B: $91- 100	2P/2B: $91- 128		
3/6-5/7 & 9/13-10/31	1P: $80- 86	2P/1B: $80- 86	2P/2B: $80- 107		
12/1-3/5 & 11/1-11/30	1P: $66- 74	2P/1B: $66- 74	2P/2B: $66- 90		

Location: 0.7 mi s of jct US 544 & US Business 17. 1250 US Hwy 17 N 29575. Fax: 803/913-5001. **Terms:** Check-in 4 pm; reserv deposit, 3 night min stay; no pets. **Facility:** 152 rooms. Rates for 4-6 persons. Check out cleaning fee, $45-$65. Handling fee imposed; 2-3 stories, no elevator; interior/exterior corridors. **Dining:** Coffee shop; 10 am-5 pm in summer; $2-$6. **All Rooms:** kitchens. **Cards:** AE, DS, MC, VI. *(See color ad below)* 🛏 🛏 [CTV] [X] [D]

RESTAURANTS

CHARLESTON CAFE

◆◆ Continental

Lunch: $4-$11 **Dinner:** $8-$32 **Phone:** 803/238-2200 53

Location: Just e of US Business 17. 815 Surfside Dr 29575. **Hours:** 11:30 am-2:30 & 5:30-9 pm. Closed: 1/1, 11/26, 12/25, Sun & Mon. **Reservations:** suggested; on weekends. **Features:** casual dress; children's menu; health conscious menu; carryout; cocktails & lounge; entertainment. Upscale food in intimate atmosphere of small dining rooms. **Cards:** AE, CB, DI, DS, MC, VI.

EL CERRO GRANDE, SOUTH STRAND

◆◆ Mexican

Dinner: $5-$8 **Phone:** 803/238-1239 54

Location: In front of Wal-Mart. 1880 US 17 N 29575. **Hours:** 11 am-3 & 5-10 pm. **Reservations:** suggested; groups only. **Features:** casual dress; cocktails. **Cards:** DI, MC, VI.

NIBIL'S

◆ Seafood

Lunch: $4-$12 **Dinner:** $6-$17 **Phone:** 803/238-5080 52

Location: Ocean front at Surfside Dr, 0.7 mi s from US Business 17, on surfside pier. 11 S Ocean Blvd 29575. **Hours:** 6:30 am-9 pm, Sun-3 pm. Closed: 12/1-2/28. **Reservations:** accepted; dinner only. **Features:** casual dress; children's menu; carryout; beer & wine only; entertainment. Simple but cozy on the pier. Fresh seafood dinners, also surf & turf. Thurs is Irish Night with corned beef & cabbage. Smoke free premises. [X]

GREENVILLE—58,300

Airport Accommodations

Listings for these establishments are found under the heading for the city in which they are located.

Greenville-Spartanburg

- **Comfort Suites - Greenville**, 3 mi w of terminal/GREER
- Greenville/Spartanburg Airport Marriott, 4.8 mi sw of airport/GREENVILLE
- Hampton Inn, 5.3 mi sw of airport/GREENVILLE
- Holiday Inn Express Airport Hotel, 4.5 mi sw of airport/GREENVILLE
- **Microtel Inn Greenville**, 4 mi w of terminal/GREENVILLE
- Wingate Inn Airport, 4.5 mi sw/GREENVILLE

LODGINGS

COMFORT INN EXECUTIVE CENTER — Rates Subject to Change — **Phone:** 864/271-0060
◆◆
All Year [BP]   1P: $55   2P/1B: $62   2P/2B: $62   XP: $5   F18
Motel   **Location:** At jct I-385 & N Pleasantburg Dr, exit 40 B. 540 N Pleasantburg Dr 29607. **Fax:** 864/242-4096. **Terms:** Sr. discount; no pets. **Facility:** 191 rooms. 2 stories; exterior corridors. **Dining:** Restaurant; 6:30-10 am, Sat & Sun 7-11 am; serving breakfast only. **All Rooms:** free & pay movies. **Cards:** AE, CB, DI, DS, MC, VI.

COURTYARD BY MARRIOTT — Rates Subject to Change — **Phone:** 864/234-0300
◆◆◆
Sun-Thurs   1P: $85   2P/1B: $85   2P/2B: $85
Fri & Sat   1P: $53- 80   2P/1B: $53- 80   2P/2B: $53- 80
Motel   **Location:** Off I-385 at Haywood Rd, exit 39. 70 Orchard Park Dr 29615. **Fax:** 864/234-0296. **Terms:** Sr. discount; no pets. **Facility:** 146 rooms. Rates for up to 4 persons; 3 stories; interior corridors. **Dining:** Restaurant; 6:30-10 am, Sat & Sun 7-11 am. **All Rooms:** free & pay movies. **Cards:** AE, CB, DI, DS, JCB, MC. *(See color ad below)*

DAYS INN — Rates Subject to Change — **Phone:** 864/288-6221
◆◆
All Year [CP]   1P: $50- 105   2P/1B: $55- 110   2P/2B: $55- 110   XP: $5   F18
Motel   **Location:** 0.4 mi sw of I-385, exit 37. 831 Congaree Rd 29607. **Fax:** 864/288-2778. **Terms:** Sr. discount; pets, $10 extra charge. **Facility:** 124 rooms. 5 stories; interior corridors. **All Rooms:** free movies. **Cards:** AE, CB, DI, DS, JCB, MC, VI.

EMBASSY SUITES RESORT HOTEL GOLF AND CONFERENCE CENTER — Rates Subject to Change — **Phone:** 864/676-9090
◆◆◆
Sun-Thurs [BP]   1P: $114   2P/1B: $124   2P/2B: $124   XP: $10   F18
Fri & Sat [BP]   1P: $89   2P/1B: $89   2P/2B: $89   XP: $10   F18
Suite Hotel   **Location:** 1.6 mi ne of I-85, exit 46B. 670 Verdae Blvd 29607. **Fax:** 864/676-0669. **Terms:** Sr. discount; no pets. **Facility:** 268 rooms. 9 stories; interior corridors. **Dining:** Restaurant; 6-9:30 am, 11-2 & 5-11 pm, Sun brunch 11 am-2 pm; $8-$20. **All Rooms:** free & pay movies. **Cards:** AE, CB, DI, DS, JCB, MC, VI.

FAIRFIELD INN — **Phone:** 864/234-9916
All Year   1P: $49- 59   2P/1B: $49- 59   2P/2B: $49- 59
Motel   Too new to rate; **Location:** 1 mi w on Pelham Rd from jct I-85, exit 54, to Beacon Dr. Fisherman Lane 29615. **Facility:** 95 rooms. Scheduled to open October 1997; 4 stories; interior corridors. **Dining:** Restaurant nearby. **Some Rooms:** whirlpools. **Cards:** AE, DI, DS, MC, VI. **Special Amenities:** Free breakfast and free local telephone calls.

FAIRFIELD INN BY MARRIOTT — Rates Subject to Change — **Phone:** 864/297-9996
◆◆◆
Sun-Thurs [CP]   1P: $53   2P/1B: $59   2P/2B: $59   XP: $3   F18
Fri & Sat [CP]   1P: $48   2P/1B: $48   2P/2B: $48
Motel   **Location:** I-385, exit 37. 60 Roper Mountain Rd 29607. **Fax:** 864/297-9996. **Terms:** Sr. discount; reserv deposit; no pets. **Facility:** 132 rooms. 3 stories; interior/exterior corridors. **All Rooms:** free & pay movies. **Cards:** AE, CB, DI, DS, JCB, MC, VI. *(See color ad below)*

GREENVILLE HILTON AND TOWERS — Rates Subject to Change — **Phone:** 864/232-4747
◆◆◆
Sun-Thurs   1P: $129   2P/1B: $144   2P/2B: $144   XP: $20   F14
Fri & Sat   1P: $79   2P/1B: $79   2P/2B: $79   XP: $20   F14
Hotel   **Location:** I-385 at Haywood Rd, exit 39. 45 W Orchard Park Dr 29615. **Fax:** 864/235-6248. **Terms:** Sr. discount; no pets. **Facility:** 256 rooms. 9 stories; interior corridors. **Dining:** Dining room; 6:30 am-2:30 & 5-11 pm; $10-$22. **All Rooms:** free & pay movies. **Cards:** AE, CB, DI, DS, MC, VI. *(See color ad p 18)*

GREENVILLE/SPARTANBURG AIRPORT MARRIOTT
◆◆◆   Sun-Thurs [EP]   Rates Subject to Change   **Phone:** 864/297-0300
Hotel   Fri & Sat [BP]   1P: $125- 135   2P/1B: $129- 139   2P/2B: $129- 139   XP: $10   F18
   1P: $79   2P/1B: $79   2P/2B: $79
Location: 0.3 mi ne of I-85, exit 54. 1 Parkway E 29615. Fax: 864/281-0801. **Terms:** Sr. discount; no pets.
Facility: 204 rooms. 7 stories; interior corridors. **Dining:** Restaurant; 6:30 am-10 pm; $9-$18. **All Rooms:** free & pay
movies. **Cards:** AE, DI, DS, JCB, MC, VI.

HAMPTON INN
◆◆◆   All Year [CP]   Rates Subject to Change   **Phone:** 864/288-3500
Motel   1P: $62- 67   2P/1B: $71- 75   2P/2B: $71- 75
Location: 0.8 mi nw of I-85, exit 54. 47 Fisherman Ln 29615. Fax: 864/234-0728. **Terms:** No pets.
Facility: 140 rooms. Rates for up to 4 persons; 3 stories; interior corridors. **All Rooms:** free movies.
Cards: AE, CB, DI, DS, MC, VI.   Roll in showers.

HAMPTON INN
◆◆◆   All Year [CP]   Rates Subject to Change   **Phone:** 864/288-1200
Motel   1P: $60- 65   2P/1B: $68- 73   2P/2B: $68- 73
Location: 0.3 mi s of I-385, exit 39. 246 Congaree Rd 29607. Fax: 864/288-5667. **Terms:** Sr. discount; no
pets. **Facility:** 123 rooms. Rates for up to 4 persons; 4 stories; interior corridors. **All Rooms:** free & pay
movies. **Cards:** AE, CB, DI, DS, MC, VI.

HOLIDAY INN EXPRESS AIRPORT HOTEL
◆◆   All Year [CP]   Rates Subject to Change   **Phone:** 864/297-5353
Motel   1P: $59   2P/1B: $59   2P/2B: $59
Location: At jct I-85 & Pelham Rd, exit 54. 5009 Pelham Rd 29615. Fax: 864/297-5353. **Terms:** Small pets
only, $25 extra charge. **Facility:** 150 rooms. Rates for up to 4 persons; 2 stories; exterior corridors.
All Rooms: free & pay movies. **Cards:** DI, DS, MC, VI. *(See color ad below)*

HOLIDAY INN I-85
◆◆◆   Fri-Sun   Rates Subject to Change   **Phone:** 864/277-8921
Motor Inn   Mon-Thurs   1P: $85   2P/1B: $85   2P/2B: $85
   1P: $78   2P/1B: $78   2P/2B: $78
Location: Jct I-85 & US 25, exit 45A. 4295 Augusta Rd 29605. Fax: 864/299-6066. **Terms:** Sr. discount;
reserv deposit; small pets only. **Facility:** 155 rooms. Rates for up to 4 persons; 5 stories; interior corridors. **Dining:** Dining
room; 6:30 am-2 & 5-10 pm; $8-$13. **All Rooms:** free & pay movies. **Cards:** AE, CB, DI, DS, JCB, MC, VI.
     Roll in showers.

Double your pleasure with AAA Plus.

HOLIDAY INN SELECT GREENVILLE

Phone: 864/297-6300

(AAA) (SAVE)

		1P:	2P/1B:	2P/2B:
Mon-Thurs		$120	$120	$120
Fri-Sun		$80	$80	

♦♦♦ **Location:** On I-385 at jct Roper Mountain Rd, exit 37. 851 Congaree Rd 29607. Fax: 864/234-0747.
Motor Inn **Terms:** Package plans; no pets. **Facility:** 208 rooms. Lobby in courtyard style with skylight. Rooms range in size from compact to spacious, all with very good amenities. Rates for up to 4 persons; 6 stories; interior corridors; luxury level rooms; whirlpool. **Dining & Entertainment:** Restaurant; 6:30 am-11 pm; $9-$17; cocktails/lounge. **Services:** valet laundry; area transportation. **All Rooms:** coffeemakers, free & pay movies, combo or shower baths. **Some Rooms:** Fee: refrigerators. **Cards:** AE, CB, DI, DS, JCB, MC, VI. **Special Amenities:** Free local telephone calls and free newspaper. (See ad p 555)   Roll in showers. 🚗 📶 ⊁ ⊞ CTV ⓕ ✕ 🔊 D S

HOWARD JOHNSON LODGE & SUITES

Phone: 864/288-6900

♦♦

	Rates Subject to Change	1P:	2P/1B:	2P/2B:	XP:	F18
All Year [CP]		$41- 44	$49- 54	$49- 54	$5	F18

Motel **Location:** Just n of I-85, exit 48B. 2756 Laurens Rd 29607. Fax: 864/288-5935. **Terms:** Sr. discount; small pets only, $10 extra charge. **Facility:** 114 rooms. 4 stories; interior corridors. **All Rooms:** free movies. **Cards:** AE, DI, DS, MC, VI.   🐾 🚗 CTV ✕ D

HYATT REGENCY GREENVILLE

Phone: 864/235-1234

(AAA) (SAVE)

	1P:	2P/1B:	2P/2B:	XP:	F18
Sun-Thurs	$139	$164	$164	$25	F18
Fri & Sat	$94	$94	$94	$25	F18

♦♦♦ **Location:** Center; Beattie St at N Main St. 220 N Main St 29601. Fax: 864/232-7584. **Terms:** No pets.
Hotel **Facility:** 327 rooms. Interior courtyard with fountain, gardens & very large skylights. Spacious rooms with large windows. 8 stories; interior corridors; whirlpool. Fee: parking. **Dining & Entertainment:** Dining room; 6:30 am-11 pm; $10-$20; cocktails/lounge. **Services:** valet laundry; area transportation. **All Rooms:** free & pay movies. **Some Rooms:** coffeemakers, microwaves, refrigerators, whirlpools. **Cards:** AE, CB, DI, DS, MC, VI.   🚗 📶 ⊁ ⊞ CTV ✕ 🔊 D S

LA QUINTA INN

Phone: 864/297-3500

♦♦♦

	Rates Subject to Change	1P:	2P/1B:	2P/2B:	XP:	F18
All Year [CP]		$55- 62	$68	$61	$6	F18

Motel **Location:** On SR 146 at jct I-85, exit 51 Woodruff Rd. 31 Old Country Rd 29607. Fax: 864/458-9818. **Terms:** Small pets only. **Facility:** 122 rooms. 2 stories; exterior corridors. **All Rooms:** free movies. **Cards:** AE, CB, DI, DS, MC, VI.   🐾 🚗 CTV ✕ 🔊 D

MICROTEL INN GREENVILLE

Phone: 864/297-7866

(AAA)

	Guaranteed Rates	1P:	2P/1B:	2P/2B:	XP:	F18
9/29-11/2		$45- 54	$49- 59	$49- 59		F18
12/1-9/28 & 11/3-11/30		$41- 50	$45- 55	$45- 55	$5	

Motel Too new to rate; **Location:** At jct I-85, exit 54 & Pelham Rd. 20 Interstate Court 29615. Fax: 864/297-7883. **Terms:** Sr. discount; no pets. **Facility:** 129 rooms. Scheduled to open May 1997; 3 stories; interior corridors. **All Rooms:** Fee: movies. **Cards:** AE, DI, DS, MC, VI.   Roll in showers. CTV ✕ D

PETTIGRU PLACE BED & BREAKFAST

Phone: 864/242-4529

♦♦♦

	Rates Subject to Change	1P:	2P/1B:	2P/2B:
All Year [BP]		$90- 160	$90- 160	$170

Historic Bed & Breakfast **Location:** Just off Business Rt I-385N; w on Williams St. 302 Pettigru St 29601. Fax: 864/242-1231. **Terms:** Age restrictions may apply; check-in 4 pm; no pets. **Facility:** 5 rooms. 2 stories; interior corridors; smoke free premises. **Cards:** AE, DI, DS, MC, VI.   CTV ✕ D

THE PHOENIX, GREENVILLE'S INN

Phone: 864/233-4651

♦♦♦

	Rates Subject to Change	1P:	2P/1B:	2P/2B:
All Year		$58- 120	$65- 127	$65- 127

Motor Inn **Location:** On SR 291; 0.5 mi s of jct I-385. 246 N Pleasantburg Dr 29607 (PO Box 5064, Station B, 29606). Fax: 864/233-4651. **Terms:** Sr. discount; small pets only. **Facility:** 186 rooms. Rates for up to 4 persons; 2 stories; exterior corridors. **Dining:** Dining room; also, The Palms, see separate listing. **All Rooms:** free movies. **Cards:** AE, CB, DI, DS, MC, VI.   🐾 🚗 ⊁ CTV ✕ 🔊 D

RAMADA LIMITED

Phone: 864/277-3734

♦

	Rates Subject to Change	1P:	2P/1B:	2P/2B:	XP:	F17
4/1-11/30 [CP]		$39- 44	$44- 49	$44- 49	$5	F17
12/1-3/31 [CP]		$41	$46	$46	$5	F17

Motel **Location:** 0.5 mi n of I-85, exit 45B, on SR 291. 1314 S Pleasantburg Dr 29605. Fax: 864/277-3734. **Terms:** Sr. discount; small pets only, $25 extra charge. **Facility:** 119 rooms. 2 stories; exterior corridors. **All Rooms:** free & pay movies. **Cards:** AE, CB, DI, DS, JCB, MC, VI.   🐾 🚗 CTV ✕ D

RED ROOF INN

Phone: 864/297-4458

♦

	Rates Subject to Change	1P:	2P/1B:	2P/2B:	XP:	F18
5/1-10/31		$43- 49	$48- 53	$53- 57	$5	F18
3/1-4/30		$40- 46	$45- 50	$50- 54	$5	F18
12/1-2/28 & 11/1-11/30		$37- 43	$41- 46	$46- 50	$4-5	F18

Motel **Location:** On s frontage Rd, just s of I-85, exit 48A. 2801 Laurens Rd 29607. Fax: 864/297-9800. **Terms:** Small pets only. **Facility:** 108 rooms. 2 stories; exterior corridors. **All Rooms:** free movies. **Cards:** AE, CB, DI, DS, MC, VI.   🐾 CTV ✕ D

RESIDENCE INN BY MARRIOTT

Phone: 864/297-0099

♦♦♦

	Rates Subject to Change	1P:	2P/1B:	2P/2B:
All Year		$99- 119	$99	$119

Apartment Motel **Location:** Off I-385 at Haywood Rd, exit 39. 48 McPrice Ct 29615. Fax: 864/288-8203. **Terms:** Sr. discount; reserv deposit; pets, $100 fee, also $5 extra charge. **Facility:** 96 rooms. 2 stories; exterior corridors. **All Rooms:** free movies. **Cards:** AE, CB, DI, DS, JCB, MC, VI.   🐾 🚗 CTV ✕ 🔊 D

WINGATE INN AIRPORT

Phone: 864/281-1281

♦♦♦

	Rates Subject to Change	1P:	2P/1B:	2P/2B:	XP:	F12
All Year [CP]		$79	$85	$85	$6	F12

Motel **Location:** Just ne of I-85 exit 54, Pelham Rd. 33 Beacon Dr 29615. **Terms:** Sr. discount; no pets. **Facility:** 120 rooms. 4 stories; interior corridors. **All Rooms:** free movies. **Cards:** AE, DI, DS, MC, VI.

(See color ad p 557)   🚗 ⊁ CTV ✕ D S

RESTAURANTS

NIPPON CENTER YAGOTO

Dinner: $14-$40   **Phone: 864/288-8471**

♦♦♦ **Location:** 1 mi se of I-385, exit 37; behind Haywood Mall. 500 Conagaree Rd 29607. **Hours:** 6 pm-9:30 pm.
Ethnic Closed major holidays & Sun. **Reservations:** suggested. **Features:** cocktails & lounge; a la carte. Amidst planted gardens, waterfall & raked gravel garden. The center houses various dining areas from Tatami rooms to regular seating area. Traditional Japanese architecture & upscale casual atmosphere. **Cards:** AE, CB, DI, DS, JCB, MC, VI.   ✕

THE PALMS   **Lunch:** $7-$13   **Dinner:** $17-$23   **Phone:** 864/370-9181
◆◆◆ **Location:** On SR 291; 0.5 mi s of jct I-385; in The Phoenix, Greenville's Inn. 246 N Pleasantburg Dr 29606.
Continental **Hours:** 6 am-10 pm, Sun 7 am-10:30 pm. Closed: 12/24 & 12/25. **Reservations:** required.
Features: semi-formal attire; cocktails & lounge; entertainment; a la carte. Fine dining in a setting of refined country elegance. Selection of creative, artistic meat & seafood dishes incorporating French & regional American influences. Jackets requested for dinner. Smoke free premises. **Cards:** AE, CB, DI, DS, MC, VI.   ⊠

PETER DAVID'S FINE CUISINE   **Lunch:** $6-$10   **Dinner:** $11-$25   **Phone:** 864/242-0404
◆◆ **Location:** Just s of E Faris Rd; in River Oaks Shopping Center. 921 Grove Rd 29650. **Hours:** 11:30
Continental am-2:30 & 6-10 pm. Closed: Sun & 12/25. **Reservations:** suggested. **Features:** cocktails & lounge. Casual, upscale dining in an elegant setting. Varied meat & poultry items with upgraded presentations incorporating European & American influences. Lighter fare, salads & sandwiches at lunch. **Cards:** AE, DI, MC, VI.   ⊠

RENE'S FISHMARKET RESTAURANT   **Lunch:** $7-$11   **Dinner:** $12-$24   **Phone:** 864/297-3456
◆◆ **Location:** I-385 exit 39, 1.2 mi w. 301 Haywood Rd 29607. **Hours:** 11:30 am-2:30 & 5:30-10:30 pm, Sat
Seafood from 5:30 pm. Closed major holidays & Sun (except Mothers Day). **Reservations:** suggested.
Features: casual dress; children's menu; carryout; cocktails & lounge; a la carte. **Cards:** AE, DI, DS, MC, VI.   ⊠

RISTORANTE BERGAMO   **Dinner:** $9-$21   **Phone:** 864/271-8667
◆◆◆ **Location:** Center; Main St at Coffie St. 100 N Main St 29601. **Hours:** 6 pm-9:30 pm. Closed major holidays,
Nouvelle Italian Sun & Mon. **Reservations:** suggested. **Features:** casual dress; cocktails & lounge; a la carte. Casual dining in bistro ambience & contemporary urban decor. Menu offers a selection of Italian specialties interpreted with a New American flair. **Cards:** AE, CB, DI, DS, MC, VI.   ⊠

S & S CAFETERIA   **Phone:** 864/233-3339
◆ **Location:** Off I-385, exit SR 291N, 0.5 mi n. 1037 N Pleasantburg Dr 29607. **Hours:** 11 am-2 & 4:30-8 pm,
American Fri & Sat-8:30 pm. Closed: 12/25. **Features:** casual dress; health conscious menu items; carryout. Wide variety of home-style regional foods. **Cards:** AE, MC, VI.   ⊠

SEVEN OAKS RESTAURANT Historical   **Dinner:** $16-$24   **Phone:** 864/232-1895
◆◆◆ **Location:** Just off Business Rt I-385; just s of auditorium. 104 Broadus Ave 29601. **Hours:** 6 pm-10 pm.
Continental Closed major holidays, Sun & 12/24. **Features:** cocktails; a la carte. Elegant dining atmosphere in restored historic mansion. **Cards:** AE, CB, DI, DS, MC, VI.   ⊠

STAX'S PEPPERMILL   **Lunch:** $8-$13   **Dinner:** $16-$30   **Phone:** 864/288-9320
◆◆◆ **Location:** Off I-385, exit 39 (Haywood Rd); in T J Maxx Shopping Center. 30 Orchard Park Dr 29615.
Continental **Hours:** 11:30 am-2 & 5:30-11 pm, Mon from 5:30 pm, Fri 11:30 am-2 & 5:30-midnight, Sat 5:30 pm-midnight.
Closed major holidays & Sun. **Reservations:** suggested. **Features:** casual dress; cocktails & lounge. Refined candlelight dining with casual upscale atmosphere. Lunch menu offers lighter fare with less complex preparation. The dinner menu features meat & seafood dishes inspired by local & international flavours & styles. **Cards:** AE, CB, DI, DS, MC, VI.   ⊠

GREENWOOD—20,800

LODGINGS

COMFORT INN   **Phone:** 864/223-2838
ⓐ SAVE All Year [CP]   **1P:** $57- 67   **2P/1B:** $62- 72   **2P/2B:** $62   **XP:** $5   **F12**
Location: On SR 72 bypass, 2 mi e of US 25. 1215 NE Hwy 72 bypass 29649. **Fax:** 864/942-0119.
◆◆◆ **Terms:** No pets. **Facility:** 83 rooms. Simply-furnished guest rooms. Suites $89-$100, single or double occu-
Motel pancy; 2 stories; exterior corridors; whirlpool, small outdoor pool. **Dining & Entertainment:** Cocktail lounge; restaurant nearby. **Services:** complimentary evening beverages, Mon-Fri; valet laundry.
All Rooms: coffeemakers, microwaves, refrigerators. **Fee:** movies. **Cards:** AE, DI, DS, JCB, MC, VI. **Special Amenities:** Free breakfast and free local telephone calls.   🍳 🛁 CTV ⊠ D

ECONO LODGE   **Phone:** 864/229-5329
ⓐ SAVE 4/1-10/31 [CP]   **1P:** $41- 43   **2P/1B:** $42- 46   **2P/2B:** $47- 49   **XP:** $5   **F12**
12/1-3/31 & 11/1-11/30 [CP]   **1P:** $36- 42   **2P/1B:** $40- 44   **2P/2B:** $44- 46   **XP:** $5   **F12**
◆◆ **Location:** 0.5 mi s of jct SR 72 & US 221. 719 Bypass 25 NE 29646. **Fax:** 864/229-4484. **Terms:** Small pets
Motel only, $25 dep req. **Facility:** 50 rooms. 2 whirlpool rms, $58 up to 2 persons; 2 stories; exterior corridors.
Dining: Restaurant nearby. **All Rooms:** free movies. **Some Rooms:** microwaves, refrigerators.
Fee: coffeemakers. **Cards:** AE, DI, DS, JCB, MC, VI. **Special Amenities:** Free breakfast and free local telephone calls.   🛏 🛁 CTV ⊠ D

HAMPTON INN GREENWOOD   Rates Subject to Change   **Phone:** 864/388-9595
◆◆◆   All Year [CP]   1P: $59- 62 2P/1B: $66- 69 2P/2B: $66- 69
Motel   **Location:** Between SR 254 & US 221/SR 72. 1624 Bypass 72 NE 29649. Fax: 864/388-9585. **Terms:** No pets. **Facility:** 75 rooms. Suites $82 single, $89 double; 3 stories; interior corridors. **All Rooms:** free movies.
Cards: AE, DI, DS, JCB, MC, VI.   Roll in showers. [icons]

INN ON THE SQUARE   Rates Subject to Change   **Phone:** 864/223-4488
◆◆◆   All Year   1P: $66- 76 2P/1B: $66- 76 2P/2B: $76   XP: $15   F
Motor Inn   **Location:** Center; corner Main St. 104 Court St 29646. Fax: 864/223-7067. **Terms:** Sr. discount; no pets. **Facility:** 46 rooms. 3 stories; interior corridors. **Dining:** Restaurant; 7 am-10 pm, Sat from 5:30 pm; closed Sun; $13-$20. **All Rooms:** free movies. **Cards:** AE, CB, DI, DS, MC, VI.   [icons]

THE JAMESON INN   Rates Subject to Change   **Phone:** 864/942-0002
◆◆◆   All Year [CP]   1P: $56   2P/1B: $60   2P/2B: $60   XP: $4
Motel   **Location:** On Bypass 72 NE, just e of jct US 254. 109 Enterprise Ct 29649. Fax: 864/227-0040. **Terms:** No pets. **Facility:** 64 rooms. Suites $80-135, single or double occupancy; 2 stories; exterior corridors.
All Rooms: free movies. **Cards:** AE, DI, DS, MC, VI.   Roll in showers. [icons]

GREER—10,300

LODGINGS

COMFORT INN   **Phone:** 864/848-4995
[AAA] [SAVE]   All Year [CP]   1P: $42- 65 2P/1B: $47- 65 2P/2B: $55   XP: $6   F18
◆◆◆   **Location:** 1.1 mi ne on US 29 from jct SR 101/SR 290. 611 W Wade Hampton Blvd 29650.
Motel   Fax: 864/848-4995. **Terms:** No pets. **Facility:** 62 rooms. In semi-rural & wooded area. Room sizes range from compact to more spacious, some with good amenities. 2 stories; interior/exterior corridors. **Services:** valet laundry. **All Rooms:** free movies, combo or shower baths. **Some Rooms:** microwaves, whirlpools.
Fee: refrigerators. **Cards:** AE, CB, DI, DS, JCB, MC, VI. **Special Amenities:** Free breakfast and free local telephone calls.   Roll in showers. [icons]

COMFORT SUITES - GREENVILLE   **Phone:** 864/213-9331
[AAA] [SAVE]   All Year [CP]   1P: $69- 129 2P/1B: $69- 129 2P/2B: $69- 129 XP: $5   F18
◆◆◆   **Location:** From jct I-85, exit 54, 0.4 mi on The Parkway, 0.2 mi on Parkway Rd East. 2681 Dry Pocket Rd
Suite Motel   29615. Fax: 864/213-9336. **Terms:** Weekly/monthly rates; package plans; pets, $25 dep req. **Facility:** 83 rooms. 1996 construction. Very attractive guest rooms & lovely public areas. 3 stories; interior corridors; whirlpool. **Services:** valet laundry; area transportation, to health club/downtown. **All Rooms:** coffeemakers, microwaves, free & pay movies, refrigerators. **Some Rooms:** whirlpools. **Cards:** AE, DI, DS, MC, VI. **Special Amenities:** Free breakfast and free local telephone calls. *(See color ad below)*   Roll in showers. [icons]

SUPER 8 MOTEL   Rates Subject to Change   **Phone:** 864/848-1626
◆◆   All Year [CP]   1P: $45- 50 2P/1B: $45- 50 2P/2B: $50- 55 XP: $5   F10
Motel   **Location:** I-85, exit 60. 1515 Hwy 101 29651. Fax: 864/848-3092. **Terms:** Sr. discount; reserv deposit, 3 day notice; no pets. **Facility:** 61 rooms. 2 stories; interior corridors. **All Rooms:** free movies. **Cards:** AE, DI, DS, MC, VI.   Roll in showers. [icons]

HARDEEVILLE—1,600

LODGINGS

COMFORT INN   **Phone:** 803/784-2188
[AAA] [SAVE]   12/1-2/28 & 3/21-11/30 [CP]   1P: $50- 80 2P/1B: $50- 80 2P/2B: $50- 80 XP: $6   F16
◆◆◆   3/1-3/20 [CP]   1P: $70   2P/1B: $75   2P/2B: $75   XP: $6   F16
Motel   **Location:** I-95 exit 5; 0.3 mi n on US 17. US 17 & I-95 29927 (PO Box 544). Fax: 803/784-2188. **Terms:** No pets. **Facility:** 99 rooms. 2 stories; interior/exterior corridors; whirlpool. **Dining:** Restaurant nearby.
All Rooms: free movies. **Some Rooms:** coffeemakers, microwaves, refrigerators. Fee: whirlpools.
Cards: AE, CB, DI, DS, JCB, MC, VI. **Special Amenities:** Free breakfast and free local telephone calls.
(See ad p 559)   [icons]

DAYS INN STATELINE   **Phone:** 803/784-2281
[AAA] [SAVE]   3/10-3/25   1P: $52- 85 2P/1B: $54- 87 2P/2B: $56- 89 XP: $6   F17
◆◆   12/1-3/9 & 3/26-11/30   1P: $34- 52 2P/1B: $38- 60 2P/2B: $38- 60 XP: $6   F17
Motor Inn   **Location:** I-95 exit 5 & US 17. (PO Box 1150, 29927). Fax: 803/784-5250. **Terms:** Reserv deposit, 3 day notice; weekly/monthly rates; small pets only, $5 extra charge. **Facility:** 120 rooms. Rooms nicely furnished & decorated. 2 stories; exterior corridors. **Dining:** Restaurant; 24 hours; $4-$12. **All Rooms:** free movies, combo or shower baths. **Some Rooms:** coffeemakers. **Cards:** AE, CB, DI, DS, JCB, MC, VI. **Special Amenities:** Early check-in/late check-out and free local telephone calls.   [icons]

HOLIDAY INN EXPRESS
◆◆◆ All Year [CP]   1P: $59   2P/1B: $59   2P/2B: $59   XP: $5   F18
Motel   **Location:** I-95 exit 5 & US 17N, 0.8 mi n on US 17. PO Box 613 29927. Fax: 803/784-6102. **Terms:** Sr.
discount; no pets. **Facility:** 112 rooms. 2 stories; exterior corridors. **All Rooms:** free movies. **Cards:** AE, CB,
DI, DS, MC, VI.
Phone: 803/784-2221
🛏 CTV ✕ D S

HOWARD JOHNSON LODGE
AAA SAVE All Year   1P: $30- 49 2P/1B: $36- 64 2P/2B: $36- 64 XP: $5   F17
◆◆   **Location:** On US 17; at jct I-95, exit 5. 29927 (PO Box 1107). Fax: 803/784-2271. **Terms:** Pets, $5 extra
Motor Inn charge. **Facility:** 128 rooms. 2 stories; interior corridors; wading pool. **Dining:** Restaurant; 6 am-2 & 5-10
pm; $4-$8. **All Rooms:** free movies. **Some Rooms:** Fee: refrigerators. **Cards:** AE, CB, DI, DS, MC, VI.
Special Amenities: Early check-in/late check-out and free local telephone calls.
Phone: 803/784-2271
🐾 🛏 CTV ✕ D

RAMADA LIMITED
AAA SAVE 3/1-8/31 [CP]   1P: $40   2P/1B: $45   2P/2B: $45   XP: $5   F18
       12/1-2/28 & 9/1-11/30 [CP] 1P: $35   2P/1B: $40   2P/2B: $40   XP: $5   F18
◆◆   **Location:** I-95 exit 8 & US 278. (PO Box 1429, 29927). Fax: 803/784-2729. **Terms:** Reserv deposit; small
Motel   pets only, $5 extra charge. **Facility:** 61 rooms. Nicely decorated & tastefully furnished rooms. Handling fee im-
posed; 2 stories; exterior corridors. **Dining:** Coffee shop nearby. **All Rooms:** free movies.
Some Rooms: refrigerators. **Cards:** AE, DI, DS, MC, VI. **Special Amenities:** Free breakfast and free local telephone
calls.
Phone: 803/784-3192
🐾 CTV ✕ D

HARTSVILLE—8,400

LODGINGS

LANDMARK INN
AAA SAVE All Year   1P: $60- 65 2P/1B: $67- 72 2P/2B: $65- 75 XP: $5   F16
◆◆◆   **Location:** 2 mi se on SR 151 business at jct US 15 bypass. 1301 S 4th St 29550 (PO Drawer 370).
Motor Inn Fax: 803/332-2611. **Terms:** Small pets only. **Facility:** 136 rooms. 2 stories; exterior corridors. **Dining:** Dining
room; 6-9 am, 11:30-2 & 5-9 pm, Sun 11 am-2 pm; $9-$18. **All Rooms:** free movies. **Cards:** AE, CB, DI,
DS, MC, VI.
Phone: 803/332-2611
🐾 🛏 CTV ✕ D

MISSOURI INN
◆◆◆   All Year [CP]   Guaranteed Rates   1P: $75   2P/1B: $85   2P/2B: $85   XP: $10   D
Historic Bed **Location:** From US 15 business route & 5th St, 0.3 mi e; opposite Coker College. 314 E Home Ave 29550.
& Breakfast Fax: 803/383-9553. **Terms:** No pets. **Facility:** 5 rooms. 2 stories; interior corridors; designated smoking area.
Cards: AE, MC, VI.
Phone: 803/383-9553
CTV ✕ D

HILTON HEAD ISLAND—23,700

LODGINGS

CAROLINA CLUB   Rates Subject to Change
◆◆◆   All Year Weekly   2P/2B: $795-1250
Condo   **Location:** In Shipyard Plantation. Southwind Dr 29938 (PO Box 8048). Fax: 803/785-6552. **Terms:** Check-in
Complex 5 pm; no pets. **Facility:** 35 rooms. Exterior corridors. **All Rooms:** kitchens, free movies. **Cards:** MC, VI.
(See ad p 568)
Phone: 803/842-6556
🎿 CTV D

COASTAL HOME & VILLA RENTALS   Rates Subject to Change
◆◆◆   3/28-4/17 & 6/6-8/14 Weekly   2P/1B: $615- 785 2P/2B: $645-1675
Condo   3/14-3/27, 4/18-6/5 &
Complex 8/15-9/4 Weekly   2P/1B: $500- 625 2P/2B: $525-1200
       9/5-10/23 Weekly   2P/1B: $450- 550 2P/2B: $475-1100
       12/1-3/13 & 10/24-11/30
       Weekly   2P/1B: $355- 450 2P/2B: $375- 950
Location: Off US 278 in the Coastal Building, just before the Sea Pines Cir on right side of street. 1036 Hwy 278 29928.
Fax: 803/785-6010. **Terms:** Check-in 4 pm, check-out 9:30 am; reserv deposit, 30 day notice; 3 night min stay; no pets.
Facility: 125 rooms. 5 stories; exterior corridors. **All Rooms:** kitchens. **Cards:** DS, MC, VI. (See color ad p 560)
Phone: 803/785-6990
🎿 CTV D

COMFORT INN & SUITES   Phone: 803/842-6662
AAA SAVE   3/1-10/31 [CP]   1P: $60- 100   2P/1B: $65- 120 2P/2B: $70- 120 XP: $10   F18
            12/1-2/28 & 11/1-11/30 [CP] 1P: $40- 60   2P/1B: $45- 65 2P/2B: $50- 65 XP: $10   F18
◆◆◆   **Location:** Via US 278E to Sea Pines Cir, 0.3 mi n via Pope Ave & S Forest Beach Dr. 2 Tanglewood Dr
Motor Inn   29928. Fax: 803/842-6664. **Terms:** Check-in 4 pm; AP, BP, EP avail; package plans; small pets only, $20
extra charge. **Facility:** 150 rooms. Some rooms with balcony. Attractively appointed. 5 stories; interior corridors. Fee: miniature golf, golf privileges; waterslide. **Dining:** Restaurant; 7 am-10 pm; $8-$15; cocktails. **Services:** Fee: coin laundry. **All Rooms:** coffeemakers, free & pay movies. **Some Rooms:** microwaves, refrigerators. **Cards:** AE, DI, DS, JCB, MC, VI. **Special Amenities:** Free breakfast and free local telephone calls. *(See color ad below)*

CROWNE PLAZA RESORT HILTON HEAD ISLAND   Phone: 803/842-2400
[AAA] [SAVE]   2/27-6/16 & 6/17-11/14   1P: $215- 260   2P/1B: $214- 259   2P/2B: $214- 259   XP: $15   F18
◆◆◆◆   12/1-2/26 & 11/15-11/30   1P: $120- 150   2P/1B: $119- 149   2P/2B: $119- 149   XP: $15   F18
Resort Hotel   **Location:** US 278 to Shipyard Plantation. Entrance to e of US 278. 130 Shipyard Dr 29928.
            Fax: 803/842-9975. **Terms:** Check-in 4 pm; package plans, Sun-Thurs; no pets. **Facility:** 340 rooms. Very nice
            public areas. The rooms are very nicely decorated & furnished. Some rooms with view of a Carolina lagoon &
pool area. 5 stories; interior corridors; beach, wading pool, saunas, whirlpools. Fee: 81 holes golf; 20 tennis courts (8
lighted). **Dining & Entertainment:** Dining room, cafeteria; 6 am-midnight; $9-$22; cocktails/lounge; entertainment.
Services: valet laundry; area transportation, to golf course; valet parking. Fee: massage. **Recreation:** children's program,
nature trails, social program; swimming, surf fishing. Fee: bicycles. **All Rooms:** coffeemakers, free & pay movies, safes,
combo or shower baths. **Some Rooms:** refrigerators. Fee: VCP's. **Cards:** AE, CB, DI, DS, JCB, MC, VI.
Special Amenities: Free newspaper. *(See ad p 563)*   Roll in showers.

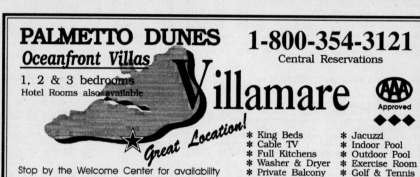

Going to the Caribbean?
Ask for the AAA Caribbean TravelBook, Including Bermuda.

DISNEY'S HILTON HEAD ISLAND RESORT
◆◆◆
Resort
Cottage

3/31-4/21 & 6/16-10/26	2P/1B: $165- 215	2P/2B: $250	
3/1-3/30 & 4/22-6/15	2P/1B: $135- 175	2P/2B: $185	
12/1-2/28 & 10/27-11/30	2P/1B: $99- 135	2P/2B: $155	

Rates Subject to Change   **Phone: 803/341-4100**

Location: Off US 278 in Shelter Cove. 22 Harbourside Ln 29928. Fax: 803/341-4130. **Terms:** Check-in 4 pm; no pets. **Facility:** 123 rooms. 5 three-bedroom grand villas $450, in winter $350; sleeps up to 12 persons. 76 two-bedroom units for up to 8 persons; 4 stories; exterior corridors. **Dining:** Cafeteria; $4-$10. **All Rooms:** free movies. **Some Rooms:** 21 efficiencies, 102 kitchens. **Cards:** AE, MC, VI. *(See color ad p 561)*

Roll in showers. ⬛ CTV ⬛ D S

FAIRFIELD INN BY MARRIOTT
◆◆◆
Motel

Rates Subject to Change   **Phone: 803/842-4800**

3/15-8/29 [CP]	1P: $55- 84	2P/1B: $61- 84	2P/2B: $63- 84	XP: $7-10	F18
2/15-3/14 [CP]	1P: $46- 66	2P/1B: $51- 77	2P/2B: $53- 77	XP: $7-10	F18
8/30-10/31 [CP]	1P: $52- 60	2P/1B: $58- 68	2P/2B: $58- 68	XP: $7-10	F18
12/1-2/14 & 11/1-11/30 [CP]	1P: $41- 50	2P/1B: $49- 59	2P/2B: $49- 59	XP: $7-10	F18

Location: Just e of Shelter Cove & Palmetto Dunes entrance via US 278. 9 Marina Side Dr 29928. Fax: 803/842-4800. **Terms:** Reserv deposit; no pets. **Facility:** 119 rooms. Weekend rates in season, $10 extra charge; 3 stories; interior/exterior corridors. **All Rooms:** Fee: movies. **Cards:** AE, CB, DI, DS, MC, VI.

⬛ CTV ⬛ ⬛ D S

FOUR POINTS HOTEL BY ITT SHERATON
AAA SAVE
◆◆◆
Motel

Phone: 803/842-3100

2/27-11/14	1P: $119- 199	2P/1B: $119- 199	2P/2B: $119- 199	XP: $10	F18
12/1-2/26 & 11/15-11/30	1P: $59- 119	2P/1B: $59- 119	2P/2B: $59- 119	XP: $10	F18

Location: Via US 278E to Sea Pines Cir, 0.3 mi n via Pope Ave, then 0.5 mi s on S Forest Beach Dr. 36 S Forest Beach Dr 29928 (PO Box 6748). Fax: 803/785-6928. **Terms:** Reserv deposit; package plans; no pets. **Facility:** 139 rooms. Across from ocean. Handling fee imposed; 5 stories; interior corridors; beach access. Fee: golf privileges; 6 lighted tennis courts. **Dining & Entertainment:** Cafeteria; 11 am-1 & 5-9 pm; $4-$13; cocktails/lounge. **Services:** Fee: coin laundry. **Recreation:** Fee: bicycles. **All Rooms:** coffeemakers, free movies, refrigerators. **Some Rooms:** 72 efficiencies, microwaves. Fee: whirlpools. **Cards:** AE, CB, DI, DS, JCB, MC, VI. **Special Amenities:** Free newspaper. *(See color ad below)*

⬛ ⬛ CTV ⬛ D S

HAMPTON INN
◆◆◆
Motel

Rates Subject to Change   **Phone: 803/681-7900**

2/4-3/30 [CP]	1P: $62- 85	2P/1B: $67- 90	2P/2B: $67- 90
3/31-9/3 [CP]	1P: $69- 90	2P/1B: $75- 95	2P/2B: $75- 85
12/1-2/3 & 9/4-11/30 [CP]	1P: $60- 75	2P/1B: $67- 80	2P/2B: $67- 80

Location: Off US 278; on Airport Rd. 1 Dillon Rd 29926. Fax: 803/681-4330. **Terms:** No pets. **Facility:** 124 rooms. Rates higher on weekends 5/26-9/9; 2 stories; interior corridors. **All Rooms:** free movies. **Cards:** AE, DI, DS, MC, VI.

⬛ ⬛ CTV ⬛ D S

So Many Diamonds.
So Little To Pay.

**BED & BREAKFAST
OCEANFRONT ON
HILTON HEAD ISLAND**

$79*/$139-169*
NOV.-FEB.   MAR.-OCT.

A Four-Diamond retreat on 12 miles of white sand beach. The Crowne Plaza® Resort Hilton Head Island is a tropical paradise at an unbeatable price for our exclusive AAA Bed & Breakfast Package.

With your package, you'll enjoy:

- Luxurious accommodations.
- Full American breakfast.
- Gated 24-hour security at Shipyard Plantation.
- Complimentary valet parking and use of Health Club.
- Two restaurants, nightclub and poolside bar.
- Shipyard Golf Club, Port Royal Golf Club, and Van der Meer Shipyard Racquet Club.
- Daily newspaper and coffee in lobby.
- In-room coffeemaker, hairdryer, safe, and 26-inch color TV.
- No hidden "service fees."

CROWNE PLAZA® RESORT
HILTON HEAD ISLAND
AT SHIPYARD PLANTATION
800-334-1881

*Prices are per room per night; single or double occupancy; Sunday through Thursday nights only; subject to restricted availability. Other special AAA discounts available on selected weekends. Advance reservations requested.

HILTON HEAD ISLAND BEACH & TENNIS RESORT
◆◆◆
Condo
Complex

	Guaranteed Rates		
5/28-9/5	2P/2B:	$89-	199
3/1-5/27 & 9/6-10/31	2P/2B:	$79-	159
1/1-2/28	2P/2B:	$69-	130
12/1-12/31 & 11/1-11/30	2P/2B:	$59-	125

Phone: 803/842-4402

Location: Via US 278. 40 Folly Field Rd 29928. Fax: 803/842-3323. **Terms:** Sr. discount; check-in 4 pm; reserv deposit, 3 day notice; no pets. **Facility:** 200 rooms. 3-5 stories; interior/exterior corridors. **Dining:** Restaurant; 8 am-2 & 5-10 pm; $8-$16. **All Rooms:** free movies. **Cards:** AE, DS, MC, VI. *(See color ad below)*

🛥 (CTV) ✕ (D) (S)

HILTON HEAD ISLAND HILTON RESORT **Phone:** 803/842-8000

(AAA) (SAVE)

◆◆◆◆

Resort Motor Inn

5/23-8/23	1P: $169- 239	2P/1B: $169- 239	2P/2B: $169- 239	XP: $10-15 F18
2/28-5/22 & 8/24-11/22	1P: $139- 219	2P/1B: $139- 219	2P/2B: $139- 219	XP: $10-15 F18
12/1-2/27 & 11/23-11/30	1P: $69- 134	2P/1B: $69- 134	2P/2B: $69- 134	XP: $10-15 F18

Location: On US 278 in Palmetto Dunes Resort. 23 Ocean Ln 29938 (PO Box 6165). Fax: 803/842-4988. **Terms:** Check-in 4 pm; weekly/monthly rates; MAP avail; package plans; no pets. **Facility:** 324 rooms. All rooms with balcony or patio. Large, luxurious units. 20 oceanfront suites, $375 for up to 4 person; $200 off season; 5 stories; interior/exterior corridors; oceanfront; beach, wading pool, saunas, whirlpools; playground. Fee: 54 holes golf; 25 tennis courts (6 lighted); inline skates. **Dining & Entertainment:** Dining room, cafeteria, deli; 7 am-10 pm; $8-$22; cocktails/lounge; also, Mostly Seafood, see separate listing; entertainment. **Services:** area transportation, to Palemetto Dunes area; valet parking. Fee: coin laundry. **Recreation:** children's program, recreation program; swimming, fishing. Rental: canoeing, paddleboats, sailboats; bicycles. **All Rooms:** coffeemakers, efficiencies, microwaves, free & pay movies, refrigerators, safes. **Cards:** AE, CB, DI, DS, MC, VI. **Special Amenities:** Free newspaper.
(See ad p 564 & color ad p 18) 🛌 🍴 ♿ CTV ✕ 🏊 D S

HOLIDAY INN EXPRESS **Phone:** 803/842-8888

◆◆

Motel

	Rates Subject to Change			
3/1-4/30 & 5/1-9/6 [CP]	1P: $71- 77	2P/1B: $71- 77	2P/2B: $71- 77	XP: $5 F19
12/1-2/26 & 9/7-11/30 [CP]	1P: $44- 49	2P/1B: $44- 49	2P/2B: $44- 49	XP: $5 F19

Location: Via US 278 to Pope Ave, 0.8 mi from traffic circle. 40 Waterside Dr 29928. Fax: 803/842-5948. **Terms:** Check-in 4 pm; no pets. **Facility:** 92 rooms. 3 stories; exterior corridors. **All Rooms:** free movies. **Cards:** AE, CB, DI, DS, MC, VI. 🛌 CTV ✕ D

HOLIDAY INN OCEANFRONT RESORT **Phone:** 803/785-5126

(AAA) (SAVE)

◆◆◆

Hotel

2/27-11/14	1P: $139- 239	2P/1B: $139- 239	2P/2B: $139- 239	XP: $10 F18
12/1-2/26 & 11/15-11/30	1P: $79- 139	2P/1B: $79- 139	2P/2B: $79- 139	XP: $10 F18

Location: Via US 278; Pope Ave at Coligny Cir. 1 S Forest Beach Dr 29928. Fax: 803/785-6678. **Terms:** Reserv deposit; BP avail; package plans; no pets. **Facility:** 201 rooms. Oceanfront grounds. Handling fee imposed; 5 stories; interior corridors; beach, wading pool; playground. Fee: golf privileges. **Dining & Entertainment:** Dining room; 7 am-2 & 5:30-10 pm; $8-$18; cocktails/lounge. **Services:** Fee: coin laundry. **Recreation:** children's program; swimming. Rental: bicycles. **All Rooms:** coffeemakers, free & pay movies, combo or shower baths. **Some Rooms:** Fee: refrigerators. **Cards:** AE, CB, DI, DS, JCB, MC, VI. **Special Amenities:** Free newspaper. *(See color ad below)* 🛌 🍴 CTV ✕ 🏊 D

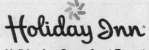

HYATT REGENCY HILTON HEAD RESORT

Phone: 803/785-1234

(AAA) SAVE

2/13-11/21	1P: $185- 265	2P/1B: $185- 265	2P/2B: $185- 265	XP: $25	F18
12/1-2/12 & 11/22-11/30	1P: $115- 155	2P/1B: $115- 155	2P/2B: $115- 155	XP: $25	F18

◆◆◆◆
Resort Hotel

Location: Via US 278, in Palmetto Dunes Resort area. 1 Hyatt Cir 29938 (PO Box 6167). **Fax:** 803/842-4695. **Terms:** Check-in 4 pm; package plans; no pets. **Facility:** 505 rooms. All rooms with balcony. 5-10 stories; interior corridors; oceanfront; luxury level rooms; beach, wading pool, saunas, whirlpools, 2 pools (1 heated indoor); aerobics & exercise instruction. Fee: 54 holes golf; 25 tennis courts (6 lighted). **Dining & Entertainment:** 2 dining rooms, coffee shop; 7 am-11 pm; $9-$22; cocktails/lounge; also, Hemingway's, see separate listing; entertainment. **Services:** valet laundry. Fee: massage; valet parking. **Recreation:** children's program, recreation program; swimming, fishing, surf fishing. Rental: paddleboats, sailboats; bicycles. **All Rooms:** coffeemakers, free & pay movies, combo or shower baths. Fee: safes. **Some Rooms:** refrigerators. **Cards:** AE, CB, DI, DS, MC, VI.

🅿️ 🎴 🛏️ CTV ✕ 🅰️ D S

THE ISLAND CLUB OF HILTON HEAD BY HILTON HEAD VACATION RENTALS

Phone: 803/686-3400

(AAA) SAVE

◆◆◆
Cottage

3/23-4/25 & 5/16-8/22 Weekly		2P/1B: $778	2P/2B: $956-1335
3/1-3/22, 4/26-5/15 & 8/23-10/31 Weekly		2P/1B: $585	2P/2B: $717-1002
12/1-2/28 & 11/1-11/30 Weekly		2P/1B: $506	2P/2B: $622- 868

Location: Off US 278, in the Plaza at Shelter Cove Shopping Center. Suite N Plaza at Shelter Cove 29928. **Fax:** 803/686-3701. **Terms:** Check-in 4 pm; reserv deposit, 30 day notice; package plans; 3 night min stay, off season; no pets. **Facility:** 65 rooms. Nicely appointed villas, some with an ocean view & some with a view of a lagoon. 40 two-bedroom units. 3-bedroom units, $1495 weekly in season. Handling fee imposed; 5 stories; exterior corridors; beach, wading pool, whirlpool; 9 tennis courts (2 lighted). Fee: golf privileges. **Services:** guest laundry. **Recreation:** children's program, nature program, recreation program, social program; swimming. Fee: bicycles. **All Rooms:** kitchens, microwaves, refrigerators, VCP's. **Cards:** AE, DS, MC, VI. **Special Amenities: Free local telephone calls.** *(See color ad below)*

🅿️ 🎴 🛏️ CTV ✕ D

MAIN STREET INN

Phone: 803/681-3001

(AAA) SAVE

◆◆◆◆
Bed & Breakfast

3/16-11/15 [BP]	2P/1B: $195- 325	2P/2B: $195	XP: $35
12/1-3/15 & 11/16-11/30 [BP]	2P/1B: $125- 255	2P/2B: $125	XP: $35

Location: Off US 278 3.3 mi e. 2200 Main St 29926 (PO Box 23886, 29925). **Fax:** 803/681-5541. **Terms:** Age restrictions may apply; reserv deposit, 14 day notice; package plans; no pets. **Facility:** 34 rooms. In a quiet area of the Island. All rooms are lavishly furnished & tastefully decorated. Very comforting public areas. A beautiful garden & courtyard. 4 rooms with fireplace. Handling fee imposed; 3 stories; exterior corridors; smoke free premises; whirlpool, small lap pool. Fee: golf & tennis privileges. **Dining & Entertainment:** Cocktail lounge; 24-hour room service; afternoon tea; restaurant nearby. **Services:** valet laundry. Fee: massage. **All Rooms:** refrigerators. **Some Rooms:** VCP's, whirlpools. **Cards:** AE, DS, MC, VI. **Special Amenities: Early check-in/late check-out and free room upgrade (subject to availability with advanced reservations).** *(See ad below)*

🎴 CTV ✕ D S

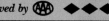

MOTEL 6 - 1129
Ⓐⓐⓐ
◆
Motel

Guaranteed Rates
All Year   1P: $49- 59 2P/1B: $59- 69 2P/2B: $59- 69 XP: $3   F17
Location: On US 278, between Palmetto Dunes & Shipyard Plantation. 830 William Hilton Pkwy 29928.
Fax: 803/842-9543. **Terms:** Sr. discount; small pets only. **Facility:** 116 rooms. 1 story; exterior corridors.
All Rooms: free movies. **Cards:** AE, DI, DS, MC, VI.   Roll in showers.
Phone: 803/785-2700
🐾 🛏 CTV ✕ 🚫 Ⓓ

PALMETTO DUNES RESORT
◆◆◆
Resort
Complex

Rates Subject to Change
3/10-9/2   1P: $110- 170
9/3-10/31   1P: $105- 160
12/1-3/9 & 11/1-11/30   1P: $80- 115
2P/2B: $121- 251
2P/2B: $126- 221
2P/2B: $101- 201
Phone: 803/785-1161
Location: On US 278. 29938 (PO Box 5606). Fax: 803/686-2877. **Terms:** Check-in 4 pm; reserv deposit, 14 day notice; no pets. **Facility:** 480 rooms. 2 to 6-bedroom units avail, 3-bedroom in season $200-$416; 5 stories; exterior corridors. **Dining:** 7 am-10 pm; $7-$25. **All Rooms:** kitchens. **Cards:** AE, MC, VI. *(See color ad below)*   CTV ✕ Ⓓ

RADISSON SUITE RESORT
◆◆◆
Suite Motor Inn

Rates Subject to Change
3/1-11/30 [CP]   1P: $119- 179 2P/1B: $119- 179 2P/2B: $119- 179 XP: $15   F18
3/12-2/28 [CP]   1P: $99   2P/1B: $99   2P/2B: $99   XP: $15   F18
Phone: 803/686-5700
Location: Off US 278 in Central Park Complex. 12 Park Ln 29928. Fax: 803/686-3952. **Terms:** Sr. discount; reserv deposit; no pets. **Facility:** 156 rooms. Handling fee imposed; 3 stories; interior corridors. **Dining:** Restaurant; 11 am-10 pm; $8-$18. **All Rooms:** kitchens, free & pay movies. **Cards:** AE, CB, DI, DS, MC, VI.   🛏 ⊬ CTV ✕ Ⓓ Ⓢ

RED ROOF INN-HILTON HEAD
◆◆
Motel

Rates Subject to Change
5/1-9/30   1P: $58- 65 2P/1B: $65- 70 2P/2B: $70- 76 XP: $5 F18
3/15-4/30   1P: $52- 62 2P/1B: $65- 68 2P/2B: $68- 72 XP: $5 F18
12/1-3/14 & 10/1-11/30 1P: $40- 45 2P/1B: $48- 55 2P/2B: $58- 65 XP: $5 F18
Phone: 803/686-6808
Location: On US 278; between Shipyard Plantation & Palmetto Dunes. 5 Regency Pkwy 29928. Fax: 803/842-3352.
Terms: Small pets only. **Facility:** 112 rooms. 2 stories; exterior corridors. **All Rooms:** free movies. **Cards:** AE, CB, DI, DS, MC, VI.
🐾 🛏 CTV ✕ 🚫 Ⓓ Ⓢ

ROYAL DUNES RESORT
◆◆◆
Condo
Complex

Guaranteed Rates
3/29-4/25 & 6/7-8/22 Weekly
4/26-6/6 & 8/23-10/31 Weekly
12/1-3/28 & 11/1-11/30 Weekly
2P/2B:$1200
2P/2B:$1050
2P/2B: $850
Phone: 803/681-9718
Location: 1 mi off US 278; in Port Royal Plantation. 8 Wimbledon Ct 29928. Fax: 803/689-1997. **Terms:** Check-in 4 pm; reserv deposit, 30 day notice; no pets. **Facility:** 56 rooms. Handling fee imposed; 4 stories; interior/exterior corridors. **Cards:** DS, MC, VI.   🛏 CTV Ⓓ Ⓢ

SEA PINES RESORT ◆◆◆ Resort Complex

Rates Subject to Change

Phone: 803/785-3333

5/31-8/15	1P: $145- 200	2P/2B: $165- 235
8/16-10/31	1P: $125- 175	2P/2B: $160- 210
3/11-5/30	1P: $125- 195	2P/2B: $160- 210
12/1-3/10 & 11/1-11/30	1P: $85- 120	2P/2B: $110- 145

Location: Via US 278. (PO Box 7000, 29938). Fax: 803/842-1475. **Terms:** Check-in 4 pm; reserv deposit, 14 day notice; no pets. **Facility:** 400 rooms. Rates are based on 4 night min stay. 3-bedroom villas $165-235 in season. Handling fee imposed; 5 stories; exterior corridors. **Dining:** Dining room, 5 restaurants; 7 am-10 pm; $7-$27. **All Rooms:** kitchens. **Cards:** AE, DI, DS, MC, VI. (See color ad p 567)   [CTV]

SHONEY'S INN ◆◆◆ Motor Inn

Rates Subject to Change

Phone: 803/681-3655

4/1-10/31	1P:	$72	2P/1B:	$78- 89	2P/2B:	$72- 89	XP: $6	F12
12/1-3/31 & 11/1-11/30	1P:	$54	2P/1B:	$54- 65	2P/2B:	$54- 65	XP: $6	F12

Location: On US 278, just e of Island Bridge on n side of road. 200 Museum St 29926. Fax: 803/681-3655. **Terms:** Sr. discount; reserv deposit, 7 day notice; small pets only, $25 extra charge. **Facility:** 136 rooms. 2 stories; exterior corridors. **Dining:** Restaurant; 7 am-10 pm, Sat & Sun-11 pm; $5-$10. **All Rooms:** free movies. **Cards:** AE, CB, DI, DS, MC, VI.   [🐾][🖨][CTV][✕][📶][D]

SOUTHWIND II ◆◆◆ Condo Complex

Rates Subject to Change

Phone: 803/842-6556

All Year Weekly   2P/2B: $795-1250

Location: In Shipyard Plantation. Rd 29938 (PO Box 8048). Fax: 803/785-6552. **Terms:** Check-in 5 pm; reserv deposit, 60 day notice; no pets. **Facility:** 24 rooms. 2 stories; exterior corridors. **All Rooms:** kitchens, free movies. **Cards:** MC, VI. (See ad below)   [🖨][CTV][D]

SPINNAKER AT SHIPYARD [AAA][SAVE] ◆◆◆ Cottage

Phone: 803/842-6556

3/21-4/24 & 5/30-8/21 Weekly		2P/2B:$1250
2/28-3/20, 4/25-5/29 & 8/22-9/11 Weekly 9/12-10/30 Weekly		2P/2B:$1150 2P/2B:$1050
12/1-2/27 & 10/31-11/30 Weekly		2P/2B: $975

Location: US 278 to New Orleans Rd, just e. 14 New Orleans Rd, Suite 2 29938 (PO Box 8048). Fax: 803/785-6552. **Terms:** Reserv deposit, 30 day notice; daily/monthly rates; package plans; no pets. **Facility:** 48 rooms. Units overlooking fairway or small ponds. Very nicely furnished units. Rates for up to 6 persons. Handling fee imposed; 2 stories; exterior corridors; whirlpool. **Services:** guest laundry. **All Rooms:** kitchens, microwaves, free movies, refrigerators, whirlpools. **Cards:** MC, VI. **Special Amenities:** Free local telephone calls. (See ad below)   [🖨][CTV][D]

VILLAMARE [AAA][SAVE] ◆◆◆ Condo Motel

Phone: 803/842-6212

3/1-9/15	2P/1B: $180- 220	2P/2B: $260- 340
12/1-12/31 & 9/16-11/30	2P/1B: $140- 180	2P/2B: $180- 240
1/1-2/28	2P/1B: $90- 120	2P/2B: $120- 160

Location: Via US 278 to Pope Ave, 1.3 mi from traffic circle in Coligny Plaza Welcome Center. 6 Lagoon Rd 29928. Fax: 803/785-2147. **Terms:** Check-in 4 pm; reserv deposit, 21 day notice, handling fee imposed; monthly rates; package plans; no pets. **Facility:** 41 rooms. All units with balcony & view of ocean. 25 two-bedroom units. 4 three-bedroom units $1895-$2395; 9/16-12/1, $1295-$1795; 12/2-2/28, $1095-$1395; rates for up to 6 persons; 3 stories; exterior corridors; oceanfront; sauna, whirlpools. Fee: golf privileges; 26 tennis courts (10 lighted). **Services:** guest laundry. **All Rooms:** kitchens, microwaves, refrigerators. **Some Rooms:** Fee: VCP's, whirlpools. **Cards:** AE, DS, MC, VI. **Special Amenities:** Free local telephone calls and free room upgrade (subject to availability with advanced reservations). (See ad p 561 & color ad p 566)   [🖨][🖨][CTV][✕][D]

THE WESTIN RESORT, HILTON HEAD ISLAND [AAA][SAVE] ◆◆◆◆ Resort Hotel

Phone: 803/681-4000

3/2-11/13	1P: $255- 355	2P/1B: $255- 355	XP: $20	F18
12/1-3/1 & 11/14-11/30	1P: $130- 220	2P/1B: $130- 220	XP: $20	F18

Location: 1 mi off US 278, in Port Royal Plantation. 2 Grass Lawn Ave 29928. Fax: 803/681-1087. **Terms:** Check-in 4 pm; reserv deposit, 3 day notice; $5 service charge; MAP avail; package plans; no pets. **Facility:** 412 rooms. All rooms with balcony; some with spectacular Atlantic Ocean view. Pool area dotted with charming sculpture gardens & a swan pond. Handling fee imposed; 5 stories; interior corridors; luxury level rooms; beach, saunas, steamrooms, whirlpools; playground. Fee: 54 holes golf; 16 tennis courts (6 lighted); aerobics. **Dining & Entertainment:** Dining room, 2 restaurants, cafeteria; 6:30 am-10:30 pm; $8-$26; cocktails/lounge; entertainment 3/1-10/1; afternoon tea 3-5 pm 11/1-3/31; also, The Barony Grill, see separate listing. **Services:** valet laundry; area transportation, shopping, golf, resorts. Fee: childcare; massage; valet parking. **Recreation:** children's program, nature program, recreation program, social program; swimming, charter fishing, surf fishing. Fee: kids night out, T'ai Chi; sailboats, windsurfing, aqua aerobics. Rental: bicycles. **All Rooms:** honor bars, coffeemakers, free & pay movies, safes. **Some Rooms:** refrigerators, whirlpools. Fee: VCP's. **Cards:** AE, CB, DI, MC, VI. **Special Amenities:** Early check-in/late check-out and free local telephone calls.   [🖨][🖨][🐾][🏋][🏋][CTV][✕][D][S]

RESTAURANTS

AMIGOS CAFE 'Y CANTINA **Lunch:** $3-$6 **Dinner:** $3-$7 **Phone:** 803/785-8226
◆
Location: From Sea Pines Circle/US 278, 0.5 mi in the Circle Center. 70 Pope Ave 29928. **Hours:** 11 am-9
Mexican
pm. Closed: 11/26 & 12/25. **Features:** casual dress; children's menu; carryout; beer & wine only; a la carte.
A small cozy cantina decor, serving authentic dishes from the Coast of Baja. A self serve type service with
paper plates & plastic utensils. **Cards:** DS, MC, VI.

THE BARONY GRILL **Dinner:** $19-$24 **Phone:** 803/681-4000
ⒶⒶⒶ
Location: 1 mi off US 278, in Port Royal Plantation; in The Westin Resort, Hilton Head Island. 2 Grass Lawn
◆◆◆◆
Ave 29928. **Hours:** 5:30-10 pm. Closed: Sun & Mon. **Reservations:** suggested. **Features:** casual dress;
Steak and
health conscious menu items; cocktails; fee for valet parking; a la carte. Intimate dining room with a "resort
Seafood
casual" atmosphere. Wide selection of contemporary cuisine to include meat, pasta, seafood with a bistro
flair, full wine room & tasting avail. Smoke free premises. **Cards:** AE, CB, DI, DS, JCB, MC, VI. 🚫 ✖

CAFE AT WEXFORD **Lunch:** $6-$8 **Dinner:** $16-$19 **Phone:** 803/686-5969
◆◆
Location: 0.9 mi w of the Sea Pines Circle, on US 278. Village at Wexford J6 29928. **Hours:** 11:30 am-2 &
French
6-10 pm. Closed: 12/25. **Reservations:** required; for dinner. **Features:** casual dress; Sunday brunch;
carryout; cocktails; minimum charge-$8. Featuring a southern country French cuisine served in a nice, comfy
atmosphere. **Cards:** AE, DI, MC, VI.

HARBOURMASTER'S **Dinner:** $14-$22 **Phone:** 803/785-3030
◆◆◆
Location: Off US 278 across from Palmetto Dunes; on harbour in Shelter Cove. 1 Shelter Cove Ln 29938.
Continental
Hours: 5 pm-10 pm. Closed: Sun & 1/1-2/1. **Reservations:** required. **Features:** casual dress; cocktails &
lounge; a la carte. Inviting bay-front atmosphere featuring fresh seafood entrees as well as a variety of meat
& pasta. **Cards:** AE, CB, DI, MC, VI. ✖

HEMINGWAY'S **Dinner:** $17-$24 **Phone:** 803/785-1234
◆◆◆
Location: Via US 278, in Palmetto Dunes Resort area; in Hyatt Regency Hilton Head Resort. **Hours:** 5
Steak and
pm-10 pm. **Reservations:** suggested. **Features:** early bird specials; health conscious menu; cocktails &
Seafood
lounge; entertainment; fee for valet parking; a la carte. Oceanfront dining in a casual "Key West"
atmosphere. **Cards:** AE, DI, DS, MC, VI. ✖

KINGFISHER/LAPOLA'S **Dinner:** $10-$24 **Phone:** 803/785-4442
◆◆
Location: Off US 278 opposite Palmetto Dunes in Shelter Cove Harbour. 8 Harbour Ln 29938. **Hours:** 5
Steak and
pm-10 pm. Closed: 12/25. **Reservations:** suggested. **Features:** casual dress; early bird specials; cocktails &
Seafood
lounge; a la carte. Many tables with view of the Shelter Cove Harbor, great view of sunsets. A menu
featuring many fresh seafood items as well as steak. Lapola's upstairs features fresh fish & an Italian menu.
Cards: AE, DS, MC, VI. ✖

MOSTLY SEAFOOD **Dinner:** $8-$23 **Phone:** 803/842-8500
ⒶⒶⒶ
Location: On US 278 in Palmetto Dunes Resort; in Hilton Head Island Hilton Resort. 23 Ocean Ln 29938.
◆◆◆
Hours: 5:30 pm-10 pm. **Reservations:** suggested. **Features:** children's menu; cocktails & lounge; valet
Seafood
parking; a la carte. Innovative fresh seafood menu; also Angus steak, chicken, pasta & a variety of wines by
the glass. Smoke free premises. **Cards:** AE, CB, DI, DS, MC, VI. ✖

THE NANTUCKET SEAFOOD HOUSE **Dinner:** $6-$25 **Phone:** 803/686-6339
◆◆◆
Location: 0.5 mi n of Sea Pines Circle. 26 New Orleans Rd 29928. **Hours:** 4:30 pm-10 pm. Closed major
Steak and
holidays. **Reservations:** suggested. **Features:** casual dress; children's menu; carryout; cocktails. Most of the
Seafood
menu is flown in from Boston. **Cards:** AE, DS, MC, VI. ✖

STARFIRE CONTEMPORARY BISTRO **Dinner:** $14-$20 **Phone:** 803/785-3434
◆◆◆
Location: From 278 to New Orleans Rd, e in the Orleans Plaza. 37 New Orleans Dr 29928. **Hours:** 6
American
pm-10 pm. Closed: Sun & 11/26. **Reservations:** suggested. **Features:** casual dress; carryout; cocktails; a la
carte. Featuring modern American cuisine with emphasis on fresh regional produce & seafood. The foods
are excellent in taste & creativity. The dining room atmosphere is warm & contemporary. Smoke free premises. **Cards:** AE,
DI, MC, VI.

TRUFFLES CAFE **Lunch:** $3-$9 **Dinner:** $9-$15 **Phone:** 803/671-6136
◆◆
Location: In Sea Pines Resort, from traffic circle, 2.8 mi on Greenwood Dr to circle bear first right for 0.3 mi.
American
79 Lighthouse Rd, Sea Pines Ctr 29928. **Hours:** 11 am-10 pm. Closed: 11/26 & 12/25. **Features:** casual
dress; children's menu; carryout; cocktails & lounge. A comfortable & casual setting, featuring fresh seafood
entrees as well as pasta & meat entrees. Smoking permitted in bar only. A $3 gate fee to enter Sea Pines Resort. Large
selection of wine by the glass. Smoke free premises. **Cards:** AE, DS, MC, VI. ✖

TWO ELEVEN PARK WINE & BISTRO **Dinner:** $11-$19 **Phone:** 803/686-5212
◆◆◆
Location: 0.3 mi e of Sea Pines Circle, in the Park Plaza near the cinema off Greenwood Dr. 24 Park Plaza
Regional
29928. **Hours:** 5:30 pm-11 pm, light fare to 12:30 am. Closed: Sun. **Reservations:** accepted.
American
Features: casual dress; children's menu; carryout; cocktails & lounge; a la carte. Featuring "fusion cuisine,"
a style of cooking with American, Southern & Italian influences. Fresh seafood avail as well as pasta, meat &
boutique pizza. Over 75 wines by the glass. **Cards:** AE, CB, DI, DS, MC, VI. ✖

HOLLYWOOD—*see Charleston & Vicinity p. 458.*

HONEA PATH—3,800

LODGING

SUGARFOOT CASTLE, A BED & BREAKFAST Rates Subject to Change **Phone:** 864/369-6565
◆◆ All Year [CP] **1P:** $63 **2P/1B:** $68 **2P/2B:** $68
Historic Bed
Location: 0.3 mi s on S Main St from jct US 76, 178 & SR 252. 211 S Main St 29654. **Terms:** Age
& Breakfast
restrictions may apply; check-in 4 pm; reserv deposit, 7 day notice; 2 night min stay; no pets. **Facility:** 3 rooms.
2 stories; interior corridors; smoke free premises. **Cards:** MC, VI. CTV ✖ Ⓓ

ISLE OF PALMS—*See Charleston & Vicinity p. 458.*

JOHNS ISLAND—See Charleston & Vicinity p. 459.

KIAWAH ISLAND—See Charleston & Vicinity p. 459.

LADSON—See Charleston & Vicinity p. 460.

LANCASTER—8,900

LODGINGS

BEST WESTERN-LANCASTER   Phone: 803/283-1200
🛆🛆🛆 [SAVE]   All Year [CP]   1P: $39- 50 2P/1B: $39- 50 2P/2B: $50- 60 XP: $5   F12
♦♦♦   **Location:** 1 mi w of jct US 521. 1201 Hwy 9 bypass 29720. Fax: 803/286-8873. **Terms:** Reserv deposit; no
Motel pets. **Facility:** 60 rooms. Inviting lobby & tastefully decorated rooms. Suites, $55-$75; 2 stories; exterior corri-
       dors; small pool. **Dining:** Restaurant nearby. **Services:** Fee: coin laundry. **All Rooms:** free movies,
       refrigerators. **Some Rooms:** Fee: VCP's, whirlpools. **Cards:** AE, CB, DI, DS, JCB, MC, VI.
Special Amenities: Free breakfast and free newspaper.   🛆 CTV ✕ D

THE JAMESON INN   Rates Subject to Change   Phone: 803/283-1188
♦♦♦   All Year [CP]   1P: $46   2P/1B: $50   2P/2B: $50   XP: $4   F12
Motel **Location:** On SR 9 bypass, 1 mi w of jct US 521. 114 Commerce Blvd 29720. Fax: 803/286-1028.
       Terms: No pets. **Facility:** 42 rooms. 2 stories; exterior corridors. **All Rooms:** free movies. **Cards:** AE, DI,
DS, MC, VI.   🛥 CTV 🛆 ✕ D

LANDRUM—2,300

LODGING

THE RED HORSE INN   Rates Subject to Change   Phone: 864/895-4968
Cottage All Year [CP]   1P: $85   2P/1B: $85   2P/2B: $85   XP: $10
       Too new to rate; **Location:** 1 mi w on SR 11 from jct SR 14, 1 mi s on Tugaloo Rd to N Campbell Rd. 310 N
Campbell Rd 29356. **Terms:** Check-in 4 pm; reserv deposit, 7 day notice; small pets only. **Facility:** 5 rooms. Scheduled to
open September 1997. Handling fee imposed; exterior corridors. **All Rooms:** kitchens.   🐾 ✕ D

LATTA—1,600

LODGING

ABINGDON MANOR   Rates Subject to Change   Phone: 803/752-5090
♦♦♦♦   All Year [BP]   1P: $95   2P/1B: $95   2P/2B: $95   XP: $25
Historic Bed **Location:** From jct SR 917 & US 301, 0.4 mi n on US 301, just w on Academy, then left & 1st house on
& Breakfast   right. 307 Church St 29565. **Terms:** Age restrictions may apply; reserv deposit, 3 day notice; no pets.
       Facility: 5 rooms. 1 room suite, $120; 2 stories; interior corridors; designated smoking area.
All Rooms: free movies. **Cards:** AE, DI, DS, MC, VI.   CTV ✕ D

LAURENS—9,700

RESTAURANT

GRAYSTONE STEAK HOUSE   Dinner: $13-$22   Phone: 864/984-5521
🛆🛆   **Location:** On US 221, 1.3 mi s of jct US 76. 1100 S Harper St 29360. **Hours:** 5:30 pm-10 pm. Closed major
       holidays, Sun & 7/1-7/7. **Reservations:** suggested. **Features:** casual dress; children's menu; early bird
♦♦   specials; carryout; salad bar; cocktails. Informal dining in a charming mansion with candlelit dining rooms.
Steak and Rack of lamb also featured as well as daily chef's specialties. A local favorite since 1969. **Cards:** AE, DI, DS,
Seafood MC, VI.   ✕

LEXINGTON—3,300

LODGING

COMFORT INN LEXINGTON   Phone: 803/359-3099
🛆🛆 [SAVE] 4/1-4/30 [CP]   1P: $60- 65 2P/1B: $60- 65 2P/2B: $75- 90 XP: $5   F18
       3/1-3/31 & 5/1-10/31 [CP]   1P: $45- 50 2P/1B: $50- 54 2P/2B: $60- 80 XP: $5   F18
♦♦♦   12/1-2/28 & 11/1-11/30 [CP] 1P: $44- 48 2P/1B: $46- 51 2P/2B: $51   XP: $5   F18
Motel **Location:** 3.5 mi s on US 1 from I-20 exit 58. 328 W Main St 29072. Fax: 803/359-3099. **Terms:** No pets.
       Facility: 62 rooms. Located in a small rural town just minutes from scenic 50,000 acre Lake Murray. 6 deluxe
suites, $75; 2 stories; exterior corridors. **Dining:** Restaurant nearby. **All Rooms:** coffeemakers, microwaves, free movies,
refrigerators. **Some Rooms:** 6 efficiencies, no utensils, whirlpools. **Cards:** AE, CB, DI, DS, MC, VI. **Special Amenities:**
Free breakfast and free local telephone calls.   🛥 🛆 CTV ✕ 🐕 D S

RESTAURANT

RESTAURANT AT CINNAMON HILL Historical   Lunch: $6-$9   Dinner: $11-$18   Phone: 803/957-8297
🛆🛆   **Location:** On SR 6, 0.5 mi n of I-20, exit 55; 1 mi s of jct US 1 & SR 6. 808 S Lake Dr 29071. **Hours:** 11:30
       am-2 & 6-10 pm, Sun 10 am-2 pm. Closed major holidays. **Reservations:** suggested. **Features:** casual
♦♦   dress; Sunday brunch; carryout; cocktails. A charming Victorian home circa 1892. Cozy, rustic dining rooms.
American Also lunch buffet. **Cards:** AE, MC, VI.   ✕

LITCHFIELD BEACH—See The Grand Strand p. 483.

LITTLE RIVER—See The Grand Strand p. 483.

MANNING—4,400

LODGINGS

COMFORT INN   Phone: 803/473-7550
🛆🛆 [SAVE] All Year [CP]   1P: $40- 49 2P/1B: $45- 59 2P/2B: $59- 70 XP: $5   F18
       Location: Jct I-95 & SR 261, exit 119. 29102 (PO Box 57). Fax: 803/473-7553. **Terms:** Weekly rates; pets.
♦♦   **Facility:** 60 rooms. 2 stories; exterior corridors; small pool. **Dining:** Coffee shop nearby. **All Rooms:** free
Motel movies. **Some Rooms:** Fee: VCP's. **Cards:** AE, CB, DI, DS, JCB, MC, VI. **Special Amenities:** Free
       breakfast and free local telephone calls.   🐾 CTV ✕ D

DAYS INN OF MANNING
◆◆
Motor Inn
Rates Subject to Change
All Year   1P: $26- 48   2P/1B: $30- 48   2P/2B: $30- 48   XP: $5   D12
Location: I-95, exit 115 at jct US 301. Rt 5, I-95 & US 301 29102. **Fax:** 803/473-4058. **Terms:** Sr. discount; pets, $5 extra charge. **Facility:** 120 rooms. 2 stories; exterior corridors. **Dining:** Restaurant; 6 am-9 pm; $3-$7. **All Rooms:** free movies. **Cards:** AE, CB, DI, DS, MC, VI.
Phone: 803/473-2596
🛏 🛍 CTV ✕ D

MANNING ECONOMY INN
AAA
◆◆
Motel
Rates Subject to Change
All Year [CP]   1P: $30- 44   2P/1B: $32- 48   2P/2B: $32- 50   XP: $5   F12
Location: Jct I-95 & SR 261, exit 119. 29102 (PO Box 490). **Terms:** Sr. discount; reserv deposit; small pets only. **Facility:** 57 rooms. 2 stories; exterior corridors. **All Rooms:** free movies. **Cards:** AE, DS, MC, VI.
Phone: 803/473-4021
🛏 🛍 CTV ✕ D

MARION—7,700

LODGING

COMFORT INN
◆◆◆
Motel
Guaranteed Rates
All Year [CP]   1P: $41- 100   2P/1B: $51- 100   2P/2B: $46- 100   XP: $5   F18
Location: US 76 & US 501 bypass 29571 (PO Box 925). **Fax:** 803/423-4276. **Terms:** Sr. discount; reserv deposit; no pets. **Facility:** 55 rooms. 2 stories; interior corridors. **All Rooms:** free movies. **Cards:** AE, CB, DI, DS, JCB, MC, VI.
Phone: 803/423-0516
CTV ✕ D

MCCLELLANVILLE—*See Charleston & Vicinity p. 460.*

MCCORMICK—1,660

LODGING

FANNIE KATE'S COUNTRY INN & RESTAURANT
◆◆◆
Historic
Country Inn
Rates Subject to Change
All Year   1P: $45- 75   2P/1B: $65- 75   XP: $10
Location: Center, just w of jct US 221 & 378. 127 S Main St 29835. **Fax:** 864/465-0057. **Terms:** No pets. **Facility:** 8 rooms. 3 stories; interior corridors; designated smoking area. **Dining:** Restaurant; 8 am-2 & 5-10 pm; $5-$16. **Cards:** AE, DS, MC, VI.
Phone: 864/465-0061
✕ D S

MOUNT PLEASANT—*See Charleston & Vicinity p. 460.*

MURRELLS INLET—*See The Grand Strand p. 483.*

MYRTLE BEACH—*See The Grand Strand p. 484.*

GREATER MYRTLE BEACH—*See The Grand Strand p. 540.*

NEWBERRY—10,500

LODGING

BEST WESTERN NEWBERRY INN
AAA SAVE
◆◆
Motor Inn
All Year [CP]   1P: $38   2P/1B: $43   2P/2B: $48   XP: $6   F12
Location: On SR 34 at jct I-26, exit 74. 11701 S Carolina Hwy 34 29108. **Fax:** 803/276-9851. **Terms:** Weekly/monthly rates; package plans; small pets only. **Facility:** 113 rooms. Pleasant rooms. Suites $80-90, single or double occupancy; 1-2 stories; exterior corridors. **Dining & Entertainment:** Restaurant; 5 am-9 pm, Sun from 7 am-3 pm; $5-$16; cocktails/lounge. **Services:** valet laundry. **Recreation:** small playground. **All Rooms:** free movies. **Some Rooms:** microwaves, refrigerators, VCP's. **Cards:** AE, DI, DS, MC, VI. **Special Amenities:** Free breakfast.
Phone: 803/276-5850
🛏 🛍 📶 🏋 CTV ✕ D

NORTH AUGUSTA—15,400

LODGING

ROSEMARY HALL & LOOKAWAY HALL-A CONSUL COURT INN
AAA SAVE
◆◆◆◆
Historic Bed
& Breakfast
All Year [BP]   1P: $75- 195   2P/1B: $75- 195   2P/2B: $195   XP: $15   F10
Location: From I-20 exit 1 & SR 230 e for 3.3 mi to US 25/Georgia Ave then s 0.5 mi, turn right onto Carolina Ave. 804 Carolina Ave 29841. **Fax:** 803/278-4877. **Terms:** Age restrictions may apply; package plans; no pets. **Facility:** 23 rooms. 2 large homes built circa 1900 with excellent manicured grounds. The public areas are splendid with original antiques. The rooms are tastefully decorated & furnished with period antiques. 2 stories; interior corridors; smoke free premises. **Dining:** Cocktail service avail; afternoon tea; restaurant nearby. **Services:** valet laundry. **All Rooms:** combo or shower baths. **Some Rooms:** Fee: whirlpools. **Cards:** AE, CB, DI, DS, MC, VI. **Special Amenities:** Free breakfast and preferred room (subject to availability with advanced reservations). *(See ad below)*
Phone: 803/278-6222
🏋 🏋 CTV ✕ D S

RESTAURANT

S & S CAFETERIA　　　　　　　　　　　　　　　　　　　　　　**Phone: 803/279-7882**
◆　　　**Location:** On US 25 at jct Martintown Rd; in North Augusta Plaza Shopping Center. 352 E Martintown Rd
American　　29841. **Hours:** 11 am-2:15 & 5-8 pm. Closed: 12/25. **Features:** casual dress; children's menu; carryout. ⊠

NORTH CHARLESTON—*See Charleston & Vicinity p. 463.*

NORTH MYRTLE BEACH—*See The Grand Strand p. 547.*

ORANGEBURG—13,700

LODGINGS

BEST WESTERN INN OF ORANGEBURG　　　Rates Subject to Change　　　**Phone: 803/534-7630**
AAA　　　All Year [CP]　　　1P: $33- 41　2P/1B: $38- 47　2P/2B: $38- 47　XP: $6　F12
◆◆◆　　**Location:** 2 blks s on US 301 & 601. 826 John C Calhoun Dr 29115. Fax: 803/534-7630. **Terms:** Sr.
Motel　　discount; pets, $8 extra charge. **Facility:** 104 rooms. 2-3 stories; exterior corridors. **All Rooms:** free movies.
　　　　Cards: AE, CB, DI, DS, MC, VI. *(See color ad below)*　　　　　　　🐾 ⌂ CTV ⊠ Ⓓ

COMFORT INN　　　　　　　　　　　　　　　　　　　　　　　**Phone: 803/531-9200**
AAA SAVE　All Year [CP]　　　1P: $50- 65　2P/1B: $50- 75　2P/2B: $55- 75　XP: $6　F17
◆◆◆　　**Location:** On US 601 at jct I-26, exit 145A. 3671 St Matthews Rd 29118. Fax: 803/536-4400. **Terms:** No
Motel　　pets. **Facility:** 60 rooms. Attractive public areas. Nicely appointed & decorated rooms. 2 stories; exterior cor-
　　　　ridors. **Dining & Entertainment:** Cocktails/lounge. **Services:** Fee: coin laundry. **All Rooms:** coffeemakers,
microwaves, free movies, refrigerators, combo or shower baths. **Some Rooms:** Fee: whirlpools. **Cards:** AE,
CB, DI, DS, MC, VI. **Special Amenities:** Free breakfast and free local telephone calls. ⌂ 🐾 CTV ⊠ Ⓐ Ⓓ Ⓢ

HOLIDAY INN　　　　　　　　　　　　　　　　　　　　　　　**Phone: 803/531-4600**
AAA SAVE　All Year　　　1P: $54- 64　2P/1B: $62- 74　2P/2B: $61- 74　XP: $8　F19
◆◆◆　　**Location:** 0.8 mi w on US 301 & 601. 1415 John C Calhoun Dr 29115. Fax: 803/516-0187. **Terms:** Pets.
Motor Inn　**Facility:** 161 rooms. 2 stories; exterior corridors. **Dining & Entertainment:** Dining room; 6:30 am-2 & 5-9
　　　　pm, Sat & Sun 7 am-2 & 5:30-9 pm; $7-$13; cocktails/lounge. **Services:** valet laundry. **All Rooms:** free &
pay movies. **Some Rooms:** Fee: whirlpools. **Cards:** AE, CB, DI, DS, JCB, MC, VI. **Special Amenities:**
Early check-in/late check-out and preferred room (subject to availability with advanced reservations).
　　　　　　　　　　　　　　　　　　　　　🐾 ⌂ 🐾 CTV ⊠ Ⓐ Ⓓ

HOWARD JOHNSON　　　　　　　　　　　　　　　　　　　　　**Phone: 803/531-4900**
AAA SAVE　All Year [CP]　　　1P: $46- 60　2P/1B: $46- 60　2P/2B: $50- 70　XP: $5　F10
◆◆　　　**Location:** From I-26 exit 145A, 0.3 mi from exit. 3608 St Mathews Rd 29115. Fax: 803/531-4922.
Motel　　**Terms:** Reserv deposit; weekly rates; no pets. **Facility:** 55 rooms. Nicely decorated rooms. 2 stories; exterior
　　　　corridors; small pool. **Dining:** Coffee shop nearby. **All Rooms:** free movies, combo or shower baths.
Some Rooms: microwaves, refrigerators, whirlpools. **Cards:** AE, CB, DI, DS, MC, VI. **Special Amenities:**
Free breakfast and free local telephone calls.　　　　　　　　　　CTV ⊠ Ⓓ

ORANGEBURG DAYS INN
Phone: 803/531-2590
(AAA) [SAVE]   All Year [CP]   1P: $50   2P/1B: $55- 75   2P/2B: $55- 75   XP: $6   F13
◆ ◆   **Location:** On US 601 at jct I-26, exit 145A. 3691 St Matthews Rd 29118. Fax: 803/531-2829. **Terms:** No
Motel   pets. **Facility:** 74 rooms. 2 stories; exterior corridors. **All Rooms:** free movies. **Some Rooms:** refrigerators, whirlpools. **Cards:** AE, CB, DI, DS, JCB, MC, VI. **Special Amenities:** Free breakfast and free local telephone calls.   [icons]

PAGELAND—2,700

LODGING

THE VILLAGER MOTEL
Rates Subject to Change   Phone: 803/672-7225
(AAA)   All Year   1P: $30   2P/1B: $33   2P/2B: $38   XP: $6
◆ ◆   **Location:** 0.5 mi n on US 601. 703 N Pearl St 29728. Fax: 803/672-5593. **Terms:** Reserv deposit; no pets.
Motel   **Facility:** 14 rooms. 1 story; exterior corridors. **All Rooms:** free movies. **Cards:** AE, DS, MC, VI.   [icons]

PAWLEYS ISLAND—See The Grand Strand p. 551.

PICKENS—3,000

LODGINGS

LAUREL MOUNTAIN MOTEL
Rates Subject to Change   Phone: 864/878-8500
◆◆◆   10/15-11/30   1P: $75   2P/1B: $75   2P/2B: $75   XP: $10   F16
Motel   12/1-10/14   1P: $65   2P/1B: $65   2P/2B: $65   XP: $10   F16
Location: On SR 11, 0.5 mi e of Table Rock State Park. 129 Hiawatha Tr 29671. Fax: 864/878-5269.
Terms: Sr. discount; reserv deposit, 7 day notice; no pets. **Facility:** 5 rooms. Handling fee imposed; 1 story; exterior corridors; smoke free premises. **Some Rooms:** efficiency. **Cards:** MC, VI.   [icons]

THE SCHELL HAUS, A RESORT BED & BREAKFAST
Rates Subject to Change   Phone: 864/878-0078
◆◆◆   All Year [BP]   1P: $80- 150   2P/1B: $80- 150
Bed &   **Location:** On SR 11, 0.5 mi e of Table Rock State Park. 117 Hiawatha Tr 29671. Fax: 864/878-0066.
Breakfast   **Terms:** Sr. discount; reserv deposit, 7 day notice; no pets. **Facility:** 6 rooms. 2 stories; interior corridors; smoke free premises. **Cards:** MC, VI.   [icons]

POINT SOUTH

LODGINGS

DAYS INN POINT SOUTH
Phone: 803/726-8156
(AAA) [SAVE]   3/1-5/1 & 6/15-9/1   1P: $44   2P/1B: $50   2P/2B: $52   XP: $6   F18
◆◆◆   12/1-2/28, 5/2-6/14 &
Motor Inn   9/2-11/30   1P: $40   2P/1B: $44   2P/2B: $46   XP: $6   F18
Location: Jct US 17 & I-95, exit 33 29945 (Rt 1 Box 52 D, YEMASSEE). Fax: 803/726-6124. **Terms:** Weekly rates; BP avail; small pets only, $3 extra charge. **Facility:** 117 rooms. 2 stories; exterior corridors; miniature golf; wading pool. **Dining:** Restaurant; 5:30 am-9:30 & 5:30-9:30 pm; $5-$10; wine/beer only. **Services:** Fee: coin laundry. **All Rooms:** free movies. **Cards:** AE, CB, DI, DS, JCB, MC, VI. **Special Amenities:** Free local telephone calls and free room upgrade (subject to availability with advanced reservations).   [icons]

HOLIDAY INN EXPRESS
Rates Subject to Change   Phone: 803/726-9400
◆◆◆   All Year [CP]   1P: $49- 54   2P/1B: $49- 54   2P/2B: $49- 54   XP: $5
Motel   **Location:** I-95 exit 33 & US 17. 40 Frampton Dr 29945 (PO Box 1730, YEMASSEE). Fax: 803/726-4556.
Terms: Sr. discount; small pets only. **Facility:** 53 rooms. 2 stories; interior corridors. **All Rooms:** free movies. **Cards:** AE, CB, DI, DS, JCB, MC, VI.   Roll in showers.   [icons]

RICHBURG—400

LODGINGS

DAYS INN
Phone: 803/789-5555
(AAA) [SAVE]   3/1-8/31 [CP]   1P: $31- 55   2P/1B: $31- 65   2P/2B: $31- 65   XP: $5   F13
◆ ◆   12/1-2/28 & 9/1-11/30 [CP]   1P: $31- 45   2P/1B: $31- 55   2P/2B: $31- 55   XP: $5   F13
Motel   **Location:** I-77 exit 65 & SR 9, just s. 3217 Lancaster Hwy 29730. Fax: 803/789-5502.
Terms: Weekly/monthly rates; pets, $3 extra charge. **Facility:** 47 rooms. 2 stories. **Dining:** Restaurant nearby. **All Rooms:** free movies. **Some Rooms:** microwaves, refrigerators. Fee: whirlpools. **Cards:** AE, CB, DI, DS, MC, VI. **Special Amenities:** Early check-in/late check-out and free breakfast.   [icons]

ECONO LODGE
Phone: 803/789-3000
(AAA) [SAVE]   All Year [CP]   1P: $30- 95   2P/1B: $30- 95   2P/2B: $36- 95   XP: $5   F18
◆ ◆   **Location:** I-77, exit 65. 29729 (Rt 1 Box 182). Fax: 803/789-3000. **Terms:** Weekly rates; small pets only.
Motel   **Facility:** 72 rooms. Pleasant family oriented property. 2 stories; exterior corridors. **Dining:** Restaurant nearby. **All Rooms:** free movies. **Some Rooms:** coffeemakers. **Cards:** AE, CB, DI, DS, JCB, MC, VI. **Special Amenities:** Free breakfast and free local telephone calls. *(See color ad p 575)*   [icons]

RELAX INN
Phone: 803/789-6363
(AAA) [SAVE]   5/1-9/30   1P: $35   2P/1B: $37   2P/2B: $39   XP: $5
◆   12/1-4/30 & 10/1-11/30   1P: $30   2P/1B: $33   2P/2B: $35   XP: $5
Motel   **Location:** I-77, exit 65. 3200 Lancaster Hwy 29729. **Terms:** Reserv deposit; weekly/monthly rates; pets, $5 extra charge. **Facility:** 30 rooms. Handling fee imposed; 2 stories; exterior corridors. **Dining:** Restaurant nearby. **All Rooms:** free movies. **Cards:** AE, CB, DI, DS, MC, VI. **Special Amenities:** Free local telephone calls and free room upgrade (subject to availability with advanced reservations).   [icons]

SUPER 8 MOTEL
Phone: 803/789-7888
(AAA) [SAVE]   All Year [CP]   1P: $41   2P/1B: $45   2P/2B: $45   XP: $4   F12
◆ ◆   **Location:** I-77 exit 65 & SR 9N. 29729 (Rt 1 Box 181 C). Fax: 803/789-5692. **Terms:** Pets, $3 extra charge.
Motel   **Facility:** 58 rooms. Nicely decorated & furnished rooms. 2 stories; exterior corridors; small pool. **Dining:** Restaurant nearby. **All Rooms:** free movies. **Some Rooms:** microwaves, refrigerators. Fee: whirlpools. **Cards:** AE, CB, DI, DS, JCB, MC, VI. **Special Amenities:** Free local telephone calls and free newspaper.   [icons]

RESTAURANT

THE FRONT PORCH RESTAURANT
◆
American

Lunch: $5   **Dinner:** $6-$10   **Phone:** 803/789-5029
Location: Exit 65 off I-77, just w on SR 9. 3427 S Gaston Rd 29729. **Hours:** 11 am-9 pm, Sat & Sun from 7 am. Closed: 7/4, 9/1 & 12/24-12/26. **Features:** casual dress; children's menu; carryout. Southern home style cooking served in a charming log house. Good variety of daily entree specials & sandwiches. Smoke free premises.   ⊠

RIDGELAND—1,100

LODGINGS

COMFORT INN
AAA SAVE
◆◆◆
Motel

Phone: 803/726-2121
All Year [CP]   1P: $43- 86   2P/1B: $49- 86   2P/2B: $49- 86   XP: $6   F18
Location: I-95 & US 278 exit 21. (PO Drawer 1389, 29936). Fax: 803/726-2121. **Terms:** Pets. **Facility:** 100 rooms. Attractive public areas. 2 stories; interior/exterior corridors. **Dining:** Restaurant nearby. **All Rooms:** Fee: movies. **Some Rooms:** microwaves, refrigerators. Fee: whirlpools. **Cards:** AE, CB, DI, DS, JCB, MC, VI. **Special Amenities:** Early check-in/late check-out and free breakfast.
🛏 🖈 🖈 🛉 CTV ⊠ 🎾 D

ECONO LODGE
◆◆
Motel

Phone: 803/726-5553
Guaranteed Rates
All Year   1P: $40- 45   2P/1B: $45- 47   2P/2B: $45   XP: $5   F18
Location: I-95 & US 278 exit 21. 516 E Main St 29936. Fax: 803/726-8780. **Terms:** Sr. discount; small pets only. **Facility:** 77 rooms. 4 whirlpool rms, $75-$80; 2 stories; exterior corridors. **All Rooms:** free movies.
Cards: AE, CB, DI, DS, JCB, MC, VI.   Roll in showers. 🛏 CTV ⊠ D

RIDGE SPRING—900

LODGING

SOUTHWOOD MANOR
◆◆
Historic Bed
& Breakfast

Phone: 803/685-5100
Rates Subject to Change
All Year [BP]   1P: $65   2P/1B: $75- 125   2P/2B: $75   XP: $10   F6
Location: 1 mi e of town centre. 100 E Main St 29129 (PO Box 434). Fax: 803/685-5100. **Terms:** Sr. discount; pets, in carriers, horses boarded. **Facility:** 4 rooms. 2 stories; interior corridors; designated smoking area. **Cards:** AE, DS, MC, VI.
🛏 🖈 ⊠ D

ROCK HILL—41,600

LODGINGS

BEST WESTERN INN
AAA SAVE
◆◆◆
Motor Inn

Phone: 803/329-1330
All Year   1P: $42- 55   2P/1B: $46- 64   2P/2B: $46- 64   XP: $5   F14
Location: From I-77 exit 82B, 0.6 mi w on US 21 to US 21 bypass. 1106 N Anderson Rd 29730. Fax: 803/329-1330. **Terms:** Reserv deposit, 7 day notice, handling fee imposed; BP, CP avail; pets, $10 extra charge. **Facility:** 60 rooms. 2 stories; interior corridors; whirlpool. **Dining & Entertainment:** Restaurant; 6:30 am-10 & 5:30-10 pm, closed Sun; $5-$16; cocktails/lounge. **All Rooms:** free & pay movies. **Some Rooms:** coffeemakers, refrigerators. **Cards:** AE, DI, DS, MC, VI. **Special Amenities:** Free local telephone calls.
(See ad below)   🛏 🖈 🛉 CTV ⊠ D

THE BOOK & THE SPINDLE
◆◆◆
Historic Bed
& Breakfast

Phone: 803/328-1913
Rates Subject to Change
All Year [CP]   1P: $55- 65   2P/1B: $60- 75   2P/2B: $55- 70   XP: $7
Location: From I-77 exit 82B, 3.5 mi s on US 21; opposite Winthrop University. 626 Oakland Ave 29730. **Terms:** Reserv deposit; small pets only. **Facility:** 4 rooms. 2 stories; interior corridors. **Some Rooms:** 2 kitchens. **Cards:** AE, DS, MC, VI.
🛏 CTV

COMFORT INN
AAA SAVE
◆◆
Motel

Phone: 803/329-2171
All Year [CP]   1P: $45- 60   2P/1B: $50- 60   2P/2B: $52- 60   XP: $5   F18
Location: Off I-77, exit 82B. 875 Riverview Rd 29730. Fax: 803/329-2171. **Terms:** No pets. **Facility:** 101 rooms. 2 stories; exterior corridors. **Dining:** Coffee shop nearby. **Services:** Fee: coin laundry. **All Rooms:** free movies. **Some Rooms:** microwaves, refrigerators. **Cards:** AE, DI, DS, MC, VI. **Special Amenities:** Free local telephone calls and free newspaper.
🖈 CTV ⊠ D

COUNTRY INN & SUITES BY CARLSON
Motel

Phone: 803/329-5151
Rates Subject to Change
All Year [CP]   1P: $69- 90   2P/1B: $69- 99   2P/2B: $69- 99   XP: $7   F18
Too new to rate; **Location:** From I77 take exit 82B, 2nd left. 865 Patriot Pkwy 29730. **Terms:** Sr. discount; reserv deposit; no pets. **Facility:** 43 rooms. 3 suites with hot tub, $125. Scheduled to open August 1997; 3 stories; interior corridors. **Cards:** AE, DI, DS, MC, VI.
🖈 CTV ⊠ S

DAYS INN

Phone: 803/329-7466

All Year [CP]   1P: $26- 120   2P/1B: $31- 120   2P/2B: $56- 120   XP: $5
Location: US 21 & I-77, exit 82B. 914 Riverview Rd 29730. Fax: 803/366-4472. **Terms:** No pets.
Facility: 113 rooms. 3 stories; exterior corridors. **Dining:** Coffee shop; 6 am-10 & 5-10 pm; $4-$9.
All Rooms: free movies. **Cards:** AE, CB, DI, DS, JCB, MC, VI. **Special Amenities:** Free breakfast and
free local telephone calls.

Motel

EAST MAIN GUEST HOUSE

Rates Subject to Change   **Phone: 803/366-1161**

Historic Bed
& Breakfast

All Year [CP]   1P: $51- 67   2P/1B: $69- 79   2P/2B: $59
Location: From I-77, exit 77; 1.5 mi n on US 21/US Business 21 to Main St then 1 mi n. 600 E Main St
29730. Fax: 803/366-1161. **Terms:** Sr. discount; age restrictions may apply; reserv deposit; no pets.
Facility: 3 rooms. 2 stories; interior corridors; smoke free premises. **Cards:** AE, VI.

ECONO LODGE

Phone: 803/329-3232

3/2-10/1 [CP]   1P: $34- 95   2P/1B: $34- 95   2P/2B: $34- 95   XP: $6   F17
12/1-3/1 & 10/2-11/30 [CP]   1P: $30- 45   2P/1B: $30- 45   2P/2B: $30- 45   XP: $6   F17
Location: I-77 exit 82B & US 21. 962 Riverview Rd 29730. Fax: 803/328-6288. **Terms:** Weekly rates; small
pets only, $5 extra charge. **Facility:** 105 rooms. 2 stories; exterior corridors. **Dining:** Restaurant nearby.
All Rooms: free movies. **Some Rooms:** coffeemakers. **Cards:** AE, CB, DI, DS, JCB, MC, VI.
Special Amenities: Free breakfast and free room upgrade (subject to availability with advanced reservations).
(See color ad below)

Motel

HAMPTON INN

Rates Subject to Change   **Phone: 803/325-1100**

Motel

All Year [CP]   1P: $79- 99   2P/1B: $79- 99   2P/2B: $79- 99   XP: $5   D12
Location: At jct I-77, exit 79 & Dave Lyle Blvd; adjacent to Galleria Mall. 2111 Tabor Dr 29730.
Fax: 803/325-7814. **Terms:** No pets. **Facility:** 162 rooms. 5 stories; interior corridors. **All Rooms:** free
movies. **Some Rooms:** 38 efficiencies. **Cards:** AE, DI, DS, MC, VI. *(See color ad below)*

HOLIDAY INN

Phone: 803/329-1122

Motor Inn

Fri & Sat 4/1-10/5 [BP]   1P: $55   2P/1B: $55   2P/2B: $60   XP: $5   F19
12/1-3/31, Sun-Thurs
4/1-10/5 & 10/6-11/30 [BP]   1P: $49   2P/1B: $49   2P/2B: $54   XP: $5   F19
Location: I-77 exit 82A. 2640 N Cherry Rd 29730. Fax: 803/329-1072. **Terms:** Reserv deposit; small pets
only. **Facility:** 126 rooms. 2 stories; interior corridors. **Dining & Entertainment:** Restaurant; 6:30 am-11 &
5:30-10 pm; $8-$15; cocktails/lounge. **Services:** Fee: coin laundry. **All Rooms:** coffeemakers, free movies.
Some Rooms: refrigerators. Fee: whirlpools. **Cards:** AE, CB, DI, DS, JCB, MC.

RAMADA LIMITED

Phone: 803/329-7900

All Year [CP]   1P: $45   2P/1B: $45   2P/2B: $50   XP: $5   F18
Location: Off I-77 exit 82B. 911 Riverview Rd 29730. Fax: 803/329-7980. **Terms:** No pets. **Facility:** 56 rooms.
Nicely furnished & decorated rooms. 2 stories; exterior corridors. **Dining:** Restaurant nearby.
All Rooms: free movies, combo or shower baths. **Some Rooms:** refrigerators. **Cards:** AE, CB, DI, DS, MC,
VI. **Special Amenities:** Early check-in/late check-out.

Motel

RESTAURANT

JACKSON'S CAFETERIA   **Phone:** 803/366-68
◆   **Location:** From US 21, s on Oakland Ave/Ebenezer Rd; in Village Square Shopping Center. 1734 Ebene
American   Rd 29732. **Hours:** 11 am-2 & 5-8 pm, Sun-2 pm. Closed major holidays. **Features:** casual dress; carryo
         Family owned & operated. Friendly gathering spot in a small town.

ST. GEORGE—*See Charleston & Vicinity p. 465.*

SANTEE—600

LODGINGS

BEST WESTERN SANTEE INN   **Phone:** 803/854-30
Ⓐ Ⓢ   All Year [CP]   1P: $50- 65 2P/1B: $50- 65 2P/2B: $50- 65 XP: $5   F
◆◆◆   **Location:** Jct I-95 & SR 6, exit 98. 29142 (PO Box 188). Fax: 803/854-3093. **Terms:** Reserv deposit;
Motor Inn   pets. **Facility:** 108 rooms. 1 story; exterior corridors. **Dining:** Verandah Restaurant, see separate listir
         All Rooms: free movies. **Some Rooms:** Fee: whirlpools. **Cards:** AE, CB, DI, DS, MC,
         Special Amenities: Free breakfast and free local telephone calls. *(See color ad p 577)*

CLARK'S INN   **Phone:** 803/854-21
Ⓐ   All Year   **Guaranteed Rates**
         1P: $32- 46 2P/1B: $37- 50 2P/2B: $37- 50 XP: $5   F
◆◆   **Location:** On SR 6 at jct I-95, exit 98. 114 Bradford Blvd 29142. Fax: 803/854-2004. **Terms:** Sr. discount;
Motor Inn   pets. **Facility:** 75 rooms. 2 stories; exterior corridors. **Dining:** Restaurant; 6 am-10 pm; $5-$16; restaura
         see separate listing. **All Rooms:** free movies. **Cards:** AE, CB, DI, DS, MC, VI. *(See color ad below)*

COMFORT INN   **Phone:** 803/854-32
Ⓐ Ⓢ   All Year [CP]   1P: $45- 99 2P/1B: $45- 99 2P/2B: $45- 99 XP: $6   F
◆◆◆   **Location:** I-95 exit 98 & SR 6. 265 Britain St 29142. Fax: 803/854-3221. **Terms:** Small pets only, $10 ex
Motel   charge. **Facility:** 62 rooms. 2 stories; exterior corridors. **Dining:** Restaurant nearby. **All Rooms:** free movie
         Some Rooms: microwaves, refrigerators. Fee: whirlpools. **Cards:** AE, CB, DI, DS, JCB, MC,
         Special Amenities: Free local telephone calls and free newspaper.

DAYS INN   **Phone:** 803/854-21
◆◆   All Year [BP]   **Guaranteed Rates**
Motor Inn   1P: $42- 55   2P/2B: $48- 61 XP: $6   F
         Location: At jct I-95 & SR 6, exit 98. 9078 Old Hwy 6 29142 (PO Box 9). Fax: 803/854-2835. **Terms:** S
         discount; small pets only, $6 extra charge. **Facility:** 120 rooms. 2 stories; exterior corrido
Dining: Restaurant; 5 pm-9 pm; $5-$8. **All Rooms:** free movies. **Cards:** AE, CB, DI, DS, MC, VI. *(See ad p 412)*

HOLIDAY INN
◆◆◆   Guaranteed Rates   **Phone:** 803/854-2121
All Year   1P: $50   2P/1B: $53   2P/2B: $53   XP: $3   F18
Motor Inn   **Location:** I-95, exit 98. 427 Bass Dr 29142 (PO Box 27). Fax: 803/854-3558. **Terms:** Sr. discount; no pets.
Facility: 168 rooms. Free green fees with room. Handling fee imposed; 2 stories; exterior corridors.
Dining: Dining room; 6 am-2 & 5-10 pm; $7-$18. **All Rooms:** free movies. **Cards:** AE, CB, DI, DS, MC.
(See color ad p 576)

🛏 CTV ✖ D

RAMADA INN   **Phone:** 803/854-2191
⬡ SAVE   5/16-7/31 [BP]   1P: $60   2P/2B: $70   XP: $10   F12
          8/1-11/30 [BP]   1P: $50   2P/2B: $60   XP: $10   F12
◆◆◆   12/1-5/15 [BP]   1P: $48   2P/2B: $58   XP: $10   F12
Motor Inn   **Location:** On SR 6 at jct I-95, exit 98. 123 Mall Dr 29142 (PO Box 501). Fax: 803/854-4825.
Terms: Package plans; pets. **Facility:** 117 rooms. 2 stories; exterior corridors; putting green; wading pool.
Fee: golf privileges. **Dining & Entertainment:** Dining room; 6 am-10 pm; $5-$10; cocktails/lounge; entertainment.
Services: Fee: coin laundry. **All Rooms:** coffeemakers, free movies. **Some Rooms:** Fee: whirlpools. **Cards:** AE, CB, DI,
DS, JCB, MC, VI. **Special Amenities:** Free local telephone calls and free newspaper. 🐕 🛏 🛎 CTV ✖ D

SANTEE ECONOMY INN   **Phone:** 803/854-2107
⬡ SAVE   All Year   1P: $30- 40   2P/1B: $30- 40   2P/2B: $30- 40   XP: $4   F12
          Location: On US 15 & 301; 0.3 mi w of I-95 & SR 6, exit 98. 626 Bass Dr 29142 (PO Box 125).
◆   **Terms:** Small pets only. **Facility:** 42 rooms. Hillside location. Most are ground level rooms. 1 two-bedroom unit.
Motel   1-2 stories; exterior corridors; playground. **Dining:** Restaurant nearby. **All Rooms:** free movies, combo or
shower baths. **Cards:** AE, CB, DI, MC, VI. **Special Amenities:** Early check-in/late check-out and
preferred room (subject to availability with advanced reservations). 🐕 🛏 CTV D

SUPER 8 MOTEL   Rates Subject to Change   **Phone:** 803/854-3456
◆◆   All Year [CP]   1P: $26   2P/1B: $28   2P/2B: $30   XP: $5   F12
Motel   **Location:** Off jct I-95, exit 98; 0.3 mi e on SR 6. 9125 Old hwy 6 29142. Fax: 803/854-4875. **Terms:** Sr.
discount; pets. **Facility:** 42 rooms. 1 story; exterior corridors. **All Rooms:** free movies. **Cards:** AE, CB, DI,
DS, MC, VI.   🐕 CTV ✖ D

RESTAURANTS

CLARK'S RESTAURANT   **Lunch:** $4-$9   **Dinner:** $4-$16   **Phone:** 803/854-2101
◆◆   **Location:** On SR 6 at jct I-95, exit 98; adjacent to Clark's Inn. 29142. **Hours:** 6 am-10 pm. Closed: 12/25.
American   **Features:** casual dress; children's menu; carryout; cocktails. senior discount. Family dining since 1946.
Cards: AE, DI, DS, MC, VI.   ✖

VERANDAH RESTAURANT   **Dinner:** $8-$16   **Phone:** 803/854-4695
◆◆   **Location:** Jct I-95 & SR 6, exit 98; in Best Western Santee Inn. Hwy 6E 29142. **Hours:** 5 pm-9:30 pm.
American   Closed: 12/25. **Reservations:** suggested. **Features:** casual dress; children's menu; carryout; beer & wine
only. Family dining. Traditional southern dishes. **Cards:** AE, MC, VI.   ✖

SIMPSONVILLE—11,700

LODGING

COMFORT INN   Rates Subject to Change   **Phone:** 864/963-2777
◆◆   All Year [CP]   1P: $49- 95   2P/1B: $55- 95   2P/2B: $55- 95   XP: $5   F12
Motel   **Location:** At jct I-385, exit 27. 600 Fairview Rd 29680. Fax: 864/963-2777. **Terms:** Reserv deposit; no pets.
Facility: 82 rooms. 2 stories; exterior corridors. **All Rooms:** free movies. **Some Rooms:** 4 efficiencies.
Cards: AE, DI, DS, JCB, MC, VI.   CTV ✖ 🕹 D

SOUTH OF THE BORDER

LODGING

SOUTH OF THE BORDER MOTOR HOTEL   **Phone:** 803/774-2411
⬡ SAVE   All Year   1P: $30- 60   2P/1B: $39- 65   2P/2B: $39- 65   XP: $5   F12
          Location: I-95 & US 301 exit 1A. 29536 (PO Box 1328, DILLON). Fax: 803/774-0904. **Terms:** Weekly rates;
◆◆◆   pets. **Facility:** 300 rooms. All rooms covered parking, mix of styles & decors. 1 story; exterior corridors; wading
Motor Inn   pool, sauna, whirlpool; 1 lighted tennis court; playground. Fee: miniature golf; kennel for pets, mini
amusement park, tanning bed. **Dining & Entertainment:** 2 restaurants, 2 coffee shops, deli; 24 hours;
$4-$17; cocktails; also, The Peddler Steakhouse, see separate listing; nightclub. **Services:** Fee: coin laundry.
Recreation: jogging. **All Rooms:** free movies, refrigerators. **Some Rooms:** coffeemakers, 4 efficiencies, microwaves,
whirlpools. **Cards:** AE, CB, DI, DS, MC, VI. *(See color ad p 579)*   🐕 🛏 🛎 🛎 CTV ✖ D

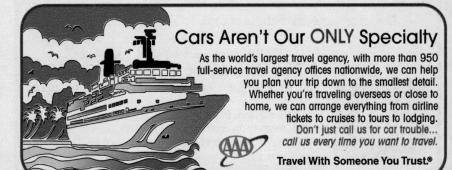

RESTAURANT

THE PEDDLER STEAKHOUSE Dinner: $12-$18 **Phone:** 803/774-314
AAA **Location:** I-95 & US 301 exit 1A; in South of the Border Motor Hotel. 29536. **Hours:** 5 pm-10:30 pr
◆◆ Closed: 11/26 & 12/24. **Features:** casual dress; children's menu; carryout; salad bar; cocktails. Featurin
American freshly cut steak at table side. **Cards:** AE, MC, VI. ☒

SPARTANBURG—43,500

LODGINGS

BEST WESTERN SPARTAN INN & CONFERENCE CENTER Rates Subject to Change **Phone:** 864/578-540
◆◆ All Year [BP] 1P: $52- 85 2P/1B: $52- 85 2P/2B: $52- 85 XP: $6 F1
Motor Inn **Location:** I-85 exit 75, Boiling Springs Rd, Business Rt 85, exit 6. 700 Sunbeam Rd 2930.
Fax: 864/578-4001. **Terms:** Sr. discount; small pets only. **Facility:** 121 rooms. 2 stories; exterior corridors
Dining: Dining room; 6:30 am-10 & 5-9 pm, Sat 8 am-11 & 5-9 pm; closed Sun; $6-$12. **All Rooms:** free movie
Cards: AE, CB, DI, DS, MC, VI. ⌂ ➘ 🅲🆃🆅 ☒ 🎵

COMFORT INN AT WACCAMAW **Phone:** 864/576-299
AAA SAVE Fri & Sat 6/1-10/31 [CP] 1P: $66 2P/1B: $66 2P/2B: $66 XP: $6 D1
12/1-5/31, Sun-Thurs
◆◆ 6/1-10/31 & 11/1-11/30 [CP] 1P: $46 2P/1B: $50 2P/2B: $51- 56 XP: $6 D1
Motel **Location:** I-26 & New Cut Rd, exit 17. 2070 New Cut Rd 29303. Fax: 864/576-2992. **Terms:** Package plans
no pets. **Facility:** 99 rooms. 2 stories; exterior corridors; small pool. **Dining:** Restaurant nearb
Services: valet laundry. **All Rooms:** free movies. **Some Rooms:** coffeemakers, microwaves, refrigerators, whirlpools
Cards: AE, CB, DI, DS, JCB, MC, VI. **Special Amenities:** Early check-in/late check-out and free breakfast.
(See ad below) 🅲🆃🆅 ☒ 🎵 🅳

COURTYARD BY MARRIOTT Rates Subject to Change **Phone:** 864/585-240
◆◆◆ Sun-Thurs 1P: $77 2P/1B: $77 2P/2B: $90
Motel Fri & Sat 1P: $54 2P/1B: $54 2P/2B: $54
Location: Jct Business I-85 & Hearon Cir, US 56 exit 4. 110 Mobile Dr 29303. Fax: 864/585-812
Terms: Sr. discount; no pets. **Facility:** 108 rooms. 3 stories; interior corridors. **Dining:** Coffee shop; 6:30-10:30 am, Sat
Sun 7-11 am. **All Rooms:** free & pay movies. **Cards:** AE, DI, DS, MC, VI. (See color ad below) ➘ 🅲🆃🆅 ☒ 🎵 🅳 🆂

DAYS INN-WACCAMAW Rates Subject to Change **Phone:** 864/576-730
◆◆ Fri & Sat [CP] 1P: $49- 65 2P/1B: $52- 70 2P/2B: $52- 70 XP: $5 F1
Motel Sun-Thurs [CP] 1P: $44- 53 2P/1B: $49- 59 2P/2B: $49- 59 XP: $5 F1
Location: I-26 & New Cut Rd, exit 17. 101 Outlet Rd 29301. Fax: 864/574-4286. **Terms:** Sr. discount; reser
deposit; no pets. **Facility:** 82 rooms. 2 stories; exterior corridors. **All Rooms:** free & pay movies. **Cards:** AE, CB, DI, DS
JCB, MC, VI. ➘ 🅲🆃🆅 ☒ 🎵 🅳

FAIRFIELD INN BY MARRIOTT   Phone: 864/542-0333
AAA SAVE   Sun-Thurs [CP]   1P: $60   2P/1B: $60   2P/2B: $60
           Fri & Sat [CP]   1P: $55   2P/1B: $55   2P/2B: $55
Motel   Too new to rate; **Location:** Jct I-85 business route & US 56 Hearon Circle exit 4-B to Howard Gap Rd. 160
Simuel Rd 29303. Fax: 864/598-9646. **Terms:** No pets. **Facility:** 92 rooms. Scheduled to open May 1997; 4
stories; interior corridors; whirlpool. **Dining:** Restaurant nearby. **Services:** Fee: coin laundry. **All Rooms:** combo or shower
baths. Fee: movies. **Some Rooms:** microwaves, refrigerators, whirlpools. **Cards:** AE, DI, DS, MC, VI. **Special Amenities:**
Free breakfast and free local telephone calls. (See color ad p 580)   Roll in showers.   🚗 📶 🛢 CTV ✕ D S

HAMPTON INN   Rates Subject to Change   Phone: 864/576-6080
◆◆◆   All Year [CP]   1P: $53- 57 2P/1B: $58- 62 2P/2B: $62   XP: $8   F18
Motel   **Location:** Business I-85, exit 1; 0.3 mi sw of jct I-26. 4930 College Dr 29301. Fax: 864/587-8901.
         Terms: Reserv deposit; no pets. **Facility:** 112 rooms. 2 stories; exterior corridors. **All Rooms:** free & pay
movies. **Cards:** AE, CB, DI, DS, MC, VI.   🚗 CTV ✕ 🎦 D

HOLIDAY INN SPARTANBURG WEST   Guaranteed Rates   Phone: 864/576-5220
◆◆◆   All Year   1P: $49- 80 2P/1B: $49- 80 2P/2B: $49- 80
Motor Inn **Location:** At jct I-26 exit 19 & Business I-85, exit 2 Sigsbee Rd. 200 International Dr 29301.
         Fax: 864/574-1243. **Terms:** Sr. discount; no pets. **Facility:** 224 rooms. 2-3 stories; interior/exterior corridors.
Dining: Dining room; 6:30 am-1:30 & 5-10:30 pm, Sat & Sun 6:30-noon & 5-10:30 pm; $6-$13. **All Rooms:** free & pay
movies. **Cards:** AE, CB, DI, DS, JCB, MC. (See ad below)   Roll in showers.   🚗 CTV ✕ 🎦 D

HOWARD JOHNSON EXPRESS INN   Rates Subject to Change   Phone: 864/576-0042
◆◆   5/1-10/31 [CP]   1P: $55- 66 2P/1B: $66- 67 2P/2B: $66- 67 XP: $5   F17
Motel   12/1-4/30 & 11/1-11/30 [CP] 1P: $49- 55 2P/1B: $55- 60 2P/2B: $55- 60 XP: $5   F17
         Location: I-26 & New Cut Rd, exit 17. 6690 Pottery Rd 29301. Fax: 864/576-4070. **Terms:** Reserv deposit;
no pets. **Facility:** 52 rooms. 3 stories; interior corridors. **All Rooms:** free movies. **Cards:** AE, DI, DS, MC, VI.
                                                                                 CTV ✕ D S

THE QUALITY HOTEL & CONFERENCE CENTER   Phone: 864/503-0780
AAA SAVE   All Year   1P: $52- 70 2P/1B: $69- 80 2P/2B: $59- 75 XP: $5-10   F18
         Location: At jct Business I-85 & Hearon Cir, exit 4. 7136 Asheville Hwy 29303. Fax: 864/503-0780.
◆◆◆   **Terms:** Reserv deposit, 10 day notice; BP avail; pets, $10 extra charge. **Facility:** 143 rooms. 6 stories; inte-
Motor Inn rior corridors. **Dining & Entertainment:** Dining room; 6:30 am-10 pm, Sun-9 pm; $5-$16; cocktails/lounge.
         Services: valet laundry. **All Rooms:** coffeemakers, free & pay movies. **Some Rooms:** whirlpools.
Fee: microwaves, refrigerators. **Cards:** AE, CB, DI, DS, JCB, MC, VI. **Special Amenities:** Free breakfast and free local
telephone calls.   🛏 🚗 📶 🛢 CTV ✕ D

RAMADA INN   Phone: 864/503-9048
AAA SAVE   All Year   1P: $59   2P/1B: $65   2P/2B: $65   XP: $7   F19
         Location: I-85 business route exit 4, 0.4 mi n on Frontage Rd. 1000 Hearon Cir 29303. Fax: 864/503-0576.
◆◆◆   **Terms:** Small pets only. **Facility:** 138 rooms. 2 stories; interior/exterior corridors. **Dining:** Coffee shop; 6
Motor Inn am-10 & 11-2 pm; $5-$7. **All Rooms:** free movies. **Some Rooms:** microwaves, refrigerators. **Cards:** AE,
CB, DI, DS, JCB, MC, VI. **Special Amenities:** Free breakfast and free newspaper.
                                                            🛏 🚗 📶 CTV ✕ D

SLEEP INN   Rates Subject to Change   Phone: 864/595-4040
◆◆   Fri & Sat 4/1-10/31 [CP] 1P: $65   2P/1B: $65   2P/2B: $65   XP: $6   F18
Motel   Sun-Thurs 4/1-10/31 [CP] 1P: $59   2P/1B: $64   2P/2B: $64   XP: $6   F18
         12/1-3/31 & 11/1-11/30 [CP] 1P: $51   2P/1B: $58   2P/2B: $58   XP: $6   F18
Location: I-26 exit 22 & SR 296, then w. 501 S Blacksktock Rd 29301. Fax: 864/595-4050. **Terms:** Sr. discount; no pets.
Facility: 63 rooms. 3 stories; interior corridors. **All Rooms:** free movies. **Cards:** AE, CB, DI, DS, JCB, MC, VI.
                                                                                 CTV ✕ D S

WILSON WORLD HOTEL & SUITES   Rates Subject to Change   Phone: 864/574-2111
AAA   All Year   1P: $79- 89 2P/1B: $79- 89 2P/2B: $79- 99 XP: $5   F18
         Location: Jct Business I-85 & I-26, exit 2C off Business 85, exit 19B off I-26. 9027 Fairforest Rd 29301.
◆◆◆   Fax: 864/576-7602. **Terms:** Sr. discount; reserv deposit; **Facility:** 200 rooms. 5 stories; interior corridors.
Motor Inn **Dining:** Restaurant; 6:30-10 am, 11-2 & 5-10 pm; $8-$15. **All Rooms:** free & pay movies. **Cards:** AE, CB,
DI, DS, MC, VI.   🚗 CTV ✕ 🎦 D S

RESTAURANT

HARRY'S ON MORGAN SQUARE   **Lunch:** $5-$9   **Dinner:** $12-$20   **Phone:** 803/583-8121
Ⓐ   **Location:** Downtown between St John (US 29) & W Main sts. 116 Magnolia St 29306. **Hours:** 11:30
am-2:30 & 5-10 pm, Sat from 5 pm. Closed major holidays & Sun. **Reservations:** suggested.
◆◆   **Features:** casual dress; cocktails & lounge. Featuring beef, poultry, veal & pasta entrees with complimenting
Continental   wine selection. **Cards:** AE, DI, DS, MC, VI.   ☒

SULLIVANS ISLAND—*See Charleston & Vicinity p. 465.*

SUMMERVILLE—*See Charleston & Vicinity p. 465.*

SUMTER—41,900   ## LODGINGS
THE BED & BREAKFAST OF SUMTER   Rates Subject to Change   **Phone:** 803/773-2903
◆◆◆   All Year [BP]   1P: $65   2P/1B: $75   2P/2B: $75   XP: $15
Historic Bed   **Location:** From US 521/US 378N Washington St, 0.5 mi w on W Hampton. 6 Park Ave 29150.
& Breakfast   **Fax:** 803/775-6943. **Terms:** Age restrictions may apply; no pets. **Facility:** 5 rooms. 2 stories; interior corridors;
smoke free premises. **Cards:** DS, MC, VI.   ☒ Ⓓ

CALHOUN STREET BED & BREAKFAST   Guaranteed Rates   **Phone:** 803/775-7035
◆◆◆   All Year [BP]   1P: $55   2P/1B: $65- 75 2P/2B: $65   XP: $10
Historic Bed   **Location:** From jct US 76 & 521, 0.4 mi w. 302 W Calhoun St 29150. **Fax:** 803/778-0934. **Terms:** Check-in
& Breakfast   4 pm; reserv deposit; no pets. **Facility:** 4 rooms. 2 stories; interior corridors; smoke free premises.
Cards: MC, VI.   ☒ Ⓓ

HAMPTON INN   **Phone:** 803/469-2222
Ⓐ ⓢ   All Year [CP]   1P: $65- 69 2P/1B: $70- 74 2P/2B: $70- 74
◆◆◆   **Location:** On US 76 & 378, 0.5 mi w of jct US 76, 378, 521 & Business Rt 76. 1370 Broad St Extension
Motel   29150. **Fax:** 803/469-2315. **Terms:** Reserv deposit; no pets. **Facility:** 73 rooms. All rooms with hair dryer, iron
& ironing board. 3 stories; interior corridors; sauna, whirlpool. **Dining:** Restaurant nearby.
All Rooms: coffeemakers, microwaves, free movies, refrigerators, combo or shower baths, VCP's.
Some Rooms: Fee: whirlpools. **Cards:** AE, CB, DI, DS, MC. **Special Amenities: Free breakfast and free local telephone
calls.**   ⊘ ⊘ ⊘ ⊘ ☒ Ⓓ Ⓢ

HOLIDAY INN   **Phone:** 803/469-9001
Ⓐ ⓢ   All Year [BP]   1P: $55- 89 2P/1B: $55- 89 2P/2B: $55- 89
◆◆◆   **Location:** On US 76 & 378, 0.5 mi w of jct US 76, 378, 521 & Business Rt 76. 2390 Broad St 29150-1000.
Motor Inn   **Fax:** 803/469-9070. **Terms:** Weekly/monthly rates; no pets. **Facility:** 124 rooms. 2 stories; interior corridors.
Dining & Entertainment: Restaurant; 6:30-9:30 am, 11-2 & 5:30-10 pm; $7-$15; cocktails/lounge.
Services: valet laundry. **All Rooms:** coffeemakers, free & pay movies. **Some Rooms:** refrigerators.
Cards: AE, CB, DI, DS, JCB, MC, VI. **Special Amenities: Free breakfast and free local telephone calls.**
⊘ ⊘ ⊘ ☒ Ⓓ

MAGNOLIA HOUSE   Rates Subject to Change   **Phone:** 803/775-6694
◆◆◆   All Year [BP]   1P: $65   2P/1B: $75   2P/2B: $75
Historic Bed   **Location:** US 521/US 378 N Washington St, w on Calhoun, right on Church St. 230 Church St 29150.
& Breakfast   **Terms:** Age restrictions may apply; reserv deposit; no pets. **Facility:** 4 rooms. Two room suite-$125; 2 stories;
interior corridors; smoke free premises. **Cards:** AE, DI, MC, VI.   ☒ Ⓓ

RAMADA INN   **Phone:** 803/775-2323
Ⓐ ⓢ   All Year [BP]   1P: $49- 69 2P/1B: $56- 76 2P/2B: $62- 76 XP: $9   F18
◆◆   **Location:** 0.5 mi n on US 76 & 521 business route. 226 N Washington St 29150 (PO Box 520, 29151).
Motor Inn   **Fax:** 803/773-9500. **Terms:** Package plans; small pets only. **Facility:** 125 rooms. 2-3 stories; exterior corridors;
putting green. **Dining & Entertainment:** Dining room; 6:30 am-2 & 6-9 pm; $6-$15; cocktails/lounge.
Services: valet laundry. **All Rooms:** coffeemakers, free movies. **Some Rooms:** kitchen. Fee: microwaves,
refrigerators. **Cards:** AE, CB, DI, DS, JCB, MC, VI. **Special Amenities: Free breakfast.**   ⊘ ⊘ ⊘ ☒ Ⓓ Ⓓ

TRAVELERS INN   **Phone:** 803/469-9210
Ⓐ ⓢ   All Year [CP]   1P: $36- 41 2P/1B: $36- 41 2P/2B: $36- 49 XP: $5   F12
◆◆   **Location:** 1 mi w; jct US 521, 76 & SR 120. US 521 & 76 at Broad St 29151 (PO Box 2731).
Motel   **Fax:** 803/469-4306. **Terms:** Weekly rates; pets, $3-$5 extra charge. **Facility:** 104 rooms. 2 stories; interior
corridors. **All Rooms:** free movies. **Some Rooms:** refrigerators. **Cards:** AE, CB, DI, DS, MC, VI.
Special Amenities: Free breakfast and free local telephone calls.   ⊘ ⊘ ⊘ ☒ Ⓓ

SURFSIDE BEACH—*See The Grand Strand p. 552.*

UNION—9,800

LODGING
THE INN AT MERRIDUN   Guaranteed Rates   **Phone:** 864/427-7052
◆◆   All Year [BP]   2P/1B: $85- 105   XP: $15
Historic Bed   **Location:** Just off SR 49 (Rice Ave); 0.8 mi e of jct US 176 & 215. 100 Merridun Pl 29379.
& Breakfast   **Fax:** 864/429-0373. **Terms:** Age restrictions may apply; reserv deposit, 3 day notice; no pets. **Facility:** 5
rooms. 2 stories; interior corridors; smoke free premises. **Cards:** AE, DS, MC, VI.   ⊘ ☒ Ⓓ

WALTERBORO—5,500

LODGINGS
BEST WESTERN WALTERBORO INN   **Phone:** 803/538-3600
Ⓐ ⓢ   12/1-12/31 [CP]   1P: $49- 59 2P/1B: $50- 65 2P/2B: $50- 70 XP: $6   F12
◆◆   1/1-11/30 [CP]   1P: $45- 55 2P/1B: $50- 60 2P/2B: $45- 65 XP: $6   F12
Motel   **Location:** Jct I-95 & SR 63, exit 53. 1140 Sniders Hwy 29488 (PO Box 1085). **Fax:** 803/538-3600.
Terms: Pets. **Facility:** 114 rooms. 2 stories; exterior corridors. **Dining:** Restaurant nearby. **All Rooms:** free
& pay movies. **Cards:** AE, CB, DI, DS, MC, VI. **Special Amenities: Free breakfast and free local
telephone calls.**   ⊘ ⊘ ⊘ ☒ Ⓓ

COMFORT INN
Phone: 803-538-5403

AAA SAVE

◆ ◆

Motel

5/1-8/15 [CP]	1P: $37-	41	2P/1B:	$47-	51	2P/2B: $49-	65 XP: $6	F12
12/16-2/28 [CP]	1P: $37-	43	2P/1B:	$47-	53	2P/2B: $55-	62 XP: $6	F12
3/1-4/30 [CP]	1P: $39-	43	2P/1B:	$49-	53	2P/2B: $52-	59 XP: $6	F12
12/1-12/15 & 8/16-11/30 [CP]	1P: $37-	41	2P/1B:	$47-	51	2P/2B: $47-	55 XP: $6	F12

Location: At jct I-95 & SR 63, exit 53. 1109 Snider's Hwy 29488. Fax: 803/538-3847. **Terms:** Reserv deposit, 3 day notice; small pets only. **Facility:** 106 rooms. 2 stories; exterior corridors; wading pool; playground. **Dining & Entertainment:** Cocktails/lounge; restaurant nearby. **Some Rooms:** microwaves, refrigerators. Fee: whirlpools. **Cards:** AE, CB, DI, DS, MC, VI. **Special Amenities: Free breakfast and free local telephone calls.** 🐄 ➾ 📶 CTV ✕ D

DAYS INN
Phone: 803-538-2933

◆ ◆ ◆

Motel

Rates Subject to Change
All Year [CP]   1P: $38- 75 2P/1B: $38- 75 2P/2B: $42- 85 XP: $5   F12
Location: At jct I-95 & SR 63N, exit 53. I-95 & US 63 29488 (Rt 4, Box 890). Fax: 803/538-2158. **Terms:** No pets. **Facility:** 61 rooms. 2 stories; exterior corridors. **Cards:** AE, DI, DS, MC, VI. ➾ CTV ✕ D

HAMPTON INN
Phone: 803-538-2300

◆ ◆ ◆

Motel

Rates Subject to Change
All Year [CP]   1P: $60- 75 2P/1B: $62- 85 2P/2B: $62- 85 XP: $5   F18
Location: I-95 & SR 63, exit 53. (Rt 4, Box 889, 29488). Fax: 803/538-5202. **Terms:** Sr. discount; no pets. **Facility:** 62 rooms. 2 stories; exterior corridors. **All Rooms:** free movies. **Some Rooms:** A/C. **Cards:** AE, DI, DS, MC, VI. ➾ CTV ✕ D S

HOLIDAY INN
Phone: 803-538-5473

◆ ◆

Motor Inn

Rates Subject to Change
All Year [BP]   1P: $49   2P/1B: $49   2P/2B: $49   XP: $8   F18
Location: At jct I-95 & SR 63, exit 53. 1120 Snider's Hwy 29488 (PO BOX 889). Fax: 803/538-5473. **Terms:** Sr. discount; small pets only, $10 extra charge. **Facility:** 171 rooms. 2 stories; exterior corridors. **Dining:** Dining room; 6 am-2 & 5-10 pm; $6-$12. **All Rooms:** free & pay movies. **Cards:** AE, DI, DS, MC, VI. *(See color ad below)* 🐄 ➾ CTV ✕ D

HOWARD JOHNSON
Phone: 803-538-3948

AAA SAVE

◆ ◆

Motel

All Year [CP]   1P: $27- 40 2P/1B: $32- 49 2P/2B: $37- 59 XP: $3   F15
Location: I-95 exit 57 & SR 64. 1305 Bells Hwy 29488. Fax: 803/538-7363. **Terms:** No pets. **Facility:** 61 rooms. 2 stories; exterior corridors. **Dining:** Coffee shop nearby. **Cards:** AE, DS, MC, VI. **Special Amenities: Free breakfast and free local telephone calls.** ➾ CTV ✕ D

RICE PLANTERS INN
Phone: 803-538-8964

AAA SAVE

◆

Motel

All Year   1P: $24   2P/1B: $31   2P/2B: $34   XP: $3   F12
Location: Jct I-95 & SR 63, exit 53. 29488 (PO Box 529). **Terms:** Weekly rates; small pets only. **Facility:** 76 rooms. 2 stories; exterior corridors. **Dining:** Restaurant nearby. **Cards:** AE, DS, MC, VI. 🐄 ➾ CTV ✕ D

SOUTHERN INN
Phone: 803-538-2280

AAA SAVE

◆ ◆

Motel

All Year   1P: $28- 35 2P/1B: $32- 39 2P/2B: $35- 45 XP: $4
Location: Jct I-95 & SR 64, exit 57. 1306 Bells Hwy 29488. Fax: 803/538-8201. **Terms:** Reserv deposit; weekly rates; no pets. **Facility:** 32 rooms. 2 stories; exterior corridors; small pool. **Dining:** Coffee shop nearby. **Cards:** AE, CB, DI, DS, MC, VI. **Special Amenities: Free local telephone calls and preferred room (subject to availability with advanced reservations).** CTV ✕ D

SUPER 8 MOTEL
Phone: 803-538-5383

AAA

◆ ◆

Motel

Rates Subject to Change
All Year [CP]   1P: $36- 55 2P/1B: $36- 55 2P/2B: $36- 55 XP: $5   F
Location: On Hwy 64 at jct I-95, exit 57. 29488 (Rt 3, Box 760). Fax: 803/538-5853. **Terms:** Sr. discount; small pets only, in smoking rooms. **Facility:** 45 rooms. 2 stories; exterior corridors. **All Rooms:** free movies. **Cards:** AE, DS, MC, VI. 🐄 ➾ CTV ✕ D

THUNDERBIRD INN
Phone: 803-538-2503

AAA SAVE

◆

Motel

All Year   1P: $24   2P/1B: $31   2P/2B: $34   XP: $4   F12
Location: Jct I-95 & SR 63, exit 53. 29488 (PO Box 815). **Terms:** Small pets only. **Facility:** 42 rooms. 2 stories; exterior corridors. **Dining:** Restaurant nearby. **All Rooms:** free movies. **Cards:** AE, DI, DS, MC, VI. **Special Amenities: Free local telephone calls and preferred room (subject to availability with advanced reservations).** 🐄 CTV ✕ D

WEST COLUMBIA—10,600   (See map p. 468; index p. 467)

LODGINGS

BEST WESTERN COLUMBIA WEST   Phone: 803/796-9400   **57**
AAA SAVE   All Year [CP]   1P: $45   2P/1B: $50   2P/2B: $50   XP: $5   F16
◆◆   **Location:** On SR 302 at jct I-26, exit 113 on frontage road; 2.5 mi e of airport. 100 Cherokee Ln 29169.
Motel   Fax: 803/739-6820. **Terms:** No pets. **Facility:** 118 rooms. King rooms with data ports. Comfortable rooms with pleasant decor. Picnic area. Lawn games. 4 stories; exterior corridors. **Dining & Entertainment:** Cocktail lounge. **Services:** valet laundry. **Recreation:** nature trails. **All Rooms:** free movies.
Some Rooms: coffeemakers, microwaves, refrigerators. **Cards:** AE, CB, DI, DS, MC, VI. **Special Amenities:** Free breakfast and free newspaper.

COMFORT INN-AIRPORT   Phone: 803/796-0044   **58**
AAA SAVE   All Year [CP]   1P: $55   2P/2B: $60   XP: $5   F18
◆◆◆   **Location:** From I-26 exit 113, 0.3 mi s on Airport Blvd. 110 Branch Rd 29169 (PO Box 2736).
Motel   Fax: 803/796-0044. **Terms:** No pets. **Facility:** 62 rooms. 2 stories; exterior corridors. **Dining:** Restaurant nearby. **Services:** Fee: coin laundry. **All Rooms:** coffeemakers, microwaves, free movies, refrigerators, combo or shower baths. **Some Rooms:** 2 efficiencies. Fee: whirlpools. **Cards:** AE, DI, DS, MC, VI.
Special Amenities: Free breakfast and free newspaper.   Roll in showers.

HAMPTON INN AIRPORT   Rates Subject to Change   Phone: 803/791-8940   **55**
◆◆◆   All Year [CP]   1P: $57- 66   2P/1B: $63- 74   2P/2B: $62- 70   XP: $8   F18
Motel   **Location:** At jct I-26 & US 378, exit 110. 1094 Chris Dr 29169. Fax: 803/739-2291. **Terms:** No pets.
MC, VI.   **Facility:** 121 rooms. 4 stories; interior corridors. **All Rooms:** free & pay movies. **Cards:** AE, CB, DI, DS, MC, VI.

HOLIDAY INN COLUMBIA AIRPORT   Rates Subject to Change   Phone: 803/794-9440   **56**
◆◆◆   All Year   1P: $66   2P/1B: $66   2P/2B: $66   XP: $7   F18
Motor Inn   **Location:** On US 1 at jct I-26; exit 111B. 500 Chris Dr 29169. Fax: 803/794-9449. **Terms:** Sr. discount; small pets only. **Facility:** 148 rooms. 2 stories; exterior corridors. **Dining:** Dining room; 6:30 am-12:30 & 6-10 pm;
$7-$12. **All Rooms:** free & pay movies. **Cards:** AE, CB, DI, DS, JCB, MC, VI. *(See ad p 472)*

RAMADA INN WEST   Phone: 803/796-2700   **61**
AAA SAVE   All Year [CP]   1P: $60- 73   2P/1B: $67- 83   2P/2B: $53- 83   XP: $8
◆◆   **Location:** At jct I-26 & US 378, exit 110. 114 McSwain Dr 29169. Fax: 803/796-0166. **Terms:** BP avail; no pets. **Facility:** 100 rooms. 10 whirlpool rms, extra charge; 2 stories; interior/exterior corridors; wading pool,
Motor Inn   whirlpool; playground. **Dining & Entertainment:** Dining room; 6 am-10 pm; $5-$15; cocktails/lounge; entertainment. **Services:** Fee: coin laundry. **All Rooms:** free movies. **Some Rooms:** radios.
Fee: microwaves, refrigerators. **Cards:** AE, CB, DI, DS, JCB, MC, VI. **Special Amenities:** Early check-in/late check-out and free breakfast.

WINNSBORO—3,500

LODGINGS

DAYS INN   Phone: 803/635-1447
AAA SAVE   All Year [CP]   1P: $25- 44   2P/1B: $25- 44   2P/2B: $34- 44   XP: $5   F13
◆◆   **Location:** On US 321, at jct SR 34 & 213; from jct I-77 6 mi w on SR 34. Hwy 321 & 34 Bypass 29180
Motel   (Route 3, Box 10). Fax: 803/635-1447. **Terms:** Weekly rates; small pets only, $5 extra charge. **Facility:** 45 rooms. Quiet location. 1 two-bedroom unit. 2-bedroom suite, $60-85; 2 stories; exterior corridors. **Dining:** Restaurant nearby. **Services:** valet laundry. **All Rooms:** free movies. **Some Rooms:** coffeemakers, efficiency, no utensils, microwaves, whirlpools. **Cards:** AE, CB, DI, DS, JCB, MC, VI. **Special Amenities:** Free breakfast and preferred room (subject to availability with advanced reservations).

FAIRFIELD MOTEL   Phone: 803/635-4681
AAA SAVE   All Year   1P: $35   2P/1B: $35   2P/2B: $39   XP: $4   F12
◆◆   **Location:** 1 mi se on US 321 bypass; 1.3 mi n of SR 34 & 321. 115 S 321 Bypass 29180.
Motel   Fax: 803/635-2736. **Terms:** Reserv deposit, 4 day notice; weekly/monthly rates; pets. **Facility:** 62 rooms. 2 stories; exterior corridors. **Dining:** Restaurant nearby. **All Rooms:** free movies.
Some Rooms: microwaves, radios, refrigerators. **Cards:** AE, DS, MC, VI.

RESTAURANT

NEWS & HERALD TAVERN   Lunch: $5-$7   Dinner: $7-$15   Phone: 803/635-1331
◆◆   **Location:** E of Congress St; behind town clock. 114 E Washington 29180. **Hours:** 11 am-2 & 5-9:30 pm, Fri
American   & Sat-10:30 pm. Closed major holidays, Sun & Mon for lunch. **Reservations:** accepted. **Features:** casual dress; children's menu; carryout; cocktails & lounge; a la carte. Daily specials featured. **Cards:** MC, VI.

YEMASSEE—700

LODGING

SUPER 8 MOTEL   Rates Subject to Change   Phone: 803/589-2177
◆   All Year   1P: $24   2P/1B: $29   2P/2B: $38   XP: $5   F10
Motel   **Location:** I-95 exit 38. Rt 2, Box 600 29945. Fax: 803/589-2008. **Terms:** Sr. discount; reserv deposit; pets, $3 extra charge. **Facility:** 38 rooms. 2 stories; exterior corridors. **All Rooms:** free movies. **Cards:** AE, DS, MC, VI.

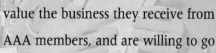

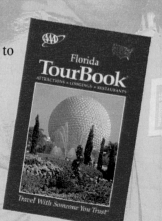

For Your Information

Three handy sections to help make your vacation planning easier.

AAA CLUBS AND BRANCH OFFICES

Need a sheet map or Triptik map? Run out of travelers checks? Want the latest update on local road conditions? All this information and more awaits you at more than 1,000 AAA and CAA clubs and offices across the United States and Canada—a boon for travelers in an unfamiliar state, province or city. Each listing provides the office address, phone number and hours of service.

TEMPERATURE CHART

Knowing what clothes to pack for a trip can make the difference between pleasant vacationing and unpleasant surprises. Use the temperature chart to help determine your on-the-road wardrobe. The chart, found in each TourBook, lists average monthly maximum and minimum temperatures for representative cities.

DRIVING DISTANCES MAP

For safety's sake, it makes sense to take regular breaks while driving on the open road. The driving distances map is a quick and useful reference for trip planning—from a 1-day excursion to a cross-country jaunt. It provides both the mileage and the average driving time (excluding stops) between towns and cities located throughout a state or province.

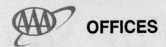 **OFFICES**

Cities with main offices are listed in **BOLD TYPE** and toll-free member service numbers in *ITALIC TYPE*. All are closed Saturdays, Sundays and holidays unless otherwise indicated.

The type of service provided is designated below the name of the city where the office is located:

Auto travel services, including books/maps, marked maps and on-demand Triptik maps ✚
Auto travel services, including books/maps, marked maps, but no on-demand Triptik maps ●
Provides books/maps only. No marked maps or on-demand Triptik maps available ■
Travel agency services ▲

GEORGIA

ROSWELL—AAA Auto Club South, 4540B Roswell Road, 30342. Mon-Fri 8:30-6:30. (404) 843-4500.✚▲

AUGUSTA—AAA Auto Club South, 3601 Walton Way Extension, 30909. Mon-Fri 8:30-5:30. (706) 738-6611.✚▲

COLUMBUS—AAA Auto Club South, 2449 Airport Thruway, 31904. Mon-Fri 8:30-5:30. (706) 324-7121.✚▲

JONESBORO—AAA Auto Club South, 696 Morrow Ind Blvd #3A, 30236. Mon-Fri 8:30-6, Sat 10-2. (770) 961-8085.■▲

MACON—AAA Auto Club South, 3586 Riverside Drive, 31210. Mon-Fri 8:30-5:30. (912) 471-0800.✚▲

MARIETTA—AAA Auto Club South, 4101 Roswell Rd NE #301, 30062. Mon-Fri 8:30-6:30. (770) 565-5700.✚▲

NORCROSS—AAA Auto Club South, 5450 Peachtree Pky Ste F1, 30092. Mon-Fri 8:30-6, Sat 9-5, Sun 10:30-5. (770) 448-7024.●▲

SAVANNAH—AAA Auto Club South, 712 Mall Boulevard, 31406-4879. Mon-Fri 8:30-5:30. (912) 352-8222.✚▲

TUCKER—AAA Auto Club South, 2200 Northlake Pky #129, 30084-4099. Mon-Fri 8:30-6:30. (770) 939-7520.✚▲

NORTH CAROLINA

ASHEVILLE—AAA Carolinas, 660-A Merrimon Avenue, 28804-3543. Mon-Fri 8-6. (704) 253-5376, *(800) 477-4222.*✚▲

CHARLOTTE—AAA Carolinas, 900 East Boulevard, 28203. Mon-Fri 8:30-5:30, Sat 9-1. (704) 319-4222.✚▲

CHARLOTTE—AAA Carolinas, 6600 Executive Circle Dr., 28212. Mon-Fri 8-6, Sat 9-1. (704) 569-3600, *(800) 477-4222.*✚▲

CHARLOTTE—AAA Carolinas, 8662 J W Clay Blvd #3, 28262. Mon-Fri 8-6, Sat 9-1. (704) 548-1334.✚▲

DURHAM—AAA Carolinas, 3909 University Drive, 27707. Mon-Fri 8-6. (919) 489-3306, *(800) 477-4222.*✚▲

FAYETTEVILLE—AAA Carolinas, 3801 Sycamore Dairy Road, 28303. Mon-Fri 8-6. (910) 864-3115, *(800) 477-4222.*✚▲

GASTONIA—AAA Carolinas, 1427 East Franklin Blvd, 28054. Mon-Fri 8-6, Sat 9-1. (704) 864-3434, *(800) 477-4222.*✚▲

GREENSBORO—AAA Carolinas, 14-A Oak Branch Drive, 27407-2145. Mon-Fri 8-6. (910) 852-0506, *(800) 477-4222.*✚▲

HENDERSONVILLE—AAA Carolinas, 136 S King St Ste D, 28792. Mon-Fri 8-6. (704) 697-8778.✚▲

HIGH POINT—AAA Carolinas, 820 North Elm Street, 27262. Mon-Fri 8-6. (910) 882-8126, *(800) 477-4222.*✚▲

MATTHEWS—AAA Carolinas, 2326A Matthews TP, 28105. Mon-Fri 8-6, Sat 9-1. (704) 844-2996.✚▲

PINEVILLE—AAA Carolinas, 9443 Pineville-Matthews, 28134. Mon-Fri 8-6, Sat 9-1. (704) 541-7409, *(800) 477-4222.*✚▲

RALEIGH—AAA Carolinas, 6677 Falls of the Neuse, 27615. Mon-Fri 8-6. (919) 848-1800.▲

RALEIGH—AAA Carolinas, 2301 Blue Ridge Road, 27607. Mon-Fri 8-6. (919) 832-0543, *(800) 477-4222.*✚▲

ROCKY MOUNT—AAA Carolinas, 3613 Sunset Ave, 27804. Mon-Fri 8-6. (919) 443-7117, *(800) 765-7117.*✚▲

WILMINGTON—AAA Carolinas, 3501 Oleandor Drive #3, 28403. Mon-Fri 8-6. (910) 763-8446, *(800) 477-4222.*✚▲

WINSTON-SALEM—AAA Winston-Salem, 1396 Westgate Center, 27103. Mon-Fri 8:30-5. (910) 744-1200.✚▲

SOUTH CAROLINA

AIKEN—AAA Carolinas, 3066 Whiskey Road, 29803. Mon-Fri 8-6. (803) 642-8377.✚▲

CHARLESTON—AAA Carolinas, 1975K Magwood Road, 29414. Mon-Fri 8-6. (803) 766-2394, *(800) 477-4222.*✚▲

COLUMBIA—AAA Carolinas, 810 Dutch Square Blvd, 29210. Mon-Fri 8-6. (803) 798-9205, *(800) 477-4222.*✚▲

GREENVILLE—AAA Carolinas, 430 Haywood Road #1, 29607. Mon-Fri 8-6. (803) 297-9988, *(800) 477-4222.*✚▲

MOUNT PLEASANT—AAA Carolinas, 320-A West Coleman Blvd, 29464. Mon-Fri 8-6. (803) 856-4607.✚▲

MYRTLE BEACH—AAA Carolinas, 7745 N Kings Hwy, 29572. Mon-Fri 8-6. (803) 692-9601, *(800) 477-4222.*✚▲

SPARTANBURG—AAA Carolinas, 818 East Main Street, 29302-1748. Mon-Fri 8-6. (803) 583-2766, *(800) 477-4222.*✚▲

Temperature Averages - Maximum/Minimum
From the records of the National Weather Service

	JAN.	FEB.	MAR.	APR.	MAY	JUNE	JULY	AUG.	SEPT.	OCT.	NOV.	DEC.
GEORGIA												
Atlanta	54/36	57/37	63/41	72/50	81/59	87/66	88/69	88/68	83/63	74/52	62/40	53/35
Augusta	59/36	62/37	67/43	77/50	84/59	91/67	91/70	91/69	87/64	78/52	68/40	59/35
Columbus	59/37	61/38	67/43	76/51	85/60	91/68	92/71	91/70	87/65	78/53	67/42	59/36
Macon	60/38	63/39	69/45	78/53	87/61	93/69	93/71	92/70	88/65	79/54	68/43	60/38
Savannah	63/41	64/42	70/47	77/54	85/62	90/69	91/71	91/71	86/67	78/56	69/46	63/40
NORTH CAROLINA												
Asheville	49/30	51/31	57/36	68/44	76/53	83/60	85/64	84/63	79/57	69/46	57/36	50/30
Cape Hatteras	52/40	54/40	58/44	66/52	75/61	82/69	84/72	84/72	80/68	71/59	63/50	55/42
Charlotte	53/33	56/34	62/39	72/49	80/58	88/66	89/69	88/68	83/62	74/50	63/39	53/33
Raleigh	52/31	54/32	61/38	72/47	79/56	86/64	87/68	88/67	82/60	73/48	62/38	52/31
Winston-Salem	50/32	52/32	59/37	70/47	79/56	87/65	88/68	87/67	81/62	72/49	60/38	50/32
SOUTH CAROLINA												
Charleston	59/44	60/44	65/50	73/58	81/66	86/73	88/75	88/75	83/70	75/61	66/50	59/44
Columbia	58/36	61/36	67/42	76/51	85/60	92/70	93/71	92/70	86/65	77/52	67/41	58/35
Florence	58/37	60/37	67/43	76/51	84/60	90/68	91/70	90/70	85/64	77/53	67/43	58/36
Spartanburg	53/35	55/35	62/40	72/50	81/59	88/67	89/69	88/68	82/63	73/52	62/41	53/34

When you're on the road, look for the AAA emblem—
it's your assurance of a quality hotel, motel or resort.

You can trust the AAA emblem as a good signal
to turn in for a comfortable night's sleep.

Americans on the road turn to us.

 Travel With Someone You Trust.®

590

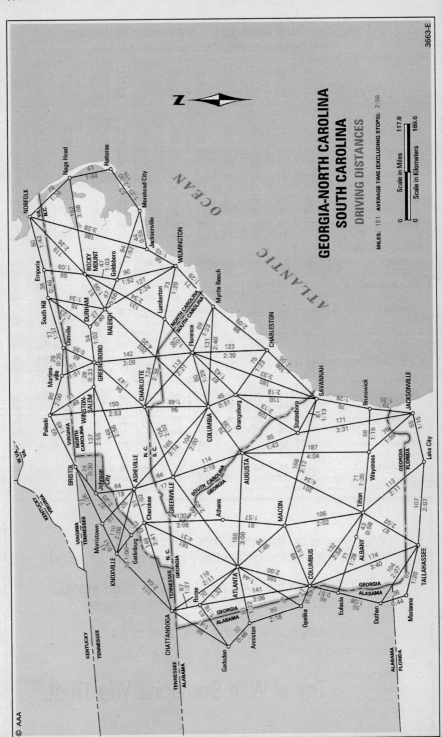

GEORGIA-NORTH CAROLINA SOUTH CAROLINA
DRIVING DISTANCES

MILES: 151 AVERAGE TIME (EXCLUDING STOPS): 2:56

Scale in Miles 0 117.8

Scale in Kilometers 0 189.6

3663-E

© AAA

Indexes

The following indexes are designed to make your travel planning easier and your travel experience more enjoyable.

POINTS OF INTEREST INDEX

The Points of Interest Index lists attractions and events described in more detail in the Attractions section of the TourBook. The categories of the index make it possible to discover potential vacation destinations or routes with concentrations of attractions, events or activities of a specific type—making it easier to tailor a trip to your interests. To read about a particular index entry, simply note its page number and turn to the corresponding location in the descriptive text.

AAA/CAA uses nearly 200 specific points of interest categories, ranging from Amusement & Theme Parks to Zoological Parks & Exhibits. Also categorized are 15 types of events, 13 types of exhibits and collections and 10 types of sports events.

Index entries appear in the TourBook as an attraction listing, as a town or place listing, or in the general text of a referenced town or place. A ★ denotes a point of interest of unusually high quality. Standard U.S. postal abbreviations have been used for the names of states and Canadian provinces. See the Index Abbreviations box for other abbreviations used.

🞨 ATTRACTION ADMISSION DISCOUNT INDEX

A Show Your Card & Save icon appearing in an attraction listing indicates that a discount is offered to holders of a AAA/CAA membership card, AAA MasterCard, AAA VISA or international Show Your Card & Save discount card.

BED & BREAKFAST LODGINGS INDEX

This index is provided as a convenience to members interested in readily identifying this type of property. Some bed and breakfasts listed might have historical significance. Those properties also are referenced in the Historical Lodgings & Restaurants Index.

COUNTRY INNS INDEX

Some of the country inns listed might have historical significance. Those properties also are referenced in the Historical Lodgings & Restaurants Index. Country inns with Continental [CP] or Full breakfast [BP] in the room rate may also be considered bed and breakfast operations.

HISTORICAL LODGINGS & RESTAURANTS INDEX

The historical lodgings in this index can also be considered bed and breakfast operations if Continental [CP] or Full breakfast [BP] is included in the room rate. See the individual accommodation listing under the town heading for details.

RESORTS INDEX

Many establishments are located in resort areas; however, the resorts in this index have extensive on-premises recreational facilities. See the individual accommodation listing under the town heading for details.

POINTS OF INTEREST INDEX

INDEX ABBREVIATIONS

HISTORIC BUILDINGS & HOUSES

MUSIC EVENTS

MUSIC HALLS & OPERA HOUSES

NATURAL PHENOMENA

NATURE CENTERS

NATURE TRAILS

NAUTICAL TOURS

OBSERVATORIES

PAINTINGS

VISITOR INFORMATION

WALKING TOURS

WATERFALLS

🄂 ATTRACTION ADMISSION DISCOUNT INDEX

BED & BREAKFAST LODGINGS INDEX

Some bed and breakfasts listed below might have historical significance. Those properties are also referenced in the Historical index. The indication that continental [CP] or full breakfast [BP] is included in the room rate reflects whether a property is a Bed-and-Breakfast facility.

GEORGIA

Accommodations

NORTH CAROLINA

Accommodations

SOUTH CAROLINA

Accommodations

BED & BREAKFAST LODGINGS (cont'd)

COUNTRY INNS INDEX

Some of the following country inns can also be considered as bed-and-breakfast operations. The indication that continental [CP] or full breakfast [BP] is included in the room rate reflects whether a property is a Bed-and-Breakfast facility.

GEORGIA

Accommodations

NORTH CAROLINA

Accommodations

Restaurant

SOUTH CAROLINA

Accommodations

HISTORICAL LODGINGS & RESTAURANTS INDEX

Some of the following historical lodgings can also be considered as bed-and-breakfast operations. The indication that continental [CP] or full breakfast [BP] is included in the room rate reflects whether a property is a Bed-and-Breakfast facility.

GEORGIA

Accommodations

HISTORICAL LODGINGS & RESTAURANTS (cont'd)

The Kehoe House .... Savannah 294
The Partridge Inn .... Augusta 249
The Pittman House .... Commerce 262
The Whitlock Inn Bed &
    Breakfast .... Marietta 238
The Windsor Hotel .... Americus 185
The Woodruff Bed & Breakfast Inn .... Atlanta North 217

Restaurants

Another Thyme Cafe .... Washington 311
Beall's 1860 .... Macon 282
Bludau's at the 1839 Goetchius
    House .... Columbus 261
Hug's Country Edition Restaurant .... Madison 283
Mr John B's, A Historic Restaurant .... Crabapple 230
Oak Tree Victorian Restaurant .... Hamilton 273
Rudolph's on Green Street .... Gainesville 269
The Depot at Covington .... Covington 264
The Grand Dining Room .... Americus 185
The Grand Dining Room .... Jekyll Island 272
The Grand Old House Restaurant .... Thomasville 305
The Olde Pink House .... Savannah 296
The Pirates' House .... Savannah 296
The Public House .... Roswell 244
The Statesboro Inn Restaurant .... Statesboro 303
Villa D' Este Ristorante Italiano .... Roswell 244

NORTH CAROLINA

Accommodations

Abington Green Bed & Breakfast Inn .... Asheville 314
Albemarle Inn .... Asheville 314
Applewood Manor Inn .... Asheville 316
Arrowhead Inn Bed and Breakfast .... Durham 357
Augustus T Zevely Inn .... Winston-Salem 427
Beaufort House .... Asheville 316
Brookstown Inn .... Winston-Salem 427
Carolina Inn .... Chapel Hill 334
Cedar Crest Victorian Inn .... Asheville 318
Cedar Hill Farm Bed & Breakfast .... Statesville 418
Claddagh Inn .... Hendersonville 375
Delamar Inn .... Beaufort 327
Echo Mountain Inn .... Hendersonville 375
First Colony Inn .... Nags Head 400
Flint Street Inns .... Asheville 319
Governor Eden Inn .... Edenton 362
Greenwood Bed & Breakfast .... Greensboro 372
Harmony House Inn .... New Bern 394
Hillsborough House Inn .... Hillsborough 379
Historic Vance Hotel .... Statesville 419
Holly Inn .... Pinehurst 402
Huntington Hall Bed & Breakfast .... Murphy 394
Hylehurst Bed & Breakfast Inn .... Winston-Salem 428
Inn at the Bryant House .... Aberdeen 312
King's Arms Inn .... New Bern 394
Lady Anne's Victorian Bed &
    Breakfast .... Winston-Salem 429
Lovill House Inn .... Boone 330
Miss Betty's Bed & Breakfast Inn .... Wilson 426
Morehead Inn .... Charlotte 338
Mountain Brook Cottages .... Sylva 420
New Berne House Inn .... New Bern 394
Pecan Tree Inn .... Beaufort 327
Pinebridge Inn .... Spruce Pine 418
Radisson Prince Charles Hotel and
    Suites .... Fayetteville 366
Richmond Hill Inn .... Asheville 324
River Forest Manor .... Belhaven 327
Rosehill Inn .... Wilmington 425
Rowan Oak House .... Salisbury 415
Sunset Inn Bed and Breakfast .... Rocky Mount 413
Taylor House Inn .... Wilmington 425
The Aerie .... New Bern 394
The Banner Elk Inn Bed &
    Breakfast .... Banner Elk 327
The Bouldin House B & B-High
    Point .... Archdale 313
The Colby House .... Asheville 318
The Curran House .... Wilmington 425
The Dunhill Hotel .... Charlotte 337
The Greystone Inn .... Lake Toxaway 383
The Henry F Shaffner
    B & B Inn .... Winston-Salem 428
The Homeplace Bed &
    Breakfast .... Greater Charlotte 348

The Inn at Bingham School .... Carrboro 332
The Inn At Webbley .... Shelby 417
The Inn Uptown .... Charlotte 338
The Lodge On Lake Lure .... Lake Lure 383
The Magnolia Inn .... Magnolia 389
The Manor Inn .... Pinehurst 402
The Oaks Bed & Breakfast .... Saluda 415
The Oakwood Inn Bed & Breakfast .... Raleigh 407
The Pines Plantation Inn .... Mount Gilead 393
The Waverly Inn .... Hendersonville 376
The Worth House .... Wilmington 426
The Wright Inn & Carriage House .... Asheville 324
Weaverville Featherbed &
    Breakfast .... Weaverville 422
Weldon Place Inn .... Weldon 423
William Thomas House Bed &
    Breakfast .... Raleigh 408

Restaurants

42nd St. Oyster Bar & Seafood
    Grill .... Raleigh 408
Carolina Crossroads .... Chapel Hill 335
Expressions .... Hendersonville 376
Henderson House .... New Bern 395
McNinch House .... Charlotte 339
Michael's .... Winston-Salem 429
Salem Tavern Dining Room .... Winston-Salem 430
The Central House .... Highlands 378
The Colonial Inn .... Hillsborough 379
The Harvey Mansion Historic Inn .... New Bern 395
The Vintage House
    Restaurant .... Hickory 377
Zevely House .... Winston-Salem 430

SOUTH CAROLINA

Accommodations

1790 House .... Georgetown 482
1837 Bed & Breakfast .... Charleston 441
27 State Street Bed & Breakfast .... Charleston 446
Abingdon Manor .... Latta 570
Ashley Inn Bed & Breakfast .... Charleston 438
Battery Carriage House Inn (1843) .... Charleston 438
Beaufort Inn .... Beaufort 434
Belvedere Bed & Breakfast .... Charleston 438
Brasington House Bed & Breakfast .... Charleston 439
Calhoun Street Bed & Breakfast .... Sumter 582
Cannonboro Inn Bed & Breakfast .... Charleston 439
Cassina Point Plantation .... Edisto Island 457
Charleston's Vendue Inn .... Charleston 439
Chestnut Cottage Bed & Breakfast .... Columbia 469
Claussen's Inn .... Columbia 470
Croft Magnolia Inn .... Darlington 475
Du Pre House .... Georgetown 482
East Main Guest House .... Rock Hill 575
Ehrhardt Hall .... Ehrhardt 477
Fannie Kate's Country Inn &
    Restaurant .... Mccormick 571
Francis Marion Hotel .... Charleston 442
Fulton Lane Inn .... Charleston 442
Guilds Inn .... Mount Pleasant 460
Hampton Inn Historic District .... Charleston 442
Indigo Inn .... Charleston 444
John Rutledge House Inn .... Charleston 445
Kings Courtyard Inn .... Charleston 445
King's Inn at Georgetown .... Georgetown 482
Magnolia Inn .... Sumter 582
Maison DuPre' .... Charleston 445
Missouri Inn .... Hartsville 559
Pettigru Place Bed & Breakfast .... Greenville 556
Planters Inn .... Charleston 445
Rosemary Hall & Lookaway Hall-A
    Consul Court Inn .... North Augusta 571
Southwood Manor .... Ridge Spring 574
Sugarfoot Castle, A Bed &
    Breakfast .... Honea Path 569
The Anchorage Inn .... Charleston 437
The Bed & Breakfast of Sumter .... Sumter 582
The Book & the Spindle .... Rock Hill 574
The Breeden Inn & Carriage
    House .... Bennettsville 435
The Elliott House Inn .... Charleston 441
The Inn at Merridun .... Union 582
The Inn on Main .... Edgefield 477
The Lodge Alley Inn .... Charleston 445

HISTORICAL LODGINGS & RESTAURANTS (cont'd)

Restaurants

RESORTS INDEX

Many establishments are located in resort areas; however, the following places have extensive on-premises recreational facilities:

GEORGIA

Accommodations

NORTH CAROLINA

Accommodations

SOUTH CAROLINA

Accommodations

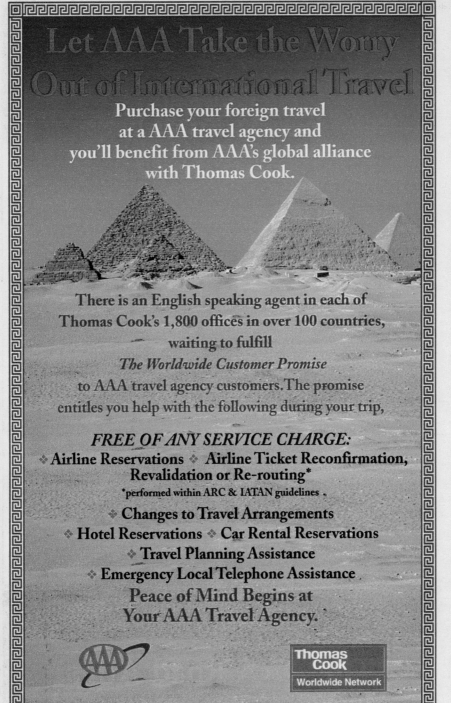

LODGING CLASSIFICATIONS

B&B – Bed & Breakfast, smaller establishment, personal attention, rooms individually decorated, at home feeling, breakfast included, limited parking.

COMPLEX– Combination of two or more classifications.

COTTAGE – Individual cabin or villa usually containing one housekeeping unit. May have separate living room/bedroom. Not required to offer daily housekeeping service.

COUNTRY INN– Larger operation than a B&B, decor may include antiques, dining room where breakfast and dinner are served.

HOTEL – Multistory building provides full service. Usually includes food service, conference space, pool and exercise equipment, room service and convenience shops. Limited or offsite parking.

LODGE – Two or more stories with all facilities in one building, usually has food and beverage service.

MOTEL – Usually one to two stories offering limited service. Food service limited to a snack bar.

MOTOR INN – Offers moderate service, building two or more stories. Usually has recreational facilities and food service. May have limited meeting space. Ample parking.

RANCH – Any classification featuring outdoor, Western-style recreation. Facilities may vary in size.

SUBCLASSIFICATIONS

APARTMENT – Four or more stories with over half of rental units equipped for housekeeping; includes kitchen, living and sleeping areas. Apartment may not offer full daily maid service.

CONDOMINIUM – Destination property located in a resort area. Units include bedroom, kitchen and living room. Not required to offer full daily maid service.

HISTORIC – Restored structures more than 50 years old. Reflects the ambiance of yesteryear. Rooms may lack some modern amenities, often shared baths. Owner operated and food service usually available.

RESORT – Applies to any other type of lodging, vacation atmosphere with extensive recreational facilities. Rates may include meals.

SUITE – Bedroom(s) and living room, which may or may not be closed off from bedroom.

REMEMBER

AAA inspectors assign ratings by evaluating lodging establishments based on their classification.

Thus, "Hotels" are rated in comparison to other "Hotels," etc.

Refer to all the details in the introductory material preceding the lodging section of the TourBook®.

Take a
Gilded Age Excursion to
America's
Largest Home™

In the heart of
Asheville, North Carolina's
Blue Ridge Mountains, there
is a place George Vanderbilt
called home.

Bask in the splendor of this
magnificent 250–room château.
Stroll through the vast Gardens
and trails. Taste the fruits of
Biltmore's vineyards at the
most visited Winery in the
nation. Enjoy our 7 shops
and 3 restaurants.

This vacation, take a Gilded
Age excursion to Biltmore.

Biltmore Estate®
Asheville, North Carolina
800-922-0036
www.biltmore.com

Photography J. Valentine

TOURBOOKMARK

◆◆◆◆◆ Luxurious, World-Class

◆◆◆◆ Top Class, Excellent Service

◆◆◆ Very Comfortable, Well-Appointed

◆◆ Comfortable, Pleasant and Casual

◆ Basic Comfort, Unpretentious but Good

- Pets Allowed
- Outdoor Swimming Pool
- Indoor Swimming Pool
- Dataports and/or Business Services
- Airport Transportation
- Exercise/Whirlpool/Sauna Facilities
- ECTV Extended Cable TV
- CTV Cable TV
- Fully Accessible
- Semi-Accessible
- Non-Smoking Available
- Hearing Impaired
- S Fire Protection Sprinklers
- D Smoke Detectors
- SAVE Official appointment lodging offering special savings
- AAA OFFICIAL APPOINTMENT

Call property for detailed information about fees & restrictions relating to the above symbols.

Biltmore Estate®
800-922-0036
www.biltmore.com